World Literature
and Its Times

VOLUME 3

British and Irish
Literature and Its
Times; Celtic Migrations
to the Reform Bill
(Beginnings-1830s)

World Literature and Its Times

Profiles of Notable Literary Works and the
Historical Events That Influenced Them

Joyce Moss • Lorraine Valestuk

GALE GROUP

Detroit
New York
San Francisco
London
Boston
Woodbridge, CT

World Literature and Its Times

Profiles of Notable Literary
Works and the Historical
Events That Influenced Them

VOLUME 3

**British and Irish Literature
and Its Times**

JOYCE MOSS • LORRAINE VALESTUK

STAFF

Michael L. LaBlanc, *Production Editor*

Maria Franklin, *Permissions Manager*
Julie Juengling, *Permissions Assistant*

Mary Beth Trimper, *Manager, Composition and Electronic Prepress*
Evi Seoud, *Assistant Manager, Composition Purchasing and Electronic Prepress*

Kenn Zorn, *Product Design Manager*
Pamela A. E. Galbreath, *Senior Art Director*
Michael Logusz, *Graphic Artist*

Barbara J. Yarrow, *Graphic Services Supervisor*
Randy Bassett, *Image Database Supervisor*
Robert Duncan, *Imaging Specialist*
Pamela A. Reed, *Imaging Coordinator*
Dean Dauphinais, *Senior Image Editor*
Robyn V. Young, *Senior Image Editor*
Kelly A. Quin, *Image Editor*

ISBN 0-7876-3728-9

Printed in the United States of America
10 9 8 7 6 5 4 3 2

Library of Congress Cataloguing-in-Publication Data

Moss, Joyce, 1951-
British and Irish literature and its times: Celtic migrations to the Reform Bill (beginnings—1830s / Joyce Moss, Lorraine Valestuk.
    p. cm.—(World literature and its times; v. 3)
    Includes bibliographical references and index.
    ISBN 0-7876-3728-9 (alk. paper)
    1. English literature—History and criticism. 2. English literature—Irish authors—History and criticism. 3. Literature and history—Great Britain. 4. Literature and history—Ireland. I. Valestuk, Lorraine, 1963- II. Title. III. Series.

PR25 .M627 2000
820.9—dc21

00–060998
CIP
Rev.

Contents

General Preface

⁓

The world at the turn of the twenty-first century is a shrinking sphere. Innovative modes of transmission make communication from one continent to another almost instantaneous, encouraging the development of an increasingly global society, heightening the urgency of the need for mutual understanding. At the foundation of *World Literature and Its Times* is the belief that within a people's literature are keys to their perspectives, their emotions, and the formative events that have brought them to the present point.

As manifested in their literary works, societies experience phenomena that are in some respects universal and in other respects tied to time and place. T. S. Eliot's poem *The Wasteland,* for example, is set in Europe in the early 1920s, when the region was rife with the disenchantment of the post-World War I era. Coincidentally, Juan Rulfo's novel *Pedro Páramo,* set in Latin America over a spread of decades that includes the 1920s, features a protagonist whose last name means "bleak plain" or "wasteland." The two literary works, though written oceans apart, conjure a remarkably similar atmosphere. Likewise Aphra Behn's novel *Oroonoko,* set largely in the British colony of Surinam in the early 1660s, and Miguel Barnet's *Biography of a Runaway Slave,* beginning in 1860 in the Spanish colony of Cuba, both feature defiant slaves. The plots in this case take place two centuries apart, suggesting that time, as well as place, is of little consequence. A close look at the two slaves, however—and the two

wastelands referred to above—exposes illuminating differences, which are indeed tied to the times and places in which the respective works are set.

World Literature and Its Times regards both fiction and nonfiction as rich mediums for understanding the differences, as well as the similarities, among people and societies. In its view, full understanding of a literary work demands attention to events and attitudes of the period in which a work takes place and of the one in which it is written. The series therefore examines a wide range of novels, short stories, biographies, speeches, poems, and plays by contextualizing a work in these two periods. Each volume covers some 50 literary works that span a mix of centuries and genres. The literary work itself takes center stage, with its contents determining which issues—social, political, psychological, economic, or cultural—are covered in a given entry. Every entry discusses the relevant issues apart from the literary work, making connections to it when merited, and allowing for comparisons between the literary and the historical realities. Close attention is given as well to the literary work itself, in the interest of extracting historical understandings from it.

Of course, the function of literature is not necessarily to represent history accurately. Nevertheless the images and ideas promoted by a powerful literary work—be it Miguel de Cervantes's *The Adventures of Don Quixote* (Spain), Nadine Gordimer's *Burgher's Daughter* (South Africa), or

John Dryden's "Mac Flecknoe" (Great Britain)—leave impressions that are commonly taken to be historical. In taking literature as fact, one risks acquiring a mistaken notion of history. Based on powerful impressions evoked in Shakespeare's *Antony and Cleopatra,* for example, and other such works people often presume Cleopatra to have been Egyptian by birth, when she was not. To adjust for such discrepancies, this series distinguishes between historical fact and literary impressions.

On the other hand, literary works can broaden our understanding of history. They are able to convey more than the cut-and-dried record, by portraying events in a way that captures the fears and challenges of a period or by drawing attention to groups of people who are generally left out of standard histories. This is well illustrated with writings that concern the position of women in different societies—for example, Flora Nwapa's novel *Efuru* (Nigeria) or Mary Wollstonecraft's essay *A Vindication of the Rights of Woman* (Britain). Literature, as illustrated by these works, engages in a vigorous dialog with other forms of communication. It often defies stereotypes by featuring characters or ideas that are contrary to preconceptions. In fact, many of the literary works covered in this series feature characters and ideas that attack or upset deeply engrained stereotypes of their day, from Friar Bartolomé de Las Casas's *A Short Account of the Destruction of the Indies* (mid-1500s Latin America) to Samuel Richardson's *Pamela* (early-1700s Britain), to Mongo Beti's *Mission to Kala* (mid-1900s Cameroon Republic).

Even nonfiction must be anchored in its place and times to derive its full value. Octavio Paz's essay *The Labyrinth of Solitude* explains the character of contemporary Mexicans as a product of historical experience; the entry on the essay amplifies this experience. A second entry, on Albert Memmi's *Pillar of Salt,* uses the less direct genre of biography to describe the life of a Tunisian Jew during the Nazi occupation of North Africa. A third entry, on *The Diary of Samuel Pepys,* reflects attitudes about fidelity to one's spouse that were undoubtedly influenced by the licentious behavior of the king and upper-class society in 1660s England.

The task of reconstructing the historical context of a literary work can be problematic. An author may present events out of chronological order, as Carlos Fuentes does in *The Death of Artemio Cruz* (Mexico), or may create works that feature legendary heroes who defy attempts to fit them neatly into a specific time slot (such as the warrior Beowulf of Denmark, glorified in England's epic poetry; or the emperor Sunjata of Mali in the Western Sudan). In the first case, *World Literature and Its Times* unscrambles the plot, providing a linear rendering of events and associated historical information. In the second, the series profiles customs particular to the culture in which the epic is set and written, arming the reader with details that inform the hero's adventures. The approach sheds light on the relationship between fact and fiction, both of which are shown to provide insight into a people and their epics. As always, this approach is taken with a warm appreciation for the beauty of a literary work independent of historical facts, but also in the belief that ultimate regard is shown for that work by placing it in the context of pertinent events.

Beyond this underlying belief, the series is founded on the notion that a command of world literature bolsters knowledge of the writings produced by one's own society. Long before the present century, fiction and nonfiction writers from different locations influenced one another through trends and strategies in their literatures. In our postcolonial age, such cross-fertilization has quickened. Latin American literature, having been influenced by French and Spanish trends among others, itself influences Chinese writers of today. Likewise, Africa's literary tradition has affected and been affected by France's, and the same relationship holds true for the writings of India and Great Britain. The degree of such literary intermixture promises only to multiply given our increasingly global society. In the process, world literature and its landmark texts gain even greater significance, attaining the potential to promote understanding not only of others, but also of ourselves.

The Selection of Literary Works

The works chosen for *British and Irish Literature and Its Times* have been carefully selected by professors in the field at the universities detailed in the Acknowledgements. Keeping the literature-history connection in mind, the team made its selections based on a combination of factors: how frequently a literary work is studied, how closely it is tied to pivotal events in the past or present, and how strong and enduring its appeal has been to readers in and out of the society that produced it. Attention has been paid to literary works set from prehistorical to Victorian times that have met with critical and/or popular acclaim. There has also been a careful effort to include works from different reaches of the British Isles, to represent female as well as male authors, and to cover a mix of genres, from the short tale, to epic poetry, blank verse, and sonnets, to various types of plays (comedy, history, tragedy, and ballad opera), to essays, biographies, and the novel. The inclusion of selected works at the expense of others has been made with this range of concerns in mind.

Format and Arrangement of Entries

The volumes in *World Literature and Its Times* are arranged geographically. *World Literature and Its Times 3* and *World Literature and Its Times 4* are devoted to British and Irish literature and its times. The volumes are divided chronologically according to when the literary works are set. Covered in the *World Literature and Its Times 3* are works set from the Celtic migrations into the region to the early nineteenth century Reform Bill. *World Literature and Its Times 4* features works set from the Victorian Era to the present. Within a volume, entries are arranged alphabetically by title of the literary work. Each entry is organized as follows:

1. **Introduction**—identifying information in three parts:

   The literary work—specifies the genre, the place and time period in which the work is set, when it was written and/or first published, and, if applicable, when it was first translated.

   Synopsis—summarizes the storyline or contents of the work.

   Introductory paragraph—introduces the literary work in relation to the author's life.

2. **Events in History at the Time the Literary Work Takes Place**—describes social and political events that relate to the plot or contents of the literary work. The section may discuss background information as well as relevant events during the period in which the work is set. Subsections vary depending on the literary work. Taking a deductive approach, the section starts with events in history and telescopes inward to events in the literary work.

3. **The Literary Work in Focus**—summarizes in detail the plot or contents of the work, describes how it illuminates history,

and identifies sources used by the author. After the summary of the work comes a subsection focusing on an aspect of the literature that illuminates our understanding of events or attitudes of the period. This subsection takes an inductive approach, starting with the literary work, and broadening outward to events in history. It is followed by a third subsection specifying sources that inspired elements of the work and discussing its literary context, or relation to other works.

4. **Events in History at the Time the Literary Work Was Written**—describes social, political, and/or literary events in the author's lifetime that relate to the plot or contents of a work. Also discussed in this section are the reviews or reception accorded the literary work.

5. **For More Information**—provides a list of all sources that have been cited in the entry as well as sources for further reading about the different issues or personalities featured in the entry.

If the literary work is set and written in the same time period, sections 2 and 4 of the entry on that work ("Events in History at the Time the Literary Work Takes Place" and "Events in History at the Time the Literary Work Was Written") are combined into the single section "Events in History at the Time of the Literary Work."

Additional Features

Whenever possible, primary source material is provided through quotations in the text and material in sidebars. There are also sidebars with historical details that amplify issues raised in the text, and with anecdotes that provide a fuller understanding of the temporal context. Timelines appear in various entries to summarize intricate periods of history. Finally, historically relevant illustrations enrich and further clarify information in the entries.

Comments and Suggestions

Your comments on this series and suggestions for future editions are welcome. Please write: Editors, *World Literature and Its Times,* The Gale Group, Inc., 27500 Drake Road, Farmington Hills, Michigan 48331-3535.

Acknowledgments

World Literature and Its Times 3: British and Irish Literature and Its Times is a collaborative effort that evolved through several stages of development, each of which was monitored by a team of experts in British and Irish Literature. A special thank you goes to Matthew Brosamer of the University of California at Los Angeles, Department of English; Margaret Ferguson of the University of California at Davis, Department of English; Benjamin Hudson of the University of Pennsylvania, Department of History; and Robert Sumpter of Mira Costa High School, History Department for their careful review of the Chronology and Introduction that begin the volume. For their incisive participation in selecting the literary works to cover in the volume, the editors extend deep appreciation to the following professors:

Lynn Batten, University of California at Los Angeles, Department of English

Peter Manning, State University of New York at Stony Brook, Chair, Department of English

Anne Mellor, University of California at Los Angeles, Department of English

Joseph Nagy, University of California at Los Angeles, Department of English

Jonathan Post, University of California at Los Angeles, Department of English

David Rodes, University of California at Los Angeles, Department of English

Karen Rowe, University of California at Los Angeles, Department of English

Susan Staves, Brandeis University, Department of English

The following professors carefully reviewed the entries to insure accuracy and completeness of information. Sincere gratitude is extended to these professors:

Michael Allen, University of California at Los Angeles, Department of English

Lynn Batten, University of California at Los Angeles, Department of English

John Bowers, University of Nevada, Department of English

Julia Brown, Boston University, Department of English

Patrick Cheney, Pennsylvania State University, Department of English

Stuart Curran, University of Pennsylvania, Department of English

Lynn Fauth, Oxnard Community College, Department of Letters

Margaret Ferguson, University of California at Davis, Department of English

Laura Franey, Millsaps College, Department of English

Lisa A. Freeman, University of Chicago, Department of English

Corrinne Harol, University of Utah, Department of English

Acknowledg-ments

Jerrold Hogle, University of Arizona, Department of English

Benjamin Hudson, Pennsylvania State University, Department of History

Arthur Little, University of California at Los Angeles, Department of English

Peter Manning, State University of New York at Stony Brook, Chair, Department of English

Edwin McCann, University of Southern California, Director, School of Philosophy

Claire McEachern, University of California at Los Angeles, Department of English

Mitzi Myers, University of California at Los Angeles, Department of English

Joseph Nagy, University of California at Los Angeles, Department of English

Maximillian Novak, University of California at Los Angeles, Department of English

Felicity Nussbaum, University of California at Los Angeles, Department of English

Jonathan Post, University of California at Los Angeles, Department of English

David Rodes, University of California at Los Angeles, Department of English

Karen Rowe, University of California at Los Angeles, Department of English

Eve Saunders, Concordia University, Montreal, Canada

James Winn, Boston University, Chair, Department of English

For their painstaking research and composition, the editors thank the writers whose names appear at the close of the entries that they contributed. A complete listing follows:

Kimberly Ball, M.A. candidate, University of California at Berkeley

Matthew Brosamer, Lecturer, University of California at Los Angeles

Jim Caufield, Ph.D. candidate, University of California at Los Angeles

Junehee Chung, Ph.D. candidate, University of California at Los Angeles

Terence Davis, B. A., University of California at Los Angeles; professional writer

Laura Franey, Assistant Professor, Millsaps College

Christine Gallant, Professor, Georgia State University

Martin Griffin, Ph.D. candidate, University of California at Los Angeles

Elisabeth Rose Gruner, Associate Professor, University of Richmond

Albert Labriola, Professor, Duquesne University

Jacob Littleton, Ph.D. candidate, University of California at Los Angeles

Pamela S. Loy, Ph.D., University of California at Santa Barbara; professional writer

Jeff Morris, Assistant Professor, Carroll College

Joseph Nagy, Professor, University of California at Los Angeles

Meredith Neuman, Ph.D. candidate, University of California at Los Angeles

Danielle Price, Ph.D., University of California at Los Angeles

Monica Riordan, B.A., University of California at Los Angeles; professional writer

Susan Staves, Professor, Brandeis University
Carolyn Turgeon, M.A., University of California at Los Angeles; professional writer

Eleanor Ty, Associate Professor, Wilfrid Laurier University, Canada

Lawrence Warner, Visiting Research Fellow, Australian National University

Colin Wells, M.A., Oxford University; professional writer

Deep appreciation is extended to Michael LaBlanc of the Gale Group for his careful editing and to Deborah Morad and Joyce Nakamura of the Gale Group for their painstaking compilation of illustrations. Anne Leach indexed the volume with great sensitivity to readers and subject matter. Lastly, the editors express gratitude to Nomi Kleinmuntz and Monica Riordan for their deft copy editing, and to Lisa Blai for her proficient word processing and organizational management.

Introduction

"Your Roman-Saxon-Danish-Norman English," quipped Daniel Defoe acidly in his 1701 poem *The True-Born Englishman*. The barb was a response to disparaging remarks about England's king, William of Orange, and some of his followers, who were Dutch, not English, and it alludes to the blend that defines the English people and their literature, a mixture that mushrooms into an even richer amalgamation when one includes Scotland, Wales, and Ireland. Inhabiting the region before the invasion of the Romans in 55 B.C.E. were British Celts, who began what in time would become a Celtic-Roman-Saxon-Danish-Norman-British-and-Irish literary continuum. The continuum harks back to the oral tales of the British Celts, or to two branches who migrated to the region from mainland Europe: the Goidelic (or *Gaelic*) Celts moved into Ireland, then Scotland; the Brythonic Celts (historical source of the term *Britain*) settled in Wales and other parts of the isles.

It was in the Middle Ages that scribes first recorded the oral tales of the British Celts, penning other literature too and in a mix of languages, adding Latin, French, and English to the varieties used by the Celts. Gradually a national consciousness developed, out of diverse building blocks. The departure of the Roman army in 409 C.E. paved the way for Anglo-Saxon conquests. A few hundred years later Scandinavians—the "Danish" of Defoe's quip—began their invasions, which would continue for centuries (as reflected in *The Battle of Maldon*). The Danish Scandinavians vanquished three kingdoms, plundered countless monasteries, whose documents they destroyed, and established a society of their own in the isles. In 878, a local Saxon ruler (Alfred) finally managed to push back the Danes and to consolidate the Anglo-Saxon kingdom that today's historians identify as Britain's first "national" monarchy, the House of Wessex. Subsequently the Danes regained control for a time, during which *Beowulf* may have found its way into manuscript form. Still the Anglo-Saxon kingdom survived, but only briefly, collapsing after the Norman invasion in 1066.

Originally from Scandinavia, the Normans had settled in France a few generations earlier. They resettled in England after 1066, remaining intimately involved in French politics, becoming embroiled in conflicts with the French king over lordship of English possessions in France. The conflicts kept erupting into warfare, with the Normans growing so militant that they began to think of themselves as English rather than French. Meanwhile, the Normans kept a steady hold on the British Isles, introducing some traditions and adopting others. In time the Normans claimed English as their language rather than French, a gradual process that quickened around 1350 and was virtually complete by 1450.

Medieval writing in various languages contributed greatly to the evolution of cultural identities in the region. In addition to recording tales of the Celts, writers under Anglo-Saxon and Norman rule composed "histories," some of which were mythical. Around 1135, Geoffrey of Monmouth wrote a history of the kings of Britain (*Historia Regum Britannie*) that endowed the region with a legendary past. The work traced Britain's kingship back to Brutus, a descendant of the Trojan founders of Rome, claiming that he arrived in Britain about 1170 B.C.E., defeated giants, and then founded New Troy, or London. The work goes on to recount rulers who succeeded Brutus, through the celebrated King Arthur, up to the invasions of the Anglo-Saxons. It is a mythical, unverifiable account, which Europe nevertheless embraced and medieval writers preserved. Their tales promoted chivalry and related ideals, focusing especially on Arthur (see *Sir Gawain and the Green Knight* and *Le Morte d'Arthur*). Meanwhile, other writers were recording the tales of the Celts, which likewise included Arthur, but with some different traits (as noted in the entry on *The Mabinogion*).

From the start, literature intersected with history, reflecting and helping to shape government, inter-regional policy, religion, ethics, family life, and more in the British Isles. Across genres, writers used literary works to critique, entertain, and document the times in which they were set, addressing issues such as the ones that follow, which resurfaced over the centuries.

- **Evolution of monarchy and Parliament—** *Richard II* (1300s); *Henry V* (1400s); *The Faerie Queen* (1500s); *Gulliver's Travels* (1600s-1700s)
- **Inter-regional relations—***The Mabinogion* (500-1200); *Rob Roy* (1700s); *Castle Rackrent* (1700s)
- **Male-female relations—***The Eve of St. Agnes* (1200s); *Songs and Sonnets* (1500s-1600s); *The Diary of Samuel Pepys* (1600s)
- **Pursuit of knowledge—***Dr. Faustus* (1500s); *An Essay Concerning Human Understanding* (1600s); *Frankenstein* (1700s)
- **Rise of the common man and woman—** *Piers Plowman* (1300s); *Pamela* (1700s)
- **Individual's relation to Christianity—** *Paradise Lost* (beginning of time); *Le Morte D'Arthur* (400s); *The Pilgrim's Progress* (1600s)
- **Slavery and British empire—***Oroonoko* (1600s); *Songs of Innocence and Experience* (1700s)
- **Social class consciousness—***The Duchess of Malfi* (1400s); *The History of Tom Jones* (1700s); *Wuthering Heights* (1700s)

Of course, how such issues were addressed depended largely on when a literary work was written. The Wife of Bath in Geoffrey Chaucer's *The Canterbury Tales* (written c. 1387-1400) argues that, contrary to popular opinion in her day, widows are entitled to remarry and enjoy physical intimacy with a man. Four centuries later, Mary Wollstonecraft's *A Vindication of the Rights of Woman* (1792) ventures outside the matrimonial sphere, making the shocking proposal for the time that women be educated alongside men. Both works champion women's rights, but the nature of these rights depends on the era.

The religious passions of the 1400s continued into the 1500s, a formative century in which England's Church broke off from Rome, despite stubborn resistance from English priests. Henry VIII, England's monarch, took the Pope's place as religious head of the new Church of England (Anglican Church). After this disharmony came friction within the kingdom between Anglicans and Puritans, who dissented from the Anglican Church. The disharmony climaxed in a civil war, which led to a brief overthrow of the monarchy for a republican government (1649-60), then a restoration of the monarchy—but with a significant change. Many English subjects no longer felt that their monarch ruled by divine right, as indicated by their interference with the royal line of succession in 1688. Parliament, exercising more say in government than ever before, placed two Protestants on the throne—William of Orange, referred to in the first line of this introduction, and his wife Mary.

Meanwhile, Ireland remained Catholic, posing a threat to England's Protestant establishment. The establishment's fear was that the Catholic countries of France and Spain would use Ireland as a base to invade England, so precautions were taken. In the sixteenth and seventeenth centuries, Queen Elizabeth, King James, and republican ruler Oliver Cromwell brought Ireland under English control through military force and renewed colonization (achieved by transplanting of English lords into Ireland). Other parts of the Isles fell under English control too, sooner than Ireland. England annexed Wales by an Act of Union in 1536, while Scotland united with England in a similar act in 1707, losing its separate parliament but gaining a share in English prosperity, as suggested in *Rob Roy*. Still, Ireland remained distinct, until 1800, when another Act of Union finally absorbed its parliament into England's. Meanwhile, as indicated, Ireland's oral and written traditions had from the start contributed to the regional literary continuum. Jonathan Swift's writings, for example, fit neatly into the continuum after Chaucer's and before Wollstonecraft's; like their works, his critiqued aspects of the regional status quo.

Swift used satire, a deft instrument in the hands of Irish and British writers alike around this time. Of course, Chaucer had used it to great effect much earlier. Now, in the late seventeenth to early eighteenth century, writers further developed the genre, using satire to critique both society and specific individuals. In his poem "Mac Flecknoe," John Dryden employed satire to disastrous effect, against playwright and poet Thomas Shadwell, damaging his reputation for centuries to come. The poet Alexander Pope likewise satirized a personal dispute between two families in his mock epic *The Rape of the Lock.* Around the same time, general social satire came into vogue in witty comedies such as William Congreve's *The Way of the World,* which concerns love and marriage and was followed later in the century by renowned comedies in the same vein (*She Stoops to Conquer* and *The Rivals*). Images of slavery abounded in the plays of Congreve's day, with love and marriage depicted as a type of bondage (the wife-slave image in these plays has been connected to the rise of abolitionist sentiments in England). Though she was a dramatist of the day, Aphra Behn invoked another genre altogether to literally tackle the subject of bondage; atypically for the period, her novel *Oroonoko* (1688) concerns slavery in part of the British Empire—Surinam, South America. Until the twentieth century, her novel would mostly be ignored, largely, it is thought, because of Behn's gender.

The novel itself was a new genre, just emerging around the turn of the eighteenth century. Satire was still in vogue at the time. Joseph Addison, who along with Richard Steele issued the periodical *The Spectator* (1711-14), abhorred satire aimed at individuals. It threw darts, he said, that poisoned reputations. In the end, though, Addison and Steele were not the ones to squash the penchant for satire. Rather it declined with the rise of the novel, whose origins have been located by some in Samuel Richardson's *Pamela* (1740) and Henry Fielding's *Tom Jones* (1749). Others argue that Behn's *Oroonoko* (1688) and Daniel Defoe's *Robinson Crusoe* (1719) had already initiated the genre. In any case, all four authors are associated with the rise of the novel, which set out to portray varieties of human experience with fidelity to reality. Adding greatly to these varieties were works by female writers who followed Aphra Behn (for example, Maria Edgeworth's *Castle Rackrent,* Jane Austen's *Sense and Sensibility,* Emily Brontë's *Wuthering Heights,* and George Eliot's *Middlemarch*). "I know something now of my Irish subjects," King George is reported to have said after reading Edgeworth's *Castle Rackrent.*

Interrupting the stream of realistic tales was the gothic novel, which concerned itself with terror or horror. Probably most renowned among the gothic novels of terror is Anne Radcliffe's *The Mysteries of Udolpho,* a novel set in the late sixteenth century that has a villain who commits diabolical acts, but has no genuinely supernatural characters. The villain is simply a malevolent human being. That malevolent people sometimes orchestrated events to satisfy their evil desires had long been acknowledged in literature. There were a bevy of plays around 1600 that featured ill-intentioned characters, among them, Thomas Kyd's *The Spanish Tragedy* (1596), William Shakespeare's *Macbeth* (1606), and John Webster's *The Duchess of Malfi* (1613). The villains are nobles, driven by a thirst for revenge or personal power.

Literature set at the end of the eighteenth century addressed evil too, but differently. A cataclysmic event occurred in 1789—the French Revolution, in which commoners seized control of government from the nobles. England was meanwhile in the midst of a vigorous Industrial Revolution, which drew rural dwellers into cities and gave rise to a burgeoning middle class, and to workers who aspired to climb into it. People began to view society as a set of competing social strata, and literature changed in keeping with the political and economic developments. In the 1790s the Romantic movement emerged, featuring poems in everyday language that expressed emotional reactions to racism (William Blake's *Songs of Innocence and of Experience*), poor vagrants (William Wordsworth and Samuel Taylor Coleridge's *Lyrical Ballads*), and exploited workers (Percy Bysshe Shelley's "England in 1819"). Again, this focus was not altogether new, but its nature changed. Two hundred years earlier Shakespeare's *King Lear* had lamented the plight of the poor in an era filled with religious sermons and a poor law that mandated charity. Blake's *Songs of Innocence and of Experience* ("The Human Abstract") made a similar lament, but tied it to inequities in his society and to his contemporaries' responsibility for them—"Pity would be no more / If we did not make somebody poor." From writings set in prehistorical times to the pre-Victorian 1830s, literary works such as these both reflected and advanced the social dialogue.

Chronology of Relevant Events

British and Irish Literature and Its Times

THE BUILDING OF BRITAIN AND IRELAND

The peopling of the British Isles occurred over a span of several millennia. Anthropological evidence suggests that the first settlers may have arrived in Ireland during the Bronze Age and that the "Beaker Folk"—so called because of their distinctively shaped drinking cups or "beakers"—settled in Great Britain around 2000 B.C.E. After the Beaker Folk came perhaps the most populous settlers to appear in the British Isles, the Celts, who arrived in waves from the first millennium B.C.E. Their migration was followed by the invasions of different peoples—the Romans, the Anglo-Saxons, Vikings, and finally, the Normans, each of whom left a significant cultural impression that contributed to the development of traditions on the Isles. Monks distinguished themselves as early historians of this developmental phase.

Historical Events	Related Literary Works
8000 B.C.E. 8000-1750 B.C.E. First people arrive in Ireland across land bridge from Scotland; Beaker Folk arrive in Britain; Stonehenge is built.	
1000-55 B.C.E. Celtic peoples arrive and settle in Britain and Ireland	*King Lear* by William Shakespeare; *The Mabinogion; The Táin (The Cattle Raid of Cooley)*
55-54 B.C.E. Julius Caesar leads two expeditions into Britain	
43 C.E. Roman conquest of Britain begins; Londinium (London) founded	*Antony and Cleopatra* by William Shakespeare
50 48-79 Southeastern Britain is conquered, Roman roads constructed	
60-62 Queen Boudicca raises revolt against the Romans in East Anglia; Romans suppress revolt but suffer severe losses	

Historical Events	Related Literary Works
122-33 Romans build defensive barrier, Hadrian's Wall, to protect northwestern frontier of Britain from invaders	
407-10 Roman army withdraws from Britain	
427-500s Invasions by Angles, Saxons, and Jutes; Britons try to fight invaders; founding of Anglo-Saxon kingdoms begins	*Le Morte D'Arthur* by Sir Thomas Malory
500 Members of the Irish kingdom of Dál Riata cross to today's Scotland	
547 British monk Gildas writes *De Excidio Britanniae* (Concerning the Fall of Britain), outlining early history involving the Britons and Saxons; the tract criticizes various individuals for their behavior	
731-32 Bede completes his *Historia ecclesiastica* (Ecclesiastical History of the English People), a record of events in Britain from Caesar's invasion in 55 B.C.E. to 731 C.E.	
786-95 First Viking raids; Norsemen arrive on Lambay Island off the Dublin Coast	
800-1014 Viking settlements in Ireland evolve into towns	
802 Welsh monk Nennius writes *Historia Brittonum* (History of the Britons), including the alleged founding of Britain by Brutus and mentioning Arthur, a British commander	*Le Morte D'Arthur* by Sir Thomas Malory
842-58 Under leadership of Kenneth Mac Alpin, Scots assimilate Picts to form what will become the kingdom of Scotland	
860s-70s Viking army overruns parts of England, including Northumbria and East Anglia	
871-99 Reign of Saxon king Alfred the Great, who defeats Vikings (Danes) on land and sea; Alfred agrees to a boundary that confines Vikings to area of northern and central England called the Danelaw	
899-924 Alfred's son, Edward, conquers the southern Danelaw	
937 Edward's son Athelstan conquers the northern Danelaw	
976-1014 Brian Boru conquers and unifies most of Ireland, becoming High King	
991 August 11—The Vikings defeat the English forces, led by Byrhtnoth, at the Battle of Maldon	*The Battle of Maldon*
1014 Brian Boru, High King of Ireland, is killed after victory over Vikings in the battle of Clontarf	
1017-35 Cnut of Denmark defeats Aethelred's son Edmund, becomes uncontested king of England, reigning as well over Denmark and, from c. 1028, over Norway	*Beowulf*
1040 Mac Bethad Mac Findláech (Macbeth) kills Donnchad (Duncan), begins peaceful 17-year reign as king of Scotland	
1057 Macbeth is killed by Malcolm	*Macbeth* by William Shakespeare
1066 William of Normandy defeats and kills King Harold II at the Battle of Hastings and is crowned William I (the Conqueror) of England.	

The numbers 500, 800, and 1000 appear as markers along the timeline.

THE MIDDLE ENGLISH ERA
FROM THE NORMAN CONQUEST TO THE TUDOR ACCESSION

The aftermath of the Norman Conquest saw the establishment of a centralized government in England. The heirs of William the Conqueror safeguarded this centralized government even when succession struggles, such as the one between Stephen of Blois and Mathilda of Anjou, threatened to tear the realm apart. In retrospect, the founding of the House of Anjou, or Plantagenet, as it was later called, produced a royal dynasty that brought England some of its most glorious triumphs (English victories over France at the Battles of Crécy and Agincourt) and its most dismal failures (the loss of Normandy during the reign of John I and the loss of France less than 50 years after Agincourt). Rivalries among the Plantagenets and their successors led to bloody civil wars and the shocking depositions of the anointed kings Richard II and Henry VI. Two powerful factions, the Yorkists and the Lancastrians, battled intermittently over the English throne for 30 years before Richard III, a Yorkist, was killed at the Battle of Bosworth Field. The leader of the Lancastrian faction, Henry Tudor, became the new king and the founder of his own royal dynasty.

1066-87 William I centralizes authority of the English Crown and establishes a Norman aristocracy

1087 *The Domesday Book,* a survey of English landholdings, is completed; William I dies; William II accedes to the throne

1106 Henry I, successor to William II, conquers Normandy for himself, establishing England's first foothold in France

1135 Henry I dies, naming his daughter Mathilda as successor; his nephew Stephen of Blois argues that an oath of allegiance to Mathilda was forced and so is void; Stephen seizes the throne

c. 1138 Geoffrey of Monmouth completes *Historia Regum Britanniae* (History of the Kings of Britain), spreads myth that Britain was founded by Brutus, a descendant of the hero Aeneas from the fallen city of Troy, creates the Arthur adapted by subsequent writers of Arthurian romance

Sir Gawain and the Green Knight; Le Morte D'Arthur by Sir Thomas Malory

1138-49 Mathilda attempts to take the English throne from Stephen, sparking a decade of bitter civil war that ends with Mathilda being forced to leave England

1152 Henry of Anjou, son of Mathilda and Count Geoffrey of Anjou, marries Eleanor of Aquitaine, after her marriage to Louis VII of France is annulled

1154-89 Reign of Henry II, Mathilda's son and first ruler of House of Plantagenet (or of Anjou)

1190-92 Richard I ("The Lionhearted") leads third crusade, later (1199) dies of an arrow wound while attempting to take a treasure from his vassal

1200 c. 1200 Layamon's *Brut* appears, containing the first treatment of King Arthur in English; poem is an English translation of a French adaptation of Geoffrey of Monmouth's *Historia,* which was written in Latin

1199-1216 Reign of John I, Richard's brother, who loses Normandy to Philip II of France

1215 King John signs the Magna Carta-a decree to protect feudal rights against royal abuse; establishes the idea that no one is above the law, even the king; establishes trial by jury

Historical Events	Related Literary Works
c. 1225 University at Cambridge is founded by students from Oxford, whose own founding is often placed at 1167	
1283 Edward I conquers Wales	
1296-1305 Scotland is militarily occupied by England; William Wallace commands Scottish resistance at battles of Stirling Bridge (1297) and Falkirk (1298)	
1300 1300s The Age of Chivalry, which began in the 1100s, flourishes; a code of conduct for knights becomes idealized as French romances are introduced into England	*Sir Gawain and the Green Knight*
1301 Edward of Caernarvon, the royal heir, becomes the first English Prince of Wales	
1314 Scots decisively defeat the English at Bannockburn	
1337 England's Edward III issues claim to French throne; Hundred Years' War between England and France begins	
1346 Edward, the Black Prince of Wales, the son of Edward III, defeats the French at Crécy	
1349 England is ravaged by the "Black Death," an epidemic of the bubonic plague	
1350-1450 Rise of English as a literary language in England, replacing French	*The Canterbury Tales* by Geoffrey Chaucer
1360 Edward III signs a peace treaty with the French; English kings continue to style themselves as kings of France	
1376-77 Edward, Black Prince of Wales, dies; his young son inherits the throne from Edward III as Richard II	
1381 Peasants' Revolt—possibly the most significant popular rebellion in English history—occurs; the revolt is suppressed and its leader, Wat Tyler, is killed by the Lord Mayor of London	*Piers Plowman* by William Langland
1388 As a result of the Black Death, Parliament enacts the Statutes of Laborers, to control prices, prevent laborers from reneging on their contracts, and force "the idle" to work	
1388-89 Lords Appellant lead "Merciless Parliament" to purge the government of Richard II's handpicked advisors and supporters	
1399 Richard II seizes the estate of his deceased uncle, John of Gaunt	
1399-1413 Henry, duke of Bolingbroke, son of John of Gaunt, revolts against Richard II, deposing him and reigning as Henry IV, first ruler of the House of Lancaster	
1400 1400 Richard II dies in Pontefract Castle, probably early this year	*Richard II* by William Shakespeare
1400-1409 Owen Glendower leads last Welsh revolts against England; English suppress uprisings in other regions too	
1411 St. Andrews University is founded in Scotland	
1415-20 Henry V defeats French at Battle of Agincourt; five years later, he signs Treaty of Troyes, designating him France's next king, and weds Catherine, daughter of French king Charles VI	*Henry V* by William Shakespeare
1422 Henry V dies of dysentery; his infant son, Henry VI, succeeds him as king of England	
1429-31 Joan of Arc has the French Dauphin crowned as Charles VII at Rheims; she is later captured, sold to the English, put on trial, found guilty by a mainly English court, and burned at the stake	

Historical Events	Related Literary Works
1453 English are expelled from most of France at the close of the Hundred Years' War; they retain the city of Calais.	
1455-85 War of the Roses, a civil war between Houses of Lancaster and York, begins; the most intense fighting occurs in 1460-61	
1461-83 Edward of York defeats the Lancastrians, wins throne, and reigns as Edward IV	
1477-91 William Caxton produces first books in England with printing press	*Le Morte D'Arthur* by Sir Thomas Malory
1483 Richard, duke of Gloucester, usurps throne from Edward V and is crowned Richard III	
1485 Richard III is killed in battle at Bosworth Field; Henry Tudor claims English throne, reigning as Henry VII, the first Tudor king	

THE EVOLUTION OF BRITISH GOVERNMENT FROM ABSOLUTE MONARCHY TO THE REGENCY

Although the Tudor dynasty was to be short-lived, its five monarchs left an indelible stamp on the nation. Shrewd, ruthless, and intensely proud of their Welsh ancestry, the Tudors ruled as absolute monarchs. They demonstrated a sure grasp of practical politics, not hesitating to introduce shattering political and religious changes. After the Tudors came the Stuart dynasty, whose rule saw the eruption of civil war. Tension had mounted between monarchs determined to reign absolutely and parliaments that were equally determined not to renounce any hard-won legislative powers. The defeat of the Royalists in the Civil War led to the outlawing of the monarchy altogether. From 1649 to 1660, England was ruled as a republic, whose government collapsed after the death its leader Oliver Cromwell, which led to the restoration of the monarchy under the Stuart king Charles II. The king, however, had less authority than before. Parliamentary power grew, leading to the rise of England's first political parties, the Whigs and Tories, and to interference with the royal succession in 1688 when William of Orange and Mary took the throne at Parliament's behest. The following year, a Bill of Rights affirmed parliamentary power, limited the authority of the Crown, and established a constitutional monarchy. Accepting the redefinition of their roles, the remaining Stuart monarchs and the succeeding Hanoverians ruled without interruption, except for a brief interval when the madness of George III necessitated that his eldest son, the Prince of Wales, reign in his stead as Prince Regent.

1500

1485-1509 Reign of Henry VII, who strengthens Crown against nobles; lingering Yorkist threat is eliiminated

1487 Court of the Star Chamber gains prominence as a court with special prerogatives; later it becomes greatly hated because of perceived abuses (this court is abolished in 1640)

1509 Accession of Henry VIII

1534 Act of Supremacy makes Henry VIII head of the Church of England, sanctioning an authority he has exercised for more than two years

1536 and 1542-43 Acts of Union integrate England and Wales; Wales first receives representation in Parliament in 1542

Historical Events	Related Literary Works
1547-53 Reign of Edward VI, who pursues his father's religious policy, upholding England's break with the Roman Catholic Church	
1553-58 Reign of Mary I, who attempts to reinstate Catholicism as the official religion	
1558 England loses city of Calais, its last possession in France	
1558-1603 Reign of Elizabeth I, the "Virgin Queen," who resolves sectarian disputes and fosters strong sense of English nationalism	*The Faerie Queene* by Edmund Spenser
1567 Mary, queen of Scots, flees intrigue in Scotland and seeks refuge in England	
1571 English government uncovers the Ridolfi Plot, in which Spanish troops have planned to invade England and replace Elizabeth with her Catholic cousin, Mary, queen of Scots.	
1577 Raphael Holinshed writes *The Chronicles of England, Scotland, and Ireland*	*Henry V, King Lear, Macbeth,* and *Richard II* by William Shakespeare
1587 Mary, queen of Scots, is executed after English agents discover evidence of a plot, led by Anthony Babington, to kill Queen Elizabeth and place Mary on the throne	
1588 English ships defeat the Spanish Armada, badly crippled by a storm at sea; victory breaks Spanish monopoly on empire, opens up the New World to English settlement	
1599-1601 Elizabeth I puts down revolt led by the earl of Essex, who is later executed	
1603-25 After death of Elizabeth I, James I (James VI of Scotland, son of Mary, queen of Scots) succeeds to English throne; James becomes the first monarch to rule England and Scotland simultaneously	*Macbeth* by William Shakespeare
1605 Band of Catholics attempt to kill James and blow up English Parliament in the Gunpowder Plot	
1610-15 Arbella Stuart, cousin to James I, secretly weds William Seymour, who has distant claim to throne; imprisoned in the Tower of London, Arbella commits suicide	*The Duchess of Malfi* by John Webster
1625 Accession of Charles I	
1628 Parliament forces Charles I to sign Petition of Right, broadening Parliament's powers	
1629 Charles I dissolves Parliament, attempts to govern without a legislative body	
1640-53 "Long Parliament" convenes, places severe curbs on royal power	
1641 Publication of *Leviathan* by Thomas Hobbes, which justifies absolute sovereignty and authoritarian government	
1642-46 Charles I rejects parliamentary demands; Civil War erupts between Cavaliers or Royalists, who favor king, and Roundheads (named for their short, cropped hair), who favor Parliamentarians; Puritans dominate in Roundhead army	*Paradise Lost* by John Milton
1642-60 Puritans close theaters; players go "underground," performing short entertainments, called drolls	
1648-52 Second Civil War ends in conquest of Ireland and Scotland by armies of Oliver Cromwell	
1649 Charles I is executed by the Parliamentarians	
1649-60 Interregnum, period of republican rule, has two main phases: in 1649-53 England operates as a Commonwealth run by a Council of State, in 1653-58 as a Protectorate under Oliver Cromwell	

1600

1650

Historical Events	Related Literary Works
1660 Under protection of General George Monck, a free election is held and Parliament recalls the late king's eldest son to be monarch; Charles II is restored to the English throne	*The Diary of Samuel Pepys* by Samuel Pepys
1678-81 The Popish Plot—Titus Oates alleges a Jesuit plot to murder Charles II, leading to the arrest and execution of suspected conspirators; the Whig party attempts to bar the king's brother, James, from the royal succession, in favor of Charles's illegitimate son, the duke of Monmouth.	
1680s Whigs and Tories struggle for dominance of Parliament	"Mac Flecknoe" by John Dryden
1685 Accession of Catholic James II	
1688 "Glorious Revolution"—in a bloodless revolt, English Protestants offer crown to William of Orange and his wife Mary, Protestant daughter of James II	
1689 Bill of Rights limits the Crown's authority, affirms parliamentary power, and establishes a constitutional monarchy	*An Essay on Human Understanding* by John Locke
1702-14 Reign of Queen Anne, the last Stuart monarch	*Gulliver's Travels* by Jonathan Swift
1707 Act of Union between England and Scotland—the nation becomes known as Great Britain	
1711 Joseph Addison and Sir Richard Steele found *The Spectator*, a periodical that offers cultural commentary and moral instruction while avoiding partisan politics	*The Spectator* by Joseph Addison and Sir Richard Steele
1714 George I of the House of Hanover succeeds Queen Anne	
1715 First Jacobite uprising—The "Old Pretender," son of James II, supported by Scots, attempts to regain throne	*Rob Roy* by Sir Walter Scott
1721-42 Robert Walpole becomes first British Prime Minister, serving George I and George II	*Gulliver's Travels* by Jonathan Swift; *The Beggar's Opera* by John Gay
1727-60 Reign of George II	
1745-46 Second Jacobite uprising—"Bonnie Prince" Charlie attempts to reclaim British throne for the Stuarts; he is defeated at Culloden and flees to France; Scottish resistance ends	*The History of Tom Jones* by Henry Fielding
1760 Accession of George III	
1776 Scotland's Adam Smith writes *Wealth of Nations*, promotes laissez faire and free trade, attacks mercantile doctrine of the day	
1780 Gordon Riots—Parliament passes a Roman Catholic relief measure, leading to mob violence and widespread destruction, including burning of Newgate Prison; riots deal severe blow to parliamentary reform	*Songs of Innocence and of Experience* by William Blake
1788 George III suffers outbreak of madness, recovers but leaves political administration under William Pitt the Younger intact	
1810 George III suffers incurable attack of madness	
1811-20 The Regency—George, Prince of Wales, becomes Prince Regent by parliamentary act, ruling England in his father's stead; after death of George III, the Prince Regent is crowned George IV	

1700

1750

1800

RELIGION AND SCIENCE

The Roman Catholic Church would dominate many aspects of British and Irish daily life from c. 200 C.E., when it was introduced to Britain, until 1534 when Henry VIII broke with Rome and established the Church of England, with himself as its head. This break with Rome was the culmination of centuries of conflict between England's Church and its kings. (As early as 1170, Thomas Becket was assassinated on the orders of King Henry II because Henry objected to Becket's attempts to keep the Church independent of royal control.) The Protestant Reformation spread throughout England, Scotland, and Wales, but failed to take root in Ireland, a circumstance that led to centuries of bitter religious strife. England remained committed to Protestantism, despite Mary I's attempt to reestablish Catholicism as the official religion, the later accession of the Catholic Stuart monarchs, and bloody civil wars. In fact, anti-Catholic feeling continued to run high, with Catholics being denied the right to worship as they chose or to hold public office. The late eighteenth and early nineteenth centuries saw a relaxation of this rigid stance with the passage of the Catholic Relief Act and the Catholic Emancipation Act of 1829. Meanwhile, the Enlightenment—an intellectual movement exploring new political, scientific, and philosophic developmentsCbegan to spread throughout Europe in the late seventeenth century, contributing to works as diverse as the gravitational theories of Sir Isaac Newton and the philosophical essays of John Locke.

Historical Events	Related Literary Works
200 c. 200 C.E. Christianity is introduced into Britain	
313 C.E. Christianity is tolerated throughout the Roman Empire, including Britain; Roman emperor Constantine issues Edict of Milan, saying Christianity can be practiced freely	
mid 400s The missionary St. Patrick converts Gaelic kings to Christianity in Ireland	
c. 450 Anglo-Saxon pagans invade; Christian church in Britain is driven underground	
c. 450-64 Christian church in Britain veers from Roman practices, develops Celtic identity	
597 St. Augustine preaches Christianity to the Anglo-Saxons; conversion begins	
664 Synod of Whitby resolves differences between Celtic and Roman Catholic Church, makes Roman practices supreme throughout England	
731 In his *Historia ecclesiastica* (Ecclesiastical History of the English People), Bede documents the spread of Christianity in England	
1000 1170 Assassination of Thomas Becket, Archbishop of Canterbury	*The Canterbury Tales* by Geoffrey Chaucer
1290 Edward I decrees that all Jews be expelled from England	
1380s Disciples of John Wyclif start translating Holy Scripture into English	*Piers Plowman* by William Langland
1500 1500s Intellectual movement known as humanism, emphasizing dignity of the individual and worth of earthly life, takes hold in England	*Dr. Faustus* by Christopher Marlowe
1534-40 Protestant Reformation begins in England; Henry VIII breaks with the Roman Catholic Church and establishes the Church of England, with himself as head	*Pilgrim's Progress* by John Bunyan

Historical Events	Related Literary Works
1535 Sir Thomas More is executed for refusing to swear an oath to the new royal succession or acknowledge Henry VIII as supreme head of the English Church	
1547-53 Protestantism becomes the official faith in England during reign of Edward VI	
1553-58 Reign of Mary I, eldest daughter of Henry VIII; "Bloody" Mary marries Philip II of Spain and attempts to restore Catholicism as official faith of England; Protestant heretics are burned, increasing anti-Spanish and anti-Catholic feelings	
1558-59 Elizabeth I ascends throne, establishes moderate Protestantism as official religion of England; Elizabethan Act of Supremacy demands oath from officials acknowledging queen as supreme head of the church	*The Faerie Queene* by Edmund Spenser
1560 John Knox, leader of Scottish Protestant Reformation and a follower of Martin Luther and John Calvin, becomes minister of High Kirk (Church) of St. Giles in Edinburgh	
1563 Elizabethan Settlement is completed; its Thirty-nine Articles define the Anglican Church doctrine	
1569 German humanist Heinrich Cornelius Agrippa von Nettesheim's work *Of the Vanitie and uncertaintie of artes and sciences*, which repudiates science and the occult, is translated into English	*Dr. Faustus* by Christopher Marlowe
1570 Louis Lavater writes *De Spectris*, which becomes one of the most prominent Protestant books on supernatural occurrences	*The Mysteries of Udolpho* by Ann Radcliffe
1580s Changes in the English theater—professional actors replace clerics and other amateurs; Protestant authorities in London are hostile to professional actors and regard new playhouses as sinful places	
1580s-1603 Parliamentary Acts fine Catholics , 20 for each absence from Anglican services; English Catholic priests are arrested as traitors if found in the country; 183 Catholics are executed for their faith	
1593-94 William Harrington and Henry Donne are arrested after Harrington is suspected of being a Catholic priest; under torture, Donne betrays Harrington, who is later disembowelled; Donne dies of plague	*Songs and Sonnets* by John Donne
1600 1605 Catholic extremists are accused of trying to blow up the Houses of Parliament in the Gunpowder Plot	*Macbeth* by William Shakespeare
1611 Publication of the King James Bible	
1614 John Donne, a Catholic, converts and becomes an Anglican priest	*Songs and Sonnets* by John Donne
1642-48 Religious differences between the Royalists (mainly Catholic) and Roundheads (Protestants, mainly Puritan) help fuel the English Civil War	*Paradise Lost* by John Milton
1650 1650s Expansion of Puritan sects during the Interregnum years	*Paradise Lost* by John Milton; *The Pilgrim's Progress* by John Bunyan
1655-56 Rabbi Menasseh Ben Israel petitions the Commonwealth of England on the legal readmission of Jews into England; Whitehall Conference decides to allow Jews to reside in England "on an unofficial basis"	
1660 Authority of established Church of England is restored after accession of Charles II	
1661 John Bunyan is arrested for lay preaching and imprisoned for 12 years	*The Pilgrim's Progress* by John Bunyan

Historical Events	Related Literary Works
1662 Parliament reimposes Book of Common Prayer on all ministers and congregations; founding of the Royal Society for the Advancement of Science	
1664 Religious meetings that do not follow forms of the Church of England are declared illegal	
1673 Test Act prohibits non-Anglicans from holding public office	
1679-81 Exclusion crisis: Lord Shaftesbury introduces bills to exclude James, duke of York, from succession to the throne, on the grounds of James's Catholicism	"Mac Flecknoe" by John Dryden
1680s-90s Beginning of the Enlightenment—European movement exploring new philosophical, scientific, and political developments; movement celebrates reason and the power of people to improve the human condition	*Gulliver's Travels* by Jonathan Swift
1684-87 Isaac Newton proposes his laws of motion and theory of gravity	
1687 James II issues Declaration of Indulgence, suspending Test Act and penal laws against Catholics and Dissenters—those who refuse to worship in accordance with all the principles of the Anglican Church	
1689 Toleration Act grants religious freedom to Dissenters; Dissenters, Roman Catholics, and Jews are still excluded from political participation and from universities	
1690 John Locke proposes that the mind of newborn humans is a "tabula rasa" (blank slate), ideas are formed by experience, the mind uses words to stand for ideas, and all knowledge results from the interplay of ideas	*An Essay Concerning Human Understanding* by John Locke; *Pamela* by Samuel Richardson
1695 Penal laws forbid Catholics in Ireland from keeping weapons	
1700 1704 Act to Prevent the Further Growth of Popery prohibits Catholics from buying land, inheriting it from Protestants, or taking leases for more than 31 years	*Castle Rackrent* by Maria Edgeworth
1740s Methodist movement begins to grow rapidly, in opposition to the long-established practices of the Anglican Church	
1780s-90s The number of religious Dissenters or Nonconformists—so called because their beliefs did not conform to the tenets of the Church of England—increases among university students, especially those attending Cambridge; scientists conduct experiments involving electricity	*Frankenstein* by Mary Shelley
1787 Religious leaders argue that England cannot be a moral leader if slave trade continues; Thomas Clarkson founds Committee for Effecting the Abolition of the Slave Trade	*Songs of Innocence and of Experience* by William Blake
1800 1802 Sir Humphrey Davy delivers *A Discourse, Introductory to a Course of Lectures On Chemistry* at newly founded Royal Institution; Erasmus Darwin writes *The Temple of Nature*, a discussion on the origins of life	*Frankenstein* by Mary Shelley
1829 Catholic Emancipation Act eliminates most discrimination against Catholics in Britain and Ireland; Catholics can now hold all government offices except those of lord chancellor of England, lord lieutenant of Ireland, and the monarchy	

THE AGE OF EXPLORATION AND FOREIGN RELATIONS

England's Age of Exploration began in earnest with the founding of the Company of Merchant Adventurers during the later years of Edward VI's brief reign (1547-53). Until then, Portugal and Spain had been the dominant European explorers, launching naval expeditions that led to the discovery of the so-called New World in the late fifteenth century. Entering into this new enterprise with gusto, the English explored both Asia and the Americas. Francis Drake, one of Queen Elizabeth's favored courtiers, circumnavigated the globe and on his return was knighted by the queen herself on the deck of his ship, *The Golden Hind.* Another favorite, Sir Walter Raleigh, set out to establish a colony in North America at Roanoke. Meanwhile, England competed with its longtime enemy Spain and its new rival, the Netherlands, for commercial resources—including gold, ivory, spices, tea, and slaves—in Africa, India, and Asia. Much of the eighteenth century saw England at war with the Netherlands, France, Spain, and even its own colonies in North America. By the time the American colonies achieved independence, England had gained enough territory and wealth overseas to sustain this loss. A new threat surfaced in the last two decades of the eighteenth century during the French Revolution. Much of Europe felt exhilarated, then dismayed, by the Revolution, which gave rise to Napoleon Bonaparte and the Reign of Terror. In 1793 France declared war on Britain, beginning a fight that—save for a brief interval of peace in 1814Cwould persist for 22 years, until Napoleon's defeat by British and Allied troops at the Battle of Waterloo.

1500

1547-53 Reign of Edward VI; English Age of Exploration begins with the founding of the Company of Merchant Adventurers; English start to explore Asia and North America

1560s-90s English privateers conduct raids on Spanish ships; rivalry between the two nations mounts; English and Dutch piracy escalates in the Mediterranean Sea while banditry flourishes in northern Italy

The Mysteries of Udolpho by Ann Radcliffe; *The Spanish Tragedy* by Thomas Kyd

1570 Publication of Roger Ascham's treatise *The Schoolmaster*, which criticizes the Italian influence on English travelers

Volpone by Ben Jonson

1577-80 Francis Drake circumnavigates the globe and is knighted by Queen Elizabeth

1585-87 Sir Walter Raleigh attempts to establish Roanoke Colony; two attempts at colonization there founder

1588 England's victory in the Spanish Armada breaks Spanish monopoly on New World, opens it up to permanent English settlement

1599-1623 East India Company is founded, concentrates trade on the Indian subcontinent

1600

1600s-50s British build forts in West Africa and compete with Dutch and Portuguese for African gold and slaves

Oroonoko by Aphra Behn

1603 James I becomes king of England, supports explorations in the Americas, entertains hopes of empire

Antony and Cleopatra by William Shakespeare

1604 James I negotiates peace with Spain

1607 Jamestown settlement founded in Virginia colony

1623 East India Company begins to concentrate on trade with India

Historical Events	Related Literary Works
1650 1651-63 England passes Navigation Acts to enforce idea that colonies exist only to benefit mother country, restricts trade between colonies and other European nations	
1652-54 First Anglo-Dutch War: under Oliver Cromwell and naval strategist Admiral Robert Blake, England successfully challenges Dutch commercial preeminence	
1665-67 Second Anglo-Dutch War erupts after British navy attacks New Amsterdam in North America; war ends inconclusively; peace of Breda restores existing situation before conflict but allows England to retain New Amsterdam, later renamed New York	*The Diary of Samuel Pepys* by Samuel Pepys
1689-90 *Two Treatises of Government* by England's John Locke justifies revolution; it argues that government is bestowed by the consent of the governed; if their trust is broken, they have the right to withdraw power from their rulers	
1689-97 War of the League of Augsburg—European nations, including England, form secret league to restrain the territorial advances of France; Treaty of Ryswick compels France to surrender much of its territory in Lorraine	
1697 William Dampier sails to Australia, publishes *New Voyage round the World,* which renews British interest in the Pacific	*Gulliver's Travels* by Jonathan Swift
1700 1702-13 England engaged in War of Spanish Succession against France and Spain; John Churchill, duke of Marlborough, wins famous victory at Battle of Blenheim (1704)	
1709 East India Company achieves trade monopoly with China	*The Rape of the Lock* by Alexander Pope
1711 Britain negotiates a separate peace with France—conditions include France ceding territories such as Gibraltar and Minorca to Britain and giving up rights to African slave trade with Spanish South America; Britain becomes the world's leading naval, commercial, and colonial power	
1713-1807 Britain traffics in slaves, is considered world's largest slave trader	*Wuthering Heights* by Emily Brontë
1718 Parliament passes Transportation Act, allowing for punishment of criminals by exile to colonies	*Moll Flanders* by Daniel Defoe
1719-20 South Sea Company has trading privileges in the Americas, plans to take over three-fifths of the national debt; a speculation craze follows, the company collapses, thousands of investors are ruined	
1740-48 War of the Austrian Succession, France loses Louisburg in North America to the British, and the British lose Madras in India to the French in 1746, get it back in 1748	
1750 1756-57 After the governor of Bengal imprisons British soldiers in Black Hole of Calcutta, British retaliate with a punitive expedition led by Robert Clive; Clive wins control of Bengal at Battle of Plassey	
1756-63 Seven Years' War—Britain defeats France, gains sovereignty in North America by the conditions of the Peace of Paris	
1770s-1800s Abolitionist movement in Britain gathers momentum; Britain extends its rule over most of India	*Sense and Sensibility* by Jane Austen; *Songs of Innocence and of Experience* by William Blake
1772 Mansfield decision—Lord Mansfield rules that slavery is not legal within England	
1775-83 American War for Independence; Britain ultimately cedes the 13 colonies	*The Life of Samuel Johnson* by James Boswell

Historical Events	Related Literary Works
1781 Aboard the *Zong*, a slave-ship, 133 slaves are murdered by being thrown overboard, outraging abolitionists	
1784 East India Act places political activities of British East India Company under control of British government, leaves company's commercial activities relatively untouched	
1788 Dolben's Act limits number of slaves transported on ships	
1789-92 The French Revolution begins with the storming of the Bastille; English radicals enthusiastically support the uprising and hope for similar political changes at home	*Lyrical Ballads* by William Wordsworth and Samuel Taylor Coleridge; *A Vindication of the Rights of Woman* by Mary Wollstonecraft
1793-1815 Fearing the spread of the French Revolution, England wages war with France	
1805 British naval forces led by Admiral Horatio Nelson defeat French at the Battle of Trafalgar at Trafalgar	
1807 Britain outlaws the slave trade	
1812-15 War between Britain and the United States confirms American independence	
1814 Dutch cede Cape Town, South Africa, to the British; Paris falls to Allies (Britain, Russia, Prussia, and Austria) in Napoleonic Wars; Allies exile Napoleon to Elba and restore Louis XVIII to French throne, meet at Congress of Vienna to reorganize Europe	*Don Juan* by George Gordon, Lord Byron
1815 Napoleon escapes Elba and returns to France, gathering supporters; his "Hundred Days" of freedom end with his defeat at Waterloo by a combined British-Prussian force, led by the duke of Wellington	*Vanity Fair* by William Makepeace Thackeray
1823 Anti-Slavery Society forms; abolition achieved in the British Empire in 1834	

(margin: 1800)

IRISH SOCIAL AND POLITICAL HISTORY
FROM THE NORMAN INVASION TO THE ACT OF UNION

The relationship between Britain and Ireland has long been a thorny one, from the Anglo-Norman Invasion in 1170 to the present day. In 1171 Henry II, the first English king to personally appear in Ireland, established English lordship over the area, and colonization began. By the close of the thirteenth century England may have ruled as much as two-thirds of Ireland. It lost much of this power in succeeding years, but Henry VIII reestablished the authority of the English sovereign over Ireland in the early sixteenth century. In 1536 he gained recognition as head of the Church of Ireland and in 1541 as *king* (rather than *lord*) of Ireland. But, if they were obligated to acknowledge English political sovereignty, the Irish resisted the Protestantism that was spreading through Britain. Despite efforts by the Tudor monarchs, the Reformation failed to take root in Ireland, contributing to centuries of strife. Nor did the Irish cease to fight for their freedom from the English—rebellions and revolts flared throughout the sixteenth and seventeenth centuries. The Tudor monarchs meanwhile renewed efforts to colonize Ireland. In the mid-seventeenth century, Irish Catholics suffered a serious blow when Oliver Cromwell invaded and exiled Catholic landowners—who held 59 per cent of Irish land—to Connaught. After the Irish sided with England's king James II in the era of the Glorious Revolution of 1688, England confiscated more Irish lands and passed penal laws aimed at Irish Catholics. England's harshness towards Ireland did not abate until the passage of the Catholic Relief Acts in 1780. Following another failed Irish revolt in 1798, an Act of Union in 1800 brought Great Britain and Ireland together as the United Kingdom.

	Historical Events	Related Literary Works
1150	1169-72 Normans conquer Ireland	*The Táin (The Cattle Raid of Cooley)*
	1170-71 Earl of Pembroke ("Strongbow") and Norman army arrive in Ireland, capture Waterford, then Dublin, becomes lord of Leinster	
	c. 1170-1270 Colonization results in settlement of Irish rural areas and towns by Anglo-Normans	
	1171 England's Henry II arrives with license from the pope to invade Ireland to reform its Church; Henry accepts homage from Norman victors; Strongbow recognizes him as overlord of his Irish holdings	
	1315-18 Edward Bruce of Scotland successfully invades Ireland, proclaims self King of Ireland; after his death in battle, Ireland once again falls under English rule	
	1366 England institutes Statute of Kilkenny, a series of repressive measures intended to prevent Anglo-Normans in Ireland from adopting the ways of the Irish	
	1394-95, 1399 Richard II travels to Ireland to suppress Irish revolts; his second expedition is inconclusive and he loses his own throne as a result of his absence from England	*Richard II* by William Shakespeare
	1449-50 Richard, duke of York, wins submission of many Irish and English rebels to English king (Henry VI)	
	1495 Poynings' Law decrees that the Irish Parliament obtain prior English approval of proposed legislation	
1500	1536 Henry VIII is officially made head of the Church of Ireland	
	1541 Irish Parliament first acknowledges England's king, Henry VIII, to also be king of Ireland	
	1553-58 Mary I of England confiscates the property of Irish rebels, giving it to loyal English lords in Ireland	
	1556 The English settle colonists in Ireland, establish "plantations" there	
	1558 Accession of Elizabeth I; Protestant Reformation fails to take root in Ireland	
	1570s Private colonization efforts undertaken by English in Ireland	
	1570s-1603 Elizabeth I suppresses numerous Irish revolts; English law enforced throughout Ireland, especially in Ulster	*Henry V* by William Shakespeare
	1590s Plantation scheme results in mass transfer of Irish lands to English; government plans to settle 20,000 English on lands in Munster; Munster revolts; truce in 1599	
	1594-1607 English suppress rebellion in Ulster. The leaders of the revolts, the earls of Tyrone and Tyrconnell, flee Ireland	
1600	1641 Catholic-Gaelic rebellion calling for the return of confiscated lands erupts; Old English Catholics in Ireland join movement; uprising ravages crops, precipitates famine; Catholics hold 59 per cent of land in Ireland	
	1649-50 Oliver Cromwell arrives in Ireland, captures Drogheda and Wexford; he levies harsh repressive measures against Catholics and exiles Catholic landowners to Connaught, a mountainous region in western Ireland	
	1688-91 Irish support James II in his bid to keep English throne; after his defeat, England confiscates more Irish lands	
	1690-91 William of Orange defeats Catholic armies at Aughrim, they surrender at Limerick; key leaders of Catholic Ireland emigrate	

	Historical Events	Related Literary Works
	1695-1728 Series of penal laws aimed at Catholics are enacted, banning Catholics from teaching, voting, and so forth.	*Castle Rackrent* by Maria Edgeworth
1700	1713 Jonathan Swift is made Dean of St. Patrick's Cathedral in Dublin	
	1714 Catholics hold only 7 per cent of land in Ireland	
	1724 Jonathan Swift helps direct Irish resistance to English oppression, publishing—under the pseudonym "M. B. Drapier"—a series of letters to persuade the Irish to refuse 100,000 in copper coins from England that would debase their own currency	
	1729 Swift publishes *A Modest Proposal,* a satiric essay that critiques authorities by offering an absurd solution to Irish poverty—breed poor children for profit and for food	
	1740 Potato crisis stimulates widespread famine	
	1774-93 Catholic Relief Acts allow Irish Catholics to buy land, practice law, vote, and marry Protestants	*The Rivals* by Richard Brinsley Sheridan
	1780 Colonial trade opens to Irish goods	
	1782 Irish Parliament wins legislative independence from Britain	*Castle Rackrent* by Maria Edgeworth
	1796-98 Inspired by the French Revolution, the United Irishmen plot and stage a revolt, which ultimately fails; its leaders are imprisoned or executed.	
1800	1800 Act of Union between Great Britain and Ireland forms the United Kingdom and abolishes the Irish Parliament	
	1803 Robert Emmet leads failed uprising against the English, is executed along with 21 others	
	1829 Final Catholic Relief Act allows Catholics to sit in parliament	

INDUSTRIAL AND RURAL ENGLAND FROM THE ENCLOSURE ACTS TO THE FIRST RAILWAYS

The very topography of Great Britain underwent rapid change in the mid-eighteenth century when Parliament started passing enclosure acts. Fields and farmlands that had been common grounds for public use were partitioned off into private holdings. The Industrial Revolution, which began in the 1760s with James Watt's invention of the steam engine, transformed England even more dramatically; machinery replaced hand-labor, factories supplanted cottage industries, and mill towns sprang up in northern and central England, to which a new laboring population migrated in search of work. Slums and tenements arose to house these migrant laborers, whose workday tended to begin at dawn and end well after dusk. Although the passage of such measures as Hanway's Act in 1788 and the Health and Morals of Apprentices Acts in 1802 alleviated some of the worst abuses in the urban labor force, workers' situations remained generally grim. Because of the Napoleonic Wars and England's associated fear of revolution, workers' attempts to better their situation met with little success. Efforts to protest abysmal working conditions and meager pay tended to meet with harsh punishment by the law, even when the protest was essentially peaceful.

	Historical Events	Related Literary Works
1750	1750-1830 Parliament passes more than 4,000 enclosure acts transferring communal land into private holdings	*Lyrical Ballads* by William Wordsworth and Samuel Taylor Coleridge; *She Stoops to Conquer* by Oliver Goldsmith
	1760 Jonas Hanway and D. Porter campaign against the exploitation of children as chimney Sweeps	
	1760s-1830s Industrial Revolution transforms England from an agrarian, handicraft-based economy into an urban, machine-driven economy; factories and mill towns are built in northern and central England	*Frankenstein* by Mary Shelley
	1760-71 Duke of Bridgewater constructs canals to link industrial centers to local coal field and each other	
	1766-90 Textile industry is revolutionized by invention of the spinning jenny, spinning frame, and power loom	
	1769 James Watt patents the steam engine	
	1788 Hanways Act for the Better Regulation of Chimney Sweepers and Their Apprentices is passed, raising the minimum age for sweeps to eight years old and adding a primitive licensing system	*Songs of Innocence and of Experience* by William Blake
1800	1802 Health and Morals of Apprentices Act restricts child labor in cotton mills to those over nine years old and reduces workday to 12 hours	
	1811 Luddite riots—textile workers protest the new machinery in the textile industry, smash textile looms	
	1815 Corn Laws passed to protect British agricultural interests from competition by raising tariff on imported grain	
	1819 August 16—100,000 millworkers gather in St. Peters Field to demonstrate for higher wages and listen to Radical speaker Henry Hunt; armed militia, who arrive to arrest Hunt, kill 11 and injure hundreds; incident is called "Peterloo" Massacre	"England in 1819" and Other Poems by Percy Bysshe Shelley; *The Mask of Anarchy*
	1825 The Darlington and Stockton Railway, the worlds first passenger railway, opens; trade unions are legalized	
	1830 Liverpool and Manchester Railway opens	

SOCIAL CHANGE AND FAMILY LIFE
FROM THE BIRTH OF ELIZABETH I TO THE REFORM BILL

From the sixteenth to the eighteenth century, family life in England changed significantly. Henry VIII's bid to divorce Catherine of Aragon and marry Anne Boleyn redefined even a royal marriage as a dissoluble institution. In the end, the marriage was annulled. Resistance to divorce continued for centuries. On the whole, divorce by private parliamentary act was seldom granted to any but the wealthy and titled during the seventeenth and eighteenth centuries. Other family dynamics, however, were changing: relationships between parents and children became less formal and rigid as the nuclear family and the individual gained importance in the 1700s. These transitions developed against a background of broader social changes: London grew into a true metropolis and cultural capital of the world; the crime rate rose, as did the number of laws to combat crime; schools were established and literacy grew; and, in the aftermath of the Industrial Revolution, an increasingly populous and influential middle class—merchants, inventors, and investors—developed and eventually wrested power from the landed aristocracy. There was a parliamentary act that marked this shift in power—the Reform Bill of 1832.

Historical Events	Related Literary Works
1500	
1533 English Ecclesiastical Court under Thomas Cranmer, archbishop of Canterbury, grants Henry VIII an ecclesiastical annulment to marry Anne Boleyn; Elizabeth I is born	
1540-1660 Elders usually control family unit, dictating children's marital partner; children show deference to parental authority	*King Lear* by William Shakespeare
1591 Sir Philip Sidney revives popularity of the Petrarchan love sonnet in England with *Astrophel and Stella*	*Songs and Sonnets* by John Donne
1600 1601 Poor Law Act mandates that each parish be responsible for its own poor	*King Lear* by William Shakespeare
1604 Canonical law prohibits remarriage of divorced persons	
1643-45 John Milton publishes pamphlets arguing for the legitimacy of divorce and *Areopagitica* to defend freedom of the press	
1650 1650-1750 Growth of public sphere—London becomes a social metropolis; newspapers, coffee houses, and clubs are established	*The Rape of the Lock* by Alexander Pope; *The Spectator* by Joseph Addison and Sir Richard Steele; *The Way of the World* by William Congreve
1650s Puritans impose anti-recreational measures, suppressing stage plays, horseracing, and brothels; adultery becomes punishable by death	
1660-85 King Charles II becomes notorious for keeping mistresses, court life is licentious; extramarital affairs increase in the upper class	*Diary of Samuel Pepys* by Samuel Pepys; *Moll Flanders* by Daniel Defoe; *The Way of the World* by William Congreve
1660s-1800 Child-rearing theories range from Locke's argument that at birth children's minds are "blank slates" to be shaped by adults, to Rousseau's view that children are naturally good but corrupted by society	*An Essay on Human Understanding* by John Locke; *Songs of Innocence and of Experience* by William Blake
1665-66 The Great Plague, the last major epidemic of bubonic plague, breaks out; the Great Fire of London consumes much of the city	*The Diary of Samuel Pepys* by Samuel Pepys
1670-1799 Private Act of Parliament grants 130 divorces, most instituted by husbands	
1688-1820 London underworld develops; capital statutes increase; death becomes the usual sentence for theft of property	*The Beggar's Opera* by John Gay; *Moll Flanders* by Daniel Defoe
1700 1700s Nuclear family gains importance; young people are increasingly granted the right to approve or refuse potential spouses	*The Rivals* by Richard Brinsley Sheridan; *She Stoops to Conquer* by Oliver Goldsmith; *The Way of the World* by William Congreve; *Wuthering Heights* by Emily Brontë
1700s-50s Gradual rise in literacy occurs; by mid-century, about half of England's married couples can sign their names; many of the elite have their children educated at home	*Pamela* by Samuel Richardson; *Tom Jones* by Henry Fielding
1702 First daily newspaper in England appears	
1705 Richard "Beau" Nash arrives in Bath, reorganizes and renovates city into thriving "spa" town	*The Rivals* by Richard Brinsley Sheridan
1724 Prostitutes abound in London; Society for the Suppression of Vice tries to close down brothels	*Moll Flanders* by Daniel Defoe
1724-25 Arrests and executions of the thief Jack Sheppard and the crime organizer Jonathan Wild take place at Tyburn	*The Beggar's Opera* by John Gay
1736-1760s Gentleman's clubs become the rage, serving as gambling dens, places of intellectual exchange, sources of patronage	
1739 Captain Thomas Coram establishes London's Foundling Hospital	*Tom Jones* by Henry Fielding
1750 1750s-1820s Medieval revival gathers momentum, manifesting itself in art, architecture, and literature; the "bluestockings" —intellectual women—organize social gatherings to discuss intellectual matters	*The Eve of St. Agnes* by John Keats; *Don Juan* by George Gordon, Lord Byron; *The Mysteries of Udolpho* by Ann Radcliffe

Historical Events	Related Literary Works
1753 In an attempt to curb clandestine marriages, Parliament passes the Hardwicke Marriage Act, making parental consent mandatory for everyone under the age of 21	*She Stoops to Conquer* by Oliver Goldsmith
1755 Samuel Johnson publishes the first *Dictionary of the English Language*	*The Life of Samuel Johnson* by James Boswell
1760s-1830s As Industrial Revolution progresses, a new class of urban workers and middle-class investors emerges	*Middlemarch* by George Eliot:;*Vanity Fair* by William Makepeace Thackeray
1776 First comprehensive bill for parliamentary reform is proposed and rejected	
1783 Public hangings at Tyburn cease	
1780s-90s Romantic movement begins in art and literature, highlighting the individual's emotional responses to nature and society	*Lyrical Ballads* by William Wordsworth and Samuel Taylor Coleridge;*Songs of Innocence and Experience* by William Blake
1790s-1815 Apprehensive over revolution in France, the British government prohibits public meetings, suspends habeas corpus, and tries reformers as war criminals; cost of living increases, especially for the poor	
1789 French Revolution inspires philosophical inquiries into the rights of men—and women	*A Vindication of the Rights of Woman* by Mary Wollstonecraft
1800s Repressive attitudes toward sexual activity increase; segregation of the sexes results	*The Eve of St. Agnes* by John Keats
1811-20 Regency period—upper classes enjoy prosperity and leisure; country-house life flourishes	*Sense and Sensibility* by Jane Austen
1820s-30s Gradual shift in power from the landed aristocrats to the mercantile middle class takes place	
1826 Sir Robert Peel, Home Secretary, reforms penal code	
1832 Passage of the first Reform Bill extends voting franchise and eliminates "rotten boroughs" in parliamentary elections	*Middlemarch* by George Eliot; *Vanity Fair* by William Makepeace Thackeray

1800

Contents by Title

Contents by Title

Contents by Author

Contents by Author

Photo Credits

Cleopatra, (standing near rug), painting by J. L. Gerome. New York Public Library Picture Collection. —From William Shakespeare's *Antony and Cleopatra,* from Gallerie des Personnages . . ., photograph. Special Collections Library, University of Michigan. Reproduced by permission. —Vikings (disembarking on the Normandy coast), engraving. The Bettmann Archive. —Viking Ships, engraving. Hulton Getty/Archive Photos. Reproduced by permission. —*The Begger's Opera,* Act III, engraving by William Hogarth. Burstein Collection/CORBIS. Reproduced by permission. —Prisoner sitting in cell at Newgate Prison. Corbis Corporation. Reproduced by permission. —Beowulf, Paet Pegarde, manuscript page, Middle English script. Photograph. —Beowulf shears the head off Grendel, illustration. Corbis-Bettmann. Reproduced by permission. —Pilgrim's steps leading up to Trinity Chapel in Canterbury Cathedral, photograph. Angelo Hornak/CORBIS. Reproduced by permission. —Death register, tallying victims of the Great Plague of London, photograph. Nicole Duplaix/CORBIS. Reproduced by permission. —Great Fire of London, lithograph by Sir Christopher Wren. Historical Picture Archive/CORBIS. Reproduced by permission. —Byron, Lord George Gordon (sitting, wearing dressing gown, slippers), illustration. The Bettmann Archive. Reproduced by permission. —Slave market at Constantinople, painting. Corbis Corporation. Reproduced by permission. —A title page for *The Historie of the Damnable Life*

and Deserved Death of Doctor John Faustus, 1592 edition, translated into english by P. F. Gent, facsimile reproduced in Ghent. Universite Faculte de Philosophi et Lettres. Recueil de Travaux Publies. no. 24, p. xxiii, photograph. The Department of Rare Books and Special Collections, The University of Michigan Library. Reproduced by permission.

From a theatre production of "Doctor Faustus" by Christopher Marlowe, Marne Maitland as Faustus and Peter Coke as Mephistopheles, Mephistopheles is standing behind Faustus who is holding a opened book, photograph. CORBIS/Hulton-Deutsch Collection. Reproduced by permission. —Title page from the book *The Duchess of Malfi* by John Webster, 1623. Photograph. —Helen Mirren, as Duchess, holding hands with Bob Hoskins, a scene from the theatrical production of *The Duchess of Malfi.* Hulton-Deutsch Collection/CORBIS. Reproduced by permission. —Shelley, Percy B. (facing front, shirt open at neck), engraving. The Library of Congress. —Political cartoon "Manchester Heroes," depicting the massacre by soldiers of people who have come to listen to speeches calling for the reform of Parliament, women and children falling beneath the hooves and swords, St. Peter's Fields. Hulton Getty/Archive Photos. Reproduced by permission. —Locke, John (oval format, three-quarter view from his left), painting. The Library of Congress. —Issac Newton, presiding at Royal Society meeting, in Cane Court, engraving. Bettmann/CORBIS. Reproduced by permission.

Title page from *Faerie Queen,* first edition, by Edmund Spenser, printed for William Ponsonbie. Bettmann/CORBIS. Reproduced by permission. —Queen Elizabeth visiting Hunsdon House, engraving. Bettmann/CORBIS. Reproduced by permission.

Vitruvian Man, famous drawing of nude man with arms extended at different angles, within a circle, drawing by Leonardo da Vinci (ink and paper have turned brownish). Corbis Corporation. Reproduced by permission. —Brock, Charles E., illustrator. From an illustration in *Gulliver's Travels,* by Jonathan Swift. Macmillan and Co., 1894. —Brock, Charles E., illustrator. From an illustration in *Gulliver's Travels,* by Jonathan Swift. Macmillan and Co., 1894. —Sir Thomas Erpingham rallying troops at Battle of Agincourt, engraving. Bettmann/CORBIS. Reproduced by permission. —Branagh, Kenneth and Brian Blessed (on battleground), in the movie *Henry V,* 1989, photograph. The Kobal Collection. Reproduced by permission. —Stuart, Prince Charles Edward (oval format, red uniform), engraving. Archive Photos, Inc. Reproduced by permission. —Unwed mothers turning over their babies to nurse in Founding Hospital, illustration. Bettmann/CORBIS. Reproduced by permission. —Scene from *King Lear,* illustration by Robert Smirke. —Scene from *King Lear,* illustration by Robert Smirke. —Johnson, Samuel (wearing curled wig, dark clothing, coarse features), engraving by Charles Townley. The Library of Congress. —Fireworks celebrating the end of the Seven Years' War, in London. Bettmann/CORBIS. Reproduced by permission. —From an illustration for Samuel Taylor Coleridge's *The Rime of the Ancient Mariner* illustrated by Gustave Dore. Dover Publications, 1970. Copyright 1970 by Dover Publications, Inc. All rights reserved. Reproduced by permission of the publisher.

Tintern Abbey, illustration. Archive Photos, Inc. Reproduced by permission. —From a illustration of William Shakespeare's *Macbeth.* Macbeth and Lady Macbeth are holding each other as the witches look on, that appeared in Amédée Pichot book Galerie des personnages de Shakespeare . . ., Paris, 1844, p. 33, photograph. Reproduced by the permission of the Department of Rare Books and Special Collections Library, University of Michigan Library. Reproduced by permission. —The Gun Powder Conspiracy, illustration. Bettmann/CORBIS. Reproduced by permission. —"Mac Flecknoe—A Satyr," poem by John Dryden, manuscript page. —Thomas Shadwell, photograph. Michael Nicholson/CORBIS. Reproduced by permission. —Victorian woman, reading to girl, illustration. Hulton-Deutsch Collection/CORBIS. Reproduced by permission. —*A Harlot's Progress Plate 1: Ensnared by a Procuress,* engraving by William Hogarth. Burstein Collection/CORBIS. Reproduced by permission. —Robin Wright, as Moll Flanders, in the 1995 film *Moll Flanders,* directed by Pen Densham, photograph MGM. The Kobal Collection. Reproduced by permission. —King Arthur, Tapestry. Francis G. Mayer/CORBIS. Reproduced by permission. —Interior of gothic church, looking east, National Gallery Collection; by kind permission of the Trustees of the National Gallery, London/CORBIS. Reproduced by permission. —Carisbroooke Castle, phototgraph. Abbie Enock; Travel Ink/CORBIS. Reproduced by permission. —Behn, Aphra (pearl necklace, hair in sausage curls), engraving. —Savigny, as Oroonoko, illustration. Hulton-Deutsch Collection/CORBIS. Reproduced by permission. —Pamela writing in dressing room, engraving by Louis Truchy. Historical Picture Archive/CORBIS. Reproduced by permission.

Title page from *An Apology for the Life of Mrs. Shamela Andrews,* by Henry Fielding. Special Collections Library, The University of Michigan. Reproduced by permission. —Engraving of Michael and Gabriel having battle with Satan and his Angels, Messiah on his chariot descending from the clouds, from *The Riverside Milton,* edited by Roy Flannagan. Copyright 2000 by Houghton Mifflin Company. —Michael leading Adam and Eve from Paradise, with his fiery sword behind him, Cherubs, above, taking their places to stand guard, from *The Riverside Milton,* edited by Roy Flannagan. Copyright 2000 by Houghton Mifflin Company. Reproduced by permission of the publisher. —Wat Tyler, being dragged to his death, photograph. Bettmann/CORBIS. Reproduced by permission. —Title page from Wm. Langlands *Piers Plowman,* Special Collections Library, The University of Michigan. Reproduced by permission. —John Bunyan, in Bedford Jail, reciting portions of *The Pilgrim's Progress* to his friends. Bettmann/CORBIS. Reproduced by permission. —Frontispiece and title page from *The Pilgrim's Progress* by John Bunyan. Corbis Corporation. Reproduced by permission. —Richard II, meeting peasants, manuscript illumination. Archivo Iconografico, S. A./CORBIS. Reproduced by permission. —Bernhard, Matt with others, in a scene from a theater production of William Shakespeare's *Richard II,* photograph by Ken

Holmes. Copyright GreenStage. Reproduced by permission. —Roman Baths, photograph. Bob Krist/CORBIS. Reproduced by permission. —Dueling scenes from 18th century manual, photograph. Bettmann/CORBIS. Reproduced by permission. —Neeson, Liam and Andrew Keir (on horseback with troops), in the movie *Rob Roy,* 1995, photograph by Tom Collins. The Kobal Collection. Copyright 1995 United Artists Pictures Inc. Reproduced by permission. —Stronachlachar Hotel on Loch Katrine, photograph. Alan Towse, Ecoscene/CORBIS. Reproduced by permission.

Kate Winslett far left, Emma Thompson (far right), two unidentified actresses, seated on blanket having a picnic, from the movie version of *Sense and Sensibility,* written by Jane Austen. The Kobal Collection. Reproduced by permission. —Wedding banquet, photograph. Leonard de Selva/CORBIS. Reproduced by permission. —Lillie Langtry, scene from the theatrical production of *She Stoops to Conquer.* Hulton-Deutsch Collection/CORBIS. Reproduced by permission. —Lady and Suitor, print by Dupin. Historical Picture Archive/CORBIS. Reproduced by permission. —King Arthur and the Knights of the Round Table, illustration. Archive Photos. Reproduced by permission. —13th century Venetian manuscript page, depicting knights dueling for lady's hand. Tomsich, Gustavo/CORBIS. Reproduced by permission. —Donne, John (1573-1631), Writers, Effigies, St. Pau'ls Cathedral, photograph. Adam Woolfitt/CORBIS. Reproduced by permission. —Queen Elizabeth knighting Sir Francis Drake, on board the *Golden Hind,* at Deptford, engraving by F. Fraenkel, from drawing by Sir John Gilbert. Baldwin H. Ward & Kathryn C. Ward/CORBIS. Reproduced by permission. —Blake, William, illustrator. From an illustration in William Blake at the Huntington, by Robert N. Essick. Harry N. Abrams Inc., Publishers, and The Henry E. Huntington Library and Art Gallery, 1994. Copyright 1994. The Henry E. Huntington Library and Art Gallery. —*The Chimney Sweep,* by Jonathan Eastman Johnson. Christies Images/CORBIS. Reproduced by permission.

Ferdinand and Isabella of Spain, print. Historical Picture Archive/CORBIS. Reproduced by permission. —Fleet of the Spanish Armada, hand-tinted illustration. Bettmann/CORBIS Reproduced by permission. —Steele, Sir Richard (in oval frame, long curled wig), engraving. The Library of Congress. —Addison, Joseph (body turned to his left), print. —Queen Maeve, image. Mary Evans Picture Library. Reproduced by permission. —Queen Maeve and the Druid, Druid warning Maeve about Cuchulain, image. Mary Evans Picture Library. Reproduced by permission. —Godwin, Mary Wollstonecraft, (profile), illustration. Corbis Bettmann. Reproduced by permission. —Women in French Revolution invade assembly demanding death penalty for members of the aristocracy, Woodcut. Bettmann/CORBIS. Reproduced by permission. —Kingsley, Ben (with unidentified man and Paul Scofield) in *Volpone,* photograph. Copyright Donald Cooper/PHOTOSTAGE. Reproduced by permission. —Tree-lined gardens at Royal Palace of St. James. Histroical Picture Archive/CORBIS. Reproduced by permission. —Fritz Weaver, standing behind Nancy Wickwire, in a scene from the film *The Way of the World.* Bettmann/CORBIS. Reproduced by permission. —Brontë Family Parsonage, photograph. Patrick Ward/CORBIS. Reproduced by permission. —Farmhouses on Yorkshire Moors, photograph. Patrcik Ward/CORBIS. Reproduced by permission.

Antony and Cleopatra

by

William Shakespeare

THE LITERARY WORK

A play set primarily in Egypt and Italy during the 30s B.C.E.; written c. 1606-07; published in 1623.

SYNOPSIS

Octavian (or Octavius) Caesar and Mark Antony rule the Roman world in an uneasy alliance that falls apart when Antony pursues a love affair with Cleopatra, queen of Egypt.

Scholars believe that Shakespeare wrote *Antony and Cleopatra* in late 1606 or early 1607, shortly after writing **King Lear** and **Macbeth** (also covered in *WLAIT 3: British and Irish Literature and Its Times*). Shakespeare, then in his early forties, had been a working playwright for about a decade and a half. The most ambitious of the three plays that the playwright based on Roman history (the other two being *Coriolanus* and *Julius Caesar*), *Antony and Cleopatra* spans a wider range of time and space than any of Shakespeare's works, compressing 12 years into action that shifts rapidly among Egypt, Italy, Greece, and other sites in the Mediterranean world. Though set in these far-flung places, the play invokes a foundation myth of the British themselves. According to this myth, Rome's founder, Aeneas, had a descendant, Brut or Brit (hence the name Britain), who led survivors of the Trojan War from Rome north to found London, or New Troy. By Shakespeare's day this myth had become entrenched. Thus, many of the English saw themselves as successors to Troy and as descendants of the Roman empire.

Events in History at the Time the Play Takes Place

Collapse of the Roman Republic. In the century before the birth of Christ, Rome's system of republican government began to disintegrate as a series of strong military leaders struggled over political power and the ever-growing financial rewards that came with it. Vast sums of money were waiting to be made by Roman governors of the areas that had fallen under Rome's control beginning in the third century B.C.E. With this huge financial incentive, the traditional Roman ideals of public service and senatorial rule gradually gave way to self-interest and rule by force.

By mid-century, the rising star of Roman politics was Julius Caesar, who made his fortune by becoming governor, in 61 B.C.E., of the province of Spain and, a few years later, of Cisalpine and Transalpine Gaul (today's northern Italy and southern France). Caesar had obtained his lucrative governorships by allying himself with the two richest generals of the day, Crassus and Pompey the Great. Together, these three military strongmen made up the so-called "first triumvirate" (*triumvir* being Latin for one of three men who share political office). According to their agreement, Pompey would govern Spain, Caesar would rule Gaul (he immediately began conquering new territory here), and Crassus would oversee the eastern province of Asia (roughly today's Turkey). As customary, the alliance was sealed by political marriages, most notably Pompey's to Caesar's daughter Julia.

In 54 B.C.E., however, Julia died. The following year Crassus led a rash expedition against Parthia, an empire roughly comprising today's Iran and Iraq. Crassus was captured and killed in the fray, leaving Caesar and Pompey to share power. Without the link of marriage, however, there was little to preserve the alliance of these two generals. By 49 B.C.E. Pompey had won control of the Senate in Rome, and Caesar's supporters were forced to flee the city. Among these supporters was young Mark Antony, a lieutenant of Caesar's in the earlier Gallic campaign. Caesar marched on Rome from Gaul, and civil war broke out between the two generals and their supporters.

CLEOPATRA'S NOSE

~

Historians argue about whether or not Cleopatra was physically attractive. The seventeenth-century philosopher Blaise Pascal observed that if Cleopatra's nose had been shorter, world history would have turned out very differently. In other words, if the Egyptian queen had been less attractive, the careers of Julius Caesar, Mark Antony, and Octavian Caesar would have followed different paths, and Rome may never have become an empire. To be sure, Shakespeare's play takes place at a momentous time in Roman history—the end of republican rule and the beginning of imperial rule. At the time, there was some question about where the center of this empire would be—would it be in Rome, or if Cleopatra had her way, in Alexandria? Clearly she wielded a degree of personal power that made this a possibility. The Greek historian Plutarch (c. 50 C.E.-120 C.E.) attributes her ability to captivate Antony not so much by to beauty as to her intelligence, wit, and charm:

> Now her beauty, as it is reported, was not so passing as unmatchable of other women, nor yet such as upon present view did enamour men with her; but so sweet was her company and conversation that a man could not possibly but be taken. And, besides her beauty, the good grace she had to talk and discourse, her courteous nature that tempered her words and deeds was a spur that pricked to the quick. Furthermore, besides all these, her voice and words were marvellous pleasant; for her tongue was an instrument of music to divers sports and pastimes. . . . (Plutarch in Neill, p. 333)

Civil war. The struggle between Caesar and Pompey was fought in a series of battles that ranged over the entire breadth of the Roman world. Pompey had a huge advantage in resources, with large and experienced armies in both Spain and the eastern provinces of Greece and Asia. However, Caesar's force, though far smaller, was closer to Italy—and faster, because Caesar had trained his men to move very rapidly in his earlier campaigns. With Antony's help, Caesar drove Pompey from Italy in a two-month lightning campaign. Then, leaving Antony in charge of Italy, Caesar moved quickly to Spain and defeated Pompey's forces there, before pursuing Pompey to Greece. The decisive battle was fought in Greece at Pharsalus in 48 B.C.E., where Pompey was again defeated. With Caesar in pursuit, Pompey fled once more, this time to Egypt, where he was murdered by two men hoping to win Caesar's favor.

Cleopatra and Egypt. Though nominally an independent country, Egypt and its rulers, the Ptolemies, had been dominated by Rome since the middle of the second century B.C.E. Pompey fled there because he had struck up a political alliance with Egypt's King Ptolemy XIII, who was embroiled at the time in a struggle for power with his sister-bride and co-ruler, Cleopatra VII. After Caesar arrived in pursuit of Pompey (who had been assassinated four days earlier), the 21-year-old queen approached him, determined to win over the victor in the civil war, since he was likely to be Rome's new ruler. Caesar, at this time in his mid-fifties, took her as his lover, and the two lived for a short time in the royal palace. Later she bore a son whom she and others acknowledged as Caesar's, calling him Caesarion ("Little Caesar"). Caesar defeated and killed Ptolemy XIII and confirmed Cleopatra as queen of Egypt. In his lifetime, Julius Caesar would act as personal patron to Cleopatra. Later, Caesar's descendant Octavian (called Octavius Caesar in Shakespeare's play) won sole rule of Rome, and made Egypt an imperial rather than a senatorial province, thereby placing it and its wealth under his direct control rather than that of the Senate.

Its fertile fields watered by the yearly flood of the Nile, ancient Egypt was an immensely wealthy land, of high value to the Roman world: for centuries, Egypt would supply much of the Roman Empire's wheat. High value was also placed on the spices and precious metals that came from Egypt. This practical value was matched by the aura of exotic mystery that enshrouded its ancient culture. For the early Ro-

From the painting, *Cleopatra and Caesar,* 1866, by Jean-Léon Gérôme.

mans, as for the Elizabethans, Egypt symbolized passion and romance. For both cultures, however, this association also had a dark side, with connotations of decadence and self-indulgence. It was considered "the night side of nature, passionate, cruel, superstitious, barbaric, dissolute" (Frye in Rose, p. 116).

Coins of the era show Cleopatra to have had a broad forehead, a sensitive mouth, a distinctive nose, and a determined chin. A daughter of the Ptolemy dynasty, she was not, as is often assumed, Egyptian, but rather of Macedonian (Greek) descent. Cleopatra did, however, learn Egyptian ways. Furthermore, she contrived to restore the glory of her dynasty in Egypt by ingratiating herself to her Roman overlords and re-

covering the lost dominions of Syria and Palestine. Thus, her interest in Caesar and his would-be successor Antony had an unadulterated political edge to it.

Caesar's assassination. After leaving Egypt, Caesar returned to Rome and celebrated a magnificent triumph (the ancient victory procession of Roman tradition). The civil war dragged on, however, with Pompey's sons rallying the dead leader's troops and supporters. After defeating Pompeian forces in Africa at Thapsus (46 B.C.E.), Caesar put down a rebellion in Spain led by Pompey's eldest son, who died in defeat in the war's bloodiest battle at Munda in late 45 B.C.E. Having finally consolidated his control of Rome, Caesar returned again and assumed dictatorial control for life. Caesar planned a large expedition against Parthia to avenge the defeat of Crassus, but within a few months, before he could mount the expedition, he was assassinated in the famous conspiracy on the Ides of March (March 15), 44 B.C.E. Cleopatra is said to have been in Rome at the time. She returned to Egypt and awaited the emergence of Caesar's successor.

CAESAR'S LEGACY

Roman tradition had always despised monarchy as a form of government. Caesar's assassins, a group of senators that included some of his friends and supporters, believed that they were taking the only step possible to restore Rome's republican government and steer her away from autocratic rule by a single all-powerful figure. In assuming such power as he now had, Caesar had stepped perilously close to the line separating autocratic from republican rule. He had begun styling himself *imperator* or "commander," a temporary title that only the Senate was traditionally allowed to bestow. Later, this word would take on the meaning of "emperor." Then, about a month before the assassination, Caesar had himself appointed "dictator in perpetuity," again appropriating a traditional title (the Roman office of dictator was a temporary emergency measure, strictly limited in its powers) in a dangerously nontraditional way. At the same time, Caesar, always popular among the people of Rome, made great progress in attacking some of Rome's most pressing social problems, and apparently ended the political chaos that had dominated events of the past decades. With the return of this chaos after his assassination, the example of autocratic rule Caesar had provided grew ever more attractive. By capitalizing on Romans' war-weariness, Octavian Caesar was able to overcome their traditional hatred of monarchy and thus to achieve what his great-uncle had not: sole rule of Rome. He became the first emperor of the Roman realm, taking the lofty new name Augustus (meaning "exalted" and "sacred") in 27 B.C.E.

The second triumvirate. Caesar's assassins spared his chief lieutenant, Mark Antony, who occupied the high office of consul at the time of the murder. Taking the initiative, Antony was able to stir popular opinion against the assassins, two of whom—Brutus and Cassius—were forced to retreat to Greece. While Antony then pursued another conspirator to Cisalpine Gaul, his domi-

nance was undercut in Rome by the orator Cicero, who attacked Antony in a series of speeches to the Senate. Antony, said Cicero repeatedly, should have been murdered too. Meanwhile, in the Senate, Cicero promoted Julius Caesar's young heir, his great-nephew and adopted son Octavian. With senatorial support, Octavian—still not yet 20 years old—defeated Antony in battle in Gaul. Antony then retreated, but he was joined by another old partisan of Julius Caesar's, Lepidus. Growing aware that the Senate was merely using him to control Antony, Octavian then allied himself with Antony and Lepidus, leaving the Senate no choice but to ratify the alliance legally, creating the so-called second triumvirate.

Reverting to a practice commonly employed by Roman strongmen before Julius Caesar, the three immediately issued death warrants for their enemies, arresting and executing some 300 senators and 2,000 other Roman citizens. Julius Caesar had been famous for clemency toward his enemies, some of whom had thus survived to conspire in his murder. From the standpoint of a would-be autocrat, such leniency was a mistake that the careful Octavian would not repeat on his climb to supreme power. Antony and Octavian then pursued the republican leaders Brutus and Cassius to Greece, defeating them at Philippi in Macedonia (42 B.C.E.), whereupon the two defeated leaders committed suicide in traditional Roman fashion, by falling on their swords.

Lepidus, a feeble man whose place in the triumvirate was due to simple chance, was given the relatively unimportant province of Spain. Real power was divided between Octavian, who took charge of Italy and most of the west, and Antony, who assumed responsibility for the eastern provinces and a planned campaign against the Parthians. Proceeding to Tarsus, a city on the southeastern coast of today's Turkey, Antony heard reports that Cleopatra had supported Brutus and Cassius. When he summoned her from Egypt, the young queen quickly cleared herself of the accusation and proceeded to charm Antony. Returning with her to her capital, Alexandria, Antony spent the winter of 41-40 B.C.E. there as her lover. At the time he was about 40 years old; she was 28. Their affair, though interrupted, would last for 11 years and produce three children. Some historians maintain that Antony and Cleopatra entered into an Egyptian marriage; if so, it was invalid in Rome, whose law forbade citizens to marry foreigners.

Early in 40 B.C.E. Antony was forced to return to Italy when, unbeknownst to him, his wife Fulvia and brother Lucius attempted to lead a revolt against Octavian. At the same time, word came that Parthia had invaded Roman territory in Syria. Octavian quickly suppressed Fulvia and Lucius's revolt and drove the two from Rome. Arriving in Italy, Antony met Octavian, and the triumvirs reaffirmed their alliance; to cement the pact, Antony married Octavian's sister Octavia (Fulvia having died in the interim). They also concluded a treaty with Pompey the Great's surviving son, Sextus Pompeius (the Pompey of *Antony and Cleopatra*), whose naval dominance had allowed him to attack Roman shipping. In 36 B.C.E. Octavian and Lepidus, aided by Octavian's skilled admiral Agrippa, destroyed Pompey's fleet in a battle near Sicily. Lepidus then tried to win a larger share of the power, but his own troops refused to back him. Octavian spared Lepidus's life but forced him to retire; no longer would Lepidus be a weak but buffering presence between Antony and Octavian.

Defeat and suicide. In the meantime, Antony returned to the east, campaigning in Greece, from where he sent Octavia back to Italy. He himself then went on to Syria, where he planned to campaign against the Parthians—and to meet Cleopatra again. They resumed their affair, encouraged by strong political as well as personal motives. Cleopatra needed Roman support to safeguard her government and fulfill her hopes of expanding Egyptian power, while Antony drew heavily on Egypt's wealth to mount his Parthian campaign. The campaign itself, however, met with defeat, and Antony was forced to retreat from Syria with heavy casualties (36 B.C.E.). His affair with Cleopatra would nonetheless continue, lasting for the remaining years of their lives, during which the couple would live together. Not only did Antony acknowledge his two sons and daughter by Cleopatra, in 34 B.C.E. he also declared Caesarion was her legitimate son by Julius Caesar. The declaration was an obvious provocation to Octavian, Caesar's adopted son. Antony also divided up much of the eastern Roman Empire among Cleopatra, Caesarion, and his own children by her.

Meanwhile, Antony's relations with Octavian foundered, and each made the population under his control swear separate allegiance to himself. Octavian mounted an increasing propaganda campaign, in which he portrayed Antony as having betrayed Roman traditions under the influence of Cleopatra's "charms and amorous poisons" (Plutarch in Neill, p. 344). In this campaign, Octavian blamed Antony for bestowing Roman possessions on a foreign woman, and claimed that Antony intended to move the center of the empire from Rome to Alexandria. The triumvirate was allowed to officially expire in 33 B.C.E., and the next year Antony divorced Octavia. This was the final straw for Octavian, who declared war not directly on Antony, but on Cleopatra. Octavian stressed the threat that Egypt posed to Rome, holding up Antony as an example of a Roman already corrupted by Egyptian mores.

"A VALIANT AND WISE CAPTAIN"

Plutarch, the Greek historian and biographer, who wrote his account some 150 years after the actual events, was Shakespeare's major source for *Antony and Cleopatra*. He offers a high opinion of Antony's abilities as a soldier and leader:

> Antonius did many acts of a valiant and wise captain . . . and he was also thought a worthy man of all the soldiers in the Roman's camp. . . . Furthermore, things that seem intolerable in other men, as to boast commonly, to jest with one or other, to drink like a good fellow with everybody, to sit with soldiers when they dine, and to eat and drink with them soldierlike—it is incredible what wonderful love it won him amongst them. . . . But besides all this, that which most procured his rising and advancement was his liberality, who gave all to the soldiers and kept nothing for himself. (Plutarch in Neill, pp. 327-28)

Later historians concur that Antony was an able general, an admirable leader, and far more likeable that his rival Octavian. His positive traits endeared him to Rome, but the historical Antony also had qualities perceived as faults, at least by supporters of his rival, Octavian, whose interpretation of events was the one lodged in records of the times. The philosopher and orator Cicero, for one, characterized Antony as lustful and drunken; others called him coarse and half-educated. Antony has been especially faulted for the cruelty with which he engaged in "prescriptions," or the execution of political enemies. Together he and Octavian arranged a massacre of their political foes, executing some 2,000 business and army men and 300 senators. Though not the sole perpetrator of the massacre, Antony was particularly blamed for the murder of Cicero, whose severed head and hands he had publicly displayed.

Octavian crossed to Actium in Greek waters, where Antony had deployed his and Cleopatra's combined navies. Cleopatra herself appeared,

Antony and Cleopatra

An engraving of Antony and Cleopatra.

much to the chagrin of the Romans, who thought the battlefield was hardly a place for a woman, a view that Cleopatra ignored. Octavian and Agrippa had several hundred ships, as did Antony and Cleopatra. Likewise, both sides had tens of thousands of infantry. In the end, Agrippa managed to blockade Antony and Cleopatra's combined forces. A naval battle was fought at Actium, where on September 2, 31 B.C.E., Agrippa's expertise led to a decisive defeat of the lovers' forces, and they fled to Alexandria. Cleopatra broke through the blockade and made for the Egyptian capital, as did Antony, with only about a fourth of the fleet. In Antony's absence, his forces surrendered, Octavian won the battle, and Actium, lost before it was fought, went down in history as a pivotal battle, for it determined that the ancient Roman world would be ruled from Rome, not from the east. As for the two lovers, they remained in Egypt for nearly a year. There are differing accounts of exactly what transpired after Actium. A number of histories say Octavian pursued Antony, who fought and briefly defeated Octavian's front line in Egypt; but Antony suffered too many liabilities to continue waging war, among them the defection of his troops (Mommsen, p. 79). In retrospect, the contest had been decided at Actium, whose loss portended the two lovers' defeat. In the summer of 30 B.C.E., while still at large, they both committed suicide.

The Play in Focus

Plot summary. The play opens in Egypt in 40 B.C.E., four years after Julius Caesar's assassination. Two of Antony's soldiers are complaining that his infatuation with Cleopatra has made him less manly and caused him to neglect his duty. Antony and Cleopatra enter, and her whimsical domination of him seems to confirm the soldiers' complaints; messengers have arrived from Rome, and Antony seems uninterested in what they have to say. After Cleopatra's loyal maid, Charmian, consults a soothsayer (who tells her she will outlive her mistress), Cleopatra and Antony receive another messenger, who tells them of Fulvia's revolt with Antony's brother Lucius against Octavius (the play's "Caesar"). Moments later Antony, this time alone, receives another messenger, who informs him that Fulvia has died. Antony tells his right-hand man Enobarbus that the news compels his return to Rome, for the message also says that Sextus Pompeius (Pompey in the play) is challenging Caesar at sea. Antony and Cleopatra quarrel violently about his departure as he tells her of Fulvia's death.

In Rome, Caesar and Lepidus discuss news of Antony's affair with Cleopatra—Caesar unfavorably describes him as "not more manlike / Than Cleopatra, nor the Queen of Ptolemy / More womanly than he" (Shakespeare, *Antony and Cleopatra,* 1.4.5-7). A brief scene in Egypt reveals Cleopatra's boredom without Antony, then the scene shifts to Sicily, where Pompey and his advisors plan their campaign against the triumvirs. Both Pompey and Caesar have assumed that Antony is still in Egypt, but we see Pompey's impressed surprise on hearing of his imminent arrival in Rome, as he comments that Antony's "soldiership is twice the other twain" (*Antony and Cleopatra,* 2.1.33-34).

After a quarrel that the flattering Lepidus smoothes over, Antony and Caesar reconfirm their alliance by agreeing that Antony will marry Octavia, and the triumvirs prepare to open negotiations with Pompey. Enobarbus, Agrippa, and Maecenas—the right-hand men of Antony, Caesar, and Pompey, respectively—talk together, and Enobarbus describes the splendor of Antony and Cleopatra's first meeting, at which Cleopatra arrived on a magnificent barge. Antony will have to leave her after marrying Octavia, Maecenas says. Enobarbus's response is emphatic:

> Never. He will not.
> Age cannot wither her, nor custom stale
> Her infinite variety. Other women cloy

The appetites they feed, but she makes hungry
Where most she satisfies.
(*Antony and Cleopatra*, 2.2.244-48)

In Egypt, Cleopatra receives the news of the marriage with a violent explosion of temper at the messenger who brings it.

The triumvirs sign the treaty with Pompey; then the generals and their staffs celebrate with repeated toasts before Caesar characteristically breaks up the party. Antony departs for Athens with Octavia, and we see Cleopatra treating kindly the same messenger she earlier abused—this time he has described Octavia as plain in appearance. In Athens, Antony learns that Caesar, ignoring the treaty with Pompey, has attacked him. Caesar has also publicly insulted Antony, who sends Octavia back to Italy to mediate between them while he prepares for war. Meanwhile, we learn, Caesar imprisons Lepidus and strips him of his position as triumvir.

In Rome, Caesar complains of the public honors and the Roman territory Antony has given Caesarion and Antony's own children by Cleopatra. Caesar is further angered by his sister Octavia's unceremonious arrival, which he takes as a humiliation for her and a political snub to himself. In Egypt, Enobarbus pleads with Cleopatra not to take part personally in the war to come, but to remain in Alexandria. Expressing surprise at the speed of Caesar's movements, Antony plans to meet him in a naval battle, knowing that his own naval strength is inferior but feeling that Caesar has deliberately challenged him to do so. Enobarbus objects that Antony is stronger than Caesar by land, and should therefore wait for a land battle, but Antony refuses.

In a series of brief scenes, we learn that Cleopatra's flagship has fled the battle, and that Antony has followed, leaving his leaderless crews to surrender. The dejected Cleopatra begs Antony's forgiveness, saying she had no idea he would follow her ship. "Egypt," he answers, "thou knew'st too well / My heart was to thy rudder tied by th' strings, / And thou shouldst tow me after" (*Antony and Cleopatra*, 3.11.56-58). Yet one of her tears, he continues, is worth more than all they have lost by the defeat.

Caesar rejects Antony's terms of surrender, instead sending an ambassador to Cleopatra promising leniency if she betrays Antony. Antony has the ambassador whipped. Enobarbus joins the many soldiers and officers who have deserted Antony, but regrets his decision when Antony generously sends Enobarbus's abandoned spoils along to Caesar's camp. As war resumes, Antony's land forces win a brief victory, but dared once

more into a reckless sea battle, he sees his ships surrender to Caesar. Thinking Cleopatra has betrayed him by accepting Caesar's offer, he resolves to kill her. At this point, Cleopatra, knowing of his anger and hoping to dissuade him from murder, sends a messenger with word of her death.

SOOTHSAYERS, DEMONS, SPIRITS, AND ANGELS

In both Plutarch's *Life of Antony* and Shakespeare's *Antony and Cleopatra*, Mark Antony is approached by a soothsayer who warns him against Octavian Caesar. In both the Roman and Elizabethan worlds, many people believed that the world was inhabited by spirits that interfered in human affairs. The word for such a spirit in Greek (the language Plutarch wrote in) is *daimon,* from which comes the English "demon." A major difference, however, is that in pre-Christian Rome, these "demons" were not necessarily viewed as evil. They were divinities that served as intermediaries between gods and humankind. Some of these demons would be assigned to an individual at birth to provide guidance in that person's intellectual and marital endeavors. In a passage Shakespeare followed closely, Plutarch tells of Antony's soothsayer warning him to keep as far away from young Octavian as he could: "Your guardian spirit," he warned Antony, "stands in awe of his, and although by itself it is proud and full of mettle, it becomes cowed and daunted in the presence of Caesar's" (Plutarch, p. 300).

Antony resolves to die, but his loyal servant Eros refuses to help him commit suicide, plunging his sword into himself instead. Antony then stabs himself, but does not do the job cleanly; as he lingers near death Cleopatra—now afraid that he will do exactly what he has in fact done—sends word that she is alive after all. She has Antony brought to the monument where she is hiding from Caesar, and there he dies in her arms. Afterward, Cleopatra pretends to negotiate with Caesar, but she merely wishes to buy time to arrange her own death, thus denying him the privilege of leading her through Rome in a triumph. She has a servant smuggle in several asps in a basket of figs, and dies after repeatedly clasping one of the poisonous serpents to her breast. Impressed by her resolve, Caesar orders the two lovers to be buried together.

The image of Rome and Egypt. In his depiction of these historical events, Shakespeare embroiders a theme that was present in the Roman view of them as well: the identification of Egypt with sensuality and femininity, and of Rome with discipline and manliness. Egypt is a place of feasting and drinking, a place where Cleopatra's servants (including eunuchs) continually banter in sexual terms, where gestures are grand and impulsive, and, above all, where the feminine quite literally rules. Rome, by contrast, is all male: serious, achieving, a place where big decisions are made. The only woman we see in the Roman world is the lifeless Octavia, who (like her brother) "is of a holy, cold, and / still conversation" (*Antony and Cleopatra,* 2.6.121-22). On stage, Egypt's laughter contrasts sharply with Rome's gravity, a fact that Cleopatra comments on with regard to Antony: "He was disposed to mirth; but on the sudden / A Roman thought hath struck him" (*Antony and Cleopatra,* 1.2.81-82). The two places represent separate views of the world, which are mutually exclusive. By contrasting the motivations of the play's characters, Shakespeare also explores these two conflicting worldviews and their clashing values.

VIEWS OF ROMAN WOMEN

~

There are strong-willed females in *Antony and Cleopatra,* just as there were in Roman history, though the women's public activity centered around that of the men in their lives. Scholars point to Roman women such as the famous Cornelia, daughter of the general Scipio Africanus, wife of the politician Tiberius Sempronius Gracchus, and mother of the famous reformers Tiberius and Gaius Gracchus. Educated, cultured, and powerful, she has been seen as a model of emancipated Roman womanhood. Yet, like the "dull" and "sober" Octavia (*Antony and Cleopatra,* 5.2.54,55), Cornelia is known because of the Roman men to whom she was daughter, wife, and mother. Similarly, Mark Antony's wife Fulvia leads a revolt—but in her husband's political interests, not her own. Perhaps one reason the Romans perceived Cleopatra as threatening was that (unlike Roman women) she enjoyed power without reference to a male figure; after the death of her brother, she ruled alone, manipulating Roman men as she needed for her own purposes. In fact, Octavian, who himself apparently never succumbed to Cleopatra's charms, is said to have incited the fighting spirit in his troops by warning them that if Cleopatra ruled the empire, they would lose male privileges.

Antony, earlier the epitome of the hard Roman warrior, is in the end impelled by his own passionate nature to embrace the softer world of Egypt. Caesar vividly recalls Antony's toughness in the Gallic campaigns that followed Julius Caesar's assassination: surviving on horse's urine and bark in the winter, Antony was able to eat "strange flesh / Which some did die to look on. And all this— / It wounds thine honor that I speak it now— / Was borne so like a soldier that thy cheek / So much as lanked [grew thin] not" (*Antony and Cleopatra,* 1.4.67-71). This description contrasts sharply with the sumptuous feasts that Enobarbus and others describe Antony enjoying in Egypt, where the lovers think nothing of laying out "eight wild boars roasted whole at a breakfast, / and but twelve persons there" (*Antony and Cleopatra,* 2.2.189-90). Later, Enobarbus calls Cleopatra herself Antony's "Egyptian dish" (*Antony and Cleopatra,* 2.6.125). After Antony's death, Cleopatra delivers a characteristically hyperbolic eulogy that brings to mind Caesar's earlier praise for the soldier Antony's wintry self-denial. Ironically Cleopatra's eulogy is couched in terms of limitless abundance: "His legs bestrid the ocean; his reared arm / Crested the world . . . . / For his bounty / There was no winter in't; an Antony it was / That grew the more by reaping" (*Antony and Cleopatra,* 5.2.83-89). Whereas the Roman view, embodied by the puritanical Octavius, sees Antony as the victim of a sad decline, the Egyptian view, exemplified by Cleopatra, sees him as triumphantly transcendent——not only of Roman custom, but of mortal limitations as well.

Cleopatra, too, finds transcendence in death, which is her paradoxically Roman moment. Throughout the play she is fickle and tempestuous: "I am quickly ill and well," she says during her first quarrel with Antony (*Antony and Cleopatra,* 1.3.72). This would certainly not be news to the messenger she alternately berates and flatters. Associated repeatedly with the changeable moon, symbol of inconstancy, as she prepares herself for death she changes her very nature: "My resolution's placed, and I have nothing / Of woman in me. Now from head to foot / I am marble-constant; now the fleeting moon / No planet is of mine" (*Antony and Cleopatra,* 5.2.239-41). Having transcended herself, in dying she transcends life itself and the sensual material world that contains it: "I have / Immortal longings in me. Now no more / The juice of Egypt's grape shall moist this lip. . . . / I am fire and air; my other elements / I give to baser life" (*Antony and Cleopatra,* 5.2.280-90).

SHAKESPEARE AND PLUTARCH

Most of the changes Shakespeare made to Plutarch's version of events are in the depiction of character, which Shakespeare heightened or softened for dramatic effect. For example, Plutarch portrays Octavia more favorably than Shakespeare does, and includes details that show Antony's often cruel side, which Shakespeare leaves out. But though Shakespeare changed some details of Plutarch's *Life of Antony*, he followed the Greek author very closely, often using the same or similar words as he had found in North's influential translation (see below). The most famous passage is Enobarbus's speech relating Cleopatra's arrival on her royal barge:

Plutarch	**Shakespeare**
. . . her barge . . . the poop whereof was of gold, the sails of purple, and the oars of silver, which kept stroke in rowing after the sound of the music of flutes. . . . And now for the person of herself: she was laid under a pavilion of cloth-of-gold of tissue, apparelled and attired like the goddess Venus commonly drawn in picture: and . . . on either hand of her, pretty fair boys apparelled as painters do set forth god Cupid, with litle fans in their hands, with which they fanned wind upon her. . . . (Plutarch in Neill, p. 332)	The barge she sat in, like a burnished throne, / Burned on the water; the poop was beaten gold; / Purple the sails, and so perfumed that / The winds were lovesick with them; the oars were silver, / Which to the tune of flutes kept stroke, and made / The water they beat to follow faster, / As amorous of their strokes. For her own person, / It beggared all description: she did lie / In her pavilion, cloth-of-gold of tissue, / O'erpicturing that Venus where we see the fancy outwork nature. On each side her / Stood pretty dimpled boys, like smiling cupids, / with divers-coloured fans, whose wind did seem / To glow the delicate cheeks which they did cool. . . . (*Antony and Cleopatra*, 2.2.201-14)

Sources and literary context. Antony and Cleopatra seem to have passed into literary legend almost the moment they died, along with the symbolic associations discussed above. For example, Virgil, the poet of Octavius Caesar's reign (after he took the title "Augustus"), makes use of the famous lovers in the *Aeneid* in order to unfavorably compare Antony with Aeneas, who (unlike Antony) resisted the charms of an African queen, Dido, and was not tempted from his duty (to found Rome). Augustus, also in contrast to Antony, manfully resisted the temptation, Virgil implies, and fulfilled his duty as Rome's (new) founder. Like any educated Elizabethan, Shakespeare was highly familiar with Virgil, and verbal echoes of the *Aeneid* appear frequently in *Antony and Cleopatra*.

Shakespeare's most important source for *Antony and Cleopatra*, however, was the Greek writer Plutarch (c. 50 C.E.-120 C.E.), whom he also used for *Julius Caesar, Coriolanus,* and several other plays. Plutarch was an immensely popular source in the Renaissance. More than any other single writer, it was Plutarch who shaped (not always with great accuracy) the Renaissance conception of the ancient world. His *Parallel Lives of the Greeks and the Romans,* of which the life of Antony is the longest, offers biographical sketches of great figures from Greek and Roman history, replete with vivid details and moralizing judgments. Shakespeare read Plutarch not in the original Greek, but in a 1579 translation by Sir Thomas North (which was in turn based on a French version of

1559 by Jacques Amyot). North's translation was also the source for other Elizabethan treatments of the Antony and Cleopatra story, such as the plays *Antonius* (1592), a translation by Mary Sidney of a French tragedy by Robert Garnier, and *Cleopatra* (1594) by Samuel Daniel, both of which also influenced Shakespeare's play. North's Plutarch was popular reading in Elizabethan England, and Shakespeare could count on at least part of his audience being familiar with many of the stories and characters from it.

Events in History at the Time the Play Was Written

James I of England. When Shakespeare wrote *Julius Caesar* (to which *Antony and Cleopatra* can be seen as a sequel) in 1599, the aging Queen Elizabeth reportedly expressed displeasure at the play's implications that regicide may have some justification. Scholars have suggested that this may be why Shakespeare avoided following *Julius Caesar* immediately with another Roman play. In 1603, however, Elizabeth died and James I, of the rival house of Stuart, became king of England. For James, the idea of empire had a special meaning. Styling himself "Emperor of Great Britain," the king wished to bring to his realm the same peace that Augustus had brought to the Roman world. The new king drew overt parallels between himself and Augustus (Octavian Caesar). His coronation medal proclaimed him Caesar Augustus of Britain, and for his triumphal arrival in London in March 1604 he had a ceremonial altar built with the inscription "Augustus novus" (designating himself the new Augustus). King James had imperial ambitions for Britain that bring to mind the Roman Empire. Over the objections of Parliament, James—who was in fact James VI of Scotland—supported the unification of Scotland and England (an ambition that would not be realized during his reign) and also the expansion of English interest in the Americas.

Both Augustus and James contended with powerful women, who in some respects resembled each other. James would probably have enjoyed several allusions in the play to some of the well-known foibles of his predecessor. Like Cleopatra, Elizabeth too had a magnificent royal barge; and when Cleopatra manhandles an unfortunate messenger or threatens to give her servant "bloody teeth" (*Antony and Cleopatra*, 1.5.70), aristocratic audience members would perhaps have been reminded that Elizabeth's behavior was rumored to have been similar at times.

However, the play can also be seen as evoking some of the English queen's strengths. For example, by dramatizing Cleopatra's political acumen, it may have evoked sentimental memories of Elizabeth's gifts too.

Reception. *Antony and Cleopatra* has evoked a wide range of critical response, from those who condemn it as one of Shakespeare's worst plays to those, with G. Wilson Knight, who rate it as "probably the subtlest and greatest play in Shakespeare" (Knight in Neill, p. 1). Early critics, measuring it against Aristotle's unities of time, place, and action, predictably enough tended to be highly unfavorable. Few, if any, of Shakespeare's plays disregard Aristotelian unities to the extent that *Antony and Cleopatra* does. In 1709 Nicholas Rowe (the first to divide the text into the scenes and acts in use today) cited its "great many faults" in this regard (Rowe in Wilders, p. 14). In the Romantic period, however, a new aesthetic permitted a greater appreciation of the play's sprawling action and immense stylistic variety. Keats called it his favorite among Shakespeare's plays, and for Coleridge too it was "the most wonderful." Coleridge, in an influential essay, led the way in bringing it back into popularity. Citing its "happy valiancy of style," he proclaimed that "*feliciter audax* [gracefully bold] is the motto for its style comparatively with his other works, even as it is the general motto of all of his works compared with those of other poets" (Coleridge in Brown, p. 29).

—Colin Wells

For More Information

Boardman, John, Jasper Griffin, and Oswyn Murray, eds. *The Roman World*. Oxford: Oxford University Press, 1986.

Brown, John Russell. *Shakespeare: Antony and Cleopatra: A Selection of Critical Essays*. London: Macmillan, 1968.

Grant, Michael. *History of Rome*. New York: Scribners, 1978.

Madelaine, Richard, ed. *Shakespeare in Production: Antony and Cleopatra*. Cambridge: Cambridge University Press, 1998.

Mommsen, Theodor. *A History of Rome under the Emperors*. Ed. Thomas Widemann. London: Routledge, 1996.

Neill, Michael, ed. *The Tragedy of Antony and Cleopatra*. Oxford: Oxford University Press, 1994.

Plutarch. *Plutarch's Lives of the Noble Grecians and Romans*. Vol. 6. Trans. Sir Thomas North. Stratford-Upon-Avon: Shakespeare Head Press, 1928.

Pomeroy, Sarah B. *Goddesses, Whores, Wives, and Slaves: Women in Classical Antiquity.* New York: Schocken, 1975.

Pugliatti, Paola. *Shakespeare the Historian.* London: Macmillan, 1996.

Rose, Mark, ed. *Twentieth Century Interpretations of Antony and Cleopatra: A Collection of Critical Essays.* Englewood Cliffs, N.J.: Prentice-Hall, 1977.

Shakespeare, William. *Antony and Cleopatra.* Ed. A. R. Braunmuller. New York: Penguin, 1999.

Wilders, John, ed. *Antony and Cleopatra,* by William Shakespeare. The Arden Shakespeare. London: Routledge, 1995.

The Battle of Maldon

as translated by
Michael Alexander

The author of *The Battle of Maldon* is unknown, though many have speculated that he may have participated in the battle itself. His intention was twofold—to document a specific battle between his English countrymen and an army of Viking invaders, and to celebrate the heroic virtues exhibited by the English soldiers in the face of annihilation. As such, he looked at both the immediate past (the poem was probably written very shortly after the battle itself in 991) and at the age-old cultural legacy of the Germanic warrior, the origins of which stretched far back to the time before the forefathers of the English crossed the English Channel in the fifth century to occupy a land inhabited by the Anglo-Saxons. The army that faced the Viking threat in 991 was no tribal band; the Anglo-Saxon society that suffered annual plundering by Scandinavian raiders was cultured and literate, and had been for many centuries. The English were known throughout Europe as exemplars of Christian scholarship and learning, in direct contrast to the Scandinavian raiders, who were despised as brutish and uncivilized pagans. Nevertheless, the English and their Viking foes descended from a common Germanic culture, and their codes of military conduct were very similar. Despite the firmly established Christianity of the English, on the battlefield they held fast to the same ancient standards of conduct that motivated their opponents—faithfulness to their leaders unto death, selfless bravery, and fierce delight in killing their foes.

THE POEM

A poem set in England on August 11, 991; probably written in the 990s; first published in 1726.

SYNOPSIS

The English lord Byrhtnoth leads an army to confront an invading force of Vikings; after a heroic battle, he is slain and the English army is defeated.

Events in History at the Time of the Poem

The Battle of Maldon in history and legend. In the late tenth century, England was accustomed to annual raids by organized groups of Scandinavian warriors. Such raids had in fact been going on for two centuries. Known now as Vikings, the warriors were called "Danes" in England at that time, even though their bases of operation extended beyond Denmark throughout Scandinavia. While often brutally violent, their raids were generally not conducted for purposes of conquest; rather, the Vikings sought gain—they would plunder towns and monasteries, taking away anything portable and valuable. Often they offered to spare the lives and property of their victims in exchange for gold, and the English frequently accepted these offers, since the Vikings had demonstrated a tendency to carry off not only material goods on their raids, but also

Vikings disembarking to raid England.

people to be sold as slaves. This was the threat facing Byrhtnoth, ealdorman of Essex, in the year 991. Leader of the English force, Byrhtnoth was the country's most powerful nobleman, next to the king.

The town of Maldon is situated northeast of London, a short distance up the Blackwater River (called the Pant in the poem) from the coast. Maldon is not mentioned in the poem (modern editors gave it the title *The Battle of Maldon*), but the town was probably the object of the Vikings' expedition. One of their raiding parties landed on Northey Island in the estuary of the river (between the ocean and Maldon), judging it to be a safe locus for collecting their forces at a prudent distance from the fortifications of Maldon. Upon learning of their arrival, Byrhtnoth, as the military commander of highest rank in the area, gathered an army and set out to confront them. His decision to face the invaders on foot was not out of the ordinary; the English army used cavalry in battle on occasion, but this was the exception rather than the rule. Another factor in his decision to lead foot soldiers may have been the marshy ground near the estuary, which would have made cavalry maneuvers difficult. The Vikings offered Byrhtnoth

peace in exchange for gold, which the defiant Byrhtnoth rejected. Instead the battle was joined and the English force utterly defeated. Its defeat had something to do with the readiness of Englishmen in the next several years to buy off raiders with the gold they sought, rather than oppose them militarily.

Other details about the battle are provided by Latin and English historical records, some roughly contemporary with the battle, and some from much later; the most important of these are the *Anglo-Saxon Chronicle* (a year-by-year account of noteworthy events kept by English monks throughout the later Anglo-Saxon era), the *Vita Oswaldi* (an early-eleventh-century biography of Oswald, bishop of York), and the *Liber Eliensis* (a late-twelfth-century history of the monastery of Ely). The date of the battle can be determined from a record of Byrhtnoth's death, recorded as August 11, 991, in an early-eleventh-century calendar of Winchester (Scragg, p. 10). The *Anglo-Saxon Chronicle* contains in its several versions a fair amount of corroborating information, although the discrepancies among these versions have caused historians to treat the Maldon material with caution. Still, we learn that the Viking forces may have been led by Olaf Tryggvason, who later became king of Norway and the hero of an Old Norse saga; one version of the chronicle reads for the year 993 (a mistake for 991):

> In this year Olaf came with 93 ships to Folkestone, and ravaged round about it, and then from there went to Sandwich, and so from there to Ipswich, and overran it all, and so to Maldon. And Ealdorman Byrhtnoth came against them there and with his army fought against them; and they killed the ealdorman there and gained control of the field.
>
> (Greenfield and Calder, pp. 150-51)

The chronicle reports the size of the Viking army to be variously 93 or 94 ships, which would make the number of Viking soldiers 2000 to 2500 (Gordon, p. 11). However, many scholars believe that these chronicle entries conflate the events of 991 with a later Viking raid, so the exact size of the invading force remains uncertain. The *Vita Oswaldi* tells of Byrhtnoth's unusual physical size, his advanced age, and his piety, and says that despite their victory the Vikings had barely enough men left after the battle to man their ships. The Viking leader, Olaf, had not yet converted to Christianity; thus, the battle did not just pit the English against an enemy, but a specifically pagan enemy.

However, the *Vita Oswaldi* also mistakes the date of the battle by several years. This and its highly exaggerated style have led to its information being treated with suspicion. The *Liber Eliensis* contains a lengthy account of the battle—or, rather, battles. It is possible that the author knew *The Battle of Maldon*, because of certain echoes of verbal detail, but in the *Eliensis* account the simple narrative of the poem describes not one battle but two; in the first, Byrhtnoth decisively defeats the Vikings, but then is persuaded to accept their challenge for a rematch four years later. The second battle lasts two weeks, and Byrhtnoth is killed along with his men. Clearly, the Battle of Maldon, while relatively insignificant in terms of the overall English-Viking strife, evolved over the years into an event emblematic of the English heroic ideal. Byrhtnoth may have lost the fight, but for the English he stood for all that was most noble and admirable about their national character.

Byrhtnoth. One of the remarkable things about *The Battle of Maldon* is how much we know about its hero, Byrhtnoth. He was an important man in late-tenth-century England, and had been for decades. He was an ealdorman, one of four or five noblemen in the kingdom whose stature was second only to the king. An ealdorman's authority was regional; Byrhtnoth was responsible for Essex, in which the town of Maldon was located. Thus, when the Vikings made their appearance there, it was only natural that he would be called upon to lead the defensive forces. He moved in the highest circles; his wife's sister married King Edmund of England around 945, and both his father and his father-in-law held the title of ealdorman of Essex before him. When he succeeded to the title in 956, he already had held an important political and military position in England for some time, and his 35 years of service as ealdorman would be markedly successful. He enjoyed the friendship of kings and other ealdormen, especially Aethelwine, ealdorman of East Anglia. Together they promoted the interests of the "reformed" monasteries, which practiced a stricter form of religious observance than had been common before a wave of reform swept through many English monasteries in the mid-tenth century, under the leadership of Dunstan, archbishop of Canterbury. In 975, when King Edgar (who had supported the reform movement) died, the then-senior ealdorman Aelfhere of Mercia sought to return the monasteries to their former,

less strict, mode of observance. Byrhtnoth and Aethelwine stood firm in opposition, and their victory in this matter (accomplished with the threat of violence) greatly increased Byrhtnoth's stature.

By 991, Aethelwine was gravely ill, and Byrhtnoth stood alone as the most powerful ealdorman in the kingdom (Scragg, p. 18). He was a wealthy landowner with estates throughout England, and was a great financial supporter of religious houses and monasteries. The monastery at Ely alone received 13 properties upon his death, and he also left generous bequests to Ramsey, Mersea, Abingdon, and Christ Church, Cambridge (Scragg, p. 15).

FROM THE *VITA OSWALDI*

After not many months had elapsed [since a battle in Wessex where the Danes were beaten], another heroic battle occurred in the east of this famous region. The renowned ealdorman, Byrhtnoth, was in charge of the battle along with his fellow warriors. Who can trust that his style is elegant enough to describe how gloriously, how bravely, how courageously Byrhtnoth urged his war captains into the battle-line? He stood there, his tall height eminent above the rest. . . . With his right hand he struck again and again, oblivious of the gray hair (like swan's down) on his head; for his alms and holy masses strengthened him. With his left hand he defended himself, mindless of his failing body; for his prayers and good deeds supported him. When he, the field's noble general, saw the enemy charging down and his own men fighting bravely—killing many of the enemy—he began to fight for his country with all his might. An uncountable number of the Danes and our own men fell; Byrhtnoth himself fell and the rest fled. The Danes were so incredibly wounded that they could scarcely man their boats. (Calder and Allen, pp. 188-89)

Thus, the Battle of Maldon, while strategically a relatively minor incident in the long history of English-Viking conflict, must have shocked the nation. Byrhtnoth was not young (he was probably about 65 when the battle took place), but he was the premier military commander that the English possessed, and his death was a great loss. The chroniclers of Ely and Ramsey made much of the battle and Byrhtnoth's martial valor; their exaggerations are perhaps to be expected, in view of his longstanding patronage of these monasteries. The Ely account says that after the battle, the Vikings took away Byrhtnoth's head in triumph. He was buried in the church at Ely (the tombs of important persons were often within the church), where he remained until 1769, when a building project disinterred his body. It was reported that no skull could be found, that the collarbone had been nearly cut in two, and

---

THE CHARACTER OF BYRHTNOTH, FROM THE *LIBER ELIENSIS*

There follows a memorable account of Byrhtnoth, a remarkable and famous man, whose life and deeds receive no small praise in the English histories. . . . Because of the extraordinary wisdom and bodily strength with which he firmly defended himself and his men, everyone called him "ealdorman" in English, that is, an elder or leader. He was eloquent in speech, robust in strength, large of body, unremitting in war and campaigns against the kingdom's enemies, and bold beyond measure, neither regarding nor fearing death. Moreover, he honored Holy Church and God's ministers everywhere and gave the whole of his patrimony for their use. He always made himself a bulwark for the religious orders against those who tried to cause trouble in holy places. . . . As long as he lived, he devoted his life to defending his country's liberty, and he was totally committed to the standard that he would rather die than injuries to his country go unavenged. (Calder and Allen, pp. 190-91)

---

that the bones were those of a man 6 feet 9 inches in height (Scragg, p. 20).

The Vikings. Since classical antiquity, the peoples of northern Europe had been known as wide-ranging seafarers and tradesmen. The Roman historian Tacitus, writing in the first century C.E., remarked on both their skill as shipbuilders and the unique design of their ships, which allowed them to land virtually anywhere, without needing to find a harbor. This enabled them to travel not only over the ocean, but far inland. No site on the coast or on a navigable river was safe—a fact made abundantly clear throughout Europe when, beginning in the late eighth century, the Vikings burst forth from Scandinavia to kill, burn, and plunder virtually at will.

Ireland and the British Isles were hit first, but in the course of the ninth century Viking raiders made attacks throughout Europe and the East. They ransacked Paris, burned Hamburg, harried the Moslem caliphate in Spain, attacked Italy, and reached as far east as Kiev, Novgorod, and Constantinople. For the most part the Vikings did not remain in the territories of their victims. Viking kingdoms were established in Ireland and northern England, and the Normandy region of France still bears the name of the Vikings ("north-men") who settled there, but these were the exception rather than the rule. Again, the practice of the Vikings was to raid rather than to decisively conquer. Their object was wealth, and their tactics were admirably suited to this goal. The mere rumor of their arrival sent people into a panic, prompting the local citizenry to hand over to the Viking force all their valuables, grateful to escape with their lives. The Vikings seemed ever ready to resort to violence if necessary, usually without warning. A particularly vivid account of the Viking attack on Constantinople in 860 is recorded in Russian and Byzantine chronicles. Constantinople was by far the largest, wealthiest, and most cultured city in all of Christendom at the time. On June 18, 860, some 200 Viking ships suddenly appeared, staging a surprise attack. Nearby monasteries were sacked without opposition. The Vikings' timing was perfect—the emperor was on campaign with his army, engaged in one of an endless series of battles against Moslems. Photius, the supreme bishop of the eastern Christian Church, lamented the calamity:

> Woe is me that I see a fierce and savage tribe fearlessly poured round the city, ravaging the suburbs, destroying everything, ruining everything—fields, houses, herds, beasts of burden, women, old men, youths—thrusting their swords through everything, taking pity on nothing, sparing nothing. The destruction is universal. Like a locust in a cornfield, like mildew in a vineyard, or rather like a whirlwind or a typhoon or a torrent or I know not what to say, it fell upon our land and has annihilated whole generations of inhabitants.
> (Photius in Logan, pp. 189-90)

Such were the raids that the Vikings carried out, or threatened to carry out, in England virtually every year for two centuries.

By the late tenth century, the Viking attacks had tapered off somewhat. In fact, Maldon was

Viking longships.

one of the last battles fought on English soil against a force of pagan Vikings raiders. Soon afterwards, the kings of Norway and Denmark converted to Christianity, and (perhaps more importantly) entered mainstream European political and military activity. The Scandinavians still were formidable opponents—the Danish king Cnut conquered and ruled England from 1016-1035—but their Viking raids ended.

The heroic ideal. The values expressed in *The Battle of Maldon* are part of a code of behavior that stretches far back into the prehistory of the Germanic peoples. There are two operative principles: first, that a warrior should exhibit absolute bravery on the battlefield, and indifference to his own fate; and second, that he should defend his leader unto death—surviving a battle in which one's leader perished was considered the ultimate disgrace. These principles inform virtually every action described in the poem.

Ancient historians agree that these values permeated primitive Germanic society; in a famous passage from his *Germania*, the first century C.E. Roman historian Tacitus comments: "to survive the leader and retreat from the battlefield is a lifelong disgrace and infamy" for the Germanic warrior (Woolf, p. 63). Julius Caesar, Sallust, Ammianus Marcellinus, and other ancient Roman writers express similar evaluations of the "barbaric" peoples to the north, noting with amazement their ferocity, indifference to pain and death, and determination not to survive their fallen leaders in battle. That such values should appear virtually unchanged in a people fully civilized (by Western standards) and Christianized a millennium later shows how deeply embedded in their culture these values were. It is instructive to note that Byrhtnoth dies a little over halfway through the poem; the remainder consists of speeches by the surviving English warriors about their determination to fight on until they too are killed. Such standards of conduct were more than simple ideals—they defined the essence of what it meant to be a warrior.

The Poem in Focus

Plot summary. Due to the loss of some of the original manuscript, *The Battle of Maldon* begins in the middle of a sentence, and also ends abruptly, before its original conclusion. Most scholars believe, however, that not more than a page or two was lost at either end, in view of the fact that the description of virtually the entire battle remains intact, from the initial contact with the Vikings to the death of Byrhtnoth and the last stand of his retainers. The first lines of the poem as we have it tell of the English army releasing their horses, and proceeding to meet their foe on foot. In a sporting mood, one soldier releases his hawk for a bit of hunting before the battle, while another advances grimly; "he made good his boast / to stand fast in fight before his lord" (*The Battle of Maldon*, p. 102). Byrhtnoth

---

THE ANGLO-SAXON ARMY

The force commanded by Byrhtnoth was in all likelihood a typical Anglo-Saxon military force, variously called a *here* or a *fyrd* in eleventh-century records. It consisted of a commander, an elite force of usually aristocratic *thegns* (lieutenants to the commander, usually bound in personal as well as military service to him), and an army composed of both freemen (landowning farmers) and peasants. Most were armed with swords, shields, and spears, but since each person had the responsibility of arming himself, and both weapons and armor were expensive, it was the nobility who came to battle best equipped. Indeed, the Bayeux Tapestry—a large embroidered pictorial account of the Battle of Hastings (1066), in which the English were defeated by the Norman army of William the Conqueror—depicts a number of English soldiers fighting with only clubs and stone-headed sticks (Hollister, p. 31). Nevertheless, large fyrds were effective and highly mobile military forces, and they often included archers as well as mounted cavalry. They could execute complex tactical maneuvers, borne of centuries of keeping Scandinavian invaders at bay. It has even been suggested that Byrhtnoth's fatal decision to allow the Vikings across the causeway to the mainland was part of a larger strategic policy: if the Vikings had decided to sail away due to the unfavorable conditions for battle at Maldon, they might have gone on to attack areas less well defended.

---

addresses his troops, instructing them on proper battle formation, and encouraging them to fight without fear.

The Vikings, who have landed on an island in the middle of the river Pant, send an emissary to parley with the English on the other shore. Calling across the river, the Viking emissary threatens violence unless a ransom is paid:

> The swift-striking seafarers send me to thee,
> bid me say that thou send for thy safety
> rings, bracelets. Better for you

that you stay straightaway our onslaught with
    tribute
than that we should share bitter strife.
                            (*Maldon*, pp. 102-103)

This challenge enrages Byrhtnoth, who answers: "Hearest 'ou [thou], seaman, what this folk sayeth? / Spears shall be all the tribute they send you, / viper-stained spears and the swords of forebears" (*Maldon*, p. 103). Ordering his army to the bank of the river, Byrhtnoth is confronted by rushing water; at high tide, there is no way to march to the Vikings' encampment on the island. Impatiently the two sides wait for ebb tide, passing the time by ineffectually shooting arrows at each other.

Finally the tide goes out, exposing a narrow causeway between the island and the riverbank. The Vikings immediately prepare to advance across it, but are compelled to go single-file, due to the narrowness of the causeway. Byrhtnoth orders the warrior Wulfstan to hold the causeway against the invaders. With the support of two fellow English soldiers, Wulfstan strikes to the ground the first Viking to step onto the causeway. Realizing their tactical disadvantage, the Vikings "began to plead with craft," and ask to be allowed safe passage across the causeway before the battle commences (*Maldon*, p. 104). Byrhtnoth agrees, "overswayed by his heart's arrogance / to allow overmuch land to that loath nation" and calls out to the Vikings: "The ground is cleared for you: come quickly to us, / gather to battle. God alone knows / who shall carry the wielding of this waste ground" (*Maldon*, p. 104).

As the enemy advances, Byrhtnoth again instructs and encourages his men, while crows and eagles circle, waiting to feast on carrion. The armies clash furiously, with losses on both sides. Wulfmaer, a kinsman of Byrhtnoth, is wounded, but the English warrior Edward has better luck, for he kills his opponent. Byrhtnoth again encourages his men (not forgetting to thank Edward for his valor), and wades into the battle. A spear flies through the air and wounds him. In a fury he attacks the Viking who threw the spear, killing him with a mighty blow that passes through armor to lodge in the enemy's heart. Laughing, Byrhtnoth calls aloud his thanks for "the day's work the Lord had dealt him" (*Maldon*, p. 106). Suddenly a spear soars through the air and strikes him. Wulfmaer pulls the spear out and throws it back at its owner, killing him. Another Viking comes forward, trying to rob Byrhtnoth of his valuable weapons and armor; Byrhtnoth strikes at him with his sword, but the blow is checked by another Viking, who disables Byrhtnoth's sword-arm. Now powerless, Byrhtnoth nevertheless continues to encourage his men and, looking to heaven, he prays. The English leader is then cut down by the enemy. He has company in death; Wulfmaer and another faithful warrior fall at his side.

The loss of Byrhtnoth would not necessarily have been disastrous for the English army if Godric had not deserted. Leaping on Byrhtnoth's riderless horse, he fled the battlefield with his brothers Godwine and Godwiy, as well as a number of others who "wheeled from the war to the wood's fastness, / sought shelter and saved their lives" (*Maldon*, p. 107). Many in the English ranks see the familiar horse retreating, and, believing the rider to be Byrhtnoth, follow suit. The diminished army is now in considerable peril. On an earlier day, notes the poem, Byrhtnoth had been warned by his lieutenant Offa that "many gathered there who were making brave speeches / would not hold in the hour of need" (*Maldon*, p. 107). A faithful remnant now remains, each man vowing to fight to the end. The young warrior Aelfwine calls out: "'Remember the speeches spoken over mead, / battle-vows on the bench, the boasts we vaunted, / heroes in hall, against the harsh war-trial! / Now shall be proven the prowess of the man'" (*Maldon*, p. 108). He advances into the fray, and kills a Viking with his spear. Responding to Aelfwine's heartening words, Offa brandishes his own spear and speaks:

> Now that the Earl who led us
> lies on the earth, we all need
> each and every thane to urge forth the other
> warriors to the war while weapon lives
> quick in hand, hardened blade, spear or good
> sword.
>
> (*Maldon*, p. 108)

Lifting his shield, Leofsunu vows not to give up a foot of ground to the enemy—he will avenge his fallen lord. Dunnere too proclaims his determination: "A man cannot linger when his lord lies / unavenged among Vikings, cannot value breath" (*Maldon*, p. 109). Others voice similar resolve; the death of Byrhtnoth must be avenged at all costs.

The battle begins to turn. Offa kills his foe, but blows rain down on him, and he falls to the ground, dead at Byrhtnoth's side. Wistan kills three men before the breath leaves Offa's body, but other Englishmen fall. Still the beleaguered English call out words of encouragement to each other; in the poem's most memorable passage, the aged warrior Byrhtwold declares:

> Courage shall grow keener, clearer the will,
> the heart fiercer, as our force faileth.
> Here our lord lies levelled in the dust,
> the man all marred: he shall mourn to the end
> who thinks to wend off from this war-play
>   now.
> Though I am white with winters I will not
>   away,
> for I think to lodge me alongside my dear one,
> lay me down by my lord's right hand.
>
> (*Maldon*, p. 111)

The poem's final lines tell that Godric (not, the poet assures us, the Godric who ran away) attacks the enemy, until he too is cut down.

Ofermod. By far the most perplexing interpretive problem of the poem centers around a single word: the Old English term *ofermod*. Occurring in line 89 of the poem, it refers to Byrhtnoth's state of mind when he allows the Vikings to cross the causeway prior to the battle. The section of the poem in which the word appears is as follows:

> Tha se eorl ongan   for his ofermode
> alyfan landes to fela   lathere theode . . .
>
> (Scragg, p. 60)

A literal translation would be: "Then the earl began, because of his *ofermod*, to allow too much land to the hateful people." Since the Vikings are victorious because they were allowed to cross to the mainland, and since *ofermod* describes why Byrhtnoth did this, it is critical to the poem's meaning to understand the word. Its two components have Modern English descendants; *ofer* simply means "over," and *mod* survives now as "mood," but in Old English it had more of a sense of "spirit" or "mind." Thus, *ofermod* ("over-mood") could simply be translated as "high-spiritedness," but that is not what the word means in the other instances in which it occurs in Old English. In these other instances (an Old English paraphrase of the Bible's Book of Genesis, a text called *Instructions for Christians,* and an eleventh-century Latin-English glossary) the word means the sin of pride (Gneuss, pp. 126-27). That this word is applied to Byrhtnoth in line 89 of the poem brings many readers up short; is he not the hero of the poem? Is the defeat, then, all his fault—a fault made all the worse because it stems not from error of judgment but outright sin? Such a judgment would seem to call into question all the praise given him throughout the rest of the poem. Since the overall presentation of Byrhtnoth's character in the poem is that of an admirable man who is worthy of the respect and devotion of his soldiers, some have seen his ofermod as something of a heroic flaw. The Anglo-Saxons were capable of admitting serious character flaws in their heroes while at the same time admiring them for those very flaws. Certain qualities unacceptable in normal men (such as arrogance, boastfulness, reckless bravery, and so on) were considered to be almost inevitable byproducts of the heroic character. In a way, this makes perfect sense—Byrhtnoth is the only person mighty enough to defeat Byrhtnoth.

Sources and literary context. Most scholars believe that *The Battle of Maldon* is our earliest and best account of the battle—that it is a primary historical document as well as a carefully-crafted poetic artifact. Its source, then, is the battle itself. Whether the author was present at the battle or relied on the testimony of eyewitnesses, the basic material of his narrative was the historical battle fought in 991. This does not mean, though, that the poem lacks a literary context—far from it. *The Battle of Maldon* was composed in a style already centuries old, and one of the most characteristic features of this style is a highly standardized body of descriptive terms or formulas. In the earliest days of Germanic alliterative poetry (presumably before it was ever written down), poets employed such formulas both as an aid to memory and as a means by which they could, in a sense, recompose the poem every time they recited it. Certain groups of words appropriate to given contexts could be retained by the poet in his memory, and applied to episodes of the poem at will during a performance. Thus, a ship could be called a "foamy-necked floater," a sword a "battle-hardened edge," and a hero a "victory-bright warrior" in poems throughout the poet's repertoire, and such formulas would probably be expected by the audience in much the same way as modern moviegoers might expect the hero of an action film to be handsome and fit.

The Battle of Maldon exhibits a number of epic verbal formulas found in other Old English poems, primarily **Beowulf** (also in *WLAIT 3: British and Irish Literature and Its Times*). For example, in line 163 Byrhtnoth's sword is described as "brad and bruneccg"; this same construction (meaning "broad and bright-bladed") appears in line 1546 of *Beowulf*, in reference to a knife (Scragg, p. 62). Other shared formulas link *The Battle of Maldon* to the Old English poems *Exodus* and *Judith* (verse adaptations based on the narratives found in the Old Testament) and to *Andreas*, an Old English epic about the missionary activities of St. Andrew. By the time *The Bat-*

tle of Maldon was written, this mode of composition was in the past, but formulaic patterns were still very much evident in later Old English verse. Writers of the time invoked these epic formulas because this was how poetry was expected to sound, rather than as an aid to memorized performance. Works like *The Battle of Maldon*, *Andreas*, and *Beowulf* are clearly the products of a sophisticated and literate culture, but highly elaborate patterns of verbal formulas abound. In the case of the longer poems, repetitive images and verbal patterns extending over hundreds of lines may be discerned, patterns that would be extremely difficult for a listener to grasp, but could readily be apprehended by a reader. Such patterns of repetition also appear in *The Battle of Maldon*, despite its brevity; for example, line 42 reads "Byrhtnoth mathelode, bord hafenode" (Scragg, p. 58) which means "Byrhtnoth spoke, raised [his] shield." At this point, Byrhtnoth is giving his scornful reply to the Viking herald's challenge before the battle commences. Much later in the poem, line 309 reads "Byrhtwold mathelode, bord hafenode," the same action being attributed to the aged warrior Byrhtwold, who is showing courageous defiance in the face of certain death (Scragg, p. 67). The lines are clearly meant to echo one another. Such verbal echoes are in keeping with the age-old literary traditions of the Anglo-Saxon people, while the careful repetition of words (separated by 166 lines) that appear nowhere else in the poem clearly makes a literary point—that the spirit of warlike ferocity lives on in Byrhtnoth's men despite his death. As the English soldiers themselves make clear, it is not their individual fates that matter, but rather their single-minded adherence to a heroic ideal that valued courage and loyalty above all else.

Reception and impact. The manuscript from which the text of *The Battle of Maldon* derives no longer exists; it was consumed in the fire that swept through the library of the British antiquary Sir Robert Cotton in 1731, the same fire that damaged the *Beowulf* manuscript. It seems that when Cotton acquired the manuscript it was already incomplete, and no record of it exists before its appearance in the Cottonian collection. Fortunately, a transcript of it was made in 1725 by John Elphinston, a curator of Cotton's library. The historian Thomas Hearne published the text in 1726 as an appendix to the monastic chronicle of John of Glastonbury, and this was the only authority for *The Battle of Maldon* until the early 1930s, when the Elphinston transcript was discovered. This transcript has been the basis of all subsequent editions.

The content of *The Battle of Maldon* in the history of English literature is distinctive. Very little Old English verse deals with events contemporary to its composition. Works like *Beowulf, Deor,* and *Widsith* involve the distant, mythical past, and other poems celebrate the lives of long-dead figures from sacred history, such as the Roman martyr Juliana, Helen (the mother of the Roman Emperor Constantine), and the English hermit Guthlac, who died in 714. Only *The Battle of Maldon* (and *The Battle of Brunanburh*, which celebrates an English victory over Danish and Scottish forces in 937) provide insight into how an Anglo-Saxon poet might view his own age in the light of Germanic literary and cultural tradition. A great number of Latin and vernacular religious prose texts survive from the later Anglo-Saxon period, and their view of warfare and the pursuit of martial glory is for the most part negative; churchmen saw the warlike aspects of the English national character as a fault, and sought to suppress it by preaching the Christian virtues of humility, tolerance, and meekness. The poet of *The Battle of Maldon* saw things differently. For him, Byrhtnoth's heartfelt religiosity and bellicose spirit could coexist admirably. This is recognized by most critics, but the extent to which the poem may also contain implied criticisms of Byrhtnoth is a matter of some debate.

The hero's *ofermod*, or pride, has been variously interpreted as a moral failing, a tactical error, and a heroic virtue; thus, depending upon how one translates this word, he could be an arrogant and blameworthy sinner, an unwise military commander, or a fair-minded warrior who does not wish to wield an unfair advantage over his opponents. Further, some have seen the immediate narrative juxtaposition of his killing his opponent (and then laughingly thanking God for the victory) with his receiving the spear-wound that leads to his death as an indication that his joy in bloodshed is inappropriate to a Christian. On the other hand, his final prayer as he lies dying on the battlefield is devoid of irony; he thanks God for a long and happy life, and prays for salvation. Clearly the poet still viewed Byrhtnoth as heroic, if flawed; in the words of J. R. R. Tolkien, "Byrhtnoth was wrong, and he died for his folly. But it was a noble error, or the error of a noble" (Tolkien, p. 16). Tolkien's view of Byrhtnoth is as about as negative as one can find among major critics, and even he notes that the poem cannot be read as a wholehearted con-demnation of Byrhtnoth. The evaluation of the poem's most recent editor strikes a middle ground:

> The poet makes a moral comment on Byrht-noth's decision to allow the Vikings too much land, and he makes another, through his structure, on the tragedy of a man cut down at the moment of his triumph. But ultimately the audience is called upon to admire the hero, commanding, fighting, and dying bravely with God on his lips.
>
> (Scragg, pp. 39-40)

Important too is how *The Battle of Maldon* provides a commentary of sorts on the Old English epic *Beowulf*, and vice versa. Critics have long seen parallels between the fates of Byrhtnoth and Beowulf; both live lengthy and illustrious lives as able and respected defenders of their people, and both are killed in old age as a result of questionable judgment, with dire consequences for the very people they sought to protect. Beowulf insists on facing a dragon alone—a brave deed to be sure, but one that leads to his death and the certain destruction of his people. Byrhtnoth, through his *ofermod*, gives the Vikings a needless tactical advantage; and the result is the destruction of the English army. Both poems also illustrate failures of the heroic ideal; Godric and his brothers flee the battlefield to save their lives, to the poet's manifest scorn, and Beowulf is twice abandoned by faithless warriors. That two Christian Anglo-Saxon poets from (perhaps) roughly the same era would apply the same standards of behavior to a legendary hero of pagan antiquity and a contemporary governor-general tells a great deal about the self-image of this society. Their Christianity was by no means a simple veneer; it is important to remember that Byrhtnoth's last words are not warlike or defiant, but prayerful—his eyes are not on the enemy, but on God. Still, the heroic past was in a profound way fully present to them, and provided a sense of legitimacy to personal acts of warlike heroism and self-sacrifice.

—Matthew Brosamer

For More Information

The Battle of Maldon. Trans. Michael Alexander. In *The Earliest English Poems*, 3d ed. London: Penguin, 1991.

Calder, Daniel, and Michael J. B. Allen, trans. and ed. *Sources and Analogues of Old English Poetry: The Major Latin Sources in Translation.* Cambridge, England: D.S. Brewer, 1976.

Gneuss, Helmut. "*The Battle of Maldon* 89: Byrhtnoth's *Ofermod* Once Again." *Studies in Philology* 73 (April 1976): 117-37.

Gordon, E.V., ed. *The Battle of Maldon.* New York: Appleton-Century-Crofts, 1966.

Greenfield, Stanley. *The Interpretation of Old English Poems.* London: Routledge, 1972.

Greenfield, Stanley, and Daniel Calder. *A New Critical History of Old English Literature.* 2d ed. New York: New York University Press, 1986.

Hollister, C. Warren. *Anglo-Saxon Military Institutions on the Eve of the Norman Conquest.* Oxford, England: Clarendon, 1962.

Jones, Gwyn. *A History of the Vikings.* Oxford, England: Oxford University Press, 1984.

Logan, F. Donald. *The Vikings in History.* 2nd ed. London: Routledge, 1992.

Scragg, D. G., ed. *The Battle of Maldon.* Manchester, N.Y.: Manchester University Press, 1981.

Tolkien, J. R. R. "The Homecoming of Beorhtnoth, Beorhthelm's Son." *Essays and Studies* 6 (n.s.) (1953): 1-18.

Woolf, Rosemary. "The Ideal of Men Dying with the Lord in the *Germania* and in *The Battle of Maldon.*" *Anglo-Saxon England* 5 (1976): 63-81.

The Beggar's Opera

by
John Gay

Born in Devonshire in 1685, John Gay was educated at the local grammar school, then apprenticed to a silk merchant in London after the early deaths of both parents. In his spare time, Gay wrote verse, publishing *Wine*, a satiric poem on the joys of drinking, in 1708. After negotiating an early release from his apprenticeship, Gay became private secretary to an old schoolmate, Aaron Hill, a professional writer with ties to the theater. Hill introduced Gay to literary circles, in which he met Jonathan Swift and Alexander Pope, to whom Gay dedicated what came to be considered his first important poem, *Rural Sports* (1713). On account of his wit and lively temperament, Gay was well liked by many of London's leading authors. They helped him secure positions and patrons, including the duke and duchess of Queensbury, to finance his art. Meanwhile, Gay turned his hand to writing plays, including *The Wife of Bath* (1713), based on Chaucer's **The Canterbury Tales** (also in *WLAIT 3: British and Irish Literature and Its Times*); *The What D'Ye Call It* (1715), a broad comic farce; and *Three Hours After Marriage* (1717), a satiric comedy about contemporary authors that Gay wrote with Pope and John Arbuthnot. Although some of these plays were well received, Gay did not achieve great popular success as a playwright until *The Beggar's Opera*. Widely considered to be his masterpiece, this innovative "ballad opera" was performed at Lincoln's Inn Fields (a London theater) on January 29, 1728, and enjoyed a record-breaking initial run of 62 performances. Set among the thieves and prostitutes of Lon-

THE LITERARY WORK

A ballad opera, set in the London underworld during the early eighteenth century; published in 1728.

SYNOPSIS

Low domestic comedy and political satire mix in this tale of a dashing highwayman, a double-crossing informer, and the highwayman's romance with the informer's daughter.

don's underworld, *The Beggar's Opera* delighted audiences with its keen satire and skillful setting of popular ballad tunes to new lyrics and contexts.

Events in History at the Time of the Ballad Opera

Crime, punishment, and the London underworld. Historian George Rudé divides the populous "lower orders" of eighteenth-century London into the following four categories: master craftsmen and small shopkeepers; skilled journeymen and apprentices; semiskilled and unskilled laborers; and the indigent, the unemployed, and the criminal classes (Rudé, p. 83). While the exact number of persons comprising the last category is not known, it has been estimated that near the end of the century about 115,000 people—something like 12 percent of the city's population—made up the London "underworld" (Rudé, p. 83).

Gay's ballad opera (essentially a play set to folk music) focuses exclusively on the denizens of the underworld—the thieves, prostitutes, and informers whose trades flourished during the early decades of the eighteenth century but whose futures were almost invariably cut short when they were apprehended by the law. Criminal courts of the time dealt harshly with members of the underworld, especially thieves, many of whom paid for their crimes with their lives. Historian Douglas Hay observes that

---

DEATH AT TYBURN

From 1388 until 1783, most London hangings took place at Tyburn. The Tyburn is a small tributary of the Thames; the term "Tyburn" became associated with the Middlesex Gallows—also known as "Tyburn Tree"—which were located on the Tyburn's west bank. The gallows were near the crossroads of Edgeware and Bayswater Roads in London, at the northeast corner of Hyde Park. The public was invited, even encouraged, to watch people get hanged, in hopes that the gruesome spectacle would deter future criminals. The eight "hanging days" of the year during which executions were scheduled were public holidays. Crowds would fill the streets from Newgate to Tyburn to observe the condemned as they traveled by cart to Tyburn Tree, a gallows so large that 21 bodies could hang suspended from it at one time. Some prisoners would be greeted with cheers and even toasted along their way by partisan spectators; others were greeted with jeers, derision, and loud demands that they be dispatched as quickly as possible. Child-and-wife murderers and "thief-takers," like Jonathan Wild, received no sympathy from the crowds, but highwaymen "whose only crime was to have robbed the rich, were often cheered and toasted as heroes of the day" (Rudé, p. 94). In *The Beggar's Opera*, Polly Peachum sentimentally envisions just such an ending for her husband, Macheath, should he be captured and condemned: "Methinks I see him already in the cart, sweeter and more lovely than the nosegay in his hand. I hear the crowd extolling his resolution and intrepidity. . . . I see him at the tree! The whole circle are in tears! Even butchers weep!" (Gay, *The Beggar's Opera*, pp. 26-27). Often after the hanging, the family of the deceased had to fight to claim the body before surgeons took it away for dissection and research.

---

the rulers of eighteenth-century England cherished the death sentence. . . . In place of police . . . propertied Englishmen had a fat and swelling sheaf of laws which threatened thieves with death. . . . One account suggests the number of capital statutes grew from about 50 to over 200 between the years 1688 and 1820. Almost all of them concerned offences against property. (Hay, pp. 17-18)

Although some offenders might be given the lesser sentence of "transportation"—exile to American, Australian, or West Indian plantations for a period of 7 or 14 years—many of them were sentenced to death by public hanging.

Public executions were not, however, always an effective deterrent to crime. Criminals who were hanged or transported were speedily replaced by others just as rapacious. In the early eighteenth century, a thriving organized crime network was formed by Jonathan Wild, an erstwhile merchant who learned the criminal trade during a stint in debtors' prison. After his release, Wild used his new skills to achieve the highest status in the London underworld. Indeed, Wild led a complicated double life: in one capacity, he served as a "thief-taker," a sort of unofficial policeman who helped the law arrest criminals and who provided evidence against those criminals at their trials. If the offender was convicted, Wild received 40 pounds for his services. In another capacity, Wild instructed criminals in his organization as to where and what they could steal. He would subsequently serve as a "fence" for the stolen loot—after receiving it from his gang, he would sell it to the public or back to the original owners at a profit. In time, Wild commanded a large organization of thieves and felons, from whom he expected complete loyalty. Criminals who ignored or resisted Wild's organization frequently found themselves betrayed to the law by Wild himself.

Wild was not the only colorful figure in the London underworld. Jack Sheppard, a Cockney "housebreaker," achieved notoriety as a thief in his own right and as one of Wild's targets. In February 1724, Sheppard was captured and imprisoned in St. Giles's Roundhouse, but he promptly escaped. Wild was then recruited in his capacity as "Thief-Taker General" to recapture Sheppard. He succeeded in doing so in May, but within the week Sheppard escaped from New Prison, where he had been incarcerated. He remained at large until July when he was again captured by Wild; tried and condemned to death, Sheppard nonetheless managed to escape from his cell in Newgate Prison on August 30, the night his death warrant arrived. Wild's men caught him again ten days later; this time Sheppard was incarcerated in the "Castle," the strongest room in Newgate, and loaded down with fetters and manacles. Incredibly, he escaped five nights later, breaking his chains, forcing open several padlocked doors, and, at last, climbing down a wall to freedom. A determined Wild renewed his pursuit of Sheppard, who was finally apprehended in a Drury Lane gin shop towards the end of October. Imprisoned once more in Newgate, Sheppard was loaded down with 300 pounds of iron until his execution at Tyburn on November 16, which was reportedly witnessed by 200,000 people. Ironically, Wild's obsessive pursuit of Sheppard damaged his own popularity with both the authorities and the denizens of the underworld. Less than a year later, he himself was arrested on a minor felony charge; former associates came forward with evidence of his various criminal misdeeds, and the man who styled himself "Thief-Taker General" was tried, condemned, and hanged at Tyburn on May 24, 1725. The dramatist Gay followed the careers of both Wild and Sheppard with interest, eventually using them as models for the characters of Peachum and Macheath in *The Beggar's Opera*.

But Gay also had grander objects in mind for his satire.

Corruption in high places. *The Beggar's Opera* targets not only such low-lifes as Jonathan Wild and Jack Sheppard but also more elevated figures, including Sir Robert Walpole, the British prime minister during the reigns of George I and George II. Walpole was a strong and capable statesman, and England enjoyed a lengthy period of peace and prosperity during his administration. At the same time, however, he actively participated in the ongoing corruption of the House of Commons by "buying" journalists and members of Parliament to help keep his party, the Whigs, in power. Walpole is said to have been "coarse in morals and uncouth in manners, a heavy drinker, generous to his friends and indifferent to his opponents" (Schultz, p. 178). Walpole's enemies accused him of lining his pockets at his country's expense, especially after an ill-fated speculation scheme crashed in 1720.

According to the plan, the South Sea Company, formed in 1711 as a rival to the Bank of England and the East India Company, would take charge of a large portion of England's national debt. A joint-stock venture, the South Sea Company set out to profit from trade in South America, where it did garner a monopoly in the slave market and also part of the market for European goods. But such faraway trade boded ill for quick profits, which was the aim of many of the company's shareholders. From the start, the South Sea Company was plagued by selfish manipulation—its directors bribed officials with stock and allowed members of Parliament and the king's court to buy many shares. Reassured because the government appeared to be investing in the company, average citizens sold their own assets to buy stock, first in this venture and then in many others. In fact, a speculation craze struck England early in 1720. Pay-offs to government officials continued, new stocks were issued, and prices soared as much as 1,000 percent before the market collapsed in August 1720 (Schultz, p. 177). In the end, many—including John Gay—who had invested heavily in the South Sea Company suffered grievously when their stocks plummeted. Average citizens faced financial ruin.

Walpole himself had invested in the South Sea Company, but he escaped disaster through the advice of his banker, Robert Jacomb. Untarnished by the scheme's collapse, Walpole used his skill and political connections to extricate some of his Whig cronies from charges of corruption, infuriating the Tory opposition. During his tenure as prime minister (1721-42), he also leveraged such things as pensions and official appointments in exchange for parliamentary support.

In *The Beggar's Opera*, Walpole's practices of bribery and influence-peddling are satirized in Gay's portrayal of Peachum, the treacherous informer who works both sides of the law and pockets the profits. Contemporary audiences also spotted allusions to Walpole in the triangle between Macheath, Polly, and Lucy, which mirrored Walpole's own extramarital affair with Maria Skerret, and in the last-minute reprieve of Macheath on the scaffold, which paralleled Walpole's own narrow escape from dismissal from office upon the ascension of George II in 1727. Perhaps in part because of the savaging he endured in *The Beggar's Opera*, Walpole legislated the 1737 Licensing Act, which reduced to three—Drury Lane, Covent Garden, and Haymarket—the number of London theaters. The ban was not lifted until 1843.

Prostitution. Although Gay concentrates most of the action in *The Beggar's Opera* on the criminal activities of Peachum, Lockit, and Macheath, he also directs his attention to their female compa-

The Beggar's Opera, Act III, from a painting of 1729-31 by William Hogarth.

triots in the London underworld—the prostitutes. During the seventeenth and eighteenth centuries, prostitutes plied their trade in public venues where large crowds could be found, including parks and even churches. Meanwhile, Covent Garden, a fashionable area in London, became the site of many houses of ill repute; as Rudé writes, "to evade the law, the houses masqueraded under the ostensibly respectable (and legitimate) labels of tavern, coffee house or 'bagnio' [public bath]" (Rudé, p. 72). The precincts from Charing Cross to Drury Lane were the most popular areas for London prostitutes.

> Tourists . . . could purchase Harris's New Atlantic, a guidebook to London's harlots, detailing addresses, physical characteristics and specialties. . . . But, in free-market London, prostitutes were chiefly to be picked up on the streets on which . . . women were available . . . "got up in any way you like, dressed, bound up, hitched up, tight-laced, loose, painted, done up or raw, scented, in silk or wool, with or without sugar. . . ." (Porter, p. 171)

Conditions in London brothels varied. Some establishments catered to an upper-class clientele, so the procuresses took special pains to please their aristocratic customers, plying them with food and wine and allowing them the opportunity to accept or reject the girl chosen for

them. Other brothels were grittier, serving those with less money and social status. Whatever their working conditions, prostitutes in houses were obliged to give a portion—up to one-half—of their earnings to the procuress, as well as pay for their own board and clothing (Scott, p. 96).

While prostitutes' lives often ended in poverty, squalor, and disease, the trade of prostitution continued to flourish throughout the eighteenth century, because it remained one of the only professions in which women could earn an independent living: "Prostitution was one of the few ways a woman could make it on her own, and if she had intelligence, sophistication, talent, and the right contacts, she could go far. Most failed because they lacked the contacts. Often the woman's family pulled strings for her to become the mistress to a powerful man, since in such a position, she could do much in return" (Bullough, p. 187). Some determined prostitutes who lacked such advantageous connections found another means of scaling the social ladder: they became actresses on the theater stage, where their looks and talent could garner them wealthy lovers and protectors. A century earlier, Nell Gwyn had worked her way up from brothel servant to actress to mistress of King Charles II. Ironically, the staging of *The Beggar's Opera* brought about a similar development—Lavinia

Fenton, the first to fill the role of Polly Peachum on stage, caught the eye of the duke of Bolton during one performance; the smitten duke made her his mistress, and, some time later, his wife.

English versus Italian opera. *The Beggar's Opera* would probably never have been written without the growing popularity of operas among English audiences. The opera form had first taken hold in England in the previous century towards the end of the Interregnum (1649-60), the period in which the royal family was exiled and the Puritans under Oliver Cromwell governed England. Although the Puritans had closed the theaters and banned the staging of plays, some people managed to circumvent this ban by presenting, in private houses, dramatic works that required musical accompaniment from beginning to end. This form, known as the "English dramatic opera," persisted until 1660, when the monarchy was restored and the theaters reopened. After 1660, the English dramatic opera underwent some changes—music became intermittent rather than continuous, and dialogue could now be spoken instead of sung, since plays were no longer banned.

During the early eighteenth century, however, English dramatic operas were supplanted by lavish Italian operas. Literary scholar Peter Elfed Lewis observes that, by the time Gay wrote *The Beggar's Opera*, "'opera' in England had become virtually synonymous with Italian opera, a theatrical form characterized by great dignity and seriousness and peopled with mythological figures or personages of high rank from the distant past" (Lewis, pp. 8-9). George Friedrich Handel, the German composer, came to London in 1710 by way of Italy and was immediately commissioned to write an Italian opera. His *Rinaldo* (1711) marked the first in a string of successful operas that he composed for English audiences. Meanwhile, the popularity of Italian opera as a genre continue to escalate—the new Queen's Theater was the principal venue for Italian opera in England and became known as the Opera House. Meanwhile, leading Italian singers, including feuding sopranos Francesca Cuzzoni and Faustina Bordoni, were paid hefty sums to perform in England and were treated like major celebrities once they arrived.

Italian opera, however, was not universally loved—some English intellectuals ridiculed everything from the tradition of the male castrati singers to the temper tantrums of divas to the lavish scope of some operatic productions. Critics such as Joseph Addison and John Dennis even believed that the taste for Italian opera threatened the future of English drama and music.

Unlike many of his contemporaries, Gay did not dislike Italian opera; he wrote an operatic libretto for Handel's *Acis and Galatea* some ten years before composing *The Beggar's Opera*. Nonetheless, he too was alarmed by the ways in which Italian opera was overshadowing English music and by the slavish worship of the genre, and sought to provide uncritical audiences with a corrective. Gay's boldest stroke by far was to set *The Beggar's Opera* not among gods and goddesses or other heroic personages in some suitably lofty atmosphere, as in Italian operatic tradition, but among thieves and whores in the seamy London underworld. Throughout his mock epic production, Gay spoofs many of the conventions of Italian opera—from the impassioned bickering between "divas" Polly Peachum and Lucy Lockit over Macheath's affections (which culminate in Lucy's unsuccessful attempt to poison her rival) to Macheath's own less than heroic reaction to his impending execution, which is to drink heavily and lament the loss of his many mistresses.

The Ballad Opera in Focus

Plot summary. *The Beggar's Opera* opens with a short introduction in which the beggar who composed the opera attempts to stage his work before a player, explaining, "I have introduced the similes that are in all your celebrated operas: the swallow, the moth, the bee, the ship, the flower, etc. Besides, I have a prison scene, which the ladies always reckon charmingly pathetic" (*The Beggar's Opera*, p. 5). The player agrees to watch the opera, and he and the beggar withdraw as the performance begins.

The curtain rises as Mr. Peachum, an informer and a fence for stolen goods, reckons up his account and sings of his profession: "Through all the employments of life / Each neighbor abuses his brother; / Whore and rogue they call husband and wife; / All professions be-rogue one another" (*The Beggar's Opera*, p. 6). Declaring himself to be as honest as any lawyer or statesman, Peachum discusses with Filch, one of his apprentice pickpockets, the fates of thieves who have worked for him but have now been arrested. Those who excelled in their trade Peachum plans to help by bribing jailers and law officers; those who did not earn sufficient profit Peachum will abandon to their fates—hanging or transportation.

Print of an unidentified inmate at Newgate Prison, c. 1850.

In the middle of this conversation, Mrs. Peachum enters to discuss Captain Macheath, a dashing highwayman and sometime associate of Peachum's, who has begun courting their daughter, Polly. The news displeases Peachum, especially when he learns that Polly wants to marry Macheath: "Gamesters and highwaymen are generally very good to their whores, but they are very devils to their wives" (*The Beggar's Opera*, p. 13). The Peachums resolve to dissuade Polly from wedding Macheath, but their resolution comes too late—Polly enters and reveals that she and Macheath are already married. Horrified, the Peachums berate their daughter, warning her that Macheath's gambling and philandering will be her ruin. Fearing that Macheath will betray them to the law so he can acquire Polly's fortune, the Peachums urge Polly to be a dutiful daughter and inform on her husband first. Polly, however, vows that she loves Macheath and will never betray him. Later Polly eavesdrops on her parents and learns they mean to have Macheath arrested. When the highwayman comes to visit his bride, Polly warns him of her parents' plans. After singing a tender duet, the loving couple decides that Macheath should go into hiding for a few weeks until Polly can persuade her parents to relent.

In the second act, Macheath meets his gang of robbers at a tavern near Newgate and tells them that they must meet at their private quarters for the next few weeks because he has fallen out with Peachum. The highwayman hopes to make Peachum believe he has left the gang and thus pave the way for reconciliation. The robbers agree to obey their leader's instructions, then depart on their separate errands. Alone in the tavern, Macheath reflects on the irresistible joys of women. To his delight, a bevy of prostitutes and female pickpockets joins him in the tavern for drinks and dalliance. While the highwayman is thus distracted, two of the prostitutes relieve him of his pistols and alert a watching Peachum, who then rushes in with some constables to arrest the astonished, enraged Macheath.

In Newgate prison, Macheath pays Lockit, the principal jailer, to fit him with a lightweight set of chains before he is led off to his cell. Alone, the highwayman bemoans his fate and laments that his imprisonment has brought him into proximity with Lockit's daughter, Lucy, whom he had also promised to marry. A vengeful—and pregnant—Lucy then enters and upbraids her former lover, vowing to watch his sufferings with enjoyment. Macheath quickly claims that Polly Peachum means nothing to him and vows to fulfill his promises to Lucy who, despite herself, is softened by his apparent ardor.

Meanwhile, Peachum and Lockit agree to divide the reward for Macheath's capture between them, but Peachum's faith in his partner's honesty is shaken when he discovers that one of his men has been convicted, in spite of the bribe Peachum gave Lockit to set him free. Peachum and Lockit quarrel violently but reconcile after realizing that each has enough evidence to hang the other. After Peachum leaves the prison, Lucy approaches her father to plead with him for Macheath's life. Lockit remains adamant—the highwayman must hang, and he advises his daughter to "do like other widows: buy yourself weeds, and be cheerful" (*The Beggar's Opera*, p. 51).

Visiting Macheath's cell, Lucy sadly relates her father's hard-heartedness but agrees to consider the highwayman's suggestion that Lockit might be bought off. While they plan this new strategy, Polly enters to visit her husband in jail. The two young women exchange hostilities and demand that Macheath choose between them. Needing Lucy's assistance to escape from jail, Macheath spurns Polly, who is dragged off, lamenting, by Peachum. Left alone with Lucy, Macheath persuades her to steal her father's keys and release him from his cell, promising to send for her as soon as the search for him cools.

As the third act begins, Macheath has escaped, leaving behind a furious Lockit and a humiliated Lucy, who now suspects she was duped by her former lover. Believing that Peachum means to cheat him out of his share of the reward money, Lockit schemes to turn the tables on his partner. Meanwhile, Macheath meets with two of his men at a gaming house, where they discuss future robberies. Macheath arranges for them to meet again that evening in another den where he can point out a likely victim.

Peachum and Lockit, meeting to discuss the division of some loot, learn from Mrs. Diana Trapes, a procuress, that Macheath is currently with one of her whores, Mrs. Coaxer. As the two men eagerly set off to recapture Macheath, Polly calls upon Lucy at Newgate. The two women bemoan their shabby treatment by Macheath, and a jealous Lucy serves Polly poisoned wine. Suspicious of Lucy, Polly refuses to drink, dropping the glass on the floor when she beholds Macheath being brought back to prison by Peachum and Lockit.

Although Polly and Lucy both plead for Macheath's life, their fathers refuse to listen. Macheath himself, while despondent over his fate, seems almost relieved that his matrimonial woes will soon be ended by his execution: "Contented I die. 'Tis the better for you. / Here ends all dispute the rest of our lives, / For this way at once I please all my wives" (*The Beggar's Opera*, p. 77).

Sentenced to death by hanging, Macheath broods on the laws that consign poor criminals like himself to death but allow rich criminals to buy their way out of punishment:

> Since laws were made for ev'ry degree,
> To curb vice in others, as well as me,
> I wonder we ha'nt better company
>   Upon Tyburn tree!
> But gold from law can take out the sting;
> And if rich men, like us, were to swing,
> 'Twould thin the land, such numbers to string
>   Upon Tyburn tree!
>   (*The Beggar's Opera*, p. 79)

Receiving a visit from two of his men, Macheath reveals that he was betrayed by one of his own gang, Jemmy Twitcher. The highwayman urges his gang members to trust no one and beseeches them to see that Peachum and Lockit are brought to the gallows. Polly and Lucy visit, still vying for Macheath's love; the jailer enters with the news that four more wives have appeared at the prison, each with a child. Appalled, Macheath asks to be led out to the gallows.

At this juncture, *The Beggar's Opera* is interrupted by another dialogue between the beggar and the player. The player is dismayed to hear that the beggar means to end the production with Macheath's hanging. The beggar explains that he wished to show "strict poetical justice" by having the opera end with Macheath's execution and the likely deaths and transportations of the other characters; the player, however, insists that "an opera must end happily . . . to comply with the taste of the town" (*The Beggar's Opera*, p. 82). The beggar agrees and hastily changes the ending. As the opera resumes, Macheath receives a last-minute reprieve, thanks to the pleas of the London rabble, and is reunited with Polly, whom he has legitimately married. The opera concludes with a dance as Macheath finds other partners for his former lovers.

Aristocrats and criminals. The eighteenth century saw the publication of numerous satirical works, including Jonathan Swift's *Gulliver's Travels* (1726; also in *WLAIT 3: British and Irish Literature and Its Times*) and Alexander Pope's *The Dunciad* (1728). What *Gulliver's Travels* did for contemporary travelogues and *The Dunciad* did for epic poetry, *The Beggar's Opera* does for opera, juxtaposing "high" and "low" elements to create the mock-heroic tone so praised by wits of the eighteenth century.

The very title of *The Beggar's Opera* reveals Gay's satirical intent by suggesting that a beggar—in the person of a starving poet—could in fact compose a work as exalted as an opera. The satirical tone continues as Gay links noble sentiments with characters who represent the very dregs of society. For example, Matt of the Mint, one of Macheath's gang, gives a speech that seems to express the openhanded philosophy of true aristocrats:

> The world is avaricious, and I hate avarice. A covetous fellow, like a jackdaw, steals what he was never made to enjoy, for the sake of hiding it. These are the robbers of mankind, for money was made for the freehearted and generous, and where is the injury of taking from another what he hath not the heart to make use of?
>   (*The Beggar's Opera*, p. 32)

Similarly, Macheath gives money to members of his gang when they fail to find success on the road: "When my friends are in difficulties, I am always glad that my fortune can be serviceable to them. You see, gentlemen, I am not a mere court friend, who professes everything and will do nothing" (*The Beggar's Opera*, p. 63). The true generosity of these thieves is contrasted with the empty promises of aristocrats in Macheath's subsequent song: "The modes of the court so common are grown, / That a true friend can hardly be met; / Friendship for interest is but a loan, / Which they let out for what they can get" (*The Beggar's Opera*, p. 63).

But while Macheath and his gang are represented as more honest than genuine aristocrats and certainly more appealing than the conniving Peachum and Lockit, Gay never forgets that they are criminals nonetheless. Moreover, Macheath may be the king of highwaymen, but his flaws—including womanizing, drinking, and gambling—are as common among aristocrats as among thieves. Mrs. Peachum scolds Polly for her rash decision to wed Macheath, demanding: "Can you support the expense of a husband, hussy, in gaming, drinking, and whoring? . . . If you must be married, could you introduce nobody into our family but a highwayman? Why, thou foolish jade, thou wilt be as ill-used and as much neglected, as if thou hadst married a lord!" (*The Beggar's Opera*, pp. 18-19). The vices of the aristocracy and the underworld are continually connected in Gay's opera.

The purported virtues of the aristocracy—propriety, chastity, decorum—are likewise mocked. Polly herself, despite her role as the opera's innocent, loyal heroine, displays a hard-headed awareness of the world and how it works, declaring to Peachum: "I know as well as any of the fine ladies how to make the most of myself and of my man too. A woman knows how to be mercenary, though she hath never been in a court or at an assembly. We have it in our natures, Papa" (*The Beggar's Opera*, p. 17). In such a context, Polly's victory over her pregnant rival, Lucy Lockit, appears not as the triumph of virtue over vice but rather the triumph of calculating pragmatism over heedless romanticism. Polly "wins" Macheath not because she is more pure than Lucy, but because she is shrewd enough to use marriage as a bargaining chip. Yet, in this regard, Gay implies, Polly and her parents are no different from the gentry, whose ways they mimic. Historian G. M. Trevelyan writes: "In the upper and middle classes, husbands were often found for girls on the principles of frank barter" (Trevelyan, p. 18). Therefore, Polly's declaration that she did not marry Macheath "(as 'tis the fashion), coolly and deliberately for honor or money" but for love leads Mrs. Peachum to lament: "Love him! Worse and worse! I thought the girl had been better bred!" (*The Beggar's Opera*, p. 20). The hollowness of upper-class ideals of honor and chastity is further suggested when Mrs. Peachum remarks to Mr. Peachum: "If she had had only an intrigue with the fellow, why the very best families have excused and huddled up a frailty of that sort. 'Tis marriage, husband, that makes it a blemish" (*The Beggar's Opera*, p. 22).

While the principle of marriage as an economic arrangement was the norm among the upper and middle classes during Gay's lifetime, the eighteenth century, overall, was a time of transition, during which "an ever-increasing proportion of ordinary marriages were the outcome of mutual affection" (Trevelyan, p. 20). In time, marriage for love became neither a disgrace nor an anomaly, though financial considerations remained, more often than not, a factor.

Sources and literary context. The seed for *The Beggar's Opera* may have been sown as early as 1716, when Gay's friend, Jonathan Swift, suggested that Gay write "a Newgate pastoral, among the whores and thieves there" (Swift in Winton, *Dictionary of Literary Biography*, p. 193). Certainly Gay's experiences as a London apprentice provided him with inspiration for such a project. Moreover, Gay drew upon real-life models for his main characters. Peachum and Macheath were based, respectively, on Jonathan Wild and Jack Sheppard, notorious figures in the London underworld. Like Peachum, Wild ran an efficient crime organization: he instructed members of his gang where and what to steal, collected the stolen goods from them at a profit, then "retrieved" and returned those goods to their original owners for a sizeable fee. And while Sheppard was a house burglar rather than a highwayman, his charisma and ability to escape from various prisons no doubt played a part in Gay's characterization of Macheath. Both Sheppard and Wild had been arrested and executed by the time *The Beggar's Opera* premiered in 1728.

Gay also mined contemporary performers in the theater for material. The rivalry between Polly Peachum and Lucy Lockit was inspired by the quarrels between Francesca Cuzzoni and Faustina Bordoni, two reigning divas of the Italian opera. Journalists eagerly chronicled the on- and off-stage spats of these dueling prima donnas, including a scratching, hair-pulling altercation that took place during a performance of Buononcini's *Astayanax* in the spring of 1727.

By the time *The Beggar's Opera* was first performed, London audiences had acquired a taste not only for opera but for satire and farce as well. The main attraction on a playbill was usually followed by a short, farcical afterpiece; moreover, music and dance numbers, such as those found in British pantomimes, were frequently scheduled between acts of the play. Gay exploited all these forms—opera, farce, pantomime—in *The Beggar's Opera*, ultimately producing an entirely new art form: the ballad opera. Unlike operas, which contained florid original airs written by the composer, Gay used a variety of familiar English, Scottish, and Welsh tunes, for which he wrote new lyrics. Many of these tunes originated from folksongs, others were drawing-room and street ballads—most were of recent composition and thus familiar to audiences. For these familiar tunes, Gay provided new, often bawdy or wittily over-stylized lyrics. In retrospect, *The Beggar's Opera* did not, as hoped by some, spawn a new tradition of English opera; nonetheless, it made a lasting contribution to musical theater.

> With time and modification [the ballad opera] form has been extended to such diverse works as the Singspiele of Mozart, the Savoy operas, and the collaborations of Rogers and Hammerstein. The historical consequences of Gay's play have been more extensive. Its melodies, a collection of spirited and sometimes hauntingly beautiful songs drawn mainly from English music, contributed as much to the developing interest in popular poetry and music as did the later *Reliques* of Bishop Percy and the earlier critiques of "Chevy Chase" by Addison. Today, *The Beggar's Opera* is for most students, the principal locus of seventeenth- and eighteenth-century popular music.
>
> (Roberts in Gay, p. xv)

Thus, traditional tunes such as "Greensleeves" and "Bonny Dundee" were given new life in *The Beggar's Opera* when transformed, respectively, into songs with lyrics such as "Since laws were made for ev'ry degree" and "The charge is prepared; the lawyers are met."

Reception. A few days after *The Beggar's Opera* premiered at Lincoln's Inn Fields, the *Daily Journal* enthusiastically praised "Mr. Gay's new English opera, written in a manner wholly new, and very entertaining," adding, "there were present then, as well as last night, a prodigious concourse of nobility and gentry, and no theatrical performance for these many years has met with so much applause" (Nokes, p. 418). Another newspaper, *The Craftsman*, reported that Gay's work "has met with a general Applause, insomuch that the Waggs say it has made *Rich* [the manager of Lincoln's Inn Fields] very *Gay*, and probably will make *Gay* very *Rich*" (Winton, *John Gay and the London Theatre*, p. 99). Gay's satiric thrusts did

not go unnoticed, either—his good friend, Jonathan Swift, wrote thus in *The Intelligencer*:

> This *Comedy* contains likewise a *Satyr*, which, without enquiring whether it affects the present Age, may possibly be useful in Times to come. I mean, where the Author takes the Occasion of comparing those *common Robbers of the Publick*, and their several Stratagems of betraying, undermining and hanging each other, to the several Arts of *Politicians* in Times of Corruption.
>
> (Swift in Gay, "Introduction," p. xxv)

The Beggar's Opera did have its detractors. Literary critic and author John Dennis (whom Gay had parodied as "Sir Tremendous" in *Three Hours After Marriage*) called it "a low and licentious piece," while an anonymous pamphleteer wrote that "thieving and the highway are edged-tools to play with, and they ought by no means to be set in a gay or ridiculous light to the mob" (Nokes, p. 443). Despite such censure, *The Beggar's Opera* remained a success, outperforming most of the productions mounted by rival theaters during its run. Its sequel, *Polly* (1729), was not so lucky; it was banned by the Lord Chamberlain and was available only by subscription.

FROM MACHEATH TO MACK THE KNIFE

~

*T*he *Beggar's Opera* spawned many imitations, such as Henry Fielding's *The Grub Street Opera* and Charles Coffey's *The Devil to Pay*, which similarly exploited street songs and broadside ballads. Few of these productions achieved the success enjoyed by Gay's work. *The Grub Street Opera* did not even make it onto the stage, vanishing mysteriously before production in 1731. Some 200 years later, however, in 1928, Bertolt Brecht successfully adapted *The Beggar's Opera* for modern audiences with his *Die Dreigroschenoper* (*The Threepenny Opera*). Brecht retained Gay's plot and most of his characters, though in altered forms, but his collaborator, Kurt Weill, composed a new score inspired by modern jazz.

The popularity of *The Beggar's Opera* was perhaps due to its very Englishness—manifested by Gay's use of British folk-tunes—which audiences, who had been sated on Italian operas, found refreshing. *Thievery-a-la-Mode*, a pamphlet circulated in June 1728, noted approvingly that *The Beggar's Opera* satirized "the inconsistencies and unnatural conduct of the Italian opera, which tho' they charm the eye with gay dresses and fine scenes, and delight the ear with sound, have nothing in them either to reform the manners or improve the mind, the original institutions of the stage" (Nokes, pp. 424-25). Swift sounded a similar note, claiming that *The Beggar's Opera* had revealed "the unnatural taste for Italian music among us which is wholly unsuitable to our Northern climate, and the genius of the people, whereby we are over-run with Italian effeminacy and Italian nonsense" (Swift in Nokes, p. 430). In 1791, John Ireland summed up what he felt to be Gay's contribution to the English theater: "Gay must be allowed the praise of having attempted to stem Italia's liquid stream which at that time meandered through every alley, street and square in the metropolis—the honor of having almost silenced the effeminate song of that absurd, exotic Italian opera" (Ireland in Nokes, pp. 425-26).

—Pamela S. Loy

For More Information

Bullough, Vern, and Bonnie Bullough. *Women and Prostitution: A Social History.* New York: Prometheus, 1987.

Gay, John. *The Beggar's Opera.* Ed. Edgar V. Roberts. Lincoln: University of Nebraska Press, 1969.

Hay, Douglas. *Albion's Fatal Tree: Crime and Society in Eighteenth-Century England.* New York: Pantheon, 1975.

Lewis, Peter Elfed. *John Gay: The Beggar's Opera.* London: Edward Arnold, 1976.

Nokes, David. *John Gay: A Profession of Friendship.* Oxford: Oxford University Press, 1995.

Porter, Roy. *London: A Social History.* Cambridge: Harvard University Press, 1994.

Rudé, George. *Hanoverian London: 1714-1808.* Berkeley: University of California Press, 1971.

Scott, George Ryley. *A History of Prostitution from Antiquity to the Present Day.* London: Torchstream, 1954.

Schultz, Harold J. *British History.* 4th ed. New York: HarperPerennial, 1992.

Trevelyan, G. M. *Illustrated English Social History.* Vol. 3. London: Longmans, 1942.

Winton, Calhoun. "John Gay." In *Dictionary of Literary Biography.* Vol. 84. Ed. Paula R. Backscheider. Detroit: Gale, 1989.

———. *John Gay and the London Theatre.* Lexington: University Press of Kentucky, 1993.

Beowulf

as translated by
Seamus Heaney

Little is known about the circumstances of the composition of *Beowulf*: not only is the author unknown, but scholars are in wide disagreement about when the poem was written. Until a generation ago the prevailing opinion was that a date somewhere in the eighth century was likely, but dates in the range of the seventh to the tenth centuries have been proposed. This makes any detailed investigation of the author's cultural and literary background problematic. However, much more is known about the unique surviving copy of *Beowulf*; while the poem is concerned with events in pagan Scandinavian history and legend, it survives in a manuscript of English origin, written in the early eleventh century. These facts could argue for either an early or late date of composition; England in the early eleventh century was ruled by the Danish king Cnut, which, if the early-eleventh-century date of authorship is accepted, could help to explain the poem's distinctly pro-Danish quality. But the Danish subject matter also fits with an eighth-century date, when relations between the English and the Danes were cordial, due primarily to their shared linguistic and cultural past, and active trade. There was at this time a sense of kinship among the Germanic peoples; the Angles and Saxons (who became the English), the Danes, and the Swedes spoke closely related languages, had a shared awareness of racial history, and, before their conversions to Christianity, worshiped essentially the same gods. In the ninth and tenth centuries, however, England was repeatedly subject to violent incursions by Scandi-

---

THE LITERARY WORK

A poem in Old English, set in sixth-century Scandinavia; its date of composition is unknown; the surviving manuscript was written in the early eleventh century; first published in 1815.

SYNOPSIS

The Scandinavian hero, Beowulf, battles monsters, wins a throne, and, while he lives, holds his people's enemies at bay.

---

navian raiders (the Vikings), which has led some scholars to argue against dating the poem from that era. Despite the uncertainty about when the poem was composed, and the anonymity of the author, one can speculate with some confidence about his religious and cultural background. Most scholars agree that the poet was Christian, possibly even a churchman, but nevertheless inclined to sympathize with the pagan, heroic past of his Germanic forefathers.

Events in History at the Time the Poem Takes Place

Settlement, feud, and transition: the Germanic peoples. *Beowulf* narrates datable historical events (such as the Geatish king Hygelac's raid into Frisia) that place its action firmly in the early sixth century. This was an age of settlement,

First page of the *Beowulf* manuscript.

feud, and transition for the Germanic peoples. The Roman Empire had fallen to Germanic invaders in the relatively recent past (the traditional date is 476), but had been moribund for many years before its final dissolution. Its deterioration created something of a power vacuum, which allowed the various Germanic peoples to move into areas formerly under Roman sovereignty. Franks, Goths, Danes, Frisians, Angles, and many other groups struggled for dominance in a Europe newly vulnerable to conquest. Opportunities for wealth—whether by trade or plunder—were great, leading to the intensification of traditional rivalries among these people, and the emergence of new ones. Complicating this scenario was the longstanding practice of the blood-feud, which dictated that an injury done to one's family required compensation, either in blood or money. Time made no difference; ancient grudges could flare into open warfare at a moment's notice, and the subsequent bloodshed prepared the way for new feuds. This never-ending cycle of violence is portrayed in great detail in *Beowulf*.

Myth or history? The modern distinction between historical truth and the fictions of myth and imaginative literature does not necessarily apply to works like *Beowulf*. For the Germanic peoples of the early Middle Ages, their history and legends were inseparable, and possessed similar qualities of truth, in that they provided a sense of national origin and identity. It was for them less important to place their foundational myths in a specific time and place than it was to show how these stories contributed to their notion of collective worth and significance. The events of *Beowulf* take place in history, but also in the mythic past, where magic, legendary characters, and founders of nations all operate together in a time that is simply long ago—or "once upon a time," in the classic language of folklore. The royal genealogies of the Germanic peoples usually include both pagan gods and figures from biblical history; for example, the *Langfethgatal*, a twelfth-century listing of Denmark's kings, includes legendary and semi-legendary figures—among them, Japheth (a son of Noah), a number of Greek gods and heroes, and the chief Germanic god, Odin (Garmonsway and Simpson, pp. 119-20). Historical works of this age usually begin with the creation of the world; this is not simply in order to begin at the beginning, but to situate recent events within a larger context that emphasizes issues of origin and destiny. *Beowulf* begins with an account of the founding of the Danish royal line by Scyld Scefing, a quasi-legendary figure; such mythic origins strengthen the dynastic legitimacy of Hrothgar. Likewise, the classic figure of Germanic myth, Wayland the Smith, is mentioned in *Beowulf* not because he is important in any historical sense, but because he was an armorer and sword-maker of magical skill, and linking his name to the weapons in the poem gives them a transcendent antiquity that they would not otherwise possess. The poet is not attempting to portray realistic, historical characters of the past any more than Virgil tries to paint a historically accurate picture of the Bronze Age in the *Aeneid*, or Shakespeare classical Rome in *Julius Caesar*. The historical setting of *Beowulf* is, more than anything else, a venue for heroic action. What is important about this time for the poet is the presence of legendary figures from the ancient past, a past in which heroes could still perform superhuman feats, where monsters still walked the earth, and Christianity had not yet come to lighten the bleak spirit of the Germanic peoples.

The Poem in Focus

Plot summary. *Beowulf* proceeds nonlinearly: the central story of Beowulf and his battles with monsters is told from beginning to end, but at many points a future event is anticipated or a past event recounted (like the "flashback" technique in cinema). The chronologically displaced narrative then serves as a commentary on the present action. Moreover, while the story of Beowulf and his heroism is the core of the poem, the tale contains multiple—often lengthy—digressions, involving kings, warriors, and battles whose relation to the basic story is often only symbolic. For example, a brief account is given of the wicked Danish king Heremod, not because he plays a part in Beowulf's tale, but because of the contrast he provides to the poem's exemplary kings Hrothgar, and, later, Beowulf himself.

The poem begins with the funeral of Scyld ("Shield") Scefing, great-grandfather of Hrothgar and founder of the Danish dynasty. Hrothgar's own rule is so successful that he decides to build a "great mead hall / meant to be a wonder of the world forever" (*Beowulf*, lines 69-70), and so Heorot is built—a great hall befitting the glory of an illustrious king.

With the account of its construction, however, comes a prophecy of its ultimate fate: "The hall towered, / its gables wide and awaiting / a barbarous burning" in a war between the Danes and Hrothgar's son-in-law (*Beowulf*, lines 81-83). Its present danger, though, is in the form of a "grim demon" named Grendel, who has been disturbed by the sounds of singing and merriment emanating from it (*Beowulf*, line 100). "[H]aunting the marches, marauding round the heath / and the desolate fens," this monstrous outcast descends from Cain, the first murderer (*Beowulf*, lines 102-104). Infuriated by the sounds of human happiness, he breaks into Heorot one night: "greedy and grim, he grabbed thirty men / . . . and rushed to his lair / . . . blundering back with the butchered corpses" (*Beowulf* 122-25). The Danes consider various plans, and even sacrifice to their pagan gods, to the narrator's evident displeasure. Their efforts are in vain. The attacks continue every night for 12 years.

> All were endangered; young and old
> were hunted down by that dark death-shadow
> who lurked and swooped in the long nights
> on the misty moors. . . .
> (*Beowulf*, lines 159-62).

Across the sea, in the homeland of the Geats (probably on the southern end of modern-day Sweden), a great warrior in the retinue of King Hygelac hears of the slaughter and decides to help. Beowulf assembles a group of 15 men, and

An illustrative interpretation of Beowulf preparing to decapitate Grendel.

HEOROT

The description of Heorot in *Beowulf* was probably meant to mirror the great buildings or "halls" of the Anglo-Saxon age, although exaggerated and idealized to a considerable degree. Archaeologists have found evidence of no structure from the Anglo-Saxon age as grand and richly decorated as Heorot, but large royal halls did exist. One such hall was the palace of King Edwin of Northumbria, who ruled in the north of England in the early seventh century. It was more than 100 feet long, and, like Heorot, stood among smaller outlying buildings that probably served as sleeping quarters for the royal family and noble guests. Less distinguished guests and retainers slept in the central hall itself, on raised platforms set against the walls. Built of timber, these halls were carefully decorated; the poem's reference to a "patterned floor" perhaps looks back to the intricate mosaic floors of the Roman villas common in England centuries before (*Beowulf*, line 725). The great central room served as throne-room (Anglo-Saxon thrones were also made of wood), a meeting place, and a dining room for celebrations. Thus, the large hall in which Hrothgar feasts is the same room in which the warriors sleep at night, and in which Grendel conducts his slaughter.

they sail to Denmark. Beowulf's offer of assistance is accepted, and that evening there is a feast in his honor. Night falls, and the Geats await Grendel. Beowulf puts aside his sword and removes his armor, declaring that he will fight the monster unarmed. Suddenly Grendel bursts in: seizing a man, the monster "bolted down his blood / and gorged on him lumps" (*Beowulf*, lines 741-42). Grendel then encounters Beowulf. After a mighty struggle that rocks Heorot, Beowulf rips off the monster's arm. Grendel flees to his lair at the bottom of the lake, where he drowns.

The next day everyone rejoices, and Beowulf hangs up Grendel's arm in the hall. A court minstrel praises Beowulf, and sings an old song of the legendary Sigemund and his battle with a dragon. He also mentions Heremod, a Danish king of a dynasty prior to Hrothgar's, who was cruel and greedy, and brought death to his people. Hrothgar orders Heorot to be newly decorated, and a great feast is given. At the feast, a minstrel sings about the events at Finnsburh, a famous incident from the Danes' past.

THE FINNSBURH FRAGMENT

The account of this incident in *Beowulf* is somewhat sketchy (probably because it was so well-known), but the missing historical details are supplied by a short Old English poem known as "The Finnsburh Fragment." In 452, the Danish lord Hnaef, whose sister Hildeburh is married to the Frisian king Finn, pays a seemingly friendly visit to Frisia. (The marriage, an attempt to make peace between two hostile peoples, is resoundingly unsuccessful.) As Hnaef and his men sleep, they are attacked by Finn and his men. Hnaef is killed, but the Frisians suffer such heavy losses that a stalemate ensues. Hengest, a loyal follower of Hnaef, takes charge of the remaining Danish forces. Finn offers Hengest a truce: the Danes accept him as their lord, and the Frisians, in turn, will treat the Danes as fellow countrymen. Furthermore, the Frisians will not seek revenge for the losses they have suffered. The truce does not hold, and the Danes avenge their losses. This episode may allude to the future struggles between the Danes and the Heathobards (whose enmity will also involve a failed diplomatic marriage). It may likewise foreshadow the Geatish king Hygelac's ill-advised raid into Frisia, in which he will be killed.

Wealhtheow, Hrothgar's wife and queen of the Danes, mentions to her husband that she is aware of his inclination to adopt Beowulf as his son. She gently advises against this, and points out that he already has a son and heir in Hrethric. She then presents Beowulf with a valuable gold collar, which the narrator tells us will be worn by Hygelac on his fatal raid into Frisia. The entertainment over, everyone retires for the night. Beowulf does not sleep in the main hall, but in another building.

Later that evening, Grendel's "grief-racked and ravenous" mother breaks into Heorot, retrieves Grendel's arm, and carries off Aeschere, Hrothgar's beloved friend (*Beowulf*, line 1278). Beowulf promises to avenge Aeschere's death. A party of Danes and Geats ride to the lake where the creature lives: "the overhanging bank / is a maze of tree-roots mirrored in its surface. / At night there, something uncanny happens: / the water burns" (*Beowulf*, lines 1363-66). Along the way, they find Aeschere's head. This time Beowulf arms himself fully, putting on a helmet and chain mail, and borrowing an ancient and noble sword. Beowulf dives into the serpent-infested depths, and swims downward for most of the day before meeting Grendel's mother. She seizes him, and only his chain mail prevents her from clawing him to death. Dragged down to her underwater dwelling, Beowulf finds himself in a fire-lit hall. He draws his sword, and swings at her to no avail; the sword cannot harm her. She tries to stab him, but is again foiled by his armor. He sees among her treasures a marvelous sword. He "took a firm hold of the hilt and swung / the blade in an arc, a resolute blow / that bit deep into her neck-bone / and severed it entirely" (*Beowulf*, lines 1564-67). Finding Grendel's body nearby, he cuts off his head, whereupon the blade of the sword melts away. He swims to the surface, taking with him the hilt of the sword and Grendel's head. At the shore only the Geats remain; the Danes have all returned home in despair. On the journey back to Heorot the head of Grendel is borne on a spear-point, a burden requiring the strength of four men.

Once back at Heorot, Beowulf presents Hrothgar with the sword hilt. The king, realizing that Beowulf will probably one day rule the Geats, gives him advice on the proper conduct of a ruler. Be good and generous to your people, he urges, and warns Beowulf against the pride and greed that consumed Heremod:

O flower of warriors, beware of that trap.
Choose, dear Beowulf, the better part,
eternal rewards. Do not give way to pride.

For a brief while your strength is in bloom
but it fades quickly; and soon there will follow
illness or the sword to lay you low. . . .
            (*Beowulf*, lines 1758-63)

Beowulf receives many valuable gifts, then departs with the Geats amid a flurry of mutual promises to render aid as needed in the future.

Upon his return to Geatland, Beowulf gives King Hygelac the treasure he received from Hrothgar, and recounts his adventures. He makes a prophecy, taking up a thread dropped earlier in the narrator's account of the building of Heorot. Hrothgar will give his daughter Freawaru in marriage to the Heathobard prince Ingeld. This attempt at making peace between the Danes and Heathobards, who are longtime enemies, will fail, and Denmark will be engulfed in war. Hygelac rewards Beowulf handsomely for his bravery. The queenly graces of his wife, Hygd, are noted, and compared to the wickedness of the infamous Queen Modthrytho, who was made to behave properly only by being married to the great King Offa.

The narrative now begins to cover a great deal of time very quickly. The fates of Hygelac and his son Heardred are briefly alluded to—Hygelac is killed while raiding Frisia, and Heardred is killed by the Swedish king Onela, an act that constitutes just one event in the long and bloody feud between Geats and Swedes. After Heardred's death Beowulf assumes the kingship, and rules ably for 50 years, during which time it is only though his overwhelming prowess that the Geats avoid being decimated by the Swedes. The story of the long feud between the Swedish and Geatish kingdoms is told in fragments (and not in chronological order) throughout the final third of the poem. The following paragraph is a summary of the story's main points.

Haethcyn, son of the Geatish king Hrethel, accidentally kills his elder brother Herebeald. King Hrethel dies of grief, and Haethcyn becomes monarch. The Swedes now view the Geats as vulnerable, a people with a new and untried ruler. Othere and Onela, sons of the Swedish king Ongentheow, attack the Geats. King Haethcyn and his younger brother, Hygelac, retaliate by attacking Ongentheow in Sweden. Haethcyn, Ongentheow, and Othere are killed, whereupon Onela becomes king of the Swedes. Meanwhile, Hygelac ascends to the Geatish throne and rashly invades Frisia. He is killed, but Beowulf (who had accompanied him) escapes. Hygelac's widow, Hygd, offers the Geatish kingship to Beowulf, believing that her son Heardred is not worthy of

the throne. Beowulf refuses, and Heardred becomes king. Meanwhile, in Sweden, Othere's sons, Eanmund and Eadgils, rebel against their uncle, King Onela. The rebels flee to Geatland and obtain sanctuary with Heardred. Refusing to tolerate this, Onela invades and kills Heardred. Onela then permits Beowulf to assume the throne of the Geats and returns to Sweden. His Swedish foe Eanmund has been killed by a Geatish faction, but the brother, Eadgils, with the assistance of an army provided by Beowulf, survives to invade Sweden and kill Onela.

WOMEN IN *BEOWULF*

Women in early Germanic society were in a much better position than in the later Middle Ages. Especially between wealthy families, marriages were generally arranged with the welfare of the woman in mind, so the husband had a financial interest in maintaining a strong, happy union. A woman could divorce her husband and take her father's money home with her if she chose, and could maintain property separate from her husband's even after marriage. Still, women were often pawns in high-stakes political maneuvering between important clans and kingdoms, and the results could be disastrous. In the Finnsburh episode, the marriage of Hildeburh to Finn is contracted to ensure peace between the Danes and the Frisians. When war breaks out, Hildeburh loses her husband, brother, and son. A similar fate awaits Hrothgar's daughter Freawaru, who will be married to Ingeld, a Heathobard. The Danes and the Heathobards were traditional enemies, and Beowulf predicts a tragic result from the union. However, the women of *Beowulf* are by no means passive; Hygelac's queen, Hygd, is in a position to offer the Geatish throne to Beowulf after her husband's death, even though her son Heardred is still alive. The Danish queen, Wealhtheow, also plays an active political role; she gently reproves Hrothgar for planning to adopt Beowulf as his heir, since this might affect the ability of her sons to attain the throne after Hrothgar's death. Pressing the point, she even goes on to ask Beowulf to provide counsel and assistance to her sons as needed—with the clear implication that the Danish throne will remain in her family.

Eadgils now sits on the Swedish throne, but is no friend to the Geats, since his brother Eanmund died not only in Geatland, but at the hands of a kinsman of Beowulf. At this point, the only thing keeping the Geats from the Swedish menace is the might of Beowulf. Now an old man, he is suddenly confronted with a new threat: a dragon has begun to fly about the land of the Geats, spewing fire from above. A thief has stolen a cup from an ancient mound of buried treasure that the dragon regards as his. The treasure, speculates the narrator in one of the poem's most famous passages (generally known as the "Lay of the Last Survivor"), must have been hidden by the last member of a once-glorious race, who, rather than see the treasure of his people scattered and plundered, buried it underground: "Now earth, hold what earls once held / and heroes can no more; . . . / I am left with nobody / to bear a sword or burnish plated goblets" (*Beowulf*, lines 2247-53).

The dragon, who hoards his treasure, is driven to murderous rage by the loss of the cup. "The hoard-guardian / scorched the ground as he scoured and hunted / for the trespasser" (*Beowulf*, lines 2294-96). Among the burned dwellings is Beowulf's royal hall. Knowing that a wooden shield will not work against a fire-breathing dragon, Beowulf has a large iron shield specially forged, and journeys to the dragon's cave in the company of 11 warriors and (to show the way) the thief who had provoked the dragon's wrath. Announcing that he will fight the dragon alone, Beowulf enters the stone-arched gateway of the dragon's lair. He calls a challenge to the dragon and readies himself for battle. The dragon blasts him with fire, and Beowulf's shield barely protects him. By this time everyone outside has fled in terror except for Wiglaf, who bears the sword and armor of the dead Eanmund, given to his father Weohstan by Onela. Remembering his vows of loyalty to Beowulf, Wiglaf rushes to his side. Beowulf strikes the dragon's skull with his sword, but the sword snaps from the force of the blow. Once more the dragon breathes fire, and this time sinks its fangs into Beowulf's neck. Wiglaf takes advantage of this opportunity to plunge his own sword into the dragon's belly. Severely wounded, the monster is no longer a match for Beowulf, who stabs it to death. Beowulf knows that he has purchased victory with his life; he feels poison bubbling in his veins. Expressing regret that he has no son to whom he can leave his armor, and happiness that he has ruled well, he asks Wiglaf to bring the dragon's treasure to him. This done, he gazes sadly upon it, although he is glad that at the end he is able to bestow such wealth on his people. He bids farewell to Wiglaf, and dies.

Wiglaf emerges from the cave, and the cowardly warriors slink back from the forest. After rebuking them, Wiglaf sends a messenger back to the Geatish encampment to announce the death of the dragon—and the king. The messenger's speech also relays the last details of the Geat-Swede hostilities, along with a dire prophecy of Swedish aggression now that Beowulf is no more. The messenger notes other dangers, too; the Frisians and their Frankish allies will remember Hygelac's raid, and will probably attack as well. Beowulf is cremated on an elaborate funeral pyre, decked with armor and helmets. He and the remains of the pyre are entombed with treasure in a great barrow on the coastland. At the poem's end the Geats say that "of all the kings upon the earth / he was the man most gracious and fairminded, / kindest to his people and keenest to win fame" (*Beowulf*, lines 3180-82).

The duties of lord, retainer, and family. The society depicted in *Beowulf* is an essentially military one, with each kingdom dedicated to consolidating and expanding its king's hegemony. Integral to this system was a series of highly personal relationships between the king and each of his men. These warriors (also called retainers, thanes, or earls) derived benefits from being in a king's retinue—they could be given weapons, armor, and precious objects, but perhaps more importantly they received a sense of lordship and community. There was no one more wretched in Anglo-Saxon society than an outcast, a man without a lord and a band of fellow warriors; in fact, the word "wretch" derives from the Old English word *wrecca*, meaning "outcast" or "exile." In return, a retainer was expected to render helpful advice and exhibit absolute loyalty to his lord; cowardice and treachery were the ultimate sins. The lord, on the other hand, was expected to protect his men from their enemies, and to generously share the spoils of war. The essence of the evil king Heremod's wickedness was that he did neither: he kept his treasure to himself, and killed Danish warriors in his own hall. For this, he himself became a friendless exile, and was ultimately killed by his enemies.

However, if retainers were bound to defend their lords to the death, lords did not necessarily see their kingship as an obligation to prefer their peoples' interests to their own. The kings in *Beowulf* maintain a personal sense of bravery, autonomy, and destiny often apart from the welfare of their kingdoms, and it is at times difficult to determine how the poet wished his readers to evaluate them in this context. For example, Hygelac's raid into Frisia was clearly rash; the narrator tells us "[f]ate swept him away / because of his proud need to provoke / a feud with the Frisians," and the consequences for the Geats were dire indeed (*Beowulf*, 1206-1208). But pride was one of the proper attributes of a noble king, and there is less criticism (explicit or implied) of Hygelac in the poem than one might expect, given the circumstances of his failed expedition. Beowulf too must be judged in light of this standard. His response to the dragon's attack on his people and kingdom will be an exclusively personal one; he views the dragon's aggression as an affront to him as an individual, and resolves to fight alone. But he is able to defeat the dragon only with help, and Wiglaf's assistance comes too late to save the king's life. Clearly Beowulf's death will be even more catastrophic for the Geats than that of Hygelac; there is a strong implication that they will be overrun by the Swedes and Frisians, and annihilated. Wiglaf has fulfilled his obligation to Beowulf, but has Beowulf fulfilled his obligation to the Geats? Is the reader meant to fault Beowulf for seeking personal glory at the cost of the Geats' welfare? These questions are fundamental to any understanding of the poem. It must be noted, too, that the final word in the text (*lofgeornost*) is applied to the dead hero, and means "keenest to win fame."

Christianity and heroic values: a contradiction? The pagan society depicted in *Beowulf*, like the Christian society in which the author lived, was based on a system of mutual obligation between lord and retainer. The Anglo-Saxon world that produced *Beowulf* was Christianized, but retained many of the elements of the society depicted in the poem; a Christian retainer in eighth- (or eleventh-) century England was bound to a Christian lord by the same code of conduct, and could expect the same benefits from his lord, as a pagan retainer in the poem. Works such as the *Anglo-Saxon Chronicle* (a year-to-year history of England maintained by monastic chroniclers from the fifth until the early twelfth century), the *History of the English Church and People* (731) by the English monk Bede, the ninth-century *Life of King Alfred* by Asser, and others all bear witness to the preeminence of this idealized code among the English before and after their conversion. For the *Beowulf* poet, Christianity was an imperative not because it changed the character and behavior of the people in any essential way, but because Christ was the true Lord—a Christian maintained fidelity to his religion for the same reason that he owed complete fidelity to his king. Christian observance was an obligation imposed

by the truth of the faith, and by the oath of allegiance taken at baptism. Paganism was wrong because the pagan gods were wicked, and a retainer was under no obligation to serve a wicked lord. Falling back into pagan observance after baptism was worse still; rather than simply following an evil lord, the lapsed Christian was guilty of treachery. Thus, Christianity among the Anglo-Saxons exhibited the same social economy that knitted together pagan society. Lordship, and the obligations imposed by it on lord and retainer, were still fundamental—the difference was that a Christian now had to exhibit loyalty to two lords, one in heaven and one on earth.

The union between the new religion and the old heroic code was not always seamless, however. Christianity emphasized qualities of otherworldliness, humility, and detachment from earthly riches and honor, and nothing could run more counter to traditional Germanic values. A pagan lord was expected to be strong, domineering, and wealthy from years of plundering the lands of his neighbors. Insults were avenged with breathtaking violence, and feuds were carried over from generation to generation by the hatred of sons for their fathers' enemies. Christian missionaries in Anglo-Saxon England converted pagan kings, but were less successful in quelling paganism's violent and acquisitive tendencies. And it seems that the newly-converted English retained an appetite for the old pagan tales as well. There were exceptions; Bede writes in his *History* of the early-seventh-century English king Oswald, who was both a mighty lord and an exemplary Christian: "Although he wielded supreme power, Oswald was always wonderfully humble, kindly, and generous to the poor and strangers" (Bede, p. 147). For the most part, though, the Christian ideal was more professed than practiced. This tension is exhibited in *Beowulf* in a number of ways. The Danes practice idolatry when confronted by Grendel, but the narrator's criticism is brief; they presumably do not know any better, and their offense is one of ignorance rather than wickedness. Grendel is said to have descended from Cain, the primordial murderer; his wickedness is thus given a specifically biblical context, with the clear implication that he is to be judged by Christian standards. Beowulf, too, operates within a Christian system of values, albeit primarily on the symbolic level. It is perhaps no accident that as he approaches the dragon's lair, he is accompanied by 12 men—the number of Christ's apostles. His descent into the fiery dragon's lair has also been likened to Christ's descent into Hell—the period between Jesus's death and resurrection when he is said to have released the Jewish patriarchs from their bondage. One should not attempt to push these parallels too far, however; *Beowulf* is not an allegory, and Beowulf is not Christ. The extent to which his death mirrors Christ's passion should be viewed as a poetic illustration of his extraordinary virtue, but the areas in which he falls short may represent the flaws of the old heroic code. He sacrifices himself for his people, true—but his death brings only their destruction. The dragon is dead, but the Swedes and Frisians are massing on the borders. The *Beowulf* poet presented pagan heroism at its best, but he makes it clear that it is insufficient.

Sources and literary context. The story of Beowulf is told nowhere else. There are no earlier (or later) versions of the Beowulf story, and indeed no references at all to Beowulf and his fights with the monsters, apart from a few tantalizing but frustrating texts like the charter (931) of King Aethelstan, which defines the boundaries for a land grant thus: "from there north over the hill . . . to the fence of Beowa's patch . . . then to the long meadow, and from there to Grendel's Mere" (Garmonsway and Simpson, p. 301). There are also references in other documents to such places as "Grendel's Gate," "Grendel's Mire," "Grendel's Pit," and the like. The existence of such texts hints that the Beowulf story (or some version of it) was well-known enough in Anglo-Saxon times to engender place names. The story as we have it may be of purely English origin, despite its Scandinavian subject.

Characters from the poem other than Beowulf appear frequently in Germanic literature. References to the members of the Danish royal family (Heremod, Scyld, Beowulf [the son of Scyld], Healfdane, Hrothgar, Hrothulf, Halga, and Hrethric) abound in Old Norse literature of the tenth through thirteenth centuries; also found are references to the Swedish, Geatish, Heathobard, Angle (or English), Frisian, and Gothic characters who populate *Beowulf*. For example, the seventh-century Old English poem "Widsith" contains a brief account of Hrothgar and his nephew Hrothulf (called Hrothwulf here):

> Very long did Hrothwulf and Hrothgar,
> nephew and uncle, keep peace as kinsmen
> together, after they had driven off the tribe of
> the Vikings and humbled Ingeld's battle-array,
> hewing down the host of the Heathobards at
> Heorot.
>
> (Garmonsway and Simpson, pp. 127-28)

This text supports the hint given in *Beowulf* that Hrothulf will eventually betray the Danes; he and Hrothgar kept peace "very long," the implication being that this peace eventually ended. It is clear that the *Beowulf* poet was placing his story in the midst of a well-defined context of history and legend.

Other aspects of the poem are reflected elsewhere as well. Wayland the Smith—whom Beowulf credits with making his mailshirt—was a legendary armorer of magical ability, and was as familiar to the Anglo-Saxons as was Hercules to the ancient Greeks. The legendary adventures of Sigemund and the Waelsings (or Volsungs) appear extensively in Old Norse literature, and a stone carving (c. 1000) found in England illustrates a scene from the story. The story of Sigemund and his sister is one of the best known in Germanic legend, and it is entirely appropriate that it be recited at Heorot by Hrothgar's minstrel. We find descriptions of pagan funerals like Beowulf's in the writings of the sixth-century historian Jordanes, who describes the funeral of Attila the Hun; in *The Travels of ibn Fadlan*, the memoir of a tenth-century Arab traveler who lived for a while among a group of Swedes; and in a number of thirteenth-century Danish and Icelandic texts.

As mentioned, the *Beowulf* poet was probably a churchman, acquainted with the Roman classics and the writings of the Church fathers. Echoes of Virgil's *Aeneid*, Boethius's *The Consolation of Philosophy*, St. Paul's letters, and certain theological writings of St. Augustine of Hippo have all been heard in *Beowulf*; these texts would have been included in any monastic library in Anglo-Saxon England, and it is reasonable to suppose that the *Beowulf* poet had read them. Another important text is the early eighth-century *History of the English Church and People*, by the Venerable Bede, a monk of the monastery of Jarrow. It describes the religious and political history of the English from the Roman occupation to Bede's own day, paying special attention to the process of conversion undergone by England's various pagan rulers. England was divided into a number of small kingdoms in those days, and so there were many to convert. Important to *Beowulf* are the descriptions of how these men, despite their apparently sincere conversions, remained tied to the ancient Germanic codes of conduct. However, reflections of these works in *Beowulf* are merely echoes, not sources per se; the poet does not use this material directly. Rather, there is more of a sense of common ground, of thematic congruity, between portions of *Beowulf* and certain Roman and Christian texts.

Events in History at the Time the Poem Was Written

The rise of Christianity in England. After the collapse of the Roman Empire, Britannia, a former Roman province, suffered incursions from the Germanic peoples. Britannia was later called "England" after the Angles, who, together with the Saxons, settled the area in the fifth century. It is their Anglo-Saxon culture and language (also called "Old English") that produced *Beowulf*. The Angles and Saxons were pagan, but Christianity had existed in England since the first century C.E. and the new rulers of England did not succeed in exterminating it entirely. Roman civilization and urban life was effectively obliterated in England, but Christian communities survived in outlying villages and monasteries. This older Celtic form of English Christianity was gradually absorbed by the newer Roman Christianity instituted by St. Augustine of Canterbury (d. 605), who is traditionally credited with reintroducing Christianity to England by converting Ethelbert, king of Kent, in 597. By the end of the seventh century the rulers and inhabitants of England were overwhelmingly Christian. In 664 the Synod of Whitby united the various independent English Churches under Roman observance, and from then until the Reformation the Church in England was one with the rest of Latin Christendom. England was a major European center of Christian and classical learning, and its missionaries and scholars traveled throughout Europe, converting pagans, establishing monasteries and schools, and disseminating literate culture. The English churchman Alcuin (735-804) inspired what is now known as the "Carolingian Renaissance," setting up a number of important libraries and schools in France for the Holy Roman Emperor Charlemagne, and serving as his official adviser on religious and educational issues. The oldest manuscript of the Latin Bible is of English provenance, probably copied c. 690-700 at Jarrow, and many important early liturgical books came from English monasteries as well. The theological, homiletic, rhetorical, and scientific writings of churchmen such as Bede, Aldhelm, and Alcuin were known throughout the West, and their authority was regarded to be little inferior to that of the Church fathers themselves. Despite its thoroughgoing Christianity, however, England was a society very much in tune with its Germanic roots. Bede was the most prominent churchman of his day, and wrote in Latin, but on his deathbed he composed his "Death Song" in traditional Old English alliterative verse. Aldhelm wrote highly ornate and complex Latin poetry, but was said to have composed Old English verse of equal quality; none has survived. English monks were forever being warned to avoid the pagan epic poems that they obviously loved so much. But if there was a tension within these churchmen, it was a relatively benign one; Christianity had been established for so long that the old poems were more of a possible distraction than a spiritual danger. It was in many ways a golden age, but one that was soon to come to an end.

The Scandinavian invasions. The Scandinavian peoples of what are now Denmark, Sweden, and Norway had been great seafarers and traders since the height of the Roman Empire, but for reasons that are still unclear, in the late eighth century they exploded into western Europe, in wave after wave of brutal aggression. These campaigns continued, off and on, for more than 200 years. At the time, the chroniclers of their depredations usually called them Danes or Northmen, but we now know them as Vikings. (The term "Vikings" properly refers just to the raiders, not to all Northmen.)

The Vikings first attacked England in 793, sacking the monastery at Lindisfarne. A second attack in 875 was even worse, and the monks all fled or were killed. The Vikings attacked at will throughout England and France, killing all who opposed them, taking captives to be sold into slavery, despoiling churches and monasteries, and burning towns. Monasteries, parishes, and dioceses throughout England were depopulated, and many ceased to exist. England had periods of respite, most prominently during the reign of King Alfred the Great (849-99), but after his death the Vikings returned many times. In fact, the final series of Danish invasions culminated in the installation of a Danish king on the English throne. By this time, however, the Danes were a different people. King Cnut (or Canute) reigned from 1016-1035, and he was generally quite popular, though not at first; as warlike as his Danish ancestors, he invaded England and plundered several cities before subduing most of northern England. The English king Ethelred fought him ably in the south, but died in 1016, and Cnut was elected king by the *witena gemot* (a body of nobles and counselors). Parts of England remained loyal to Edmund, the son of

Ethelred, but a few months later Edmund too died, and Cnut ruled unchallenged. He was not English, and so had no vested interest in favoring one English lord over another, and managed to remain above—and even dampen—their continual feuding. He was an able defender of the realm, and just in his administration. He also was a devout Christian; he endowed many monasteries, secured the possessions of the English Church, and even went on a pilgrimage to Rome. It was probably in his reign that the *Beowulf* manuscript was written, and the presence of a Dane on the English throne may explain why a poem with so much Danish content was produced in England at this time.

Reception. What happened to the *Beowulf* manuscript between the time of its creation and the early seventeenth century is anybody's guess. It was acquired by Sir Robert Cotton at about this time, and in 1705 it was read (if barely understood) by Humfrey Wanley, an assistant librarian at the Bodleian library at Oxford. The Danish scholar Jonsson Thorkelin made a translation of *Beowulf* into Latin in 1815, and this introduced the poem to Europe as a whole. In the nineteenth century, advances in philology allowed the language of the poem to be understood better than before, and scholars were able to situate it within a specific cultural and linguistic context. Early criticism of *Beowulf* tended to see it as a composite poem, with a mixture of Christian and pagan elements; thus, in 1887 F. A. Blackburn could confidently write, "It is admitted by all critics that the Beowulf [sic] is essentially a heathen poem; that its materials are drawn from tales composed before the conversion of the Angles and Saxons to Christianity; and that there was a time when these tales were repeated without the Christian reflections and allusions that are found in the poem that has reached us" (Blackburn, p. 205).

Things began to change in the twentieth century, as more sensitive and nuanced readings began to emerge. The most influential of these early attempts was made by J.R.R. Tolkien, now best known as the author of *The Lord of the Rings*, but throughout his life a first-rank scholar of medieval Germanic literature and philology. In his famous essay "*Beowulf*: The Monsters and the Critics," he argued that the poem should be read as a poem, not as a mirror of racial nostalgia, not as a disfigured artifact from the mythic past, and

not, in short, as anything other than the sophisticated creation of a gifted poet. "*Beowulf*," he writes, "has been used as a quarry of fact and fancy far more assiduously than it has been studied as a work of art" (Tolkien, p. 246). Since the publication of Tolkien's essay, his advice has generally been heeded, though the number of books and articles on the poem has reached staggering proportions, and readings have been proposed from across the ideological spectrum. The dating controversy is still unsettled, and the extent to which the poem's Christian content determines its meaning is still energetically debated.

Recently the poem has enjoyed a new translation by the Nobel-laureate Irish poet Seamus Heaney (used for the purposes of this entry). His version, which was given the Whitbread Award in Great Britain, uses a powerfully spare diction and vocabulary in an effort to mirror the plain-spoken quality of the Old English original. Critics have for the most part been lavish in their praise, seeing Heaney's simple language as an artful means of bringing to the forefront the poem's structural and thematic complexities, while retaining its original vigor.

—Matthew Brosamer

For More Information

Baker, Peter S., ed. *Beowulf: Basic Readings*. New York: Garland, 1995.

Bede. *A History of the English Church and People*. Trans. Leo Sherley-Price. Baltimore: Penguin, 1955.

Beowulf. Trans. Seamus Heaney. New York: Farrar, Straus and Giroux, 2000.

Blackburn, A. F. "The Christian Coloring in the Beowulf." *PMLA* 12 (1897): 205-25.

Garmonsway, George Norman, and Jacqueline Simpson, eds. *Beowulf and its Analogues*. London: J. M. Dent & Sons, 1968.

Kiernan, Kevin S. *Beowulf and the Beowulf Manuscript*. New Brunswick: Rutgers University Press, 1981.

Nicholson, Lewis E., ed. *An Anthology of Beowulf Criticism*. Notre Dame: University of Notre Dame Press, 1963.

Niles, John D. *Beowulf: The Poem and its Tradition*. Cambridge: Harvard University Press, 1983.

Stenton, Sir Frank. *Anglo-Saxon England*. 3d. ed. Oxford: Oxford University Press, 1971.

Tolkien, J. R. R. *Beowulf: The Monsters and the Critics*. Proceedings of the British Academy 22 (1936): 245-95.

The Canterbury Tales

by

Geoffrey Chaucer

Geoffrey Chaucer is by far the best-known poet of the English Middle Ages, and it is primarily in *The Canterbury Tales* that his fame rests. His lifetime (c. 1340-1400) spanned some of the most tumultuous events of the era. He saw the ravages of the Black Death (1348), in which over one-third of Europe's population was wiped out. He may have witnessed the destruction wrought in London by the Peasants' Revolt (1381), as his apartment sat directly over the city gate through which the rebellious thousands poured, bent on a campaign of arson and destruction that culminated in the beheading of the archbishop of Canterbury. And he participated in several of the battles between the English and French that would later be called the Hundred Years' War (1337-1453). A high-ranking official in the king's service, he was by turns a courier, soldier, diplomat (and possibly spy), customs inspector, overseer of building projects, forest officer, and member of Parliament. He also traveled widely; his errands in the king's service took him to France and Italy on several occasions, and even to Spain. Entirely separate from his official duties was his work as a poet. Probably beginning with short love poems, he soon began composing more ambitious works, such as *The Book of the Duchess* (c. 1368-72), a poem expressing the grief of the duke of Lancaster for his dead wife, and *Troilus and Criseyde* (c. 1382-86), a romance-epic of the Trojan War. His last work (left unfinished at his death) was *The Canterbury Tales*. Most of these tales were composed relatively late in Chaucer's life, but some were composed separately years

> ## THE LITERARY WORK
>
> A collection of tales set in ancient and medieval times, mainly in Europe; first published in 1478.
>
> ## SYNOPSIS
>
> In the late fourteenth century, a group of pilgrims entertain each other with stories while traveling from London to Canterbury.

before, and given a place in *The Canterbury Tales* simply by being assigned a pilgrim-narrator. Showing extraordinary variety in form and content, the tales are both a mirror of Chaucer's wide-ranging experience as an unusually well-read poet and important royal official, and a uniquely complex representation of fourteenth-century life, literature, and ideas.

Events in History at the Time of the Tales

Estates satire. Much as a professional comedian now will have vast repertoires of doctor jokes, lawyer jokes, and so on, medieval satirists were wont to poke fun at various professions, attributing certain stereotypical qualities to each of these "estates" of society. Medieval estates satire was a flourishing genre, and Chaucer was its most noteworthy practitioner in fourteenth-century England. For centuries society had been perceived as divided into three parts: those who worked, those who prayed, and those who fought. Given that there were a great many more professions than peasant, priest, and soldier, the reality was, of course, far more complex, but satirists nevertheless applied a similarly formulaic approach to the wide diversity of callings they saw around them. This is manifest in the "General Prologue" to *The Canterbury Tales*. The Miller is a thief because society commonly viewed millers as thieves (they held regional monopolies on the grinding of grain into flour, and were thought to habitually give short weight), and the comic potential of their rascality is exploited to the fullest in "The Reeve's Tale." Pardoners had a terrible reputation as unprincipled con-men, who would abuse their holy calling by selling fraudulent pardons for sin and trafficking in bogus relics. Cooks were drunkards who sold contaminated food; merchants engaged in usury and financial double-dealing; summoners were corrupt extortionists; friars were greedy and duplicitous seducers; widows were sex-crazed—the list of stereotypes goes on and on. Chaucer's satirical presentation of these and other professions should therefore be viewed not so much as a mirror of society (although it is that as well), but as a combination of literary realism and the tradition of estates satire. His purpose was entertainment and moral instruction, not sociology, and his creation of vivid and lifelike characters who nevertheless acted as traditional caricatures of their professions owes as much to this age-old literary technique as to his sharp eye for individuality and realism.

The role of the Church. The Church played a substantial role in most aspects of fourteenth-century life. A significant portion of the land and wealth in England was owned or controlled by either the local diocese or the religious orders (such as monks, nuns, and friars), each of which acted as a corporation in its own right, able to buy, sell, and inherit property, and to increase its holdings insofar as it was able. On the economic level alone, therefore, the power of the Church was considerable. As a legal entity the Church had sweeping influence over the lives of Christians (essentially everyone in fourteenth-century England, since the Jews had been expelled generations before), because it maintained authority over entire spheres of activity that were regulated by canon (church) law. There were two judicial systems in place, civil and ecclesiastical. While the Civil Courts adjudicated affairs involving theft, murder, treason, poaching, and the like, the church courts held sway in matters relating to marriage (such as adultery and bigamy), the Church (failing to pay tithes, stealing from church property), and deviant beliefs and practices (heresy and witchcraft). Also, all churchmen (and women) were for the most part responsible only to the church courts, and could be tried nowhere else. This added up to a great deal of power; for example, since inheritance disputes often pivoted on whether or not a marriage was valid or an heir legitimate, the decision of the church court on such issues could determine an aristocratic or even royal succession, or bestow title to vast landholdings. Furthermore, throughout the fourteenth century a large part of the English population (a standard estimate is 25 percent) was in holy orders, and so subject to church law only. Chaucer's tales represent the two legal systems in the persons of the Man of Law, a distinguished lawyer in the civil courts, and the Summoner, a corrupt instrument of the ecclesiastical court's power. The Summoner takes bribes to let adulterers alone.

Many other institutions, such as schools and universities, were also controlled by churchmen. Even the crusades were under papal auspices. But it was the day-to-day interaction between Church and individual that seems to have interested Chaucer most—the friar who appears at one's doorstep with a ready homily and an outstretched palm, the pardoner who offers remission of God's punishment for sin, the nuns who teach young ladies how to behave, the parson who watches carefully over the spiritual welfare of his parishioners—all these people made the Church a living and immediate presence in the lives of medieval Englishmen to an extent that is difficult to imagine now. The call to penance and moral reform was an important aspect of this presence, and it came from numerous sources.

By church law, every Christian had to undergo the sacrament of penance at least once a year; penance involved confessing one's sins to a priest, who would then (if he determined that the confession was complete and sincere) offer absolution and God's forgiveness. This absolution could, in fact, be obtained from more than one source; normally confession would be made to one's parish priest, but wandering friars could also hear confessions, and as there was a popular notion that the penance imposed by the friars was less severe than that of the secular clergy, bad feelings arose between these competing branches of the clergy. According to the moral theology of the time (fully articulated in Chaucer's "Parson's Tale," a lengthy treatise on penance), true penitence consisted of three stages: contrition of heart, confession of mouth, and satisfaction in deed. This "satisfaction" was the penance performed by the sinner; it consisted of making things right (such as restoring a stolen item to the lawful owner), but there was a punitive aspect as well. The sinner had to perform some action as evidence of his or her contrition. This could (and often did) involve simply giving money to the Church, which prompted a spirited competition for penitent sinners.

Pilgrimage in fourteenth-century England. Another way in which a penitent sinner could demonstrate contrition was to go on pilgrimage. Pilgrimage destinations were holy places, usually dedicated to the veneration of a particular saint, whose relics (physical remains of the saint, such as a hand, skull, clothing, or even a complete body) were enshrined there. The shrine to St. Thomas Becket in Canterbury was in many ways typical; one could see the bloodstained floor of the cathedral where Becket had been martyred in 1170, collect water from a well near the shrine that was believed to have curative powers, and buy trinkets and souvenirs from vendors. Upon arriving at the site, the pilgrim would request that the saint intercede with God on his or her behalf. The petitions were varied; some sought forgiveness for sin, some wished to recognize the saint's help in curing an ailment, and some hoped that the saint would miraculously intervene to correct a problem, such as illness, childlessness, or reversal of fortune.

Pilgrimage was a popular activity in fourteenth-century Europe, and it is not difficult to imagine that in a society without formal vacations (in the modern sense), pilgrimages provided a much-needed element of variety and relief from workday tedium. That it served as an outlet helps explain why the institution of pilgrimage, however pious in design, was frequently criticized by moralists, who regarded it as an occasion for loose talk, drunkenness, and debauchery. Far from the watchful eyes of family and parish priest, pilgrims were often viewed like rowdy conventioneers are now—perhaps quite upright at home, but not on their best behavior when on the road. It was for this reason that members of religious orders were generally forbidden to go on pilgrimage without the express permission of their superiors. The reality was probably much as Chaucer represents it; pilgrims came from all walks of life, and the truly pious (such as the Parson) rode in company with revelers (the Miller), scholars (the Clerk), and conmen (the Pardoner), each seeking God or worldly gratification in his or her own way.

The steps to Trinity Chapel in Canterbury Cathedral, worn down through the years by the feet of pilgrims.

Pilgrimage also had a symbolic dimension. Life, according to a medieval homiletic commonplace, was a pilgrimage—each person sets off at birth on the pilgrimage of his soul, and the destination is not of this world: it is the heavenly Jerusalem, and eternal bliss in the company of God. The Parson says as much in the prologue to his tale:

> Jesus in mercy send
> Me wit to guide your way one further stage
> Upon that perfect, glorious pilgrimage
> Called the celestial, to Jerusalem.
> (Chaucer, *The Canterbury Tales*, p. 502)

For the intensely holy Parson, the earthly pilgrimage to Canterbury is just a pale reflection of the real pilgrimage, the only one that truly matters. Many critics believe that even though *The Canterbury Tales* was left unfinished, Chaucer meant "The Parson's Tale" to complete the work, and that its emphasis on penance, avoidance of sin, and spiritual renewal summed up his own beliefs about the nature of pilgrimage. The pilgrims never arrive at Canterbury, but the work concludes with a vision of heaven—the end of the road for all true pilgrims.

Pagan antiquity. The world of classical antiquity loomed large in the England of Chaucer's day. For the Middle Ages, the achievements of the

Greeks and especially the Romans were almost beyond wonder. Chaucer had been to Italy, and would have seen the architectural remains of a civilization that, though long dead, remained in many ways a model for all that was good and noble. He could read the works of the Roman poets Virgil, Ovid, Statius, and Lucan—this, for him, was literature of a sort that could never be duplicated. It possessed that essential quality of "authority"; its merits (poetic art, wisdom, and relevance to the human condition) were permanent and unassailable. For Chaucer and his contemporaries, the world had diminished since the Golden Age of Greece and Rome, and nothing like it would be seen again. The medical and scientific teachings of Aristotle and Galen, the moral wisdom of Seneca, the rhetorical skill of Cicero, the literary genius of Ovid—in virtually every field of human endeavor the ancients were thought to have blazed a trail that later generations could only follow.

The Christian Middle Ages did see one advantage that it possessed over the classical past— the possibility of salvation. The noble Greeks and Romans, however accomplished, were benighted by their lack of revealed religious truth, and could never achieve happiness in the afterlife. This was cause for some unease. How could a people so mighty and admirable be now collectively damned to hell, and was it not an affront to God to hold these people in such high esteem? Various attempts were made to circumvent this problem; there were venerable legends about the pagan Romans and Christianity. For example, the emperor Trajan (53-117 C.E.) a just ruler though not a Christian, was said to have been resurrected from the dead and converted, so that he could attain salvation. The poet Virgil (70-19 B.C.E.) was thought to be a prophet of Christianity, who had embedded a prediction of Christ's birth in one of his *Eclogues,* and Dante (1265-1321) in his *Inferno* invented a special circle of hell for "virtuous pagans" (such as Plato and Aristotle) who were denied heaven because they did not know Christ, but were nevertheless spared torment in recognition of their merits. Chaucer's solution was to apply a philosophical and moral standard to his pagan characters that was both Christian and non-Christian, a standard derived from the thought of Boethius (c. 480-524 C.E.), a Roman magistrate under the Gothic emperor Theodoric. Unjustly accused of treason, he was imprisoned and eventually put to death with great cruelty. An eminent man of letters (his translations of Aristotle into Latin were used throughout the early Middle Ages in Europe), he composed while in prison *The Consolation of Philosophy*, a dialogue between himself and Lady Philosophy. His fictionalized self was so miserable and embittered by his fall from grace that his reason was clouded. Lady Philosophy (who personified the loftiest possible achievements of the human mind) explained to him his irrationality—his misery was not due to his imprisonment and death sentence, but to his failure to understand the workings of fortune and divine providence. Fortune, explains Lady Philosophy, is the working of chance in the world. To rely on worldly success for happiness is foolish because ill-fortune or the plots of one's enemies can take it all away in an instant. It is far better, she argues, to ignore the gifts of fortune—good or bad—and simply trust in God's providence, which must necessarily proceed towards a larger, ultimate good. Boethius (himself a Christian) inserted no Christian dogma into the *Consolation*; rather, Lady Philosophy builds her argument on reason alone, on philosophy rather than theology. Boethius's work was critically important to Chaucer in that it provided a reasonable ethical framework for the tales that Chaucer set in pagan antiquity; the characters in these tales could not benefit from Christian revelation, but they could think and reason their way to a close approximation of it.

The Tales in Focus

Contents overview. The overall narrative format of *The Canterbury Tales* is fairly simple; a group of pilgrims gather at the Tabard Inn in Southwerk (just across the Thames River from London), readying themselves for a pilgrimage to the shrine of Thomas Becket in Canterbury. Martyred in 1170, Becket was especially venerated as a saint who would intercede on behalf of the sick, and his shrine was the most popular pilgrimage destination in fourteenth-century England. The narrator of the "General Prologue" to *The Canterbury Tales* (a pilgrim named Geoffrey Chaucer— a nonjudgmental yet perceptive fictional version of the poet himself) states that since he is going to give an account of his journey, it is reasonable to briefly introduce each of his fellow pilgrims. This he does in the *Prologue*, and it is through these portraits that critical judgements are often made about the tales the pilgrims tell.

Before leaving the inn, the pilgrims agree that each will tell four tales—two on the way to Canterbury and two on the return journey—and that he or she who tells the best tale will be rewarded back at the inn with a supper, paid for by the rest of the company. This ambitious plan is never realized; no pilgrim except Chaucer tells more than one tale, and many remain silent. *The Canterbury Tales* is thus, as we now possess it, unfinished.

The tales fall into many different genres but touch repeatedly on certain themes and subjects of evident interest to Chaucer, and the tales summarized below have been chosen with this in mind. "The Miller's Tale" is a fabliau (as are the Reeve's, Summoner's, Merchant's, and Shipman's tales), a genre originating in France generations before Chaucer's lifetime, characterized by low humor usually of a sexual and/or scatological nature. While these qualities remain in Chaucer's fabliaux, (especially in "The Miller's Tale") they exist side-by-side with more serious meditations on man's place in a fallen world, guided by God but goaded by the devil. The Wife of Bath gives a lengthy prologue to her tale in which she recounts the history of her five marriages, and explains in great detail her thoughts on matrimony, love, and the position of women in a man's world. In her tale, she takes up these same themes in the genre of an Arthurian Romance (though little in the way of Arthurian chivalry is evident) about a rapist knight who learns the error of his ways. "The Franklin's Tale" is a Breton *lai*, another genre of French origin, in which characters inhabit the pre-Christian world of ancient Brittany; these stories generally exhibit elements of magic and folklore. This tale emphasizes themes of marital honor and fidelity, and explores the possibilities for virtuous action in a world in which Christian revelation is absent. Finally, "The Nun's Priest's Tale" is a mixture of two genres: the beast fable, in which animals both wise and foolish speak and act as humans, and the beast epic, in which speaking animals act in satirical counterpoint to human models. The tale involves a rooster and a hen—a married couple who learnedly discuss the significance of the rooster's dream of being carried off to his death by a fearsome marauder. Later, the marauder appears in the form of a fox.

Plot summaries. *The Miller's Tale.* Set in contemporary Oxford, this tale involves an old carpenter (John), his beautiful young wife (Alison), and their boarder, a clever student (Nicholas). John is a jealous man, and ever fearful that he will be made a cuckold, so he watches Alison closely—with just cause. So overcome is Nicholas with her beauty that he propositions her; she wants to acquiesce but is afraid of John. Nicholas promises that he will find a way to dupe the old

man, and they part in high expectation. Soon after, Alison attends church, and is espied by Absolon, the parish clerk—a ridiculous, foppishly dressed young man who loves music, singing, and taverns, but is squeamish about farting. He immediately falls in love with her. He brings her beer and money, but to no avail—she scorns him.

One day when John is off at work, Nicholas hits upon a plan to make his dreams about Alison come true. He retires to his room, telling Alison to profess ignorance if John asks where he is. John returns home, and after wondering for a while where Nicholas could be, sends a servant to his room to fetch him. The servant returns alone, saying that Nicholas is lying in a dead faint. John runs up and rouses him, and Nicholas breathlessly tells him that he has discovered through astrology that a second flood will come, drowning the whole world and everyone in it. John despairs, but Nicholas tells him that there is a way out—they can prepare three tubs (one for John, one for Alison, and one for Nicholas) and tie them to the rafters of the ceiling. On the fateful night, they will sleep in the tubs, and when the water rises to a sufficient level, they will cut holes in the roof, and float away in safety. John gratefully agrees to the plan, and the tubs are prepared.

Several nights later, with John safely in his tub, Alison and Nicholas lie in bed together, enjoying the fruits of Nicholas's cleverness. Suddenly Absolon appears at the bedroom window, ready to try his luck again with Alison. He pleads his case with such obstinacy that she finally agrees to give him a kiss if he will only go away. While Nicholas kneels down in readiness at the window, Alison sticks her buttocks out into the pitch-black night, and Absolon kisses her there, with gusto. Realizing what has happened, he frantically rubs at his mouth with dirt and woodchips, while Alison laughingly shuts the window.

Absolon is black with rage and vows vengeance. Going across the village to the blacksmith's shop, he borrows a coulter—a large, sharp, bladed instrument that fits on the front of a plow. The end of the coulter is red-hot from the blacksmith's forge. Absolon carries it back to the window, and again professes his love for Alison—this time promising her a gold ring in return for a kiss. Nicholas hears this proposal, sticks his buttocks out the window, and farts on Absolon with such force that the clerk is almost blinded. Nevertheless, he is ready with the coulter, and jabs it a hand's breadth into Nicholas's posterior. Nicholas's screams for water, which wakes John, who (thinking that the cries of "water" refer to the oncoming flood) cuts the ropes that hold his tub to the roof beam, and crashes to the floor, breaking his arm. The townspeople rush in at the commotion, and, perceiving the entire situation, laugh heartily at the discomfiture of the three men. The tale ends with Alison suffering no harm whatsoever.

The Wife of Bath's Prologue and The Wife of Bath's Tale. The Wife of Bath is unique among the Canterbury pilgrims in that her prologue is much longer than her tale. In the prologue, she gives a spirited account of her life insofar as it relates to men—specifically, the five husbands she has successively married since the age of 12. She begins by defending multiple marriages (i.e., remarriage after the death of a spouse) and attacking those who argue that a widow should remain single until death. Since the law allows her to remarry, she insists, she will do so as she pleases. Furthermore, she maintains, since church law gives each spouse authority over the other's body, she will demand sex from her husbands incessantly, whether they wish it or not; her husbands are her debtors and her slaves, to whom she has applied the "whip" regularly (*The Canterbury Tales*, p. 279). For the Wife of Bath, marriage has been a constant struggle for power and autonomy, and she has used every means at her disposal to keep her husbands under her thumb. Her first three husbands were rich and old, and she kept them in a constant state of jealousy and sexual exhaustion until they died. Her fourth was a profligate reveler, and was unfaithful to her, but she avenged herself on him by drinking and celebrating without him, and making him jealous. Even before he died she had selected a likely fifth, and sure enough, at the funeral Jankyn appeared, and she was so smitten with him and his well-shaped legs that she married him in a matter of weeks. At the time Jankyn was a young man of 20, and she a wealthy widow of 40, but this bothered her not a bit; she loved him best of all, though they fought constantly. She declares that he pleased her sexually more than anyone before, but in another way gave her grief. What bothered her most was that he had a *Book of Wicked Wives*, and would read aloud from it to annoy her. This book was an anthology of misogynist and antimatrimonial literature, full of stories about men brought to ruin and despair by their wives' misconduct. One evening she could stand it no longer; she leapt up, tore three pages from the book, and struck him on the cheek so hard that he fell back into the fire. Enraged, he got up

and struck her on the side of the head, whereupon she fell stunned to the floor. Faintly she called out that still she loved him, and would like a kiss before she died. Horrified at what he had done, Jankyn knelt down, and she punched him in the face. All ended well, she concludes; forever after, he obeyed her in every respect.

"The Wife of Bath's Tale" recapitulates many of the themes in her prologue. A young knight of King Arthur's court sees a maiden walking before him, and rapes her. For this crime he is sentenced to death, but Queen Guinevere and the ladies of the court convince Arthur to put the knight's fate in their hands. The queen tells the knight that he has a year and a day to discover what it is that women most want; if he finds the correct answer, he will save his life. The knight has no choice but to agree, and sets off.

After searching far and wide, and receiving many opinions, the knight turns back in despair; no one knows what women want. Suddenly in a forest he sees a company of women dancing. As he approaches, they vanish and in their place sits the ugliest woman he has ever seen. When he tells her that unless he can learn what women most desire he will be killed, she says that she will tell him if he promises to do the next thing she asks. He agrees, and they go together to Arthur's court. Upon their arrival the queen and ladies of the court are summoned, and the knight gives the answer the woman has taught him: that women want to be the masters of their husbands. No lady of the court can disagree with this, and the knight is spared.

At once the ugly woman leaps to her feet, tells the court that she gave the correct answer to the knight in exchange for his agreement to do what she asks, and calls upon the queen to compel him to marry her. The knight begs for mercy—anything but that, he says—but there is no gainsaying the woman's rights, and they are married amid great joy and celebration. That night, when he is brought to her bed, the knight is woeful; he writhes to and fro, and will not touch her. She wonders at his standoffishness; do all of King Arthur's knights act in this way to their wives? But she is so ugly, so old, and so low-born, he answers. She then explains to him at great length that being ugly, poor, old, and low-born are not necessarily bad qualities, especially in a wife—for example, he will never have to worry about her being unfaithful. Still, she continues, in view of his manifest desires, she will give him a choice; he can either have her foul, old, and faithful to him, or young and beautiful, in which case he must take his chances. After agonizing over the choice, he finally decides to leave it up to her. This being the correct answer, she is magically transformed into a beautiful young woman, who promises to be true to him forever.

The Franklin's Tale. In ancient Brittany (a region of northwest France), there lived a knight named Arveragus who loved a lady named Dorigen. His love was so ardent that after a while, despite the fact that she came from a more aristocratic family than he, she consented to marry him. He promised to obey her in all matters, as long as they maintained a public image of his being in charge. She, in turn, promised to be his true, humble wife. The Franklin here interjects his approval of this arrangement; mutual surrendering of mastery to the other, he believes, is the key to a successful marriage.

Shortly after the marriage, Averagus departs for England to win fame and honor in knightly pursuits. Dorigen is heartbroken at his departure, and will not be consoled. She walks along the cliffs by the ocean in a frenzy of grief and looks down at the rocky shoreline. Imagining Averagus sailing back to her only to be dashed to pieces, she cries out to God—all things are made for a good reason, she admits, but why has he made these horrible rocks? How could divine providence countenance such a fiendish creation?

After a time, her friends prevail upon her to attend a garden party, and there she meets Aurelius, a young squire who is madly in love with her. Gathering his courage, he approaches her and asks if he might obtain her love. Somewhat shocked at this request, she nevertheless jokingly promises that if he will remove the rocks from the coast, one by one, she will give him what he desires. Despairing, he returns home to languish in sorrow—this is surely an impossibility, he believes. His brother, pitying his anguish, remembers a scholar he knew back at the university in Orleans, a man learned in magic. Together they set out, hoping that he can accomplish the impossible. The scholar meets them on the road, tells them that he already knows their errand, and invites them to dinner at his house. There they are entertained with a variety of extraordinary magical feats, and determine that if anyone can accomplish this task, he can. The scholar accepts the commission, but his fee will be a thousand pounds (over a million dollars in modern currency). For Aurelius no price is too great, and he happily agrees.

The three men return to Brittany, and the scholar, after much deliberation and calculation,

fulfills his mission—the rocks disappear. Aurelius finds Dorigen and, reminding her of her promise, tells her that the rocks are gone. In despair she runs to Arveragus (who has since returned from England) and confesses everything. Unhappily he says that a promise is a promise—she must be true to her word—but he will kill her if she ever tells anyone about it. Disheveled and weeping, she sets out to find Aurelius. He meets her on the way and asks her where she is going. To keep her promise, she tells him, "as my husband bade, / To keep my plighted word, alas, alas!" (*The Canterbury Tales*, p. 446). Taken aback by her grief and unwillingness, Aurelius releases her from her promise. She joyfully returns home, and Aurelius sadly goes to pay the scholar. Giving him 500 pounds, he asks for a few years to make up the remainder. Aurelius promises to make good his debt, though it will render him a pauper. After hearing what has happened with Dorigen, the scholar forgives Aurelius his debt. The tale closes with the Franklin asking the Canterbury pilgrims a question: Who was the most generous? Arveragus for commanding his wife to keep her word, Aurelius for not compelling Dorigen to submit to his lust, or the scholar for forgiving Aurelius's debt?

The Nun's Priest's Tale. A poor widow lives on a small farm, subsisting on meager fare derived from poultry, three cows, three pigs, and a sheep. Ruling over the henhouse is a magnificent rooster named Chaunticleer, who studies astrology so as to know the exact time to crow each morning. He has seven hens as wives, but he is especially devoted to Pertelote, the most beautiful of them all. Early one morning, as he roosts next to her, he begins to groan in his sleep. When Pertelote scolds him, he explains that he has had a bad dream; in his dream, a frightening houndlike beast, with glowing eyes, reddish-yellow fur, and black-tipped ears and tail, snatched and tried to kill him. His wife has little patience for this story. In scorn she upbraids him as a coward. Is he a man or not? Why does he take heed of dreams? They are vanities, false and meaningless. This all comes from bad digestion, she claims—perhaps he needs a laxative. Chaunticleer responds with a lengthy and scholarly defense of dreams as legitimate indicators of truth. Finishing his discourse, he tells Pertelote to speak no more of laxatives, and quotes to her a Latin proverb: *mulier est hominis confusio*, which he mistranslates as "woman is man's delight and all his bliss"—it actually means "woman is man's destruction" (*The Canterbury Tales*, p. 239). He then flies down from his perch to search for grain in the yard, and makes love to Pertelote 20 times before morning is done.

The Nun's Priest now expostulates with great vehemence about the momentousness of Chaunticleer's decision to descend from the

MORAL STORIES OR LECHEROUS LAYS?

At the end of *The Canterbury Tales* lies Chaucer's "retraction"—a brief statement of regret for all his sinful poems, in which he asks his readers to pray for his soul. He is happy to have composed moral works (such as his translation of Boethius), but he renounces his "many a song and many a lecherous lay" and all those works which "tend towards sin" (*The Canterbury Tales*, p. 505). Was he fully serious? Many scholars think not, noting that writing such a statement (called a palinode) was an established convention among medieval poets. Important too is the idea that profound and moral truths may be contained within humorous tales, even of the coarsest sort. Viewed in this way, a seemingly vulgar or silly tale might not necessarily "tend towards sin" if its surface narrative symbolically indicates such truths. Of use here is a bit of literary advice from St. Paul, who says (in Romans 15:4) that instruction may be found in all that is written. Any story could be a vehicle for wisdom and holiness as long as the reader was properly informed. Thus, at the end of "The Nun's Priest's Tale," the narrator says:

> . . . if you think my story is absurd,
> A foolish trifle of a beast and a bird,
> A fable of a fox, a cock, a hen,
> Take hold upon the moral, gentlemen.
> St. Paul himself, a saint of great discerning,
> Says that all things are written for our learning;
> So take the grain and let the chaff be still.
>
> (*The Canterbury Tales*, p. 247)

If a tale is read in this manner, whatever is frivolous in it, which cannot nourish the spirit, can be dismissed. The remaining wisdom of "The Nun's Priest's Tale," hidden behind symbol, might be something like this: Chaunticleer is the human soul. Distracted by feminine beauty (Pertelote), he is vulnerable to the devil (Daun Russell). Similarly illuminating readings may be extracted from Chaucer's other humorous tales, which has led many readers to conclude that he meant them to be taken quite seriously.

perch—did God preordain this act? Did Chaunticleer do it of his own free will? Alas that he did, for a traitorous murderer, a recreant worse than Judas, lurks about the farm. A fox, named Daun Russell, has designs upon the barnyard fowl. He races into the yard, and the hens all cry alarm—Chaunticleer is about to flee, but the fox amiably tells him not to be afraid. He has heard tell of Chaunticleer's wonderful singing voice, and would he be so kind as to crow for Daun Russell? Flattered beyond reason, Chaunticleer stays and crows resoundingly. Daun Russell takes this opportunity to grab Chaunticleer by the throat and carry him off. The farm erupts in chaos, with the poor widow and her daughters crying out and chasing after the fox, and the animals running about in high excitement. Chaunticleer, in a flash of inspiration, suggests to the fox that he turn and mock his pursuers. Pleased with the idea, Daun Russell does so, giving Chaunticleer the opportunity to escape and fly into a tree. The fox begs him to come down, but Chaunticleer has learned his lesson.

The battle of the sexes. Most of *The Canterbury Tales* involve sexual politics in some manner; whether between lovers, spouses, or romantic rivals, the tensions and difficulties inherent in sexual relationships provide Chaucer with much of his narrative momentum. Chaucer is unusual among writers of his time in that he is far more likely to represent both sides of the struggle fairly, and to portray his female characters as realistically as his male characters, rather than as personified stereotypes of preconceived feminine attributes. Consequently his tales underscore the struggle undergone by women to make their way in a world dominated by men. Still, the reader must keep in mind that people of both sexes in the fourteenth century (whether fictional characters or poets) were conditioned from birth to position themselves in a male-dominated society. The relations between the sexes in *The Canterbury Tales* must be seen in this light. The Wife of Bath (to choose the most obvious example) was not a feminist in the same way that she was not a baseball fan—neither institution had been invented yet.

Attitudes about women in the fourteenth century derived from a wide variety of sources, most of them hostile. From the ancient world came the misogynist verse of Horace, Juvenal, and Ovid; the tradition in Roman law that a woman was in most respects a social inferior; and the medical/biological writings of Aristotle, Galen, Soranus, and others that described the relationships between women's biological "defects" and their alleged mental shortcomings, such as the incapacity for logic, a tendency towards hysteria, and so on. To this the ancient and medieval Church added the notion that women were spiritually deficient as well. They were less able to resist temptation (it was Eve who sinned first, not Adam), and they were inconstant as well as sexually predatory. Moreover, their second-class status had divine sanction: Christ became man, not woman, and so the entire priestly hierarchy of the Church was denied them. St. Paul too was quite clear on the proper role of women—they should be modest and obedient to their husbands, and ought never to speak in Church. Interestingly, this view of women was for the most part predicated on their various possible relationships with men—that is, as a wife, an adulteress, a nag, a temptress, and so on. Women who renounced men and sex were considered to be capable of the highest degrees of sainthood—indeed, the premiere exemplar of human virtue (apart from Christ himself, who, being God, had something of an advantage) was the immaculate and sinless Virgin Mary, a woman. Thus, misogynist writings from late antiquity through the Middle Ages tended to disparage women, the conviction being that they were bad for men. An excellent example of this idea is the treatise *Against Jovinian* by St. Jerome. Jovinian was a writer (a contemporary of Jerome) who held that the married state was in no way inferior to that of a professed virgin, and that the claims being made for virginity as a necessary adjunct to true holiness were unfounded. In response, Jerome wrote a scathing attack on Jovinian, which asserted not only that virginity was the morally superior state, but that women were essentially dangerous.

It was unwise, taught Jerome, to marry women. Making a fundamental contribution to medieval antimatrimonial literature, Jerome quoted at length from a treatise (*The Book on Marriage*) that he claims was written by Theophrastus (c. 372-288 B.C.E.), an ancient philosopher who followed the school of Aristotle. This text condemns marriage in wholly practical and intellectual terms—to marry is to renounce happiness, financial stability, the life of the mind, the respect and company of one's friends, and any possibility of independence and self-determination. A wife will nag, scold, demand praise, find fault, and generally make her husband's life a living hell. A host of examples from Greek and Roman history are cited to support this argument. The following ex-

ample is typical: "We read of a certain Roman noble who, when his friends found fault with him for having divorced a beautiful, chaste, and rich wife, stretched out his foot and said to them, 'And the shoe before you looks new and elegant, yet no one but myself knows where it pinches'" (Blamires, p. 73). By the late Middle Ages, misogynist and antimatrimonial literature swelled from these beginnings to vast proportions, and almost constituted a genre unto itself. Jankyn's *Book of Wicked Wives*, which contained these and similar writings, would have found many keen readers in Chaucer's day.

Chaucer presents counter-arguments to these views in two ways: by creating characters such as the Wife of Bath to disagree with them, and by writing stories in which they are shown to be either false or balanced by equally unappealing portraits of men. The Wife of Bath knows Jerome and Theophrastus, as well as a fair number of their medieval followers, and is prepared to take them on. Men, she says, are miserly, brutal, suspicious, and (when they get old) laughably inadequate in bed. How can women be blamed for chafing at the miseries of being married to them? And, she demands, what is wrong with sex? Jerome and other churchmen may disparage the wedded state and idealize virgins, but she will oppose them on two counts—first, being married is not sinful, but only imperfect in relation to virginity; and second, marriage is always permissible to the unmarried, even the four-times widowed. Since she does not aspire to the perfect state, she will happily and vigorously pur-

---

FROM ST. JEROME: *AGAINST JOVINIAN*

"We must take note of the Apostle's [i.e., St. Paul's] good sense. He did not say, 'it is good not to have a wife,' but, 'it is good not to touch a woman': as though there were danger in the touch. . . . Just as he who touches fire is instantly burned, so by mere touch the peculiar nature of man and woman is perceived, and the difference of sex is understood. . . . Hence it was that our Joseph, because the Egyptian woman wished to touch him, fled from her hands, and, as if he had been bitten by a mad dog and feared the spreading poison, threw away the cloak which she had touched. [Joseph repulsed the advances of Potiphar's wife, pulling himself from her grasp so that she tore his clothes; later she alleged attempted rape]" (Genesis 39:7). (St. Jerome in Blamires, p. 65)

sue her marital goals in the full (and correct, according to church teaching) knowledge that she is committing no sin. God made sexual organs and the pleasure they generate for a reason, and far be it from her to find fault with that.

Other indications that the misogynist position was not necessarily universal may be found in Chaucer's fabliaux. The women in "The Miller's Tale" and "The Merchant's Tale" fulfill all the traditional stereotypes: they lie, scheme, hold their husbands in contempt, and ultimately cuckold them. The husbands, on the other hand, are little better: they foolishly wed young and attractive wives despite their advanced age, they marry for dishonorable motives, and their obsessive jealously makes their cuckoldry an inevitable conclusion. This fundamentally destabilizes the antimatrimonial position, which is based on the idea that men are in a secure, wise, and noble state before they are married—here, the men are worthless to begin with. John in "The Miller's Tale" is not just a fool who marries a wife he cannot satisfy and who believes Nicholas's absurd prediction that the world will be drowned. He is a selfish man who is happy to keep silent about the supposed oncoming flood (he has no thought for the lives of his servants or neighbors), as long as he will be able to save his most valuable possession—his beautiful young wife. He appears to deserve his fate, and the reader feels no outrage at his injured rights as a husband.

Sources and literary context. Scholars have come to some measure of agreement about Chaucer's range of reading, and the possible source texts for *The Canterbury Tales*. The Bible and other early Christian writings figure prominently, though Chaucer encountered many of them in excerpted form. The Roman poets Virgil, Ovid, and Statius show their influence regularly in Chaucer. Ovid's *Metamorphoses* was the standard repository of mythological narrative for the medieval world, and Statius was considered an epic poet on par with Virgil himself—the longest of *The Canterbury Tales*, the romance-epic "The Knight's Tale," was adapted from Statius's *Thebaid*, via the *Teseida* of Boccaccio. Works by Seneca and (to a lesser extent) Cicero were known to Chaucer, and appear in his writings primarily in the form of moral maxims and brief cautionary tales within a larger narrative.

The bulk of Chaucer's source material, however, derived not from the ancient world but from the literature of the Middle Ages, in French, Italian, and Latin. The thirteenth-century *Romance of the Rose* (begun by Guillaume de Lorris and com-

pleted by Jean de Meun) was a pervasive influence; echoes of it appear in virtually every story in *The Canterbury Tales*. Chaucer's fabliaux were all probably of French origin, although since these tales were anonymous and widely disseminated in varying versions (many of which are now lost), it is difficult to identify a specific source for any given fabliau. Among Italian writers, Petrarch (1304-74) provided the basis for "The Clerk's Tale," and Boccaccio's influence is difficult to overestimate. His *Teseida* was transformed into "The Knight's Tale," and his *Filocolo* is a likely source for "The Franklin's Tale." Chaucer's use of medieval Latin literature includes such standard reference works as the *Speculum historiale* and *Speculum naturale* (Mirror of History and Mirror of Nature), two widely disseminated encyclopedias by the Dominican friar Vincent of Beauvais (1190-1264), and the *Legenda aurea* (Golden Legend) of Jacobus de Voragine (1230-1298), a massive collection of saints' lives. With their respective treatises on penance and on the virtues and vices, two Dominican friars of the thirteenth century (Raymond of Pennaforte and William Peraldus) provided the source texts for "The Parson's Tale," which is not a tale at all, but a lengthy discussion of sin and its remedies.

There is no known source for "The Miller's Tale." Since it is a fabliau, scholars generally assume that Chaucer adapted it from a French original, but if he did, this original has been lost. There exists a Flemish version of the story that is roughly contemporaneous with "The Miller's Tale," and it is possible that they derive from the same source, but the differences between the tales are many. In the Flemish story the woman is not a young wife, but an unmarried prostitute, and the man hanging from the tub in the ceiling is not her husband, but another customer. There are other versions as well (in German, English, and Italian), but they are much later than "The Miller's Tale," and probably not immediately descended from Chaucer's source.

The "Wife of Bath's Prologue" is made up of a variety of standard early Christian and medieval texts that say women are corrupting and marriage is unwise. The main sources are Jerome's *Against Jovinian*, Theophrastus's *Golden Book of Marriage*, Walter Map's *Letter of Valerius to Rufinus, Against Marriage* (c. 1180), and the portraits of the Old Woman and The Jealous Man in the *Roman de la Rose*. The situation is less clear with the sources for "The Wife of Bath's Tale." Chaucer's friend and contemporary John Gower wrote a similar version of the tale in his *Confessio Amantis* called

"The Tale of Florent," and two later poems entitled *The Marriage of Sir Gawaine* and *The Weddynge of Sir Gawen and Dame Ragnell* also tell the same general story, but the relationships among these versions is uncertain.

The basic story of "The Franklin's Tale" is found in two works of Boccaccio's *Decameron* as well as in his *Filocolo*. The version in the *Filocolo* is closer to that of Chaucer, and most scholars believe that Chaucer used it as his source. However, he made substantial changes. Rather than removing rocks from the ocean, the task the sources gives to the young lover (called Taralfo in Boccaccio's version) is to produce a blooming garden in January. Chaucer's story involves such issues as the problem of evil, divine providence, and the nature of magic, none of which appear in Boccaccio. Also, Chaucer makes use of the writings of Jerome in "The Franklin's Tale." When Dorigen is facing the unwelcome prospect of keeping her word to Aurelius, she meditates on a lengthy catalog of women who chose death over unchastity; this catalog is taken from Jerome's *Against Jovinian*.

The basic story told by Chaucer in "The Nun's Priest's Tale" is an old one, probably derived from some version of the Old French beast epic *Roman de Renart*. Why Chaucer chose to name his fox Daun Russell instead of Reynard (the standard name for foxes in medieval beast epics) is unclear, but he got the name Chaunticleer from the *Roman*. The *Roman* is nevertheless a source in name only. The parody of an academic debate on dreams, the discussion of predestination versus free will, the overblown apostrophes on treason and flattery—these are Chaucer's own. For the dream lore in "The Nun's Priest's Tale," Chaucer drew on two standard works—the *Commentary on the Dream of Scipio* by the Roman author Macrobius (c. 400) and a commentary on the *Book of Wisdom* by Robert Holcot (d. 1349).

Reception. Chaucer was well known as a poet even in his own day, as shown by references in contemporary works to his preeminent skill as a versifier. This fame fairly exploded after his death, to the extent that the history of fifteenth-century literature can be seen as, more than anything else, an attempt to follow in his footsteps. He was revered as a master, and many poets even wrote "Canterbury" tales of their own, in an effort to complete Chaucer's work. Thus, we have a "Plowman's Tale" (supposedly told by the Parson's brother, to whom Chaucer gave no tale), and a lively account of what happened when everyone arrived at Canterbury and the Pardoner got into trouble with a barmaid. While we now know that these works are not by Chaucer, they are a clear indication of his stature as a poet in the century after his death. Chaucer's fame would endure in subsequent centuries, as shown by his impact on later authors in this volume. Edmund Spenser modeled the language of his **Faerie Queene** (also in *WLAIT 3: British and Irish Literature and Its Times*) after Chaucer's English. Also, William Shakespeare drew on "The Knight's Tale" for his plays *A Midsummer Night's Dream* and *Two Noble Kinsmen*. Finally, John Dryden and Alexander Pope adapted and modernized various tales by Chaucer, helping, like other writers before and after them, to ensconce him as the "Father of English Literature."

—Matthew Brosamer

For More Information

Benson, Larry, and Theodore Andersson, eds. and trans. *The Literary Context of Chaucer's Fabliaux: Texts and Translations*. Indianapolis: Bobbs-Merrill, 1971.

Benson, Larry, ed. *The Riverside Chaucer*. 3d ed. Boston: Houghton Mifflin, 1987.

Blamires, Alcuin. *Woman Defamed and Woman Defended: An Anthology of Medieval Texts*. Oxford, England: Oxford University Press, 1992.

Bryan, W. F., and G. Dempster, eds. *Sources and Analogues of Chaucer's Canterbury Tales*. Chicago: The University Press, 1941.

Chaucer, Geoffrey. *The Canterbury Tales*. Trans. Nevill Coghill. Baltimore: Penguin, 1952.

Cooper, Helen. *The Canterbury Tales*. The Oxford Guides to Chaucer. Oxford, England: Clarendon, 1989.

Brewer, Derek, ed. *Geoffrey Chaucer*. London: Bell, 1974.

Kelly, Henry Ansgar. *Love and Marriage in the Age of Chaucer*. Ithaca, N.Y.: Cornell University Press, 1975.

Mann, Jill. *Chaucer and Medieval Estates Satire: The Literature of Social Classes and the General Prologue to "The Canterbury Tales."* Cambridge: Cambridge University Press, 1973.

Pearsall, Derek. *The Canterbury Tales*. London: George Allen & Unwin, 1985.

——. *The Life of Geoffrey Chaucer: A Critical Biography*. Oxford, Engalnd: Blackwell, 1992.

Castle Rackrent:
An Hibernian Tale taken from facts and from the manners of the Irish squires before the year 1782

by

Maria Edgeworth

Maria Edgeworth (1767-1849) came to live in Ireland at the age of 15. The year was 1782, the same one in which Ireland achieved a short-lived parliamentary independence from English rule, and a year earlier than the setting of her first (widely considered her best) novel, *Castle Rackrent*. The Anglo-Irish Edgeworth family had held Irish lands since the reign of James I, somehow managing to maintain them despite a history of inept Edgeworths who, in the manner of the Rackrents, did their best to gamble, drink, and mismanage the estate away. In contrast, Maria's father, Richard Lovell Edgeworth, was a conscientious landlord and a political progressive, reforming age-old feudal practices that oppressed tenants and made estates unprofitable. Richard Lovell Edgeworth was also a brilliant inventor and educational theorist who took great pains to educate his daughter. The two collaborated on works of educational theory (*Practical Education*; *Professional Education*) that are considered to be among the most important contributions to contemporary instruction. Also, based on her father's ideas, Maria wrote stories designed to educate and improve children (*The Parent's Assistant, Early Lessons, Moral Tales, Popular Tales*), and even her novels for adults show a strong didactic strain. *Castle Rackrent*, the first of four novels she would write concerning the Anglo-Irish in Ireland (including *Ennui, The Absentee*, and *Ormond*), instructs through counter-example, showing quite clearly how not to run an estate. But the novel can also be read as a nuanced commentary on relations between Irish and

> ### THE LITERARY WORK
> A novel spanning three generations; purported to be set before 1782 in an unspecified region of the Irish countryside; published in 1800.
>
> ### SYNOPSIS
> A servant narrates the downfall of the family he serves as they lose their ancestral estate through personal vice and gross mismanagement.

Anglo-Irish, Catholic and Protestant, tenant and landlord, servant and master, wife and husband.

Events in History at the Time the Novel Takes Place

Irish and English. *Castle Rackrent* is set in an Ireland under English rule. Before English rule, Ireland was a country of competing minor kings frequently engaged in warfare with one another; the "High King" of Ireland was so in name only. Internal strife and lack of central political authority made Ireland vulnerable to unified England. This chaos was, moreover, reflected in the structure of the Irish Church. The Irish Church was founded in the fifth century by the most famous of Irish missionaries, St. Patrick. Because of Ireland's lack of central political authority, the Church in Ireland developed along lines different from those that delineated the Church in the rest of Europe; Irish ecclesiastic authority was divided between the abbots of Ireland's many monasteries rather than being concentrated in a hierarchy of bishops as it was elsewhere. Following the fall of Rome, the Irish Church lost communication with the Roman papacy for 400 years, and Irish Christianity developed its own customs that ran counter to Roman law. In Ireland, priests could marry, abbots need not be ordained, and many ecclesiastic offices were hereditary. By the twelfth century, the papacy, claiming authority over all temporal rulers, had regained control of the Church in continental Europe and Britain, and now turned its attention to reforming heretical Ireland. Pope Adrian IV (the first English pope) realized that without a strong central political power there could be no guarantor of papal authority in Ireland. So in 1155, he issued a papal bull, entitled *Laudabiliter*, declaring that England's King Henry II was "Lord of Ireland." Fourteen years later, Henry II decided to assert this title.

In 1169 Diarmuid MacMurrough, an Irish king facing the rebellion of his subjects, sought the help of Richard de Clare, a powerful Anglo-Norman magnate residing in Wales. De Clare, more commonly known as "Strongbow," came to MacMurrough's aid and successfully put down the revolt, staying on afterwards to marry MacMurrough's daughter and inherit his kingdom when the Irish king died a few years later. The gaining of an independent kingdom by a powerful vassal worried Henry II, and in 1171 the English king came to Ireland to finally claim his title as 'Lord.' Strongbow, along with the Irish kings, swore fealty to Henry, who demanded that henceforth the Irish kings pay him tribute. In return, Strongbow and other Anglo-Normans (English descendants of immigrants from Normandy, who had conquered England a century earlier) would be granted large tracts of land in Ireland, in return for which they had to render military service. Henry himself claimed the area around Dublin, which came to be known as the "English Pale," as the exclusive province of the English Crown.

Henry met no resistance in his enterprise: the Anglo-Normans were glad to have the backing of the English Crown in the midst of Irish chaos, the Irish Church welcomed the strength that they believed closer ties to Rome and a powerful English king would bring, and most importantly, the Irish kings acquiesced. At this point, they had no sense that Ireland was a nation that should be ruled by the Irish. Their concerns were, rather,

confined to the local level, with individuals focusing on the constant struggle to maintain authority over their small contested kingdoms. Henry II was just another more powerful king demanding fealty.

The Anglo-Irish. Anglo-Norman settlers continued to expand the territory that Henry II originally granted them, and by 1250 they controlled three-fourths of Ireland. These Anglo-Normans, along with other immigrants from England, established English-style feudalism in the lands they controlled, and in 1264 founded the first Irish Parliament, modeled on the English system but with limited representation only from the Anglo-Norman regions and the English Pale. Over time, the descendants of English settlers in Ireland developed a sense of identity as neither English nor Irish, but Anglo-Irish. Although the native Irish would always greatly outnumber the Anglo-Irish, the latter would dominate Ireland, owning most of the land and occupying all positions of power in the colonial government and the official Church.

Ireland under English rule was a classic colonial society fueled by racial tension. Although many Anglo-Irish intermarried with the Irish and adopted the native language and customs, for the most part the Anglo-Irish regarded their English heritage as a badge of superiority, holding the native Irish in contempt. Two factions developed within the ranks of Anglo-Irish: the so-called "Old English," the original colonists who settled Ireland in the early days of Henry II, and the "New English," the colonists who came to Ireland in later centuries. One of the main differences between the two was religion: by and large, the "Old English" were Catholic while the "New English" were Protestant, or more specifically, Anglican.

In Ireland as in Britain under Anglican rule, Protestants (Presbyterians, Quakers, Baptists, and others) who did not conform to the Anglican Church were labeled "Dissenters," and suffered privations. In Ireland, Dissenters were not part of the power elite, but they did share to some extent in the privileges that distinguished Protestant from Catholic. In this entry, the term "Protestant" should be understood to refer to Anglicans in the main, but also to include, to a lesser degree, non-Anglican Protestants.

Catholic and Protestant. After Henry II established English rule, Ireland was left largely to its own devices. It was for a long time considered an unprofitable, backward colony, and the Wars of the Roses (1455-87) distracted English monarchs from affairs across the Irish Sea. Once Henry VIII broke with the Catholic Church to form the Anglican Church, however, Ireland became a threat to English security. Because of their nation's Catholicism, Irish rebels could attract powerful Catholic allies from the continent, and England's Catholic opponents could always count on a safe harbor in Ireland as long as the Irish remained largely loyal to the pope. This situation led Queen Elizabeth I to bring Ireland under closer English control. She initiated a program of "plantation," seizing the large landholdings of Irish Catholic rebels and giving them to loyal Protestant English subjects; the Catholic tenants on these lands were also replaced with Protestants. In the following centuries the native Irish were evicted out of hand, many exiled to the rocky and unproductive lands of Connaught in the west of Ireland, their plots given to Protestant British settlers. There were not enough British immigrants to work the land, however, and the native Irish slowly came back as tenants and laborers for the new Protestant Anglo-Irish landowners. The divide between Protestant and Catholic assumed a greater significance than in Britain or the rest of Europe. Like the Protestant settlers themselves, Protestantism was in Ireland an English import, associated with the colonial power. The vast majority of the native Irish resisted this power and remained Catholic.

In the Williamite War (1689-91), Irish Catholics supported England's Catholic King James II, while Irish Protestants supported the Protestant contestant for the English throne, William of Orange. After James's defeat, Catholics were punished for their support of James by the confiscation of yet more land, which Protestant immigrants received. Because of their ever-increasing land holdings, Protestants dominated the Irish Parliament and all other sectors of Irish public life, a situation known as the "Protestant Ascendancy"—the label was also applied to the Anglo-Irish Protestants who benefited from this situation. During the Ascendancy, the Irish Parliament passed Penal Laws similar to the anti-Catholic legislation that had been in effect for some time in England. These laws denied Catholics the vote, prevented them from holding government office, and barred them from the legal professions and armed services. Catholics were not allowed to bear arms, establish schools, or send their children abroad for an education. They could no longer buy land, and what lands they retained had to be divided equally among the owner's sons when the owner died—thus the Protestant elite tried to break up Catholic estates into small, unprofitable pieces. Eldest sons could, however, gain possession of the entire family estate by becoming Protestant, and thus the Penal Laws led to the conversion of many "Old English" land-owning Catholics to Protestantism.

A subject people. The Irish Parliament came into being in the thirteenth century under the domination of the Anglo-Irish. One of its first acts was to prohibit wearing native Irish dress. Later centuries saw the passage of subsequent laws in a similar spirit, such as the Statutes of Kilkenny, which prohibited the Anglo-Irish from marrying Irish people and from speaking the Irish language. Such laws reveal an ongoing anxiety over the separation of Anglo-Irish and Irish; they also point to the existence of that which they prohibit—many Anglo-Irish, particularly the "Old English" who had come to Ireland in the twelfth and thirteenth centuries, did intermarry with the native Irish, frequently adopting native language and customs. Yet despite this apparent cultural assimilation, on a political level, boundaries between Anglo-Irish and Irish were maintained. Only Anglo-Irish could serve in the Irish Parliament, and the court system was restricted to Anglo-Irish as well. Under Henry VIII in the mid-sixteenth century, Catholic priests were forbidden to perform the Mass, and prayer books in English replaced native-language worship in the official Irish Church. Thus, the native Irish were excluded by virtue of race, language, and faith from the Anglo-Irish colonial government, legal system, and Church.

Over the centuries of English rule, the native Irish resisted this situation, but for a long time the lack of unity among a people who had never considered themselves a nation made throwing off the English yoke impossible, though several attempts were essayed. In one such attempt, with help from Spain, a confederation of Irish chiefs headed by Hugh O'Neill sought to oust the English but were defeated by English forces in 1603. Facing punishment, many of these chiefs fled to France in the so-called "Flight of the Earls," leaving behind large land holdings in Ulster that the English Crown quickly claimed. These lands were designated plantations, and British subjects were invited to settle them while native Irish were driven out. The Flight of the Earls left a vacuum in Irish leadership and is emblematic of Ireland's plight under English rule. Native Irish families who held power in the days before English rule lost their lands piecemeal to Anglo-Norman settlers, or were deprived of them under anti-Catholic laws, or had them confiscated if they dared challenge British colonial power. To avoid persecution, many emigrated to France and other Catholic countries on the European continent. Native Irish had to abandon their homeland if they wanted to pursue careers in the Church, law, or politics. Thus by the eighteenth century, to be native Irish was for the most part to be poor, disenfranchised, and landless, a tenant or cottier on an estate owned by the English or Anglo-Irish.

The landlord system. By the eighteenth century, 5,000 Protestant Anglo-Irish families (like the Edgeworths) controlled 95 percent of Ireland's profitable lands. Under this system, land was no longer Irish property, and Irish society was divided into relatively inflexible classes. There were the Anglo-Irish landlords and the Irish tenants, separated by differences in culture, religion, and language.

Many Anglo-Irish landlords acquired a bad name for themselves by choosing to spend the profits from their properties on luxuries and high-status homes rather than reinvesting in the land. Absentee landlords in particular were seen as parasites on (or rather off) the land. In *Castle Rackrent*, one such absentee landlord leaves the affairs of the estate in the hands of a middle man, a new class of tenant who "took large farms on long leases from gentlemen of landed property, and let the land again in small portions to the poor, as under tenants, at exorbitant rents" (Edgeworth, *Castle Rackrent*, footnote, p. 20). Middle men were common on Anglo-Irish estates. More common still were land agents (such as the novel's Jason Quirk), representatives who collected rents, maintained records, and enforced the various property rights for both absentee and resident landlords. Both middle men and land agents served to widen the perceived divide between Anglo-Irish landlords and their tenants, lessening the sense of obligation felt on either side.

The situation of tenants under this system was varied, but for the most part poor. Only 5 to 10 percent of tenants were "strong farmers" with over 30 acres, enough to allow them a measure of prosperity. The rest of the tenants had less than 30 acres, most of them much less, and the majority of people living on the land were not even tenants proper, but rather cottiers. Cottiers received the use of a small piece of land in re-

turn for their services either to a tenant or to the landlord himself, and generally lived in conditions of wretched poverty. Large cottier families crowded into dilapidated one-room shacks and struggled to feed themselves off their meager land-holdings.

A population explosion between 1725 and 1785 increased the strain on this system. Taking advantage of the land shortage, landowners raised their rents, prompting tenant farmers, in turn, to sublease more of their land than in the past in hopes of earning enough to meet their financial obligations. The vicious cycle of runaway rent and the subsequent subdivision of the land had disastrous consequences for the Irish economy. The real productive value of the land declined while more and more people were trying to eke out a living on a fixed acreage.

Independence? For much of its history, the Irish Parliament was beholden not only to the English Crown but also to the British Parliament, a situation that many Anglo-Irish deplored but lacked the power or unity to change. Then in the eighteenth century, the American Revolution necessitated the removal of English troops from Ireland to fight in North America. To defend themselves against possible invasion from France, who had joined the Revolution in 1778, the Anglo-Irish organized their own volunteer army in Ireland. With troops to back them up, Anglo-Irish demands for parliamentary independence were taken more seriously, and in 1782, a new constitution was ratified establishing the independence of the Irish Parliament. Maria Edgeworth sets her novel before this date, which at the time seemed to be a landmark in Irish history. High hopes attended the newly independent Irish Parliament, at least for the Protestant Ascendancy, who had orchestrated it and would be the only ones to receive greater power. Native Irish, Catholics, and Dissenters, on the other hand, had no share in the "independence." Powerless, they would rise up to demand complete autonomy from Britain in the rebellion of 1798.

The Novel in Focus

Plot summary. Thady Quirk, the novel's narrator, presents himself as "honest Thady," unquestioningly loyal retainer to the Rackrent family at Castle Rackrent, an Irish country estate (*Castle Rackrent*, p. 7). He proclaims the narrative that follows to be "the Memoirs of the Rackrent Family," undertaken by himself "out of friendship for the family" (*Castle Rackrent*, p. 7). Thady's gossipy narrative is divided into two sections: the initial one recounts the character and deeds of the first three masters of Castle Rackrent (Sir Patrick, Sir Murtagh, and Sir Kit) under whom Thady and his forebears have served; the second gives a more detailed description of the estate's final Rackrent owner, Sir Conolly, and of how he loses everything through waste and mismanagement. The "editor" of Thady's memoirs, in reality also the author, offers a preface, a postscript, a glossary of Irish terms, and scholarly footnotes throughout "for the information of the ignorant English reader" (Castle Rackrent, p. 4).

Thady's tale begins with Sir Patrick, who had to change his surname from O'Shaughlin ("one of the most ancient in the kingdom") to Rackrent in order to inherit the estate from his cousin, Sir Tallyhoo Rackrent (Castle Rackrent, p. 8). Sir Patrick is a sociable spendthrift who fills his house with liquor and landed gentlemen and dies as he lived—inebriated and oblivious to his accumulating debts. His funeral draws nobility from near and far, but is interrupted by a group of creditors who seize the body for debt. Sir Patrick's heir, Sir Murtagh, takes the opportunity to renege on his father's financial obligations "on account of this affront to the body" (Castle Rackrent, p. 12). It is rumored, however, that Sir Murtagh himself orchestrated the seizure of the corpse so that he would have an honorable excuse for refusing to pay.

Sir Murtagh, who has inherited none of his father's profligacy or generosity, soon proves to be not above such suspicions. Avaricious and litigious, he is a good match for his wife, whose maiden name is Skinflint. Between the two of them, they call in every age-old feudal obligation from their tenants, who are required to constantly supply the Rackrents with free labor and gifts of livestock, agricultural produce, and cloth—items owed, by ancient tradition, in addition to the stipulated rent. Meanwhile Sir Murtagh amuses himself by engaging in numerous lawsuits with the neighbors over property rights. One day, a volatile argument with his wife over a property issue causes Sir Murtagh to burst a blood vessel and die. His wife receives a generous jointure, or inherited yearly income, and exits the estate, leaving behind no children and not even a candle or a piece of linen cloth, for all had been purchased with her own money.

Sir Murtagh's brother, Sir Kit, becomes new owner of the estate. Thady loves him at first sight, observing that "money to him was no more than dirt," as the young squire tosses him a guinea

(Castle Rackrent, p. 20). All will be well, Thady thinks, if Sir Kit stays, but when the sporting season is over the new master leaves for Bath, putting care of the estate into the hands of a ruthless middle man. The middle man squeezes the tenants for every penny he can get, while Sir Kit sends home increasingly desperate demands for cash to fund his taste for gambling. Meanwhile,

JEWS IN EIGHTEENTH-CENTURY IRELAND

Sir Kit marries a Jewish heiress in Castle Rackrent who stubbornly refuses to give him her diamond cross. She tenaciously holds onto this symbol of Christianity, a curious detail that makes one wonder if more than the cross's monetary value is at stake. Reviewing the history of Jews in the British Isles provides clues to understanding her behavior. Expelled from Britain in 1290, professed Jews were allowed to return in the mid-seventeenth century and began to filter into England and then Ireland. By the mid-eighteenth century, about 8,000 Jews constituted .1 percent of England's population. The community in Dublin grew to 40 families in the mid-to-late eighteenth century, most of them employed in the jewelry trade. Although Jews had been permitted to resettle in the region, hostility against them persisted, as reflected in the repeal eight months after its passage of the Jew Bill, or Jewish Naturalization Act of 1753, which would have allowed Parliament to naturalize professing Jews. More hostility surfaced as the century progressed. In 1780 in Dublin, Sir John Blaquiere introduced a bill for the naturalization of all foreign settlers except Jews, denigrating them as money grabbers who brought ruin wherever they went. The Irish Naturalization Act of 1784 specifically excluded Jews, remaining in effect through the time of the novel (it would be repealed in 1816). Dublin's Christian society accepted some of the richer Jews into its fold, and a few Christian champions came to the fore who contested Blaquiere's stereotype; an anonymous writer to Freeman's Journal (March 23, 1780), for example, argued that the Irish Jews were hard-working and thrifty, and deserved respect. But such champions were outnumbered by the intolerant denigrators and proselytizers. Throughout the eighteenth century, missionaries prevailed on Dublin's Jews to convert to Christianity. Certainly conversion allowed individual Jews to avail themselves of opportunities, rights, and privileges otherwise denied them. By the end of the century, Dublin's Jewish community had neared extinction as a result of conversions, intermarriage, and emigration.

Thady's son, Jason, begins to work with the middle man, helping him copy the accounts and learning the business. When a part of the estate goes up for sale, Jason makes a bid for it. With the middle man's connivance and the help of Thady, Jason takes advantage of Sir Kit's lack of knowledge in such matters, and gets the land at a bargain price. Sir Kit soon hits bottom, and in order to solve his financial woes marries a rich Jewish heiress in England and brings her to Castle Rackrent to live.

Sir Kit's new wife proves stubborn, however, and will not relinquish a magnificent diamond cross for Sir Kit to sell, so, to make her more amenable, Sir Kit locks her in her room for seven years. Reports of a mysterious illness as the reason for his wife's confinement make handsome Sir Kit an attractive marriage prospect, and three hopeful candidates vie for his attention. Sir Kit takes advantage of the situation to dally with all three, and in consequence is called out by three outraged brothers to a series of duels, in one of which he is killed. Afterward, Lady Rackrent, alive and well with jewels and fortune intact, is set free and returns to England, which concludes the first part of *Castle Rackrent*. Once again the master and mistress of Castle Rackrent have produced no heirs.

The second part of *Castle Rackrent* is the "History of Sir Conolly Rackrent," Sir Kit's distant relative (*Castle Rackrent*, p. 38). Also called "Sir Condy," this new master of Rackrent springs from a less exalted branch of the family. He grew up playing in the streets with and receiving help in his lessons from Thady's son, Jason. Having no fortune of his own, Sir Condy was educated for a career in law, but shows no aptitude for it or any other practical matter. Thady tells how Condy never really applied himself to his studies because, "seeing how Sir Kit and the Jewish lived together," he set his hopes on inheriting the Rackrent estate, and even accepted loans from several tenants on the strength of this expectation (*Castle Rackrent*, p. 40). Sir Condy's vices are drink and an unwillingness to apply himself to business matters. As owner of the estate, he lives up to the family tradition of falling into debt.

Unlike his two predecessors, however, Sir Condy does not make a marriage calculated for monetary gain. Such concerns play no part in his decision between the two women who want to be his wife: Isabella Moneygawl, a young Anglo-Irish woman for whom Sir Condy feels little affection, but who flatters his ego by defying her wealthy family for him; and lowly but attractive Judy M'Quirk, Thady's relative, a native Irishwoman who won Sir Condy's heart some time ago. In a drunken moment, Sir Condy settles the matter with a coin toss, which turns out in Isabella's favor. Though her family is rich, they withhold her dowry, disapproving of the match, but Isabella anyway maintains the costly lifestyle to which she is accustomed, adding to her husband's mounting debts. Just before he is to be arrested for debts outstanding to the local wine merchant, Sir Condy manages to win a seat in Parliament, which gains him temporary legal immunity.

At the election celebration, Thady falls into conversation with the man sent to arrest Sir Condy, happening to mention to him the full extent of his master's financial embarrassment. The man connives with Thady's son, Jason, who by this time has become agent of the Rackrent estate and an attorney, to buy up all of Sir Condy's outstanding debts and enforce them simultaneously, compelling Sir Condy to sign over Castle Rackrent to Jason. Facing the protests of an angry mob of tenants who fear the methods of their new landlord as much as they regret the ruin of Sir Condy, Jason makes a minor concession. He allows Sir Condy to stay on at the hunting lodge, a small building on the estate. Isabella deserts her husband for the comfort of the Moneygawl home, while, "grieved and sick at heart for my poor master," Thady follows Sir Condy into a life of reduced circumstances (*Castle Rackrent*, p. 77).

It turns out, however, that Jason does not have complete title to Castle Rackrent. Before signing the estate away, Sir Condy stipulated that Isabella receive a jointure of £500 yearly from the estate before any payment of his debts. It seems this act of generosity might save Sir Condy, for Isabella is ill, and should she die before him, the jointure will pass back to Sir Condy. Hearing of this monetary prospect, Judy M'Quirk makes another bid for Sir Condy's affections. Sir Condy, however, demonstrates his lack of business savvy once again. He sells Jason his right to the jointure for a mere 300 guineas up front, at which point Judy M'Quirk tries to attract Jason, but to no avail.

Finally, in a reckless drinking bout with old friends, Sir Condy bets his last guinea that he can consume in one draught all the whiskey punch that Sir Patrick's great drinking horn can contain. Sir Condy is, alas, no Sir Patrick and, after swallowing the drink, he drops dead. Thady wraps up the fall of the Rackrent family in typically understated fashion—"He had but a very poor funeral, after all" (*Castle Rackrent*, p. 96).

Duplicity and subversion in *Castle Rackrent*. Much is made of the mantle "honest Thady" wears in the opening paragraph of *Castle Rackrent*. In a lengthy footnote, the editor gives an account of the mantle's antiquity as an item of apparel in the great nations of Israel, Greece, and Rome, then goes on to quote Edmund Spenser, who describes the mantle as "a fit house for an outlaw, a meet bed for a rebel, and an apt cloak for a thief" (*Castle Rackrent*, p. 8). The mantle is also a fitting symbol for the duplicity that many readers have ascribed to "honest Thady" and his narration of improbable praise for the series of pathetic and culpable landlords who comprise the Rackrent family.

Citing Thady's assistance to his son in obtaining his first piece of Rackrent property, and Thady's supposedly inadvertent betrayal of Sir Condy by revealing the full extent of his master's debts to the wine merchant's man, literary critic James Newcomer sees Thady as a willing agent conspiring in the Rackrents' downfall. After all, the Quirk family ultimately benefits from the Rackrents' loss. Likewise, Robert Tracy does not take Thady's memoir at face value: "Thady presents himself as another literary cliché, the faithful Irish servant. In inventing him, Edgeworth examined the process by which the colonized subject simultaneously feigns loyalty, manipulates his rulers, and subverts their control" (Tracy, p. 17). Tracy even suggests that Thady makes Sir Condy the inept landlord he becomes. In the second part of *Castle Rackrent*, Thady mentions that he once told tales about the family to Condy when he was a boy, and Tracy speculates that the first part of *Castle Rackrent* is a specimen of the sort of stories Condy heard, stories praising the various vices and foolish acts of former Rackrents and encouraging young Condy to emulate them, to his ruin and the Quirks' gain.

Other literary critics challenge the validity of such interpretations. Vera Kreilkamp, for example, insists that "Thady's behavior and speech do not suggest that he is a master of irony and a calculating opportunist," but rather that he has "a deeply impaired sense of identity and is torn by his loyalties to conflicting worlds" (Kreilkamp, p. 40). In a similar vein, Elizabeth Harden explains Thady's praise of folly in the following terms: "Thady's loyalty to the family is the honor of a peasant's code of values, and his opinions of the landlords depend on their treatment of him" (Harden, p. 101). Readers may find it difficult to understand Thady's praise, but, according to these critics, this does not mean that praise is false.

Critics also point to Edgeworth's own duplicity, because she presents the novel as set "Before the Year 1782," while incidents in the novel indicate that it actually treats a later period. We may deduce from the fact that Thady "thought to make him a priest," that Jason Quirk is Catholic, and yet his purchase of any portion of the Rackrent estate would have been impossible in Ireland before 1782, since the Penal Laws still prohibited Catholics from buying land at this time. If Jason converts to Protestantism somewhere along the way, it is strange that Thady passes over this significant event in silence. Anthony Mortimer suggests that this inconsistency reflects Edgeworth's desire to deny the influence of Ireland's past on Ireland's future. It is the very absence of the Catholic question from *Castle Rackrent* that calls attention to the importance of the Protestant/Catholic dichotomy in the Irish landlord system, and the inability of the Anglo-Irish, or at least the liberal Anglo-Irish, to face the fact that their own power stemmed from the persecution of Irish Catholics. It should be remembered that Edgeworth presents the mantle as simultaneously a venerable cultural object linking Ireland with the very foundations of Western civilization, and as a tool of subversion used by outlaws, rebels, and thieves. This dual image may reflect Edgeworth's own assessment of the qualities of duplicity and subversion then considered intrinsic to the native Irish. Giraldus Cambrensis (Gerald of Wales), twelfth-century historian and apologist for the Anglo-Norman conquest of Ireland, expresses the stereotype thus:

> For this hostile race is always plotting some kind of treachery under cover of peace. . . . This wily race must be feared far more for its guile than its capacity to fight, for its pretended quiescence than for its fiery passions, for its honeyed flattery than for its bitter abuse, for its venom than for its prowess in battle, for its treachery than for its readiness to attack, and for its feigned friendship than for its contemptible hostility.
>
> (Giraldus Cambrensis in Ranelagh, p. 39)

If Thady is indeed two-faced, this trait may be morally deplorable, but it enabled his family to survive and prosper, just as the traits of duplicity and subversion were necessary for the survival of native Irish culture under English rule.

Sources and literary context. Maria Edgeworth based her novel's narrator, Thady Quirk, on John

Langan, the Edgeworth family steward whose native Irish dialect and character so struck Maria that she began to write a family history as he would tell it. "He seemed," she said, "to stand beside me and dictate; and I wrote as fast as my pen could go, the characters all imaginary" (*Castle Rackrent*, p. xi). Although the rest of the characters in the novel are supposed to be imaginary, they could easily have been based on Maria Edgeworth's own ancestors, whose vice and mismanagement is documented in a family memoir, *The Black Book of Edgeworthstown*. The imprisonment of Sir Kit's wife was based upon a real event about which Maria Edgeworth read in *Gentleman's Magazine* of 1789: Elizabeth Malyn, Lady Cathcart, was imprisoned by her husband Colonel Hugh Macguire in their house in the Irish countryside for 20 years (a legal practice until 1891) for refusing to surrender her property and jewels.

The reality that the book is supposed to mirror, however, is general rather than specific. Maria Edgeworth offers *Castle Rackrent* as "a specimen of manners and characters," which she was in an excellent position to observe in the Ireland of her day (*Castle Rackrent*, p. 97). Edgeworth's experience as her father's accountant would have exposed her to the harsh economic realities of tenants and cottiers, while the discussions of contemporary politics she and her father shared gave her a depth of understanding of class conflict and national events that distinguishes her fiction from that of many other contemporary women authors. *Castle Rackrent* is considered the first regional novel in the English language. It is also regarded as the first Anglo-Irish novel, the first "Big House" novel, and the first colonial novel, all of which would become important genres in English literature as the nineteenth century progressed.

Events in History at the Time the Novel Was Written

Insurrection of 1798. Maria Edgeworth started writing *Castle Rackrent's* first section sometime in the mid-1790s, completing it by the end of 1797. She completed the second section sometime between 1797 and 1799, adding the preface and glossary in 1799, and publishing the novel in 1800. In 1798, before she wrote the preface or glossary, and possibly before she completed the second section of *Castle Rackrent*, an event occurred that had profound significance for the course of Irish history, and perhaps for the course of the novel: the rebellion of the United Irishmen.

The United Irishmen were originally a nationalist group of Dissenters and radical Anglicans led by Theobald Wolfe Tone in the north of Ireland. They formed in the late eighteenth century, driven by the desire for independent nationhood and an egalitarian society, drawing inspiration from the American and French Revolutions. The United Irishmen called for independence from Britain and an end to religious persecution for all Irish people, ideas whose time had apparently come, as the group quickly spread throughout the country, expanding its ranks to include Catholics as well as Protestants. Confronted by growing unrest, the Anglo-Irish government made a concession, and in 1793 passed the Catholic Relief Act, giving the right to vote and enter the professions to those Catholics who owned property. This was clearly not enough, and when later that year the leaders of revolutionary France vowed to come to the aid of any people who wished to overthrow a tyrannical government, the United Irishmen began to plot a revolution. In 1798 government spies got wind of the group's plans and conducted mass arrests, torturing those even suspected of belonging to the rebel organization. In protest the United Irishmen killed government officials, landlords, and sometimes those who were guilty merely of being Protestants. The rebellion was soon put down, but the atrocities had been great on both sides.

Due to Richard Lovell Edgeworth's humane landlordship and liberal politics, his family and their estate were spared the depredations of the United Irishmen, but the Edgeworths were forced to flee the battle that spilled onto their lands, taking refuge in the county town of Longford. There, Richard Lovell Edgeworth was accused of conspiring with the rebels, and barely escaped being lynched by a terrified loyalist mob. Edgeworth was an exceptional man in many ways and he deplored the brutality of the British troops in putting down the uprising, yet, as a member of the Anglo-Irish gentry, even he could not support the rebels in their cause. He supported an end to religious persecution, to be sure, but he, like the rest of the Protestant Ascendancy, could not endorse a complete break with England. Ireland in the eyes of the Anglo-Irish was in many ways a savage land of superstition, violence, and ignorance. They thought that without England, Ireland would be chaos, and the Edgeworths, who placed high value on the human ability to reason and to improve the condition of society, could not countenance chaos.

Maria Edgeworth made a conscious decision not to represent in fiction the political turbulence she had witnessed in life. "The people," she observed in 1834, when the strife worsened, "would only break the glass, and curse the fool who held the mirror up to nature—distorted nature in a fever" (Edgeworth in Harden, p. 94). Yet the rebellion of 1798 is reflected in *Castle Rackrent*. Before publishing the novel in 1800, Edgeworth and her father had just returned from a tour of England and doubtless saw that English opinion in the wake of 1798 was already too inclined against the Irish, and that the depictions in *Castle Rackrent* would only add fuel to this negative fire. Thus her placement of the novel's setting to the period "before 1782," and her constant insistence that the novel treats former times and manners, implies that the ills of Ireland under the landlord system belonged to the bad old days prior to parliamentary independence. The first part of the novel, completed before the events of 1798, depicts corrupt landlords who stay in power despite their faults. In the second section, however, which may have been completed after the uprising, the Rackrents are replaced by the native Irish. The spirit of feudalism, represented by Thady's obsequious worship of "the family," with its sentimental appeal and its devastating flaws, is likewise replaced by a straightforward capitalist relationship between the tenants of Castle Rackrent and their new, completely practical landlord, Jason Quirk.

Union with England. The 1798 display of revolutionary violence convinced many members of the Ascendancy that independence from England, even the parliamentary independence they had achieved in 1782, was folly. To maintain their power, the Anglo-Irish needed English support. The Ascendancy was split between those who desired Union with England, which meant abandoning the Irish Parliament as an institution and instead sending representatives to the English Parliament, and those who believed Ireland must maintain parliamentary independence despite the internal threat. Although Richard Lovell Edgeworth supported Union, he voted against it on principle, because the vote had been so obviously rigged with bribes in Union's favor. Nonetheless, the Act of Union passed, and in 1800 the 500-year-old Irish Parliament was dissolved.

Those, like Richard Lovell Edgeworth, who supported the union with England, had hoped it would remove Ireland's colonial status, elevating Ireland to an equal partnership with England. Such hopes were not fulfilled. Even after Union, Ireland maintained a second-class colonial status with respect to England, and the vast Catholic native-Irish majority of the population remained excluded from power. In contrast to her father's unremitting optimism, Maria Edgeworth expresses some prescient doubt as to the ultimate outcome of the impending union in the postscript of *Castle Rackrent*: "It is a problem of difficult solution to determine, whether an Union will hasten or retard the amelioration of this country" (*Castle Rackrent*, p. 97).

FROM THE GENERAL PREFACE TO THE 1829 EDITION OF THE WAVERLEY NOVELS

Without being so presumptuous as to hope to emulate the rich humor, pathetic tenderness, and admirable tact, which pervade the works of my accomplished friend, I felt that something might be attempted for my own country, of the same kind with that which Miss Edgeworth so fortunately achieved for Ireland—something which might introduce her natives to those of the sister kingdom in a more favorable light than they had been placed hitherto, and tend to produce sympathy for their virtues, and indulgence for their foibles.

(Scott in Newcomer, pp. 16-17)

Reviews. *Castle Rackrent* was an instant commercial success. The novel, originally published anonymously, even gained the admiration of King George III, who is said to have exclaimed "I know something now of my Irish subjects" after reading it (George III in Butler, p. 359). While Jane Austen would later receive only £450 for her novel *Emma*, Maria Edgeworth would receive £2,000 for a single work after the success of *Castle Rackrent* and her later novels. Critics of the day barely noticed *Castle Rackrent*, but this was typical for the turn of the eighteenth century, when novels held a relatively low status and were largely dismissed as frivolous entertainment. What reviews the novel did receive were modestly favorable, with criticism focusing on the novel's seemingly limited and eccentric view of Irish life. Contemporary critics thought Edgeworth's subsequent novels gave a more mature treatment of Irish society that bore a greater relevance to the real world, although later critics would praise *Castle Rackrent* above all the author's other works.

Edgeworth had many notable admirers in the literary world. Sir Walter Scott was perhaps her most famous, acknowledging her influence on his work in his postscript to *Waverley* (1814). Her other admirers included Lord Byron, Ivan Turgenev, and Jane Austen, a fan of Edgeworth's later novel *Belinda* (1801), who sent Edgeworth an advance copy of her novel *Emma*.

—Kimberly Ball and Monica Riordan

For More Information

Bilger, Audrey. *Laughing Feminism: Subversive Comedy in Frances Burney, Maria Edgeworth, and Jane Austen.* Detroit: Wayne State University Press, 1998.

Butler, Marilyn. *Maria Edgeworth: A Literary Biography.* Oxford: Clarendon, 1972.

Edgeworth, Maria. *Castle Rackrent: An Hibernian tale taken from facts and from the manners of the Irish squires before the year 1782.* Ed. George Watson. Oxford: Oxford University Press, 1991.

Harden, Elizabeth. *Maria Edgeworth.* Boston: Twayne, 1984.

Hyman, Louis. *The Jews of Ireland: From Earliest Times to the Year 1910.* London: Jewish Historical Society of England and Israel Universities Press, 1972.

MacDonagh, Oliver. *The Nineteenth Century Novel and Irish Social History.* Dublin: National University of Ireland, 1971.

McCormack, W. J. *Ascendancy and Tradition in Anglo-Irish Literary History from 1789-1939.* Oxford: Clarendon, 1985.

Maguire, W. A. "*Castle Nugent* and *Castle Rackrent*: Fact and Fiction in Maria Edgeworth." *Eighteenth Century Ireland* 11 (1996): 146-59.

Mortimer, Anthony. "Castle Rackrent and Its Historical Contents." *Etudes Irlandaises,* 9 (December 1984): 107-23.

Newcomer, James. *Maria Edgeworth, the Novelist: 1767-1849. A Bicentennial Study.* Fort Worth: Texas Christian University Press, 1967.

Ranelagh, John O'Beirne. *A Short History of Ireland.* 2d ed. Cambridge: Cambridge University Press, 1994.

Tracy, Robert. *The Unappeasable Host: Studies in Irish Identities.* Dublin: University College Dublin Press, 1998.

The Diary of Samuel Pepys

by

Samuel Pepys

Born in 1633, Samuel Pepys (pronounced "peeps") was the son of a tailor who brought the family to London when Samuel was a boy. In 1660, just months after Pepys began his diary, Admiral Edward Montagu, a well-connected cousin by marriage, invited the young man to sail as his secretary on a historic journey to the Netherlands, where Montagu was to join the party escorting King Charles II back to England. Pepys thus enjoyed a personal part in the Restoration, the event that ended 18 years of Puritan rule and royal exile (the Interregnum) and returned the monarchy to power in England. During the 1660s, helped by his powerful cousin, Pepys won a series of important positions in the office of naval administration. By the end of the Second Anglo-Dutch War (1665-67), Pepys's valuable service had earned the trust of both King Charles II and his brother James, the duke of York and Lord High Admiral (later King James II). Though poor eyesight forced him to discontinue his diary in 1669, Pepys's career continued to flourish, culminating in his appointment as Secretary of the Admiralty in 1684 under Charles II, a position he retained after James II succeeded to the throne in 1685. After James II's overthrow in 1688, however, Pepys—until then one of the most powerful men in England—was forced to retire. He died in 1703, having helped transform the English navy into a large and well-equipped professional fighting force that would dominate the seas for two centuries. The early stages of this achievement can clearly be seen in the diary—along with the vivid personal touches that give

---

THE LITERARY WORK

A personal diary recording the daily events of life in London from January 1, 1660 through May 31, 1669; first published in 1825.

SYNOPSIS

Tracing his rise from young unknown civil servant to powerful administrative official of the English Royal Navy, Samuel Pepys's secret diary offers not only an insider's view of important historical events, but also the frankest details of a life marked by curiosity, energy, passion, and sheer pleasure in being alive.

---

this remarkable writer a rare place in both literature and history.

Events in History at the Time the Diary Was Written

The Restoration. The Puritan minority that dominated English politics during the Interregnum had drawn its political strength from its dynamic leader, Oliver Cromwell, who in turn drew much of his support from the army. Cromwell's death in 1658 had left a leadership vacuum in which the various factions held in check by his personal authority—Puritans, republicans, influential city officials in London, royalists, and others—now vied for power. By mid-1659 the reins of government had fallen by default into the hands of the so-called Rump Parliament, the remnant of the legitimately elected Parliament after it had been purged by the Puritans. But the Rump lacked the support to govern effectively; and by 1660, amid political chaos, many English had begun to long for what only a few years earlier had been unthinkable: the return of the monarchy.

The greatest power lay with the army, and the most powerful part of the army was stationed in Scotland and commanded by General George Monck, a former royalist general who had also served under Cromwell. On January 1, 1660, the day Pepys began his diary, Monck crossed with his troops south into England and marched on London. Though he intended at first to preserve the Rump against other commanders who threatened it, on arriving in London Monck soon realized that the Rump was incapable of governing the deeply divided country. Monck reversed the earlier purges, restoring the elected members who had been expelled from Parliament. This restored Parliament dissolved itself in February, and the new elections—as most expected—brought a royalist majority.

On May 1, 1660, a week after it convened, the new Parliament was read a statement from King Charles II, who was in exile at Breda in the Netherlands. Charles's Declaration of Breda prudently promised religious toleration, a general amnesty for most anti-royalists, and back pay for the army; a week later, Parliament restored Charles II to the throne. Three days after that, on May 11, an English naval fleet weighed anchor for the Netherlands, arriving two days later. On May 23 the royal party met the fleet officers, and King Charles II, with his brother James, who was newly appointed Lord High Admiral, set sail for England on the *Naseby*. Also on board the flagship was the 27-year-old Pepys, who enjoyed the king's stories and became known by name to James. Landing in Dover on May 26, Charles II made a triumphant journey to London, cheered by crowds along the way: as Pepys recorded, "The Shouting and joy expressed by all is past imagination" (Pepys, *The Shorter Pepys*, p. 51).

War with the Dutch. Although the Netherlands had provided Charles with a refuge during his exile, hostilities that arose between the English and the Dutch during the Interregnum soon also came to dominate the restored king's foreign policy. These hostilities grew out of a long commercial rivalry between the two seafaring peoples. In the first half of the seventeenth century—a century often called the "golden age" of Dutch

commercial expansion—Dutch merchants had opened European markets in such trade items as timber from the Baltic; sugar, tobacco, coffee, and indigo dye from the Americas; cotton from the Middle East; and spices from Asia. From the 1650s, however, English merchants increasingly challenged Dutch commercial preeminence, leading to the First Anglo-Dutch War (1652-54), which was won by the English under Cromwell and his leading naval strategist, Admiral Robert Blake.

One immediate cause of that war had been the Navigation Act of 1651, by which the English restricted all trade between England and its colonies to English ships or to ships belonging to the country of origin. Soon after the Restoration, Parliament enacted a similar but more specific measure, the Navigation Act of 1660, which named the particular items (timber and other naval supplies, plus sugar, tobacco, cottons, and dyes, for example) that non-English ships were forbidden to carry between England and its colonies. Three years later, the Navigation Act of 1663 banned the shipping of any European goods to the colonies except through England and Wales. These measures aimed to increase the English share of world commerce primarily at the expense of the Dutch, and (despite his good treatment at Dutch hands) Charles strongly supported these restrictions.

Such aggressive policies also reflected a desire on the part of Charles and some of his advisors to show that they could match the military record of the Cromwell years. English aggression soon led to fighting in America and Africa. In 1664, for example, the English navy attacked stations of the Dutch East India Company in West Africa in an attempt to loosen Dutch control of the lucrative slave trade; in the same year, the English also seized New Amsterdam, the principle Dutch city in North America, renaming it New York. The attacks were the immediate cause of the Second Anglo-Dutch War, which broke out in February 1665.

At first, the war went well for the English, with an English fleet under the king's brother, James, routing the Dutch at the battle of Lowestoft in June 1665. The English failed to follow up the victory, however, and in early June of the following year they were badly defeated in the Four Days Battle in the English Channel. An English victory in the Battle of St. James Day at the end of July was once again not followed up, although a few weeks later a small English force sneaked into a Dutch harbor and burned more than 100 merchant vessels. Peace negotiations were opened at Breda in early 1667, but while they were going on the Dutch sailed boldly up the broad Medway River, which forms a natural harbor where it flows into the sea near London, and attacked the English fleet at anchor. Three English ships were burned and the English flagship *Royal Charles* (as the *Naseby* had been renamed) was captured and towed away. So complete and so public was the humiliation that Pepys—by now in charge of supplying the navy—feared that angry London crowds might attack the Naval Office where he worked. Despite this demoralizing catastrophe, however, the war was inconclusive: the Peace of Breda, reached soon afterward, restored the situation before the conflict, and the English were allowed to retain possession of New York.

The plague and the Great Fire. Two natural disasters had also added to the English woes during the war with the Dutch. In the summer of 1665, soon after the war broke out, bubonic plague struck in London, killing more than 30,000 people at its peak in September alone before abating sharply in December, by which time it had claimed an estimated 75,000 victims. Summer heat and dirty, narrow streets infested with plague-carrying rats made the city a miserable as well as a dangerous place. Often at night the only sound heard on the deserted streets was the rumble of the cart collecting the bodies of plague victims, which were buried in mass graves. Houses infected by the plague were marked by a red cross painted on the door with the words "Lord have mercy on us" inscribed next to it. One house struck early in the outbreak was that of Pepys's neighbor, a Dr. Burnett, who "gained great goodwill among the neighbors" by shutting himself in as soon he self-diagnosed the illness (*Pepys*, p. 496). The plague fell most heavily on the crowded urban poor, as most who could afford to leave London did so. King Charles moved the court from London, for example, and Pepys found lodgings for his wife Elizabeth in nearby Woolwich, where he joined her as often as work permitted.

No sooner was the dispirited city beginning to recover from the plague than, in September 1666, it was ravaged over five days by the worst fire in its history. The blaze erupted early on Sunday, September 2, in the king's bakery in Pudding Lane, near London Bridge, and was fanned by a strong east wind that drove the flames westward along the Thames toward the main part of the city. Nearly all of the city's buildings were

The bubonic plague swept through London in 1665, killing an estimated 75,000 people. This extract from a 1665 London death register tallies a weekly accumulation of plague victims.

made of wood, and by the time the fire was extinguished on Thursday it had consumed over 13,000 houses and nearly 100 churches. Among the churches destroyed was the old St. Paul's Cathedral, soon to be rebuilt by the architect Sir Christopher Wren; the replacement remains one of London's great landmarks. Wren and others (including Pepys's friend John Evelyn and the scientist Robert Hooke) drew up elaborate plans to rebuild the demolished city on a grander scale and submitted them to the king. In the end, however, the city was rebuilt along pretty much the same lines as before, except that the streets were widened, the height of buildings was limited, and Charles ordered the buildings themselves to be constructed of brick or stone rather than wood.

Pepys witnessed the Great Fire—indeed, he helped to fight it—and his description remains the most important historical source for it as well as comprising some of the diary's most moving passages. The fire left tens of thousands homeless and an unknown number of dead; as with the plague, the urban poor suffered most. Pepys writes of "poor people staying in their houses as long as till the very fire touched them, and then running into boats or clambering from one pair of stair by the waterside to another" to escape the flames (*Pepys*, p. 660). Also like the plague, the Great Fire seemed to many to be a punishment from God; to those who sought a reason for God's wrath, the licentiousness of the royal court supplied one. (Both Charles and James were notorious womanizers—Charles ultimately acknowledged 17 bastard children—and the hedonistic atmosphere that pervaded Restoration court life sprang from their example.) The naval disaster on the Medway amplified this growing discon-

A lithograph by Sir Christopher Wren, c. 1808, depicting the Great Fire of London.

tent with court excesses, and as the Second-Anglo Dutch War drew to a close in 1667, the public demanded action. All eyes now turned to those responsible for the conduct of the war—and particularly to those responsible for running the navy.

Pepys and the Royal Navy. Pepys had entered service at the Naval Office in 1660 as Clerk of the Acts of the Navy Board, a position won for him by his cousin, Admiral Edward Montagu. Montagu was by then one of Charles's chief naval commanders; others included George Monck, Sir William Penn (father of Pennsylvania's founder), and Sir William Coventry. Pepys worked daily with these experienced veterans, all of whom figure prominently in the diary, learning constantly and taking on more and more important duties and positions. The navy in which they served had been created largely during the Interregnum, when the English had for the first time built ships specially for a standing navy and employed regularly paid officers and recruits to man them, rather than commandeering merchant ships and their crews as needed. Over his long career, Pepys would build on this foundation, creating an effective and essentially modern institutional framework to support virtually every aspect of a standing professional naval force.

Although this accomplishment came after Pepys discontinued the diary, his daily record does outline the first decade of his extraordinary career. As Clerk of the Acts, Pepys began as a secretary recording the decisions and actions of the Navy Board (the civilian administrative arm of the navy) and writing its correspondence. Reorganizing the board's office, Pepys streamlined procedures and mastered every detail of the board's workings. By 1662, Coventry referred to him as "the life of this office" (*Pepys*, p. 220). That same year Pepys's growing administrative abilities won him a coveted appointment to the Tangier Committee, an important position because the navy was then planning to construct a massive breakwater at this North African port (*Pepys*, p. 220). When war broke out in 1665, Pepys was rapidly promoted to Treasurer of the Tangier Committee. And later that year he also won the crucial position of Surveyor-General of the Victualling, which put him in charge of supplying food for the navy's crews. In practice, however, Pepys not only managed the victualling but also oversaw the acquisition of all other naval supplies, the construction of new vessels and repair of old ones, and the recruitment and pay of the crews. As Pepys reports, his energy and expertise led no less a figure than Monck to praise him as "the right hand of the navy" (*Pepys*, p. 484).

When the war ended, Parliament formed two investigative committees to assign blame for its having gone badly: the Committee for Miscarriages and the Committee for Accounts (later called the Brooke House Committee). Pepys was summoned almost immediately to be questioned about the Medway disaster by the former. He was thoroughly prepared, with reams of notes and files at hand for reference. In front of the entire House of Commons, he gave evidence in what those present called the best address they had ever heard before that legislative body. Pepys's successful defense lent great credibility to the Navy Board and confirmed him as its leading expert. When he was called later by the Brooke House Committee, he also succeeded in exonerating himself. That, however, occurred in 1670. By then Pepys had discontinued his diary but continued his career, well on his way to what one scholar calls "his single greatest achievement, the professionalizing of the naval officer" (Ollard, p. 107).

Patronage, class, and sexual attitudes. In seventeenth-century England, such careers were open to men of Pepys's background only through the patronage, or sponsorship, of more powerful figures. Relations between patron and protégé could be highly complex, interweaving attitudes towards class, power, and social propriety. In August 1663, for example, Pepys found out that his patron, Admiral Montagu (by then created Lord Sandwich), was having an affair with a younger woman of dubious reputation. Bothered by Sandwich's scandalous behavior, that November Pepys composed "my great letter of reproof" to Sandwich, criticizing him for casting aside his honor and jeopardizing his place at court and thus, by implication, Pepys's career as well (*Pepys*, p. 322). Copying the entire letter into the diary, he nervously awaited the results of his boldness, though Sandwich's response turned out to be mild and Pepys's relationship with Sandwich was not immediately damaged. Even so, the astute Pepys found an additional patron in Sir William Coventry, another naval commander whose star was rising, and who in 1666 proposed him for the job of Surveyor-General of the Victualling. By then, Sandwich had made several missteps in the war against the Dutch that did indeed threaten his position; Coventry gradually replaced Sandwich in sponsoring Pepys's career.

Like the nuances of patronage, sexual attitudes were informed by class distinctions. Lord Sandwich, patron to Pepys, tried to seduce Pepys's wife, not a shocking development since a wife was commonly expected to make her body available to her husband's superior. Pepys himself engaged in sexual affairs with women beneath him on the social scale—maids, servants, shopgirls, or subordinates' wives. Indeed, even as Pepys lectured his patron, he carried on an affair with a young married woman, Mrs. Bagwell, whom he seduced by promising to advance her husband's career. Pepys's misgivings about such behavior generally reflected religious convention and fear of disclosure rather than concern for women whose positions left them vulnerable to sexual predation:

> God forgive me, I was sorry to hear that Sir W. Pens [Penn's] maid Betty was gone away yesterday, for I was in hopes to have had a bout with her before she had gone, she being very pretty. I have also a mind to my own wench, but I dare not, for fear she should prove honest and refuse and then tell my wife.
>
> (*Pepys*, p. 217)

By contrast, Pepys reserved his romantic admiration for sexually inaccessible women of higher social rank—even if he knew them to be promiscuous. "Strange it is," he admitted, that he saw the beautiful Lady Castlemayne (one of Charles II's lovers) through a haze of fanciful reverence "though I know well enough she is a whore" (*Pepys*, pp. 213-14).

Not only did the king's sexual excesses set an example; they also reflected a loosening of morals and a relaxation of attitudes toward sexuality in Restoration England. Encouraging this shift was the belief by all types of Protestants that marriage partners owed each other mutual comfort, including sexual responsiveness. The view gave a positive spin to the sexual act, in contrast to the traditional or old-fashioned Catholic regard for it as just a necessity for procreation. By the middle of the seventeenth century, the English in general had accepted this newly legitimate view of sex within marriage. Sex for men outside marriage gained more acceptance too, in a more or less clandestine way, depending on the man. A double standard prevailed, with marriage manuals advising the upper-class wife to overlook her husband's infidelities. Concerned about harm done to the male body by abstinence as well as excess, doctors recommended moderate sexual activity. Moderation was necessary, they said, because a man needed to preserve a certain amount of semen to stay in good health. Also his strength when his children were conceived determined how hearty they would be. A sexually exhausted father would not do. Such advice, combined with the fear of venereal disease, encouraged men to more frequently engage in activities such as the fondling of a woman's private parts than in actual sexual consummation. The evidence suggests that such fondling was acceptable to a wide range of women in late seventeenth-century London, of various classes and marital statuses.

This liberal environment resulted in great measure from England's reaction to the austere 1650s. During the Interregnum, the Puritans had invoked policies that curbed pleasures, from closing theaters and brothels, to limiting the number of alehouses, to making adultery punishable by death. The restoration of royal rule saw a major backlash against this attempt to prescribe private behavior. Early in the century the law shamed sexual offenders, exposing and punishing them by having them stand in white sheets before a congregation or in a market-day square. After 1660 the country dispensed with such "shame punishments," separating to a large degree issues of sexual immorality from the law.

The Diary in Focus

Contents summary. Samuel Pepys, 26 years old as he begins his diary, prefaces the work with a brief summary of his personal situation and that of the nation before his first entry for January 1, 1660: he is in good health; he lives in London with his wife Elizabeth and their servant Jane; the Rump Parliament has assembled; Monck is in Scotland but may march south to ensure free elections; Pepys himself works as a clerk for Mr. George Downing, an official in the Exchequer (after whom Downing Street was later named). January 1 is a Sunday, and the simple, homey occurrences of this first entry reflect Pepys's light schedule (later the pressure of business will intrude even on Sunday, his Sabbath). He and his wife sleep late, attend a sermon, and dine at home on turkey (which his wife burns her hand preparing). In the afternoon Pepys tends to his personal finances; then he and his wife visit Pepys's father, eating supper there before coming home and going to bed. Entries for January and February register frequent meetings with friends during the day (several times Pepys explicitly says he has little to do at work), supply details of Pepys's home and family life, and follow unfolding political events.

In his entry for March 3, Pepys notes that his cousin Montagu has been appointed "one of the

generalls-at-sea, and Monke the other" (*Pepys*, p. 24). Three days later Montagu takes Pepys aside to discuss the young man's career. He then offers Pepys his patronage and asks him to be his secretary as the political climate shifts towards restoring the king:

> [He told me that] he would use all his own and all the interest of his friends that he hath in England to do me good. And asked me whether I could without too much inconvenience go to sea as his Secretary, and bade me think of it. He also begin [sic] to talk of things of state, and told me that he should now want one at sea in that capacity that he might trust in. . . . He told me also that he did believe the King would come in. . . . Everybody now drink [sic] the King's health without any fear, whereas before it was very private that a man dare do it.
> (*Pepys*, pp. 25-26)

On March 22 Pepys buys new clothes and notes that people are already treating him with deference or offering him favors and gifts. He prays that he will not become overly proud because of his new status. The next day he moves onto the flagship *Swiftsure* with Montagu, occupying the best of the cabins allotted to his patron, and sets up his writing equipment. On April 2 Montagu shifts his flag to the *Naseby*, and Pepys transfers to that vessel with him; the fleet sails for the Netherlands on May 11; and on May 23 Charles II and the future James II board the *Naseby*, where on the return voyage Charles entertains Pepys and others with the story of his narrow escape after the Battle of Worcester (during an attempt to regain the throne in 1651). On May 25 Pepys describes the king's landing at Dover and his jubilant welcome: "Infinite the Croud [sic] of people and the gallantry of the Horsmen [sic], Citizens, and Noblemen of all sorts" (*Pepys*, p. 50).

In the coming months Pepys begins his job as Clerk of the Acts (June); purchases a fine new cloak with gold buttons and a silk suit, both of which please him mightily (July 1); moves to a new house at the Navy Office in Seething Lane and hires a boy named Will Hewer—later a close friend and confidant—as a servant (July 17 and 18); attends a footrace in Hyde Park (August); and enjoys a sexual liaison with a woman whom he meets at his old house (September). During this time he confers constantly with Montagu (whom Charles II created earl of Sandwich in July), Coventry, Penn, and others, and above all learns the ropes at the Navy Office: "For this month or two, it is not imaginable how busy my head hath been," Pepys declares in August

(*Pepys*, p. 70). In October he goes to see the anti-royalist plotter Major-General Harrison "hanged, drawn, and quartered . . . he looking as cheerfully as any man could do in that condition"; Pepys notes that as a boy he had seen King Charles I executed (in 1649) and now has seen the first blood drawn in revenge of that regicide (*Pepys*, p. 86).

A highlight of the following year, 1661, is Charles II's coronation at Westminster on April 23, a crowded and impressive pageant that Pepys describes at length, and after which he and several companions are sick from drinking too much wine. By his twenty-ninth birthday on February 23, 1662, Pepys has reason to be satisfied at his improved place in the world: he is "in very good health and like to live and get an estate; and if I have a heart to be contented, I think I may reckon myself as happy a man as any is in the world—for which God be praised" (*Pepys*, p. 180). Despite his now increased income, however, he continues to be strict about expenses and castigates himself frequently for being stingy with his wife. In the evenings he enjoys playing the lute and especially the flageolet, a small flutelike instrument; he and his wife often attend the theater, and he also relishes drinking wine with friends until late at night. These latter two pastimes he views as indulgences and repeatedly vows to quit. He also takes encouragement from his deepening involvement at work:

> My mind is now in a wonderful condition of quiet and content, more than ever in all my life—since minding the business of my office, which I have done most constantly; and I find it to be the very effect of my late oaths against wine and plays; which, if God please, I will keep constant in. For now my business is a delight to me and brings me great credit, and my purse increases too.
>
> (*Pepys*, p. 209)

Always eager to acquire new areas of expertise, in July 1662 Pepys engages a mathematics tutor to teach him the multiplication tables and other skills that might help him at work. That August he learns from Montagu of his appointment to the Tangier Committee (*Pepys*, p. 220).

While Pepys consistently includes revealing and often brutally honest personal details in his account of the days' events, the middle years of the decade are dominated by the war, the plague, and the Great Fire. The war and the plague run through the daily entries like a thread, whereas the Great Fire stands out for the concentration of narrative focus that Pepys brings to bear on it.

Pepys's maid wakes him at 3 o'clock the morning of September 2, 1666, with the news that a fire is burning in the city. He looks out the window, then goes back to sleep. Up at seven again, he hears that more than 300 houses have now been burnt. He goes out to look around and sees the blaze threatening people and homes, with "nobody in my sight endeavoring to quench it, but to remove their goods and leave all to the fire" (*Pepys*, p. 660). He hurries to the royal residence at Whitehall and notifies the king's attendants:

> I was called for and did tell the King and the Duke of York what I saw, and that unless his Majesty did command houses to be pulled down nothing could stop the fire. They seemed much troubled, and the King commanded me to go to the Lord Mayor from him and command him to spare no houses but to pull down before the fire every way.
>
> (*Pepys*, p. 660)

MAJOR EVENTS IN THE DIARY

1660 January 1: begins diary. March 9: becomes secretary to Montagu. May: goes with Montagu to the Netherlands, accompanies Charles II to England. June 29: appointed Clerk of the Acts of the Navy Board.

1661 April 23: attends coronation of Charles II.

1662 November 20: appointed to Tangier Committee.

1663 November 17: writes letter reproving Montagu.

1664 March 15: brother Tom dies.

1665 February 15: elected Fellow of the Royal Society. February 22: Second Dutch War begins. March 20: appointed Treasurer of Tangier Committee. May-December: plague in London. December 4: appointed Surveyor-General of the Victualling.

1666 September 2-5: Great Fire of London.

1667 June 10-13: Dutch raid the Medway.

1668 March 5: defends Navy Board before House of Commons. October 25: wife Elizabeth catches Pepys having sex with their maid, Deb Willet.

1669 May 31: discontinues diary.

(Adapted from *Pepys*, pp. xli-xliii)

Pepys finds the panic-stricken Lord Mayor "like a man spent, with a handkercher [sic] about his neck. To the King's message, he cried like a fainting woman, 'Lord, what can I do?'" (*Pepys*, p. 660). People trying to save their belongings jam the streets, boats taking on goods crowd the Thames, and many items float loose on the water. Pepys himself goes out on the river in a small boat, "so near the fire as we could for smoke; and all over the Thames, with one's face in the wind you were almost burned with a shower of Fire-drops" (*Pepys*, p. 662).

Pepys's prodigious energy is paradoxically reflected in the quickening pace and longer entries of the diary's last few years. He gives the impression that the busier he becomes at work, the more energy he has for chasing women, adding books to his now impressive library, attending plays and concerts, and above all pausing to take delight in the small details of life. These last happy years of the diary are overshadowed by two storm clouds, however: Pepys's turbulent relations with his wife, and the growing trouble he has with his eyes. On October 25, 1668, Elizabeth discovers Pepys having sex with their young maid, Deb Willett—as Pepys puts it in the idiosyncratic mix of English and Spanish that he uses for sexual details, "imbracing the girl con my hand sub su coats" (*Pepys*, p. 950). Pepys feels remorse for the anguish he has caused both women, writing that the incident has led to "the greatest falling out with my poor wife, and through my folly with the girl, that ever I had; and I have reason to be sorry and ashamed of it—and more, to be troubled for the poor girl's sake" (*Pepys*, p. 954). At the same time, Pepys's eyes have become increasingly painful when he reads or writes, causing him to fear eventual blindness. It is this affliction that causes him, on May 31, 1669, to lay down his pen for the last time. Though his fears of blindness proved unfounded (his eyes, probably strained from hours of writing in poor light, recovered), he never resumed the diary.

Pepys's passions. Pepys's unusual curiosity and enthusiasm led him in so many directions that his interests can be seen as a cultural catalogue of his times. Music, plays, and books feature constantly in the diary's pages, as do records of the lively discussions about them that Pepys had with his wide circle of friends. As his fortune increased he also began collecting prints, though the prizes of his collection—a group of prints by Rembrandt Van Rijn (1606-69)—were acquired after he stopped the diary. In addition to the arts, Pepys also followed the rapid scientific advances of his day and was elected a fellow of the recently formed Royal Society in 1665 (later

he would serve as the president of this early scientific organization).

After the restrictions of Puritan rule, Pepys and his peers relished the free rein they could give to their taste for the arts. An accomplished musician, Pepys composed and sang, as well as played the lute, flageolet, recorder, and viol. Upper-class life in Restoration London offered frequent concerts and other musical performances, and Pepys attended avidly, recording his reactions in detail. In one of the diary's most famous passages, he sees a play called *The Virgin Martyr*, which does not particularly impress him. Written by Philip Massinger and Thomas Dekker and first performed in 1620, the play concerns the love of a Roman princess for a governor's son, and his love for another, Dorothea, whose daring conversion in these pre-Christian times ends with her being tortured to death. Apart from his reaction to the play itself, the music "ravished me; and endeed, in a word, did wrap up my soul so that it made me really sick" (*Pepys*, p. 882). Pepys also says of *The Virgin Martyr* that this occasion is "the first time it hath been acted a great while" (*Pepys*, p. 882). Public performances of plays were banned under the Puritans, from 1642 to the Restoration in 1660, when the English theater began a major revival. Other Elizabethan plays Pepys saw include Shakespeare's *A Midsummer Night's Dream, Othello*, and *Hamlet*. Of Restoration-era plays, a favorite was John Dryden's comedy *Sir Martin Marr-all*.

Pepys's third great love was literature and book collecting, and the diary is replete with passages in which Pepys browses through bookshops. In seventeenth-century London booksellers published books as well as sold them, although the two functions were just beginning to be separated. In fact, one of the six booksellers Pepys frequents in the diary, Henry Herringman, was the first to quit the retail book business and concentrate on publishing alone. Pepys's book collection contained some 3,000 books: to house them, he commissioned dockyard carpenters to build special oak bookcases; free-standing and enclosed by glass doors, the bookcases are thought to be the earliest of their kind. Pepys had 12 of them built over the years, starting in 1666.

Literary context. Although diaries (like other forms of autobiographical writing) have been kept in some form or another since ancient times, during the Renaissance a new emphasis on the individual encouraged diarists to keep fuller and more intimate records than had been common in earlier times. By the seventeenth century in

England, the Protestant Reformation's spirit of self-examination had influenced religious autobiographies, such as John Bunyan's *Grace Abounding to the Chief of Sinners* (1666). While Pepys's own self-examination differs from such public statements of faith in being both secular and private, clearly the diarist's attitudes have been shaped by a similar confessional spirit—even if it is only to himself that he confesses.

Pepys wrote his diary in shorthand, adopting a system developed in the 1620s by Thomas Shelton, one of four seventeenth-century developers of such time-saving writing systems. Pepys learned the Shelton system, which after a brief vogue failed to gain lasting popularity, while he was an undergraduate at Cambridge. Except for proper names, virtually the entire diary was written in shorthand. Pepys worked on it regularly but without a schedule: sometimes he kept it up day-by-day, sometimes he caught up on three or four days at a time. But virtually every day has its own ample entry, tracing his day from start to finish. Although he often made rough drafts and then copied them into the diary itself, he usually did not edit the entries to any substantial degree later, and he wrote in full regular prose. Nowhere does Pepys indicate his reasons for keeping this uniquely comprehensive and revealing diary, but they are surely related to his passion for observation and his talent for record-keeping.

The other famous diary of the Restoration era was kept by Pepys's friend John Evelyn (1620-1706), a writer, scientist, and gardener who was also one of those to draw up plans for rebuilding London after the Great Fire. Evelyn kept a lifelong diary that, like Pepys's, is a major historical source for the period. The two met and became friends after Pepys began his diary; in contrast with Pepys's private journal, however, Evelyn's is highly selective, self-consciously literary, heavily edited, and expressly meant to be read by his descendants. Other diarists of the Restoration included the scientist Robert Hooke (also a friend of Pepys's), but Hooke's entries, while regular, often consist of no more than brief notes.

Publication. Pepys's original diary can still be found in the Pepys Library at Magdalene College, Cambridge, where Pepys's entire collection has remained intact in the same shelves he had built for it. The diary takes up six large leather-bound volumes, which sit on the second shelf of the first bookcase. Pepys bequeathed his library to his old college, and the diaries went virtually unnoticed until 1818, when interest in them was stirred by the successful publication of John Evelyn's diary. The head of the college asked his uncle, William Grenville, who could read Shelton's shorthand and also happened to be a leading British politician, to transcribe a few pages of Pepys's work. Using these pages as an aid, a student named John Smith undertook the massive job of transcribing the entire six volumes (leaving out the erotic passages). Another of Grenville's nephews, Lord Braybrook, published a selection from Smith's 54 notebooks in 1825, and this became an overnight success. Braybrook published a third edition in 1848-49, which ensured the diary's popularity with Victorian readers. The full text was not transcribed and published until 1970-77, under the supervision of the distinguished Pepys scholars William Matthews and Robert Latham.

—Colin Wells

For More Information

Brome, Vincent. *The Other Pepys*. London: Weidenfeld and Nicholson, 1992.

Hill, Christopher. *The Century of Revolution: 1603-1714*. New York: Norton, 1980.

Hutton, Ronald. *The Restoration: A Political and Religious History of England and Wales 1658-1667*. Oxford, England: Oxford University Press, 1985.

Lockyer, Roger. *Tudor & Stuart Britain 1471-1714*. Harlow, England: Longman, 1964.

Miller, John. *The Restoration and the England of Charles II*. Harlow, England: Addison Wesley Longman, 1997.

Ollard, Richard. *Pepys: A Biography*. Oxford, England: Oxford University Press, 1985.

Pepys, Samuel. *The Shorter Pepys*. Ed. Robert Latham. Berkeley: University of California Press, 1985.

Rivington, Charles A. *Pepys and the Booksellers*. York: Sessions Book Trust, 1992.

Stone, Lawrence. *The Family, Sex and Marriage in England 1500-1800*. New York: Harper and Row, 1979.

Taylor, Ivan E. *Samuel Pepys*. Boston: Twayne, 1989.

Don Juan

by
George Gordon, Lord Byron

THE LITERARY WORK

A satirical poem set in Spain, Greece, Russia, and England during the late eighteenth century; published, serially, from 1819 to 1824.

SYNOPSIS

A handsome young Spaniard embarks on a series of amorous adventures in his native country and abroad.

Born in 1788, George Gordon became the sixth Baron Byron at age ten, after his great-uncle's death. The new Lord Byron was educated at Harrow and Trinity College, Cambridge; in 1807, he published his first book of poems, *Hours of Idleness,* which received mildly favorable notices from most literary magazines but one scathing critique from the influential *Edinburgh Review.* Stung, Byron launched a counterattack in his first satirical poem, "English Bards and Scotch Reviewers" (1809), which was influenced by Alexander Pope's *The Dunciad.* Soon after his satire's publication, Byron embarked on a Grand Tour of Europe, which provided him with the material for his romance, *Childe Harold's Pilgrimage.* The first two cantos of that poem became an instant success when they appeared in print in 1812 and Byron himself became famous overnight. A disastrous marriage in 1815, followed by a scandalous separation one year later, tarnished the poet's reputation and in 1816 Byron left England, never to return. While living abroad in Switzerland and Italy, Byron continued to write, producing two more cantos of *Childe Harold's Pilgrimage*, the dramatic poem *Manfred*, and the epic satire, *Don Juan.* Although contemporary critics denounced *Don Juan* as immoral, modern scholars consider it to be Byron's masterpiece, a comic tour-de-force of formidable scope and range.

Events in History at the Time the Poem Takes Place

Don Juan—history and legend. While it is unclear whether Don Juan Tenorio—as he was most often called—was a real person, the dashing seducer had been a familiar figure in Spanish and Italian folk legend as early as the seventeenth century. In 1630, Tirso de Molina, a Spanish monk, became the first to dramatize Don Juan's exploits in his play *El burlador de Sevilla y convidado de piedra* ("The rake of Seville and the stone guest"). In the play, Don Juan engages in a series of romantic intrigues, seducing and abandoning several women. In one entanglement, Don Juan slays Don Gonzalo, the father of his intended victim. Towards the end of the play, Don Juan flippantly invites the stone statue of the murdered man to dine with him. To his surprise, "Don Gonzalo" accepts the invitation and reciprocates with one of his own. During the latter encounter, the statue challenges Don Juan to a handshake; meeting the challenge, the astonished Don Juan finds himself cast into hell before he can confess his misdeeds to a priest.

Lord Byron

Tirso's play inspired many later treatments of the legend, including Jean-Baptiste Moliere's play, *Dom Juan ou le festin de pierre* (1665) and Wolfgang Amadeus Mozart's famous opera, *Don Giovanni*, which was first performed in Prague in 1787. Significantly, the Don Juan legend underwent considerable changes as it traveled from Spain to other parts of Europe. Tirso's Don Juan had been a true libertine—a religious freethinker as well as a dissolute rake—whose ultimate damnation was due as much to his blasphemy as to the sexual indiscretions that flouted faith and convention. Literary scholar Moyra Haslett observes that, in Tirso's play and in the earliest versions that followed, "Don Juan's greatest offence is his presumption that God's mercy can be taken for granted and will be available to him whenever he wishes to repent. And it is for this that he is finally punished" (Haslett, p. 8). However, after the story became very popular among the troupes of the *commedia dell'arte* in Italy, the legend's comic aspects gradually overshadowed the religious and moral themes. Don Juan became a figure of fun, rather than menace, a fitting subject for puppet-shows, farces, and even pantomimes (the precursor to modern musicals). London audiences were especially partial to pantomimic treatments of Don Juan, such as *Don John; or the Libertine Destroyed*, offered by Drury Lane in 1782, and the similarly named *Don Juan; or the Libertine Destroyed: A tragic Pantomimical*

Ballet, first performed at the Royalty Theatre in 1788, the year, coincidentally, of Byron's birth. While it is unclear which, if any, of these productions influenced Byron's poem, the poet was certainly aware of Don Juan's familiarity to audiences and of his popularity in the pantomimic medium, humorously declaring in Canto 1, "I want a hero. . . / I'll therefore take our ancient friend Don Juan— / We all have seen him, in the pantomime, / Sent to the devil somewhat ere his time" (Byron, *Don Juan*, 1.6-8).

Catherine the Great. Don Juan's interaction with Catherine the Great represents one of the more historical interludes in Byron's poem. Born in 1729, Sophia Augusta Frederica—of the principality of Anhalt-Zerbst—was betrothed in 1744 to Grand Duke Peter Feodorovich, nephew of Empress Elizabeth of Russia and heir presumptive to the Russian throne. In an attempt to please her mother-in-law, Sophia took the name Ekaterina (Catherine) Alekseevna before her marriage in 1745. The royal couple soon became estranged; Peter was less well educated than Catherine and showed a tendency towards madness. After the birth of her son, Paul, in 1754, Catherine became involved in politics, opposing her husband's pro-Lutheran and pro-Prussian policies.

On January 5, 1762, the Grand Duke ascended to the Russian throne as Peter III; matters between Peter and Catherine further deteriorated when he threatened her with divorce on the grounds of her infidelity. His accusations were justified; during her life, Catherine was to take many lovers, including Gregory Potemkin and Alexander Lanskoy, on whom she showered titles, lands, and wealth. The empress responded to her husband's threats six months later, while Peter was away from court. Conspirators led by Gregory Orlov, Catherine's current lover, and backed by the Imperial Guard issued a pronouncement that stripped Peter of his powers and made Catherine empress in her own right. The deposed emperor was secluded in a country house at Ropcha, where he was murdered in July 1762, probably with Catherine's approval.

Reigning as Catherine II, the new empress was considered, overall, an able ruler—an enlightened despot who transformed Russia into a great power. Her domestic policies were not completely successful, however. Early in her reign, Catherine convened a legislative commission of 565 representatives—from every class except the serfs—and tried to introduce new, modernized laws. The commission was ultimately dismissed

BYRON AND THE SKEPTICAL TRADITION

Various modern critics have noted the influence of such skeptical thinkers as David Hume, the Scottish philosopher, and Michel de Montaigne, the French essayist, in *Don Juan*. Indeed, in the poem's later cantos, Byron, through the medium of his garrulous narrator, frequently expresses the main philosophical tenet of skepticism: that true knowledge of anything is uncertain. Quoting Montaigne's motto "Que sçais-je?" ("What do I know?"), the narrator explores the skeptics' position "[t]hat all is dubious which man may attain . . . / There's no such thing as certainty, that's plain / As any of Mortality's conditions: / So little do we know what we're about in / This world, I doubt if doubt itself be doubting" (*Don Juan*, 9.131, 133-36). Later in the poem, the narrator expands upon his theme, arguing that "He who doubts all things, nothing can deny" and calling into question the very nature of reality itself: "But what's reality? Who has its clue? / Philosophy? No; she too much rejects. / Religion? Yes; but which of all her sects?" (*Don Juan*, 15.701, 710-12). Don Juan's refusal to acknowledge any certainties—whether in love, thought, or faith—contributed, as much as its bawdiness, to the poem's hostile reception by contemporary critics. The influential *Blackwood's Magazine* denounced *Don Juan* as a "filthy and impious poem" and its author as "no longer a human being, even in his frailties; but a cool unconcerned fiend" (Eisler, p. 647). Byron, however, fought back in Canto 7 of *Don Juan*, listing the names of other controversial thinkers in his own defense:

> They accuse me—*Me*—the present writer of
>   The present poem—of—I know not what,—
> A tendency to under-rate and scoff
>   At human power and virtue, and all that:
> And this they say in language rather rough.
>   Good God! I wonder what they would be at!
> I say no more than has been said in Dante's
> Verse, and by Solomon and by Cervantes.
>
> By Swift, by Machiavel, by Rochefoucalt,
>   By Fenelon, by Luther, and by Plato:
> By Tillotson, and Wesley and Rousseau,
>   Who knew this life was not worth a potato.
> 'Tis not their fault, nor mine, if this be so—
>   For my part, I pretend not to be Cato,
> Nor even Diogenes—we live and die,
> But which is best, you know no more than I.
>
> (*Don Juan*, 7.17-32)

18 months later, without the implementation of a single new law. The empress did, however, introduce some administrative reforms, especially at the level of local government. After a peasant rebellion in 1773-74, Catherine increased the number of *gubernias*—the territorial units into which Russia was divided—from 20 to 51, and separated the administrative, financial, and judicial functions of each provincial government.

Catherine's foreign policy achievements were more spectacular. Her success in that arena included the acquisition of a large portion of Poland, including Lithuania and Kurland. The empress also went to war with Turkey on two occasions (1769-74 and 1787-91), strengthening Russia's hold on the Black Sea coast from the Kerch Straits to the Dniester River, thus securing a natural frontier to the south and another outlet to the sea.

One pivotal Russian victory during the second war with Turkey was Marshal Alexander Suvorov's 1790 capture of Ismail (Izmail), a key Turkish fortress on the Danube. The siege was immensely costly, however—an estimated 20,000 Russians died in the storming of Ismail (Coughlan, p. 309). Byron vividly describes the carnage of the siege of Ismail in *Don Juan*: "Three thousand cannon threw up their emetic, / And thirty thousand musquets flung their pills / Like hail, to make a bloody diuretic./ Mortality! thou hast thy monthly bills" (*Don Juan*, 7.89-92). Juan,

who has joined the Russian army, and his fellow soldiers wallow "in the bloody mire / Of dead and dying thousands" and stumble over fallen comrades "sprawling in [their] gore" (*Don Juan*, 7.153-54, 160). In St. Petersburgh, however, Catherine herself remains untouched by the horrors of the war, rejoicing when Juan brings her the dispatch regarding Ismail's fall: "Great joy was hers, or rather joys; the first / Was a ta'en city—thirty thousand slain./ Glory and triumph o'er her aspect burst. . . / Those quenched a moment her Ambition's thirst" (*Don Juan*, 9.465-67, 469). Byron also satirizes Catherine's promiscuity, as the empress becomes immediately infatuated with the messenger, Juan himself: "Besides, the Empress sometimes liked a boy, / And had just buried the fair-faced Lanskoi" (*Don Juan*, 9.375-76).

Bluestockings. Among Byron's favorite targets in *Don Juan* are the group of intellectual Englishwomen commonly known in the eighteenth and nineteenth centuries as "bluestockings." While never a formal society, the bluestockings organized social gatherings to discuss literature and other intellectual matters, to which they invited various men of letters and members of the aristocracy. Fanny Burney, a British novelist and one of the original bluestockings, explained that the term came into existence when one lady, a Mrs. Vesey, invited Ben Stillingfleet, a learned man, to attend one of her parties. Stillingfleet initially declined, saying he lacked the proper garments, but was told by Mrs. Vesey to come "in his blue stockings" which he was wearing at the time. Stillingfleet obeyed, and the group was nicknamed the Bluestocking Society, in his honor. The bluestockings were frequently satirized— most often by men—as affected, pretentious women who lacked any true understanding of literary and political matters. In Canto 11 of *Don Juan*, Byron, who despised bluestockings, not least because he numbered his estranged wife among them, describes how Juan, newly arrived in England, is immediately accosted by these "learned ladies": "The Blues, that tender tribe, who sigh o'er sonnets. . . / Advanced in all their azure's highest hue: / They talked bad French of Spanish, and upon its / Late authors asked him for a hint or two" (*Don Juan*, 11.393-98).

BYRON'S MARRIAGE

As a glamorous celebrity of Regency England, Byron attracted more than his share of feminine attention. He embarked on a series of affairs with several fashionable beauties, including the countess of Oxford and the flighty, scandalous Lady Caroline Lamb. However, he chose as his bride Anne Isabella (Annabella) Milbanke, a pious, proper, and rather priggish young woman with a passion for mathematics, which prompted Byron to label her as a "bluestocking." Despite their different personalities, the couple married with the best of intentions. Byron hoped his wife's virtuous ways might reform him, and Annabella hoped she might succeed in changing her husband. Not surprisingly, the marriage was a disaster, lasting only a year. Byron found Annabella's prim naiveté annoying, and she in turn was shocked by his volatile moods, eccentricities, and his relationship with his half-sister, Augusta Leigh. Lady Byron returned to her parents' house in January 1816, taking her infant daughter, Augusta Ada Byron, with her. On April 21, 1816, Byron signed a deed of formal separation, leaving England forever two days later. The Byrons never saw each other again, and the poet's bitterness over his failed marriage resurfaces continually throughout *Don Juan*. Indeed, many of Byron's gibes at "bluestockings" are directed at Annabella. In designating a series of commandments for his readers, Byron declares, "Thou shalt not bear false witness, like 'the Blues', / (There's one, at least, is very fond of this)", referring to Lady Byron's attempts to have him proven mad when their marriage foundered.

The Poem in Focus

Plot summary. The poem begins with an account of Don Juan's childhood in Seville, as the only son of rakish Don Jóse and reserved, intel-

A Turkish slave trader negotiates the sale of two female slaves at a market in Constantinople, the same city where Don Juan is sold into slavery.

lectual Donna Inez. The domestic strife of this ill-matched pair reaches a crisis when Donna Inez attempts to have her husband declared insane. Matters deteriorate until divorce seems inevitable, but then Don Jóse unexpectedly dies of a fever. As Juan's sole guardian, Donna Inez attempts to rear her son in the strictest propriety. At 16, however, the naive Juan falls in love with one of his mother's friends, the 23-year-old Donna Julia, who is married to a much older husband. The two have a brief affair that ends when Don Alfonso, Julia's husband, catches them together in her bedroom. Donna Inez sends Juan abroad to "mend his former morals"; Julia is sent into a convent (*Don Juan*, 1.1523).

The ship carrying Juan soon encounters a storm, however, and suffers heavy damages, forcing the survivors to take to the lifeboats. The shipwreck and ensuing hardships take their toll on the sailors, some of whom resort to cannibalism after the rations run out (the first victim is Juan's tutor, Pedrillo) only to die raving in a mad frenzy. Others succumb to drought, thirst, and exposure; ultimately, only four, including Juan himself, are left when land is finally sighted. In their haste, the survivors overturn the boat, and only Juan manages to swim ashore. He is found and secretly nursed by Haidée, the beautiful daughter of a Greek pirate. As Juan recov-

ers, he and Haidée fall in love but their idyll is cut short by her father, who has Juan carried off in chains to be sold as a slave in Constantinople. Haidée suffers a seizure and dies of grief.

In the slave market, Juan and a fellow prisoner, an Englishman named Johnson, are purchased by Gulbeyaz, fourth wife of the sultan of Constantinople. Both are brought to the palace by Baba, a eunuch, who disguises Juan as a girl to bring him before the sultana, who wishes him to become her lover. Although an outraged Juan initially spurns Gulbeyaz's aggressive advances, he begins to soften towards her when she bursts into tears. A surprise visit by the sultan himself interrupts this encounter, and "Juanna" is quickly concealed in the harem with several other girls, all of whom feel strangely drawn to their new companion. The next morning, Gulbeyaz flies into a rage when she learns Juan spent the night in the harem. The sultana's jealousy necessitates Juan's flight from the palace, accompanied by the harem girls and his fellow prisoner, Johnson.

Having made good their escape, Juan and Johnson join the Russian army, which is currently besieging the Turkish city of Ismail. Although the military campaign is marred by incompetence and savagery, Juan distinguishes himself in the fighting and even rescues a young girl, Leila, from the carnage when the city falls.

He is then sent to St. Petersburg with dispatches for the Russian empress, Catherine the Great; Leila accompanies him.

At the Russian court, handsome Juan captures the empress's fancy and she soon makes him one of her favorites, conferring lands, wealth, and influence upon him. Catherine's assiduous attentions, however, prove to be too much for Juan, who first becomes "a little dissipated," then falls gravely ill (*Don Juan*, 10.179). The royal physicians prescribe a change of climate to ensure his recovery; the empress reluctantly agrees to send him to England as an emissary. With Leila once more in tow, Juan departs Russia in great style and luxury.

Safely landed in England, Juan and Leila travel by carriage across the countryside towards London. To his surprise, Juan becomes the victim of an attempted robbery on his way to town; he shoots one of the thieves, and the rest flee in confusion. Juan then proceeds to London, where his looks, accomplishments, and glamorous reputation secure him an immediate place in English high society. After finding a suitable guardian for Leila, Juan experiences the pleasures of the season, then departs London for a country house party at the estate of his new friends, Lord Henry Amundeville and his wife Adeline. Scandalized by the provocative behavior that another houseguest, the duchess of Fitz-Fulke, displays towards Juan, Lady Adeline, known for her beauty and virtue, determines to find him a suitable bride. However, she is inexplicably displeased when Juan seems taken with Aurora Raby, a beautiful young girl with a spotless reputation: "She marvell'd 'what he saw in such a baby / As that prim, silent, cold Aurora Raby?'" (*Don Juan*, 15.391-92).

Meanwhile, Juan's sojourn at the Amundeville estate is disrupted by the nocturnal sighting of a ghostly figure in a black cowl, which vanishes as mysteriously as it appears. Unnerved, Juan confesses his experience to his hosts, who surmise that he has seen the "Black Friar" who haunts the house. That night, however, Juan once again encounters the ghost but makes a shocking discovery when he confronts it: "Back fell the sable frock and dreary cowl, / And they revealed—alas that ere they should! / In full, voluptuous, but *not o'ergrown* bulk, / The phantom of her frolic Grace—Fitz-Fulke!" (*Don Juan*, 16.1029-32). The poem concludes on an unresolved note when Juan and the Duchess appear at breakfast the following morning, both haggard and wan from the night's adventure.

The tale of Don Juan's exploits becomes somewhat incidental, however, to the digressions of the poem's garrulous, worldly narrator—often identified as Byron himself—who continually departs from the plot, either to comment satirically upon the characters' situations or, more frequently, to pursue a variety of social, political, and philosophical tangents. Some of the digressions are deliberately frivolous, however. For example, at one point during the Juan and Haidée idyll, the narrator embarks on a rapturous description of the joys of wine and women:

> Man, being reasonable, must get drunk;
> The best of life is but intoxication:
> Glory, the grape, love, gold, in these are sunk
> The hopes of all men, and of every nation;
> Without their sap, how branchless were the trunk
> Of life's strange tree, so fruitful on occasion:
> But to return,—Get very drunk; and when
> You wake with head-ache, you shall see what then.
>
> (*Don Juan*, 2.1425-32)

After praising "hock and soda water" as a cure for hangovers, the narrator recalls himself to Don Juan's story with a start: "The coast—I think it was the coast I / Was just describing—Yes it was the coast—" (*Don Juan*, 2.1434, 1441-42). The narrator is well aware of his own loquacity, confessing, "If I have any fault, it is digression— / Leaving my people to proceed alone / While I soliloquize beyond expression" (*Don Juan*, 3.858-60). Despite this artless admission, the digressions continue throughout the poem.

As the poem progresses, the digressions themselves become more serious and, at times, more scathing. In the cantos dealing with the siege of Ismail, the narrator delivers a blistering commentary on the horrors of war and the extravagant waste of human life:

> There was an end of Ismail—hapless town!
> Far flashed her burning towers o'er Danube's stream,
> And redly ran his blushing waters down.
> The horrid war-whoop and the shriller scream
> Rose still; but fainter were the thunders grown:
> Of forty thousand who had manned the wall,
> Some hundreds breathed—the rest were silent all!
>
> (*Don Juan*, 8.1010-16)

Even Juan, whom the narrator has previously regarded with amused indulgence, comes under fire for his own part in the slaughter; his chance rescue of Leila is cynically described by the narrator as "one good action in the midst of crimes" which "[i]s 'quite refreshing,' in the affected phrase / Of these ambrosial, Pharasaic times, / With all their pretty milk-and-water ways" (*Don Juan*, 8.713-16). The narrator further raises the question of whether "some transient trace of pity" that resulted in a few victims being spared can really mitigate the atrocities committed "in one annihilated city, / Where thousand loves, and ties, and duties grow?" (*Don Juan*, 8.985, 989-90). At such moments in *Don Juan*, the narrator's perspective—worldly, cynical, questioning everything from the standpoint of mature age and wider experience—takes precedence over the more facile impressions of the eponymous hero: "Juan's participation [in the siege] . . . consists of alert excitement, constant activity, and moments of pity. The narrator's relationship with events is of far greater interest to the reader for he presents a much more complete picture of the battle than Juan can comprehend. . . . The reader reacts with the narrator and looks to him rather than to Juan for directions here" (Beatty, pp. 38-39).

A "hero" for the age. While Byron's earlier poems, such as *The Corsair* and *Childe Harold's Pilgrimage*, featured tortured, brooding heroes with dark pasts and darker secrets, *Don Juan* represents a departure from that tradition in every way. Indeed, Byron has not so much adapted the Don Juan legend as turned it inside-out. The wicked, dashing seducer of Tirso's play and Mozart's opera has been replaced by "a stripling of sixteen" who, in the first of his adventures, is led astray by the older Donna Julia (*Don Juan*, 1.658). Juan's passivity during that episode becomes representative of his conduct in later affairs; in Byron's poem, the women are always the aggressors, and Juan merely responds to their advances. Consequently, his misadventures are seldom presented as his fault or responsibility. After Juan's affair with Haidée ends with her death and his enslavement, the voluble narrator laments how "a gentleman so rich in the world's goods /. . .is suddenly to sea sent, / Wounded and chain'd, so that he cannot move, / And all because a lady fell in love" (*Don Juan*, 4.403, 406-408).

Byron's demystification of the Don Juan legend is attributable to many factors, not least of which is the poet's own desire to create something new. In the opening verses of *Don Juan*, the narrator declares emphatically, "I want a hero: an uncommon want, / When every year and month sends for a new one, / Till, after cloying the gazettes with cant, / The age discovers he is not the true one" (*Don Juan*, 1.1-4). After proposing and rejecting a slew of contemporary celebrities, the narrator declares, "I condemn none, / But can't find any in the present age / Fit for my poem (that is, for my new one); / So as I said, I'll take my friend, Don Juan" (*Don Juan*, 1.37-40). Byron's Juan (intentionally pronounced "Joo-un" for the sake of rhyme), therefore, is reinvented as an Everyman figure, traveling through an often confusing modern world. As literary scholar David Perkins observes, "Indeed, [Juan's] character is remarkably generalized. We can list traits—courage, kindliness, generosity, idealism—but the upshot seems to be that he is an average sort of fellow subject to average instincts and illusions" (Perkins, p. 829).

BYRON'S RHYMES

In the first canto of *Don Juan*, Byron sets out his plans for his poem, declaring, "Prose poets like blank verse, I'm fond of rhyme, / Good workmen never quarrel with their tools" (*Don Juan*, 1.1605-06). Indeed, Byron's fondness for rhyme and his determination that his stanzas should be seen and heard to rhyme contribute to the comic tone of *Don Juan*. For example, orthodox pronunciations of Spanish names are deliberately twisted for the sake of preserving Byron's meter and rhyme scheme—thus, in the poem, "Juan" is pronounced as "Joo-un" to rhyme with "true one" and "new one", "Inez" as "Eye-nez" to rhyme with "fine as," and "Guadalquivir" as "Gwadalquiver" to rhyme with "river." Byron's use of "Hudibrastic rhyme"—the practice of rhyming a polysyllabic word with an unexpected series of monosyllabic words (introduced in Samuel Butler's 1663 satirical poem, *Hudibras*)—could be even more deadly, as demonstrated by this infamous couplet: "But—Oh! ye lords of ladies intellectual, / Inform us truly, have they not henpecked you all?" (*Don Juan*, 1.175-76).

Yet Juan's very "averageness" throws into sharp relief the societies into which he is introduced and the personalities with which he must interact. The character's youth and blandness also provide a necessary contrast to the narrator's distinctive voice and views. Byron's emphasis in *Don Juan* is less on the heroic than on the human, less on the romantic than the real. Nettled by his publisher's criticism of *Don Juan*, Byron responded irritably: "So you and Mr. Foscolo, etc., want me to undertake what you call a 'great work?' an Epic poem, I suppose, or some such pyramid. I'll try no such thing. . . You have so many 'divine' poems, is it nothing to have written a *Human* one? without any of your worn-out machinery. . . . Since you want length, you shall have enough of *Juan*, for I'll make 50 cantos" (Byron in Perkins, p. 934). Despite hostile reactions to *Don Juan*, Byron continued to work on his poem for the rest of his life, confiding to his publisher about Juan's further adventures:

> To how many cantos this may extend I know not nor whether (even if I live) I shall complete it; but this was my notion: I meant to have made him a Cavalier Servente in Italy and a cause for divorce in England, and a sentimental "Werther-faced man" in Germany, so as to show

the different ridicules of the society in each of those countries. . . . But I had not quite fixed on whether to make him end in Hell, or in an unhappy marriage, not knowing which would be the severest. The Spanish tradition says Hell: but it is probably only an Allegory of the other state.

> (Byron in Perkins, pp. 940-41)

Sources and literary context. Byron drew from history to provide the events and characters in *Don Juan*. His excoriating depiction of the siege of Ismail, for example, was taken from Marquis Gabriel de Castelnau's account, *Essai sur l'histoire ancienne et moderne de la Russie* (1820), though Byron emphasized the horror, rather than the glory, of the campaign. Byron also mined his own life for inspiration, often to devastating effect. For example, Donna Inez, Juan's mother, is a thinly veiled portrait of Annabella Milbanke, Byron's estranged wife, who also "was a learned lady, famed / For every branch of every science ever known" (*Don Juan*, 10.73-74). Moreover, the unhappy marriage between Don Jóse and Donna Inez parallels that of the Byrons; in the poem, Inez mimics her real-life counterpart by attempting to prove that her husband is mad. Despite these semi-autobiographical details, however, Byron avoids identifying himself too closely with any of his characters. Even the narrator, whose voice resembles Byron's own, maintains the fiction that he is distinct from both Juan and Byron, declaring during his comments on the disastrous marriage of Juan's parents: "I'm a plain man, and in a single station" (*Don Juan*, 1.174). This pretense, however, becomes harder to sustain during later cantos of the poem, especially when the narrator's perceptions as an older, more sophisticated man of the 1820s overshadow those of young, callow Juan, living in the 1790s.

Despite its somewhat misogynistic remarks, *Don Juan* sprang from more than Byron's lingering anger over his failed marriage. Some incidents of the poem appear to be drawn from more amusing moments in Byron's life; in Canto 16, Byron borrows the ghost said to haunt his own estate of Newstead Abbey—which housed the black-robed Order of Canons Regular 400 years earlier—to create the "Black Friar" who roams the halls of the Amundevilles' stately home. In a casual swipe at Gothic romance, however, Byron reveals the "Black Friar" legend as a ruse concocted by an amorous houseguest to facilitate sexual conquest, a theme also explored in Keats's **"The Eve of St. Agnes"** (also in *WLAIT 3: British Literature and Its Times*). Similarly, a cross-

---

A SCANDALOUS LIFE

Throughout *Don Juan*, the line between fiction and reality continually blurs, as the narrator becomes less of an imaginary construct and increasingly like Byron himself. Indeed, Byron ascribes many of his own exploits to his characters, such as swimming the Hellespont (an athletic feat on which Byron prided himself) and rescuing a Turkish girl from being drowned (an incident that inspired an earlier poem, *The Giaour*). Byron's incestuous feelings for his half-sister Augusta were also exploited in *Manfred*, through the title character's tortured memories of Astarte, a kinswoman whose exact relationship to Manfred is continually hinted at, but never explicitly revealed. Other scandals, however, did not make their way into Byron's poetry but remained confined to his private correspondence and his memoirs (the manuscript of these memoirs was later burned by his squeamish publisher, John Murray). These other scandals include his brief entanglement with Percy Bysshe Shelley's erratic sister-in-law, Claire Clairmont, which resulted in the birth of an illegitimate daughter, Allegra; and his spell of promiscuity after leaving England, during which Byron had sexual relations with, by his estimation, some 200 partners. In 1819, Byron fell in love with 19-year-old Countess Teresa Guiccioli, whom he called his "last Passion" (Byron in Parker, p. 80). After Teresa was granted a separation from her much older husband in July 1820, she and Byron lived in close proximity in Ravenna, seeing each other frequently. Despite its tempestuous beginnings, the relationship between Teresa and Byron settled into comfortable domesticity; they remained together until his death in 1824.

dressed Juan's comic adventures in a Turkish harem could be interpreted as Byron poking fun at his own success with such Oriental romances as *The Giaour* and *The Corsair*.

Other of Byron's jabs at contemporary literary movements were more pointed. Throughout his poetic career, Byron clashed frequently with William Wordsworth, Samuel Taylor Coleridge, and Robert Southey, whom he derisively referred to as the "Lakers" because all three lived in the Lake District in Northern England. Byron took particular exception to Wordsworth's rejection of the eighteenth-century poets Byron admired—specifically, John Dryden and Alexander Pope—and exhortations that poetry should devote itself to the mundane and commonplace aspects of life. Rejecting in turn the aesthetics of his contemporaries, Byron turned to the Italian poets of the Renaissance for inspiration, borrowing for *Don Juan* "the colloquial idiom, the volubility, the brisk and easy handling of ottava rima (a stanza of eight pentameter lines rhyming *ababbabcc*), the profuse incident, the wandering plot, and above all, the medley of realism and romance, of sentiment and buffoonery" (Perkins, p. 829). Perkins contends, "That Byron happened upon these writers is one of the most significant accidents in literary history; only with their help did he achieve full expression of his complex personality" (Perkins, p. 829). Byron's particular sensibility and unusual choice of models renders *Don Juan* unique in the canon of Romantic literature. Modern poet and scholar Derek Parker sums up: "The force of Byron's political and social opinions, the force of his satire, the romance of his personality, the extraordinary cleverness of his metrical and rhyming schemes, came together finally in *Don Juan*. . . . It was the first, and almost the last poem of its kind" (Parker, p. 127).

Events in History at the Time the Poem Was Written

Europe after the Napoleonic Wars. For the better part of 22 years—from 1793 to 1815—England was at war with France, observing with alarm the excesses of the French Revolution and the meteoric rise to power of Napoleon Bonaparte, who became emperor of France in 1804. In the decade that followed, England watched in alarm as Napoleon's seemingly invincible army seized Rome, Amsterdam, and Hamburg. France's victories on land, however, were countered by England's might at sea; Admiral Horatio Nelson handed Napoleon a major defeat during the naval battle of Trafalgar in 1805.

Ultimately, Napoleon overextended himself with an ill-advised invasion of Moscow in 1812, where the rigors of a Russian winter took their toll on French troops, which were forced to retreat. Napoleon also suffered a string of costly defeats that weakened his power base even further. In

BYRON AND THE "LAKERS"

Byron's animosity toward the Lake District poets had as much to do with politics as with poetics. As an outspoken liberal of the Whig party, Byron supported such causes as Catholic emancipation and labor reform. He even delivered an eloquent speech in the House of Lords on behalf of Nottingham weavers who were rioting to protest the mechanization of their profession. Byron's liberalism also made him sympathetic to the principles underlying the French Revolution, even though he deplored the savage excesses that ultimately damaged those principles. By contrast, Wordsworth, Coleridge, and Southey, who had supported the French Revolution in its early years, were deeply disillusioned when the event failed to fulfill their hopes. In their middle age, the Lake poets adopted increasingly conservative positions, becoming staunch supporters of England's reactionary Tory government. Byron, who despised "turncoats," seldom bypassed the opportunity to criticize what he saw as the Lakers' hypocrisy. Most of Byron's bile was reserved for Robert Southey, who was appointed poet laureate in 1813, and vilified Byron as the head of "The Satanic School of Poetry" in his preface to *A Vision of Judgement* (1821), a fulsome occasional poem on the death of King George III. Byron had earlier ridiculed Southey in his "Dedication to Don Juan"; he responded even more trenchantly with his own *The Vision of Judgement*, a parody so biting that Byron's publisher, John Murray, refused to print it. Branding Southey as a hypocrite, toady, and mediocre poet, Byron wrote:

> He had written praises of a regicide;
> He had written praises of all kings whatever;
> He had written for republics far and wide,
> And then against them bitterer than ever . . .
> He had written much blank verse and blanker prose,
> And more of both than anybody knows.
>
> (Byron in Perkins, p. 922)

John Hunt, editor of *The Liberal*, eventually published the poem in 1822, and, as a result, was indicted for libel of the king and his royal patrons a few months later.

1814, Paris fell to allied troops from England, Russia, Prussia, and Austria; the allies exiled Napoleon to Elba and restored Louis XVIII to the French throne. The former emperor escaped Elba in 1815 and attempted a comeback, only to be conclusively defeated at the Battle of Waterloo. He was then imprisoned on the island of St. Helena, where he died in 1821.

After Napoleon's exile to Elba, representatives of Britain, Russia, Prussia, Austria, and France met at the Congress of Vienna in 1814, to reorganize Europe. Diplomats from smaller allied countries—Spain, Portugal, Sweden—also attended. Despite quarrels between the allies over land and boundaries, the following conditions were ultimately agreed upon: Prussia received 2/5 of Saxony, along with territorial compensations in Westphalia and the Rhineland; Poland was divided among Russia, Austria, and Prussia; and Russia acquired most of the duchy of Warsaw as a separate kingdom under Russian sovereignty.

While these agreements strengthened unity among the allies and the final peace settlement preserved Europe from any major wars until the outbreak of World War I in 1914, not everyone approved of the terms established in the Congress of Vienna. British liberals, including Byron, Shelley, and Leigh Hunt, were disgusted by what they saw as a victory for tyrannical kings of Europe, whose reactionary regimes were upheld by the acquisition of new territories and the alliance with Britain. In the "Dedication" to *Don Juan*, Byron attacks Lord Castlereagh, who represented Britain at the Congress of Vienna, as "a tinkering slavemaker, who mends old chains, / With God and man's abhorrence for its gains" (*Don Juan*, "Dedication," lines 111-12). Similarly harsh words are leveled at the duke of Wellington, who commanded the British troops at Waterloo, and was hailed as a hero by his country. Byron, however, was less impressed, declaring in one of his lengthiest digressions in *Don Juan*:

> Never had mortal Man such opportunity,
> Except Napoleon, or abused it more:
> You might have freed fall'n Europe from the
>   Unity
> Of Tyrants, and been blest from shore to
>   shore:
> And now—What is your fame? Shall the
>   Muse tune it ye? Now—that the rabble's
>   first vain shouts are o'er?
>   (*Don Juan*, 9.65-70)

Byron's criticisms of England, its traditions, and its "heroes" become increasingly more pronounced as the poem progresses and Juan himself arrives in England.

Reviews. Not surprisingly, in light of Byron's fall from grace, critical response to *Don Juan* was hostile. Contemporary reviewers in England refused to judge poem and poet separately; Byron was attacked as much for his lifestyle as for his poetry. An anonymous review in the influential *Blackwood's Magazine* stated: "[T]he poet has devoted his powers to the worst of purposes and passions. . . . The moral strain of the whole poem is pitched in the lowest key—and if the genius of the author lifts him now and then out of his pollution, it seems as if he regretted the elevation and made all haste to descend again" (Trueblood, p. 27). The reviewer for *The British Critic* was even more censorious, declaring, "The versification and morality are about upon a par" and dismissing *Don Juan*, overall, as "a narrative of degrading debauchery in doggerel rhyme" (Trueblood, p. 30).

Despite these harsh comments on Byron's lack of morality, a significant number of critics found praiseworthy elements in *Don Juan* itself. The same *Blackwood's Magazine* review that condemned Byron's lack of morality praised the poem's breezy style and ambitious scope, terming *Don Juan* "the most admirable specimen of the mixture of ease, strength, gaiety, and seriousness extant in the whole body of English poetry," and stated that "Lord Byron has never written anything more decisively and triumphantly expressive of the greatness of his genius" (Trueblood, p. 27). Another critic, writing for the *New Monthly Magazine*, declared regretfully, "We cannot read these passages [in *Don Juan*] without being touched by their exquisite beauty, and wishing that a poet so full of the true inspiration had devoted his powers to the cause of virtue" (Trueblood, p. 35). A review in *The Edinburgh Magazine* recognized and even cautiously commended Byron's satiric bent in *Don Juan*: "In spite of all his faults, Byron has a noble sympathy with liberty, and a just abhorrence of the leagued and crowned oppressors of the earth" (Trueblood, p. 57).

The scandal caused by early cantos of *Don Juan* soon led John Murray to reconsider publishing later sections of the poem. From Canto 6 on, *Don Juan* was published by John Hunt, Leigh Hunt's brother and editor of *The Liberal*. Although Hunt was a less reputable figure in the publishing world than Murray and although most major journals ignored those later cantos, the poem continued to sell widely, often in cheap, pirated editions. But perhaps the last word on *Don Juan* should be pronounced by Byron himself. Never reluctant to promote his own work, the irrepressible poet appealed to a friend: "As to 'Don Juan,' confess, confess—you dog and be candid. . . it may be bawdy, but is it not good English? It may be profligate but is it not *life*, is it not *the thing*?" (Byron in Perkins, p. 938).

—Pamela S. Loy

For More Information

Beatty, Bernard. *Byron's Don Juan*. London: Croom Helm, 1985.

Christensen, Jerome. *Lord Byron's Strength: Romantic Writing and Commercial Society*. Baltimore: Johns Hopkins University Press, 1993.

Coughlan, Robert. *Elizabeth and Catherine: Empresses of All the Russias*. New York: G. P. Putnam's Sons, 1974.

Eisler, Benita. *Byron: Child of Passion, Fool of Fame*. New York: Alfred A. Knopf, 1999.

Erickson, Carolly. *Our Tempestuous Day: A History of Regency England*. New York: William Morrow, 1986.

Haslett, Moyra. *Byron's Don Juan and the Don Juan Legend*. Oxford: Clarendon, 1997.

McGann, Jerome J., ed. *The Oxford Authors: Byron*. Oxford: Oxford University Press, 1986.

———. *Don Juan in Context*. Chicago: University of Chicago Press, 1976.

Manning, Peter J. *Byron and His Fictions*. Detroit: Wayne State University Press, 1978.

Parker, Derek. *Byron and His World*. New York: Viking, 1968.

Perkins, David, ed. *English Romantic Writers*. San Diego: Harcourt Brace Jovanovich, 1967.

Trueblood, Paul Graham. *The Flowering of Byron's Genius: Studies in Byron's Don Juan*. Palo Alto: Stanford University Press, 1945.

Wu, Duncan, ed. *A Companion to Romanticism*. Oxford: Blackwell, 1998.

Dr. Faustus

by

Christopher Marlowe

Elizabethan playwright Christopher Marlowe (1564-1593) is often called the most influential English dramatist before Shakespeare. The son of a modestly successful shoemaker, Marlowe was born and raised in Canterbury, England. He was educated there and at Corpus Christi College, Cambridge, where he received his B.A. degree in 1584 and his M.A. degree in 1587. Because very little is known about his life, the order in which he wrote his plays is uncertain. Possibly while still at Cambridge he collaborated with a younger friend, Thomas Nashe, in writing *Dido, Queen of Carthage*. Scholars believe that Marlowe wrote two other plays while still at Cambridge: *Tamburlaine the Great* and its sequel, *Tamburlaine, Part II*, both of which opened to extraordinary success in London before the end of 1587. For the next six years, Marlowe lived in London and enjoyed unprecedented popularity with theatergoers. In 1593, when he was only 29 years old, he was killed in a tavern brawl. Aside from *Dr. Faustus*, his plays include *The Massacre at Paris*, *Edward II*, and *The Jew of Malta*. He also wrote poems, the best known of which are "Hero and Leander" and "The Passionate Shepherd to His Love." Generally reckoned Marlowe's greatest play, *Dr. Faustus* is often discussed in relation to his other major tragedies, *Tamburlaine the Great* and *The Jew of Malta*. All three plays focus on characters who overreach the norms of human ambition in various fields of endeavor: the Mongol conqueror Tamburlaine in earthly power, the Jew of Malta in riches, and Faustus (a historical figure reputed

---

THE LITERARY WORK

A play set in Germany in the early sixteenth century; written c. 1589-93; first recorded performance in 1594; published in London in 1604.

SYNOPSIS

A German sorcerer sells his soul to the devil in exchange, he thinks, for knowledge and magical power.

---

to be a magician) in knowledge and magical power.

Events in History at the Time the Play Takes Place

Medieval and Renaissance approaches to knowledge. By the early sixteenth century, the Renaissance had reached northern Europe from its origins in fourteenth-century Italy. While the impulses that gave rise to the Renaissance are complex, most historians agree that the movement brought a new emphasis on human capabilities and particularly on the potential of the individual. Speaking broadly, medieval thought, by contrast, had stressed the acceptance of received authority, particularly that of the Catholic Church, and had demanded conformity to the Church's traditional beliefs. These beliefs set precise limits to humankind's place in nature and to the knowledge about nature that it was deemed appropriate for humans to possess. Any attempt to transcend these limits risked becoming the sin of pride.

Aside from the obvious model of Adam and Eve, who had been expelled from Eden for tasting the forbidden fruit of knowledge, there was a risk of sin in seeking knowledge. Knowledge was regarded as something certain and finite, a body of concepts that had been handed down either from God or from authorities approved by the Church. People regarded knowledge as a legacy, something to be preserved and maintained, not increased. Maintaining it, in part, meant interpreting it properly. Thus, the major intellectual movement of medieval Europe, scholasticism, was primarily concerned with interpreting the authorities by examining the appropriate texts and by discussing their meaning. There were highly developed techniques for doing both of these things: close reading (*lectio*) was followed by formal debate (*disputatio*), in which students argued both sides of a question. Most often, the *disputatio* centered on how to interpret a passage of scripture or theology, or focused on some precise theological point (a notorious topic being how many angels could fit on the head of a pin). Scholastic techniques themselves were based largely on one of the greatest authorities outside the Church, the Greek philosopher Aristotle (fourth century B.C.E.). In works such as the *Analytics*, Aristotle had formulated the rules of reasoning, known as logic, that were used in the disputatio.

Renaissance intellectuals chafed at what they saw as the narrow confines of these scholastic techniques for approaching knowledge. As Marlowe's play opens, Faustus, a scholar, is dissatisfied with the *Analytics* and the *disputatio*, expressing boredom with the Church-approved texts of Aristotle (such as the *Analytics*), whose rediscovery in the twelfth century had helped found scholasticism. As a man of the Renaissance, Faustus is more interested in semi-legendary characters from the heroic past, such as Helen of Troy or Alexander the Great. It was precisely this sort of human interest in the ancient world—a literary, historical, and aesthetic interest—that began during the Renaissance to supplant the largely theological concerns of medieval scholasticism.

Science and occultism in Renaissance thought. Along with their impatience at scholastic techniques, thinkers during the Renaissance also began to question the old conception of knowledge as certain and finite. Like the explorers who were pushing the boundaries of their known world during this same period, scientific pioneers devoted themselves to seeking new frontiers of knowledge rather than simply mastering old territory. Yet there was a psychological penalty for giving up the certainty that came with dealing with only received authorities. Occult belief systems seemed to offer a shortcut to understanding and, more importantly, controlling a world not only of broader horizons but also of less certain convictions.

The appeal of the occult was bolstered by the fact that it too had its ancient authorities, often the same ones that humanists were using for literary or scientific purposes. The Greek mathematician Pythagoras (sixth century B.C.E.), for example, invested numbers with mystical powers. Similarly, the ideas of Plato were immensely influential not just in philosophy but in mysticism as well; rediscovered and reinterpreted by the Florentine humanist Marsilio Ficino (1433-1499), they found their way into the mainstream of occult studies. Ficino's works, for example, stressed Plato's doctrine of the immortality of the soul, and emphasized contemplation as a way of bringing the soul to the divine, and the exercise of a music-based magic and medicine. A century later Ficino's magical neoplatonism would influence German students of the occult such as Cornelius Agrippa, whose career became entwined in legend with that of the historical Faust. Spells and incantations (which Marlowe shows Faustus reading from old books) were another way magicians could utilize ancient authority. A common way of using such verbal formulas was in attempting magically to raise the spirits of the dead, just as Marlowe's Faustus conjures the ghosts of Helen and Alexander.

Neither medieval nor Renaissance thinkers drew clear distinctions between science and magic, and people often attributed magical powers to those who those who had acquired scientific or other learning. For example, medieval sages such as the scientist and philosopher Roger Bacon (c. 1214-1292) and the physician and alchemist Pietro d'Abano (c. 1250-1316), both mentioned in Marlowe's play, were by the time of the Renaissance popularly considered to have been magicians. In both eras, astrology was studied alongside astronomy, for example, and alchemy (which attempted to transform common elements into rare ones, usually gold) alongside the physical sciences. During the Renaissance, as interest in science grew, fascination with the occult grew with it.

At the same time, religious leaders often opposed both occult and scientific knowledge. They viewed the former as overstepping the knowledge that God permitted humans to possess, thus inviting the sin of pride; but they also realized that the new science was challenging Church-approved doctrines. Nicolaus Copernicus's heliocentric model of the universe, for example, was opposed by both Catholic and Protestant leaders because it overturned the traditional geocentric system of Ptolemy and Aristotle, which the Church had incorporated into its doctrine centuries earlier.

The Faust legend and the Protestant Reformation. By the lifetime of the mysterious figure known variously as George or Johann Faust (Faustus in Latin), occultism had come to constitute a significant strand of Renaissance humanism. Little is known about the historical Faust, but he is thought to have been an astrologer and alchemist who lived in Germany and died sometime around 1540. He had a reputation as an evil man who had declared that the devil was his *Schwager*, or comrade. After his death legends arose of how he had made a contract with the devil, exchanging his immortal soul for knowledge and magical power.

Yet the historical Faust also seems to have won the respect of such illustrious contemporaries as the religious reformers Martin Luther and Philip Melanchthon, two major leaders of the Protestant Reformation in Germany. It was in Wittenberg, where the fictional Faustus (and perhaps the historical Faust) studied theology at the famous university, that Martin Luther initiated the Protestant split with the Roman Catholic Church in 1517. While conflicts between Protestants and Catholics would continue throughout Europe for centuries, Protestantism rapidly won wide support in Germany. Overt hostility to Catholicism in the popular German Faust tales can be seen, for example, when Faust uses magic to make a fool of the pope. Most Protestants differed from Catholic doctrine in their belief that faith alone (and not good works) was necessary for salvation; even so, Protestants maintained, salvation came from the independent grace of God, who had foreordained which souls would be saved. The age's preoccupation with such issues is reflected in the tales that arose around the historical Faust, in which Faust's deliberate denial of faith and consequent damnation seem both freely chosen and yet also inescapably predestined.

The Play in Focus

Plot summary. As first published in 1604, *Dr. Faustus* contains 13 scenes with no act divisions;

a prologue and an epilogue are delivered by the Chorus. Most of the speeches of Faustus and other characters of high status are in blank verse (unrhymed iambic pentameter); the speeches of lowly characters like the servant Wagner are in regular prose. In the prologue the Chorus explains that the play will not be about war, love, or bold deeds, but about the fortunes, good and bad, of Faustus. He was born of humble parents in Roda, Germany, and brought up by relatives in Wittenberg. There he attended the university, where he studied theology and attained the degree of Doctor of Divinity. He excelled everyone in disputation on matters of theology until he became swollen with pride and, like Icarus of classical mythology, flew too high and fell to his ruin. (Using wings of feathers and wax crafted by his father, the boy Icarus flew too close to the sun, whereupon the wax melted and he fell into the sea and drowned.) Glutted with learning, Faustus fed his appetite for knowledge by turning to necromancy or magic, which became the sweetest thing in the world to him.

As Scene One opens, Faustus sits in his study

CORNELIUS AGRIPPA

The career of the German humanist Heinrich Cornelius Agrippa von Nettesheim (1486-1535) illustrates the connections between magic and other aspects of Renaissance humanism. A contemporary of the historical Faust, Agrippa studied science, medicine, and philosophy as well as such diverse occult traditions as the Jewish Kabbala, neoplatonic mysticism, Pythagorean numerology, alchemy, and magic. In his book *On the Occult Philosophy* (1531), he followed other Renaissance humanists, notably Italy's Pico della Mirandola (1463-94), in proclaiming kabbalistic and magic practices as a way of reaching true knowledge of God and nature. Yet shortly afterward he repudiated both science and the occult, attacking them in a work translated into English in 1569 as *Of the Vanitie and Uncertaintie of Artes and Sciences*. After his death, Agrippa's reputed feats of magic blended with tales of the historical Faust; Marlowe has his fictional Faustus mention Agrippa as a model whose knowledge he hopes to emulate.

and considers what he has learned. Having mastered Aristotle and the disputatio, he longs for "a greater subject" to fit his genius (Marlowe, *Dr. Faustus*, 1.11). He knows philosophy and the works of Galen (the ancient Greek medical authority used by medieval physicians); in fact, his medical skills have saved whole cities from the plague. Yet he is still a man and cannot make other men immortal, which would be a medical feat worth something. As for the field of law, it is fit only for "a mercenary drudge" and is "too servile and illiberal for me" (*Dr. Faustus*, 1.35-36). "Divinitie is best" he proclaims, but quotes two passages from scripture that suggest that all men are sinful and must eventually die (*Dr. Faustus*, 1.37). No, he decides, what he most desires is to study the secret books of magicians:

> O what a world of profit and delight,
> Of power, of honor, of omnipotence
> Is promised to the studious Artizan?
> . . .
> A sound Magician is a mighty god:
> Heere Faustus trie thy braines to gaine a
>   deitie.
>
> (Dr. Faustus, 1.52-63)

Faustus tells his servant Wagner to summon his friends Valdes and Cornelius, who can help him. Wagner exits, and as Faustus waits he is visited by a Good Angel and an Evil Angel. The Good Angel warns him to lay his study of secret books aside and concentrate on the scriptures, before his soul is tempted and he incurs the wrath of God. The Evil Angel urges him, "Go forward *Faustus* in that famous *arte*, / Wherein all nature's treasury is containd" (*Dr. Faustus*, 1.74-75). The angels exit, and Faustus fantasizes about the material and intellectual rewards that magic will bring him. "Shall I make spirits fetch me what I please, / Resolve me of all ambiguities, / Performe what desperate enterprise I will?" he wonders (*Dr. Faustus*, 1.79-81). He will get gold from India, pearls from the oceans, delicious foods from the newly discovered Americas; he will have spirits read him books of exotic philosophy and divulge to him the secrets of foreign kings. He will also win political might, becoming sole monarch of the land and commanding the spirits to invent powerful new weapons of war for him.

Valdes and Cornelius enter, and Faustus tells them that they have finally won him over to magic. Once again he rejects philosophy, law, medicine, and divinity: "Tis Magicke, Magicke that hath ravisht mee," he declares (*Dr. Faustus*, 1.110). He will be as great a magician as Agrippa, whose skill in conjuring the spirits of the dead brought him honor throughout Europe. Valdes assures him that the combination of the magic books, Faustus's genius, and his own and Cornelius's experience will soon put the whole world

under their power. Cornelius claims that the basic principles of magic are not so difficult to learn, and they will bring Faustus great fame and wealth. They exit to eat dinner, after which they will begin to conjure spirits.

In the second scene two scholars arrive and ask Wagner where his master is. Wagner comically avoids answering the question directly, instead using nonsensical scholastic reasoning to argue that the two are "dunces" for asking it in the first place (*Dr. Faustus*, 2.18). The scholars are afraid that Faustus has "falne into that damned art" of magic, for which Valdes and Cornelius are known; they plan to inform the rector of the university, who may be able to "reclaime" Faustus (*Dr. Faustus*, 2.32-33, 36).

In the next scene Faustus begins conjuring. He utters a Latin incantation rejecting the Holy Trinity and hailing an infernal trinity of Lucifer and the devils Beelzebub and Demigorgon, and then summons the devil Mephastophilis. Mephastophilis appears but is so ugly that Faustus sends him back, commanding him to reappear in the form of a friar. When Mephastophilis does so, Faustus assumes that the devil has come to do his bidding. Mephastophilis instead says that he follows only Lucifer's commands: it was not Faustus's summons that brought him so much as the abjuration of the Holy Trinity, which is "the shortest cut for conjuring" and always brings devils hoping to capture the abjurer's soul (*Dr. Faustus*, 3.52). Faustus asks about Lucifer, the prince of devils. Mephastophilis tells him that Lucifer was once God's most dearly loved angel, until his "aspiring pride and insolence" caused God to throw him "from the face of heaven" (*Dr. Faustus*, 3.67, 68). Mephastophilis and other devils are those who conspired against God with Lucifer and were thus cast out with him. Where were they cast? Faustus asks. To hell, Mephastophilis answers. Faustus persists: then why is Mephastophilis now out of hell? Hell is not so much a place, the devil replies, as it is the absence of heaven. Faustus scorns Mephastophilis's passionate longing for the "joyes of heaven" and advises him to learn some of Faustus's own "manly fortitude" (*Dr. Faustus*, 3.84-85). He then sends Mephastophilis back to Lucifer with an offer: if Lucifer will grant whatever Faustus asks for 24 years, Faustus will afterward surrender his soul to Lucifer in exchange. He tells the devil to meet him in his study at midnight with an answer. Mephastophilis leaves and Faustus imagines all the power that his bargain with Lucifer will bring him.

In Scene Four, as in the play's other comedic scenes, Wagner and a clown (a rustic simpleton) offer a comic parallel to the action in the preceding scene. Thus, Wagner comments that the unemployed clown is so desperate that he would probably sell his soul to the devil for a shoulder of mutton. He then asks the clown to be his servant, or else Wagner will turn all of the lice on him into familiars (spirit allies in animal form) and have them tear the clown apart. Wagner then summons two devils, Baliol and Belcher, who come and terrify the clown. The clown agrees to serve Wagner if Wagner will teach him how to conjure the devils, whom he hopes can turn him into a flea so that he can tickle a pretty girl.

In his study in Scene Five, Faustus wavers, wondering if it is too late for him to be saved. The Good Angel and the Evil Angel return: the Good Angel warns Faustus to leave magic behind and think of heaven, while the Evil Angel lures him again with honor and wealth. His head filled with thoughts of riches, Faustus summons Mephastophilis, who arrives with the news that Lucifer has agreed to the deal that Faustus proposed—but Faustus must sign a contract with his own blood. As Faustus signs the contract, the Latin words *Homo fuge* (Man, flee!) appear on his arm. Declaring that he does not believe in hell or in any kind of suffering after death, Faustus says that he feels "wanton and lascivious" and commands Mephastophilis to find him a wife (*Dr. Faustus*, 5.144). Mephastophilis declares that marriage is meaningless and offers to bring Faustus a paramour rather than a wife. Faustus instead demands three books: one of spells and incantations for conjuring spirits, one to tell him the motions of the stars and planets, and one with knowledge of every kind of plant.

Faustus then begins to repent at having foresworn the joys of heaven, but Mephastophilis assures him that heaven is not "such a glorious thing" after all (*Dr. Faustus*, 5.188). The Good and Evil Angels again reappear: the Good Angel urges Faustus to repent, but the Evil Angel tells him that God can never pity him now. After the angels exit, Faustus contemplates killing himself. He again asks for information about the heavens, but Mephastophilis's answers fail to satisfy him. When Faustus asks who made the world, Mephastophilis refuses to tell him, saying that the answer goes "against our kingdom": instead of pondering such questions, Mephastophilis tells him, he should "Think on hell, Faustus, for thou art damned" (*Dr. Faustus*, 5.255, 56). Again the two angels reappear, and again the Good An-

gel says that it is not too late for Faustus to repent. When Faustus calls on Christ to save his soul, Lucifer appears and warns Faustus that by thinking of Christ he is breaking his promise. Lucifer distracts Faustus by showing him the seven deadly sins (pride, covetousness, wrath, envy, gluttony, sloth, and lechery), who enter and parade across the stage. In a brief comic scene, Robin, an ostler (the attendant at an inn who cares for horses), steals one of Faustus's magic books; with his friend Rafe, he plans to use the book to magically control women and to conjure in the devil's name.

In several subsequent scenes, Faustus is shown exercising his magical powers through Mephastophilis, who does his bidding obediently. In one scene, Faustus and Mephastophilis have traveled through the Alps to Rome, where Faustus becomes invisible. He proceeds to play tricks on the pope and a group of friars, snatching away the delicacies on which the pope is feasting, and smacking the pope on the ear. A brief comic scene then shows Robin and Rafe accidentally conjuring Mephastophilis, who frightens them by lighting fireworks on their backs. In a scene set at the court of the German Emperor Charles V, Faustus impresses the emperor by conjuring the shades of Alexander the Great and his paramour. When a knight at the court makes fun of him, Faustus punishes him by making a pair of horns appear on his head. In a later scene at the court of a duke and duchess, Faustus asks the duchess if there is any delicacy she desires. When she tells him she would love some ripe grapes even though they are out of season, Faustus sends Mephastophilis on a lightning journey to India for the fruit, which she declares are the best grapes she has ever tasted.

Such scenes take place over the 24 years that remain to Faustus under his contract with Lucifer. Finally, following a speech by Wagner, who says that he believes his master is preparing for death, Faustus conjures the shade of Helen of Troy for some scholars who wonder what this legendary Greek beauty looked like. After she parades across the stage and the grateful scholars leave, an old man enters and warns Faustus to repent, to seek mercy instead of falling prey to the sin of despair. Just as Faustus begins to do so, Mephastophilis appears and threatens him with torture. Faustus asks Lucifer's pardon and entreats Mephastophilis to bring back Helen of Troy to be his paramour, so that she can distract him from thoughts of repentance. Referring to the Trojan War that was fought over Helen's kid-

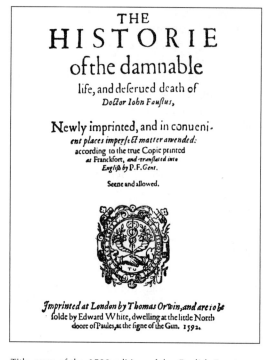

THE
HISTORIE
of the damnable
life, and deferued death of
Doctor Iohn Fauftus,

Newly imprinted, and in conueni-
ent places imperfect matter amended:
according to the true Copic printed
at Franckfort, and tranflated into
English by P.F.Gent.

Seene and allowed.

*Imprinted at London by Thomas Orwin, and are to be
folde by Edward White, dwelling at the little North
doore of Paules, at the figne of the Gun.* **1592.**

Title page of the 1592 edition of the *English Faust-book,* a translation of the German work that was Marlowe's source for *Dr. Faustus.*

napping, Faustus declares that she will be all the heaven he needs:

> Was this the face that lancht a thousand
>   shippes,
> And burnt the topleffe Towres of *Ilium?*
> Sweete *Helen*, make me immortall with a kisse:
>   . . .
> Here wil I dwel, for heaven be in these lips.
> (*Dr. Faustus*, 12.81-86)

As devils enter to torment the old man, he curses Faustus, but the old man's faith remains firm that he himself will end up with God in heaven.

In the play's final scene, Faustus enters again with the scholars, telling them of his despair and dismissing their suggestions that it is not too late for him to repent. He advises them to leave for their own sakes as the moment of his damnation approaches. They do so, and the clock strikes eleven: Faustus has "but one bare hower [hour] to live" (*Dr. Faustus*, 14.62). In a long final speech, he beseeches time to stand still and then, as the clock strikes eleven-thirty, he asks God to put some end to his suffering, even if he has to endure a hundred thousand years of damnation. The clock strikes twelve and Faustus pleads, "My God, my God, looke not so fierce on me" as Mephastophilis appears and takes him off to hell. In the brief epilogue, the Chorus admonishes the

audience to avoid Faustus's fate, warning them not to inquire into "unlawful things, / whose deepness doth intise such forward wits, / To practice more than heavenly power permits" (*Dr. Faustus*, Epilogue, 6-8).

An appetite for certainty. As the audience learns in the opening scene, Faustus's main reason for wanting magical powers is intellectual curiosity. He expresses this motivation as a desire for certainty: magic, he imagines, will "resolve me of all ambiguities" (*Dr. Faustus*, 1.80). Yet when he asks about the motions of the planets, for example, the few certain answers that Mephastophilis gives him are uninformative and superficial. Faustus quickly loses interest in asking deep questions and for the rest of the play he seems more interested in performing tricks than probing the mysteries of the universe.

Faustus's disappointment at the unforeseen limitations he encounters finds a historical parallel in the career of Cornelius Agrippa (1486-1535), the German magician, philosopher, and scientist that Faustus claims as a role model in Scene One. Like Faustus, in his book *On the Occult Philosophy* Agrippa professes ambivalent and even contradictory rationales for learning magic. On the one hand he praises it as a noble path to truth, while on the other he openly extols the uses of charms and spells for achieving worldly or self-serving ends such as wealth, political power, revenge, or love. In another book, however, *Of the Vanitie and Uncertaintie of Artes and Sciences,* Agrippa bitterly rejects both science and the occult, describing himself and other magicians as fraudulent hucksters who have preyed on people's gullibility in order to advance their own interests. Science is no better, Agrippa asserts: occult and scientific knowledge are alike in their vanity and uselessness.

"Agrippa's life and works," writes scholar John S. Mebane, remind us "that those who long most intensely for certain knowledge are often those who ultimately despair of attaining truth through systematic inquiry" (Mebane, p. 70). This normal intellectual hunger for certainty, Mebane continues, was exacerbated by the circumstances in which sixteenth-century intellectuals found themselves:

> In the sixteenth century, the reaction against the new learning and against occult philosophy came not solely from those who were consistently conservatives or reactionaries, but from scholars who previously had taken pride in their command of the arts and sciences. . . . The conflicts of Agrippa's life are in many ways those

From a stage production of *Dr. Faustus,* starring Marne Maitland as Faustus and Peter Coke as Mephastophilis.

of the Renaissance itself. . . . Agrippa's career suggests to us that works such as Marlowe's *Dr. Faustus* . . . are no more incoherent than the very lives of those individuals whose intellectual and spiritual turmoil such works of art are designed to reflect.

(Mebane, pp. 71-72)

While religious certainty had been shaken by movements such as humanism and the Reformation, scientific knowledge had not yet developed to the point that it was able to offer sure answers on its own. In this light, Agrippa's (and Faustus's) disillusionment with intellectual endeavor can be seen as a form of anxiety that arose from the collapse of one system of knowledge before another developed sufficiently to take its place.

Sources and literary context. Marlowe drew extensively on only one literary source for *Dr. Faustus,* a prose narrative commonly called the *English Faust-book,* or *E.F.B.* Published under the title *The History of the Damnable Life and Deserved Death of Dr. John Faustus,* this book was a free and sometimes inaccurate translation of an anonymous German volume called *The History of Dr. Johann Faust.* The German original, also known as the *Faustbuch,* was published in 1587; the earliest surviving edition of the English version is dated 1592, but it is believed that Marlowe used an earlier edition published perhaps in 1588 or 1589. The author of the *Faustbuch* collected a number of popular medieval folktales and recast them with Faust as the central character. Marlowe followed the *English Faust-book* closely, drawing on it for the play's overall structure as well as for many of its details, including the depiction of Mephostophiles (as the name is spelled in the E.F.B.), Faustus's questions about astronomy, his magical tricks on the pope, and the procuring of grapes for the duchess. A more general literary source was the medieval tradition of Christian morality plays, simple dramatizations of religious themes performed in church settings. The appearance of the Good and Evil Angels, a common device in morality plays, is Marlowe's most conspicuous borrowing from this popular tradition.

In the early 1590s, a number of other plays about magicians were successfully produced for the London stage. Scholars who favor an early date for *Dr. Faustus* (1588 or 1589) see it as originating, rather than following, this trend. More significantly, the play is seen as one of the earliest English tragedies, and the first to revive the sense of a grand struggle between tragic fate and free will that characterized ancient Greek tragedy. Marlowe thus adapted the Protestant preoccupation with faith and predestination to the tragic stage: critics also describe the play as the first Christian tragedy, insofar as the conflict is over a human soul rather than a social or political issue (as in Greek tragedy).

Events in History at the Time the Play Was Written

The Reformation and the rise of Elizabethan theater. Protestantism was introduced to England in 1534 by the decision of Henry VIII to remove the English Church from papal control. At first, morality plays continued to be staged in churches much as before, but soon the English Church began repressing them as reminders of Catholicism. By the early decades of Elizabeth I's reign (1558-1603), theater in England was undergoing rapid change, forced out into the secular world where its appeal soon reached wider audiences. By the 1580s, when Marlowe began writing his dramas, professional actors had replaced the clerics and other amateurs who traditionally performed the stage productions of the medieval world. At the same time, however, Protestant authorities in the city of London were hostile to these professionals and to the new playhouses, which they viewed as sinful places on a par with gambling houses and brothels.

In the face of opposition by zealous Protestant reformers, the theater companies often sought the patronage and protection of wealthy and powerful men. One of the earliest was the company with which Christopher Marlowe was professionally associated, the Admiral's Men, formed in 1576 under the protection of Lord (later Admiral) Charles Howard. As Marlowe and others recognized, despite the reformers' opposition, the playhouses' rapidly growing audiences offered immense opportunities for talented actors and writers. A compromise with the reformers was reached by the late 1580s, when Queen Elizabeth authorized the Master of the Revels, the official in charge of court entertainments, to act as a censor of theatrical manuscripts. Owing to its religiously sensitive subject matter, *Dr. Faustus* seems to have been particularly heavily censored. This has created severe problems for those attempting to determine the play's original text.

Publication and impact. It is unclear whether Marlowe actually wrote the play down as we have it, or whether the text was written down from the memories of actors or audience members. The play's first recorded performance, by the Admiral's Men, took place on September 30, 1594, but most scholars believe it had been produced before that. The earliest printed version dates from a decade later, in 1604, when Thomas Bushell published it as *The Tragicall Historie of D. Faustus*. Scholars call this version the "A" text, to distinguish it from a very different version, the "B" text, published by John Wright in 1616 with significant additions and changes. While some disagreement remains, and there are discrepancies and clear gaps in the text, most scholars accept the A text (on which this entry is based) as the more authoritative.

Both the German and English Faust-books reflected the popular appeal of the Faust legend, but it would be Marlowe's play that transformed the story of the man who sold his soul for knowledge into an enduring modern myth. Translated into German, simple versions of Marlowe's play became a staple of puppet shows in Germany for 200 years. The story has since been treated by other writers, notably by the German Romantic poet Johann Wolfgang von Goethe (1749-1832), but also by other poets and by prose writers, including Thomas Mann and Heinrich Heine. It has also inspired composers such as Hector Berlioz and Charles François Gounod, as well as artists ranging from the French Romantic painter Eugene Delacroix to German Expressionist Max Beckmann.

—Colin Wells

For More Information

Bloom, Harold. *Christopher Marlowe*. Modern Critical Views. New York: Chelsea House, 1986.

Bloom, Harold. *Christopher Marlowe's Dr. Faustus*. Modern Critical Interpretations. New York: Chelsea House, 1988.

Empson, William. *Faustus and the Censor: The English Faust-book and Marlowe's Dr. Faustus*. Oxford: Blackwell, 1987.

Gatti, Hilary. *The Renaissance Drama of Knowledge: Giordano Bruno in England*. London: Routledge, 1989.

Healy, Thomas. *Christopher Marlowe*. Plymouth, England: Northcote, 1994.

Marlowe, Christopher. *The Complete Works of Christopher Marlowe: Volume II: Dr. Faustus*. Ed. Roma Gill. Oxford: Oxford University Press, 1990.

Mebane, John S. *Renaissance Magic and the Return of the Golden Age: The Occult Tradition and Marlowe, Jonson, and Shakespeare*. Lincoln: University of Nebraska Press, 1989.

Thomas, Vivien, and William Tydeman. *Christopher Marlowe: The Plays and Their Sources*. London: Routledge, 1994.

Traister, Barbara Howard. *Heavenly Necromancers: The Magician in English Renaissance Drama*. Colombia: University of Missouri Press, 1984.

The Duchess of Malfi

by
John Webster

~

John Webster was born in London around 1578, the son of a cart-maker. Probably he was educated at the Merchant Taylors School, and certainly he received legal training at the Middle Temple, one of London's law schools. In both of his professions, cartwright and lawyer, he was exposed to the theater: the Merchant Taylors organized many civic entertainments in London, while the Temple law schools were famous for their private theatricals. Webster began his career as a playwright in 1602. For a number of years, he collaborated on the writing of comedies, tragicomedies, and public processions. His first tragedy, *The White Devil*, performed in 1612, was a failure onstage; his next, *The Duchess of Malfi*, has distinguished itself as one of the great tragedies of the age. Webster's last years are clouded in obscurity. He seems to have died some time in the 1630s, leaving behind drama that conveys the darkness and pessimism of late Renaissance England.

Events in History at the Time the Play Takes Place

The real duchess of Malfi. Webster's tragedy is based on a factual scandal, often told in collections of stories throughout the sixteenth century. In 1490 Giovanna d'Aragona married Alfonso Piccolomini. She was 12 years old and a granddaughter of Ferdinand I, Aragonian king of Naples until 1494; Piccolomini was nephew to Pope Pius II and heir to the newly created duchy of Amalfi. She bore him a daughter, and was

---

THE LITERARY WORK

A play set in Amalfi, Italy, at the end of the fifteenth century; first performed in England in 1613, and published in 1623.

SYNOPSIS

An Italian duchess marries a commoner, incurring the wrath of her brothers; they kill both the duchess and her husband before becoming victims of their own diabolical scheme.

---

pregnant with a son when he died of gout in 1498. The next year the duchess delivered her son and the infant inherited the duchy, which Giovanna ruled as regent.

Giovanna's world was one in which women of all but the lowest class were kept in seclusion from infancy until they reached marriageable age, around 12 or 13. The young woman at this point became a commodity, a bargaining chip, as Giovanna had been. Aristocratic families of this time used marriage as an economic and political tool: matrimony cemented alliances, created blocs of power, and established women in positions that would sustain them (since upper-class women of the era did not work). An aristocratic family, even one of no more than ordinary ambition, could hardly afford not to position a daughter's marriage so that it benefited them.

Once married, young noblewomen of prosperous fifteenth-century Italy hired nurses and servants to tend their homes and children, which gave them the luxury of leisure time. They began using this leisure to forge new contacts and otherwise improve themselves, joining literary salons, for example, social gatherings in which they ventured opinions. Leisure "created the opportunity for personality to flourish," albeit usually in less inflammatory ways than in Webster's play (Plumb, p. 134). This is the point to which noblewomen had progressed by the time of Duchess Giovanna's widowhood.

Into the midst of her opulent surroundings, the widowed duchess invited a man named Antonio Bologna to come and work as her major-domo (the highly-placed servant responsible for running her estate.) Antonio was a commoner, although of a well-respected family. He had served as major-domo to Federico, the last Aragonian king in Naples; after Frederico's death in exile in 1504, Antonio returned to Naples, where he became employed by Giovanna d'Aragona. Still a young woman, she fell desperately in love with her employee, whom she married in secret that year.

She was taking a significant gamble. The marriage combined two related offenses, from which it is hard to pick the more grievous. First, marrying without her family's consent would inevitably draw their wrath on her head. It was almost unheard of for a person of Giovanna's rank to pick her own mate, even in the case of re-marriage, a fairly common event in fifteenth-century Italy. The requirement that the family be consulted applied to men as well as to women; nevertheless, a heavier condemnation would fall upon any woman who dared to do what Giovanna had done. Antonio did not become duke of Amalfi because of the marriage; indeed, he got nothing from the union except a secret wife. However, a woman at this time was assumed to remain under the power of some man or other for her whole life, passing from her father to her husband and (if father and husband were dead) her nearest male relatives. By marrying without consulting her brothers, Giovanna had deprived them of their legal right to pick a husband of whom they approved. And, at least as bad, she had not even married an aristocrat. Kinswoman to a king, she had stooped to marry the king's servant, a man whose family was reputable only as long as its members stayed in their proper place.

Giovanna had good reason to hide her marriage: as soon as it was discovered, she would almost certainly have to resign her noble title—or

worse. Who could say what the consequences of Giovanna's decision would be for her low-born husband or herself? There was a great deal of ambiguity about the legal status of women; despite official limits, some women had managed to grow quite powerful. As an aristocratic widow, the duchess was far from helpless. However, by flouting convention so boldly, Giovanna practically guaranteed a catastrophic conclusion to her marriage.

With craft and secrecy, the newlyweds managed to conceal their union for a few years—long enough for the duchess to bear three children. Their suspicions finally aroused, her brothers set spies on the pair. Antonio took the children to Ancona; the duchess stayed behind for a time but, growing unbearably lonely, she followed, on the pretext that she was making a religious pilgrimage to nearby Loreto. From Loreto, she took her retinue to Ancona, where she announced to her staff that she planned to renounce her title and live privately with Antonio. Her shocked servants deserted her; one hastened to inform the brothers, while the rest returned to the palace at Amalfi.

Giving up her title solved the family's major problem: with Giovanna out of the way, another member of the family could serve as regent to the still-young duke of Amalfi. Her children with Antonio would be barred from succession to the title. However, the wrath of her brothers went beyond the problems of lineage. In their view, the duchess had broken ranks with the family, and needed to be punished. One brother put pressure on Cardinal Gonzaga, legate of Ancona, to banish Antonio; but Antonio and Giovanna had prepared for this, and took up residence with a friend of Antonio's in the city of Siena. From here too they were expelled due to the brothers' influence.

But this time they did not escape so luckily. On the way to Venice, they were overtaken by soldiers on horseback. These soldiers demanded that the duchess accompany them. She reassured her husband that her brothers would not hurt her, and along with her two younger children, went with the soldiers. After this point, probably in the summer of 1512, neither she nor the two children were ever heard from again. Whether quickly dispatched, or imprisoned for life, the duchess met a tragic end, almost certainly the victim of her brothers' vengeance.

Antonio did not escape either. He made it to Milan with his eldest son and lived there, under the protection of powerful friends, for a year and a half. But one day in October 1513, he was stabbed to death by a soldier named Daniele de Bozolo and three accomplices. All four escaped and were never prosecuted for the murder.

The story of this fateful love had wide currency in Europe in the sixteenth century, largely due to the efforts of a man named "Delio," who witnessed Antonio's murder. This "Delio" was almost certainly Matteo Bandello, a Neapolitan storyteller and poet, whose *Novelle* (books of short stories published in 1554) were a treasure-trove for later novelists and playwrights. Most of Bandello's stories concerned men who pursued other men's wives and daughters. Incestuous liaisons, bloody vendettas, and violent punishments for scandalous affairs filled the pages of his books. Bandello seems to have heard Antonio's story from a mutual friend, and become acquainted with the unhappy husband; however, it was purely by chance that he was present in the streets of Milan at the very moment that Antonio died. It was Bandello who ensured that, while the brothers never faced legal retribution for their crimes, they would live in infamy as literary symbols of pride and cruelty.

Naples and the kings of Aragon. Fifteenth-century Italy was a collection of city-states that operated as separate units, recognizing no ruler above their own individual ones, a situation that sheds light on the importance that the duchess's brothers attached to control of Amalfi. The duchess herself hails from Naples, the largest urban center in southern Italy at the time. Like the rest of the peninsula, Naples underwent turmoil both politically and culturally. Naples was, in many ways, the most oppressive and reactionary city-state, in terms of its political structure. It retained all the features of high feudalism, which focused most wealth and power in the hands of a few noblemen and the king of Naples, while the majority of the population eked out a living from the poor soil of southern Italy. Not content with their individual power and wealth, the nobles plotted against each other continually. Political violence was as common in Naples as anywhere in Italy at the time. One Neapolitan queen had three husbands assassinated before she herself was dispatched by her fourth. In light, then, of the violence endemic to her original home ground, the kingdom of Naples, the story of Giovanna d'Aragona is not an anomaly, but rather a fairly standard intrigue for the time.

Until the middle of the thirteenth century, the Naples region and the island of Sicily (the two were politically linked) were ruled as part of the Holy Roman Empire. When the Holy Roman Emperor Frederick II died in 1250 C.E., the pope invited the French royal family, the Anjous, to assume dominion over the region. Three decades later, in 1282, the civil unrest known as the Sicilian Vespers drove the Anjous from Sicily; the royal family of Aragon, a region in Spain, took over the island.

AMALFI

Amalfi is a small city on the Tyrrhenian coast of southern Italy. Today its population is only slightly higher than 3,000; it was once far larger. In 849 C.E., the navy of Amalfi defeated Arab invaders. In the wake of this triumph, Amalfi became one of the preeminent trading towns of southern Italy, a position it retained for over three centuries. Its prosperity was slowly eroded by the ascendance of Venice; much of the trade of the Tyrrhenian coast was siphoned north. Then, in 1343, the coast was devastated by an earthquake, followed by a tidal wave that washed away half of Amalfi and destroyed its harbor. Amalfi never recovered its former glory. By the late thirteenth century, it was one of many satellite states with a noble lord who pledged allegiance to Naples. Today, the only vestige of its medieval glory is a traditional boat race that pits Amalfi against the other "maritime states," Genoa and Venice.

From 1282 until 1504, the politics of southern Italy were dominated by the struggle between the houses of Anjou and Aragon: the former retained control of mainland southern Italy, while the latter maintained their stronghold on Sicily, from where they attempted to undercut the Anjous. Despite intermittent unrest, the early fourteenth century was a glittering period in Naples. The political violence did not prevent the city-state from being one of the great centers of learning and culture. Such distinguished writers and artists as Francesco Petrarch, Giotto, and Giovanni Boccaccio all visited the court of Naples. Having established himself as one of the most powerful politicians of his day, Robert of Anjou (1292-1350), the king of Naples, and his court received extended visits from some of these artists and writers. Robert numbered Petrarch and Boccaccio among his admirers.

When Robert died in 1350, the region suffered an almost immediate collapse, prompted less by the great man's death than by the twin forces of disease (the plague) and economic hardship (the depression that gripped much of Europe in the fourteenth century). Naples was especially hard-hit by the latter. In contrast to other areas that had developed trade or manufacture, it had remained devoted to agricultural products, and when the demand for these dried up, the economy had little else to sustain it. Naples's political life deteriorated as well. Between 1350 and 1442, the city-state suffered from a string of violent, corrupt, and tyrannical kings and queens, a situation exacerbated by the continual rebelliousness of the principal barons.

THE CIVIL WEDDING AND *THE DUCHESS OF MALFI*

Among the charges that Ferdinand levels against his sister is the claim that she is, in fact, not even married. Because she was not wed in a church by a priest, he says that her relationship with Antonio is adulterous, and a sin for which she will be damned. Ferdinand's accusation is only half correct. While a church wedding was the only guaranteed way to gain society's full support of a marriage, it was not the only way to marry. The duchess weds Antonio *per verba de presenti*: in essence, this involves a promise by two people to marry, in the presence of a witness. Official religious dogma held that these marriages, although sinful, were legally binding. Such couples, while occasionally subject to mild punishment for not respecting marriage as a sacrament, had the rights of all married couples. Theirs was considered a civil marriage. To the extent that the duchess is involved in an unlawful marriage, in that hers is a marriage outside the Church, it would be the job of the ecclesiastical courts to prosecute her. But the Church is represented in the play by the cardinal, a man who keeps mistresses, hires murderers, and casually advises Bosola to suborn a priest to determine Antonio's whereabouts. His corrupt ways reinforce an issue with which the play is preoccupied: the hypocrisy of eminent but opportunistic courtiers and churchmen. Even if the duchess has sinned in the eyes of the Church by entering into such a marriage, it is hard to imagine who in the play would be competent to judge her.

In 1443 peace was restored by means of war. Alfonso, the Aragonian king of Sicily, backed by powerful northern Italian families, conquered Naples and drove the Anjous from Italy. He then established an Aragonian counterpart to the golden monarchy of Robert of Anjou. A shrewd and charismatic leader, with a knack for making profitable alliances, Alfonso managed to keep his nobles in check, and patronized universities and artists in Naples and Sicily. His successors were less skilled. Between 1458 and 1494, civil unrest returned to the region, which may explain the behavior of the duchess of Malfi's brothers. In 1494, France's Charles VIII marched easily into Naples. Two decades followed in which control shifted from French to Aragonian hands; after a brief period in which the two attempted to share control, Ferdinand, king of Spain, established a hold on the region that would last for over two centuries.

Historians generally agree that the political struggle for Naples and Sicily at the end of the fifteenth century brought an end to the Renaissance in Italy. The fighting drew foreign armies onto Italian soil, where they would stay, in one form or another, until the middle of the nineteenth century. The French and Spanish struggle over Naples revealed the weaknesses of Italy's political structure, in which a number of city-states guarded their independence so jealously that they could not unite even to fight a common foe.

The Play in Focus

Plot summary. The play opens with a visit by the duchess's two brothers, Ferdinand and the cardinal, to her palace at Amalfi. Antonio, the major-domo, and Delio, his friend, look on as a man named Bosola harangues the cardinal. Seven years earlier, Bosola had assassinated someone for the cardinal; he was caught and sentenced to seven years on the prison-galleys. Released at last, he has sought out the cardinal for support or further employment, but the cardinal shuns him. Bosola is still lurking in the shadows when the duchess enters. Her brothers charge her never to remarry. Ferdinand in particular reveals how obsessively jealous he is of his sister's chastity, which means more to him than just his power over her behavior. Before his departure, Ferdinand hires Bosola, ostensibly to act as the master of horses in the duchess's household, but really to be Ferdinand's spy there.

After the brothers take their leave, the duchess (now alone) calls for Antonio under the pretext that she wants him to write her will. As she dictates it, however, she reveals that the will is actually a contract of marriage between herself and Antonio. She then offers the startled Antonio a ring, informing him, "'Twas my wedding ring, / And I did vow never to part with it, / But to my second husband" (1.2.323-25). With Cariola, her serving-maid, as witness, the two are legally married in a civil ceremony.

Act 2 begins some months later: the duchess, her marriage to Antonio still a safely guarded secret, is attempting to hide the fact that she is pregnant. The suspicious Bosola offers her apricots, a fruit that pregnant women were supposed to crave. The duchess devours them, and if this were not enough to confirm Bosola's suspicions, she almost instantly goes into labor.

To conceal the impending birth, Antonio and his friend Delio contrive an elaborate ruse. They claim that a great many valuables are missing, and to discover the thief, they confine all servants to their quarters until morning, when a search will be conducted. This allows the midwives to come and go unnoticed. Bosola sneaks out of his quarters, but he is discovered by Antonio and the two men quarrel. Suspecting that Bosola is a spy, Antonio accuses him of poisoning the apricots he gave the duchess. Bosola, still ignorant of Antonio's real status in the household, makes several vague counteraccusations against him. Antonio manages to steer Bosola away from the duchess's rooms, but drops a paper on which is written the horoscope of his newborn son. Although the paper does not reveal that Antonio is the boy's father, Bosola's discovery of it confirms his suspicions. Bosola then carries this information to Rome, where Ferdinand and the cardinal live.

Meanwhile, in Rome, the cardinal is entertaining his mistress, Julia, wife to an old courtier named Castruchio. The lovers are interrupted by two messengers. First, Antonio's friend Delio arrives to warn Julia that her husband is returning to Rome from Malfi. Delio had wished to marry Julia, and now wishes her to be his mistress. While she is rejecting his suit, another messenger arrives: Castruchio delivers Bosola's news, to Ferdinand. Nearly insane with rage, Ferdinand shares the news with the cardinal, but decides to do nothing until he knows the name of the duchess's lover: "Till I know who leaps my sister, I'll not stir: / That known, I'll find scorpions to string my whips" (duchess, 2.5.77-78).

Act 3 opens more than two years later. The duchess and Antonio have managed to conceal their marriage, despite having two more children. The duchess now receives another visit from Ferdinand. Hiding his rage, Ferdinand announces that he has found a new husband for the duchess:

the great Count Malateste. His true feelings of jealousy and anger emerge in an encounter with Bosola. Later, when Ferdinand enters his sister's room, Antonio barely escapes unseen, as Ferdinand angrily upbraids both the duchess and her unknown husband, whom Ferdinand correctly assumes is listening. Still, Ferdinand merely threatens the duchess with his dagger. Vowing never to see his sister again, he rushes from her room and speeds back to Rome.

ASTROLOGY

Belief in astrology was widespread in the Renaissance; people quite commonly thought that it could be useful in predicting an individual's life. Astrology plays a crucial role in one scene in *The Duchess of Malfi*. When Antonio meets Bosola on the night the duchess gives birth, he tells the spy that he has been "setting a figure for the Duchess's jewels," that is, casting a horoscope to gain information about the thief (*Duchess*, 2.3.20). People believed that according to a complicated system of significations, the alignment of planets and stars revealed everything from a thief's physical appearance, to his whereabouts, to if (or when) the stolen items would be returned.

In reality, no jewels were stolen, but Antonio has been applying his astrology: he has cast a horoscope for his son. The news is dismal: "The Lord of the first house, being combust in the ascendant [i.e., very near the rising sun], signifies short life: and Mars being in a human sign [Virgo], join'd to the tail of the Dragon, in the eight house, doth threaten a violent death" (*Duchess*, 2.3.57-63). According to scholar Johnstone Parr, this is not an accurate horoscope for midnight on December 19, 1504. It does, however, reveal that Webster was familiar with the technical aspects of astrology, for the signs of short life and violent death that it mentions are, in fact, substantiated by the Greek astrological authority Claudius Ptolemy. Ironically this child with the horrifying horoscope is the only member of the duchess's family to survive the fifth act, though the horoscope makes one wonder how long he will outlive his parents.

Fearing discovery, Antonio and the duchess concoct a desperate plan. She announces to the household that Antonio was caught defrauding her and has fled, a story that allows Antonio to escape to Ancona without people suspecting that he is her husband. Unfortunately, the duchess divulges the plan to Bosola, who has tricked her into trusting him by his violent defense of Antonio's honesty. The spy then advises the duchess to feign a pilgrimage to Loreto, and from there to join her husband in Ancona. Then he follows Ferdinand to Rome to deliver this information.

After Bosola betrays the duchess's marriage to Ferdinand, it is made public. At Loreto, where he is resigning his cardinal's seat to become a soldier, the cardinal publicly repudiates his sister and brother-in-law, who have come to beg his help. Ferdinand's influence has caused them to be banished from the state of Ancona; further, the pope has stripped the duchess of her title, and the majority of her servants have abandoned her. As they ponder where to go, Bosola arrives with a letter from Ferdinand that reads, "Send Antonio to me; I want his head in a business. I stand engaged for your husband for several debts at Naples: let not that trouble him, I had rather have his heart than his money" (*Duchess*, 3.5.27-35). Antonio and the duchess are not deceived by the veiled threats in the letter; they refuse the offer, and decide to separate temporarily. But shortly after Antonio departs for Milan, Bosola returns with a troop of soldiers and carries the duchess away to be a prisoner at her own palace in Malfi.

Later, Ferdinand comes to visit his imprisoned sister, ostensibly, according to Bosola, to attempt a reconciliation. Entering her darkened room, Ferdinand offers her a hand, which the duchess is supposed to assume is his own but which is actually a dead man's severed hand. When Ferdinand calls for light, the duchess discovers his grisly deception, and then sees, behind a screen, hanging wax figures that Bosola tells her are the corpses of her husband and child. Although Ferdinand's goal is to drive the duchess insane, she remains calm, loyal to her dead husband, and unrepentant. She maintains her composure even after Ferdinand empties the inmates of the local madhouse into her palace. When Bosola, disguised as the man who will dig her grave, taunts her with the futility of her life, she answers merely, "I am Duchess of Malfi still" (*Duchess*, 4.2.138). Finally, assassins strangle the duchess, her children, and her maidservant Cariola. When he sees the corpses, Ferdinand is stricken with remorse and blames Bosola, telling him that he should have carried the duchess to a hidden monastery rather than follow the insane orders that he himself, Ferdinand, had given. Ferdinand then swears that Bosola will gain nothing from his crimes. Stunned by his master's ingratitude,

Bosola experiences an awakening of his conscience. After Ferdinand leaves, Bosola respectfully disposes of the duchess's body and goes to Milan, where the cardinal and Ferdinand are to meet.

Act 5 opens in Milan, when the tide seems to have turned against the murderous brothers. Although Ferdinand and the cardinal continue to harass Antonio, they themselves are falling apart. Ferdinand has gone totally insane, and now suffers from lycanthropy (he thinks that he is a werewolf)—a disease believed by Renaissance medical experts to result from an excess of jealousy or another melancholic emotion. Bosola arrives, hoping yet to wrest some material benefit from the cardinal, despite his earlier moral awakening. He promises to assassinate Antonio. But what he really wants is proof of the cardinal's complicity in the death of the duchess. He obtains this proof through Julia, the cardinal's mistress, who has long loved Bosola. After confessing his guilt to her, the cardinal poisons Julia. Bosola agrees to help dispose of Julia's body; but after the cardinal has left the stage, Bosola declares that he means to save Antonio, not kill him. Unbeknownst to him, however, Antonio plans to visit the cardinal that night and either gain clemency or be killed by him.

That night, the cardinal anxiously awaits the arrival of Bosola to dispose of Julia's corpse. Sneaking in, Bosola overhears the mad Ferdinand muttering about strangulation; misunderstanding his insane rambling, Bosola assumes—not incorrectly—that a plot is laid for his life. In the darkness, he stabs a man he believes has come to assassinate him, then learns, to his horror, that it is Antonio. Fate has condemned Bosola to commit the one act he wished to avoid. In retaliation for this mischance, Bosola finds and accusingly kills the cardinal: "Thou took'st from Justice her most equal balance, / And left her naught but the sword" (*Duchess*, 5.5.38-9). The noise of the fray attracts the insane Ferdinand, who stabs both the cardinal and Bosola. As he dies, Bosola kills Ferdinand, and tells Delio, who arrives with Antonio's only surviving son, what has transpired. Appalled by the tragedy, Delio resolves to "make noble use / Of this great ruin" and see that Antonio's and the duchess's son inherits her title to Malfi (*Duchess*, 5.5.109-10). Delio delivers a final eulogy: "Integrity of life is fame's best friend, / Which nobly, beyond death, shall crown the end" (*Duchess*, 5.5.119-20).

The duchess, rank, and remarriage. Critical evaluation of Webster's title character has tended to hinge on varying readings of two cultural commonplaces of the Renaissance: second marriages were improper (especially for women) and marriages should respect class lines. The play is noticeably, perhaps deliberately, ambiguous in its moral judgments. If the reader believes that Webster endorsed the cultural strictures against class-breaking and second marriages, then the duchess is immoral, improvident, and driven to tragedy by her own lusts. If, on the other hand, the reader believes that Webster was critical of those strictures, then the duchess is almost an early feminist heroine.

Neither of these two strictures was rigidly observed. The arguments against second marriages were usually practical, rather than moral or legal. Treatises on marriage warned men that marrying a widow might cause serious problems: the wife might idealize her late husband, and would probably be molded to the dead husband's requirements, making her unmanageable. If the widow had children, they were likely to create problems: even if there were no conflict of personality between stepchild and new husband, the second marriage made issues of inheritance and succession more complicated. It was also often claimed that widows were naturally lusty. Unlike virgins, who were believed to be afraid of men, widows had experienced sex; when a widow wed again, especially a younger man, it was often assumed she did it to resume sexual activity.

Lisa Jardine has argued that the disapproval of remarriage was based in economic reality. Among the upper classes and aristocracy, the wedding of a daughter was expensive: as part of her dowry, the bride would probably carry some portion of her birth-family's estate into her husband's family. This land, and the wealth that went with it, did not return to the original family—unless the bride's husband died before her, in which case she usually inherited her husband's estate and often resumed a primary connection to her birth family. (In the play, Ferdinand admits that his schemes against his widowed sister spring from greed; he hopes to inherit her property when she dies.) Multiple marriages prevented the return of dowry property to its family of origin, and threatened further dissolution of large estates.

If such attitudes were universally held in the Renaissance, argue some literary historians, then Webster meant his audience to condemn the duchess (Leech, p. 108). However, opinion was far from unanimous on the issue of remarriage. Many treatises on marriage did condemn second marriages (among them Jeremy Taylor's *Holy Living*), but many others did not. And even those who frowned on remarriage in principle accepted it as an inevitable practice; after pointing out that widows' usual motive for second marriages was lust, one commentator concludes that, "if they cannot avoid the prickes of nature . . . it is better to marry than burn" (Wadsworth, p. 396). There were eminent humanists at the time the play takes place—Cornelius Agrippa (1486-1535), for example—who accepted the practice; in his own time Webster might also have assumed a certain empathy for his heroine. But exactly what he thought of her is difficult to determine.

A VOGUE FOR "MACHIAVELLIAN" TACTICS

Webster, like other dramatists of his day, conceived of politics and power in a manner greatly influenced by *The Prince* (1513) by Italy's Niccolò Machiavelli. A handbook for rulers, *The Prince* speaks of setting aside moral values if doing so is necessary to achieve a higher purpose, such as driving foreign powers from Italy. Cruelty is sometimes advisable, but only for the common good, a caveat that French, English, and other readers mostly ignored. By the early 1600s, *Machiavelli* had taken on a sinister meaning, as had *politic* and *Machiavellism*, implying "scheming, crafty, villainous, and apt to kill in a treacherous way, usually by poison." English dramatists seized on the implication, incorporating it into plays that met a popular demand for tales of horror and intrigue staged in Italy. Including comedy as well as tragedy, examples of such plays are Ben Jonson's **Volpone** (1606; also in *WLAIT 3: British and Irish Literature and Its Times*), Webster's *The White Devil* (1612) and *The Duchess of Malfi* (1623), and Philip Massinger's *The Duke of Milan* (1623).

From the Renaissance perspective, the duchess is guilty of any number of crimes, ranging from disobedience to lying to fornication. The duchess of Webster's play is far from blameless, but at the same time, the depiction seems to take pains to distance her from common stereotypes about remarrying widows. She is not lustful and genuinely loves her husband. Similarly, Antonio takes on the persona not of a social climber, but of a decent man who is destroyed by his encounter with nobility. Perhaps most importantly,

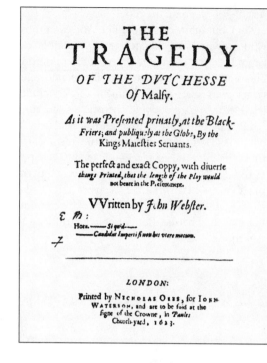

THE TRAGEDY

OF THE DVTCHESSE Of Malfy.

As it was Prefented privatly, at the Black-Friers; and publiquely at the Globe, By the Kings Maiefties Seruants.

The perfect and exact Coppy, with diuerfe things Printed, that the length of the Play would not beare in the Prefentment.

VVritten by *John Webfter.*

Hora.──── *Si quid* ────
──── *Candidus Imperti fi non his vtere mecum.*

LONDON:

Printed by Nicholas Okes, for John Waterson, and are to be fold at the figne of the Crowne, in *Paules* Church-yard, 1 6 2 3.

Title page of the 1623 edition of *The Duchess of Malfi.*

the play makes the conduct of the duchess's accusers far more evil than the worst interpretation one can assign to her own behavior. If it is wrong for her to remarry, it is certainly far more wrong for the cardinal to keep a mistress; if she should not have married below herself, Ferdinand most certainly should not have hounded her to death. Bosola, even as he serves Ferdinand for hope of gain, condemns the brothers roundly. Yet the play remains silent about the morality or immorality of the duchess.

On the other hand, a marriage like that of the duchess to a commoner-servant would most likely impress Webster's audience as a clear-cut travesty of accepted social order. In the intellectual universe of the Renaissance, social place was thought to be prescribed by God, and upper-class culture frowned with utmost severity on anomalies in this divinely ordained social order. Marriage across classes cast doubt on the lower-class partner (who was assumed to be ambitious) and on the upper-class partner (who was assumed to have forgotten the dignity of his or her high place). But the class system was sometimes negotiable.

In spite of the Renaissance emphasis on proper degree in marriage, it cannot be stated that unions across classes were never accepted. Marriages between nobles and commoners were

not frequent, but they occurred often enough for us to trace their impact, and there is substantial evidence that they were accepted. In 1515 Henry VIII's sister Mary wed the duke of Suffolk; the marriage would have been considered beneath her because she was the widow of Louis XII, late king of France. Yet no one harassed the couple about the union, and their daughter was included in the line of succession after Henry VIII died. This daughter, Frances Brandon, inherited the duchy of Suffolk. Eventually she married her secretary, a man 16 years younger, which prompted an exasperated outcry from Queen Elizabeth—but no official punishment. Indeed, Brandon remained a respected member of the court. It seems clear that, despite oft-repeated norms of behavior, Renaissance England was willing to accept at least some deviations from what was expected of a marriage.

Sources and literary context. The ultimate source for the story of Giovanna d'Aragona was a story by Matteo Bandello, an Italian poet and writer of novellas, who may have known Antonio personally. Webster probably knew the story third-hand; it passed through French, in the form of François Belleforest's *Histoires Tragiques*, to English in William Painter's *Palace of Pleasure*. Unlike Bandello and Webster, Belleforest and Painter condemn the duchess explicitly. Webster's main change to the story was the character of Bosola. In Bandello's original, Bozolo is the name of the man who kills Antonio, but he has no other role in the plot. Webster's enlargement of this character is probably the result of a contemporary vogue for malcontents: characters who are driven by disgust at their surroundings into acts of violence and revenge. Prominent characters of this type include Hamlet in Shakespeare's *Hamlet*, Vindice in Middleton or Tourneur's *The Revenger's Tragedy*, and Malevole in John Marston's *The Malcontent*. Webster probably took the idea of using wax figures to represent corpses in the play from an episode in Sir Philip Sidney's *Arcadia*. Less directly, like other dramatists of his day, Webster was influenced by interpretations of writings by Italy's Niccolò Machiavelli, whose advice to rulers had been distorted to rationalize cruelty.

Events in History at the Time the Play Was Written

Arbella Stuart's marriage. As he wrote *The Duchess of Malfi*, Webster was probably following the developing drama of Arbella Stuart. This

Helen Mirren, as the Duchess of Malfi, holds the hand of her co-star Bob Hoskins in a 1981 production of John Webster's play at the Roundhouse in London.

story was among the chief news items of the early 1610s, and while its parallels to Webster's plays are not close enough to suggest a definite influence, they are still striking.

Arbella Stuart was cousin to King James, and a figure of some prominence. During Elizabeth's reign, she was often mentioned as a possible successor to the throne, a claim that seems to have worried James. As her closest male relative, and her sovereign, he was responsible for arranging a marriage for her, but hesitated to grant her permission to marry despite the possibility of many worthy matches. Over 30, with the end of her childbearing years approaching, Arbella finally obtained permission to marry in 1610; but when James learned that she intended to marry William Seymour, he forbade the match. Publicly, he asserted that a match with Seymour, the second son of an earl, would be beneath Arbella; privately, he must have worried about the fact that Seymour had a tenuous claim to the throne dating from Henry VIII's time. The offspring of such a union might pose a challenge for James's children. The couple defied the king's word, and were married secretly in late 1610. They were arrested and imprisoned separately, but escaped (with Arbella dressed as a man) and made their way to France. Unfortunately Arbella was captured off the coast of Calais; she refused to

land in France until she had word that her husband was safe. The authorities took her to the Tower of London, where in 1615 she died (apparently of suicide by starvation). During the years of her imprisonment, the precise time when Webster was working on the play, rumors swirled through London: Arbella had had a baby in confinement; she was going mad; James was trying to break her spirit. There are obvious parallels between these rumors and events in *The Duchess of Malfi*.

Public response to Arbella's plight is quite telling about Renaissance attitudes to marriage. There was a great deal of public criticism, not only of the marriage, but also of the deception behind it. Although Arbella was never charged with any crime, the king's lawyers asserted that she had broken an old law forbidding those of royal blood to marry without permission, and that she was a ward of the court who did not have the right to choose for herself. Thus, underneath all of her other crimes, lay an initial disobedience against patriarchal authority.

Although these charges were probably widely accepted by many, scorn of Arbella existed side by side with sympathy for her. The report of the Florentine ambassador on public reaction to news of the escape reveals how widespread this sympathy was:

From the least to the greatest, every one rejoiced over this escape and showed so great an affection to the Lady Arbella that it nearly surpassed convenience, and the people said aloud, "May God protect her!" "Can it be true that, because she got married, so great a lady has to be so ill treated? See, now she will be able to enjoy her liberty and live with her husband, in spite of everybody." (Steen, p. 73)

If Webster expected his audience to feel sympathy for the duchess's plight, the response to Arbella must have seemed to him an auspicious sign.

Reviews. *The Duchess of Malfi* was performed at the indoor Blackfriars Theatre and the larger outdoor Globe Theatre. Little is known about individual reactions at the time. The play appears seems to have been fairly popular until the end of the seventeenth century when it was performed less frequently. Like many Renaissance plays, *The Duchess of Malfi* was rediscovered by early-nineteenth-century critics. Their debate over the play's merits gave rise to questions still discussed, such as whether the duchess is admirable or blameworthy. The element of the grotesque added controversy about whether to perform the play. Even in the twentieth century, reviewers were prone to make such assertions as, "Masterpiece of poetic drama though it be . . . such things as are done in this play are not suitable for the stage. The play may be read—it should not be acted" (Mcluskie, p. 38). But on the whole, the twentieth century lauded Webster's work as a daring blend of the grotesque and the psychologically realistic.

—Jacob Littleton

For More Information

Forker, Charles. *The Skull Beneath the Skin.* Carbondale: Southern Illinois University Press, 1986.

Hearder, Harry. Italy: *A Short History.* Cambridge, England: Cambridge University Press, 1990.

Leech, Clifford. *John Webster: a Critical Study.* London, 1951.

McLuskie, Kathleen, and Jennifer Uglow, eds. *The Duchess of Malfi,* by John Webster. Bristol: Bristol Classical Press, 1995.

Parr, Johnstone. *Tamburlaine's Malady, and Other Essays on Astrology in Elizabethan Drama.* University, Alabama: University of Alabama Press, 1953.

Plumb, J. H. *The Italian Renaissance.* Boston: Houghton Mifflin, 1987.

Steen, Sara. "The Crime of Marriage: Arbella Stuart and *The Duchess of Malfi.*" *Sixteenth Century Journal* 22:1 (1991): 62-75.

Wadsworth, Frank. "Webster's *Duchess of Malfi* in the Light of Some Contemporary Ideas on Marriage and Remarriage." *Philological Quarterly* 35 (1956): 394-407.

Webster, John. *The Duchess of Malfi.* Ed. Elizabeth Brennan. London: New Mermaids, 1993.

"England in 1819" and Other Poems

by

Percy Bysshe Shelley

THE LITERARY WORKS

Three poems set in England during the 1810s; all three were written in 1819; "The Mask of Anarchy" was published in 1832; "England in 1819" and "Song to the Men of England" were published in 1839.

SYNOPSIS

Triggered by the Manchester Massacre in 1819, the poems protest government in the Regency era and call for revolution. The first poem describes the corrupt monarchy; the remaining two call upon England's oppressed workers to rise up against employers.

Percy Bysshe Shelley was born in 1792 at Field Place, near Horsham, Sussex, into a conservative landowning aristocratic family, but most of his writing was devoted to spreading his vision of a free-thinking, universal brotherhood. He attended Oxford University but was expelled for publishing *The Necessity of Atheism*. In 1811 he married Harriet Westbrook, with whom he had two children. He published his first long Radical poem, *Queen Mab*, in 1813. Involved in Radical political activities in Ireland and then Wales, he fled Wales for London in 1813. Here he met the well-known, liberal social philosopher William Godwin, and also Godwin's daughter, Mary, whose mother was the famed feminist Mary Wollstonecraft (see **Vindication of the Rights of Woman,** also in *WLAIT 3: British and Irish Literature and Its Times*). Mary Godwin and Shelley became a couple, going off to continental Europe, where they lived near the Romantic poet Lord Byron. In 1816 Harriet Shelley drowned herself and Percy Shelley married Mary Godwin. The next year the British courts denied him custody of his two children by Harriet; the bitterness of this experience prompted him to leave England for good and settle in Italy. He died here in 1822 at the age of 30, victim of a drowning accident.

Although Shelley never completed his formal education, he voraciously read classical Greek and Western literature, philosophy, history, and contemporary sciences. Also, he eagerly followed the social and political events that were unfolding in England at the time, penning political po-ems such as *Queen Mab, The Revolt of Islam,* and the three poems featured in this entry, which comment on the social revolution taking place in England during this era.

Events in History at the Time of the Poems

The Napoleonic Wars and the British monarchy. The stage of the French Revolution known as the "Reign of Terror"—when thousands of counterrevolutionaries were guillotined along with the French royal family—provoked consternation among England's aristocracy. It seemed very likely that the Revolution might

Percy B. Shelley

cross the British Channel, and that the British monarchy might meet the same fate as that of the French royal family, who had been executed publicly. In 1793 France declared war on Britain, and the Napoleonic Wars began. Napoleon Bonaparte seized power in 1799 and established a military dictatorship in France; he then began his series of conquests of neighboring states—Switzerland, Italy, Holland, Germany. As the war progressed, the British enacted increasingly conservative, restrictive laws in order to control any possible sedition at home. Lasting for over a decade, the Napoleonic Wars finally ended in 1815, with Napoleon's decisive defeat at the Battle of Waterloo.

During the Napoleonic Wars, the British monarchy itself fragmented and changed shape, and Shelley's sonnet, "England in 1819," caustically draws upon the details of this change. King George III had the first of several attacks of madness in 1788, and was declared insane in 1811; his son George, the Prince of Wales, ruled as Regent until 1820 (hence the term "Regency England"). In that year George III died and the Prince of Wales took the throne as George IV.

George III may have been high-handed and stubbornly authoritative (which cost England its American colonies), as well as fat, moralistic, and dull, but he had strengths that the Prince Regent definitely lacked. George III was also squarely

middle class in his emphasis on thrift and domestic virtue, and he remained happily married to Queen Charlotte, who bore him 15 children. His three eldest sons were all profligate and corrupt, each with a long line of royal mistresses. The third, George, who became Prince Regent, was the most extravagant of all. In 1798, George reluctantly married his cousin, Princess Caroline, to settle his debts of thousands of pounds. Nine months later, after the birth of a daughter, Charlotte, he formally separated from Caroline, and from then on he openly carried on a series of royal affairs. He loved to eat, and his increasing girth showed it; he also loved to give wildly expensive parties for the London aristocracy (one banquet in 1817 featured more than 100 gourmet dishes).

The working-class experience in Regency England. At the other end of the social scale, the laborers, artisans, and the poor grew increasingly desperate as their wages dropped or they were forced out of work altogether by the Industrial Revolution (a series of technological and social changes that transformed England from a primarily agricultural nation into an urban manufacturing power; these changes quickened between 1750 and 1850). Shelley's companion poems, "Song to the Men of England" and "The Mask of Anarchy," are full of the particulars of the contemporary working-class experience during this period.

Traditionally, artisan trades such as spinning and weaving had been "cottage industries," with whole families laboring at home. But during the first few decades of the nineteenth century, the machines of the factory mills relentlessly replaced the handwork of the artisans, producing more goods at a more rapid rate. So in a market flooded with cheaper goods, fewer workers were needed to produce them, and unemployment increased exponentially. As more and more workers became available, the masters (employers) reduced the wages of those who did work. Often the workers were paid in scrip to be used only in the factory stores (which featured inflated prices) rather than in coin. The most depressed trade was that of weaving, as the artisan weavers were rapidly replaced by the power looms of the cotton mills.

Factory masters also required laborers to work longer hours in shifts at the factories: the average length of a working day was 14 hours. Child labor was essential to the mills, and it was not until 1819 that an act was passed limiting the time that children could spend working in the cotton mills to 12 hours a day. This was the first, though inadequate, parliamentary reform of the laborers' working conditions. The factory shifts destroyed the workers' family lives in other ways: whereas parents and children had formerly worked together at home to craft their goods, now they worked at the mills on different shifts.

Ever since the coming of the Industrial Revolution, workers in different trades had attempted to organize into unions, although unionists could be prosecuted for conspiracy. The Combination Acts, first passed in 1799 and 1800, sentenced unionists to prison terms. By 1817 it had become alarmingly clear to authorities that the organizing of trade unions was spreading. It was also clear that the union movement was coming into contact with radicals who called for universal suffrage, or the right of all Englishmen to vote for parliamentary representatives.

There was an increasing number of demonstrations, and sometimes strikes, by workers in different English manufacturing cities. In Manchester the spinners went on strike in 1818, followed by the bricksetters, dyers, and carpenters in 1819. In that same year the miners marched in Dewsbury, and the framework-knitters demonstrated in Nottingham. As a result, the Combination Acts were more rigorously enforced. Shelley's "Song to the Men of England" is addressed to the workers who are afraid to organize into trade unions.

Other earlier government measures had increased the workers' misery. In the late eighteenth century, the rural landowners sped up the "enclosing" of areas on their estates that had traditionally been held in common by the rural poor; this common land henceforth became a private part of the landowner's estate. The government passed enclosure laws to enforce this action; Parliament was in favor of it because higher taxes could thus be levied on the landowners. The enclosed lands had been areas where the poor could plant small gardens for food, or keep some chickens and a cow to supply eggs and milk. Now, the poor either starved, or worked for low wages in the cotton mills or mines.

The plight of the poor was made even more desperate during the Napoleonic Wars; grain could not be imported, which kept the cost of bread high. In 1815, when the wars ended, the government passed the Corn Laws (not repealed until 1846), which kept the cost of grain artificially high by raising the tariff on imported grain to protect English farmers, or landowners, from foreign competition. Since bread was made from grain, this only drove the cost of the staple food of the poor upward. At one point, it was cheaper to buy a pint of gin than a loaf of bread. During 1815 there were riots to prevent the exportation of grain and also to protest the high cost of grain; riots by the unemployed to destroy factory machinery; and still more riots by weavers, miners, and other workers in reaction to the reduction of their wages. In 1816 the first of a series of food riots took place, as 1,500 farm laborers, carrying spiked sticks and flags with the slogan "Bread or Blood," set the barns of their landlords on fire. The government responded with predictable military force, set up a Special Commission to investigate, and hanged several of the rioters. Then in 1817 habeas corpus (the law that prevented imprisonment without a charge and guaranteed a speedy trial) was suspended for the first time in centuries.

CLASS SUFFRAGE IN THE NINETEENTH CENTURY

One of the main causes of social unrest during the Romantic period was the fact that suffrage, or the right to vote for parliamentary representatives, was restricted to aristocratic landowners until the first Reform Bill was passed in 1832. The early decades of the nineteenth century saw a continuing shift in the population from the rural areas to the large manufacturing cities; yet these urban English citizens had no parliamentary representation, whether middle-class factory owners or workers. As urban conditions grew increasingly desperate, the conservative landowning members of Parliament stiffened their resistance to any kind of labor reform. The first Reform Bill of 1832 extended franchise to middle-class property owners. But aristocratic landowners and middle-class property owners all shrank from allowing unpropertied workers to vote for parliamentary representatives, who could then make laws affecting those with property. Radical workers joined the Chartist movement in the mid 1830s; in 1836 they drew up a "Charter" with a petition to parliament calling for "universal suffrage" that would extend the vote to all Englishmen. In 1838 the Charter was formally adopted by unionists. The government responded by jailing many Chartists, and others fled the country. In 1840 Chartism organized into the National Charter Association, and continued to agitate for parliamentary consideration of their petition. The House of Commons rejected their petition in 1848. Suffrage was not extended to the working classes until the second Reform Bill in 1867.

Shelley's poem *The Masque of Anarchy* was inspired by the Manchester Massacre of 1819, depicted in this political cartoon.

Radical culture in Regency England. The Radicals opposed the conservative, harsh repression of the monarchy and the parliament. The Radicals were to be found among the English working-class artisans and laborers, as well as among the intellectuals and writers—both middle class or, in the cases of Byron and Shelley, aristocratic.

The movement for parliamentary reform in England extended back to the 1770s. In the 1790s, the movement grew stronger among the London artisans and the rural working-class societies that studied the works of the Radical Thomas Paine (including *Rights of Man* [1791] and *Age of Reason* [1793]). Later, rural working-class Radicals would read religious tracts, histories, and Radical periodicals; or the illiterate workers would meet weekly in a pub where William Cobbett's Radical pamphlet, *Political Register,* would be read to them.

Working-class Radical leaders began agitating to extend the vote to all men, whether propertied or not; and the Hampden Clubs were formed in 1812 to bring the reform movement out into the open. These clubs sprang up in large towns all over England, and continued until 1820; their working-class members resolved to achieve reform by securing suffrage, rather than by rioting.

To the aristocratic, propertied English citizens who did have the vote, the idea of extending suffrage to all classes (of men) was appalling, even terrifying.

There was also an active Radical press that supported working-class protest. Some pamphlets and weekly periodicals, like Cobbett's *Political Register,* were designed to reach a working class audience; others were aimed at a middle-class and aristocratic audience, most notably Leigh Hunt's *The Examiner.* Founded in 1808, this weekly became widely read for its literary reviews, incisive political articles, and contributions by major Radical writers such as William Hazlitt, Byron, and Shelley.

Radical publishers always ran the risk of imprisonment for political libel; so many of them received prison terms that it became a badge of honor. Both Cobbett and Hunt spent time in prison under this charge—Hunt for his article attacking George III, with an irreverent aside on his weight. When habeas corpus was suspended in 1817, Radical leaders fled, and Cobbett left England.

The Manchester Massacre: Peterloo. "On August 16, 1819, about 100,000 millworkers and their families gathered in St. Peter's Field outside a cotton mill in Manchester, both to demonstrate for higher wages and to hear the Radical orator Henry Hunt (no relation to Leigh Hunt) speaking for universal suffrage. The demonstration was to be peaceful, so the workers were unarmed and whole families attended with their children. Local authorities sent a saber-armed militia on horseback to arrest Hunt. After he had been carried off, they turned on the tightly packed crowd to cut down the people who were frantically stampeding to escape. One witness described the scene ten minutes later:

> Over the whole field, were strewed caps, bonnets, hats, shawls, and shoes, and other parts of male and female dress; trampled, torn, and bloody. The yeomanry had dismounted—some were easing their horses' girth, others adjusting their accoutrements; and some were wiping their sabers. Several mounds of human beings still remained where they had fallen, crushed down and smothered. Some of these were still groaning—others with staring eyes, were gasping for breath, and others would never breathe more.(Bamford in Hollis, pp. 100-101)

Records show that 11 workers were killed; 571 were injured on the field, and of these, 161 cases came from saber wounds and the rest were due to trampling by either the panicked crowd or the horses' hooves of the militia. More than 100 of the injured were women or girls. Probably there were scores more who did not report their injuries for fear of later retaliation (Thompson, p. 687).

The massacre outraged the working class and much of the middle class, and it served to mobilize Radical organization. It came to be known as "Peterloo" in a sardonic reference to the Battle of Waterloo that defeated Napoleon, the military victory of which England was so proud. Shelley was in Italy at the time, but his response to the event was the same as that of the Radicals in England.

The Poems in Focus

Contents summary. "England in 1819." This poem may follow the general form of the sonnet, being 14 lines of iambic pentameter with a concluding couplet, but its rhyme pattern is neither Shakespearean, Spenserian, nor Petrarchan; it is instead *ababab cdcdcc ee.* It is an unconventional sonnet grammatically too, for the first 12 lines list the nouns that constitute the subject of "are" in line 13.

England in 1819

An old, mad, blind, despised and dying king;
Princes, the dregs of their dull race, who flow
Through public scorn-mud from a muddy
　　spring;
Rulers, who neither see, nor feel, nor know,
But leech-like to their fainting country cling,
Till they drop, blind in blood, without a
　　blow;
A people starved and stabbed in the untilled
　　field;
An army which liberticide and prey
Makes as a two-edged sword to all who wield;
Golden and sanguine laws which tempt and
　　slay;
Religion Christless, Godless—a book sealed;
A Senate—Time's worst statute unrepealed,
Are graves from which a glorious Phantom
　　may
Burst to illumine our tempestuous day.

All the nouns in lines 1 through 12 are the "graves" of line 13. These nouns describe the monarchy and the workers of England in 1819; all are dying, affected by the decaying Regency monarchy—the insane, dying George III and his scandal-ridden sons, with their expensive, tax-supported extravagances (they "leech-like to their fainting country cling" ["England in 1819," line 5]). Nineteenth-century physicians used leeches on patients to draw off the poisonous blood that was supposed to cause illness; Shelley visualizes the fat princes as leeches who have gorged themselves on blood and then fallen off the patient. The "blood" is not only the exorbitant taxes that the government has drawn from the people during the war years but, more immediately, the blood of those who have just been "stabbed" in the Manchester Massacre ("England in 1819," lines 6-7). The millworkers there were demonstrating for higher wages because they were "starving," and they did so in St. Peter's Field, which was "untilled" because the factory had taken over productive farmland ("England in 1819," line 7).

To a reader at the time, the poem from lines 8-14, which predicts a revolutionary backlash, would have recalled the Glorious Revolution of 1688-89, in which James II was deposed. The "army" that advanced on horseback with sabers to kill the peacefully demonstrating workers was "a two-edged sword," for it would provoke English workers into a reprisal ("England in 1819," lines 8-9). Nor was there any justice available in the Parliament, whose members accepted bribes ("golden laws"), and where, by law, Catholics were forbidden to hold office ("Time's worst statute unrepealed") ("England in 1819," lines 10, 12).

The first 12 lines portray Shelley's present-day England, and the concluding couplet predicts its future. The king, the Prince Regent, the workers who died at Peterloo, the Manchester militia, the parliamentary laws forbidding suffrage to workers and Catholics—all of these are "graves" ("England in 1819," line 13). But out of these graves may "burst" a spirit, or "glorious Phantom" to guide England in 1819 ("England in 1819," lines 14, 13). The word *glorious* alludes to the Glorious Revolution. The image of the spirit rising from the grave is a millennial one. Shelley is predicting an imminent, apocalyptic war between the English people and their rulers.

"Song to the Men of England." This "song" is addressed to the English workers, whether farm laborers, miners, or factory hands. Shelley asks them why they work so hard for such low wages when their masters and ruling monarchy do no work themselves. The metaphor underlying the first three stanzas is that of the bee colony, where the worker bees busy themselves creating the honey for the colony and building the hive, while the male drones' only work is to fertilize the Queen bee. It is a particularly telling metaphor for the monarchy, alluding to the well-known sexual excesses of the Prince Regent and his two eldest royal brothers, and more specifically to Queen Caroline's well-known love affairs.

The workers, the "Bees of England," make weapons and chains for their rulers to use against them, weave the robes for the aristocracy to wear, toil in the mines for coal and tin, and plant the crops that the wealthy landowners eat ("Song to the Men of England," line 9). The workers, counsels Shelley, should continue laboring, but should keep their products for themselves, and they should use the arms they forge in self-defense. But, afraid to do this, they return to their hovels while the wealthy live in "halls" ("Song," line 26). When the workers do demonstrate, the "steel" of the militia slashes them ("Song," line 28). And so, out of fear, the workers stop resisting; they build their own "tomb," and weave their own "winding-sheet" (the burial cloth for the dead) because of their refusal to rebel ("Song," lines 30, 31). They literally work themselves to death, while England becomes their "sepulchre" or burial vault ("Song," line 32).

"The Mask of Anarchy." The poet is "asleep in Italy," when he has a dream-vision about England, a dream that the rest of the poem relates ("The Mask of Anarchy," line 1). He sees a line of figures, all abstractions. (The word *mask* in the title is a pun, for it could mean a facial covering that hides one's true identity, or it could refer to the seventeenth-century aristocratic theatrical performances known as "masques" that had a procession of allegorical figures.) The first three figures take the shape of the people from contemporary English government most closely connected with governmental repression. First there is "Murder," who looks like Lord Castlereagh, the conservative Foreign Secretary from 1812-1822 who brutally suppressed the United Irish Rebellion ("Mask," lines 5, 6). He is followed by "seven blood-hounds" who are fed by the "human hearts" that he throws to them ("Mask," lines 8, 12). The next is "Fraud," in the form of Lord Eldon, weeping huge tears that become "millstones," which crush the "little children" playing around his feet ("Mask," lines 13, 14, 16, 17). Eldon was Lord Chancellor (or presiding officer of the House of Lords), famous for weeping in court; he was also the judge who deprived Shelley of the custody of his children. The third figure is "Hypocrisy," which appears as Lord Sidmouth, the Home Secretary whose cruel policies against labor unrest—supported by Castlereagh—helped to spark Peterloo ("Mask," line 24).

Bishops, lawyers, and peers (or noblemen) are next in the procession. The last figure to appear is "Anarchy," who rides "a white horse" and looks like "Death in the Apocalypse" ("Mask," lines 30-31, 34). Anarchy wears a crown and holds a scepter, and his brow is marked, "I am God, and King, and Law" ("Mask," line 36). By "King," Shelley does not literally mean the monarch, but rather that Anarchy rules the country, for the Peterloo Massacre shows that the country has no form of moral authority or control. Peterloo violated the longstanding English constitutional rights of peaceful assembly and free speech. The skeleton-like figure of Anarchy rides over England ("Mask," lines 35-39). Anarchy is surrounded by "a mighty troop" of soldiers who are trampling the multitude, waving swords, and riding through England drunkenly until they come to London ("Mask," lines 40-41, 44, 47-48). There these "hired murderers" address Anarchy as their "God, and Law, and King," and ask for further work and for money ("Mask," lines 60-61). The implication is that these royal forces are really mercenaries, professional soldiers who hire themselves out to foreign armies, and are not really English soldiers. Lawyers and priests (these would be priests of the established Church of England, not Catholic priests) also bow to Anarchy as their God and king.

Anarchy advances through London past "his" Palace, and is about to meet the Parliament when a maiden, Hope, rushes past him ("Mask," line 79). She lies down in the street in front of Anarchy's horse and expects to be trampled and killed, but instead the figure of Freedom arises. Small at first, it grows larger and more powerful, clothed in armor. It passes over the multitude, and in its wake Anarchy lies dead and the "murderers" whom Anarchy employed also are trampled to dust ("Mask," line 134). The "sons of England" revive in the new light, and listen to the words spoken by Hope ("Mask," line 140).

The rest of the poem gives Hope's long address to the "sons of England." First she advises them to join together to "shake [off] your chains" ("Mask," line 153). Then she tells them that if they do not yet know what Freedom is, they certainly know "slavery" ("Mask," line 157), which is seen in the daily experience of workers in the different trades. They labor for low wages in the mills, or on farms, or in the mines ("Mask," line 165). They see their families starve while the aris-

tocracy feasts at banquets ("Mask," lines 172-73). They are forced to accept scrip or paper money for their wages ("Mask," lines 176-80). And when they do hold peaceful demonstrations, they are murdered as they were at Peterloo ("Mask," lines 188-92).

However, Hope will describe Freedom for these workers, since they have never known it. Freedom is "bread" for the laborer who can now come from work to a united family in a "happy home" ("Mask," line 220). Freedom is Justice, where money and rank have no effect; Freedom is Wisdom, under which all religions are allowed; Freedom is Peace, which would never brook the expense and human cost of the Napoleonic wars; Freedom is Love, which makes the rich give their goods to the poor. ("Mask," lines 230-32; 234-35; 239-41).

Hope then calls for another unarmed demonstration in St. Peter's Field outside Manchester,

JUDICIAL CORRUPTION AND RELIGIOUS REPRESSION

It was clear by the end of the Regency period in 1820 that reform was urgently needed at all levels: in parliamentary representation, in labor conditions, in the court system and penal code, and in the Church (Murray, p. 266). Seats in the House of Commons were openly bought and sold, and bribery was an assumed part of the proceedings. Parliamentary seats were even advertised (Murray, pp. 267-68). The penal code included public floggings for petty thefts, and public executions, with about 150 kinds of felony warranting capital punishment. Prisoners' situations while serving their sentences differed drastically according to their means. Those with wealth and/or position were allowed private rooms, visitors, and special meals (Murray, p. 276). At that time, neither dissenters, Catholics, nor Quakers could hold parliamentary seats. In 1828, Dissenters from the Church of England were put on an equal basis with members of the Church; in 1829, the Catholic Emancipation Bill was passed; and during the early 1830s Quakers were admitted to Parliament.

but this time she calls on all the English poor—working or unemployed—to gather, not just the millworkers. They will come from prisons and workhouses, as well as the factories and mines, to assemble and declare that God made them free ("Mask," line 275). The "tyrants," "troops," and "charged artillery" may attack them again

("Mask," lines 303-07). This time, however, the poor will not flee but will stand and face the horsemen in passive resistance, for they will be supported by the "old laws of England" that guarantee the rights of free speech and of peaceful assembly ("Mask," line 331).

The "tyrants" may again slash and stab them, but their resistance should be the passive one of the martyr. This time, the "tyrants" afterward will meet the scorn from "every woman in the land" and from the genuine soldiers who have fought for England in the recent wars ("Mask," lines 356-57). Their slaughter of the poor will cause such universal contempt in the Nation that Hope's concluding words to the workers will become the hymn for all who are oppressed. These concluding words command the poor to join together "like Lions" ("Mask," line 368). This refers not only to the ferocity of the beast, but to the fact that the lion is emblematic of England, and thus suggests that these impoverished citizens are the truest Englishmen.

Inciting action. The intended audience of the three poems examined in this entry was different from that of Shelley's other poems. His other works are dense with allusions to philosophy, especially idealistic skepticism, as well as contemporary discoveries in the empirical sciences of physics, optics, astronomy, anatomy, and botany. Metrically complex, these other poems are startlingly original in the freshness of their images and the music of their alliteration. Their audience is Shelley's peers, similarly educated and skilled in reading difficult poetry. But the poems under consideration here were written to be read by the middle class and, particularly, the working-class Radicals who were agitating for trade unions and for parliamentary reform. More than that, these poems were not written to *describe* utopian social change in the future but to *cause* social reform in the present. The verse urges the workers to "forge arms—in your defence to bear" ("Song," line 24).

"England in 1819" could be read by either class of Radicals, but probably was aimed more at the middle class. It uses the literary form of the sonnet, associated with literary tradition but here subverted into something decidedly nontraditional in its rhyme pattern and its run-on quatrains. Its references to the workers at Peterloo as "a people" suggest a distance from them ("England in 1819," line 7). Its allusions to corruptions in the law are more likely to be caught by middle-class Radicals. The poem portrays the

contemporary situation of England, but does not call for any action.

This is not the case with the other two poems under discussion here, which seem to have been aimed at the working-class readers who would immediately recognize the truth of Shelley's portrayal of their daily experiences. Many of them would have participated in some of the earlier labor demonstrations and would especially empathize with Shelley's graphic allusions to the details of Peterloo. One can imagine such readers in the Hampden Clubs settling down to read "The Mask of Anarchy," or a unionist chanting "Song to the Men of England" to an enthusiastic crowd at a local tavern. Both poems have the simple phrasing, the straightforward rhymes, and the musical cadences of the anonymous broadside ballads sold on the streets to the working class.

"Song to the Men of England" is directly addressed to "you" workers or "bees of England." The first five stanzas seem designed to raise resentment at the masters, or capitalists, who do no work themselves but gain all the benefits. The sixth stanza urges a course of action for the workers, and the concluding two stanzas powerfully predict the death that awaits the workers if they do not act.

"The Mask of Anarchy" more closely resembles the Radical literature that was aimed at the literate working-class reader. Shelley is clearly not one of the workers, for he is "in Italy" when he has his "vision" of the Tory politicians and Peterloo. But he is the middle-class or aristocratic Radical sympathizer whose backing gave a sense of moral support to the working-class Radicals. There is a grim kind of humor in the descriptions of Castlereagh hiding human hearts beneath "his wide cloak" to feed his following hounds, Eldon weeping tears that become "millstones" that "knock out" the brains of the children around his feet, and Sidmouth riding along on a crocodile. The final figure of Anarchy in the procession, compared directly to one of the Four Horsemen of the Apocalypse, would have at once alerted such a reader to the possibility that these historical figures could be signs of the "Last Days."

Hope's long recital (stanzas 40-51) of the details from working-class life that comprise their state of "slavery" seems calculated to make the reader more and more indignant. It is notable that the details are taken from the working-class experience of all the trades, showing that Shelley is appealing to an entire class and not just the factory workers. The final third of the poem is devoted to a replaying of Peterloo for the reader, only this time with a different ending. The workers still are cut down by the sabers and bayonets; the horses still trample them; but this time they stand "with folded arms and looks" ("Mask," line 321), shaming the attacking militia with their resolute courage. This shame follows the militia as they leave the field, and all Englishmen scorn them for their cowardice in attacking unarmed families who have peacefully assembled.

Working-class Radical leaders were urging the workers to resist passively by seeking parliamentary reform, rather than by violent riots. The conclusion to Shelley's poem follows this path of moderation.

Sources and literary context. "The Mask of Anarchy" draws upon many of the conventions common to Radical poems, tracts, pamphlets, and cartoons of the time. It is a didactic poem, for it is trying to persuade the workers of the necessity for a resistance to authority that is passive and not violent. Radical literature often dramatized the lessons to be taught, as Shelley does with his narrative of Hope and her closing re-enactment of Peterloo. The dream-vision was also a fairly common device. The phrasing and language is simple and almost naive in places, which also characterized much of the Radical literature written to be read by the working class. The figure of Liberty, which Hope sees, often appeared in literature of the Radical culture and in political cartoons, and was considered a Radical emblem. Finally, the idea of passive resistance was much in the style of popular protest then; the Radicals believed that an active political resistance was dangerous because it would serve only as a pretext for government violence.

Another source for these poems is the biblical book of Revelation, which details the events of the end of the world. Both the sonnet "England in 1819" and the longer poem "The Mask of Anarchy" employ apocalyptic images. The concluding couplet for the sonnet has, as its background, the apocalyptic belief that the righteous will rise from their graves after the Last Judgment. Shelley portrays Anarchy much as John portrays Death in Revelation: "Behold a pale horse: and his name that sat on him was Death" (Rev.:6.8). Shelley writes: "Last came Anarchy; he rode / On a white horse splashed with blood / He was pale even to the lips" ("Mask," lines 30-32). Also "seven blood-hounds" follow Castlereagh, and seven is a number associated

with the Last Days before the Apocalypse that runs through Revelation ("Mask," line 8).

There was a rise in millenarianism among the working class in the 1790s, a surge that persisted well into the nineteenth century. Many believed that they were living in the "last days" before the Apocalypse. Apocalyptic literature has often sprung up among oppressed peoples—the ancient Persians, the Jews, and the early Christians, for example—living in some horrifying period of history when it seems that the righteous are being crushed by the overwhelmingly powerful. It seemed that way to the English working poor, who were experiencing the fragmentation of their families, endless hard labor, starvation, and the terrors of the early years of the Napoleonic Wars. Having been raised on the Bible, a great many working-class readers knew the Revelation of John, which portrays the Apocalypse vividly. In the 1790s the dramatist Thomas Holcroft wrote *New Jerusalem,* and other millenarian pamphlets appeared (Thompson, pp. 116-17). Millenarianism is central to William Blake's later minor and major prophetic poems, especially, of course, his major prophecy "Jerusalem," which concludes with the beginning of the actual Apocalypse.

Publication and reception. Although these three poems were inspired by the events of 1819, none of them was published until more than a decade later. "England in 1819" was sent to Leigh Hunt in 1819 with the note, "I don't expect you to publish it, but you may show it to whom you please" (Shelley, p. 375). Indeed, Hunt did not publish it. "England in 1819" and "Song to the Men of England" were not published until 1839, when they appeared in Mary Shelley's first collected edition of her husband's works. By that time, Queen Victoria had ascended to the throne, Viscount Melbourne had become prime minister, and the liberal Whigs dominated English politics.

Shelley sent "The Mask of Anarchy" to Hunt in 1819 to be published in *The Examiner,* but it was not published immediately. Hunt had already served a prison term for libel. Publishing Shelley's poem in 1819 would have guaranteed some kind of government prosecution for the publisher, from heavy fines to prison to possible exile. Hunt waited to publish "The Mask of Anarchy" until 1832, after Shelley had died and in the year that the first Reform Bill was passed.

For literary scholars and readers, "England in 1819" has served as a summation and indictment of this entire decade of class struggle. The two other companion poems have had more of the fate that Shelley would have wished. Both have become cherished songs of protest for the British socialist movement, with "Song to the Men of England" used as one of its anthems. George Bernard Shaw greatly admired Shelley's works as a precursor to socialism. He recorded that in 1892, the one hundredth anniversary of Shelley's birth, there was a celebratory meeting in a working-class hall in East London. Shaw wrote: "The President of the National Secular Society recited Shelley's 'Men of England,' which brought the meeting to an end amid thunders of applause;" and that year also, in a meeting of the Aberdeen Trades Council, a speaker "thrilled his audience with a dramatic rendering of some sonorous verses from Shelley's "Masque of Anarchy" (Shaw in Foote, p. 247).

—Christine Gallant

For More Information

Behrendt, Stephen C. *Shelley and His Audiences.* Lincoln: University of Nebraska Press, 1989.

Cox, Jeffrey N. *Poetry and Politics in the Cockney School: Keats, Shelley, and Their Circle.* Cambridge: Cambridge University Press, 1998.

Dawson, P. M. S. *The Unacknowledged Legislator: Shelley and Politics.* Oxford: Clarendon, 1980.

Foote, Paul. *Red Shelley.* London: Sidgwick & Jackson, 1980.

Gaull, Marilyn. *English Romanticism: The Human Context.* New York: Norton, 1988.

Hollis, Patricia, ed. *Class and Conflict in Nineteenth-Century England.* London: Routledge & Kegan Paul, 1973.

Holmes, Richard. *Shelley: The Pursuit.* New York: Dutton, 1975.

Houtchens, Lawrence Huston, and Carolyn Washburn Houtchens, eds. *Leigh Hunt's Political and Occasional Essays.* New York: Columbia University Press, 1962.

Murray, Venetia. *An Elegant Madness: High Society in Regency England.* New York: Viking, 1999.

Rule, John. *The Labouring Classes in Early Industrial England 1750-1850.* London: Longman, 1986.

Shelley, Percy Bysshe. *The Poetical Works of Shelley.* Cambridge Edition. Ed. Newell F. Ford. Boston: Houghton Mifflin, 1975.

Thompson, E. P. *The Making of the English Working Class.* New York: Random House, 1964.

An Essay Concerning Human Understanding

by
John Locke

Commonly acknowledged to be the most influential philosopher writing in English, John Locke (1632-1704) was a thinker whose career spanned a wide range of fields. His skills included those of educator, scientist, physician, diplomat, economist, theologian, civil servant, and political theorist. Locke played each of these roles at various times in his professional life. He spent one year as a lecturer at Oxford University, where he had been an undergraduate in the 1650s. In 1666 Locke accepted a position as personal physician to Anthony Ashley Cooper, later the earl of Shaftesbury. The two men became friends, and as Shaftesbury became embroiled in a political struggle with King Charles II during the 1670s, he came to rely on Locke for political as well as medical advice. In 1675, for reasons of health, Locke moved to France, where he read the highly influential philosophical works of René Descartes (1596-1650). He returned to England in 1679, just as Shaftesbury's conflict with the king was coming to a head. With Shaftesbury's political defeat in 1681 and flight to Holland the following year, Locke's own position in England became insecure, and he too fled to Holland in 1683. Locke had begun writing *An Essay Concerning Human Understanding* in 1671, and in Holland he resumed the project in earnest. Returning to England in 1688, he finished the book, published it in 1690, and continued to refine it in accord with the dynamic intellectual exchanges of his time.

THE LITERARY WORK

An essay in four books written in Holland and England in the late 1600s; published in London in 1690.

SYNOPSIS

A philosophical inquiry into the origins, nature, and limits of human knowledge, the essay refutes the belief that humans are born with some ideas (such as God) already formed in their minds. It proposes that all ideas are formed by experience, that the mind uses words to stand for ideas, and that all knowledge results from the interplay of ideas.

Events in History at the Time of the Essay

Cartesian rationalism. In the first half of the seventeenth century, the French philosopher René Descartes revolutionized European thought with the apparently simple declaration: *Cogito ergo sum* ("I think, therefore I am"). The notion underlying this statement is that all things are subject to doubt—except for the act of doubting, or reasoning, itself, and thus the mind that reasons or doubts. Reason, for Descartes, is the faculty of mind capable of establishing certain knowledge (a point that Locke's essay would dispute). On this foundation, Descartes, and the Jewish Spaniard from Amsterdam, Baruch Spinoza

John Locke

(1632-77), as well as others, built the intellectual structure of seventeenth-century rationalism, which ultimately posited that reason was not only the basis of existence but also the source of all knowledge. Any truth, the rationalists maintained, could be arrived at by the independent exercise of reason alone, without external verification—that is, without referring to the outside world as it is perceived by the senses.

Also crucial to the rationalists' argument was Descartes's doctrine of innate ideas, which held (in keeping with the independence of reason) that certain important ideas exist in the human mind from birth and therefore are fully formed before any perceptions of the outside world might bring them into being. Indeed, in some rationalist writings these innate ideas are the starting points from which reason articulates any given truth. The doctrine of innate ideas was widely accepted by the time Locke began work on *An Essay,* and he devotes Book I (of the four books that comprise the work) to refuting it.

Francis Bacon and induction. While the rationalists (most of whom lived on the European continent) developed their view of how humans know and understand things, a few English thinkers were moving in a very different, and in some ways opposite, direction. This English tradition is commonly held to have originated in the thought of Sir Francis Bacon (1561-1626),

the essayist, lawyer, scientist, philosopher, and statesman who played important roles in the administrations of Elizabeth I (ruled 1558-1603) and her successor, James I (ruled 1603-1625). In contrast to the rationalists' use of innate ideas as a starting point for knowledge, Bacon proposed instead that the freely inquiring mind is, in the famous Latin phrase, a *tabula rasa*—a "blank slate"—on which such knowledge as the world itself supplies is impartially recorded. In other words, knowledge is properly acquired precisely *without* preexisting ideas, by a process Bacon called "induction": the accumulation of perceived sensory data to the point at which the perceiver can then extract general principles, or underlying truths, that give shape or meaning to this data.

Bacon's technique of induction would help give rise to the philosophical position known as "empiricism." In contrast to rationalism, empiricism holds that all knowledge derives from the senses, through their perception of the outside world. Locke and other English philosophers and scientists of the seventeenth century regarded Bacon as their intellectual father; Locke's *Essay* has been regarded by some as the definitive statement of the empiricist position.

The new experimental science. The philosophical debate in the seventeenth century over the origins and nature of knowledge took place in the context of the scientific revolution that had begun in the sixteenth century. Starting with the work of astronomers Nicholas Copernicus (1473-1543), Johannes Kepler (1571-1630), and Galileo Galilei (1564-1642), scientists had brought new techniques into play that changed forever humanity's view of the universe and our place in it. This new scientific approach was based on both observation (for example, Galileo's use of the telescope) and reason (for example, Copernicus's conclusion that the planets revolve around the sun). Taking the new approach a step further, Galileo brought observation and reason together in the crucial innovation of a scientific method—the experiment.

While Francis Bacon had not been a very accomplished scientist himself (in particular, he ignored the potential of mathematics in describing nature), he did bring some valuable and refreshing new approaches to the practice of science. Aware of Galileo's work in Italy, Bacon took up the new experimental method and integrated it into his larger theory, which included the logic of induction. It was in his advocacy of experiments, not in his espousal of induction, that Bacon's contributions were most valuable to later generations of scientists.

Indeed, induction threatened to hobble the experimental method, for part of Bacon's inductive method was to reject the predictive hypothesis as an explanatory tool. Hypotheses, Bacon believed, could only cloud the gathering of pure data by introducing preconceptions into the mind of the scientist. (Bacon's reasoning ignores the inescapable fact that an experiment must have some hypothesis, even if it is unstated, otherwise the experiment would be aimless.) In his rejection of hypotheses, Bacon was reacting against the pure rationalism of medieval Scholasticism, which had relied on speculative hypotheses unchecked by sensory data and therefore ungrounded in physical reality. Bacon's radical rejection of this outmoded tradition was so attractive to his followers that generations of English scientists believed, falsely, that they were practicing pure induction. *"Hypotheses non fingo"* ("I frame no hypotheses"), claimed the most brilliant of them, the Englishman whom the opening pages of Locke's Essay calls "the incomparable Mr Newton" (Newton, p. 371; Locke, *Essay Concerning Human Understanding*, p. 11).

Isaac Newton and the Royal Society. In the genius of Isaac Newton (1642-1727), the scientific revolution begun by Copernicus found its culmination. A mathematical genius as well as a formidable experimentalist, Newton combined the strongest elements of the rationalist and empiricist traditions. Newton's laws of motion put the physics experiments of Galileo on sound theoretical footing, and his related law of gravity did the same for the astronomical ideas of Copernicus and Kepler. To express his theories mathematically, Newton invented a new mathematical language, the calculus (which was independently invented in mainland Europe by the rationalist G. W. von Leibniz). Newton published his findings in the *Philosophiae Naturalis Principia Mathematica* (Mathematical Principles of Natural Philosophy, commonly called the *Principia*) in 1687, as Locke was completing the *Essay*.

Locke and Newton both belonged to the first scientific association in England (and one of the first in Europe), the Royal Society of London for the Promotion of Natural Knowledge. The Royal Society, now a conservative bastion of the scientific community, was at the cutting edge of the new experimental method when it was founded in 1660. Locke was elected to the Royal Society

in 1668, and Newton in 1671. Among the society's founding members were the father of modern chemistry, Robert Boyle; the microscopist, physicist, and inventor Robert Hooke; and the architect Christopher Wren. Locke also engaged in intellectual exchanges with scientists outside the Royal Society, such as physician Thomas Sydenham (1624-89), a founder of modern clinical

---

GREEK ORIGINS

~

The opposing viewpoints of rationalism and empiricism both originate in the writings of the Greek philosophers of the fifth and fourth centuries B.C.E. Plato stressed what he called "ideas," universal truths that exist in perfect form apart from, and beyond the reach of, the senses. In *Phaedo*, Plato suggested that concepts such as equality, for example, cannot be apprehended by the senses and must therefore exist in the soul before the birth of the body. Plato proposed his theories in reaction to the fifth-century B.C.E. Greek philosophers known as the Sophists, who had discounted the power of reason in favor of practical observation. Plato's student Aristotle, while exalting the role of reason, also championed observation and experience, comparing the mind to a blank slate in his work *On the Soul*.

---

medicine, and Dutch astronomer, physicist, and mathematician Christian Huygens (1629-95).

These and other scientists were carrying on a complex program of experiment and observation, which gave rise to an energetic debate about scientific methods. Boyle and Hooke, for example, championed the usefulness of carefully tested hypotheses; Hooke, in fact, engaged in a bitter dispute with Newton partly over Newton's claim not to have framed any hypotheses. Locke himself accepted the validity of framing a hypothesis, while at the same time endorsing a Baconian reliance on observation: "He, that would not deceive himself, ought to build his hypothesis on matter of fact, and make it out by sensible [sensory] experience" (*Essay*, p. 113).

The problem was partly one of language: what exactly was meant by words like *hypothesis*? In the seventeenth century, scientific terms had not yet been carefully defined and were consequently used in many different, even contradictory, ways. Today, scientists distinguish between *hypothesis*,

Isaac Newton presides over a meeting of the Royal Society. As members of the society, Locke and Newton were exposed to cutting-edge developments in the scientific experimental method.

an unconfirmed explanatory proposition; *theory,* a set of propositions that entails certain observational consequences and is to some degree confirmed; and scientific *law,* a general proposition that is highly confirmed. (Newton's mathematical description of gravitation is accepted as a *law.*) While these are modern definitions, Locke too addresses such linguistic issues, devoting Book III of the *Essay* to language and meaning, which he recognizes as basic to the process of understanding.

Politics, religion, and science. Locke was ten years old when the English Civil War (1642-49) broke out; he came of age during the war and the following eleven-year period in which Oliver Cromwell and Parliament ruled England as a "commonwealth," having deposed and executed King Charles I in 1649. Called the Interregnum, this period ended with the restoration of King Charles II in 1660. Cromwell and his strongest supporters in Parliament were Puritans, and many of the scientific attitudes of the age can be thought of as springing from the same profound questioning of received authority that led the Puritans to dispute the status quo in government (like the divine right of kings) and in religion (like the necessity of ecclesiastic hierarchy). Locke's own religious views are generally char-

acterized as Puritan. A willingness to question authority is central not only to his philosophical thought but to his highly influential political thought, as well.

After Charles II took the throne, the opposition to strong royal power was manifested in the formation of the Whig party, which opposed the Tories, or the party of the king. The Whigs engineered the removal of Charles II's brother and successor, the Catholic King James II, in 1688; this so-called Glorious or Bloodless Revolution installed the Dutch Protestant Prince William of Orange and his wife Mary (James's Protestant daughter) as joint rulers of England. Locke's friend and employer Shaftesbury was a leader of the Whigs and, on account of his writings, Locke himself is often viewed as the formulator of Whig political theory. Shaftesbury died in Holland in 1683, and Locke returned from Holland with Mary after the Whig victory in 1688. It was in this political environment that he was able to finish and publish the *Essay* and his other major works.

The Essay in Focus

Contents summary. The four parts of the *Essay* are titled as follows: "Book I, Of Innate Notions"; "Book II, Of Ideas"; "Book III, Of Words"; "Book IV, Of Knowledge and Opinion."

Book I begins with a brief introduction that states Locke's purpose: "to inquire into the original, certainty, and extent of human knowledge; together with the grounds and degrees of belief, opinion and assent" (*Essay*, p. 55). The book will examine, in turn, three main subjects: first, the origins of the ideas that come into our minds and of which we are conscious; second, the knowledge that we think we gain from those ideas, how certain that knowledge is, what evidence it is based on, and how far it extends; and, finally, faith and opinion, by which Locke means our assent to propositions of whose truth we have no certain knowledge.

Locke then proceeds to his arguments against the existence of "innate principles" or "notions" (*Essay*, p. 59). First, Locke asserts that "children and idiots" do not possess the ideas that are claimed to be innate, for example simple propositions such as "Whatever is, is" (*Essay*, p. 60). This is enough to prove that such ideas cannot be inborn, for if they were, children would have them. If not innate, he asks, how do ideas come into our minds? There is only one way possible: gradually and through the senses. "The senses at first let in particular ideas, and furnish the yet empty cabinet: and the mind by degrees growing familiar with some of them, they are lodged in the memory" (*Essay*, p. 65). A child can tell sweet from bitter long before it knows the difference between the general concepts of sweetness and bitterness; it learns the concepts from the sensory experience of tasting sweet and bitter things repeatedly over time. The mistake made by those who endorse innate ideas is to assume that simply because certain concepts (such as sweetness or bitterness) seem universal, those concepts must be inborn; what the supporters of innate ideas do not realize is that common experience could also supply them.

In Book II ("Of Ideas") Locke begins by tackling the question of how that process works. In a famous passage, he supposes the mind to be like

> white paper, void of all characters, without any ideas; how comes it to be furnished? Whence comes it by that vast store, which the busy and boundless fancy of man has painted on it, with an almost endless variety? Whence has it all the materials of reason and knowledge? To this I answer in one word, from *experience*: in that, all our knowledge is founded, and from that it ultimately derives itself.
>
> (*Essay*, p. 109)

There are two ways in which experience provides the ideas that furnish our minds: some ideas (sweetness, for example) come into it directly from sensation; other ideas arise from the mind's own operation (doubting or believing, for example) and come into it through what Locke calls "reflection" (*Essay*, p. 109). Both kinds of ideas, which Locke groups together as "simple ideas," vary from person to person, depending on what sorts of things people come into contact with (sensation) in their environments and how their own minds operate (reflection) (*Essay*, p. 121). What Locke calls "complex ideas" (for example, horse, gold, beauty, or the universe) are formed by combining simple ideas in various ways (*Essay*, p. 159). What distinguishes a complex idea is that it can be broken down into its component ideas, yet it still exists as a nameable bundle of ideas in its own right. All our ideas, even the most complicated, arise from such combinations of simple ideas, which, in turn, are derived from either sensation or reflection.

LOCKE'S *TWO TREATISES OF GOVERNMENT*

Locke's political ideas were published in his *Two Treatises of Government* (1690), in which he asserts that legitimate government is based on a social contract between persons in nature, whereby each agrees to transfer his or her executive power to a central government and so becomes a citizen of a civil society. The contract relies on the consent of the governed. It follows that if the ruler fails to promote justice, the subjects have the right, even the duty, to revolt. Aside from formulating the Whigs' liberal political agenda for the century to come, Locke's political thought provided the theoretical basis for the American Revolution. Also articulated in the treatises were concepts such as the separation of powers (through checks and balances between branches of government) that inspired the framers of the United States Constitution.

Locke goes on to consider worldly objects that produce sensations (which in turn create ideas in the mind). Material objects can possess two kinds of qualities, he says, which he calls primary and secondary: primary qualities are those that are inherent in an object itself, such as its size, shape, texture, or the movement of its parts; secondary qualities are those that vary according to how they are perceived, such as sound, taste, smell, or color. Perception itself is a mental phenomenon, Locke continues, so that secondary qualities depend on the mind of the perceiver as well as on his senses. For the remainder of Book II, Locke considers the various ways that the qualities of objects—their perception by the senses and the mind, and the ideas that result—can combine to form other more sophisticated ideas. He discusses some of the basic and more sophisticated ideas in detail (philosophers still find much of his analysis relevant today). Major examples include thinking, pleasure, pain, power, cause and effect, identity, madness, truth, and falseness. The simple ideas of pleasure and pain, for example, can combine in different ways to form more complex ideas—passions such as love, hatred, desire, or joy.

At the beginning of Book III ("Of Words"), Locke declares that God has given humans the capacity for making articulate sounds, which allows people to take an idea that they experience and give it a name—that is, to use a word for it. Human words, then, are "names which stand for ideas" (*Essay*, p. 361). It is through the use of these names that people communicate their ideas to each other, rather than through the ideas themselves, which remain "invisible, hidden from others, nor can of themselves be made to appear" (*Essay*, p. 363). Yet these invisible ideas are still fundamentally traceable to sensory experience, and Locke suggests that all words, including those for abstract concepts, have their origins in the concrete:

> *Spirit,* in its primary signification, is breath; *angel,* a messenger: and I doubt not, but if we could trace them to their sources, we should find, in all languages, the names, which stand for things that fall not under our senses, to have had their first rise from sensible ideas.
>
> (*Essay*, p. 362)

In contrast to the medieval Scholastic theory that words represent the "real essences" of what they signify, Locke proposes that words represent general ideas constructed by us, which are "nominal essences." *Gold,* for example, does not represent a real essence, but a nominal, agreed-upon essence based on defining attributes, such as yellow, malleable, fusible, and soluble. It is a general word for a complex idea, a category people who use the word have agreed on for convenience (*Essay*, p. 374). Definition, Locke goes on, "is nothing else, but *showing the meaning of one word by several other not synonymous terms*" (*Essay*, p. 378). But, he adds, words for "simple ideas, and those only, *are incapable of being defined,*" since simple ideas are those that cannot be broken down into other ideas, separate com-

ponents, which would be necessary in order to create a definition (*Essay*, p. 378). Language is not perfect, Locke cautions, and "the very nature of words, makes it almost unavoidable, for many of them to be doubtful and uncertain in their significations" (*Essay*, p. 424). Taking advantage of such ambiguities, people often abuse language, using words inconsistently or distorting their meanings so that their audiences are misled. Such abuse can be either deliberate or negligent.

Having laid the groundwork that he believes necessary for a discussion of knowledge, in Book IV ("Of Knowledge and Opinion") Locke arrives at the essay's climax. "Knowledge," he states at the outset, is nothing but "*the perception of the connexion and agreement, or disagreement and repugnancy of any of our ideas. In this alone it consists*" (*Essay*, p. 467). The agreement or disagreement between ideas can be "intuitive"—that is, when we perceive it without recourse to intermediate ideas—or "demonstrative"—that is, when we perceive it only through the mediation of other ideas (*Essay*, p. 471). A third and less sophisticated kind of knowledge, which Locke calls "sensitive knowledge," comes directly from our experience of "particular external objects" (*Essay*, p. 477-78). Outside of these three kinds of knowledge, anything else we think we know merely amounts to "faith" or "opinion" (*Essay*, p. 477). Furthermore, because our ideas themselves are beset by doubts and uncertainties, "*the extent of our knowledge* comes not only short of the reality of things, but even of the extent of our own ideas" (*Essay*, p. 479). Thus, in most cases, certain knowledge is illusory, though probable knowledge (a conclusion whose likelihood is sufficient to compel assent) may be commonly attained.

Locke stipulates two areas of knowledge that are exceptions to this prevailing uncertainty: mathematics and morality, in both of which he asserts that knowledge is certain. This is because both moral and mathematical ideas are "archetypes" of themselves, a term Locke uses but does not define (*Essay*, p. 501). Indeed, he further claims, any time an idea is the archetype of itself—or conforms exactly to that archetype—then and only then is certainty possible. Knowledge, which comes from ideas, thus depends for its accuracy on the accuracy of those ideas. Similarly, truth as well "*is about ideas agreeing to things*" (*Essay*, p. 511). From these assertions Locke argues that individuals should not accept what others tell them to be true or certain without attempting independently to verify such statements themselves. Yet within these limitations people can and often must act as if something were true, even if it cannot be strictly verified. We may thus offer limited assent to any proposition that is consistent with our own observations and "comes attested to by the reports of all who mention it" (*Essay*, p. 584).

Locke defines "reason" as "the discovery of the certainty or probability of such propositions or truths, which the mind arrives at . . . by sensation or reflection"; "faith," by contrast, is "the assent to any proposition, not thus made out by the deductions of reason; but upon the credit of the proposer, as coming from God, in some extraordinary way of communication" (*Essay*, p. 608). Faith is less certain than reason, he says, and propositions on faith should not be accepted where they run contrary to reason. It is easy for a believer to be led astray, so special care should be given in assenting to matters of faith. *"Belief,"* Locke cautions, *"is no proof of revelation"* (*Essay*, p. 621).

Still, Locke allows, fewer people assent to erroneous opinions than is commonly imagined. He puts all of human knowledge within three categories:

> *First,* the nature of things, as they are in themselves, their relations, and their manner of operation: or *secondly,* that which man himself ought to do [how he ought to behave], for the attainment of any end, especially happiness: or *thirdly,* the ways and means, whereby the knowledge of both the one and the other of these, are attained and communicated.
> (*Essay*, p. 634)

The first he calls *"natural philosophy,"* the second *"ethics,"* and the last *"the doctrine of signs"* (*Essay*, pp. 634-35). These three areas, he concludes, make up "the three great provinces of the intellectual world, wholly separate and distinct one from another" (*Essay*, p. 635).

Rationalism, empiricism, and probability. While Locke has sometimes been called the father of empiricism, his approach to epistemology, or the study of thought, also contains elements that clearly come from the European rationalist tradition. Locke's identification of mathematics as an area of certain knowledge, for example, confirms the validity of this central feature of rationalist doctrine. Yet mathematics itself was expanding from a medium perceived as transmitting certainty to one capable as well of expressing probability. Scholars have identified this shift as "helping to shape a mathematics more suited to scientific inquiry"; a major feature of the new experimental science was a movement away from casting conclusions as certain fact to presenting them as more or less probable depending on circumstances (Shapiro, p. 38). The emphasis on probability rather than certainty remains essential to the practice of science today.

Locke devotes an important chapter in Book IV to probability, which he calls *"the appearance of agreement upon fallible proofs"* (*Essay*, p. 577). Agreement between ideas, it will be recalled, constitutes knowledge in Locke's scheme; probability, then, is the appearance of such agreement on less than clinching evidence. Infallible proof, as Locke has striven to demonstrate, is, in practice, hard to come by:

> Most of the propositions we think, reason, discourse, nay act upon, are such, as we cannot have undoubted knowledge of their truth: yet some of them border so near upon certainty, that we make no doubt at all about them; but *assent* to them as firmly, and act, according to that assent, as resolutely, as if they were infallibly demonstrated, and that our knowledge of them was certain and perfect.
> (*Essay*, p. 578)

The rest of Book IV, Locke continues, will be dedicated to exploring in detail the "degrees" of such probability, "from the very neighborhood of certainty . . . even to the confines of impossibility" (*Essay*, p. 578).

Scientists today tend to accept the world as a slippery place, in which absolute statements are to be regarded with suspicion and in which theories about how nature works must be treated as provisional rather than final. This realization lies at the core of the scientific revolution that reached its climax in Locke's lifetime. Neither Descartes's rigid rationalism nor Bacon's rigid reliance on sense could be made to fit the new science, whose practitioners were forced to recognize that both reason and the senses could easily be deceived by the natural world's immense complexities. Locke's achievement lies in his attempt to map the gray areas that emerged, as acquiring knowledge became less a matter of resting on absolutes—on pure reason alone, or pure experience, or pure certainty, or pure speculation—and more a matter of disciplined selection from a varied yet structured palette of choices once regarded as absolutes.

Sources and literary context. Locke was not the first to recognize the illusory nature of certainty and the importance of probability. In this he followed the French scientist, philosopher, and mathematician Pierre Gassendi (1592-1655), who also stressed the probable nature of knowledge. Gassendi's approach combined elements of rationalism and empiricism. He rejected Descartes's innate ideas, emphasizing the senses and induction as primary sources of knowledge; yet he followed Descartes in relying on mathematics and accepting deduction, that is, drawing a conclusion by reasoning from given premises rather than by direct observation. Locke read both an edition of Descartes's *Meditations* (1642) that contained an appendix of Gassendi's criticisms and Gassendi's own *Disquisitio Metaphysica* (Metaphysical Disquisition; 1644). His thinking was deeply influenced by these works, which, for example, suggested that ideas that enter the mind through the senses can combine to form other ideas that might appear to have arisen purely from reason.

Of course, Descartes also directly influenced Locke. Though not mentioning the French philosopher by name, Locke tacitly recognizes the importance of Descartes's ideas over and over, whether by rebutting them, adopting them outright, or adapting them to his own thought. He spends Book I rejecting Cartesian innate ideas, while his distinction among intuitive, demonstrative, and sensitive knowledge is taken directly from Descartes, and his concerns with the "original," "certainty," and "extent" of human knowledge, as well as with "ideas," reflect central Cartesian concepts to which Locke takes his own approach.

Locke did not work in a vacuum; his thought represents a synthesis of ideas that were very much in the air during an age of intense intellectual activity. His *Essay's* four books are prefaced by an introductory "Epistle to the Reader," in which Locke sets out his reasons for embarking on the project. He relates how, in discussing a subject (he does not specify what it was), he and several friends found themselves rapidly mired in doubts and uncertainties:

> After we had a while puzzled ourselves . . . it came into my thoughts . . . that, before we set ourselves on inquiries of that nature, it was necessary to examine our own abilities, and see what objects our understandings were, or were not fitted to deal with.
>
> (*Essay*, p. 8)

Locke jotted down a few notes for the next meeting with his friends; these became the first drafts of the *Essay*, the rest of which was later "written by incoherent parcels; and, after long intervals of neglect, resumed again" (*Essay*, p. 8). Using imagery (the "commonwealth") borrowed from the Interregnum, Locke also refers to the scientific revolution in which his friends and contemporaries were engaged:

> The commonwealth of learning, is not at this time without its master-builders, whose mighty designs, in advancing the sciences, will leave lasting monuments to the admiration of posterity . . . in an age that produces such masters, as the great Huygenius [the Dutch physicist who discovered Saturn's rings and was among the first to use pendulums in clocks], and the incomparable Mr Newton . . . 'tis ambition enough to be employed as an under-laborer in clearing ground a little, and removing

---

LOCKE AND EIGHTEENTH-CENTURY LITERATURE

There is a direct correspondence between ideas in Locke's *An Essay Concerning Human Understanding* and literature produced a few decades later. One Lockean notion invoked by these writers is that animals, like humans, can reason, albeit on a lower level. Jonathan Swift in **Gulliver's Travels** (1726; also in *WLAIT 3: British and Irish Literature and Its Times*) carries this notion to extremes, depicting animals that are more worthy of admiration than humans. At one point, Locke's essay speaks of a blind man who says he understands the meaning of *scarlet*, whereupon a friend asks him to define it. *Scarlet*, explains the blind man, is like the sound of the trumpet; thus, he approximates what the color means—all that can be done, teaches the essay, when relying on words. Henry Fielding invokes this same blind man in *Tom Jones* (1749; also in *WLAIT 3: British and Irish Literature and Its Times*): "To treat of the effects of love to you must be as absurd as to discourse on colours to a man born blind" (*Fielding in MacLean*, p. 107). Finally, Laurence Sterne applied Locke's teachings in *Tristram Shandy* (1759-67), whose narrator, for example, doubts what, if anything, he can know for certain and links the passage of time to the train or succession of ideas in one's mind. It took a few decades, then, for Locke's teachings to manifest themselves in fictional literary works, but the impact was ultimately very widespread. Especially from 1725 to 1765, England seemed to embrace Locke's ideas about human understanding, despite the sometimes difficult-to-grasp logic and style that some readers associated with Locke's writing.

some of the rubbish that lies in the way to knowledge.

(*Essay*, p. 11)

Much of this "rubbish," he continues, has been left by the pedantic and often "frivolous" use of abstruse scientific terms, which make science "unfit" for "polite conversation" (*Essay*, p. 11). Such scholarly jargon masks ignorance, hinders knowledge, and promotes vagueness. With his *Essay*, Locke hoped to "break in upon the sanctuary of vanity and ignorance" by explaining the nature of knowledge and understanding in plain, everyday language (*Essay*, p. 11).

Reception and impact. The first edition of the *Essay* was actually published in December 1689, though (following common publishers' practice) it was dated 1690. It was followed by four other editions, in which Locke responded to criticisms and added new material, until the fifth edition of 1706, published two years after his death. Despite its length and difficulty, the *Essay* made an immediate impact on the English and European intellectual scene, and soon other works of philosophy began citing it heavily. In 1692, for example, in the preface to his own book, *Dioptrica Nova*, William Molyneux, a doctor from Dublin, Ireland, echoed Locke's own praise of Newton in the following assessment of Locke's contribution to logic:

> To none do we owe for a greater advancement in this part of philosophy than to the incomparable Mr. Locke, who, in his *Essay Concerning Human Understanding*, has rectified more received mistakes, and delivered more profound truths . . . than are to be met in all the volumes of the Ancients.
>
> (Molyneux in Cranston, *John Locke*, p. 359)

Locke wrote thanking Molyneux, and the two struck up a friendship that lasted until Molyneux's death; in fact, Molyneux's criticisms and suggestions were among those to which Locke responded in later editions of the *Essay*.

Not everyone was so complimentary, though. There was a general rivalry going on at the time between poets and philosophers. On the one hand, poets showed little patience for the seemingly trivial investigations of philosophers; on the other hand, philosophers showed little tolerance for the "romantic exaggerations" of the poets. John Dryden, leading poet of Locke's age, disparaged philosophers; so to a degree did novelist Jonathan Swift, as shown in his ***Gulliver's Travels*** (also in *WLAIT 3: British and Irish Literature and Its Times*). The minds of the scientists and philosophers in Laputa, points out *Gulliver's Travels,* "are so taken up with intense speculations, that they neither can speak nor attend to the discourses of others, without being roused by some external taction upon the organs of speech and hearing" (*Swift in MacLean,* p. 9).

The church too took issue with philosophical notions of the time. The most strident negative criticisms came from Edward Stillingfleet, the Bishop of Worcester, who accused Locke of denying the dogma of the Trinity, prompting a lengthy debate in print, which is sometimes included as an appendix to the *Essay*. So upset were the pundits at Oxford University that they invoked measures in 1703 to prevent students from reading the essay. Within a few decades, though, resistance would diminish and champions of the essay would come to the fore; notable among them was Joseph Addison, the guiding hand behind the influential daily journal ***The Spectator*** (also in *WLAIT 3: British and Irish Literature and Its Times*). *The Spectator* began in 1711 to reproduce what it perceived as the finest ideas of its age, among them those contained in the excerpts that it published of Locke's essay.

The impact of the *Essay* can be readily traced in such European movements as the Enlightenment, as well as in the tradition of British empiricism. This school of philosophical thought was taken up by George Berkeley (1685-1753) and continued into the twentieth century (in the work of Bertrand Russell and others). English literature too was deeply affected by Locke's writings, beginning in the eighteenth century and continuing in later works, such as the 1811 Jane Austen novel ***Sense and Sensibility*** (also in *WLAIT 3: British and Irish Literature and Its Times*).

—Colin Wells

For More Information

Chappell, Vere, ed. *The Cambridge Companion to Locke.* Cambridge: Cambridge University Press, 1994.

Cranston, Maurice. *John Locke.* London: Longmans, 1966.

———. Introduction to *Locke's Essay Concerning Human Understanding*, by John Locke. New York: Collier, 1965.

Gibson, James. *Locke's Theory of Knowledge and its Historical Relations.* Cambridge: Cambridge University Press, 1968.

Jones, R. F. *Ancients and Moderns.* St. Louis: Washington University Studies, 1961.

Locke, John. *An Essay Concerning Human Under-*

standing. 1706. Reprint, London: Penguin Books, 1997.

MacLean, Russell. *John Locke and English Literature of the Eighteenth Century.* New York: Russell [and] Russell, 1962.

McCann, Edwin William. *Locke's Theory of Essence.* Ann Arbor, Mich.: Xerox University Microfilms, 1975.

Newton, Isaac. *Mathematical Principles of Natural Philosophy and His System of the World.* Trans. Florian Cajori and Andrew Mott. Berkeley: University of California Press, 1934.

Shapiro, Barbara J. *Probability and Certainty in Seventeenth Century England: A Study of the Relationships Between Natural Science, Religion, History, Law and Literature.* Princeton: Princeton University Press, 1983.

Yolton, John. *Locke and the Way of Ideas.* Oxford: Oxford University Press, 1954.

Zook, Melinda S. *Radical Whigs and Conspiratorial Politics in Late Stuart England.* University Park, Penn.: Pennsylvania State University Press, 1999.

"The Eve of St. Agnes"

by

John Keats

~

<table>
<tr><td>

THE LITERARY WORK

A poem set in England during an unspecified medieval time; published in 1820.

SYNOPSIS

A young man uses the trappings of an ancient legend to win his beloved, the daughter of a rival family.

</td></tr>
</table>

Born in 1795, John Keats was the eldest son of Thomas Keats, head stableman at a London livery stable, and of Frances Jennings, the stable owner's daughter. Thomas Keats eventually inherited the prosperous business from his father-in-law. His son John attended Reverend John Clarke's private school at Enfield, where he was befriended by Charles Cowden Clarke, the headmaster's son, who encouraged John Keats's love of reading and later introduced him to the works of great poets. When Keats was eight, his father was killed in a riding accident; his mother died of tuberculosis six years later. The four Keats children became the wards of Richard Abbey, an unscrupulous tea merchant who later embezzled the funds left in trust for the children. Abbey removed John from school at age 15 and apprenticed him to Thomas Hammond, an apothecary-surgeon in Edmondton. In 1815 Keats studied medicine at Guy's Hospital in London, qualifying as an apothecary-surgeon the following year. But after meeting such literary figures as Leigh Hunt, Charles Lamb, William Hazlitt, and Percy Bysshe Shelley, he abandoned his new profession to become a poet. Published in 1817, Keats's first book of verse, *Poems,* garnered mixed reviews. His second, more ambitious work, *Endymion,* appeared in 1818 and was savaged by critics. Dissatisfied with *Endymion* himself, Keats immersed himself in other projects, determined to create a new kind of poetry that would compare favorably to the great works of William Shakespeare and John Milton. Between January and September of 1819, Keats produced most of his major poems—"The Eve of St. Agnes," "Lamia," "La Belle Dame Sans Merci," and the great odes, including "Ode on a Grecian Urn." They were published the following year. Keats's contemporaries praised "The Eve of St. Agnes" for its colorful imagery and lyrical beauty; it has since been distinguished as one of the poet's masterpieces, perhaps his most successful narrative poem.

Events in History at the Time the Poem Takes Place

The legend of St. Agnes. Keats's poem seems to take place sometime between the fourteenth and sixteenth centuries, when England was mostly Catholic and such figures as St. Agnes and St. Mark were still openly worshipped. Little is actually known about the real St. Agnes, except that she was one of the earliest Christian martyrs, who lived in Rome and was killed for her faith around 305 C.E. An early account of her martyrdom—attributed to St. Augustine of Hippo—describes Agnes as a beautiful maiden of 13 who rejected all her Roman suitors, including Eutropius, the governor's son, for God. According to legend, the governor offered Agnes lands and honors if she would marry his son, then threatened her with torture when she refused. Unmoved, Agnes remained true to her calling and the enraged governor ordered her stripped naked and led to a brothel. But Agnes's hair suddenly grew longer, covering her shame, and an angel appeared in the brothel and clothed her in pure white garments. Eutropius attempted to approach Agnes in the brothel but was struck blind for his offense. After curing him, Agnes was accused of witchcraft and sentenced to burn at the stake. The flames, however, would not touch her, and finally she was executed in the Roman manner by being stabbed in the throat. Her body was buried by the street Via Nomentana in Rome; a church was built over her grave circa 354.

DREAMS AND THE ROMANTIC IMAGINATION

The Romantics—writers and artists of the early nineteenth century who emphasized nature, spontaneity, and emotion in their works—were fascinated by imagination, which they believed to be the driving force behind poetic creation. Their fascination often translated into a keen interest in the nature of dreams, visions, and the supernatural, all of which were mined for inspiration. Mary Shelley, for example, drew upon a vivid nightmare to create her novel *Frankenstein* (also in *WLAIT 3: British and Irish Literature and Its Times*). Some authors even cultivated a dreamlike state by deliberately ingesting opium or laudanum; Samuel Taylor Coleridge's poem "Kubla Khan" was allegedly composed while the poet was in the throes of an opium delusion. Keats himself, mulling over the association between imagination and dreams, argued, "The Imagination may be compared to Adam's dream—he awoke and found it truth" (Keats in Perkins, p. 1208). The comment was a reference to Adam's dream of Eve's creation in Milton's *Paradise Lost* (also in *WLAIT 3: British and Irish Literature and Its Times*). Likewise the phenomenon he describes fits Madeline's situation in *The Eve of St. Agnes:* she dreams of love and passion, and on waking experiences the reality of both.

Because of her steadfastness and purity, Agnes became the patron saint of young virgins, her feast day falling on January 21. During the early days of the Catholic Church, the prayer "Agnus Dei" ("Lamb of God") was chanted on St. Agnes Day; two lambs were sacrificed and their wool saved to be woven by nuns. In the Middle Ages, a legend developed claiming that on St. Agnes's Eve (January 20) a virgin could learn the identity of her future husband by fasting for 24 hours, then lying on her back in bed. Her true love would appear before her in a dream, kiss her, and feast with her. The poem turns entirely on this conceit; Keats's heroine, Madeline, mulls over how, on St. Agnes's Eve, "Young virgins might have visions of delight, / And soft adorings from their loves receive / Upon the honeyed middle of the night, / If ceremonies due they did aright" (Keats, "Eve of St. Agnes," lines. 47-50). Keats emphasizes Madeline's innocence by continually associating her with the virgin saint; he refers to her as "St. Agnes' charmed maid" and describes how, on retiring to her chamber, she sees "in fancy, fair St. Agnes in her bed" ("Eve of St. Agnes," lines 192, 233).

Courtly love. Although "The Eve of St. Agnes" concentrates on atmosphere and emotion rather than on historical events, Keats nonetheless presents an accurate portrayal of the medieval courtly lover in the poem's yearning hero, Porphyro. The conventions of courtly love—a predominantly aristocratic and literary phenomenon—were established in the twelfth century by a French clerk, who wrote in *The Art of Courtly Love* : "Love is a certain inborn suffering derived from the sight of and excessive meditation on the beauty of the opposite sex, which causes each one to wish above all things the embraces of the other and by common desire to carry out all of love's precept in the other's embrace" (Capellanus in Matthews, p. 60).

While these symptoms were common to both sexes, the most recognized form of courtly love involved the man's swearing his total devotion and service to one woman, who was often not his wife. Historian Mark Girouard notes, "The accepted symbol of medieval courtly love was the knight kneeling at the feet of his mistress, as a superior and adored being. . . . Medieval courtly love could vary from the worship of an untouchable mistress by her adoring swain to passionately physical love affairs" (Girouard, pp. 199, 204). Keats's depiction of Porphyro corresponds closely to these descriptions. Hiding in the shadows, the lovestruck young man "implores / All saints to give him sight of Madeline / But for one moment in the tedious hours, / That he might gaze and worship all unseen; / Perhaps speak, kneel, touch, kiss—in sooth such things have been" ("St. Agnes," lines 77-81). Alone with Madeline, Porphyro initially maintains the same worshipful pose, declaring, "Thou art my heaven, and I thine eremite" ("St. Agnes," lines 277). But Porphyro and Madeline's lovemaking moves their relationship into the realm of the "passionately physical."

Marriage and the medieval woman. While the philosophy of courtly love placed women on pedestals and depicted them almost as celestial beings, for most medieval women life was far more earthbound. The daughters of aristocratic families were destined to become either wives or nuns: "a father or a rich male relative provided an upper-class girl with either a dowry to buy her a husband or a contribution to gain her entrance into a convent" (Bornstein, p. 47). It seems logical to conclude that these are the only two options open to Madeline, who is a baron's daughter.

Marriage during medieval times had little to do with romantic love and nearly everything to do with lands, wealth, and alliance, especially for upper-class families. Moreover, a young girl tended to wed the man selected for her by her fathers or guardian, who would be sure to settle a sizable dowry on her when she married, to preserve family dignity and pride: "Even in the lowest ranks of society a bride was expected to bring something with her besides her person when she entered her husband's house" (Power, p. 41).

Many marriages and betrothals were arranged when both parties were in their cradles; infant heiresses were particularly desired as brides. Children could marry at the age of seven but those marriages could be voided as long as the girl was under 12 and the boy under 14. The youth of the wedded couple was not necessarily an impediment to a successful marriage; a young husband and wife started out with few preconceived ideas or preferences, and so matured together.

Chastity was a virtue husbands confidently expected from their wives.

> Virginity was exalted for young girls, who were told to preserve their sexual purity and modesty before marriage. Chastity was exalted for wives, who were told to use sex only for procreation or to satisfy their husbands' needs and to remain absolutely faithful to their husbands. Chastity

The medieval concept of courtly love, illustrated in this duel between two suitors, fit very well with nineteenth-century treatments of women as virtuous, almost celestial beings.

> was proclaimed as the most important virtue for a woman and the foundation for her honor.
> (Bornstein, p. 29)

Certainly, the type of sexual experimentation of which Madeline secretly dreams in Keats's poem would be roundly condemned in the Middle Ages, as would her disobedience in eloping with Porphyro, the suitor whose family is bitterly at odds with her own.

The Poem in Focus

Plot summary . The poem begins on a cold winter's night—the St. Agnes's Eve of the title—as a lone beadsman (a person praying the rosary) prays for the dead in a deserted chapel. Within the nearby Great Hall, however, a feast is being held; among the noble guests is Madeline, a beautiful young girl. In accordance with the traditions of St. Agnes, Madeline fasts and avoids speech and eye contact with her would-be suitors, hoping to see her true love in her dreams.

One ardent suitor, Porphyro, has traveled across the moors to court Madeline, despite the vicious feud that exists between their families.

Angela, Madeline's old nurse and Porphyro's only ally, hides him from his enemies, and tells him of Madeline's observance of St. Agnes's customs. On learning this, Porphyro concocts a plan to enter Madeline's chamber "and there hide / Him in a closet, of such privacy / That he might see her beauty unespied, / And win perhaps that night a peerless bride" ("St. Agnes," lines 164-67). Initially dismayed by Porphyro's intention to use St. Agnes's rituals to his own advantage, Angela consents to help him after he assures her he will not harm Madeline.

Hidden in the closet, Porphyro watches, entranced, as Madeline enters her room, prays, then removes her costly clothes and jewels. Madeline climbs into bed, falls asleep, and dreams. At this point Porphyro steals from the closet and quickly prepares a sumptuous feast, then serenades Madeline with her own lute to wake her.

Awakened from her sleep, Madeline is jarred by the discontinuity between dream and reality: "There was a painful change, that nigh expell'd / The blisses of her dream, so pure and deep: / At which fair Madeline began to weep / And moan forth witless words with many a sigh" ("St. Agnes," lines 300-303). Finding the Porphyro of the waking world to be "pallid, chill, and drear," Madeline implores him to assume the persona of her dream lover again: "Give me that voice again, my Porphyro! / Those looks immortal, those complainings dear!" ("St. Agnes," lines 311-13). Porphyro approaches Madeline's bed, merging dream with reality by consummating their passion: "Into her dream he melted, as the rose / Blended its odour with the violet" ("St. Agnes," lines 320-21).

After their sexual encounter, Madeline struggles with ambivalent feelings, fearing Porphyro's desertion. He assures her that she is his bride and that he means to take her away with him. The lovers steal downstairs in the dark and find the revelers in a drunken sleep. Leaving their enemies behind, Porphyro and Madeline flee unhindered into the storm. The poem returns to its opening mood of silence, chill, and gloom as the revelers suffer nightmares, old Angela dies "palsy-twitch'd," and the lone "Beadsman," his prayers completed, "For aye unsought for" sleeps "among his ashes cold" ("St. Agnes," lines 376, 378).

Sex and sexuality. In Keats's own time, upper-class sexual attitudes and practices were undergoing change. From around 1670 to 1810 society had adopted a generally permissive, indulgent attitude toward sensual pleasure. En-couraging this attitude was the spread of Protestantism, which disagreed with the Catholic idea that sexual relations should be for procreation only. According to the Protestant view, marriage partners owed each other mutual comfort, and this involved sexual satisfaction. Other developments of the century also contributed to the trend, among them the ideas of French philosophers—such as Claude Adrien Helvitius (1715-71)—who held that passion and pleasure should be the guiding principles of life. Also influential were the writings of English philosopher John Locke. Locke's *Essay on Human Understanding* (also in *WLAIT 3: British and Irish Literature and Its Times*) stressed the importance of sensation to human knowledge, a notion that many of Locke's readers accepted and then connected to physical as well as emotional and mental experiences.

Discarding former inhibitions, people began to openly acknowledge the needs of the human body. The eighteenth century saw pornography become openly popular for the first time. Originally published in 1773, *Covent Garden Magazine or Amorous Repository* printed not only sexually titillating stories but also the advertisements of prostitutes. In 1795 *The Ranger's Magazine, or the Man of Fashion's Companion* began publication, printing a monthly list of prostitutes, descriptions of court cases having to do with adultery, and other such news. Pornographic pictures also found their way into respectable society, with the English caricaturist Thomas Rowlandson producing such prints for the Prince Regent around 1812.

In the 1770s, *The Lady's Magazine* warned its female readers that although sexual attraction was transitory, it was integral to marriage and an aspect of the union that the wife should strive to maintain. However, this same decade saw the beginning of a backlash in the form of newly repressive attitudes towards sex. These attitudes gained force and spread rapidly in the early 1800s. Segregation of the sexes was encouraged in many social situations, to shield virtuous women from possible corruption. Indeed the old language of courtly love would not have seemed amiss in certain nineteenth-century circles. "Men spoke of the women they respected as superhuman, angelic beings, pure and untainted, uncorrupted by any stain of vice. . . . [I]t was only natural for men to want to keep them pure by screening them off from contamination. Hence . . . the increasing segregation of women from worldly pastimes" (Erickson, p. 191). Keats himself came into conflict with this particular way of thinking. While writing about the controversial sexual encounter between Porphyro and Madeline in "The Eve of St. Agnes," he argued with friends about how explicit this passage should be. At one point, he wrote three additional stanzas providing more details of Porphyro and Madeline's lovemaking; his friend Richard Woodhouse reacted negatively, declaring that the alteration would "render the poem unfit for ladies, & indeed scarcely to be mentioned to them among the 'things that are'" (Woodhouse in Hill, p. 60). Keats heatedly responded that "he [should] despise a man who would be such a eunuch in sentiment as to leave a maid, with that Character about her, in such a situation and [should] despise himself to write about it" (Woodhouse in Hill, p. 60). He furthermore argued that Porphyro merely behaved as any normal man would when confronted by Madeline's beauty. Ultimately, however, Keats followed his friends' advice and left the description of the encounter more ambiguous.

In either version, "The Eve of St. Agnes" grapples with thorny issues of maturity and sexuality. The young lovers, Porphyro and Madeline, are caught in the age-old dance between men and women, desiring yet fearing to claim their adult sexuality. Porphyro's conduct is particularly ambiguous—at first, he desires only to "kneel, touch, kiss", but once hidden in Madeline's closet, he becomes a voyeur, secretly watching the object of his desire undress:

> Anon his heart revives; her vespers done,
> Of all its wreathed pearls her hair she frees;
> Unclasps her warmed jewels one by one;
> Loosens her fragrant boddice; by degrees
> Her rich attire creeps rustling to her knees."
>
> ("St. Agnes," lines 81, 226-230)

Later, spreading out the St. Agnes feast and singing in Madeline's ear to awaken her, he is as much seducer as would-be suitor, manipulating old legends to suit his purpose.

Madeline's own behavior is also somewhat problematic. Literary critic Jack Stillinger contends, "There are reasons why we ought not entirely to sympathise with Madeline. She is a victim of deception, to be sure, but of deception not so much by Porphyro as by herself and the superstition she trusts in" (Stillinger in Hill, p. 157). Stillinger draws attention to a stanza Keats decided to omit from the final printed version of the poem; in this verse, Madeline anticipates "a dizzy stream" of pleasures—"palpable almost"— in her dream, but fully expects "to wake again /

Warm in the virgin morn, no weeping Magdalen" (Keats, p. 214, note 6). While Madeline follows St. Agnes Eve rituals in hopes of receiving a vision of her future husband, it is the vision, not the reality, she appears to desire most. She wants to experience the pleasures but not the consequences of sexual experience. Her reaction to the loss of her virginity is mixed, at best:

> No dream, alas! alas! and woe is mine!
> Porphyro will leave me here to fade and
>   pine.—
> Cruel! what traitor could thee hither bring?
> I curse not, for my heart is lost in thine,
> Though thou forsakest a deceived thing;—
> A dove forlorn and lost with sick unpruned
>   wing.
>
> ("St. Agnes", lines 328-33)

"A TEMPEST FELL": WHAT KEATS LEFT OUT

See while she speaks his arms encroaching slow
Have zoned her, heart to heart,—loud, loud, the dark winds blow!. . .

For on the midnight came a tempest fell;
More sooth, for that his quick rejoinder flows
Into her burning ear and still the spell
Unbroken guards her in serene repose.
With her wild dream he mingled as the rose
Marrieth its odour to a violet.
Still, still she dreams, louder the frost wind blows!

(Keats in Stillinger, p. 457)

Seduced and believing herself deceived, Madeline fears abandonment by her lover; Porphyro's promises of marriage and a new home quell those fears, but significantly, Keats provides no guarantee of "happily ever after" for these lovers, whose tale ends with their flight into "an elfin-storm from faery land" ("St. Agnes," line 343).

Sources and literary context. Keats first received the idea for his poem from a friend, Isabella Jones, who told him about the legend of St. Agnes's Eve. He brooded over the story for some time, drawing inspiration from many different sources: Spenser's *The Faerie Queen* (also in *WLAIT 3: British and Irish Literature and Its Times*), numerous Gothic tales, and three French romances—"Flores et Blanche-Fleur," "Cléomades et Claremonde," and "Pierre de Provence et la Belle Maguelone." These diverse influences all shaped the finished poem; told in the graceful nine-line stanzas made famous in Spenser's epic, "The Eve of St. Agnes" relates a tale of feuding families and star-crossed love reminiscent of *Romeo and Juliet*, rich with imagery evoking both the modern Gothic and the medieval.

SPENSER AND THE ROMANTICS

Edmund Spenser, the Elizabethan poet, experienced a renaissance of his own when his epic romance *The Faerie Queen* was reprinted nine times during the eighteenth century. Many Romantics thrilled to the adventures of Spenser's Redcrosse Knight and other courtly heroes and heroines. However, Spenser's most visible legacy to the Romantics seems to be the elaborate stanza he devised for his romance. The Spenserian stanza is nine lines long with an interlocking rhyme scheme— *ababbcbcc*; the first eight lines are written in iambic pentameter, and the ninth line contains an extra iambic foot, called an Alexandrine. Many Romantics were fascinated by this metrical form and attempted to use it in their own works. Keats's "The Eve of St. Agnes," Shelley's *Adonais*, and Byron's *Childe Harold's Pilgrimage* were all composed in Spenserian stanzas.

Keats's composition of "The Eve of St. Agnes" also grew out of the "medieval revival" in painting, architecture, and literature, which gained momentum during the Romantic period (c. 1789-1832). Throughout much of the eighteenth century, the Middle Ages and everything connected to them—art, history, and literature—were held in disdain by "modern" Englishmen, who were quick to condemn the supposed barbarism and violence of their medieval past, expressing their preference for the rational temperament and polished manners of the present day. Nonetheless, a growing fascination with medievalism began at the end of the century. At first, this fascination took mostly an antiquarian turn, with historical enthusiasts seeking physical artifacts of the Middle Ages, such as manuscripts and ancient ruins. Medieval antiquarians played a significant role in resurrecting Gothic architecture, which made a comeback in the eighteenth century. While the Gothic revival had its ludicrous moments, such as the craze for sham ruins created by landowners seeking to add a picturesque note of decay to their estates, it also fueled further interest in medieval history, literature, and

life. Literary scholar Alice Chandler observes, "The very irregularity, asymmetry, and plenitude of Gothic architecture came to be a sign of its organic structure and thus of its closeness to nature. Towards the end of the eighteenth century, medieval people became associated with the natural and thereby with the heroic, the vital, and the creative" (Chandler, p. 9). To supremely jaded denizens of the super-rational eighteenth-century, medieval people "were thought to be closer to their feelings and freer and more unconstrained than modern man" (Chandler, p. 9).

Given the Romantics' attraction to nature, to which they turned for solace after witnessing increasing industrialism and the horrors of a violent revolution in France, it was perhaps inevitable that they should eventually be drawn to the vigor and freedom they perceived in the Middle Ages. Reprintings of such medieval romances as Sir Thomas Malory's *Le Morte D'Arthur* (also in *WLAIT 3: British and Irish Literature and Its Times*) and Edmund Spenser's *The Faerie Queen,* inspired many nineteenth-century authors to compose works set in medieval times and works rich with period details. Chief among such writings were the wildly popular historical novels of Sir Walter Scott (see **Rob Roy,** also in *WLAIT 3: British and Irish Literature and Its Times*). Coleridge, too, used medieval settings and atmosphere in such poems as "Christabel" and the lesser known "Ballad of the Dark Ladie." Keats's "The Eve of St. Agnes" likewise strove for an atmospheric effect, concentrating mainly on evoking the rich textures and colors of medieval times, as in the description of Madeline's chamber window:

> A casement high and triple-arch'd there was
> All garlanded with carven imag'ries
> Of fruits and flowers, and bunches of knotgrass,
> And diamonded with panes of quaint device
> Innumerable of stains and splendid dyes.
> ("St. Agnes," lines 208-212)

Keats's direct appeal to the readers' senses, as in his mouthwatering descriptions of the "jellies soother than the creamy curd, / And lucent syrops, tinct with cinnamon" that Porphyro provides for the feast, remain his most striking contribution to this tradition of neo-medievalist literature ("St. Agnes," lines 266-67).

Events in History at the Time the Poem Was Written

Courtship, marriage, and sex in nineteenth-century England. While less colorful or romantic than Porphyro and Madeline's flight across the moors, elopements did, in fact, take place in the England of Keats's day. Eager couples who wished to avoid formalities or expenditures—such as marriage licenses—could travel to the village of Gretna Green in Scotland and simply pledge themselves to each other in the presence of a witness, usually the village blacksmith. Despite being perfectly legal, marriage "over the anvil" was considered more improper than romantic and the custom would be curbed somewhat when a 21-day residency requirement before marriage was imposed in 1856.

In general, however, courtship and marriage tended to be more prosaically handled in Keats's time. A young girl of the middle to upper classes generally came "out" into society when she was 17 or 18; families that could afford such extravagances usually tried to give their daughters a "London season." Beginning after Easter, the "season" was "a dizzying three-month whirl of parties, balls, and social events" that, for many, "revolved around the deadly serious business of marrying off the young girls of the family to eligible and wealthy young men" (Pool, p. 52). A girl might have more than one season if her family's budget could afford it, but if she had not secured an offer of marriage within two or three seasons, she was considered a failure. A woman still unmarried by 30 was regarded as "on the shelf" and doomed to remain a spinster.

Men seeking wives took the marriage market quite seriously and were careful not to commit themselves until they were certain of their choice. Dancing with the same young woman more than twice at a ball could be considered tantamount to a declaration of marriage or, at least, serious romantic intent. Unmarried men and women also attempted to avoid being found together unchaperoned, lest their decisions be made for them by the possible scandal.

After a man proposed, he was expected to inform the parents of his future bride of his intentions, and acquaint them with his own financial circumstances and ability to provide for his wife. His future bride's parents, in turn, were obligated, to the best of their knowledge, to state their daughter's own fortune—which became the husband's property after marriage. Financial considerations were important to both families. Lawyers acting on behalf of the bride and groom would habitually negotiate a marriage settlement, addressing such concerns as spending money ("pin money") for the wife, "portions" for future children, and a "jointure"—in the form of money or

property—to be bequeathed to the wife on her husband's death. These transactions would take place well before the engaged couple walked down the aisle.

The marriage itself could be carried out in several ways, through the publishing of banns—an inexpensive procedure in which the couple's wedding was announced three Sundays in a row from the parish pulpit—or through the acquisition of a marriage license from a local clergyman, which would allow a couple to marry in any parish in which one of them had lived for 15 days. The well-to-do could also pay for a special license from the archbishop of Canterbury that allowed a couple to marry anywhere and anytime.

While the nineteenth-century middle- to upper-class Englishman was often sexually experienced before marriage—many engaged in affairs with domestic servants and prostitutes—his female counterpart was raised to be innocent and ignorant of such matters.

> In proper middle- and upper-class circles, for example, women were supposed to have no sexual contact before marriage—a hand around the waist, a kiss, and a fervent pressing of the hand was probably the accepted limit in most cases. . . . The consequence of this prudery was that women often came to their wedding nights ignorant and terrified. (Pool, p. 187)

The sexual double standard became only more pronounced as the century progressed. During the imminent Victorian age (1837-1901), daughters got little if any advice from their middle- and upper-class mothers on what to expect on their wedding nights.

The youngest Romantic. Along with Wordsworth, Coleridge, Byron, and Shelley, Keats is considered one of the major poets of the Romantic period. As the youngest and perhaps the most impressionable of the Romantics, Keats entered into various debates regarding poetry's true purpose, formulating and revising numerous theories. He was "astonishingly quick to enter with gusto into ideas, to explore them by adopting and believing in them, however transiently" (Perkins, p. 1116). Throughout his brief career as a poet, Keats experimented with different aesthetics and approaches, perhaps seeking a synthesis between the objective grandeur of older models—namely, Shakespeare and Milton—with the subjective introspection and intuition of Wordsworth and other Romantic writers. By 1820—the year in which "The Eve of St. Agnes" was published—Keats had clarified particular insights that characterize much of his major work. One literary historian observes:

> The strength of [Keats's later] poems is that they give complete and powerful expression to the natural human longing for a better world, a more perfect love, a lasting intensity of happiness, and yet they also remain faithful to the critical intelligence that forces us to acknowledge that dreams are only dreams and that in the sole world we know values are tragically in conflict. (Perkins, pp. 1117-18)

Reviews. "The Eve of St. Agnes" was included for publication in Keats's 1820 volume, entitled *Lamia, Isabella, The Eve of St. Agnes, and Other Poems*. Unlike *Endymion*, this collection met with a mostly favorable reception; an anonymous critic writing for the *Monthly Review* declared, "This little volume must and ought to attract attention, for it displays the ore of true poetic genius, though mingled with a large portion of dross" (Schwartz, p. 202). Several reviewers noted the new direction Keats appeared to be taking in his work. The poet Leigh Hunt, Keats's acquaintance, wrote in *The Indicator* that Keats had reached his prime: "The author's versification is now perfected, the exuberances of his imagination restrained, and a calm power, the surest and loftiest of all power, takes place of the impatient workings of the younger god within him. . . . Mr. Keats undoubtedly takes his seat with the oldest and best of our living poets" (Hunt in Schwartz, p. 227).

Among the individual poems in the volume, much attention was devoted to Keats's Miltonic poem, "Hyperion" (inspired by Milton's epic, *Paradise Lost*), and the Grecian romance, "Lamia." However, "The Eve of St. Agnes" was also singled out for its richness and beauty. In his review, Hunt quoted the verses describing Madeline kneeling in prayer before a stained glass window and exclaimed, "Is not this perfectly beautiful?" (Hunt in Schwartz, p. 223). A critic for the *Monthly Magazine* was likewise impressed by this "exquisite scene," noting, "A soft religious light is shed over the whole story" (Schwartz, p. 261).

It was during the Victorian Age (1837-1901), however, that "The Eve of St. Agnes" came into

its own, along with Keats's own poetic reputation. The poet Algernon Charles Swinburne observed that "[The Eve of St. Agnes] stands out among all famous poems as a perfect and unsurpassable study in pure colour and clear melody" (Swinburne in Hill, p. 62). And William Michael Rossetti, brother to painter-poet Dante Gabriel Rossetti and poet Christina Rossetti and one of Keats's early biographers, declared, "The power of 'The Eve of St. Agnes'. . . lies in the delicate transfusion of making sight and emotion into sound. . . . Perhaps no reader has ever risen from 'The Eve of St. Agnes' dissatisfied" (Rossetti in Hill, pp. 63-64).

—Pamela S. Loy

For More Information

Bate, Walter Jackson. *John Keats*. Cambridge, Mass.: Belknap Press, 1963.

Bornstein, Diane. *The Lady in the Tower: Medieval Courtesy Literature for Women*. Hamden: Archon, 1983.

Erickson, Carolly. *Our Tempestuous Day: A History of Regency England*. New York: William Morrow, 1986.

Girouard, Mark. *The Return to Camelot: Chivalry and the English Gentleman*. New Haven: Yale University Press, 1981.

Hill, John Spencer. *Keats: The Narrative Poems*. London: Macmillan, 1983.

Keats, John. "The Eve of St. Agnes." *The Works of John Keats*. Hertfordshire: Wordsworth Editions, 1994.

Matthews, John. *The Arthurian Tradition*. Shaftesbury: Elemental Books, 1994.

Perkins, David, ed. *English Romantic Writers*. San Diego: Harcourt Brace Jovanovich, 1967.

Pool, Daniel. *What Jane Austen Ate and Charles Dickens Knew: From Fox-Hunting to Whist—the Facts of Daily Life in 19th-Century England*. New York: Touchstone, 1993.

Power, Eileen. *Medieval Women*. Cambridge: Cambridge University Press, 1975.

Schwartz, Lewis M., ed. *Keats Reviewed by His Contemporaries: A Collection of Notices from the Years 1816-1821*. Metuchen, N.J.: Scarecrow, 1973.

Stillinger, Jack, ed. *Complete Poems by John Keats*. Cambridge: Bellknap, 1978.

Stone, Lawrence. *The Family, Sex and Marriage in England 1500-1800*. New York: Harper and Row, 1979.

The Faerie Queene

by

Edmund Spenser

THE LITERARY WORK

An epic poem set in the mythical time and place of Faerie Land; the first three books were published in 1590, and an additional set of three in 1596.

SYNOPSIS

The Faerie Queene chronicles the adventures of various knights, each the champion of a specific moral virtue, in the service of Gloriana, the Queen of the Faeries.

Born in the early 1550s, Edmund Spenser began his education at the Merchant Taylor's school in London. He later attended Cambridge on a sizar's scholarship, which was awarded to poor but deserving students. After leaving Cambridge with his M.A. in 1576, Spenser anonymously published *The Shepheardes Calender* (1579), a collection of pastoral poems that established him as a new and important voice in English poetry. Next came Spenser's masterpiece, *The Faerie Queene,* the first three books of which were published in 1590. By this time Spenser had pursued various appointments in the English administration of Ireland and had obtained a 3,000-acre estate in Munster. His duties did not appear to slow his literary output, for he continued to publish many books of poetry throughout the mid-1590s. The most significant of these were *Amoretti* and *Epithalamion* (1595), which loosely represented his courtship and marriage to Elizabeth Boyle, and the second edition of *The Faerie Queene,* which included three new books along with those of the first edition. Not long after this, Spenser's home in Ireland was destroyed in an Irish rebellion. He returned to England shortly before his death in 1599. Of all his writings, *The Faerie Queene* remains his most significant for its synthesis of literary traditions and its awareness of England's emerging identity as a national power.

Events in History at the Time of the Poem

Emergent nationalism and movement toward empire. Throughout the latter half of the sixteenth century, English intellectuals and educators called for a poetry that would put England on the cultural map of Europe, and, perhaps more than any other work of its time, *The Faerie Queene* fulfilled that demand. The need for such a work had grown out of England's recognition of its nascent greatness. Long on the political, economic, and cultural fringes of Europe, England had become aware of itself as a growing power that was playing a more significant role in

THE FAERIE
QVEENE.

Difpofed into twelue books,
Fafhioning
XII. Morall vertues.

LONDON
Printed for William Ponfonbie.
1590.

Title page of the first edition of *The Faerie Queene*, printed in London in 1590.

the affairs of the Continent than in the past. Its monarch, Elizabeth I, had brought a new degree of stability to the nation, although religious and political tensions seethed under the surface of civil life. English trade continued to prosper, and along with it a presence on the seas that not only made voyages of discovery possible, but established England as second only to Spain in military might.

When Elizabeth ascended the throne in 1558, she faced a nation torn by religious disputes that spilled over—as they did throughout Europe at this time—into internal politics and international relations. Elizabeth's father, Henry VIII, had wanted to divorce the Spanish Catherine of Aragon because she seemed unable to produce a male heir for him. When the Pope refused to grant what he wished, Henry divorced the Catholic Church instead, proclaiming himself the Supreme Head of the Church of England. He confiscated Church property and instituted an ecclesiastical structure that would tend to the peoples' souls in the manners to which they were accustomed, while consolidating royal power rather than contesting it.

At first, the Church of England sought to remain Catholic in all respects but its governance.

However, this proved nearly impossible to do. Instead, it became the rallying point for sectarian controversy and international intrigue. Citizens loyal to the Pope had thought the changes had gone too far, while those inspired by the works of Martin Luther and John Calvin thought they had not gone far enough. Both camps found allies on the Continent: the Catholics with France and Spain, the Protestants with the Netherlands, Geneva (highly Calvinist), and Saxony (highly Lutheran).

Much was at stake in the controversy. Although Henry did not appear to intend it as such, his separation of England from the Catholic Church was a watershed moment in which a nation state asserted its independence from spiritual, moral, and ecclesiastical rule. But the move came at quite a cost. Henry had to enforce his change by inaugurating an Oath of Supremacy; subjects took this oath to affirm their recognition of the monarch as the Supreme Head of the Church of England. When citizens of note refused to sign, like Henry's chancellor the leading humanist Thomas More, they were publicly executed.

When Henry's daughter Mary came to the throne, after the feeble and short reign of Edward (Henry's only son), the new queen attempted to return England to Catholicism. It was too late, however. Popular resistance against the papacy prompted Mary to burn people at the stake about 300 times to enforce her will, and this only plunged the nation into an increasingly bitter controversy that would not reach a significant resolution until the English Civil War of 1642. During her reign, Elizabeth balanced these tensions by asserting the importance of the English nation over sectarian strife, which was certainly a great achievement.

Elizabeth learned the importance of maintaining a middle ground in the years before she became queen. She was closely watched for signs of her true leanings, and in 1554 her half sister Mary came close to confirming a case of treason against her. While Mary was alive, Elizabeth carefully maintained an outward conformity to Catholicism, while secretly courting leaders of the more popular Protestant cause. She also knew the importance of being in favor with the populace, for her claim to the throne was not strong. In fact, all the Tudors had a rather weak claim to the throne, and Mary, who had declared Elizabeth illegitimate because she was the daughter of Henry VIII's second wife, had made the claim seem even more flimsy. Indeed, many

Queen Elizabeth was the inspiration for Gloriana, to whom Spenser dedicated his epic poem.

argued that Elizabeth's cousin Mary Queen of Scots had a stronger right to the English throne. Nevertheless, Elizabeth succeeded her half sister, bringing with her a strong sense of England's fears and hopes.

Early in her reign, Elizabeth's attentiveness to her country's needs was perhaps most clearly seen in her response to pressures to marry. Not only did her subjects want a clear succession to the throne, but they also believed that a woman's intellect and capacity to rule was weaker than a man's, which meant that Elizabeth needed a husband to guide her reign. At the same time, many of the most eligible suitors to Elizabeth's hand, such as the French duke of Anjou, were Catholic and so raised fears of domination and the reinstatement of unpopular religious rule by foreign powers. In the end, after many suitors and countless evasions, Elizabeth claimed herself espoused to her nation.

While Elizabeth's autonomy helped secure the nation against the unwelcome foreign influence of France or Spain, there were still many internal and external threats. From within, most threats centered around Mary Queen of Scots. Her long affiliation with hard-line French Catholics led to conflict with John Knox, a Puritan preacher who led a popular Scottish revolt against Mary. Mary was forced to seek refuge with her English cousin in 1568. Her presence in England as both a royal guest and a political prisoner became a lightning rod for Catholic plots, most of which conspired to assassinate Elizabeth and crown Mary in her place. For years, Elizabeth's counselors urged the queen to do away with this rival, but she refused. Finally, in 1586, agents of Elizabeth intercepted letters that revealed Mary's knowledge of a plot against Elizabeth's life led by Anthony Babington. With so much clear evidence of the threat that Mary posed, Elizabeth ordered the execution.

Armada. Mary's execution in 1587 precipitated what was to be England's greatest moment of danger and its greatest victory. With Mary dead, King Philip of Spain took up the Catholic cause to vindicate the faith by restoring England to Catholicism. Although he had once offered Elizabeth his hand in marriage if she were to change her religion, he had grown accustomed to fighting the English, who had allied themselves with Protestants in the Netherlands. In 1588 he attempted to attack England itself. He raised a massive armada of about 130 ships, 8,000 sailors, and 19,000 soldiers, hoping to establish a beachhead on the Isle of Wight and to incite the largely Catholic north of England to insurrection. Both of these hopes failed as an English fleet of less than 100 vessels, aided by a terrible storm, managed to scatter the Spanish forces.

The English regarded this victory as divine affirmation of its queen, of England's security, and, in general, of its unique and important place in human history.

Over these years England had many other things to celebrate as well. Despite the numerous conspiracies, religious tensions, and worries about succession, England enjoyed a great deal of prosperity. Its monarchy grew stronger, not only because of the wealth generated by Henry VIII's confiscation of Church properties, but also because of customs fees on an increasingly thriving mercantile trade. Elizabeth kept England largely isolated from the religious wars that decimated the Continent, and in this atmosphere trade prospered, especially the wool and iron trade. On the high seas, England enjoyed even more treasure as its vessels privateered those of the Spanish. England also began to establish itself in exploration; Sir Francis Drake circumnavigated the globe between 1577 and 1580, while one of the queen's favorites, Sir Walter Raleigh, promoted voyages to the New World and urged the Crown to establish colonies. Elizabeth was less than enthusiastic, not only because of her tightness with money, but also because she encountered enough trouble attempting to establish a strong English presence in Ireland. Nevertheless, England was looking toward expansion, and although some urged it, the nation had to wait almost a century to realize its potential in Asia, as well as the Americas.

The cult of the Virgin Queen. In *The Faerie Queene*, whose very title glorifies Queen Elizabeth, Spenser offers "mirrours more then one" in which the Queen could see herself: she could choose to identify with *The Faerie Queene* Glorianna, or with Belphoebe, a virgin huntress modeled on the Roman goddess Diana (Spenser, *The Faerie Queene*, 3.Proem.5). In the former, she could see reflections of her might as a monarch, in the latter "her rare chastitee" (*The Faerie Queene*, 3.Proem.5). Moreover, at the same time that the poem invites Elizabeth to admire these representations, it asks her to leave off for a moment her admiration of Cynthia, another name for the goddess Diana, which Sir Walter Raleigh used to portray Elizabeth. In these gestures, Spenser is engaging in the complex and sometimes competitive struggle to gain the queen's ear, and perhaps her favor. These displays belong to a phenomenon called the "Cult of Elizabeth," or the "Cult of the Virgin Queen"— pageants, tournaments, dramas, speeches, and poems that allegorized Elizabeth—usually as

goddess—and her courtiers—usually as suffering, lovelorn youths. While on the surface entertaining, these allegories sometimes cloaked serious political intentions.

The cult has its origin in sixteenth-century assumptions about gender, monarchy, and power. In the male-dominated world of sixteenth-century England, a female monarch created a great deal of anxiety, especially after the disastrous rule of Mary. As mentioned, women were regarded as intellectually and morally inferior to men, and therefore in need of male governance. But with a female as the supreme ruler of all subjects, there was no sanctioned medium through which she could be influenced, save the role of husband, and this had been ruled out. Elizabeth sought to have her subjects understand that she, a woman, could be sufficiently virtuous and self-governing to rule effectively on her own. In the early weeks of her reign, she had a speech read to her privy council and to Parliament that indicated how these male leaders were to regard her: "In the end this shal be for me sufficient that a marble stone shall declare that a Quene, having raigned such a time lyved and dyed a virgin" (Frye, p. 15). Of course this did not hinder her counselors and Parliament from urging her to marry, but as time went on, they not only accepted her virginal status but began to regard it as the source of England's unique strength. Moreover, her much touted virginity provided them with a role through which they could approach her in opulent, allegorical fictions.

Almost every procession and public occasion included displays in which Elizabeth's subjects expressed their desires for political or military positions—often through cultic images of the queen. In 1579, for example, the poet Sir Philip Sidney collaborated on an entertainment called *The Four Foster Children of Desire*. A hybrid of drama and tournament, or joust, it figured Elizabeth as Desire, who was unattainable because of her virtue and the protection of her foster children. While the fiction is, on the surface, benign, it most certainly had a political edge when performed before Elizabeth and the duke of Anjou on his last attempt at marriage negotiations. In this light, Protestant politics were being forwarded in the guise of entertainment.

The most lavish display of the cult of Elizabeth occurred four years earlier, in 1575, when Elizabeth visited Robert Dudley, the earl of Leicester, at Kenilworth Castle. Dudley had long been one of Elizabeth's favorites, but a troubled past and his reputation for unreliability kept his sphere of influence in Elizabeth's reign rather limited. Seeking to expand his role in the realm, most likely in the direction of assisting the Dutch Protestants against Catholic Spain, Dudley displayed his great devotion to Elizabeth in shows and entertainments spanning three weeks. Upon her arrival she was greeted with a tableau of the Lady of the Lake who had been imprisoned since the days of Arthur and could only be freed by a "maid" (a reference to Elizabeth) whose powers were greater than those of the Roman goddesses Diana and Juno. She also saw an impressive fireworks display that included charges that passed under the water and appeared to be extinguished, only to rise out of the water and blaze until finally consumed. The following day, a poem interpreted the display to mean that no "cold answers" by the queen could quench Dudley's "desire" (Gascoigne, pp. 91-131).

Many other performances followed, all of which were designed to put Dudley and Elizabeth's relationship before the public in hopes that Elizabeth would adopt a more aggressive military posture in the Spanish-Dutch controversy that would center on Dudley's generalship. Of course, the power to create these depictions of the queen rested not only with her courtiers, but with Elizabeth herself. At Kenilworth, for instance, the queen apparently censored some of the entertainments because they raised the long-dead issue of a marriage with Dudley. Thus, it was acceptable to appeal to the queen in ways that befit the quasi-deific image of her, but not in ways that concerned a romantic relationship between her and Dudley. The images surrounding the cult of Elizabeth, in which she might appear as Cynthia, Diana, Deborah, Astraea, Belphoebe, and in many other guises, were part of a complex game between queen and subjects, and this game kept her femininity, her chastity, and her power constantly in view.

The Poem in Focus

Plot summary. Spenser sets his poem in the ancient days of the mythical land of Faerie, at a time when Gloriana, the queen of Faeries, is holding a 12-day feast. On each day, an occasion arises that requires a knight to undertake an adventure, each of which is thematically linked to a moral virtue (temperance, chastity, friendship) that is explored through a book of the poem. These books have their own plot lines, though some plots and characters bridge the gap from one book to another. A knight whose tale is virtually complete may make a cameo appearance as a minor character in later tales.

Book 1 concerns the Redcrosse knight, or holiness, whose quest begins when a maid comes to the court of the Faerie Queene asking for a knight to rescue her parents' land from a dragon. In Book 2, Sir Guyon, the champion of temperance, seeks to capture the evil enchantress Acrasia, who has murdered the parents of a young child. Book 3, which explores the virtue of chastity, centers on the female knight, Britomart, whose quest is double: to rescue a lady from the enchanter Busirane, and to find Artegall, who is destined to be her husband. Of all the books, Book 4 (Friendship) is the most singular in that it continues the many unresolved story lines of Book 3, features two knights instead of one, and yet gives the two knights, who are the champions of friendship, little presence in the plot. Book 5, the legend of Justice, features Artegall, whose task it is to rescue Irena from the great injustices of Grantorto. Last, in a legend of courtesy, Sir Calidore seeks to capture the Blatant Beast, whose bite marks the wounded (both deserving and undeserving victims of rumor) with shame and dishonor. Of the five, the two most frequently read books are 1 and 3.

Book 1—The Legend of Holiness. In the court of the Faerie Queene, a young maid named Una appears, riding on a white ass and wearing the black clothes of mourning. She tells the court that her parents' land has been ravaged by a huge dragon, and she seeks a knight to rid the land of this beast. Accompanying her is a dwarf, who leads a war horse carrying an empty suit of armor, which has one red cross on the shield and one on the breastplate. The lady identifies this as the armor of a Christian and explains that it is necessary for success in the quest. A young rustic (named Redcrosse) takes up the armor and sets out with Una and the dwarf to meet the dragon.

Along the way, Redcrosse meets with many adventures that develop an allegory relating not only to the basic story of sin and grace shared by every Christian, but also to the religious struggles in Spenser's England. Redcrosse and Una enter a forest with a bewildering array of paths and soon lose their way. They come upon a cave occupied by Errour, a monster shaped like a serpent from the waist down and a woman from the waist up. As Redcrosse attempts to slay Errour, he is wrapped up in her coils and almost strangled. Una reminds him to "add faith unto your force," and with this he is able to defeat Errour, but only after unleashing her offspring (*The Faerie Queene*, 1.1.19). Following this dubious victory, Redcrosse and Una find their way to the hermitage of Archimago, who outwardly appears to be a holy man but is actually a sorcerer. He conjures up two spirits, one of which he makes identical to Una and the other he makes look like a young man. He shows Redcrosse the sight of this false Una making love to the young man, and Redcrosse, disillusioned, abandons the true Una.

Travelling with the dwarf, Redcrosse fights three Saracen knights, and in the process takes up with a new damsel. Although he knows her as Fidessa (faithfulness), she is really Duessa, who is associated with the Whore of Babylon and the Antichrist. For his victories over the Saracen knights, he finds shallow glory in the House of Pride, where he witnesses a procession of the seven deadly sins, led by Queen Lucifera. When, however, the dwarf discovers the torture and murder taking place in the House of Pride, he tells Redcrosse, who leaves both the House and Duessa behind. Duessa, however, catches up with him beside the banks of a stream. Weakened by his trials, Redcrosse takes off his armor and begins to woo Duessa, but his courting is interrupted by the giant Orgoglio, who captures him and takes Duessa for himself.

As Redcrosse slips further into sin, Una searches for him while confronting many dangers of her own. She is almost raped by one of the Saracen knights, but is saved by a troop of satyrs and fauns. Here she is no more free than before as they attempt to worship her in their misguided way. However, she finds an ally in Satyrane, who promises to help her locate Redcrosse. He helps her to escape the pagan band, but soon gets drawn into a bloody fight with the knight who had tried to assault Una. She quietly slips away during their fight, then meets up with the dwarf, who informs her of Redcrosse's imprisonment. Together, they chance upon Prince Arthur, who in Spenser's poem was seeking the court of Gloriana before he became the familiar King Arthur of Camelot. Arthur rescues the knight Redcrosse from the giant's dungeon and leaves the physically wasted knight to Una's care. After Arthur departs, Una and Redcrosse come upon the cave of an individual named Despair, who nearly succeeds in getting Redcrosse to take his own life.

With his physical and spiritual downfall complete, Redcrosse is delivered by Una to the House of Holiness, where he regains strength for his fight with the dragon. The battle lasts three days, which equates it with the three days of Christ's temptations and the three days during which he descended into Hell. The fight is also fought on the familiar biblical terrain of Eden. After the first day, Redcrosse falls into the streams flowing from the well of life, whose waters wash away sin. After the second day, he is restored by the tree of life, which stands near the tree of knowledge. Thus renewed, he rescues the kingdom on the third day by slaying the dragon through its mouth.

The king and queen of Eden betroth Una to Redcrosse, but Archimago and Duessa intervene one last time in an attempt to drive the two apart. The villains' true identities and schemes are discovered, however, and it is proclaimed that Redcrosse and Una will marry after he completes his seven years of service to the Faerie Queene.

Book 3—The Legend of Chastity. Whereas the narrative of Book 1 is fairly linear, Book 3 is marked by multiple plot lines, though Britomart's quest is the clear center of the book. It opens with two knights—Guyon, the champion of temperance from Book 2, and Prince Arthur—traveling through the land of Faerie. They come upon a third knight, whom Guyon challenges to a joust. The stranger unseats Guyon, but Arthur makes peace. The poet identifies the stranger as Britomart, a female knight who is seeking the one she is destined to marry. No sooner is she identified than a woman riding a white horse bursts through the brush, chased by a "foster" (forest dweller) who is trying to rape her. Guyon and Arthur rush after the lady, while Arthur's squire, Timias, pursues the foster.

Britomart, true to the steady virtue of chastity, chooses not to participate in this trial of male desire and returns to her quest alone. She comes to the fields surrounding the Castle Joyeous, where knights must pledge their loyalty and service to the mistress of the castle, Malecasta, or face a challenge from her knights. Such a challenge is underway as the Redcrosse knight refuses to swear loyalty to any other lady but Una. While he is beset by six knights, Britomart enters the battle and handily rescues Redcrosse.

After the battle, Malecasta receives both knights at her castle. While they are being entertained, Redcrosse takes off his armor, but Britomart refuses, and her female identity remains hidden. That night, Malecasta, who still thinks Britomart is a male knight, tries to seduce her, causing Britomart to leap out of bed and hold a surprised and screaming Malecasta at sword-point. In the melee that follows, Britomart receives a light wound, but because everyone fears her prowess, she and Redcrosse leave the castle with little trouble. As the pair set forth, Britomart tells how she came to see her destined lover, Artegall, in Merlin's mirror, and how Merlin had told her of the great destiny of their progeny, who would one day rule Britain.

Eventually the two knights part, and Britomart finds her way to a rocky shoreline and complains bitterly about her inability to find Artegall. While she is complaining, a knight appears and warns her to leave the shore or fight. Frustrated by her fruitless search and disdainful of this challenge, she chooses to fight and badly wounds her opponent. This knight is Marinell, whose mother had learned in a prophecy that he was to receive a deep wound from a woman's hands, and has long forbade her son to have any contact with women. Nonetheless, Florimell, the woman almost raped at the beginning of the story, loves him and was in fact trying to find him when the foster assaulted her.

At about this point the narrative shifts from Britomart to a dazzling array of interlinked stories, all of which show different shades of romantic love. Arthur and Guyon are still chasing Florimell, and Arthur's squire Timias pursues the foster. The foster and two others ambush Timias, and although Timias manages to kill them, he is seriously wounded. As providence would have it, the nymph Belphoebe happens by and, taking pity on the squire, brings him to her bower and nurses him back to health. He falls in love with Belphoebe, but so praises her chastity that he finds his own desires frustrated. Meanwhile, a tale of beastly lust is told as Florimell continues to flee, until her horse lies down in exhaustion. On foot now, Florimell finds a cottage belonging to a witch and her son. The son courts Florimell, which sets her off again. She makes her way to the seashore and takes refuge with an old fisherman in a boat. He attempts to rape her, but she is then rescued by the shape-shifting Roman god Proteus and taken to his lair under the sea. In an attempt to console her son, the witch creates a false Florimell, around whom another set of misadventures occurs. Jealousy and adultery are displayed in the tale of old Malbecco and his young wife Hellenore. A young knight named Paridell seduces Hellenore and later carries her off. At this point in the narrative, Britomart returns as a guest in Malbecco's house. She defeats Paridell in a fight and returns to her search for Artegall.

Instead of finding Artegall, however, Britomart finds a knight crying on the ground. When she inquires, she learns that the knight, Sir Scudamour, is grieving over the abduction of his lady, Amoret, by the sorcerer Busirane. Busirane's castle is surrounded by a wall of fire that Sir Scudamour cannot penetrate. Britomart manages to get through and enter the castle, but for a long time is unable to find any occupants. Eventually a door opens and out comes a courtly procession that depicts images of the suffering and damage caused by lust. At the end of the procession, Britomart sees Lady Amoret, bound to a pillar at the waist. Before her sits the sorcerer Busirane, writing with blood taken from Amoret's heart. As he is about to stab Amoret with a dagger, Britomart strikes him down and captures him. The reunion of Amoret and Scudamour ends the book, while many other plot lines, including Britomart's search for Artegall, remain to be concluded in other books of *The Faerie Queene*.

Religious strife in the legend of holiness. In the poem's allegory, Spenser openly aligns many of Redcrosse's enemies with Catholicism, whose more zealous adherents had created trouble for Elizabeth throughout her reign. When Redcrosse strangles Errour, the monster vomits papers and books that scholars identify as Catholic tracts. The sorcerer Archimago's language is also telling:

> For that old man of pleasing wordes had
> store,
> And well could file his tongue as smoth as
> glas;
> He told of Saintes and Popes, and evermore
> He strowd an *Ave-Mary* after and before.
> (*The Faerie Queene*, 1.1.35)

Archimago uses his beguiling language to speak about things that Protestants objected to in the Catholic faith. Duessa, too, is identified with Catholicism. When the giant Orgoglio captures Redcrosse, the whore Duessa responds to Orgoglio's favors, receiving from him the three-tiered crown of the Pope, which symbolizes his rule over the world. To make the Catholic connection even more diabolical, Spenser has Orgoglio give her a terrifying beast to ride. This image, of a woman riding a monstrous beast, drawn from the New Testament Book of Revelations (17:3-18), is that of the Whore of Babylon, which Protestants saw figured in the Catholic Church.

Another important feature in Spenser's allegory of Catholicism is the consistent depiction of treachery, which alludes to the covert nature of Catholic opposition to Elizabeth's rule.

Archimago, for example, reveals his malevolent side only after Redcrosse and Una go to sleep. Similarly Duessa assumes a disguise and a false name, Fidessa, which shows the falsity of her faith. After Prince Arthur defeats Orgoglio and frees Redcrosse, Duessa is disrobed to reveal a loathsome hag whose outward ugliness mirrors her spiritual corruption. But the duplicity of these characters is most strikingly depicted in the final canto, when Duessa, whom many scholars have associated with Mary Queen of Scots, has Archimago, disguised as a messenger, provide false letters to claim that Redcrosse is betrothed to the daughter of the Western Emperor (Catholic Rome). Here the various kinds of duplicity and treason in the poem evoke the subterfuge discovered in the many plots to bring down Elizabeth and place Mary on the throne.

Beyond the vilification of the Catholic cause, in the poem Spenser affirms the core ideals of a moderate Protestantism. To the Protestant mind, Catholicism placed too much emphasis on the efficacy of human power to secure salvation. To varying degrees, Protestants rejected the importance of the priesthood in administering the sacraments that led to salvation, and they questioned whether the human activity surrounding penance, confession, and good deeds had in themselves the power to save. As Redcrosse prepares to enter the House of Holinesse, the narrator defines a relationship between "spiritual foes" and human power:

> Ne let the man ascribe it to his skill,
> That thorough grace hath gained victory.
> If any strength we have, it is to ill,
> But all the good is Gods, both power and eke
>   [also] will.
>
> (*The Faerie Queene*, 1.10.1)

By claiming that God's grace alone has the power to bring salvation, the poem links its ideas of holiness with the Protestant emphasis on grace through faith alone. Indeed, Redcrosse's first spiritual guide within the House of Holinesse is "Fidelia," or faith. Out of faith comes the grace to practice Christian virtues of penance, charity, mercy, and prayer.

The cult of Elizabeth in the legend of chastity. Since Book 3 represents the virtue closest to the mystique of Queen Elizabeth, it naturally includes some of Spenser's most intense engagements with the cult of the virgin queen. This distinct fusion of political will and erotic desire especially shapes the Belphoebe-Timias episode, which allegorizes the relationship between Eliz-

abeth and Spenser's patron, Sir Walter Raleigh. In this allegory, Timias's fight with the "fosters," or foresters, depicts Raleigh's role in putting down the Desmond Rebellion, which took place in Ireland from 1579 to 1583, when Raleigh was a captain in the English Army. In one instance, Raleigh and a few of his men were approaching a ford, when rebels ambushed them. Raleigh got across successfully, but the man behind him fell off his horse in the middle of the crossing while being pursued by the rebels. With others in the company too far back to help, Raleigh wheeled around and scattered the rebels, allowing his soldier to safely regain his horse. Although the rebels outnumbered Raleigh and his men, he managed to face the rebels down and proceed on safely. Spenser celebrates his patron's martial heroism when Timias is ambushed at a ford:

> The gentle Squire came ryding that same way,
> Unweeting of their wile and reason bad,
> And through the ford to passen did assay;
> But that fierce foster, which late fled away,
> Stoutly forth stepping on the further shore,
> Him boldly bad his passage there to stay.
>
> (*The Faerie Queene*, 3.5.18)

While Raleigh's fight at the ford did not result in any loss of life, Timias kills three fosters, which alludes to Raleigh's role in the execution of the rebellion's three leaders, the earl of Desmond and his two brothers (Bednarz, pp. 53-55).

Having asserted his patron's faithful service to the Crown through Timias, Spenser then unites the wounded squire with Belphoebe, whom he has earlier introduced as a "mirror" of the Queen's chastity. Belphoebe finds herself immediately attracted to Timias and, in accordance with her virtue, is startled by her attraction:

> . . . when that Lady bright
> Beside all hope with melting eyes did vew,
> All suddeinly abasht she chaunged hew,
> And with sterne horrour backward gan to
>   start.
>
> (*The Faerie Queene*, 3.5.30)

Her pity for Timias wins out, and she revives him with medicinal herbs (the poem mentions tobacco, a New World discovery associated with Raleigh). As Timias recovers, he asks—in line with the deifying tendencies of the cult of Elizabeth—if Belphoebe is a goddess or an angel. Blushing, she claims to be a maid. With the help of her hunting companions, who have now caught up with her, Belphoebe takes Timias to her dwelling. Spenser likens her abode to a "stately Theatre," evoking Elizabeth's court with the word "stately" and the performative qualities of courtly life with the word "Theatre" (*The Faerie Queene*, 3.5.39). Speaking the language of the cult of Elizabeth, Timias complains of his thwarted desires and broods anxiously over his fitness to offer due service to Belphoebe. As with many of the court entertainments in Elizabeth's day, Spenser's Timias-Belphoebe story promotes a deserving courtier whose expressions of ardor translate into a bid for preferment.

Sources and literary context. So ambitious were Spenser's plans for *The Faerie Queene* that the poet synthesized into the epic almost every important work of literature he would have known. In its conception as "historicall fiction" divided into 12 books of 12 cantos each, Spenser draws upon the great epics of ancient Greece and Rome: Homer's *Illiad* and *Odyssey*, and *Virgil's Aeneid*. The latter was especially important in that it celebrated the establishment of the Roman Empire, which Spenser hoped England would one day emulate. In choosing Arthurian legend as the landscape of his historical fiction, Spenser seeks to sum up his own nation's achievements in the genre of romance. The poet's debt to Chaucer is also evident throughout the epic, but perhaps most clear in Spenser's choice of stanza. His unique and very difficult nine-line form in some ways hearkens to, but exceeds, the eight-line stanza that Chaucer used in *Troilus and Criseyde*. In the names of many characters and in the similarity of some plot lines, Spenser also sought to emulate the great Italian romance-epics of Ariosto's *Orlando Furioso* and Tasso's *Gerusalemme Liberata*. In his prefatory letter to Raleigh, Spenser claims that his idea to fashion each book around a virtue derives from a list of 12 virtues found in Aristotle's writing. Although no such list has ever been identified in the philosopher's works, the exact identity of such a source is not as important as the intent signified by Spenser: to harmonize classical moral virtues with Christian ones, and to synthesize a philosophical system with poetic insight. Such literary ambition and exuberance has rarely been equaled.

In the literary culture of his own day, Spenser's *The Faerie Queene* occupies a unique and preeminent place. Most writers in Spenser's day were either "amateurs" or "professionals." Amateurs tended to be aristocrats who wrote to display their intellectual and linguistic gifts. They circulated their works in manuscript, showed no interest in writing for money, and did not think of printing their works. Sir Philip Sidney, the author of *Astrophel and Stella*, *The New Arcadia*, and *The Defence of Poetry*, exemplifies the amateur trend in Elizabethan literature. Professionals like Shakespeare wrote to make money, usually by selling their plays for a one-time fee to theater companies, though they also sought to make a profit from publishing. But Spenser—by writing an epic that celebrates the English nation, promotes empire, and incites readers to virtuous action through moral examples—was claiming to occupy a status different from either the amateur or the professional: that of the laureate poet, whose ambition is to be *the* great national poet whose work has a significant relationship to that nation's identity. The genre most fit for the laureate was the epic, and that Spenser's laureate status was recognized is clear when a contemporary called Spenser "our Virgil" (Helgerson, p. 26).

THE LETTER TO RALEIGH

~

Spenser included a letter to his patron, Sir Walter Raleigh, in the 1590 edition of *The Faerie Queene*, in order to help readers better understand the poem and avoid the "gealous opinions and misconstructions" of misinterpretation (*The Faerie Queene*, p. 737). He tells Raleigh that the poem's "generall end" is "to fashion a gentleman or noble person in vertuous and gentle discipline," and that he follows Homer and others in giving examples of "a good governour and a vertuous man" (*The Faerie Queene*, p. 737). Spenser's profession of literature's power to shape the moral lives of noteworthy people echoes the shift toward humanist education, which had been long underway in England and throughout Europe. During the Renaissance, educators sustained the medieval curriculum of the *trivium* (the disciplines of grammar, rhetoric, and logic) and the *quadrivium* (mathematics, music, geometry, and astronomy), but shifted its focus. Whereas medieval education emphasized logic and preparing individuals for the Church, humanist educators favored rhetoric and preparing individuals for civic leadership. Spenser goes on to defend his allegorical method as a means of delighting his readers, and thus inducing them to his more important moral intent. Spenser's letter was removed from the 1596 edition of the *The Faerie Queene*, perhaps because Raleigh had fallen out of favor with the queen. Nevertheless, the letter has remained important for the light it sheds on Spenser's literary and cultural motivations.

Reception and impact. Though the particular circumstances are unknown, scholars agree that when Spenser visited London in 1590, he had some opportunity to present *The Faerie Queene* to Elizabeth. Later, in February 1591, he received from the Crown a life pension of 50 pounds a year, an extraordinary reward for a work of literature in his day. Beyond that, it is difficult to gauge the work's critical reception, though it is widely thought that the work was well received. Spenser published the second edition of *The Faerie Queene* in 1596, and posthumous editions published in 1609 and 1611 indicate a steady, long-term demand for the poem.

In relation to future generations, Spenser's impact shows most clearly in John Milton, whose poetic ambitions easily rival Spenser's. In his great treatise against censorship, the *Areopagitica,* Milton calls his predecessor "our sage and serious poet Spenser, whom I dare be known as a better teacher than Scotus or Aquinas" (Milton, p. 728). No extended commentary on Spenser's works occurs until 1715, and the literary tastes of the eighteenth century kept interest in the poet low. His work would receive much higher acclaim from the Romantics of the nineteenth century, with their interest in Arthurian legend and imaginative expansiveness.

—Jeff Morris

For More Information

Adams, Robert M. *The Land and Literature of England: An Historical Account.* New York: Norton, 1983.

Bednarz, James. "Raleigh in Spenser's Historical Allegory." *Spenser Studies 4* (1983): 49-70.

Cheney, Patrick. *Spenser's Famous Flight: A Renaissance Idea of a Literary Career.* Toronto: University of Toronto Press, 1993.

Frye, Susan. *Elizabeth I: The Competition for Representation.* Oxford: Oxford University Press, 1993.

Gascoigne, George. "The Princelly Pleasures at Kenelworth Castle." In *The Complete Works of George Gascoigne.* Vol. 2. Ed. John W. Cunliffe. Grosse Pointe: Scholarly Press, 1969.

Giamatti, A. Bartlett. *Play of Double Senses: Spenser's Faerie Queene.* New York: Norton, 1990.

Heale, Elizabeth. *The Faerie Queene: A Reader's Guide.* Cambridge: Cambridge University Press, 1987.

Helgerson, Richard. *Self-Crowned Laureates: Spenser, Jonson, Milton, and the Literary System.* Berkeley: University of California Press, 1983.

Milton, John. *Complete Poems and Major Prose.* Ed. Merritt Y. Hughes. Indianapolis: Bobbs-Merrill, 1957.

Montrose, Louis. "The Elizabethan Subject and the Spenserian Text." *In Literary Theory/Renaissance Texts.* Baltimore: Johns Hopkins University Press, 1986.

Spenser, Edmund. *The Faerie Queene.* Ed. A. C. Hamilton. New York: Longman, 1977.

Strong, Roy. *The Cult of Elizabeth: Elizabethan Portraiture and Pageantry.* London: Thames and Hudson, 1977.

Frankenstein

by

Mary Shelley

THE LITERARY WORK

A novel set in Switzerland, Germany, Russia, and Britain in the late eighteenth century; first published in England in 1818.

SYNOPSIS

Determined to create human life, a scientist named Frankenstein produces a monstrous man and then abandons him. Desperate for love and guidance, the rejected creature turns violent, killing those closest to Frankenstein and haunting his creator until his death.

Born in London in 1797, Mary Shelley was the daughter of William Godwin and Mary Wollestonecraft, both of them writers and revolutionaries famous for their radical ideas. Godwin was primarily a political philosopher, and Wollstonecraft was an early feminist who died 11 days after Mary Shelley's birth (see ***A Vindication of the Rights of Woman,*** also in *WLAIT 3: British and Irish Literature and Its Times*). Raised by Godwin and his new wife, Mary grew up in an intellectual, open environment, where ideas and the arts flourished and idealistic admirers crowded around the family table. One of her father's admirers, the Romantic poet Percy Bysshe Shelley, fell in love with the beautiful young intellectual, and the two eloped in 1814, when Mary was 16, despite the fact that Shelley was already married. The next decade of Mary's life was marked by tragedy: her first child was born in 1815 and died shortly after; Mary's half-sister, Fanny Imlay, and Percy's wife, Harriet, both committed suicide the following year; Mary and Percy's second child, William, died as a young boy. Mary lost her third child as well, and, after giving birth to the one child who would survive, Percy Florence, went on to suffer a dangerous miscarriage. Then, in 1822, Percy Shelley, whom Mary had married in 1816, drowned in the Gulf of Spezia. Mary, who was not yet 25 at the time, would spend her 30 remaining years living modestly. Indeed, Mary's greatest success would be *Frankenstein,* written when she was only 19 and conceived after a night of telling ghost stories in the Alps with Percy, the poet Lord Byron, and By-

ron's doctor, John Polidori. The resulting tale of an overly ambitious scientist and his monstrous creation has come to be known as one of the greatest horror stories ever written and continues to be relevant today because of the questions it raises about science's dangerous potential.

Events in History at the Time of the Novel

The French Revolution. Part of the enduring importance of *Frankenstein* can be seen in the way it tapped into the concerns of its age, combining the central dualities of a culture in which reason and science were "displacing religion as centers of value" (Levine and Knoepflmacher in Crook, p. 59). The late eighteenth century (when the novel is set) and early nineteenth cen-

British imperialism, stretching towards the Arctic regions during the early nineteenth century, is satirized in this political cartoon. Shelley's novel captures the empire's wanderlust in the adventure-seeking explorer Robert Walton.

tury (when it was written) were times of momentous change and upheaval in Europe; between 1770 and 1830 Europe's link to its feudal past was severed, and the continent moved decisively into the modern age. The French Revolution was only the most dramatic of these changes, inspiring people around the world with its rhetoric of freedom and liberty—of overthrowing the old guard in order to create a new, more just world. In the first few years of the Revolution, between 1789 and 1791, everything seemed to have changed in France, and much of Europe celebrated. As described in 1824 by the English poet Robert Southey "Nothing was dreamt of but the regeneration of the human race" (Southey in Travers, p. 1).

In retrospect, the French Revolution was the first major political event in what historians call the modern period. Ancient structures of power were torn down, feudal rights diminished, the relationship between the church and state was renegotiated, and groups long denied any political representation became empowered. The implications of the Revolution were even more far-reaching; the revolutionary concepts of "the people" and their rights set off a vigorous optimism outside France, and the replacement of traditional state-sanctioned religious power established the tone for an age that would increasingly find its main source of moral values in patriotism and democracy rather than in religion. More than anything, however, the French Revolution provided the example of a society completely undone and then refashioned in a newer, brighter hue. Though the Revolution ultimately ended violently, disintegrating into the infamous Reign of Terror and the continual upheavals of the Napoleonic Wars, its possibilities colored the imagination of an entire age—for better or for worse.

The Industrial Revolution. The Industrial Revolution was as utterly transforming as the French Revolution, restructuring society in ways irreversible and profound. Industrialization in general has altered how people live, where they live, what they value, and how they define their lives; indeed, it was "the most fundamental force in world history in both the nineteenth and the twentieth centuries" (Stearns, p. 1). The Industrial Revolution began, more or less, in the eighteenth century in western Europe, and in Britain in particular. Before 1700 Western technology was firmly anchored in agricultural modes of production, despite advancements in such fields as metallurgy, textile manufacturing, and the harnessing of energy. During the eighteenth century, those developments began to take a shape that would eventually lead to a complete overhaul of society.

In Britain, agricultural advances took place at the same time that huge strides in science allowed for a variety of new technologies. By the 1730s a string of inventions had begun to shift the cotton industry towards a more efficient factory system. More inventions followed, including the perfection of the steam engine by James Watt in the 1760s. By the end of the century the production of cotton was rapidly increasing. The new machines required workers to cluster in factories rather than work in their homes, contributing to the larger trend of urbanization that was changing the face of Britain in the late eighteenth century. Britain's cotton capital, Manchester, grew from a town of roughly 25,000 in 1772 to a city of 367,232 in 1851. Cities all over Britain exploded as people became less reliant on large farms and estates, and more dependent on industry. Families were forced into the cities in increasing numbers, but the lives they found there were not always pleasant. The early revolution was fueled by the labor of men, women, and children who were often severely underpaid and mistreated. Tremendous hardships seemed inevitable given the massive restructuring of society along lines so untested and uncharted. Never before had so much seemed possible; yet never before had the future of mankind seemed so bleak and unsure.

Science at the turn of the nineteenth century.
The dual sense of possibility and dread that characterizes *Frankenstein* and the age in which it was written owed much to the scientific advances of the time. Though the so-called Scientific Revolution had begun in the late seventeenth century, it was only in the later eighteenth that science began to take on the prestige and value in popular culture that made it an important part of people's lives. Indeed, public awareness of developments in science increased steadily in this period. The Frenchman Bernard de Fontenelle helped to popularize scientific progress with a series of publications, while in England a wide market opened up for scientific textbooks and scientific books geared towards the general reader. Museums specializing in scientific apparatus or natural history appeared, and lectures devoted to scientific topics became increasingly popular. Though science became fashionable and lent a sense of optimism and excitement to the age, only rarely was the layman's knowledge profound. With the increasing specialization of subject areas, and the growing use of mathematics in scientific study, advanced knowledge was becoming more difficult to acquire. Instead, phenomena—in areas such as stargazing, mesmerism, and electricity—attracted the public's attention more than the actual scientific processes behind them.

Especially captivating were the advances made in the study of electricity, a topic that would greatly influence the writing of *Frankenstein*. The eighteenth century saw a number of developments in this field of study, from the construction of the first machine to generate electricity in 1706 to the invention of the dry pile and battery of cells in 1800. A multitude of theories, many of them wrong, were put forward to explain electrical phenomena; in 1791, for instance, Luigi Galvani came out with the results of his long study of "animal electricity," or "galvanism," theorizing that electricity is intrinsic to animal tissues. Galvani made headlines when, in 1802, one of his disciples applied a Voltaic pile connected by metallic wires to the head of a recently killed

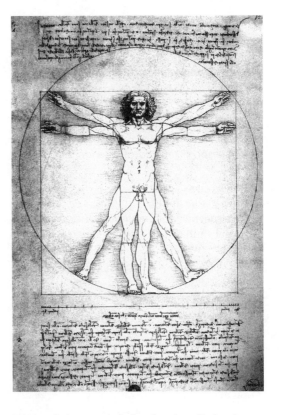

Writing during a period of profound medical and scientific discovery, young Shelley gave birth to a protagonist fascinated by the human anatomy. Depicted here is an eighteenth-century diagram based on Leonardo Da Vinci's drawing of the proportions of the human figure, showing the real-life fascination.

ox. At the same moment the ox's "eyes were seen to open, the ears to shake, the tongue to be agitated, and the nostrils to swell, in the same manner as those of the living animal" (Aldani in Mellor, p. 105). In 1803 a more lurid demonstration took place, in which galvanic electricity was applied to the corpse of a recently hanged criminal, whose "jaw began to quiver . . . adjoining muscles . . . horribly contorted, and . . . left eye actually opened" (Aldani in Mellor, p. 105). Events like these were widely reported and discussed throughout Europe in the early nineteenth century.

The most popular science of the early nineteenth century, however, appears to have been that of Erasmus Darwin (1731-1802), Charles's grandfather, who wrote two encyclopedic technical works—*Zoonomia; or The Laws of Organic Life* and *Phytologia*—as well as the two long poems *The Botanic Garden* and *The Temple of Nature*. While most scientists had viewed the universe as perfect, fixed, and divinely ordered well into the eighteenth century, Erasmus Darwin and others began weakening this view by the beginning of the nineteenth. By 1803 Darwin accepted that the earth must once have been covered by water, and that all life must therefore have evolved from the sea. One of the earliest theorists of evolution, Erasmus Darwin believed that life was spontaneously being generated at every moment, and that sexual reproduction was the most advanced method of creation; as he wrote in *The Temple of Nature,* "the most perfect orders of animals are propagated by sexual intercourse only" (Darwin in Mellor, p. 98). This idea has a great resonance in *Frankenstein;* Victor Frankenstein substitutes paternal, solitary propagation for sexual reproduction, thus "[reversing] the evolutionary ladder described by Darwin" (Mellor, p. 100).

Another scientist who heavily influenced the writing of Shelley's novel was Sir Humphry Davy, who, like Darwin, was a poet as well as a scientist. In 1802 Davy gave a famous introductory lecture to a chemistry course at the newly founded Royal Institution. This lecture was published almost immediately afterwards and titled *A Discourse, Introductory to a Course of Lectures on Chemistry,* from which many of the reasons for Victor Frankenstein's fascination with chemistry seem to have been derived. In a celebratory tone, Davy argues that chemistry is the basis for most of the other sciences; "the phenomena of combustion, of the solution of different substances in water, of the agencies of fire; the production of rain, hail, and snow, and the conversion of dead matter into living matter by vegetable organs, all belong to chemistry" (Davy in Mellor, p. 92). Chemistry, Davy goes on to say, has acquainted the scientist with the different ways in which the external world relates, thus endowing him with the power to change and modify nature, "not simply as a scholar, passive and seeking only to understand her operations, but rather as a master, active with his own instruments" (Davy in Mellor, p. 93). It is this optimism that characterizes many of the general attitudes toward science and industry in the late eighteenth and early nineteenth centuries; and, as Anne Mellor argues, it is this optimism that Mary Shelley, in Frankenstein, sees as profoundly dangerous (Mellor, p. 93).

Science and religion. The scientific changes that began taking place during the latter part of the eighteenth century had serious implications for religious thought and practice. Typically, the modern period is seen as, among other things, a process of increasing secularization, greatly promoted by the scientific discoveries that so in-

flamed the population during the Romantic period. Indeed, during this period any comfortable alignment between science and religion was undermined by the proliferation of new fields and specialties, as well as by discoveries that displaced Isaac Newton's conception of the universe as perfectly mirroring God's order.

By the time of Newton's death in 1727, an easy alliance between science (called "natural philosophy" until the early nineteenth century) and the Anglican Church had been well established. Newton's natural philosophy had supported the design argument of natural theology, delineating the order and laws of nature, God's "second book," and so had been sanctioned by the Church (Yeo, p. 320). This vision was of a world made up of inert corpuscles of matter that moved only as a result of divine forces. The advances in science during the Romantic period—often called a second scientific revolution, one to rival the revolution associated with Newton and other seventeenth-century scientists—created a variety of fields and disciplines that could no longer support, in total, this unified Newtonian vision. Furthermore, attitudes were shifting steadily. The influential theologian and scientist Joseph Priestley, for instance, did not regard matter as passive and inert, but, rather, as containing its own inherent force. This was a view the Newtonians had always feared, for it either equated God with nature, or excluded God from it entirely.

Despite the fact that the alliance between natural philosophy, the Church, and the Royal Society, which had dominated scientific study in Newton's day, was weakened by the scientific advancements of the Romantic period, religion and science remained intricately linked throughout this period. Religious orthodoxy declined somewhat, and the advancements made less sure the grounds for belief, but actual atheism was very uncommon during this time. Even those most critical of the Newtonian universe were by no means atheists. Priestley's books on science and theology were shelved side by side at the Bristol library.

Romanticism. Romanticism is typically seen as a movement that started roughly at the time of the French Revolution. While somewhat difficult to define, the movement was inextricably linked to the political changes and revolutionary fervor of its age. Romantic thinkers objected to traditional ideas and artistic practices, rejecting the Enlightenment philosophies that had characterized most of the eighteenth century with their unshakable faith in human reason and the ability of men to grasp the reality of the world. To those attempting to define the world in the wake of this extreme optimism and rationalism, such reliance on human reason seemed too reductive, too uninterested in the transcendent and the otherworldly. Romanticism instead emphasized emotion and sensation over abstract reason, the subjective and personal over the objective, and the irrational over the rational. In relation to Shelley's novel, Romanticism can be seen as a rejection of the kind of eighteenth-century rationalism and materialism that characterize Victor Frankenstein's science. Indeed, Victor Frankenstein can be viewed as an example of eighteenth-century optimism carried too far. Romanticism, on the other hand, took issue with this commitment to science and materialism; at odds with this vision of the world, the Romantic protagonist both raged against the confines of his society and transcended them.

Part of the Romantic project was to point to the limitations of science, and to illuminate those aspects of experience that an overly reasoned science tended to neglect. Intuition and imagination were just as important as reason, the Romantics argued, and yet were excluded from scientific analysis—as were inner experiences like the appreciation of nature or beauty. Indeed, the misery accompanying the Industrial Revolution demonstrated to many Romantic writers the limitations of science as a means to salvation and happiness.

The Novel in Focus

Plot summary. *Frankenstein* opens with a frame story, told in a series of letters written by Robert Walton, an ambitious young explorer aboard a polar expedition sailing Arctic waters in the hope of finding either a passage to the North Pole or the secret of the magnet. Walton's ambition for glory and his faith in humanity's potential for discovery are unchecked; he is the scientist filled with his own power, asking "what can stop the determined heart and resolved will of man?" (*Frankenstein*, p. 8). His enthusiasm for the great venture is marred only by his lack of a friend. He finds that friend in Victor Frankenstein.

One day the sailors, making their way through the waters north of Russia, are forced to wait for the ice surrounding them to break. In the distance they catch sight of a shape being pulled across the ice in a dogsled. The shape disappears, but the next morning Robert Walton goes on deck to find his sailors convincing a bedraggled, paranoid man to leave another sled and come aboard the ship. Walton is surprised to see that the man is a fellow European. Once the stranger, Victor Frankenstein, is nursed back to health, he agrees to tell Walton how he ended up in his near-death state; this story makes up the rest of the novel.

EXPLORING THE ARCTIC

Since the late 1500s, when explorers set out to find a trade route across the North Pole, until April 6, 1909, when Robert Peary, his assistant Matthew Henson, and four Inuit completed a final sprint across the ice, the North Pole eluded explorers and adventurers. An obsession that cost many their ties to family and even their lives, the search for a passage to the North Pole occupied men of all kinds. In 1607 Henry Hudson of Britain's Muscovy Company sought passage over the North Pole to Asia, only to be stopped by a wall of ice. In 1773 the Phipps expedition, mounted by Britain's Royal Society and Admiralty, and also stopped by ice, determined that no simple sea route existed. Around the time *Frankenstein* was written, Britain's secretary of the Admiralty, John Barrow, began a series of naval expeditions to find a route to China that would pass between the islands of Arctic Canada—a search that continued until Sir John Franklin, leading an expedition in 1845, disappeared without a trace. Robert Walton's passion in the novel, then, is reflected in countless tales of real men who sacrificed everything in search of the same passage.

Victor Frankenstein begins his narration with the story of his childhood: how his family was distinguished and loving, and how they lived in Geneva, where they formed a stable part of established society. Victor's closest companions were Elizabeth—his adopted sister, whom, it was understood, he would one day marry—and his best friend, Henry Clerval. While Elizabeth fills her days with the "aerial creations of the poets," and Henry immerses himself in tales of chivalry and romance, Victor delights in investigating the causes of things; "the world was to me a secret which I desired to divine" (*Frankenstein*, p. 22). At age 13 Victor discovers the work of the medieval alchemists, which opens an entire new world to him. Though his father disparages this study, carefully explaining to Victor that modern science possesses far greater powers than the medieval, Victor's enthusiasm is not dampened. He proceeds to become a passionate disciple of the alchemists and occultists of old. Then, at age 15, Victor witnesses a violent thunderstorm, during which the oak in front of his house is utterly destroyed by lightning. It happens that a natural philosopher is visiting the family, and he explains to them his ideas on electricity and galvanism. These ideas throw Victor into a fresh passion and course of study that eventually leads him to a German university, where he immerses himself in this new science that can "penetrate into the recesses of nature and show how she works in her hiding-places" (*Frankenstein*, p. 33).

In Ingolstadt, Germany, Victor does little but read, with passion, books on natural philosophy and chemistry. For the first two years Victor does not even visit Geneva—being too "engaged, heart and soul, in the pursuit of discoveries which I hoped to make" (*Frankenstein*, p. 35). More and more the question haunts him: "Whence, I often asked myself, did the principle of life proceed?" (*Frankenstein*, p. 36). As his studies turn more in this direction, he begins spending nights in the churchyard examining dead bodies. Then, suddenly, in the middle of all this darkness "a sudden light" breaks in on him and he discovers the secret of "bestowing animation on lifeless matter" (*Frankenstein*, p. 37). From dissecting rooms and slaughterhouses Victor gathers up his materials, then locks himself into his solitary chamber to create a living man. It is on a dreary night in November that, with a jolt of electricity, Victor finally infuses life into the painstakingly formed man lying at his feet. After all his work, by the "glimmer of the half-extinguished light," Victor beholds the "yellow eye of the creature open" (*Frankenstein*, p. 42).

The scientist's reaction is one of horror as he sees that his beautiful creation, now filled with life, is wretched and monstrous to behold—the yellow skin barely covering veins and muscle, the eyes watery, the lips straight and black. "Now that I had finished," Victor narrates, "the beauty of the dream vanished, and breathless horror and disgust filled my heart" (*Frankenstein*, p. 42). Victor flees the room, and in his feverish wanderings runs into his old friend Henry Clerval, who has come to Ingolstadt to study Oriental literature and languages. Clerval notes how thin and wasted Victor has become, but Victor does not reveal the reason for his sickness. When he returns to his chamber, Victor finds, to his intense relief, that the creature has vanished. A nervous fever possesses Victor for many months, during which time Clerval nurses him back to health.

During his recovery, Victor once again enters into contact with Elizabeth and his family, and makes plans to return to Geneva. What finally draws him there is grim news indeed. A letter from his father arrives detailing the murder of Victor's young brother, William. There is a suspect—Justine Moritz, a kind young woman who has been adopted by the Frankenstein family. She appears to be the murderer because a possession of William's has been found in her pocket. In the midst of his grieving, Victor catches sight of a horrible figure running through the trees and realizes instantly that the creature is the one responsible for the murder of William and the framing of Justine. Fearing that no one will believe his wild tale, and convincing himself that Justine could not possibly be convicted anyway, Victor does not speak up. He remains silent even as the evidence points more and more towards Justine's guilt, and even when she is convicted of William's murder and executed. In anguish, Victor blames himself for both deaths.

It does not take long for the creature to approach Victor, revealing himself one day at the base of Mount Blanc. Victor reacts with rage and hatred at the sight of the "vile insect" and "abhorred monster," but the monster implores Victor to hear his story. Finally, Victor agrees, and the creature begins to speak (*Frankenstein*, p. 83). His tale is a sad one.

The monster speaks of waking in Victor's apartment with no language or knowledge of the world, then retreating into the woods to wander helplessly, searching for food and warmth, and finally taking shelter in a shack alongside a little cottage. Realizing that his appearance provokes only hatred and fear wherever he goes, he hides in his shelter, observing the family who lives in the cottage, learning their language and reading from a stack of books he comes upon. The monster waits one year before revealing himself to this family, whom he has grown to love, hoping that he can appeal to the blind father's sympathy. But once again he is reviled and rejected. When the children walk in upon their father conversing with such a monstrous figure, the son attacks the creature and the entire family flees. Full of despair, the creature longs desperately for someone to love. Realizing he will never find such a person in normal society, he determines to hunt down his creator and request that a female companion be made in the same mold as he. The creature finds some of Victor's papers in his clothing, which help lead him to Victor's family. In his travels he is again unfairly rebuffed by those he encounters. The creature begins to grow bitter and to seek "a deep and deadly revenge" that would "compensate for the outrages and anguish I had endured" (*Frankenstein*, p. 126). It is in this mood that he comes across beautiful little William, who shrieks at the sight of the creature and threatens that his father will punish the "hideous monster" (*Frankenstein*, p. 127). Thus begins the creature's murderous hatred of mankind and of his creator, leading him to kill William and then frame the innocent Justine for his murder.

Now, says the creature, all he wants is what is due him: a companion with whom he can flee society forever. Feeling he has no other choice, Victor agrees, and the creature leaves. Victor does not begin on this venture immediately, however. He journeys to England, then takes a long tour of the country with Henry Clerval before setting up a laboratory in Scotland to begin his project. Finally, having almost completed the creature's female companion, Victor looks up to catch sight of the creature grinning at the window. In horror, and vowing not to repeat his first mistake, Victor destroys his own work as the creature looks on in rage and grief. The creature promises revenge: "Your hours," he tells Victor, "will pass in dread and misery"; also he warns his creator, "I shall be with you on your wedding-night" (*Frankenstein*, pp. 152-53). Victor leaves the island and learns that the creature has murdered Clerval, but still the scientist does not take his creature's words seriously enough to delay getting married to Elizabeth. Victor returns to Geneva and makes the arrangements. Despite his precautions, Elizabeth is murdered on the night of their wedding.

In grief and frenzy, Victor now vows his own revenge, and thus begins a cat-and-mouse game between the creator and his creation in which Victor pursues the creature and the creature enables his pursuit, leading Victor towards the North Pole. It is here that Victor, near death, is rescued by Robert Walton. Having finished his strange, long story, Victor finally dies. Walton hears a noise, then leaves; when he returns to his cabin, he finds the creature standing over the body of Frankenstein, heartbroken and filled with remorse. "Once," the creature says, "I falsely hoped to meet with beings who, pardoning my outward form, would love me for the excellent qualities which I was capable of unfolding. . . . But now crime has degraded me beneath the meanest animal. . . . It is even so; the fallen angel becomes a malignant devil. Yet even that enemy of God and man had friends and associates in his desolation; I am alone" (*Frankenstein*, p. 204). The creature tells Walton that he will travel north and ascend a funeral pile, exulting "in the agony of the torturing flames"; with these words he jumps from the ship and onto an ice raft lying close by, soon to be "borne away by the waves and lost in darkness and distance" (*Frankenstein*, pp. 205-206).

Gravediggers, corpses, and anatomists. Victor Frankenstein's midnight prowlings in "unhallowed damps of the grave," where he "disturbed, with profane fingers, the tremendous secrets of the human frame," might seem merely the product of a Gothic imagination or classic horror novel (*Frankenstein*, p. 39). The truth is, however, that bodysnatching was widespread in Mary Shelley's time, and, what is more, the graveyard in which Shelley's mother was buried, the St. Pancras parish churchyard, was a "well-known haunt of bodysnatchers" (Richardson, p. xiii). The bodysnatching era, as it has come to be known, can be seen as a dark underside to the wild scientific discoveries and expansion of the Romantic age. Before this time, the scientist's legal access to corpses had been limited to the gallows, from which the bodies of executed murderers would be turned over to science as an extension of the criminal's punishment. Because execution was a fairly common punishment for an assortment of crimes, this promise of bodily mutilation and dissection made the murderer's punishment that much more severe.

In the eighteenth century, rising interests in human anatomy, physiology, and medicine increased the demand for corpses. This demand led almost inevitably to a thriving black market in corpses and the widespread practice of grave robbing. Around the time of the novel, all medical education was private, and surgeons and anatomists had to take it upon themselves to procure the corpses needed for instruction. These scientists often paid good money for stolen corpses and, after dismembering them, even sold them to their students for a profit. Historically, it seems likely that the first bodysnatchers were anatomists or surgeons and their students. In the late seventeenth century, for instance, an observer commented that the disappearance of an executed gypsy's body was probably due to some surgeon "to make anatomical dissection on" (Richardson, p. 54). In the early eighteenth century a clause for surgeon trainees at the Edinburgh College of Surgeons forbade students' involvement in grave exhumation, and later students were known to accompany professional bodysnatchers to the graveyards. By the early nineteenth century, it appears that bodysnatching was almost solely performed by professionals—those doing it only for purposes of money—rather than by the scientists themselves, mostly because of public outrage over body and corpse stealing.

In Mary Shelley's time, no buried corpse in the country was secure from the bodysnatcher. These bodysnatchers—or, as they were also known, "resurrectionists"—almost always worked in small gangs, with one person standing lookout while the rest dug open the graves. Freshly filled graves made digging easy, and the bodysnatchers' tools were usually simple: shovels, a sack, perhaps a hook. The most accessible graves were the mass graves that held the urban poor. As one bodysnatcher explained in 1828 before the Select Committee on Anatomy, "I like to get those [bodies] of poor people buried from the workhouses, because, instead of working for one subject, you may get three or four" (Richardson, p. 60). These paupers' graves were often left open, the corpses in them exposed, until they were completely filled, thus making the bodysnatcher's job relatively simple.

Bodysnatchers bore the brunt of public scorn and punishment for these acts, but, eventually, anatomists too would be convicted for their participation. In 1831 a new bill, known as the Anatomy Act, was introduced to Parliament, recommending that the government itself procure the bodies of paupers and criminals for scientific use. This new bill, which remains the basis of modern law on the subject, effectively ended the bodysnatching era.

Sources and literary context. The story of *Frankenstein*'s origin is famous: during an 1816 vacation to the Alps and after a night of reading ghost stories aloud, the Shelleys and their friends, Lord Byron and his doctor, Polidori, each agreed to write a story of his or her own. While the three men promptly began their tales, all of which were quickly abandoned, Mary struggled to think of a story that would "rival those which had excited us to this task" and "make the reader dread to look round, . . . curdle the blood, and quicken the beatings of the heart" (*Frankenstein*, pp. xxiii-xxiv). Day after day passed with no result. Then one night, after listening to Byron and Shelley discuss the work of Erasmus Darwin and the possibility of animating corpses, Mary could not

sleep. Instead, as she writes in her introduction to *Frankenstein,*

> My imagination unbidden, possessed and guided me. . . . I saw—with shut eyes, but acute mental vision—I saw the pale student of unhallowed arts kneeling beside the thing he had put together. I saw the hideous phantasm of a man stretched out, and then, on the working of some powerful engine, show signs of life and stir with an easy, half-vital motion. Frightful must it be, for supremely frightful would be the effect of any human endeavour to mock the stupendous mechanism of the Creator of the world. . . . The idea so possessed my mind that a thrill of fear ran through me. . . . On the morrow I announced that I had *thought of a story*. I began that day with the words "It was a dreary night of November."
>
> (*Frankenstein*, p. xxv)

Percy Shelley encouraged Mary to develop the story into a longer tale, on which she worked steadily throughout the summer and following fall. Her work was disrupted that winter by the suicides of both Fanny Imlay, Mary's half-sister, and Percy's wife Harriet. Taking up the work again in early 1817, Mary finished the book by April.

Frankenstein had many literary and intellectual influences. Its original title, *Frankenstein, or the Modern Prometheus,* shows the influence of Greek myths about the god Prometheus, who supposedly shaped human beings from clay and brought them fire. Various Romantic writers invoked the Prometheus image, Shelley uniquely by tying it to the scientist-creator. Also influential on *Frankenstein* were the works of individuals such as William Godwin, John Milton, Jean Jacques Rousseau, and Samuel Taylor Coleridge and the other Romantic poets. The novel was most heavily situated within the Gothic tradition said to have begun with Horace Walpole's 1765 novel, *Castle of Otranto*. This influence is not surprising: In the two years before writing Frankenstein, Mary Shelley read Anne Radcliffe's **The Mysteries of Udolpho** (also in *WLAIT 3: British and Irish Literature and Its Times*) and *The Italian*, in addition to numerous other Gothic novels. Their influence is clear, even though the "mouldering abbey is transformed into Victor's laboratory," the ghost into Victor's creature, and the villain's pursuit of the heroine into the creature's pursuit of Victor (Crook, p. 58). Traditional Gothic conventions include creaking castles, evil aristocratic villains, and images of death and decay, including rotting chains, corpses, graveyards, and suggestions of the supernatural. Despite its lack of ghosts and haunted mansions, *Frankenstein* shares the spookiness and thrilling darkness definitive of the genre. It shares also the sense of crossing lines or boundaries and of otherworldliness. The enormous popularity of the Gothic novel had actually passed by 1816, but the genre, with its emphasis on darkness, madness, the supernatural, and strange passions, has never been fully dead.

Reception. The first edition of *Frankenstein* was published anonymously, though it included a dedication to William Godwin that provided a clue to the author's identity. This first edition received a mixed reception. Out of the nine journals to evaluate the novel in 1818, four gave it overwhelmingly negative reviews. *The Quarterly Review*, for instance, announced that "taste and judgment alike revolt at this kind of writing . . . the greater the ability with which it is executed the worse it is—it inculcates no lesson of conduct, manner or morality; it cannot mend, and will not even amuse its readers, unless their tastes have been deplorably vitiated" (*The Quarterly Review* in Baldick, p. 57). Despite the severity of such criticism, the book was almost immediately a popular success. It also received some critical acclaim from the eminent novelist Walter Scott, who complimented the author's "uncommon powers of poetic imagination" (Scott in MacDonald and Scherf, p. 35). The novel inspired its first stage adaptation only five years later with the production of Richard Brinsley Peake's *Presumption; or The Fate of Frankenstein*. By 1826, 14 more dramatizations had been based on Shelley's story. Subsequent generations would continue to receive the novel enthusiastically. In 1931 Universal Studios' film version of *Frankenstein*, starring Boris Karloff, cemented the image of the mad scientist and his hideous progeny. Along with numerous other retellings, the film has ensured *Frankenstein's* enduring fame.

—Carolyn Turgeon

For More Information

Baldick, Chris. *In Frankenstein's Shadow: Myth, Monstrosity and Nineteenth-Century Writing*. Oxford, England: Clarendon Press, 1987.

Barbour, Ian G. *Religion and Science*. San Francisco: HarperSanFrancisco, 1997.

Black, Jeremy. *Eighteenth-Century Europe*. 2nd ed. New York: St. Martin's, 1999.

Capelotti, P. J. *By Airship to the North Pole*. New Brunswick, N.J.: Rutgers University Press, 1999.

Crook, Nora. "Mary Shelley, Author of *Frankenstein*." In *A Companion to the Gothic*. Ed. David Punter. Oxford: Blackwell, 2000.

MacDonald, D. L., and Kathleen Scherf. "Introduction." *Frankenstein; or The Modern Prometheus*, by Mary Shelley. Orchard Park, N.Y.: Broadview Press, 1994.

Mellor, Anne K. *Mary Shelley: Her Life, Her Fictions, Her Monsters*. New York: Routledge, 1988.

Richardson, Ruth. *Death, Dissection and the Destitute*. New York: Routledge & Kegan Paul, 1987.

Shelley, Mary. *Frankenstein*. New York: Bantam, 1991.

Stearns, Peter N. *The Industrial Revolution in World History*. Second edition. Boulder, Colo.: Westview, 1998.

Travers, Martin. *An Introduction to Modern European Literature*. New York: St. Martin's, 1998.

Yeo, Richard. "Natural Philosophy (Science)." In *The Romantic Age: British Culture 1776-1832*. Ed. Iain McCalman. Oxford: Oxford University Press, 1999.

Gulliver's Travels

by

Jonathan Swift

J onathan Swift is generally recognized as the English language's most accomplished prose satirist. Born of an Anglo-Irish family in Dublin, Ireland, in 1667, he worked in England for ten years (1689-99) as private secretary to the British statesman Sir William Temple, becoming ordained as a priest in the Anglican Church in 1696. In 1704 Swift published his first major work, *A Tale of a Tub*, a sharp, ironic attack on corruption in religion and letters. Over the next several years, he published numerous shorter works—essays, articles, pamphlets—on political, religious, and social issues. In 1710, when the Tory party won political power from the Whigs, Tory leaders induced Swift to change sides (he had been a Whig), and for four years he was a leading propagandist for the Tory cause. His political influence ended when the Whigs regained control in 1714, and Swift returned to Ireland, where he became Dean of St. Patrick's Cathedral in Dublin. He wrote little for the next six years, beginning *Gulliver's Travels* in 1721, while at the same time resuming work on other more overtly political subjects (as in *The Drapier's Letters* and *A Modest Proposal*). It was *Gulliver's Travels*, however, that won him his widest audience. The narrative has enjoyed an unusual double life— the entire work as a sophisticated satire of politics and human nature, and Part I alone as a timeless children's fantasy.

THE LITERARY WORK

A satirical narrative set in various fictional kingdoms between 1699 and 1715; first published in 1726 as *Travels Into Several Remote Nations of the World*.

SYNOPSIS

Lemuel Gulliver, a young Englishman, takes sea journeys to Lilliput, where people are six inches tall; to Brobdingnag, where people are giants; to Laputa, a flying island of scientists and philosophers, and its neighboring kingdoms; and to the land of the Houyhnhnms, wise and rational horses who use humanlike brutes as domestic animals.

Events in History at the Time of the Narrative

The Glorious Revolution. During the 1680s, the English political landscape experienced a series of upheavals that would determine its rough outlines for decades to come. This disruption culminated in 1688 with the "Bloodless" or "Glorious" Revolution, in which the English Parliament replaced James II, England's last Catholic king, with his Protestant daughter, Mary, and her hus-

Half-title page from an 1894 edition of *Travels Into Several Remote Nations of the World,* the original title of Gulliver's Travels.

band, Prince William of Orange, who became King William III of England. As in 1660 when Charles II had been restored to the throne, Parliament again asserted its right to decide the succession of the English throne, but this time it did so in a way that would have lasting constitutional implications. The offer of the crown to William and Mary was made on conditions—listed in a Bill of Rights—that limited the Crown's power. Among other provisions, Catholics were barred from occupying the throne; the king was no longer allowed to suspend laws that banned non-Anglicans from filling government positions (including Parliament), nor was he allowed to impose levies or to keep a standing army without Parliament's consent; and parliamentary elections and proceedings were to be free of interference by the Crown or the courts. Finally, should William and Mary remain childless, after their deaths the crown was to pass to Mary's younger sister, Anne.

The party system: Whigs and Tories. A new and important factor in both the revolution itself and the constitutional settlement that followed it was the role of political parties. Two parties, the

Whigs and the Tories, had emerged during the 1670s in a Parliament that was often divided over a set of related issues. By the turn of the century, these complex issues included the legal status of the Anglican Church, the constitutional position of the monarch, the direction of foreign policy, and management of the economy.

The revolution was largely the work of radical Whigs. Tory opposition sprang from a belief in the divine right of kings, the tenet that monarchs get their right to rule from God rather than from their subjects, which compelled support for the legitimate Stuart heir. Yet Tory unity was difficult, because many Tories also supported the supremacy of the Anglican Church, and James II was Catholic. The Tory party stood for tradition, but its political power was enfeebled when these two strong, contradictory traditions clashed.

In general, the Whigs wanted to limit the official role of the Anglican Church and the power of the Crown, pursue an aggressive war policy against France and Spain (England's major colonial rivals), and encourage the development of colonialism's potentially vast economic benefits. Accordingly, it was those who would benefit from such policies—merchants, bankers, businessmen, and others in the religiously diverse and increasingly wealthy middle class—who tended to make up the Whigs' power base. Tory wealth, by contrast, generally came from land, not cash. Tories stood for the power of the king and the sanctity of legitimate royal succession, a sea-based military strategy rather than the Whigs' expensive land campaigns, and a minimalist approach to risky colonial endeavors. The Tories also stood for the Anglican Church, particularly the High Church, or conservative branch, whose members championed traditional rites and church hierarchy. Members of the less conservative Low Church, which stressed instead a follower's biblical faith and piety, tended to become Whigs, as did Dissenters (Protestants who refused to belong to the Anglican Church). The Tory and Whig parties became known as the High-Church and Low-Church parties, respectively, an association alluded to in *Gulliver's Travels*: in Lilliput, there are more High Heels than Low Heels but the Low Heels have all the power, just as in England in 1726, there were more Tories than Whigs, but the Whigs had control of the government.

The early political parties, however, were still new and had not yet developed the discipline and structure they would later possess. The divisions between them were often blurred. For example, to varying degrees many Tories acknowledged a need for reform, and the Glorious Revolution could not have occurred without their often reluctant cooperation. Similarly, a Whig who was also an ardent Anglican might support the Anglican Church's monopoly on public life (so-called "Test Acts" theoretically excluded non-Anglicans from serving in public office). Indeed, staunch Anglican Jonathan Swift expressed just such support while writing on behalf of the Whigs during the first decade of the eighteenth century.

Scotland and Ireland. Along with helping to establish the party system, the Glorious Revolution also cemented England's political control over her two Celtic neighbors, Scotland and Ireland. Groups in both kingdoms had offered support to the deposed Catholic monarch James II after his flight from England, Scotland out of loyalty to its own Stuart dynasty (to which James belonged), and largely Catholic Ireland out of religious sympathy. James's supporters, in both places, were called Jacobites (from *Jacobus*, Latin for "James"). By the end of 1691, the English under William and Mary had subdued the Jacobite forces and had effectively taken over Scotland and Ireland. In 1707, the Act of Union united Scotland and England; the Scottish Parliament was abolished and Scottish members of Parliament were incorporated into the new Parliament of Great Britain in London.

England's protectionist trade policies excluded non-English vessels and merchants from trade with the colonies, which had crippled the Irish colonial economy; the burden of similar exclusion was the major factor that drove Scotland into union. From the English viewpoint, union with Scotland was a strategic advantage, for an autonomous Scotland had been a continual threat to English interests. Lacking such strategic value in English eyes, Ireland fared less well, and her parliament's appeal for union in 1703 was rejected by the English. Ireland would thus continue both to retain a degree of independence and to endure exploitation.

War with France. Jacobite rebellion in Scotland and especially in Ireland was supported by France, England's long-time enemy, which was enjoying military ascendancy in Europe under its powerful king, Louis XIV. Between 1689 and 1697, England and its allies—the Netherlands, the Holy Roman Empire, and Spain—faced France in the inconclusive "War of the Grand Alliance." In 1700 the Spanish Hapsburg emperor Charles II died without an heir, and war again broke out over who would control Spain and its vast colonial empire, which France's Louis claimed for his grandson Philip V. This "War of the Spanish Succession" (1701-14) took place on a much larger scale than the previous conflict, and again saw Britain allied with other powers against French might. Owing largely to the skilled generalship of John Churchill, duke of Marlborough, the allies won a series of land victories in Europe, most significantly at Blenheim (1704) and Ramillies (1706). Though Philip V controlled Spain and its colonies when the war was officially concluded at the Peace of Utrecht in 1714, French power was decisively curtailed. Some critics have seen these wars between France and Britain reflected in the struggle between Lilliput and its neighbor Blefescu in *Gulliver's Travels.*

Queen Anne (1702-14). Mary died in 1694, and when William died in 1702, the throne passed

---

IRISH PATRIOT

Meeting in Dublin but subordinate to London, the Irish Parliament was entirely Protestant and represented the interests of the "Anglo-Irish," the Protestant descendents of English immigrants to Ireland. As an Anglican, a member of the Anglo-Irish ruling class, and a frequent resident of England, Swift might be expected to have supported England's policies in Ireland. Yet the Anglo-Irish often bridled at England's exploitative economic measures, and while writing *Gulliver's Travels* in Ireland in the 1720s, Swift also began penning protests against English rule that won him wide popularity as an Irish patriot. Best known are *The Drapier's Letters* (1724-25) and *A Modest Proposal for Preventing the Children of Poor People from Being a Burthen to Their Parents or Country, and for Making Them Beneficial to the Publick* (1729), in which he ironically suggests ways for the rich to cook and eat the children of the poor, thus alleviating the problems of hunger and poverty all at once.

---

to Mary's younger sister Anne, who would be the last of the Stuart monarchs. Though William III had brought Britain into the war, Anne pursued it vigorously. Determined to keep the Crown above the party strife that now dominated Parliament, Anne tried to steer clear of favoring either Whigs or Tories in choosing her ministers.

In the end, however, this proved impossible; her very attempts often inflamed party passions.

The most influential minister at the beginning of Anne's reign was Sidney Godolphin, whose sympathies slowly shifted from the Tories to the Whigs as he worked to win from the Whig-dominated Parliament the financial support necessary for John Churchill to pursue the expensive war against France. His informal partnership with Godolphin led Churchill, who similarly started with Tory leanings, to move also to the Whig side. A close friendship between the queen and Sarah Churchill, the duchess of Marlborough, combined with the duke of Marlborough's military success and the war's great popularity, ensured the ascendancy of Whig politicians during the first part of Anne's reign.

By 1707, however, Queen Anne's friendship with Sarah Churchill had begun to cool, and her

EXPLORATION AND COLONIALISM

From the fifteenth through the eighteenth centuries, European nations explored the globe and established colonial outposts from China and India to the Caribbean and the Americas. The eighteenth century would see the rise of a global British Empire, consisting of colonies whose role was to send raw materials to Britain, where they would be turned into finished products. Among the people administering these colonies were Crown officials on behalf of private trading companies, and the corruption of both was legendary. Far from any official oversight, the officials were easily bribed in exchange for trading and other privileges. Near the end of *Gulliver's Travels*, Gulliver delivers a polemic against the rapacity and corruption of colonial practices.

personal dislike of many of the Whig leaders started to undermine her willingness to cooperate with them. Over the next few years, as early successes in the war gave way to stalemate, popular support for the Whigs' aggressive war aims also declined sharply. By 1710, the party divide had become clearer than at any time before: the Whigs were the party of war, the Tories the party of peace. In that year, with the war now highly unpopular, Queen Anne dismissed Godolphin and her other Whig ministers and replaced them with a group of moderates led by Robert Harley, soon to be made earl of Oxford. Though Harley tried to preserve his independence from party af-

filiation, partisan conflict forced him into the Tory camp, just as it had earlier forced Godolfin and Marlborough toward the Whigs.

The Tories' separate peace. The Tories' chief goal was to end the war, and accordingly Harley opened negotiations with the French almost immediately. These negotiations, kept secret from Britain's allies, resulted in Britain and France's signing a separate peace in 1711 under terms that were highly advantageous to Britain. British territorial gains included Gibraltar and Minorca in Spain; the Hudson Bay, Newfoundland, and Nova Scotia in Canada; and the island of St. Kitts in the Caribbean Sea. The new territory provided British merchants with greater access to Mediterranean and Caribbean trade, supplied the British Navy with ports from which to protect the merchant fleet, and allowed British fishermen to ply the rich fishing banks of the western North Atlantic Ocean; in addition, Britain gained a monopoly on the lucrative slave trade with South America. Britain thus emerged from the war as the leading colonial, commercial, and naval power in Europe. Britain's allies, by contrast, felt betrayed by Britain's withdrawal from the war, which dragged on until they too agreed on terms in the 1714 Peace of Utrecht.

George I, the Whig resurgence, and Robert Walpole. With the war over, the big question in British politics became the succession: who would follow the aging, ill, and Protestant Anne (none of whose 15 children had survived) as Britain's monarch? Tories were bitterly divided on the issue, with some holding out for the Catholic Stuart, James III, but many more supporting another descendent of James I, the German Protestant Prince George of Hanover. (George's mother, Sophia, had been designated to inherit the English throne by the 1701 Act of Settlement but she died a couple months before Anne, and George was her eldest son.) The Whigs, by contrast, were solidly united behind George, who duly succeeded to the British throne as George I on Anne's death in 1714.

The Tories had realized with concern that George was a natural ally for the Whigs. As a Lutheran Protestant, he could be expected to oppose the Anglican grip on public life. As not only a British monarch but also a German ruler with interests abroad, he was likely to favor an activist foreign policy. Both of these attitudes reflected Whig, not Tory, values. Tory fears were realized when George dismissed the Tory administration and installed Whig ministers instead. Among them

Gulliver awoke to find that the Lilliputians had tied him down.

was a skilled and ruthless young politician named Robert Walpole, who became a junior minister and then left the administration to form a power base in Parliament. When Whig leaders were tainted by financial scandal in 1720, Walpole seized the opportunity to take control of the party.

Walpole showed financial prowess, extracting himself from scandal and then dominating the government. He flagrantly exercised patronage, gaining a reputation as an intriguer who bought off opponents with government positions. Critics lambasted him for promoting corruption. In the 1720s, Walpole became "the subject of a continuous campaign of opposition vilification, especially in the press. The newspapers, pamphlets and caricatures" compared him to "the Devil himself. He was caricatured as a highwayman, tartar chief, child murderer, dancing master, boot-licer, despoiler of Magna Carta, serpent, and a host of other unsavoury roles" (Hill, p. 11). Many were convinced that his policies promoted an unstable, unethical regime. Moreover, he was given to ostentation, and in relation to this trait, boasted a mansion and a collection of paintings envied through much of Europe.

Especially infuriating to Swift was the doctrine Walpole seemed to invoke that the government had the right to insure its own survival at the expense of its subjects' freedom, property, and legal rights. Walpole showed particular disregard

for the rights of artists, invoking a Stamp Act and a seditious libel law to censor publishers, and appealing also to the Lord Chamberlain to restrain theater performances that were hostile to him. Certainly he was a target of literary poets, such as Alexander Pope, and novelists, like Swift himself, who satirized Walpole in *Gulliver's Travels*.

Despite the unceasing attacks, Walpole dominated British politics for over two decades, until his resignation in 1742. In retrospect, historians have pronounced him a deft administrator and politician. He developed the cabinet system in England and helped transform the House of Commons into the center of power. He is also credited with inventing the modern position of prime minister: that of majority party leader, head of government, and leading royal advisor with responsibilities to Parliament. But Walpole's was a transitional time in government, and in the early eighteenth century, his achievements were not nearly as apparent as his violation of individual rights and promotion of corrupt politics.

The Novel in Focus

Plot summary. *Gulliver's Travels* is narrated by Gulliver and takes place in four parts, each purporting to recount one of his journeys. In Part 1, "A Voyage to Lilliput," Gulliver, a young doctor, accepts a position as ship's surgeon on a merchant vessel bound for the South Sea and sets sail in spring 1699. That fall, driven onto a rock by high winds, the ship is destroyed. Gulliver, the sole survivor, swims aimlessly until, just as his energy is spent, he touches bottom and finally struggles onto an unknown shore. Exhausted, he lies down and falls asleep. When he awakes, he finds himself unable to move—his arms and legs are fastened to the ground, and his head is tied down by his long hair. Soon he feels something on his body, and glancing downward with difficulty he sees standing on his chest "a human creature not six inches high" who is soon followed by a small crowd of similar miniature people (Swift, *Gulliver's Travels*, p. 16). Gulliver tries to get up, but is peppered with arrows that feel like needles. Subdued, he lies moaning in pain. After lying still for some time, he begins to communicate, signing that he is hungry and thirsty. The tiny people bring him food and drink: entire joints of roast meat smaller than larks' wings, loaves of bread no bigger than bullets that he eats three at a time, whole casks of wine that he drains in one shot. Soon he feels the need to urinate: "which I very plentifully did, to the great astonishment of the people," who flee

---

THE SOUTH SEA BUBBLE

The early pages of *Gulliver's Travels* would have reminded contemporary readers of the financial scandal that cleared Robert Walpole's path to power: the bursting of the so-called "South Sea Bubble" in 1720. Founded in 1711 to reap the benefits of the peace settlement with France, the South Sea Company prospered from the African slave trade. Then in 1719 the company proposed that it take over much of the massive national debt held by the Bank of England (which the Whigs had founded in 1694 to fund war with France). Securing support from the Whig administration by bribing its leaders with gifts of stock, the company rode a wave of speculation that pushed its stock from £120 to £1,000 between January and August 1720. Then in September this investment bubble burst, creating a national crisis in which many wealthy families were ruined, the money supply dried up, and the bribed leaders were forced to resign in disgrace. A few months later, Swift began *Gulliver's Travels*. Like Gulliver, Britain had been taken for a ride to the South Sea, a prosperous voyage—until it ended on the rocks.

"to avoid the torrent which fell with such noise and violence from me" (*Gulliver's Travels*, p. 20). They transport him, still restrained, on a wheeled cart to their city and chain him inside a temple. There he is visited by the emperor of Lilliput, as he learns the place is called. Lilliputian scholars are assigned to teach him their language and customs, and he is soon able to communicate freely.

The satire emerges through aspects of Gulliver's stay in Lilliput and of life in early 1700s England. Lilliput's emperor (comparable to King George I) has ministers who are chosen by their ability to do acrobatic tricks on a tightrope or, from Gulliver's perspective, a thread. The best of them is Flimnap, the Treasurer (often equated with Robert Walpole). Second best is Reldresal, who befriends Gulliver, even though the Lilliputans are repeatedly shown as fearful, awestruck, or revolted by Gulliver's huge relative size. As Gulliver becomes more and more involved with the Lilliputian court circle and especially the emperor, we learn that Lilliputian politics are actually torn by a number of bitter party disputes. For example, those who wear high heels (comparable to the Tories) intransigently oppose those who wear low heels (comparable to the Whigs). The emperor has only low-heel ministers as his advisors; his son and heir wears one of each, which causes him to wobble when he walks. (In real life, King George I's son was friendlier to the Tories than his father was.) Another rancorous dispute, which has acquired religious overtones, divides those who open their eggs at the small end and those who open them at the big end. Small-Endians (who are like English Protestants) currently prevail in Lilliput, forcing many Big-Endians (like English Catholics) to seek refuge on the nearby island of Blefescu (analogous to mostly Catholic France) and leading to a long-running war between the two kingdoms.

When the emperor reveals that Blefuscu is about to launch a great naval invasion against Lilliput, Gulliver volunteers to help. He wades to Blefuscu, attaches cables to the Blefuscudian ships, and hauls them back to Lilliput. Gulliver balks, however, when the Lilliputian emperor wants him to help conquer the Blefuscudians outright and force them to crack their eggs at the small end: "I plainly protested, that I would never be the instrument of bringing a free and brave people into slavery" (*Gulliver's Travels*, p. 51). Soon afterward, when a violent fire breaks out in the royal palace and threatens the empress's chambers, Gulliver extinguishes the fire by urinating on the flaming building. Urination within the palace walls is a capital offence, however, and the enraged empress (comparable to Queen Anne) vows revenge; the episode marks the beginning of Gulliver's alienation from the Lilliputians. When he learns that the emperor and his advisors plan to starve him to death, Gulliver flees to Blefuscu. (The parallel here is that many Tories fled from England to France after George I and the Whigs took power.) A few days later, Gulliver finds a human-sized boat washed ashore and uses it to leave Blefuscu. Soon he is picked up by an English ship and returns home, arriving in April 1702.

Part 2, "A Voyage to Brobdingnag," begins two months later when, "condemned by nature and fortune to an active and restless life," Gulliver again takes a position on a merchant vessel and leaves his wife and two children, bound for India (*Gulliver's Travels*, p. 85). Blown off course by a storm, the ship wanders for a year, until land is spotted and a party sent ashore. Gulliver goes with them to explore on his own while the men look for water, but is stranded when he sees "a huge creature" chasing them back out to sea (*Gulliver's Travels*, p. 87). After hiding in a field of giant wheat, Gulliver is captured by a gigantic laborer, who turns him over to his similarly colossal employer, a farmer. The situation is now reversed: Gulliver is the puny, awestruck witness of huge, frightening, often unattractive people, whose skin blemishes and gaping pores disgust him just as his frequently did the Lilliputians. Gulliver again rapidly picks up the language, learning that the place is called Brobdingnag. Cared for and befriended by the farmer's nine-year-old daughter, Glumdalclitch, he is soon being taken around to nearby towns by the farmer, who is able to make a good living charging admission to view him as a freak of nature. Exhausted by the heavy schedule, he is relieved when the farmer takes him to the capital city and the queen offers to purchase him, letting Glumdalclitch remain as his caretaker. Gulliver proves a popular diversion at court, though he tangles repeatedly with the queen's dwarf, who seems to feel that Gulliver threatens his own situation. The Brobdingnagian king inquires about England and Europe, and Gulliver tries to portray English customs and politics in a positive light. He has some difficulty, which is not eased by the king's vast amusement at the presumption of such tiny creatures to take their affairs so seriously. Their conversations cloak a critique of English society:

> He was perfectly astonished with the historical account I gave him of our affairs during the last century; protesting it was only a heap of conspiracies, rebellions, murders, massacres, revolutions, banishments; the very worst effects that avarice . . . cruelty . . . envy . . . ambition could produce. . . . "My little friend . . . you have clearly proved that ignorance, idleness, and vice, are the proper ingredients for qualifying a legislator. That laws are best explained, interpreted, and applied by those whose interest and abilities lie in perverting, confounding and eluding them."
>
> (*Gulliver's Travels*, pp. 139-40)

Gulliver has several close calls on this trip. He is taken up to a high rooftop by a pet monkey, for example, and nearly drowned in a pitcher of cream by the jealous dwarf. Finally, the little box he lives in is picked up by a giant eagle and dropped in the ocean, where an English ship happens by and brings him on board. He reaches England in June 1706, where he has great difficulty readjusting to human scale.

Part 3, "A Voyage to Laputa, Balnibarbi, Glubbdubdrib, and Japan," begins as Gulliver accepts another position as ship's surgeon, though

---

THE "LITTLE FAMILY"

In Brobdingnag Gulliver inspires great curiosity among his giant hosts, who exhibit him as a sort of circus sideshow. Midgets and human freaks, as well as monkeys and puppets, were common entertainments for the English in the eighteenth century. Gulliver fears that the Brobdingnagians will find him a mate to bear his children; in fact, such a family was put on display in 1712 in London. The exhibit, which became known as the "Little Family," featured a man who was only three feet tall, his pregnant wife, and their little horse.

---

he has trouble persuading his neglected wife and children to let him take the job. Setting out in August 1706 for the East Indies, the ship arrives in Asian waters the following April. There it is attacked and boarded by Dutch pirates, who cast Gulliver adrift in a small boat with just a few days' provisions. Spotting some islands in the distance, Gulliver makes for them, ending up on the farthest one, which is rocky and almost barren. Suddenly he is amazed to see "a vast opake [opaque] body" blotting out the sun, a circular "island in the air" (in some respects, analogous to England) that floats slowly along, and on which he can make out human inhabitants who seem able to guide its course (*Gulliver's Travels*, p. 167). They let down a chain and pull him up. He is immediately struck by their bizarre appearance: their heads lean to the side, one eye looks up and the other "inward," and their clothes are "adorned with the figures of suns, moons, and stars, interwoven with those of fiddles, flutes, harps, trumpets, guittars, harpsicords, and many more instruments of musick, unknown to us in Europe" (*Gulliver's Travels*, p. 169). He learns that the island is called Laputa, and that its inhabitants' lives are dominated by astronomy, mathematics, and music. They spend their time in abstract musings, being so lost in thought that they must be attended by "flappers," whose job it is to tap their mouths and ears

lightly with special sticks in order to keep their minds on what they're saying or hearing.

Guided by its king, who controls the island's flight through magnetic forces, Laputa floats over an island called Balnibarbi. There, influenced by the Laputans, the people have been seized by a mania for "projecting," which (the reader soon realizes) means coming up with intricate, unfinished schemes for doing useless things with a maximum of wasted effort. At a special academy one "projector," for example, has a plan to extract sunbeams from cucumbers and store it in vials, to help the king's garden during cloudy weather. One hopes to take human excrement and turn it back into food; another works on "a new method for building houses, by beginning at the roof" and working down, taking as his model the bee and the spider (*Gulliver's Travels*, p. 192). There is a complex machine for grinding out words at random in order to make new books on science, philosophy, and other subjects.

Gulliver then visits two more islands: Glubbdubdrib, where the people are sorcerers and conjure up famous figures from history for him to meet; and Luggnagg, where he encounters the wretched Struldbruggs, who have immortality without lasting youth, so that their bodies and minds simply become more and more decrepit. Leaving Luggnagg, Gulliver makes a brief visit to Japan before returning to England in April 1710.

Part 4, "A Voyage to the Country of the Houyhnhnms," is Gulliver's final journey, which he undertakes in September 1710. This time he is made captain of his own ship, but his disaffected crew mutiny and put him ashore and leave him as soon as they can. Moving inland, he comes upon some grotesque and ugly Yahoos, which surround him threateningly until a horse approaches and they flee. The horse examines him curiously; another arrives and Gulliver soon realizes that they are conversing in a manner that seems highly "orderly and rational" (*Gulliver's Travels*, p. 240). The two gentle horses escort him to a house, which Gulliver slowly realizes belongs to the first horse, a dapple-grey, to whom the other horses seem to defer. Out in the yard are a number of the grotesque creatures, which a shocked Gulliver believes to be humans—wild, dirty, unclothed, and dumb, but still recognizable. The first word he learns is the horses' name for these humanlike beings, whom they call "Yahoos" and use in the some of the same ways that Europeans use horses. The horses themselves are Houyhnhnms, and it is in their calm, well-

---

SATIRICAL TARGET PRACTICE—ENGLAND'S ROYAL SOCIETY

In Swift's day, literary men especially laughed at what they saw as the antics of the institution known in England as the Royal Society. The society, formed in 1660, dedicated itself to experiments that would promote knowledge. The problem, from the point of view of Swift and his contemporaries, was its emphasis on seemingly impractical inventions and on the study of the trivial or obvious. The society gave rise to experiments to determine that air was necessary for life, for example, and to discover the anatomy of a flea. That learned men should spend valuable time on such concerns inspired ridicule. Joseph Addison and Richard Steele "derided the Fellows [of the Royal Society] as being of little wit, dull and without learning, kept out of the real world, that is the political world, because they were distracted by playing with such toys as scientific instruments, more interested in insects . . . than in man, society and God" (Hall, p. 167). The derision was lodged publicly in the journals the *Tatler* and the ***Spectator*** (also in *WLAIT 3: British and Irish Literature and Its Times*). It became fashionable to laugh at the Fellows, though this did not suggest a complete dismissal of the value of experiment. Swift "would have agreed wholeheartedly with the King of Brobdingnag, who "gave it for his Opinion; that whoever could make two Ears of corn, or two Blades of Gras to grow upon a spot of ground where only one grew before; would . . . do more essential Service to his Country, than the whole Race of Politicians put together" (Downie and Swift in Downie, p. 281).

ordered society that Gulliver, whom they see as a uniquely intelligent Yahoo, finds true happiness. Like the Brobdingnagians, the Houyhnhnms are curious about European ways, and particularly about English politics, which Gulliver again finds himself uncomfortable explaining. As in Brobdingnag, the conversation here constitutes a critique of English society.

> He asked me what were the usual causes or motives, that made one country go to war with another. . . . Sometimes the ambition of princes, who never think they have land or people enough to govern: sometimes the corruption of ministers, who engage their master in a war, in order to stifle or divert the clamour of the subjects against their evil administration. . . . A *soldier* is a Yahoo hired to kill in cold blood as many of his own species, who have never offended him, as possibly he can. . . . I was going on to more particulars, when my master commanded me silence. . . . He said . . . when a creature pretending to reason, could be capable of such enormities, he dreaded lest the corruption of that faculty, might be worse than brutality itself. He seemed therefore confident, that instead of reason, we were only possessed of some quality fitted to increase our natural vices. . . .
>
> (*Gulliver's Travels*, pp. 261-64)

Gulliver begins to adopt the Houyhnhnms' outlook and to think of Europeans as savage Yahoos. Having lived among the Houyhnhnms for five years, he is heartbroken when their General Council orders him to leave. Considering a plan to exterminate the Yahoos, they fear that Gulliver might incite a rebellion. He sets out in a small boat and is picked up by a Portuguese ship, whose generous and kindly captain looks after the unhappy and disgusted traveler. In December 1715 he finally returns to England and his family, but five years later, as he begins to write his account of his voyages, he still cannot stand to be touched by his wife or children, whom he continues to see as Yahoos. Instead, he buys two horses and spends hours every day talking to them. He ends his account with a diatribe against human pride.

Perspective and reason. Among Gulliver's most useful qualities at the start of his adventures is his openness to the language and customs of the people he encounters, a flexibility that helps him adapt to strange situations with often surprising ease. Yet each new perspective he adopts seems to chip away at his own, so that he appears less and less able to evaluate the behavior that he en-counters. Instead, he simply accepts it uncritically. In Lilliput, for example, while taking the Lilliputians more seriously than the reader knows he should, he does at least refuse the emperor's request to vanquish the Blefuscudians; later he admires the obviously nonsensical schemes of the "projectors" and still later is undisturbed by the Houyhnhnms' plans to exterminate the Yahoos. His long, self-inflicted ordeal changes him from a seemingly well-adjusted, if already credulous, young man to a ranting misanthrope who is clearly mentally unbalanced. Gulliver loses his prodigious elasticity: stretching too easily, he can no longer snap back.

This process provides the narrative framework for Swift's caustically ironic treatment of his main two satirical targets, human nature and human politics. It also provides the common bull's-eye that these targets share, which is the belief in reason as our defining characteristic. Starting in the seventeenth century, philosophers such as René Descartes (1596-1650) and John Locke (1632-1704) had ushered in what is commonly called the Enlightenment or the Age of Reason. We are rational animals, claimed these and other Enlightenment figures: reason plays the central role in determining both our nature and our political institutions. By contrast, in an often quoted letter, Swift gives a clear summary of his overall aim in writing *Gulliver's Travels*: "proving the falsity of the definition *animale rationale;* and to show that it should only be *rationis capax*" (*Gulliver's Travels*, p. xxxi). In other words, Swift wished to show that man was not a "rational animal," as the Enlightenment writers would have it, but simply "capable of reason" at moments. Significantly, it is after visiting the most superhumanly (or, as some critics have argued, inhumanly) rational beings on his itinerary, the Houyhnhnms, that Gulliver has the most trouble snapping back to a human existence and a human perspective. It is part of the irony that too heavy an exposure to reason makes Gulliver lose his own; he is least rational when he thinks himself most, and has lost his perspective just when he is most certain of it.

Sources and literary context. While Swift was writing for the Tories in London, he and his friends Gay and Pope (along with a few others) founded the Scriblerus Club, in which the idea was to create a collaborative work of satire. Tenuous evidence suggests that Swift may have used some of this material for *Gulliver's Travels*. More certain is that Swift drew on an array of models in choosing the form his work would take. Swift and other satirists of his day looked to classical forerunners, such as the Greek Menippus (third century B.C.E.) and the Roman Lucian (second century C.E.). In their works and those of their followers could be found devices such as fantastic journeys, utopian parodies, and conversations with the spirits of famous figures in history. For Lilliput and Brobdingnag, the most obvious inspiration is the masterpiece of the French writer François Rabelais (c. 1494-1553), *Gargantua and Pantagruel*, which features giants and comic inversions of scale, along with much scatological humor and sharp irony. Cyrano de Bergerac's satirical fantasies *Comic History of the Estates and Empires of the Moon* (1656) and *Comic History of the Estates and Empires of the Sun* (1657) have the hero being exhibited for money by a race of giants; the hero also encounters a race of birds on the sun who judge humanity and find it wanting, much like Swift's Houyhnhnms. A growing number of travel books (about which Gulliver complains) had appeared by the time Swift wrote *Gulliver's Travels*, from Richard Hakluyt's *The Principal Navigations, Voyages, Traffiques and Discoveries of the English Nation* (1589) to William Dampier's *A New Voyage Round the World* (1697). Maps were also increasingly available in this age of commercial exploration, and Swift (who never traveled further than Ireland) is careful to keep his geography accurate, which heightens the effect of his fictional settings. Finally, there were popular shipwreck tales: a true account by Alexander Selkirk, who in 1704 was left on a deserted island by pirates and was not rescued for five years; and Daniel Defoe's *Robinson Crusoe* (1719), based on Selkirk's book.

Reception. The success of *Gulliver's Travels* was immediate and lasting, with a reported 10,000 copies sold in its first week and a steady readership ever since. As John Gay reported in a letter from London to Swift in Ireland:

> About ten days ago a book was published here of the travels of one Gulliver, which hath been the conversation of the whole town ever since: the whole impression sold in a week; and nothing is more diverting than to hear the different opinions people give of it, though all agree in liking it extremely. . . . From the highest to the lowest it is universally read, from the cabinet council to the nursery.
>
> (Gay in Bellamy, p. 10)

Samuel Johnson wrote that "it was received with such avidity, that the price of the first edition was raised before the second could be made; it was read by the high and the low, the learned and the illiterate" (Johnson in Bellamy, p. 12). Despite its huge popular success, some critics were shocked by the portrayal of the Yahoos—a word which, like "Lilliputian," has entered standard English. Ironically, this is the section that has become the favorite of modern scholars.

—Colin Wells

For More Information

Bellamy, Liz. *Jonathan Swift's Gulliver's Travels.* London: Simon & Schuster, 1992.

Black, Jeremy. *The Politics of Britain, 1688-1800.* Manchester: University of Manchester Press, 1993.

Downie, J. A. *Jonathan Swift Political Writer.* London: Routledge & Kegan Paul, 1984.

Hall, Marie Boas. *Promoting Experimental Learning: Experiment and the Royal Society 1660-1727.* Cambridge: Cambridge University Press, 1991.

Hill, Brian W. *Sir Robert Walpole: Sole and Prime Minister.* London: Hamish Hamilton, 1989.

Knowles, Ronald. *Gulliver's Travels: The Politics of Satire.* New York: Twayne, 1996.

Black, Jeremy. *Robert Walpole and the Nature of Politics in Early Eighteenth-Century Britain.* London: Macmillan, 1990.

Erskine-Hill, Howard. *Swift: Gulliver's Travels.* Cambridge: Cambridge University Press, 1993.

Lockyer, Roger. *Tudor & Stuart Britain 1471-1714.* Harlow, England: Longman, 1964.

Swift, Jonathan. *Gulliver's Travels.* New York: Knopf, 1991.

Henry V

by

William Shakespeare

~

By 1598, near the end of his first decade as a playwright, William Shakespeare had written a number of plays that dramatized England's recent past. These plays concerned the struggles for control of the English throne that ravaged the country between 1399 and 1485. *Henry V* was the last of this set of plays to be written, and the only one that does not concentrate on the seizure of the English throne; rather, the triumphant reign of King Henry V, with its crowning jewel, the subjugation of the French at the Battle of Agincourt, provides the focus of the play. The play highlights a critical stage in the consolidation of authority under the English monarch.

Events in History at the Time the Play Takes Place

The struggle for the English Crown. The reign of Henry V (1413-1422) constitutes one of the high points of the English monarchy. It was a period of triumph: Henry's subjugation of France in three successful campaigns filled England with pride for centuries. Heightening the glories of Henry's reign were the political and social instabilities that both preceded and succeeded his rule.

Trouble began with the death of Edward III, England's king from 1327 to 1377. Edward III ruled effectively, and left a large family, but his heir, Edward the Black Prince (so called for his black armor), predeceased his father. The next heir was the Black Prince's son, Richard, who as-

---

> ## THE LITERARY WORK
>
> A play set in England and France in 1415; first performed and published around 1598.
>
> ## SYNOPSIS
>
> A young English king leads his nation to victory in a war against France.

---

cended the throne on the death of his grandfather, in 1377. (See *Richard II*, also in *WLAIT 3: British and Irish Literature and Its Times*.) Headstrong, extravagant, and suspicious, Richard abused his authority: he squandered the money Parliament allowed him to collect in taxes and alienated the nobility by eliminating perceived threats. Not only did he exile the future Henry IV, as well as the earls of Warwick, Derby, and Nottingham, but Richard also had the earl of Arundel executed, murdered the duke of Gloucester, and placed his trust in advisors disliked by the rest of the aristocracy. He also waged an Irish campaign that was both costly and time-consuming. When Henry Bolingbroke rose against the king in 1399, Richard was forced to abdicate; Bolingbroke became Henry IV.

Henry IV's seizure of the crown inaugurated a century of nearly perpetual trouble. His deposition of Richard showed the rest of the nobility (many with plausible claims to the throne) that action, not birthright, made a man a king; he consequently spent much of his 14-year reign fending off power-hungry nobles. He established a firm enough reign to leave his son the throne, but Henry V was handed a thorny legacy. Henry's reign would be relatively brief, less than ten years. In this time, he would stabilize the rule of his family, the House of Lancaster, by leading England to victory over France.

DIVINE RIGHT OF KINGS

Henry IV's usurpation of the throne defied a long-established political doctrine: the divine right of kings. Since the Middle Ages, Christian Europe generally believed that government was inspired and approved by God. According to the tenets of divine right, monarchs ruled by the will of God and were accountable to Him alone; monarchy itself was a divinely ordained institution; hereditary right could not be abolished; and subjects were charged by God to obey their sovereign, even if they believed he was wicked and corrupt. To rise up against an "anointed king"—so called because of the precious oils rubbed upon him during the sacred ceremony of his coronation—was to offend against God. In *Henry IV*, Parts 1 and 2, and *Henry V*, the shadow of Richard II's deposition and murder hangs heavily over his successors—Henry IV is continually haunted by the memory of his deed, as is his son, Henry V, when he, in turn, ascends the throne. Beset by anxieties and fearing an English defeat at Agincourt, Henry V fervently prays for strength and God's mercy for past sins:

> Not today, O lord,
> O, not today, think upon the fault
> My father made in compassing the crown!
> I Richard's body have interrèd new;
> And on it have bestowed more contrite tears
> Than from it issued forcèd drops of blood.
> (Shakespeare, *Henry V*, 4.1.285-290)

Dynastic successions. The "Hundred Years' War" refers to the series of wars between England and France that took place from 1338 to 1453. In the late twelfth century the English king Henry II married Eleanor of Aquitaine, former wife of the French king Louis VII; with Eleanor came rights to her duchy, the large and fertile province of Aquitaine in southern France. Her English descendants inherited this rich prize, and reaped the benefits of favorable trade with it. However, the province, while officially English, was governed by the French, who pre-dictably favored French interests, so the English perpetually feared the loss of this wealthy trade. For their part, the French monarchs tried to expel the English: "Every French king for 200 years had tried by war, confiscation, or treaty to regain Aquitaine. The quarrel was . . . bound for war" (Tuchman, p. 72).

If Aquitaine was the reason for the war between England and France, the tangled web of dynastic succession provided the pretext. In 1314 Philip IV of France died, leaving four children. Three sons succeeded him, but each died quickly and without a male heir. His fourth child, Isabella, married the English king Edward II and mothered Edward III, who was thus a strong candidate for the French throne. The French, unwilling to accept the sovereignty of an English king over French soil, chose instead Philip VI, nephew of Philip IV. Edward III, the French court ruled, could not assume the throne because of the Salic Law, an ordinance that forbade the French throne from being inherited through a woman.

However, the Salic Law was based on a deliberate misreading of French history. According to the French, the authority for the law was King Pharamond, the legendary founder of France, and the "Salic land" was France itself. The English correctly noted, however, that the "Salic land" was not France but a region of Germany between the Elbe and Sala rivers that had been conquered by France in 805 C.E.—four centuries after Pharamond was said to have lived. Moreover, French kings continually used relationships to women to justify their reigns: Pepin, Hugh Capet, and Hugh's son Louis X (St. Louis) all justified usurpations by claiming a superior title to the throne derived from a mother or wife. Thus, the English kings felt that it was perfectly legitimate to dishonor the politically based law.

In 1337 Edward III assaulted France. This first war ended inconclusively, with a truce, in 1342. In 1346 the English tried again. Outnumbered and on foreign soil, they seemed to have little chance of success; few, not even the English themselves, expected the spectacular triumph in the offing.

On August 26, 1346, the two armies met at Crécy. Edward was not trying to fight but to lead the English army to the safety of Flanders. Intercepted by the French, he had no choice but to attempt a battle. His being boxed into this corner turned out to be fortunate for the English— when the battle was over, they were victorious: 4,000 French soldiers, including many of the most famous French knights, lay dead. English casualties were a fraction of this amount, numbering only a few hundred.

After the victory, Edward led his army north to the port town of Calais. He conquered it, but only after a year-long siege that drained the English treasury and sapped his army's will to continue fighting. This, and the catastrophe of the Great Plague, interrupted the war. A treaty was signed in 1348. However, the loss of Calais, which would remain in English hands until 1558, and other such blows to French dignity (throughout *Henry V*, Englishmen taunt the French with references to Crécy), ensured that the war would continue.

In 1356 renewed hostilities culminated in the Battle of Poitiers. Despite once again being badly outnumbered—with 8,000 men to 16,000 French soldiers—the English army under Edward the Black Prince won, and captured the French king. The king's ransom brought England gold, valuables, and nearly a third of France; however, it proved difficult to hold on to this new wealth. The people in England's new dominions thought of themselves as French, and were unwilling to be ruled by foreigners. Meanwhile, at home, Edward III's rule began to fray under scandal, fiscal discontent, and the disgrace of many of his ministers. The nation was distracted from foreign affairs by the succession crisis that followed Edward's death—not until Henry V took the throne in 1413 was an English king able to renew the war in an ambitious way.

History's Henry. Born in 1387, Henry V spent his youth in the manner typical of a child in an extremely wealthy family. He learned to hunt, fight, and dance; he was trained to run a great estate. He was, in fact, a special favorite of Richard II, the king his father would dethrone. This usurpation changed Henry's life. Instead of living and dying a wealthy, less significant member of the royal family, he became successor to the throne and defender of his father's tenuous rule. Henry's real schooling occurred in the saddle as he helped put down rebellions in Yorkshire, Scotland, and Wales between 1400 and 1407.

With his father's reign secure by 1408, Henry, or Prince Hal, as he was called, settled into London life. It was then, and not in his adolescence, as Shakespeare implies, that he acquired his reputation as a rake. His wildness seems to have endeared him to the people of London, who saw it as proof of an active spirit. There was tension between father and son, which sprang from Hal's popularity; Henry IV feared his son's growing influence, especially since the prince disagreed with his father on various points of policy. Shortly before his death, the king called his son to account. Hal rode to the palace accompanied by his crowd of boisterous, well-armed knights; London gathered to cheer his defiance. Inside, however, he showed another face: he swore loyalty to his father and was as good as his word.

THE SALIC LAW

The Salic Law was not invented to keep Edward III from taking the Crown of France. However, it was recently minted jurisprudence, politically motivated, and without warrant in the political history of France. In 1318, after the death of the French king Philip IV's eldest son, Louis X, Philip's next eldest son took the throne as Philip V. Inconveniently for Philip, Louis had left a four-year-old daughter, Jeanne. To provide a retroactive justification for his coronation, Philip convoked an assembly of statesmen and jurists, who, predictably, approved Philip's accession on the principle that women could neither rule France nor inherit the throne (to pass on to a husband or son). This law would be used in 1328 to invalidate Edward III's claim to France, and again in 1413 to reject Henry V's.

When he took the throne in 1413, Henry V abruptly extricated himself from his old circle. Thereafter, his advisors were sober, trustworthy men. He also showed political genius in placating his father's enemies, restoring many to power, and funding charities and religious houses. When the time came for war, he led with confidence and conducted battle brilliantly; at the negotiating table, he bargained astutely.

In retrospect, Henry V appears to have possessed many of the virtues befitting a medieval king (generosity, piety, courage in war, skill in peace) and comparatively few of the usual black marks (capriciousness, tyranny, indecision). Given his many political successes, it was not surprising that English chroniclers, such as Edward Hall and Raphael Holinshed, presented him as a heroic, larger-than-life figure, a depiction further popularized by Elizabethan playwrights, including Shakespeare. Indeed, of all the British kings, real and mythical, perhaps only King Arthur has lived more vividly in the British memory than Henry V.

An English nobleman rallies his troops at the Battle of Agincourt.

Henry V in the Hundred Years' War. Henry V's successes in France were as glorious as his great-grandfather Edward III's, although more fleeting. He conducted three successful campaigns in France. The first (1415) culminated with the English triumph at Agincourt (see below). The second (1415-1419) solidified Henry's rule over Normandy. The third (1420) followed the treaty of Troyes, which made Henry heir to the French throne; it aimed to secure the south of France, which remained loyal to the French king's natural son, but was cut short by Henry's untimely death.

Henry landed with a force of close to 10,000 men late in the summer of 1415. He immediately besieged Harfleur, a strategically important city in Normandy. Harfleur held out for more than a month. It was forced to surrender when reinforcements from Paris failed to arrive, but the English had little reason to feel encouraged. The prospect of conquering a whole nation, town by town, was daunting; even worse, winter was fast approaching, and fever had incapacitated much of the English army. Henry marched his army northwest, hoping to reach the safe haven of Calais (still an English possession). Believing that

the main army of France lay far to the south, he expected an easy march.

But the massive French army had already trekked north, and now stood between the English and Calais. Henry tried every means to avoid battle: he even offered to surrender Harfleur and pay for the damage of the siege. Aware of their superiority, the French pressed into battle, a huge mistake on their part. On October 25, 1415, the two armies clashed near the village of Agincourt. At the end of the day-long battle, the elite of the French army had been killed, the army itself put to flight, and French morale devastated. The English were victorious.

Agincourt. Three times in less than 100 years, vastly larger and better-rested French armies, fighting on home soil for the fate of their own land, were beaten by English forces so conscious of their own inferiority that, each time, they tried to avoid battle. Crécy, Poitiers, and Agincourt seemed to be miraculous English victories.

But however miraculous they seemed, practical realities of the time can explain them. In many ways the French advantage was a hollow supposition, a perception that did little more than make the French lax in preparing for battle. First, from 1327 on, France's leadership had been split by rancor, conflicting motives, and mutual distrust. At the time of Agincourt, France was embroiled in a lethal struggle for control of the Crown. The aging Charles VI experienced long bouts of insanity. His sons battled the duke of Burgundy for the right to succeed their father, so that Henry's army often tramped through the countryside unhindered, while French forces fought each other around Paris.

The key to French failure, however, was strategic rather than political. The French understood an army as a convocation of different groups of armed men, each under the leadership of an aristocrat who was often unwilling to follow the orders of the king and his marshals. At key points in each of the three battles, some of these armed groups simply did not fight, whether because of poor communication, resentment, or a disagreement over strategy. English forces, though organized on the same principles, operated more efficiently: they were alert to fighting a formidable opponent, were relatively unified in their leadership, and knew that they could not count on support in the countryside if they retreated.

Most importantly, the French still believed that battle was a chivalric struggle between well-armed noblemen. French leaders wanted to conduct battle as a group of individual fights between French and English knights. Generally the loser in such a fight would be killed only accidentally: he was much more valuable for the ransom he could bring if taken prisoner. French knights tended to disdain the commoners or hired soldiers who fought with spears or bows. In their view, such rabble were good only to provide support for the mounted knight. The French army had troops of archers for support, but it did not always use them, believing that it could break the English defenses with a cavalry charge.

When battle was joined, French knights would ride forward pell-mell, hoping first to strike terror into the hearts of the English commoners (who stood ready with spears as the first defense) and then to find a suitable English knight to fight. At Crécy, at Poitiers, and most resoundingly at Agincourt, the disorganized mass of French knights was cut down by a hail of arrows from England's archers, which slowed their charge and gave the English soldiers on the front line a chance to stop it altogether.

The English did battle differently. Some years before his first campaign, Edward III had outlawed all sport for young men except archery. By the time they got to Crécy, England's archers were the most skilled in Europe. They furthermore used a longbow, a lighter and more quickly fired weapon than the crossbow used by the French. Also, the defensive positions that the English had to adopt because of their numerical inferiority favored the effective deployment of banks of archers. In the end, their willingness to use bowmen was the real key to England's success. The mounted knight who had dominated warfare throughout the Middle Ages proved vulnerable to a knot of commoners with cheap, easily made weapons. France lost three dukes, 90 counts, and 1,500 knights at Agincourt, along with thousands of commoners. English losses totaled 500, only three of whom had noble titles.

An Englishman on the French throne? After Agincourt, Henry took his army home for the winter and did not return to France for two years. This was not unusual: medieval armies lacked the means for fighting until one side surrendered unconditionally; indeed they lacked even the concept of systematic war. Armies roamed around until a key battle was fought, at which point a truce would enforce peace until hostilities were resumed, often years later. In his second campaign of 1417-1419 (not represented by Shakespeare), Henry conquered much of Normandy by siege, while, for much of the time, the

French were busy fighting domestic battles around Paris. By the beginning of 1420, Normandy had been subdued, and Henry was the ruler of a third of France. Paris lay ahead.

The next stage was diplomatic rather than military. Henry laid siege to Paris, the home of the French kings, but the French were in no shape to resist. The two main powers of France, the Burgundians and the forces of the Dauphin (the heir to the French throne), could not overlook their hatred of each other even with a conqueror at their gates, and Henry took advantage of the situation to capture the crown for himself. In May 1420, the Treaty of Troyes ended the war. By the terms of the treaty, the Dauphin was disinherited (he fled to the south of France, where he was still well supported). Charles VII remained king of France until his death, at which time Henry would take the throne. The treaty was sealed with a marriage: Henry wed Charles's daughter, Catherine. In January 1421 Henry returned to England with a new kingdom and a queen.

In five years of fighting, Henry established himself as a military and political genius—one of the greatest fighting kings of the Middle Ages. In fact, he would be the last great fighting king of the Middle Ages. When he returned to France late in 1421 to renew his battle with the Dauphin, Henry was 35. In the middle of an inconclusive campaign, Henry fell ill, probably of dysentery. He died in August 1422, and with him died English hopes for domination of France. As successful as he was, Henry fought a type of war whose time had passed. The period of armed conquest on medieval lines was drawing to a close. Conditions allowed England to win France using tactics of the Middle Ages, but not to keep it.

The Play in Focus

Plot summary. *Henry V* opens as two high-ranking clerics discuss a bill currently being proposed in Parliament. The bill would strip the Church of any lands that the king feels are being misused and return them to the Crown. To forestall the ratification of this proposal, the clerics decide to encourage Henry's ambitions for the French throne. Henry has already announced his claim to dukedoms in France to the French king and is now considering war.

The king enters, and the two clerics explain to him why the Salic Law is invalid. The king calls for his counselors; they too approve an assault on France. Finally Henry calls for the

CLERICAL ABUSES

The bill mentioned in the opening scene of *Henry V* was an actual piece of legislation considered but shelved by Parliament in Henry IV's reign. When Henry V took the throne, the measure (which would allow the king to confiscate Church lands almost at will if he could document abuses, or misuse of funds) was once more brought before Parliament. High-ranking officials of the Catholic Church enjoyed wealth and power equal to those of the richest aristocrats in the land. The bishop of Winchester, for instance, commanded a yearly income of close to £4000 at a time when the average worker earned far less than a £100 a year. Such examples made the Church a target of ever-increasing resentment from both the common people and the king. Church officials were widely perceived as corrupt predators. Shady practices went all the way up the Church hierarchy: clerics of rank were often appointed to posts in parishes that they never visited, collecting a salary for the position without doing any work at all. In England, protest against such practices went under the name of Lollardism. Lollards, led by John Wycliffe, pressed simple but ambitious demands: an end to corruption in the Church, a reduced role for priests in the spiritual life of common people, and the printing of the Bible in English rather than Latin. Occasionally the protesters shamed a bishop or two, but for the most part they only suffered persecution for their pains. Meanwhile, the kings of the fifteenth century had reasons of their own to target the Church. The late Middle Ages witnessed an increased concentration of wealth in the hands of a few noble families, called magnates. Magnates owned vast estates in widely scattered parts of Britain; they commanded large personal armies and wielded tremendous political influence. At any time, an ambitious magnate could threaten the power of the monarch. Henry IV himself had begun as a magnate; after deposing Richard II, he had to put down the rebellions of other powerful landowners. It was essential for the king to remain stronger than the most powerful magnates. One way to do so was by taking power from the Church. Since the Church held most of its wealth in the form of grants from the king, the legal mechanism for this stripping already existed: all that was needed was a pretext. The Lancastrian kings found this pretext in the complaints of the Lollards.

French ambassadors who have been awaiting an audience. They bring a message from the Dauphin (the French heir to the throne) in reply to Henry's claim to the French dukedoms. The Dauphin not only spurns the claim (as might be expected), he also sends a gift: tennis balls. The tennis balls are meant to ridicule Henry, not only for his youth but for his past, which was spent in the pursuit of frivolous pleasures rather than serious statecraft. This insult merely confirms what has already been decided: the English will attack France.

The scene shifts to a tavern in London, where the companions of Henry's ill-spent youth—Nym, Bardolph, and Pistol—are watching over the deathbed of the king's former friend, the drunken and cowardly Sir John Falstaff. Falstaff dies, signaling the demise of Henry's youthful ways. From now on, he is wholly the noble and martial king. Nym, Bardolph, and Pistol will follow him to war, however; they provide both comic relief and the perspective of commoners on the battlefield.

Before the army can sail for France, Henry has to deal with a potentially inauspicious sign: he has caught three traitors who planned to kill him in exchange for money from the French. Henry arranges a drama. He asks the traitors what penalty he should impose on a soldier caught slandering him. All three traitors urge the utmost severity. Henry announces he will be lenient nonetheless, then hands the men papers in which

Kenneth Branagh and Brian Blessed in a scene from the 1989 film version of *Henry V*.

they are charged with treason against their king. The traitors fall to their knees, confessing their guilt and begging forgiveness for their souls, but not for their bodies. They are then arrested and taken to be executed.

In the middle of Act 2, the French court makes its first appearance. The king, while defying the English threat, is cautious, but the Dauphin is arrogantly reckless. The constable of the French army warns the Dauphin that the English are a major force. However, when the English ambassador enters, his offers of peaceable negotiation are rejected.

The scene shifts at once to the midst of the Battle of Harfleur. Henry spurs his men to victory; after a brief scene of battle, he is shown behaving honorably to the subjected citizens of the city. Enlivening the Harfleur scene is a brief argument involving a Welshman (Fluellen), a Scot (Jamy), and an Irishman (Macmorris); this episode demonstrates the clashing personalities—despite their common aim—of the king's forces, and allows for some fun with their different accents.

After a brief scene that displays the continued arrogance of the French court, Shakespeare moves ahead to the evening before Agincourt. In the French camp, all are bold and optimistic; they argue about horses, mistresses, and other unmartial topics. The English camp, by contrast, apprehensively awaits the day to come. A disguised Henry wanders through the camp to gauge the mood of his men. While in disguise, he quarrels with a common soldier; they agree to resume their fight after the battle, and exchange gloves so they will be able to recognize each other. Despite this light distraction, Henry is ill at ease, wondering if his cause is just and lamenting the men who will die in its pursuit.

This somber atmosphere departs with the morning. The next scene is pure English triumph as Henry rallies his troops with a rousing speech and informs the French herald that he will not permit himself to be ransomed should he be taken. As the battle rages, messengers from both sides report the various English successes; even the cowardly Pistol is shown taking a prisoner.

BRITISH UNITY

The scene in *Henry V* in which members of each nation of the British Isles (England, Scotland, Ireland, and Wales) are shown working together—albeit somewhat contentiously—to conquer Harfleur is not entirely accurate as historical fact. While natives of the three nations that were more or less subject to England undoubtedly aided the English cause, the nations themselves were restive under the English yoke. From the time of Edward III, war against France nearly always meant war against Scotland. In fact, shortly after Troyes, Henry V's forces captured and hanged 20 Scottish soldiers fighting for the French. Scottish lords generally took advantage of anything that distracted England to begin border raids or declare themselves free of English control. Ireland was similarly intransigent and accepted English supremacy only at the point of a sword. And Shakespeare's audience would have been keenly aware that Henry's father had faced a serious challenge to his authority in Wales from Owen Glendower, a warlord who harassed the English border for years in the name of Welsh autonomy. But if some liberty is taken in how loyal the other nations of the British Isles were, the play acknowledges their honor, especially in the Welsh character Fluellen. Fluellen is portrayed as brave and steadfast, though he is made somewhat ridiculous by the way he speaks and his loyalty is exploited when Henry charges him to wear a certain glove in his cap. Believing himself to have received a great honor, Fluellen obeys, only to be astonished when Williams, a common English soldier and the glove's owner, attacks him. Unbeknownst to Fluellen, Williams and a disguised King Henry had earlier quarreled, then traded gloves to help them find each other in order to resume the quarrel later. In returning Williams's blows, Fluellen unwittingly becomes part of a royal prank.

The French, by contrast, are lacking in bravery and run from the fray. Later, Henry is enraged to learn that French soldiers have massacred the pages set to watch the English tents; in retaliation, he orders all French prisoners killed. The last desperate onslaught of the French is repulsed; after a counting of the dead on both sides, the battle is over. Afterwards, Henry locates the man with whom he exchanged gloves, discloses the joke, and then returns the glove—filled with gold coins.

Shakespeare glides over the five years that separate Agincourt from the Treaty of Troyes. The last scene shows the negotiations leading to the treaty, and also switches from the martial to the marital; in a scene made comic by the princess's poor English, and by Henry's task of wooing his enemy's daughter, the king attempts, and eventually wins, Princess Catherine's heart. The rest—Henry's untimely death and his son's failures—are briefly alluded to in an epilogue, but the play itself ends on this celebratory note.

The character of Henry. In a popular legend, Henry spent his youth in frivolity and dissolution; he was said to have haunted taverns and brothels, and kept company with thieves and gamblers. But, just as his father faced the challenge of open rebellion, "Prince Hal" transfigured himself, throwing off his old associates and becoming a paragon of royal virtue. He was thus a mix of social height and social baseness; the skill and pride that accompanied his nobility was salted with an understanding of commoners gleaned from his youth. This combination paid off in France, where he led not as a king interested in advancing his own ambitions, but as the head of a unified nation. So, at least, runs the tale according to Shakespeare who, owing to a paucity of information, had to invent many details of Henry's personality.

Shakespeare's Henry V is an ambiguous character who has stirred controversy among a number of modern critics. The character's defenders contend that, whatever his flaws, *Henry V* represents an ideal monarch of Shakespeare's day, citing as evidence the justness of Henry's claim to France, his adroit handling of the three English traitors, his willingness to listen—while disguised—to the complaints and fears of common soldiers on the night before Agincourt, and his ability to rouse his troops to greater efforts in battle with the stirring declaration that "he today that sheds his blood with me / Shall be my brother. Be he ne'er so vile, / This day shall gentle his condition" (*Henry V*, 4.3.62-64). By contrast, the character's detractors charge that greed was Henry's motive for going to war with France, cite his killing of the French prisoners at Agincourt as proof of his belief in the superiority of brute force, and complain about his "awkward" wooing of Princess Katherine. It savors more, they say, of the boastful, triumphant king than the ardent lover: "I love France so well that I will not part with a village of it—I will have it all mine. And, Kate, when France is mine and I am yours, then yours is France and you are mine" (*Henry V*, 5.2.173-76).

Behind the controversy is the question of Henry's true motives. History shows that, by today's standards, not all Henry's actions were admirable. More than once, he proved himself capable of brutal treatment. Early in his reign, Henry put down a Lollard rebellion. It is reported that during a public burning of a Lollard, the condemned man began to scream for mercy. Henry ordered the fires extinguished and asked the man if he would recant his beliefs. When the man refused, Henry ordered the fires relit. He was no less severe when he discovered that an old friend and advisor, Sir John Oldcastle, was a leader of the Lollards. (Oldcastle was the original name used for the character Falstaff; it was changed when Oldcastle's descendants complained.) Henry had Oldcastle arrested, and eventually sent him to the stake with his followers.

Again in the French wars, Henry showed a capacity for ruthlessness. At Agincourt, he ordered all French captives slaughtered; while not unprecedented, this move went against the grain of medieval warfare. Armed combat was a formal, play-by-the-rules affair; once an opponent had cried mercy, the victor was normally bound to take care of him. Shakespeare, following the historians he consulted, presents the Agincourt slaughter as just revenge for French perfidy in stealing from the English army's tents and killing the pages on guard there. Modern historians are more inclined to suspect a tactical motive, inasmuch as the great number of French captives was a liability to the English as long as battle continued.

According to this last view, Henry did what was strategically necessary. Modern historians have similarly argued that Henry married France's Katherine because he recognized that the only way England could hold on to French lands, which rightfully belonged to it, was for Henry to rule France and be accepted by the people there. Finally, modern historians have described Henry as a man of "sincere piety" (Har-

riss, p. 202). His attack on the Lollards and defense of the Church establishment earned him, thought others in his time, "divine support" in the war against France, which gave them confidence in him (Allmand in Harriss, p. 120). Much about Henry remains elusive, but clearly he was adroit not only at soldiering but also at public relations. "Research has shown that for much of his reign Henry had the practical support of the majority of the highest nobility of the land"; he amassed popular support too, with the help of sermons such as one before his last trip to France, in which the king was called England's "maistur mariner," an appeal for the concept of a monarch and his kingdom united in war against an enemy, and under holy auspices (Allmand in Harriss, pp. 121, 122). Henry himself did much to further this concept. As king, Henry commanded a confidence in his person and purpose that enabled him to bring the "realm order, economy, unity, and respect for the crown" (Harriss, p. 209). In other respects, the man's character remains ambiguous, as it is in Shakespeare's play.

Sources and literary context. For *Henry V*, Shakespeare consulted his usual source: the historical chronicles of Raphael Holinshed, who was himself indebted to the writings of fellow historian Edward Hall. Some passages in Shakespeare's play, such as the discussion of the Salic Law, follow Holinshed argument for argument. In addition, Shakespeare took incidents and ideas from the markedly inferior but popular anonymous play *The Famous Victories of Henry the Fifth* (1598): this play contains many of the same episodes, and also juxtaposes weighty affairs of state with the soldiering of working-class recruits. For the scene in which Henry strolls through his camp in disguise, Shakespeare was probably indebted to a genre of plays popular in the 1590s, in which a ruler disguises himself to discover the true feelings of his subjects.

Events in History at the Time the Play Was Written

From Henry VI to Shakespeare's world. The marriage of Henry V to Katherine, daughter of French king Charles VI, seemed to guarantee that an Englishman would soon rule France. The promise was barely realized, with one such monarch. Henry VI was crowned French king in 1431, the only Englishman ever crowned on French soil, but his long reign (1431-61) was deeply troubled. Nine months old when his father died, he was never able to shake the influence of the English nobility, who ruled with a free hand during his minority. He reigned poorly, struggling to control nobles who moved ever closer to open rebellion; in 1461 he was deposed by the duke of York. By this time, the Dauphin, who had been disinherited by the Treaty of Troyes, ruled France. England had been utterly expelled; he accomplished this reversal mostly because of more effective military leadership (including Joan of Arc), and partly because the English were unable to pay the immense cost of foreign occupation. The gains of Henry V proved costly and impossible to sustain. In the end, his untimely death led to the loss of England's foothold in France and eventually plunged England into civil strife.

In 1455, a period of civil war began that was to last for three decades. The Wars of the Roses pitted two factions of nobles against each other—the Lancastrians, led by Henry VI, and the Yorkists, led by the future Edward IV (the war was named after the floral badges worn by each side: red for Lancaster, and white for York). The deposing of Henry VI by Edward IV brought a Yorkist to the throne. But the change did not result in peace: the wars continued until the duke of Richmond defeated Richard III in 1485, becoming Henry VII, first king in the Tudor dynasty of Shakespeare's day. Henry VII identified with the Lancastrians (he was descended from the second husband of Henry V's widow), and his marriage to the Yorkist princess Elizabeth unified the two families.

Shakespeare's England, which faced threats to stability in its own era, looked back on the confused events that plagued the fifteenth century with fear: the unrest reminded the people how easily personal ambition and disrespect for tradition could lead to civil chaos. However, from those horrible years shone a single ray of light: the reign of Henry V. "Good King Harry" was remembered with warm nostalgia, a nostalgia no doubt made the warmer by the coldness with which Shakespeare's contemporaries viewed the other kings of the late medieval period. *Henry V* reflected more than just affection for the past, though; it also indicated apprehension about the future. Among other perils, England in the late 1590s, in which the play was written, experienced 400 percent inflation, Irish wars, and succession anxiety. Elizabeth I had reigned for nearly 40 years; her refusal to marry and beget heirs had left the question of succession open. Who would

reign and how peacefully? Would the country bleed?

The discontented soldier. After he is beaten by Fluellen, Pistol announces that he will quit the soldier's life and live by robbery. This decision reflects a concern, widespread in Shakespeare's day, about the fate of the common soldier after his military career ended. Whether rightly or wrongly, many in sixteenth-century England believed that the ranks of highwaymen, bandits, and confidence artists were swollen with former soldiers.

In Henry's time, war was a highly individual affair. The king commanded his vassals; the vassals brought varying numbers of foot-soldiers, for whom they were responsible. While payment for services could be erratic, the common soldier could generally be assured some form of support from the feudal state to which he would return. He might even be enriched by the fruits of pillage or (more rarely) ransom. The decline of feudalism during the Tudor monarchies tended to remove this security. Returning veterans were, like many displaced people, likely to fall through the gaps in a society whose poverty laws were a tattered patchwork of good intentions. Unlike other displaced persons in this society, veterans had weapons and the ability to use them. As soldiers, they had learned that violence brought wealth. Discharged from service, the poor soldier could easily become a beggar, robber, or thug. In fact, many beggars attempted to gain sympathy by claiming the respect due to a veteran, and people of the time assumed that it just took one desperate night for a beggar to become a thief. While actual numbers are hard to come by, the literature of the period is full of portrayals of the swaggering, intimidating military bully.

Reviews. Although *Henry V* was first performed in 1599, the earliest recorded criticism does not appear until well into the seventeenth century. In 1691 Gerard Langbaine noted a historical parallel between the play and England in Queen Elizabeth's day: "This play was writ during the time that [the earl of] *Essex* was General in *Ireland,* as you may see in the beginning of the [fifth] Act, where our Poet, by a pretty Turn, compliments *Essex,* and seems to foretell Victory to her Majesties Forces against the Rebels" (Langbaine in Scott, p. 185). Other critics singled out characters and the execution of various scenes. Fluellen became a favorite; Charles Gildon called the character "extreamly [sic] comical, and yet so very happily touch'd, that at the same time when he makes us laugh, he makes us value his Character" (Gildon in Scott, p. 187). Gildon also praised Henry V as "very noble" and complimented some of his speeches as "very fine" (Gildon in Scott, pp. 186-187). Gildon was less impressed by the wooing scene between Henry and Katherine, which he described as "extravagantly silly and unnatural" (Gildon in Scott, p. 187). In the late eighteenth century, Samuel Johnson had a similar opinion: "The character of the King is well-supported, except in his courtship." In Johnson's view, "the great defect of this play is the emptiness and narrowness of the last act," but apart from this, *Henry V* "has many scenes of high dignity, and many of easy merriment" (Johnson in Scott, p. 190).

—Jacob Littleton

For More Information

Earle, Peter. *The Life and Times of Henry V.* London: Weidenfeld and Nicolson, 1993.

Greenblatt, Stephen. *Shakespearean Negotiations.* Berkeley: University of California Press, 1988.

Harriss, G. L., ed. *Henry V: The Practice of Kingship.* Oxford, England: Oxford University Press, 1985.

Holinshed, Raphael. *Shakespeare's Holinshed.* 1587. Ed. Richard Hosley. New York: G. P. Putnam's, 1968.

Labarge, Margaret. *Henry V.* London: Secker and Warburg, 1975.

Morgan, Kenneth. *The Oxford History of Britain.* Oxford, England: Oxford University Press, 1998.

Saccio, Peter. *Shakespeare's English Kings: History, Chronicle, and Drama.* New York: Oxford University Press, 1977.

Scott, Mark W. ed. *Shakesperean Criticism.* Vol. 5. Detroit: Gale Research Company, 1987.

Shakespeare, William. *King Henry V.* Ed. Claire McEachern. New York: Penguin, 1999.

Sprague, A. C. *Shakespeare's Histories: Plays for the Stage.* London: Society for Theatre Research, 1964.

Tuchman, Barbara. *A Distant Mirror.* New York: Bantam, 1978.

The History of Tom Jones: A Foundling

by

Henry Fielding

Henry Fielding was born in 1707 into a family with aristocratic connections. His father, Edmund, had ancestors who were earls, and his mother, Sarah, was daughter of the judge Sir Henry Gould. Their son Henry attended the elite Eton College, but then found himself forced to earn a living in his early twenties when a disputed inheritance claim left him without support. At this point, the young Fielding turned to playwriting and political journalism. In all, he would write some 25 plays, many satirizing the political corruption of the times. So scathing was his ridicule of corrupt government ministers, particularly of the powerful prime minister Sir Robert Walpole, that Parliament passed the 1737 Licensing Act, by which all new plays had to be approved and licensed by the lord chamberlain before production. This exercise in government censorship effectively ended Fielding's career as a dramatist, so he turned to political journalism, writing in the service of Whig opposition leaders Lord John Russell (fourth duke of Bedford) and Lord George Lyttleton (to whom *Tom Jones* is dedicated). After an abortive 1728 elopement with an heiress, Fielding courted and married Charlotte Cradock in 1734. She died 10 years later, and in 1747 he married Mary Daniel, who had been his wife's maid. He embarked during his first marriage on his career as a novelist, publishing first *An Apology for the Life of Mrs. Shamela Andrews* (1741), a spoof on Samuel Richardson's **Pamela** (also in *WLAIT 3: British and Irish Literature and Its Times*). Next came *The History of the Adventures of Joseph Andrews and of His Friend Mr.*

THE LITERARY WORK

A novel set in England in 1745 during the Jacobite rebellion; published in 1749.

SYNOPSIS

Tom Jones, purportedly illegitimate, overcomes the evil machinations of his half-brother, Master Blifil, in order finally to attain his birthright and the hand of Sophia Western.

Abraham Adams (1742). In 1748 Fielding was appointed magistrate for Westminster and Middlesex, in which capacity he established a reputation for justice in the suppression of crime. The following year he published his third novel, *Tom Jones*, which uses gentle satire to expose the follies, vanities, and vices of virtually every social class in mid-eighteenth century England.

Events in History at the Time of the Novel

Women's place in English society. Fielding's literary career, from his first published plays in 1727 until his death in 1754, coincided with an era when social and economic changes were causing profound upheaval in English life. The gradual emergence of a powerful middle class, which paralleled the first stirrings of centralized factory production, led to an intense scrutiny and reform of many long-accepted standards of morality. Not least among these changes was the status of women in society. In particular the role of marriage raised debatable questions: Should marriage be based on love or on purely economic considerations? Do parents have the right to choose marriage partners for their children? Since the mid-seventeenth century, there had been a trend toward greater autonomy for children in choosing marriage partners, except for the wealthiest classes, among whom considerations of property continued to determine alliances. But by Fielding's day, middle- and lower-class marriage candidates, and even a few among the wealthier, landed classes, normally made their own choices, with parents exercising no more than the right of veto over candidates deemed too poor or ill-bred. "At the root of these changes in the power to make decisions about marriage . . . there lie . . . a new recognition of the need for personal autonomy, and a new respect for the individual pursuit of happiness" (Stone, pp. 183-84). This change has been attributed to a more indulgent regard for individual emotional integrity.

Related to the new emphasis on personal happiness is the critique in *Tom Jones* of the equation in eighteenth-century society between chastity and virtue. A sexual double standard of the time demanded strict chastity in women, particularly women of the middle and upper classes, but allowed men considerable latitude for dalliance prior to marriage and even within marriage. This is reflected in *Tom Jones,* whose hero appears to essentially have no sexual restraint. Yet he is the hero. The novel, in other words, argues against a morality that is defined solely or primarily in sexual terms, as it appears to have been in Richardson's novel *Pamela.*

Fielding's opinions on the issue of marriage were similarly progressive for his day. *Tom Jones* provides a gallery of unsatisfactory marriages plagued by a variety of moral ills: mercenary motives, avarice, jealousy, vanity, and poverty. In particular, the custom of forced marriage—still practiced, as noted, among the moneyed classes, who judged the desirability of a marriage solely on considerations of wealth and property—receives some of Fielding's most savage satire. Fielding considered such forced marriages little more than legalized rape.

Social class in eighteenth-century England. While Fielding was a forceful opponent of marriages arranged for mercenary reasons of property or title, and *Tom Jones* clearly contrasts the old and new views of marriage, the novel's so-

cial conservatism is equally unmistakable. Fielding, who identified with the interests of the aristocratic ruling class, was less concerned than some of his contemporaries with social mobility; events, particularly in his novels but also in his plays, tend to work themselves out in the direction of preserving the hierarchical class structure of his day. Eighteenth-century England was a rigidly stratified class-based society, with the royalty and aristocracy at the top of the social hierarchy, the landed gentry or squirearchy below them, followed by an increasingly prosperous and powerful urban middle class of lawyers, bankers, merchants, and manufacturers. Underneath them came small tradesmen and artisans, small freeholders of farms, and, at the bottom, landless farmhands, factory workers, and assorted urban laborers.

Fielding's novels do not explicitly challenge this social structure or its associated inequalities. His heroes, whatever their personal status and class might seem to be, always arrive at wealth and gentility by the end of the novel, and *Tom Jones* is no exception. The protagonist, Tom, becomes an acceptable mate for the upper-class Sophia only when his authentic well-born status is revealed. If he had remained a penniless bastard, his ending would no doubt have been far less happy. The novel appears to endorse England's stratified society as the most desirable pattern, but the novel does find fault with particular injustices in the interest of ridding that pattern of its offenses. As a novelist, and also in his role as a magistrate, Fielding was zealous in his aim of reforming the manners of his age, particularly the vices of petty theft, prostitution, and especially the domestic violence characteristic of many forced marriages. As one social historian explains, "Mistreatment of women by their husbands was commonplace. Severe beatings, often routinely administered on whim, were outside the pale of the law. Only when they ended in murder was the brutality deemed to be criminal" (McLynn, p. 102).

Fielding's latitudinarian ethics. *Tom Jones,* however humorous, was written by Fielding as Christian censor of the manners and morals of his age. The novel's moral message is directly related to seventeenth- and eighteenth-century latitudinarian Christianity. This was a branch of the Anglican Church known as the "Broad Church," in contrast to the "High Church" (which emphasized tradition, ceremony, and hierarchy) and the "Low Church" (which emphasized the centrality of biblical faith, piety, and personal conversion). In its own emphasis on good nature and charity, latitudinarian Christianity derives from the teachings of such Low Church divines as Isaac Barrow, John Tillotson, Samuel Clarke, and Benjamin Hoadly. Basic to the latitudinarian position was a belief in the essential goodness of human nature and in the importance of charity as the cardinal virtue. Good nature became the core of latitudinarian Christianity, which had as its goal the practical betterment of society, as well as the salvation of individual souls. The latitudinarians emphasized the human potential for perfection, if only the pressures of corrupt customs and biased education could be removed. This conviction served as the rationale that undergirded Fielding's social satire.

Latitudinarian Christianity was strongly influenced in England by the development of natural religion. The earliest representative of natural religion in England was early seventeenth-century Deism; in Fielding's time, its leading spokespersons were Anthony Ashley Cooper, third earl of Shaftesbury (1671-1713), and Henry St. John, Viscount Bolingbroke (1678-1751). These men believed that religious knowledge is innate to human beings and can be acquired through reason alone. They denied all supernatural revelation and the authority of the Bible and of specific church teachings as genuine sources of religious truth. Fielding himself was not a Deist; he remained a staunch Broad-Church Anglican, but he was influenced, like most intellectuals of his age, by the efforts of natural religion to unite the best of Christian ethics, classical philosophy, and the new scientific knowledge. The influence of natural religion resulted in a growing emphasis on works rather than faith. Christians were those who behaved like Christians, and charity was the most obvious expression of religious devotion.

The theological doctrines of all the main churches were affected by latitudinarian tendencies in the eighteenth century. Mainstream dissent from the Anglican Church, once the driving force behind the Puritan revolution, visibly declined in English popular life and retreated, at least for the moment, to its traditional support among the urban middle class. The branch of Anglicanism known as the High Church continued its somewhat erratic work in the rural areas, dependent as ever on the residence and personal commitment of a portion of its clergy. In the towns and smaller cities, the High Church contingent was all too prone to withdraw, or to appeal—as its competitors, the Dissenters did—to polite middle-class congregations who could af-

ford to supplement the income of churchmen in poorer parishes, and to beautify or rebuild churches.

In *Tom Jones*, Fielding opposes his latitudinarian ethics to other doctrines then prevalent among religious controversialists, particularly the doctrine of total depravity found both in the ethics of self-interest espoused by Thomas Hobbes and the Calvinist theology then gaining renewed strength with the rise of Methodism in England. Both Hobbes and the Calvinists as-

---

RELIGION IN EIGHTEENTH-CENTURY ENGLAND

In the age when Fielding wrote *Tom Jones*, advances in science were threatening the traditional authority of the Bible and the Church. Characters in the novel embody particular religious and philosophical positions that reflect schisms of the age:

Conservative Christian: This stance includes Calvinists, Methodists, most Nonconformists, and some Anglicans (followers of the mainstream Church of England). According to its beliefs, people are saved solely by faith in Christ. They are basically immoral, and faith is more important than reason. In *Tom Jones*, Thwackum (whose name means "hit them") represents this stance.

Deist: Included in this category are religious skeptics. The stance is a philosophy and so does not concern itself with salvation. Its followers do not believe in the Bible, but claim that God can be known by reason. In *Tom Jones*, Square (whose name means a "rationally constructed geometric form") represents this stance.

Liberal Christian: This stance includes latitudinarians, a branch of the Anglican Church that rejected miracles and expressed confidence in human nature and its ability to improve society. Also including some other Anglicans, this stance achieves a mean between the extremes of Conservative Christian and Deist, and exercises great license in regard to who can be saved. A pagan with a good heart has a better chance than a vicious Christian, according to Fielding, who falls into this category.

---

serted the essential selfishness and depravity of human nature, and this attitude is reproduced in *Tom Jones*, particularly in the characters of the Man of the Hill and the chaplain Thwackum. The Man of the Hill has retreated from human society because of its wickedness and greed, but when Tom happens to save him from thieves, he agrees to tell his story. The novel leaves him isolated in his misanthropy. Thwackum illustrates the callous streak in strict Calvinist notions of innate depravity, and the novel leaves him preaching his hard-hearted gospel in an obscure vicarage.

ENGLISH POLITICS IN THE EIGHTEENTH CENTURY

Jacobite: A loyal supporter of the Catholic king James II and his claim as the legitimate heir to the throne of England. Many Roman Catholics and High-Church Tories were Jacobites or sympathized with the Stuarts (James's lineage). Support for the Jacobite cause posed a more or less serious threat of a Stuart restoration from 1688 until 1745, and thereafter survived in Ireland, Scotland, and Wales.

Whigs: Members of a political group identified with some powerful aristocratic families and the financial interests of the wealthy middle classes. Whig membership was largely drawn from Low Churchmen and Dissenters, and they monopolized parliamentary politics for most of the century. Whig policies were strongly anti-Catholic, anti-Jacobite, and anti-French.

Tories: Members of a political group that supported the hereditary right of James II, despite his Roman Catholic faith. Tory membership was often identified with High-Church Anglicanism, the aristocracy, and the squirearchy (or country gentry). Although powerless in Parliament after the ascension of George I in 1714, Tories continued to dominate local borough politics and administration well into the nineteenth century.

Squirearchy: The class of landed gentry that comprised the backbone of Tory and Jacobite conservatism. The squirearchy was often satirized by the urban Whigs in the stock figure of the "Country Tory" or "Booby Squire," stereotyped as a backwoods country gentleman of rough manners and an excessive fondness for fox hunting and ale drinking.

(Cleary, pp. 264-72)

The "Forty-Five." The historical setting for *Tom Jones* is the era of the last Jacobite rebellion in 1745, commonly known in English history as the "Forty-Five." Its background begins with the House of Stuart, which had ruled England since the ascension of James I in 1603.

The Rise and Fall of the House of Stuart

1603 James I (James VI of Scotland) inaugurates rule of the House of Stuart on the English throne.

1642 Civil war erupts, leads to execution of Charles I in 1649.

1649-60 Era of Puritan rule consists of two periods: 1) the Commonwealth (1649-53), in which Parliament retained nominal control, though Oliver Cromwell wielded ultimate power; 2) the Protectorate, in which Cromwell ruled as Lord Protector, advised by a council of state.

1660-85 England restores the monarchy. Charles II, a Stuart, assumes the throne.

1685-88 James II, a Stuart and a Roman Catholic, rules England, fathers a son.

1688 English Protestants, rejecting the prospect of a Catholic successor, depose James II and award reign to William III of Orange and his wife Mary (James II's Protestant daughter).

The deposed James II fled to France, where he was supported in exile by France's Louis XIV. When James II died in 1701, his son James Edward Stuart, known as the Old Pretender, was proclaimed James III by Louis XIV and treated as the legitimate king of England. Supported by French forces, the Old Pretender made several halfhearted attempts to gain the English throne. Succeeding William and Mary on the throne was Queen Anne, Mary's younger sister. Anne ruled England from 1702 to 1714, leaving no heir. At this point, the English Parliament took the crown from the House of Stuart and gave it to George I, monarch of the German electorate of Hanover and great-grandson of James I through his mother's line. In response to what he considered the House of Hanover's usurpation of the crown, the Old Pretender invaded Scotland in 1715, but this attempt was abortive.

By the 1740s, George II was king of England, and his armies—allied with Austrian, Hanoverian, and Hessian forces—were fighting on the Continent in the War of the Austrian Succession (1740-48). Charles Edward Stuart, who was the son of James Edward Stuart and was known as the Young Pretender or Bonnie Prince Charlie, landed in Scotland in July 1745 with a handful of followers, intending to reclaim the English throne for his father. This attempt is featured in *Tom Jones*. The Young Pretender first gathered support among the Highlanders of Scotland, then scattered a loyalist army at Prestonpans and occupied Edinburgh. In the autumn, he raised his standard in England, reaching Derby by December. Here, only a few days' march from London, his luck turned and his losses mounted. Compounding the problem were the facts that his small army had been increased by only a few English recruits, and that he had left much opposition behind him. In the end, the Young Pretender reluctantly abandoned the idea of a dash upon London and returned to Scotland. Though he was able to win one more victory at Falkirk, he suffered a crushing defeat at Culloden in April 1746. This defeat ended the Jacobite threat for all time.

While *Tom Jones* is not an overtly political novel, the events of the "Forty-Five" provide a colorful background for Tom's picaresque adventures on the road. The protagonist, Tom, is himself a loyal subject of George II and even briefly joins a troop of soldiers marching north in order to repel the Stuart invader, though several other important characters in the novel are Jacobites or at least sympathetic to Bonnie Prince Charlie's cause. Squire Western, father of Tom's beloved Sophia, is a thoroughgoing Tory, the political party from which the Stuarts drew most of their support, and details about him expose his Jacobite leanings.

Prince Charles Edward Stewart, also known as Bonnie Prince Charlie, led the Jacobite rebellion in 1745.

The Novel in Focus

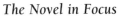

Plot summary. The wealthy and benevolent Squire Allworthy, a widower, lives in Somerset with his ill-humored and ill-favored unmarried sister Bridget. Returning home late one evening after a business trip to London, Squire Allworthy finds a baby in his bed. He is charmed with the mysterious boy, names him Tom, and becomes his guardian and provider, eventually adding the surname Jones on the assumption that the mother is Jenny Jones, a maidservant to the local schoolmaster Partridge. Soon after, both Jenny and Partridge vanish from the town, Bridget marries the devious and brutal Captain Blifil, and they have a son, Master Blifil, who is raised alongside Tom. The boys are taught by the punishing chaplain Thwackum and the philosopher Square. Squire Allworthy's household consists also of the maid Deborah Wilkins, the gamekeeper Black George Seagrim, and the gamekeeper's wife and daughters. Among the household's neighbors are the bluff and bumptious Squire Western, his sister Mrs. Western, and his daughter Sophia.

The continuous narrative of the novel begins when the hero is 19, with several preceding childhood episodes establishing him as a generous, good-natured, and high-spirited lad, in contrast to the selfish, devious, and villainous Blifil. Tom at this point recognizes that his childhood affection for his beautiful, sweet-natured neighbor Sophia (whose portrait Fielding based upon his own wife Charlotte) has grown into adult love. But Sophia is destined by her father to marry Master Blifil, whom she detests, and Tom, dejected by his imminent loss of Sophia, allows himself to be distracted by the charms of Molly Seagrim. When Molly declares that she is pregnant, Tom is prepared to do the honorable thing in the face of Squire Allworthy's displeasure, but he is released from this obligation when he learns that Molly has been very free with her favors, which she has extended even to the tutor Square.

By clever misrepresentation, the scheming young Blifil converts his uncle Squire Allworthy's affection for Tom into anger, and with the help of Thwackum and Square, he succeeds in having Tom expelled from the house. Filled with despair because he has alienated his beloved foster-father and is leaving all he cares for, Tom sets off for Bristol intending to go to sea. Meanwhile Sophia, disgusted by Blifil's courtship, escapes her father's close confinement and runs away to London with her maid, Mrs. Honour, intending to seek shelter there with her kinswoman Lady Bellaston.

Amid many colorful adventures on the road, including falling in with a troop of redcoats marching north to oppose the Stuart rebellion, Tom encounters Partridge, the former schoolmaster thought to be his father, now traveling the country as a barber-surgeon. Tom's generosity is rewarded when the alms he gives a beggar lead to his discovery of Sophia's pocketbook, a sign that she has journeyed to London, which renews Tom's hope of winning her. Unknown to Tom, he and Sophia are lodging at the same inn, but because of Partridge's loose tongue, Sophia believes that Tom (now in bed with a certain Mrs. Waters) no longer loves her, and she flees towards London. Tom follows, and in London is ensnared by the rich and amorous Lady Bellaston, who supports him as a kept lover. She and her friend Lord Fellamar, who is in lustful pursuit of Sophia, conspire to keep Tom away from his beloved, with Lord Fellamar nearly raping and abducting Sophia before the timely arrival of Squire Western.

PRESS-GANGING

≈

In *Tom Jones*, Lady Bellaston and Lord Fellamar plot to have Tom press-ganged, but the hero is jailed on suspicion of murder before their plan is executed. Impressment, also known as "crimping," involved the forcible abduction and enlistment into the military or naval service of able-bodied but unwilling men. England manned many of its warships by means of these crude and violent methods during much of the eighteenth century, and the practice flourished in port towns throughout the world until the early nineteenth century. The "recruiters" preyed to a great extent upon men from the lower classes, who were, more often than not, vagabonds or even prisoners. Usual sources of manpower were waterfront boardinghouses, brothels, and taverns whose owners often victimized their own clientele.

Partridge now reveals that Mrs. Waters is none other than Jenny Jones, supposed by many to be Tom's mother, and for a brief period Tom fears he has committed incest. Jenny reveals, however, that Tom's mother was really Bridget Allworthy (later Mrs. Blifil), who has confessed all to her brother on her deathbed, and that his father was a young gentleman long since dead. Lady Bel-

laston and Lord Fellamar conspire to have Tom press-ganged into the navy, but instead he is arrested and imprisoned after a fight in which it first appears he has killed his assailant.

Sophia cannot forgive Tom's entanglement with Lady Bellaston, and his fortunes are at their nadir. Blifil arranges for the sailors who witnessed the fight to give evidence against Tom, but, with the help of a long letter from Square to Squire Allworthy, Blifil's envious machinations, dating from their earliest boyhood, are finally revealed, and Tom is reinstated in his repentant uncle's affection. Tom meets Sophia again at last, learns that she loves him and forgives his infidelities, and receives the hearty blessing of her father. According to the dictates of his generous heart, Tom forgives all who have wronged him, including the detestable Blifil.

The foundling: nexus of English social and sexual morality. *Tom Jones* begins with Squire Allworthy's discovery of an abandoned baby who has been slipped into his bed. His natural generosity and humanity lead Squire Allworthy to care for the child and raise him as a son, but actually foundling infants often met a far different fate. In fact, by means of introducing this one little baby, Fielding deftly illuminates many of the prevailing social and sexual relations of eighteenth-century England: between males and females, parents and children, servants and masters, and gentry and commoners. The novel draws its satirical implications from the different characters' attitudes toward the infant Tom: the search for Tom's mother shows the inquisitorial climate of village life; Bridget Allworthy's behavior reflects the cagey dissembling done to maintain an image of respectability; and the maid Deborah Wilkins's hard-hearted attitude toward the foundling satirizes the hypocrisy and smug sanctimony of a self-professed Christian who can cheerfully damn both a mother and child to miserable poverty.

As indicated, economic changes in the eighteenth century were upsetting traditional social patterns. Progressive enclosure of common fields was destroying cooperative village farming in various areas, driving previously self-sufficient farm families into the ranks of landless rural laborers. Rather than starve in the country, many of these newly poor took work in factory towns or moved to London, swelling its urban underclass. This rapid population growth exacerbated poverty, which adversely affected illegitimate children:

One consequence of the rise in the proportion of the propertyless in the society was a rise in the rates of illegitimate to legitimate births. . . . The rise in bastardy inevitably stimulated some deliberate infanticide and a great deal of abandonment, for the plight of an unmarried mother without means of support was bad enough to encourage a few desperate women to murder their newly born infants and many more to leave them in the streets either to die or to be looked after by a charitable passer-by, the parish workhouse, or a foundling hospital. (Stone, pp. 296-97)

Illegitimacy was rapidly rising in eighteenth-century England, even though the social ramifications for the parents were disastrous. Communities traditionally supported illegitimate children through the parish poor rate—that is, the local charity tax—but they also pressured the father to marry the mother. Legislation passed in 1733 added legal pressures to those of the community, making any man whom the mother identified as the father of her illegitimate child liable for child-support payments. Meanwhile, women who bore children out of wedlock were ostracized by the community and left to fend for themselves as best they could. In his role as local magistrate, Squire Allworthy predicts that this fate will befall Jenny Jones, Tom's presumed mother, when he tells her that by her "crime" she will be "rendered infamous, and driven, like Lepers of old, out of Society; at least from the Society of all but wicked and reprobate Persons; for no others will associate with you" (Fielding, *Tom Jones*, vol. 1, p. 52). The typical fate of a "fallen woman" was to be driven into prostitution, as Squire Allworthy obliquely insinuates in the novel, and she bore the greatest part of the guilt involved: "For by the Laws of Custom the whole Shame, with all its dreadful Consequences, falls entirely upon her" (*Tom Jones*, vol. 1, p. 52).

The voice of community censure is embodied in the person of Mrs. Deborah Wilkins, Squire Allworthy's "elderly Woman Servant," whose "pure Eyes" size up the infant Tom's situation immediately: "I hope your Worship will send out your Warrant to take up the Hussy its Mother (for she must be one of the neighborhood) and I should be glad to see her committed to *Bridewel*, and whipt at the Cart's Tail. Indeed, such wicked Sluts cannot be too severely punished" (*Tom Jones*, vol. 1, p. 40). Located in London, Bridewell was a women's reformatory, and by English law, the mother of a bastard child chargeable to the parish could be committed by order of two justices to this prison (or house of correction), there

An increase in the rate of child abandonment in the eighteenth century led to the establishment of the London Foundling Hospital depicted in this illustration.

to be corporally punished and set to work for the term of one year. The "proper" Mrs. Wilkins advises Squire Allworthy to dispose of the child in this way:

Faugh, how it stinks! It doth not smell like a Christian. If I might be so bold to give my Advice, I would have it put in a Basket, and sent out and laid at the Church-Warden's Door. It is a good Night, only a little rainy and windy; and if it was well wrapt up, and put in a warm Basket, it is two to one but it lives till it is found in the Morning. But if it should not, we have discharged our Duty in taking proper care of it; and it is, perhaps, better for such Creatures to die in a state of Innocence, than to grow up and imitate their Mothers; for nothing better can be expected of them.

(*Tom Jones*, vol. 1, p. 41)

This is the voice of Christian charity and duty, the object of Fielding's relentless satire.

In London, the rate of child abandonment led in 1741 to the establishment of the London Foundling Hospital. The hospital's resources were limited, and when it began to accept children from anywhere in England in 1756, it was overwhelmed with more than 15,000 foundlings in the first four years, 10,000 of whom died. "Although many of this growing mass of abandoned children were illegitimate, a majority seem to have been legitimate children of couples who were financially unable to support them. Abandonment of infants was thus a product partly of rising rates of bastardy, but still more of a deepening economic crisis for the very poor" (Stone, pp. 298-99). Accounts of the abuse and exploitation suffered by abandoned children in the eighteenth century make some of the most harrowing reading in the chronicles of English social history. The typical fate of foundlings "lucky" enough to survive infancy was dark indeed:

> For the few who survived, the prospect was a grim one. The older females were frequently handed over to "a master who is either vicious or cruel: in the one case they fall victim to his irregular passions; and in the other are subjected, with unreasonable severity, to tasks too hard to be performed." These were the lucky ones, others being virtually enslaved by criminals and trained for a life of prostitution if female or of robbery and pick-pocketing if male. Some had their teeth torn out to serve as artificial teeth for the rich; others were deliberately maimed by beggars to arouse compassion and extract alms. Even this latter crime was one upon which the law looked with a remarkably tolerant eye. In 1761 a beggar woman, convicted of deliberately "putting out the eyes of children with whom she went about the country" in order to attract pity and alms, was sentenced to no more than two years imprisonment. (Stone, p. 298)

Fielding was well aware of the horrors faced by foundling children, and reacted with a moral outrage that helped inspire the writing of *Tom Jones*.

Sources and literary context. Fielding drew on the picaresque tradition of Miguel de Cervantes's *Don Quixote* (1605) as a primary model for *Tom Jones*. As in the Spanish classic, many of the comic events in *Tom Jones* occur in wayside inns, where a variety of characters are juxtaposed for satiric effect. Not only are the landlords and landladies of these inns and alehouses lampooned for their petty avarice and nosiness, but chambermaids and stewards, coachmen and postilions, constables and thieves, clergymen and peddlers, doctors and lawyers, soldiers and sailors, and, of course, upper-class ladies and beaux all receive satiric lashings for their follies and vices, particularly for hypocrisy, greed, and calculating self-interest.

Fielding had perfected his technique as a comic dramatist through the 1730s, writing popularly successful plays such as *Tom Thumb* (1730)

and *Pasquin* (1736). The witty dialogue in *Tom Jones* reflects his genius as a dramatist, as do the novel's many memorable characters and the artfully contrived comic situations. Fielding's characters show a debt to the classical Greco-Roman dramatic tradition, particularly the stock characters invented by the Greek philosopher Theophrastus and the conventional plots of Roman comedy, which feature "humorous" characters—individuals ruled by a dominant "humor," such as the lecherous man, the avaricious man, or the superstitious man. The influence of the English satirical tradition is also apparent in occasional allusions to Samuel Butler's *Hudibras* (1663), Jonathan Swift's *A Tale of a Tub* (1703), and Alexander Pope's **The Rape of the Lock** (1714) (also in *WLAIT 3: British and Irish Literature and Its Times*). For example, Fielding recommends always reading *Tom Jones* with "a Tankard of good Ale," citing as his authority Butler's opinion that not the muses but ale is the true source of inspiration for both authors and readers (*Tom Jones*, Vol. 1, pp. 150-51).

Among Fielding's contemporaries were writers who contributed to the newly emerging genre of the novel, including Daniel Defoe and Samuel Richardson (see **Moll Flanders** and **Pamela; or Virtue Rewarded,** also in *WLAIT 3: British and Irish Literature and Its Times*). The circumstantial manner in which Defoe's and Richardson's novels imitate reality was essential to the new, empirical approach to the world invoked by scientists of the Royal Society. (The Royal Society's approach to truth was through the amassing, weighing, and measuring of particulars.)

Fielding, while embracing the empirical approach to some extent, in other respects diverged from the style of Defoe and Richardson. To a certain degree, Fielding remained loyal to the classical tradition of Plato and Aristotle, who taught that the highest reality transcends the realm of shadowy particulars in which daily life is lived. This highest reality is found in the essential forms of things and in generalized representative types; the artist must penetrate through particulars to the general, through what is accidental to what is universal. Thus, Fielding's characters, though they have a life and integrity of their own, can also be read as tokens of a reality larger than themselves, and his novels can be seen as highly schematic paradigms of the human condition. As the novel itself says, the subject of Tom Jones "is no other than HUMAN NATURE" (*Tom Jones*, vol. 1, p. 77).

Reception. *Tom Jones* was an immediate popular success and has long retained its preeminent place in the canon of English literature. According to Samuel Taylor Coleridge (see **Lyrical Ballads,** also in *WLAIT 3: British and Irish Literature and Its Times*), *Tom Jones* had one of "the three most perfect plots ever planned" (Coleridge in Blanchard, p. 321). The opinion of an anonymous reviewer in the April 1751 issue of *The Magazine of Magazines* is typical:

> Whosoever is acquainted with his [Fielding's] writings must confess that there is no body so . . . capable of representing virtue in its own amiable dress, or vice in its native deformity, that has such a thorough insight into the causes and effects of things, is such a master of character, and so able to draw the picture of an author, and a reader of every kind. (Blanchard, pp. 77-78)

Some contemporary critics, such as Samuel Johnson and Samuel Richardson, criticized the "low" characters in the novel, but their opinions merely reflect the critical dogmatism of the eighteenth century, when standards of decorum held that the deeds of innkeepers and servants—to say nothing of impoverished bastards—could never make suitable reading for modest and pious ladies. In spite of relentless disparagement by moralizing critics, *Tom Jones* nevertheless earned its author the highest praises from, among others, the English historian Edward Gibbon, who pronounced *Tom Jones* to be an "exquisite picture of human manners" that would endure (Gibbon in Blanchard, p. 234).

—Jim Caufield

For More Information

Battestin, Martin C. *A Henry Fielding Companion.* Westport, Conn.: Greenwood, 2000.

———. *Henry Fielding: A Life.* London: Routledge, 1989.

Blanchard, Frederic T. *Fielding the Novelist: A Study in Historical Criticism.* New Haven, Conn.: Yale University Press, 1926.

Cleary, Thomas R. *Henry Fielding: Political Writer.* Waterloo, Ont.: Wilfrid Laurier University Press, 1984.

Fielding, Henry. *The History of Tom Jones: A Foundling.* 2 vols. Ed. Fredson Bowers. Oxford, England: Clarendon, 1974.

Harrison, Bernard. *Henry Fielding's Tom Jones: The Novelist as Moral Philosopher.* London: University of Sussex Press, 1975.

McLynn, Frank. *Crime and Punishment in Eighteenth-Century England.* London: Routledge, 1989.

Paulson, Ronald. *The Life of Henry Fielding.* London: Blackwell, 2000.

Smallwood, Angela J. *Fielding and the Woman Question: The Novels of Henry Fielding and Feminist Debate 1700-1750.* New York: St. Martin's, 1989.

Stone, Lawrence. *The Family, Sex and Marriage in England 1500-1800.* New York: Harper, 1979.

Thomas, Donald Sherrel. *Henry Fielding.* London: Weidenfeld and Nicolson, 1990.

Vickery, Amanda. *The Gentleman's Daughter: Women's Lives in Georgian England.* New Haven, Conn.: Yale University Press, 1998.

King Lear

by
William Shakespeare

William Shakespeare (1564-1616) was about 41 years old when he wrote *King Lear*, the tragedy that many deem his greatest. He created the play to be performed for King James, who had assumed the English throne shortly before, in 1603. Featured in the tragedy is a ruler who in some ways diverged sharply from James. James showed a commitment to peace and to preserving the integrity of and even unifying Britain, in contrast to Lear's fatal division of his kingdom, which prompted bloodshed and war. Shakespeare wrote this tragedy well after the halfway point of his two-decade career, at a time when his acting company, the King's Men, was cementing its position as London's preeminent theatrical troupe. Shortly thereafter, he would stop writing tragedies altogether. *King Lear* is therefore one of Shakespeare's last great statements on the tragic potential in human life. Set in a kingdom of ancient Britain, the play is also one of his wildest, darkest, and most anarchic.

Events in History at the Time the Play Takes Place

Layers of time. The exact time period in which *King Lear* takes place remains imprecise. One of Shakespeare's sources, Raphael Holinshed's *Chronicles of England, Scotland, and Ireland* (1587), places the story of King Lear at around 800 B.C.E., but the play shows few traces of early times. In fact, the handful of historical details that are in the play does not correspond to our

THE LITERARY WORK

A tragic play set in ancient Britain around 800 B.C.E.; written c. 1605; first performed in 1606; published in 1608.

SYNOPSIS

An aging king's decision to abdicate and divide his kingdom among his three daughters leads to tragedy for the entire royal family.

understanding of life among the early Britons of the first millennium B.C.E. Anachronisms surface that are characteristic of medieval rather than ancient Britain, the influence perhaps of Holinshed's source, the *Historia Regum Britanniae* (History of the Kings of Britain, c. 1135) by Geoffrey of Monmouth, which Shakespeare himself may have read. Even more prominent in *King Lear* are the reflections of social conditions and controversies from Shakespeare's own age. Perhaps because of its dearth of historical detail, many have "seen the play primarily in relation to the Jacobean age," that is, the age of King James (Foakes in Shakespeare, p. 13). Given the complication of three chronological layers—ancient, medieval, and Jacobean—the following survey moves from life among the ancient Britons as we understand it today, to the legendary history of King Lear as Shakespeare knew it, to the era of King James as it relates to the play.

Celtic life. Not organized into a single kingdom, the ancient British Celts, or Britons, consisted rather of individual peoples loosely affiliated by language and culture. These peoples immigrated into Britain in successive waves, from the early to the late first thousand years B.C.E., with the last major group appearing sometime before 100 B.C.E., ahead of the Roman arrival in 55 B.C.E. These ancient British Celts are the first group in Britain about whom historians have been able to glean some detailed information.

ANACHRONISTIC HUSBANDS

Among other anachronisms, Cordelia's suitors are the king of France and the duke of Burgundy, but neither France nor the duchy of Burgundy existed in 800 B.C. The region that would become France was known then as Gaul, and pre-Christian Burgundy did not exist as a separate area, but simply as part of Gaul. Likewise, ancient Britain did not have a duke of Cornwall or of Albany—the duchy of Cornwall dates from 1337 and the first duke of Albany from 1458. But the two titles had particular resonance in the court of King James, who had two sons in these very positions: his son Charles had been made duke of Albany in 1600; his son Henry, duke of Cornwall in 1603.

Most of the Celts were settled farmers and herders. Their settlements were small and widely dispersed, with much of the population raising food for sustenance. But they also had a fairly well-developed system of trade and were skilled at working in iron, leather, gold, and clay to create goods for exchange (metal money was not in use by the ancient Celts before they came under the influnce of the Romans). Society esteemed military prowess, especially the young warrior-hero who succeeded in single combat. Also esteemed was intellectual prowess. The people boasted a highly developed oral literature. Heroes were well versed in the traditional knowledge and storytellers transmitted important information—codes of law, genealogies, and epic stories. However, the Britons were pre-literate; the various letters sent in *King Lear* are among the play's many anachronisms.

The Britons were not unified under a single ruler. Instead, the basic unit of society was the large or small settlement, and its basic unit was the family. Society consisted of four classes: the king, nobles, free commoners, and the "unfree" (including, among other groups, slaves). While kingship was hereditary, it did not necessarily fall to the eldest son; any male relative of the current king could be designated his successor. In the noble class were druids, priests who intervened between the people and their pagan gods. Most of the free commoners were farmers and craftsmen. A woman did not enjoy the same rights as a man; her powers were limited, though the specific parameters remain unknown.

The Celts did not have the implicitly feudal system of government present in *King Lear*. Each Celtic clan owned its own land, which could not be withdrawn from the clan, though it could be lost by agreement or sale. In any case, land was not dispensed by a king in exchange for services, as it was under feudalism. The Celts did have another institution, "clientship," by which a lord would provide a commodity (for example, land, military protection, or some other benefit) to a client in exchange for a service (crops, or military service, or hospitality). But the relationship was more cooperative and less dependent than in feudal society.

The Celts reached their historical pinnacle just before they were conquered by the Romans and then by Germanic tribes. Overrun twice, the Celts of continental Europe receded into the historical background. It was mainly on the British Isles that independent Celtic peoples survived, among groups inhabiting areas of Ireland, Scotland, and Wales.

From clientship to feudalism. As indicated, the few historical references in *King Lear* reflect life not in ancient but in medieval England, when society was based on feudalism. The institution first appeared on the island after its invasion by the Normans in 1066. In a feudal system, the king owns all the land and bestows it on tenants-in-chiefs, that is, lesser nobles than himself, in exchange for political and military service. The system came to England about 1070 B.C.E., when William the Conqueror introduced a professional army based on the mounted knight. He peopled this army with the help of his tenants-in-chief, who in exchange for a land grant, provided him with a specific number of armored knights for a certain amount of time each year. To secure the arrangement from generation to generation, society practiced primogeniture, which meant a tenant's inheritance passed *undivided* to his eldest son. This preserved continuity in the services owed to the king. If a man had no son, feudal law dictated that his inheritance should be divided among his daughters, a custom that promised them a lower standard of living than the one in which they had been raised.

Legendary history as Shakespeare knew it. Lear is a legendary king, whose existence remains unproven. Holinshed's *Chronicles,* which documents the legendary history, identifies Lear as a descendant of Brutus, the alleged founder of the first British kingdom. A survivor of the Trojan War, Brutus's forefather, Aeneas, is said to have gone to Italy, which led to his founding of Rome, and to Brutus's subsequent trek northward to found a kingdom in Britain. In other words, Britain, like Rome, was the descendant of the doomed city of Troy. According to the *Chronicles,* Brutus first appeared on the island around 250 years before Lear, conquered a giant people there, established a kingdom, and governed it for 15 years. Before his death, he divided the island among his three sons. His eldest son, Locrine, ruled England next; followed by Locrine's son Maden, followed by his son Mempricius, and so on through the generations (to Ebranke, Brute Greeneshield, Leill, Ludhurdibr, and then Bladud) until Lear, who became the tenth one to reign.

Described as an especially noble monarch, Lear governed England in great wealth, establishing the town Leicester (then called Caerleir). He had three daughters whom he loved dearly, favoring especially his youngest, Cordelia. In his old age, he seized upon the idea of having the three express their affection for him to determine which of them should be his successor. Cordelia's answer vexed him so greatly that he married his two eldest daughters to the dukes of Cornwall and Albany, informing them that they could divide all his land between them after his death; half of this inheritance they were to receive immediately. Cordelia, on the other hand, was to receive nothing. Yet a king of Gaul (supposedly ruled by 12 kings at the time) desired her anyway and married her.

Unwilling to bide their time until his death, Cornwall and Albany rose against Lear. They seized the governance of the land from him, granting him an allowance that they reduced over time. Heartbroken, Lear grieved especially over the unkindness of his two daughters, who begrudged him everything. Finally, he fled into Gaul, where before seeing him, Cordelia sent ahead money so that he could attire himself and retain servants as befit his status. Welcoming him at court, she and her husband listened to the wrongs he had suffered, then raised an army to help him reclaim the land. War followed, leading to Cornwall and Albany's deaths and Lear and Cordelia's victory. Restored to his kingdom, Lear ruled for two or three more years, then died. Afterwards, Cordelia became queen, ruling Britain honorably for five years, during which her husband passed away. Her sisters' sons, chafing under the rule of a woman, finally rebelled and imprisoned her, whereupon she committed suicide. So ends the legendary history, which Shakespeare adapts and diverges from in significant ways, complicating the plot with a subplot and with historical elements from his own time.

The Play in Focus

Plot summary. *King Lear* has a double storyline, involving two sets of characters who interconnect. The main plot features Lear and his daughters; the subplot, the earl of Gloucester and his sons. At the beginning of the play, the earl of Kent, a trusted advisor to Lear, talks with Gloucester about the impending division of Lear's kingdom among his sons-in-law, the dukes of Albany and Cornwall. Interrupting the conversation, Gloucester's bastard son, Edmund, appears and meets Kent. Despite his abilities, Edmund will inherit nothing from his father; Gloucester's estate is slated to go to his eldest and legitimate son, Edgar.

Lear, his daughters, and their retinue enter. The king announces that today he will decide the issue of Cordelia's marriage: she has two suitors, the duke of Burgundy and the king of France. But first, he will divide the kingdom among his heirs as their dowries, awarding the choicest portion to whichever daughter merits it best and loves him most. Goneril and Regan each claim to love Lear more than life itself, and so are rewarded with large, fertile thirds of the kingdom. Lear then turns to Cordelia, his favorite and the one with whom he hopes to live after abdicating. But she refuses to flatter him, saying only that she loves him "according to my bond, no more nor less" (Shakespeare, *King Lear,* 1.1.93). Enraged and uncomprehending, Lear instantly disinherits Cordelia. "With my two daughters' dowers," he tells Cornwall and Albany, "digest this third" (*King Lear,* 1.1.129). When trusty Kent attempts to defend the disinherited Cordelia, Lear banishes him too. The duke of Burgundy and the king of France enter, and Lear tells them of this sudden change in Cordelia's fortune. Burgundy withdraws his proposal, but

Illustration from Act 4, Scene 7 of *King Lear,* including Cordelia, Lear, and Kent.

France accepts Cordelia even without a dowry. Taking leave of her sisters, Cordelia, who knows their true natures, admonishes them to care for their father. Alone, Goneril and Regan discuss Lear's age and fitful ways; they resolve to form a united front against his capricious temper.

Elsewhere, the bastard Edmund vows to do whatever it takes to win Gloucester's patrimony, including turning his father against his legitimate son, Edgar. After Gloucester enters, Edmund presents him with a letter—supposedly from Edgar—seeking assistance from Edmund in killing their father. Alarmed, the credulous earl asks Edmund to look into the matter, then leaves. A solitary Edmund rejoices in the success of his plan thus far and, when Edgar enters, tells him their father is murderously angry with him and advises him to flee.

Meanwhile, Lear has been staying with Goneril, who shows exasperation at her father's supposedly unruly retinue of knights, and at Lear's continuing exercise of the very rights he gave away. Hoping to anger him into leaving her house, Goneril encourages her servant Oswald to be less attentive and deferential to the king and his company. Elsewhere in the house, the banished Kent, disguised as the servant Caius, applies for a position waiting on Lear. Pleased

by the blunt speech and forthright manner of "Caius," Lear takes the servant on. Kent, as Caius, meets Lear's outspoken fool, who engages the old king in a set of serious jests that probe into the folly of his giving up his power. The fool's criticisms of the king's shortsightedness prove justified when Goneril angrily demands that her father dismiss half of his 100 knights. Furious, Lear storms out of her home, vowing to take refuge with Regan. He is unaware, however, that his elder daughters have discussed the issue, and Regan is likewise prepared to curtail his "privileges."

Meanwhile, Gloucester, now convinced that Edgar is plotting his death, plans to arrest his son. Edmund warns Edgar to flee, while pretending, for Gloucester's sake, to attempt his capture. Alarmed, the unsuspecting Edgar obeys. Edmund then wounds himself and presents the injury to Gloucester as proof of Edgar's murderous intent. Thoroughly taken in, Gloucester vows to make Edmund his heir. Now a fugitive, Edgar disguises himself as Poor Tom o' Bedlam, a mad beggar.

Not finding Regan at home, Lear and his followers continue on to Gloucester's castle. Regan and Cornwall have arrived there ahead of him, ostensibly to seek advice from the old earl. Kent, whom the king has sent before him with a message for Regan, encounters Goneril's servant Oswald, and they quarrel. In the midst of the altercation, Regan and her husband Cornwall enter; displeased by Kent's rough manner, they have him put in the stocks as punishment.

Lear arrives at Gloucester's castle to find his servant Caius (really Kent) in the stocks, and Regan and Cornwall unwilling to see the king. At this point, Lear loses his temper. Regan and Goneril appear together and form a united front against him, demanding that he give up his entire retinue and submit to their authority. Heartbroken and defiant, Lear curses them and storms out of the castle with his fool as a storm approaches. Gloucester releases Kent from the stocks and offers to help him find the missing king. Later, Kent informs a trustworthy knight that a power struggle between Cornwall and Albany is imminent and sends a message with him to Cordelia in France, informing her of the new developments.

Out in the storm, Lear begins to go mad— "My wits begin to turn" (*King Lear,* 3.2.68). He exhorts the forces of nature to rise up and destroy his ungrateful daughters for their mistreatment of him. The fool sensibly notes that only those out of doors, meaning themselves, are going to be harmed by the rain. Kent, as Caius, enters, and leads them to shelter, a lean-to against the castle walls. There, Lear and the fool discover Edgar, half-naked and gibbering in his own disguise as Poor Tom. The deranged Lear quickly enters into a bizarre colloquy with Poor Tom, seeing in the supposed beggar's condition a reflection of his own woes: "Didst thou give all to thy daughters? And art thou come to this?" (*King Lear*, 3.4.50-51). Edgar maintains his masquerade, claiming to have once been "a servingman, proud in heart and mind, that curled my hair, wore gloves in my cap, served the lust of my mistress' heart, and did the act of darkness with her" (*King Lear*, 3.4.83-86). As Poor Tom, he raves about the demons that now torment him.

Meanwhile, Gloucester informs Edmund that a French army has landed at Dover, intending to restore Lear to power. Even though this is treason to England's new rulers, the loyal Gloucester ventures forth to send Lear on to his rescuers at Dover. Edmund betrays his father to Cornwall for his own advancement. Unaware of this latest treachery, Gloucester locates the disguised Kent on the heath and arranges for him to take Lear to Cordelia's forces at Dover. Returning home, Gloucester is ambushed by an enraged Regan and Cornwall, who bind him, accuse him of treason, and gouge out his eyes. Horrified by the monstrous act, a servant tries to stop Cornwall, losing his life but mortally wounding Cornwall in the process. Conscious now of Edmund's betrayal, the blinded Gloucester is thrown outdoors. He encounters Edgar, still disguised as Poor Tom, who, stricken by his father's injuries, leads the despairing earl to Dover.

Cornwall's death inaugurates the disintegration of Goneril and Regan's power. Disillusioned by his wife's cruelty to her father, Albany turns against Goneril, who has anyway settled her affections elsewhere. Goneril falls in love with Edmund and secretly plans to eliminate the mild-mannered Albany. Regan too falls in love with Edmund.

Meanwhile, at Dover, Cordelia prepares for war and searches for her father, who has escaped his keepers and is running madly through the fields. Edgar and Gloucester reach Dover, where Edgar cures his father's suicidal despair by pretending to lead him to the cliffs, then letting him "jump" and informing him of his "miraculous" survival. Unaware of the ruse, Gloucester resigns himself to life for the time being. Just then, a deranged Lear, decked in weeds, enters. Still tee-

tering between sanity and madness, Lear recognizes Gloucester, and they have a brief, poignant reunion before madness overtakes the king once more. Finally, some of Cordelia's attendants enter and lead Lear to safety. Journeying onward, Gloucester and Edgar encounter Oswald, sent to kill the blinded earl, but Edgar slays the steward instead, finding on his body a letter from Goneril asking Edmund to kill Albany.

Cordelia and a remorseful, now lucid Lear finally reunite at Dover, while Goneril and Regan muster their army for battle against the French forces. By now, Edmund has captivated the widowed Regan as well as Goneril. He tries to decide which sister he wants and, as a commander

---

THE WISDOM OF FOOLS

Lear's fool would have been a familiar figure to Shakespeare's audiences. Indeed, the figure of the court fool dates back to ancient times, and their absurd antics while in the service of their masters have been recorded in history. Tradition taught that fools were touched by God, because some had a physical or mental impairment, and therefore deserved privileges. However, the vast majority of professional fools had no handicap at all, but were skillful masters of a repertoire of bawdy songs, acrobatics, repartee, and/or clever jests. From medieval times, fools were often employed to provide entertainment for noble and royal houses. They were expected to gibe at and question, as well as amuse, their masters, the way Lear's fool does in the play. In Shakespeare's day, King James himself had a fool, Archie Armstrong, who was treated indulgently and enjoyed great license.

---

of the sisters' army, makes his own plans to kill Lear and Cordelia, even though Albany has promised to spare them.

The battle is joined, and the French are defeated. Lear and Cordelia suffer capture and imprisonment, but try to take comfort in each other's presence. Fearing the sympathy his prisoners will evoke in the people, Edmund charges a captain to sneak into Lear and Cordelia's cell and kill them. Meanwhile, dissension erupts in the victors' camp: Regan and Goneril quarrel over Edmund, whom Albany summarily accuses of treason. Astonished, Edmund demands to know who has laid this charge. Edgar appears, his identity still hidden, and challenges Edmund to sin-

Illustration from Act 5, Scene 3 of *King Lear.*

gle combat. Invoking the "rule of knighthood," Edmund accepts the challenge and they fight (*King Lear*, 5.3.143). Edmund is mortally wounded, whereupon Edgar reveals his true identity and informs his half-brother of their father's recent death. Acknowledging his crimes, Edmund resigns himself to death. More tumult follows as Kent arrives on the scene and messengers announce that Goneril has poisoned Regan and stabbed herself on witnessing Edmund's defeat. Their bodies are brought forth and laid beside the dying Edmund, who at the last moment admits his plot to kill Lear and Cordelia. But even as Albany dispatches a messenger to countermand Edmund's order, Lear enters, bearing the dead Cordelia in his arms. Having lost his tenuous hold on sanity again, the brokenhearted king does not seem to notice Goneril and Regan's corpses or the now undisguised Kent's presence. Lamenting the death of his beloved Cordelia, Lear expires over her body. Left to tend the realm under the shadow of this apocalypse are two battered survivors, Edgar and Albany: "The oldest hath borne most; we that are young/ Shall never see so much, nor live so long" (*King Lear*, 5.3.332-33).

Changing world views. The "late eclipses in the sun and moon portend no good to us," observes Gloucester, blaming the heavens for earthly discord and showing a pagan fear of supernatural forces that he does not understand (*King Lear*, 1.2.103-104). Out of earshot, his son Edmund disagrees:

> This is the excellent foppery of the world, that, when we are sick in fortune, often the surfeits of our own behaviour, we make guilty of our disasters the sun, the moon, and stars . . .
> I should have been that I am had the maidenliest star in the firmament twinkled on my bastardizing.
>
> (*King Lear,* 1.2.124-32)

The two attitudes reflect the view Shakespeare's world held of earlier, pagan society, as well as religious controversies of Shakespeare's own era. Society in his day regarded pagans as superstitious and fearful, or atheistic, or saved by a commitment to truth and similar virtues (Elton, p. 115). In the above instance, Gloucester embodies the superstitious; Edmund, the atheistic. Aside from this difference, the two also reflect an emerging skepticism in Shakespeare's day in relation, for example, to how the Bible explained creation. "Nothing can be made out of nothing," says Lear in the play (*King Lear*, 1.4.130). Clearly a pagan, Lear invokes various gods in the play, but he also utters a line that might have easily been voiced by Renaissance skeptics, such as Thomas Harriot (1560-1621) who questioned God's creation of the world out of nothing. A mathematician, Harriot "did not like . . . the old storie of the Creation of the world. He could not beleeve the old position" (Aubrey in Elton, p. 187).

Other debates in Shakespeare's day concerned astrology (whose validity the general public first began to doubt in the early seventeenth century), the existence of miracles, and possession by evil spirits. Through Edgar's character in *King Lear,* "demonic possession and "miracles" are shown to be frauds" (Elton, p. 93). As Poor Tom, Edgar raves about demonic possession. But he is an avowed dissembler; the audience knows he is faking it. He likewise dissembles about the so-called miracle of his father's survival when he fools the old man into thinking he has jumped from the cliffs at Dover. "Thy life's a miracle," says Edgar, knowing full well that it is a miracle he manufactured (*King Lear,* 4.6.55). In his own writings, King James condemned belief in miracles and other superstitions, so that by addressing them in the play, Shakespeare spoke directly to the monarch's concerns.

Sources and literary context. Shakespeare drew on the drama as well as the history of his day for sources, most notably the anonymous play *The True Chronicle History of King Leir* (c. 1590). He also, as indicated, drew on Raphael Holinshed's *Chronicles of England, Scotland and Ireland* (1587), which took its account of Lear from Geoffrey of Monmouth's *Historia Regum Britanniae* (c. 1135). Apart from these sources, Shakespeare's main plot may have been partly inspired by a contemporary event. In the early 1600s, Brian Annesley, a former courtier of Queen Elizabeth, suffered a "distemperature of mind and memory," and the eldest of his three daughters, Grace, planned to have him declared insane and "altogether unfit to govern himself or his estate" (Wildegos in Bullough, p. 309). Annesley's youngest daughter, Cordell, intervened, writing to one of King James's chief ministers, Lord Cecil, on her father's behalf. Cecil came to the rescue, and Annesley lived out his days in the care of a friend (Sir James Croft). Annesley died in 1604, willing most of his possessions to Cordell. From this real-life incident, Shakespeare may have derived the idea of Lear's madness, which has no precedent in the earlier plays or histories.

The subplot of Gloucester is adapted from Sir Philip Sidney's *Arcadia* (1590), a knightly romance that was among the most popular of Renaissance England. In the second book of *Arcadia,* the heroes encounter a young man named Leonatus leading his blind father. This father had

been king of Paphlagonia until he was tricked, deposed, and blinded by his bastard son Plexirtus. Left to wander, the former king encounters Leonatus, the legitimate son he had abandoned. The parallel with the Gloucester plot is clear, although Leonatus is not disguised. Again, a real-life incident may have been influential. In 1604-1605, Sir Robert Dudley, the bastard son of a favorite in Queen Elizabeth's court, tried to certify his legitimacy in court. His father had not admitted marriage to his mother so as not to anger the queen. The case, which Dudley lost, created a stir in England. Finally, Edgar's masquerade as Tom o'Bedlam in the play was Shakespeare's invention, although he drew on Samuel Harsnett's *Declaration of Egregious Popishe Impostures* (1603) to furnish details of Tom's professed punishment by demons.

Events in History at the Time the Play Was Written

England's poor. At the time *King Lear* was written, almost half of England's population consisted of the poor. There were the visible poor (maimed soldiers, the sick, survivors of natural disasters like fire, and households overburdened with children), and there were the invisible poor—average, humble families who labored for an insufficient pittance. "When they have worke," said a 1638 report on the laboring poor in Hertfordshire, "the wages given them is so small that it hardly sufficeth to buy the poore man and his familye breed," and so people starved (Bridenbaugh, p. 376). The result was intense suffering, an escalating problem since the 1590s, aggravated by depressions and crop failures. In the cloth trade, unemployed spinners would take to the road, wandering through town and country, begging for scraps. On farms, crop failures led to food shortages that, in turn, led to starvation and sometimes death for children. This kind of suffering had become widespread by Shakespeare's day and "must be understood entirely apart from the better-known problem of the visible poor" (Bridenbaugh, p. 377).

The growing population, along with other developments, exacerbated the situation from the sixteenth to early seventeenth centuries, causing consternation among government authorities and churchmen alike. To stop people from starving—and rioting—poor laws were passed in 1598 and 1601. Each parish, according to the poor laws, had to take responsibility for its own poor. The laws authorized the parish to levy rates on parish dwellers for relief of the destitute, the amount depending on the value of each property, in accord with the Anglican tenet that everyone is responsible for almsgiving according to his or her ability. Attempts were made to contain the number of poor in a parish, using methods like

---

BEDLAM BEGGARS

The origin of the Bedlam beggar harks back to c. 1247 when the priory of Saint Mary of Bethlehem was first built in London. By 1402, the priory was being used as a hospital for the insane, and the institution came to be called "Bedlam," a corruption of "Bethlehem." By Shakespeare's day, the term referred not only to discharged mental patients licensed to beg, but also to those who feigned madness and prior institutionalization. They "commonly walked 'bare-legged and bare-armed,' and called themselves Poor Tom" (Foakes in Shakespeare, p. 238). In *King Lear*, Edgar, in his disguise as Poor Tom, professes possession by demons—Flibbertigibbet, Modo, Mahu, Frateretto, and Hoppedance are fiends who prey upon him. The image plays on a superstitious belief that an addled person was possessed by evil spirits.

---

the census to limit the number of recipients on poor relief. Vagrants and recent arrivals in a community would be sent back to their home parishes.

For the most part, society frowned on vagrants like *King Lear*'s Poor Tom, believing that idleness drove them to "seek their meate . . . with Begging, Filching, and Stealing' when they should be laboring" (Bridenbaugh, p. 385). In fact, vagrancy was an offense whose perpetrators suffered punishments such as branding (with a *V*) and ear-boring, two penalties prescribed by laws in 1572 and 1604. There was widespread fear in society of the criminal vagrant, which made people reluctant to give alms to any vagrant. The general perception was that vagrants were shiftless, despite the reality that many of them did not avoid labor but were itinerant laborers or temporary workers. At the same time, a growing faction of society showed genuine concern for the poor, and sought reform. Homilies, or sermons of the era, exhorted worshippers to "open their hand unto their brethren that were pore" and admonished those who "have great plentie of meats and drinkes, great store of moth-eaten apparel," but will not "part with any peece of your super-

fluities to helpe and succor the poore, hungry, & naked" (homilies in Elton, p. 227). There were people who heeded the homilies, and attempted to improve conditions. Some communities established almshouses, but such efforts were mostly directed at the visible poor. Still, the countryside remained riddled with unidentified impoverished, respectable persons whom neither the poor laws nor the reformers ever detected. In sum, a large share of the era's misery "passed unnoticed," which brings to mind King Lear's self-recrimination for the poverty he never knew existed until he himself experienced it (Bridenbaugh, p. 376):

> . . . Oh, I have ta'en
> Too little care of this. Take physic, pomp,
> Expose thyself to feel what wretches feel,
> That thou may shake the superflux to them,
> And show the heavens more just.
>
> (*King Lear*, 3.4.34-38)

Addled parents and defiant children. From about the 1580s, England began to take a heightened interest in suicide, the insane, and milder mental and emotional disturbances such as melancholy. Bethlehem (also spelled *Bethlem*) Hospital became infamous for its inmates, thanks in no small part to Jacobean playwrights. In reality, it was far less imposing than its image suggested. The asylum, called *Bedlam* in the popular vernacular, was actually a small structure housing fewer than 30 inmates, who "languished there for years, living in squalid conditions without adequate medical treatment" (MacDonald, p. 2).

Courts were fairly scrupulous about who was declared mentally deranged. They usually appointed relatives or friends to care for an insane landowner. And before the insane man's property could be turned over to a guardian, a jury had to declare that the man was too deranged to manage his estate and had been for a year or longer. King James himself took special interest in the insane, instructing the courts to make sure such unfortunates were "freely committed to their best and nearest friends, that can receive no benefit by their death" and that committees be "bound to answer for . . . the very just value of their estates . . . for the benefit of such lunatic (if he recover) or of the next heir" (James in MacDonald, p. 5). As suggested by this edict, insanity was considered a temporary state, a perception that sheds light on Lear's moments of lucidity in Shakespeare's play. When a madman recovered, taught the law, his property ought to be restored to him, minus the amount expended on his care. Paupers who were mad received attention too. By the time *King Lear* was written, the government had ordered parishes to consider the impoverished insane as part of the so-called deserving poor, who, like the physically disabled, could not work through no fault of their own.

What was thought to cause lunacy in early 1600s England? Exhibiting superstitions of the age, people pointed to witchcraft, possession by the devil, and astrology. Physicians invoked more rational explanations, tracing mental disorders to emotional disturbances, which they, in turn, traced to family issues—unrequited love, marital disharmony, the death of a child, perhaps even "filial ingratitude" (*King Lear*, 3.4.12-15).

"It is the duty of the child," taught Alexander Nowell, dean of St. Paul's in London, "to frame their life according to the will of their father" (Nowell in Greaves, p. 282). Catholic and Protestant families alike raised children to revere and obey their elders, and to relieve parents in times of economic or physical distress. Of course, there were exceptions—uncaring children who shirked their duties to elderly or infirm parents, as Lear's daughters do. But generally children fulfilled their obligations to parents, which must have made Goneril and Regan's spurning of Lear seem particularly egregious to the audience in Shakespeare's day.

Aside from family strife, emotional disturbances were seen as the consequence of old age. The aged, it was thought, became children again, difficult to please, easily angered, given to talking to themselves. When Goneril speaks of her father's "unruly waywardness," which "infirm and choleric years bring with them," she invokes this perception of the elderly (*King Lear*, 1.1.299-300). Interestingly, children like Goneril who challenged parental authority were considered delusional themselves. People actually spoke of the defiant child as being "brainsick" (MacDonald, p. 165).

From disunity to the promise of unity. In contrast to the divisiveness featured in *King Lear*, King James stressed the importance of unity in Britain. Referring back to the legendary first British kingdom and the friction that ensued after Brutus divided it among his heirs, James admonished his son, Prince Henry, to refrain from dividing it further:

> And in case it please God to prouide you to all these three Kingdomes, make your eldest son Isaac, leauing him all your kingdomes; and prouide the rest with priuate possessions: Otherwayes by deuiding your kingdomes, yee

shall leaue the see of diuision and discord among your posteritie; as befell to this Ile, by the diuision and assignement thereof, to the three sones of Brutus. . . .

> (James in Shakespeare, p. 15)

James even tried to repair this initial division, proposing that Scotland and England unite into one kingdom. The goal would not be reached in his lifetime; it would take another hundred years before Scotland joined with England in the Act of Union (1707). Still, James acquired an image as unifier. Among other indications of this image was a show performed in London in 1605. Called *The Triumphs of Reunited Britannia,* the show celebrated the inauguration of London's new mayor (Sir Leonard Holliday). It also suggested that the separate crowns of England and Scotland had merged in King James. Recalling the legendary history of King Brutus (or "Brute"), it recapitulated how his division of Britain among his three sons had led to disharmony and war. From this retrospective, the show telescoped forward to 1605, at which point its legendary characters "step out of time to celebrate the fact that the chaos they created has been reduced to order by the 'new Brute', King James" (Dutton, p. 133). Thus, in dealing with the division of a kingdom, *King Lear* addresses a topic of discussion in early seventeenth-century England.

Reception. *King Lear* is recorded as having been performed at the court of King James in 1606. The earliest surviving critical commentary on the play, however, does not appear until 1681, when Nahum Tate, an Irish playwright, explained, in a letter to a friend, his reasons for revising Shakespeare's tragedy for the seventeenth-century stage:

> I found the whole [of *King Lear*] to answer your Account of it, a Heap of Jewels, unstrung and unpolisht; yet so dazling in their Disorder, that I soon perceiv'd I had seiz'd a Treasure. 'Twas my good fortune to light on one Expedient to rectifie what is wanting in the Regularity and Probability of the Tale, which was to run through the whole A *Love* betwixt *Edgar* and *Cordelia,* that never chang'd word with each other in the Original.

> (Tate in Harris and Scott, p. 93)

Tate's revisions included "making the Tale conclude in a Success to the innocent distrest persons: Otherwise I must have incumbred the Stage with dead Bodies" (Tate in Harris and Scott, p. 93). Surprisingly, Tate's changes were so successful that for the next 150 years his version of *King Lear* was performed far more frequently than Shakespeare's.

Joseph Addison, the eighteenth-century essayist, disagreed with Tate's changes. Tate's version of *King Lear* had, in Addison's view, "lost half its beauty" (Addison in Harris and Scott, p. 94). Nineteenth-century intellectuals concurred, expressing a strong preference for Shakespeare's original, for which William Hazlitt expressed awe and wonder:

> It is then the best of Shakespear's plays, for it is the one in which he is most in earnest. . . . This depth of nature, this force of passion, this tug and war of the elements of our being, this firm faith in filial piety, and the giddy anarchy and whirling tumult of the thoughts at finding this prop failing it, the contrast between the fixed, immoveable basis of natural affection, and the rapid, irregular starts of imagination, suddenly wrenched from all its accustomed holds and resting places in the soul, this is what Shakespear has given, and what nobody else but he could give.
>
> (Hazlitt in Harris and Scott, p. 108)

—Jacob Littleton and Joyce Moss

For More Information

Bridenbaugh, Carl. *Vexed and Troubled Englishmen 1590-1642*. New York: Oxford University Press, 1968.

Bullough, Geoffrey, ed. *Narrative and Dramatic Sources of Shakespeare*. Vol. 7. London: Routledge and Kegan Paul, 1973.

Dutton, Richard. *William Shakespeare: A Literary Life*. London: Macmillan, 1989.

Elton, William R. *King Lear and the Gods*. San Marino, Calif.: The Huntington Library, 1966.

Greaves, Richard L. *Society and Religion in Elizabethan England*. Minneapolis: University of Minnesota Press, 1981.

Harris, Laurie Lanzen, and Mark W. Scott, eds. *Shakespearean Criticism*. Vol. 2. Detroit: Gale Research, 1985.

Holinshed, Raphael. Holinshed's *Chronicles of England, Scotlande, and Irelande*. Vol. 1. 1587. London: J. Johnson, 1807.

MacDonald, Michael. *Mystical Bedlam: Madness, Anxiety, and Healing in Seventeenth-Century England*. Cambridge: Cambridge University Press, 1981.

Mack, Maynard. *King Lear in Our Time*. Berkeley: University of California Press, 1965.

Ross, Anne. *Everyday Life of the Pagan Celts*. London: B. T. Batsford, 1970.

Salgado, Gamini. *The Elizabethan Underworld*. New York: St. Martin's, 1992.

Shakespeare, William. *King Lear*. Ed. R. A. Foakes. The Arden Shakespeare. London: Thomson Learning, 1997.

The Life of Samuel Johnson

by
James Boswell

James Boswell (1740-1795) was a young, fun-loving, aristocratic, would-be man-about-town when he came to London from his native Scotland in 1762. He soon became a compulsive writer, beginning a detailed journal in which he recorded virtually every significant event or conversation of his daily life. Among the many London celebrities the 22-year-old Boswell sought out was the 53-year-old literary giant Samuel Johnson (1709-84), whom he met in May 1763. The two then began a friendship that lasted until Johnson's death. Outside of his journals (discovered in the twentieth century) and his writings about Johnson, Boswell's best known literary work is *An Account of Corsica* (1768), in which he describes the Italian island and its struggles for independence from Genoa. In 1773, Boswell and Johnson traveled to the Scottish highlands and the Hebrides, a voyage that Boswell later immortalized in the *Journal of a Tour to the Hebrides with Samuel Johnson, LL.D.* Based on his (heavily revised) diary of the trip, the *Journal* was published in 1785, the year after Johnson's death, and is considered by some to be Boswell's masterpiece. *The Life of Samuel Johnson,* regarded by many as the finest biography ever written, has given the world an unforgettable portrait of Samuel Johnson. Johnson was a prolific writer—a poet, a lexicographer, a biographer, a playwright, and an essayist—yet Boswell's biography focuses not on Johnson's works but on the personality and the opinions of the leading literary figure of his day.

THE LITERARY WORK

A biography set in eighteenth-century England and Scotland; first published in London in 1791.

SYNOPSIS

The poor son of a bookseller, Samuel Johnson becomes the leading literary figure of his generation. He wins renown for his witty conversation and vigorous, combative intellect—traits that his younger friend James Boswell depicts in vivid, dramatic, often humorous detail.

Events in History at the Time of the Biography

Whigs and Tories, Hanoverians and Jacobites. Samuel Johnson was born during the reign of England's last Stuart monarch, Queen Anne (ruled 1702-14), the daughter of James II. A Catholic, James II had been overthrown in 1688, in favor of his elder daughter Mary, a Protestant, and her Dutch husband, Prince William of Orange. The pair ruled Britain jointly until Mary's death in 1694. On William's death in 1702, Mary's younger sister Anne, also a Protestant, succeeded to the throne, but faced the threat of continuing attempts by her male Catholic Stuart relatives to reclaim the monarchy. Supporters of these attempts, who backed first James II and then his son and grandson (James and Charles,

Samuel Johnson

respectively), were called "Jacobites" (from *Jacobus*, Latin for James).

Closely involved in these events was the emergence of political parties, the Whigs and the Tories. Most Jacobites were Tories (though not all Tories were Jacobites). Generally more conservative than the Whigs, they represented the landed aristocracy and gentry. Tories tended to espouse values regarded as "traditional": the divine right of kings through legitimate succession, strong distinctions of social rank, and the supremacy of the Established or Anglican Church. Samuel Johnson, a lifelong Tory, appears to have been a devout Anglican and a Jacobite, as well as a staunch advocate of social rank, an assessment that is open to some debate. In any case, the Whigs, by contrast, represented the growing middle class: merchants, bankers, and other businessmen, whose wealth was based on cash rather than land and who sometimes had little sympathy for conventional distinctions of social rank. They were often non-Anglicans (called Dissenters or Nonconformists) and tended to support the power of Parliament over that of the monarch. With the exception of a brief period during the reign of Queen Anne, the Whigs dominated British politics for most of the eighteenth century.

The Whigs found a natural ally in George Ludwig, elector of Hanover. (An elector was a prince entitled to elect the emperor of the Holy Roman Empire.) Though a German prince, he was also the closest Protestant Stuart relative in the line of succession, and on Anne's death in 1714, the Whigs secured the British throne for him. Despite sporadic Jacobite opposition, the Hanoverian dynasty would hold the throne until 1837.

Old and Young Pretenders. The first Jacobite rebellion under the Hanoverians occurred in 1715, only a year after George I came to the throne. James II's son, James Francis Edward Stuart (often called "the Old Pretender" or James III, though he was never crowned), landed with troops in Scotland in December of that year. Within a few months, however, he was forced to flee as the uprising collapsed. James's son Charles Edward Stuart, called "the Young Pretender" or "Bonnie Prince Charlie," revived the Jacobite cause with a final rebellion 30 years later, in 1745-46, which also ended in failure and flight. These Jacobite revolts had the glamorous air of a lost cause that pitted a "true" principle—the legitimate succession of the monarchy—against overwhelming odds. In fact, *The True Briton* was the name of the leading Jacobite journal, a phrase that Samuel Johnson echoed in the poem "London" (1738), his earliest literary success, which was also a violent attack on the Whigs. "Here let those reign, whom Pensions can incite," Johnson wrote, implying that the Whigs who controlled the king and his court kept power through the distribution of pensions, or annual subsidies given by the king (Johnson in Clark, p. 145). Another of Johnson's early works was an anonymously published biography of the poet Richard Savage, who had celebrated the 1715 revolt and attacked the Hanoverian succession in several poems written at the time of the revolt. Savage died in jail in 1743.

Religion played a complex and ambivalent role in the Jacobite struggle. The Stuarts' Catholicism brought them support from France and Ireland, Catholic lands that also had political reasons for opposing England. In contrast, the strongly Presbyterian Scotland supported the Jacobites solely for national reasons—the Stuarts had originally been Scotland's royal house. Similarly, the Stuarts' Catholicism did not necessarily preclude support for them in Protestant England; Anglicans could present themselves as supporting their divinely sanctioned monarch *despite* religion rather than because of it. This helped the English Jacobites perpetuate their cause by allowing them to claim a certain disinterested moral superiority, but in the end it also

Fireworks in London celebrate the end of the Seven Years' War.

limited Jacobite support in England, whose populace included many that refused to back a Catholic ruler. One of the Jacobites' major strengths was thus also their greatest weakness.

The Seven Years' War The Jacobite cause was only one factor in Britain's long-running conflict with France, a struggle that was renewed in the middle of the eighteenth century after several decades of uneasy peace. Indeed, Bonnie Prince Charlie's rebellion of 1745-46 (which included an abortive French invasion of England that ended when the French ships were wrecked in a storm) was only one campaign in a Europewide conflict, the War of Austrian Succession (1740-48). This war, in which France, Prussia, and Spain opposed Britain, Austria, and Holland, proved inconclusive. Far more decisive was the war that followed, in which France and Britain (and their respective allies) again opposed each other. Called the "Seven Years' War" in Europe, where it lasted from 1756-63, it is known as the "French and Indian War" in North America, where battles were fought beginning in 1754. As its two branches indicate, this war's consequences reached well beyond Europe. However, the contest boiled down to one between Britain and France, each with its vast colonial possessions. Britain won decisively, and took not only

France's North American territory in Canada, but also French possessions in India. This was the final stage in Britain's emergence as the world's leading naval and colonial power.

The Seven Years' War also marked the end of significant support for Jacobite aspirations in Britain. Instead, a new patriotic fervor grew out of Britain's victories and her expanded global influence, a fervor that was given a boost in 1760 by the death of King George II and the accession of his son George III, who was the first of the Hanoverian monarchs to be regarded as an Englishman rather than a German. Writing in the 1770s, Johnson voiced the proud sentiments of many former Jacobites, as well as those of the Whigs who had led the nation through the war: Britain had won a great triumph in which "France was disgraced and overpowered in every quarter of the globe . . . and the name of an Englishman was reverenced through Europe" (Johnson in Clark, p. 190).

The American Revolution. In the aftermath of the Seven Years' War, Britain's colonies in the United States of America grew steadily more dissatisfied with British rule, particularly when measures such as the Stamp Act (1765) imposed a heavy tax that was unpopular with the colonists. While the British government intended the tax to help defray the cost of defending the colonies (as Britain had in the Seven Years' War), the colonists resented being taxed when they were not represented in Parliament. "No taxation without representation" was the famous cry, to which many Englishmen responded with sympathy. Johnson found himself in a minority among his friends when he published a vituperative attack on the colonists entitled "Taxation no Tyranny" (1775); the piece was commissioned by government ministers, but even they were compelled to tone it down before publication. Far from his earlier Jacobite refusal to acknowledge the Hanoverians' right to the throne, Johnson now castigated the colonists for denying "the authority of their lawful sovereign" (Johnson in Clark, p. 226). His rigid hostility to America and Americans (amus-

ingly recounted by Boswell) continued after the surrender of General Cornwallis, the British commander, to U.S. General George Washington at Yorktown in 1781.

Boswell and Johnson together. In arguing about America with Johnson, Boswell held fast to his own opinions, but at other times he is said to have shown "traces of conscious submissiveness and unconscious resentment" toward his friend (Brady, p. 163). For the most part, though, theirs was a warm, familiar relationship. Johnson, 31 years older than Boswell, became his mentor. The son of noted jurist Lord Auchinleck, Boswell would eventually become a lawyer himself, then forego this avocation to write and rewrite *The Life of Samuel Johnson*.

Boswell admired Johnson for his writings and for his ability to put his finger precisely on the pulse of a matter and speak his mind. For his part, Johnson relished Boswell's mental quickness and good humor, though at first Boswell struck him as a confused and rather lonely young man. In fact, the friendship had a deep emotional component for both parties, Johnson gratified by Boswell's unflagging interest in him and Boswell by his mentor's deep affection. So often did Boswell seek reassurance of it that Johnson was in fact moved to grumble: "You always seem to call for tenderness. My regard for you is greater almost than I have words to express, but I do not choose to be always repeating it" (Johnson in Brady, p. 161). Drawn to drink and women, Boswell looked up to Johnson, admonishing himself in his journals to develop strength of mind and character, to "be Johnson" (Bate, p. 361). Over the years the two discussed love, drink, sex, melancholy, uses of the orange peel, the source of the English language. Boswell is believed to have taken notes on their talks for entries in his journal, which covered these and other matters. Sometimes he probably drew off from company to jot down what had just been said, but mostly he made memos at night of the goings-on of the day, coming back to them later to write full-blown entries. He wrote up his entry for October 1, 1776, for example, on October 17, 1776, working from notes—"as I allways do" (Johnson in Scott, p. 35).

Close but not without ripples, the 21-year friendship saw moments of disharmony. Boswell risked rebuke to hear his mentor speak on various subjects, and Johnson delivered it up, sometimes treating the younger man roughly. Annoyed by his questions, Johnson once declared that Boswell's company was enough to drive a

LONDON IN THE "AGE OF JOHNSON"

"When a man is tired of London," Boswell records Johnson as saying, "he is tired of life; for there is in London all that life can afford" (Boswell, *The Life of Samuel Johnson*, p. 233). The three decades from roughly 1750 to 1780, often called the "Age of Johnson," brought dramatic changes to the writer's beloved city. Its population was booming, and would double over the eighteenth century—from an estimated 500,000 in 1700 to well over a million in 1800. Before 1750, only London Bridge spanned the Thames River, so that ferries and barges constantly crossed from one side to the other, limiting passenger and cargo transportation within the city itself. Beginning in 1750 with Westminster Bridge, half a dozen new bridges were built, allowing greater expansion to the south; new docks went up in the east, as well as new housing in the north and the stylish west. By the end of the Seven Years' War in 1763 (incidentally the year in which Boswell met Johnson), London could claim to be the world's financial capital. Always important in English social life, it now enjoyed an uncontested preeminence in literature and the arts as well as in politics and finance. At the center of the city's glittering cultural life Johnson reigned supreme. His friends included fashionable portrait painter Sir Joshua Reynolds, playwright Oliver Goldsmith, historian Edward Gibbon, political writer Edmund Burke, and actor David Garrick. They formed the Literary Club, meeting for dinner and long (often combative) discussions on politics and other matters at one of the city's many lively coffee houses or taverns.

man out of his own house. Boswell mostly tolerated such outbursts and ultimately the friendship endured. One day the two touched on the topic of biography. Boswell wondered whether a biographer should mention his subject's vices and personal idiosyncrasies. In Johnson's opinion, this would be a questionable practice. Clearly *The Life of Samuel Johnson* delves into Johnson's idiosyncrasies, though to what degree Boswell's high esteem for Johnson affects the objectivity of the portrait remains unknown.

The Biography in Focus

Contents summary. Samuel Johnson was born in Lichfield, Staffordshire, on September 18, 1709. His parents were not young when he was born and would have only one other child, Nathaniel, who died at age 24. Samuel's father, Michael Johnson, was a marginally successful bookseller who owned a shop in Lichfield and also opened a stall in the nearby city of Birmingham every market day. It is widely believed that Johnson's lifelong tendency toward depression, or "a vile melancholy" came from his father (*Samuel Johnson*, p. 35). From his mother, Sarah Ford, "a woman of distinguished understanding" and piety, he developed a strong religious faith (*Samuel Johnson*, p. 36). The precocious little boy also displayed "that jealous independence of spirit, and impetuosity of temper, which never forsook him" when he turned on and pummeled "as well as his strength would permit" a school teacher who protectively tried once to escort him home because of his severe near-sightedness (*Samuel Johnson*, p. 38). Aside from his poor vision, as a boy Johnson also contracted scrofula (tuberculosis of the lymph glands), known as the "king's evil" because the touch of a monarch was thought to cure it. His mother actually took her son to London, where she succeeded in having him touched by Queen Anne, but to no avail. The disease left him blind in one eye and disfigured by facial scars.

In school Johnson's imposing intelligence and prodigious memory were matched only by his laziness. He would often put off his work until the last minute and then do it all in a single spurt. Though he was uncommonly large, his poor sight kept him from joining his friends in games—which suited his laziness, as he told Boswell later. It did not, however, stop him from exploring the books in his father's store, where he read randomly but voraciously, as he told Boswell, "all ancient writers, all manly" (*Samuel*

Johnson, p. 43). His father did not have enough money to send him to university, but a wealthy schoolmate of his promised to support him there, so at 19 he entered Pembroke College, Oxford. A teacher at the college told him that his undirected reading had made Johnson "the best qualified for the University that he had ever known come there" (*Samuel Johnson*, p. 43). "Johnson knew more books than any man alive," the same teacher later told Boswell (*Samuel Johnson*, p. 46). However, he rarely read a book all the way through, possessing an uncanny talent for dipping into it and "seizing at once what was valuable," as Boswell puts it (*Samuel Johnson*, p. 46). He used this technique throughout his life. He particularly loved to read poetry and composed poems himself.

JOHNSON AND AMERICANS

Like many of his countrymen, Boswell sympathized with the American cause, but Johnson could be counted on to erupt into torrents of abuse when the subject arose in conversation: "Sir, they are a race of convicts, and ought to be thankful for any thing we allow them short of hanging" (*Samuel Johnson*, p. 176); "I am willing to love all mankind, *except an American*" (*Samuel Johnson*, p. 247).

His friend, however, failed to honor the promise to support him, and after three years Johnson was forced to leave Oxford. His father, now insolvent, could not help him financially, and Johnson found menial work in a local school. Quitting the unpleasant job after a few months, he drifted, staying with a friend in Birmingham for six months and then renting a room there before returning to Lichfield in 1734. He set up a private school near Lichfield, but the only students he attracted in the year-and-a-half of its existence were David Garrick, the future famous actor, and his brother George, plus one other boy. He wed a widow named Elizabeth Porter, who was nearly twice his age, and the marriage lasted until her death in 1752. Apparently "Tetty" was not particularly well liked by some of Johnson's friends: "I have seen Garrick exhibit [imitate] her," Boswell reports, "by his exquisite talent for mimickry, so as to excite the heartiest bursts of laughter" (*Samuel Johnson*, p. 52). After the failure of his school, Johnson decided to try his luck in London; by coincidence Garrick went to the city at the same time to finish his education and become a lawyer, though he soon gave up those plans for the stage. Johnson was working on a play called *Irene* (about a Christian slave girl in the court of a Turkish sultan), which he tried unsuccessfully to get produced. It would not be performed until 1749 when Garrick, by then in charge of the prestigious Drury Lane Theater, produced it.

Johnson found work writing articles for a popular periodical called *The Gentleman's Magazine,* which provided income while he worked on other projects, like his poem "London," which was published in 1738. Then in 1744 he published his biography of Richard Savage, collecting the old Jacobite's life story as he and Savage, both in a state of poverty, wandered the streets of London.

JOHNSON'S *DICTIONARY OF THE ENGLISH LANGUAGE*

~

Johnson's was the first English dictionary that attempted to be comprehensive and precise in its definitions, while incorporating quotations from well-known authors to illustrate them. It was modeled on a French dictionary produced by the French Academy, which (Boswell relates) took its 40 members 40 years to finish. When Boswell asked how Johnson could intend to do it in three years, Johnson replied, "Let me see; forty times forty is sixteen hundred. As three to sixteen hundred, so is the proportion of an Englishman to a Frenchman" (*Samuel Johnson,* p. 60). While the *Dictionary* is a work of serious lexicography, Johnson's personality crept into some of the best known definitions: *oats,* for example, are "a grain, which in England is generally given to horses, but in Scotland supports the people" *excise* is defined as "a hateful tax levied upon commodities" and a *lexicographer* is "a writer of dictionaries, a harmless drudge" (*Samuel Johnson,* pp. 345, 81).

Johnson's modest publishing success was far outstripped by the meteoric rise of Garrick, who shot to fame and fortune almost overnight. During the years of the Jacobite rebellion (1745-46), Johnson published little, an inactivity that Boswell supposes may have been out of "sympathetick anxiety" with the revolt (*Samuel Johnson,* p. 58). Or, Boswell goes on, Johnson may already have been planning the compendium that would consume much of his time in coming years: his "arduous and important work, his DICTIONARY

OF THE ENGLISH LANGUAGE" (*Samuel Johnson,* p. 59). A group of booksellers gave him an advance for the work, but the expenses (he had to hire six copyists to help compile it) left little for him to live on. Still, work on the dictionary kept him busy for some years; when finally published in 1755, it brought him the fame and literary reputation he sought.

Johnson continued other projects while working on the *Dictionary,* publishing a poem, "The Vanity of Human Wishes," in 1749. In that year he also got into a dispute with Garrick over his play, *Irene,* which Garrick wished to edit for production. The play was a flop despite Garrick's editing, but Johnson took his failure philosophically, saying that the public knew best. The following year he began a periodical in the tradition of *The Tatler* and *The Spectator* (famous magazines of an earlier generation), calling it *The Rambler.* Johnson wrote the magazine alone, putting out two editions a week for two years, from March 1750 to March 1752. In the same month that he ended the magazine, Johnson's beloved wife died, leaving him (as his servant Francis Barber told Boswell) "in great affliction" (*Samuel Johnson,* p. 71).

The success of his *Dictionary* in 1755 brought him an honorary Master's degree from Oxford as well as immediate fame. However, Johnson still had very little income, having long since spent all of the advance he had received for the *Dictionary.* He continued writing articles for various periodicals, and resumed work on an older project for which he had been unable to find financial support—an annotated edition of Shakespeare. In 1757 he began another periodical, *The Idler,* which Boswell describes as having "less body and more spirit" than *The Rambler;* in some of the issues, Johnson addresses his own laziness, describing "the miseries of idleness, with the lively sensations of one who has felt them" (*Samuel Johnson,* p. 85). Like those in the earlier periodical, these pieces were usually hastily written at the last minute.

Johnson's mother died in 1759, when he was 50 and she was 90; it distressed him that he had not been to see her for several years, though he had diligently sent her money that he could hardly afford. Soon afterward, hoping to settle his mother's debts and also pay for her funeral, Johnson wrote *Rasselas, Prince of Abyssinia,* completing the short novel during the evenings of a single week. (Although Boswell does not describe the novel's reception, it became and remains Johnson's most widely read work.) In 1762, two years after coming to the throne, King George II bestowed on Johnson an annual pension of £300 a year, enough to live on modestly. Johnson wondered if it was proper to accept the customary honor for public service, since in his *Dictionary* he had sardonically defined *pension* as "pay given to a state hireling for treason to his country" (*Samuel Johnson,* p. 345). Joshua Reynolds, the painter, assured him that his definitions hardly applied to him personally.

The following year, 1763, was for the 22-year-old Boswell "a memorable year; for in it I had the happiness to obtain the acquaintance of that extraordinary man whose memoirs I am now writing" (*Samuel Johnson,* p. 93). From this point, the account becomes much more detailed, so that the last 20 years of Johnson's life take up two thirds of the book. The tone of the biography changes as Boswell's personal observations play a larger part, and he relates scene after scene of entertaining Johnsonian conversation. Their first meeting, however, was anything but auspicious. The Scottish Boswell, aware of Johnson's well-known prejudice against his native land, was self-conscious and awkward, and the big, bearlike Johnson got off several witticisms at Boswell's expense. Boswell relates his own embarrassment without flinching, as is typical of his technique throughout the biography, in which he is willing to show himself openly, almost enthusiastically, in an unflattering light. Despite his discomfiture, Boswell called on Johnson a few days later. He found the famous writer's apartment, furniture, and clothing "sufficiently uncouth . . . but these slovenly particularities were forgotten the moment he began to talk" (*Samuel Johnson,* p. 97). Johnson welcomed him, and the two soon became friends. As he had hoped, Boswell found himself joining Johnson and his literary friends for long evenings of wine and talk at the Mitre tavern or the Turk's Head coffee house, Johnson's favorite haunts. But Boswell's father put an end to his dissipated but enjoyable life in London by enjoining his son to study for the law; agreeing, Boswell made plans to go abroad to study and travel. He persuaded Johnson to see him off, and the two journeyed to Harwich, where Boswell embarked for Holland. They made their goodbyes and promised to write. "As the vessel put out to sea, I kept my eyes on him for a considerable time, while he remained rolling his majestick frame in his usual manner: and at last I perceived him walk back into the town, and he disappeared" (*Samuel Johnson,* p. 122).

It was in 1764, while Boswell was traveling in Europe, that Johnson and his friends founded the Literary Club, meeting weekly at the Turk's Head. Using Johnson's daily journal as his guide, Boswell records Johnson's growing dissatisfaction with his own laziness since receiving the pension. The following year, Johnson met a couple, the Thrales, with whom he became intimate friends. Henry Thrale, a well known brewer, and his vivacious wife Hester, lived in a magnificent house just outside London at Streatham, where Johnson would often go for long visits. In that same year, 1765, he also published his long-awaited edition of Shakespeare. Boswell returned in February. In 1767 "one of the most remarkable events of Johnson's life" occurred: he enjoyed a long conversation with the king, who sought him out while Johnson was conducting research in the royal library (*Samuel Johnson,* p. 133). "I find it does a man good to be talked to by his Sovereign," Johnson reported to his fascinated friends, after recounting the conversation in detail (*Samuel Johnson,* p. 136).

"I REFUTE IT *THUS*"

One of the most famous passages in *The Life of Samuel Johnson* concisely illustrates Johnson's trenchant wit. Johnson and Boswell were discussing the philosophical ideas of George Berkeley, who questioned the objective existence of matter, when Boswell remarked that Berkeley's argument was hard to refute. "I shall never forget the alacrity with which Johnson answered," Boswell writes, "striking his foot with mighty force against a large stone, till he rebounded from it, 'I refute it *thus*.'" (*Samuel Johnson,* p. 122)

In 1773 Johnson joined Boswell for a strenuous tour of Scotland, which Johnson enjoyed despite his famous bias against the Scots. Boswell refers the reader to his *Journal of a Tour to the Hebrides* for further information. Johnson and Boswell continued their social rounds through the 1770s, which Boswell reports in vignette after small vignette: conversations on literature, art, politics, death (which Johnson feared immensely), and drinking (Johnson had begun abstaining, saying that he found moderate drinking impossible). A characteristic episode occurred in 1776, when Boswell brought Johnson together at a dinner party with another friend of his, the radical politician John Wilkes. The two men were polar opposites in every respect, and had attacked each other in print, but they had never met. Knowing that Johnson would probably refuse to meet Wilkes if approached directly, Boswell took advantage of Johnson's "spirit of contradiction" and relayed the invitation to the dinner party, but pretended to remember at the last minute that Wilkes would be there as well, suggesting that perhaps Johnson would prefer not to attend after all (*Samuel Johnson,* p. 217). As Boswell had hoped, Johnson then insisted on going—which he did, getting along very well with Wilkes, with whom he enjoyed several jokes at Boswell's expense.

Johnson wrote little until 1779-81, when he produced his last major work, *The Lives of the Poets,* consisting of biographic and critical sketches of the major English poets. In 1783 Johnson suffered a stroke and his health began declining sharply, though his conversation, Boswell assures us, was as vigorous and lively as ever. Samuel Johnson died on December 13, 1784, at age 75.

A question of "character". The critic Ralph W. Rader observes that "the subject of Boswell's life is not the life of Johnson but the character of Johnson as revealed in the facts of his life" (Rader in Bloom, p. 11). "Character" is indeed a central concept of the biography, both in the sense of personality (as above) and in the older sense of social reputation, or status. It is in this latter sense that Boswell uses the word most often. For example, in discussing whether Christian values permit dueling over honor, Johnson argued that "a man may shoot a man who invades his character, as he may shoot him who invades his house" (*Samuel Johnson,* p. 299). In another conversation, Boswell wondered why Johnson, with his great talents, was not dissatisfied that "he was not called to some great office, nor had attained to great wealth"; Johnson, irritated, responded that the subject was inappropriate: "Nobody . . . has a right to talk in this manner, to bring before a man his own character . . ." (*Samuel Johnson,* p. 287).

"Character" in this sense is thus closely linked to social status, which in British society was most often determined by class. Johnson's lowly origins did not prevent him from holding highly conservative views about the value of social rank, which he firmly believed was a social necessity. Responding to the idea that social distinctions should be based on merit alone, Johnson replied dismissively:

Why, Sir, mankind have found that this cannot be. Were that to be the only distinction among mankind, we should soon quarrel about the degrees of it. Were all distinctions abolished, the strongest would not long acquiesce, but would endeavor to obtain a superiority by their bodily strength. . . . A man is born to hereditary rank; or his being appointed to certain offices, gives him a certain rank. Subordination tends greatly to human happiness. . . .
(*Samuel Johnson,* p. 111)

This description does allow for flexibility in social "subordination," for some recognition of merit in the assignment of status. The stage career of Johnson's lifelong friend David Garrick offers a colorful example. When Garrick began his career, "players" (as actors were called) occupied a low rung on the social ladder. By the time of his death in 1779, Garrick's own great wealth and celebrity had brought his profession greater respectability. As Johnson put it, "Here is a man who has advanced the dignity of his profession. Garrick has made a player a higher character" (*Samuel Johnson,* p. 241).

Garrick's personal "character," of course, has little to do with his public "character" but the same cannot be said of Johnson, whose public reputation derived directly from his brilliant, quirky personality, as expressed in both his writings and his life. While generous, frank, moral, and compassionate on the outside, Johnson, as shown in Boswell's biography, was a privately troubled man, given to constant self-recrimination and gloominess. Johnson himself faults his tendency to keep scrutinizing his own behavior—"I resolve," he wrote in his diary for September 18, 1764, "[t]o drive out vain scruples. . . . God help me . . . to combat scruples" (Johnson in Bate, p. 381). It is Boswell's understanding of the deep connection between the man's public and private "characters" that lends his portrait of Johnson such force.

Sources and literary context. Boswell's primary source for *The Life of Samuel Johnson* was Johnson himself, and the most vivid scenes are those in which Boswell is present. Boswell relied upon his extensive journals, and he included numerous letters between Johnson and himself in his text. He also interviewed others and used any notes or correspondence, usually quoting verbatim, that they had saved in order to fill in gaps in his knowledge. The genre of biography was developing rapidly in the eighteenth century, as exemplified by the biographical works of Johnson himself and others, and

Boswell stands squarely within this tradition, even as he expands the possibilities inherent in it (by including letters, for example, or the notes of others). Johnson's reputation was such that even during his lifetime it was clear that he would be an apt subject for biography. Within a few years of his death, two of his friends, the former Hester Lynch Thrale (who had remarried an Italian singer named Piozzi after her husband's death) and Sir John Hawkins, published their own versions of Johnson's life. Hawkins had known Johnson longer than Boswell, and Hester Lynch Piozzi had known him more intimately. Lynch Piozzi's *Anecdotes of the Late Samuel Johnson* appeared in 1786, and Hawkins's *Life of Samuel Johnson* in 1787. In trying to find a publisher for his own much more detailed book, Boswell was admonished that the two earlier works had saturated the market and that the public was losing interest. Several times in *The Life of Samuel Johnson*, Boswell slights both authors, describing them unflatteringly, correcting their versions of events.

Boswell himself sought to portray Johnson differently from the others, by writing his life in scenes, like a drama. In keeping with the effort, he took some dramatic license—exaggerating Johnson's use of "Sir" at the beginning of a remark, for example, and calling him Dr. Johnson, when "Mr." was the title Johnson himself seems to have preferred. The effort turned out to be an unceasing endeavor; the apparently unsatisfied Boswell released a second edition of the biography in 1793, and was hard at work on a third when he died in 1795.

Publication and reception. Since its publication, some critics of *The Life of Samuel Johnson* have insisted that its worth resides solely in the greatness of its subject, and that Boswell's contribution was merely that of a sort of secretary. Many more, however, have seen Boswell as a great artist and writer in his own right. By the 1830s there were critics, like the historian Thomas B. Macaulay, who claimed that Boswell's portrait surpassed the historical Johnson himself in interest:

Boswell's book has done for him [Johnson] more than the best of his own books could do. The memory of other authors is kept alive by their works. But the memory of Johnson keeps many of his works alive. The old philosopher is still among us in the brown coat with the metal buttons, and the shirt which ought to be at wash, blinking, puffing, rolling his head, drumming with his fingers, tearing his meat like a tiger, and swallowing his tea in oceans. No human being who has been more than seventy years in the grave is so well known to us. (Macaulay in Clingham, p. 3)

—Colin Wells

For More Information

Bate, W. Jackson. *Samuel Johnson*. New York: Harcourt, Brace, Jovanovich, 1977.

Black, Jeremy. *The Politics of Britain, 1688-1800*. Manchester: Manchester University Press, 1993.

———. *An Illustrated History of Eighteenth Century Britain, 1688-1793*. Manchester: Manchester University Press, 1996.

Bloom, Harold, ed. *James Boswell's Life of Samuel Johnson*. Modern Critical Interpretations. New York: Chelsea House, 1986.

Boswell, James. *The Life of Samuel Johnson*. Ed. Christopher Hibbert. London: Penguin, 1986.

Brady, Frank. *James Boswell: The Later Years 1769-1755*. New York: McGraw-Hill, 1984.

Clark, J.C.D. *Samuel Johnson: Literature, Religion, and English Cultural Politics from the Restoration to Romanticism*. Cambridge: Cambridge University Press, 1994.

Clingham, Greg. *Boswell: The Life of Samuel Johnson*. Cambridge: Cambridge University Press, 1992.

Hibbert, Christopher. *The Personal History of Samuel Johnson*. London: Longman, 1971.

Hyde, Mary Morley Crapo. *The Impossible Friendship: Boswell and Mrs. Thrale*. Cambridge, Mass., Harvard University Press, 1972.

Lipking, Lawrence I. *Samuel Johnson: The Life of an Author*. Cambridge: Harvard University Press, 1998.

Scott, Geoffrey. "The Making of the Life of Johnson as Shown in Boswell's Fist Notes." In *Twentieth Century Interpretations of Boswell's Life of Johnson*. Ed. James L. Clifford. Englewood Cliffs, N.J.: Prentice Hall, 1970.

Lyrical
Ballads

by

William Wordsworth and Samuel Taylor Coleridge

Born in West Cumberland, England, in 1770, William Wordsworth was educated at a local school in Hawkshead in the heart of the English Lake District, and later at St. John's College, Cambridge. In 1791 he traveled to France, where he became an ardent advocate of the French Revolution, then in its earliest and most idealistic stages. He also became romantically involved with a Frenchwoman, Annette Vallon, who bore him an illegitimate daughter. They planned to wed, but lack of money forced Wordsworth to return to England in December 1792. Guilt over the separation and disillusionment with the direction that the Revolution had taken drove Wordsworth to the brink of an emotional breakdown. Turning to poetry as an escape, he published *Descriptive Sketches* (1793), which recounts his tour of the Swiss Alps. In 1795 Wordsworth received a legacy from a friend that enabled him to pursue a career as a poet; he also met Samuel Taylor Coleridge. Born in Devonshire in 1772, Coleridge attended Jesus College, Cambridge. He was a voracious reader, devouring libraries of books, and was more a philosopher than a poet. Oppressed by debt and despondent over a brother's death, he dropped out of Cambridge in his third year of college, served briefly in a cavalry regiment, and then met Wordsworth. He also became politically active, advocating Utopian schemes and promoting a sort of nonviolent revolution to eradicate social and political barriers in England. His radicalism was channeled into poetry as the 1790s progressed. In 1798 Coleridge and Wordsworth published—anony-

---

THE LITERARY WORK

A collection of 23 poems set in rural England during the late eighteenth century; first published anonymously in 1798.

SYNOPSIS

Conveyed through the poems are emotional responses to the natural and supernatural in conversational verse. The initial poem, Coleridge's "The Rime of the Ancient Mariner," concerns a supernatural curse; the final one, Wordsworth's "Lines Composed a Few Miles Above Tintern Abbey," features a changing relationship to the natural world.

---

mously—a small volume of their work, *Lyrical Ballads, with a Few Other Poems*, which launched a revolutionary movement in poetry.

Events in History at the Time of the Poems

From Neoclassicism to Romanticism. From 1660 to the 1789 outbreak of the French Revolution, the type of literature dominating England was Neoclassicism; the term stems from the intense admiration that seventeenth- and eighteenth-century authors held for the "classical" writers of ancient Greece and Rome, who were considered models to imitate. Neoclassic poets shared:

1) A reverence for tradition, often paired with a distrust of innovation

2) The conception of literature as an art that could be perfected only by study and practice

3) The belief that poetry should hold a mirror up to nature and should provide instruction as well as aesthetic pleasure

4) An emphasis on shared human experiences

5) The acceptance of man as a limited being who must resign himself to his place in the natural hierarchy and submit to God's superior wisdom and authority

A shift away from Neoclassicism became noticeable toward the end of the eighteenth century, after William Blake and Robert Burns published poems in a very different style than that employed by earlier eighteenth-century poets, such as Alexander Pope, and found a significant following among contemporary readers (see Blake's *Songs of Innocence and Songs of Experience*, and Pope's *Rape of the Lock*, also in *WLAIT 3: British and Irish Literature and Its Times*). Other poets soon followed Blake's lead, breaking new literary ground.

In contrast to the Neoclassic poets, the "Romantics" developed a new school of writing with its own set of shared characteristics:

1) A preference for poetic innovation over adherence to tradition

2) The belief that the composition of poetry should be spontaneous and natural

3) An emphasis on landscape and nature, especially as they affect the poet's perceptions

4) The choice of the self or social outcasts as poetic subjects

5) The conception of man as a being of limitless potential and aspirations whose failures could be considered as glorious as his successes

Many of these Romantic characteristics can be observed in the poems in *Lyrical Ballads*; Coleridge's "The Rime of the Ancient Mariner" and Wordsworth's "The Mad Mother" both feature outcasts as their protagonists, while Wordsworth's "Lines Composed a Few Miles Above Tintern Abbey" explores the emotional and spiritual effects that revisiting a well-loved landscape has upon the mind of the poet.

Politically, the Romantic movement has been linked to the outbreak of the French Revolution in 1789. At first English liberals and radicals supported the popular revolution. A new age of "liberty, equality, and fraternity" seemed about to dawn and many young Englishmen, including

William Wordsworth, eagerly lent their efforts to the cause. But the carnage of France's 1792-94 Reign of Terror (in which the revolutionaries guillotined tens of thousands of alleged opponents) and the ascent of Napoleon Bonaparte as emperor diminished hopes of social equality in Wordsworth and his contemporaries. Still, the dream of fresh beginnings persisted, leading to a new literary tradition that would dominate the next three decades. This tradition was part and parcel of the revolutionary spirit in an age during which old idols were toppled, new ideas and doctrines introduced, and bold experiments performed.

The "Great Chain of Being." The Neoclassic poets and their eighteenth-century contemporaries subscribed to the theological concept of the Great Chain of Being, which stipulated that the universe held every possible kind and variety of life, that each species differed from the next by the least possible degree, and that all of creation was arranged in a hierarchy, extending from the least to the greatest species, all the way up to God Himself. According to this model, humans occupied a middle position, above the animals but below the angels: all creatures—especially humanity—were expected to accept their divinely allotted place in God's scheme and not attempt to reach beyond their position with vain aspirations.

In *Lyrical Ballads*, these tenets are subtly but continually challenged, most notably in "The Rime of the Ancient Mariner." The Mariner's thoughtless and wanton shooting of the albatross results in as rigorous a punishment—for him and his shipmates—as if the bird were indeed the "Christian soul" to which the sailors have compared it (Coleridge, "Rime," line 65). Moreover, the Mariner's redemption does not begin until he learns to reverence what he has formerly despised—the "thousand thousand slimy things" of the deep, which are nonetheless God's creatures, too ("Rime," line 238). In his final injunction to his captive listener, the Mariner implicitly dismisses the belief that one form of life is superior to another, in the lines, "He prayeth well, who loveth well / Both man and bird and beast" ("Rime," lines 611-12).

Religious temper of the times. During the 1740s, a new religious movement developed in opposition to the Anglican Church. Called the Methodist movement, it was led by John Wesley, an English theologian educated at Oxford, and it emphasized the importance of faith over good works as the road to salvation. Although Anglican clerics and members of the upper classes were often repelled by the emotionalism and zeal aroused by Methodist preachers, the new religious awakening flourished, reinvigorating both the Anglican Church and some of the Dissenters' sects, which diverged from it. During the 1780s and 1790s, Methodism was growing among university students, especially at Cambridge.

Many of these students objected to the Test Acts, which stipulated that scholars who wished to receive a university degree had to subscribe to the Thirty-nine Articles of the Anglican faith. Rejection of Anglican doctrines contributed to a resurgence of Unitarianism around this time, a creed that emphasized the role of reason in religion and presented an increasingly scientific view of the universe. Main tenets of eighteenth-century Unitarianism stressed the oneness or unipersonality of God, the humanity—rather than divinity—of Jesus, and the importance of man's rational faculty.

Many young intellectuals embraced Unitarianism, including Coleridge early in his university career. To be a Unitarian at the time implied certain other traits pertaining to the follower, namely that one sympathized with the French Revolution and opposed aristocracy. "Radicalism in politics and rationalism in religion went hand in hand" (Willey, p. 16). In 1794 Coleridge made a full conversion to Unitarianism, enthusiastically supporting—even propagandizing—its agenda. For a time, he and the poet Robert Southey planned to found a democratic community based on Unitarian ideals in the United States. The scheme fell through, but not before Coleridge had committed himself to marrying Sara Fricker, the sister of Southey's own fiancée. The marriage later foundered, as did Coleridge's belief in Unitarianism, but at the time that *Lyrical Ballads* was being composed, Coleridge's faith was still intact.

In general, Coleridge developed a concept of nature as an entity comprised "of living intelligent forces, seen sometimes as parts of a divine mind which transcend[s] them and sometimes as agents of that mind, but always as working to fulfill divine purpose" (Piper, pp. 86-87). Scholars trace this concept to his Unitarianism. In "The Rime of the Ancient Mariner," even the spirits of the polar region are presented as thinking beings with clearly defined purposes, a view that the Mariner, despite his delirium, acknowledges and understands: "Under the keel nine fathom deep / From the land of mist and snow / The spirit

An illustration by Gustave Doré of the line "It ate the food it ne'er had eat," from Coleridge's "The Rime of the Ancient Mariner."

slid: and it was he / That made the ship to go" ("Rime," lines 377-80).

Rural and industrial England. *Lyrical Ballads* struck a chord with contemporary readers for several reasons, in part because it evoked the natural world and a rural way of life that was rapidly vanishing. Since the mid-eighteenth century, the Industrial Revolution had been ushering in dramatic economic and social changes. James Watt's invention of the steam engine in 1765 introduced a power source that would replace wind and water. In the textile and other industries, machines began to replace manual labor. Mill towns and factories arose in northern and central England, where a new laboring population gathered in search of work, inhabiting slums and tenements that sprang up to shelter the newly arrived workers.

The advance of technology, as well as other changes, impinged on the lives of many rural dwellers. New machines led to the end of home and cottage industries. Meanwhile, enclosures of open-field and communally worked lands, creating new private holdings, drove many small farmers out of rural areas. Such enclosures had been taking place for centuries, unofficially, but the pace quickened from 1761 to 1801. Parliament passed 1,1479 acts that legislated the enclosure of some 2.4 million acres, threatening to wipe out small farmers and rural laborers in the designated areas (Mahoney, p. 67). As stone walls and hedges partitioned off lands that had once been cultivated by communities, many rural dwellers were left with two choices: to migrate to the industrial towns or to eke out a living as farm workers on subsistence wages.

Meanwhile, the war between England and France—which had begun in 1793—helped drive up the cost of living. "Between 1790 and 1795 the price of oats rose 75 percent, that of a loaf of bread doubled in the country and tripled in London, and that of a pound of potatoes quadrupled. . . . These economic factors . . . were catastrophic for the rural poor" (Johnston, p. 478). At the time, Wordsworth was setting up a household with his sister Dorothy in the rural town of Racedown. "The country people here," he told his friend William Mathews, "are wretchedly poor" (Wordsworth in Johnston, p. 478). Perhaps because of their wretched poverty, the "country people" of Racedown and, later, Somersetshire attained a powerful hold on Wordsworth's imagination, as manifested in *Lyrical Ballads*. "Simon Lee" tells of an old huntsman and his wife who have fallen on hard times since the death of his master:

> A scrap of land they have, but they
> Are poorest of the poor.
> This scrap of land he from the heath
> Enclosed when he was stronger;
> But what avails the land to them,
> When they can till no longer?
> (Wordsworth, "Simon Lee," lines 59-64).

The Poems in Focus

Contents summary. *Lyrical Ballads* is prefaced with an "Advertisement" that identifies the collected poems as experiments: "They were written chiefly with a view to ascertain how far the language of conversation in the middle and lower classes of society is adapted to the purposes of poetic pleasure" (Wordsworth and Coleridge, *Lyrical Ballads*, p. 7). The poems themselves concentrate on humble subjects and rustic settings, although a few explore the mythical and supernatural. Of the total 23 poems, Coleridge contributed only four. Framing the initial 1798 edition are Coleridge's "The Rime of the Ancient

Mariner" and Wordsworth's "Lines Composed a Few Miles Above Tintern Abbey."

"The Rime of the Ancient Mariner." The poem begins as an ancient mariner approaches a guest at a wedding and begins to tell him a tale. Although the wedding guest tries to fend the mariner off, he mesmerizes the guest into submission: "He holds him with his glittering eye— / The Wedding Guest stood still / And listens like a three year's child; / The Mariner hath his will" ("Rime," lines 17-20).

The mariner continues with his tale, relating how his ship sailed to the equator, then was driven toward the South Pole by a storm, where it drifted through freezing mists, past arctic wastelands. An albatross flies toward the ship, and the crew, taking the bird's appearance as a good omen, receives it hospitably. When the ice breaks, allowing the ship to pass through and resume a northward course, the albatross follows. The mariner shoots the bird with his crossbow.

Fearing an ill omen, the crew initially cries out against the mariner's killing of the albatross, but when the wind holds and the sun rises, they agree that the killing was justified, making themselves complicit in the deed. As they near the equator, the wind dies down and the ship is becalmed. Parched with thirst and convinced that they are being pursued by a vengeful spirit, the angry crew hangs the body of the albatross around the mariner's neck, as a sign of his guilt.

Sometime later, the mariner spies a shape approaching them and manages to call out to his shipmates. Hoping for rescue, all are horrified when they behold a ghostly ship drawing near, with only two spectral inhabitants on board—a man who looks like Death himself and an even more terrifying woman: "Her skin was white as leprosy, / The Night-Mare LIFE-IN-DEATH was she, / Who thicks man's blood with gold" ("Rime," lines 192-94). Death and Life-in-Death throw dice for the ship's crew, the latter winning the mariner. The ghost-ship vanishes at sunset and as the moon rises, the mariner's shipmates drop dead, leaving him the sole survivor: "And every soul, it passed me by, / Like the whizz of my crossbow!" ("Rime," lines 222-23).

In the present, the wedding guest fears he is being held captive by a spirit, but the mariner reassuringly affirms that he is a living man and continues his story. On board ship, surrounded by the corpses of his comrades, the mariner experiences agonies of loneliness and self-loathing: "The many men, so beautiful! / And they all dead did lie: / And a thousand, thousand slimy things / Lived on; and so did I" ("Rime," lines 236-39). Desolate, the mariner tries in vain to pray and yearns for death, but to no avail. After seven days and nights, he sees two water snakes swimming in the deep and is struck by their beauty:

A spring of love gushed from my heart,
And I blessed them unaware . . .
The self-same moment I could pray;
And from my neck so free
The Albatross fell off, and sank
Like lead into the sea.
("Rime," lines 284-85, 288-91)

Exhausted, the mariner sinks into a healing slumber, awakening to find himself drenched in rain: the drought has ended. Suddenly, the ship's sails fill and the ship, so long becalmed, begins to move. To the mariner's astonishment, the bodies of his shipmates arise and begin to pilot the vessel. The mariner realizes that spirits have inhabited the corpses of the dead crew. The ship sails smoothly on until it reaches the equator, then stops abruptly; the mariner swoons, falling to the deck. Returning gradually to consciousness, he hears "two voices in the air" discussing his situation and learns that he has been given a long, heavy penance by the Spirit of the South Pole for shooting the albatross, and his punishment is not yet over ("Rime," line 397).

Meanwhile, the ship has sped northward while the mariner lay unconscious; the speed slackens when he regains his senses, but the mariner can nonetheless see that the ship is approaching his own land and safe harbor and is overjoyed. Just as the ship nears the bay, the mariner sees that his shipmates' bodies have again collapsed on the deck, but "[a] man all light, a seraph man / On every corse [corpse] there stood" ("Rime," lines 490-91). The sound of oars breaks the silence; the mariner sees a boat carrying a pilot, the pilot's boy, and the local hermit, who lives in the wood by the sea. When the ship suddenly sinks, casting the mariner into the water, the pilot comes to the rescue, pulling him into the boat. The mariner's presence, however, disturbs his rescuers, sending the pilot into a fit and the pilot's boy into a mad frenzy. Once on land, the mariner pleads with the hermit to shrive his soul. Compelled by a "woeful agony" to relate his tale of misfortune to the hermit, the mariner at last finds himself free, but only for the present: "Since then, at an uncertain hour, / That agony returns: / And till my ghastly tale is told / This heart within me burns" ("Rime," lines 582-85).

The mariner informs the wedding guest that he always knows the person to whom he must tell his tale and, before taking his leave, urges him to love and honor all God's creatures: "He prayeth best, who loveth best / All things both great and small; / For the dear God who loveth us, / He made and loveth all" ("Rime," lines 614-17).

Alone and much shaken by what he has heard, the wedding guest leaves the festivities: "He went like one that hath been stunned, / And is of sense forlorn: / A sadder and a wiser man, / He rose the morrow morn" ("Rime," lines 622-25).

"Lines Composed a Few Miles Above Tintern Abbey." The poem begins as Wordsworth revisits—after a 5-year absence—one of his favorite places, the banks of the Wye River, a few miles above the ruins of Tintern Abbey:

Once again
Do I behold these steep and lofty cliffs
Which on a wild secluded scene impress
Thoughts of a more deep seclusion: and connect
The landscape with the quiet of the sky.
(Wordsworth, "Tintern Abbey," lines 4-8)

Traces of civilization intrude on the serene scene, not all of them happy.

These hedge-rows; hardly hedge-rows, little lines
Of supportive wood runs wild; these pastoral farms
Green to the very door; and wreathes of smoke
Sent up, in silence, from among the trees,
With some uncertain notice, as might seem,
Of vagrant dwellers in the houseless woods,
Or of some hermit's cave, where by his fire
The hermit sits alone.
("Tintern Abbey," lines 18-23)

The scene stimulates Wordsworth's memory. Recalling his recent sojourns "in lonely rooms, and mid the din / Of towns and cities," he reflects on how his memories of nature brought him "sensations sweet, / Felt in the blood and felt along the heart" ("Tintern Abbey," lines 25-26, 27-28).

Returning to the present, Wordsworth gazes on the scene before him, storing up memories for the future. He thinks back to the time when he first visited this spot as a boy and "bounded o'er the mountains, by the sides / Of the deep rivers, and the lonely streams, / Wherever nature led . . . / I cannot paint / What then I was" ("Tintern Abbey," lines 68-70, 75-76). Despite having outgrown the "aching joys" and "dizzy raptures" of boyhood, the adult Wordsworth nonetheless believes that he has received "abundant recom-

Wordsworth composed his poem a few miles above Tintern Abbey, seen here.

pense" through a more mature appreciation of what nature has to offer:

> For I have learned
> To look on nature, not as in the hour
> Of thoughtless youth, but hearing oftentimes
> The still, sad music of humanity,
> Not harsh nor grating, though of ample power
> To chasten and subdue.
> ("Tintern Abbey," lines 88-93)

THE BALLAD STANZA

The publication of Bishop Thomas Percy's *Reliques of Ancient Poetry* (1765) revived the ballad as a poetic genre and inspired countless modern imitators, including Wordsworth and Coleridge. Popular ballads were generally written in quatrains in alternating four- and three-stress iambic (an unstressed syllable preceding a stressed syllable) lines. Generally, the second and fourth lines—and occasionally, the first and third—rhymed. While not all of the *Lyrical Ballads* use the ballad stanza, the form can be seen in Wordsworth's "We Are Seven" and Coleridge's "The Rime of the Ancient Mariner": "Alóne, alóne, all, áll alóne, / Alóne on a wíde wíde séa! / And néver a sáint took píty ón / My sóul in ágony!" ("Rime," lines 232-35)

Grateful for this heightened understanding, Wordsworth hails nature as "the anchor of my purest thoughts, the nurse, / The guide, the guardian of my heart, and soul / Of all my moral being" ("Tintern Abbey," lines 109-11).

Moreover, Wordsworth contends, he can experience vicariously the childlike joy his companion and younger sister, Dorothy, still feels: "In thy voice I catch / The language of my former heart, and read / My former pleasures in the shooting lights / Of thy wild eyes" ("Tintern Abbey," lines 116-19). Wordsworth enjoins Nature to bestow upon his sister the same blessings and teachings he has received, then maintains that not even his death can sunder him and Dorothy, who are connected through their love of nature as well as blood. He concludes his address to her by stating that "these steep woods and lofty cliffs, / And this green pastoral landscape, were to me / More dear, both for themselves, and for thy sake" ("Tintern Abbey," lines 157-59).

Beginning with the "Ancient Mariner" and ending with "Tintern Abbey" infused the 1798 *Lyrical Ballads* with a progression. Haunted by his experience, the mariner endures alienation from society (the wedding party) that he imposes on his listener, the wedding guest, who is rendered "sadder" but "wiser" by this encounter. The collection builds from this alienation to "Tintern Abbey," in which the speaker, who, since the first edition was anonymous, might easily be presumed to be the same for both poems, finds consolation and joy in nature and in his satisfying intimacy with his sister.

Nature and the supernatural. Several years after the publication of *Lyrical Ballads*, Coleridge described in his *Biographia Literaria* the creative decisions that he and Wordsworth made while compiling their project:

> It was agreed that my endeavours should be directed to persons and characters supernatural. . . . Mr. Wordsworth, on the other hand, was to propose to himself as his object to give the charm of novelty to things of every day.
>
> (Coleridge in Abrams, II, p. 388)

Despite this seemingly polarized division of labor, the natural and the supernatural continually intertwine in the poems of both Wordsworth and Coleridge. While "The Rime of the Ancient Mariner" is undeniably a tale of imagination and the supernatural, Coleridge nonetheless maintains a connection to the everyday world and its wonders. Before the mariner's adventure takes on its nightmarish cast after his shooting of the albatross, for example, he witnesses nature's stark beauty while voyaging through the polar seas: "And now there came both mist and snow, / And it grew wondrous cold: / And ice, mast-high, came floating by, / As green as emerald" ("Rime," lines 51-54).

While Coleridge provides a wealth of sensory details in mapping out a supernatural landscape, Wordsworth uses a minimum of detail to convey an overall impression of peace and tranquility; his description of the natural landscape is as serene as Coleridge's is restless. However, Wordsworth too reveals a sense of the interconnection of nature and the supernatural. "Tintern Abbey" may lack the ghostly apparitions of "Rime," but Wordsworth imbues nature itself with a living spirit that has the power to teach and inspire:

> And I have felt
> A presence that disturbs me with the joy
> Of elevated thoughts; a sense sublime
> Of something far more deeply interfused,
> Whose dwelling is the light of setting suns,
> And the round ocean and the living air,
> And the blue sky, and in the mind of man:
> A motion and a spirit, that impels
> All thinking things, all objects of all thought,
> And rolls through all things.
>
> ("Tintern Abbey," lines 93-102)

Although the terms "Romantic poet" and "nature poet" seem to be synonymous, Wordsworth and Coleridge were indebted to such pre-Romantic poets as William Cowper (1731-1800), Oliver Goldsmith (1730-74), Thomas Gray (1716-71), and James Thomson (1700-48). Often called the "poets of sensibility" for their intense responsiveness to extremes of beauty and ugliness, these writers set the trend of eighteenth-century nature poetry. Thomson, who grew up in the Scottish countryside and did not see London until he was 25, was considered the first and most popular nature poet of his time. His poem "The Seasons" became an emulated model: "Generations of readers learned to look at the external world through Thomson's eyes and with the

---

WREATHES OF SMOKE AND VAGRANT DWELLERS

An atmosphere of tranquil solitude hangs over the Tintern Abbey of Wordsworth's poem. But the air harbors disturbing traces of contemporary history, too. Adversity prompts beggars and the miserable poor—the vagrants of Wordsworth's poem—to take respite in the abbey's ruins. Intruding also on the peace are wreathes of smoke, traces of an encroaching industrialization. Wordsworth lamented the intrusion of factories, railroads, and the like into rural areas such as his Lake District. As for the poem's reference to beggars, when read in conjunction with the other *Lyrical Ballads*—points out Peter Manning—one perceives the sense of "social injustice" that the vagrant brings to "Wordsworth's meditative landscape" (Manning, p. 24). England was witness to many social injustices connected to events of the time, from the French Revolution, to the enclosure acts, to the American Revolution. As a result of this last revolution, poor rural dwellers, such as the husband of the "Female Vagrant" (in the *Lyrical Ballads* poem of that name), were conscripted into the British army to put down the rebellion. Wordsworth's and Coleridge's feelings about contemporary events found their way into *Lyrical Ballads*, under less-than-ideal conditions. In 1797, the British government feared a naval invasion by the French. Coleridge, who had published political pamphlets and preached in Unitarian pulpits, became known for his republican and socially liberal sympathies, and the government jumped to conclusions. It assumed, mistakenly, that Coleridge and his friends were helping France to plan such an invasion, and so "dispatched its own spy to keep track of their doings." (Fry, p. 6)

emotions which he had taught them to feel. The *eye* dominates the *literature* of external nature during the eighteenth century as the imagination was to do in the poetry of Wordsworth" (Abrams, I, p. 2471).

"MY DEAR, DEAR SISTER!"

~

Dorothy Wordsworth (1771-1855), the only girl among the five Wordsworth children, was born 21 months after William, to whom she was devoted. The Wordsworths' mother died when Dorothy was seven, and the children were separated, the boys attending boarding school while Dorothy lived with various relatives, seeing her brothers only during their summer vacations. After William received a bequest from his friend Raisley Calvert in 1795, the 24-year-old Dorothy set up housekeeping with her brother. They soon became fast friends with Coleridge, forming a familiar threesome. Dorothy herself had writing talent. For several years, she kept journals, one at Alfoxden in 1798—the year *Lyrical Ballads* was published. Modern scholars consider her journals invaluable for various reasons, including their record of natural scenes that would later be immortalized in her brother's poetry and the intimate details they provide of his daily life.

From "Autumn" by James Thomson, a Poet of Sensibility

Now black and deep the night begins to fall,
A shade immense! sunk in the quenching
   gloom,
Magnificent and vast, are heaven and earth.
Order confounded lies, all beauty void,
Distinction lost, and gay variety
One universal blot. . . .
Drear is the state of the benighted wretch
Who then bewildered wanders through the
   dark. . . .
  (Thomson in Abrams, *Autumn,* lines 1138-46)

From "The Thorn" by William Wordsworth, a Romantic Poet

There is a thorn; it looks so old,
In truth you'd find it hard to say,
How it could ever have been young,
It looks so old and grey.

. . .

Now would you see this aged thorn . . .
You must take care and chuse your time . . .
. . . for oft there sits . . .
A woman in a scarlet cloak,

And to herself she cries,
"Oh misery! oh misery!
"Oh woe is me! oh misery!"
  (Wordsworth, "The Thorn," lines 1-4, 57-69)

While the nature poetry of Thomson and his contemporaries concentrated on accurately conveying the beauties of the external world, that of Wordsworth and Coleridge dealt more with the poet's *response* to the external world: "Romantic 'nature poems' are in fact meditative poems, in which the presented scene usually serves to raise an emotional problem or personal crisis. . . . In addition, Romantic poems habitually imbue the landscape with human life, passion, and expressiveness" (Abrams, II, p. 8). Wordsworth and Coleridge's achievement was to transform the poetry of natural description by turning the eye, previously trained upon the external world, *inward* upon the soul. By connecting the natural world to human responses to it, nature became an extension of the poet's own imagination or, as Wordsworth was later to describe it, "that *inward* eye / Which is the bliss of solitude" (Wordsworth in Abrams, II, p. 207).

Literary partnership. While history does not record the exact details of the first meeting between Wordsworth and Coleridge, after making each other's acquaintance in 1795, the two men quickly became indispensable to each other. Their personalities and temperaments were complementary:

> Coleridge, with his enormous reading, his scholarship, his religious enthusiasm, his knowledge of classical and European literatures, his scientific interests, his emotional approach to politics, was a man of speculation, restless enquiry and self-questioning. While Wordsworth, with his passionate response to the natural world, was a man of physical experience and steadily accumulating moral certainties by which ideas might be judged and settled.
>
> (Holmes, p. 151)

Coleridge's wide-ranging intellectual interests at first made him the dominant partner in the relationship with Wordsworth, although their positions would eventually reverse themselves. Both, however, had an unerring sense of what the other needed most. Coleridge supplied Wordsworth with unfailing admiration for his writing, and helped shape its direction, while Wordsworth provided emotional support by validating Coleridge's sense of himself and his own genius.

In the three years between their first meeting and the publication of *Lyrical Ballads*, Wordsworth and Coleridge spent much of their time together. Often accompanied by Wordsworth's sister, Dorothy, the two men took long walks through the countryside, picnicked, read poetry aloud, and avidly discussed their own potential contribution to literature. Coleridge believed Wordsworth to be the premier poet of the era, though Coleridge himself was more prolific in 1797 "and his conversational style of writing influenced Wordsworth rather than the other way around" (Fry, p. 5).

> With the fervor of high-minded youth, they talked of making the world better through their poetry. They hoped in that time of national crisis and pessimism to bring to men, disillusioned by the French Revolutionary idea, the secret they had discovered of the principle of joy in the universe. They would preach no political or social reform; and, in order to reach men, they would cast out of their writing all poetic diction and return to directness, sincerity, and basic human emotions.
>
> (Noyes, p. 23)

Although they shared similar goals, Wordsworth and Coleridge soon discovered they were incapable of collaborating on a single poem. At first, Wordsworth suggested the killing of the albatross and even penned a few lines of "The Rime of the Ancient Mariner," but he quickly sensed that Coleridge had his own ideas of how the poem ought to develop and so dropped out of the project. Nonetheless, the two poets continued to rely on each other's feedback and suggestions. By the summer of 1798, most of the poems that comprise *Lyrical Ballads* had been completed and offered to Joseph Cottle of Bristol for publication. Wordsworth's "Lines Composed a Few Miles Above Tintern Abbey," however, was an exception, a last-minute contribution, added just as the other poems were going to press. Neither poet suspected that their poorly received literary experiment would ultimately lay the foundation for much of modern poetry.

Ironically, *Lyrical Ballads* marked both the beginning and the end of the poets' literary partnership. Wordsworth, the more driven of the pair, even came to dislike "The Rime of the Ancient Mariner," blaming it for the hostile reviews *Lyrical Ballads* received after its initial publication. He moved the poem to next-to-last in the 1800 edition and also convinced Coleridge to modernize its diction, then continued to do so

himself for later editions. (Sometime after 1805, Coleridge wrote explanatory glosses for the poem, included in most editions today.) In 1810 the two quarreled bitterly over the married Coleridge's doomed infatuation with Sara Hutchinson—Wordsworth's sister-in-law—and Coleridge's growing addiction to opium, which interfered with his productivity as a poet; the breach was not mended until nearly 20 years later.

Sources and literary context. Wordsworth rarely attempted to disguise the autobiographical nature of his poems. Many of his contributions to *Lyrical Ballads* were based on real-life encounters; Wordsworth's meetings with an old man who had been the huntsman to the squires of Alfoxden and a young girl living in the Wye Valley provided the inspiration for "Simon Lee" and "We Are Seven," respectively. Of the deeply personal "Lines Composed a Few Miles Above Tintern Abbey," Wordsworth wrote:

> No poem of mine was composed under circumstances more pleasant for me to remember than this. I began it upon leaving Tintern, after crossing the Wye, and concluded it just as I was entering Bristol in the evening after a ramble of 4 or 5 days, with my sister. Not a line of it was altered, and not any part of it written down till I reached Bristol.
>
> (Wordsworth in Abrams, II, p. 151)

TINTERN ABBEY

Visiting architectural ruins was a favorite pastime of nineteenth-century British travelers. Tintern Abbey, to which Wordsworth refers in the title of his poem, was founded in 1131 by Walter de Clare for Cistercian monks who had emigrated from France. Like many small monasteries, the abbey was dissolved under Henry VIII in 1537, after England broke from the Roman Catholic Church. By Wordsworth's time, the roofless, fourteenth-century church was all that remained of the original edifice. The building's graceful proportions and attractive natural setting (Tintern Abbey was located south of Monmouth on the west bank of the Wye River) endeared it to Wordsworth. Although the poet never mentions the abbey itself in his poem, his title and praise of the surrounding region—the "steep woods and lofty cliffs" and "green pastoral landscape"—contributed to the ruin's popularity as a tourist attraction. ("Tintern Abbey," lines 158-59)

By contrast, Coleridge's poems in *Lyrical Ballads* were based more on his own imaginings. While "The Nightingale" was similar in tone and subject to Wordsworth's poems, "The Foster-Mother's Tale" and "The Dungeon" were both taken from the unfinished play *Osorio*, on which Coleridge was working. "The Rime of the Ancient Mariner" can be tied to several influences: John Cruikshank, a friend and neighbor of Coleridge's, had told him of a dream he once had about "a skeleton ship, with figures on it" (Cruikshank in Bate, p. 51). Coleridge himself had meanwhile been thinking of outcast figures in literature, such as the Wandering Jew. Finally, Wordsworth had been reading Captain George Shelvocke's *Voyage Round the World by the way of the Great South Sea* (1726), which mentioned that a man who killed an albatross—a bird of good omen—could incur the vengeance of the spirits who inhabited the Antarctic region. Also from Wordsworth came the idea of resurrecting the dead bodies to sail the ship.

LITERARY MILESTONE

"The 1798 *Lyrical Ballads* . . . is considered one of the most important turning points in English literary history. It was a challenge to conventional tastes both in politics and literature: the focus on rustic persons and themes, together with the implicit attack on the artificial poetic diction of most eighteenth-century poetry . . . presented the reading public with fare that seemed starkly new." (Fry, p. 11)

Although the foundation for a new poetic tradition had been tentatively laid by the poets of sensibility mentioned above, Wordsworth and Coleridge were the ones to propel poetry in a new direction for the next 30 years. Rejecting ancient Greek and Roman models, they turned instead to rustic ballads—such as those found in Bishop Thomas Percy's *Reliques* and the Scots dialect poems of Robert Burns—and to their own subjective experience for inspiration. In this, they were greatly influenced by John Locke's ***An Essay Concerning Human Understanding***, which described sensation as the basis of knowledge, and by Addison and Steele's periodical ***The Spectator***, which popularized Locke's notions about how the imagination interacts with the world to shape one's experience of it (both works also in

WLAIT 3: British and Irish Literature and Its Times). All these influences led to the project, whose aims Wordsworth would clarify in his famous "Preface to *Lyrical Ballads*" of 1800. "All good poetry," says the Preface, "is the spontaneous overflow of powerful feelings" and the poet himself "is a man speaking to men" (Wordsworth in Abrams, II, pp. 160, 164).

Reviews. In retrospect, *Lyrical Ballads* is a literary milestone, but the majority of critics hardly recognized this at the time. On its first appearance in print, the collection received some scathing reviews. Noting that Wordworth's "Advertisement" for *Lyrical Ballads* revealed that the poems were intended as experiments, Robert Southey curtly declared in *The Critical Review*, "The 'experiment,' we think, has failed, not because the language of conversation is little adapted to 'the purposes of poetic pleasure,' but because it has been tried on uninteresting subjects" (Southey in Jones and Tydeman, p. 54). Southey singled out individual poems for blame or praise, remarking of Wordsworth's "The Idiot Boy," "No tale less deserved the labour that appears to have been bestowed upon this" (Southey in Jones and Tydeman, p. 53). He was similarly unenthusiastic about Coleridge's "The Rime of the Ancient Mariner": "Many of the stanzas are laboriously beautiful; but in connection they are absurd or unintelligible. . . . Genius has here been employed in producing a poem of little merit" (Southey in Jones and Tydeman, p. 53). Southey did admire what he saw as the "superior powers" of Wordsworth's "Tintern Abbey": "On reading this production, it is possible not to lament that he should have condescended to write such pieces as 'The Last of the Flock,' 'The Convict,' and most of the ballads" (Southey in Jones and Tydeman, p. 54). Finally, in the *Edinburgh Review*, Southey tied the ballads to the historical moment, reprovingly, it seems: "They are filled with horror and compassion at the sight of poor men spending their blood in the quarrels of princes, and brutifying their sublime capabilities in the drudgery of unremitting labour. . . . The present vicious constitution of society alone is responsible for all these enormities" (Southey in Manning, p. 24).

Charles Burney, writing for *The Monthly Review*, had somewhat warmer praise for *Lyrical Ballads*, noting of the authors' use of the ballad form, "The style and versification are those of our ancient ditties but much polished, and more constantly excellent" (Burney in Jones and Tydeman, p. 56). While Burney expressed views similar to

Southey's on "The Rime of the Ancient Mariner," calling it "the strangest story of a cock and a bull that we ever saw on paper," he nonetheless conceded that "there are in it poetical touches of an exquisite kind" (Burney in Jones and Tydeman, p. 55). Burney also called "Lines Composed a Few Miles Above Tintern Abbey" the "reflections of no common mind; poetical, beautiful, and philosophical" (Burney in Jones and Tydeman, p. 57). Despite reservations about the authors' choice of subjects—the rural poor, mad, and dispossessed—and the collection's melancholy tone, Burney concluded, "So much genius and originality are discovered in this publication, that we wish to see another from the same hand, written on more elevated subjects and in a more cheerful disposition" (Burney in Jones and Tydeman, p. 57).

Significantly, neither Southey nor Burney perceived the appeal *Lyrical Ballads* would hold for readers, nor did they foresee the new direction that poetry would take as a result of this poetic experiment. But William Hazlitt, who would become one of the most influential critics of the Romantic period, recorded his own reaction to some of the poems in *Lyrical Ballads* after meeting Wordsworth at Alfoxden in 1798:

> I was not critically or skeptically inclined. I saw touches of truth and nature, and took the rest for granted . . . [but] the sense of a new style and a new spirit in poetry came over me. It had to me something of the effect that arises from the turning up of the fresh soil, or of the first welcome breath of Spring. (Hazlitt in Noyes, p. 46)

—Pamela S. Loy

For More Information

Abrams, M. H., ed. *The Norton Anthology of English Literature*. 2 vols. 5th ed. New York: W. W. Norton, 1986.

Bate, Walter Jackson. *Coleridge*. New York: Macmillan, 1968.

Fry, Paul H., ed. *The Rime of the Ancient Mariner*, by Samuel Taylor Coleridge. Boston: Bedford/St. Martin's, 1999.

Holmes, Richard. *Coleridge: Early Visions*. New York: Viking, 1989.

Johnston, Kenneth R. *The Hidden Wordsworth: Poet, Lover, Rebel, Spy*. New York: W. W. Norton, 1998.

Jones, Alun R., and William Tydeman, eds. *Lyrical Ballads: A Casebook*. London: Macmillan, 1979.

Mahoney, John L. *William Wordsworth: A Poetic Life*. New York: Fordham University Press, 1997.

Manning, Peter J. "Troubling the Borders: *Lyrical Ballads* 1798 and 1998." *The Wordsworth Circle* 30, no. 1 (winter 1999): 22-27.

Noyes, Russell. *William Wordsworth*. Boston: Twayne, 1991.

Piper, H. W. *The Active Universe: Pantheism and the Concept of Imagination in the English Romantic Poets*. London: Athlone, 1962.

Willey, Basil. *Samuel Taylor Coleridge*. New York: W. W. Norton, 1972.

Wordsworth, William, and Samuel Taylor Coleridge. *Lyrical Ballads*. 1798. Reprint, London: Methuen, 1968.

The Mabinogion

as translated by Patrick Ford

In 1849 Lady Charlotte Guest translated into English a group of 11 Welsh tales and dubbed the ensemble *The Mabinogion*, a convenient, if inaccurate, title that has come to designate the 11 as a whole. The term is the plural of *mabinogi*, a label applied to four of the stories. The relation among these stories, called the "Four Branches of the Mabinogi," remains a subject of considerable debate. Known as *Pedair Cainc* in Welsh, the "Four Branches" may refer to genealogical connections among the characters featured in the four separate stories, or perhaps even to different phases in the life of the figure of Pryderi, king of the south of Wales, who appears in each of the four tales. He is conceived, born, kidnapped, and named in the first; appears as a minor character who goes on an expedition in the second; regains some of his prominence in the third; and dies early in the fourth. Scholars have speculated that the ubiquitous Pryderi may be equivalent to the mysterious Mabon (featured in "Culhwch and Olwen"), both of whom tend to disappear or languish in captivity. This possible equivalence makes an explanation of the term *mabinogi* as "lore about Mabon" attractive. On the basis of language and content, scholars have generally dated the composition of the earliest versions of the texts to the second half of the eleventh century ("Culhwch and Olwen"; contains a reference to William, the eleventh-century Norman conqueror of England). The tales were composed in Welsh, a language still widely spoken in Wales. Here, in the second half of the first millennium, C.E., surviving elements of a Celtic civilization,

THE LITERARY WORK

Eleven prose tales set in Britain at various times between 500 B.C.E. and 1200 C.E.; written in Welsh in the eleventh and twelfth centuries; published in English in 1849.

SYNOPSIS

In four tales known as the "Four Branches of the Mabinogi," members of semidivine, mythical families interact, marry, give birth, perform acts of heroism and trickery, and die. In a fifth tale, "Culhwch and Olwen," with the help of the legendary Arthur, a young prince undertakes a set of monumental tasks to win the hand of the maiden he loves—a giant's daughter.

originally extending throughout Britain, developed into a people with their own distinctive culture. A legacy of this culture, *The Mabinogion* is a treasure-trove of medieval Welsh literature that provides clues to the workings of ancient British society.

Events in History at the Time the Tales Take Place

The world of the ancient Britons. The peoples of ancient Britain (late first millennium, B.C.E.) spoke Celtic languages and shared a Celtic cultural heritage that stretched all the way from Asia

Minor (Turkey) to the Iberian peninsula to Ireland. In the north of Britain were the Picts, predecessors of the Irish Celts. These Irish Celts immigrated to the islands and coast of the British northwest in the second half of the first millennium, C.E., ultimately to absorb the Picts and form the kingdom later known as Scotland. In the south of Britain were various British Celtic tribes, or Britons, ruled by kings and forming loose federations.

The lives of the early Britons, ancestors of the Welsh, were probably very similar to what we would find across the sea in Ireland during the same period. Society consisted of fortified communities dependent on agriculture and herding, ruled over by chieftains, and populated by extended kin groups. Wealth was measured in livestock as well as land, and status in the higher echelons of society was estimated according to pedigree and the number of followers a man had in his retinue. In upper-class society, men cultivated the art of warfare; the prominence of single combats between kings and/or champions in *The Mabinogion* reflects the value attached to individual prowess and martial enterprise in the culture. But battle was not the only way for an individual to excel in ancient Britain. Poetry and other forms of verbal artistry and lore, including the ability to "war with words" (which encompassed insult and satire), were highly prized in Celtic society as well.

The families of the ancient British were probably patriarchal, with authority resting in the hands of the elder males, although, as we see from the story of Rhiannon (told in the "First Branch of the Mabinogi"), aristocratic women had some control over their lives and could influence the actions of their spouses. In the upper classes, children (such as Pryderi of the First Branch and Lleu of the Fourth Branch) usually spent their childhood in fosterage with families of equal or higher rank—that is, they were raised by and in a family other than the one into which they were born. This custom forged strong ties among the powerful elite in society.

All these features of ancient British society still obtained in eleventh- and twelfth-century Wales. However, the gradual triumph of Christianity in Britain during the latter part of the Roman period (third to fifth centuries, C.E.) eradicated much of the original religion or muted it into forms of narrative, custom, and belief that were unthreatening to the new faith. The gods of ancient Britain, like those of the pre-Christian Irish, were probably organized into various pantheons or families, and different locations and tribes had their own localized divinities, both male and female. In the "Four Branches of the Mabinogi," characters who are children of the ancestral Llyr ("Sea") contrast with others who are children of Dôn ("Craft"), and both groups most likely derive from families of pre-Christian gods. Also featured in the First Branch are denizens of a supernatural kingdom, the kingdom of Annwn ("Un-World" or "Deep World"), which points to another lingering tradition about these ancient divinities.

Celtic life after the Romans. With the appearance of Roman military might in the first century, C.E., the British peoples became (in some cases, unruly) subjects of the Roman administrative state, which was centered in newly established military camps, towns, and cities (such as London and Chester) as well as in the rural villas of Roman administrators and Romanized Britons. Christianity, one of the cultural influences imported via the Romanization of Britain, established itself firmly in what had previously been a pagan country. Then, in 383, the Roman legions left the Britons behind to seize control of the Western empire under the leadership of one of their generals, the Spaniard Magnus Maximus, who briefly became emperor. (This historical character is the source for Macsen Wledig in one of *The Mabinogion* tales, "The Dream of Macsen".) By the time the Romans left, the Britons were essentially a Christian people. However, the new Christian religion, like Romanization in general, made less headway among some groups—among the Picts and other tribes in the northern part of the British island and along the coast of the areas that would become Cornwall and Wales.

In the vacuum left by the departure of the Romans, Germanic peoples, some of whom had come to Britain as mercenaries, took advantage of the situation. The Angles, Saxons, and Jutes (who spoke languages that were the ancestors of English, and are known collectively as Anglo-Saxons) conquered much of Britain in the fifth and sixth centuries. The conquerors absorbed some British Celts into the new Anglo-Saxon kingdoms and drove others into a portion of southwestern Scotland (called Strathclyde), into the peninsulas of Wales and Cornwall, and across the English Channel into Brittany (then called Armorica), where even today a British Celtic language is spoken (Breton). The Cornish were conquered by the Anglo-Saxons by the end of the first millennium, C.E., but their language too survived down to early modern times.

After the profound changes brought about by the arrival of the Anglo-Saxons and the displacement of the British Celts, it took a few centuries for a sense of collective identity to develop in Wales. Signaling this collective identity was an increasing use of the term *Cymry* ("Fellow Countrymen") among Welsh writers of the eleventh and twelfth centuries to designate their people. Even beyond this period, however, the Welsh (an Anglo-Saxon term meaning "strangers" or "slaves") saw themselves as the rightful heirs to Britain and looked back wistfully to the time when the land was theirs.

In the sixth and seventh centuries, Christianity came to the Anglo-Saxons through the Britons and the Irish (in Scotland), and through missionaries sent by Rome. Thus, there was a growing religious affinity among peoples of the British Isles, but this did not lessen the struggle over boundaries between the Anglo-Saxons and the Welsh, which continued into the eleventh century. At that time, Wales west of Offa's Dyke (constructed by the Anglo-Saxons in the eighth century and recognized on both sides as the dividing line between the two peoples) was essentially divided into three kingdoms, or centers of power: Gwynedd in the north, Powys in the center, and Dyfed (Deheubarth) in the south.

There were other, smaller kingdoms as well, and the relations among the Welsh rulers were never very stable. Often, one king or aspirant to the throne would ally himself with the Anglo-Saxons (or later, with the Normans) against his Welsh rivals. Especially along the coast, the Welsh were often harried by the Vikings who had established their own kingdom in Ireland. Meanwhile, some Welsh kings and dynastic families enjoyed close relations with their Irish counterparts, a fact reflected perhaps in the events of the "Second Branch of the Mabinogi." (Gruffudd ap Cynan of Gwynedd, for instance, one of the longest-lived Welsh kings of the late eleventh/early twelfth centuries, was the son of an Irish-Viking princess and spent time in exile in Ireland.) Around 1050 the king of Gwynedd—Gruffudd ap Llywelyn (Gruffudd son of Llywelyn)—succeeded in unifying the Welsh more than any previous king, and also in repelling the encroaching Anglo-Saxons, but he was slain in 1063. When the Normans invaded England in 1066, its king Harold Godwinson (who had conducted a successful military campaign against Gruffudd and exploited the power vacuum left in the wake of the death of Gruffudd ap Llywelyn), was acknowledged as overlord by the various Welsh kings.

The Tale in Focus

Plot summary. *The First Branch*. In the vague, pre-Roman times in which these stories are set, a king named Pwyll Pendefic rules over the kingdom of southern Wales, known as Dyfed. While hunting by himself, he accidentally insults the honor of Arawn, the king of the otherworldly kingdom of Annwn. Arawn obligates Pwyll to take his place in the otherworld for a year and to fight an important duel in defense of Arawn's kingship in a year's time. Pwyll accomplishes his mission successfully, spending his time in the lavish otherworldly court in the shape of Arawn, sleeping chastely with Arawn's wife, and slaying Arawn's rival for the throne. Thereby the king of Dyfed wins the lasting friendship of his otherworldly colleague, as well as the title "Head of Annwn."

In the second part of the story, Pwyll and his men, while sitting on a mound famous for the unusual occurrences that happen upon it, encounter a supernatural female riding by on a horse. None of Pwyll's men, whom he sends to determine the maiden's identity, can catch up with her. When Pwyll himself rides after her, the woman, named Rhiannon, finally does stop and reveals her errand. She is in love with Pwyll, Rhiannon explains, even though she has not met him before, but is shortly to be given in marriage to a man she does not love. Rhiannon coaches the instantly amorous Pwyll as to how to win her before it is too late. Despite some complications brought about by Rhiannon's former suitor, Pwyll and Rhiannon in the end are married, and she goes to live with him.

In the third part of the story, a child is finally born to Rhiannon and Pwyll, after some time and considerable anxiety on the part of Pwyll's subjects over whether their king will have an heir after all. The baby, however, is mysteriously stolen on the night of his birth, and the women who were supposed to guard him but fell asleep concoct the story that Rhiannon ate her own newborn son. Unable to refute the monstrous charge, Rhiannon accepts the punishment of having to sit at the entrance to Pwyll's court, tell her story to anyone who does not know it, and offer to carry visitors into the court on her back. (In fact, the text tells us, no visitor allows her to do so.) The story switches back to the night of the boy's birth, and to the home of Teyrnon, a former member of Pwyll's retinue, whose mare has just foaled. As Teyrnon inspects the newborn colt, a great claw reaches in to grab it, but Teyrnon cuts the arm off at the elbow. When he goes outside to investigate further, he does not find the owner of the arm but instead a baby swaddled in silk. Teyrnon and his wife adopt the child, who grows up to be a fine-looking youth, bearing a striking resemblance to Pwyll. Teyrnon, putting two and two together, realizes that this must be Pwyll's lost son and takes him to the court of Dyfed, where the youth is reunited with his parents, and Rhiannon is released from her punishment. The young man, who had been named Gwri by his foster parents, is renamed Pryderi ("Anxiety") in memory of his mother's ordeal and vindication. In due time, Pwyll passes away, and Pryderi inherits the throne of Dyfed.

The Second Branch. The events of the Second Branch take place after those of the First Branch. The tale opens on the northwestern coast of Wales on the rock of Harddlech, where Bendigeidfran son of Llyr, the king of all of Britain, and his brother Manawydan and sister Branwen are looking out over the Irish Sea. A fleet approaches, carrying Matholwch, the king of Ireland, who offers marriage to Branwen. The offer is accepted, to everyone's satisfaction—except that of Efnisien, Bendigeidfran's half-brother. To protest the alliance that was formed without his consent, Efnisien mutilates Matholwch's horses, an insult that nearly impels the Irish party to leave in anger. Bendigeidfran intercepts them, explaining that he was not responsible for the outrage, and gives in compensation many more horses than the Irish brought with them, and a cauldron that revives the dead.

Matholwch and his men finally return to Ireland with Branwen, who is at first received cordially by the Irish. After a while, however, the memory of the insult suffered by Matholwch turns the Irish against Branwen, who is reduced to a scullery maid. She sends a message via a trained starling to her brother the king, who gathers the forces of Britain and invades Ireland. The Irish are immediately intimidated by the British and, aided by the diplomacy of Branwen, sue for peace, offering to turn the kingship over to Gwern, the son of Matholwch and Branwen. Despite an attempt on the part of the Irish to ambush their British "guests" (a plot foiled by the wily Efnisien), the two enemy hosts sit down to a feast together, where the heir to the Irish throne, Gwern, is introduced to his mother's relatives. Pandemonium results when Efnisien tosses Gwern into the fire, where he burns to death. In the ensuing battle between the British and the Irish, Efnisien sacrifices himself by sneaking into the cauldron of revival, which the

Irish are using to regenerate their fallen troops, and bursting it, as well as his own heart, in a final heroic act of exertion. Only seven Britons and Branwen survive the cataclysmic battle, which wipes out the Irish forces. One of the survivors, Bendigeidfran, who is mortally wounded, orders that his head be cut off, and that his men (who include Manawydan, his brother, and Pryderi of the First Branch) return to Britain and proceed with his head to Harddlech, and then to the island of Gwales off the southern coast of Wales. At both of these places, Bendigeidfran assures them, they will be magically fed, comforted, entertained, and protected from the ravages of time in the company of the head. When they finally leave Gwales, they are to proceed to the royal site of London, where the head is to be buried in a hill, as a means of magically protecting Britain against invasion. Branwen, realizing the enormity of the destruction that has been brought about on her account, dies of a broken heart. The rest of the party discovers that Bendigeidfran's son, to whom had been entrusted the kingship in his father's absence, has also died of a broken heart, and the throne has been usurped by Caswallon, son of Beli (seemingly a member of a rival family). Nonetheless, the seven from Ireland carry on, obeying their king's instructions, enjoying the feasts in Harddlech and Gwales, and finally transporting Bendigeidfran's head to its prescribed resting place. The text ends with an account of how Ireland was repopulated by five pregnant women, the only natives to have survived the devastating battle with the British.

The Third Branch. In the aftermath of the invasion of Ireland, the return to Britain, and the prolonged pleasure of the supernatural feast of Bendigeidfran's head, Pryderi suggests that his fellow survivor Manawydan marry Pryderi's widowed mother Rhiannon and settle down in southern Wales. Manawydan agrees, and the wedding is celebrated with an expedition to the same mysterious mound that figures in the First Branch. While Manawydan, Rhiannon, Pryderi, and Pryderi's wife, Cigfa, are sitting on this mound, the country around them is magically turned into a deserted wasteland. The couples go to England, around the border country of Hereford, to seek their fortunes as craftsmen. Manawydan and Pwyll succeed at the crafts to which they apply themselves, but return to Wales for fear of reprisal from the jealous English craftsmen. Later, while on a hunt, Pryderi is lured into a fort, where he is magically trapped. His mother Rhiannon goes in after him, and suffers the same fate, after which the fort disappears. Perplexed and bereft of their spouses, Manawydan and Cigfa return to England, where Manawydan once again succeeds as a craftsman, but once again decides that it would be best to retreat to Wales. He becomes a farmer and grows a crop of wheat, but finds that in the night the wheat is stolen mysteriously. Standing guard over his last patch of wheat, Manawydan discovers the culprits: a horde of mice. He drives them away and catches a pregnant mouse. About to execute it by hanging, Manawydan is met by a series of figures who implore him to spare the mouse. These passersby finally reveal themselves to be the same person—namely, the pregnant mouse's supernatural husband, who had enchanted Pryderi and Rhiannon, and then transformed himself, his wife, and his men into mice, in order to take revenge on behalf of his kinsman, the suitor from whom Pwyll had rescued Rhiannon in the First Branch. After Manawydan releases the lady mouse, the wasteland turns back into Wales, and Pryderi and Rhiannon are released.

The Fourth Branch. The northern kingdom of Gwynedd is ruled by Math, son of Mathonwy, who, except in wartime, always keeps his feet in the lap of a virgin. Math's nephew, Gilfaethwy, falls madly in love with his uncle's footholder, and his desire is detected by his brother, the magical trickster Gwydion, who concocts a plan to divert Math and allow Gilfaethwy to satisfy his desire. In the guise of traveling poets Gwydion and Gilfaethwy travel to the kingdom of South Wales, to the court of King Pryderi, son of Pwyll. They offer to give him beautifully equipped horses and hounds, created by Gwydion out of mushrooms, in exchange for the pigs that Pryderi has received from Annwn (in gratitude for Pwyll's deeds, described in the First Branch). Pryderi agrees and gives them the pigs, seemingly the first domesticated pigs known to humankind, and Gwydion and Gilfaethwy hurry back north—the magical spell that created the horses and the hounds will soon wear off. When he sees that he has been cheated, Pryderi collects an army and sets out to attack Gwynedd and to recover his pigs. While Math is on the battlefield rising to the challenge (he in fact slays Pryderi), Gilfaethwy rapes the footholder. Gwydion and Gilfaethwy then flee. When they finally return to Math's court to ask for forgiveness, they are turned into animals, different species for each of three years, and in the guise of animals Gwydion and Gilfaethwy give birth to animal children. After his three years of punishment, Gwydion, now

rehabilitated, offers to help Math find a new virginal footholder, suggesting his own sister, Aranrhod. Math, testing her virginity, asks her to step over his magic wand. When she does so, two items drop from her: a boy—whom Math baptizes and names Dylan, and who immediately flees into the waters of the ocean, where he spends the rest of his life—and "something," which only Gwydion notices, and which he hides in a chest under his bed. This "something" grows into another child, whom Gwydion takes and shows to Aranrhod. Her reaction, however, is hardly maternal: she curses the boy, saying that he will only receive a name and arms through her (of course, she has no intention of giving him either), and that he shall never have a human wife. Through the magic and trickery of Gwydion, Aranrhod unwittingly does name and arm her offspring, after he grows into a young man. (The name he receives is "Lleu," which means "bright.") And when Lleu is of an age to marry, Gwydion and Math create for him a woman made out of flowers, called Bloedeuwedd ("Flower Face"). This artificial wife, unfortunately, turns out to be treacherous, and she goads her lover, a hunter named Gronw Pebyr, into slaying Lleu, after she learns the secret of how he might be slain. As he is killed, Lleu is turned into an eagle and flies away. The faithful Gwydion does not rest until he finds this eagle, perched on a tree and dropping pieces of his rotting flesh, and through his magic transforms it back into Lleu. Gwydion tracks down Bloedeuwedd and punishes her by turning her into the first owl, to be hated by all other birds, while Lleu has his revenge on Gronw Pebyr. The text ends with the statement that Lleu ruled over Gwynedd, presumably after the death of Math.

Culhwch and Olwen. Culhwch, a young Welsh prince, refuses the proposal of his conniving stepmother to marry her daughter. As a result, she spitefully imposes upon him the magical condition of being hopelessly in love with Olwen, the daughter of the giant Yspaddaden. Culhwch's father advises the lovelorn lad to seek the assistance of Arthur, Culhwch's cousin, in finding the maiden, whom Culhwch has never met. At Arthur's court (seemingly in Cornwall) Culhwch invokes the names of all the male and female members of Arthur's retinue in the interest of asking for his cousin's help, which is generously given. As Arthur says to his right-hand man Cei, when he rejects Cei's advice not to admit his young cousin into the court, "We are nobles as long as anyone seeks us out; the greater the favor we bestow, the greater shall be our nobility, our fame, and our honor" (Mabinogion, p. 125).

After Arthur's men help Culhwch find Olwen (not an easy task), Culhwch formally asks the giant Yspaddaden for her hand. Taking an instant dislike to his prospective son-in-law, Yspaddaden says that he will consent only after Culhwch has accomplished 27 daunting tasks. Most have to do with preparing for the wedding. For instance, Culhwch is to obtain the cauldron of the Irish king's steward to cook the wedding feast, and locate and free the imprisoned huntsman Mabon, whose services will be required in the hunting of Twrch Trwyth (a gigantic boar), but whose whereabouts are known only to the most ancient of animals. Arthur and his men accomplish these deeds for Culhwch, although the text does not actually account for all of them. The quest turns momentarily ominous early on, when Cei angrily leaves Arthur and drops out of the story after Arthur teases that the giant whom Cei had just treacherously slain after plucking out his beard (one of Yspaddaden's requests—the whiskers are to be made into a leash, for use with a dog in the hunt for the boar) would have bested Cei if the fight had been fair. The most difficult and protracted deed is the obtaining of the comb and shears to be found on the head of the boar. (Yspaddaden wants them for his pre-wedding preparations.) Arthur's hunt for this animal, who was a human king turned into a boar by God in punishment for his sins, takes Arthur and his men to Ireland and throughout Wales and Cornwall. The comb and shears are finally won, but the boar escapes. The last of the tasks to be accomplished is the obtaining of "the blood of the pitch black witch, daughter of the bright-white witch from the Valley of Grief in Hell's back country" (Mabinogion, p. 156). The blood will be used as a softener for Yspaddaden's whiskers, so that they can be trimmed properly. Overcoming the witch and obtaining her blood proves more difficult than Arthur and his men thought; for the first time taking care of the task on his own instead of delegating it to his men, Arthur himself kills her: "Then Arthur made for the entrance to the cave; from there he threw Carnwennan his knife at the witch and cut her in half until she was twin tubs", that is, two bloody halves (Mabinogion, p. 157). Presented with all of these accomplishments and prizes, Yspaddaden has no choice but to surrender his daughter. After he is shaved by one of Arthur's men, who also removes the giant's "flesh and skin down to the bone, and his two ears", Yspaddaden declares that it is time

for him to die (Mabinogion, p. 157). He is promptly dispatched, although not by Culhwch (who has been barely active throughout the questing part of the story) or Arthur, but by Goreu ("Best"), a young warrior whose brothers had all been killed by the giant, and who emerges as a new hero in Arthur's circle in the course of this story.

Varieties of Celtic heroism. In contrast to Ireland's medieval *The Táin* or *Cattle Raid of Cooley* (also in *WLAIT 3: British and Irish Literature and Its Times*), which centers on a single and singular hero (Cú Chulainn), in these earliest of Welsh tales is a fascinating variety of heroic behavior and identity. The heroes in *The Mabinogion* range from the initially impetuous Pwyll of the First Branch, to the cautious Manawydan of the Third, to the forthright Bendigeidfran of the Second Branch, and the devious Gwydion of the Fourth. While these Welsh heroes are magicians (Math and Gwydion) and fighters (Pwyll), they are also peace-loving rulers (Bendigeidfran) and entrepreneurial craftsmen (Manawydan and Pryderi). They identify closely with subjects and kingdom (Bendigeidfran's head becomes a talisman for all of Britain), but they also exhibit antisocial tendencies (the "villainous hero" Efnisien, who mutilates his future brother-in-law's horses and throws his nephew into the fire but also sacrifices his own life for the good of his fellow Britons). The Welsh heroes of the "Four Branches" know how to use the power of speech (Gwydion can pass as a storyteller; Branwen can teach birds to talk), yet they know too the value of silence and of keeping secrets (Pwyll goes "undercover" in the otherworld). There are moreover heroines as well as heroes in this story world, whose adventures demonstrate acutely the dangerous alternation between power and powerlessness that characterizes all heroic careers. Rhiannon and Branwen are helpless at key points in their stories, but no more so than is the hero Lleu in the hands of his treacherous wife Blodeuwedd, or Pryderi both at the beginning of his heroic career, when he is kidnapped, and at the end, when he is outwitted and slain by the wily Gwydion.

The world of Arthur as reflected in "Culhwch and Olwen" partakes of the same heroic ethos, emphasizing a similar set of virtues. And yet there is something different about Arthur's world. In the "Four Branches," despite the occasional intervention of or foray into the otherworld, life is firmly grounded in the realities of human society, and framed with human responsibilities (such as child-bearing) and restraints (such as death). "Culhwch and Olwen" features the seemingly constant, almost restless movement of Arthur and his men, their willingness to undertake adventure and accept challenges, and Arthur's penchant for freeing captives and those upon whom paralyzing limitations have been imposed (such as the hapless Culhwch, who would never have found Olwen without Arthur's help). These features evoke a fantasy world of sorts, an imaginative environment of risk-taking and escape from mundane consequences. It is perhaps the timeless, deep-seated yearning for such a way of life that accounts in part for the perennial popularity of Arthurian story. Together with the "Four Branches," then, "Culhwch and Olwen" evokes aspects of the wishful and supernatural, and of everyday life among early Britons.

The mystique of Arthur. Doubtless the preservation of Arthurian tradition in "Culhwch and Olwen" was motivated to some extent by politics, as well as by the desire to showcase and perhaps critique one of the most popular figures in the legendary lore of the British Celts. Was there a historical Arthur? This is a question we will probably never be able to answer definitively, given the meagerness of the evidence about Britain of the fifth and sixth centuries, the putative period in which Arthur lived. The sixth-century British monk Gildas speaks of a Romano-British aristocrat "Ambrosius Aurelianus" who, in the period just before Gildas's birth (500?) led his fellow Britons in a successful counterattack against the encroaching Anglo-Saxons; considerably later sources identify this Ambrosius with Arthur.

The earliest reference we have to an actual, recognizable "Arthur" comes in the ninth-century Latin compilation known as *The History of Britons* (*Historia Britonum*, attributed to Nennius) and the tenth- or eleventh-century *Welsh Annals,* which speak of Arthur as a battalion leader (*dux bellorum*) who led the British in a series of successful battles against the Anglo-Saxon invaders but was finally slain in the Battle of Camlann. *The History* also speaks of an Ambrosius, a wondrous prophetic boy who is nearly killed as a human sacrifice by a wicked king. The twelfth-century writer Geoffrey of Monmouth identifies this figure with Merlin (from the Welsh name Myrddin), a great prophet of northern British Celtic and Welsh tradition, who is brought into the Arthurian orbit for the first time in Geoffrey's *History of the Kings of Britain* (*Historia Regum Britanniae*, c. 1135). There are also references to be

found to Arthur and to Myrddin in obscure poems written in early medieval Welsh in the late first millennium, C.E., but it is an ongoing challenge to scholars of Welsh to reconstruct stories out of these poems and references.

Then we have "Culhwch and Olwen," from the eleventh or early twelfth century. This is the very earliest extant example of an Arthurian

---

A PENCHANT FOR PEACEMAKING

Interwoven into "Culhwch and Olwen" is the story of Creiddylad, which features Arthur's penchant for peacemaking, a trait that resurfaces in later Arthurian tales outside Wales:

A little while before that, Creiddylad daughter of Lludd . . . went off with Gwythr son of Greidawl. But before he could sleep with her, Gwyn son of Nudd, came and took her by force. Gwythur son of Greidawl gathered a host and came to attack Gwyn son of Nudd. Gwyn won the battle and took Greid son of Eri . . . Nwython, and Cyledyr Wylt the wild, his son. He killed Nwython, cut out his heart and forced Cyledyr to eat his father's heart; because of that Cyledyr went mad.

Arthur heard about that and came to the North. He summoned Gwyn son of Nudd to him, released his nobles from his prison, and made peace between Gwyn son of Nudd, and Gwythr son of Greidawl. This is the peace that was concluded: to leave the maiden unmolested by either party in her father's house, and a battle between Gwyn and Gwythr every May first, forever, until Judgment Day, from that day forth. The one that conquered on Judgment Day would get the maiden.

(Ford, *Mabinogi*, p. 151).

---

heroic story. Certainly the impression left by the tale, particularly the listing of the members of Arthur's court and various passing references to other stories involving Arthur and his men, is that "Culhwch and Olwen" is only the tip of an iceberg. The outline of its main story is familiar from the world of folktales—a young man sets forth in search of a hard-to-win bride and along the way wins the assistance of supernatural or unusually talented helpers. It is also familiar from the quest-driven world of later Arthurian romance, which is full of knights rescuing, and falling in love with, damsels in distress held captive by ogreish fathers, husbands, or would-be lovers.

What is especially curious about the Arthur of this text, as of virtually all the glimpses we have of Arthur before Geoffrey's work, is that he is not characterized as a king. This may be a reflection of the amorphous nature of kingship or its nomenclature in early medieval Wales, but it may also point toward a fundamental aspect of Arthur's function. Perhaps he serves in British Celtic story more as a leader of potentially heroic young men, who helps them achieve their rites of passage from childhood to adulthood, than as a "king" in the sense of a ruler who basically stays at home in his court or works to expand his kingdom through conquest. (In contrast to the British Celtic image, this second view is in essence the Arthur of Geoffrey of Monmouth, and of later popular imagination, medieval and modern.) Moreover, Arthur bears what was originally a Roman name (Artorius), as do some of the prominent heroes associated with him (such as Cai, from Caius). But there is very little else about the Arthur of "Culhwch and Olwen" that would strike us as "Roman" or as reminiscent of the classical world. He seems very much the British chieftain and warrior, primarily engaged in feasting, going off on warlike adventures, and hunting.

Other elements of this early tale surface in later ones. Already to be found in "Culhwch and Olwen" are Arthur's famous sword, Caledfwlch (known in later, non-Welsh tradition as "Excalibur") and his wife Gwenhwyfar (a Welsh name later turned into "Guenevere"), but there is no mention of "Camelot," the name of Arthur's renowned dwelling, which seems to be a later, non-Celtic invention. Also, alongside the generosity and courage Arthur exhibits in our story, there is also a dark side to him that surfaces in later Arthurian story, exemplified in the ominous rift between Arthur and his loyal sidekick Cei, which (the text says) would last through Arthur's hour of greatest need. A story interwoven into the text of "Culhwch and Olwen," having to do with the perennial struggle between two heroic males over possession of the woman Creiddylad, is perhaps meant to remind us of the instability of Arthur's own marriage, as described in Welsh tradition and also, more famously, in the later French story of the tragic love between Arthur's queen Guenevere and Lancelot, his favorite knight. Guenevere/Gwenhwyfar's infidelity or vulnerability to sexual predators is intimated in Welsh Arthurian tradition, although not explicitly in "Culhwch and Olwen." Also another early Welsh text, "The Wonders of Britain," refers to a story about Arthur's killing of his own son. Already in its Celtic phase of development, then, Arthurian story featured, amidst its fantasies of independence from social restrictions and pres-

sures, troubling episodes of conjugal and familial strife.

Literary context. All 11 *Mabinogion* tales are preserved, together with other literary compositions, in two fourteenth-century manuscripts, *The White Book of Rhydderch* and *The Red Book of Hergest*. Moreover, individual *Mabinogion* tales or portions thereof are to be found in other Welsh manuscripts, some earlier than the fourteenth century. Had this ensemble of texts not survived, our knowledge of the content of storytelling in medieval Wales would be sketchy at best. It would have depended on the often obscure poems that have survived from early (pre-twelfth-century) medieval Wales, scattered allusions to characters and tales in the vast repertoire of poetry that comes to us from the later medieval periods of Welsh (twelfth-sixteenth centuries), the traditions recorded in the Welsh medieval collection known as *The Triads of the Isle of Britain*, and the unreliable reports of Welsh legend in the works of medieval British authors such as Geoffrey's *History of the Kings of Britain*. Written in Latin, Geoffrey's work arguably launched the international career of Arthur as a figure of story and a paragon of sovereignty and knightly valor. His work is predated by *The Mabinogion's* "Culhwch and Olwen," but even with it as a source, scholars are still uncertain about the origins and evolution of the Arthurian cycle.

Scholars have suggested that in its tendency to catalog and to exaggerate the capabilities and peculiarities of its major and minor characters, our text may be imitating or even parodying the techniques of the oral storyteller. In any case, Welsh oral tradition plays a much more important role as source for our text than any known work of literature in Welsh, Latin, or any of the other languages spoken in or around Wales.

Events in History at the Time the Tales Were Written

A threatened identity. In the latter part of the eleventh century, when the "Four Branches" and "Culhwch and Olwen" were probably written down, England was invaded by the Normans (Northmen or Vikings who had settled in a part of France still bearing their name—Normandy). The Normans defeated the Anglo-Saxons in 1066, becoming the leading military force on the island. Soon the new conquerors turned their attention to Wales, and an on- again-off-again war between them and the Welsh commenced, lasting for more than 200 years. Initially, the Normans left the task of dealing with these difficult neighbors to certain trusted nobles who virtually conquered and set up their own mini-kingdoms in Wales (in an area called the "March," which included Hereford, the setting in the Third Branch that is identified as "England"). The Welsh rebelled, the Normans counterattacked, and the Welsh recuperated, with the result that, except for the northeastern territory and the southern coastline of Wales, most of the land remained in Welsh lands, albeit under threat of Norman attack. Great kings emerged in the twelfth century in Wales, who, while acknowledging the overlordship of the Norman king of England, maintained their independence, such as Owain Gwynedd, Madog ap Maredudd of Powys, and Rhys ap Gruffudd of Deheubarth.

Feudalism—the notion that one's status derives from allegiance to a lord, as opposed to the native Welsh notion that status depends on one's kin-group—began to make headway in Wales in the twelfth and thirteenth centuries through contact with the Normans, as did the French language and the influence of French literature. The hopes of the Welsh to maintain their independence in the face of Anglo-Norman military might would be dashed, however, in 1283 (after *The Mabinogion* was composed) with the death in battle of Llywelyn ap Gruffudd, the celebrated king of Gwynedd who came very close to unifying Wales, and with the conquest of Wales by Edward I of England. Down to recent times, Welsh poets, expressing the aspirations of a conquered yet defiant people, have prophesied the coming of a new champion of the Welsh—a new Llywelyn or a new Arthur—who will lead them to freedom from the English. The rise of the Tudor kings of England who came to power in the late fifteenth century and were of Welsh stock ("Tudor" is a Welsh name) gave hope to some of the Welsh that their nation would be vindicated. In fact, the opposite happened, with the Acts of Union of 1536 and 1542 doing away with the last vestiges of Welsh autonomy.

Life in medieval Wales. Wales of the eleventh and twelfth centuries had a rural economy, dependent on agriculture and herding, and on forests rich with game, although some of the towns or military headquarters established by the Romans during their occupation continued to function as centers of trade, political power, and cultural activity, as did the towns that developed around the monasteries established in the second half of the first millennium, C.E., and later. Society was stratified, with a land-owning aristocratic class (*uchelwyr*) at the top and a large population of tenant farmers of varying degrees of independence forming the base. The freemen, including the aristocracy, fought and feasted, while the unfree worked the land. Territorially and politically, Wales was divided into a north and south, Gwynedd and Dyfed respectively, with the territory of Powys in the middle, and in the course of medieval Welsh history there were further political subdivisions. Kings were often not called such (the term *arglwydd,* or "leader" was more frequently used than *brenhin,* "king"), but dominion was often held within what could be called dynastic families, with succession from generation to generation often determined by a show of power rather than by fixed rules of inheritance. A noble aspiring to leadership gathered a retinue of loyal fellow nobles around himself, among whom the poet was an important and functional figure. This social reality is reflected in "Culhwch and Olwen" in the size of Arthur's retinue, and on the extent to which he depends on them to accomplish the tasks that Arthur agrees to perform on behalf of his cousin Culhwch.

Literature in Welsh was produced under the patronage of churches and monasteries, which in addition to cultivating the study of biblical and classical (Latin) texts supported the activities of the "native" learned classes, including poets, genealogists, and specialists in traditional law. The monasteries depended on the cooperation and patronage of powerful lords, just as the latter derived prestige and authority from the support of the church, a political agenda reflected in the literature. The majority of texts surviving from medieval Wales are Welsh poems written in praise of the nobles who supported the poetic profession and depended on the good "public relations" these poems generated for them. Welsh poetry of this period is very complex in its metrical schemes and recondite in its vocabulary and syntax. In "The Dream of Rhonabwy" from *The Mabinogion*, the inaccessibility of this poetry is gently mocked: "And thereupon, lo, bards coming to chant a song to Arthur. But never a man was there might understand that song save Cadyrieith [a linguistically gifted member of Arthur's retinue] himself, except that it was in praise of Arthur" (Jones and Jones, p. 151). While the creators of literature in medieval Wales were very much observers of their times, these learned writers were also nostalgia-driven, intent on preserving in a literary form the glory of a bygone age peopled by larger-than-life ancestral figures, both Welsh and British.

Impact. Some details of the "Four Branches" are echoed in the medieval Welsh "Triads" compilations and in the vast body of court poetry, prophetic verse, and love lyrics composed in Wales between the twelfth and fifteenth centuries. Given the nature of the literary evidence, however, it is difficult to determine just how popular these stories and characters were in later medieval Welsh storytelling tradition. Traces of the "Four Branches" can be found in modern Welsh folk tradition, and popular culture today has embraced these stories enthusiastically. (Comic books in Welsh featuring stories from *The Mabinogion* are available, for example.)

Outside Wales, the "Four Branches" had to wait until they were translated into other European languages in the nineteenth century to become widely known. In the twentieth-century, novelists such as Evangeline Walton (who wrote a quartet of novels based on *The Mabinogion*) and Lloyd Alexander (author of *The Black Cauldron*) and designers of games (such as "Dungeons and Dragons") have mined the "Four Branches" for ideas and inspiration. There is no evidence that "Culhwch and Olwen" was ever known outside Wales. Still, somehow the salient details and general story patterns of Arthurian tradition, which are very much on display in "Culhwch and Olwen," were introduced into the lore of the Normans and, through them, into the medieval French-speaking world as well as into all the major literary traditions of medieval Europe. The popularity of the tales of Arthur continued un-abated through the seventeenth century, when this tradition was temporarily eclipsed by other literary passions in England. Arthurian lore made a remarkable comeback, however, in the nineteenth century, in no small part generated by new editions of medieval Arthurian texts (including Lady Charlotte Guest's 1849 translation of *The Mabinogion*). Given the availability of Welsh Arthurian texts in translation, and the ever-increasing interest in Arthur's British Celtic roots, it was virtually impossible for nineteenth- and twentieth-century artists who invoked this tradition—for instance, writers such as Alfred Tennyson (in *Idylls of the King*) and filmmakers such as John Boorman (*Excalibur*)—to ignore the fundamental Celtic dimension to the figure of Arthur.

—Joseph F. Nagy

For More Information

Davies, R. R. *The Age of Conquest: Wales 1063-1415.* Oxford, England: Oxford University Press, 1991.

Ford, Patrick, K., trans. *The Mabinogi and Other Medieval Welsh Tales.* Berkeley: University of California Press, 1977.

Gerald of Wales. *The Journey through Wales and The Description of Wales,* Trans. Lewis Thorpe. Harmondsworth, U.K.: Penguin, 1978.

Jones, Gwyn, and Thomas Jones, trans. *The Mabinogion.* 2d revised ed. London: J. M. Dent and Charles E. Tuttle, 1989.

Stephens, Meic, ed. *New Companion to the Literature of Wales.* Cardiff: University of Wales Press, 1998.

Wilhelm, James J., ed. *The Romance of Arthur: An Anthology of Medieval Texts in Translation.* New York: Garland Press, 1994.

Macbeth

by
William Shakespeare

THE LITERARY WORK

A play set in Scotland in the mid-eleventh century; written and first performed c. 1606, published in 1623.

SYNOPSIS

A Scottish warrior kills the king to take his throne, which leads to chaos, bloodshed, and tragedy.

Although the facts are continually in dispute, tradition has it that William Shakespeare was born in Stratford in 1564, a child of the provincial middle class. He moved to London in the 1580s and joined the burgeoning world of the London theater, first as an actor and director, then as a playwright. Between 1588 and 1611, he produced close to 40 plays. *Macbeth* belongs to the end of Shakespeare's "tragic period," the years between 1600 and 1606 when he produced the five tragedies that are usually called his greatest work: *Hamlet, King Lear, Othello, Antony* and *Cleopatra*, and *Macbeth*. Written and performed—perhaps coincidentally—around the time of the accession (1603) of King James I of England, who also happened to be King James VI of Scotland, the play treats the issue of royal succession and offers a rare example of Renaissance English ideas about Scotland.

Events in History at the Time the Play Takes Place

The political background to *Macbeth*. *Macbeth* is set in mid-eleventh-century Scotland, a time of intense political and social transition. Around 500 C.E. the Scots navigated the 13 miles of the North Channel separating the northeastern Irish kingdom of Dál Riata (today's county Antrim) from Britain and became one of five distinct groups of medieval peoples who occupied what is now Scotland. The Scots tussled with the other groups throughout the centuries in an endless succession of battles and won only with difficulty the lands that Macbeth would rule in the mid-eleventh century. Among their rivals were the Picts who lived north of the firths of Clyde and Forth and in the northern Hebrides, Orkneys, and Shetlands; the Britons who inhabited today's Galloway, Cumberland, and Strathclyde (i.e., to the south and west); the Angles, who originated in Germany and Denmark, who lived in Northumbria (to the south and east); and later the Vikings who inhabited the northern and western isles. Having first set foot on the western coast of present-day Scotland (probably around the Mull of Kintyre), the Scots moved into the lands occupied by these other groups. By the mid-ninth century, all these people had been mingling and vying for prominence for centuries.

Under Kenneth mac Alpin (ruled 842-58), the Scots finally completed their conquest of the Picts; the political entity that arose from this situation was the foundation of the later kingdom of the Scots. It stretched almost completely across Scotland north of the Forth-Clyde isthmus, except for some of the northern islands, which were occupied by the Vikings. These Scandinavians were tenacious in their attacks upon Scotland. As Shakespeare's play opens, a Danish army under "Sveno" is attacking the Scots. In fact, the Scandinavian threat is often cited by historians as one of the reasons why the Scots felt such a need to consolidate their power by assimilating the Picts. From the mid-ninth century onward, the Scandinavians did not merely come as raiders, they came to stay, and settled in the northern islands and in Caithness, at the northernmost point of Scotland. The Scottish kings often forged alliances with them, and the players in *Macbeth* all had strong Scandinavian connections. Macbeth himself had Scandinavian cousins. His cousin Malcolm mac Malbrigte had given his daughter to Sigurd, the lord of Orkney, and she produced a son, Thorfinn, who would plague Macbeth's kingship—the two seem to have fought at least one major battle, which Macbeth lost. Because of his complicated lineage, Thorfinn was actually one of the most powerful men in Scotland. He ruled the Orkneys, Shetlands, and possibly part of the Hebrides; also he claimed Caithness and Sutherland by hereditary right from his maternal grandfather. His position in a way exemplifies the intricate web of alliances and genealogies by which Scotland was held together and, sometimes, by which its existence was threatened.

To the south, the Scots had other, related problems. By 1018 they had defeated the Northumbrians at Carham and had won all the territory as far south as the River Tweed, a boundary that still divides Scotland from England. Sometime after 1018, the Scots made Strathclyde a client kingdom, which meant that it was subject to the Scottish kings. The rule of Strathclyde was made hereditary for whoever was the heir to the Scottish throne. But the situation was far from stable. The Angles of Northumbria in particular were a constant source of anxiety to the Scottish kings, and the complex power plays between the Scots, the Angles in Northumbria, and the Danes based in Dublin form the wider political backdrop of Shakespeare's play.

Yet *Macbeth* is above all else a family drama, as were all political disputes in Scotland. The leading families were bound to one another in a practically unfathomable series of alliances and feuds. Macbeth and Duncan were certainly related, even if they were not, in fact, first-cousins.

The Dál Riata royal family that first came from the Irish kingdom of the same name to Scotland was of the dynasty of Cenél nGabráin; they moved into the heartland of what would become the Scottish kingdom. A second Dál Riata lineage, Cenél Loairn, moved north and settled in a region of northern Britain (which included Macbeth's home province of Moray); the region stretched from the Atlantic Ocean to the North Sea and from Ross to the river Dee—a huge, wild territory separated from the rest of Scotland by the Grampian mountains. From nearly the beginning of the Dál Riata migration, the two lineages would in an important sense be separate from one another (indeed they fought battles against each other). But, through intermarriage, political expediency (usually having to do with Viking incursions), and the peculiarities of the Scottish succession (see below), the two lines nevertheless often entered into an uneasy alliance.

The king of Moray. In Shakespeare's play, Macbeth is referred to incorrectly as the thane of Glamis and/or of Cawdor. His real title was king of Cenél Loairn or king of Moray, and this is a distinction that makes all the difference for an appropriate historical understanding of what really transpired between Macbeth and Duncan. The two kingly dynasties—Cenél nGabráin and Cenél Loairn—had competed for primacy in Dál Riata and continued their competition when they moved into the east. By the tenth century they were competing for primacy over all of Scotland (Hudson, p. 146).

The leaders of the two royal families were often at serious odds with each other. A royal ancestor of Duncan, Malcolm I (died 954) attacked Moray in the mid-tenth century and killed the king, named Cellach. Malcolm's son, Dub ("the Dark"), was slain in Moray in 966; a later legend claims that his body was hidden under a bridge, and the sun refused to shine until it was recovered. Malcolm's other son, Kenneth I, Duncan's great-grandfather, succeeded in having his overlordship acknowledged by his rivals of Cenél Loairn, and he is described as high king of the Scots on his death in 995. His supremacy was continued by his son Malcolm II, who was called the "king of the Mounth" (the mountain chain that marks Moray's southern border) in an important historical document. Macbeth's father, Findláech, who was king of Cenél Loairn, or king of Moray, probably was married to one of Malcolm's female relatives (possibly a daughter or a sister) in what was most likely a politically motivated marriage meant to solder peace between the two royal dynasties of Cenél nGabráin and Cenél Loairn (Hudson, p. 137). Even after Macbeth's eventual downfall, the dynasty of Cenél nGabráin could not tame Moray, and political unrest continued in the area for at least another century and a half.

The changing rules of Scottish kingship. *Macbeth* turns on the question of kingship, which was in a state of transition during the eleventh century. In practice, kingship among the Scots had alternated among the adult male members of the royal family who possessed the necessary genealogical qualifications. The kingship could be passed laterally—that is, from brother to brother, or cousin to cousin, or uncle to nephew—as well as from father to son or grandson. The candidates for king were to be drawn from the ranks of men whose father had himself been king (but was not necessarily the current king). The sharing of the kingship among branches of the dynasty was an effort to prevent the family from becoming embroiled in a feud, with all its attendant dangers. When one branch of the family felt powerful enough to exclude its kinsmen, the succession would pass lineally rather than laterally. A novelty, however, was introduced when Malcolm II appointed his grandson Duncan as his heir (technically, his *tanaise*, which is Gaelic for "the second" or "expected one"). Duncan's ascension to the throne illustrated the power of his grandfather and the hold his family had on the kingship of Cenél nGabráin. He claimed his royal title through his mother rather than his father, who was a cleric. Thus Shakespeare's play, which laments the unnatural act perpetrated by Macbeth in taking the kingship from Duncan, does not reflect the actual political situation in eleventh-century Scotland: Duncan was himself inappropriately the king, according to the usual method of selecting a king.

Scottish kings were very powerful figures who had authority in all legislative, military, fiscal, and judicial matters. A king had a main fortress, but he also traveled about the country, visiting different fortifications and the powerful men who lived in them and who represented their province in dealings with the king. These men were called *mormaers* (or "great stewards"); such a man was often of royal lineage and was the *toisech* ("leader" or "chief") of a particular family and the area it inhabited. In the Anglo-Saxon lands that had been annexed to the Scots' domain there were also thanes, or minor officials appointed by the king. Thanages tended over time to become hereditary positions. The word "thane" (from the Anglo-Saxon *thegn*, or "one who serves") was not used to describe the office in Macbeth's day. Responsibility for running royal estates was in the hands of the *rechtaire* ("steward"), who assisted the *exactores* ("tax gatherers") in collecting *cáin* (tribute) and "conveth" (food and housing for the king and his followers when he was in the area). These services were necessary in view of the king's habit of visiting royal estates; such a visit occurs in the first act of Shakespeare's play when Duncan visits Macbeth's castle.

MURDER MOST USUAL

Although Shakespeare's play portrays Macbeth's killing of Duncan as an abnormal act, Scottish history from the mid-tenth to mid-eleventh century is full of slain kings. Two of them died in Moray: Dub probably in 966 and, of course, Duncan in 1040. But this is just the tip of the iceberg. The usual custom was for a king to appoint a *tanaise*—an heir-designate—while he himself was still alive. This effort towards a peaceful change of power counted for little in the civil wars that ravaged both Scottish royal families. Cousin murdered cousin, and nephew killed uncle as branches of the royal families fought for supremacy from the latter tenth century to the early eleventh century. Thus, while the men in Duncan's retinue bewail the horror, the "murder and treason" that have befallen Scotland with the slaying of the king in Shakespeare's play, in real-life Scotland no one was likely to have been much surprised by any of it (*Macbeth*, 2.3.69).

The kingship of Duncan. The reign of the historical Duncan offered much room for improvement; in real life, his removal from the kingship would not have been much cause for wonder. The grandson of the ruthless Malcolm II, Duncan (or Donnchad) had been appointed as the king's heir, which, as mentioned, went against usual succession custom. Duncan succeeded to his kingship in 1034. His path to the throne had been smoothed by assassinations that his grandfather had prescribed on his behalf. This had created an atmosphere of unease and mistrust among Duncan's nobles, which could account for the general failure of his reign; a contemporary poem (the "Prophecy of Berchan") ridicules him as a hypochondriac and suggests that his maladies would be his claim to fame. In any case, Duncan became king mostly because it was his grandfather's will that he be king, not because he was commonly held by his peers to be the best candidate of his generation; historians speculate that his accession "did not . . . gain wide acceptance" (Lynch, p. 49). His historical reputation is that of a very inept military leader. He led a disastrous raid on the city of Durham in Northumbria in 1039/40, from which he retreated, having lost badly. He then seems to have turned his eyes northward and to have gone into Moray on his royal circuit, a display of the royal presence that was intended to overawe his subordinate king. While on that progress he was killed by Macbeth on August 16, 1040. His exact age at death is unknown, but he was young (a contemporary chronicle describes him of immature age). Certainly he was a far cry from the gentle, wise, and aged king of Shakespeare's imagination. In the matter of ambition, however, Shakespeare understood his man correctly: Macbeth took advantage of Duncan's unpopularity and weakness to kill him and seize the overlordship of all the Scots.

The real Macbeths. Macbeth (or Mac Bethad Mac Findláech) appears frequently in historical documents of the time, although never in much detail, and it is difficult to piece together his life and his career. The "Prophecy of Berchan" asserts that he was fair-haired and slender with a ruddy complexion. His early life, we know, was overshadowed by civil war among the Cenél Loairn. Macbeth was the son of Findláech (or Finlay), king of Cenél Loairn, who was slain by Macbeth's cousins Malcolm and Gillacomgàin in 1020, when Macbeth was probably quite young. Macbeth himself became king in 1029, following Malcolm's death. Soon after, as attested by both English and Scandinavian records, Macbeth submitted to Cnut the Great, king of the Danes and the English.

Macbeth is the first Scots prince for whom we know the name of his wife: Gruoch. Her prior husband was Macbeth's cousin and rival for power Gillacomgáin, who had been a mormaer to his brother Malcolm. Gillacomgáin was killed along with his men in a fire in 1032; historians do not know with certainty that Macbeth was responsible, but he did marry Gruoch shortly thereafter, in what is generally taken as a show of unity. We know almost nothing of Gruoch but that she was descended from royal blood of Cenél nGabráin. Upon marrying her, Macbeth adopted her son by Gillacomgain, Lulach; this may indicate that he was interested in calming the political strife in Moray. Gruoch herself had a gripe

with Malcolm II and his family—the former king had killed her grandfather, Kenneth III, and her nephew (in 1033). She was aristocratic, powerful, and doubtless vengeful when it came to Malcolm and Duncan; in this regard, Shakespeare's portrait of her is accurate. The real Lady Macbeth was furthermore a patroness of the Church. Her donation of lands at Kirkness, in Fife, are remembered in the register of the church of St. Andrews. She and Macbeth were likewise patrons of the arts.

Macbeth killed Duncan in 1040, near Elgin, which is well within Moray's borders. This act alone was not enough to have made him king of the rival dynasty of Cenél nGabráin, and high king of all the Scots—he would have needed to demonstrate the proper ancestral credentials and to have been enthroned at Scone. Duncan's sons Malcolm and Donald fled Scotland in 1042—Donald to Ireland, and Malcolm to England, to his kinsman Siward, earl of Northumbria. Malcolm eventually solicited the help of the English king Edward the Confessor to regain the Scottish throne, just as in Shakespeare's play. Macbeth's inability—or unwillingness—to kill the pair led to his own death in 1057. Evidence is scant, but Macbeth ruled peacefully and well for nearly two decades before the dynastic infighting and intrigue that characterized Scottish politics once again overtook him. He even made a lengthy pilgrimage to Rome in 1050, a sign to many historians that Scotland was at peace at that time. If so, it was not to last long. The Northumbrians under Siward attacked on behalf of Malcolm in 1054 and defeated Macbeth. Malcolm was reinstated in his home territory as Macbeth's underking, and he set his sights on the kingship of all of Scotland. In mid-August 1057 Malcolm challenged Macbeth to battle at Lumphanan, north of the river Dee. Macbeth won the battle but was seriously wounded and bled to death at Scone on August 16, 17 years to the day after he had killed Duncan (Hudson, p. 144). After Macbeth's death, Lulach, whom Macbeth had probably made his underking in Moray, succeeded to the throne. Lulach held on for a brief period of months and was killed by Malcolm in March 1058; this death marked the end of Cenél Loairn's aspirations to the kingship of all Scots. We do not know what happened to Gruoch.

The Play in Focus

Plot summary. *Macbeth* opens on an ominous note. Duncan, king of Scotland, is receiving news of battle from a wounded soldier. The battle is, in fact, a rebellion: Scottish warriors, among them the thane of Cawdor, are rising up against Duncan. Rosse, another thane, enters to announce that the rebellion has been subdued, and that the credit for the victory belongs to Macbeth. Duncan decides that, as a reward for valor, Macbeth will be made the new thane of Cawdor.

Now the scene shifts to a forest, where Macbeth and his fellow warrior Banquo are returning from the battle. They come across three "weird sisters," witches or supernatural creatures. The witches greet Macbeth as the thane of Cawdor and say that he is fated to become king. Understandably amazed, Macbeth and Banquo ask for more information; the witches, however, say only that Banquo will not be a king, but that his children will rule. As the witches vanish, Rosse finds Macbeth and tells him that he is now thane of Cawdor. Shocked at the quick fulfillment of the prophecy, Macbeth falls into a soliloquy in which he reveals that he is already thinking of killing his king.

Of course, Duncan knows nothing of this when he decides to visit Macbeth at the latter's home. His arrival is preceded by Macbeth's first conversation with his wife, who has received a letter from him about the prophecy, and who is filled with deadly excitement over the possibilities:

> The raven himself is hoarse
> That croaks the fatal entrance of Duncan
> Under my battlements. Come, you spirits
> That tend on mortal thoughts, unsex me here
> And fill me from the crown to the toe topfull
> Of direst cruelty. . . .
> . . . Come, thick night,
> And pale thee in the dunnest smoke of hell,
> That my keen knife see not the wound it
>   makes,
> Nor heaven peep through the blanket of the
>   dark,
> To cry, "Hold, hold."
>
> (*Macbeth*, 1.5.37-52)

Her intent fully formed, Lady Macbeth urges Macbeth to kill Duncan and fulfill the prophecy, but he is undecided. After dinner, they argue the situation: Lady Macbeth tries to get her husband to adopt ruthless violence, but Macbeth, at least at first, points out that the king has honored him and is a guest in their house. However, his objections are overridden by his wife's taunting urgency and by his own desire for glory. In the depths of the night, he steals away to slay Duncan.

Macbeth and Lady Macbeth hold on to each other in this imaginative illustration of Shakepeare's characters.

Macbeth kills Duncan after his wife drugs the king's attendants; afterward, Macbeth places bloody daggers in their hands. He is sorry almost at once, but Lady Macbeth, while shocked by the amount of blood, remains composed. A knocking is heard, and the scene shifts. Downstairs, the warrior Macduff has arrived. He greets Macbeth and asks to see the king; it is Macduff who finds Duncan's body. As he raises the house with his cries, Macbeth kills the king's sleeping attendants, whom he plans to blame for the murder. Lady Macbeth swoons—or pretends to; as the others attend her, Duncan's two sons, Malcolm and Donalbain, speak to each other. They decide to flee, Malcolm to England, and Donalbain to Ireland: they know that whoever killed Duncan will soon set his sights on them.

In the chaos and sorrow that follow Duncan's death, strange happenings disrupt the normal flow of nature. Duncan's horses eat each other; owls kills hawks. Most ominously, day refuses to come. In this dark confusion, the flight of the king's sons throws suspicion on them. Macbeth is named king of this turbulent and peaceless land. A few days pass, and Macbeth plans to kill Banquo. All the witches' prophesies have come true; but the guilty king believes he can circumvent the one that says that Banquo's children will ascend to the monarchy. He hires murderers to assail Banquo and his son Fleance as they are out hunting before dinner at the royal palace. Although the murderers manage to kill Banquo, Fleance escapes.

At the banquet that night, Macbeth's brief kingship reaches its zenith and immediately begins to decline. As he prepares to eat with the assembled thanes of Scotland, Macbeth sees Banquo's ghost. The apparition makes itself visible only to the king, but Macbeth cannot hide his horror. Despite Lady Macbeth's attempt to explain it as a meaningless attack of nerves, a number of thanes begin to connect Macbeth's strange behavior with the horrible events that continue to plague the land.

THE KING'S HEALING TOUCH

The scene in England includes a brief reference to a notable legend of the English monarchy. After Malcolm and Macduff reach an agreement, Macduff asks if King Edward will see them. He is told that the king is attending those afflicted with scrofula, an inflammation of the joints called "the king's disease" because the king's touch was supposed to heal it. This belief lasted from the Middle Ages to the late eighteenth century. Within the play, the image of the English king piously helping his afflicted subjects serves to underscore Macbeth's deep villainy. In its political context, however, the idea was somewhat sensitive. The new English king, James I, was uncomfortable with the idea of the touch. Theologically, he distrusted the implication that the king was capable of miracles, and politically, he tended anyway to limit his public appearances.

As the next scene opens, the situation has decidedly changed. Macduff has gone to England to find Malcolm and to rally support for a war against Macbeth. Macbeth prepares for war, and he seeks out the witches for more information. The witches give him what seems to be good news: they tell him he will not be harmed by any man "of woman born," and will not lose his throne until "Great Birnam Wood to high Dunsinan Hill / Shall come against him" (*Macbeth*, 4.1.107-108). But they also give him bad news, in the form of a pageant of all the kings who will

follow Macbeth, all descended from Banquo. Yet Macbeth cannot accept this evidence. After the witches vanish, he promises to be bloody and quick for whatever little time is left to him.

His first act is to have Macduff's wife and children killed. Meanwhile, in England, Macduff has found Malcolm at the court of Edward the Confessor. He tries to persuade the exiled prince to join the fight against Macbeth. At first, Malcolm refuses; he claims he is unfit to be king, and would be even worse than Macbeth. When Macduff laments the future of a country with such kings, Malcolm tells the truth; he was only testing Macduff, unsure of the thane's honesty. Of course he will join the fight, and he will also bring aid from the English court.

Act 5 unfolds rapidly. The forces massed against Macbeth have beaten him back to his last fortress, at Dunsinane. Locked inside, Lady Macbeth (absent since Act 3) is going insane. This woman who stood fast through bloody murder has succumbed to her guilt; she sees her hands stained with blood that cannot be washed away. Macbeth is convinced he cannot be conquered until Birnam Wood rises up and moves to his castle; still, he is in despair. Weighed down by his crimes, and possessed with an acid awareness of the futility of his ambition, he says in a famous soliloquy that life is only "a tale / Told by an idiot, full of sound and fury / Signifying nothing" (*Macbeth*, 5.5.25-27). Outside, Malcolm gives the order that seals Macbeth's fate: each soldier is to camouflage himself with boughs cut from the trees of Birnam Wood as they move to Dunsinane. When a sentry tells Macbeth of their approach, he knows he is doomed. He learns that his wife has just died, then swears he will fight until he himself is killed.

Scenes of battle follow. Macbeth encounters Macduff; as they fight, Macbeth tells him of the witches' prophesy, that he cannot be killed by any man of woman born. Macduff scoffs because he himself was "from his mother's womb / Untimely ripped," delivered by Caesarian section from his dying mother (*Macbeth*, 5.8.15-16). Macduff kills Macbeth offstage and returns with the slain tyrant's head, one of the bloodiest stage directions in Shakespeare's body of works. Malcolm is named king, but the audience knows that, in the long run, Fleance's children will peacefully succeed him.

***Macbeth*, royal play?** *Macbeth* is Shakespeare's only play concerning Scottish history, and it was written in the first few years after the death of Queen Elizabeth made King James VI of Scotland

King James I of England. Many critics have suggested that these two facts are related, and that Shakespeare was prompted to consider Scottish history by the sudden ascension of a Scottish king to the English throne. Certainly, little had been written about Scotland in English literature for a while, with the exception of some prejudiced and scurrilous pieces (see Literary Context, below) now rendered hugely inappropriate. "When Scotland's King James became England's King James in March 1603, his accession made a Shakespearean Scottish play commercially viable and creatively attractive. King James and his Scottishness created an occasion, and at some point Shakespeare and the King's Men apparently seized the popular, commercial moment" (Braunmuller in Shakespeare, p. 8).

It seems likely that *Macbeth* was at least partly inspired by King James's accession. However, those critics who have suggested that *Macbeth* was an attempt to gain the favor of the king himself are on less steady ground. They ignore the fact that, in several ways, the play is actually dangerous, and perhaps even insulting to the king. Obviously, *Macbeth* is crammed with corrupt politics, blood-stained acts, deception and cruelty; the overall impression is of a brutal, almost primitive land ruled only by force and the sword. In itself, this pessimistic view is not remarkable; Shakespeare's plays on English history are much the same (although they are not tragic). However, there are no redeeming Scottish characters in the play: of the "good" characters in *Macbeth,* Banquo stands by while he suspects Duncan's life is in danger, Malcolm and Donalbain flee at the first sign of danger, and Macduff leaves his family exposed to Macbeth's cruelty. The play's unabated darkness prevents any glow, with the result that Scotland itself seems bleak, dark, and primitive.

In fact, the reader whose knowledge of the Renaissance view of Scotland is limited to this play will be led far astray. *Macbeth*'s obsessive focus on the turbulence of Scottish politics prevents it from portraying the full splendor of what was, in fact, a nation as advanced and cultured as England itself. While Scotland was smaller, less populous, and in places more barren than its southern neighbor, it had a long tradition of learning, arts, and culture. Its monasteries and universities made Scotland part of the cultural map of Europe in medieval times, and Scotland arguably experienced the Renaissance before England; during the fifteenth century, when English poetry languished in a post-Chaucerian lull, talented and erudite poets such as Robert Henryson (?1430-1506), William Dunbar (?1465-?1530), and Gavin Douglas (?1475-1522) inaugurated a golden age of literature in Scotland. King James VI/I himself was a late product of this Scottish Renaissance; he was a scholar who, by the time he ascended the English throne, had composed important treatises on statesmanship (*Basilikon Doron* [1599]) and on witchcraft (*The Daemonologie* [1597]).

Macbeth ignores these facts about the Scottish past—facts that certainly would have been flattering to James. Instead, the play ends on a note of British imperialism: Malcolm's first act as king is to "ennoble" his thanes by giving them the English title of "earl." Shakespeare's perspective on Scotland may well have pleased an English crowd; but it is hard to see how it would have flattered a Scottish king.

Sources and literary context. Shakespeare's main source for the story of *Macbeth* was Raphael Holinshed's *Chronicles,* a history of the British Isles produced during Tudor times. He also seems to have consulted a number of Scottish chronicles. Shakespeare follows Holinshed's account fairly closely, although Holinshed's Duncan is young, while Shakespeare's is aged. More significantly, Shakespeare turns Macbeth's rule from a long and generally successful one, to a short, dismal fiasco. In addition, the playwright borrows details from other parts of the chronicles: Lady Macbeth's prodding, for instance, is taken from the account of Donwald, an earlier king whose wife incited him to murder. The witches themselves are from the Macbeth story as told by Holinshed:

> It fortuned as Macbeth and Banquo journeyed towards Forres, where the king then lay, they went sporting by the way together without other company . . . there met them three women in strange and wild apparel, resembling creatures of elder world, whom when they attentively beheld, wondering much at the sight, the first of them spake and said; All hail Macbeth, thane of Glammis . . . The second of them said; All hail Macbeth, thane of Cawdor. But the third said; All haile Macbeth that hereafter shall be king of Scotland. (Holinshed in Bullough, p. 495)

Macbeth is a tragedy influenced in almost equal measure by the heroic tragedies of the 1590s and the darker, generally more pessimistic tragedies of the 1600s. Like the great tragic heroes of the 1590s, Macbeth is an over-reacher, and the audience is emotionally invested in him

Depiction of Catholic co-conspirators in the Gunpowder Plot.

even as it abhors his actions. In this, he is reminiscent of such heroes as the protagonist of Christopher Marlowe's **Dr. Faustus** (also in *WLAIT 3: British and Irish Literature and Its Times*). But Macbeth has some affinity as well with the more sordid, scheming heroes of early Jacobean tragedies; like the heroes of such plays as *The Revenger's Tragedy* and *The Changeling,* he tries to succeed by intrigue and private murder. In fact, he opens the play as a bold warrior, but soon moves to scheming plots.

Events in History at the Time the Play Was Written

The Gowrie Conspiracy. Murder and mayhem in Scottish politics was not confined to the shadowy past. King James I of England was himself involved in a murky incident that may or may not have involved an attempt on his life. At the time, he was still King James VI of Scotland. On August 5, 1600, he went suddenly to Perth, accompanied by the 19-year-old Alexander Ruthven, a young man whose 22-year-old brother was John Ruthven, earl of Gowrie. The elder Ruthven had recently made very public statements against James. No one knows precisely what happened next, or why, but the result was that both brothers were killed that day. James claimed that the Gowries made an attempt on his life (a kidnapping attempt is more likely), but his version was not widely accepted, and many people voiced the opinion that the king had in fact had the young men killed. Some 18

years earlier, their father, William, earl of Gowrie, had been involved in a raid to seize James, only to be executed for treason.

All these years later, James was supposedly out hunting when young Alexander Ruthven told him an intriguing story of the capture of a suspicious stranger with a pot full of foreign gold, who was being held prisoner in his brother Lord Gowrie's house in Perth. The king set off with Ruthven to Lord Gowrie's house in Perth to examine the stranger. He accompanied Alexander to a small room in a turret, where instead of the stranger he found himself confronted with a dagger-wielding man in armor. A struggle followed, during which the panicky king screamed words like "treason" and "murder," until an attendant rushed in and killed the two. So went the king's story, which many of his ministers and courtiers simply would not believe (Bevan, p. 61). Certainly James's reputation was damaged by the incident. A mere month later, a pamphlet published in Edinburgh, entitled "Gowries Conspiracie," supported James's version of events and was quickly sent to London to be published. The speed with which his official version was made public suggests "a propaganda war and/or contemporary anxieties about attacks on monarchs" (Braunmuller in Shakespeare, p. 2). Queen Elizabeth herself seems to have doubted the veracity of James's account.

In 1604, a year after James had become king of England and two years before Shakespeare wrote *Macbeth*, James's own troupe of actors performed *The Tragedie of Gowrie*, but the play was suppressed after only two performances. Doubtless, it intended to be supportive of England's new king, but the monarch was clearly taking no chances with his public image. There was too much controversy about the event.

Witchcraft. In 1590 James VI of Scotland traveled to Denmark to meet and marry the Danish princess, Anne. There, he came into contact with Continental theories about witchcraft, which were more lurid and fantastic than English ideas. That same year, in Scotland, he interrogated several accused witches at a trial in North Berwick; the women involved were accused of plotting his death by conjuring a storm to sink his ship on his voyage home from Denmark, and at least one of them was burned at the stake (Bevan, p. 48). James wrote a book on witches in 1597, called *The Daemonologie*, in which he introduced to Scotland the ideas he had heard about witches in the Danish court.

> These beliefs included not merely the witch's contracting her or his soul to the devil, but a demonic "pact" that involved sexual intercourse with Satan, . . . the "black Mass" and other inverted religious practices, and numerous activities such as stealing and eating children, exhuming bodies, parodying baptism using cats and other animals, flying through the air, and sailing the sea in sieves. (Braunmuller in Shakespeare, p. 30)

During the 1590s, persecution and prosecution of witches (who were overwhelmingly women) increased in both England and Scotland; this atmosphere surely pervades *Macbeth*.

Nonetheless, the history of witchcraft in the Renaissance is much less picturesque than the weird hags of Shakespeare's play might suggest. The Church of England tended to discourage belief in witches, considering it superstition; notwithstanding the Salem witch trials in the American colonies a century later, Protestants usually de-emphasized the possibility of miracles in earthly life. This, however, did not prevent the average person from believing in charms and potions, and each village or neighborhood had its wise woman or man who could concoct love potions, hint about the future, or heal sick pets. Such "white" magic was an accepted part of most communities, even if the Church did not approve.

Quite different was the treatment of "black magic"—practiced not for the community, but against it). To be accused of witchcraft was no light matter. Sixteenth- to seventeenth-century statutes made hanging the maximum punishment (witches in England were never burned). Prosecution for witchcraft depended on witness testimony (which was often prejudiced). In comparison to some other lands, England condemned relatively few witches. Between 1558 and 1736, only 500 people were tried for the crime in its most populous counties; 109 were convicted and hanged. By comparison, 900 were burned as witches in the single French province of Lorraine between 1580 and 1595. The witches were generally accused of rather homespun evils: making a woman infertile, or ruining a crop, or haunting another person's dreams. Few accusers were bold or fearful enough to assert that a witch could control the weather, a power that *Macbeth's* witches claim in the play.

Shakespeare got the idea for witches from his source; but he makes them a larger part of his story. This seems to have been a response to a popular vogue partly inspired by the king himself, whose *The Daemonologie* asserted the reality

THE GUNPOWDER PLOT

In 1605 England was rocked by an alleged assassination attempt, the Gunpowder Plot (a conspiracy to kill James I while he addressed Parliament). The conspirators, a group of Catholics opposed to the Protestant monarchy, had formulated a plan to kill not only the king but also his family and dozens of government officials by blowing up Parliament House. The conspirators set out to dig a tunnel into the basement of the Parliament building, place gunpowder in the vaults, then explode them. Before they could fully execute their plan, the conspirators were found out, then arrested, drawn, and quartered. Among them was Robert Catesby, a young nobleman whose involvement came as a shock to James, since he had regarded Catesby as a loyal subject, much as the Duncan of Shakespeare's play seems to have regarded Macbeth. Scholars speculate, however, that Catesby was the model not for Macbeth, but for the earlier thane of Cawdor, another rebellious lord.

of witches. Producers of *Macbeth* after Shakespeare enhanced the role of the witches, adding to their number and providing them elaborate costumes and dances; ironically, at the same time the prosecution of witchcraft was in marked decline in England. The trend would continue, leading to the abolition of the statutes against witchcraft in 1736.

Reviews. *Macbeth* survives only in the Folio collection of Shakespeare's work. It was never printed in a cheaper quarto version, an oblique indicator of a popular play. Otherwise, there is little indication of the play's reception among its original audiences. *Macbeth* grew in popularity as the seventeenth century progressed; a heavily revised version by William Davenant (almost operatic in its emphasis on song and spectacle) was frequently performed during the Restoration era. The chief eighteenth-century critic of Shakespeare, Samuel Johnson, both praised and criticized *Macbeth* (see **The Life of Samuel Johnson,** also in *WLAIT 3: British and Irish Literature and Its Times*).

> [The play is] deservedly celebrated for the propriety of its fictions, and solemnity, grandeur, and variety of its action; but it has no nice discriminations of character, the events are too great to admit the influence of particular dispositions, and the course of the action necessarily determines the conduct of the agents. (Johnson, p. 360)

During the late-eighteenth and early-nineteenth-century Gothic era, *Macbeth's* use of the supernatural would gain new appreciation. Later in the nineteenth century, during the Victorian era, audiences would inaugurate a fascination with the aggressive behavior of Lady Macbeth. The play has since remained among the most frequently performed in the world.

—Jacob Littleton

For More Information>

Aitchison, Nick. *Macbeth: Man and Myth.* Gloucestershire: Sutton, 1999.

Barrow, G. W. S. *Kingship and Unity: Scotland 1000-1306.* London: Edward Arnold, 1981.

Bevan, Bryan. *King James VI of Scotland and I of England.* London: Rubicon, 1996.

Hudson, Benjamin T. *Kings of Celtic Scotland.* New York: Greenwood, 1994.

Johnson, Samuel. *Collected Works.* Oxford: Oxford University Press, 1984.

Lynch, Michael. *Scotland: A New History.* London: Pimlico, 1992.

Mackie, J. D. *A History of Scotland.* 2d ed. Eds. Bruce Lenman and Geoffrey Parker. London: Penguin, 1978.

Morgan, Kenneth. *Oxford Illustrated History of Britain.* Oxford: Oxford University Press, 1984.

Purkiss, Diane. *The Witch in History.* London: Routledge, 1996.

Sadler, John. *Scottish Battles.* Edingburgh: Cannongate, 1996.

Shakespeare, William. *Macbeth.* Ed. A. R. Braunmuller. The New Cambridge Shakespeare. Cambridge: Cambridge University Press, 1997.

Thomas, Keith. *Religion and the Decline of Magic.* Oxford: Oxford University Press, 1973.

"Mac Flecknoe"

by

John Dryden

~

Critic, playwright, poet, and translator, John Dryden (1631-1700) so dominated the literary scene of the later seventeenth century that it is often referred to as "the Age of Dryden." Dryden himself explicitly took on the responsibility of speaking for his age in a pioneering work of literary criticism, *An Essay of Dramatic Poesy* (1668), in which he called himself *Neander*, Greek for "New Man." The year before, he had published the poem "Annus Mirabilis" ("Year of Wonders"), which celebrated the English spirit as manifested in two events of 1666: a naval victory over the Dutch, and recovery after the Great Fire of London. This and other poems on matters of public or political importance won him the honor of being named poet laureate by King Charles II in 1668. Yet most of Dryden's literary output in the 1660s and 1670s was for the theater. As the author of nearly 30 plays, he led the way in the revival of the English drama during the reign of Charles II (1660-85). Only in the late 1670s, as he was nearing 50, did Dryden begin writing the satiric poems for which he is best known today. In the political satires "Absalom and Achitophel" (1681) and "The Medall" (1682), he attacked the enemies of the king; and in "Mac Flecknoe," written earlier but published later, he lambasted rival playwright Thomas Shadwell, with whom he had earlier clashed on literary issues.

THE LITERARY WORK

A satiric poem set in London; written c. 1676; published in 1682 (pirated edition) and 1684 (authorized edition).

SYNOPSIS

Dryden lampoons his political and literary antagonist, the playwright Thomas Shadwell, by depicting him as heir to the throne of literary dullness left him by the notoriously bad poet Richard Flecknoe.

Events in History at the Time of the Poem

Restoration of the monarchy. In 1660 King Charles II returned from exile to reclaim the English throne, 11 years after his father's execution at the end of the English Civil War and the beginning of the Puritan interregnum (parliamentary rule) under Oliver Cromwell. While Charles was enthusiastically welcomed by his subjects, the restored monarchy was not the powerful institution it had been before the Civil War. The king's powers were limited by restrictive laws that Parliament had forced Charles I to accept before he was deposed and that continued in

314

Mac Flecknoe
A
Satyr. By Mr Dryden.

All human things are subject to decay,
And when Fate Sumons, Monarchs must obey;
This Flecknoe found, who like Augustus young
Was call'd to Empire, & had govern'd long;
In Prose, & Verse, was held w'thout dispute,
Through all y'e Realmes of Nonsense, absolute.
This Aged Prince, now flourishing in peace,
And blest w'th Issue of a large encrease;

Wou

Manuscript page from *"Mac Flecknoe—A Satyr."*

force after the Restoration. Earlier, for example, monarchs had recourse to secret courts, such as the Star Chamber, and they could also arrest members of Parliament without cause. These and similar royal prerogatives were now abolished. Most important, the king could no longer impose taxes without Parliament's approval. Charming, resourceful, and politically savvy, King Charles II would be forced to spend much of his time and energy contending with Parliament for the royal treasury to remain solvent.

Charles, however, had another source of revenue, if a politically risky one. He had spent much of his exile in France, under the protection of that country's powerful and ambitious Louis XIV, who was also his first cousin. Influenced in his tastes by French culture and envious of Louis XIV's broad royal prerogatives, Charles saw the French king as a natural ally. In 1670 he signed the Treaty of Dover, under the terms of which he agreed to assist France in war against Holland. In a secret version of the treaty, Charles, who had long had Catholic sympathies, agreed to declare himself a Catholic in return for a large cash payment from France. Furthermore, in 1669, the year before the treaty, Charles's younger brother James, the duke of York, had told the king that he himself

had converted to Catholicism. While Charles ultimately acknowledged 17 illegitimate children (a fact to which Dryden humorously alludes in "Mac Flecknoe"), he had no legitimate heir, so that James was next in the line of succession. If James's Catholicism became known, there would certainly be deep unrest.

Religious tensions. Despite the king's buoyant return, religious tensions in English society persisted, and they built up steadily during the 1660s and 1670s. There were three main religious groups in the country: the Anglicans, the majority group, who belonged to the Church of England (also called the Established Church), generally an ally of the Crown; the Dissenters, or the smaller Protestant sects that flourished in England outside the Anglican Church and viewed Anglican practices as too close to Catholicism (these included the various Puritan groups); and the Catholics, those who had clung to the original faith after the Protestant Reformation of the previous century.

Early in Charles's reign, the Anglican Church moved aggressively to reassert the supremacy it had lost during the years of Puritan rule. Its aim was to crush both the Catholics and the Dissenters. From 1661 to 1665 Parliament passed a series of severe laws called the Clarendon Code that proscribed non-Anglican worship. The Act of Uniformity (1662) imposed the Anglican *Book of Common Prayer* on all ministers; the Conventicle Act (1664) banned non-Anglican religious meetings; and the Five Mile Act (1665) prohibited those ministers who did not subscribe to the Act of Uniformity from living in or even going within five miles of the towns where they had earlier held services. The climax to such measures came in 1673, when Parliament passed the first Test Act, which prohibited all non-Anglicans from holding public office. It was at this point that Charles II's brother, James, was forced to reveal his conversion and to resign his position as Lord of the Admiralty.

While Protestant Anglicans and Dissenters often opposed each other, both could agree upon their shared fear of and hostility toward the Catholics. Catholicism was associated with foreign domination (by the pope, for example, or the French) and with strongly monarchical or absolutist forms of government, as in the case of Louis XIV. Tainted by such associations, English Catholics' patriotism was easily doubted. Many English tended to view Catholicism as a dire threat to individual freedom, which they prided themselves on having carefully nurtured for centuries by means of hard-won parliamentary checks on royal power. Fed by Charles's Catholic and French sympathies, by the revelation of James's Catholicism, and by the knowledge that the militarily powerful French would support any Catholic claimant to the English throne, anti-Catholic fears grew steadily during the first two decades of Charles II's rule. The fears dictated views about other aspects of life; most Londoners were certain that Catholics had started the Great Fire in 1666. The inconclusive Third Anglo-Dutch War (1672-1674), which resulted from England's obligations under the Treaty of Dover, heightened the city's atmosphere of suspicion, particularly in the stridently anti-French, anti-Catholic House of Commons, which felt betrayed by Charles's alliance with the French. Such tensions led Dryden to describe London as "much to fears inclined" in "Mac Flecknoe" ("Mac Flecknoe," line 65).

Emerging political parties. By the time Dryden was writing "Mac Flecknoe," these religious differences had begun to polarize the English political world in a way that was new. Within just a few years—after the poem was written but before its publication in 1682—English politics would give rise to the first modern political parties, the Whigs and the Tories. The parties would crystallize around the attempt by the king's opponents to exclude the Catholic James from succeeding to the throne after Charles's death. The resulting battle, called the Exclusion Crisis, involved a number of parliamentary elections. The king several times dissolved Parliament, hoping to increase the number of his supporters and to forestall attempts to exclude James from the succession. While local issues remained at the forefront of such elections, the larger issue of exclusion emerged as a principle around which two organized, opposing sides took shape. The exclusionists came to be called "Whigs" (after Scottish outlaws called Whiggamores) and the antiexclusionists were known as "Tories" (originally used for Irish robbers); each of the names was adopted after first being bandied about insultingly by the other side. Both parties had acknowledged leaders; both gradually acquired a rudimentary central organization; and both slowly developed ideologically consistent positions on other issues as well.

Though such distinctions were not yet as clear-cut as they would later become, in general the Tories could be characterized as more conservative and the Whigs as more radical. Above

Thomas Shadwell

all, Tories supported the king and the principle of legitimate succession. The Tory power base was the traditional landed elites, for Tories were often aristocrats whose wealth was based on large estates and who allied themselves with the local Anglican church leaders. They also often tended to be more hostile to Dissenters than to Catholics, and if an English Catholic was active politically, he was likely to be a Tory. (Dryden, for example, a staunch Tory, converted from Anglicanism to Catholicism in the mid-1680s.) By contrast, the Whigs drew on a broader, more varied power base, comprising disparate interests outside the establishment. Above all, they represented the newly emerging commercial middle class—tradesmen, merchants, and shopkeepers whose growing wealth was based on cash, not land. Also the Whigs attracted both Dissenters and "republicans" (those who had supported Cromwell's Puritan regime for ideological rather than religious reasons).

These new party allegiances not only encompassed political and economic issues but shaped, and were shaped by, broader cultural and aesthetic values as well. While not the ostensible substance of the disagreement between the Tory John Dryden and the Whig Thomas Shadwell, political concerns can be vaguely but certainly discerned in the literary feud that developed between these two Restoration playwrights, whose respective political affiliations paralleled their literary tastes and standards.

In "Absalom and Achitophel" (1681), Dryden attacked—at the request of Charles II—Lord Shaftesbury, one of Charles II's former ministers, who allied with Charles's illegitimate son, the duke of Monmouth, against the succession of James, the duke of York. Shadwell replied with the much less successful *The Medal of John Bayes: A Satire Against Folly and Knavery* (1682). Dryden countered not only with the scathing denunciation of Shadwell that is "Mac-Flecknoe" but with an unflattering portrait of his opponent as Og in Part II of "Absalom and Achitophel" (1682).

RESTORATION DRAMA

The Puritans had banned theatrical performances in 1642, but when Charles II was restored in 1660, the institution of theater was restored as well. Yet the tragedies and comedies that flourished during the Restoration period did so on a smaller scale than their Elizabethan or Jacobean predecessors. Dryden, though not considered a great playwright by modern critics, was adept at pleasing audiences, and did so with grand heroic tragedies in verse, and refined, amoral, and chatty comedies of wit or manners. Opposing this school of comedy was the comedy of humors, in which characters stood for a particular mood or quality, and were usually named in such a way as to evoke their characteristic "humor." Sir Formal Trifle, for example, is a vacuous speechifyer in *The Virtuoso* (1676), a play by Dryden's rival Thomas Shadwell, the defender of humors comedy.

Thomas Shadwell, playwright. Thomas Shadwell (1642?-92), the hapless victim of "Mac Flecknoe," was born in Norfolk to a well established if not very wealthy family and educated at Cambridge. He left that university before taking a degree and in 1658 entered the Middle Temple in London to study law. The details of his life are somewhat sketchy, but the following fact is not in dispute: before Dryden published "Mac Flecknoe," Shadwell was considered by many to be one of the most important living English playwrights. His reputation has not yet recovered. According to one Shadwell scholar,

Because most critics have read Dryden and not Shadwell or because they have not penetrated

"Mac Flecknoe's" deceptive premise about Shadwell's opposition to wit or because they have been pleased with the fiction, they have accepted and promulgated the satire's facetious conclusions. . . . It appears "Mac Flecknoe" has been so convincing that habitually just and perceptive critics lose control on describing or evaluating Shadwell. . . .

(Kunz, pp. 13-16)

Shadwell's first play, a comedy of humors entitled *The Sullen Lovers or, The Impertinents* (1668) was a success. The great diarist Samuel Pepys (see *The Diary of Samuel Pepys*, also in *WLAIT 3: British and Irish Literature and Its Times*) attended many early performances of the play; over the course of watching it multiple times Pepys goes from finding Shadwell's drama "tedious, and no design at all in it," to "contemptible," to "a pretty good play," to "a play which pleases me well still" (Pepys in Borgman, pp. 17-18). His change in attitude has a lot to do with the evident pleasure that other theatergoers, from the king himself to the common folk, take in the play. Shadwell did in fact enjoy the favor of upper-class patrons (prominently, the duke of Newcastle) throughout his career and was a favorite among the masses as well. He followed *The Sullen Lovers* with a host of other plays: later in 1668 with *The Royal Shepherdess* (a pastoral tragi-comedy); in 1670 with *The Humorists* (a comedy); in 1671 with *The Miser* (a comedy); and, before the end of 1682, with 10 other plays of varying success. Shortly after "Mac Flecknoe" was published, Shadwell's career went into something of a decline. His next play, a comedy entitled *The Squire of Alsatia*, would not be produced until 1688, although he would write and translate poetry in the interim. *The Squire of Alsatia* was a success, and Shadwell's fortunes picked up. Thanks to his patron, the earl of Dorset, Shadwell became poet laureate on March 9, 1689, a position he would retain until his death in 1692.

Dryden and Shadwell—the literary feud. There was a subtitle on the pirated (unauthorized) version of "Mac Flecknoe" that appeared in 1682: "A SATYR UPON THE *TRUE-BLEW-PROTESTANT* POET, T. S. BY THE AUTHOR OF *ABSALOM [and] ACHITOPHEL*" (Oden, p. 283). Clearly the publisher hoped to cash in on the conflict inherent in juxtaposing Shadwell's extreme and well-known Whiggism ("true-blew-Protestant poet") with the strongly Tory views espoused so devastatingly in "Absalom and Achitophel." But the feud itself, more literary than political, had been running for a decade before the writing of "Mac Flecknoe" around 1676. The shots on both sides had been fired off largely in the prologues, epilogues, prefaces, and dedications to plays written between 1667 and 1676.

Apart from their political quarrels, and jabs at each other's personal appearances, characters, and proclivities, the major points of contention between the two writers were:

- the literary assessment of the playwright Ben Jonson (1572-1637)
- the relative merits of the comedy of wit, championed by Dryden, as compared with the comedy of humors, practiced by Jonson and championed by Shadwell ("humor" here refers to a driving character trait or emotion—envy, for example, or anger)
- the proper purpose of comedy itself, which Dryden believed was to divert and to delight, but which Shadwell insisted was to instruct morally

Literary historians trace the origins of the quarrel to 1667, when Dryden published a prologue to his adaptation of Shakespeare's *The Tempest,* in which he compared Jonson unfavorably with Shakespeare. "Labouring" Jonson, Dryden wrote, had "crept" below such geniuses as his older contemporary Shakespeare (Dryden in Oden, p. 6). The following year, in his *Essay of Dramatic Poesy,* Dryden praised Jonson as "the most learned and judicious Writer any theater ever had," but went on to assert that "one cannot say he wanted [lacked] wit, but rather that he was frugal of it" (Dryden in Oden, p. 16). Now, these may seem like mild criticisms, but Shadwell and others of his circle idealized Jonson and would tolerate not even the slightest detraction from their hero's reputation. Shadwell responded in the preface of his own very Jonsonian play *The Sullen Lovers* (1668) by defending Jonson,

whom I think all Drammatick *Poets* ought to imitate, though none are like to come near; he being the only person that appears to me to have made perfect Representations of Humane Life . . . though I have known some of late so Insolent to say that Ben *Johnson* [sic] wrote his best *Playes* without wit.
(Shadwell in Oden, p. 24)

The last part of this quote is clearly a reference to (if a distortion of) Dryden's earlier comments in his *Essay of Dramatic Poesy.* Shadwell went on in this work to attack Dryden's plays as "that Indecent way of Writing" because they showed characters behaving improperly— "Swearing, Drinking, Whoring" (Shadwell in Oden, p. 24). The following year, Shadwell enlarged upon his condemnation of Dryden's type of dramatic writing in his preface to *The Royal Shepherdess,* asserting as well that a poet who aims above all to please the audience (which Dryden maintained was his goal) "loses the dignity of a Poet, and becomes as little as a Jugler, or a Rope-Dancer" (Shadwell in Oden, p. 32).

In 1671 the play *The Rehearsal* by George Villiers, duke of Buckingham, satirized rhymed heroic drama and included a character named Mr. Bayes, who recognizably mocked Dryden himself. Although Dryden as a shareholder in the theater concern known as the King's Company actually profited from this play, its ridicule signaled the waning of the vogue for grand heroic plays. Around this same time Shadwell produced *The Humorists,* whose characters included the foolish poet "Drybob," another caricature of Dyden. (In this era, "dry bob" meant a harmless blow, or a form of sexual impotence.) As the 1670s progressed, Shadwell continued to fire off barbs at Dryden in prologues to such plays as *Epsom-Wells* (1672) and *Psyche* (1675). Finally, in the dedication to *The Virtuoso* (1676), Shadwell derided "some Women and some Men of Feminine understandings, who like slight plays onely, that represent a little tattle sort of Conversation like their own" (Shadwell in Oden, p. 157). It was this attack, some scholars have suggested, that provided the final provocation for the hammer blow that was "Mac Flecknoe." Shadwell also wrote the following inflammatory remark:

That there are a great many faults in the conduct of this Play, I am not ignorant. But I (having no Pension but from the Theatre, which is either unwilling or unable to reward a Man sufficiently for so much pains as correct Comedies require) cannot allot my whole time to the writing of Plays, but am forced to mind some other business of Advantage. (Had I as much Money, and as much time for it) I might, perhaps, write as Correct a Comedy as any of my Contemporaries. (Shadwell in Winn, p. 289)

Dryden took umbrage at all this, given his modest salary as poet laureate (£200 for 1675) and other financial circumstances that in fact inhibited his literary pursuits. The "false picture of a well-fed Laureate enjoying the leisure of a profitable pension," was probably the incendiary incident that gave rise to "Mac Flecknoe" (Winn, p. 290).

"Mac Flecknoe"

Plot summary. Following common practice in such satirical literary skirmishes, Dryden never mentions Shadwell by name, but instead refers only to "Sh—." This transparent pretense paid lip service to the idea of protecting the identity of the victim (who was, in fact, readily identifiable), and made those who could identify the victim feel as if they were in on a secret joke. In this case, using "Sh—" also allows Dryden to perpetrate a number of scatological puns equating his victim with excrement, a major theme in the poem.

The poem itself is relatively short, amounting to 217 lines. It begins with a description of the aging Flecknoe, monarch of "all the realms of Nonsense," who (like King Charles II) must settle the question of his succession:

> All human things are subject to decay,
> And when fate summons, monarchs must
> obey.
> This Flecknoe found, who like Augustus,
> young
> Was called to empire, and had governed long;
> In prose and verse, was owned, without
> dispute,
> Through all the realms of Nonsense, absolute.
> ("Mac Flecknoe," lines 1-6)

Now nearing the end of his reign and blessed (also like Charles) "with issue of a large increase," Flecknoe ponders which of his many sons should inherit his throne and "wage immortal war with wit," the enemy of Nonsense ("Mac Flecknoe," lines 8 and 12). Only the one who most resembles the monarch himself is fit to rule, Flecknoe cries:

> Sh— alone my perfect image bears,
> Mature in dullness beyond his years:
> Sh— alone, of all my sons, is he
> Who stands confirmed in full stupidity.
> The rest to some faint meaning make pretence,
> But Sh— never deviates into sense.
> ("Mac Flecknoe," lines 15-18)

Even Sh—'s "goodly fabric"—that is, his fat body—seems majestic to Flecknoe ("Mac Flecknoe," line 25). Like Old Testament prophets prefiguring Christ, earlier bad authors, such as Thomas Heywood (c. 1570-1641) and James Shirley (1596-1666), prefigure Sh—; even Flecknoe himself, like John the Baptist, was merely sent "but to prepare thy way" ("Mac Flecknoe," line 32). Flecknoe recalls that, as Sh—'s barge preceded his own in a royal procession down the River Thames, Sh—'s lute playing brought calls

of his name from Pissing Alley (a street in London) and A— Hall (probably Ashton Hall, owned by Colonel Edmund Ashton, a friend of Shadwell's). Little fish flocked around the boat in the same way as they crowded around the bits of floating sewage in the river, and, in strumming the lute, Sh—kept better time even than the mechanical meter of his play *Psyche*. Flecknoe ends his speech weeping "for joy / In silent raptures of the hopeful boy" ("Mac Flecknoe," lines 60-61). While every consideration says that Sh— is meant for "anointed dullness," the strongest argument is to be found in his plays ("Mac Flecknoe," line 63).

Near the walls around the fair city of Augusta (London) is an old ruined building, once a watchtower but now the site of several brothels. Nearby is an acting school, the Nursery, where tomorrow's queens, heroes, whores, and emperors are trained. Plays by the great John Fletcher (1579-1625) are not performed there; nor are those by the greater Ben Jonson. The clowns Simkin and Panton often practice their verbal tricks at the Nursery, though. This is the site Flecknoe has chosen for Sh—'s coronation, since Thomas Dekker (c. 1572-1632), a bad playwright, long ago foretold that a mighty prince would reign there, born to be "a scourge of wit, and a flail of sense," a virtuoso of "true dullness" ("Mac Flecknoe," lines 89-90). The news of the coronation spreads throughout the city, or at least through that neighborhood. Instead of Persian carpets, the "imperial way" is strewn with the "scattered limbs of mangled poets" ("Mac Flecknoe," lines 98-99). The books of ignored writers come out from the bookshops to attend the ceremony, books whose pages have been used to wrap pies and wipe bottoms: there are many works by Heywood, Shirley, and John Ogilby (1600-76), but "loads of Sh— almost choked the way" ("Mac Flecknoe," line 103). Cheated publishers make up the ceremonial guards, with Henry Herringman (Dryden's and Shadwell's publisher until 1678) commanding them.

Then Flecknoe himself appears, high up on a throne of his own works. Next to him is Sh—, who is compared not only with Aeneas's son Ascanius, "Rome's other hope," but also with Hannibal, Rome's great enemy ("Mac Flecknoe," line 109). Just as Hannibal swore eternal enmity to Rome, so now does Sh— swear that he will always maintain "true dullness" and keep up the fight against wit and sense ("Mac Flecknoe," line 115). Acting as both king and priest, Flecknoe prepares the oil with which to anoint his heir. In Sh—'s left hand, Flecknoe puts a mug of ale, instead of the ball that English monarchs hold at coronation; in Sh—'s right hand, Flecknoe puts a copy of his own awful play *Love's Kingdom,* in place of the English monarch's scepter. Around Sh—'s temples he spreads a garland of sleep-inducing poppies (Shadwell was an opium addict), and there are reports later that say 12 owls flew overhead exactly at that moment, just as Rome's founder Romulus saw 12 vultures at the site of the future city. The ceremony and the omens of coming might are cheered by the admiring crowd.

Fighting the urge to make a speech, Flecknoe shakes his hair; droplets of sweat fly from his forehead onto Sh— as Flecknoe gives in and begins speaking prophetically. May Sh— reign from Ireland to far Barbadoes, he proclaims, and may his mighty pen stretch even beyond *Love's Kingdom.* Let others teach success, he says, addressing Sh— after the crowd roars its approval, but you learn from me how to go through labor without giving birth and how to work hard without producing anything. Other playwrights' characters may betray their author's wit in their own follies on stage, he says; the fools in your plays will always prove that you yourself are senseless, too. Don't steal your fools from other writers but make them out of your own dullness, so that future ages will see your originality. And if you want empty, flowery rhetoric, don't work at it but trust your own nature. Sir Formal Trifle (a fatuous orator from Shadwell's *The Virtuoso*) will always be with you, whether you want him or not. Nor should you be seduced into following Jonson, who wouldn't really like your plays anyway, but instead you should acknowledge me, Flecknoe, as your true artistic father. When did Jonson attack arts he didn't understand? When did Jonson inject vulgar non sequiturs into his dialogue, or produce a situation comedy when he had promised a real play? When did he steal whole scenes from Fletcher, the way you do from George Etherege (c. 1635-c. 1692, an eminent Restoration playwright)? Comparing Jonson's work to yours is like comparing oil to water; the oil floats above, while your territory is down on the bottom. Your mind is bent toward dullness, which makes your writings lean that way, too. Your only resemblance to Jonson is that you both had mountainous stomachs, but yours is full of wind, not sense, making you a huge wine cask of a body but only a small keg of wit. Your verse, like mine, drones weakly: your tragedies make

people laugh, while your comedies put them to sleep; your satires are toothless, and the poison in your heart loses its venom when it touches your pen. Your genius is not in sharp satire but in soft anagrams or acrostics, where you can make puns and play mechanically with the shape of the words on the page (as in George Herbert's famous poems "Easter Wings" and "The Altar"):

> Leave writing plays, and choose for thy command
> Some peaceful province in acrostic land.
> There thou may'st wings display and altars raise,
> And torture one poor word ten thousand ways.
> ("Mac Flecknoe," lines 205-208)

Or write your own songs and sing them yourself, playing your lute.

But Flecknoe's last words are hardly audible, for two characters from *The Virtuoso* have recreated a trick from that play and opened a trap door under his feet. Down goes "the yet declaiming bard," while his coarse mantle is "borne upwards by a subterranean wind" ("Mac Flecknoe," lines 213-15). It settles on his heir, bringing the poem to an abrupt conclusion "The mantle fell to the young prophet's part / With double portion of his father's art" ("Mac Flecknoe," lines 216-17).

Dullness: the intersection of politics and criticism. "Mac Flecknoe" hinges on the idea of dullness; the word itself appears eight times in the brief poem, always in reference to Sh—. For Dryden, however, dullness was not only the defining characteristic of Shadwell and his literary output, but it was also the most potentially dangerous aspect of all writers who share Shadwell's literary values. In Dryden's view, nothing less than the survival of art and culture was at stake in the battle against dullness. Dryden was a Tory because he saw the king as fighting in the front lines of that battle, indeed as having rescued the nation from dullness:

> At his return, he found a Nation lost as much in Barbarism as in Rebellion. And as the excellency of his Nature forgave the one, so the excellency of his manners reform'd the other. The desire of imitating so great a pattern, first waken'd the dull and heavy spirits of the *English,* from their natural reserv'dness: loosen'd them, from their stiff forms of conversation; and made them easy and plyant with each other in discourse. Thus, our way of living became more free: and the fire of the English *wit,* which was before stifled under a constrained melancholy way of breeding, began first to display its force.
> (Dryden in Oden, p. 102)

Dryden thus explicitly links freedom with the throwing off of dullness, and therefore also links it with wit; furthermore, he attributes the injection of freedom and wit into English culture directly to Charles II.

Ranged against freedom and wit is the panoply of Whiggishness, as embodied by Shadwell, the monarch of dullness. Even the setting of "Mac Flecknoe" in the city center, London's commercial district, has political overtones. As one critic has noted, "Dryden's placing of the action in the mercantile center of London indicates the important and truly dangerous natural alliance he saw between Whigs, the mercantile middle classes, sedition, and bad art" (Wykes, pp. 180-81). It is this larger preoccupation that lies behind the more overtly political and topical concerns in the poem with coronations, succession, and legitimate rule. For Dryden, dullness threatened to undo the invigorating atmosphere of the Restoration itself.

"ABSALOM AND ACHITOPHEL"

Dryden changed the course of history with his masterful poem "Absalom and Achitophel," published shortly before "Mac Flecknoe," in 1681 at the height of the Exclusion Crisis. The poem turned the tide of public opinion against the Whigs and in favor of the king, thus allowing James, duke of York, to succeed to the throne on Charles's death in 1685. The poem capitalizes on parallels between the events of the Exclusion Crisis and the Biblical story of King David and his son Absalom, who is induced to revolt against his father by the king's treacherous advisor Achitophel. Particularly damning was Dryden's portrait of Charles's advisor Shaftesbury as the false Achitophel, "a name to all succeeding ages cursed":

> For close designs, and crooked counsels fit;
> Sagacious, bold and turbulent of wit;
> Restless, unfixed in principles and place;
> In power unpleased, impatient of disgrace;
> A fiery soul, which working out its way,
> Fretted the pygmy body to decay.
>
> ("Absalom and Achitophel," lines 150-57)

Sources and literary context. "Mac Flecknoe" represents the earliest example in English of a mock heroic or mock epic poem, a genre that would become influential among later writers. The mock epic takes the elevated style and dic-

tion of epic poetry and applies them to trivial or unworthy subjects, using the resulting disparity to make its humorous point. As the recurring references to Rome in "Mac Flecknoe" suggest, Dryden lived in an age that was preoccupied with ancient civilizations, particularly that of Rome, which many English saw their own nation as resembling or even emanating from. According to a medieval myth, a descendant of the Roman hero Aeneas, whose name was Brut or Brit (hence "Britain"), had led survivors from the Trojan War to found London, or New Troy. By Dryden's time, historians were challenging this myth, but it nonetheless had a tenacious hold on people, many of whom saw themselves as descendants of the Roman Empire.

Like all English gentlemen in this period, Dryden received a classical education in Greek and Latin literature. His ancient models can be found in the epics of Homer (the *Iliad* and the *Odyssey*) and Virgil (the *Aeneid*), with which he was intimately familiar. (Later he would translate the works of Virgil, including the *Aeneid,* from Latin into English.) Dryden found a more recent model in a 1667 English epic by John Milton, ***Paradise Lost*** (also in *WLAIT 3: British and Irish Literature and Its Times*), which dealt with the Biblical theme of the Fall of Man after Eve's temptation in the garden of Eden. Milton had worked in relative obscurity, and Dryden was among the first to recognize the magnitude of his poetic achievement, which may have been imposing enough to deflect Dryden from attempting a grand English epic of his own. Echoes from Milton's important work subtly pervade "Mac Flecknoe," as they do Dryden's other poetry.

Dryden's immediate inspiration for using the conventions of epic poetry to deprecate an unworthy subject can be found in the French mock epic *Le Lutrin* (1667), by Nicolas Boileau (1636-1711). "He writes it in the French Heroique Verse, and calls it an Heroique Poem: his Subject is Trivial, but the Verse is Noble," Dryden noted (Dryden in Miner, p. 196).

On a more superficial level, Dryden's sources for the poem include the works of Shadwell himself (to which Dryden frequently refers), as well as works of literary forebears (such as Jonson), most of whom are mentioned above. Again, the immediate catalyst for "Mac Flecknoe" seems to have been Shadwell's *The Virtuoso,* in which Shadwell excuses any faults by complaining that he does not have the luxury of writing on the pension awarded to others. Directed at Dryden, the barb probably inspired the retort that became "Mac Flecknoe."

Publication and impact. The exact date "Mac Flecknoe" was composed remains controversial, but recent scholarship suggests that it was almost certainly written as early as 1676. The poem circulated in manuscript for years before being published (some 15 manuscripts are known to have survived). Though very much an "in-joke" (owing to its highly allusive nature), it was popular enough to be pirated in 1682. Dryden himself authorized its anonymous publication in 1684 in *Miscellany Poems*, a poetry anthology published by Jacob Tonson in London. Yet not until 1693, the year after Shadwell's death, did Dryden publicly acknowledge authorship of both "Mac Flecknoe" and "Absalom and Achitophel," the poems now considered his two finest works.

As critics point out, were it not for "Mac Flecknoe," Thomas Shadwell would today be generally recognized as one of the three or four most significant Restoration playwrights—not a brilliant writer, certainly, but a competent one. As it is, his name has become a byword for literary stupidity, so devastating was the poem's impact on his reputation. The force of Dryden's satiric portrait inspired a number of imitators, notably the most brilliant poet of the early eighteenth century, Alexander Pope (1688-1744), whose mock epic *The Dunciad* openly takes "Mac Flecknoe" as its model in its excoriation of dullness.

—Colin Wells

Ashley, Maurice. *England in the Seventeenth Century.* Harmondsworth, England: Penguin, 1977.

Borgman, Albert S. *Thomas Shadwell: His Life and Comedies.* New York: New York University Press, 1928.

Dryden, John. "Mac Flecknoe." In *John Dryden: Selected Poems.* Ed. Christopher S. Nasaar. Harlow, England: Longman, 1987.

———. *Of Dramatic Poesie: An Essay.* Ed. John L. Mahoney. 1666. Reprint, Indianapolis: Bobbs-Merrill, 1965.

Hill, Christopher. *The Century of Revolution, 1603-1704.* New York: Norton, 1980.

Kunz, Don R. *The Drama of Thomas Shadwell.* Vol. 1. Salzburg: Institute Für Englische Sprache und Literatur, 1972.

Lockyer, Roger. *Tudor [and] Stuart Britain 1471-1714.* Harlow, England: Longman, 1964.

McFadden, George. *Dryden: The Public Writer, 1660-1685.* Princeton: Princeton University Press, 1978.

Miner, Earl, ed. *John Dryden.* Athens, Ohio: Ohio University Press, 1975.

Oden, Richard L., ed. *Dryden and Shadwell: The Literary Controversy and Mac Flecknoe, (1668-1679).* Delmar, New York: Scholars' Facsimiles and Reprints, 1977.

Winn, James A. *John Dryden and His World.* New Haven: Yale University Press, 1987.

Wykes, David. *A Preface to Dryden.* London: Longman, 1977.

Middlemarch: A Study of Provincial Life

by
George Eliot

George Eliot (the pen name of Mary Anne Evans) was born November 22, 1819, at South Farm, Arbury, Warwickshire, as the third child of land agent Robert Evans and Christiana Evans. The strong evangelical piety inculcated in her during childhood would stay with her until she encountered the ideas of the freethinker Charles Bray and his circle in the 1840s. In 1846 she translated the work of the radical biblical scholar D. F. Strauss and would later translate the works of theologians Ludwig Andreas Feuerbach and Baruch Spinoza. Settling in London in 1851, she exercised further intellectual influence as subeditor of *The Westminster Review*. In 1853 Eliot's friend Herbert Spencer introduced her to George Henry Lewes, one of the founders of the radical weekly *The Leader*. A man of liberal views, Lewes lived apart from his wife, who had borne a child by another man; because he had condoned her adultery, he was unable to sue for divorce. George Eliot and Lewes decided to live together openly and maintained a deep commitment to each other until his death in 1878. Two years later, she married an old friend, John Walter Cross, who was 21 years her junior, but died that same year on December 22. Encouraged by Lewes, Eliot had begun to publish fiction in 1857. *Middlemarch*, the sixth of her seven novels, is often considered her masterpiece because of its scope, variety, and the brilliance of its psychological analysis of provincial English life.

THE LITERARY WORK

A novel set in an English provincial town between 1829 and 1831; written in 1869-72; published in bimonthly and monthly installments from 1871-72.

SYNOPSIS

The novel traces the fate of high ideals in an English provincial town, as focused in the consciousness of a young woman.

Events in History at the Time of the Novel

The Industrial Revolution and rise of the middle class. The nineteenth century saw the growth of the British middle class. It emerged as a direct result of the Industrial Revolution, which began in Britain roughly between the 1760s-80s and concluded with the building of the railways and the advent of heavy industry in the 1840s. During this period, England's economy changed from one that was agrarian-based and handicraft-oriented, in which workers bought raw materials and produced goods at home in their cottages ("cottage industries"), to one dominated by urban, machine-driven manufacture (the "factory system"). As more factories appeared, two classes of workers began to emerge—the working class whose members produced the goods, and the group that

The nineteenth centiry saw the growth of the British middle class, a consequence of the Industrial Revolution, which lasted for nearly a century, ending with the building of the railways and the advent of heavy industry in the 1840s.

political economist Karl Marx would later describe as "capitalists," because they possessed the money or capital to buy the machines and buildings. The bankers, bureaucrats, and manufacturers—who comprised the capitalist faction of English society—came to be grouped with middle-class small farmers, shopkeepers, merchants, and skilled artisans, since the wealth of all these groups took the form of money and not land. Given mass production's dramatic increases in output and sales, the middle class managed to gain considerable wealth and power at the expense of the landed aristocracy and its agricultural concerns.

The increasing importance of the middle class is reflected by a concern in *Middlemarch* for the choice of vocation of its major characters. Now that society had become more fluid and shifting, relying increasingly on class distinctions rather than those of inherited rank, the choice of a profession gained importance. The experiences of the novel's Tertius Lydgate, Will Ladislaw, and Fred Vincy all illustrate the challenges experienced by young men of the early nineteenth century in finding an appropriate vocation when their "only capital [is] in their brains" (Eliot, *Middlemarch*, p. 201).

Along with the middle class's growing economic power came social power as well. Even the strictly hierarchical social structure of England's rural areas was affected. At the beginning of the century, the landed aristocracy, old and powerful families with hereditary titles and huge estates, occupied the top of this hierarchy. Ranked next were the local gentry, who had smaller properties that were nonetheless large enough to have tenants. Clergymen, high-ranking military officers, and barristers also belonged to this rank. Next came the yeoman farmers, the independent landowners with their large or small holdings, the bankers, and then the lesser tradesfolk and artisans. At the very bottom were the working poor and farm laborers.

With the arrival of industrialization, some of these rankings began to change. Although the local landed gentry still held the most respected positions in provincial society, families that possessed considerable amounts of capital rather than land were also gaining esteem and influence. In the novel, Mr. Vincy, who manufactures ribbons, and Nicholas Bulstrode, Middlemarch's banker, belong to this up-and-coming class. They are deemed important enough for Brooke, a member of the landed gentry who wants to run for Parliament, to invite them to dinner in the hopes of winning their political support. The shifting balance of power among the classes is also evident when Peter Featherstone, a gentleman farmer whose social position is one step below that of the landed gentry, accuses his nephew Fred Vincy of preferring his other uncle Mr. Bulstrode to himself; the small landowner feels threatened by the power of the capitalist.

Public health reform. Because the rise of railways and factories encouraged the concentration of an urban population, English provincial towns and cities grew rapidly around the time *Middlemarch* takes place. Between 1821 and 1831 the population of Manchester increased by 44.9 percent, that of Leeds by 47.3 percent, that of Bradford by 65.5 percent, and that of Liverpool by 45.8 percent (Briggs, p. 86). With the rise of cities came overcrowding and unhealthy working and living conditions that led activists to push for reform. Public health and sanitation became priorities in both urban and rural areas. In 1832 the Sadler Committee secured a parliamentary investigation of conditions in the textile factories. The investigation led to the Act of 1833, which limited the hours of employment for women and children in textile work. In 1842 Sir Edwin Chadwick initiated another investigation into the sanitary conditions of factories, and in 1855 Florence Nightingale reported on the state of rural hygiene. This was the nascent age of medical reform, with advances in both medical practice and

research. In Eliot's novel, Tertius Lydgate pushes for rural health reform around 1830—well ahead of Nightingale's efforts, making him a harbinger of changes soon to come. In real life, even earlier efforts at health reform produced revolutionary results. Edward Jenner, for example, had discovered and administered the first vaccinations in 1798.

TWO FLEDGLING PROFESSIONS

Neither surgeons nor journalists were highly esteemed in early-nineteenth-century society. In *Middlemarch*, Tertius Lydgate aspires to elevate his status and influence as a country surgeon by applying his skills as a scientist to his practice. Meanwhile, Mr. Vincy has reservations about his daughter Rosamond's engagement to Lydgate, since doctors occupied a lower financial status than wealthy manufacturers at the time. Newspaper editors suffered similar circumstances. Even editors of national papers rarely earned a living from full-time occupation in the field. Thus, Will Ladislaw's relatives are horrified when he agrees to serve as a newspaper editor in *Middlemarch*. His cousin, Mr. Casaubon, a member of the landed gentry, deems it unfitting for a relative of his to take up such a lowly occupation.

Political unrest and the age of revolution. Nineteenth-century English politics were heavily influenced by the ideology of the French Revolution (1789-93). In 1789, members of the French bourgeoisie called a meeting of the National Assembly and asserted their demands in a "Declaration of the Rights of Man and Citizens." This was a manifesto that protested noble privilege and hierarchy, but without supporting a democratic or egalitarian society. Although the first article proclaimed that "Men are born and live free and equal under the law," the Declaration also provided for the existence of social distinctions, for the bourgeoisie considered private property a natural, inalienable, and inviolable right.

The struggle between bourgeois and aristocratic powers continued into the nineteenth century, and in 1830 France was again thrown into turmoil when Charles X tried to curtail the powers fought so hard for in 1789. The July Revolution erupted when the king attempted to dissolve Parliament, abolish freedom of the press, and decrease the voting population. This revolution marked the defeat of the aristocrats by the middle class and ended with the king's being deposed. The overthrow of the French royal family triggered risings in Belgium (1830) and Poland (1830-31), and agitations in parts of Italy and Germany. Its effects also reached England: "The Reform Act of 1832 corresponds to the July Revolution of 1830 in France, and had indeed been powerfully stimulated by the news from Paris. . . . [T]his period is probably the only one in modern history when political events in Britain ran parallel with those on the continent, to the point where something not unlike a revolutionary situation might have developed in 1831-2 but for the restraint of both Whig and Tory [political] parties" (Hobsbawm, pp. 110-11).

Reform Bill of 1832. *Middlemarch* takes place between September 30, 1829, and the end of May 1832, during England's struggle for political reform, which culminated in the passage of the First Reform Bill in June 1832. As the middle class grew, so did its desire to protect its commercial and industrial interests. This desire was exacerbated by inequalities in parliamentary representation between rural areas and the rapidly growing cities. Even though rural England was more and more thinly populated, rural votes counted towards representation in Parliament, while many of the newer manufacturing cities with large, growing populations were not represented at all. Since the rural areas were for the most part controlled by aristocratic landowners and the cities were controlled by the middle class, its members found their political powers severely limited by the existing laws. Identified with the Whig party, the middle class launched a campaign to press for a bill that would allow them more political representation. At the beginning of the novel, the upper-class Tories—Dunder Arthur Wellesley, the duke of Wellington, Sir Robert Peel, and King George IV—are in control; conservatives, they manage to hold out against the forces of reform. However, with the death of George IV in June 1830 and the assumption of power by the Whigs under Lord Charles Grey as prime minister in November 1830, reform of some kind became inevitable.

The first great Reform Bill was introduced by Lord John Russell in March 1831. When it passed the second reading by only one vote, Lord Grey asked for a dissolution of Parliament to make his case to the rest of the country. The dissolution, which took place on April 22, marks the end of the last Parliament to be successful in blocking

reform, with the reformers eventually winning 90 seats. In the spring of 1832, after passing in the House of Commons, the Reform Bill went to the House of Lords. The House threw out the bill on May 7, 1832, at which point *Middlemarch* ends. But in a few weeks the same bill would be passed (June 7, 1832) under pressure of near rebellion.

The passage of the Reform Bill of 1832 by Grey's Whig government proved to be a hallmark in parliamentary reform. Seats were redistributed in favor of growing industrial cities, and qualifications were amended to give the right to vote to smaller property holders and all freeholders who owned at least 10 pounds. The bill disfranchised 56 boroughs, among them the so-called "rotten boroughs," which had very small populations (or none at all), and those known as "pocket boroughs," in which the number of representatives had been controlled by aristocratic landowners. It also gave representation to 42 cities and towns that had previously lacked it, among them Manchester, Birmingham, Sheffield, and Leeds. On the whole, the bill transferred political power from the landowning aristocrats to the middle class and subordinated the House of Lords to the popular will. It was the first of three major measures in the nineteenth century to liberalize parliamentary representation. Benjamin Disraeli and the Conservatives would pass the Reform Bill of 1867, which enfranchised working men in the towns and more than doubled the electorate, and in 1885 the electorate would again be doubled by enfranchising even more workers and agricultural laborers.

The Novel in Focus

Principal Characters

Dorothea Brooke A well-born, idealistic young woman

Edward Casaubon Her middle-aged husband, an Anglican clergyman and classical scholar

Will Ladislaw Casaubon's poor relation, who falls in love with Dorothea

Tertius Lydgate A newly arrived young doctor with good family connections

Rosamond Vincy Lydgate's wife and the daughter of the leading manufacturer in Middlemarch

Fred Vincy Rosamond's brother, who hopes to inherit property from his uncle, a gentleman farmer

Mary Garth Fred's childhood sweetheart, the daughter of a struggling land agent

Celia Brooke Dorothea's younger, more conventional sister

Sir James Chettam Celia's husband and Dorothea's former suitor
Brooke Dorothea and Celia's bachelor uncle and guardian
Nicholas Bulstrode Philanthropic banker who uses his money to further his religious beliefs

Plot summary. *Prelude*—George Eliot's Prelude introduces the novel's narrator as well as its most comprehensive theme: the scarcity of opportunity in the modern world for exceptional individuals to fulfill their promise. The narrator meditates on the life of St. Teresa, who lived 300 years before the novel opens, suggesting that there are "later-born Theresas" who instead of reforming a religious order never accomplished anything great because they are "helped by no coherent social faith and order" (*Middlemarch*, p. xiii). Eliot's narrator will guide us through this disappointing world, enfolding its action in compassionate psychological analysis.

Book 1—Miss Brooke. The novel is set in Middlemarch, a town in England's rural Midlands, and its environs. The heroine Dorothea Brooke and her sister Celia have only recently come to live at Tipton Grange, the estate of their uncle, Mr. Brooke. Beautiful and well-born, Dorothea has intellectual and spiritual ideals and ambitions that distinguish her from other women, most particularly her more conventional sister. "Open, ardent, and not in the least self-admiring," she is "enamoured of intensity and greatness" (*Middlemarch*, pp. 1, 3). Blinded by these ideals, she chooses to marry the elderly scholar and clergyman, Edward Casaubon, rector and owner of the prosperous Lowick estate, naively imagining that he has brilliant scholarly work before him to which she can devote herself.

Dorothea soon meets Casaubon's second cousin, Will Ladislaw, whose grandmother was disinherited for marrying a Polish political patriot. He is a footloose and artistic young man who refuses to choose a profession. Casaubon dislikes Will because the young man is critical of the scholar's patient and cautious approach to his work.

At this point, the novel introduces the principle family in town society, the Vincys. Mr. Vincy is the leading manufacturer of Middlemarch. His family is financially comfortable and socially ambitious; they have sent their oldest son, Fred, to Oxford, and their daughter, Rosamond, to a lady's school, where she can mingle with the children of gentility. Fred has just returned after failing his exams and acquiring the expensive habits of a gentleman. The current

hope is that Mrs. Vincy's brother, Peter Featherstone, an ailing old bachelor gentleman farmer, will make Fred the heir to his land and property at Stone Court. However, Fred is in a quandary because he has a gambling debt that he cannot pay, and the security is being held by Caleb Garth, whose daughter, Mary, is Fred's childhood sweetheart and present-day love. Caleb, a land agent, is not doing well enough in business for him to lose the money. Aside from her connection to Fred, Mary has another tie to the Vincy family. She nurses and otherwise cares for their uncle Featherstone to help her own family out.

Book 2—Old and Young. Another prominent businessman in Middlemarch, the banker Nicholas Bulstrode, uses his position in town to assert his personal religious views. He has just

---

ELIOT'S "RELIGION OF HUMANITY"

By Eliot's day, rational philosophy and modern science had made it more and more difficult for thinking people to accept the biblical story of creation and the traditional idea of a transcendent deity. Contrary to the biblical story that man was created in God's image, Darwin's *Origin of the Species* (1859) maintained that man and ape possess a common ancestor. Well acquainted with the advances in science and philosophy, George Eliot set out to reinvent meaningful existence in an age in which people were no longer bound together by a common, coherent social faith and order. How do we do our daily duty when God is no longer an accessible myth? How do we reconstruct the bonds of sympathy that were once so prominent in family and village? *Middlemarch* attempts to replace conventional religion with a so-called religion of humanity, in which faith and morality are to be found in the interdependent web of concerns that exist in the human community. We see a wide range of Anglican clergymen in *Middlemarch* (the conservative Cadwallader, the liberal Farebrother, and the evangelical Tyke), but none possess the spirituality of the heroine. In Book 8, Chapter 80, when Dorothea emerges from her great moral struggle, she looks out of her window at dawn to see figures moving in the distance: "She was part of that involuntary, palpitating life, and could neither look out on it from her luxurious shelter as a mere spectator, nor hide her eyes in selfish complaining." Her sense of "vivid sympathetic experience" now returned to her, she goes forth to help save Lydgate's reputation and marriage (*Middlemarch*, p. 544).

Middlemarch

offered a young doctor, Tertius Lydgate, the position of head superintendent at his new fever hospital in exchange for Lydgate's support of Bulstrode's choice for the old infirmary's chaplain. Unlike Fred, who cannot decide on a profession, Lydgate shows an intellectual passion for his medical practice akin to romantic love. Although he comes from a good family, Lydgate is an orphan whose father was a military man and left little provision for his children. Eager to be a medical and scientific reformer, he hopes that by working in the country he will "keep away from the range of London intrigues, jealousies, and social truckling, and win celebrity, however slowly, as Jenner [the discoverer of the vaccination] had done, by the independent value of his work" (*Middlemarch*, p. 100). These idealistic views about country politics are soon tested when Lydgate finds himself forced to cast the deciding vote for the infirmary chaplain; according to his bargain, he chooses Bulstrode's candidate against his friend Reverend Farebrother, identifying himself as one of Bulstrode's party.

Meanwhile, Dorothea Brooke is on her honeymoon in Rome, where she encounters Will Ladislaw. They soon become friends, and Will, who has fallen in love with Dorothea, decides he will return to England and choose a profession in hopes of winning her approval. Dorothea herself is disappointed with married life. Casaubon, who is much older and dispassionate by nature, is unable or unwilling to educate her about his intellectual pursuits and does not appreciate her affectionate nature. The couple has their first disagreement when Dorothea inadvertently wounds her husband by mentioning that she hopes he will soon begin to write his book.

Book 3—Waiting for Death. Back in Middlemarch, Fred falls ill with typhoid fever, and Rosamond suggests that they contact Lydgate for help. Once Fred is safely out of danger, the illness provides an excuse for Rosamond to flirt with Lydgate, which the neighbors notice. When Lydgate hears rumors of her engagement, however, he tries to avoid the Vincys, only in the end to impulsively engage himself to Rosamond when he sees her cry.

The Casaubons are by this time home from Rome and learn that Celia and the conventional Sir James Chettam have become engaged. Dorothea and Casaubon soon have another disagreement, this time over Will's visiting them, and Casaubon grows ill. Lydgate, who is called in to doctor the old scholar, warns that Casaubon must not overwork himself and ought to avoid

any mental agitation because of his heart. Dorothea asks her uncle to write Ladislaw not to come to Lowick, but Mr. Brooke instead secretly invites Ladislaw to his estate. He hopes that Will can help him with the newspaper he has purchased, the "Middlemarch Pioneer," to further his political ambitions for a seat in Parliament. Meanwhile, Casaubon is not the only one in his village who is seriously ill. Peter Featherstone's relatives have gathered around his deathbed, but it is his caretaker, Mary Garth, who is with him when he dies. He commands her to burn one of two wills he has made, but Mary refuses to do so, even if her refusal is likely to harm her sweetheart Fred's prospects, because burning the will may lay her open to suspicion.

Book 4—Three Love Problems. Featherstone's relatives gather to read his will, only to discover that most of the property, including his Stone Court home, has been bequeathed to a Joshua Rigg, an illegitimate son. In other words, his death has not enriched the Vincys. This disappointment makes Mr. Vincy unhappy about Rosamond's impending marriage to Lydgate, since the young doctor's practice is not established. Lydgate himself is financially naive and starts to spend beyond his means.

In the countryside, Dorothea's uncle has the landed gentry in an uproar because of his determination to win a seat in Parliament and support the Reform Bill, although he is notorious throughout the area as "a damned bad landlord" (*Middlemarch*, p. 247). It is only when Mr. Brooke must talk with an angry tenant who threatens him with the "Rinform" (in other words, "reform") that he decides to let the land agent Mr. Garth (Mary Garth's father) have a hand in the management of his estate (*Middlemarch*, p. 274). In the meantime, Ladislaw has accepted a position as editor of the local paper bought by Mr. Brooke to further his political ambitions, a job that Casaubon believes is beneath the family's dignity. Dorothea proceeds to add fuel to the fire, unintentionally angering Casaubon when she suggests that he give half his inheritance to Will. The book ends as Casaubon, insecure but proud, worries that Dorothea has become critical of his scholarly efforts, and blames Ladislaw for this turn of events. Casaubon also suspects that Ladislaw is scheming to marry Dorothea after his death.

Book 5—The Dead Hand. Dorothea consults Lydgate about her husband's health. The doctor takes the opportunity to ask her for a contribution to the new hospital. He mentions that jealousy and prejudice among the other practitioners is making support scarce; also, the town is suspicious of Lydgate's new methods. The young doctor refuses to prescribe unnecessary drugs, which makes him unpopular with the town's apothecaries. He also supports all kinds of new scientific practices, including autopsies and the improvement of hygiene; patients who prefer tried-and-true methods have become wary of him, and Lydgate's rival doctors are defensive because his insistence on reform implies a criticism of their established ways. The young doctor receives little sympathy at home, either—Rosamond, his new wife, admits, "I often wish you had not been a medical man," adding that his cousins think he has sunk in rank because of his profession (*Middlemarch*, p. 316).

It seems that the town is more interested in political than medical reform. At least Ladislaw is keeping himself busy, and he has begun to enjoy his work at the paper. Dorothea, however, finds that she does not like the uninspiring tasks that her husband gives her as work. Ever since Casaubon has learned that he could die at any moment, he has become more demanding of her time. When he tries to extract a promise from her that if he dies, she will carry out all his wishes, Dorothea hesitates. In the end, she reluctantly decides to comply, but before she can tell him, she finds him dead. Soon after the funeral, Dorothea discovers that her husband's will includes a recently added codicil prohibiting her from marrying Ladislaw on pain of losing Casaubon's property. The news only causes Dorothea to yearn for Ladislaw.

In Middlemarch, the townsmen are more interested in politics than in the landed gentry's problems. Ladislaw has been busy coaching Dorothea's uncle Brooke, who nonetheless delivers such a poor speech that it ends his political career. Brooke decides to give up the paper, which prompts Ladislaw to move from political journalism into politics; he predicts that "political writing, political speaking, would get a higher value now public life was going to be wider and more national, and they might give him such distinction that he would not seem to be asking Dorothea to step down to him" (*Middlemarch*, p. 351). These hopes of moving up socially will soon be dashed, however. Mr. Bulstrode, now the owner of Stone Court, has just been paid a visit by an acquaintance from the past, an alcoholic drifter named John Raffles. Raffles demands money to keep quiet about how Bulstrode once prevented a stepdaughter of his

(who would later become Ladislaw's mother) from inheriting some money.

Book 6—The Widow and the Wife. Fred Vincy finally decides on a career; he will learn the land business from Caleb Garth. Fred's sister, however, has been faring less well. Rosamond has lost the child she was carrying because she disobeyed Lydgate and went riding with one of his upper-class relatives. Lydgate is also worried about their growing debt, but Rosamond shows little sympathy for the problem and only suggests that they ask her father for money or leave Middlemarch for London, which Lydgate refuses to do. Meanwhile, Raffles accosts Ladislaw with information about his mother: she ran away from her family when she found out they were Jewish pawnbrokers. Bulstrode has a guilty conscience because her disappearance made it possible for him to acquire the entire fortune and he made no attempt to contact her. To ease his conscience, he offers Ladislaw money, which the young man rejects as morally tainted because of the association with Jewish pawnbroking. Discouraged by the news concerning his family, he visits Dorothea again. During the conversation, Dorothea realizes that Ladislaw loves her and feels elated, but she keeps her love for him to herself. This part ends with Will leaving Middlemarch.

Book 7—Two Temptations. Lydgate's money troubles have worsened. His attempts to discuss economizing with Rosamond only alienate her from him. Rosamond arranges everything as she pleases, countermanding Lydgate's efforts to find a buyer for their house and writing to Sir Godwin Lydgate, Tertius's well-to-do uncle, for money. In desperation, Lydgate finally asks Bulstrode for the money. The banker complies, but the deed will come back to haunt Lydgate. Raffles has become very ill from an attack of alcohol poisoning, and Bulstrode decides to loan Lydgate money to put him under obligation in case Raffles says something incriminating about Bulstrode to Dr. Lydgate. Also Bulstrode neglects to tell Raffles's attendant about the doctor's orders not to let Raffles take alcohol, which anyway was a controversial prescription for the time. Raffles dies. Bulstrode believes that his secret is now safe, but rumors have already spread among the townspeople. They ostracize Bulstrode and also Lydgate, whom they believe has been bribed to keep silent.

Book 8—Sunset and Sunrise. When Rosamond finds out about the scandal, she remains unsympathetic and fantasizes about falling in love with Ladislaw. Only Dorothea tells Lydgate that she believes he is innocent, and Lydgate is touched. The two commiserate, and she sympathetically asserts, "There is no sorrow I have thought more about than that—to love what is great, and try to reach it, and yet to fail" (*Middlemarch*, p. 527). All her life she has had the ambition to accomplish something that would help others less fortunate than herself, but she has not been able to find out how to do so. She offers to help him with the hospital. But Lydgate confesses that his wife does not want to stay in Middlemarch, and he is having trouble communicating with her anyway. Dorothea then offers to speak with Rosamond.

JEWS IN VICTORIAN ENGLAND

Toward the end of the novel, Middlemarch discovers that young Will Ladislaw has, in the words of one of its inhabitants, "a queer genealogy" that includes "a grafting of the Jew pawnbroker" (*Middlemarch*, p. 497). During this period, Jews in England were still primarily dependent on the finance trades. The wealthiest of Jewish families worked as stock brokers, merchant bankers, and large-scale merchants. Most Jewish families, however, did not possess anywhere near the kind of wealth that Ladislaw's grandparents had achieved; the vast majority were immigrants from Central Europe who were struggling to make ends meet (Lipman, pp. 27-34).

Uneasiness with minorities in nineteenth-century England is evident in the novel. The clergyman who mentions this news about Ladislaw's heritage goes on to observe that "there's no knowing what a mixture will turn out beforehand. Some sorts of dirt serve to clarify," while another townsman expresses his hostility towards "[a]ny cursed alien blood, Jew, Corsican, or Gypsy" (*Middlemarch*, p. 497). Discrimination moreover was legally condoned. Jews could not legally carry on retail trade in the city of London until 1830, and professing Jews could not exercise the parliamentary franchise until 1835. Only with the Jewish Relief Act of 1858 did the House of Commons finally dispense with the Christian words of the admission oath, thus allowing Jews to hold seats in Parliament.

After Lydgate leaves, Dorothea forms a plan to loan him the money he borrowed from Bulstrode and to deliver the check when she visits Rosamond. When she visits Rosamond the next day, however, she finds Ladislaw holding Rosa-

mond's hands and assumes the worst, although Ladislaw visits Rosamond only because he is friends with Lydgate and enjoys playing music with her. Ladislaw is horrified and Dorothea leaves immediately in shock and humiliation. After a night of great moral struggle, however, she decides that it is her duty to go back and offer Rosamond her sympathy about Lydgate's disgrace. Touched by Dorothea's generosity, and in a rare moment of unselfishness, Rosamond tells Dorothea how innocent her relationship with Ladislaw really is. When Ladislaw comes to see Dorothea again, the two decide that they love each other so much that they will get married in spite of his parentage, his poverty, and what Middlemarch thinks.

Finale. Mr. Bulstrode gives Stone Court to his wife, and she decides to ask Mr. Garth to adopt his original plan with respect to having Fred help manage the property. Fred Vincy becomes a successful farmer, and Mary publishes a children's book. The Lydgates move to London where the doctor builds a successful medical practice among the rich, but he dies when he is only 50, having "always regarded himself as a failure" because he never realized his scientific ambitions. (*Middlemarch*, p. 575). Although Dorothea is happily married to Ladislaw, who becomes a member of Parliament, "Dorothea herself had no dreams of being praised above other women, feeling that there was always something better which she might have done, if she had only been better and known better" (*Middlemarch*, p. 575). Despite these disappointments, the novel ends by affirming the incalculably diffusive effect of the unhistoric acts of goodness by people like Dorothea, who "lived faithfully a hidden life and rest in unvisited tombs" (*Middlemarch*, p. 578).

Gender and class. In *Middlemarch*, conventional attitudes about gender roles and class identity lead to poor marital choices. As an unmarried woman not yet in control of her property, Dorothea longs "for the time when she would be of age and have some command of money for generous schemes" (*Middlemarch*, p. 2). She realizes that her sphere for doing good is limited to that of the home, but she hopes to circumvent these limitations by serving as a helpmate to a man who does the kind of work in which she believes. Dorothea chooses Edward Casaubon as her husband because, compared to the other potential suitors available to her in her small social circle, he comes closest to caring for the spiritual and intellectual matters most important to her. Having unsuccessfully searched for a purpose to her life, she rejoices that "[n]ow she would be able to devote herself to large yet definite duties; now she would be allowed to live continually in the light of a mind that she could reverence" (*Middlemarch*, p. 28).

Dorothea soon discovers that her idealism is misplaced. Casaubon is trying to write a religious history, the "Key to All Mythologies," which proves "that all the mythical systems or erratic mythical fragments in the world were corruptions of a tradition originally revealed" (*Middlemarch*, p. 14). As Will Ladislaw points out to Dorothea, Casaubon's efforts are hopelessly wasted "as so much English scholarship is, for want of knowing what is being done by the rest of the world"—he is referring to new German scholarship with which Eliot herself was familiar (*Middlemarch*, p. 144). Casaubon himself holds conventional views about women; he marries Dorothea because he deems her intelligent enough to help him with his studies and to admire him, but not knowledgeable enough to make him feel insecure.

Likewise, Lydgate's conventional views of women cause him to marry Rosamond Vincy; he prefers women that he believes to be passive and helpless, and finds he does not care for the more intellectual Dorothea initially because "it is troublesome to talk to such women" (*Middlemarch*, p. 63). He assumes that if a woman does not express her thoughts, she cannot possess any complicated ones. Little does he know that Rosamond only pretends to be passive in order to get what she desires. Lydgate does not realize that she is attracted to him primarily because of her aspirations to become part of the landed gentry, with which he is associated because of his heritage. She feels ashamed of being middle class. "Rosamond felt that she might have been happier if she had not been the daughter of a Middlemarch manufacturer. She disliked anything which reminded her that her mother's father had been an innkeeper" (*Middlemarch*, p. 69). When Lydgate finds that they are in debt and tries to economize, Rosamond refuses to cooperate because she does not want to lose her dreams of social position. But the way she resists is not by arguing with him—her supposed passivity allows her to not have to communicate; she simply ignores his orders and does as she pleases. Yet, even well after Lydgate realizes this about her, he cannot help treating her as weaker than himself: "He wished to excuse everything in her if he could but it was inevitable that in that excusing mood he should think of her as if she

were an animal of another and feebler species." Nevertheless, "she had mastered him" (*Middlemarch*, p. 461).

Sources and literary context. The origins of *Middlemarch* date from early in 1869 when Eliot began writing a story about Tertius Lydgate confronting the fictional town of the novel. Set during the years of Eliot's childhood in Coventry and the surrounding Warwickshire of England's midlands near where she was raised, much of the depiction of town and country life belongs to the writer's own personal memories. The character Caleb Garth, for example, holds the same occupation as Eliot's own father, that of a land agent.

However, Eliot also did considerable research in areas she was less familiar with, scientific and medical reform as well as political history, as evidenced in a small notebook titled *Quarry for "Middlemarch"* that she used while writing the novel. She learned about late-eighteenth-century French scientists such as the pathologist Francois Bichat, the physician and surgeon Francois Broussais, the chemist Francois Raspail, and the physician Rene Laennec from the English translation of Renouard's *History of Medicine* (1856) and from J. R. Russell's *History and Heroes of the Art of Medicine* (1861). Eliot also read *The Lancet*, a medical journal, as well as specific articles dealing with medical issues, to follow the controversies and developments that interested the scientific community of her day. Work, however, progressed slowly and in December 1870 she began to write another story called "Miss Brooke." This story grew in complexity and length, and in the spring of 1871, Eliot decided to merge the two tales into a novel, which became so long that George Lewes decided it could not be sold as a "triple-decker" novel, the three-part form typical of the Victorian novel. Instead he published it in eight parts, dividing the novel into small, affordable installments.

Events in History at the Time the Novel Was Written

Post-reform malaise. *Middlemarch* reflects the atmosphere of malaise felt by many people, particularly intellectuals, as they contemplated the reforming zeal of the 1820s and 1830s to produce a significantly better society. In 1859 John Stuart Mill had published *On Liberty*, a work that expresses the political philosopher's anxieties about the rise of democratic individualism. Such a society will be better for the average person, he argues, but not for the person of extraordinary

A nineteenth-century woman sits reading with a young girl. Female readers were condoned in Eliot's day. Female writers were more controversial.

talent. The "tyranny of public opinion" that Mill feared would rule modern democracy finds a parallel in the ascendance of mediocrity in Middlemarch society. At the end of *Middlemarch*, we learn that neither Dorothea nor Lydgate realize their ambitions or abilities. This is the result perhaps of circumstances in Eliot's own time. The 1820s and 1830s were a period of great optimism, but the period in which George Eliot wrote the novel was not.

The "Woman Question." George Eliot wrote *Middlemarch* in 1869-71, at a time when women were beginning to write and publish their work for money in increasing numbers. Among other English female writers of the day were Elizabeth Barrett Browning, Christina Rossetti, and Charlotte and Emily Brontë (see **Wuthering Heights**, also in *WLAIT 3: British and Irish Literature and Its Times*). It was also the period in which the controversy over "The Woman Question," the political and economic rights of women, gained a new intensity. In 1869, political economist John Stuart Mill wrote *The Subjection of Women*, which warns of the dangers of not allowing women more opportunity. The next year, 1870, saw the passing of the Married Women's Property Act, which removed some of the legal in-

equalities between the sexes in Britain. But work for women outside the home remained an exception in the Victorian era. Mainstream Victorian society believed women and men must occupy separate spheres because they have distinct natures, distinct capacities, and hence distinct tasks. The traditional ideal required that a woman be admired for skills that made her an agreeable hostess and an effective housewife and mother.

Thus, considerable disagreement among even literary men developed when an increasing number of women chose to write and publish fiction. Opinions ranged from the poet Robert Southey's discouraging advice to Charlotte Brontë that "literature cannot be the business of a woman's life, and it ought not to be," to the enthusiastic support of literary critic and biographer G. H. Lewes, the man who would soon become George Eliot's life companion (Southey in Gay, p. 330). In an essay entitled "The Lady Novelists" Lewes argues that "the advent of female literature promises woman's view of life, woman's experience; in other words, a new element" because of her "greater affectionateness, her greater range and depth of emotional experience" (Lewes in Gay, pp. 331-32). This comment obviously reflects another stereotype of the day, albeit a positive one: accepting the belief that the sexes belong in separate spheres because they possess different but complementary natural capacities, Lewes asserts that a woman's special emotional sensitivity should make her a worthy writer of fiction.

Eliot, who did not personally experience much of the criticism that Victorian society directed at women writers, nevertheless wrote essays on women's rights and women writers. In 1855, a sympathetic essay on Margaret Fuller and Mary Wollstonecraft (see **A Vindication of the Rights of Woman,** also in *WLAIT 3: British and Irish Literature and Its Times*) praises the two writers for bringing attention to "the fact, that, while men have a horror of such faculty or culture in the other sex as tends to place it on a level with their own, they are really in a state of subjection to ignorant and feeble-minded women" (Eliot, *Essays,* pp. 203-204).

However, in her essay on "Silly Novels by Lady Novelists" in 1856, Eliot ridicules the unrealistically beautiful, gifted, and religious heroines so common in women's fiction for living in a society that presents no serious problems for its inhabitants. Instead, she encourages woman writers to keep to higher literary standards, asserting that "women can produce novels not only fine, but among the very finest" (Eliot, *Essays*, pp. 323-24).

Like many of the women writers of her day, George Eliot chose to publish her fiction under a male pseudonym even though she did not need to do so for the same reasons that other women did; by the time she wrote her first works of fiction, she was already well respected as an intellectual and did not have to worry that male reviewers would slight her work because she was a woman. Rather, it was Lewes, who also served as Eliot's literary agent, who thought that the mystery of a pen name might be helpful for both critical and marketing purposes.

Reception. *Middlemarch* was a commercial success, and praise was unanimous. *The Telegraph* reported it "almost profane to speak of ordinary novels in the same breath with George Eliot's" and there were favourable reviews by the *Edinburgh Review*, the *Quarterly*, the *Fortnightly*, the *Spectator*, and the *Athenaeum* (Haight, p. 444). Given the breadth of topics covered in the novel, the reasons for the acclaim also tended to vary considerably. In his review for the *Fortnightly* from January 19, 1873, Sidney Colvin was impressed by "a medical habit in the writer" (Colvin in Hornback, p. 651). Edith Simcox wrote in the *Academy* of the "perfect realistic truth to a profoundly imaginative psychological study" (Simcox in Haight, p. 444). The flaws perceived in the book were also diverse. Many found the novel pessimistic. Probably the most famous criticism of the book came from the young Henry James, writing in *The Galaxy* in March, 1873: in his eyes the novel was "a treasure-house of detail, but . . . an indifferent whole" (James in Hornback, p. 652). In particular, critics challenged the ending, especially the passages in the penultimate paragraph in which the narrator appears to blame society for Dorothea's difficulties (Eliot removed much of the passage from her subsequent editions). However, some 30 years later in 1919, writer Virginia Woolf would praise rather than criticize this seriousness, calling *Middlemarch* "one of the few English novels written for grownup people" (Woolf, p. 168).

—Junehee Chung

For More Information

Beaty, Jerome. "History by Indirection: The Era of Reform in *Middlemarch*." *Victorian Studies* 1 (1957-58): 173-79.

Briggs, Asa. *Victorian Cities*. Berkeley, Calif.: University of California Press, 1963.

Eliot, George. *Middlemarch*. Ed. Bert G. Hornback. New York: W. W. Norton, 1977.

———. *Essays of George Eliot*. Ed. Thomas Pinney. London: Routledge and Kegan Paul, 1963.

Furst, Lilian R. "Struggling for Medical Reform in *Middlemarch*." *Nineteenth-Century Literature* 48:3 (December 1993): 341-61.

Gay, Peter. *The Bourgeois Experience, Victoria to Freud*. Vol. 3., *The Cultivation of Hatred*. New York: W. W. Norton, 1993.

Haight, Gordon S. *George Eliot: A Biography*. New York: Oxford University Press, 1968.

Hobsbawm, Eric. *The Age of Revolution, 1789-1848*. New York: Vintage, 1962.

Hornback, Bert G. *Middlemarch: A Novel of Reform*. Boston: Twayne, 1988.

Lipman, V. D. *Social History of the Jews in England, 1850–1950*. London: Watts, 1954.

Woolf, Virginia. "George Eliot." In *The Common Reader*. First Series. Ed. Andrew McNeillie. London: The Hogarth Press, 1984.

Wright, T. R. *George Eliot's Middlemarch*. Hemel Hempstead, Hertfordshire: Harvester Wheatsheaf, 1991.

Moll Flanders

by
Daniel Defoe

THE LITERARY WORK

A novel set in London and North America at the end of the seventeenth century; published in England in 1722.

SYNOPSIS

A lower-class Englishwoman lives a long life filled with crime, peril, and adventure, then settles into a pious old age.

Daniel Defoe was born in 1660, the son of a candlemaker in London. He originally intended to become a tradesman, but his incompetence with money (nearly all of his businesses failed) and strong interest in public affairs led him to his real vocation: writing. Beginning in 1700, he produced a torrent of pamphlets, newspaper articles, poems, and books on subjects ranging from accounts of true crimes to the history of the devil. Amazingly prolific, and often working just one step ahead of his creditors, Defoe transformed such genres as political commentary and journalism: he practically invented the English newspaper with his work for the *Review*, which he founded and published and of which he was sole author for nine years. Not surprisingly, given these conditions, Defoe's writing is brisk, efficient, and concerned with contemporary life in all its variety. He brought these qualities to *Moll Flanders*, a novel that reflects his nonfiction writings on such contemporary topics as crime, prostitution, colonization, and the nature of marriage.

Events in History at the Time the Novel Takes Place

Women of ill repute. Though Moll Flanders is never, by modern standards, a prostitute, in seventeenth- to eighteenth-century terms she is branded as such. On a number of occasions in the novel, she becomes a mistress, or kept woman—in other words, a whore of high status. Her series of relationships with men highlights the common problems that led many women of the period to make a living with their bodies, and her matter-of-fact acceptance of her behavior indicates how readily extramarital sex (in exchange for financial support) was accepted in late-seventeenth-century England.

Actually, the late seventeenth century was a golden age for English prostitution. Of course, there were earlier and later advantageous periods too. Prostitutes had faced few legal troubles from 1161 to 1548, when London's bordellos were licensed by the bishop of Winchester, and the practice proliferated in nineteenth-century Victorian London, which had some 3,000 brothels. But the years between 1660 and 1700 were a high-water mark for the profession: at no other time were prostitutes, as a class, so socially visible, nor was there ever a time when the highest class of prostitutes, such as the courtesans of King Charles II, were so celebrated and influential. The period following Charles's restoration to

An engraving of 1731–32 by William Hogarth, depicting a harlot's progress as she is ensnared by a procuress.

the English throne in 1660 is known as one of the most cheerfully amoral in the history of England. Extramarital liaisons not only flourished, but actually became a source of public entertainment in the form of widely circulated gossip. Poets and playwrights celebrated the ideal of the rake, the young man of leisure who devotes himself to conquering as many women as he can. The most successful prostitutes and madams were nearly as famous as the preeminent politicians, so much so that in 1668 two famous bawds, Elizabeth Cresswell and Damaris Page, addressed a satirical pamphlet to the king's favorite courtesan: "The Poor Whore's Petition to the Most Splendid Illustrious Serene and Eminent Lady of Pleasure, the Countess of Castlemaine" (Burford, p. 83).

Lack of options was the principal force driving women to this recourse. Women raised on public charity, as Moll is, nearly always found it difficult to locate men willing to marry them, and only rich women could be secure without entering into a marriage. Women did have opportunities to work, but jobs that were legal did not pay very well, and many (such as hotel work, domestic service, and even acting) carried their own sexual dangers. People generally assumed, often correctly, that actresses, for example, were also available as prostitutes. Of her few options, the woman in financial trouble was likely to decide that prostitution, while immoral, was the most comfortable as well as the most lucrative alternative—especially when society nodded so indulgently at the profession. Women who moved to London from the countryside were especially vulnerable; when the city failed to provide them with honest work, they did not have a network of family or friends to keep them from poverty.

Even marriage was no guarantee of security. Moll is married five times, and at the end of each marriage she finds herself in renewed dire straits. She comes to realize that, in marriage, a woman is considered property or a status symbol more than a companion or even a sex object. She concludes that "marriages were here the Consequences of politick Schemes for forming Interests, and carrying on Business, and that Love had no share, or but very little in the Matter . . . any other Qualification, whether of Body or Mind, had no power to recommend: That money only made a Woman agreeable . . . Money was the thing" (Defoe, *Moll Flanders*, pp. 53-54).

Moll is at least partly right. Marriage for love was gaining ground in English society, but the old view—marriage as an alliance to maintain or promote social status—still held considerable sway. The case of Priss Fotheringham, a lower-class madam of the Stuart period, shows that Moll's conclusion is not unreasonable for her circumstances and time. Fotheringham was married while very young to a man who not only beat her, but also forced her to prostitute herself. She abandoned this man and began to represent herself as a widow, eventually marrying a halbardier (a type of soldier). But while her pimping husband was easy to escape, the lure of easy money was not; Priss set herself up as a prostitute again, with her new husband's aid. Before long, she had established a thriving brothel, the Six Windmills, mentioned in many topical tracts of the period as a notorious den of vice. While marriage, then, was the surest route for a woman to achieve financial stability, it by no means eliminated the danger of entering the "world's oldest profession" —a bad husband could drive a woman to prostitution even more quickly than no husband. Damaris Page, a great bawd for seamen, found many of her prostitutes among women whose husbands had been drafted into the British Navy, and who faced an indefinite period without a wage-earner to support them. Perhaps worst-off were impoverished widows: too old to attract a new husband easily, but with children in need of food and clothing, a widow was apt to turn to the tenuous financial support provided by so-called "temporary husbands."

At certain points, Moll is very close to the financial trouble that might have forced her into the lowest class of prostitute, the common street-walker. Like the real Priss Fotheringham, she marries poorly, to a man who spends all her money and leaves her destitute. Defoe spares his heroine the fate of the streetwalker, however, and instead Moll turns into a prostitute of a very different ilk. Neither streetwalker nor bawd, she becomes the exclusive mistress of her employer's son, and later of a man whose legal wife has gone insane. In modern times, this relationship has been excluded from the definition of prostitution, but in the heavily Christian eighteenth century, it was simply whoredom with a kinder face. Moll is quite clearly dependent on both her lovers, and they treat her as a pseudo-wife; in short, they give her money for the privilege of sex.

RIBALD DITTIES

~

During the reign of Charles II, performers filled the streets of London singing ribald lyrics that reflected the public's impressions of the king's latest lovers. Lady Castlemaine, famous for her boundless libido and her undisguised ambition to sustain her official position as royal mistress, became the frequent target of sexually suggestive ditties. The earl of Rochester penned one verse that captured popular opinion of the day about how thoroughly she dominated the hopelessly infatuated Charles II: "Nor are his high Desires above his Strength; / His sceptre and his _____ are of a length. / And she that plays with one, may sway the other, / And make him little wiser than his Brother [James II]." (Masters, p. 69)

The kept woman was the princess of prostitutes; she was treated with respect, lived opulently, and (if she was careful) could amass enough to live on when she had grown old or could no longer find a lover to support her. Those who were not provident in this way often turned to procuring young women for their rich friends. Though it is impossible to identify the number of kept women at the end of the seventeenth century, it was certainly a common option for women. Many female lovers of high-placed aristocrats and politicians even became public figures in their own right, both celebrated and reviled. In undertaking her line of work, Moll is following a path set by King Charles himself, whose many mistresses, as noted, became subject matter for songs, newspapers, and pamphlets.

Criminal punishment. Moll Flanders's life, from beginning to end, is framed by the law. She enters the world in Newgate Prison, London's notorious jail for all sorts of social undesirables—from juvenile pickpockets to homicidal madmen. Throughout her career as a criminal, she constantly faces the specter of punishment, and finally is expelled from England to the English colony in Virginia. To understand the novel, then, it is necessary to understand the punishment a criminal risked.

NEWGATE

~

Nothing symbolized official punishment more frighteningly than Newgate Prison, the place where Moll Flanders is born. Established in the twelfth century, by the end of the eighteenth century Newgate had grown to a two-winged, four-story building capable of holding more than 600 prisoners. The prison was notorious for disease, disorder, and discontent. Prisoners, except those condemned to death, mixed freely, men with women and petty criminals with hardened murderers. Its main halls remained cast in semi-darkness, the air was dank, and food and water were always inadequate. Sanitation consisted of filthy, rarely cleaned pots in the corner of each long cell; more inmates died from "jail fever" than were carried to the gallows. The jail was split, as it had been for centuries, along class lines: inmates with adequate money were allowed to buy their own food and clothing and could bribe the guards for privileges, while the poorer criminals were left to rot in their own filth. Despite the grim conditions, Newgate inspired a kind of ghastly camaraderie among inmates, who, complained critics of the prison, diced and whored as freely as they would have in the outside world.

The picture of law and punishment in late-seventeenth-century England is far from pretty. Legal theorists had not yet developed ideas of rehabilitating criminals so that they would commit no more crimes. A criminal was not a person to be saved, but, rather, a wrongdoer deserving strict punishment, which was usually physical, often brutally so. Sentences for prostitution included the pillory (in which the convict, hands and feet bound in wood, was put on display for a set period of time in a central square), ducking (in which a convict was repeatedly immersed in water), and even caging (in which the unlucky

person was placed in a cage). Common to all these sentences was carting (being carried through the streets) and public humiliation. The punishment exposed the criminal to ridicule, which crowds of Londoners readily supplied, jeering and throwing rotten fruit.

Moll is also a thief, an occupation fraught with more ominous penalties. By the middle of the eighteenth century, close to 150 crimes were punishable by death, including nearly all crimes that involved theft of property. Worse, this ultimate price was imposed even on first-time offenders; every time a thief plied his trade, he or she had to be prepared, in principle, to lay down his or her life for the item stolen. In practice, far more convicts were sentenced to die than were actually put to death. Legal theorists held that capital punishment should be attached to a wide variety of crimes to demonstrate the power of the state but meted out to only a fraction of each type of criminal. Any convict who could find an advocate, or who had friends willing to plead on his or her behalf, stood a good chance of being pardoned. In the novel, Moll finds a minister willing to plead on her behalf. This remedy had to be found quickly: a capital criminal could not count on a lengthy stay in prison; if a pardon did not come soon, the cart to the gallows would. Public executions were an almost daily occurrence throughout the period.

In sum, punishment tended to be both brutal and somewhat random; the state castigated freely, but inconsistently. Eighteenth-century criminologists had little sense of how to prevent crime from occurring; their only strategy was to make the criminal's life as uncomfortable as possible. Although the modern myth of a brutal England, where life was cheap and public executions the main entertainment, is undeniably overstated, it does reflect a truth about the way crime was perceived in the period: the culprit deserved physical abuse and ought to be made a spectacle.

The Novel in Focus

Plot summary. *Moll Flanders,* like all of Daniel Defoe's novels, is quick-paced and full of action. Moll narrates and, like her creator, proves to be much more interested in facts and actions than quiet contemplation. Her life is both long and varied, with every brief period of security surrounded by struggles involving penury and the law: Moll is rich, then poor, then rich again, her fortunes seemingly directed by pure chance rather than by her own formidable will.

Robin Wright as Moll Flanders in the 1996 movie production of Defoe's enduring tale.

Moll's mother is a professional thief. At 18 months, Moll loses her mother, who is transported to the colony of Virginia, a fate often visited upon convicted felons who escape the death penalty. Moll spends her early childhood in various settings, eventually settling into the home of the mayor of Colchester.

When Moll reaches 14, however, her benefactress dies, and Moll must fend for herself once more. She finds employment as a domestic servant in the home of a rich widow with growing children, and suffers the indignity of waiting on young girls to whom she feels absolutely superior in all but wealth. While the girls irritate her, she loses her virginity to her employer's eldest son, and lives for a time as his secret mistress. In the end, though, it is the youngest son, Robin,

who proposes to her. This sets an alternating pattern that will recur throughout Moll's life: a period of criminal or immoral behavior, followed by a period of happy respectability.

Even this early on, Moll shows the adaptability and practicality that will be her defining features. She accepts Robin's offer, and they live happily together in London. Robin dies after five years, however, and, left to her own devices, Moll makes her biggest matrimonial error, wedding a draper (a seller of cloth) who quickly spends all the money she had saved and ends up in debtor's prison. Rather than work to free him, Moll moves to a boarding house and begins calling herself a widow.

Next Moll meets and marries a ship's captain, and the two decide to move to Virginia, where

Moll feels she will be able to make a fresh start. Instead of a new beginning, however, she is forced to confront her past in the person of her mother, who, it will be recalled, was transported to Virginia before Moll's second birthday. The joy of this occasion is significantly dampened by the discovery that Moll's mother is also her husband's mother; Moll has unwittingly married, and born children for, her half-brother. The marriage is discreetly dissolved, and Moll eventually returns to England, where she settles in Bath and becomes a mistress once more, falling in love with a man whose wife is insane. Moll and this man live together for six years, during which she bears him four children, each sent out to be nursed at birth so that she can continue her duties as mistress. When, after six years, the man develops a conscience and ends the relationship, Moll is not unduly upset; she convinces him to leave her with 50 pounds, and in return, she promises not to bother him again. Adding this amount to the 450 pounds she has managed to save, Moll takes stock of her worldly possessions (some silver, some clothes, and plenty of linens) and faces her future alone once again.

DEFOE'S FULL TITLE

Eighteenth-century readers expected titles to provide a reasonably full description of a book's contents; in the case of *Moll Flanders*, this was no easy feat. The title page of the first edition reads, "The Fortunes and Misfortunes of the Infamous Moll Flanders, who was born in Newgate, and during a life of continued variety, for threescore years, besides her childhood, was twelve years a Whore, five times a wife (thereof once to her own brother), twelve years a Thief, eight years a transported Felon in Virginia, at last grew rich, lived honest, and died a penitent. Written from her own Memorandums."

Longing for a settled home, but having no idea how to find it, Moll lives frugally, the terror of poverty always present. She meets a man, Jemmy, who represents himself as a wealthy gentleman of Lancashire, and she hints that she too has great wealth. As the two approach marriage, she discovers the truth: the man is simply a highwayman and confidence man by trade. She reveals to him that she, too, is not wealthy. Both corrupt but good-natured, they live together for a time in great happiness. When Jemmy decides to

revert to his first love, highway robbery, however, Moll returns to London.

Back in London, Moll marries a bank clerk she has known for some time and for five years, until his death, she lives a completely virtuous life. After he dies, she sells her property and once more rents rooms in a boarding house. Then one day she asserts that the devil has persuaded her to steal items from an apothecary's shop. Still reeling from that theft, she steals a necklace from a schoolgirl. In short order, Moll has embarked on the next phase of her life: a career as a thief. She prowls the streets and fairs of London, picking pockets and snatching up unwatched goods. After an apprenticeship in which she teaches herself the art of theft, this career takes off. At an advanced age (she is now over 50), Moll becomes the richest thief in England.

One day Moll is caught trying to steal silk from a clothier, which ends her 12-year career as a thief. She is committed to Newgate, the very jailhouse in which she was born. There she sees Jemmy, her former husband, who has likewise been convicted of robbery. Both are sentenced to die, but manage to get their sentences commuted. Moll will be transported to Virginia, as her mother had been; accompanied by Jemmy, whom she accepts as her husband once again, she embarks on her second trip to the colonies.

Moll and Jemmy do not live very much like felons in the New World. They commit themselves to honest lives, though they fund those lives with the goods they acquired through robbery. They establish a plantation in Maryland and soon have a farm of 50 acres. But their good fortune does not end here: when Moll goes to visit her brother and former husband, she learns that their mother has died. Prospering in the New World just as Moll is now doing, she willed Moll a great plantation in Virginia. Now doubly wealthy, Moll and Jemmy settle into the quiet life of colonial planters. All the tumult of years spent in often-unlawful acquisition is over. When she is 70, Moll returns to England, followed by her husband. They decide to spend the rest of their lives in strict piety, in atonement for their many sins.

Money, charity, and individualism. One of the most curious features of *Moll Flanders* is its heroine's meticulous attention to her pocketbook. The novel is punctuated with lists of Moll's possessions, and at key moments she is as much concerned with her material wealth as with her state of mind. The revelation of Moll and Jemmy's mutual deception about their financial status is a poignant moment; Moll blurs the line between matters of money and matters of the heart: "Nothing that ever befel me in my Life sunk so deep into my Heart as this Farewel . . . for I would have gone with him thro' the World, if I had beg'd my Bread. I felt in my Pocket, and there I found ten Guineas, his Gold Watch, and two little Rings" (*Moll Flanders*, p. 120). Moll no sooner expresses her sorrow over the loss of a man she says she wouldn't mind begging for, than she feels the valuables in her pocket and is reminded of the only security that seems to exist for a woman like her: money at hand. This is not accidental. Moll's preoccupation with financial well-being reflects her own tenuous position in life, as well as the conditions of the time in which Defoe wrote.

Defoe was a Nonconformist, a member of a Protestant denomination (such as Quaker, Baptist, or, in Defoe's case, Presbyterian) that would not swear allegiance to the Anglican Church. After the Glorious Revolution of 1688, Nonconformists lobbied successfully for an end to the official persecution they had suffered under King James II from 1685 to 1688; they would no longer be faced with fines or jail time for not attending Anglican services. They still paid a price, however, if they did not swear loyalty to the Anglican Church. They could not advance in politics or law, or pursue a clerical career, and they could not attend the universities. Because of these limitations, many Nonconformists—who tended to be urban and middle-class anyway—congregated in the limited fields left open to them; they were skilled workmen and manufacturers, shopkeepers, and merchants. Defoe originally intended to become a tradesman, and even though his incompetence with money prevented him from realizing the ambition, he remained profoundly interested in financial questions throughout his career. He produced numerous tracts on important trade questions of the day and touted positive trade relations as the key to a country's wealth. Even his books on the proper conduct of marriage emphasize how important financial stability is to emotional happiness. In short, his own experience predisposed him to create characters who were motivated by the pursuit of wealth. Defoe's other famous hero, Robinson Crusoe, is even thriftier and more obsessed with money than Moll.

Defoe was, in this regard, no more than a child of his times. The early eighteenth century witnessed the beginning of the great age of British mercantilism. Naval wars with Holland in the previous century had established England as the predominant sea power in northern Europe, and the development of international travel, especially the regularization of the long sea routes to India, made England's preeminent position worth countless millions in goods and money. Furthermore, modern capitalism was beginning to take shape. The Glorious Revolution of 1688, in which the English took the throne from the Catholic King James II and gave it to the Protestant William and Mary, finally dispensed with the idea of the king as divinely empowered. From now on Parliament would command the country, with elected officials protecting the interests of England's middle-class mercantile leaders, who conducted brisk, efficient trade and constituted the commercial backbone of the country. By the turn of the eighteenth century, conditions were favorable for an explosion of mercantile endeavors, which is precisely what would occur after the financial crash of the 1720s. England would recover, then enjoy a period of widespread prosperity.

MARRIAGE FOR LOVE—FACT OR FICTION?

How common was it for a rich son like the novel's Robin to marry a domestic servant like Moll? This remains unknown, but it was certainly far rarer than the sexual exploitation of female servants, "whose virtue was always uncertain and was constantly under attack" (Stone, p. 381). Since marriage for love was on the rise, a trend Defoe himself heartily supported, such a match is not inconceivable, but the question is whether early-eighteenth-century fiction such as his *Moll Flanders* and Samuel Richardson's **Pamela** (also in *WLAIT 3: British and Irish Literature and Its Times*) reflected or promoted such a love match. In both novels, an upper-class man defies social convention by marrying a lower-class woman, realistic insofar as this was far more likely than an upper-class woman's wedding a lower-class man.

One of the chief consequences of the country's shift to a new commercial orientation was that a person's individual identity acquired a financial component. Most people continued to define themselves according to their traditional existence: a farmer was still a farmer; a baron, still a baron. A large proportion of the population, however, found itself deprived of association with a particular piece of land or a traditional occupation—especially in London, which experienced exponential growth and phenomenal change between 1600 and 1740. Indeed, the city became the place to go if one wanted to change identities. It promised escape from the narrowness of rural life, whether by amassing a fortune in the burgeoning city or simply by taking on a new name.

THE DEVIL MADE ME DO IT

In Defoe's novel, Moll blames the devil for her initial theft. For people of the time, this was no frivolous claim. Defoe himself genuinely believed that the devil made people commit immoral acts, as reflected in his *The History of the Devil, Ancient and Modern*:

But I return to the Devil's managing our wicked part; for this he does with most exquisite ability . . . he thrusts our vices into our virtues by which he mixes the clean and the unclean. . . . Here, indeed, I should enter into a long detail of involuntary wickedness, which . . . is neither more nor less that the Devil in everybody; aye in every one of you.

(Defoe, *The History of the Devil*, p. 190)

This assumption of new identities affects Moll Flanders. She is a product of social decay—she is born fatherless, and her mother is a convict sent to the Virginia colony. Thus, Moll is raised without a traditional identity—a situation made worse by the fact that she is a woman, and hence unable to pursue most vocations open to men. Defoe's novel portrays the state of mind that results from such an origin. Moll's place in society has to be earned, and she must work hard for it. No wonder that, at moments of crisis, she takes stock of her situation not by referring to what she has learned or what insights she has gained, but by taking a quick scan of her bank account. For her, possessions signify identity. The more she has, the freer and therefore happier she is; the more desperate her straits, the more desperately she behaves to get her money back. Horrified by having entertained the thought of killing a child for a gold necklace, Moll reflects, "Poverty, as I have said, harden'd my Heart, and my own Necessities made me regardless of any thing" (*Moll Flanders*, p. 152).

The effect can be disturbing. Far from a unified, consistent character, Moll appears to be a bundle of roles and effects—now a loving wife, now a cunning thief. She flips from one side to the other without acknowledging any inconstancy, as if being moral were simply a different kind of racket. Her behavior in this regard mirrors contradictions in the social, moral, and religious prescriptions of her day. The world Moll lived in was a conflicted society, pious at times, yet men commonly had mistresses and people were becoming obsessed with material accomplishment. Individual morality was in a state of flux as life grew increasingly secularized. For the poor, a painful disparity existed between human aspiration and the reality of the world in which they lived. The gap between what a woman like Moll could hope for and the paucity of opportunities that could liberate her from her status was nearly unbridgeable.

Sources and literary context. *Moll Flanders* is based on the lives of two famous criminals, Moll King, who stole gold watches from ladies in church, and Callico Sarah. The relationships to these two female criminals are rather loose, however, and for most of his actual details Defoe is indebted to a genre of which he himself was a practitioner, the criminal biography. The criminal biography is characterized by a mixture of wonder at the criminal's accomplishments and bold exploits, and stern condemnations of wrongdoing in the abstract—both of which are present in *Moll Flanders*. Taking inventory of a theft—the silver tableware, the silk handkerchiefs, the cash—Moll is overwhelmed by emotion: "I was under such dreadful Impressions of Fear, and in such Terror of Mind, tho' I was perfectly safe, that . . . I cried most vehemently; Lord, said I, what am I now? A Thief!" (*Moll Flanders*, p. 150). Another feature of the criminal biography is sensational incident—the anecdote of a specific crime that thrills by its dramatic detail and the nearness of disaster. The moment in which Moll contemplates killing the little girl for her necklace is an example. Aside from criminal biography, Defoe is indebted to the techniques of journalism he himself practiced; the novel's tone is brisk, detailed, and without frills. Moll Flanders is considered the first major plebeian heroine in English literature. Before 1722 no significant literary work had portrayed the misfortunes of a vulnerable woman in contemporary society with such intelligent and sympathetic understanding. Most writers before Defoe had created scornful presentations of the criminal or had treated characters who represented defiled humanity as a subject for comedy. The roller-coaster ride of Moll Flanders's life in Defoe's eyes, however, is more than a moral tale or an entertaining adventure. The novel seems to resonate with the words Defoe once wrote about his own life: .

No man has tasted differing fortunes more,
And thirteen times I have been rich and poor.
(Moll Flanders, p. 338)

Events in History at the Time the Novel Was Written

Reformation of manners. Though he published Moll Flanders in 1722, Defoe sets the novel in the seventeenth century; Moll stops her tale in 1682, some three decades before Defoe actually wrote it. In most ways, this gap does not make a substantial difference in respect to the culture of England. In 1722, as in 1682, crime was rampant and penalties were harsh; although under the reign of another king (George I), England was fundamentally the same.

In one very important way, however, the culture underwent profound change. In the regulation of sexual mores, the 1680s marked the end of an era; for Moll to "retire" in that year to a life of penitence accentuates the change.

With the death of Charles II in 1685 came the end of the first stage of the Restoration. During his exile in France, Charles had acquired habits of sensual indulgence, love of pleasure, and relatively loose morality that he brought back when he was restored to the English court. The English nation, tired of the restraint enforced by the Puritans who had ruled before Charles, welcomed this jolly king. In a matter of years, England had one of the most flagrantly corrupt courts in Europe. Prominent nobles practically got away with murder; when one wild aristocrat incited a riot by defecating from a balcony onto a crowd in the street below, the king himself paid the fine. The licentiousness of Charles's court was most evident in sexual matters. Not only were his mistresses famous, but courtly bawds helped facilitate extramarital affairs between adulterous nobles and citizens.

Charles's lusty reign reached its end in the 1680s—the same decade in which Moll decides to repudiate her past. In the wake of Charles's reign came a predictable backlash. First James II and then William and Mary attempted to "clean house"—if not to squash vice, then at least to force it into hiding once more. These early ef-forts were scattershot and had limited success. But in the early 1690s, an anti-vice campaign of a different stripe, motivated not by royal fiat but rather by genuine public feeling, surfaced.

This effort was headed by groups called the Societies for the Reformation of Morals. The beginnings of the movement are unclear; it seems that most of the early adherents belonged to prayer circles, and many were ministers. Whatever their origin, they were disgusted by what they saw as the lax morals of the English people and were bent on improving them. Their initial weapon was simple tale telling: private individuals who noticed such behavior as solicitation, swearing, or drunkenness were expected to detain the perpetrator and find the nearest authority. Many early members of the movement were shopkeepers who wished to clean up their neighborhoods, and so, unsurprisingly, most of the first detainees were drunks, vagrants, or prostitutes. People could also be called on such crimes as Moll commits: fornication and thievery.

LOWER-CLASS MARRIAGE PRACTICES

In Moll Flanders, Moll's acceptance of Jemmy as her husband once again testifies to how easy it was for those without property to contract marriage in early-eighteenth-century society. The marriage itself consisted not of a church ceremony, but of a mutual agreement between the two parties. A couple could just exchange oral promises (called spousals), then live together, and church law would consider the marriage legally binding. This remained the case until a half century after the novel takes place, when the 1753 Marriage Act required a church ceremony for a marriage to be valid.

It is not surprising that the Societies faced many initial problems. In the first place, the very mechanism for enforcing laws against lewd or immoral behavior had broken down. Before the Civil War, a prostitute, adulterer, or Sabbath-breaker—indeed, almost anyone who had broken a moral rather than social law—was tried in ecclesiastical court in front of a jury of clerics. These clerics, who could dispense whatever justice they thought necessary, were quick to punish moral sins with whipping or public humiliation. If Moll had ever been charged for bigamy, adultery, or other anti-Christian sexual behavior, she would have been taken to such an ecclesiastical court. But the ecclesiastical courts had broken down by the time Moll reaches middle age in the novel, and the Puritans eventually did away with them altogether. The result was a wealth of old statutes regulating all sorts of moral behavior, but no court accustomed to prosecuting such cases. The Societies helped break down judicial unwillingness to prosecute moral crimes simply by forcing the epidemic of such crimes on the courts' attention.

EIGHTEENTH-CENTURY HIGHWAYMEN

In the novel, Moll's husband Jemmy is a late-seventeenth-century highwayman. The profession flourished even more in the early eighteenth century, with the highwayman becoming the criminal scourge of England. In his play *The Beggar's Opera*, a work about the 1720s (also in *WLAIT 3: British and Irish Literature and Its Times*), John Gay portrays the highwayman as a dashing Robin-Hood-style outlaw. To some degree, highwaymen lived up to their reputation—exhibiting politeness to women, not brandishing their guns directly at victims, sometimes returning a favorite stolen item—but plenty of roughshod highwaymen belied the romantic image. The average culprit took to the road with a few pistols, a black mask over his eyes, and a silk kerchief over his face. If he worked alone, he concentrated on robbing coaches. A pistol in one hand, a hat in the other, he would demand the passengers' purses, their watches, their silver buckles. Highway crime peaked in early 1720s England, growing so pervasive that do-gooders leafleted the homes of the rich, warning them not to embark on a journey without £10 and a watch to pay the thief.

A more significant obstacle proved to be the hostility of the general populace to the Societies' aims. While the majority of street-level criminals obviously did not appreciate being turned in, plenty of seemingly upstanding citizens also resisted the movement. Many "respectable" citizens were secretly engaged in corrupt business practices or were in cahoots with criminal elements and resented the Societies' interference with their illegal and lucrative sidelines. In the first decade of the eighteenth century, a Society worker was stabbed to death while attempting to shut down a brothel—by the very soldiers he had brought to help him carry out the arrests. Police officers too were as likely to be corrupt as cooperative,

many having augmented their meager pay by collecting kickbacks from bawds and pimps.

What may be surprising is that the Societies for the Reformation of Morals actually had a significant impact. Over their three decades of operation, the Societies brought to trial thousands of cases of corrupt behavior that would otherwise have gone unreported. Though it is unlikely that the Societies significantly improved the morals of corrupt people, they undoubtedly helped force such behavior back underground, or at least into the less-publicized corners of London. No longer would society at large shout the names of a hundred famous bawds in every public place; no longer would the stage feature plays presenting fornication as a social game. No wonder, then, that Defoe chose the free-swinging previous century for Moll's tale of debauchery.

Criminal transportation. Defoe's treatment of Moll's time in Virginia is far from realistic. While English convicts were indeed sent to Virginia in great numbers, none of them—so far as history records—stepped immediately into the comfortable wealth that Moll and Jemmy enjoy. The life of the transported convict was harsh, often even unlivable.

The groundwork for criminal transportation was laid in 1597 by an Elizabethan statute that provided for the banishment of rogues and vagabonds. This law was strengthened in 1615 by James I, who authorized pardons for condemned felons, on condition of banishment to the New World. The number of felons transported was miniscule until 1718, when Parliament passed the Transportation Act, which allowed for the systematic exile of criminals as a punishment for crime. A plan evolved to send large numbers of convicts to work as servants in America, which would relieve overpopulation in England and at the same time populate the new colonies.

Between 1718 and 1775 roughly 30,000 convicts were transported; two-thirds landed in Virginia or Maryland, with the rest ending up in the West Indies. Though relatively few of the convicts were rogues or prostitutes of Moll's type, there were enough to prompt law-abiding colonists to attempt to stop the importation of hardened criminals. Surviving court records show, however, that convicts committed very few crimes once in the New World. Most were debtors, rebels from Ireland or Scotland, forgers, or thieves. Those convicted of a minor crime in England were sentenced to seven years of labor, while felons, the greatest number of whom had committed grand larceny, received fourteen years.

Though English citizens viewed America as a land of economic plenty with vast expanses of abundant wilderness, the New World still generated fears of barbarism and isolation for the convicts. Virginia was considered a cold, disgraceful place. And for many, America seemed like the remotest corner of the world, "a primitive land on the outer margins of the British empire" (Ekirch, p. 64). Most of the convicts hated to uproot their lives; their crimes had made them outcasts in English society, and all they had were their families. Once transported out of England, there was no guarantee they would ever see their loved ones again.

Transportation may have offered the convict a chance to start life anew, but only because there were few options. Faced with the unpalatable alternative of hanging, a large number of the condemned anxiously applied for transportation pardons. Moll greets the prospect of her life in America with mixed emotions: "I had now a certainty of Life indeed, but with the hard Conditions of being order'd for Transportation, which indeed was a hard Condition in it self, but not when comparatively considered" (*Moll Flanders*, pp. 229-30).

There was certainly no allowance made for convicts to bring their stolen wealth with them as Moll does, although for this to have happened was not out of the question. Until the mid-eighteenth century, transportation was conducted privately; once a convict had been sentenced to go to Virginia, it was up to the jailer to find a merchant willing to transport him or her and to locate colonists who needed servants. At any stage in the process, corruption could occur, or bureaucracy cause a slip in the transmission of prisoners.

Once in the New World, convicts faced an entire continent of open territory, to which they could escape if they had the will; they were indentured, but not imprisoned. Some no doubt did just this. Most criminals, taken from their natural environs and left without money or possessions in a foreign land, however, tended to remain with their new masters. The treatment the convicts received varied, but was nearly always harsh. They worked in fields or factories, and as domestic servants. The law rarely dictated minimum standards for housing or feeding them, so many no doubt suffered harsh conditions. As records indicate, they sometimes rebelled. Contemporary accounts of riots staged by indentured servants suggest that hardened criminals were the instigators.

Reviews. During his own day, and for two centuries after, Defoe was better known as a journalist and nonfiction writer than as a novelist. For this reason *Moll Flanders* received comparatively little critical attention until the twentieth century. The novel was, however, an immediate popular success in Defoe's day, due primarily to its scandalous content. The novel is presumed to have had a lower-class readership, as shown by a popular rhyme of the day: "Down in the kitchen, honest Dick and Doll [common names for servants] / Are studying Colonel Jack and Flanders Moll" (*Moll Flanders*, p. 325).

Although Defoe's novels were written earlier than those of Samuel Richardson, Richardson's have traditionally been considered the first English novels. Some attribute this to Defoe's lack of a coherent plot structure or sufficient character development. In the twentieth century, however, Defoe received attention as a praiseworthy novelist for his dramatic sense of the individual scene, for his lively presentation of the lower classes of his day, and for the valuable record of other aspects of life then. In the case of *Moll Flanders,* this attention ultimately gives rise to the question, "How many writers can lay claim to greater skill in narrative? Defoe carries his plot forward in time, develops Moll's character in her environment, gives us a vivid sense of the kinds of robberies that were occurring. . . . And all of this is accomplished . . . while . . . amusing us and giving us a slight chill of horror" (Novak, pp. 97-98).

—Carolyn Turgeon

For More Information

Andrews, Allen. *The Royal Whore.* London: Hutchinson, 1971.

Akroyd, Peter. *Evil London.* London: Wolf, 1973.

Bristow, Edward. *Virtue and Vice.* London: Gill and Macmillan, 1977.

Burford, E. J., and Joy Wotton. *Private Vices, Public Virtues.* London: Robert Hale, 1995.

Defoe, Daniel. *The History of the Devil, Ancient and Modern.* Philadelphia: H. [and] P. Price, 1802.

———. *Moll Flanders.* Ed. Edward H. Kelly. New York: W. W. Norton, 1959.

Ekirch, A. Roger. *Bound For America.* Oxford: Clarendon, 1987.

Masters, Brian. *The Mistresses of Charles II.* London: Blond & Briggs, 1979.

Novak, Maximillian E. *Realism, Myth, and History in Defoe's Fiction.* Lincoln: University of Nebraska Press, 1983.

Sharpe, J. A. *Crime in Early Modern England.* London: Longman, 1984.

Smith, E. J. *Colonists in Bondage.* Cambridge: Harvard University Press, 1947.

Stone, Lawrence. *The Family, Sex and Marriage in England 1500-1800.* New York: Harper, 1979.

Le Morte D'Arthur

by

Sir Thomas Malory

While there were a number of men named Thomas Malory in late-fifteenth-century England, no evidence has come to light that definitively links the author of *Le Morte D'Arthur* (also known as the *Morte Darthur* and the *Morte D'Arthur*) with any one of them. What the author tells us about himself is scanty; he says that his name is Sir Thomas Malory, that he is a knight and a prisoner, and that he finished his book in the ninth year of the reign of King Edward IV—that is, in 1469 or 1470. He wrote no other work that is known. Since the late nineteenth century critics have for the most part believed that he was Sir Thomas Malory of Newbold Revel in Warwickshire, though substantial objections have been raised to this identification, primarily because the Warwickshire Malory seems to have been a man of habitual and extreme violence. He was indeed an imprisoned knight, but his crimes of "rape, church-robbery, extortion and attempted murder" seem very much at odds with the Christian and chivalric attitudes expressed by the author of the *Morte D'Arthur* (Field, *Life and Times,* p. 5). Nevertheless, it is clear that the author Malory (whoever he was exactly) knew two things extremely well—the vast body of Arthurian literature that came down to him, and the business of warfare. The vivid, bloody, and technically detailed battle descriptions in *Le Morte D'Arthur* argue that his title "Sir" was more than an honorific; he was probably a knight by profession, and accustomed to warfare. The occupation, coupled with his mastery of French and English literary

> ### THE LITERARY WORK
>
> A romance-epic set in the mythic England of King Arthur (c. 450 C.E.); first published in 1485.
>
> ### SYNOPSIS
>
> Arthur attains the English throne and establishes the Round Table. He and his knights undergo many glorious adventures before all is destroyed in a climactic civil war, brought on by adultery, treachery, and blind vengeance.

sources for the story of Arthur, made him well qualified to retell this story in a manner that reflected both his profound admiration for the age of Camelot described in Arthurian literature, and his evident pessimism about the capacity of his contemporaries for wise and stable government.

Events in History at the Time the Romance-Epic Takes Place

England in the fifth century. Malory was aware of the time in which the historical King Arthur was said to have lived—a full millennium before his own age. He did not doubt (as some modern historians do) that Arthur ever existed. If Arthur did exist, he probably lived in the time in which Malory thought he did—the late fifth century C.E. This period was one of turmoil for England (then called Britannia); existing for centuries as a civilized Roman province, it had recently been abandoned by the Roman army because of the barbarian invasions that threatened the heart of Rome. The people left behind were British but also fully Roman, and their society was similar to those of other long-settled regions of the empire—indeed, it was in many ways more prosperous. There were some rather large cities (one of the largest, Londinium, survives as modern-day London), which were connected by an elaborate system of well-constructed roads, a number of which remain in use to this day. Serving as centers of military and civil administration, commerce, law, and religion, these cities were supported by extensive rural farmlands. Some farms were vast estates owned by noblemen and worked by slaves; others were smaller household farms operated by (for example) retired soldiers, who often received plots of land as a reward for faithful service. So fertile was the land that British grain was exported widely, along with metals from the rich Roman mining operations in Britain. The military was long a major presence, with the fortresses of Roman legions situated in strategic urban locations throughout the island. Resembling the army of a modern first-world country far more than that of the Round Table under Malory's King Arthur, the Roman military was heavily and hierarchically regimented, with a set chain of command. The knights of Roman Britain were very different from the highly individualized knights of Camelot; they were simply officers in the army and served as part of a disciplined force that had kept the peace for centuries.

The departure of the Romans' protective shield left the native British population to their own devices and to the depredations of Germanic invaders from northern Europe. These invaders would eventually prevail—in fact, the name "England" comes from the Angles, one of these Germanic peoples, along with the Saxons and Jutes, who invaded and eventually settled Britain. But there was a time in which the forces of Romano-British civilization fought against the forces that sought to destroy them, and for a while they were successful. Arthur, if he ever lived, was probably a leader of these native British people. Whatever the truth of history, it was soon almost entirely lost, and what remained became shrouded in legend. No British historical chronicle survives from the age in which Arthur may have lived; the first historical work in which he is mentioned is the *Historia Britonum*

(The History of the Britons, c. 796) of Nennius, who portrays him as a mighty leader of the British forces that fought the Saxons in 452. The Arthur of Nennius is formidable, but he is not a king, and he bears next to no resemblance to the Arthur portrayed in the literature of the later Middle Ages. The Arthur of Malory owes much to another work, the *Historia Regum Britanniae* (History of the Kings of Britain, c. 1135) of Geoffrey of Monmouth, who was responsible for creating the Arthur adapted by all subsequent writers of Arthurian romance. Geoffrey probably invented almost all the details. His near-contemporary William of Newburgh had severe doubts about the truth of his narrative, writing (c. 1198): "[He] disguised under the honorable name of history, thanks to his Latinity, the fables about Arthur which he took from the ancient fictions of the Britons and increased out of his own head" (William of Newburgh in Loomis, p. 72). Nevertheless, Geoffrey's work came to be accepted as legitimate historical truth throughout Europe, and was avidly read and copied. From Geoffrey's work grew century after century of Arthurian literature—none of it having much to do with the fifth century. The defining ethos of the Arthurian myth—chivalry—had yet to be invented, and the prevailing concern was that of civilization (that is, Rome) versus barbarism. One quality bridges the gap, however, and that is loyalty to one's lord, over and against treason, rebellion, and anarchy.

Loyalty and lordship. In periods of civil disturbance, it is crucial to know who one's allies are, and upon whom one can rely in the face of a mortal foe. This knowledge can be difficult, since lawlessness breeds ambition, and opportunities present themselves for personal advancement at the expense of duty and loyalty. From what we know of the time following the withdrawal of Roman imperial government from Britain, such behavior was largely responsible for the breakdown of society. With no Roman legions to enforce the law and protect the rights of the citizenry, numerous petty warlords tried to seize power. A large portion of the Roman army had been made up of mercenary Germanic soldiers, and many of these stayed behind in Britain, soon to be joined by their countrymen from across the English Channel. They too sought to dominate, and the country collapsed into anarchy. Attempts were made to stabilize the situation through marriage alliances and treaties, but these collapsed in the mad rush to power. It was in this context that the genuine Arthur (some historians believe) succeeded in bringing stable rule to Britain for a time. He did so by winning the loyalty of his followers and by ruling justly in exchange for that loyalty. Of course, his enemies also commanded troops loyal to them, but there is no evidence that their aims went beyond the desire to rule, to dominate others. Arthur, it seems, represented the Roman mode of rule—a lordship informed to some degree by a sense of responsibility to law, order, and fairness. His followers, in turn, exhibited a quality of loyalty that transcended the simply personal; they obeyed Arthur, but their allegiance looked beyond him to the ideals he represented.

This notion of a political legitimacy based as much on ideology as on personal loyalty can be seen clearly in *Le Morte D'Arthur*. Malory's Arthur represents a concept of lordship that holds a king accountable to standards of just rule, even at the expense of his personal power. Arthur manages to attract the best knights of Christendom to the Round Table and to command their loyalty, precisely because of this ideology. Wicked rulers like the Roman emperor Lucius (who invades England early in Arthur's reign) seek only power and wealth, while Arthur extends his dominions to bring justice and law to regions that lack it. King Mark of Cornwall is another negative example of a king in *Le Morte D'Arthur*; angered because his wife Isoud and Sir Tristram love each other, King Mark is continually plotting to have Tristram (also spelled Tristan) murdered. Mark's conduct in this regard is at several points called "treason," with the clear implication that even a king is subject to a higher law—a law that it is "treasonable" to flout. When King Arthur is confronted with evidence of his wife Guinevere's adultery with Lancelot, he unhappily condemns her to death— not because he wants to, but because this is what the law demands. Mark, in the face of similar evidence of Tristram and Isoud's adultery, resorts to stealth and ambush. It is this illegal conduct, despite his kingship and the lovers' guilt, that makes him a traitor against the rules of law, chivalry, and lordship.

Arthur is by these standards an exemplary king; he rules, but does not consider himself above the law. He presides not over a group of self-seeking warlords, but over the knights of the Round Table—a table that by design has no head position, no seat of distinction that might prompt ambition. He joyfully sends his best knights forth on a quest for the Holy Grail, in full awareness that many of them will die and thereby diminish the strength of his realm, because he believes

Fourteenth-century tapestry depicting King Arthur.

that his legitimacy ultimately derives from God. The oath of chivalry taken by his knights (which is entirely absent in the early medieval Arthurian materials) also owes much to this fundamental notion of lordly responsibility; both Arthur and his subject knights are bound by its rules, and he earns their loyalty because he subjects himself to its standards of noble behavior. Their loyalty is, in turn, based on this same code; a treacherous knight is guilty of an offense against chivalry itself, over and above the strictly legal dimension of his crime. This is made abundantly clear in the fate of one Sir Rauf Grey, who in 1463 was found guilty of treason. The chronicler Richard Grafton described in 1568 the punishment he suffered: "[he] was disgraded of the high order of knighthood by cutting off his gilt spurs, rending his coat of arms, and breaking his sword over his head; and finally, his body was shortened by the length of his head" (Benson, p. 148). A common traitor would simply have been executed—brutally, and without fanfare. Grey's knighthood made it necessary that the punishment fully show how grossly he had erred, not only as an Englishman who betrayed his king, but as a faithless knight who violated the most basic rule of chivalry.

The Romance-Epic in Focus

Plot summary. *Le Morte D'Arthur* begins, as it ends, in treachery, adultery, and bloodshed. Uther Pendragon, king of England, is at war with the duke of Cornwall. During a truce, he invites the duke and his wife, Igraine, to his court, but upon their arrival, Uther develops a passionate lust for Igraine. So forward are his advances that Igraine tells her husband, and they stealthily depart. The furious Uther prepares for war, but the duke has two castles well provisioned for siege—Tintagel, in which he deposits Igrain, and Terrabil, in which he secures himself. Uther's lust is made known to the magician Merlin, who tells Uther that he can fulfill his desire, on the condition that the child born of Uther's union with Igraine be given to Merlin to raise as he sees fit. Uther swears that he will do so, and that night gains entrance into Tintagel, having been magically transformed into the likeness of the duke. Igraine, believing him to be her husband, welcomes him into her bed, and that night Arthur is conceived. The duke is killed in battle, and Uther marries Igraine. Arthur is born and handed over to Merlin, who deposits him with Sir Ector, a well-regarded knight, to be reared. Uther reigns

amid violence and civil war for a time, but then dies. The kingdom is on the point of anarchy when Merlin summons all the nobles of the realm to London, promising a miraculous revelation of England's future king.

All are gathered for Mass at the greatest church of the city, when suddenly a marvel is perceived in the churchyard. An anvil rests upon a large block of marble, both pierced through by a sword adorned with the following words: "Whoso pulleth out this sword of this stone and anvil, is rightwise king born of all England" (*Morte D'Arthur*, vol. 1, p. 16). All attempt this feat, and none succeed except the youthful Arthur. While many proclaim him king, others object; but with the help of Merlin's sage advice and magic, the rebels are defeated. Arthur then sits securely on the throne. But the seeds of his kingdom's eventual downfall have already been planted. Arthur's half-sisters, Morgan le Fay and Morgause (daughters of Igraine and the duke of Cornwall), have long held Arthur in enmity because his father killed theirs. Morgan has since become a necromancer and directs her magical arts against Arthur. Morgause has married King Lot of Orkney and given birth to four sons (Gawain, Agravain, Gaheris, and Gareth). They eventually become famous knights of the Round Table, which does not stop them from playing active roles in Arthur's destruction. Immediately after Arthur consolidates his rule, Morgause seduces him. From this incestuous union is born Mordred, who will in the end (as Merlin prophesies) rebel against Arthur and kill him. Merlin chastises Arthur for this conduct, but nevertheless provides him with a weapon that will sustain him for many years. Leading him to an otherworldly lake, he shows him an arm reaching up from below the water's surface, holding a sword and scabbard. They row out to the sword, and Arthur takes it up—it is Excalibur, an enchanted sword of great power, and its scabbard magically prevents the wearer from bleeding. Fearful of Merlin's prophecy about what will come of his union with Morgause (and not knowing the child's identity or whereabouts), Arthur has all children born to the nobility on May 1 (the date was given to him by Merlin) placed in a ship, which he sets adrift. It breaks up on the coast, and all the children perish—except Mordred, who is found and raised by a stranger.

Arthur falls in love with and marries Guinevere, despite Merlin's warning that she will eventually love Lancelot. From Guinevere's father, Arthur retrieves the Round Table (which originally belonged to Arthur's father, Uther) and establishes it in London. Twenty-eight knights take seats at the table, and as they begin to have their own adventures, the fame and might of Arthur's kingdom grows. The Round Table (due to its shape, with no position of authority) allows the knights to sit as equals, and as more are added to its ranks it becomes an international symbol of chivalry, honor, and magnificence. Foreign kings invade and are repulsed until Arthur becomes the greatest king in Christendom. However, not all is well. Morgan succeeds in stealing the magic scabbard and substituting a copy, and Merlin falls in love with a young enchantress who encourages his affections so that she can learn the secrets of his magic. Finally tiring of him, she imprisons him in a cave, and he is forever lost to Arthur.

Lancelot arrives at Arthur's court and is given a seat at the Round Table. He rapidly establishes himself as the greatest knight in the world. None can withstand him on the battlefield or in tournaments. Moreover, he is a peerless model of knightly courtesy. He and Guinevere commit adultery, and from this point all his feats of prowess are performed in her honor. Knight after knight is defeated and sent to court to present himself to the queen; each must thenceforth do as she commands. Oddly, this arouses few suspicions, and the affair is kept secret for many years. Though his love of Guinevere is adulterous (and treasonable), Lancelot nevertheless holds Arthur in high honor and remains devoted in his service. Regarding his love for Guinevere as permanent and almost holy, he dismisses the overtures of all women who fall in love with him—except one. Lady Elaine is the daughter of King Pelles, a descendant of Joseph of Arimathea, the follower of Jesus who brought the Holy Grail (the cup used at the Last Supper) out of Jerusalem centuries before. She loves Lancelot, and King Pelles supports her designs because he knows that from Lancelot and Elaine will be born Galahad, a knight of perfect virtue who will find the Holy Grail. By enchantment Lancelot is made to think that Elaine is Guinevere, and spends the night with her. He forgives her the deception, but feels unhappy about betraying Guinevere. Only his closest friends learn of the tryst. Elaine afterward bears a son, and he is raised as a knight.

Some years later, Galahad arrives at Camelot. Guinevere thinks that he looks very much like Lancelot. At the Round Table, at a seat ever vacant, is found written in letters of gold Galahad's name; this is the Siege Perilous, the seat reserved

Illustrations from a fifteenth-century manuscript representing the legend of King Arthur.

(by magic, on pain of death) for the best knight in the world. Galahad takes his seat, and through various manifestations (including a visit by a prophetic hermit, the appearance of a magic sword, and a vision of the Holy Grail itself, floating through the dining room at Camelot) it becomes clear to all that now is the time for the Round Table knights to embark on a quest to find the Holy Grail. Thus, 150 knights prepare for departure. Another hermit appears and warns them not to bring any women with them, and to confess their sins before they go. Arthur (who, as king, must stay behind) is joyful at the glorious nature of the adventure, but fears that the Round Table will never again meet at its full strength. The knights each depart by separate ways.

The knights meet with considerable difficulty; enemies confront them at every turn and offer battle. Some are demons in disguise; some are other Round Table knights not recognized in time to avoid battle. In any case, the result of the battle is a symbolic moral judgment of the knight's character. Often there is a hermit nearby, who will explain the significance and symbolism of an event to the knight who has just undergone it. Morally flawed knights simply blunder around in the wilderness, fighting (and often losing) battle after battle, never to find the Grail. Gawain, for instance, gets nowhere. In direct contrast to his portrait in ***Sir Gawain and the Green Knight*** (also in *WLAIT 3: British and Irish Literature and Its Times*), he is depicted here as an irascible knight who seduces maidens and has a habit of cutting off people's heads first and asking questions later. The quest for the Grail shows him for what he is in Malory's work—a knight unworthy of such a sacred goal. As was made clear from the beginning, it is Galahad who is destined to attain the Grail, and he does, in company with two other knights of considerable (but lesser) moral virtue—Sir Percival and Sir Bors. They bear the Grail east and are granted a series of holy and mystical visions. Galahad is now too exalted to remain on earth, and his soul ascends to glory in heaven. Percival (who like Galahad is a virgin) becomes a hermit and lives for a while before also dying in sanctity. Bors returns to Camelot to tell the story.

With the quest over, life at Camelot soon returns to normal. Lancelot did not succeed in attaining the Grail because (as was made clear to him through various supernatural agencies at the time) of his sin with Guinevere. He was granted the grace to get as far as he did only because of his genuine contrition. His vow to avoid future sin does not last long, however, and he and Guinevere soon fall back into their adulterous ways. Enemies are at work as well; Mordred (now a Round Table knight) and his half-brother Agravain suspect that Lancelot and Guinevere are committing adultery, and they plot to expose this crime to the king. The lovers are surprised together in bed; Agravain, Mordred, and 12 knights (all heavily armed) appear at the door of the bedchamber, loudly crying treason and demanding entrance. Lancelot, naked but armed with a sword, kills Agravain and the 12 knights (Mordred survives) and makes his escape. Arthur grieves for the loss of the Round Table's unity, but his duty as king is clear. Guinevere is condemned to be burned at the stake. As she is about to be executed, Lancelot arrives with a company of knights loyal to him, and a fierce battle ensues. Guinevere is rescued, but Gaheris and Gareth (who bear Lancelot no malice, but obey the command of Arthur to stand at his side) are unknowingly killed by Lancelot. Gawain did not mind the death of Agravain, since he had been warned against plotting to expose the adulterers, but now is prostrate with grief at the deaths of his two remaining brothers. He vows vengeance against Lancelot. Arthur too is intent on revenge, and the royal army besieges Joyous Gard, the castle where Lancelot has taken refuge with the queen and his army. There commences a series of bloody battles. Many die on both sides, though Lancelot is careful never to kill Arthur. The pope in Rome finally has enough of Christian killing Christian, and compels Arthur to accept a treaty—Lancelot will depart for his native France, never to return, and Arthur will be reconciled to the queen. This is accomplished, but Gawain's desire for vengeance is such that he persuades Arthur to invade France. Lancelot, now ruler of all France, is a formidable opponent with no wish to fight Arthur, but nevertheless an English army of 60,000 crosses over to France and besieges Lancelot's castle. England and Guinevere are left in the care of Mordred.

Battle is offered, but Lancelot refuses to come forth with his army and fight. Gawain taunts Lancelot so aggressively that he is soon persuaded to emerge and fight Gawain in single combat. The battle proves long and strenuous, but soon Gawain falls, seriously wounded. Lancelot refuses to kill him, and after three weeks the healed Gawain again challenges Lancelot, with the same result. Gawain heals more slowly this time, but resolves anyway to challenge Lancelot once more when news arrives from England—Mordred has usurped the throne and is bent on marrying Guinevere. Arthur returns to England with his army, and is met by a large host; Mordred has found many allies in Britain whom he has persuaded to join him in rebellion. In the initial battle, the weakened Gawain receives his death-wound. Before dying, he expresses sorrow to Arthur for all the trouble he has caused, begs Arthur to send for Lancelot to help in the war against Mordred, and writes a letter to Lancelot asking forgiveness for his vengeful conduct, and for military assistance to help Arthur. He dies and Arthur buries him with honor. That night, as Arthur prepares for the final battle with Mordred, Gawain appears to him in a dream. Gawain advises Arthur to avoid battle with Mordred until Lancelot arrives, since without Lancelot's help Arthur will surely die. The next morning Arthur arranges to meet Mordred to work out a truce; they approach each other in the area between the two armies, each having instructed his army to begin fighting if a sword is drawn. Then disaster strikes—a snake bites a knight on the foot, and he unthinkingly draws his sword to kill it. Battle is joined, and the slaughter is immense. After a time, Arthur finds himself alone on the field, except for Sir Lucan and Sir Bedevere. Spying Mordred a short distance off, he rushes at him with a spear. Mordred is impaled, but as he dies, he gives Arthur a mortal wound to the head with his sword. A dying Arthur commands Bedevere to cast his sword Excalibur into the nearby lake, and as Bedevere does so, a hand emerges from the water to receive it. Arthur then dies, and Malory speculates on the legend that he will return someday to lead England again, as suggested by the legendary inscription on Arthur's tomb: *Hic iacet Arthurus, rex quondam rexque futurus* [Here lies Arthur, once king, and future king] (*Morte D'Arthur*, vol. 2, p. 519). Hearing that Arthur and Mordred are dead, Guinevere becomes a nun, renowned for her piety. Lancelot returns to England and endures considerable grief after learning what has happened. He eventually becomes a hermit, and both he and Guinevere die in holy penitence. A number of the surviving Round Table knights go to the Holy Land to fight the infidel. Back in England, Constantine (son of Cador of Cornwall) becomes king after Arthur and rules well.

Le Morte D'Arthur is more than just an account of the reign of Arthur and of the love-triangle that brought it down. There are many other knights of the Round Table whose stories are told by Malory as well. Most prominent among these stories is that of Sir Tristram. Second only to Lancelot in knightly prowess and chivalry, Tristram dominates one of the large central sections of *Le Morte D'Arthur*. Like Lancelot, he too pursues a faithful but adulterous love, in his case for Isoud, the wife of his lord, King Mark. The lengthy and colorful exploits of Tristram, as well as those of other knights such as Gawain, Gareth, and Palomides are episodically interwoven into the basic overall plot summarized above.

The heroic model. The single most defining quality exhibited by the knights of the Round Table is their heroism. They are not ordinary men; their skill at arms, their feats of bravery, their matchless chivalry—all these attributes make them very much larger than life. This is in many ways the point of telling their stories; Malory (who seemed to regard the story of Arthur as more of a history than a work of imaginative literature) thought their deeds a worthy model of behavior—a model to be admired and emulated. This does not mean that the knights were wholly good. In fact, all were flawed in some manner, with the single exception of Galahad, and it is no accident that Galahad has little role to play in the central Arthurian story. His virtue is almost inhuman in its perfection. He does not seek worldly honor; he avoids amorous contact

with women; and his sole aim is to complete the mystical quest of the Holy Grail. Once he achieves this, he dies in religious ecstasy. He is ultimately too good for this earth. The heroism of the other knights is of a different sort. Their deeds are beyond the measure of normal men, but they struggle with the vices of lust, anger, and pride, and their extraordinary feats throw these failings into sharp relief. For Malory, they are exemplary in both a positive and a negative sense, in that their good and bad qualities are both so extreme. Bravery and strength, honor and loyalty—these are all noble traits, and the lofty example of the Round Table knights can be an ennobling influence. Conversely, the vengeful wrath of Gawain, Arthur's incest with his sister, and the calamitous adultery of Lancelot and Guinevere are not garden-variety sins; they are appalling in their wickedness and disastrous in their consequences, and thus serve as supremely potent moral lessons.

The heroic model that emerges from *Le Morte D'Arthur* is therefore somewhat problematic. How can one admire an adulterer like Lancelot? a habitual killer like Gawain? a killer of a shipload of infants like Arthur? For Malory, they nevertheless must be admired because their virtues outweigh their faults, and these virtues are beacon lights shining forth from the distant past, illuminating a fifteenth-century England that was sadly lacking in this regard. Arthur and his knights were fallible like all men (except for Galahad), and therefore recognizably human—a quality that brought them closer to men who might seek to emulate them.

Sources and literary context. At the time Malory was writing *Le Morte D'Arthur*, Arthurian literature had been phenomenally popular throughout Europe for centuries. What began in the twelfth century with Geoffrey of Monmouth's *History of the Kings of Britain* (c. 1135) rapidly mushroomed into a highly varied body of chivalric romances; by the end of the thirteenth century, nationally distinctive accounts of the exploits of Round Table knights were being produced in every region of Europe. England favored native British knights (such as Sir Gawain), while France weighed in with Lancelot, who emerged wholly from French additions to the basic Arthurian story. He first appears in *Le Chavalier de la Charrete* (c. 1181—usually known in English as *Lancelot*) of Chretien de Troyes. The high-water marks of German Arthurian literature were the *Tristram* (c. 1210) of Gottfried von Strassburg and the *Parzival* (c. 1215—a Grail-

Le Morte D'Arthur

quest narrative featuring Percival instead of Malory's Galahad) of Wolfram von Eschenbach, both modeled on French originals. Other Arthurian romances were written in Icelandic, Dutch, Spanish, and even Latin. The bulk of Arthurian literature in the Middle Ages, however, was of French origin, and it is in this French material that Malory found his sources. He refers throughout *Le Morte D'Arthur* to "the French book" as the source from which he is translating, but this is misleading on two counts: first, more than one French work served as his source (these include long prose narratives about Lancelot, Tristan, and the Grail quest); second, he also made use of English material.

It should be noted at this point that *Le Morte D'Arthur* is not a single, continuous narrative, but a collection of stories, each with its particular subject. William Caxton, who in 1485 first published the work, divided it into 21 books, some of which naturally group together in that they involve the same story arc. Eugene Vinaver, the editor of the standard critical edition of *Le Morte D'Arthur*, used as his base text not the edition of Caxton, but a manuscript discovered in 1934, thought by many to reflect more nearly Malory's original work. This text is divided into eight "tales" or "books," each treating a different part of the larger story. It is by looking at these eight divisions that Malory's use of source texts may be best apprehended, as he tends to use an (in most cases) identifiable separate body of materials for each. For example, the first book begins with Uther and takes the narrative through Arthur's gaining the throne, also detailing the adventures of several knights. It derives primarily from what modern editors call the *Suite de Merlin* (c. 1235), a lengthy surviving portion of a larger French work that recounts Arthur's parentage and birth, his early years of struggle for royal supremacy, and the events of this time that look forward to the quest for the Holy Grail. Book 2 recounts Arthur's early military campaigns. It is adapted from the English *Alliterative Morte Arthure* (c. 1400). Other sources (all French) include the *Prose Lancelot* (c. 1215-30), a long French prose narrative of Lancelot's pre-Grail adventures, which was the basis for much of the subsequent literature about him; the *Prose Tristan* (c. 1230), an early French version of the Tristan story; *La Queste del Saint Graal* ("The Quest of the Holy Grail," c. 1215-30), which Malory follows fairly closely for his version of the Grail story; and at least two thirteenth-century French prose versions of the story of Arthur's death. Mal-

ory may have used other sources as well; for example, some believe that he was influenced by the romances of Chretien de Troyes, and it will probably never be known how much other material that Malory used has been lost.

In view of this crushing weight of source texts, it would be natural to view Malory as a mere translator and compiler, but this would be wrong. He used his sources with care and deliberation, seeking always to write (as he saw it) a true history of Arthur and his knights. These sources were for him the raw material of this history, not "literary" texts (in the modern sense) to be slavishly translated. Their authority was in the stories they told, not in the way they told it, and *Le Morte D'Arthur* is very much Malory's own.

Events in History at the Time the Romance-Epic Was Written

The wars of the fifteenth century. The later fifteenth century was a time of great turmoil for England. The Wars of the Roses (1455-1485) devastated the land and people as the houses of York and Lancaster fought for political supremacy. The crown changed hands several times amid conflict of a new and brutal nature. Towns were burned and townspeople massacred, nobles were summarily executed, and mercenary armies roamed the countryside at will, their allegiance changing with the financial and military fortunes of their employers.

The Hundred Years' War (actually a series of wars, fought between England and France, the last battles of which were waged in 1453) had left idle an enormous number of experienced and hungry soldiers. When the antagonists of the Wars of the Roses began hostilities in 1455, they found a ready supply of armed combatants in such men. For the most part, these soldiers did not care whether York or Lancaster ruled England; they were trained to kill, and would kill at the bidding of whoever was paying their wages. In between employers, they would rob merchants, plunder villages, and commit other outrages more or less with impunity, because the authorities were occupied with the civil war. It was the general lawlessness of the time, as much as the Wars of the Roses themselves, that made this such a turbulent era.

It would have been natural for Englishmen to look back with nostalgia to the days of the Plantagenet kings (the ruling dynasty from 1154-1399) and even the first two Lancastrian monarchs (Henry IV [1399-1413] and Henry V

[1413-22]); those were the days, it seemed, when kings kept the peace, and their knights served out of duty and loyalty, rather than greed and self-interest. Many doubtless thought this way, but Malory's views appear to have been more complex. If the author of *Le Morte D'Arthur* was indeed the Sir Thomas Malory of Newbold Revel, then he served the conservative Lancastrian side, which stood with the landed aristocracy of the countryside, as opposed to the moneyed interests of the cities and towns, who sided with the house of York. This does not mean, however, that he can be dismissed as simply a reactionary who, seeing a decline of chivalry and honor in England, chose to seek comfort in the golden age of King Arthur. He may have thought that the Wars of the Roses brought out the worst in people, and that nobility of conduct was scarcely to be found. But for Malory it was ever thus, even in the age of King Arthur. Writing of the defection of English knights to Mordred while Arthur was busy fighting Lancelot in France, Malory laments:

> Lo ye all Englishmen, see ye not what a mischief here was? For he that was the most king and knight of the world, and most loved the fellowship of noble knights, and by him they were all upholden, now might not these Englishmen hold them content with him. Lo thus was the old custom and usage of this land; and also men say that we of this land have not yet lost ne forgotten that custom and usage. Alas, this is a great default of us Englishmen, for there may nothing please us no term.
> (*Morte D'Arthur*, vol. 2, p. 507)

Arthur's England, like the England of Malory's day, was flawed; chivalry was alive and well, but ever in conflict with the forces of disloyalty, cowardice, and treachery. The breakdown of the civil order brought on by the Wars of the Roses was comparable to the dissolution of Arthur's kingdom, with similar forces at work in both instances: fickle warriors, fallible kings, and power-hungry nobles.

Modes of war in the fifteenth century. Malory's depiction of armed combat as an incongruous blend of noble ideals and shocking brutality seems to be a fairly accurate representation of how warfare was perceived, if not necessarily practiced, in his day. The days when wars consisted primarily of combat among knights were long past, if they ever existed at all; common foot soldiers and archers decided whether battles were won or lost, and chivalric combat continued to be practiced simply because the nobility wanted to, rather than out of any legitimate tactical considerations. Knights might buckle themselves into elaborate suits of plate armor (the cost of which could outfit a small army of foot soldiers armed with bows or pikes) and ride around on the field of battle, seeking honorable engagements with similarly outfitted foes, but late-medieval weaponry such as the longbow and (increasingly) firearms could easily bring them down, and even if their initial wounds were not mortal their cumbersome armor made them easy prey for enemy infantry. Being at such a disadvantage apparently did not bother many knights. It was more important to live and fight with honor and decorum than to win the battle, or even live through it. By the close of the fifteenth century, mounted knights had ceased to be much of a factor in warfare; they were simply too vulnerable to enemy firepower. Knights of a more practical turn of mind began to reserve their heavy full-body armor for ceremonial occasions, and adapted to an increasingly modern and indiscriminately brutal style of battle.

LAWLESSNESS IN ENGLAND: FROM A PETITION ADDRESSED TO THE KING IN 1472

~

"Sovereign Lord, it is so that in divers parts of this realm, great abominable murders, robberies, extortions, oppressions and other manifold maintainences, misgovernances, forcible entries, as well upon them being in by judgement as otherwise, affrays, assaults, be committed and done by such persons as either be of great might, or else favoured under persons of great power, in such wise that their outrageous demerits as yet remain unpunished." (Bennett, p. 183)

It was not just advances in military technology that ended the days of the warrior-knight. In the fourteenth century, a knight wounded or captured on the battlefield could generally rely on his enemies to observe certain protocols. He would be treated and healed (if possible), given accommodations appropriate to his social status, and returned to his country after a ransom had been paid. According to the rules of chivalry, one's enemy was a fellow knight-in-arms, and entitled to be treated as such. Off the field of battle, men who the day before had been doing their best to kill each other could easily act as the best of friends, hunting and drinking together in high aristocratic style. In Malory's lifetime, however, things began to change. A lowborn foot soldier had no compunction against killing a knight with his longbow or pike, nor was he dissuaded by the knight's chivalric disinclination to fight against a social unequal. Moreover, such soldiers began to display a disturbing trend in behavior. They would likely as not kill any wounded knight they found in battle, and despoil him of his valuable armor, weapons, and horse. As military commanders began to take a more hard-headed approach to warfare, they did not discourage these practices among their soldiery. Chivalry was all well and good, but at the end of the battle it was better to have one's enemies dead than alive. Making this situation worse was the fact that the Wars of the Roses were civil wars—each side saw the other as guilty of treason, and each claimant to the throne saw the other as a usurper. This meant that the knights on the losing side of a battle were not simply defeated enemies, but traitors, convicted by their own actions. The penalty for treason was death, and many knights and noblemen were summarily executed on such charges. Others were imprisoned, but again, times had changed. No longer could a knight expect to be imprisoned in relative comfort, and many knights suffered miserable confinements. As noted, Malory himself was imprisoned, which has led many scholars to read an autobiographical element into a passage of *Le Morte D'Arthur* in which Tristram's captivity is described:

> So Sir Tristram endured there great pain, for sickness had undertake him, and that is the greatest pain a prisoner may have. For all the while a prisoner may have his health of body he may endure under the mercy of God and in hope of good deliverance; but when sickness toucheth a prisoner's body, then may a prisoner say all wealth is him bereft, and then he hath cause to wail and to weep. Right so did Sir Tristram when sickness had undertake him, and then he took such sorrow that he had almost slain himself.
>
> (*Morte D'Arthur*, vol. 1, pp. 453-54)

Treating a privileged class of warrior so roughly was not entirely new, but in the Wars of the Roses it seems to have been a widespread tendency, part of an overall trend—chivalry, though still practiced by individual knights, no longer governed warfare.

Persistence of chivalric ideals. If chivalry was seen as an embattled institution in fifteenth-century England, the nobility of the age (and for many generations afterwards) sought energeti-

cally to keep it alive. In Malory's day it was not at all uncommon to find knights who did their best to model themselves after the knights of the Round Table, seeking honor in single combat in warfare, in judicial duels (a duel fought to determine guilt when a knight was accused of an offense), and in tournaments—elaborate ceremonial occasions where heavily armored knights would joust on horseback. Throughout the fifteenth, sixteenth, and even early seventeenth centuries, men possessed and used full suits of armor, and engaged in highly ritualized forms of battle. In 1520, Henry VIII of England hosted an elaborate tournament known as the Field of the Cloth of Gold; the Holy Roman Emperor and the king of France (as well as a host of lesser kings and nobles) attended, and there was a magnificent display of jousting by the finest knights in Europe. In warfare such behavior also persisted. Knights on either side of a battle would formally challenge each other to single combat, and often hostilities would cease so that the bout could take place under properly ordered conditions, and so that all could watch it. In the late sixteenth century the Englishman Ben Jonson (later to find fame as a poet and playwright), while serving with an English army in Flanders, challenged an enemy soldier to single combat during a lull in the fighting. Descended as he was from an old, though impoverished, noble family, he fought in a manner of which Malory would have approved. He skillfully killed his opponent and carried the fallen warrior's arms triumphantly back to the English camp. The view that true honor could be found only in formal hand-to-hand combat continued to be held for some time, and chivalric (and judicial) combats between individuals persisted even into the nineteenth century. Late-medieval and Renaissance knights acted in this manner not so much out of theatrical exuberance (although there was surely an element of this), but in a self-conscious conviction that they were fulfilling their calling as knights. The career of Sir John Astley, Malory's contemporary, is a case in point. He was an avid collector of chivalric literature, an official at judicial duels, and an actual combatant in chivalric contests that were fought to the death. Skilled at arms, he defeated his opponents repeatedly and lived until 1486. For him, the chivalric past was fully present, and the Arthurian tales, manuals of knighthood, and other books of this sort that he owned were not the diversions of an antiquary, but useful and instructive guides to behavior. As Larry Benson notes, "[g]iven Astley's interest in chivalric matters . . . he could well have been one of the 'noble gentlemen' who urged Caxton to publish Malory's work" (Benson, p. 175).

Astley was by no means unique. It is clear that the knightly class of Malory's day saw the chivalric code, exemplified in the available literature of Arthur and the Round Table knights, as the very core of their being. It was not an issue of nostalgia or even of conservatism. Chivalry was a living and permanent institution for a class of men who saw themselves as participating, in a manner unaffected by the passage of many centuries, in the essence of what made Arthurian England great.

Reception and impact. The impact of *Le Morte D'Arthur* following its publication was immediate, in that it sustained and animated the tradition of chivalric literature in England. Such literature continued to be published for at least a century afterwards, and it found an enthusiastic readership. In 1590 Edmund Spenser's **Faerie Queene** (also in *WLAIT 3: British and Irish Literature and Its Times*) represented a still-lively taste for knightly heroism and the world of Arthurian magic, and in the mid-seventeenth century, John Milton contemplated writing a long epic poem on King Arthur before deciding to write **Paradise Lost** (also in *WLAIT 3: British and Irish Literature and Its Times*). But there were also works by people who found such narratives tiresome and ludicrous. Such works include *Don Quixote* (1605) by the Spanish writer Cervantes, which was widely read in England. The title character is a kindly knight whose foolishness and pretensions to old-style chivalry make the case that there is no place for Arthurian values in the modern world. The play *The Knight of the Burning Pestle* (first performed 1607-1608, published 1613) by Francis Beaumont voices a similar view, satirizing chivalric literature (and its audience) through the title character, a grocer who is so influenced by Arthurian romances that he tries to live as a knight-errant, with absurd results. In the nineteenth century, *Le Morte D'Arthur* regained popularity with the rise of neo-medievalism and a taste for the "gothic" in literature. Major works such as Byron's *The Corsair* and *Lara* (1814) and Tennyson's *Idyls of the King* (1842-1885) show the pervasive influence of Malory's romance-epic. It would continue to be rewritten and adapted through the twentieth century, perhaps most notably in T. H. White's bestselling novel *The Once and Future King* (1958).

—Matthew Brosamer

For More Information

Archibald, Elizabeth, and A. S. G. Edwards, eds. *A Companion to Malory*. Woodbridge, U.K.: D.S. Brewer, 1996.

Bennett, H. S. *The Pastons and their England: Studies in an Age of Transition*. Cambridge, 1932.

Benson, Larry. *Malory's Morte Darthur*. Cambridge: Harvard University Press, 1976.

Brengle, Richard L., ed. *Arthur, King of Britain: History, Romance, Chronicle & Criticism, with Texts in Modern English, from Gildas to Malory*. New York: Appleton-Century-Crofts, 1964.

Field, P.J.C. *The Life and Times of Sir Thomas Malory*. Cambridge, England: D. S. Brewer, 1993.

Field, P. J. C. *Malory: Texts and Sources*. Cambridge, England: D. S. Brewer, 1998.

Loomis, Roger Sherman, ed. *Arthurian Literature in the Middle Ages: A Collaborative History*. Oxford, England: Oxford University Press, 1959.

Lumiansky, R.M. *Malory's Originality: A Critical Study of Le Morte Darthur*. Baltimore: The Johns Hopkins Press, 1964.

Malory, Sir Thomas. *Le Morte D'Arthur*. Ed. Janet Cowen. 2 vols. New York: Penguin, 1969.

Parins, Marylyn Jackson, ed. *Malory, The Critical Heritage*. London: Routledge, 1988.

Vinaver, Eugene, ed. *The Works of Sir Thomas Malory*, by Sir Thomas Malory. 2d ed. Oxford, England: Oxford University Press, 1967.

The Mysteries of Udolpho

by
Ann Radcliffe

THE LITERARY WORK

A novel set in France and Italy in 1584; published in English in 1794.

SYNOPSIS

After the deaths of her parents, Emily St. Aubert is separated from her idyllic home and her first lover and is held prisoner in the Italian castle of Udolpho. Her escape leads to discoveries about her family history and her lover's fate.

orn in London in 1764, Ann Ward moved to Bath in 1772. There is some uncertainty about her education. She perhaps attended a school run by Harriet and Sophia Lee. Sophia, one of the earliest writers of gothic novels, may have strongly influenced Ann's future writings. It is known that Ann married the journalist-publisher William Radcliffe in 1787 and began writing with his encouragement. Within a few years she had published the romantic novels *The Castles of Athlin and Dunbayne* (1789) and *The Sicilian Romance* (1790). The publication of her third novel, *The Romance of the Forest* (1791), established her reputation as a gothic novelist, and the more successful release of *The Mysteries of Udolpho* (1794) proved her mastery of "terror," earning her the epithet "Great Enchantress" of the gothic movement (coined by English writer Thomas De Quincey). The work gained similar distinction, attaining enduring renown as the most influential Gothic novel of the eighteenth century.

Events in History at the Time the Novel Takes Place

Condottieri. After 1350 the city-states of Italy found themselves in a constant state of war. What were initially local conflicts began to spread further along the Italian peninsula, drawing in the larger city-states. Successful in trade and commerce, these city-states did not want to disrupt their burgeoning economies by sending their citizens to war. They chose instead to hire outsiders who would fight for them. In time, the practice of war became a profession in Italy, and the *condottieri,* or hired soldiers, emerged as crucial players in the military and political landscape. They differed from typical soldiers in that they usually had no partisan feelings in the conflicts for which they hired themselves out.

One of the most prominent condottieri captains, Sir John Hawkwood, was not even Italian. An Englishman fighting in France, Hawkwood came to Italy when England and France made peace and pledged his own skills and his English soldiers to Florence for a lucrative contract or *condotta.* Hawkwood's company of Englishmen played a pivotal role in Italian conflicts from the 1360s through the late 1390s.

At first, the majority of the early condottieri were foreigners, but eventually inhabitants from the Appenine and Romagna region of the Italian peninsula began to form their own mercenary armies. Soldiers would attach themselves to a popular leader, by whom they were directed into the service of any state that could settle on a price with him. These mercenary companies put themselves at the service of wealthy, but poorly defended, cities of the Italian plains, which included Padua, Parma, Venice, and Bologna.

From this new military professionalism came new forms of warfare. It grew rarer to fight in the open field because commanders began to rely on strategies of attrition, frequent skirmishing to lower enemy morale, and long sieges in which firearms and field fortifications became important factors.

THE CODE OF THE CONDOTTIERI

B ecause the involvement of the condottieri was financially rather than politically or patriotically motivated, the battles between condottieri armies often produced fewer casualties than traditional warfare. There was a mutual sympathy and an understanding between condottieri, who knew the men opposing them were fighting for the same cause they were: money. In one of Hawkwood's greatest battles against the Veronese, the total casualties amounted to 716 dead and 846 wounded. By comparison, 1,500 knights and 10,000 common soldiers died in the earlier battle of Crécy in France, and 26,000 men died in the battle of Towton during the English War of the Roses.

By employing condottieri companies, Italian city-states enjoyed the benefits of a standing army without having to pay the costs of maintaining one, but less palatable consequences resulted from the new practice too. While not actively employed, the large bands of condottieri posed a serious danger to the stability of the city-states they were hired to protect. A mercenary, Cecchino Broglio, for example, though born in the city of Piedmont, had fought successful battles for Milan. When peace was reached in Milan, Broglio launched his own raids into Florentine territory. Florence made formal protests to the leadership of Milan, who claimed they were not responsible for Broglio's conduct. As Broglio's incessant raiding continued, Florence realized the only way to stop him was to hire him. Broglio refused several offers, but finally agreed to a three-year contract to serve as the Captain-General of Florence,

which, as anticipated, ended condottieri raiding in Florentine territory.

An even greater danger to the leaders of the Italian city-states came from the incredible popularity of some condottieri captains. In the fifteenth century, Biordo Michelotti became a condottiere after being exiled from his native city of Perugia. Years later, as Perugia struggled with violent unrest, Michelotti used his own army to take control of the city. A very popular leader, he maintained control for several years, until assassins sent by papal factions murdered him, inaugurating a new period of unrest in Perugia.

The most widespread use of condottieri began in the thirteenth century and continued through the late fifteenth century, with their activities persisting on a smaller scale for many more years to come. In Radcliffe's novel, Montoni, the principal villain, raises his own band of codottieri in the late sixteenth century. He meets several condottieri captains at the gambling tables and conceives "a desire to emulate their characters, before his ruined fortunes tempted him to adopt their practices" (Radcliffe, *The Mysteries of Udolpho*, p. 379). Using the castle of Udolpho as a base of operations, Montoni quickly gathers an army of his own and launches incursions into the nearby countryside. Not only do his men pillage the helpless traveler; they also attack and plunder "the villas of several persons" (*The Mysteries of Udolpho*, p. 397). His condottieri status reveals Montoni to be motivated primarily by economics; in short, he is a hunter of fortunes.

Pirates and *banditti*. In the sixteenth century, Dutch and English shipbuilding far surpassed the techniques used in the Mediterranean Sea, partly due to the greater availability and quality of timber in northwestern Europe. Realizing that Mediterranean ships were more poorly constructed and less well armed than northern European ships, English and Dutch pirates quickly took advantage.

Meanwhile, banditry in northern Italy was becoming epidemic. After an outbreak of bubonic plague in 1576, years of famine and increasing economic hardship followed. Responding to this weakening economy, landlords and city governments increased the already soaring taxation, prompting more unrest and dissatisfaction in the lower classes. This rising discontent manifested itself in an unprecedented surge of banditry in the last two decades of the sixteenth century. In an attempt to curb this problem, the viceroy of Naples condemned 18,000 people to death but

Interior of a Gothic church.

soon realized this did nothing to discourage banditry. Government actions against the major bandit camps took on the aspect of miniature wars, with the law regaining control only when the viceroy of Naples joined with papal forces to crush the bandit movement

This sweeping criminality surfaces on several occasions in the novel. The servant Ludovico is kidnapped by pirates who have been so successful that they need the cellars below one of the homes, Chateau-le-Blanc, to store their plunder. Early in the novel, Emily and her father, Monsieur St. Aubert, worry about encountering *banditti* (bandits) in the isolated mountain passes of the Pyrenees, and later a count's family is almost murdered when it meets a group of bandits while traveling. A member of the family overhears the bandits debating whether to rob them: "While we run the chance of the wheel [an instrument of torture] . . . shall we let such a prize as this go? (*Mysteries of Udolpho*, p. 613).

Convent life. In the sixteenth century, bachelors striving to marry their way into fortune precipitated an inflation of the dowry payment from a bride's family to a groom's. Daughters had once been powerful assets for alliances with other families, but now, in view of the rising dowry, they more often became financial burdens. Women with little financial means often faced the diffi-

cult choice of marrying a man socially beneath them or remaining unmarried. At the same time, the rise of urban centers and guilds restricted the freedom of working-class men; apprentices and journeymen often stayed unmarried for years until they attained a mastership. Meanwhile, the Church gained stature as an avenue for professional advancement. Clerical orders provided one of the few opportunities for upward mobility, attracting many eligible bachelors, who disappeared from the marriage pool to enter the clergy, where they sometimes took vows of celibacy.

With so many men removed from the supply of potential husbands, a place had to be found for the growing surplus of unmarried women. Convents became a natural solution. Typically families paid a fee to have their daughters accepted into a convent, but they considered the expense a bargain compared to the escalating cost of dowries. While the majority of nuns came from upper-class families, reformed prostitutes, the mentally disabled, and destitute widows also joined some convents. Charitable contributions would pay a poor woman's way into the convent, where she repaid her benefactors by praying for them. Many such women entered convent life not because of religious devotion, but simply because, with no dowry and no chance for education or employment, the convent was their only option. Coincidentally some found fulfillment through the prayer and religious instruction that were part and parcel of convent life.

For a short while, the protagonist of Radcliffe's novel, Emily, lives in a convent near Chateau-le-Blanc. She discovers that she enjoys the tranquillity of the convent, but her primary reason for staying is practical rather than spiritual. She receives a letter that crushes her dreams of returning to live at her home, La Vallée, informing her that "her circumstances would by no means allow her to reside there, and earnestly advising her to remain, for the present, in the convent of St. Clair" (*The Mysteries of Udolpho*, p. 494).

The degree of discipline in convents varied wildly by geography, time period, the codes of the religious orders that sponsored them, and the ideals of the local authorities. At some convents, the nuns had their own money to buy whatever they wished; at others, nuns began their service with a vow of poverty and surrendered their possessions, which were liquidated to help support the convent. In Radcliffe's novel, when Emily enters the convent of St. Clair, she makes no payments or donations but is readily welcomed by the abbess. The nuns of St. Clair do no work and spend much of their idle time gossiping, but their living conditions are spartan. When Emily enters the convent, she finds herself in a tiny cell with only a bed of straw. Like many medieval and renaissance women, Emily considers remaining at the convent when she has no other options, but when she suddenly becomes a wealthy heiress, the idea of staying at St. Clair is quickly forgotten.

The Novel in Focus

Plot summary. As the novel opens, Emily St. Aubert is living an idyllic existence with her parents at La Valleé, a modest chateau set high in the Pyrenees. Monsieur St. Aubert has devoted himself to a simple life, far removed from the complications and pettiness of Paris society. One day Madame St. Aubert's locket with Emily's portrait inside mysteriously disappears. Emily later notices a romantic poem has mysteriously appeared on the wall of the tiny fishing house on their property. Otherwise, life follows a routine. Monsieur St. Aubert devotes himself to Emily's education, teaching her Latin, English, the sciences, and literature, while also trying to instill in her his own appreciation for the peace and satisfaction that a simple life brings. Emily studies diligently, following Monsieur St. Aubert's philosophy that "a well-informed mind is the best security against the contagion of folly and vice" (*The Mysteries of Udolpho*, p. 6). She adopts Monsieur St. Aubert's appreciation of the simple life, knowing she will receive only a small inheritance, as the family's fortunes have diminished due to poor investments.

The family's tranquillity is upset when Madame St. Aubert dies from a terrible fever. Emily grows additionally disconcerted when she hears her father sighing over a mysterious miniature of a woman who is not her mother. Trying to overcome his melancholy, St. Aubert takes Emily for a trip through the Pyrenees. During their travels they meet Valancourt, a young nobleman hunting in the mountains, who joins them in their travels. Spending several days with the St. Auberts, Valancourt falls in love with Emily, but he must leave her to return to his regiment because of increased hostilities in the civil wars between the French king's Catholic armies and the rebellious Protestant Huguenots.

As they reach the coast, Monsieur St. Aubert's health declines and Emily struggles to locate a doctor. They find a small village where they are welcomed by an elderly peasant. Monsieur St. Aubert is surprised to learn that they are very near to Chateau-le-Blanc, the former residence of the marquis de Villeroi. Monsieur St. Aubert wistfully recalls the marquis's wife, the marchioness de Villeroi, but gives Emily no explanation of their acquaintance. The marquis's sprawling chateau now lies abandoned. Just before he dies, Monsieur St. Aubert tells Emily that, without reading them, she must burn a collection of papers he has hidden in his study (the place where he sighed over the miniature). Emily agrees and, leaving Emily only the modest chateau at La Vallée, Monsieur St. Aubert dies. He is buried at the neighboring convent of St. Clair.

Returning to La Vallée, Emily finds her father's secret documents. She dutifully overcomes her desire to read the papers and burns them as promised. For a few months Emily continues on at La Vallée, pursuing her education and receiving Valancourt. Monsieur St. Aubert's sister, Madam Cheron, deems it improper for Emily to live at La Vallée without a chaperone, and so summons her niece to her own chateau in Tholouse.

In Tholouse, Madame Cheron forbids Emily to write Valancourt; because he has an older brother and stands to inherit nothing, Madame Cheron considers him an unworthy suitor. Also, knowing that Emily has no fortune of her own, Madame Cheron believes she should use her beauty to attract a wealthy husband from a prestigious family. Emily obeys her aunt's wishes, but Valancourt continues to visit Emily in the secluded gardens of Madame Cheron's chateau. When Madame Cheron learns that Valancourt is related to Madame Clairval, a wealthy and influential neighbor, she suddenly encourages Emily to see him and supports their plans to marry.

Meanwhile, Madame Cheron pursues a husband for herself, a seemingly wealthy Italian nobleman from Venice, whom she marries. The nobleman, Monsieur Montoni, drops his courtly façade and shows his true colors when he prohibits Emily from marrying Valancourt. He also informs Emily that they will be moving to his home in Venice. Valancourt and Emily consider eloping, but decide it would be devastating to their future plans and too detrimental to Emily's social situation. They part sadly, hoping to be reunited.

In Venice, Montoni becomes even colder toward Emily and her aunt, now Madame Montoni, when he learns that his new wife's fortune is much smaller than she led him to believe. He too has misrepresented his wealth; his Venice mansion is in dire need of repair. In an attempt to salvage his finances and ally himself with a powerful family, Montoni invites Count Morano to court Emily. Though Emily refuses the count's affections, Montoni arranges for a wedding in a few days.

Before the wedding can take place, Montoni takes his wife, her niece, and the entire household to the ancient castle of Udolpho with no explanation. At Udolpho, Emily explores the gloomy corridors with Madame Montoni's servant, Annette. Annette has learned the history of the castle from the other servants and explains that it was once owned by Signora Laurentini, a distant cousin of Montoni's. Montoni wanted to marry her, but she refused and disappeared from the castle shortly thereafter. Her body was never found, but the servants believe her ghost still walks the castle. Emily dismisses the more fantastic elements of the story, but is intrigued by the disappearance of the signora. Later, while wandering through one of the signora's old rooms, Emily finds a veiled painting. When she lifts the veil, she is terrified and faints from the shock of what she has seen.

Montoni presses Madame Montoni to sign over her French properties to him, but she refuses. Furious, Montoni spends his time repairing the castle's defenses and gathering armed condottieri in its hall. Emily enjoys the solitude of her chamber, but becomes frightened when she hears noises in the corridors and sees a strange apparition outside her window. During the stay here, Montoni and his men ride out in large numbers and return to the castle for wild celebrations. Annette spends time with Ludovico, one of the castle servants, and learns that Montoni's men are professional soldiers of fortune and have been successfully raiding nearby towns.

Emily is shocked one morning to learn that Count Morano has arrived at the castle. In the middle of the night, he comes into Emily's room and tries to abduct her, but Montoni and his men hear the commotion and burst into the room. Montoni and Morano draw swords, and Morano is severely wounded. Despite his strong desire to kill Morano, Montoni allows his servants to carry him from the castle. Emily later learns that Montoni rejected Morano's marriage suit in Venice because Morano's fortune was not so large after all.

When government troops march against Montoni's castle, Montoni sends Emily away to a secluded cottage. After a few days reminiscent of her life at La Vallée, Emily returns to Udolpho and sees that a terrible battle has taken place. Despite some damage to the castle walls, Montoni's men have won the day and driven away the government forces. Turning his attention back to Emily's aunt, Montoni demands she sign over her lands, but still she refuses. Her aunt disappears, and Emily fears foul play, then learns that her aunt has been locked in one of the towers. In a last attempt to get her properties, Montoni refuses to give his wife food, but to no avail. Madame Montoni remains obstinate, ultimately dying of starvation and fever in the tower.

Emily is heartbroken by the death of her aunt and watches sadly as Montoni's cruel soldiers bury her in the chapel. The hotly desired properties have passed to Emily, and Montoni threatens her with the same fate as her aunt if she does not surrender her rights to the land. Emily refuses at first, but when Montoni promises she will be returned to France if she signs the papers, she agrees and signs. Montoni tells her she will be returned to France in a few months, once he is sure the lands are fully in his possession.

Back in her chamber, Emily again sees a strange figure out on the battlements and hears singing in the middle of the night. Though the voice is faint, Emily believes the singer to be Valancourt and learns from Ludovico that there is a Frenchman locked in the dungeon. Certain that the man is Valancourt, Emily sends a note to him through Ludovico and is surprised to receive her mother's missing locket in return. Ludovico promises to sneak the man out of the prison.

True to his word, Ludovico brings the prisoner to Emily's chamber the next night. Emily is disappointed to see he is not Valancourt. His name is Du Pont, and he once lived very near Emily's home at La Vallée. Though they have never met, Du Pont had admired Emily from afar. He admits to having taken the locket from the fishing cottage, and also he wrote the poem on the wall. A few nights later, when Du Pont is again visiting Emily, Ludovico rushes in and tells them the castle gate has been left open while Montoni's men celebrate another successful expedition. Emily, Du Pont, Annette, and Ludovico all escape the castle and race away.

Back in France the count de Villefort, a distant relative of her father's old acquaintance, the marquis de Villeroi, removes his daughter Blanche from the convent where she has been living and takes his family to live at Chateau-le-Blanc. He hopes to restore the sprawling Chateau to its former glory. A few days later a storm nearly dashes a small ship into the rocky beach by the Chateau. The ship lands, and Emily, Du Pont, Ludovico, and Annette come ashore.

Blanche makes friends with Emily, who agrees to stay at Chateau-le-Blanc until she learns whether or not the papers Montoni forced her to sign are legally binding. Emily also writes letters to Valancourt's family, hoping they will be forwarded to his current post. Emily and Blanche explore the ruined chateau, which captivates them with its endless hallways and the chambers of the marchioness, all locked since her death 20 years earlier. The housemaid, Dorothée, remarks at Emily's resemblance to the marchioness and finally agrees to unlock the chambers. Dorothée and Emily enter the marchioness's suite of rooms and are terrified to see a figure lying on the bed. They race out of the rooms and share their story with the rest of the household.

Wanting to dispel the servants' growing fears about ghosts in the chateau, the count asks for a volunteer to spend a night in the marchioness's chambers. Ludovico bravely steps forward and locks himself in the rooms for the night. The next morning he has disappeared. Unable to solve the mystery of his disappearance, the count and his son stay in the rooms. They make it through the night, but seem shaken the next morning and refuse to divulge what they have seen.

Emily visits her father's grave at St. Clair and begins living in a small cell among the monks and nuns of that monastery and convent. One of the nuns, Sister Agnes, starts raving when she sees Emily. The other nuns explain that Sister Agnes has been demented since she came to the convent 20 years earlier. Several days later Blanche persuades Emily to return to the chateau, and, soon after, Valancourt arrives. He seems strangely melancholy during their time together and tells Emily that he no longer deserves her esteem. Confused by Valancourt's words, Emily goes to the kindly count for advice. He informs her that Valancourt is reputed to have lost his small fortune through gambling and vice in Paris. The count's own son was nearly ruined when Valancourt and his friends apparently cheated him in a game of cards. The count tells her she should send Valancourt away and accept the unblemished affections of the noble Du Pont. Devastated, Emily dismisses Valancourt and leaves for La Vallée.

A few weeks later, the count and his family leave Chateau-le-Blanc to visit Emily. They lose their way through the mountains at night and seek refuge in a ruined fort. Finding a band of hunters inside, they agree to share a meal with them. Blanche loses the group in the darkness and overhears some of the other "hunters" discussing their recent robberies. They are banditti plotting to poison the count and his group. Before Blanche can tell her father, he overpowers the bandits with the help of his servants, Du Pont, and (it turns out) Ludovico. After the fight, Ludovico explains that these same bandits are affiliated with a group of pirates who ply the Mediterranean. A network of caves link the beach with the cellars just below the marchioness's chambers back at the chateau. While Ludovico slept, the pirates came into the room through a secret door after storing their plunder in the caves and were surprised to find him there. Not wanting him to give away the secret, they kidnapped him. Ludovico also reveals that one of the pirates bragged about pretending to be a ghost when Emily and Dorothée visited the chambers.

After a brief visit at La Vallée, Emily returns with the count and Blanche to Chateau-le-Blanc. Emily visits St. Clair and learns that Sister Agnes is dying. When she says good-bye to Sister Agnes, she finds her strangely coherent. Agnes confesses to Emily that she is actually Signora Laurentini. She once loved the marquis de Villeroi, but his family did not approve of her, and he returned to France to marry the marchioness. Feeling betrayed and seething with jealousy, the signora followed him back to Chateau-le-Blanc and slowly convinced him that the marchioness had been unfaithful. Twisted by the signora's lies, the marquis poisoned the marchioness, but then he realized his mistake and left Signora Laurentini and Chateau-le-Blanc behind forever. Repenting her murderous jealousy and the loss of the marquis, who died in battle just weeks later, Signora Laurentini entered the convent of St. Clair, hiding her true identity.

Sister Agnes now tells Emily that the marchioness was the younger sister of Monsieur St. Aubert. Saddened by the tragic death of the aunt she never knew existed, Emily realizes this fact explains the mystery of St. Aubert's documents and the miniature portrait. We also learn that the veiled painting at Udolpho concealed a wax sculpture of a rotting corpse used by previous generations as a Catholic religious warning about the wages of sin. In the shadows of the chamber, Emily believed it to have been the remains of Signora Laurentini. At this point, Sister Agnes dies, leaving her considerable wealth to the current heir of the marchioness. Emily is thus newly wealthy; however, she feels saddened by all the unnecessary tragedy and her own loss of Valancourt.

The count comes to Emily and tells her he had been falsely convinced of Valancourt's treachery. While Valancourt was ruined by his own gambling, he had nothing to do with the crooked games or the loss of others' fortunes. With the reputation of Valancourt restored, Emily's newfound wealth, and his plea to her for forgiveness, nothing impedes their union. Valancourt is called back to Chateau-le-Blanc and happily reunited with Emily. As a married couple, they take possession of Emily's original home at La Vallée.

Poison in fiction and history. When Montoni retreats to the castle of Udolpho, he believes he is safe from the political treacheries and betrayals that have been smoldering in Venice. But when he makes a toast to the future endeavors of his condottieri, his wine glass shatters and we learn that it is "Venice glass, which had the quality of breaking, upon receiving poisoned liquor" (*The Mysteries of Udolpho*, p. 313). Realizing that someone is trying to kill him, Montoni imprisons the servants who poured the wine and uses this incident as an excuse to imprison Madame Montoni as well. Poison also figures prominently in the death of Emily's aunt, the former mar-

chioness de Villeroi. After the marquis agreed to Signora Laurentini's diabolical plan to murder the marchioness, "a slow poison was administered" (*The Mysteries of Udolpho*, p. 658).

In the Renaissance, poison was commonly used in political assassinations in European lands. Murderers favored poison because it concealed the identity of the killer and was difficult to detect, given the limited medical techniques of the period. The novel speculates that even if the marchioness's father suspected the plot, "the difficulty of obtaining proof deterred him from prosecuting the Marquis de Villeroi" (*The Mysteries of Udolpho*, p. 659). Similarly, Montoni eventually releases the servants he suspects of poisoning him because there is no way of proving their guilt.

Inspiration for the novel's instances of poisoning may hark back to Radcliffe's own family history. In 1672 her ancestor Cornelius De Witt was falsely accused of plotting to poison William of Orange. The story of De Witt's subsequent torture and imprisonment was widely known during Ann Radcliffe's life and may have had an influence on her frequent use of poison in *The Mysteries of Udolpho*.

Sources and literary context. With the publication of Horace Walpole's *The Castle of Otranto* in 1764, gothic fiction seized the imagination of English readers. The movement featured stories of mystery and terror, characterized by gloom, violence, and medieval settings. The term *gothic* was drawn from medieval architecture that figured so prominently in the fiction, especially the ruins and edifices that distinguished its settings. Among the most widely used gothic elements were ruined castles, sublime landscapes, shadowy dungeons, wandering ghosts, and sinister plots.

One of the first female gothic writers was Sophia Lee, who wrote *The Recess* in 1783 and ran the school that many scholars believe Ann Radcliffe attended as an adolescent. With the publication of *The Romance of the Forest* and then *The Mysteries of Udolpho*, Radcliffe gave new energy to the movement and helped make the gothic romance the most popular literary genre of the 1790s. More exactly, Radcliffe cultivated a particular type of gothic fiction, one that aimed to inspire terror, not horror. Writers of horror, argued Radcliffe, go far beyond insinuation; they graphically depict grisly deeds and grotesque apparitions. In contrast, terror restricts itself to just insinuating dreadful circumstances and perilous dangers into the reader's imagination without

Radcliffe's description of Udolpho may have been influenced by her view of Carisbrooke Castle during her visits to the Isle of Wight.

giving full details. Based usually on unseen threats, it awakens a reader's faculties to a high intensity. Terror is expansive, whereas horror constricts and freezes these same faculties, a difference Radcliffe allegedly explained in an essay attributed to her—"On the Supernatural in Poetry."

Radcliffe had not traveled outside of England at the time she wrote *The Mysteries of Udolpho*, and many of her descriptions of the beautiful landscapes of France and the romantic splendors of Italy were borrowed from travel books. William Coxe's *Travels in Switzerland* (1789) mentions the nuns of St. Clare, claiming that one of them was Agnes, the former queen of Hungary, who spent her old age in the convent. Radcliffe's own travels to England's Isle of Wight, with its famous ruins of Carisbrooke Castle and Netley Abbey, may have influenced her description of the crumbling castle of Udolpho.

The wild landscape paintings of Salvator Rosa (1615-1673) further informed Radcliffe's imagination, as did the French mythological landscape paintings of Claude Lorrain (1600-1682). Finally, her landscape descriptions are heavily indebted to the theory of the "picturesque." Popularized in her time, this theory concerned the criteria for making verbal descriptions evoke "painted" pictures in the mind (discussed in William Gilpin's *Three Essays,* 1792).

The wax figure that Emily believes to be the corpse of Signora Laurentini may have been inspired by the description of a tomb in Pierre Jean Grosley's *New Observations on Italy and Its Inhabitants:* "[in] the waxen image of a woman, made by her lover who had found her dead and buried upon his return . . . a lizard is sucking her mouth, a worm is creeping out of one of her cheeks" (Grosley in Norton, p. 73). This resembles the waxen figure Emily sees in the novel, the face of which is "partly decayed and disfigured by worms (*Mysteries of Udolpho*, p. 662).

Events in History at the Time the Novel Was Written

The gothic movement and women's rights. In 1765 William Blackstone stated in his *Commentaries on the Laws of England* that "the husband and the wife are one person in law; that is, the very being or legal existence of the woman is suspended during the marriage, or at least is incorporated and consolidated into that of the husband: under whose total protection and cover, she performs everything" (Blackstone in Hoeveler, p. 6). In eighteenth-century England, women had no rights to sue, sign contracts, or make a valid will without the consent of their husbands. When Ann Radcliffe signed the publishing contracts for *The Mysteries of Udolpho* and her other novels, her husband, William Radcliffe, had to sign them as well. A contract signed by a wife without her husband's consent had no legal validity, and a woman had no right to sell property, intellectual or otherwise.

Married women found it difficult to control any of their own real property during marriage. While a husband could not take away his wife's land or other real property, he could take all rents and other income these properties generated. By law, husbands had the right to physically punish their wives, and women had little recourse to escape bad marriages. Divorce by act of Parliament was enormously expensive and quite rare; from 1670 to 1857 only four women managed to obtain divorces this way. To gain a legal separation in the church courts, a wife had to prove that her husband was adulterous and so physically cruel as to be life threatening. If a wife left her husband without a lawful divorce, she was guilty of desertion and had no claim to any of his property—including property she had brought into the marriage. In addition, she lost all rights to custody of their children.

Among upper-class women, England's marriage laws made the well-being and safety of heiresses a major concern. Realizing that they could gain complete control of vast fortunes through a simple marriage, male suitors seduced wealthy heiresses without the consent of their families. By 1753 this problem had become so prevalent that, in an attempt to curb clandestine marriages, Parliament passed the Hardwicke Marriage Act, which made parental consent mandatory for everyone under the age of 21. Radcliffe appears to have applied such laws, with which she was familiar, to the plot of her novel. While Valancourt has Emily's true love, a clandestine marriage is his intention when he asks her to "quit Madame Montoni's house, and be conducted by him to the church of the Augustines, where a friar should wait to unite them" (*The Mysteries of Udolpho*, p. 154). Emily refuses because of "her repugnance to a clandestine marriage, her fear of emerging on the world with embarrassments" (*The Mysteries of Udolpho*, p. 155).

In such a male-dominated world, it perhaps comes as no surprise that "middle-class women writers of this period were particularly attracted to the female gothic novel because they could explore within it their fantasized overthrow of the public realm, figured as a series of ideologically constructed male 'spaces,' in favor of the creation of a new privatized, feminized world" (Hoeveler, p. 4). Novels like *The Mysteries of Udolpho* typically featured an innocent female character who eventually triumphs over a male villain—and even gets asked for forgiveness by the hero—despite oppressive strictures imposed from every side. While Emily is not married to him in the novel, her relationship with Montoni puts her in virtually the same position.

Belief in ghosts—from the novel's to Radcliffe's day. Catholic folklore of the late sixteenth century often featured ghosts. According to this folklore, the spirits of men who had died after leading sinful lives or without giving a proper confession appeared to friends or family members and asked them to pray for their salvation. These doomed spirits were consistent with the Catholic belief in purgatory, a temporary state in which the soul undergoes punishment before being allowed into Heaven. Many stories ended with the reappearance of the ghost in a more peaceful condition, an indication that the soul of the deceased was passing from purgatory into Heaven. This convenient resolution gave credence to the power of prayer and encouraged continued support to Catholic churches that took donations to pray for the souls of the departed.

Protestants—Radcliffe was one—rejected the idea of purgatory and usually attempted to refute the belief that ghosts were the spirits of the dead. In 1570 Louis Lavater wrote *De Spectris*, which became one of the most prominent Protestant books on supernatural occurrences. The book emphasized the Protestant view that spirits go directly to heaven or hell at death and do not return from either. Because their fates are sealed at death, spirits cannot walk the earth soliciting prayers for their salvation. Instead Protestants believed that ghosts, if they existed at all, were good or bad angels, most commonly bad angels sent by the devil to lure men into sin and false doctrines. These bad angels could be driven away only through prayer and the study of scripture.

For those who continued to believe in ghosts as spirits of the dead, there were certain rules to be followed while encountering a spirit. N. Taillepied, writing in France in the 1580s, advised his readers that, although "we are actually affrighted and startled in some degree at any such appearance or at a ghost," we should "not fear any the more, nor tremble and shake, but boldly say: 'If thou art of God, speak; if thou art not of God, begone'" (Taillepied in Finucane, p. 102). When Ludovico asks to have a sword during his stay in the haunted chamber, the count echoes another sixteenth-century belief by telling him, "Your sword cannot defend you against a ghost, neither can bars, or bolts; for a spirit, as you know, can glide through a keyhole as easily as through a door" (*The Mysteries of Udolpho*, p. 544).

Even after Ludovico's disappearance, the count doubts the existence of ghosts in the chateau, despite a friend's advice. "I allow it may be probable," counsels the friend, "that the spirits of the dead are permitted to return to the earth only on occasions of high import; but the present import may be your destruction" (*The Mysteries of Udolpho*, p. 571). The count continues to regard this belief as mere "superstition," which is the conclusion of this episode that Radcliffe delivers to her readers.

By Radcliffe's time the questions concerning the existence and nature of ghosts had not yet been fully answered. Samuel Johnson spent considerable time evaluating the historical evidence (see **The Life of Samuel Johnson**, also covered in *WLAIT 3: British and Irish Literature and Its Times*). Johnson came to the following conclusion: "It is

SUPERNATURAL EFFECTS, MUNDANE CAUSES

~

Incident	Explanation
Disappearance of Madame St. Aubert's locket.	Du Pont has watched Emily from afar and steals the locket from the fishing house.
A ghostly voice accosts Montoni during a meeting with his men.	Du Pont has found a secret chamber and wails through a crack in the wall.
Disappearance of Ludovico from the sealed chamber.	Pirates enter through a secret door and kidnap Ludovico.
Apparition on the battlements.	Du Pont has tried to visit Emily while briefly free of the dungeon.
Spectral singing heard for years in the forest around Chateau-le-Blanc.	The Abbess secretly allows Sister Agnes to leave the convent at night, hoping her singing will ease her troubled spirit.
Emily and Dorotheé see an apparition in the mar-	A pirate, caught by surprise in the room, pretends to be a ghost to frighten the women away.

wonderful that five thousand years have now elapsed since the creation of the world and still it is undecided whether or not there has ever been an instance of the spirit of any person appearing after death. All argument is against it; but all belief is for it" (Johnson in Finucane, p. 169). In keeping with this view, in the novel Emily experiences numerous occurrences that she is tempted to believe are supernatural. Some of these incidents are dramatically established but immediately explained. When Emily hears something strike her door and hears heavy breathing on the other side, we expect supernatural circumstances. Instead it is Annette, who has run terrified to Emily's chamber and fainted just as she reaches the door. Every other supernatural

incident has a similar explanation, though some do not come until late in the novel. Here are the key "realities" behind the novel's most "supernatural" moments.

Reception. Ann Radcliffe received £500 for the copyright of *The Mysteries of Udolpho*, an unheard-of fee for an author of the period, especially a female author. This amount was "at the time so unusually large a sum for a work of imagination" that, on being told she had received £500, old Mr. Cadell, a man "more experienced" than anyone in such matters, offered a wager of £10 "that it was not the fact" (Norton, p. 95). Ironically, Cadell's publishing firm would pay Radcliffe £800 for her next novel, *The Italian*. By comparison, more than 20 years later, Jane Austen would receive only £10 for her gothic parody *Northanger Abbey*.

The reading public was instantly fascinated by the novel: "When a family was numerous, the volumes flew, and were sometimes torn, from hand to hand, and the complaints of those whose studies were thus interrupted, were a general tribute to the genius of the author" (Scott in Norton, p. 102). Critics appeared to be just as intrigued. The *Monthly Review* raved that "a story so well contrived to hold curiosity in pleasing suspense, and at the same time to agitate the soul with strong emotions of sympathetic terror, has seldom been produced" (*Monthly Review* in Norton, p. 106). When reviews offered mild criticisms of the novel, the backlash was so severe that retractions were quickly made. After the *Critical Review* received an outraged response to its first article on the novel, it was quick to dilute its critical tone with an apology, followed by high praise indeed: "It could not be our intention to speak slightingly of a work which all must admire, and which we have no hesitation in pronouncing 'The most interesting novel in the English language'" (*Critical Review* in Norton, p. 105).

—Terence Davis

For More Information

Bruhm, Steven. *Gothic Bodies: The Politics of Pain in Romantic Fiction.* Philadelphia: University of Pennsylvania Press, 1994.

Castle, Terry. "The Spectralization of the Other" in *The Mysteries of Udolpho.* In *The New Eighteenth Century.* Ed. Laura Brown and Felicity Nussbaum. London: Methuen, 1987.

Ellis, Kate Ferguson. *The Contested Castle: Gothic Novels and the Subversion of Domestic Ideology.* Chicago: University of Illinois Press, 1989.

Finucane, R. C. *Ghosts: Appearances of the Dead & Cultural Transformation.* Amherst: Prometheus, 1996.

Gilpin, William. *Three Essays: On Picturesque Beauty; On Picturesque Travel; and On Sketching Landscape.* 3rd ed. London: Cadell and Davis, 1808.

Hoeveler, Diane Long. *Gothic Feminism: The Professionalization of Gender from Charlotte Smith to the Brontës.* University Park: Pennsylvania State University Press, 1998.

McNamara, Jo Ann Kay. *Sisters in Arms: Catholic Nuns through Two Millennia.* Cambridge: Harvard University Press, 1996.

Miles, Robert. *Ann Radcliffe: The Great Enchantress.* Manchester, N.Y.: Manchester University Press, 1995.

Norton, Rictor. *Mistress of Udolpho: The Life of Ann Radcliffe.* London: Leicester University Press, 1999.

Poovey, Mary. "Ideology in *The Mysteries of Udolpho.*" *Criticism* 21 (1979): 307-30.

Radcliffe, Ann. *The Mysteries of Udolpho.* Ed. Bonamy Dobrée. Oxford, England: Oxford University Press, 1998.

———. "On the Supernatural in Poetry." *New Monthly Magazine* 16 (1826): 145-52.

Trease, Geoffrey. *The Condottieri: Soldiers of Fortune,* New York: Holt, Rinehart, and Winston, 1971.

Oroonoko, or The Royal Slave: A True History

by

Aphra Behn

~

THE LITERARY WORK

A short novel set in Africa and South America in 1663-64; published in London in 1688.

SYNOPSIS

Oroonoko, a young African prince, is enslaved and transported from West Africa to an English plantation in Surinam. Captured after leading a slave revolt, he nobly endures torture and mutilation before being executed.

Little is known about the enigmatic Aphra Behn other than the fact that she was the first Englishwoman to write professionally. She is believed to have been born Aphra Johnson in a small town near Canterbury, England, in July 1640. In the 1660s she may (as she claims in *Oroonoko*) have traveled to Surinam, a British plantation colony on the Atlantic coast of South America. Later in that same decade, she acted as a spy in the Netherlands on behalf of the newly restored King Charles II. Returning penniless to London and having failed to persuade the government to reimburse her for the money she had spent on gathering intelligence, she seems to have served some time in debtors' prison. She began writing to pay her debts, in the end producing from 15 to 20 plays that enjoyed notable success on the London stage. The best known is *The Rover* (1677), which, like her other plays, features the intrigue and bawdiness common in Restoration drama. While she also wrote poetry, Behn is remembered today primarily for *Oroonoko*, one of the earliest examples of a new literary form—the novel.

Events in History at the Time of the Novel

Plantation settlements. In the sixteenth century, Spain still dominated European colonization of the New World. Great Britain entered the competition near the end of the sixteenth century, but early British attempts to found overseas settlements faltered. During the seventeenth century, however, the British succeeded in establishing colonies in the Americas that would provide the foundation of a world empire. With the exception of the Puritan settlements in New England (undertaken to escape religious persecution), these early colonies were plantation settlements that in certain respects resembled those the Spanish had already established. As such, they embodied a combination of commercial and patriotic aspirations: the merchants and adventurers who founded them wished to make personal profit for themselves, but they also generally shared the larger goal of securing economic self-sufficiency for Britain. They hoped that crops might be grown in the colonies and shipped back to Britain, either to be consumed or turned into finished products.

By the middle of the seventeenth century, British plantation settlements had been founded in two parts of the New World: the southern Atlantic coast of North America (i.e., Virginia,

Aphra Behn

1607; Maryland, 1632); and the islands of the Bermudas and the West Indies (i.e., Bermuda, 1609; St. Kitts, 1624; Barbados, 1625). In both regions, Britain at first grew cotton and tobacco; on Barbados and the other islands of the West Indies, however, these cash crops were soon wholly or partly replaced by sugar cane, in response to the growing desire for sugar in London.

It was from Barbados that British settlers began to colonize the nearby coast of South America in the 1650s, led by the island's former governor, Francis, Lord Willoughby of Parham. In 1651 Willoughby led a group of planters to an area between the mouth of the Amazon River in Brazil and today's Venezuela, an area that would become the colonial territory of Surinam. Willoughby and other historical individuals appear as characters in *Oroonoko*, the second part of which is set at Parham, Willoughby's sugar plantation in Surinam. During the early 1660s, when Behn herself was probably in Surinam, global commercial rivalry between the British and the Dutch intensified, leading to the Second Anglo-Dutch War (1665-67). Under the Treaty of Breda, which ended the war but not the rivalry, Surinam was ceded to the Dutch in exchange for Manhattan Island—a loss that Behn laments in *Oroonoko*. The colony was afterward known as Dutch Guiana.

Rise of the Atlantic slave trade. Well before Europeans ventured across the Atlantic Ocean, they explored and traded along the coast of Africa. Starting with the Portuguese in the early fifteenth century, Europeans came to the African coast in search of a sea route to Asia. They established supply stations for ships sailing to Asia and soon began trading with the Africans. In particular, they bought large quantities of cheap and abundant African gold from the Akan peoples—the Fanti, Ashanti, and others—who lived between the mouths of the Volta and Ankobra rivers. Part of today's Ghana, this region soon became known to the Europeans as "the Gold Coast."

Until the beginning of the seventeenth century, the Portuguese retained a virtual monopoly on trade with coastal West Africa, including the Gold Coast. Jealously guarding against encroachment by other Europeans, the Portuguese built a number of coastal fortresses that served as trading outposts. Beginning about 1600, however, first the Dutch and then the British gradually cut into the West African gold trade, eventually building their own forts or capturing those of the Portuguese. The biggest Portuguese fort, Elmina, fell to the Dutch in 1638. A few years earlier, in 1632, the British had established their own fort, Cormantine, on land leased from the local Fanti king. This is the "Coramantien" of the novel, which Behn depicts as a country ruled by Oroonoko's grandfather. The fort fell to the Dutch in 1665, during the Second Anglo-Dutch War. By the 1680s, the Dutch and the British had successfully excluded the Portuguese from trade along the Gold Coast.

In that same decade—the decade in which Behn published *Oroonoko*—another commodity was overtaking gold as the Europeans' most valuable export from the West African coast. Slavery had survived on a limited scale in the European, African, and Islamic worlds since ancient times, and a slave trade existed in Africa when the Portuguese arrived. African slavery before the Portuguese, however, was of a very different nature in that it did not stem from the kidnapping or sale of human beings but rather from their capture in war, or some negotiations that called for temporary enslavement.

Apparently as early as the eighth century slaves had been used to work on sugar plantations in the Islamic Middle East. Such plantations served as a model when the cultivation of sugar cane spread further west in the Mediterranean world. Thus a link between slavery and labor-intensive plantations—even between slavery and a specific crop, sugar cane—persisted from the Middle Ages. When, in the fifteenth century, the Portuguese discovered islands such as Madeira and Cape Verde in their explorations along the African coast, they founded sugar plantations there and began using African slaves to work them. Meanwhile, the Spanish had established the first plantations in the Americas. Portuguese traders began transporting some Africans to work on these Spanish plantations, and by the 1580s the Portuguese had established plantations of their own in need of slave labor in Brazil.

First the Dutch and then the British followed the Spanish and Portuguese in establishing plantations. The Dutch and the British afterward strove, in turn, to control the increasingly lucrative slave trade. As the plantations expanded during the seventeenth century, this trade in human beings grew on an unprecedented scale, providing a cheap, abundant, and brutally imprisoned labor supply for the economic ventures of the New World. By the end of the century, with an estimated 35,000 transported each year, slaves would overtake all other commodities as Africa's most valuable export, and the still growing slave trade would rest firmly in the hands of the British.

Events in Britain: Restoration and revolution. Dominance of the slave trade was an aspect of Britain's general rise to commercial preeminence over the course of the seventeenth century. With this expansion of British commerce came great benefits, but also social tensions that helped redraw the political landscape. Not all of the profits from commerce would find their way into the hands of the traditional titled elites like Lord Willoughby, the aristocratic proprietor of the sugar plantation in Surinam. While such aristocrats often possessed the capital to fund commercial ventures, alongside this traditional pool of affluence, a separate source of wealth was emerging. It comprised those—such as merchants, lawyers, and other businessmen or professionals—who had initially made their money from business, rather than those who inherited their wealth and enhanced it through investments. The political demands of this growing middle class lay behind many of the profound conflicts that wracked British society in the seventeenth century.

Like Behn's novel, the full title of which is *Oroonoko, or The Royal Slave: A True History*, these conflicts concerned the nature of royalty and the question of what it means to be a king. Such is-

sues, unavoidably, also involved religion. Behn was a young girl when, after the bloody English civil war, King Charles I was dethroned and beheaded in 1649 by his victorious enemies in the Puritan-dominated Parliament. After 11 years of Puritan rule (the Interregnum), some of the English recalled their dead king's son from exile in Holland and restored him to the English throne as King Charles II. The Restoration of 1660, however, did not end the struggle between Parliament and the king. Crucial to the parliamentary cause had been a loose alliance between the Puritans and the merchant class, many of whom either were Puritans themselves or shared a number of Puritan values. Even after the Restoration, merchants and others still wished to limit the Crown's power and expand Parliament's. The course of the Interregnum had convinced them that a king was a necessary evil, but one to be severely restricted and controlled by Parliament. The royalists, by contrast, upheld the principle of the "divine right of kings," which taught that a monarch's power was divinely bestowed, transmitted through a single legitimate line of succession, and (theoretically at least) absolute in nature. The right to govern as a king, believed the royalists, was inborn, not acquired, and God-given rather than conferred by society.

"CORMANTEE" SLAVES

~

Slaves taken from the Gold Coast were called Cormantees, after the English fort Cormantine (Coramantien in the novel). They were prized by slaveholders for their strength and courage. In the early 1670s English colonists in Barbados, fearing that Cormantee slaves were planning to revolt, executed some 30 of them. Like Oroonoko in the novel, these slaves are reported to have died calmly in the belief that death would bring a return to their homelands.

These clashing conceptions of monarchy again came into open conflict in the early 1680s, after Charles II's younger brother James, the next in line for the throne, publicly declared that he was a Roman Catholic. In largely Protestant England, Catholicism was widely feared for several reasons, an important one being its association in the English mind with foreign enemies such as France and Spain. During the so-called Exclusion Crisis (1679-81), Charles, who had many illegitimate children but no heir, battled successfully to prevent Parliament from excluding James from the succession. When James followed his brother to the throne (as James II) after the latter's death in 1685, the new king's efforts on behalf of Catholicism led to a backlash that ended in his overthrow only four years later, in the Glorious or Bloodless Revolution of 1688.

ROYAL PARALLELS

While *Oroonoko* may be based on real events in Africa and South America, parallels between the novel and contemporary English politics suggest that it may have prompted Behn to write the story. In poems celebrating the royal brothers Charles II and James II, Aphra Behn had already referred to each of them as "Caesar," which is the name given to Oroonoko by the English in the novel. Like Oroonoko, who revolts rather than have his child born into slavery, James too was preoccupied with the fate of his offspring and potential heir, the son whose birth precipitated the Glorious Revolution of 1688. James was also one of the "black Stuarts," as some members of the royal family were called because of their dark complexions and hair. Finally, Behn uses the phrase "the frightful Spectacle of a mangl'd King" at the end of the novel to refer to the mutilated Oroonoko, but it would also remind readers of the executed Charles I, beheaded in 1649 (Behn, *Oroonoko*, p. 65).

The Glorious Revolution was engineered largely by the same political grouping that had earlier tried and failed to exclude James from succeeding to the throne, who had become known collectively as Whigs. The Whigs included the merchants and liberal Anglicans (members of the mainstream Church of England, which was headed by the reigning monarch). Puritans and other dissenting Protestants also tended to be Whigs. Against them were the royalists, who had supported James's succession and who were now called Tories. Most Tories belonged to the Anglican Church, many as conservative members. A handful were Catholics. The Whigs and the Tories were England's first true political parties in the modern sense. Born from the events of the 1680s, they would dominate the political scene for the next century.

The Revolution itself was triggered by the birth of a male heir to the throne in June 1688,

which left the Whigs facing the prospect of another Catholic monarch. Shortly afterward, Whig leaders encouraged James's son-in-law, the Dutch Protestant prince William of Orange, to invade England. When William did so with a large army in October, James's nerve failed and he fled to France. In the settlement that followed, Parliament offered the crown jointly to William and his wife Mary, James's Protestant daughter.

Behn, a fervent royalist, wrote *Oroonoko* in the tense months before the Glorious Revolution, as it became clear that support for James's policies had eroded even among Tories. Conversely, however, few Whigs actually intended to depose England's legitimate monarch; the overture toward William had been meant rather to intimidate James into abandoning his pro-Catholic stance. Yet by the time Behn died in April 1689, William and Mary had been crowned as king and queen. In a close parallel to her novel, a man whose bloodline had predestined him for kingship had been violently removed from his royal station, to endure humiliating exile in a foreign land.

The Novel in Focus

Plot summary. Behn prefaces the novel with a dedicatory letter addressed to Richard Maitland, earl of Lauderdale, a Catholic supporter of James II who would follow the exiled king to France. "This is a true Story, of a Man Gallant enough to merit your Protection," she writes; if the tale seems made up, it is because "these Countries do, in all things, so far differ from ours, as to produce unconceivable Wonders" (*Oroonoko*, p. 7). The claim of telling a true story is repeated in the novel's opening paragraphs and often later in the work, throughout which the narrator seems to speak with Behn's own voice. She purports to have seen many of the events in Surinam herself and to have heard the rest from "the Mouth of the chief Actor in this History, the Hero himself," who also told her about his youth in Africa (*Oroonoko*, p. 8).

Before beginning the story, the narrator briefly describes Surinam's native inhabitants and how Africans are brought there to work as slaves on the sugar plantations. The British colonists, says the narrator, live with the local Indians "in perfect Amity, without daring to command 'em; but on the contrary, caress 'em with all the brotherly and friendly Affection in the World, trading with 'em for food, animal skins, and other supplies" (*Oroonoko*, p. 8). The Indians are like Adam and Eve in their modest and simple innocence. They are useful to the British, who therefore treat the Indians well and do not dare to enslave them, especially since the Indians so utterly outnumber the colonists. "Those then," she continues, "whom we make use of to work in our Plantations of Sugar are Negro's, Black-Slaves [sic] altogether" (*Oroonoko*, p. 11). (The narrator is wrong on two counts: the early British did enslave Indians; and blacks too outnumbered the British.) The African slaves are bought by colonists who strike a deal with a ship's captain, agreeing on a price per head for a certain number of slaves.

One of the places where the slaves are purchased is "*Coramantien, a Country of Blacks so called*," a "war-like and brave" kingdom that is always in conflict with some neighbor or other, and that consequently has a steady supply of prisoners to sell into slavery. The British captains pay the Coramantien generals directly for slaves, so that "the General only has all the profit" (*Oroonoko*, p. 11). The king of Coramantien is an old man with many wives and 13 sons. Each of the sons, however, has died bravely in battle, leaving a single successor, a 17-year-old grandson named Oroonoko. This young prince is already a brave and accomplished warrior, a handsome young man "adorn'd with a native Beauty so transcending all those of his gloomy Race" that even those who did not know him were struck with "Awe and Reverence," as is the narrator herself when she first meets him much later in Surinam (*Oroonoko*, p. 12). In addition to his beauty, Oroonoko possesses both a noble soul and a quick and ready intelligence. An apt pupil, he has been educated in European style by a French tutor. From the tutor he learned French, and from the many European traders in the kingdom he learned English and Spanish as well.

Oroonoko falls in love with Imoinda, the beautiful daughter of the general who has trained him to be a soldier. They agree to marry, but when Oroonoko seeks his grandfather's approval, the old man, having summoned Imoinda, falls in love with her himself. Then, according to custom, the old king sends her a veil signifying that he desires to take her into his bed, which as king he is entitled to do. Oroonoko, finding out that she has received the royal veil, flies into a rage, but is somewhat comforted when his friends assure him that the king is too old to impose himself on Imoinda sexually. One of the king's older wives befriends Oroonoko and arranges a tryst for the two lovers in Imoinda's royal apartment, during which Imoinda assures Oroonoko that she is still a virgin. When the king learns of their meeting, he becomes enraged and sells both women into slavery, with orders that they be sold off to another country, whether Christian or otherwise.

The old king tells Oroonoko that Imoinda has been put to death, thinking that his grandson will forgive him for that punishment sooner than for selling Oroonoko's beloved into slavery. The king begs Oroonoko's forgiveness, which Oroonoko grants him. After a battle in which Oroonoko's generalship brings victory to his army, Oroonoko returns to court just as an English ship arrives in port. Oroonoko knows the captain—having sold slaves to him—and when the captain invites the young prince and his friends to dinner aboard the ship, Oroonoko does not hesitate to accept. After plying his guests with wine, the English captain suddenly gives a signal and the young Africans are surrounded and clapped in irons. They have been enslaved.

Oroonoko rages like a lion in his fetters, but to no avail. He then decides to stop eating in protest at the betrayal, and when his men follow his example, the captain fears that they will all perish before he can sell them. So the captain pretends to be sorry, saying that he wants to set the Africans free and let them go at the next land they come to, but he is afraid they will take revenge. Oroonoko promises that he will not attack the captain, who, seeing that Oroonoko's men will never eat with their prince in chains, sets Oroonoko free. Keeping his promise, Oroonoko thus passes the voyage comfortably, but on arrival in Surinam the treacherous captain once again chains the young prince, who is sold off along with the others to the overseer of an English plantation. This is Parham, a plantation near where the narrator happens to be staying at the time, her father having been appointed as the colony's lieutenant governor (she says that he died on the voyage from England).

Trefry, the overseer, recognizing Oroonoko's intelligence and spirit, soon "lov'd him as his dearest brother, and shew'd him all the Civilities due to so great a Man" (*Oroonoko*, p. 35). After he hears Oroonoko's story, Trefry promises he will find a way to return him to his country. He also promises to inquire after the fate of Oroonoko's friends. Following the custom of renaming slaves, Trefry gives Oroonoko the name Caesar.

When Caesar (as he is referred to from this point on) arrives at the main house, it is as if a king or a governor is arriving, not a slave. He is assigned responsibilities like other slaves, but since "it was more for Form, than any Design, to put him to his Task, he endur'd no more of the Slave but the name" (*Oroonoko*, p. 37). When the other slaves see Caesar, they recognize him as the prince who has sold many of them into slavery themselves, and they bow down before him as if he were their king. For his part, Caesar tells them to get up and treat him as a fellow slave, for he is no better than they are. Trefry then tells Caesar that there is a beautiful young female slave by whom "most of these young *Slaves* were undone in Love," and who indeed has charmed Trefry himself as no other woman has ever done (*Oroonoko*, p. 38). She has been given the name Clemene. Why, Caesar asks, since she is a slave, has Trefry not simply forced himself on her? He was going to, Trefry answers, but her modesty stopped him cold. The next day Trefry takes Caesar to the famous beauty, and the young prince is overjoyed at suddenly seeing the face of none other than his beloved Imoinda.

The two lovers embrace ecstatically and hear each other's story, agreeing that it is better to be enslaved together than to be free apart. Leaving the reunited pair, Trefry hurries to the main house to give the news of the reunion to the narrator (who now explains that she has already become friends with Caesar and has assured him of his liberty once the governor arrives). Caesar and Clemene are married that very day to general celebration, and soon afterward Clemene becomes pregnant. Clemene's pregnancy makes Caesar all the more impatient to get her and himself freed, and he repeatedly implores Trefry to expedite the process. But the governor's expected arrival by ship fails to occur. As it seems to Caesar that delay follows delay, he begins to suspect that the whites want the baby to be born into slavery, a prospect that heightens his anxiety. The whites, in turn, grow suspicious that the increasingly sullen Caesar is planning a revolt, and the narrator herself, as his good friend, is assigned the task of sounding him out and watching him. He assures her that he will not lift his hand against the whites.

The narrator then relates several feats of prowess that Caesar performs. He kills an attacking tiger by running it through with a sword, and when another big cat seems invulnerable to hunters' bullets, he shoots it through the eye with a bow and arrow. Another time, having heard of the electric eels that can cause numbness or unconsciousness by their touch, he grabs hold of one. After being shocked into unconsciousness

and almost drowning, Caesar keeps his grip on the eel and they enjoy it for supper. And when friction arises between the whites and the local Indians, Caesar takes a party of whites, including the narrator, on a friendly journey among the Indians, with the result that good relations are restored.

Yet still the whites delay the couple's liberation. One Sunday, when the whites have been drinking and are not paying attention, Caesar assembles the 150 or so male slaves and delivers a fiery speech about the injustice of their enslavement. Why should the whites have such power over them, he asks:

> Have they Vanquish'd us Nobly in Fight? Have they Won us in Honourable Battel? And are we, by the chance of War, become their Slaves? This wou'd not anger a Noble Heart, this wou'd not animate a Souldiers soul; no, but we are Bought and Sold like Apes, or Monkeys, to be the sport of Women, Fools and Cowards; and the Support of Rogues, Runagades, that have abandoned their own Countries, for Rapin (rape), Murders, Thefts and Villainies. . . .
>
> (*Oroonoko*, p. 52)

Having roused them, Caesar then proposes a plan to escape into the wilderness, where they can survive on their own. Then they can make their way towards the sea, establish a colony of their own, defend it if necessary, and hope to obtain a ship to take them back to Africa and freedom. The slaves vow to follow him to the death, and they all take their wives and children and go off into the wilderness.

Next morning, when the slaves' absence is discovered, a party of 600 whites is assembled and sets off in pursuit, led by the colony's deputy governor, William Byam, who has pretended affection for Caesar while in reality hating him bitterly (*Oroonoko*, p. 54). The narrator despises Byam, calling him a "Fawning, fair-tongu'd fellow . . . whose Character is not fit to be mentioned with the worst of the Slaves" (*Oroonoko*, p. 54). The English catch up with the fleeing Africans, who are outnumbered and eventually surrender, leaving Caesar, Clemene, and Tuscan, a slave who has acted as Caesar's lieutenant, to fight on by themselves. Finally, Byam tricks Caesar into surrendering by promising to set him free and let him sail away on the next ship that arrives. When Caesar gives himself up, with Imoinda and Tuscan, the two men are seized by the white mob, bound to stakes, and whipped mercilessly. The white women, the narrator relates, flee from fear of the rebellious slaves, so that the narrator herself is not on hand to prevent Caesar's whipping at the hands of the mob.

Allowed to take Clemene for a walk, Caesar kills her with her consent, intending to kill himself as well after revenging himself upon Byam. There is no hope of escape and the couple cannot bear to have their child born into slavery. Caesar also fears that the whites will rape Clemene. But he lacks the strength to move after cutting Clemene's throat. Feebly he attempts to disembowel himself as he is recaptured by the white mob. The whites finish the job for him, tying him to a whipping post around which they build a fire. Caesar calmly smokes a pipe as first his genitals, then his nose and ears, and finally his arms are hacked off by the enraged whites. Only when his second arm is cut off does the pipe fall and Caesar die, without uttering a sound.

Race and nobility. *Oroonoko* fascinates critics today because it deals with complex issues—race, gender, and sexual violence—that are often linked in modern discourse but were rarely discussed together, if they were discussed at all, in early English literature. The fascination is heightened by the fact that the novel was written by a professional woman writer in an age when few women wrote at all, and no other women wrote professionally. Finally, Behn is held by many to have pioneered a literary form, the novel, that did not yet exist but would soon rise to dominate modern literature.

Book and author thus add up to an unusual and provocative combination, but one that may easily create a deceptive impression of modernity for readers today. Another aspect of her tale clearly mattered more to Behn than the "modern" themes mentioned above, but lacks the same meaning for moderns that it had for Behn and her contemporaries: that is the innate nobility of its central character. A brief consideration of Oroonoko's nobility supplies a proper context for the novel's most important "modern" theme, that of race. A reader today might applaud a white writer's characterization of a black man as noble and heroic. Yet Oroonoko's physical beauty, for example, the most visible manifestation of his nobility, is described as stemming from European-looking features (paler skin, thin lips, arched nose, and so forth). These features set him apart from other blacks, whose ugliness the narrator assumes, and place Behn firmly within her time, when other descriptions of "beautiful" blacks stressed their European features. In 1674, a French traveler to the Gold Coast likewise

praised an African who lacked "the unattractive flat nose or that large mouth that the other blacks have" (Justel in Behn, p. 77).

The sense of modernity that Behn's novel conveys comes from its apparently even-handed treatment of the races, by which both some blacks and some whites are noble and heroic and others less so. But this aspect of the novel actually has little to do with modern notions of equality. To Behn, a royalist, race simply mattered less than inborn nobility in determining someone's social rank and human worth. As Oroonoko's speech to his fellow slaves suggests, it is dishonorable and treacherous enslavement that the novel objects to, not the existence of slavery as an institution. He and his fellow slaves had not been won laudably in war; they were captured and sold like animals, and to serve ignominious masters. As enslavement of Africans became more firmly entrenched in the eighteenth century, race would take on greater significance for most whites in determining one's rank and worth than it had for Behn and some of her contemporaries.

SLAVE ESCAPES

Surinam (now often spelled Suriname) has the world's largest concentration of people who are descended from runaway slaves. Like Oroonoko in the novel, slaves who were able to escape the plantation's brutality sought refuge in the dense growth of the surrounding rain forest. Unlike the novel's hero, who is caught by a white mob, many of these escaped slaves won recognition of their independence by treaty and proudly preserved their African heritage. Today, the descendants of escaped slaves call themselves Bush Negroes and make up 5-10 percent of Surinam's population.

Sources and literary context. In the past scholars have been divided on the question of whether Aphra Behn actually visited Surinam, but recent critics have generally accepted that she did. Lord Willoughby (the owner of Parham), John Trefry (the overseer of Parham), William Byam (Surinam's deputy governor), and other characters in the novel all existed in reality and seem to have been drawn reasonably true to life. William Byam, for example, provoked complaints from Surinam planters, who found him capricious and

OROONOKO

Mrs SAVIGNY *in the Character of* OROONOKO.

Oro. *I'll turn my Face away, and do it so.*

Published Nov.r 23, 1776 by J. Lowndes & Partners

Oroonoko was adapted for the stage in the seventeenth and eighteenth centuries.

arbitrary in exercising power. How much of the tale Behn tells, then, is true? Again, scholars have been divided and documentary evidence is sparse. No records remain, for example, of any lieutenant governor appointed to Surinam who might be confirmed as Behn's father. If all of the narrator's claims are taken at face value, then Behn and her family accompanied her father to Surinam after his appointment as lieutenant governor, probably sometime in 1663. The father died on the voyage, and after arriving, Behn met a slave named Oroonoko (called Caesar). Subsequent events unfolded as related.

On the other hand, claims of truthfulness are a common literary device in fiction, and travelers' accounts had been written on which Behn may have relied. Critics skeptical of Behn's claims, for example, have suggested she drew heavily on George Warren's *An Impartial Description of Surinam upon the Continent Guinea in America* (1667). Behn may, in other words, have meant simply to report events as they actually happened, as Warren and other travelers did; or, she may have intended her readers to understand that her tale was a fiction, in which case she anticipated other early novels by decades (*Robinson Crusoe*, often cited as the "first" novel, would be

published in 1719). In between these two extremes lies any number of degrees of truth and invention, though it seems at least likely that much of the story may actually have occurred. Some critics have therefore settled for calling Behn's unusual book an autobiographical novel.

Reception. Behn was best known to her contemporaries for her often bawdy plays and frankly erotic poems, both of which were acceptable to English society when written by men but which could provoke withering censure when written by a woman. The earliest recorded reaction to *Oroonoko* comes from the playwright Thomas Southerne, who adapted the book for the stage in 1696. In the dedication he wrote that Behn "had a great Command of the Stage; and I have always wonder'd that she would bury her Favorite Hero in a *Novel,* when she might have revived him in the *Scene*" (Southerne in Behn, p. 193). Southerne put his idea into action; he himself staged *Oronooko* in 1696 (with a white Imoinda). As Restoration openness gave way to the more fastidious sensibility of the eighteenth and nineteenth centuries, Behn's works were often viewed as improper, even obscene. Yet *Oroonoko's* influence can be traced to the European ideal of the noble savage, which the novel promoted. First enunciated in the sixteenth century, in the wake of Portugal's contact with Brazilian peoples, by such writers as Desiderius Erasmus (*Praise of Folly* [1509] and François Rabelais (*Pantagruel* [1533]), this concept attributes an exalted state of innocence to primitive peoples, in contrast to the perceived corruption of the civilized world.

Not until the twentieth century, however, did Behn's highly original voice again find a real audience. Virginia Woolf, for example, praised her as a forerunner to later trailblazing female authors, such as Jane Austen (1775-1817) and George Eliot (1819-80). Woolf wrote in 1929, "All women together ought to let flowers fall upon the grave of Aphra Behn . . . for it was she who earned them the right to speak their minds" (Woolf, p. 69).

—Colin Wells

For More Information

Behn, Aphra. *Oroonoko.* Ed. Joanna Lipking. New York: Norton, 1997.

Brown, Laura. *The Romance of Empire: Oroonoko and the Trade in Slaves.* In *The New Eighteenth Century.* Ed. Felicity Nussbaum and Laura Brown. New York: Methuen, 1987.

Duffy, Maureen. *The Passionate Shepherdess: Aphra Behn 1640-89.* London: Jonathan Cape, 1977.

Ferguson, Margaret W. *Juggling the Categories of Race, Class, and Gender: Aphra Behn's* Oroonoko. In *Women, "Race," and Writing in the Early Modern Period.* Ed. Margo Hendricks and Patricia Parker. London: Routledge, 1994.

Goreau, Angeline. *Reconstructing Aphra: A Social Biography of Aphra Behn.* New York: Dial, 1980.

Klein, Herbert S. *The Atlantic Slave Trade.* Cambridge: Cambridge University Press, 1999.

Spencer, Jane. *The Rise of the Woman Novelist: From Aphra Behn to Jane Austen.* Oxford: Blackwell, 1986.

Todd, Janet, ed. *Aphra Behn Studies.* Cambridge: Cambridge University Press, 1994.

Woolf, Virginia. *A Room of One's Own.* London: Chatto & Windus, 1929.

Woodcock, George. *Aphra Behn: The English Sappho.* Montreal: Black Rose Books, 1989.

Pamela, or
Virtue Rewarded

by
Samuel Richardson

Samuel Richardson is among the most unlikely masters of English literature. He was
born in 1688 in London and apprenticed
to a printer at the age of 17. He worked hard,
married his master's daughter, and eventually became head of the printing house. In time he was
made Printer of the Journals of the House of
Commons. Richardson did not write imagina-
tively until the age of 50. While composing a
book of model letters for semiliterate people, he
heard the story of a servant who married her aristocratic employer; the conjunction of these two
factors seems to have inspired *Pamela*. The novel
was published to great acclaim in 1740 and the
aging printer found himself with a new career:
novelist. *Pamela* was followed by the sequel
Pamela in Her Exalted Condition (1741) and by
Clarissa (1748) and *Sir Charles Grandison* (1753).
While *Clarissa* is designated as Richardson's masterpiece, *Pamela* has achieved distinction as the
work that created the modern English novel.

Events in History at the Time the Novel
Takes Place

The rise of literacy. Somewhat unusually for a
servant girl of the time, Pamela is both literate
and well-read in Richardson's novel. She has
been given not just one but two routes to literacy: her deceased mistress encouraged her to
read, and her parents ran a school before economic reversals thrust them into poverty. In fact,
neither of these routes was open to most servants. England in 1740 remained a place of lim-

THE LITERARY WORK

A novel set in the English countryside in the
1730s; published in 1740.

SYNOPSIS

In letters exchanged with her parents, a
teenaged servant girl recounts how her
gentleman employer falls in love with her, has
her kidnapped, and ultimately marries her.

ited literacy—exactly how limited is debatable
since the figures are elusive. Broadly speaking,
adult male literacy rose from 25 percent in 1600
to 75 percent in 1800; the unspecified female
rate lagged behind (Hunter, p. 61). It was not
until the second half of the nineteenth century
that most working-class men and women could
read and write.

The total number of literate adults was rising
gradually in the early 1700s. By 1750 only about
half of all brides and grooms could sign their
names, a criterion of literacy. Various types of
schools existed—charitable, endowed grammar
schools; parish schools; and "dame" schools (so-
called because the teacher was a single elderly
woman). But education was neither compulsory
nor always available. There were in fact employers like Pamela's mistress in the novel who took
an active interest in their servants' education. In
real life, a Dr. Claver Morris sent one of his maids
to a local "dame" school to learn to read, as

shown in his *The Diary of a West Country Physician*, A.D. 1684-1726. For most servants, however, economic pressures could make attendance difficult, and in retrospect employers such as Dr. Morris seem to have been more the exception than the rule.

Still, to observers of the early 1700s, England appeared to be in the throes of a reading explosion. This was the age of the newspaper, the cheap pamphlet and broadside, and the first stories that would be acknowledged as English novels. (Before *Pamela*, there were around 100 stories written in the form of letters; *Pamela* was revolutionary among them because of its focus on a unified central action—the romantic relationship.) There was, then, a proliferation of material for a reading public that was growing but still small.

Two factors may account for the sense of a reading explosion. First, most popular works would have a relatively small number of readers but countless listeners, as groups of the illiterate or semiliterate gathered to hear a literate friend read from the latest work. Second, such increases in literacy as occurred were especially noticeable because they involved groups that had never been primarily associated with literacy: upper- and middle-class women, the middle classes generally, and even some members of the urban working poor.

The growth of literacy had important, eventually world-changing, consequences. The new readership lacked the classical education that was the eighteenth-century standard for full literacy; thus, its members were much less likely to glorify Greek and Latin forms and styles than were the more thoroughly educated. In time the growth of literacy quashed the close relationship between modern European and classical culture, which had been central to literary production for more than a thousand years. The new readership preferred fresh types of works: most importantly, novels and romances. Among the first fruits of this trend, *Pamela* signaled a change in the literary culture of England.

Master and servant. By the early eighteenth century, all that remained of the feudal system that had characterized medieval English society were the great families and estates of the gentry and aristocracy. As modern culture evolved, the powers of the great landowners shrank, but they did not entirely disappear. The ideal of chivalrous honor survived; and, in the management of servants on large estates, so did some echo of the feudal relation between master and peon.

This is not to say that interactions between landowning masters and their servants were feudal in any direct way. Eighteenth-century servants earned wages, and tenants paid rent rather than provided services. Neither was bound to the land the way their medieval ancestors had been; both were free to go when they had satisfied their contracts. And the reverse was also true—masters had fewer obligations to their subordinates and could dismiss them almost at will. On the other hand, landowner masters enjoyed less power than before. Their legal authority was almost gone, eradicated by the growth of central administration. Although landowners often served as justices of the peace for their areas, they now had to follow the laws of the land.

In spite of these vast changes, the relationship between masters and servants remained sentimentally feudal. From the Renaissance to the Victorian era (early 1500s-early 1800s), the domestic staff was considered part of the household, and the relationship between servant and master could resemble that between parent and child. A gentlewoman like Pamela's deceased mistress might want her servant to be a surrogate daughter rather than to just make the beds and set the table.

In addition to wages, masters were generally responsible for feeding and clothing their employees (one reason why wages tended to be low); if a servant's parents had not provided education, as few were able to do, it was up to the master to equip the servant with whatever education was necessary for the completion of tasks. For maidservants, hired mostly to execute simple domestic chores, such education was generally minimal; Pamela is a great exception. Her mistress seems to have valued her company, and therefore to have expanded her mind with reading, playing musical instruments, and dancing to make her a better companion. In this regard too, her fate differed from that of most domestics of the day. Their lives, while arguably easier than those of fieldworkers, were spent in a daily round of cleaning, serving, or cooking. And their social life tended to be centered on other servants in the household, especially when their employment was a distance from the parental home.

Theoretically servants were protected from their masters by the laws referred to earlier and by common decency; in actual practice, servants' dependent state left them exposed to the whims and desires of their masters. To disoblige one's master, even justly, was to risk losing one's hard-earned place; and, to the extent that an employer's recommendation was crucial to securing a new place, a dismissal could be devastating. An eighteenth-century handbook for servants recommends that a servant recognize "that God meant he should be very exactly observant of all his master's orders . . . that he should shrink from none of them, without a certainty that he would sin if he obeyed them; and must even then, with modesty and sorrow, express the great difficulty he is under, and the mighty concern he feels, in being forced to be disobedient" (Seaton, p. 76).

Many cases of rape took place between masters and servants. For the most part, society dismissed the ravishing of a maid by a master, regarding his behavior as only a minor sin. Few maids braved all the obstacles to take cases of rape to court, and one who did stood a small chance of having the jurymen believe her over her master. "To do so would set at risk the entire fragile nexus of authority, obedience, and deference" upon which upper-class society was built (McLynn, pp. 107-108). So, while it is true that the power of the landed gentry had waned much by the early eighteenth century, it still dwarfed the resources and actual rights of servants. Those with a grievance against their master generally found the courts, the neighboring gentry, the state, and sometimes even the Church unwilling to intervene. Such wronged servants required the wits of a Pamela Andrews to survive without damage to person or purse.

Two models of marriage. *Pamela* reflects a conflict between two very different conceptions of matrimony. The older conception was rooted in social and economic imperatives; according to this model, romantic love was a secondary consideration, nice if it happened but certainly not essential. By the middle of the sixteenth century, however, a new model grew prominent, one that stressed the emotional link between husband and wife and that idealized their relationship as the center of adult life.

The relative, sliding nature of these two conceptions must be stressed; neither was during *Pamela*'s day the sole lens through which English society viewed marriage. In part the social view of marriage rested on the assumption that a husband and wife could grow to love each other after marriage. In many cases, even supporters of marriage as a love match believed that considerations of class and wealth had to be taken into account. Nevertheless, by the time of the novel there was a striking cultural shift in favor of the emotional component, as reflected by developments in *Pamela*.

The eighteenth-century socioeconomic view of marriage is most visible among the upper classes and the gentry, partly because there is more documentary evidence, and partly because the economic stakes were higher. What evidence we have suggests that marriage among the laboring poor was largely a matter of individual choice, and thus more likely of affection. But for families with any monetary interests at all, marriage generally involved negotiations, contracts, and exchanges of money. A beneficial marriage was one that profited both sides, financially and socially. It empowered the families in additional ways, cementing alliances between political factions or business interests, or signifying the end of a feud. If a marriage promised to achieve such ends, a young man's or woman's preferences could hardly be allowed to upset the process. Practical concerns took precedence over affection

MARRIAGE OR ADULTERY?

Pamela's miraculous ascent into the ranks of the wealthy was, in terms of its times, almost purely a fairy tale. Sometimes servants did marry masters; Richardson, for instance, began as an apprentice under his future wife's father. However, in that case there was no real difference of class, only an initial difference in status; as an apprentice, Richardson could hope to rise on his own. It was much rarer for a member of the gentry to marry a servant. Moreover, for the handful of cases in which this did occur, the elevated spouse had much more difficulty blending into "the high life" than Pamela. By far, the more common occurrence was the extramarital liaison, especially between male squires (wealthy landowners) and female servants. Apparently few young girls had Pamela's mixture of piety, foresight, and self-discipline. Impelled by desire or threatened with dismissal, and often duped by false promises of marriage, many succumbed to gentle advances or to rough compulsion—with rapes turning into liaisons. If a pregnancy resulted, the best the girl could hope for was to be supported in genteel ignominy; at worst, she might be dismissed and abandoned. It is difficult to gauge how common such affairs were, although they were common enough to be universally known as a potential pitfall of servitude. No one in the novel is surprised to hear that Mr. B. has taken a liking to his mother's chambermaid; they are shocked only when they hear of the marriage.

in these matches, which were generally engineered by parents. It was understood that spouses might have to look elsewhere for love; extramarital affairs, though not approved of, were tolerated as long as they were conducted discreetly.

The model of companionate marriage linked matrimony and emotional involvement. Many historians see the origins of this model in the Reformation, the movement led by theologians, called Protestants, who began to reject Catholicism in 1517. Protestant theologians valorized marriage and accused Catholics of a perverse emphasis on sexual abstention. More exactly, Protestants did not approve of the vows of chastity required of Catholic clerics: Martin Luther, the man who began the Reformation, married monks to nuns. By the time of the novel, this renewed focus on marriage had acquired an affective component in larger society. Manuals on devotion and conduct, such as *The Young Ladies' Companion* (1740) and *The Compleat Housewife* (1734), paint an idyllic picture of husband and wife as helpmates in their spiritual, emotional, and working lives. Such ideals spread most quickly in the middle classes, those who worked for their money. As old feudal relationships evaporated and social life rebased itself on the single-family unit, new standards for gendered behavior emerged; this happened most quickly in the city, where people were furthest removed from the old rural kinship patterns. Men left their homes to work, and women managed the domestic sphere, where they took charge of home duties and child-rearing. The consequence was complementary roles in marriage; where the man left off, the woman picked up, and vice versa. Such ideals mandated that love, or at least affection, be the basis of a marriage.

Again, the two views of marriage—affective and economic—were entangled; thus, the shift from one to the other is hard to measure. The triumph of love in marriage is probably intimately connected to the political triumph of the bourgeoisie by the middle of the nineteenth century: marriage as an unadulterated economic alliance lost its preeminent position largely because the wealthy, high-society family had ceased to be so great a political or economic force.

The rise of the individual. The trend of companionate marriage reflects a more fundamental rise—a new importance attached to individual sensations, fortunes, and thoughts rather than those of a general human type or social class.

Promoting this democratic approach were ideas recently introduced by English philosopher John Locke in *Thoughts concerning Education* and ***Essay on Human Understanding*** (also in *WLAIT 3: British and Irish Literature and Its Times*). While Locke acknowledged that individuals develop intellectual understanding to varying degrees, he leveled the playing field far more than ever before, positing, for example, that at birth everyone's mind is a tabula rasa, or blank slate. In other words, we all start out equally, regardless of class or other social distinctions. (*Pamela* itself refers to *Thoughts concerning Education*, from which Pamela imbibes the concept of the young mind being a blank slate). Locke also concerned himself with individual identity, teaching that people get in touch with their separate identities by remembering their past thoughts and actions, as Pamela does in her letters and diary entries. She continually ruminates over her own actions to discover what is true and how it fits with her morals. Although Pamela is only a lowly servant, the novel elevates individual consciousness by bringing her personal identity to the fore.

The Novel in Focus

Plot summary. *Pamela* comprises a series of letters between Pamela Andrews and her parents, as well as passages from her journals. Over the course of the novel's 500 pages, Pamela's letters grow so long and detailed that the reader wonders how she found the time to write them. The frame device is essential, however: it allows Pamela to describe events as they happen, without divulging whether her tale will have a happy ending. Because the story moves forward in spurts, the reader shares Pamela's anxiety, and what is in effect a simple fairy tale develops with dramatic tension.

The story opens with a death. Pamela Andrews, a beautiful and intelligent servant girl, writes to her parents in a distant town to inform them that her mistress has died. This aged gentlewoman's last words charge her son to "remember" Pamela. This son, called Mr. B. throughout the novel, soon gives hints of how well he will take care of Pamela: he gives her leave to write letters, read books from the library, and wear some of her mistress's old clothes.

John, the servant who carries the letters to Pamela's parents, brings back to her a disquieting letter, in which her father warns her to beware of Mr. B., whose kindness the old man distrusts. She is only a poor girl and can expect nothing from a wealthy squire like Mr. B. except to be seduced and abandoned. Pamela avows that she will heed this advice, even though she herself does not see anything suspicious.

The first sign of trouble appears in connection with Mr. B.'s sister, Lady Davers. Aware of Pamela's beauty, Lady Davers wants to take the girl away. Mr. B. agrees but delays the departure and one day asks Pamela to stay. She says she would rather be with Lady Davers, and he responds by embracing and trying to kiss her. When she rebuffs him, he repents and orders her to keep silent about his advances.

Now Pamela makes a curious choice. Instead of fleeing the house, she decides she is safe enough to delay. She switches beds, though, and sleeps with the head housekeeper, Mrs. Jervis. The other servants get wind of what is going on; all of them side with Pamela, and show her as much support as possible. Meanwhile, Mr. B. has changed his approach; he criticizes Pamela and hints that he will cast her out. Discovering that she has not stayed silent but has told Mrs. Jervis of his indiscretion, he grows enraged.

> Come in fool, said he angrily, as soon as he saw me; (and snatched my hand with a pull;) you may well be ashamed to see me, after your noise and nonsense, and exposing me as you have done. (Richardson, *Pamela, or Virtue Rewarded*, p. 28)

When he confronts Pamela, an argument erupts in which she handles herself well. Nevertheless, Mr. B. resolves to cast her out, and Pamela is happy to leave. She lingers, though, seemingly for no good reason; she wants to complete a waistcoat she is embroidering for the man she claims to hate!

The day before Pamela is to leave, Mr. B. announces he will visit his sister. That night, Pamela and Mrs. Jervis discuss the squire's behavior as they fall asleep. Pamela hears a noise from the closet. As she rises to check it, out bursts Mr. B., who had concealed himself within. He claims to want only to talk, but Pamela does not believe him. She screams and faints. When she comes to, Mr. B. and Mrs. Jervis attend her solicitously, and from this moment until Pamela leaves, Mr. B. makes no more unseemly advances. He even suggests that he could arrange a marriage for Pamela with a young clergyman in his employ, but the girl refuses.

Finally the day comes when Pamela takes her leave. After a tearful farewell to each of the servants, she sets off in one of her master's coaches.

But if Pamela thinks she is going home, she soon learns otherwise; the coachman, Robin, drives her to Mr. B.'s other estate, in the isolated northern region of Lincolnshire. Richardson breaks the epistolary frame to report that Mr. B. sends a letter to Pamela's father, in which he accuses Pamela of slandering his reputation; he also says she has been carrying on an improper intrigue with the same clergyman Mr. B. had offered her, and that he, Mr. B., has imprisoned her at Lincolnshire for her own good. Her father is so distraught that he walks all night to confront Mr. B., only to be poorly comforted by the squire's assurance that he means the girl no harm. The father has little recourse: while Mr. B. does not have the legal right to kidnap Pamela, his wealth and connections make it all but impossible for the worried father to lodge a complaint. He returns home.

This brief non-epistolary excursion ends, and Pamela's voice resumes. She describes how she was carried to Lincolnshire and imprisoned there. This estate is the mirror opposite of her old home; instead of the kindly Mrs. Jervis, the housekeeper here is an ugly, corrupt old woman named Mrs. Jewkes, who torments Pamela with hard rules and smutty jokes. Soon after her arrival, Pamela experiences another shock: John, the servant who has carried her letters to her parents, admits that he showed Mr. B. everything she wrote. Apart from the shock of discovering that her employer—a man who has already grievously invaded her privacy—has had access to her personal correspondence, Pamela is unhappy because her letters were filled with frank denunciations of him. From now on, she takes special care to hide her writing.

Mr. B. writes to say he will not come to Lincolnshire until the girl gives him permission, but Pamela knows how little she can trust this promise. She determines to find a way to escape before he changes his mind. Even though she is watched closely, she manages to contract a friendship with the neighborhood parson, Mr. Williams—the same clergyman Mr. B. had offered her in marriage. Between fights with Jewkes, Pamela carries on a secret correspondence with Williams. Though younger and less experienced than he, she is much cannier and finds herself directing the parson. He appeals to the local gentry, but they refuse to intervene. Because she is poor and without social status, they feel she is not worth helping. The parson himself offers to protect Pamela by marrying her. She refuses. When his attempts to free her are found

This scene from *Pamela* is part of a series of 12 pictures painted in 1744 by Joseph Highmore, and later engraved by Louis Truchy.

out, he is roughed up and arrested by Mr. B.'s henchmen.

Pamela receives an angry letter from Mr. B., who, jealous of her friendship with Williams, accuses her of deceit and hypocrisy. She then reaches her lowest point. One night she tries to escape but falls from the garden wall. Distraught, Pamela throws some of her outer garments into a pond, hoping to make everyone think she has drowned. She considers, then rejects, suicide, and crawls to a woodshed to sleep, where she is found in the morning by a frightened Mrs. Jewkes.

This near-suicide brings Mr. B. to Lincolnshire, despite his promise. He and Pamela spend an evening together that is almost free of rancor. It is as if something has changed between them. Mr. B. clearly loves her, and she admits that she cannot hate him. But the squire is at war with his own snobbish unwillingness to marry a servant, and she will not accept him any other way. He makes her an offer that amounts to contractual concubinage, which she refuses indignantly.

What, sir, would the world say, were you to marry your harlot? That a gentleman of your rank in life should stoop, not only to the base-born Pamela, but to a base-born prostitute? Little, sir, as I know of the world, I am not to

be caught by a bait so poorly covered as this! (*Pamela*, p. 201)

He makes another attempt at rape, this one more comical than real; he disguises himself as a servant girl, Nan, and manages to sneak into Pamela's and Jewkes's room. Yet, despite his own hard language and Mrs. Jewkes's encouragement, he does not rape Pamela. She faints, and he relents once more.

After this episode, the two combatants spend time together and grow closer. Mr. B. even hints that he will propose marriage. But while he is away on a trip, Pamela receives an anonymous warning that the squire is planning a mock marriage. This warning haunts her, but she does not tell Mr. B. of her doubts; instead, at the very moment when they should be closest, she withdraws. Enraged and baffled, he sends her away. She is sorry to leave but feels it cannot be helped.

At last free after months of confinement, Pamela is desperately unhappy. At her first stop on the road home, she is overjoyed to find a letter from Mr. B. imploring her to return. She happily obliges. Back in Lincolnshire, they make plans for their wedding; he quiets her fears about the sham marriage, admitting that he had in fact planned such a trick but then abandoned it. One by one, the old rifts are bridged: Mr. B. frees

Williams from prison, and they are reconciled; Pamela and Mrs. Jewkes become as close as their different temperaments allow; Mr. B. introduces his fiancée to the local gentry who had refused to aid her, and she manages not to rebuke them. Pamela's father arrives, and is overwhelmed with joy to find that his daughter's glad tidings are correct.

The marriage takes place, and all seems to be bliss. But there is still one more hurdle to cross. Pamela won the hearts of her husband's neighbors, but her new sister-in-law, the proud Lady Davers, will not be so easily reconciled to the idea of having a servant girl for a relative. One day when Mr. B. is away, Lady Davers arrives at Lincolnshire. She abuses and torments Pamela, refusing to believe that her brother and the one-time servant are legally married. Finally Pamela escapes to a neighbor's house.

The concluding chapters concern the reconciliation of Lady Davers to her brother and his wife. When Lady Davers tells Pamela that her brother already has a child from an illegitimate affair, Mr. B. is thrown into such a rage that he swears to break off all communication. Stricken with guilt, his sister relents. In the last scene, Lady Davers asks to read the letters that compose the novel itself. She senses that they will win her heart, since they played so large a role in winning Mr. B.'s.

Saint or sinner? Plot summary can provide only the barest sense of what *Pamela* is about. The novel would be far shorter without the heroine's extended comments on everything that occurs. Pamela is among the most relentlessly contemplative characters in literature; hardly a word or event passes without her ruminating on it and finding some lesson in it. In addition to his heroine's many pages of moral commentary, Richardson appends to the novel a key of the moral lessons to be drawn from each character in the novel, major and minor. For instance, he writes, "The upper servants of great families may, from the odious character of Mrs. Jewkes, and the amicable ones of Mrs. Jervis, Mr. Longman, & c. learn what to avoid, and what to choose, to make themselves valued and esteemed by all who know them" (*Pamela*, p. 531). Richardson was clearly less interested in telling a rousing story than in providing positive examples. The struggle between Pamela and Mr. B. is as much a fight over morals as it is a love contest. The subtitle, "Virtue Rewarded," indicates the lesson to be drawn: Pamela's constant attention to moral propriety eventually overpowers Mr. B.'s illicit lust.

Richardson's novel succeeded in becoming a moral model in the author's time. *Pamela* became a byword for virtuous modesty, and the book was recommended from more than one London pulpit as edifying reading. Not everyone, however, was enchanted by Richardson's upright ingenue. Within weeks of the novel's appearance, she was at the center of a controversy that raged for years. For many readers, Pamela was not the forthright, pious girl she appeared to be, but rather a calculating hypocrite who hid her desire for Mr. B., admitting her love only when she was assured of the most favorable terms.

The first two years of the 1740s saw a stream of burlesques, pamphlets, and invective directed at Richardson's pioneering novel. An anonymous poem on Mr. B.'s first attempted rape asks, "Tho' odd the question may be thought / From one so very modest, / Yet that she would forgive the fault / To me seems much the oddest" (Kreissman, p. 24). According to such critics, Pamela mouths religion but acts like a market woman, holding out for the highest price for her only commodity: herself. And, in the eyes of these critics, Richardson himself was no better: he claimed to eschew the lascivious scenes common to earlier stories yet filled his work with luscious descriptions of Pamela and two scenes of attempted rape. Perhaps most damningly, though the novel itself says Pamela is a special case, not one to be imitated, critics argued that the romance would prompt gentlemen to think of marrying their chambermaids, and vice versa.

All such invective was topped by *Shamela*, the famous parody written by the well-educated gentleman, Henry Fielding, author of *Joseph Andrews* (1742) and **Tom Jones** (1749; also in *WLAIT 3: British and Irish Literature and Its Times*). *Shamela*, more formally known as *An Apology for the Life of Mrs. Shamela Andrews*, is a masterpiece of parody: Fielding hones in on every aspect of his target that could possibly give a reader pause, from the smug letters of commendation with which Richardson prefaces his novel, to its insistent references to Pamela's physical beauty. Most distasteful to Fielding was what he saw as *Pamela*'s crass, commercial conception of "virtue rewarded"—rewarded not with the simple joy of being virtuous, but rather with a fabulous marriage and incredible wealth. In this world, believed Fielding, nothing is for sure, and certainly not that virtuous actions will be justly rewarded; to suggest otherwise is not only misleading, but also directly counter to a morality centered on heaven. To highlight this, his Shamela is a crude

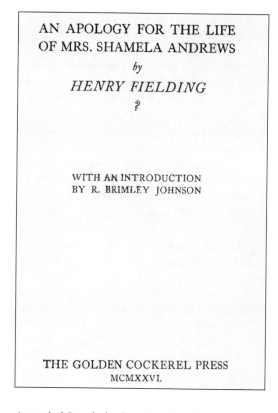

AN APOLOGY FOR THE LIFE
OF MRS. SHAMELA ANDREWS

by

HENRY FIELDING
?

WITH AN INTRODUCTION
BY R. BRIMLEY JOHNSON

THE GOLDEN COCKEREL PRESS
MCMXXVI.

A spoof of *Pamela* that has attained enduring renown, *Shamela* was originally published in 1741, not under Fielding's name but under a pseudonym (Conny Keyber).

harlot who uses a pretense of virtue to trap a Mr. B. (who gets a full name in this version—"Booby"). Her mother is a bawd and Mrs. Jervis is no better; Parson Williams is Shamela's former lover, with whom she takes up again as soon as she is safely married. The exaggerated crudity is evident in this exchange between Booby and Shamela:

> Yes (says he) "you are a d——d [damned], impudent, stinking, cursed, confounded Jade, and I have a great Mind to kick your A—. You kiss [my] — says I. A-gad, says he, and so I will; with that he caught me in his Arms, and kissed me till he made my Face all over Fire.
> (Fielding, p. 328)

Fielding closes his parody with a version of Richardson's moralizing conclusion, in which he directly states his objections: *Pamela* is filled with erotic scenes barely draped in morality; it exonerates Mr. B. and Mrs. Jewkes, who commit immoral acts; and, worst of all, it presents a ludicrous mismatch as a wonderful thing.

Obviously there was much more at stake in the controversy over *Pamela* than mere interpretation of a popular novel; the book aggravated deeply ensconced class tensions. These tensions are reflected in the difference between Fielding—a gentleman of leisure and literature—and Richardson—a hardworking mercantile man. Fielding's novels suggest an allegiance to the remnants of the social system that had organized England from its feudal beginnings. His father was the impoverished descendant of the earl of Denbigh; his mother, the daughter of a squire. Richardson represented the industrious middle classes, rising in wealth and power and impatient with the social dominance of the idle rich. In 1740 Richardson's viewpoint was, to say the least, innovative and, at most, revolutionary. Much more traditional was the outlook that society can function properly only if everyone keeps his or her God-appointed place and fulfills the tasks of that place without envy or ambition. This did not mean forestalling all change; some reforms were considered salutary to society. It did, however, mean preventing the breakdown of social division and the concomitant redistribution of power. Fielding's parody can thus be seen as an attack on the transgression of class borders. From this point of view, even a woman as bad as Shamela is acceptable in her place; it is her sudden elevation that makes her ridiculous, or even dangerous.

To be fair, Fielding's novel does not give unlimited license to the gentry; his Squire Booby is as ridiculous for stooping as Shamela is for aspiring. Implicit in the view is an explanation for servant-master liaisons—the extramarital affair may have been preferable to marriage across classes. While the former threatens individual souls, the latter threatens the social order itself.

By contrast, in *Pamela* the idea of marrying into the gentry does not frighten the heroine at all. This and other details can be construed to render her a social climber. But in the eyes of many, such ambition did not make her a pariah—quite the contrary. For Richardson, as for all the self-made people he represents, social climbing was not blameworthy, but praiseworthy. Not tied to the land as farmers or enriched by wealthy ancestors, members of the middle class labored for their sustenance and tended to believe that their hard work, discipline, thrift, and caution would be rewarded—not only in heaven but with material advancement on earth.

By the 1740s, the middle class was beginning to dominate English political and social life. While the landed gentry retained a potent place in the cultural imagination, it was commerce, manufacturing, and their middle-class agents that made the nation rich. They were therefore unwilling to accept traditional obstacles to social advancement. The English gentry did not work for its wealth—it enjoyed its prestige by accident of heredity. Should not the fruits of life go to those whose personal virtues have earned them? Richardson's novel does not indulge in bourgeois propaganda. Nevertheless, it is filled with unflattering images of the gentry: Mr. B. and Lady Davers are conceited, headstrong, self-centered, and impulsive. If Pamela ends up joining the very class she spent much of the novel criticizing, she does so only after reforming it: Mr. B. will be a rake no longer, and the proud Lady Davers is humbled. The mere fact that Richardson was able to write this parable of social change indicates how far the middle class had come. By 1740, capitalism was the engine driving English society; the land-rich gentry, while still socially preeminent, were being left behind. Richardson's novel represented the future; Fielding's response, the past.

Sources and literary context. *Pamela* is difficult to categorize. On the one hand, it is usually considered the first modern English novel; there is nothing quite like it in history, even though works of prose fiction, such as Thomas Greene's *Pandosto* (1590) and William Painter's *Palace of Pleasure* (1575) had been circulating in England for more than a century. Richardson's status as the first modern English novelist rests on two accomplishments. First, he changed the focus of the novel from free-roaming, often risqué adventures to a sober tale of ordinary people contemplating marriage. Second, Richardson introduced realism into the novel: from now on, the mainstream novel would lack the element of the fabulous and magical so common in its predecessors, such as Sidney's *Arcadia* (1590) and Lady Mary Wroth's *Urania* (1621). Clearly Pamela's was the story of a particular person rather than of general human types, "as had been common in the past" (Watt, p. 15). Moreover, her circumstances were realistic and the plot was not episodic in nature, but concerned a single line of action—romance and marriage. From Frances Burney to Jane Austen to Charles Dickens and Charlotte and Emily Brontë, novelists would pick up the Richardsonian focus on marriage across social class in their works. Inasmuch as most subsequent novelists followed Richardson's lead in these respects, Richardson created the modern novel in England.

Influences on *Pamela* are myriad, ranging from the epistolary format that had been in use for more than a century, to the books of model letters (including Richardson's own *Familiar Letters on Important Occasions*) aimed at the semiliterate. There was also a longstanding tradition of literature that revolved around the fabulous marriage. Stories about such marriages hark back not only to fairy tales but also to Greek and European romance, in which a seemingly low-born child is eventually revealed to be a prince or princess in disguise. Richardson eliminates noble origins, but only to highlight Pamela's innate nobility.

PAMELA'S NAME

In 1740 the name "Pamela" was not a common name; it was made popular by Richardson's novel. But Richardson did not make the name up. He borrowed it from one of the heroines of Sir Philip Sidney's *Arcadia*, a romance written in the 1580s. Sidney's Pamela is a genuine princess, sent into disguise as a simple shepherd girl; despite this crucial difference, the two Pamelas share personality traits that make the name equally appropriate. Both are somewhat august, self-respecting personalities, quick to rebuke any assault on their dignity. More significantly, both have a tendency to launch into long speeches on virtue, honor, and the benefits of chastity, and both are placed in situations in which they must defend their honor by their own wits. Richardson uses nomenclature to align his work with a still-popular classic, but also to suggest the differences: Sidney created a world of singing shepherds and chivalric knights, while Richardson's Pamela operates in a world of venal servants and embroidered waistcoats.

Finally, *Pamela* appeared at a time that saw the rise of sentimental literature. Championed first by Richard Steele, an essayist and playwright, sentimental works stressed moral propriety and discussed fine grades of feelings.

Reviews. *Pamela* was an astounding success; either loved or hated, Pamela Andrews was a name on everyone's lips for years. The book was commended by preachers, moralists, and many critics, including the esteemed Samuel Johnson (see *The Life of Samuel Johnson*, also in *WLAIT 3: British and Irish Literature and Its Times*). Johnson praised the genuineness of emotion in Richardson's writing, qualifying his praise:

[I]f you were to read Richardson for the story, your impatience would be so much fretted that you would hang yourself. But you must read him for the sentiment, and consider the story as only giving occasion to the sentiment.

(Johnson in Boswell, pp. 190-91)

On the other hand, *Pamela* was derided by moralists and by Fielding, and banned by the Catholic Church (presumably because of its lascivious scenes). It inspired plays, paintings, and spurious sequels. By the end of the century, the furor had died down. Richardson's novel remained popular, but at a much lower pitch. The genius of succeeding novelists such as Jane Austen, the Brontës, and Charles Dickens made Richardson's technique seem primitive and outdated. Occasionally, though, Richardson still found champions, among them Sir Walter Scott (see **Rob Roy,** also in *WLAIT 3: British and Irish Literature and Its Times*). In Scott's estimation, "No one before had dived so deeply into the human heart" (Scott in Richardson, p. xii).

—Jacob Littleton

For More Information

Armstrong, Nancy. *Desire and Domestic Fiction* . Oxford: University of Oxford Press, 1987.

Boswell, James. *The Life of Samuel Johnson*. Ed. Bergan Evans. New York: Modern Library, 1952.

Fielding, Henry. *Joseph Andrews and Shamela*. Oxford: Oxford University Press, 1980.

Hunter, J. Paul. *Before Novels*. New York: Norton, 1990.

Kreissman, Bernard. *Pamela-Shamela*. Lincoln: University of Nebraska Press, 1960.

McLynn, Frank. *Crime and Punishment in Eighteenth-century England*. London: Routledge, 1989.

Morris, Claver. *The Diary of a West Country Physician, A.D. 1684-1726*. Ed. Edmund Hobhouse. London: Simpkin, Marshall, 1934.

Richardson, Samuel. *Pamela, or Virtue Rewarded*. New York: Norton, 1958.

Seaton, Thomas. *The Conduct of Servants in Great Families*. 1720. Reprint, New York: Garland, 1985.

Stone, Lawrence. *The Family, Sex, and Marriage*. London: Weidenfeld and Nicolson, 1977.

Watt, Ian. *The Rise of the Novel: Studies in Defoe, Richardson and Fielding*. Berkeley: University of California Press, 1957.

Paradise Lost

by

John Milton

THE LITERARY WORK

An epic poem in blank verse set at the beginning of time in Heaven, Chaos (a state of turbulence where matter is in flux), Hell (a place of imprisonment at the bottom of Chaos), and earthly Paradise (whose center is the Garden of Eden); published in 1667 as 10 books, republished in 1674 as 12 books.

SYNOPSIS

The poem dramatizes Adam and Eve's expulsion from Paradise as a result of the War in Heaven between Satan and God.

Born in 1608 in London, John Milton forged a career that reflects the turmoil of English political, social, and religious life in the seventeenth century. Throughout the 1640s, civil war ravaged England as parliamentary and royalist armies battled for control of the country, a struggle that ended when the king, Charles I, was publicly beheaded in Whitehall, London, in January 1649. Milton published prose works on issues of religious and political controversy during the decade, including *Areopagitica* (1644), which defends freedom of the press. From 1649-1659, after Milton's writings attracted the attention of parliamentary leaders, he became diplomatic secretary for Oliver Cromwell's government. Although Milton had been doing less official work toward the end of the 1650s (largely because of the complete loss of his eyesight in 1652), his close connections with Cromwell's government jeopardized him in 1660, when the monarchy regained control in England and the Stuart kings were restored to the throne. After serving a few months in prison, Milton was released and suffered no further major reprisals. Meanwhile, in 1658, having earlier published a volume of verse (*Poems of Mr. John Milton, Both English and Latin,* 1645), Milton turned again to poetry. The initial version of *Paradise Lost* consisted of 10 books, but by 1674, the epic had been restructured and a few lines added so that the final version encompassed 12 books, modeled after Greek epics. In addition to using classical epic conventions to tell the Judaeo-Christian story of humanity's fall, *Paradise Lost* incorporates key features of seventeenth-century English history.

Events in History at the Time the Poem Takes Place

War in Heaven. *Paradise Lost* is set at the beginning of time. The epic's early events center upon the Christian myth of the War in Heaven and the defeat of the evil angels, based loosely on three passages from Judeo-Christian scripture: Isaiah 14:12–21, Luke 10:18, and Revelation 12:7–12. The passage from Isaiah describes Satan as "the morning star, son of the dawn," who has "fallen from the heavens," and ascribes to him an overweening pride and arrogance that stem from his rivalry with God (Isaiah 14.12):

"I will scale the heavens;
Above the stars of God
I will set up my throne;
I will take my seat on the Mount of Assembly,
    in the recesses of the North.
I will ascend above the tops of the clouds;
I will be like the Most High!"
Yet down to the nether world you go to the
    recesses of the pit!

(Isaiah 14.14–21)

Pride and vainglory, traits of Satan that find their way into *Paradise Lost*, lead to the War in Heaven and impel the fallen angel to seek vengeance for his loss by wreaking havoc on God's newly created beings, Adam and Eve. In the passage from the gospel of Luke, Jesus himself echoes the account in Isaiah of Lucifer's downfall, noting, in particular, how the rebellious angel's descent was like lightning. The passage from Revelation dramatizes the military conflict of the War in Heaven, identifying Michael as the leader of the good angels and Satan as his adversary, also called the "huge dragon," "the devil," and "the seducer of the whole world" (Revelation 12:7-12). While Milton clearly relied on the three foregoing passages from scripture, he drew from Greek myth too—for example, from the War of the Titans against Jove (recounted by authors such as Hesiod and Pindar). In the first book of *Paradise Lost* he refers to Briareos and Typhon, of the Titans and earth-born Giants who warred on Jove (Milton, *Paradise Lost,* 1.198). Jove's use of lightning to defeat Typhon and to cause his nine-day fall into Tartarus, or into a cave near Tarsus (in Asia Minor) anticipates the Son's use of thunderbolts to cause the fall of the evil angels from Heaven in Book 6 of *Paradise Lost.*

Garden of Eden. The later events of *Paradise Lost* deal with Satan's seduction of Eve in the Garden of Eden and her relationship with Adam during and immediately after their downfall. Again drawing on scripture, Milton adapts and enlarges the account in Genesis 3:1–7:

Now the serpent was more crafty than any other wild animal that the Lord God had made. He said to the woman, "Did God say, 'you shall not eat from any tree in the garden'?"

The woman said to the serpent, "We may eat of the fruit of the trees in the garden; but God said, 'You shall not eat of the fruit of the tree that is in the middle of the garden, nor shall you touch it, or you shall die'." But the serpent said to the woman, "You will not die; for God knows that when you eat of it your eyes will be opened, and you will be like God, knowing

good and evil." So when the woman saw that the tree was good for food, and that it was a delight to the eyes, and that the tree was to be desired to make one wise, she took of its fruit and ate; and she also gave some to her husband, who was with her, and he ate. Then the eyes of both were opened, and they knew that they were naked; and they sewed fig leaves together and made loincloths for themselves.

(Genesis 3:1-7)

From this brief biblical account, Milton creates a luxuriant Garden of Eden as the center of an earthly Paradise teeming with plants, fruits, flowers, rivers, birds, fish, and beasts whose interaction is harmonious. *Paradise* has been traced back to the Persian word for "park" or "enclosure." Genesis 2:8 tells us that the garden was in "the East," which in this context generally means "Mesopotamia" (Metzger and Coogan, p. 178). We are also told that four rivers flow out of the garden—Gihon, Pishon, Tigris, and Euphrates—but the first two are unknown, making it impossible to pinpoint a precise location for the earthly Paradise.

In *Paradise Lost*, Milton situates the Garden of Eden on a plateau at the summit of Paradise, and along the slope of ascent lies a "steep wilderness, whose hairy sides" are "with thicket overgrown, grotesque and wild" (*Paradise Lost,* 4.135–36). Rising from the slope, as well, are various trees—cedar, pine, fir, and palm—creating "insuperable highth of loftiest shade" (*Paradise Lost,* 4.138). Such a lush paradise has numerous precedents in classical, medieval, and Renaissance literature. Among the precedents most likely to have influenced Milton are Sumerian, Babylonian, and Assyrian myths, the most influential being the epic *Gilgamesh*, which predates the Book of Genesis by 2,000 to 3,000 years.

The Poem in Focus

Plot overview. *Paradise Lost* is divided into 12 books that function much like the chapters of a novel. The narrative begins with the defeat of Satan after his failed attempt to take control of Heaven, follows him through the stages of his successful plot to subvert God's newest creation, humankind, and ends with the expulsion of Adam and Eve from the Garden of Eden.

Like most epics, *Paradise Lost* starts in *medias res*, or in the midst of things—that is, the story is not told in strict chronological order. For example, it is only midway through the epic that the seraph (or angel) Raphael recounts the earliest events, such as the War in Heaven, but the epic's narrator recounts the consequences of that conflict, notably the punishment of the evil angels and their effort to avenge their downfall at the start of the poem, in Books 1 and 2. The following brief survey summarizes the sequence of events through the twelve books of the poem.

Book 1. The poem begins with a statement of its theme: to "assert Eternal Providence" and to "justify the ways of God to men" (*Paradise Lost,* 1.25-26). While the downfall of Adam and Eve and their loss of Eden are foreseen, the poem also emphasizes the role of the Son as the redeemer, who offers himself as a sacrifice on behalf of fallen humankind (*Paradise Lost,* 1.4). The narrator then recounts the aftermath of the War in Heaven, particularly the defeat and banishment of the fallen angels to Hell. Satan, who remains defiant, revives the fallen angels after their defeat and assembles them to plan how they will avenge their loss.

Book 2. A meeting takes place in Pandemonium, a structure built by the fallen angels in Hell. In this edifice, which resembles both a temple and a palace, Satan occupies the position of preeminence: "high on a throne of royal state" (*Paradise Lost,* 2.1). Four angels present their views concerning the options for vengeance, and there is overwhelming approval for a plan to attack the newly created race of Man, who is less than the angels "in power and excellence, but favored more" by God (*Paradise Lost,* 2.350). Satan volunteers to conduct a reconnaissance of these newly created beings. He persuades the gatekeeper, Sin, to unlock the gates of Hell and let him out. He then flies through Chaos, until he lands on the convex exterior of the cosmos, which is encased by a crystalline sphere or shell.

Book 3. Seeing what has happened, God the Father informs the Son that Satan will succeed in his plan to subvert Adam and Eve, who will fall from their state of grace. Though God foresees their downfall, he emphasizes that the fault is theirs, not his, for they are creatures whom he created with free will. Meanwhile, Satan dives through an opening in the exterior of the cosmos and flies to the brightest body in the heavens, the sun. Disguising himself as a lesser angel, he seeks information about Adam and Eve from Uriel, the seraph who is regent of the sun. Directed to earth, Satan lands within sight of Eden.

Book 4. Having assumed the shape of a cormorant, Satan perches on the Tree of Life, from which he surveys Eden. When he notices Adam and Eve, he enters the shapes of other animals;

In this scene from the 1688 edition of *Paradise Lost,* the angels Michael and Gabriel battle Satan and his angels.

and as if he were stalking prey, he approaches the human pair to overhear their conversation. He learns of their one prohibition—the divine command not to eat the fruit of the Tree of Knowledge of Good and Evil—and plans their downfall. Uriel, who was tricked into directing Satan to earth, becomes aware of the deception, and alerts Gabriel, the seraph who protects Paradise, to the intruder. Satan creeps up to Eve while she sleeps and induces her to dream.

Book 5. In her dream Eve is awakened by a voice that resembles Adam's, though it is spoken by an angelic being. (The being is none other than Satan in the guise of this angel.) Led in her dream to the Tree of Knowledge of Good and Evil, Eve is urged to eat of the forbidden fruit and does so. She then accompanies the angelic being "up to the clouds," from which she views "the earth outstretched immense" (*Paradise Lost* 5.86, 88). To warn Adam and Eve of Satan and his wiles, God the Father instructs the seraph Raphael to travel to earth. Raphael recounts how Satan, then called "Lucifer," seduced one third of the angels to revolt against God, suggesting how formidable an adversary he is to the humans.

Book 6. Raphael continues his account of Satan's revolt. After three days, the war becomes a stalemate, even though the resourceful and ingenious Satan invents gunpowder that ignites cannons. These "implements of mischief" overwhelm the good angels, whose recourse is to uproot the mountains of Heaven and to topple them onto the weapons devised by Satan (*Paradise Lost,* 6.488). To bring the three-day war to an end, the Father urges the Son to mount "the chariot of Paternal Deity," from which he will assault the evil angels (*Paradise Lost,* 6.750). Speeding toward them in the chariot, the Son discharges "ten thousand thunders" in a volley so intense that the evil angels leap from the precipice of Heaven, falling for nine days into Hell (*Paradise Lost,* 6.836).

Book 7. At Adam's request Raphael recounts the story of the Creation. Sped by a chariot through the gates of Heaven, the Son, accompanied by angels, oversees "the vast immeasurable abyss," which is "outrageous as a sea, dark, wasteful, wild" (*Paradise Lost,* 7.211–12). In a series of utterances, the Son begets one stage of the Creation after another. Plenitude, continuity, and hierarchy characterize Nature, which is full of diversity and innumerable creatures—fowl, fish, and beasts. The account focuses on the creation of humankind and the enjoinder that Adam and Eve, endowed "with sanctity of reason," should "be fruitful, multiply, and fill the earth" (*Paradise Lost,* 6.508, 531).

Book 8. Adam asks Raphael about the planets and other celestial bodies, their placement in the heavens, and their motions. But Raphael discourages such inquiry, even the query on whether the earth or the sun is the center of the universe. Instructing Adam to "be lowly wise," Raphael encourages discussion more directly relevant to the human condition (*Paradise Lost,* 8.173). Adam, complying with his teacher's guidance, affirms that it is more important to know what "before us lies in daily life" (*Paradise Lost* 8.193). Recollecting the first moments of consciousness after he was created, Adam indicates to Raphael that he felt the need for "collateral love," and "dearest amity" (*Paradise Lost,* 8.426). The subjects of Eve's creation, Adam's conjugal union with her under the direction of God, and Raphael's elaboration on the relationship of Adam and Eve conclude Book 8.

Book 9. Having infiltrated the Garden of Eden, Satan takes the form of a serpent and waits for an opportune moment to seduce humankind. Eve proposes that she and Adam divide their labors, because when they are together, they talk and become diverted from their duties to "tend plant, herb and flower" (*Paradise Lost,* 9.206). Spying Eve at work alone, Satan begins to seduce her to his purpose, leading her to the Tree of Knowledge of Good and Evil. He accuses God of preventing humankind from becoming divine, for if, contends Satan, Eve were to eat of the forbidden fruit, she would become godlike. Emboldened by this argument, Eve eats the forbidden fruit and offers it to Adam, who also eats it. Soon they quarrel, each blaming the other for their transgressions.

Book 10. The Son travels to the Garden of Eden to judge Adam and Eve. Because of their transgressions, they are to be punished in various ways: Adam will toil for his living, and Eve will experience the pain of childbirth. In the meantime, the figures of Sin and Death, who had been in Hell, have followed Satan in his journey to the earth, and now prey on Adam and Eve, as they will on all humankind to come. Satan, exulting in his successful temptation of humanity, returns to Hell, mounts his throne, and reports his triumph to the evil angels. However, he is transformed into "a monstrous serpent on his belly prone" and the evil angels become serpents too (*Paradise Lost,* 10.514). When they try to alleviate hunger and thirst by eating fruit, they chew "bitter ashes" (*Paradise Lost,* 10.566). By the end of the book, Adam and Eve experience remorse and become contrite.

Book 11. The Son presents Adam's and Eve's prayers to God, who accepts them, but ordains the couple's banishment from Paradise. The archangel Michael informs the pair of God's verdict; but to prevent them from becoming disconsolate, God has instructed his angelic emissary to foretell "to Adam what shall come in future days" (*Paradise Lost,* 11.114). The revelation is to include mention of "the covenant in the woman's seed renewed," a reference to the Virgin Mary, to whom the Son will be born in human form as Jesus (*Paradise Lost,* 11.116). While Eve is asleep, Michael takes Adam to a mountaintop, from which they view future events: Cain's slaying of Abel, various scenes of peace and war, the Flood, Noah's ark, and the resurrection of Jesus Christ.

Book 12. The vision of the future continues: the Israelites are enslaved by Egypt, liberated under the leadership of Moses, and then ruled by David, the ancestor of Jesus. In his narration, Michael emphasizes the coming of Jesus the Redeemer, and the foundation and growth of Christianity under the Apostles. Particularly highlighted is the Son's final victory over Satan.

At the "world's dissolution," the Final Judgment will occur (*Paradise Lost* 12.459). The reference here is to Doomsday, when the world will be cataclysmically destroyed and all humankind will be judged by the Son, who will determine the ultimate disposition of human souls to Heaven or Hell. After Eve awakens, she and Adam are escorted by Michael from the Garden of Eden.

Satan. Milton lived through one of the most dramatic periods in English history, a period that has been described by one historian as "the world turned upside down" (Hill, p. xv). The upheaval in Milton's era challenged the medieval worldview, in which the various social classes—commoners, clergy, nobility, and the sovereign—were rigidly stratified, one above the other. Disrupting this hierarchy was the vastly expanding middle class, including craftsmen, tradesmen, merchants, and lawyers, who settled in urban areas and whose involvement in socioeconomic culture modified traditional concepts of status. The Protestant Reformation also contributed to social instability by challenging the authority of the papacy and by encouraging people to read the Bible on their own rather than having it interpreted for them by a priest. In the early seventeenth century, many scientific discoveries, particularly Galileo's confirmation that the earth revolved around the sun, challenged traditional worldviews as well. In this climate, leftist political, religious, and military groups questioned the hegemony of the sovereign as the head of church and state. That challenge eventually resulted in the English Civil War, in which Oliver Cromwell, commander of England's army, defeated the royalists. With the beheading of King Charles I in January 1649, the Interregnum (years of English government between the reigns of monarchs) began, and Cromwell presided over the nation.

In view of the foregoing events, Satan in *Paradise Lost* may typify the defiant rebel who challenges God's absolutism, refusing to capitulate even when he privately despairs of victory. To the fallen angels who rally around him after their defeat in Heaven and downfall into Hell, Satan proclaims:

> Powers and Dominions, deities of Heaven,
> For since no deep within her gulf can hold
> Immortal vigor, though oppressed and fallen,
> I give not Heaven for lost. From this descent
> Celestial Virtues rising, will appear

> More glorious and more dread than from no
>   fall,
> And trust themselves to fear no second fate.
>   (*Paradise Lost*, 2.11–17)

In effect, Satan defines his existence by being adversarial. A number of readers considered this defiance of God to be heroic.

The basis for interpreting Satan as a hero derives from the reaction of British Romantic poets in the late eighteenth and early nineteenth century. William Blake, Percy Bysshe Shelley, and

MILTON AND WOMEN

When he was composing his epic poem, the 56-year-old Milton had already outlived two wives and was entering upon his third marriage. Milton also had published two editions of *The Doctrine and Discipline of Divorce*. Undoubtedly some of his marital experiences affected the characterization of Eve and her relationship with Adam. It seems likely, for instance, that when Eve separates from Adam in Book 9 of *Paradise Lost*, Milton may have recalled his first wife's separation from him in 1642, when she went home to her parents within two months of their marriage (she would return to him three years later). Evidently Mary Powell found Milton to be an inhospitable spouse, perhaps because she was only 17 years old, whereas he was 33. Also, Milton's studious regimen, frugal meals, little social contact with others, and antiroyalist sentiments all ran counter to Mary's upbringing. Significantly, in his divorce tracts Milton contends that the chief purpose for marriage is to alleviate loneliness. Similarly, Adam in *Paradise Lost* cites his "single imperfection"—how he is "in unity [his oneness or singularity] defective" and why he desires "collateral love, and dearest amity" (*Paradise Lost*, 8.423, 426). Such is the basis for marriage, and when the rapport of love and amity is severed, so too, Milton contends in the divorce tracts, is the marriage. Because of his personal experiences and the subordinate status of women in seventeenth-century England, Milton probably held the view concerning spousal relations that the Son himself expresses when punishing Eve after her downfall: to her "husband's will" she "shall submit" and he over her "shall rule" (*Paradise Lost*, 10.195, 196). While such may have been his general view, his poem manifests a relatively open-minded outlook on women for his time, depicting a relationship between Adam and Eve that is more mutual and reciprocal than hierarchical.

In the final climactic stanzas of Milton's poem, the angel Michael escorts Adam and Eve from the Garden of Eden, as shown in this 1688 illustration.

Lord Byron all perceived Satan as a rebel-hero, in part, perhaps, because they, like Satan, challenged traditional authority. Satan may even be seen as an allegorical rendition of Cromwell, who not only rebelled against but also overcame the Stuart king of England. But Cromwell's triumph supposedly occurred because the Stuart monarchy was an unjust rulership, an institution that appropriated power claimed by Parliament and that subjugated the people. Whereas the sovereignty of God may be construed as legitimate, a human sovereign who is an absolutist tends to become a tyrant, and a tyrant merits overthrow and punishment. In other words, Milton's poem may be distinguishing legitimate from illegitimate sovereignty. Milton himself composed several anti-monarchical tracts justifying the forcible removal of King Charles I—and his execution. Alternatively, according to William Blake, although Milton's poem glorifies Satan's heroic energy and resourcefulness, its author may have been of the devil's party without knowing it. In other words, the poem could be implying that any absolutist, even the Judeo-Christian God, is unjust, largely because decrees of salvation and damnation might be construed as arbitrary. The more likely implication, however, is that human institutions that presume to operate under the aegis of God (monarchy and the church) can be sacrilegious and corrupt.

Another point of view is developed in illustrated editions of *Paradise Lost,* the first of which appears in 1688, the year of the Glorious or Bloodless Revolution, in which the English Parliament replaced James II, England's last Catholic king, with his Protestant daughter, Mary, and her husband, Prince William of Orange, with whom she ruled jointly. In the first illustrated edition of the poem, Satan's face resembles that of a Stuart monarch, the dynastic house that the Revolution of 1688 terminated. The epic narrates how Satan elevates himself above his peers, extorting homage from them as if he were a deity. In doing so, he becomes an "idol of majesty divine," as the epic recounts, and the evil angels who worship him are idolaters (*Paradise Lost,* 6.106). These images all suggest the Stuart monarchs, whom one can identify with the idols, and the royalists who assisted them, whom one can identify with the idolaters. Further, if Milton describes the council in Hell in Book 2 of *Paradise Lost* as a parliamentary debate, this too supports the view that Satan is meant to resemble the Stuart monarchs. The devil's council offers only the pretense of debate—the consensus that finally issues from the deliberations is the same plan initially proposed by Satan, whose dominant will prevails. The same thing happened during Charles I's kingship; when Parliament did not comply with his will, he threatened to dissolve it. Moreover, Satan enthroned in Pandemonium resembles both a political and a religious leader, the two roles of the Stuart monarchs.

Sources and literary context. In writing *Paradise Lost,* Milton relied primarily on Hebraic and Christian scripture. He also incorporated extensive commentary on that scripture by the rabbis and by the Church Fathers, who were the prominent Christian interpreters in the early centuries after Christ (people like St. Augustine of Hippo and St. Jerome). To achieve the epic form of the poem, Milton consciously imitated previous long narrative poems, such as Homer's *Iliad* and *Odyssey* and Virgil's *Aeneid.* In fact, at the beginning of Book 9 of *Paradise Lost,* Milton refers to all three of these classical epics. Milton is likewise indebted to the epics of classical antiquity for the twofold themes of love and war that inform *Paradise Lost* and for numerous literary conventions and devices traditionally associated with long narrative poems, such as the invocation of the muse(s), a descent into the underworld, and epic similes (protracted comparisons and analogies). Milton depended as well on numerous medieval and Renaissance epics. Dante's the *Divine Comedy*, for example, especially the *Inferno*, influenced *Paradise Lost* in numerous ways, particularly in the topography of Hell. Indeed, one of the most renowned paradoxes in *Paradise Lost*, in which "hope never comes" to the fallen angels though it "comes to all," derives from the inscription on the portal to Dante's underworld, which counsels all who enter its confines to abandon any hope of escape (*Paradise Lost*, 1.66–67).

Events in History at the Time the Poem Was Written

Civil War, Interregnum, Restoration. Milton lived in an era of extraordinary turmoil, which derived from the clash of the Stuart sovereigns, James I and Charles I, with Parliament. This clash intensified under Charles I for several reasons:

- The tension between the king's view that his right to rule came from God (the so-called divine right of kingship) and Parliament's view that the power of the king derived from the consent of the people
- Parliament's insistence of its right to meet and not to be dissolved by royal decree when its views challenged those of the king; Parliament's reluctance to finance the king's wars against France, Spain, and the Scots
- The appointment as Archbishop of Canterbury of William Laud, who enforced a uniform mode of worship and the use of a prayer book, both of which were favored by only a small minority of the English people

Antagonizing most Englishmen, as well, was Charles I's marriage to the French Catholic princess Henrietta Maria.

In this era Milton composed numerous tracts against high-ranking clergy and the monarchy. He opposed the episcopal hierarchy in the Church of England—namely, the ecclesiastical dignitaries headed by William Laud—and disapproved of a monarchy that abridged the liberties of the people, that arrogated powers belonging to Parliament, and that conducted what was tantamount to personal rule. More radically, Milton defended regicide and paved the way for later works in which he celebrated republicanism. At the same time, he was the victim of personal abuse in polemical tracts whose authors were employed by the son of Charles I.

Between 1649 and 1660, England was not a

monarchy but a republic whose leaders experimented with national governments. First there was the Commonwealth (1649-53), under which Cromwell attempted to let others govern, then the Protectorate (1653-60), with Cromwell serving as head of state until he died in 1658. Eighteen months of strife followed before free elec-

MILTON: PRIVATE LIFE AND PUBLIC SERVICE

1642: Milton marries Mary Powell; England is on the verge of Civil War.

1643-44: The first and second editions of Milton's *The Doctrine and Discipline of Divorce* are published.

1644-45: Cromwell and his New Model Army win major battles.

1647: Cromwell's army occupies London.

1649: The Commonwealth is declared; Charles I is beheaded; Milton is appointed diplomatic secretary to the Council of State.

1652: Milton suffers total blindness; Mary Powell dies.

1653: Cromwell is named the Lord Protector.

1656: Milton marries Katherine Woodcock.

1658: Katherine Woodcock dies; Cromwell dies; Milton begins in earnest to write *Paradise Lost*, some of which may have been composed earlier.

1660: Charles II becomes king of England; Milton is arrested, but soon released from jail.

1663: Milton marries Elizabeth Minshull and probably finishes *Paradise Lost*.

1665-66: Milton escapes the plague in London by residing at a cottage in Chalfont St. Giles, Buckinghamshire.

1667: First edition of *Paradise Lost* is published.

1674: Second edition of *Paradise Lost* is published; Milton dies of gout on November 8th and is interred inside St. Giles Church in Cripplegate, London.

tions led to the recall of Charles II to the throne. England's 11 years of nonroyal rule ended. The experiment in government had failed.

Despite the military successes of Cromwell's army at home and even abroad and the tolerance for the independent religious congregations and political radicals, the Commonwealth had not been a popular government; it fell because it was unrepresentative. The Parliament in session, called the Rump (because its members remained seated while others, who were unsympathetic to the army, were purged), was a thin disguise for military despotism. Because a freely elected Parliament would have seated many members sympathetic to the return of the monarchy, Cromwell and the officers of his army devised a constitution for a government called the Protectorate, which supplanted the Commonwealth. Cromwell was made Lord Protector and Head of State. The failure of the Protectorate can be traced to the military character of the government, Cromwell's death in 1658, and the inability of his son, Richard, to elicit political support. Charles II took the throne in 1660, but his kingship was limited in its power; and within a few generations, religious toleration and the sovereignty of the people became important elements of the English constitution.

The military and political turmoil that beset the 1640s and 1650s in England informs *Paradise Lost* on many levels. The most graphic example is the War in Heaven, which occupies most of Book 6. The "spread ensigns" and "firm battalion" that assemble under the command of Satan and the cannons that discharge their fire-iron balls dramatize the tactics of infantry, artillery, and cavalry during the English Civil War (*Paradise Lost*, 6.533, 534). In Adam's dream-vision of the future, which spans Books 11 and 12, the biblical figure of Nimrod (from Genesis 10:8) typifies the military despotism that enforces political rulership:

> . . . one shall rise
> Of proud ambitious heart, who not content
> With fair equality, fraternal state,
> Will arrogate dominion undeserved
> Over his brethren, and quite dispossess
> Concord and law of nature from the earth;
> Hunting (and men not beasts shall be his
>   game)
> With war and hostile snare such as refuse
> Subjection to his empire tyrannous.
>   (*Paradise Lost*, 12.24–32)

The characterization of Nimrod may glance back at not only Charles I but also Cromwell, whose excesses Milton disliked and whose military threats and intervention can be viewed as arrogant gestures of personal rule.

Milton and Puritanism. Puritanism in mid-seventeenth-century England was a religious orientation whose adherents, by their emphasis on scripture and on the practices of early Christianity, preferred simple religious beliefs, simple forms of worship, simple methods of church organization, and a strict moral code with reference to personal conduct. Puritans objected to the vestiges of Roman Catholicism in the liturgy and prayer book of the Church of England and in the episcopal hierarchy. They also preferred to eliminate priestly vestments, rituals and ceremonies, statues, colored windows, and music from churches. They abhorred the dissolute life of the Stuart monarchs and the extravagant masques at the court of Charles I that pandered to the king's proud self-image, used garish scenery and theatrical devices, featured wantonness, and employed objectionable music. They disliked festivities, stage-plays, rural sporting games (especially when held on Sundays), maypoles, and folk dances. Doctrinally, Puritans embraced many of the views of the French reformer John Calvin.

Accordingly, Puritans were labeled Dissenters. Because they did not succeed in purifying the culture and in purging the Church of England of its excesses, which they perceived as vestiges of Roman Catholicism, some more radical Puritans broke away from the established Church and became separatists. Many separatists advocated the abolition of the priesthood and episcopacy, contending, as well, that each congregation should be independent of all others and have the right to choose its own pastor. Most important to Puritans was the right to express their religious views without oppression or persecution from the established Church, not a right they would enjoy. Instead the Laudians, or followers of the Anglican Archbishop Laud, who resented the Puritans, used civil authority to punish them. To escape the Laudians, some Puritans traveled to the colonies in America. While it may be argued that the Puritans failed in their immediate objective of reforming the established Church, a broader view will indicate that Puritanism had long-term effects: buttressing Protestantism against Catholic resurgence in England; advocating liberty of conscience; espousing religious toleration; resisting civil authority's insistence on uniform religious beliefs; and upholding the rights of the people to limit the power of a sovereign. While Milton leaned toward Puritanism, he also manifested affinity with Presbyterianism, which also emphasized the doctrines of Calvin. Initially, Milton was part of a coalition, including the Puritans, the Presbyterians, and others, that sought to reform the Church of England. But when he discovered that the Scottish Presbyterians, in particular, were striving to impose their particular beliefs as the established religion, he castigated them for hypocrisy.

Paradise Lost reflects Puritanism in several ways. If the Puritans disliked the established Church because of its resemblance to Roman Catholicism, then the papacy, in particular, evoked their hatred. Pandemonium, the temple and palace that the devils construct in Hell, resembles St. Peter's Basilica in Rome. Like St. Peter's, Pandemonium has ornate pillars, "golden architrave," "cornice" and "frieze, with bossy sculptures grav'n," and "the roof was fretted gold" even the "doors" with "their brazen folds" suggest the entrance to St. Peter's (*Paradise Lost* 1.713–17, 724).

To provide a contrast to the excesses of Roman Catholicism, Milton in *Paradise Lost* depicts the evening and morning prayers of Adam and Eve as simple and spontaneous forms of worship. Before they withdraw to their innermost bower in the Garden of Eden, Adam and Eve celebrate the beneficence of the Lord in a short prayer. The commentary that follows accentuates the couple's Puritanism:

> This said unanimous, and other rites
> Observing none, but adoration pure
> Which God likes best, into their inmost
> bower
> Handed they went.
> (*Paradise Lost*, 4.736–739)

And after they awaken, the morning prayer of Adam and Eve likewise reflects the features admired by Puritans:

> Lowly they bowed adoring, and began
> Their orisons, each morning duly paid
> In various style, for neither various style
> Nor holy rapture wanted they to praise
> Their Maker, in fit strains pronounced or
> sung
> Unmeditated, such prompt eloquence
> Flowed from their lips, in prose or numerous
> verse,
> More tuneable than needed lute or harp
> To add more sweetness.
> (*Paradise Lost*, 5.144–52)

Finally, there was a belief among Puritans, and other Protestants, that marriage was not simply for procreation—marriage partners owed each other mutual comfort and support. Manuals of the early 1700s (*The Compleat Housewife*, 1734, for example, and *The Young Ladies' Companion*, 1740) promoted the idea of husband and wife as helpmates in their spiritual, emotional, and working lives, an ideal clearly reflected in Eve's relation to Adam.

Milton and science. Much as upheavals in politics and religion characterized seventeenth-century England, so too radical changes in the field of science challenged traditional views of the design of the universe that contributed to the instability of the era. The Royal Society, an association of scholars dedicated to individual research and the collective evaluation and publication of findings, was established in 1660, about the time Milton began *Paradise Lost*. Since its founding, the Royal Society has exercised great influence on science and on scientific education. In Milton's era one of the most significant scientific findings included the verification by telescope of the Copernican or "heliocentric" (sun-centered) model of the universe.

While Milton surely knew about this model, in *Paradise Lost* he uses the Ptolemaic or "geocentric" (earth-centered) model, which dates back to the second century C.E. In the geocentric conception, the fixed earth is at the center, encompassed, in turn, by seven spheres or tracks in which the moon, Mercury, Venus, the sun, Mars, Jupiter, and Saturn revolve. The eighth sphere includes the fixed stars; the ninth, though crystalline, is watery; the tenth, called the *primum mobile* or "the first mover," imparts motion to the other spheres. Encasing the universe is a hard, crystalline shell, called the "firmament." This schema of the universe informs much of *Paradise Lost*, including the account in Book 7 of the creation of the world. Incorporated in literature and theology since at least the Middle Ages, the geocentric model of the universe was congruent with the biblical account of Creation in Genesis: God made the sun, moon, and stars revolve around the earth as a sign of his care and concern for humankind—one of the dominant themes of Milton's epic.

But scientific findings in the late sixteenth and early seventeenth centuries began to prove the truth of the heliocentric model of the universe. Such findings, which resulted from Galileo's invention of the telescope late in the sixteenth century, included topographic features of the moon (its valleys and mountains and its reflection, not radiation, of light), sunspots, the satellites of Jupiter, the peculiar form of Saturn, the phases of Venus and Mars, and the Milky Way. Galileo was persecuted by the Catholic Church in Italy, primarily because his revolutionary findings were construed as challenges to ecclesiastical authority (and also to the biblical account of the Creation). Milton, during his journey through Italy in 1638–1639, visited Galileo, who at the time was blind and under house arrest. From atop a mountain in Fiesole outside Florence, in the region of Tuscany, Milton viewed the heavens through Galileo's telescope. That experience so stimulated his imagination that Milton refers explicitly to Galileo three times in *Paradise Lost*, calling attention to the astronomer's major discoveries involving the moon and the sun. First, to highlight the "broad circumference" of Satan's shield, Milton likens it to "the moon, whose orb / Through optic glass the Tuscan artist views" (*Paradise Lost*, 1.287–88). Second, when Satan lands on the sun, Milton contends that he produced

> . . . As when by night the glass
> Of Galileo . . . observes
> Imagined lands and regions in the moon.
> (*Paradise Lost*, 5.261–63)

Sometimes the two models of the universe—the geocentric and heliocentric—are juxtaposed, but the intent does not seem to be to affirm the validity of the latter. When, for example, Adam inquires about the design of the universe, Raphael discourages such "studious abstruse thoughts" (*Paradise Lost*, 8.40). He cautions Adam:

> God to remove his ways from human sense,
> Placed heaven from earth so far, that earthly sight,
> If it presume, might err in things too high,
> And no advantage gain. What if the sun
> Be center to the world, and other stars
> By his attractive virtue and their own
> Incited, dance about him various rounds?
> (*Paradise Lost*, 8.119–25)

Raphael's admonition speaks to a human inclination toward presumption and pride in probing the mysteries of the Creation. While science as such is not rejected, Raphael admonishes scientists who are motivated by the quest for fame and self-glorification, even to the extent of seeking out "other worlds" (*Paradise Lost*, 8.175). The seraph's guidance to Adam—to "be lowly wise" and to "think only what concerns thee and thy being"—counsels obedience to God (*Paradise Lost*, 8.173–74). Another way of framing Raphael's guidance is to highlight the distinction between *scientia* (or knowledge), on the one hand, and *sapientia* (or wisdom), on the other. The latter is clearly preferable to the former. And when the latter is combined with humility, as when Raphael enjoins Adam to "be lowly wise," Milton is epitomizing his understanding of humankind's ideal relationship with God.

TO RHYME OR NOT TO RHYME

When *Paradise Lost* was first published in 1667, some readers asserted that the poem should have been composed in rhyme. Milton's revolutionary act of dispensing with the principal marker of English verse was perceived as an eccentric and possibly elitist gesture against the native rhyming tradition. Milton himself in a prefatory note to the epic explains that his "measure is English heroic verse without rhyme, as that of Homer in Greek and of Virgil in Latin" (Shawcross in Milton, pp. 249-50). Milton composed his epic in blank verse, or unrhymed iambic pentameter, a measure that includes ten syllables per line. Because the metrical foot called the iamb is disyllabic, including an unstressed and a stressed syllable, there are five iambs per line of verse. This was the same measure used by Renaissance dramatists, such as Christopher Marlowe and William Shakespeare. Milton may have chosen this measure not only because of its use by classical forbears, such as Homer and Virgil, but also because of the dramatic features of his epic. After all, Milton initially conceived of *Paradise Lost* as a drama, which was to have been called "Adam Unparadised," for which only an outline survives. He furthermore dismissed rhyme as an invention used to set off weak subject matter and meter—that is, to conceal poetic deficiencies.

> . . . a spot like which perhaps
> Astronomer in the sun's lucent orb
> Through his glazed optic tube yet never saw.
> (*Paradise Lost*, 3.588–90)

Third, to elaborate on the clearness of the firmament, Milton describes the atmosphere as ideal for the use of a telescope:

Reception. When it was first published (1667), *Paradise Lost* elicited less than glowing praise because its author was John Milton. Milton's religious and political views branded him as an unpopular author after the Restoration, so that the excellence of his greatest work went largely unheralded, except for the admiration of a few close associates, such as Andrew Marvell, who worked with Milton while he was diplomatic secretary during the Interregnum. Another admirer was John Dryden, who toward the end of the century rendered parts of *Paradise Lost* in rhymed couplets for an opera called *The State of Innocence*, which was published in 1677 but never performed.

Not until the eighteenth century did Milton's epic achieve more universal praise. In a series of essays in the literary journal called *The Spectator* (1712; also in *WLAIT 3: British and Irish Literature and Its Times*), Joseph Addison ranked *Paradise Lost* with classical epics. A generation later, in 1727, the French writer Voltaire expressed unbounded admiration for Milton and his epic. By the mid-eighteenth century, political liberalism and the Romantic movement, which involved renewed attentiveness to nature, had registered an impact on English society; in 1756 the English critic Joseph Warton focused, among other aspects, on the natural setting for the Garden of Eden in *Paradise Lost*, describing the unbridled imagination of its author as sublime. Later in the eighteenth century, however, in *The Lives of the Most Eminent English Poets* (1783), Samuel Johnson expressed a mixed reaction: though he praised Milton's imagination, he decried the images from nature as being derived more from books than from direct experience.

In the early nineteenth century, especially in the wake of the French Revolution, *Paradise Lost* evoked the admiration of William Blake, Percy Bysshe Shelley, and Lord Byron, all of whom perceived Milton's Satan as a heroic rebel and God as a tyrant.

Today, *Paradise Lost* is commonly held to be a classic of Western literature, which engages present-day topics of intense interest, such as patriarchy, humankind's relationship with God, gender relations, and environmentalism.

—Albert C. Labriola and Martin Griffin

For More Information

Empson, William. *Milton's God*. Revised ed. Corrected, with Notes and an Appendix. London: Chatto [and] Windus, 1965.

Fish, Stanley. *Surprised by Sin: The Reader in Paradise Lost*. 2nd. ed. with a new preface. Cambridge: Harvard University Press, 1997.

Flannagan, Roy, ed. *The Riverside Milton*. Boston: Houghton Mifflin, 1998.

Hanford, James Holly, and James G. Taaffe. *A Milton Handbook*. 5th ed. New York: Meredith, 1970.

Hill, Christopher. *Milton and the English Revolution*. New York: Viking, 1977.

Marjara, Harinder Singh. *Contemplation of Created Things: Science in Paradise Lost*. Toronto: University of Toronto Press, 1992.

Metzger, Bruce M., and Michael D. Coogan, eds. *The Oxford Companion to the Bible*. Oxford, England: Oxford University Press, 1993.

Milton, John. *Paradise Lost*. In *The Complete Poetry of John Milton*. Ed. John T. Shawcross. Garden City, N.Y.: Doubleday, 1971.

The New American Bible. Mission Hills, Calif.: Benziger, 1986.

Rogers, John. *The Matter of Revolution: Science, Poetry and Politics in the Age of Milton*. Ithaca, N.Y.: Cornell University Press, 1996.

Zwicker, Steven N., ed. *The Cambridge Companion to English Literature, 1650-1740*. Cambridge, England: Cambridge University Press, 1998.

Piers Plowman

by
William Langland

~

Unlike modern works that feature the author's name prominently on the cover, medieval poems were frequently written and read without much regard for the author's identity. In the case of *Piers Plowman*, we have some evidence for the poet's name; a handwritten note in an early fifteenth-century manuscript attributes the poem to "Willielm[us] de Langlond," which seems confirmed by this cryptogram in the poem itself: "'I have lived in land,' said I, 'my name is Long Will'" (Langland, *Piers Plowman*, B.15.152). Since no other information about "William Langland" has come to light, however, this name is mainly a convenience, rather than a helpful piece of historical information. All other biographical materials about the poet come from the poem itself. The opening episode of *Piers Plowman* shows a strong knowledge of the area around Malvern Hills (in south west Worcestershire), and it is clear that Langland spent much time in London as well. He was married, and was associated with the Church at the lowest levels of clerical orders, probably as an acolyte who earned his living by saying prayers for benefactors (dead or living). But writing poetry—"medd[ling] with making verses," as one character puts it (*Piers Plowman*, B.12.16)—was really Langland's life's work. Over a period stretching from as early as the 1360s—when he was in his thirties—to his death sometime after 1387 or 1388, Langland obsessively wrote and rewrote his poem. The only version we can be sure Langland believed was complete is the B text, on which the following entry is based.

THE LITERARY WORK

An alliterative Middle English poem set mainly in Malvern Hills, Westminster, and London in the fourteenth century; composed in three versions: the unfinished "A text," written c. 1368–75; the "B text," written 1377–79; and the "C text," written 1382–88.

SYNOPSIS

In a series of eight dreams (and two dreams-within-dreams), Will the Dreamer deals with concerns such as truth, reward, and charity while trying to discover how to save his soul. He seeks the embodiment of Christian living—both social and personal.

Events in History at the Time of the Poem

The crisis of kingship. On July 16, 1377, a ten-year-old boy was crowned king of England. Richard II's grandfather, Edward III, had reigned for over 50 years, but Edward's oldest son and would-be heir to the throne—Edward Prince of Wales, the beloved "Black Prince"—had died in 1376, a year before his father. The Black Prince's death dashed England's hopes for a renewal of strong leadership after King Edward's increasingly imprudent reign. During the "Hundred Years War" with France, for instance, Edward had signed a treaty in 1360, in which he ceded both his claim to the French crown and most of his territories in France, receiving in return only a ransom for King Jean II of France. In later years, a foolish policy of excessive favoritism toward a few courtiers, including his mistress, Alice Perrers, had further decreased the public's faith in the king. The crowning of Richard did little to ameliorate the situation. During Richard II's minority, England was ruled by councils who were often at odds with the young king's four surviving uncles. These instabilities culminated in 1399, when Richard's cousin, Henry of Lancaster (Henry IV), seized the throne. The strife continued in the fifteenth century's War of the Roses between two clans, the Yorks and Lancasters, who traced their ancestry to Richard II's uncles.

The Black Death and the Revolt of 1381. Feudal English society was divided into three classes, or "estates": the knights and gentry at the top, the clergy in the middle, and the peasants at the bottom. Conservative thinkers taught that God ordained society in this way and that everyone should be thankful for his or her given status. In this schema, the knights would be the leaders of society. While it was commonplace to pay lip service to the equality of all humanity before God, manual laborers were not only physically exploited by their lords, but also rhetorically denigrated as the lowest of God's creatures. The Bible seemed to promote this view. In the story of creation, Adam and Eve's eldest son, Cain, is identified as the first murderer (of his brother Abel), as well as the first to till the earth. Langland's decision to make a plowman the ideal figure of his poem is therefore a remarkable one. His exaltation of Piers registered powerfully against an accepted stereotype of the plowman as a cursed figure.

In 1348–49 disaster struck England in the form of the bubonic plague, or Black Death, which arrived from Europe on rat-infested ships. (The disease was carried by black rats and spread by their fleas.) The bubonic plague ravaged England, wiping out a third or more of the population, including half the clergy, and greatly upsetting the feudal system of labor, instigating the transition to a farm rental system. Before the Black Death, laborers worked for one baron on one manor, for the privilege of using land that was not theirs: "The lord gave use of the land—whether a baronry or a few half-acre strips; his 'man' responded with customary services which, if he was a bondsman, were often agricultural work (though they could include many other sorts of service, for example the messenger service)" (Baldwin, p. 69). However, on account of

the Black Death, the demand for labor increased so dramatically that these peasants gained more power than before in the marketplace. In other words, feudal society was breaking down. The situation led to dramatically higher wages for the laborers and a less stable pool of workers on the manors. To counter these effects, Parliament enacted the Statutes of Laborers between 1349 and 1388, which sought to control prices, to prevent laborers from reneging on their contracts, and to force "the idle" to work.

In response to these statutes and to a series of poll taxes in 1377, 1379, and 1380, a mass of laborers stormed London in June 1381. Joined by artisans and other nonpeasants, the so-called "Peasants' Revolt" brought mass destruction of property and loss of life: the archbishop of Canterbury and the treasurer of England, both major forces behind young Richard's reign, were beheaded as the king remained helplessly ensconced in the Tower of London. Leaders of the revolt issued a long list of demands, including the abolition of the poll taxes, of the Statutes of Laborers, of church-held property, and of villeinage. A villein was a feudal tenant of a lord or manor to which he was entirely subject; villeinage was the tenure by which he held some of its land. Now the rebels wanted to demolish the entire social structure, in which laborers were wholly subject to a lord. A meeting between King Richard and Wat Tyler, a leader of the rebels, resulted in the death of Tyler and the end of the revolt. But the events of June 1381, in which *Piers Plowman* played a part, had major social consequences.

Lollardy and the Great Schism. To conservative Christian thinkers like Langland, the social instabilities that prompted the revolt of 1381 were inextricably connected to the health of the Church. Langland and others saw signs of spiritual and ecclesiastical discord all around them. As Langland was writing, a major Oxford theologian, John Wyclif (or Wycliffe), offered ideas that seem to have inspired some of the rebels' thinking in 1381. A call for the distribution of the Church's property, for instance, was one of his central tenets.

Wyclif instigated a movement that has been called "the premature reformation": he urged that the Bible be translated into English and made available to all Christians, rather than just to the clergy; he condemned what he deemed features of "idolatry" in the practice of the religion—pilgrimage and the Eucharist; and he questioned the legitimacy of bishops and priests in absolving sin.

Wat Tyler, shown here being dragged to his death, was the ill-fated leader of the Peasants' Revolt of 1381.

His ideas quickly spread beyond the ivory towers of Oxford University, becoming the seedbed of a movement called "Lollardy" (an abusive term derived from the Dutch word *lollaerd,* or "mumbler") that appealed to individuals of all classes—individuals who often identified with Langland, believing him to be a kindred spirit. Regarding Lollards as a great threat, in 1382 the orthodox Church condemned Wyclif's doctrines and in 1407 it outlawed ownership of any of his writings—or any vernacular Biblical writing.

Lollardy was only one of a number of Christian "heresies" that flourished in later medieval Europe. Another, close in spirit to the Lollards, flourished among the Hussites in Bohemia in the early fifteenth century.

The orthodox Church also suffered internal strife, which captured the attention of authors like Langland and his contemporary, Geoffrey Chaucer. Western Christendom witnessed a major event at precisely the moment that Langland was producing the B text of *Piers Plowman*: the papacy, which had been centered in Avignon, France, for decades (the so-called "Babylonian Captivity"), returned to Rome.

The decades of exile had developed from a conflict between King Phillip IV of France and Pope Boniface VIII in the early fourteenth century. In effect, the French harassed Boniface so much that he had to flee Rome; he died soon thereafter, and in 1309 his successors relocated the papacy to Avignon, close to Philip's realm. The papacy's ecclesiastical and political authority waned during its period in Avignon, particularly among lands unfriendly to the French (especially England); because of this, Pope Gregory XI reestablished it in Rome in 1377.

Political antagonisms in 1378 led to a peculiar state of affairs: two popes were elected by different factions. Elected first was Pope Urban VI, and he returned to Rome, whereupon a faction of French cardinals, fearful of Italian influence, declared Urban's election null; they proceeded to elect Clement VII, the "antipope," who remained in Avignon. England supported Urban, France supported Clement, and various kingdoms throughout Europe took different sides. Known as the "Great Schism," this situation of competing popes had disastrous political, spiritual, and psychological effects on Christendom. Langland himself appears to have been despondent over the situation. Passages of the B text express great anger at the papacy—so great, in fact, that some take it as evidence that Langland wrote the B text after 1378.

Other instabilities in the Church. Lollardy and the Great Schism were perhaps the most urgent, but by no means the only, instances of Christian instability addressed by Langland and his peers. In England itself, the abuses practiced by many mendicant (that is, begging) friars aroused the indignation of Langland and Wyclif, who believed that contemporary friars had fallen far from the ideals espoused by their founder, St. Francis of Assisi. Since friars were answerable only to the Pope and not to local bishops, they could preach and perform sacraments anywhere

they liked. Antifraternalism—that is, the stereotyping of the friars as sly hustlers for money, who abused their authority and who preached poverty but lived grandly off others—were mainstays of Lollard satires, of some wonderful Chaucerian poetry, and indeed of *Piers Plowman*, which even depicts the Antichrist, who destroys Holy Church Unity as a friar. Yet it should be noted that in many ways Langland shows great affinities with Franciscan ideals, such as true mendicancy (i.e., the embracing of poverty) and missionary activity, and that it is the perceived decline from those ideals, not the institution of friars, that piques his anger.

Finally, the presence in this world of non-Christians was a major problem for Langland and many others in fourteenth-century England. Jewish communities had been expelled from England by Richard I in 1290, and it is unlikely that Langland traveled abroad where he could have encountered individuals of many faiths. Yet Langland, like many preachers and other writers, shows great concern for evangelism: the view was that the conversion of Jews and Muslims to Christianity should be a major goal of the papacy. This can be seen as a peaceful ideal, yet the corollary was severe: if these heretics refuse to believe and if they threaten Christian territories, they should be forced into submission, even death. Such was the ideology that fueled the many crusades led by Western bishops and secular leaders against the Muslims in the later Middle Ages (with little success).

In Langland's day the Turks' encroachment upon the West made these issues especially urgent. From the 1320s, the Ottomans had expanded their empire into Europe; by the 1360s they were consistently sacking cities in eastern Europe. The Battle of Kosovo in 1389 gave the Turks control over the Balkan region. Western Christians sought to repel the Turkish advance by a crusade in 1396, but the Christians were slaughtered at Nicopolis, in effect ending the crusading era.

The Poem in Focus

Contents summary. The B text of *Piers Plowman* relates a series of dreams in which Will the Dreamer either witnesses events or has discussions with a variety of figures. Most of these are allegorical personifications, either of social concepts and institutions (such as "Holy Church," "Scripture," and "Meed," the idea of reward), or of elements that make us human ("Reason" and

---

THE PURPOSE OF PILGRIMAGE

Pilgrimage is a form of religious devotion that entails journeying to a holy place. Popular destinations for pious medieval Christians included Jerusalem, where Christ was crucified, or, closer to home, the shrine of St. Thomas Becket at Canterbury Cathedral and the shrine of the Virgin Mary at Walsingham. According to the Church, pilgrimage provided a means for Christians to achieve penance after confessing their sins: this is a process Langland dramatizes in the Second Vision (although Piers the Plowman substitutes plowing the half-acre for pilgrimage). But companionship and sightseeing were, of course, other attractions of pilgrimages. People from all walks of life, from peasants to royalty, undertook these journeys. On the other hand, there were many who rejected the practice. These naysayers faulted the practice as one easily given to abuse, for it tempted Christians to seek earthly things rather than spiritual wholeness. Detractors accused it, as well, of fostering misplaced devotion, for pilgrims sometimes put their faith in the literal shrines rather than in the spiritual truths represented by these physical objects. While this attitude would later become a mainstay of Lollardy, Langland had long been against pilgrimages; Piers himself claims, "I wouldn't take a farthing's fee for Saint Thomas' shrine" (*Piers Plowman*, 5.558). In the Prologue, pilgrims do not fare well among the "fair field full of folk" (*Piers Plowman*, Prol. 17):

> Pilgrims and palmers ["professional" pilgrims] made pacts with each other
> To seek out Saint James [an important shrine in Spain] and saints at Rome. They went on their way with many wise stories,
> And had leave to lie all their lives after.
> I saw some that said they'd sought after saints:
> In every tale they told their tongues were tuned to lie
> More than to tell the truth—such talk was theirs.
>
> (*Piers Plowman*, Prol. 46-52)

"Soul"). The Dreamer's encounters with such figures can be seen as the author's struggle to understand these concepts and their role in social and individual well-being. The overarching structure is Will's search for "Truth" and his attempts to understand how to "do well, better, and best"—that is, how to live a Christian life in the face of all the failings of humanity evident in late fourteenth-century England. *Piers Plowman* B is divided into a Prologue and 20 passus, or chapters, which relate eight dreams and two dreams-within-dreams. Many of the poem's surviving manuscripts call the first two visions the *Visio* (meaning "Vision"), and the final six the *Vita of Do-Well, Do-Better, and Do-Best* (meaning the "Life of Do-Well, Do-Better, and Do-Best"). But it is possible that these rubrics originate from later scribes of the poem.

The *Visio* begins in the Prologue, in which Will falls asleep and sees "A fair field full of folk" situated between a dungeon and a tower. In Dream One, Lady Holy Church explains the meaning of his vision: "Truth" lives in the tower, while the dungeon is the Castle of Care, whose captain is Wrong, "Father of falsehood" (*Piers Plowman*, 1.64). Next, Will learns about Falsehood through the figure of Lady Meed ("reward"), who is to be married to False. When Theology objects to the marriage, a trial before the King takes place in Westminster. Meed and Conscience, to whom the King has offered Meed's hand, debate the role of rewards. To adjudicate the impasse, Reason is brought to the courts at Westminster. The King agrees with Reason that Lady Meed perverts the cause of justice. Most everyone in the court thinks she is "a cursed slut," so she mopes (*Piers Plowman*, 4.160). The King scorns her: "Through your law I believe I lose many reversions. / Meed overmasters law and much obstructs the truth" (*Piers Plowman* 4.175–76). No one marries her; by the end of the episode the issue of her marriage has given way to that of reward and its role in justice.

At this point, the Dreamer awakens and promptly falls back asleep, inaugurating the second dream. Reason preaches repentance, prompting the Seven Deadly Sins to confess their sins and undertake a pilgrimage to Truth. A plowman named Piers offers to guide them by means of the Ten Commandments and the Christian virtues. First, declares Piers, the pilgrims must help him plow his half-acre. Piers calls upon Hunger to force slackers to do their share, and Hunger offers a policy for dealing with the hungry: the indigent (those who are physically unable to work) should be given food, but the able-bodied should work for theirs. Truth sends Piers a pardon, but when a priest claims not to find any pardon written on the paper, Piers tears it in anger, announcing that he will cease plowing and instead devote his life to penance and prayers.

Dreams Three and Four constitute *The Life of Do-Well*. After his second dream, having been awakened by the argument between the priest and Piers, Will asks two friars where he might find "Do-well." The friars claim that Do-Well lives with them; Will argues with them by saying that Do-Well cannot be among sinners. The friars give an *exemplum*, that is, tell a brief story, to explain their point, but Will says, "I have no natural knowledge . . . to understand your words, / But if I may live and go on looking, I shall learn better" (*Piers Plowman*, 8.57–58). Will's third dream continues his quest. Will encounters Thought, with whom he argues about the meaning of Do-Well, Do-Better, and Do-Best. At this point, Will seems to think that the three are people or things, whereas the poem's point seems to be that one finds "Do-Well" by doing well. Will and his companion meet Wit, who says that Do-Well lives in the body and goes on to discuss the body's animating forces. Wit then offers definitions of Do-Well: almsgiving; marriage; and doing as the law teaches. The characters are joined

---

A PARDON FOR WHAT?

In the poem, Piers warns workers to labor while they may, since Hunger is coming; he gives a prophecy that "Daw the diker [will] die for hunger, / Unless God of his goodness grants us a truce" (*Piers Plowman*, 6.330-31). The next passage says "Truth heard tell of this and sent word to Piers / To take his team and till the earth, / And procured him a pardon a *poena et a culpa* ["from punishment and from guilt"], / For him and for his heirs for evermore after" (*Piers Plowman*, 7.1-4). Basically, the process of sermon, confession, repentance, and pilgrimage leads to such a pardon. However, the poem's mention of the pardon has been the center of some controversy. In the poem, Piers tears up the "pardon." One of the points of contention in his tearing it is whether he does so on the same grounds that he disapproves of pilgrimage: that is, whether he expresses the view that a person ought not to focus on paper pardons but on spiritual ones.

Piers Plowman

BRITISH/IRISH LITERATURE AND ITS TIMES   333

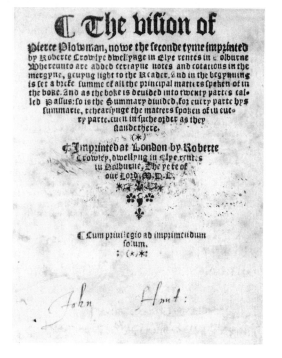

Title page of the 1550 edition of *Piers Plowman*.

by Dame Study, who upbraids the misuse of reason by her husband, Wit, and other scholars. Will then debates the value of wisdom with Clergy and Scripture. He subsequently has an "inner dream," or a dream within the dream, in which he foolishly follows Fortune. After friars refuse to help him, he discusses the nature of God's justice with Lewte (Justice), Scripture, and the Emperor Trajan, a righteous pagan. Nature then shows Will the natural world, in which humans do not act according to Reason. Will and Reason discuss the value of human and divine suffering, after which Will awakens from his inner dream and encounters a new figure, Imaginative (the power to form mental images of external things or things from the past). Imaginative questions the worth of Will's "meddling with makings" (writing poetry), which Will defends as a form of work (*Piers Plowman*, B.12.16). Imaginative says that while learning is very valuable, grace is more important, and responds affirmatively to Will's question about whether the heathen can be saved.

Will awakens and considers his dream, then falls asleep again. In his fourth dream, Conscience invites him to dine with Clergy, an academic Doctor (professor), and Patience, a pilgrim. The Doctor, Clergy, and Patience all respond to Conscience's request that they define Do-Well and Do-Better. Conscience and Patience set out on a pilgrimage together, on which they meet Hawkin, who represents "Active Life" and is the Dreamer's alter ego. Hawkin's coat, Will notices, is stained with sin; this leads Will to consider the subject of minstrelsy and poverty. Conscience says "your best coat, Hawkin, / Has many spots and stains; it should be washed" and proceeds to teach him how to do so (*Piers Plowman*, 13.313-14). Together Conscience and Patience offer to help him keep his coat clean by means of penitence and submission to God's will. Patience teaches him that Charity is found among the poor and praises patiently borne poverty. Will wakes up again.

Dreams five and six constitute *The Life of Do-Better*. The first passage recounts Will's encounter with Anima (Soul), who gives a long sermon on charity, its role in converting Jews and Muslims, and its manifestations in the history of the Church. Next, Anima teaches that charity is a tree in the heart, tended by *Liberum Arbitrium* (Free Will) on land owned by Piers Plowman. At the mention of Piers, Will swoons and has his second inner-dream, in which he sees the tree, whose symbolic significance Piers explains. The tree's apples come to symbolize figures from the Old Testament who fall under the devil's power. The Dreamer then sees the Annunciation, in which Mary learns from the angel Gabriel that she is to be the mother of the Messiah, and also sees events from the life of Christ before awakening from the inner dream. The rest of Dream Five relates Will's encounters with figures for Faith, Hope, and Charity, embodied in Abraham, Moses, and the Good Samaritan. This last figure teaches Will about the Trinity, the doctrine that in one God are three persons: Father (God the creator of the world), Son (Jesus), and spirit (the spirit of God, or the holy spirit).

Will's sixth dream occurs when he falls asleep before Palm Sunday services. He witnesses Christ entering Jerusalem and learns from Faith that Christ will take the armor of Piers Plowman to fight against Death. After Christ's crucifixion, Will descends to Hell, where the Four Daughters of God (Mercy, Peace, Truth, and Righteousness) debate about whether man can be saved from Hell. Christ arrives, and they celebrate when he does indeed free the human souls. Easter bells awaken Will, who calls his wife, Kit, and daughter, Calote, to go with him to church.

Will again falls asleep in church. In Dream Seven he envisions Piers, painted bloody and carrying a cross, coming in among the people. Conscience explains Christ's roles as knight, king, and conqueror. The Holy Spirit descends upon Piers and his fellows, distributing gifts of grace. Piers receives a plow to sow the Word of God, and a barn, which represents Holy Church Unity. Pride attacks Piers as he plows, so Conscience urges Christians into the barn, and Will awakens.

As the final dream begins, Will is disturbed; he encounters Need, who argues that Temperance is the primary Christian virtue. Falling asleep, Will dreams of the attack on Holy Church by the figure of a great adversary, the Antichrist, who is followed by friars. Will is attacked by Old Age and takes refuge in Holy Church. Kynde (Nature) and Conscience cannot thwart the entry of Friar Flatterer. Conscience announces he will go on pilgrimage to seek Piers Plowman, and cries for grace until Will awakens.

The figures of Piers the Plowman and Will the Dreamer. The implications of Langland's decision to feature a plowman in his poem were enormously powerful—so much so that John Ball, a leader of the Peasants' Revolt of 1381, cites "Piers Plowman" as if he were a historical individual rather than a poetic idealization.

Yet the details of the poem itself do not endorse the revolutionary ends that Ball and others seem to have found in it. When Piers says he will show the pilgrims the way to St. Truth after plowing a half-acre by the highway, a knight asks him to teach him to plow; Piers responds by insisting that both plowman and knight uphold their given positions:

> I shall sweat and strain and sow for us both,
> And also labor for your love all my lifetime,
> In exchange for your championing Holy
>   Church and me
> Against wasters and wicked men who would
>   destroy me.
>
> (*Piers Plowman*, 6.25-28)

The poem also affirms the centrality of the Church in English life—a role resented by the rebels, who directed their animosity against the Church by beheading the archbishop of Canterbury, Simon Sudbury, in the rising of 1381. The whole episode of the pilgrimage to Truth, as John Burrow argues in "The Action of Langland's Second Vision," dramatizes the traditional process of sermon, confession, repentance, and pilgrimage. Langland substitutes "plowing"—that is, performing one's duties faithfully—for literal pilgrimage, which he disdains. But the structure of this episode, and of many others throughout the poem, makes clear Langland's support of traditional ecclesiastical roles in society.

Moreover, Piers's reference to "wasters and wicked men" seems to accept without question the definitions of society upon which the Statutes of Laborers rested: those workers who are "true" to their lords are indeed doing their part to "plow the half-acre," while those who attempt to take advantage of the labor shortfall after the Black

---

JOHN BALL'S LETTER TO THE PEOPLE OF ESSEX, 1381— A TRANSLATION INTO MODERN ENGLISH

Ball, a leader of the Peasants' Revolt, refers to Piers Plowman as if he were real:

John the Shepherd [pseudonym for John Ball], formerly priest at Saint Mary's in York, and now of Colchestre, warmly greets John the Nameless, and John the Miller, and John Carter, and bids them to beware of guile in the town, and stand together in God's name. and *bids Piers Plowman to go to his work,* and fully chastises Hob the Robber, and take with you John Trueman and all his fellows, and no more, and obey only one leader, and no more. . . .

(italics added; *Ball in Dean*, p. 135)

Death are "wasters" who should be prosecuted (*Piers Plowman*, 6.28). Langland, to be sure, is no reactionary who blindly seeks to uphold the status quo; indeed, this and many other passages in the poem are poignant in their approach to the treatment of the destitute. Moreover, an element of *Piers Plowman* that resounds nearly as powerfully as the figure of Piers is that of the Dreamer himself, who expresses fears that his own work—the writing of his poem, an activity often likened to plowing, especially in relation to the "sowing of the Word"—might be deemed "wasteful" by those in authority (Bowers, pp. 214-15). The poem's intimate relation to such events as the Revolt of 1381 and the Statutes of Laborers show conclusively that his poem is hardly wasteful, though. It can itself be an actor in history, despite the intentions of the author.

Literary context It is impossible to identify any particular historical person or event that inspired Langland to write. Certain historical events are clearly reflected in the poem, such as the Prologue's episode of the coronation, which is clearly indebted to the ascension of Richard II in 1377 (Baldwin, pp. 78-81). But other attempts to find historical personages in the poem—such as the equation of Lady Meed with Edward III's mistress Alice Perrers, or the identification of references to the Great Schism of 1378—rest on flimsier ground.

As noted, *Piers Plowman* was an actor in social history as well as a respondent to it. Likewise, it played an active role in British literary history, initiating what came to be known as "the *Piers Plowman* tradition." This tradition consists of a series of poems from the late fourteenth and early fifteenth century that appropriate *Piers Plowman*'s imagery and alliterative style for radical political ends: *Piers the Plow-*

IMAGINATIVE BERATES THE DREAMER WILL

"And you meddle with making verse and might go say your Psalter,
And pray for them that provide your bread, for there are plenty of books
To tell men what Do-Well is, Do-Better and Do-Best both
And preachers to explain it all, of many a pair of friars."
I saw well he spoke the truth, and somewhat to excuse myself
Said, "Cato comforted his son, clerk though he was,
To solace himself sometimes: so I do when I write.
Interpose some pleasures at times among your cares.
And I've heard it said of holy men, how they now and then
Played to be more perfect in their prayers afterward.
But if there were any one who would tell me
What Do-Well and Do-Better were, and Do-Best the last,
I would never do any work but wend to Holy Church
And stay there saying prayers save when I ate or slept."

(*Piers Plowman*, B.12.16-28)

---

man's *Creed, Mum and the Sothsegger,* and *Richard the Redeless.* These poems are also heavily indebted to the Lollard movement. Many Lollard writings share with *Piers Plowman* ideologies that might be seen as urging reform in the Church, such as a replacement of literal acts like pilgrimage with a renewed emphasis on Christian vocations that God has called upon a person to perform, vocations like plowing, for example. But in many other ways, Langland was unquestionably orthodox, and thus far from Wyclif and his followers. Landland's writing, for instance, acknowledges the efficacy of the clergy in his day.

In fact, Langland's extensive rewriting of the B text (so extensive that he produced a new poem, the C text) seems in part intended to reaffirm his orthodoxy and to reclaim his work from the rebels of 1381 (Justice, pp. 232-51). It is unclear to what extent Langland's early readers recognized the presence of three different versions of *Piers Plowman*, but today we can identify their cumulative status as the most influential alliterative, satirical, and allegorical works of the English Middle Ages. In the Middle English canon, the 58 surviving manuscripts of the A, B, and C texts are second in number only to Chaucer's **Canterbury Tales,** and the range of manuscripts in which *Piers Plowman* appears along with other works indicates that it appealed to a wide variety of readers. The success of *Piers Plowman*, scholars have argued, prompted "the Alliterative Revival" of the later fourteenth and early fifteenth centuries, to which we owe such poems as **Sir Gawain and the Green Knight** (also in *WLAIT 3: British and Irish Literature and Its Times*).

Beyond its direct influence on John Ball and "the *Piers Plowman* tradition," and its indirect role in enabling a rebirth of alliterative poetry after centuries of neglect, *Piers Plowman* has not fared well. "Regretfully one must conclude that, at least after the immediate and usually Lollard imitations," asserts Anne Hudson, "*Piers Plowman* in the two and a half centuries after its composition was more honoured in the name than in the reading" (Hudson, p. 263). Yet, for those seeking to understand the English Middle Ages, *Piers Plowman* remains an illuminating work that constitutes both a reflection and an agent of social and literary history.

—Lawrence Warner

For More Information

Baldwin, Anna P. "The Historical Context." In *A Companion to "Piers Plowman."* Ed. John A. Alfrod. Berkeley: University of California Press, 1988.

Bloch, M. *Feudal Society.* Trans. L. A. Manyon. 1950. Reprint, London: Routledge and Kegan Paul, 1962.

Bowers, John M. *The Crisis of Will in "Piers Plowman."* Washington, D.C.: Catholic University Press, 1986.

Burrow, John. "The Action of Langland's Second Vision." In *Style and Symbolism in "Piers Plowman."* Ed. Robert J. Blanch. Knoxville: University of Tennessee Press, 1969.

Dean, James M., ed. *Medieval English Political Writings*. Kalamazoo, Michigan: Western Michigan University for TEAMS, 1996.

Hudson, Anne. "The Legacy of *Piers Plowman*." In *A Companion to "Piers Plowman."* Ed. John A. Alfrod. Berkeley: University of California Press, 1988.

Justice, Steven. *Writing and Rebellion: England in 1381*. Berkeley: University of California Press, 1994.

Kirk, Elizabeth D. "Langland's Plowman and the Recreation of Fourteenth-Century Religious Metaphor." *Yearbook of Langland Studies* 2 (1988): 1-21.

Langland, William. *Piers Plowman: An Alliterative Verse Translation*. Trans. E. Talbot Donaldson. Ed. Elizabeth D. Kirk and Judith H. Anderson. New York: Norton, 1990.

————. *The Vision of Piers Plowman: A Critical Edition of the B-Text*. Ed. A. V. C. Schmidt. 2d ed. Rutland, Vermont: Everyman, 1995.

McKisack, May. *The Fourteenth Century, 1307-1399*. Oxford: Clarendon, 1959.

Simpson, James. *Piers Plowman: An Introduction to the B-Text*. New York: Longman, 1990.

The Pilgrim's Progress

by

John Bunyan

J ohn Bunyan's life spanned one of the most dramatic periods in English history. He was born in Bedford in 1628, just a year before Charles I dissolved Parliament and began 11 years of "personal rule." In 1640, when economic necessity finally forced Charles I to recall Parliament, the competing interests of the aristocracy, the growing bourgeoisie, religious dissenters, and the army clashed, and by 1642 civil war had broken out. The execution of Charles I remains the most notorious incident of this period, but profound changes occurred at every level of society. This is the world in which Bunyan came of age and which formed the religious and political convictions that shaped his literary career. When the teenaged Bunyan entered the army in 1644, he must have served under antiroyalist parliamentary forces and was thus exposed to some of the most iconoclastic thought that has ever emerged in English history. Suggestions of the lasting influence of this formative period resonate throughout his writings. After a long, agonizing conversion, he was accepted into the Independent Church, a Protestant congregation, and eventually became a noted lay preacher and author of polemic religious works. When the monarchy was restored in 1660, radical Protestant sects and lay preaching were no longer tolerated; in 1661 Bunyan was arrested for lay preaching and put in jail. It was during his 12-year imprisonment that he began his most popular work, *The Pilgrim's Progress*, an allegorical tale of how an individual can successfully travel the path to salvation in a world of spiritual corruption and social injustice.

THE LITERARY WORK

An allegory set in a timeless dreamscape that resembles rural England in the seventeenth century; published in 1678.

SYNOPSIS

A Christian experiences an intense spiritual crisis that impels him to abandon his home and family in the City of Destruction (the world of sin and damnation) to seek the Celestial City (heaven).

Events in History at the Time the Allegory Takes Place

The rise of the individual in the Reformation. The events of *The Pilgrim's Progress* seem to occur outside of time or place—Bunyan frames the allegorical journey toward heaven of his representative man, Christian, in the context of a dream. Actually, the story is firmly anchored by an early, radical Protestant belief system within the landscape of social and political turmoil of the English civil wars and the subsequent restoration of the monarchy. To understand Bunyan's viewpoint, one needs to keep in mind the original meaning of the term "Protestant." It emanated from the Reformation movement, heralded in Wittenberg, Germany, in 1517 when Martin Luther nailed his Ninety-five Theses—which condemned the Roman Catholic practice of selling indulgences (remission of punishment

John Bunyan was imprisoned for 12 years, during which he began *The Pilgrim's Progress*. In this imaginative illustration, Bunyan sits in Bedford prison and recites portions of his work to friends.

for sin)—on the door of the local church. Although writing a century and a half later, Bunyan is still working out how this original "protest" against the state of the late-medieval Catholic Church affects the individual's understanding of salvation.

Corruption in the Roman Catholic Church is often cited as the reason for the Protestant Reformation, but at the heart of this revolution, which would last centuries, was the relationship of the individual to God. Reformation theologians took the concept of original sin (the idea that all people are born as sinners as a result of the fall of Adam and Eve) to its logical extreme and emphasized that performing good works in this world could not assure a heavenly reward. The Calvinist strain of Protestantism stressed the idea of predestination, that all souls are either elect (destined by God's inscrutable will to be saved) or reprobate (justly doomed to damnation because of their innate depravity). This meant that, instead of looking to the hierarchical authority of the Church, each person had to seek his or her own personal relationship with God, and, rather than solicit the intercession of saints, every person had to find evidence of the working of Christ in his or her own life.

The Reformation has been seen by some as a key component in the development of an intro-spective, subjective, "modern" self, and *The Pilgrim's Progress* certainly emphasizes such a sense of individuality. Though he meets both allies and enemies along the way and sometimes travels with a companion, Christian's journey is essentially a solitary one; ultimately he alone will be responsible for its success or failure. By the end it appears that Christian is one of God's elect, but along the way this fact does not make his path any less precarious. The dangers he faces are real, and some of the greatest pitfalls in his way are highly subjective, internalized conflicts. Christian's struggle with spiritual numbness, self-doubt, and the fear that he is not "chosen" sounds very much like a seventeenth-century Protestant conversion narrative.

Bunyan's Christian, like other seventeenth-century Protestants, benefits greatly from the proliferation of English translations of the Bible, such as the Geneva translation (1560) and the authorized King James version (1611); previously, Bibles had been published in Latin. Advances in printing technology made books much more widely accessible in the late seventeenth century. An increase in basic literacy made reading possible for more and more people, and better access to Bibles in English allowed readers to engage in independent application of Scripture to personal experience. It is significant, therefore, that *The Pilgrim's Progress* begins with a vision of Christian with a book in his hand. The dream-narrator describes Christian's reaction, saying that "as he read, he wept and trembled: and not being able longer to contain, he brake out with a lamentable cry; saying, *what shall I do?*" (Bunyan, *The Pilgrim's Progress*, p. 8). Here Bunyan is indicating the power of reading in enacting radical change—spiritual and, as it turned out, social and political as well.

The changes brought by the Reformation continued to revolutionize England well into the seventeenth century. Calvinist Protestantism taught that all people had equal opportunity and claim to salvation, and this naturally suggested a leveling of social relations and economics. In relation to the poor, the working classes, and displaced or itinerant populations, the new theology created a liberating "double sense of power—individual self-confidence and strength through unity" (Hill, *World Turned Upside Down*, p. 154). Actually "Protestantism was not a democratic creed"—from Luther's Germany to Bunyan's England the revolution concerned a certain type of "*Christian* liberty, liberty for the elect" (Hill, *World Turned Upside Down*, p. 156). But for those who felt *God's* calling, it was indeed powerful. Like Bunyan himself (who was trained as a tinker), Christian is a "common" sort of man who nevertheless takes on lords, judges, and clergy. Although often taken as a universal paradigm of spiritual journey, *The Pilgrim's Progress* is a product of seventeenth-century spiritual, social, and political concerns.

Congregation vs. parish. Just as the conservative, Presbyterian parliamentary establishment was beginning to suppress more radical groups at the turn of the 1650s, Bunyan was experiencing the first pangs of his three-year spiritual crisis, which culminated in his conversion and his joining of the Independent congregation at Bedford. The freedom with which Bunyan could embrace a congregation with selective membership was itself a sign of remarkable religious change. Bunyan's was a "gathered" Church—that is, one formed by individuals who had adequately demonstrated an authentic spiritual experience. Such congregations were fundamentally different from those of the parish system, which were automatically determined by a person's place of residence. Whereas in the earlier part of the century gathered congregations had to form on the remote soil of Holland or New England, by 1650 compulsory attendance at parish churches was abolished and independent congregations, such as Bunyan's, flourished.

The Palace Beautiful in *The Pilgrim's Progress* is an allegory of this kind of Church, "constituted by the inward call of the Holy Spirit to a group of believing men and women and not by government edict" and "accountable to God for keeping its life and that of its members pure and in accordance with their understanding of what Scripture required" (White, pp. 52, 54). When Christian is told that he must converse with and satisfy the maiden Discretion before entering the Palace Beautiful, Bunyan's allegory is reflecting the practices of the gathered Church tradition that defined his own experience. In Bunyan's vision, fellowship is helpful to the spiritual sojourner but not strictly necessary: the character Faithful goes on alone right past the Palace Beautiful and (through his martyrdom) still reaches salvation before Christian. Nonetheless, Bunyan's allegory seems to suggest that belonging to a Church is advantageous in this wicked world: the armor that Christian receives at the Palace Beautiful empowers him to fight Apollyon and the monster's claim to sovereignty over him as a resident of the City of Destruction.

Lay preaching. By 1655 Bunyan had begun to preach, first within his Independent congregation and then publicly in the area of Bedford. Lay preaching is a logical extension of the general trend toward individual conscience, a direct relationship with God and a dismantling of ecclesiastical hierarchies, but not all Protestant groups were entirely comfortable with expanded access to the pulpit. Presbyterians, for example, preferred ordained ministers and an alternative Church hierarchy made up of lay elders.

Bunyan's position seems to have been somewhere between that of the more conservative Presbyterians and that, for example, of the Quakers, who felt that any individual, even a woman, might speak publicly if the Holy Spirit so moved him or her. Bunyan objected to Quaker practices because, among other things, they valued the power of the spirit more than that of the Bible. In contrast, Bunyan subscribed to the ultimate primacy of the Bible. In *The Pilgrim's Progress*, his character the Evangelist portrays a Christian minister assuming what Bunyan deems to be the minister's proper role in the conversion experience—starting the troubled soul down the road to salvation and providing scripturally sound advice in times of crisis—although the seemingly otherworldly Evangelist cannot easily be identified as a specific social type, such as a university-educated minister. Bunyan and others like him held that what makes a minister or lay preacher an effective agent of God is not his worldly status but his spiritual calling.

Bunyan himself felt that calling and became a "mechanic preacher," an itinerant speaker who often spoke abroad and particularly to the disenfranchised. Bunyan and others like him presented a fundamental challenge to a stratified class system in which laborers and artisans were expected to keep to their station (again, Bunyan was a mere tinker) and ministers were expected to have a university education (an advantage that was not available to everyone). In his preaching, Bunyan used "plain style," a straightforward, unornamented rhetoric preferred by the Puritan clergy. He also took part in vigorous theological controversies (first and most notably against the Quakers) and published many polemical writings early in his career. So what made Bunyan and other lay preachers so troubling to the university-trained orthodoxy? In a sense, it was simply disagreement over a matter of "calling." While others felt his calling was to be a tinker, Bunyan insisted it was to spread the Gospel.

The Restoration and Bunyan's imprisonment. The final years of the 1650s saw an end to the religious toleration that fostered social and political challenges to the economic and political status quo of English society. In 1660 the monarchy was restored (in the person of Charles II, son of the executed king), along with the House of Lords and the hierarchy of the official Church of England. It was the beginning of a period of suppression and persecution of the "Dissenters," Puritans who dissented from the Church of England and who had pursued their religious beliefs more or less freely for almost two decades. Beginning in 1660 and until 1828, the Dissenters were forbidden from entering the university and Parliament, and were not supposed to gather for worship. Bunyan himself was one of many Dissenters arrested for illegal preaching. As a mechanic preacher he was deemed categorically dangerous because "[f]or the Bedfordshire gentry Bunyan's preaching, even if it did not directly incite rebellion, fanned the discontent that many felt with the restored regime and church" (Hill, *A Turbulent, Seditious, and Factious People*, p. 107).

When Bunyan was finally brought to trial, he was not officially charged for illegal preaching but (under an old Elizabethan act) for unlawful meetings. Although such a charge appeared to pertain to civil rather than religious offenses, it was clear that Bunyan was convicted for being a mechanic preacher. Originally sentenced to just three months in jail, Bunyan refused to stop preaching and was thus handed a 12-year sentence. It was a time of great hardship for him and his family but also a period of much literary activity, including the inception of *The Pilgrim's Progress*. The book opens with a reference to his imprisonment (explicitly glossed in the marginalia) during these disappointing years: "As I walk'd through the wilderness of this world, I lighted on a certain place, where was a Denn; And I laid me down in that place to sleep: And as I slept I dreamed a Dream" (*The Pilgrim's Progress*, p. 8). Just as the dream frames the story of Christian's journey, the fact of Bunyan's imprisonment (in the "Denn") frames the dream itself.

The most dramatic and famous sequence in the book, when Christian and Faithful arrive at Vanity Fair and are subsequently tried, draws on

---

BUNYAN RECOUNTS HIS TRIAL

"He [the magistrate] said, that I [Bunyan] was ignorant, and did not understand the Scriptures; for how (said he) can you understand them, when you know not the original Greek? etc.

. . . To [him] I said, that if that was his opinion, that none could understand the Scriptures, but those that had the original Greek, etc., then but a very few of the poorest sort should be saved. . . .

. . . He said there was none that heard me, but a company of foolish people.

. . . I told him that there was the wise as well as the foolish that do hear me; and again, those that are most commonly counted foolish by the world are the wisest before God. . . .

. . . He told me, that I made people neglect their calling; and that God had commanded people to work six days, and serve him on the seventh.

. . . I told him, that it was the duty of people, (both rich and poor) to look out for their souls on them days, as well as for their bodies: and that God would have his people exhort one another daily. . . .

. . . Well, said he, to conclude, but will you promise that you will not call the people together any more? And then you may be released, and go home.

. . . I told him, that I durst say no more than I had said. For I durst not leave off that work which God had called me to."

(Bunyan, *Grace Abounding*, p.p. 92–93)

Bunyan's own experience. Although the two pilgrims appear to do nothing but refrain from buying goods, and offend merely by a public display of piety, the indictment against them is *"That they were enemies to, and disturbers of their Trade; that they had made Commotions and Divisions in the Town, and had won a party to their own most dangerous Opinions, in contempt of the Law of their Prince"* (*The Pilgrim's Progress*, p. 76). This civil charge exposes a fear of popular sedition reminiscent of the atmosphere around the time of the Restoration when church / state orthodoxy and social hierarchies sought to reassert themselves. It is also significant that not only the judge but many of the offended parties at the trial are lords. The witness Pickthank testifies that Faithful "hath railed on our noble Prince *Beelzebub*, "spoke contemptibly" of the local nobility (Lord *Carnal Delight*, Lord *Desire of Vain-glory*, Sir *Having Greedy*, etc.), and "said moreover, that if all men were of his mind, if possible, there is not one of these Noble-men should have any longer a being in this Town" (*The Pilgrim's Progress*, pp. 77-78). Here the intensity of the threat (real and perceived) posed by the mechanic preacher and the corresponding reaction by the upper classes is vividly illustrated.

Intolerance. The persecution of Dissenters during the Restoration is only one example in a century peculiarly marked by intolerance. Religious and political affinities were intertwined in seventeenth-century England, and although the age was certainly harder on some groups than on others, everyone found themselves at some point or another the victim of suppression or persecution—Roman Catholics, radical and conservative Dissenters, even orthodox Anglicans. As Charles II's reign continued, the situation for Dissenters such as Bunyan sometimes got easier. In 1672, for example, Bunyan was released from prison and even licensed to preach under the Second Declaration of Indulgence. Even the declared Roman Catholic James II at times was tolerant of religious freedoms (if only to make things easier for those of his own faith). It was not until after the Glorious Revolution, however, that broad, institutionalized tolerance was attempted.

Because Christian is persecuted (as was Bunyan himself), it is tempting to read a tolerationist position into *The Pilgrim's Progress*. There is, after all, some variety to be found among the successful journeys to the Celestial City. Faithful, for example, gets there without joining in the fellowship of a gathered Church. And yet in most other ways the path is "straight and narrow"; in the end the stories of failure are more numerous than the success stories and usually more vividly drawn. The plea to "be content to follow the Religion of your Countrey, and I will follow the Religion of mine" is not uttered by Christian nor by his pious companions but by Ignorance, who is damned for his lack of proper appreciation of the straightness of the way (*The Pilgrim's Progress*, p. 101). As mentioned, Bunyan himself exhibited intolerance toward religious convictions that differed from his own; in fact, his first publication, *Some Gospel-Truths Opened* (1656), targeted the Quakers.

The Allegory in Focus

Plot summary. *The Pilgrim's Progress* is framed as a dream. In one sense the dreamer does not interject in the narrative much more than to provide transitions from one event to another ("Then I saw in my dream . . .," etc.). In another sense the dream-narrator is a constant, mysterious presence intensifying the reader's experience of witnessing the story as it unfolds rather than hearing it described in retrospect. The striking opening image thrusts the reader into the story at the very moment of Christian's spiritual crisis and decision to leave on his journey:

> I dreamed, and behold *I saw a Man clothed with Raggs standing in a certain place, with his face from his own House, a Book in his hand, and a great burden upon his Back.*
> (*The Pilgrim's Progress*, p. 8)

Christian's reading of "the Book" (the Bible) tells him that he is damned. His family is amazed at his sudden distress yet unable to understand or assist him, but the man simply known as Evangelist (who represents a guiding preacher) is able to instruct Christian on what he must do to save himself. Rebuffing the interference of both his family and neighbors, Christian flees the City of Destruction and runs towards the Wicket-gate— the first landmark on the way to the Celestial City and a sign that his conversion has begun. As soon as he sets out, however, Christian gets stuck in the marshy Slow of Dispond (or slough of depression) and is misled by Mr. Worldly-Wiseman, whose bad advice on a sort of moral shortcut nearly destroys Christian.

With the aid of the Evangelist, Christian arrives safely at the Wicket-gate, but his two near-misses are indicative of the sorts of dangers he will meet throughout the journey, which turns out to be both easier and harder than it appears. Christian's passage through the Wicket-gate and subsequent visits to the House of the Interpreter and the Palace Beautiful mark a new stage in his journey. In the House of the Interpreter—where he is shown allegorical scenes of salvation and damnation and taught how to decipher them—Christian becomes responsible for correctly "reading" the situations that he encounters along his way. Upon leaving the House of the Interpreter to resume his journey, the difference within Christian is marked by three "shining ones" who bestow the forgiveness of his sins, the change of his "Rags" for "Raiment," and the receipt of "a Roll with a Seal upon it," a sort of certificate that is both a sign of his assurance of salvation and a textual source of "refreshment" to read along the way (*The Pilgrim's Progress*, pp. 31-32). He is now a better interpreter of allegorical situations and is equipped to deal with such characters as Simple, Sloth, Presumption, Formalist, and Hypocrise—and yet Christian still falls victim to deceptive appearances and his own lapses of spiritual vigilance (such as when he falls asleep and loses his Roll). Even though he has the benefit of fellowship (at the Palace Beautiful) and traveling companions at times (first Faithful and then Hopeful), Christian's way to the Celestial City is characterized by failures as well as successes. Christian steadily improves as a spiritual "reader," but later failures will show that his understanding is never without some degree of human imperfection.

In the Valley of Humiliation, Christian confronts Apollyon, a Satanic monster and tempter of mankind who claims sovereignty over him as a subject of the City of Destruction. The dramatic battle that ensues is much more active than the cerebral skirmishes with doubt and presumption in which Christian has engaged thus far, and yet there are psychological aspects to it. He fights Apollyon with the sword and armor he receives upon leaving the Palace Beautiful, but this weaponry must also be understood figuratively as the advantage of Godly fellowship. Only after failing to trick Christian does Apollyon attack him physically, and it is **Christian's good sense that finally defeats his opponent.**

The dangers Christian encounters in the Valley of the Shadow of Death are also a mix of the physical and the psychological. When Christian sees the "two Giants, *Pope* and *Pagan*," he can pass them "without much danger" because "that *Pagan* has been dead many a *day*" and the "*Pope*" is "by reason of his age . . . grown so crazy and stiff in his joynts, that he can now do little more then sit in his Caves mouth, grinning at Pilgrims

as they go by, and biting his nails, because he cannot come at them" (*The Pilgrim's Progress*, p. 54).

And yet not all dangers along the way can be overcome with the power of spiritual understanding. At Vanity Fair (a place that effectively transforms familiar provincial festivities into a site of empty frivolities and sin), Christian and his new companion, Faithful, are arrested, beaten, and put on trial for the "*Commotions and Divisions in the Town*" occasioned by their pious detachment from the corruption of the marketplace. There is very little they can do but embrace martyrdom (*The Pilgrim's Progress*, pp. 72-80). Both Christian and Faithful secretly hope they are the one whom the Evangelist has predicted will die "yet have the better of his fellow" in death—in other words, the one who will reach heaven first through glorious martyrdom (*The Pilgrim's Progress*, p. 72). The Jury (Mr. Blindman, Mr. No-good, Mr. Malice, Mr. Love-lust, Mr. Live-loose, Mr. Heady, Mr. High-mind, Mr. Enmity, Mr. Lyar, Mr. Cruelty, Mr. Hate-light, and Mr. Implacable) delivers a predictably grim verdict under the Judge (Lord Hategood), and Faithful is put to a cruel death. Christian escapes this fate and continues his journey with a new companion, Hopeful, who comes upon his name, it seems, "by the beholding of *Christian* and *Faithful* in their words and behavior, in their sufferings at the *fair*" (*The Pilgrim's Progress*, p. 80).

Fellowship and conversation play an increasingly prominent role in the story as the work progresses. Not only do individual stories edify and give comfort to fellow pilgrims, but together the travelers can recognize and resist the bad examples, deceptions, and faulty doctrine of those whom they meet along the way. And yet even with spiritual companionship the travelers fall into the hands of the Giant Despair at Doubting-Castle. Here again is a place of mixed psychological and physical danger, where the pilgrims are tortured in mind and body. Fittingly it is Hopeful who comforts Christian when he is beaten down (literally and figuratively) by Despair, but ultimately it is the literate Christian who suddenly remembers the "*Key* in my bosom, called *Promise*" (biblical texts that offer salvation) and accomplishes their escape (*The Pilgrim's Progress*, p. 96).

Christian and Hopeful reach the last stage of the journey and the Shepherds (experienced members of a heavenly fellowship who proffer advice) give them the enigmatic reassurance that the way is "safe for those for whom it is to be safe, *but transgressors shall fall therein*" (*The Pilgrim's Progress*, p. 98). By this time, it looks as though the difficulties are over. The two pilgrims avoid the errors of Ignorance and Little-faith. However, Flatterer is disguised as an Angel of Light and ensnares Christian and Hopeful. They are released by "a shining one," who whips them for their inattention (*The Pilgrim's Progress*, pp. 109-110). The two make their way through the Inchanted Ground and come near their final destination. At last they are within sight of the Gate to the City, which lies across a deep river. The river is death, a passage that all must make. Christian, nearly paralyzed with fear and overcome by the waters, manages to cross over only with the aid of Hopeful. Once on the other side the two are welcomed into Heaven in a scene of great rejoicing. As Ignorance, who has been ferried across the river by Vain-hope, is taken away, the narrative closes with the admonition that it is just as possible for an erring soul to go to Hell from the very gates of Heaven as it is from the City of Destruction.

Teaching the reader how to read. Like Christian in the House of the Interpreter, readers of *The Pilgrim's Progress* must learn to understand allegory and apply it correctly to their own lives. Some allegories are simply more complicated than others. Like Christian, the reader may easily see why it is necessary to flee the City of Destruction and yet fail at first to understand why one must avoid Mr. Legality and his son Civility who live in the Town of Morality. Included in the allegory are Bunyan's marginal notes, which help the reader understand the subtle points and strict doctrine of the allegory. Scriptural passages function as a sort of Biblical study guide. In fact, the marginalia and scriptural passages in *The Pilgrim's Progress* were so central to the objectives of the book that Bunyan never stopped adding to them.

In some ways *The Pilgrim's Progress* is a continuation of the lay preaching that was so important to Bunyan that he went to prison rather than promise to give it up. At an even more fundamental level, the composition of an accessible text that even a minimally literate person can grasp furthers the general commitment of the Reformation to help people find spiritual enlightenment through reading. Bunyan was very successful in creating such an accessible book—*The Pilgrim's Progress* was initially popular with the poor and the working classes who had less formal education, and in later years it was consid-

ered particularly appropriate for younger readers and eventually came out in many editions for children.

Although a didactic text, *The Pilgrim's Progress* by no means offers merely a static, one-way reading process. Christian is often asked to narrate his story—such as when he must give an account of his journey to Discretion before being admitted to the Palace Beautiful. This has elements of a sort of practical catechism in that Christian must provide correct interpretations of events, but it is a highly subjective, extemporaneous performance as well. His fellow travelers, Faithful and Hopeful, also share their stories, and what they report encountering is often quite different from what Christian has experienced. In some congregational churches a successful confession of one's spiritual development was required for full membership. More generally, however, the ability to tell about one's spiritual journey created a sense of community and drew in new members, serving as a type of informal, grass-roots evangelism. Bunyan creates characters who do not so much dictate what true conversion must look like but rather provide varied examples of what it might look like. In the end Bunyan wants the reader to do more than passively receive his book. In his verse conclusion, he offers this final challenge:

> NOW Reader, I have told my Dream to thee;
> See if thou canst Interpret it to me;
> Or to thy self, or Neighbour: but take heed
> Of mis-interpreting . . .
> Put by the Curtain, look within my Vail;
> Turn up my Metaphors and do not fail:
> There, if thou seekest them, such things to find,
> As will be helpful to an honest mind.
> (*The Pilgrim's Progress*, p. 134)

Sources and literary context. The Bible, of course, is a crucial source in *The Pilgrim's Progress*; Bunyan uses scriptural language and imagery, and biblical quotations illustrate and are illuminated by every step (and misstep) Christian takes. Many have also noted the autobiographical influence in *The Pilgrim's Progress*. Not only do events such as Bunyan's imprisonment figure into the plot—the trial of Faithful, for example, can be read as a sort of allegorical parody of Bunyan's own trial—but some also read Christian's allegorical journey according to the author's own conversion story as presented in his autobiography *Grace Abounding to the Chief of Sinners*. In fact, Bunyan's own spiritual development, his theological beliefs, and literary style are all intertwined. His first wife brought books into the marriage as part of a material and spiritual dowry—Arthur Dent's *The Plaine Mans Path-way to Heaven* and Lewis Bayly's *The Practice of Piety*. Both of these books have had a profound influence on Bunyan's theology, as has Martin Luther's *Commentary on Galatians*, a work Bunyan was reputed to hold in the highest esteem.

THE SEQUEL TO *THE PILGRIM'S PROGRESS*

The Pilgrim's Progress, the Second Part was published in 1684 and is evidence of the popularity of the original. Bunyan was not merely capitalizing on his former success, however. In part Bunyan's sequel was intended to thwart the proliferation of "continuations" of the story by other people. Ironically, while counterfeited and pirated editions cut Bunyan out of profits and recognition, they offered further proof of the popular success of *The Pilgrim's Progress*.

The reception of the original is mirrored in the plot of the *Second Part* itself as the protagonist's wife, Christiana, their children, and various companions follow Christian's trail—complete with markers and monuments to the earlier journey—towards the Celestial City. The landscape, once the site of scenes of intense isolation, is now populated by many travelers who, like the reader, know the story of Christian's journey. Bunyan's sequel shows what a spiritual journey would be like if, instead of an agonized solitary experience, it was a collective popular phenomenon, one that welcomed a wider variety of travelers.

Dent's *The Plaine Mans Pathway to Heaven* contains an extended dialog between Theologus ("a Divine"), Philagathus ("an honest man"; literally "love-good"), Asunetus ("an ignorant man"), and Antilegon ("a caviller," or frivolous hairsplitter; literally "against the word"). The dialog provided Bunyan not only with a precise account of the "straight and narrow" way to heaven but also with an important literary model. Puritan Protestants were against theater in all forms, and Dent's justification of dialog was crucial for Bunyan; in his "Apology," which introduces *The Pilgrim's Progress*, he explicitly reminds the potentially offended reader *"that men (as high as Trees) will write/ Dialogue-wise; yet no Man doth them slight/ For writing so"* (*The Pilgrim's Progress*, p. 5). Other writers' examples provided literary models as well as justification.

John Foxe's 1563 *Acts and Monuments of these latter and perilous days* (popularly known as the *Book of Martyrs*), for example, which Bunyan bought and read while in jail, provided copious examples of Protestant martyrdom presented in vivid, even lurid detail. It also seems that Bunyan must have known Richard Bernard's *The Isle of Man: or, The Legall Proceeding in Man-shire against Sinne*, an extended, incredibly detailed allegory in which spiritual malefactors are sought out, arrested, tried, and convicted. Like Bunyan, Bernard provides marginal glosses to render the allegorical characters and their actions absolutely clear.

Unlike Bernard's allegory, Bunyan's does not confine itself to criminal justice. Instead, the defining metaphor is the journey as spiritual development—a literary commonplace by Bunyan's time and, ironically, equally suited to the conversion narrative and the romance (as in a tale of epic adventure). In the episode in which Christian battles Apollyon, Bunyan displays his familiarity with the popular romance tradition in which brave heroes fight dragons and other monsters in exciting combat. The influence of other popular genres, such as folktales and ballads, can also be seen throughout the story, especially in Bunyan's predilection for songs, which punctuate major episodes in the allegory.

The decision to publish. The reasons leading to Bunyan's final decision to publish *The Pilgrim's Progress* in 1678 are still not entirely clear, although relaxation of censorship was certainly a factor. Nevertheless, Bunyan still would have had to be somewhat circumspect about how he presented his more controversial ideas. Even after the Restoration had firmly taken hold, Bunyan had to keep in mind "the nervous rulers of England, who equated obstinate refusal to conform to the state church with sedition and rebellion. Jailbirds like Bunyan had to be especially careful. So we should not expect outspoken political comment in his writings; nor were politics his main concern" (Hill, *A Turbulent, Seditious, and Factious People*, p. 119). For Bunyan, patience was a necessary way to deal with Restoration censorship, but allegory was a more creative way around the same problem. Bunyan, as noted, provided his own marginal glosses to explain crucial points of the allegory, adding to his explanations in successive editions. For the modern reader further notes are required to open up the rich complexities of the apparently straightforward correspondences.

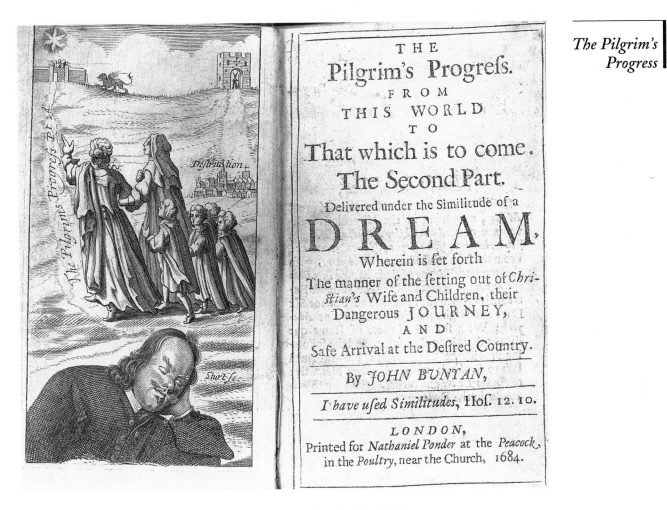

The frontispiece and title page from a 1684 edition of the sequel to *The Pilgrim's Progress*.

Impact. *The Pilgrim's Progress* has made a lasting impression on subsequent writers, especially novelists. To mention just a handful of examples in the nineteenth century, George Eliot, Charles Dickens, Louisa May Alcott, and Mark Twain all create characters who read and are affected by *The Pilgrim's Progress*. In *Little Women*, for instance, Alcott does not merely make her four heroines avid readers of Bunyan; they re-enact Christian's journey and Alcott herself at points shapes her narrative to the contours of Bunyan's book, naming chapters after famous episodes. Bunyan's book is in fact a proto-novel, one of the earliest models for popular prose fiction that emerged just before the rise of the novel in the eighteenth century. This is an ironic victory for Bunyan, who certainly would be surprised to discover his importance in the development of a secular genre historically considered to be immoral. As Christopher Hill has observed, "Just as Oliver Cromwell aimed to bring about the king-dom of God on earth and founded the British Empire, so Bunyan wanted the millennium and got the novel" (Hill, *A Turbulent, Seditious, and Factious People*, p. 368).

Reception. When it appeared in 1672, *The Pilgrim's Progress* was "an immediate and unprecedented bestseller," going through three editions in its first year and 13 editions by the time Bunyan died in 1688 (Keeble, p. 245). This is not to say that the immediate response to Bunyan's work was uncritical. Since the work was to a great extent polemical, reactions were based on content more than on literary considerations, and in addition to admirers (and even imitators) there were plenty of religious and political detractors. The popularity of the book remained high among the poor, middle, and working classes (and, as it turned out, in America), and yet "[a]mong the literati of the early eighteenth century Bunyan's popularity was taken not as proof of his excellence but as confirmation of his vulgarity, and so of his inconsequentiality" (Keeble, p. 246). This mixed response has endured for over three centuries.

Although writers such as Daniel Defoe, Jonathan Swift, and Lawrence Sterne came to appreciate Bunyan's literary merits despite prevailing dismissive attitudes, it was not until the nineteenth century that critical and popular estimations of *The Pilgrim's Progress* came closer together. On the one hand, Samuel Taylor Coleridge, Sir Walter Scott, and other Romantic writers praised Bunyan as "the embodiment of the 'heav'n-sent' or 'natural' genius" (although such praise "tended to ignore or denigrate his conscious artistry") (Forrest and Greaves, p. xi). On the other hand, it also appears that "Bunyan's reputation ascended the social scale only as the middling sort and evangelicism gained respectability in the nineteenth century" (Hill, *A Turbulent, Seditious, and Factious People*, p. 366). In any case, Bunyan's almost uniformly favorable—if rather uncritical—reputation in the 1800s flagged towards the end of the century. The twentieth century saw increased interest in the literary complexities of *The Pilgrim's Progress*, and renewed critical attention has provided an abundance of nuanced readings of the deceptively simple allegory.

—Meredith Neuman

For More Information

Bunyan, John. *Grace Abounding to the Chief of Sinners.* Harmondsworth, Middlesex: Penguin, 1987.

———. *The Pilgrim's Progress.* Oxford: Oxford University Press, 1986.

———. *The Pilgrim's Progress from this world to that which is to come.* Ed. J.B. Wharley and R. Sharrock. Oxford: Oxford University Press, 1967.

Evans, Vivienne, and Lewis Evans. *John Bunyan: His Life and Times.* Dunstable, Bedfordshire: The Book Castle, 1988.

Forrest, James F., and Richard Lee Greaves. *John Bunyan: a Reference Guide.* Boston: G. K. Hall, 1982.

Hill, Christopher. *A Turbulent, Seditious, and Factious People: John Bunyan and his Church 1628-1688.* Oxford: Clarendon Press, 1988.

———. *The World Turned Upside Down: Radical Ideas During the English Revolution.* London: Penguin, 1975.

Keeble, N. H. "'Of him thousands daily Sing and talk': Bunyan and his Reputation." In *John Bunyan Coventicle and Parnassus Tercentenary Essays.* Ed. N. H. Keeble. Oxford: Clarendon Press, 1988.

Pooley, Roger. "Grace Abounding and the New Sense of Self." In *John Bunyan and His England, 1628-88.* Ed. Anne Laurence, W. R. Owens, and Stuart Sim. London: Hambledon, 1990.

White, Barrie. "John Bunyan and the Context of Persecution, 1660-1668." In *John Bunyan and His England, 1628-88.* Ed. Anne Laurence, W. R. Owens, and Stuart Sim. London: Hambledon, 1990.

The Rape of the Lock

by
Alexander Pope

Alexander Pope, the foremost English poet of the eighteenth century, was born in London in 1688. He studied and wrote poetry from childhood, with his first published poems appearing in 1709. His first major work, a poem on the art of writing called *An Essay on Criticism,* was published in 1711. That same year, at the instigation of his friend John Caryll, he began writing for Richard Steele and Joseph Addison's **The Spectator** (also in *WLAIT 3: British and Irish Literature and Its Times*), a popular forerunner of the modern magazine. He also wrote his initial version of *The Rape of the Lock,* a poem dealing humorously with a real-life feud between leading Catholic families, the Fermors and the Petres, instigated when young Lord Petre cut off a lock of Arabella Fermor's hair. The outraged Arabella made a huge fuss over this loss, and Pope, to show the absurdity of the situation, elevated it still higher, into the realm of an epic battle, complete with heroic weapons, a dark underworld, and a glittering array of supernatural creatures who intervene in mortal affairs.

Events in History at the Time of the Poem

Rise of the first British Empire. When Pope wrote *The Rape of the Lock,* Britain was poised at the edge of new economic prosperity at home and vastly expanded influence abroad. During the reign of the last Stuart monarch, Queen Anne (1702-14), Britain fought the bloody and expensive War of the Spanish Succession against

---

> ## THE LITERARY WORK
>
> A mock-epic poem set in England in 1711; written in 1711; published in 1712, and republished with significant additions in 1714 and 1717.
>
> ## SYNOPSIS
>
> A young man steals a lock of hair from the head of a beautiful young woman.

---

longtime rival France, up to then Europe's foremost military power. The war, which lasted until 1714, broke out when France's King Louis XIV claimed the Spanish crown for his grandson Philip V, to whom the childless Habsburg king of Spain, Charles II, had left it. In so doing, Louis broke an earlier treaty by which he had agreed to the partition of Spain and its extensive colonial possessions between France and Austria. Britain therefore allied with Austria, the Netherlands, and various German principalities, the goals being to prevent the union of France and Spain and to restore the balance of power in Europe.

In 1711, the same year that Pope composed the first version of *The Rape of the Lock,* Britain negotiated a separate peace with France that confirmed Britain's control of key wartime territorial conquests abroad and also ceded to Britain exclusive rights to the lucrative African slave trade with Spanish South America. The territorial concessions included Gibraltar and Minorca in the Mediterranean (giving British merchants access to trade with the Middle East), as well as parts of Canada, France's colonial stronghold. While Philip V was allowed to rule Spain, France and Spain were not permitted to unite, and French power was dramatically curtailed. Its hard-won victories now transformed Britain into the world's leading naval, commercial, and colonial power. The so-called "first" British Empire that resulted would reach its high point after the Seven Years' War (1756-63), in which France suffered further military and colonial defeat. In *The Rape of the Lock*, Queen Anne's favorite residence, Hampton Court, provides both a venue for the poem and an emblem of Britain's rising military power: "Here Britain's Statesmen oft the Fall foredoom / Of foreign tyrants . . ." (Pope, *The Rape of the Lock*, 3.5-6).

Exotic products, expensive luxuries. The commercial advances that Britain made in the eighteenth century rested on foundations laid in the seventeenth. Trading companies like the East India Company (founded in 1600) imported spices, cotton, and silk, and, by the end of the seventeenth century, exotic new food items like coffee from the bazaars of the eastern Mediterranean region, chocolate from South America, and tea from China and later India. Pope shows all three of these new foods being consumed by the wealthy English elite in *The Rape of the Lock*. Tea is associated in the poem with Queen Anne herself, who was known to be fond of the drink and to serve it to her ministers, a practice that Pope mentions: "Here thou, great ANNA! Whom three realms obey / Dost sometimes counsel take—and sometimes Tea" (*The Rape of the Lock*, 3.7-8). (The "three realms" are England, Scotland, and Ireland, the first two of which were united as Great Britain during Anne's reign, while the Irish Parliament was subordinate to its British counterpart.) Coffee, tea, and chocolate (which the English added to hot milk and whisked into a froth, a process Pope describes in the poem) were still new and expensive luxuries in the early eighteenth century. These and other status items would become accessible to less wealthy members of society only later in the century, as global sea routes, lower tariffs, and new sources of supply in Asia and the Americas brought prices down.

All of this was made possible by the new commercial and colonial empire that Britain was in the process of building. In an essay for *The Spectator* written in 1711, Pope's friend Joseph Ad-dison commented on Britain's growing global reach:

> The single Dress of a Woman of Quality is often the Product of an hundred Climates. The Muff and the Fan come together from the different Ends of the Earth. The Scarf is sent from the Torrid Zone, and the Tippet [a kind of stole] from beneath the Pole. The Brocade Petticoat rises out of the mines of *Peru*, and the Diamond Necklace out of the Bowels of *Indostan*. . . . Our rooms are filled with Pyramids of *China*, and adorned with the workmanship of *Japan*. . . .
>
> (Addison in Bloom, p. 74)

Indeed, the collection of cosmetics, oils, and perfumes found on such a lady's dressing table comprises what Addison calls "a kind of Additional Empire," a consumer's domain of sumptuous material accoutrements (Addison in Bloom, p. 74). It is precisely these upper-class ladies that Pope depicts in *The Rape of the Lock*, as he claims explicitly in a letter to two friends of his, fashionable ladies themselves; the poem, he writes, offers "a pretty complete picture of the life of our modern ladies" in London, which he calls "this idle town" (Pope in Bloom, p. 68).

Women in eighteenth-century society. As feminist critics have pointed out, Pope's portrayal of Belinda, the poem's central character, reveals much about his society's attitudes toward women. In this time as in many others, a woman's proper role in society was defined by her relationship to men, even, among the upper classes, by her suitability as a decoration for the males around her. Essayist Richard Steele, Addison's partner in *The Spectator,* offered the opinion that right-thinking women "will in no part of their Lives want [lack] Opportunities of being shining Ornaments to their Fathers, Husbands, Brothers or Children" (Steele in Hammond, p. 81). While such sentiments are not unique to eighteenth-century Britain, some critics have suggested that the commercial revolution described above gave them a new force. Ellen Pollak, for example, quotes from the poem while linking these sentiments to the age's acquisitive imperial preoccupations:

> As a "Vessel" (II, 47) carrying all the "glitt'ring Spoil" (I, 32) of the world, she herself is identified with that world and, like nature, is to be conquered, ransacked, and possessed by commercial man. . . . "Deck'd with all that Land and Sea afford" (V,11), she is both the trophy of men's exploits and their manikin, a compulsive consumer who not only receives but testifies to British national wealth.
>
> (Pollak in Hammond, p. 78)

As suggested, the "glitt'ring Spoil" of this age's conquest and commercial exploitation ornamented only those women in the relatively small upper classes, perhaps 2 to 5 percent of the general population (Langford, p. 64). Most women in British society, like most men and many children, worked long hours at difficult or even grueling jobs. The men, though, enjoyed a measure of control and independence, albeit limited by economic circumstance. Like their upper-class counterparts, women in the lower classes were considered the property of their fathers or husbands. Domestic service, the most important area of employment for women, often involved physically arduous tasks in this preindustrial age: hauling water, washing and drying clothes by hand, disposing of human waste. In the early eighteenth century, female domestic servants comprised perhaps 15 percent of London's approximately 500,000 inhabitants (Black, pp. 56-57, 90). Aside from the arduous labor, female servants were vulnerable to sexual harassment or abuse by their masters as well as other men, and these servants had little recourse if abuse took place. One famous incident in 1729 led to the conviction of a Colonel Francis Charteris for raping a servant named Ann Bond. The case was exceptional in making it to court in the first place, however, and the conviction meant little, since Charteris was pardoned by King George II.

Servants were supposed to remain unnoticed in the background. In *The Rape of the Lock*, Belinda's maid, Betty, is mentioned by the poet only as an excuse to catalog the ways in which she beautifies her mistress for an evening of coffee, cards, and flirtation. A shadowy figure introduced as "Th' inferior Priestess" at the altar of Belinda's dressing table, Betty is defined by her subsidiary role and low social rank; her name is withheld until her part in the action is over (*The Rape of the Lock*, 1.127).

Vistas of materialism. While the industrial revolution that would materially change the nature of work was still several decades in the future, the financial revolution on which it would be based was already well underway. The Bank of England, the first modern central bank, had been founded in 1694 to help fund the government's wars with France. In addition to lending money to the government and issuing notes, the Bank of England also acted as a lender to commercial banks. All of these were important functions that would become essential to the monetary system of modern industrial economies.

While such affairs may seem far removed from the frivolous world depicted in *The Rape of the Lock*, historians have argued that this new financial system subtly but profoundly shaped the values of society by altering the way people interacted with material objects. According to this interpretation, not only did the financial revolution make possible the commercial ventures that brought exotic goods from all over the world into people's lives, it changed the very way in which those goods were perceived—and the way in which people perceived one another. Historian and critic C. E. Nicholson links the new system of money and credit to "a process whereby relations between people acquire the characteristics of being relations between things, a process during which commodities acquire an autonomy that conceals their true nature" (Nicholson in Bloom, p. 71). In *The Rape of the Lock*, as critics have observed, people are objectified and objects animated.

EIGHTEENTH-CENTURY FEMALE READERS

~

In its prescription of "acceptable" reading for women, eighteenth-century society included the works of Pope. Women encountered Pope's writings in conduct books, magazines, educational tracts, and separate collections of his work, and many liked what they read. These women, maintains one literary historian, recognized real rather than ideal women in Pope's work, identifying with the "familiar aspects of female experience" when, for example, Belinda primps for her evening out (Thomas, p. 118). Referring specifically to *The Rape of the Lock*, Judith Cowper wrote verse of her own that invited Pope to sit "in judgment o'er our fav'rite follies" (Cowper in Thomas, p. 130). On the other hand, Anne Finch, countess of Winchilsea, complained to Pope about the injustice of lines in *The Rape of the Lock* that make sport of women writers (calling the Goddess of Spleen "Parent of Vapours and Female wit, / Who give th'*Hysteric* or *Poetic* Fit," and "make some take Physic" and "others scribble Plays" (Pope in Thomas, p. 140). A poetic debate ensued, along with another, more acrimonious one between Pope and Lady Mary Wortley Montagu, whose verse remained unpublished. Poetry at the time was a male-dominated genre. Few women risked public condemnation by publishing their poems, especially those who engaged in a duel of verse.

The nascent materialism of the early eighteenth century would be boosted later in that century by the industrial revolution; and it would find a reaction, as Nicholson points out, in the ideas of Karl Marx and Friedrich Engels in the mid-nineteenth century. Pope satirized the misuse of money and credit—the basis of the capitalist system against which Marx inveighed—later in his career, in the humorous poem *Of the Use of Riches, an Epistle to Bathurst* (1732). In *The Rape of the Lock*, he alludes only indirectly to the financial world. For example, the close of business at London's Royal Exchange marks the onset of evening and the end of Belinda's long preparation for her night of cards: "The merchant from th' Exchange returns in peace / And the long labours of the Toilet cease" (*The Rape of the Lock*, 3.23-24). Here Pope uses juxtaposition to stress the connection between commerce and its material fruits, in this case the cosmetics on the dressing table.

The Poem in Focus

Plot summary. In the second version of 1714 and the final version of 1717, the poem is divided into five cantos of approximately 140-180 lines each, prefaced by a letter to Miss Arabella Fermor (whom Pope never met), the historical model for Belinda. In the letter, Pope explains the addition of "The Machinery," by which he means the spirits (sylphs, gnomes, nymphs, and salamanders) that assist the characters of the poem (and function as a mock counterpart to the gods that assist Achilles, Odysseus, Aeneas, and other classical epic heroes). He goes on to assure her—in a heavily ironic tone—that only the central incident itself is based on fact: "The Human persons are as fictitious as the Airy ones; and the character of *Belinda,* as it is now manag'd, resembles you in nothing but Beauty" (Pope, p. 2).

Canto 1 opens with parodic versions of the traditional epic statement of theme and invocation of the poet's muse. Instead of a grand subject, the poet will sing of "trivial things"; instead of asking the divine muse of poetry for assistance, the poet merely informs her that his verse is owed to a human (Pope's friend John Caryll, who asked him to write the poem):

> What dire offence from am'rous causes springs,
> What mighty contests rise from trivial things,
> I sing—This verse to *Caryll,* Muse! is due:
> This, ev'n *Belinda* may vouchsafe to view:
> Slight is the subject, but not so the praise,
> If She inspire, and He approve my lays.
> (*The Rape of the Lock*, 1.1-6)

A series of rhetorical questions then sets the stage for the narrative. Why, the poet asks, would a "well-bred Lord" assault "a gentle *Belle*" in this way; why, in the first place, would "a gentle Belle reject a Lord"; could "little men" be involved "in tasks so bold," and can "such mighty rage" be contained "in soft bosoms?" (*The Rape of the Lock*, 1.7-12).

The narrative, set during a single day, begins as Belinda, a beautiful and fashionable young lady, awakes at noon. She impatiently summons her maid before getting out of bed. In a dream before she awoke, her guardian sylph Ariel (in the form of a youth whose beauty made her blush in her sleep) has told her about the spirits, the "thousand bright Inhabitants of Air," who accompany and guard virginal young ladies (*The Rape of the Lock*, 1.28). Once they too were "inclos'd in Woman's beauteous mold," but "by a soft transition" they have given up their material bodies for "these of air" (*The Rape of the Lock*, 1.48-50). Yet, although they have given up their bodies, they have not given up the vanity, or the love of fancy coaches and card games, that they had when they were alive. Women with "fiery" tempers become salamanders, women with "soft yielding minds" become nymphs, prudish women become gnomes, and flirtatious women, "the light Coquettes," become sylphs (*The Rape of the Lock*, 1.61-65). The sylphs protect any "fair and chaste" woman "who rejects mankind" (*The Rape of the Lock*, 1.67-68). When women seem to drift aimlessly through the world, they are in fact being guided by the invisible sylphs, who help them resist the temptations of men. The dream concludes with Ariel's warning that "some dread event" is going to occur that day and that a man will be behind it (*The Rape of the Lock*, 1.109).

Woken by her lapdog, Shock, Belinda sees a love letter as soon she opens her eyes, and forgets the dream and its warning as she rereads it. Betty, her maid, arrives and begins the long process of dressing her mistress (described in terms that parallel the arming of the epic hero for battle).

Canto 2 begins with Belinda's passage on the Thames River, where her luminous beauty rivals the sun and attracts all eyes. She smiles at all of her admirers but does not play favorites. Graceful, sweet, and humble, she delicately rejects their advances without offending them. She has two carefully curled locks of hair hanging down the nape of her neck, which the poet compares to "sprindges" or snares that can entrap her admirers. One of these admirers, the Baron, spies and then covets one of these locks:

> This Nymph, to the destruction of mankind,
> Nourish'd two Locks, which hung behind
> In equal curls, and well conspir'd to deck
> With shining ringlets the smooth iv'ry neck:
> Love in these labyrinths his slaves detains,
> And mighty hearts are held in slender chains.
> With hairy sprindges we the birds betray,
> Slight lines of hair surprize the finny prey,
> Fair tresses man's imperial race insnare,
> And beauty draws us with a single hair.
> Th' advent'rous Baron the bright locks
>   admir'd,
> He saw, he wish'd, and to the prize aspir'd.
>   (*The Rape of the Lock*, 2.20-30)

The Baron plots to steal a lock of hair so he can add it to his collection of "all the trophies of his former loves" (*The Rape of the Lock*, 2.40).

As the vessel makes its way down the Thames toward Hampton Court, Ariel, the chief sylph, summons his insect-sized spirit soldiers. While other spirits, he tells them, are charged with keeping the planets in their proper orbits or protecting the British throne, the sylphs' job is just as important: to make sure powder isn't blown away in the breeze, or to keep perfume from leaking out of its jar. "Black omens," he continues, threaten the most beautiful of women today and the sylphs must be on their guard (*The Rape of the Lock*, 2.101). He gives them their assignments: one will guard her fan, another her watch; one will protect her "fav'rite Lock," and fifty will strengthen her greatest defense, her petticoat (*The Rape of the Lock*, 2.115). Sylphs who desert their post will suffer a terrible fate—being stuck in gooey make-up, for example, or ground up and whisked with the hot chocolate.

Canto 3 opens as Belinda arrives at Hampton Court in early evening, eager to begin her game of cards with the Baron and another young gentleman. Watched over by the sylphs, the game unfolds like a battle, with Belinda winning the first four tricks. The Baron recovers, taking four tricks himself, so that the outcome hinges on the ninth and final trick. Belinda takes it, winning the game, and rejoices at her victory, but too soon: the fumes of the coffee that is served after the game waft a new plan into the Baron's head. Clarissa, a sylph, unaccountably presents the Baron with a pair of scissors, "a two-edg'd weapon," with which he tries to snip off one of the locks as Belinda bends over her coffee (*The Rape of the Lock*, 3.128). The sylphs rush to the lock's defense, blowing the hair back with their

In this 1714 illustration of Canto 3 of *The Rape of the Lock,* Belinda swoons while the Baron flourishes the ravished lock of hair.

little wings and twitching Belinda's earring so that she moves her head. Worried, Ariel himself monitors her thoughts—and detects "in spite of all her art, / An earthly lover lurking at her heart" (*The Rape of the Lock*, 3.144). Suddenly, all his power vanishes and he resigns himself to fate. The Baron snips the lock, cleaving a sylph with it, though the sylph's ethereal body quickly reunites. Belinda screams in horror and rage, the Baron lets out a victory cry, and the poet wonders at "the conqu'ring force of unresisted steel" (*The Rape of the Lock*, 3.178).

Canto 4 takes the gnome Umbriel to the Cave of Spleen, a gloomy, airless underground grotto ruled by a dark goddess who embodies melancholy and resentment. (Spleen, one the four humors of medieval and Renaissance medicine, was thought to be the substance responsible for depression and anger.) Spleen's handmaids are "Ill-nature" and "Affectation" (*The Rape of the Lock*, 4.27, 31). In this "dismal dome" can be found grotesque examples of "bodies changed to various forms by Spleen": animate objects like "living Tea-pots" or talking pies, pregnant men, and young ladies turned into bottles that call for corks (*The Rape of the Lock*, 4.18, 48-54). Umbriel, who prides himself on causing irritating problems, blemishes, and embarrassments for attractive women, asks Spleen to "touch Belinda with chagrin" (*The Rape of the Lock*, 4.77). Granting his wish, Spleen gives Umbriel two gifts: a bag filled with "the force of female lungs, / Sighs, sobs, passions, and the war of tongues"; and a vial filled with "fainting fears, / Soft sorrows, melting griefs, and flowing tears" (*The Rape of the Lock*, 4.83-86).

"ENGLISH" CARD GAMES

Card games were popular among all classes but, since the cards themselves were taxed and therefore expensive, the less well-off rarely could afford to play. Many of the favorite card games in England were derived from popular ones in France or Spain, England's longtime enemies, which showed that national rivalries were no barrier to cultural diffusion. A popular Spanish import was *primero,* the ancestor of today's poker, which is mentioned by Shakespeare as being played by King Henry VIII and has been called the oldest card game played in England. From France came *piquet,* a game for two played by Charles I, who retained its French terminology out of deference to his French-born wife. The game played by Belinda in *The Rape of the Lock* was the Spanish game *ombre,* a favorite of the fashionable set in seventeenth- and eighteenth-century England. It bore a resemblance to the modern games of whist and bridge, including trump suits, bids, and taking tricks.

Returning to daylight, Umbriel finds the depressed and listless Belinda and opens the bag over her head. Thalestris, named after the mythological queen of the Amazons, stokes the anger that has been ignited in Belinda by the bag's contents. "Was it for this that you took such constant care, / The bodkin, comb and essence to prepare" (*The Rape of the Lock*, 4.97-98). To let the Baron get away with showing the prize lock of hair to his envious friends and to amazed young ladies, Thalestris urges, will mean loss of honor for Belinda. Belinda, now enraged, goes to her beau, Sir Plume, but his ineffectual stammering fails to persuade the suave Baron. As long as his "nostrils draw the vital air," the Baron vows, he will never return the lock (*The Rape of the Lock*, 4.137). Umbriel, the troublemaker, then breaks the vial, and Belinda's rage turns to sobs and tears. The lament that follows (modeled on Achilles' lament after the death of his friend Patroclus in the *Iliad*) combines epic phrases with mock-epic twists, as in the couplet with which it begins: "Forever curs't be this detested day, / Which snatched my best, my fav'rite curl away!" (*The Rape of the Lock*, 4.148-49). It would have been better, she continues, if she had lived in some remote corner of the world, away from men's admiration, where no one plays cards or drinks tea. The lament and the Canto conclude with her wish that the Baron had "been content to seize / Hairs less in sight, or any hairs but these" (*The Rape of the Lock*, 4.175-76).

In Canto 5 Clarissa, the sylph who gave the scissors to the Baron, urges Belinda to value "good sense" as highly as beauty (*The Rape of the Lock*, 5.16). Advocating the deeper qualities of merit and virtue as necessary additions to superficial beauty, Clarissa concludes: "Beauties in vain their pretty eyes may roll; / Charms strike the sight, but merit wins the soul" (*The Rape of the Lock*, 5.33-34). But Clarissa's advice falls on deaf ears, and instead (incited by Thalestris) battle breaks out among the men and women present: "All side in parties, and begin th' attack; / Fans clap, silks russle and tough whalebones crack; / Heroes and Heroines shouts confusedly rise, / And base, and treble voices strike the skies" (*The Rape of the Lock*, 5.39-42). The sylphs watch the fight and contribute a soft blow now and then; as in a pillow fight, no one is really hurt. After a while, Jove (king of the gods) weighs the wits of the men against the hair of the women. The hair is heavier, and so Jove will award the battle to the women. Belinda finds the Baron in the fray and throws a pinch of snuff up his nose, causing an epic sneeze (ironically fulfilling his earlier vow never to return the lock). Belinda prepares to finish him off with her hairpin, and he boasts that he is afraid not of death, but only of being without her. "Restore the Lock! she cries; and all around / Restore the Lock! the vaulted roofs rebound" (*The Rape of the Lock*, 5.104-105). But the lock is nowhere to be found. There are those, the poet tells us, who thought it ended up on the moon, but the Muse saw it go straight up to the stars, leaving "a radiant trail of hair" behind it (*The Rape of the Lock*, 5.128). Belinda should no longer mourn her stolen lock, the poet concludes, but should instead be content that her hair will make her name famous long after she and everyone she knows have disappeared:

When those fair suns shall set, as set they must,
And all those tresses shall be laid in dust;
This Lock, the Muse shall consecrate to fame,
And 'midst the stars, inscribe *Belinda's* name.
(*The Rape of the Lock*, 5.147-50)

In the final canto of the poem, a fight breaks out among the belles and beaux, as shown in this illustration from the 1714 edition.

The poem's spirits—not from thin air. In his letter to Arabella Fermor that prefaces *The Rape of the Lock*, Pope says: "The *Rosicrucians* are a people I must bring You acquainted with. The best account I know of them is in a French book call'd *Le Comte de Gabalis*. According to these Gentlemen, the four Elements are inhabited by Spirits, which they call Sylphs, Gnomes, Nymphs and Salamanders" (Pope, p. 2). Although Pope uses the Rosicrucian machinery of sylphs and other spirits lightheartedly in the poem, the Rosicrucian movement was treated very seriously by others, and still has adherents to this day. It is based to a large extent on the pre-Christian, Greek-influenced Egyptian philosophy of Gnosticism, which, to speak in the broadest of terms, asserts that "this world and its creator are evil, or at least alien, cut off from the higher world that is the true home of all spiritual beings" (Popkin, p. 100). The Rosicrucian movement began in early seventeenth-century Germany. Its foundational text, *Fama Fraternitatis, dess Loblichen Ordens des Rosenkreutzes*—the Declaration of the Worthy Order of the Rosy Cross—was first published in Kassel in 1614. The text discussed a secret brotherhood supposedly founded by a man named Christian Rosenkreuz, a healer who traveled widely in the East and who had brought back with him much arcane knowledge. In 1615 the *Confessio Fraternitatis* was published; it had essentially the same message as the *Fama* but also

---

FROM SARPEDON'S SPEECH IN THE *ILIAD*

Here is an excerpt from Pope's own translation of a speech from Homer's *Iliad* on which he modeled Clarissa's advice to Belinda:

> But since, alas, ignoble age must come,
> Disease, and Death's inexorable doom;
> The Life which others pay, let us bestow,
> And give to Fame what we to Nature owe;
> Brave tho' we fall; and honor'd, if we live;
> Or let us Glory gain, or Glory give!
> (*The Rape of the Lock*, p. 132)

Here is the corresponding passage from Clarissa's speech:

> But since, alas! frail beauty must decay,
> Curl'd or uncurl'd, since Locks will turn to grey;
> Since painted, or not painted, all shall fade,
> And she who scorns a man, must die a maid;
> What then remains but well our pow'r to use,
> And keep good-humour still whate'er we lose?
> (*The Rape of the Lock*, V. 25-30)

---

promised the downfall of the Pope (McIntosh, pp. xviii-xix).

The Rosicrucian movement was, in fact, militantly Protestant. It concerned itself with secret knowledge, frequently couched in the sexual terms characteristic of alchemy. The belief was that this secret knowledge, often alchemical itself, could transform the world by ushering in a new golden age in which, among other things, Catholicism and the Pope would be defeated. The movement spread quickly from Germany to England; Francis Bacon (1561-1626), the Renaissance English philosopher and statesman was obviously indebted to the *Fama*, and even King James I seems to have had some sort of passing connection with the brotherhood (McIntosh, pp. 33, 40). Pope's own use of Rosicrucian lore was amongst the earliest in English letters. The book he mentions to Arabella Fermor, *Le Comte de Gabalis*, by the Abbé Montfaucon de Villars, was first published in Paris in 1670:

> In it, the narrator describes how, in a series of conversations, the Count (the Comte of the title) expounds the theory of elemental spirits called Gnomes, Nymphs, Sylphs, and Salamanders, who govern respectively earth, water, air, and fire. He shocks the narrator by describing how these creatures mate with mortals. . . . The tone of the book is wry and rather lighthearted.
>
> (McIntosh, p. 107)

Pope himself uses the Rosicrucian lore lightheartedly, employing its spirits in his poem as if they were Greek gods aiding mortals in some great tragedy, invoking them to mock the protagonist Belinda. The poem, for example, assigns sylphs to the lofty tasks of guarding her fan, reinforcing her petticoat, and, of course, protecting her favorite lock.

If Pope's verse benefited from the teachings of the Rosicrucians, it apparently promoted them as well. There were English translations of *Le Comte de Gabalis* in 1680 and 1714, both entitled *The Count de Gabalis: Being a Diverting History of the Rosicrucian Doctrine of Spirits*. The second of these translations was in fact encouraged by the publication that same year of *The Rape of the Lock* (McIntosh, p. 108).

Sources and literary context. As mentioned, the poem was occasioned by a quarrel between two wealthy Catholic families, the Petres and the Fermors, which itself had arisen when young Lord Petre cut off a lock of Miss Arabella Fermor's hair. Pope himself did not know the families well, if at all, but his friend John Caryll was close to both. Caryll asked Pope to compose a poem that would "make a jest of it, and laugh them together again" (*The Rape of the Lock*, p. 71). Nothing more is known of the incident itself.

English writers of the late seventeenth to late eighteenth centuries showed a special fascination with classical models (of which the epic reigned supreme), and this period in English literature is often termed "neo-classical" or "Augustan." For *The Rape of the Lock*, Pope drew on his fluent and detailed knowledge of Greek and Latin epic poetry (Homer's *Iliad* and *Odyssey*; Virgil's *Aeneid*) as well as on a more recent example of the genre, Milton's English epic **Paradise Lost** (1667; also in *WLAIT 3: British and Irish Literature and Its Times*). The epic hero endured arduous journeys or ordeals, fought battles, descended into the underworld, and enjoyed romantic interludes; themes were elevated and political (the sack of Troy in the *Iliad*, the founding of Rome in the *Aeneid*, the Fall of Man in *Paradise Lost*), and the hero's quest usually involved his honor. The preoccupation with epic forms gave rise to the humorous application of those forms to subjects considered less elevated, resulting in the genre of mock-epic, which was also well established by Pope's time. Other examples of the genre include John Dryden's **Mac Flecknoe** (1682; also in *WLAIT 3: British and Irish Literature and Its Times*), and Jonathan Swift's *Battle of the Books* (1704).

Publication and reception. Written quickly, the first version of the poem was circulated among Pope's friends in 1711, the year of its composition and of the quarrel that inspired it, and was published the following year. In 1714 Pope expanded the original two cantos to five, adding the game of cards and "the machinery" of the sylphs, gnomes, and other spirits. The final version, to which the main addition was Clarissa's speech in Canto 5, was published in 1717. Pope himself declared that he added the speech in order "to open more clearly the MORAL of the Poem," though some critics have questioned how seriously he meant the statement.

Pope's contemporary Joseph Addison called *The Rape of the Lock* a work of "pure wit," praising Pope's irony and sharp social commentary (Addison in Morris, p. 102). As indicated, female contemporaries responded less approvingly; the countess of Winchilsea, for one, "deplored" Pope's satiric tone in the poem (Thomas, p. 144). Writing later in the century, Samuel Johnson asserted that *The Rape of the Lock* showed "the two most engaging powers of an author. New things are made familiar, and familiar things are made new" (Johnson in Pope, p. 105). The poem has been faulted for superficiality as well as for the difficulty of discerning Pope's own views in it (a quality that has led other critics to praise it). Despite its brevity, it has also been lauded as a work of great vividness and richness; critics have dwelt especially on its powerful evocation of the bright, sunlit beauty of Belinda and her precious items of luxury.

—Colin Wells

For More Information

Black, Jeremy. *An Illustrated History of Eighteenth Century Britain*. Manchester: Manchester University Press, 1996.

Bloom, Harold, ed. *Alexander Pope's The Rape of the Lock*. Modern Critical Interpretations. New York: Chelsea House, 1988.

Braudel, Fernand. *The Structures of Everyday Life: Civilization and Capitalism, 15th-18th Century*. Vol. 1. New York: Harper & Row, 1979.

Erskine-Hill, Howard. *The Social Milieu of Alexander Pope: Lives, Example, and the Poetic Response*. New Haven: Yale University Press, 1975.

Hammond, Brean, ed. *Pope*. New York: Longman, 1996.

Langford, Paul. *A Polite and Commercial People: England, 1727-1783*. Oxford: Clarendon Press, 1989.

Mack, Maynard. *Alexander Pope: A Life*. New York: Norton, 1986.

McIntosh, Christopher. *The Rosicrucians: The History, Mythology, and Rituals of an Esoteric Order*. York Beach, Maine: Samuel Weiser, 1997.

Morris, David B. *Alexander Pope: The Genius of Sense*. Cambridge: Harvard University Press, 1984.

Pope, Alexander. *The Rape of the Lock*. Ed. Elizabeth Gurr. Oxford Student Texts. Oxford: Oxford University Press, 1990.

Popkin, Richard H., ed. *The Columbia History of Western Philosophy*. New York: Columbia University Press, 1999.

Rogers, Pat. *Essays on Pope*. Cambridge: Cambridge University Press, 1993.

Thomas, Claudia N. *Alexander Pope and His Eighteenth-Century Women Readers*. Carbondale: Southern Illinois University Press, 1994.

Richard II

by
William Shakespeare

~

With the exceptions of *King John* and *Henry VIII*, Shakespeare's English history plays dramatize the century-long story of the Wars of the Roses, the conflict between the two royal houses of Lancaster and York that dominated English politics during the fifteenth century. Shakespeare composed the plays in an order different from that in which the actual events occurred, so that *The Tragedy of King Richard II* (known simply as *Richard II*), though written near the middle of the sequence, relates the background from which the struggle arose. The Wars of the Roses were of particular interest in Shakespeare's time, not least because they had been ended by Henry VII, the grandfather of the reigning monarch, Queen Elizabeth. Like Shakespeare's other history plays, *Richard II* addresses questions of increasingly urgent importance, since the childless Queen Elizabeth, now in her sixties, remained without a clear successor. These questions relate to the nature of monarchy and, above all, to what makes a monarch legitimate. *Richard II* balances Richard's tyrannical behavior with his unquestionable title to the throne, and Bolingbroke's effective leadership with his lawless usurpation.

Events in History at the Time the Play Takes Place

The legacy of Edward III. Richard II was only ten years old when he ascended to the throne in 1377, succeeding his grandfather, Edward III, who reigned from 1327 to 1377. Richard's fa-

THE LITERARY WORK

A play set in England in the late fourteenth century; written and first performed c. 1595; published c. 1597.

SYNOPSIS

Richard II, the king of England from 1377 to 1399, is overthrown and replaced by his cousin Bolingbroke, who becomes King Henry IV.

ther, Edward the Black Prince, the oldest of Edward III's seven sons, had died of illness the year before. The health of both Edwards was broken by years of rigorous campaigning in France, where, starting in the 1330s, Edward III had initiated the conflict that would become known as the Hundred Years' War. The war was not going well for England when Richard succeeded to the throne. Early English successes in the 1340s and 1350s (such as the Black Prince's victory at Poitiers in 1356) had given way to a French military revival starting in 1369, a resurgence that came as both Edward III and his son declined in health.

Under these difficult circumstances, influence in the government had increasingly fallen to the next oldest of Edward III's surviving sons, John of Gaunt. Fearing that Gaunt might try to usurp the throne, after Edward III's death the nobles demanded that Richard be confirmed as rightful heir. The unpopular Gaunt's influence, however,

THE PEASANTS' REVOLT

As part of Edward III's legacy, Richard inherited mounting social and religious tensions within the kingdom. In June 1381, just a few years after ascending to the throne, Richard faced the only real outbreak of social unrest in medieval English history. For decades since the outbreak of the plague (the Black Death) in 1349, the reduced population had made labor scarce and had thus driven up wages, improving the lot of free peasants, artisans, and serfs. Noble landowners had quickly responded by enacting the Statute of Labourers in 1351, which attempted to impose a maximum wage on the free peasants and artisans. The serfs, peasants whose labor was not paid but exacted by the nobles under the feudal system, now found themselves forced to work under the same customary conditions in a market in which the real value of their labor had doubled or tripled. Unrest, which had mounted during Edward III's final years, crested in 1380 when Richard's council enacted a poll tax of a shilling a head (about ten days' wages) in order to pay for the expensive and mismanaged war with France. This flat tax penalized the poor, who rose up against the landowning nobles and against the Catholic Church, which was also a major landowner and thus controlled any serfs who were tenants on its land.

Led by Wat Tyler, a peasant, and John Ball, a rebellious priest, peasants and serfs throughout southeast England attacked the manor houses of the nobles, the offices of lawyers and judges (where documents attesting to the legal status of serfs were kept), and religious edifices. Moving to London, they attacked John of Gaunt's palace, among others, and trapped Richard in the Tower of London. As the uprising spread throughout England, on his counselors' advice the 14-year-old king met the rebels. Young Richard promised them pardons as well as freedom for the serfs—promises that neither he nor his counselors had any intention of keeping. At a subsequent meeting between Richard and Wat Tyler, the rebel leader was stabbed and killed by the Lord Mayor of London; most of the other leaders were rounded up and hanged. Unrest continued to fester in repeated minor outbreaks throughout the reign. Though the events in *Richard II* take place nearly two decades after the Peasants' Revolt, Shakespeare alludes to Richard's unpopularity, having him comment bitterly on Bolingbroke's calculated "courtship to the common people / How he did seem to dive into their hearts / With humble and familiar courtesy" (Shakespeare, *Richard II*, 1.4.24-26).

continued after Richard's accession, despite Gaunt's being excluded from the ruling council set up to run the government during Richard's minority. Richard's other uncles were also excluded from the council, for similar reasons. Appointed by Parliament, the council represented the interests of the English nobles, which often conflicted with those of the monarch. Control of England now depended on control of its young king, and thus from the beginning of his reign Richard found himself caught between his ambitious uncles and Parliament's wary nobles.

The Lords Appellant As he grew older Richard sought greater independence in exercising power. He began to select his own advisors, and starting in 1383 Parliament objected repeatedly to what it regarded as the mismanagement of Richard's government. Richard, in turn, struggled to build up his own following. By 1386 the opposition centered on one of Richard's uncles, Thomas Woodstock, duke of Gloucester, a younger brother of John of Gaunt. (John himself, who had mediated between the king and his critics in the past, was away attempting to enforce a hereditary claim to territory in Spain.) Gloucester found allies in Gaunt's son Henry Bolingbroke (also spelled Bullingbrook), earl of Derby; Thomas Mowbray, earl of Nottingham; and two other earls, Warwick and Arundel. Together, these five made up the Lords Appellant, or "accusing lords." Thus, disgruntled members of the royal family allied with nobles against the king and his new advisors. After defeating the king's favorite in a skirmish at Radcot Bridge, the Lords Appellant dominated Parliament (the so-called Merciless Parliament of 1388), carrying out a year-long purge of the king's supporters.

Gloucester, Mowbray, and Bolingbroke. For two years Richard kept a low profile, but in May 1389 he declared himself of an age to rule with full independence. Gaunt returned from Spain later that year, and with his uncle's presence as a buffer Richard enjoyed nearly eight years of relatively stable and peaceful rule. His first wife, Anne of Bohemia, died in 1394, and two years later the 29-year-old Richard cemented a peace with France by marrying Princess Isabella, the 7-year-old daughter of the French king.

During this time of unprecedented harmony, however, Richard was quietly building up a second alliance of favored advisors. These included Sir John Bushy, Sir Henry Green, Sir William Bagot: the "caterpillars" of Shakespeare's play, an extended metaphorical reference to their parasitical existence in the "garden" that is England (*Richard II,* 3.4.43, 46). Richard had pardoned the five Lords Appellant, but, under circumstances that remain unknown, in 1397 he arrested three of them: his uncle Gloucester, and the earls of Warwick and Arundel. The three were convicted of treason; Warwick was sentenced to exile and Arundel to death. Gloucester, who was being held in a castle under Mowbray's charge, mysteriously died while a prisoner. It is not known whether Richard ordered his death or whether Mowbray acted on his own—willingly or unwillingly—or whether Gloucester died of poor treatment or even simply of natural causes. In *Richard II,* Richard's guilt is unstated but assumed.

Soon after Gloucester's death, Mowbray seems to have warned Bolingbroke—the other surviving appellant—that the king might revoke their pardons. Bolingbroke then turned to his father, John of Gaunt, and on Gaunt's advice accused Mowbray of treason in plotting against the king. Later, he added charges of murdering Gloucester and misappropriating funds meant for the war. (It is at this point that Shakespeare's play opens.) Mowbray denied the charges and demanded trial-by-combat, as was his right under the feudal system. Richard ordered the trial to take place, but stopped it at the last minute, in-

The Peasants' Revolt prompted a meeting between Richard II and the rebels, depicted here.

stead banishing the two disputants—for ten years in Bolingbroke's case and for life in Mowbray's. Before Bolingbroke's departure, Richard reduced his exile to six years.

Bolingbroke's Lancastrian inheritance. At the same time that the struggle between Mowbray and Bolingbroke was taking place, Richard undertook a series of harsh financial measures designed to increase his royal treasury and support his sumptuous court, the extravagance of which exceeded that of his predecessors. Most notably, he won from Parliament a lifetime grant of all customs duties on wool and leather (England's largest trade items). Also, as recorded by Shakespeare's major historical source, Raphael Holinshed, Richard forced wealthy subjects to sign "blank charters"—I.O.U.s essentially—for him to fill in at will. Elsewhere Holinshed describes Richard as "prodigall, ambitious, and much given to the pleasure of the body," qualities that would lead to the king's downfall (Holinshed in Bullough, p. 408). After Gaunt's death in 1399, Richard overstepped himself by illegally seizing the vast estate Gaunt had possessed as duke of Lancaster. He then made the further tactical error of traveling to Ireland to put down a rebel-

FACTORING IN THE ENGLISH PARLIAMENT

Richard II necessarily concerned himself with Parliament during his reign. Coming into being from 1272-1377, the English Parliament had crystallized into two separate bodies by the time he ascended the throne. The two divisions were not yet called "houses" of Parliament, but already the king had to obtain the consent of the "lords" to conduct war, and already the "commons" rather than the lords had become the branch that represented the community. Over the next 50 years, procedures would solidify, parliamentary rights would achieve recognition, and Parliament would become a forum in which to air and decide major issues affecting the realm. Usually assembling annually in Westminster Palace, Parliament was held for varying lengths of time over the years. In 1376 Parliament lasted for ten weeks while during Richard's reign it sometimes ran even longer. Its two bodies would discuss the king's affairs, grant the taxes needed to conduct them, and consider remedies for grievances that plagued the kingdom. The commons consisted of more than 250 elected representatives, not all of them residing in the areas they represented. The lords included about 100 members, nearly half of them ecclesiastics (bishops and archbishops) and the rest laymen (earls, dukes, and, thanks to Richard, marquises and barons). During his reign, Richard broadened the class of lords by his actions in relation to two of its subdivisions. The title of "baron" existed before then, but first landholding and later heredity determined who took the title. In 1387 Richard introduced a major change by ignoring these qualifications and promoting a steward of his household—John Beauchamp of Holt—to baron. Beauchamp was a fervent loyalist to Richard, whose reign by this time was fraught with the tension that manifests itself in Shakespeare's play. Richard's subjects therefore interpreted Beauchamp's entitlement as a political act. If the new baron was elated, he would not remain so for long; his fortunes ultimately plummeted. In 1388, the year Parliament purged the kingdom of Richard's supporters, its leaders would have Beauchamp beheaded. For the moment, though, Beauchamp could enjoy his new status, even if it enflamed others in the realm. So incendiary was this act of the king's, says one historian, that it may be the reason for his unpopularity: "Richard's ill repute probably attached to this method of preferment [entitling a baron], as it did to marquis," a title Richard introduced in 1385, when he made Robert de Vere England's first marquis.

(Brown in Davies, p. 115).

lion of Irish leaders against their English overlords, having quelled a similar revolt in 1394 and deeming it necessary now to consolidate the earlier victory. As one scholar puts it, this move was "reasonable policy, fatally timed," for Bolingbroke took advantage of Richard's absence to return and claim his Lancastrian inheritance (Saccio, p. 28). Many of the nobles, fearful that the confiscation of one estate left their own vulnerable to similar treatment, rallied to support Bolingbroke. By the time Richard hesitantly returned from Ireland, Bolingbroke was in a strong position—but it is still uncertain whether (as he maintained) he wanted merely to claim the inheritance that was rightfully his or whether he already had it in mind to depose Richard and take his place.

Richard's deposition and death. Lured by deceit into an ambush by Bolingbroke's ally, Northumberland, Richard was captured and taken to the Tower of London in August 1399. (Shakespeare omits the ambush, making the king's opponents more honorable and Richard more the agent of his own destruction.) On September 30 Parliament deposed Richard, and on October 13 Bolingbroke was crowned as Henry IV.

In January 1400 a few of the former king's supporters attempted to murder Bolingbroke and restore Richard to the throne, but the plot was easily foiled and the conspirators captured. Sometime in February Richard died in his cell at Pomfret Castle. One account has him starving to death; another (which Shakespeare followed) has him assassinated in order to secure Bolingbroke's place on the throne.

The Play in Focus

Plot summary. The play opens with King Richard and his uncle, John of Gaunt, in Richard's throne room, preparing to hear the accusations of Gaunt's son Bolingbroke against Thomas Mowbray, duke of Norfolk, and to hear Mowbray's defense. The two appear and, amid elaborate and courtly speeches from both, Bolingbroke accuses Mowbray of treason, misappropriation of royal funds, and of complicity in the death of Thomas Woodstock, duke of Gloucester, Gaunt's younger brother and thus also Richard's uncle. Mowbray denies the charges, but with a studied ambiguity that leaves open the possibility that he in fact arranged the slaying on Richard's orders.

Bolingbroke has issued, and Mowbray accepted, a challenge to decide the truth of the accusations in a trial-by-combat—the "chivalrous design of knightly trial" dictated by feudal custom (*Richard II*, 1.1.81). Richard forbids the trial-by-combat, tries ineffectually to reconcile the two, then reverses himself and declares a date for the tournament. As the highly ceremonial event is about to occur, however, Richard again reverses himself and brings it to a halt. Instead he has decided to banish both Bolingbroke and Mowbray, the former for ten years and the latter for life. After Gaunt expresses his grief at his son's exile, Richard commutes the sentence to six years. Gaunt and Bolingbroke bid each other farewell; Richard complains to his favorites that Bolingbroke curries favor with the common people, "As were our England in reversion his, / And he our subjects' next degree of hope" (*Richard II*, 1.4.35-36). Richard also reveals his plans to "farm our royal realm" in order to finance a planned war in Ireland and—upon hearing that John of Gaunt is ill—to appropriate his uncle's huge fortune (*Richard II*, 1.4.45).

Act 2 opens with the sick Gaunt and his younger brother the duke of York expressing grief over Richard's refusal to accept their "wholesome counsel," though Gaunt hopes that the ad-

vice of a dying man may make a greater impression on their headstrong young nephew (*Richard II*, 2.1.2). Gaunt then launches into one of the most famous speeches in Shakespeare's plays, an apostrophe in which he expresses his love for England and his outrage that Richard should spoil and ruin it for his own profit:

> This royal throne of kings, this sceptred isle,
> This earth of majesty, this seat of Mars
> This other Eden, demi-paradise . . .
> This happy breed of men, this little world,
> This precious stone set in the silver sea . . .
> This blessèd plot, this earth, this realm, this
>   England . . .
> Is now leased out, I die pronouncing it,
> Like to a tenement or pelting farm.
>   (*Richard II*, 2.1.40-60)

THE WARS OF THE ROSES

While the Wars of the Roses (1455-85) were not fought until half a century after Richard II's deposition, the dynastic struggle of which they were the culmination in fact began with Bolingbroke's rebellion. Because of the illegitimate way in which Bolingbroke had come to power, his Lancastrian descendants never enjoyed real security on the throne. In 1455 Bolingbroke's grandson, Henry VI, was challenged by Richard, duke of York—who was also descended from Edward III. Both sides won victories, but in the end both also exhausted their supply of male heirs, many of whom died in combat. The sons of Richard, duke of York, became Edward IV and Richard III, the latter of whom was defeated in 1485 at the Battle of Bosworth by the Welsh-descended Henry Tudor. As King Henry VII, Henry Tudor married a York and could claim to have ended the Wars of the Roses by uniting the two houses, both of which were branches of the powerful Plantagenet family.

Richard enters, and Gaunt reproaches him in similar terms, calling him "Landlord of England . . . not king" and openly accusing him of spilling royal blood in the murder of Gloucester (*Richard II*, 2.1.113). Gaunt exits, and only a few lines later Northumberland, a noble, enters with news of Gaunt's death. Richard immediately announces to York his intention of seizing Gaunt's estate. York, now "the last of noble Edward's sons," laments both the spilling of Gloucester's blood and the improper confiscation of Bolingbroke's "charters and customary

From a 1998 GreenStage production of *Richard II.*

rights" (*Richard II*, 2.1.171, 196). They exit, but Northumberland remains with Ross and Willoughby, two other nobles, and they discuss Gaunt's death. Northumberland reveals that he has news of Bolingbroke's impending arrival and proposes that they join him in order to "shake off our slavish yoke" and "redeem from pawn our blemished crown" (*Richard II*, 2.1.291). Ross and Willoughby agree, and the three conspirators exit.

Two of Richard's favorites, Bushy and Bagot, comfort Queen Isabella, who feels sorrow at Richard's absence in Ireland and expresses a sense of foreboding. Green, another royal favorite, enters and announces that Bolingbroke has landed at Ravenspur in northern England, where Northumberland and other nobles have flocked to his cause. York enters and worries that he is too old and weak to defend the king's interests. Indecisive, he is split between his two kinsmen, between his duty to Richard and his conscience, which tells him that the king has deeply wronged Bolingbroke. Duty prevails, barely, and York goes off to prepare a defense at Berkley Castle until Richard can return. As Bolingbroke, Northumberland, and the other rebels approach the castle, York comes out to meet them and challenges Bolingbroke's action as treason against the king. Bolingbroke defends him-

self by invoking his customary rights of inheritance. York caves in, inviting Bolingbroke into the castle.

Act 3 opens with the entrance of Bolingbroke, York, Northumberland, and other nobles, with Bushy and Green in tow as prisoners awaiting execution; the queen is at York's manor house, and Bolingbroke asks him to treat her well. The scene shifts to Richard, who has arrived from Ireland, and two of his few remaining supporters: his cousin Aumerle, son and heir to York, and the Bishop of Carlisle. In this long scene, the play's structural center, Richard alternates between joyful confidence and utter despair. Three times he plucks up his courage, and three times news of Bolingbroke's progress sends him crashing down again. The center of his confidence is the medieval conviction that, as he puts it, "The breath of worldly men cannot depose / The deputy elected by the Lord" (*Richard II*, 3.2.56-57). Yet this belief in the divine right of kings crumbles before his own inability to act, to take command, to be a king in deed as well as in name. He gives up when his supporters are still ready to fight, sitting down while they remain standing:

> For God's sake let us sit upon the ground
> And tell sad stories of the death of kings,
> How some have been deposed, some slain in
>   war,

Some haunted by the ghosts they have
   deposed,
Some poisoned by their wives, some sleeping
   killed,
All murdered. For within the hollow crown
That rounds the mortal temples of a king
Keeps Death his court. . . .
                    (*Richard II*, 3.2.155-62)

The scene ends as Richard tells Aumerle to send his followers away.

In the next scene Bolingbroke, York, and Northumberland arrive at Flint Castle, where (as Northumberland says, significantly omitting the royal title of king) "Richard . . . hath hid his head" *Richard II*, 3.3.6). Bolingbroke professes his continued allegiance to the king—with the condition that Richard end Bolingbroke's exile and restore his inheritance. Otherwise, he threatens, blood will rain "from the wounds of slaughtered Englishmen" (*Richard II*, 3.3.44). With a flourish of trumpets, Richard enters with Carlisle and Aumerle, immediately upbraiding Northumberland for not bowing in the royal presence. But he agrees to Bolingbroke's terms. In fact, in submitting he goes further than asked and ironically, it seems, suggests his own deposition: "What must the king do now? Must he submit? / The king shall do it. Must he be deposed? / The king shall be contented. Must he lose / The name of king? A God's name let it go" (*Richard II*, 3.3.143-46). A few lines later he asks, "What says King Bolingbroke? Will his majesty / Give Richard leave to live till Richard die?" (*Richard II*, 3.3.173-74). Bolingbroke, however, kneels before Richard, before leaving to escort him to London. In a brief scene, the queen overhears a gardener telling a servant of Bolingbroke's capture of the king. The gardener compares England to a garden that has been badly kept, overgrown with weeds and crawling with caterpillars (the king's flattering favorites), but the weeds have now been "plucked up root and all by Bolingbroke" (*Richard II*, 3.4.52).

Act 4 consists of a single long scene, set in Parliament, in which Richard's erstwhile supporters (Aumerle and Bagot, primarily) blame each other for Gloucester's death; Bolingbroke hears of Mowbray's death; York, in Richard's name, invites Bolingbroke to take the throne; Richard appears, is formally deposed, and is sent to the Tower. In vain, Aumerle and the Abbott of Westminster hatch an abortive plot to restore him. The scene climaxes with the deposition, in which Richard physically hands the crown to Bolingbroke. Afterward, Richard gazes on his own reflection, asking "Was this the face / Which like the sun did make beholders wink?" before shattering a mirror (*Richard II*, 4.1.282-83).

Act 5 begins with Richard and the queen meeting as he is being taken to the Tower. Northumberland enters with the news that Bolingbroke has changed his mind: Richard is to go not to the Tower but to Pomfret Castle, deep in Lancastrian lands in the north. The queen will return to France. Richard and the queen bid each other farewell tenderly. York discovers his son Aumerle's part in the plot to restore Richard and goes to warn Bolingbroke; Aumerle arrives before him and begs Bolingbroke's forgiveness. Against York's advice, but in deference to the duchess of York's pleas for her son's life, Bolingbroke agrees. Exton, a noble, is told by a servant that Bolingbroke has wished Richard dead. Exton declares, "I am the king's friend, and will rid his foe" (*Richard II*, 5.4.11).

Alone in his cell at Pomfret Castle, Richard reflects on his solitude, considering the thoughts with which he might "people this little world" in which he now finds himself (*Richard II*, 5.5.9). He seems to recognize some degree of complicity in his own passiveness: "I wasted time and now doth time waste me" (*Richard II*, 5.5.49). He is visited by a groom who wants no more than "to look upon [his] sometime royal master's face" but who tells him that his horse Barbary was ridden by Bolingbroke on coronation day without a sign of discomfort at having a new master (*Richard II*, 5.5.75). As the keeper arrives with Richard's food, Richard warns the groom to leave. When the keeper says that Exton has ordered him not to taste the food (for poison), Richard beats him, as Exton and four murderers rush in. Roused to action, Richard kills two of the murderers before Exton strikes him down. With his last words, Richard curses Exton and commends his own soul to heaven. In a brief final scene, Bolingbroke banishes Exton, yet admits that he wished Richard dead and acknowledges his own guilt.

The idea of England as a nation. Two centuries separated Shakespeare from the events of *Richard II,* and during those years England was transformed from a medieval feudal society into a modern nation-state. As the critic E. M. W. Tillyard has noted, Shakespeare uses stylized motifs throughout the play in order to lend it a "medieval feel" that would seem authentic to his audience: death as a monarch holding court, in Richard's speech quoted above, for example, or the highly ritualized ceremonial challenges traded by Mowbray and Bolingbroke in Act 1.

Knights, chivalric ritual, references to the Crusades, stately ceremonial speeches (especially in Act 1)—in Tillyard's words, the effect of such elements is "just like a medieval illumination" (Tillyard in Newlin, p. 36). Richard himself, Tillyard observes, is "the last king of the old medieval order," the last of those in the direct line of undisputed succession descended from William the Conqueror (Tillyard in Newlin p. 32). In his struggles with those who would limit his power, the historical Richard relied more than his predecessors on the medieval concept that kings rule by divine right; Shakespeare repeatedly has his Richard invoke the same principle. Bolingbroke, the usurper, represents the new order, a world in which a king in some sense would have to earn his title rather than rely solely and exclusively on the divine sanction of his birth. As a character, he anticipates the later plays in the history cycle, moving away from what Tillyard calls "the essential medievalism of *Richard II*" (Tillyard in Newlin, p. 37).

POETRY AND *RICHARD II*

Richard II was reportedly a poet himself, though not an accomplished one, and he is known to have patronized the great poets of his age, most notably Geoffrey Chaucer (who also died in 1400). On a visit to England in 1395, the French chronicler Jean Froissart presented Richard with a book of poems in French, which Richard spoke fluently. An inscription on Richard's tomb even compares him to the Greek poet Homer, leading some to speculate that the king must indeed have been a poet. Shakespeare may have had these facts in mind when creating his own character for the medieval king, a character that critics praised as the most poetic of his tragic figures before *Hamlet* (1600-1601).

The medieval world conspicuously lacked the idea of national identity; to modern historians it is precisely in his use of this idea in the play that Shakespeare imposes an Elizabethan outlook on its medieval picture. In the feudal world there was no national identity as such. Feudal allegiances were based on service to a liege lord, not on any notion of duty to one's king or country. The idea of "country" in this sense did not exist, for England in Richard II's day was a loose web of feudal obligations, only some of which were to the king. As duke of Lancaster, for example,

John of Gaunt held an absolute authority in his duchy that superseded even the king's. Gaunt's famous apostrophe to England is Elizabethan, not medieval, in its conception of England as a tight little "fortress," a "happy breed of men," a "little world" protected by the "moat defensive" of the Channel and the North Atlantic (*Richard II*, 2.1.45, 48). Such ideas had arisen only after the dramatic failure of the Spanish Armada in 1588, which had occurred a mere seven years before the play was written (and was intended by the Spanish king to secure Elizabeth's deposition). An Englishman of the fourteenth century was not primarily an Englishman—he was above all a Yorkshireman, or a Cornishman, or a Kentishman.

Even the Hundred Years' War, in which historians have often seen national feeling beginning to take shape, was waged for feudal reasons (such as the English kings' inherited claims to French land), not for anything we would recognize as national interest. Down to Edward III's time, in fact, English kings spoke French, which was part of their Norman heritage. Gaunt's view of England in the play arises from historical circumstances particular to Elizabeth's day, in which Protestant England saw itself as a new Israel, surrounded by and heroically resisting powerful Catholic enemies. Yet Shakespeare's importation of Elizabethan national sentiment into the feudal world of his history plays has been highly influential in shaping our view of the past. As historian E. R. Lander has suggested, it was in this Elizabethan context that "Shakespeare invented the long popular tradition of a nation in arms behind the king" (Lander, p. 54).

Sources and literary context. As for all of his history plays, Shakespeare's most important source for *Richard II* was Raphael Holinshed's popular *Chronicles of England, Scotlande and Irelande* (published in 1577, with a second edition in 1587). Other sources included the medieval French chronicler Jean Froissart (available in an English translation by Lord Berners in 1523-25); the early Tudor historian Edward Hall, author of an influential work entitled *The Union of the Two Noble and Illustre Fameiles of Lancastre and York* (1542; enlarged 1548, 1550); and Samuel Daniel's *The First Fowre Bookes of the Civile Warres* (an epic poem on the Wars of the Roses published starting in 1595). Though Shakespeare generally follows Holinshed's account closely, he also departs from it to serve his dramatic purposes. He invents or adapts some events and characters, compresses sequences that took place over days into single scenes, and heightens some events while omitting others. The most obvious departure from Holinshed is the part of the queen. In Holinshed, Richard's actual queen, Isabella of France, was about ten years old at the time of his deposition, but Shakespeare follows Daniel in portraying her as a mature woman. The royal couple's scenes together, and the love the queen expresses for her king, help Shakespeare develop Richard's character from the arbitrary tyrant of the first half of the play into the more sympathetic and morally aware figure of the second half. Of events that Shakespeare compresses, the most obvious example is Act 2 Scene 1, in which Gaunt gives his famous apostrophe to England, exits, and is revealed to have died only a few lines later; Richard seizes his estate; and Bolingbroke is said to be already on his way to contest the seizure.

The popularity of *Richard II* and works such as Daniel's show that the conflict between the Lancasters and Yorks could be shaped into story that would grip Elizabethan (and later) audiences. Revealingly, the white (York) or red (Lancaster) rose was only one of several heraldic symbols associated with each house, and the association was not a standard literary device until Henry VII invented the Tudor double rose (white and red) to symbolize his uniting of the two houses. Shakespeare popularized the association, which soon became a fixture of English literature, but the name "Wars of the Roses" did not come into general use until the nineteenth century.

Events in History at the Time the Play Was Written

Elizabeth and Richard II. Parallels between Elizabeth I and Richard II occurred to the queen's contemporaries strikingly early in her long reign, which lasted from 1558 until her death in 1603. Like Richard, the queen was known for surrounding herself with trusted favorites. In 1578, she apparently rebuked one of these advisors, Sir Francis Knollys, who had given her advice that (for an unknown reason) she did not like. In a letter of January 9, Knollys responded that he refused to "play the partes of King Richard the Second's men" by offering only flattery (Newlin, p. 14). Ten years later, another courtier, Henry, Lord Hunsworth, wrote in similar circumstances that he "was never one of Richard II's men" (Newlin, p. 14). Then in July 1597, almost two years after the earliest productions of *Richard II*, one of Elizabeth's courtiers, Sir Walter Raleigh,

wrote to another, Sir Robert Cecil, about a third courtier, the earl of Essex:

> I acquaynted . . . [Essex] with your letter to mee & your kynd acceptance of your enterteyne-mente, hee was also wonderful merry att ye consait of Richard the 2. I hope it shall never alter, & whereof I shalbe most gladd of as the trew way to all our good, quiett & advance-ment, and most of all for her sake whose affaires shall therby fynd better progression. (Raleigh in Newlin, p. 14)

The gist of this enigmatic reference seems to be a humorous comparison (or "consait," conceit) between Richard and Elizabeth—and that, like Richard's, Elizabeth's courtiers knew how to flatter in order to secure their own "good, quiett & advancement." The "enterteynemente" may have been a private performance of Shakespeare's play.

Censorship and rebellion. Such parallels were no doubt behind the censorship, in all printed versions of the play produced during Elizabeth's lifetime, of the long deposition scene (Act 4). Unlike Richard's, Elizabeth's title to the throne was quite shaky. Her most famous rival, Mary Queen of Scots, had been executed in 1587; like Bolingbroke, Mary was a cousin of the monarch and was close (next, in Mary's case) in line of succession. While it seems that in performances the deposition scene was retained, the deposing of a monarch was considered too volatile a subject for portrayal in the printed version.

The parallels between the two monarchs were vividly illustrated by events in February 1601, when the earl of Essex (who had fallen from favor) rebelled in an attempt to depose the queen and seize the throne himself. Significantly, his best claim to legitimacy was his descent from the same duke of Gloucester that Richard II was supposed to have had murdered. On the evening before the rebellion, the earl and his supporters commissioned a special performance of *Richard II* at the Globe theater, probably in the hope that Londoners would support Elizabeth's deposition as they did that of the play's Richard. The rebellion was quickly crushed, and the performance was used as evidence at Essex's trial. Shakespeare and his colleagues did not suffer as a result; on the contrary, on the day before Essex's execution, they performed in front of the queen. However, later that year Elizabeth was heard to remark, "I am Richard II, know ye not that?" (Newlin, p. 15).

Reception. In the same conversation, the queen referred to *Richard II* as having been performed 40 times "in open streets and houses" (Newlin,

p. 16). While no records survive, if this refers to the original production, it was an exceptionally long run for an Elizabethan play. Regardless, it is known from contemporary references that *Richard II* was one of Shakespeare's most successful plays in original production, as it has remained ever since. It was printed in three quartos in 1597 and 1598; in the latter year the author Francis Meres, surveying the state of literature in England, called it "foremost among the tragedies of the day" (Meres in Shewring, p. 24). (The term "quarto" designates not only the size of a volume—the standard paper is folded twice instead of once [folio]—but also, in Shakespeare's case, designates the plays [18] published in his lifetime.) Six passages (including three excerpts from Gaunt's apostrophe) were anthologized in the popular collection *England's Parnassus* (1600). The deposition scene was not printed until the Fourth Quarto of 1608, five years after Elizabeth's death.

—Colin Wells

For More Information

Bullough, Geoffrey, ed. *Narrative and Dramatic Sources of Shakespeare*. Vol. 3. New York: Columbia University Press, 1960.

Davies, R. G., and J. H. Denton, eds. *The English Parliament in the Middle Ages*. Manchester: Manchester University Press, 1981.

Lander, J. R. *Conflict and Stability in Fifteenth Century England*. London: Hutchinson, 1977.

Lockyer, Roger. *Tudor & Stuart Britain 1471-1714*. Harlow, England: Longman, 1964.

McKisack, May. *The Fourteenth Century*. Oxford: Oxford University Press, 1959.

Moseley, C. W. R. D. *Shakespeare's History Plays: Richard II to Henry IV, The Making of a King*. London: Penguin, 1988.

Muir, Kenneth. *The Sources of Shakespeare's Plays*. London: Methuen, 1977.

Newlin, Jeanne T., ed. *Richard II: Critical Essays*. New York: Garland, 1984.

Saccio, Peter. *Shakespeare's English Kings*. New York: Oxford University Press, 1977.

Saul, Nigel. *Richard II*. New Haven: Yale University Press, 1997.

Shakespeare, William. *King Richard II*. Ed. Andrew Gurr. New Cambridge Shakespeare. Cambridge: Cambridge University Press, 1984.

Shewring, Margaret. *King Richard II. Shakespeare in Performance Series*. New York: Manchester University Press, 1996.

The Rivals

by

Richard Brinsley Sheridan

THE LITERARY WORK

A play set in Bath in the eighteenth century; performed and published in 1775.

SYNOPSIS

A wealthy young man poses as a poor soldier to win the heart of an excessively romantic young woman.

Born in Dublin, Ireland, in 1751, Richard Brinsley Sheridan was the second son of Thomas Sheridan, an actor and theater manager, and of Frances Chamberlaine Sheridan, a playwright and novelist. His father was Irish, his mother of English ancestry, and Sheridan took pride in both heritages. The O'Sheridans, as his father's family was originally called, converted in the seventeenth century from the Catholic faith to Protestantism. As a boy, Richard attended Samuel Whyte's grammar school in Dublin, then became a student at Harrow, a famous boarding school in England. In 1768, two years after his mother's death, Sheridan left Harrow and rejoined his family, who by this time lived in Soho, England. In late 1770, the family moved to Bath, where Thomas Sheridan had founded a new Academy of Oratory, a project with which both his sons were expected to assist. During this time, Richard Sheridan met 16-year-old Elizabeth Ann Linley, a musician's daughter, reputed to be one the best singers of her day. The couple married in 1773, Sheridan defying his father, who had ordered him to forget Elizabeth and study for a career in law. Sheridan decided instead to become a playwright. In 1774 he began writing his first play, *The Rivals*, which premiered on January 17, 1775, at Covent Garden Theatre. The play was not an instant success; audiences found parts of the comedy too coarse and the whole production too long. Undaunted, Sheridan revised it. A second performance—11 nights later—fared far better, and the play enjoyed a successful run for the rest of the season. Embedded in its comedy is a satiric portrayal of high society, keenly executed by the 23-year-old Sheridan.

Events in History at the Time of the Play

High society in Bath. Sheridan's decision to have *The Rivals* take place in Bath, as opposed to London, which was a favorite setting of eighteenth-century comedies, gives his play a unique atmosphere and appeal. "Bath had a strong hold on the imagination of the time as a place of pleasure and romance. Young people longed to go there because of the many opportunities Bath offered for meeting members of the opposite sex, for dancing, flirting and perhaps falling in love" (Macklin in Sheridan, p. xviii). Sheridan, having met his future bride in Bath, could testify to the truth of its attraction for the young.

The city of Bath was set in a hollow, encircled by hills, and the Avon River flowed through the center of town. Owing to its natural hot springs, Bath had long been established as a spa; its first

Many Europeans traveled to Bath for its healing waters.

public baths were built during Roman times. In the Middle Ages, the ill and infirm came to bathe in the waters, which were thought to have healing properties. An elaborate abbey was constructed there in the fifteenth century but ultimately abandoned in the sixteenth century after Henry VIII shut down all the monasteries. During the sixteenth and seventeenth centuries, Bath became known mainly as a spa or "watering-place" again, and its popularity as a fashionable resort increased after Queen Anne visited the city in 1702, the year she ascended to the throne.

During the eighteenth century, Bath underwent major reconstruction and expansion to accommodate the increasing number of tourists flocking to the city for social or medicinal reasons. Streets were cleaned and paved, and elaborate new buildings—lodging houses, lending libraries, a hospital, a pump-room where invalids could drink the waters in peace—were constructed. The famous architect, John Wood (1705-1754), and his son, John Wood the Younger (1728-1782), designed many of these new structures, including the North and South Parades (two new streets by the river, where visitors could take leisurely walks or could frequent nearby coffee houses), the Royal Crescent (a curving terrace of elegant houses built on a hillside overlooking the city), and Assembly Rooms (where tourists gathered for parties and balls).

While the Woods and other architects transformed the city of Bath physically, Richard "Beau" Nash transformed it socially. A London dandy, Nash first arrived in Bath in 1705 and was appalled by the dirt and disorder there. When the current Master of Ceremonies, Captain Webster, was killed in a duel over a gambling dispute, Nash succeeded to the position, which entailed coordinating the community's entertainment activities and social events. The new "King of Bath" took his responsibilities very seriously, introducing a rigorous code of dress and conduct that he expected all visitors to follow. Historian George Gadd summarizes Nash's major precepts:

> Informal dress, and in particular riding boots and aprons, were banned from public assemblies. Gambling was brought under a degree of control. [Nash] forbade duelling and even the wearing of swords in the city. He insisted that balls should end on the stroke of eleven. He issued a code of rules to cover the less-clear aspects of social demeanor. . . . The strange thing is that the majority of visitors, however high their rank, accepted the rules laid down by Nash and generally with a good grace.
>
> (Gadd, p. 29)

Although Nash died in 1761, some 14 years before *The Rivals* premiered, his influence was still felt in Bath, where his code of conduct remained in effect. In the play, Jack Absolute's manservant, Fag, apprises Thomas Coachman of the unique character of Bath:

> In the morning we go to the pump-room (though neither my master nor I drink the waters); after breakfast we saunter on the parades or play a game of billiards; at night we dance: but damn the place, I'm tired of it: their regular hours stupefy me—not a fiddle nor a card after eleven!
>
> (Sheridan, *The Rivals*, p. 13)

Later, Jack himself comments on the city's anti-weapons laws when he goes to meet Sir Lucius O'Trigger in a likewise forbidden duel: "A sword seen in the streets of Bath would raise as great an alarm as a mad dog" (*The Rivals*, p. 90).

Dueling. The climax of *The Rivals* involves a duel, a practice conducted with great pomp and spectacle before the fifteenth century. By the time of *The Rivals*, though, duels were fought mainly in private to settle a quarrel between gentlemen.

Offenses meriting a formal challenge to a duel included striking or slandering one's future opponent: accusing a man of lying was considered the worst of insults. The offended party issued his challenge, either in person or by letter, and offered the offender a choice of weapons, usually swords or pistols. The duelists, accompanied by "seconds" (friends chosen to assist them), then met at the appointed time and place, where they fought until one of them was defeated or killed or both professed themselves satisfied with the outcome and called a halt to the proceedings.

One historian reckons "that in the reign of George III (1760-1820) 172 duels were recorded, in which 69 men were killed and 96 wounded, 46 of them desperately" (Rush, p. 61). No doubt Sheridan's own bloody encounter with Captain Thomas Mathews was counted among these duels. In 1772 Sheridan and his then-sweetheart, Elizabeth Linley, ran away to France—some biographers contend they were secretly wed there—to escape the unwelcome attentions being paid her by Mathews, a married acquaintance. Sheridan and Mathews fought two duels over Linley later that year; during the second, both men sustained serious wounds. Sheridan's wounds were the more severe; he was carried from the field covered in blood, his face badly beaten from the hilt of Mathews's sword, and with part of Mathews's blade sticking through his ear. To the amazement of all, he made a full recovery and even satirized dueling in *The Rivals* through his depiction of the blood-thirsty Sir Lucius O'Trigger. A veteran of several duels, Sir Lucius challenges Jack Absolute because of a jest the latter makes about Ireland, then later alarms neophyte duelist Bob Acres by advising him to let his opponent "see the broad side of your full-front" because "a [pistol] ball or two may pass clean through your body, and never do any harm at all" (*The Rivals*, p. 95).

The Irish—onstage and offstage. At the time *The Rivals* takes place, Ireland had been an English possession in all but name for more than 200 years. After breaking with the Roman Catholic Church and establishing his own Church of England, Henry VIII brought all of Ireland under the English Crown and declared himself head of the Church of Ireland as well. For generations to come, bitter disputes would rage between the Protestant English and the predominantly Catholic Irish; England, however, remained in control. From 1695 to 1728, the British Parliament enacted penal laws, oppressive statutes that prevented Catholics from voting, holding public

While Sheridan satirizes dueling in the play, he himself incurred serious wounds in 1772 when he fought two duels over his sweetheart, Elizabeth Linley.

office, serving in the military, teaching, or practicing law. Catholic priests were forbidden to conduct services unless they forswore allegiance to the Catholic Stuarts, the exiled royal family. During the eighteenth century, thousands of Irish Catholic farming families lived in poverty and near starvation, while a small number of newly rich Anglo-Irish Protestants prospered in the countryside and the town of Dublin, or as absentee landlords in England.

The sons of ambitious or well-to-do Irish families were usually sent to England to be educated, some of them becoming more English than Irish in the process. Others retained a patriotic loyalty to their native Ireland. Though of Anglo-Irish heritage and educated in England, Sheridan took a significant interest in the welfare of his native country. He, like a few others in his day, balked at old stereotypes. Over time, prejudice had given rise to an image of the average Irishman as a violent, drunken lout with a laughable accent. Another, more positive image had developed too, that of the rebellious Irish patriot. Radicals in England admired this rebellious spirit, and English edicts that penalized the Irish Catholics began changing. There was a partial reversal of the penal laws, thanks to the Catholic Relief Acts (1774-1793), first passed the year before Sheridan's play debuted. By 1793, Ireland's Catholics could buy land, practice law, vote, and marry a Protestant. But they still suffered restrictions.

They could practice law, for example, but could not become judges.

The ambivalence with which the English regarded the Irish in real life is reflected in the depiction of Irish characters in late-eighteenth-century drama. The Irish were often portrayed in keeping with the stereotype, as drunken, quarrelsome louts. But after the 1750s, they took on a softer, blander aspect. In Sheridan's first version of *The Rivals*, his Irish character, Sir Lucius, was a coarser, less attractive man, and more mercenary and bloodthirsty. The opening-night audience reacted negatively, many feeling this portrayal to be a slur on the Irish. This unfavorable reaction prompted Sheridan to reinvent the character, which he did to great effect; subsequent audiences found appealing Sir Lucius's "glib tongue, swaggering courage, and . . . good natured honor" (Auburn, p. 56). In his introduction to *The Rivals*, Sheridan wrote that he truly had not intended "any national reflection in Sir Lucius O'Trigger," but added:

> If any gentleman opposed the piece from that idea, I thank them sincerely for their opposition; and if the condemnation of this comedy (however misconceived the provocation) could have added one spark to the decaying flame of national attachment to the country supposed to be reflected on, I should have been happy in its fate; and might with truth have boasted, that it had done more real service in its failure, than the successful morality of a thousand stage-novels will ever effect.
>
> (*The Rivals*, p. 4)

Marriage. Like many eighteenth-century comedies, *The Rivals* deals with marriage, an institution that was in a state of flux at the time of the play. In earlier centuries, marriages among propertied classes were usually arranged by the parents of the future bride and groom. Wealthy, landed families sought to ally their children with mates who possessed similar or superior material advantages.

> The choice of marriage partner concerned both boys and girls and was especially important in a society where there were large financial and political stakes in marriage and where divorce was virtually impossible. Almost all children until the end of the sixteenth century were so conditioned by their upbringing and so financially helpless that they acquiesced without much objection in the matches contrived for them by their parents.
>
> (Stone, p. 182)

Children whose affections strayed in less appropriate directions, toward less suitable mar-

riage partners, were often sternly rebuked by their parents and even threatened with disinheritance if they married without parental consent.

During the seventeenth and eighteenth centuries, however, significant sociological changes, such as the increasing importance of the nuclear family, shifted the balance of power. In all but the most aristocratic families, parents were more willing to consider factors other than money and property when it came to arranging marriages, such as personal affection and physical attraction between the prospective spouses. This undoubtedly was due in part to contemporary writers and thinkers who, from the 1680s to the 1740s, advanced the cause of marriage for love by criticizing the alternative. Writing for **The Spectator** (also covered in *WLAIT 3: British and Irish Literature and Its Times*), Daniel Defoe championed the importance of personal affection: "Forcing to marry is, in the plain consequences, not only forcing to crime, but furnishing an excuse to crime," and "where there is no pre-engagement of the affection before marriage, what can be expected after it? . . . There is not one in ten of those kinds of marriages that survives" (Defoe in Stone, p. 276). Less directly, sentimental novels, which became increasingly popular in the late eighteenth century, probably encouraged (and also reflected) the shift toward marriage based on romantic love. In 1773, two years before *The Rivals* debuted, a writer for *The Lady's Magazine* complained: "There is scarce a young lady in the kingdom who has not read with avidity a great number of romances and novels, which tend to vitiate the taste" (Stone, p. 283).

In *The Rivals*, Sheridan explores several aspects of the generational conflict over arranged marriages. Flighty Lydia, who forfeits two-thirds of her vast fortune if she weds without her aunt's consent, seeks romantic guidance from the sentimental novels her maid smuggles to her. Meanwhile, the autocratic Sir Anthony Absolute threatens to disown and disinherit his son, Jack, if the latter refuses to wed the bride Sir Anthony has chosen for him. An equally furious Jack fumes that his father is a hypocrite because "he himself married for love, and was in his youth a bold intriguer, and a gay companion!" (*The Rivals*, p. 39).

The Play in Focus

Plot summary. The play begins when two servants who work for the Absolute family meet by chance on a street in Bath. Thomas, a coachman, tells Fag, a manservant, that his master—Sir Anthony Absolute—has come to Bath with a party of friends and relatives in hopes of curing his gout. Fag, who serves Sir Anthony's son, Captain Jack Absolute, confides in his fellow servant that Jack has been posing as Ensign Beverley, a penniless soldier, to court Lydia Languish, an heiress with a large fortune and a head full of romantic fantasies. The disguised Jack must also contend with Lydia's "old tough aunt," Mrs. Malaprop, who must consent to the match if Lydia is to retain her fortune (*The Rivals*, p. 12). Mystified by the captain's masquerade, Thomas nonetheless wishes him well in his courtship of Lydia; the two servants then part to attend to their separate business.

Meanwhile, at Mrs. Malaprop's lodging, Lydia greets her newly returned maid, Lucy, with demands for the latest sentimental novels. As Lucy unpacks her finds for her impatient mistress, Lydia's cousin, Julia Melville, enters. Recently a guest at Sir Anthony Absolute's Devonshire estate, Julia has traveled with the baronet to Bath to visit her family and her betrothed, Faulkland. Lydia eagerly confides in Julia the details of her own romance with "Beverley," a romance that Mrs. Malaprop has just discovered and is now attempting to thwart by confining Lydia to the house. Lydia, however, is determined to elope with her unsuitable suitor, even though she will lose most of her fortune if she marries without her aunt's consent. When Julia expresses disapproval of her cousin's caprice, Lydia points out that Julia herself is betrothed to the equally capricious Faulkland. Julia defends her beloved, saying that his whims spring from insecurity.

On learning that Sir Anthony and Mrs. Malaprop are coming up the stairs, Julia makes a quick exit and Lydia hastily hides her new novels as her aunt enters. Mrs. Malaprop once again demands that Lydia renounce Beverley but the girl refuses and is sent to her room as punishment. Sir Anthony and Mrs. Malaprop then discuss a possible betrothal between Lydia and Sir Anthony's son, Jack, whom neither aunt nor niece has met. The baronet is certain he can persuade his sometimes rebellious son to agree to the match. After Sir Anthony leaves, Mrs. Malaprop dithers over her own infatuation with Sir Lucius O'Trigger, an Irish baronet with whom she has been corresponding under the name of "Delia." Summoning Lucy, Mrs. Malaprop entrusts the maid with another letter for Sir Lucius. Alone, however, Lucy reveals that she has been playing all sides against each other—conspiring with the young lovers, betraying them to Mrs. Malaprop, deceiving Sir Lucius into thinking he was courting Lydia and not her aunt—for her own gain.

THE SENTIMENTAL NOVEL

In *The Rivals*, Lydia and her maid mention the titles of several authentic sentimental novels. While many are unknown to modern readers, a few—such as Lawrence Sterne's *The Sentimental Journey* (1768) and Tobias Smollett's *The Expedition of Humphrey Clinker* (1771) and *The Adventures of Peregrine Pickle* (1751)—survive to the present day, offering a testament to eighteenth-century popular taste. *The Adventures of Peregrine Pickle* contains a long interpolation titled "The Memoirs of a Lady of Quality, written by herself," describing a young woman's many amorous adventures. The narrator of this episode relates the colorful details of her elopement at the age of 15, in terms that would certainly have appealed to the highly romantic Lydia Languish:

> I ran upstairs in a state of trepidation, to my faithful lover, who waited for me with the most impatient and fearful suspense. At sight of me his eyes lightened with transport; he caught me in his arms, as the richest present Heaven could bestow . . . then applauding my love and resolution in the most rapturous terms, he ordered a hackney-coach to be called, and, that we might run no risk of separation, attended me to church, where we were lawfully joined in the sight of heaven.
>
> (Smollett, vol. 2, p. 40)

At his lodgings, Captain Jack Absolute learns from Fag of his father's arrival in Bath, then receives a visit from his friend and Julia's betrothed, Faulkland, who knows of his courtship of Lydia. Faulkland urges Jack to make his true identity known to both Lydia and Mrs. Malaprop, but Jack is determined not to reveal himself to Lydia until he is sure of her affection and her fortune. The conversation turns to Faulkland's own relationship with the absent Julia, about whose welfare he is deeply concerned. "O! Jack," declares Faulkland, "when delicate and feeling souls are separated, there is not a movement in the elements; not an aspiration of the breeze, but hints some cause for a lover's apprehension!" (*The Rivals*, p. 28). Jack reassures his friend that Julia is in good health and has just arrived in Bath with

Sir Anthony. Moments later, Bob Acres, a country neighbor of the Absolutes and another of Lydia's would-be suitors, calls upon Jack and sends Faulkland into a jealous frenzy by thoughtlessly describing how much Julia enjoyed herself while in Devonshire. Faulkland storms out, to Jack's amusement and Acres's confusion. Acres then confides in Jack about Lydia's suitor Beverley, unaware that they are the same man. After Acres leaves, Jack receives a visit from Sir Anthony and learns that his father has chosen a bride for him. Appalled, Jack protests that his affections are already engaged, but a furious Sir Anthony threatens him with disinheritance unless he obeys his father's wishes. Not knowing the identity of the girl and picturing some "old, wealthy hag," Jack refuses to consent to the arrangement; father and son part in anger (*The Rivals*, p. 39).

Jack soon learns, however, that Lydia is the bride Sir Anthony has chosen for him and that he has become his own rival. The captain quickly regains his place in his father's good graces with a show of penitence while privately resolving to carry on with his masquerade as Beverley for Lydia's sake. As Jack Absolute, he presents himself to Mrs. Malaprop—thus receiving her leave to court her niece—but manages to convince Lydia that he is actually Ensign Beverley posing as Jack Absolute. Mrs. Malaprop, eavesdropping on the lovers, is confused by what she hears of their conversation and fails to unravel Jack's deceit.

Elsewhere in Bath, Acres complains of Ensign Beverley to Sir Lucius, who urges him to challenge his unseen rival to a duel. Never having fought a duel, Acres feels squeamish about the prospect; nonetheless, he composes a letter of challenge, which he entrusts to his old friend Jack Absolute, to deliver to Beverley. Jack soon faces a more immediate problem when he is forced to meet Lydia in his father's company. Despite a last attempt at subterfuge, his charade collapses and Lydia discovers that her impoverished ensign really is the son of a wealthy baronet. Finally found out, Jack confesses all, but only Sir Anthony is amused. Disappointed in her dreams of a romantic elopement, Lydia bursts into tears and refuses to have anything to do with her former lover.

Later, Sir Lucius tracks Jack down and challenges him to a duel for some jest he made about Ireland. Still smarting over Lydia's rejection, a foul-tempered Jack accepts the challenge; the two men agree to meet that evening in Kingsmead Fields at six o'clock. Parting from Sir Lucius, Jack meets Faulkland, despondent over

a quarrel with Julia, and asks him to act as his second. While they are talking, a servant delivers a letter from Julia to Faulkland, who hurries off to see her. His insecurities, however, lead him to test Julia's devotion again, this time by claiming he has killed someone in a duel and must flee the country. When Julia immediately offers to accompany him, Faulkland rejoices to have "proved [her] to the quick" and resolves to repay her steadfastness with "years of tender adoration" (*The Rivals*, pp. 83-84). But, on learning that Faulkland has once more tried to test her, Julia breaks off their engagement: "I now see that it is not in your nature to be content, or confident in love. With this conviction—I never will be yours" (*The Rivals*, p. 84). Left alone, Faulkland laments his jealous folly.

Meanwhile, Lydia broods over her past romance with Beverley and sulks over Jack's deceit. Depressed over her own parting with Faulkland, Julia urges her cousin to appreciate the sincere love of a man and not to be ruled by caprice. Suddenly, Mrs. Malaprop, Fag, and David—Acres's manservant—burst into the room with the news that Jack, Acres, and Sir Lucius are all involved in a duel. Alarmed, the entire party heads to Kingsmead Fields. On his way to the duel, Jack encounters Sir Anthony, who discovers the weapons his son is carrying but fails to guess their purpose until Jack has left. Informed by David of the duel, Sir Anthony joins the others.

At Kingsmead Fields, Sir Lucius unnerves Acres by discussing gunshot wounds at length. When Jack and Faulkland arrive, the other men are astounded to learn that Jack is indeed Ensign Beverley. Acres now refuses to fight his "dear friend Jack Absolute," to the disgust of Sir Lucius, who pronounces him a coward. Drawing their swords, Jack and Sir Lucius prepare to duel but are interrupted by Sir Anthony, Mrs. Malaprop, Lydia, and the others. The last skeins of the plot unravel—Lydia confesses her love for Jack; Sir Lucius learns he has been corresponding with Mrs. Malaprop instead of Lydia and hastens to disentangle himself; and Julia, spying a penitent Faulkland, decides to forgive him after all. Sir Anthony soothes Mrs. Malaprop's wounded feelings, while Acres, relieved at not having to fight any duels, calls for fiddles and entertainment in the Bath assembly rooms to celebrate the union of the two couples.

An excess of sensibility. The composition and setting of *The Rivals* coincides with the "Age of Sensibility," the half-century or so between the

COMICAL WORDPLAY

Sheridan's use of wordplay—especially in the names of his characters—contributes greatly to the comedy in his works. Indeed, modern critics compare Sheridan's name choices to those found in Elizabethan comedies of humors, in which characters' names corresponded to their most salient traits. *The Rivals* features such characters as Sir Anthony Absolute—who is "absolute," even somewhat tyrannical, in his determination to choose his son's bride—and Lydia Languish, who "languishes" or pines over sentimental novels. Jack's manservant, Fag, toils or "fags" for him. Bob Acres, Lydia's country bumpkin suitor, has only his property or "acres" to commend him as a matrimonial catch. And the pugnacious Sir Lucius O'Trigger is always eager to pursue a quarrel (in modern parlance, he could be considered "trigger-happy"). Arguably, the most famous of Sheridan's characters in *The Rivals* is Mrs. Malaprop, whose name is derived from the French phrase *mal à propos*, meaning "inappropriate." Mrs. Malaprop's speech is consistently inappropriate: Julia observes her "select words so ingeniously misapplied, without being mispronounced" (*The Rivals*, p. 19). Mrs. Malaprop's frequent substitution of the wrong word for the one she means to use results in statements that are at once pretentious and nonsensical, such as her speech on the proper education of a young lady:

I would send her . . . to a boarding school, in order to learn a little ingenuity and artifice. Then, Sir, she should have a supercilious knowledge in accounts; and as she grew up, I would have her instructed in geometry, that she might know something of the contagious countries; but above all . . . she should be mistress of orthodoxy, that she might not mis-spell, and mis-pronounce words so shamefully as girls usually do; and likewise that she might reprehend the true meaning of what she is saying.

(*The Rivals*, p. 22)

Appropriately enough, the type of error in speech Mrs. Malaprop continually commits found its way into everyday English as the word "malapropism."

death of Alexander Pope in 1744 and the 1798 publication of William Wordsworth and Samuel Taylor Coleridge's **Lyrical Ballads** (also covered in *WLAIT 3: British and Irish Literature and Its Times*). In Sheridan's lifetime, "sensibility" was very similar to what modern readers would call "sensitivity." During the seventeenth century, writers and intellectuals tended to extol the virtues of stoicism, a Greek philosophy maintaining that human beings should be passionless and accept anything that happens as a product of divine will or the natural order. Stoicism emphasized reason and the unemotional will. Some eighteenth-century thinkers, however, came to believe that good will toward others and acute responsiveness—or "sensibility"—to another person's joys and pains were the truest indicators of a virtuous heart and gentle breeding. Those who possessed "exquisite sensibilities" were thought to be intensely affected by beauty—whether in nature or art—and could be moved to sympathetic tears at the sight of another's suffering. Of course, it was possible to carry the idea of "sensibility" too far—as Jane Austen was to argue in her novel **Sense and Sensibility** (1811; also in *WLAIT 3: British and Irish Literature and Its Times*). In fact, many eighteenth-century writers, including Sheridan, made a point of satirizing the excesses of sensibility, showing how over-reliance on the emotions—at the expense of reason—may lead to self-inflicted misery.

The two romantic subplots—Jack and Lydia, Faulkland and Julia—offer compelling contrasts to one another. In the former, Sheridan satirizes the contrived plots and impractical romanticism of the popular sentimental novels to which flighty Lydia is addicted. Such novels (Samuel Richardson's *Clarissa* is one example) generally depicted young lovers rebelling against their parents, communicating secretly by letter, contriving forbidden meetings in remote places, choosing poverty over wealth, and planning elopements that, when successfully executed, signaled the happy ending to their romance. Lydia, who devours such stories, expects Jack to comply with her fantasies, however foolish they seem. In her first scene, Lydia reveals how she has manufactured a quarrel with her lover simply to make their courtship more exciting:

> I wrote a letter to myself, to inform myself that Beverley was at that time paying his addresses to another woman. I signed it *your Friend unknown,* showed it to Beverley, charged him with his falsehood, put myself in a violent passion, and vowed I'd never see him more.
>
> (*The Rivals*, pp. 16-17)

Later, disillusioned by Jack's revelation that he is the son and heir of a wealthy baronet, Lydia pouts over their lost elopement and rhapsodizes over their former trysts:

> How often have I stolen forth in the coldest night in January, and found him in the garden, stuck like a dripping statue! There would he kneel to me in the snow, and sneeze and cough so pathetically! he shivering with cold, and I with apprehension! . . . Ah, Julia! that was something like being in love.
>
> (*The Rivals*, p. 87)

Lydia's foolishness, however, springs as much from her fear that her fortune is the real attraction for her prospective bridegroom as from her overly romantic imagination, a fear heightened by the revelation of Jack's true identity. Referring to the central meat market in London, Lydia indignantly wonders if she is to become "a mere Smithfield bargain at last," sold like a side of beef into matrimony after being duped by her betrothed in the process (*The Rivals*, p. 86). After learning that Jack's life is endangered because he accepted a challenge to a duel while on the outs with her, Lydia finally recognizes her folly and forgives her suitor for the crime of being rich and eligible.

While Sheridan depicts Lydia's faults as arising mainly from her youth and an overfondness for romantic novels, he presents a far more serious case of sensibility run amuck in Faulkland. Moody, volatile, and deeply insecure, Faulkland creates most of his own problems. Temporarily separated from his betrothed, Julia, Faulkland torments himself about her welfare: "I fear for her spirits—her health—her life. My absence

may fret her; her anxiety for my return, her fears for me, may oppress her gentle temper. And for her health—does not every hour bring me cause to be alarmed?" (*The Rivals*, p. 28). The revelation that Julia is well and has been enjoying herself in his absence not only fails to reassure Faulkland; it arouses his jealousy as well. Consequently Faulkland keeps testing Julia's devotion, first by questioning her reasons for accepting his proposal of marriage, then, more dangerously, by pretending that he must go into exile after killing his opponent in a duel. His insecurity costs him the very thing he strives to hold on to; when Julia finally decides to take him back at the end of the play, even she expresses surprise that she still wants him: "Oh! Faulkland, you have not been more faulty in your unkind treatment of me, than I am now in wanting inclination to resent it. As my heart honestly bids me place my weakness to the account of love, I should be ungenerous not to admit the same plea for yours" (*The Rivals*, pp. 100-101).

Jack and Julia provide the necessary correctives to the overwrought imaginations of their loved ones. Although Jack has willingly indulged Lydia's taste for high romance, he has no intention of living in poverty with her; indeed, he sees no reason why he and Lydia should not enjoy a marriage based on both affection and financial security. Thus, Jack's whole motive in masquerading as Ensign Beverley is to please Lydia and to "prepare her gradually for the discovery [of his true identity]" (*The Rivals*, p. 26). Similarly, Julia cherishes the hope that her steadfast love will soothe Faulkland's numerous anxieties and enable him to be happy and secure about their future. In her first scene with Lydia, Julia praises Faulkland's good qualities, calling him "too proud, too noble to be jealous," but she also perceptively analyzes the reasons for his faults: "Yet, though his pride calls for this full return [of love]—his humility makes him undervalue those qualities in him, which would entitle him to it: and not feeling why he should be lov'd to the degree he wishes, he still suspects that he is not lov'd enough" (*The Rivals*, p. 18).

In response to the play, people have expressed strong feelings about the levelheaded Jack and Julia. Sheridan himself believed that Julia's lengthy defense of Faulkland was "the only speech in the play that cannot be omitted" (Sheridan in Auburn, p. 56). Literary scholar Jack D. Durant describes Jack and Julia as "the centers of two actions, one featuring the whole man—practical, sensible, solid—the other the whole woman—gracious, lyric, sensitive" (Durant, p. 81). And, indeed, it is the saner, more emotionally balanced viewpoint of Jack and Julia that ultimately prevails over the excessive sensibilities of Lydia and Faulkland; Julia even has the last word in the play, declaring, "When hearts deserving happiness would unite their fortunes, virtue would crown them with an unfading garland of modest, hurtless flowers; but ill-judging passion will force the gaudier rose into the wreath, whose thorn offends them, when its leaves are dropped!" (The Rivals, p. 102).

Sources and literary context. By the time the 23-year-old Sheridan wrote The Rivals, he had already experienced two duels and a marriage-by-elopement in the face of parental opposition. Not surprisingly, audiences who attended the premiere of Sheridan's first play expected to see something as sensational as the author's life performed on stage. To some extent, Sheridan fulfilled those expectations: there are unmistakable autobiographical echoes in The Rivals. The young lovers, Jack and Lydia, plot an elopement and must battle overbearing guardians who wish to dictate their matrimonial choices. There is even the promise of two duels in the fifth act, though both are aborted—the first through the cowardice of an opponent, the second through the intervention of others. However, as Sheridan's biographer, Fintan O'Toole, points out: "It is no accident that The Rivals, like the Sheridans' life at the time, starts where any ordinary romantic drama would end. The young lovers . . . have already met, courted, fallen in love and agreed to marry. . . . All the complications of the plot hinge upon a mere caprice" (O'Toole, p. 89). The hazards and dangers Sheridan and his bride faced become the stuff of absurd romantic fantasies concocted by the giddy Lydia. Thus, Sheridan simultaneously exploits and satirizes his own colorful history.

Overall, the characters in The Rivals conform mostly to recognizable types in eighteenth-century comedies: the resolute hero (Jack), the innocent heroine (Lydia), the tyrannical father (Sir Anthony), and the country bumpkin (Bob Acres). Mrs. Malaprop, however, was based on Mrs. Tryfort, a character in A Journey to Bath, an unfinished play by Sheridan's mother, Frances. Like her most famous descendant, Mrs. Tryfort also misapplies the English language, invariably choosing the most inaccurate or inappropriate terms to convey her meaning.

Sheridan's play may be viewed not only as partial autobiography or satire but as a reaction to the sentimental comedies—such as Richard Steele's The Conscious Lovers (1722) and Richard Cumberland's The West Indian (1771)—dominating the stage in the late eighteenth century. The Age of Sensibility had produced a literature of sensibility that, while popular with large segments of the audience, was by no means universally loved. In his "Essay on the Theatre; or, A Comparison between Laughing and Sentimental Comedy" (1773), Oliver Goldsmith mounted an outright attack on the genre, complaining that "the virtues of private life [charity, forgiveness, benevolence] are exhibited, rather than the vices exposed; and the distresses rather than the faults of mankind make our interest in the piece" (Goldsmith in McMillin, p. 188). Warming to his theme, Goldsmith continued,

> In this manner we are likely to lose one great source of entertainment on the stage; for while the comic poet is invading the province of the tragic muse, he leaves her lovely sister quite neglected. . . . It is not easy to recover an art when once lost, and it will be but a just punishment, that when, by our being too fastidious, we have banished humour from the stage, we should ourselves be deprived of the art of laughing.
> (Goldsmith in McMillin, pp. 388-389, 390)

SHERIDAN AND THE COMPETITION

Rivalries ran high and hot between many eighteenth-century dramatists, who often attacked one another in print. Sheridan himself was later to target several rivals in his satiric farce The Critic (1779), including Richard Cumberland, a playwright known for his heavy-handed sentimental comedies and dramas. Cumberland, for his part, thoroughly resented Sheridan's success. One famous anecdote recounts how Cumberland's children pestered him to take them to see Sheridan's The School for Scandal, which had been hailed enthusiastically by critics and audiences alike. When the children laughed at the play, Cumberland pinched them, inquiring loudly, "What are you laughing at my dear little folks? You should not laugh, my angels; there is nothing to laugh at," then adding, under his breath, "Keep still, you little dunces" (Cumberland in O'Toole, p. 152). When the story got back to Sheridan, he remarked that Cumberland was very ungrateful to keep the children from laughing at his comedy: "For I went the other night to see his tragedy and laughed at it from beginning to end." (Sheridan in O'Toole, p. 152)

In the heavy hands of sentimental playwrights, comedy, Goldsmith felt, had ceased to be *funny*. Goldsmith's own artistic response to sentimental comedy was to write **She Stoops to Conquer,** a decidedly unsentimental, even farcical "laughing comedy" that debuted at Covent Garden Theatre in 1773. *The Rivals* followed closely in its footsteps; Sheridan even composed a special prologue, early in his play's run, arguing that comedy should be kept free of sentimentality. Praising the Comic Muse as "adorned with every graceful art / To charm the fancy and yet reach the heart," Sheridan asked, "Must we displace her? And instead advance / The goddess of the woeful countenance— / The sentimental muse!" (*The Rivals*, p. 8). While less bawdy and licentious than Restoration comedies of manners, *The Rivals* attempts to recapture the wit and ridicule of plays such as Congreve's **The Way of the World** (also in *WLAIT 3: British and Irish Literature and Its Times*). In keeping with the taste of contemporary audiences, however, *The Rivals* also presented characters who were fundamentally good-natured and lovable, despite their foibles. Indeed, Goldsmith and Sheridan are often credited together for reviving the "laughing comedy" as a viable genre.

Reception. The premiere of *The Rivals* took place on January 17, 1775, and was not a success. The consensus was that the play at this point was an hour too long, too poorly acted, and too crude because of the cursing and a few bawdy remarks. Apparently, several of the actors, especially Ned Shuter (Sir Anthony Absolute) and John Lee (Sir Lucius O'Trigger), gave sub-par performances. Demonstrating disapproval of Lee's performance, a spectator threw an apple at him during the fifth act, prompting the enraged actor to break character and address his tormentor: "By the powers, is it personal? Is it me or the matter?" (Lee in Sherwin, p. 116). The general consensus among the newspapers was that it was both: Lee and Sir Lucius were singled out for the most adverse criticism. The *Morning Chronicle* wondered, "What evil spirit could influence the writer and manager to assign the part of *Sir Lucius O'Trigger* to Mr. Lee, or Lee himself to receive it?" and elaborated: "The representation of Sir Lucius is indeed an affront to the common sense of an audience, and is so far from giving the manners of our brave and worthy neighbors that it scarce equals the picture of a respectable Hottentot [a European term for the Khoikhoi people of South Africa, regarded here as inferior to Europeans]" (Loftis, p. 54). *The London Packet*, by contrast,

found fault with all the roles in *The Rivals*, complaining: "The characters are not only larger than life but are rather awkwardly placed. The diction is an odd mixture of the elegant and the absurd" (O'Toole, p. 96).

After so dismal a reception, Sheridan quickly withdrew his play for substantial revisions, trimming the length, excising some of the bawdier jokes and the more ineffective witticisms, and clarifying the character of Sir Lucius by making him more of a gentleman and less of a buffoon. When *The Rivals* returned for its second performance a mere 11 nights later, Lawrence Clinch had replaced John Lee in the role of Sir Lucius. This time the play earned a warmer reception, as shown in the new reviews:

> It was almost as though the play had had a delayed impact, as if a break had been needed for its originality [unique blend of wit and absurdity with warm-heartedness and benevolence] to sink in. The reviews were by no means ecstatic, but critics now saw "great and various improvements" and "many evident traits of literary genius."
>
> (O'Toole, p. 98)

The recasting was also a success—the *London Evening Post* praised Clinch for "[making] Sir Lucius so agreeable to the audience" (Auburn, p. 193). The *Morning Post*, meanwhile, enthusiastically depicted Sheridan as a heroic figure who, "Hercules-like, even in the cradle of genius, tore the serpents asunder by the vigour of his mind, and baulked the cankered malice of his foes" (O'Toole, p. 98). Finally, David Garrick, the dominant actor of his day and a well-known theater manager, changed his apprehensive murmur of "I see this play will creep" early in the second performance of *The Rivals* to a far more positive declaration at the end, "I see this play will run" (Garrick in O'Toole, p. 98). And so it did, for the remainder of the season.

—Pamela S. Loy

For More Information

Auburn, Mark S. *Sheridan's Comedies: Their Contexts and Achievements.* Lincoln: University of Nebraska Press, 1977.

Durant, Jack D. *Richard Brinsley Sheridan.* New York: Twayne, 1975.

Gadd, David. *Georgian Summer: Bath in the Eighteenth Century.* Park Ridge: Noyes, 1972.

Kelly, Linda. *Richard Brinsley Sheridan: A Life.* London: Sinclair-Stevenson, 1997.

Loftis, John. *Sheridan and the Drama of Georgian England.* Oxford: Basil Blackwell, 1976.

McMillin, Scott, ed. *Restoration and Eighteenth-Century Comedy*. New York: Norton, 1973.

O'Toole, Fintan. *A Traitor's Kiss: The Life of Richard Brinsley Sheridan, 1751-1816*. New York: Farrar, Straus and Giroux, 1997.

Rush, Philip. *The Book of Duels*. London: George G. Harrap, 1964.

Sheridan, Richard Brinsley. *The Rivals*. Essex: Longman, 1985.

Sherwin, Oscar. *Uncorking Old Sherry: The Life and Times of Richard Brinsley Sheridan*. New York: Twayne, 1960.

Smollett, Tobias. *The Adventures of Peregrine Pickle*. 2 vols. London: J. M. Dent and Sons, 1930.

Stone, Lawrence. *The Family, Sex and Marriage in England 1500-1800*. New York: Harper and Row, 1977.

Rob Roy

by

Sir Walter Scott

~

THE LITERARY WORK

A novel set in England and Scotland in 1715; first published in London in 1818.

SYNOPSIS

Young Frank Osbaldistone journeys from London to Scotland, where he becomes embroiled in political intrigues with the Scottish outlaw Robert MacGregor, or Rob Roy.

Walter Scott (1771-1832) was born in Edinburgh, Scotland, where he grew up listening to his grandmother's tales of the Border, as the region joining southern Scotland and northern England is known. The Border tales of his childhood stayed with him as he abandoned an early legal career to pursue his real love, writing: in 1802-1803 he published a three-volume collection of Scottish Border ballads called *Minstrelsy of the Scottish Border*. Its success established his literary reputation, which was secured over the next decade by a series of highly popular narrative poems, the most successful of which was *The Lady of the Lake* (1810). The poems featured the colorful Scottish settings and romantic themes that would also distinguish his early novels, the first of which, *Waverly*, was published to immediate acclaim in 1814. Over the next 15 years, Scott wrote more than 20 historical novels, all of them, like *Waverly*, published anonymously. Starting with *Ivanhoe* (1820), set in medieval England and the most popular of all Scott's books, Scott expanded his range to include a variety of locales and historical periods. Despite *Ivanhoe's* continuing popularity, it is Scott's earlier novels, which take their settings from Scottish history, that have had the greatest impact. *Rob Roy* takes place before and during an unsuccessful uprising in 1715. In this uprising, Scottish Highland leaders such as Rob Roy (a historical figure on whom Scott based his fictional character) supported James II's Catholic son James Francis Edward Stuart in his bid for the British throne.

Events in History at the Time the Novel Takes Place

Union between Scotland and England. The Scottish unrest featured in *Rob Roy* and the other Waverly novels arose from the complex historical relationship between Scotland and England. The two kingdoms had been ruled by the same monarchs since 1603, when the Stuart monarch King James VI of Scotland had acceded to the English throne as James I of England. While this brought the Scots and English into closer contact, Scotland still retained legal and political independence from her more powerful southern neighbor. Before being removed from power in 1688, the Catholic James II (James I's grandson) had tried and failed to effect a political union between his two kingdoms. By 1707, however, under his Protestant daughter Queen Anne (ruled 1702-14), circumstances had altered, and in that year an Act of Union merged the two kingdoms as Great Britain. The Scottish Parliament was

From the 1995 film version of *Rob Roy,* starring Liam Neeson and Jessica Lange.

abolished and Scottish representatives took their places in the English Parliament at Westminster in London, making a new British Parliament. However, this so-called "incorporation" of Scottish political representation into the English system was heavily weighted in favor of the English: only 45 Scottish representatives were added to the 558 members of the House of Commons, and only 16 Scottish peers were added to the nearly 200 English peers in the House of Lords. Scotland kept her own legal system and currency, the Scottish pound, which was worth about one-twelfth of the English pound sterling.

From the Scottish viewpoint, the incentive for union was mainly economic. England provided the largest market for Scotland's major exports, which were cattle, linen, and coal; like the historical Rob Roy, Scott's fictional character is a cattle drover who drives his Highland herds south for sale in either the Lowlands or in England. English colonies in America and elsewhere also represented a significant trading opportunity for Lowland Scottish merchants, like the Glasgow businessman Nicol Jarvie in *Rob Roy.* For the English, union offered political security, since one condition was that the Scots accept the English choice of a Protestant successor to the infirm and now childless Anne. Union, the English hoped, would make it more difficult for France—England's enemy but the traditional ally of the

Catholic Stuarts—to gain a strategic foothold in the north. The first test of the union came with Anne's death in 1714.

Hanoverian succession and Jacobite resistance. Among other reasons, the Catholic James II had been removed because the predominantly Protestant English wished for a Protestant ruler; in the so-called "Glorious Revolution" of 1688, the English Parliament had replaced him with his daughter Mary and her Dutch husband William of Orange, both Protestants. William and Mary ruled jointly until Mary's death in 1694, when William took over as sole ruler. With William's death in 1702, James's younger daughter Anne had come to the throne, also a Protestant. Anne, however, was the last Protestant Stuart with a direct claim to the throne. Rather than accept Anne's Catholic younger brother, James Francis Edward Stuart, as king, the English Parliament settled the succession on a Protestant German prince, George (titled the Elector of Hanover), James I's great-grandson and James II's cousin.

The 1688 birth of Anne's younger brother, James Francis, a male Catholic heir to the throne, had prompted the Glorious Revolution against his father, James II. In 1708, the year after the union, James Francis made a first attempt to raise a revolt in Scotland and take the throne, but he and the French fleet sent to aid the revolt were defeated by bad weather as well as the English

Royal Navy. Now, with Anne's death, James Francis's supporters again rallied to his cause. These supporters (called *Jacobites*) had always been strongest in Scotland, and in the country's Highlands, traditional loyalty to the Scottish Stuarts was reinforced by the survival of Catholicism among some of the clans.

The Jacobite standard was raised in September 1715 by John Erskine Earl of Mar, a frustrated politician with no military experience, who acted without the knowledge of James himself. Mar enjoyed wide support, much of which came from his pledge to repeal the union (by now highly unpopular in Scotland), but his poor tactical skills led to the complete defeat of his forces by the government's general, John Campbell Duke of Argyll, at the battle of Sherrifmuir in November. By December, when James arrived in Scotland from France (where he lived in exile), the revolt was over; both he and Mar fled to France in February 1716.

Rob Roy MacGregor. No contemporary portraits exist of Robert MacGregor (1671-1734), but decades after MacGregor's death Scott and other writers were able to get physical descriptions from men who, as youngsters, had seen him. These reports generally describe a man of no more than average height (that is, perhaps 5'4", which was then average for a man in the Highlands), lean but muscular, with unusually broad shoulders and noticeably long, powerful arms. He had dark red hair (hence his nickname, anglicized from *Raib Ruadh* or "Rob the Red" in Gaelic) and later in life wore a beard and mustache. He is also described as direct and bluntly honest in his manner, deep voiced, and often eloquent in his speech. Like other Highland men, he wore as his main garment the plaid, a blanketlike rectangle of finely woven wool, folded and belted around the waist to leave the legs bare, then draped over the left shoulder (to leave the sword-arm free) and secured by a pin of deer bone. The plaid could be unwrapped and used as a blanket when sleeping on rugged terrain, which Highland men were accustomed to doing. Standard Highland men's attire was completed by the dirk, a long daggerlike weapon, two pistols with engraved butts, and a broadsword with a basket-handle, all worn in the belt, plus at times a shield called a *targaid*.

Alone of all the Highland clans, the MacGregors over the seventeenth century had been deprived of their ancestral lands by the legal and extralegal maneuvers of powerful enemies, particularly the mighty Campbells. At times, the Campbells even successfully urged the crown to proscribe or outlaw the very name MacGregor; coincidentally, for much of his life Rob Roy signed the name Campbell, as his mother came from a branch of that large clan. (In Scott's novel, Rob Roy is using the name Campbell when the reader first encounters him.) Despite the handicap of coming from a broken clan, Rob Roy managed by his thirties to acquire property and cattle, both of which he increased through shrewd and prudent management. He won a reputation for honesty and responsibility, so that wealthier men were willing to invest money in his cattle ventures. In 1712, however, one of his lieutenants absconded with £1,000, a substantial fortune, which Rob Roy had secured as a loan from the powerful James Graham, duke of Montrose. As Rob Roy struggled to pay back the loan honorably, the land-hungry Montrose had him declared an outlaw and seized his land.

HIGHLANDS AND LOWLANDS

Scotland's most important boundary, that between the northern Highlands and the southern Lowlands, reflects both a geographical and a cultural division. Since the Middle Ages Scots in the Lowlands have been open to English cultural influence from across the border, while Scots in the rugged and inaccessible Highlands preserved more of their original Gaelic (or Celtic) ways. Lowlanders spoke Scots, for example, a blend of English and Gaelic with French influences, which Sir Walter Scott and the authors who followed him reproduced in a stylized form in their novels; Highlanders might speak Scots (as Rob Roy does in Scott's novel) but would also speak pure Gaelic. By the early eighteenth century, the Lowlands had become, like England, heavily Protestant, while pockets of Catholicism remained in the Highlands. Highland life before the Industrial Revolution was dominated by about 90 clans, extended families that continually struggled among themselves for scarce resources. Such struggles often led to feuds between clans that spanned generations, the most famous feud being that between the Campbells and MacDonalds.

Outraged and outcast, Rob Roy then took to the career that, in his eyes, Montrose had forced upon him. As an outlaw, his principle target was the wealthy Montrose himself. He avoided robbing the poor, and indeed was known for his generosity toward them, causing some to call him a Scottish Robin Hood. In one well-known incident, an old peasant woman was threatened with eviction if she could not pay the back rent she owed to Montrose. She appealed to Rob Roy, who lent her the money—with instructions to get a full receipt from Montrose's men. After Montrose's men collected the rent, Rob Roy and his men simply ambushed them and took the money back. Interrupted briefly by service with Mar's army, Rob Roy's career as an outlaw continued until 1725, when he obtained a royal pardon for his actions against Montrose.

ROB ROY AT SHERRIFMUIR

One the most controversial episodes in the life of the real Rob Roy was his participation—or, more accurately, his lack of participation—on the Jacobite side in the battle of Sherrifmuir, the major conflict of the 1715 revolt. In his lengthy historical introduction to the 1829 edition of the novel, Scott writes that Rob Roy held his men back at the crucial moment despite Mar's orders to charge: "Though it is said that his attack might have decided the day, he could not be prevailed upon to charge. . . . Rob did not, however, neglect his own private interest on the occasion. In the confusion . . . he enriched his followers by plundering the baggage and the dead on both sides" (Scott, *Rob Roy*, pp. 28-9). Yet later scholars (such as W. H. Murray, Rob Roy's recent biographer) have concluded that Mar's tactics had already failed, and that in following the order to charge, Rob Roy would have needlessly thrown away the lives of his men. Furthermore, there was no baggage or plunder to pick up—only arms and equipment, which (Murray points out) the poorly equipped men would have been foolish to leave behind. Generally a well-informed historian, Scott in this case relied on sources based on gossip that arose after the battle.

The Novel in Focus

Plot summary. While the colorful and dramatic Rob Roy dominates the novel, he does so from behind the scenes and under other names (among them, Campbell and MacGregor). He plays a relatively small part in the action itself. The narrator is an Englishman, Frank Osbaldistone, who tells the story from the perspective of an old man addressing a much younger man, his friend Tresham, who is the son of a business partner. Thus, Frank is looking back on events that took place in 1715, when he was about 20, from the vantage point of around the year 1765.

At the beginning of Frank's story, his father has summoned him home to London from France, where the young man has been studying business practices under the tutelage of his father's French business partners. Mr. Osbaldistone hopes that Frank will one day take over the prosperous trading firm of Osbaldistone and Tresham, of which Frank's father is a founding partner. Frank, however, has been more interested in poetry than in business, and despite the kindly prompting of his father's head clerk, Owen, he is unable to answer his father's questions satisfactorily. He declares that he has no intention of going into business and instead wishes to devote himself to literature. His father gives him a month to think about it, but at the end of the month Frank has not changed his mind. His father, pointing out that Frank has no way of making a living, says that he will only support the youth if Frank will go visit the family estate in the north of England. Living there are Frank's uncle and six male cousins, one of whom Mr. Osbaldistone plans to choose as a replacement for Frank to inherit the business. Frank, as Owen sadly says, has "ruined" himself (*Rob Roy*, p. 84).

Yet as he sets out on horseback the next morning for the long journey north, Frank feels exhilarated. Stopping at an inn near the Border country, he meets an enigmatic Scot named Mr. Campbell—the first Scotchman I chanced to meet in society," as Frank puts it—whose self-confident manner and casual dominance of the conversation contrast with his coarse clothing and low occupation of cattle dealer (*Rob Roy*, p. 96).

The next day, Frank leaves the northern road to finish his journey to Osbaldistone Hall. As he approaches the "large and antiquated edifice," he comes across a group of "tall, stout young men" engaged in a fox hunt on horseback, a typical sporting activity for upper-class young men in the English countryside, but one with which Frank has had no experience (*Rob Roy*, pp. 100, 101). With them is a beautiful young lady, whose horse briefly seems to falter, giving Frank an excuse to approach as if to help her. Thus Frank meets Diana Vernon, called Die, and his cousins, the young men he saw hunting. The sparkling Die Vernon, whose unusual personality appears to Frank as a fascinating "mixture of boldness, satire, and simplicity," contrasts sharply with his loutish cousins, who seem to live only for the pleasures of sport and drinking (*Rob Roy*, p. 103). In this they take after their father, Sir Hildebrand Osbaldistone, a gruff but goodhearted country squire who, unlike his sons, "retained much of the exterior of a gentleman" (*Rob Roy*, p. 109). Frank is pleased to learn that Die Vernon, the niece of Sir Hildebrand's deceased wife, lives with the family at Osbaldistone Hall.

Only one of Frank's cousins stands out from the others, and that is Rashleigh Osbaldistone, the young man Frank's father has chosen to be his successor at the firm of Osbaldistone and Tresham. Die, who befriends Frank, informs him of Rashleigh's impending departure for London, and warns him as well to be careful of Rashleigh. She also hints that Rashleigh may know more than he should about the robbery of a government tax excise officer. Frank, who had crossed paths with the officer on his journey north, had been accused but cleared of the robbery, in which Campbell, the enigmatic Scot whom Frank encountered, also seems involved.

During his extended stay at Osbaldistone Hall, Frank finds his feelings for Diana deepening into love, and he learns as well that Die's warnings about Rashleigh were justified. Left in charge of Osbaldistone and Tresham when Mr. Osbaldistone travels to France, Rashleigh plunders the company and absconds to Scotland with the missing funds. When Frank finds out, he realizes that he must go to Glasgow to meet his father's clerk, Owen, and attempt to recover his father's fortune. He says goodbye to Die Vernon and sets out for Scotland, with Osbaldistone Hall's Scottish gardener, Andrew Fairservice, as his guide.

Arriving in Glasgow, Frank attends church with Fairservice. Suddenly a voice in his ear warns him that he is in danger in Glasgow and tells him to meet the speaker on the old bridge over the River Clyde at midnight. When Frank does so, the stranger escorts him to the infamous prison called the Tolbooth. The guard recognizes Frank's escort and greets him warmly but nervously, and they all go inside the prison, where, to Frank's amazement, he finds Owen in one of the cells. Owen recounts how he had approached one of the firm's two Glasgow trading partners, who had turned him over to the authorities when they learned that the firm could not immediately honor its debt to them. Owen had then been imprisoned under a Scottish law that allowed creditors to detain a debtor whom they believe has reason to flee the country. Owen's only recourse had been to the firm's other Glasgow partner, Mr.

Nicol Jarvie, whom he had written to that morning. Though Owen has little hope of help from Mr. Jarvie—whom Owen calls a "cross-grained crab-stock"—Jarvie himself soon appears at Owen's cell and offers his assistance by putting up Owen's bail (*Rob Roy*, p. 263). The firm owes Jarvie money as well, but the shrewd businessman doesn't see how he can be paid back if Owen is left in the Tolbooth. Jarvie then recognizes Frank's mysterious escort, who turns out to be a distant relative of his—and who reveals himself a few moments later to Frank as none other than Campbell. (Frank had not recognized Campbell until Jarvie identified him.) Frank, Jarvie, and Campbell leave the prison, and Campbell disappears across the darkened street.

CATTLE REIVING AND BLACKMAIL

The historical Rob Roy was a cattle thief and a blackmailer—and that was before he became an outlaw. Cattle theft, called *reiving*, was a perfectly honorable practice according to Highland custom. So was blackmail, which originally meant offering protection against such theft (*black* referred to the color of the cattle; *mail* was Scots for "tribute" or "rent"). Cattle were the main form of wealth in the Highlands, and as a landless and often proscribed clan, the MacGregors became especially adept at both reiving and blackmail. Like their father before them, Rob Roy and his brothers operated a "Watch," a legally sanctioned blackmail system that offered protection to cattle drovers, complete with signed contracts and written receipts. Outside the Watch, however, blackmail was technically illegal, though not uncommon. The skills required for reiving and blackmail—stealth, swordsmanship, and the handling of cattle, primarily—later stood the outlaw Rob Roy in good stead when he turned these skills on the herds of his enemy, Montrose.

The next day Frank walks through Glasgow and is startled to see Rashleigh, whom he follows and eventually approaches. After exchanging insults, they draw their swords and begin to duel but are interrupted by the sudden appearance of Campbell, who interposes himself between them and allows Rashleigh to flee. Campbell then restrains the angry Frank, explaining that to follow Rashleigh now would be to walk into a trap, for Rashleigh has prepared to have Frank charged once again with the earlier robbery of the government tax excise officer.

Up to this point, Jarvie has evaded Frank's questions about Campbell. That evening, as Frank and Owen eat dinner at Jarvie's house, Frank insists on an explanation. Campbell seems to be helping Frank. But can he be relied upon? Is he honest? "Ay," Jarvie answers in his Lowland Scots brogue, "he has a kind o' Hieland honesty" (*Rob Roy*, p. 298). Highlanders, he goes on, "are clean anither set frae the like o' huz" (clean another set from the like of us; *Rob Roy*, p. 298). There is very little law in the Highlands, Jarvie continues: usually the sword acts as prosecutor and the shield as defender. Overpopulation has left too many men with no way of making a living that a Lowlander like Jarvie would think of as honest—and all these men are armed and used to the ways of violence. Rob Campbell, however, was once a respectable drover, until his creditors seized his land and home, turning his wife out onto the hillside and, the story goes, abusing her as well. When he came home he found only desolation. That was when he took up his broadsword "and became a broken-man," turning to blackmail and reiving on a large scale (*Rob Roy*, p. 303).

THE TOLBOOTH

~

Donald MacGregor, leader of the clan MacGregor and father of the historical Rob Roy, served two years in this notorious Glasgow prison for his continued support of King James II after the Revolution of 1688. By the time he returned to his family in 1691, the prison's harsh and unsanitary conditions had broken his once robust health.

There is a political angle as well, for now that Queen Anne is dead, dissatisfaction will cause the Jacobites to rise in the Highlands and "come down on the Low Country like a flood" (*Rob Roy*, p. 305). Campbell can raise 500 men to follow him, and Jarvie suspects that he has been active in establishing communications between the Highland chiefs and the Jacobites in the Border country, including northern England. In fact, Jarvie discloses, it was Campbell, along with Rashleigh or one of Frank's other cousins, who had robbed the government tax excise officer. The cousins are all Jacobites and Catholics, and would consider the hated excise officers legitimate targets for robbery.

The funds stolen from Osbaldistone and Tresham can also aid the Jacobite cause, Jarvie explains, though less directly: they are in the form of bills of exchange. Like other companies, Frank's father's has bought forest land in the Highlands, paying with these bills, which are made out (like checks) to the sellers. With the bills missing, the Highland landowners will suffer financially, which Rashleigh hopes will drive them to join the rebellion. If Campbell is a Jacobite, Frank asks Jarvie, why would he want to help restore the missing bills? Jarvie isn't sure, but he knows that Campbell has been friendly with the Argyll family, supporters of George I, and he also knows that Campbell and the Jacobite leadership distrust each other. "The truth is," Jarvie tells Frank, "that Rob [Campbell] is for his ain [sic] hand . . . he'll take the side that suits him best" (*Rob Roy*, p. 307).

After Frank promises him a generous reward, Jarvie agrees to accompany him into the Highlands to seek Campbell out and enlist the outlaw's aid in recovering the missing bills of exchange. By this time, Campbell might even have the bills himself. The two set off from Glasgow in the morning, along with Fairservice, who has by now comically insinuated himself into a position as Frank's servant. At the end of a day's ride they cross the River Forth, which forms part of the line between the Lowlands and the Highlands, and stop at an inn for the night, where a sword fight ensues. When Frank steps outside to find Fairservice—who has fled the swordplay—the inn's landlady hands Frank a secret note from Campbell warning him against trusting the men inside the inn.

A detachment of English soldiers arrives at the inn, and the Highlanders are revealed to have been waiting for them. These Highlanders are men with grudges against Rob Roy and have been brought in to help hunt him down. The soldiers search Frank, find the letter from Rob Roy, and arrest him, Jarvie, and Fairservice. That night the Highlanders depart to seek Rob Roy; the next morning, the soldiers press on in another direction with Frank and his companions. But as they pass on a narrow track between a lake and a steep mountain, they are ambushed from front and rear. The ambushers, commanded by Helen Campbell, Rob Roy's wife, a stern and harshly beautiful woman wearing a man's plaid, do violent battle until the soldiers surrender. News comes that Rob Roy was captured that morning by the Highlander collaborators and is now being held by the English nearby, under the com-

Rob Roy's prison on Loch Katrine, Scotland.

mand of the duke of Montrose. At this point Helen Campbell cold-bloodedly executes a captive, the excise officer whom her husband had earlier robbed. She orders Frank to deliver a message to her husband's captors: free Rob Roy or she will proceed to execute her English soldier prisoners.

The duke refuses to yield and declares that the outlaw must die. Rob Roy, however, makes a daring escape. When he learns that he is suspected of helping in the escape, Frank flees too. A chance encounter on the road with Die Vernon, who is traveling with an older man, results in the recovery of the missing bills, which Die has obtained from Rashleigh—but Frank, believing that she has wed her older companion, is heartbroken. Reunited later with Rob Roy and Jarvie, Frank learns that Die has now fled the

country and that a Jacobite rebellion is about to erupt. Rashleigh, bitter because Rob Roy forced him to give Die Vernon the bills, has betrayed the Jacobites and gone over to the English. Jarvie and Frank return to Glasgow, where Frank's father has joined Owen to await Frank's safe return with the bills.

The revolt breaks out the day that Frank and his father leave Glasgow for London, where Mr. Osbaldistone joins with other companies in offering credit to the government to help prosecute the war against the Jacobite rebels. While Frank enlists in the government army, Sir Hildebrand and his sons (except for Rashleigh) fight on the Jacobite side. After his boys are killed in the failed revolt, Sir Hildebrand falls ill and, about to die himself, disinherits Rashleigh and leaves Osbaldistone Hall to Frank. When Frank arrives to take possession, he finds Die Vernon and the older man she had been traveling with hiding out in the semiabandoned house. The man, it turns out, is her father, a Jacobite aristocrat wanted by the authorities. Rashleigh learns of their presence and appears with law officers, hoping to have them all arrested as Jacobites and reclaim his inheritance. His plan is foiled by the appearance of Rob Roy, who slays Rashleigh in the ensuing fight, leaving Frank and Die free to marry and move into Osbaldistone Hall.

EMIGRATION FROM THE HIGHLANDS

The early decades of the nineteenth century brought an end to the Highland way of life even as Scott was romanticizing it. The old feudal system of "lairds" and "crofters" (lords and tenant farmers) had begun breaking down in the previous century as the population surged beyond the capacity of the land to support it. In *Rob Roy,* Jarvie complains about Highland overpopulation, though it would later become a much more serious problem than in the early eighteenth century. As with other historical issues, Scott borders on anachronism in the views that he has Jarvie espouse. It was later in the eighteenth century that emigration to colonial settlements—such as those in North America—surged, and landowning lairds, facing ruin from decreased rents, began evicting the remaining crofter families in order to devote the land to livestock. Significant numbers also began leaving the Highlands to seek jobs in Glasgow and other urban industrial centers.

"Honour" vs. "credit: Scott's two Scotlands. Like many of Scott's other novels, *Rob Roy* contrasts the older, feudal world of the Highlands with the newer, highly ordered commercial prosperity of the Lowlands. Both the historical Rob Roy and Scott's fictional character are motivated largely by the ancient concept of honor, which had a central role in Highland society, particularly in the feuds between clans; in the character of Nicol Jarvie, Scott creates a spokesman for an opposing, economically based code of social behavior. "Honour," Jarvie asserts, "is a homicide and a bloodspiller, that gangs about [goes about] making frays in the street; but Credit is a decent honest man, that sits at home and makes the pat play [the pot boil]" (*Rob Roy*, p. 297).

According to Jarvie, the catalyst for the economic expansion that he celebrates so enthusiastically throughout the novel was the union of 1707. He notes, for example, the prosperity brought by the sugar and tobacco trade from the British colonies, which the union opened to Scottish merchants: "What was ever like to gar [make] us flourish like the sugar and tobacco-trade? Will any body tell me that, and grumble at the treaty that opened us a road westawa' yonder?" (*Rob Roy*, p. 312). As historians point out, however, "it was only in the period after the 1740s that the direct economic benefits of union came to fruition" (Devine and Young, p. 25). Jarvie's attitudes thus verge on being anachronistic, insofar as they anticipate a Scotland that was only just beginning to come into being at the time in which the novel is set. But in putting these views into Jarvie's mouth, Scott is able to foreshadow historical developments with which his nineteenth-century audience would have been familiar.

Sources and literary context. Scott used a variety of historical sources for details of Rob Roy's life, including eyewitness accounts, ballads, oral traditions, and the written records of the MacGregor family. For the rebellion and the war, he drew on similar sources and on the memoirs and letters of participants, as well as on later histories, such as *A History of the Rebellion raised against his Majesty by the friends of the Popish Pretender,* by Reverend Peter Rae, of which Scott had the second edition (1746). Although he visited some of the settings in the novel, Scott spent most of his time in Edinburgh, and his familiarity with the Highlands was not extensive. His descriptions of Glasgow and of the Highlands owe much to books, especially Daniel Defoe's popular *Tour through the Whole Island of Great Britain* (1724-27), Edward Burt's *Letters from a Gentleman in the North of Scotland to His Friend in London* (1730), and Rev. Patrick Graham's *Sketches of Perthshire* (1806). Scott also peppers the novel with colorful Scottish proverbs, many of which he found in *A Complete Collection of Scottish Proverbs* (1721), by James Kelly. Earlier literary treatments of Rob Roy included a pamphlet once attributed to Defoe called *The Highland Rogue* (1723) and William Wordsworth's poem *Rob Roy's Grave* (1807), which Scott quotes from in his introduction to the 1829 edition and in the epigraph to the novel.

Like Wordsworth, Scott stands firmly within the Romantic movement in literature, which began in the 1790s and in which ethnic and national mythology had begun to play a major role by the 1810s. Scott is credited with inventing the historical novel, which is also sometimes called a "romance," a term that recalls the medieval "romances" from which the Romantic period derives its name. Like *Rob Roy* and Scott's other novels, these medieval poems of chivalric adventure featured exotic settings and heroic deeds.

Events in History at the Time the Novel Was Written

Economic expansion. In the century between the novel's setting (1715) and its composition (1817), Scotland, and especially Glasgow, had moved from the dawn of an era dominated by colonial trade to the dawn of an era that would be dominated by the industrial revolution, which was already underway when Scott wrote *Rob Roy.* During this century, developments in economic practice were accompanied by advances in economic theory, most notably in the work of Glasgow political economist and philosopher Adam Smith (1723-90). Smith's 1776 work *The Wealth of Nations*, perhaps the most influential economic treatise ever published, laid the theoretical underpinnings of modern capitalism: free trade, easy credit, a national debt, and minimal government interference in economic competition. At the time from which Frank Osbaldistone looks back on the novel's events (c. 1765), the era of colonial trade was reaching its climax. As critics have pointed out, Smith was composing his work in Glasgow at the very time that Scott portrays Frank Osbaldistone recording the events of his youth; in the novel, Osbaldistone puts Smith's economic ideas into Jarvie's mouth, but nearly a decade before Smith's birth.

Jarvie praises the civic blessings he believes the new economic practices have secured, but Scott seems to see a darker side to the forces at work in this era of expansion. Rob Roy, for example, is driven to the outlaw's life by the very economic phenomenon that Jarvie celebrates as more "honest" than honor: credit. Such concerns were highly topical in Scott's day because of an intense public debate over returning the British pound to the gold standard. It was feared that such a measure (which in fact occurred the year after the novel's publication) would result in less credit being extended. Furthermore, the missing bills of exchange that drive the novel's plot have a historical parallel not in Rob Roy's life but in Scott's. Scott himself was in financial trouble over bills of exchange in the years immediately before he wrote *Rob Roy,* and parts of the novel echo letters in which he described his troubles.

Reception. Second only to *Ivanhoe* in popularity among Scott's novels, *Rob Roy* sold out its large print run of 10,000 copies within a few weeks of publication. It has been repeatedly adapted for the stage, with a version by Isaac Pocock opening in March 1819 and becoming one of the most influential theatrical productions of the era. In general, critics have praised the novel for its characterization but expressed reservations about its plot. The part of the plot that hinges on the bills of exchange has been singled out as particularly implausible. Perhaps because the bills themselves have no historical basis, it is doubted that they would have incited the Highlanders to revolt, even had such bills played a part in their affairs.

Frank's long sojourn at Osbaldistone Hall has also been condemned as aimless and uninteresting for the reader. Yet, as the twentieth-century Scottish author John Buchan writes in his biography of Scott, once Frank crosses into Scotland, "we are in the grip of epic narrative" (Buchan, p. 183). The often comic portrayals of Andrew Fairservice and Nicol Jarvie have been compared to characters in the later novels of Charles Dickens. In their evocation of Highland mystery and romance, *Rob Roy* and the other *Waverly* novels had an impact on outsiders' perceptions of Scotland that has lasted to the present day. Indeed, it has been said that Walter Scott single-handedly created the Scottish tourist industry.

—Colin Wells

For More Information

Anderson, James. *Sir Walter Scott and History.* Edinburgh: Edina Press, 1981.

Buchan, John. *Sir Walter Scott.* London: Cassell, 1932.

Cadbury, William. "The Two Structures of Rob Roy." *Modern Language Quarterly* 29 (1968): 42-60.

Devine, T. M., and J. R. Young, eds. *Eighteenth Century Scotland: New Perspectives.* East Lothian, Scotland: Tuckwell Press, 1999.

Lauber, John. *Sir Walter Scott.* Rev. ed. Boston: G. K. Hall, 1989.

Lenman, Bruce. *The Jacobite Risings in Britain, 1689-1746.* London: Eyre Methuen, 1980.

Macinnes, Allan I. *Clanship, Commerce and the House of Stuart, 1603-1788.* East Lothian, Scotland: Tuckwell Press, 1996.

Murray, W. H. *Rob Roy MacGregor: His Life and Times.* Edinburgh: Canongate, 1993.

Scott, Sir Walter. *Rob Roy.* Ed. Ian Duncan. Oxford, England: Oxford University Press, 1998.

Sense and Sensibility

by
Jane Austen

Jane Austen was born on December 16, 1775, in Hampshire County; she was the seventh of eight children of George Austen, a clergyman of the Church of England. Austen family tradition holds that an early version of *Sense and Sensibility* (called "Elinor and Marianne") may have been written in 1795 when Austen was 20. At her own expense, Austen published the final, substantially revised *Sense and Sensibility* in London in 1811. The novel makes no reference to notable historical events but portrays social life in a period that seems contemporary with the end of the eighteenth and the beginning of the nineteenth centuries. *Sense and Sensibility* was the first of four novels—the others being *Pride and Prejudice* (1813), *Mansfield Park* (1814), and *Emma* (1816)—published in Austen's lifetime; *Northanger Abbey* and *Persuasion* were published posthumously in 1818, the year after Austen died. Austen herself never married, but, like the heroines of her novels and like many of her contemporaries, she was fascinated by marriage, especially by the kind of marriage prized by her contemporaries: marriage to a gentleman with a landed estate.

Events in History at the Time of the Novel

The gentry in early–eighteenth-century England. The dominant English political ideology between 1795 and 1811 taught that political power belonged to male landowners. These were the men thought to have the greatest stake in the

---

THE LITERARY WORK

A novel set sometime between the 1790s and 1810s in the English countryside, in the counties of Sussex and Devonshire, and in London; published in 1811.

SYNOPSIS

Two sisters, Elinor and Marianne Dashwood, genteelly born but without fortunes, find suitable husbands.

---

welfare of the nation and to be capable of an educated and disinterested consideration of the nation's good. By the Qualifications Act of 1711, still in force in 1811, country Members of Parliament (MPs) were required to possess freehold land worth £600 a year, and MPs from the town boroughs were to possess land worth £300 a year. The standard calculation figured the capital value of an estate at 20 times its annual revenue, which meant a country MP was required to have a landed estate worth about £12,000. This ideology was challenged by radicals such as Thomas Paine, in his *The Rights of Man* (1791-92), and by members of the London Corresponding Society, organized in 1792 to facilitate communication among English groups agitating for extensions of the franchise and for increased civil liberties. But the successes of the radicals in the French Revolution—from the fall of the Bastille in 1789 to the spectacle of French aristocrats being guillotined—provoked reaction in

England against radical democratic ideas of power sharing. So power continued to rest with a gentleman in possession of a good estate. Someone of social consequence with economic security, such a gentleman was an attractive object on the marriage market.

The landed aristocracy shared power with the landed gentry and with a class that has usefully been described as the "pseudo-gentry"—that is, the group of gentlemen (and their families) who lacked sufficient land to be supported by income from it but who, nevertheless, tended to share the values and (to a lesser degree) the lifestyle of the gentry. This group included military officers or clergymen (like Austen's brothers and father) and barristers. Because family estates were generally inherited by the eldest son, younger brothers from the aristocracy and the "genuine" gentry, often lacking enough capital to support themselves in leisure, frequently entered these professions along with the pseudo-gentry. Whereas an aristocratic landowner might have an annual income of somewhere between £10,000 to £100,000 a year, a gentry income was more likely to be about £1,000 or £2,000 a year, and a Church of England clergyman might have to struggle along on a few hundred pounds or even less. Austen's novels, including *Sense and Sensibility*, are dominated by characters from the gentry and pseudo-gentry.

The right to vote was tied to the possession of an estate, albeit a much smaller one. Borough qualifications varied widely, but country electors had to possess freehold property worth 40 shillings a year; tenants with leases shorter than the terms of their lives did not qualify. Modern estimates place the proportion of adult males possessing the franchise in parliamentary elections at roughly 15 percent. Women neither stood as candidates for Parliament nor voted, which was one reason contemporaries thought allowing landed property to fall into female hands was a "waste." Nor were women generally thought to have the capacity to manage landed estates.

To be a gentleman who owned a substantial landed estate was to have not only what contemporaries considered the highest form of economic security; it also gave the landowner possible access to political power and patronage and significant local power. Specifically, the landowner could select tenants for his smaller farms or village houses. A good number of country gentlemen (possessed of at least £100 a year) also served unpaid stints as local Justices of the Peace (JPs), an office for which no formal legal training was required. JPs enjoyed summary jurisdiction over a wide array of misdemeanors, including drunkenness, bastardy suits, and poaching. In exercising this jurisdiction, they could have offenders whipped, fined, or incarcerated in a local house of correction.

One form of local power frequently attached to the ownership of land could be exercised by either a man or a woman, namely, the ability to nominate a clergyman as rector of the local parish church, a right called an "advowson." In *Sense and Sensibility* Colonel Brandon possesses an advowson, which he uses to facilitate Elinor's marriage. Of 11,600 positions for rector in Church of England parishes at the end of the eighteenth century, at least 5,500 were in the power of private landowners to bestow. Landowners understood the advowson to be a useful kind of patronage they might invoke to provide for younger brothers, other male relatives, dedicated tutors or secretaries, or dependents of political allies. Advowsons would sometimes be put up for sale or auction, though not everyone approved of the practice. In fact, Jane Austen's father was the incumbent of such a living, or post, which his uncle Frank had purchased in 1770 to bestow on him.

A rector with a Church of England living was himself a man with property rights and attendant powers, although his estate and his powers were smaller than those of his landed patron. While he held the living, he had a freehold estate in the church buildings and land. A major problem for clergymen like Jane Austen's father was that control of their estates ended with their lives, reverting to their patrons and leaving their widows and children without any inheritance (beyond what they were able to save). A rector was also entitled to tithes, that is, to one-tenth of the produce of the cultivated land in the parish. Since the Church of England was the state church, all residents of a parish were legally required to pay tithes and parish poor rates, even those residents who professed other religions (about 10 percent of the total population). Jane Austen's brother George, a Church of England clergyman with two livings, in one year earned about £300 from his lands and £600 from tithes. In *Sense and Sensibility*, Colonel Brandon gives a position of this sort as a gift to Edward Ferrars, enabling him to support the wife of his choice.

Inheritance laws and practices. In English common law, landed estates descended by primogeniture, that is, the eldest son inherited the whole estate; his younger brothers and his sisters inherited nothing and were thus dependent on his decency to make some provision for them. (Property other than land statutorily descended by a formula that treated all siblings equally; this distribution formula, along with primogeniture, operated unless individuals had altered the descent by wills or trusts, which they usually did in the upper classes, though the bulk of the estate would still be settled on the eldest son.) Primogeniture was clearly understood by contemporaries to be a way of ensuring that large estates remained large enough to support an upper-class person in an upper-class way of life. It also ensured that the division between the upper classes and the lower classes was maintained. If estates had been divided equally among all siblings, they would have become progressively smaller, and the aristocracy and the gentry would have risked becoming indistinguishable from small farmers.

Nevertheless, in this period the rigid application of common-law primogeniture was generally thought to be too harsh to younger sons and to daughters. In most upper-class families, couples married with prenuptial agreements drawn up by lawyers after negotiations between the fathers of the bride and groom. These agreements were called "marriage settlements." As indicated, they commonly preserved the bulk of the estate for the eldest son but also made provisions from the estate for others. Daughters and younger sons commonly received "portions" in land or money to be paid out of the estate, collectable upon marriage or upon reaching the age of majority. Newspaper marriage announcements often specified exactly how many pounds a fortunate bride possessed as her portion (as our own announcements now specify from what colleges and professional schools a bride has graduated, allowing a perhaps more discreet calculation of how much tuition money has been spent on her education). Austen knew very well that the size of a girl's portion strongly affected her attractiveness on the contemporary marriage market, and frequently specified in her novels exactly how many thousand pounds of portion the more fortunate young women possessed. Normally a marriage settlement also provided a woman with a jointure, that is, entitlement to a yearly income for her life should her husband die before her. The amount of a woman's jointure was normally related to the amount of the portion she brought to the marriage, the portion being used as a capital sum that could support the later jointure payments;

contented and generous husbands might add to a wife's jointure during the marriage. Mrs. Jennings in *Sense and Sensibility* lives well on the income of her jointure.

Because marriage settlements were private contracts negotiated between families, their provisions were highly variable. No one, of course, could know in advance how many children would be born of a particular marriage or whether a husband would predecease his wife. Nor was it possible to predict exactly how much revenue a particular estate would be capable of generating 20 or 40 years into the future, some estate owners being both careful managers and lucky, others both spendthrift and unfortunate. Consequently, there was frequently tension between gentlemen who inherited an estate and the various other persons who had what amounted to legal liens on his estate in the form of portions, a jointure, or annuities that were supposed to be paid out of it. An heir might be short of cash through no fault of his own, or, as his dependents often suspected, too selfish or too self-indulgent to pay them what was due. Persons entitled to jointures or portions could sue for them, and there are ample records of such litigation. Yet there were practical impediments to poor people's litigating, and social and moral inhibitions about suing members of one's own family. Part of the heroines' problem in *Sense and Sensibility* is that they have a moral lien on their stepbrother's estate, derived from their relationship and from his promise to their dying father, rather than a legal lien.

Women and marriage. The higher in the social hierarchy a person was, the more limited the pool of suitable marriage partners. Royal marriages were still arranged for dynastic and political purposes, and economic considerations significantly affected aristocratic marriages as well. In the gentry and pseudo-gentry, a woman, possessed of her own reasonable portion, ideally married a gentleman possessed of a landed estate sufficient to allow the couple to live on its proceeds, or, at least, married a gentleman with a good income from his inheritance or profession. The Church, the law, and the military remained the respectable professions.

Again ideally, a young person of this class selected a marriage partner with the advice and consent of his or her parents. Young women, especially, were constantly instructed that they lacked the discernment to know whether a particular man would make a good husband; in practice, most sensibly relied on their parents and other relatives to investigate the character and prospects of suitors. The Marriage Act of 1753 required the consent of parents or guardians to the marriage of anyone under the age of 21; elopement to Scotland was the only way to avoid the provisions of this act. Sometimes, parents themselves proposed candidates for a daughter's hand, but by this time, in these classes, it was generally thought to be an abuse of parental power to attempt to coerce a daughter to marry a man who, upon acquaintance, she disliked. In effect, both parents and children had something close to veto power. A daughter would normally not marry a man of whom her parents strongly disapproved, and parents would not normally try to force a daughter to marry a man she found distasteful. Similarly, since marriages were understood to be a union of two families, a responsible and well-behaved young woman would not normally attempt to marry into a family that found her unsuitable; Lucy's clandestine engagement in *Sense and Sensibility* exemplifies bad behavior for this reason. Family discussions over a girl's marriage often involved such tactics as parents warning daughters who might be lukewarm to a particular suitor that they were unlikely to have such a good chance again or daughters pleading with fond fathers to let them marry men with less than stellar prospects. Sometimes a marriage settlement secured a "portion" (amount) on a child without making it contingent on that child's good behavior. But, because of the way marriage settlements of this period were drafted, even if a child were entitled to a marriage portion, the settlement might give a parent the power to adjust the size of the settlement or even to withhold it altogether should the child attempt to make a marriage of which the parent did not approve. Parents also had the leverage over children that came from their right to deny them the inheritance of personal property by changing their wills and by threatening to withhold money and patronage from a disobedient child. (Almost no one would have totally disinherited an eldest son, especially one like Edward Ferrars in *Sense and Sensibility*; Mrs. Ferrars's indulgence in this peculiarly English parental privilege is clearly an abuse of parental power.) Although on rare occasions society was shocked by the elopement of a gentlewoman with a footman, for the most part gentlewomen themselves were not much tempted to desire marriages with men significantly socially or economically beneath them. As Amanda Vickery remarks, "wealth and rank had an intensely ro-

mantic, as well as mercenary appeal" (Vickery, p. 44). In practice, it was the rare gentry daughter who married against her parents' opposition.

The plight of portionless daughters. Lack of sufficient money for daughters' portions was more of a problem for the gentry and pseudogentry than headstrong romantic daughters eloping with unsuitable men. There were estates whose possessors were better at spending and mortgaging than at investing and saving, estates against which decision-makers had too optimistically charged larger portions and jointures than the assets could support, and estates where demographic roulette had produced numerous children or long-lived widows. All these led to genteel daughters who had small, negligible, or unpaid portions. Families with large numbers of children—Jane Austen was one of eight children—found it especially difficult to support all of them in genteel life. At the turn of the century, settlements often used some version of a formula for charging portions on the estate that gave one year's income from the estate as a portion for a single younger child, two years' income should there be two younger children, and up to three years' income should there be a necessity for dividing it between three or more younger children. Large families often hoped for assistance in providing for younger sons and for daughters from kin or other connections, like the assistance the Austens received when their childless distant cousins, the Knights, adopted the Austens' third son, Edward, as their heir. Edward, in turn, as it was hoped such a child would do, shared his good fortune with his widowed mother and his unmarried sisters, giving them a cottage at Chawton in which to live in 1808.

Well-off gentlemen sometimes pleased themselves by marrying attractive girls with tiny portions or no portions at all, but the absence of a portion was a significant obstacle to a good gentry marriage. Despite a few notable exceptions, the lot of an unmarried gentlewoman was usually unenviable. To be a married woman, mistress of one's own household, and the mother of children was what normally made a woman a respected adult. Among the gentry and pseudogentry, a single woman counted herself fortunate if she became the mistress of the home of some male relation who lacked a wife; she was likely to dread the day when she might be forced to lose status by going out as a governess or paid lady's companion, thus becoming a sort of upper-level domestic servant, or when she had to take up a post as a teacher in a boarding school.

Women's education. The few who thought seriously about the education of gentlewomen at the turn of the nineteenth century confronted the fact that gentlewomen were primarily being educated to be the wives and mothers of gentlemen. Early feminists, from Mary Astell (1666-1731) to Catherine Macaulay (1731-91) and Mary Wollstonecraft (1759-97), had argued vigorously that women naturally possessed as much reason as men and urged that gentlewomen be educated more like gentlemen, studying philosophy, theology, literature, science, and history (see *A Vindication of the Rights of Woman,* also in *WLAIT 3: British and Irish Literature and Its Times*). These feminists lamented what they considered a superficial and "ornamental" ladies' education, which added dancing, music, drawing, and French to the basic instruction in housekeeping, morality, and Christianity that every mother was supposed to see that her daughter received. The problem, though, as these feminists acknowledged, was that, since no learned professions were open to women and women were denied roles in the governance of their country, it was hard to see what practical use educating women in classics or serious history would serve. While feminists lamented the failure to cultivate women's reason and urged that they would not be fully moral beings or adequate mothers without more rigorous education, most people probably agreed with political economist and philosopher Adam Smith that the typical ladies' education was sufficiently useful: "They are taught what their parents or guardians judge it necessary or useful for them to learn; and they are taught nothing else. Every part of their education tends evidently to some useful purpose; either to improve the natural attractions of their person, or to form their mind to reserve, to modesty, to chastity, and to economy; to render them both likely to become the mistresses of a family, and to behave properly when they have become such" (Smith, vol. 2, p. 302). The sporadic education Jane and her older sister, Cassandra, received was typical of their time and class: mostly educated at home by their mother, they were briefly sent to girls' boarding schools, once to a school run by a female family connection for a few months, and once to the Abbey School in Berkshire for less than a year. A watercolor artist was hired to instruct them at home. They could read as they liked in their father's library and benefit from the intellectual stimulation their better-educated brothers provided.

The Novel in Focus

Plot summary. *Sense and Sensibility* begins with a crisis over how inherited wealth will be distributed. Mr. and Mrs. Henry Dashwood and their three daughters have been living for ten years at Norland Park, a Sussex estate owned by Henry Dashwood's uncle. Unusually for a comedy, the novel begins with deaths: first the death of the uncle, and then, a year later, the death of Henry Dashwood himself. As was common in contemporary inheritance practices, the uncle had determined that Norland Park would be inherited in the male line, first by John Dashwood, Henry's son by his first marriage; then by John's son, Henry. At the uncle's death, Henry Dashwood, father of the heroines, inherits only the right to the income from the estate during his life. Because he enjoys the income from Norland for only one year—and because he has not saved much before coming into this inheritance—at his death he leaves his widow and his daughters only £7,000. To this, the uncle has added legacies of £1,000 each for the three daughters. The widow and the daughters thus have £10,000 between them. Conservatively invested, this would yield about £500 a year, enough for four gentlewomen to live modestly, but certainly not enough to support the more privileged life to which Norland has accustomed them. Nor is it enough to provide attractive "portions," the contemporary term for dowries, for three girls.

John Dashwood and his wife quickly move into the house he has inherited, reducing his stepmother and stepsisters to the undesirable condition of visitors in the house they had thought of as their home. Despite a promise made to his dying father to do everything in his power to make his stepmother and stepsisters comfortable, John rapidly allows his selfish wife to convince him that he cannot afford to make any additions to their capital.

Elinor at 19 and Marianne at 17 are of marriageable age; the obvious problem is how they are to marry without good portions. Three gentlemen are introduced in the first of the novel's three volumes, two of whom clearly qualify as potential husbands for the Dashwood girls: Edward Ferrars and John Willoughby, both in their twenties. The third gentleman, Colonel Brandon, in his late thirties, is less obviously a potential husband.

Kate Winslet (far left) as Marianne Dashwood and Emma Thompson (far right) as Elinor Dashwood star in this 1995 film production, directed by Ang Lee.

Edward Ferrars is Mrs. John Dashwood's brother, the elder son of a very rich and unpleasant mother. He is neither handsome, nor lively, nor conventionally ambitious. His mother wants him to go into politics, or at least the army, but "all his wishes centered in domestic comfort and the quiet of private life" (Austen, *Sense and Sensibility*, p. 49). Marianne finds Edward dull, but Elinor is attracted to his quiet manner, his intelligence, his "sentiments," and his goodness. He seems to like Elinor, but is so reserved and correct in his conduct that she is uncertain of his feelings.

Thanks to the kindness and charity of Sir John Middleton, a relative of Mrs. Dashwood's, Mrs. Dashwood and her daughters are able to settle into Barton Cottage, very near Barton Park, his estate. Sir John is a sociable country squire, fond of hunting; his wife, Lady Middleton, dotes on her children and can say nothing that is not insipid and commonplace. Her loquacious mother, Mrs. Jennings, also lives with the Middletons.

One day, running down a hill in a rainstorm with characteristic impetuosity, Marianne falls and twists her ankle. A handsome neighbor, Willoughby, rushes to her assistance, swoops her into his arms, and carries her back to Barton Cottage. Marianne quickly responds to his gallantry.

Sir John reports that Willoughby periodically stays in the neighborhood at Allenham Court, visiting the elderly Mrs. Smith, whose presumptive heir he is.

Edward's caution and correctness are contrasted to Willoughby's ardor and impulsiveness. Elinor suggests to Marianne that she would be wise to be more guarded in displaying her love for Willoughby, but Marianne insists that sincerity is preferable to reserve and that "the restraint of sentiments which were not in themselves illaudable . . . [would be] a disgraceful subjection of reason to commonplace and mistaken notions" (*Sense and Sensibility*, p. 84). Willoughby seeks chances to be alone with Marianne, becoming intimate enough to beg a lock of her hair as a keepsake. Although Willoughby has not introduced Marianne to Mrs. Smith, he drives her to Allenham to see the gardens and the house. When Elinor suggests that this excursion is improper, Marianne replies that she trusts her own feelings to tell her when she acts properly or not and that she feels no impropriety or wrong in what she has done.

A complication arrives in the person of Colonel Brandon, a respected friend of Sir John's, returned from service in India, who quickly grows fond of Marianne. Willoughby and Marianne amuse each other with witticisms at the absent colonel's expense. "Brandon," declares Willoughby, "is just the kind of man . . . whom everybody speaks well of, and nobody cares about; whom all are delighted to see, and nobody remembers to talk to" (*Sense and Sensibility,* p. 81). Later, just as the Middletons and the Dashwoods are to go on an excursion to the estate of Colonel Brandon's brother-in-law, the colonel receives a letter that forces him to cancel the excursion. He apologizes and departs immediately for London. Willoughby then departs with equal suddenness, pleading that Mrs. Smith is sending him to London to attend to her business. Edward, too, leaves after a constrained visit of only a week.

New visitors at Sir John's, Mr. and Mrs. Palmer, show the kind of ordinary but interesting pain Austen often discovers in marriages. Charlotte Palmer is a daughter of Mrs. Jennings. Her husband is an intelligent man whose temper has been soured by his marriage to a beautiful but foolish woman. Good-humored and even kind, Mrs. Palmer volubly persists in publicly interpreting her husband's coldness and rudeness to her as "droll" (*Sense and Sensibility,* p. 134).

Yet more relations of Mrs. Jennings visit, two sisters: Miss Steele, nearly 30, very plain, and Lucy Steele, about 22, pretty, and with "a smartness of air, which though it did not give actual elegance and grace, gave distinction to her person" (*Sense and Sensibility,* p. 142). Elinor pities Lucy, who has native intelligence without education, but is disgusted by her toadying to Lady Middleton. The first volume ends with a surprising revelation: Lucy confides to Elinor that she and Edward have been secretly engaged for four years. Edward proposed to her when he was a pupil studying with Lucy's uncle, Mr. Pratt. Elinor reluctantly accedes to Lucy's demand that she keep this engagement a secret.

In the second volume, neither Elinor nor Marianne having yet secured husbands, Mrs. Jennings volunteers to take them with her to London, confident that she can help them make good matches. Kind Mrs. Jennings is the widow of a man who has "traded with success in a less elegant part of town" (*Sense and Sensibility,* p. 170). As a retail tradesman, he ranked conspicuously below the gentry; nevertheless, he has provided well for his widow and for his two daughters. Mrs. Jennings is understandably, if indelicately, proud of the matches she has helped her daughters make, and determines to do as well for the Dashwood sisters.

Against Elinor's better judgment, Elinor and Marianne accept Mrs. Jennings's invitation to stay with her in London. Elinor recognizes Mrs. Jennings's basic decency, yet worries "that she is not a woman whose society can afford us pleasure, or whose protection will give us consequence" (*Sense and Sensibility,* p. 173). The role of introducing Elinor and Marianne to London society ought rightly to be played by Mr. and Mrs. John Dashwood, who ignore this obligation as they do so many others. Marianne is eager to be in London to discover what happened to Willoughby and to see him again. Given the degree of intimacy between Marianne and Willoughby and the fact that Marianne is apparently writing to him in London, Elinor suspects that they are secretly engaged. Meanwhile, Marianne, learning that Willoughby is indeed in London, anxiously but unavailingly expects him to visit her.

At a London party, Marianne accidentally discovers Willoughby with a fashionable young lady. He does his best to avoid her indiscreet advances; when she presses for an explanation, he replies coldly and withdraws. Distraught, Marianne retreats. Willoughby sends a letter announcing that he has "long been engaged elsewhere" and insisting that he never intended to convey anything beyond friendship and esteem to Marianne. Elinor finds this letter "impudently cruel"; Marianne is hysterical and grief-stricken (*Sense and Sensibility,* p. 196). Much to their surprise, Elinor and Mrs. Jennings learn that there never was an engagement between Marianne and Willoughby. Willoughby is to marry a Miss Grey, who has a portion of £50,000.

Colonel Brandon, calling on Elinor at Mrs. Jennings's London house, seeks to diminish Marianne's suffering by revealing to Elinor unhappy and embarrassing facts about his own history. When his first love, Eliza, was unwillingly married to his older brother, he retreated to India. Eliza's husband treated her badly and divorced her on grounds of adultery. She afterwards gave birth to an illegitimate child, Eliza Williams. Colonel Brandon rescued Eliza when her mother died, then placed the girl in the care of a respectable woman. At the age of 16, Eliza suddenly disappeared. We now learn that the mysterious letter calling Colonel Brandon away in the first volume contained news of little Eliza and led him to discover that she had been seduced by Willoughby, who then abandoned her and her baby. The colonel rescued them. When Elinor conveys these revelations to Marianne, they convince her that she was deluded about

Willoughby's character and cause her to begin to regard Colonel Brandon with more interest and sympathy.

After these revelations, mordant comedy is provided by Mrs. John Dashwood's London dinner party: Elinor watches Lucy Steele ingratiate herself with the proud and ill-natured Mrs. Ferrars. Although alert to the mind-numbing stupidity of the fashionable social world exemplified by this dinner party, Elinor nevertheless allows herself to be amused at the spectacle of the foolish Mrs. Ferrars and the foolish Mrs. John Dashwood behaving graciously to the obsequious Lucy—"whom of all others, had they known as much as she did [about Lucy's secret engagement to their relation], they would have been most anxious to mortify" (*Sense and Sensibility*, p. 239). Elinor has also been informed that Mrs. Ferrars would like to see Edward marry a Miss Morton, daughter of Lord Morton, who has a portion of £30,000, and that, as an inducement, she has offered Edward £1,000 a year to do so.

With some cruelty, Lucy calls on her rival Elinor to boast of her progress in Mrs. Ferrars's regard and of her confidence in Edward's affection for her. Faithful to her promise to keep Lucy's secret, Elinor has been suffering in silence. Edward himself then calls in the midst of this tête-à-tête, further trying Elinor's powers of self-control in an exceedingly awkward three-way conversation. The second volume ends with another triumph of Lucy over Elinor: John Dashwood finally sees that it is his duty to have Elinor and Marianne stay with the Dashwoods in London, but Mrs. Dashwood demurs; succumbing to Lucy's flattering attentions, she invites the Steele girls instead.

The third and final volume of *Sense and Sensibility* opens with a sudden reversal of Lucy Steele's fortunes: news of her engagement becomes public and the outraged Mrs. Ferrars and Mrs. John Dashwood turn her away. Edward refuses to marry Miss Morton and is disinherited by his mother. He has earlier expressed an interest in becoming a clergyman and is now reported to be seeking a Church living so that he can marry and support Lucy. Elinor is astonished when Colonel Brandon—not appreciating that Lucy's engagement to Edward pains Elinor—comes to her with a generous offer of a Church living worth about £200 a year for Edward. Duty requires Elinor to convey this ostensibly happy news to Edward, who receives it glumly. Edward's fashionable and foppish younger brother,

Robert, who complacently enjoys his good fortune consequent on Edward's loss of their mother's favor, laments that Edward is reduced to anything so "ridiculous" as being a country clergyman. Robert furthermore reports that he considers Lucy "the merest awkward country girl, without style, or elegance, and almost without beauty" (*Sense and Sensibility*, p. 296). Meanwhile, Edward's independent fortune of £2,000 and this new £200 a year are far less than the opulence Lucy expected to enjoy with the elder son of Mrs. Ferrars.

Elinor and Marianne, now eager to go home to Barton Cottage, accept the Palmers' offer to return by way of the Palmer estate, Cleveland. There, Marianne indulges her love for wild nature by wandering about in the damp, and succumbs to a dangerous fever. The gravity of her illness arouses general fear that she might die.

Just as Marianne recovers enough to be out of danger, an amazed Elinor receives a visit from Willoughby, who calls on her at Cleveland in an attempt to palliate his guilt. He acknowledges that he courted Marianne despite his engagement to Miss Grey and his determination not to marry a poor woman, but declares that he did, involuntarily, become attached to Marianne. He sheds new light on his abrupt departure from Allenham when he confesses that, far from being sent to London on Mrs. Smith's business, Mrs. Smith was so appalled by his seduction and abandonment of Eliza Williams that she disinherited him and sent him away.

Elinor and Marianne return to Barton Cottage. Her illness has offered Marianne an occasion for serious reflection. She admits to Elinor that she behaved badly with Willoughby and declares that she now understands the importance of actively exerting control over one's feelings. The sisters walk out to the spot where Marianne first met Willoughby. There Marianne confesses that she has not only been imprudent, but that she has been "insolent and unjust" to those who have been kind to her, especially Elinor, for whose conduct and fortitude under similarly difficult circumstances she professes admiration (*Sense and Sensibility*, p. 337). Even Mrs. Dashwood, not notably reflective, now takes some responsibility for her own imprudence as Marianne's mother and recognizes that she has been blind to Elinor's suffering and remarkable virtues.

The novel concludes with a spate of marriages, some blissful, others uncomfortably realistic. The Dashwoods are at first distressed by what seems to be the news that Edward has married Lucy.

A wedding banquet c. 1812.

However, they soon learn—to their wonderment—that it is Robert Ferrars who has married Lucy. Edward and Elinor delight in the absurd letter Lucy has sent to inform him of this sudden transfer of her affections. Mrs. Ferrars's rage at Robert inspires her to bestow £10,000 on Edward, thus enabling Edward and Elinor to marry with a reasonable income (about £720 a year). Lucy's continued campaign of flattery directed at Mrs. Ferrars in time restores Robert and herself to favor, and subjects the Ferrars and the John Dashwoods to a life of jealous and quarrelsome intimacy with each other. Willoughby lives a very ordinary life, occupying himself with his hunting dogs and horses, living with a wife who is "not always out of humour" (*Sense and Sensibility*, p. 367). At 19, Marianne marries Colonel Brandon, learning to love him and make him deservedly happy.

Colonel Brandon, wealth, and the Indies. *Sense and Sensibility,* tells us that when Brandon was a young man his family had an estate that was much encumbered, that is, burdened with debt. His father was the legal guardian of the orphaned heiress Eliza, whom he married to Brandon's brother against her inclination, presumably in part to use her money to help pay up the debt on the estate. Brandon tells Elinor that when he lost Eliza to his brother, he withdrew from Eng-

land to India by exchanging his commission in the regular army for one in the East India Company army. Returned from India, he now has the rank of colonel and is comfortably rich, in possession of a nice estate in Dorsetshire, able to support not only himself and Marianne, but also to make the generous gift of a living to Edward.

As is common in novels and plays of this period, distant parts of the British Empire like India are offstage presences, not directly represented, but referred to as places in which people die, from which people return, and—sometimes—where fortunes are made. Decades of parliamentary investigation into alleged corruption and crime by Englishmen seeking to enrich themselves in India, most famously in the impeachment trial of Warren Hastings, governor-general of India, contributed to a pervasive popular sense that there was something less than respectable, even shameful, about people who had been to India and about wealth from there. Willoughby takes advantage of this prejudice when he mocks Brandon as a man with "more money than he can spend" and as a man who knows all about "nabobs" (*Sense and Sensibility*, p. 82). "Nabob" was originally the English version of an Urdu word for the Mohammedan governors of the Mogul empire in India; it came to be used, often derisively, for English officials in

India who returned with large fortunes. Such people were ridiculed and feared, in part because they usually came from less-than-distinguished social positions, then used their fortunes to buy land, with its accompanying political and social power. For an English person to go to India in this period was a high-risk strategy not normally engaged in by the respectable or well-off because most English people who went to India died of disease or drowned before they could return home with any profits. To exchange a commission in the regular army for one in India would have seemed to many an act of desperation.

Jane Austen is characteristically coy about what Brandon did in India and what impact it had on his fortune. Some readers have assumed that he inherited his Delaford estate because his brother died, which is possible, but we are not told that his brother has died; the colonel may simply have purchased the Delaford estate, relying at least in part on money he has made in India—or he may have used money made in India to improve the condition of the family estate. Given his age when he went out to India and the expensiveness of commissions in the regular army (British army officers had to purchase their commissions), it seems likely that Brandon went to India at a rank considerably lower than colonel and rose in rank in India.

The English presence in India had officially begun in 1601 when the East India Company received its first royal charter giving it a trading monopoly there. After Robert Clive's success in 1757 at the Battle of Plassey in Bengal, Britain increasingly acquired sovereignty as well as wealth in India.

For the few fortunate men who survived long enough and had sufficient good fortune to rise to the rank of colonel in India, the financial rewards were considerable. A colonel's pay and allowances alone came to about £3,500 a year. But high-ranking officers in India also participated in the process of collecting taxes and shared in tax revenue. Officers in the British army in Europe rarely collected significant prize money after victories, but officers in the East India army regularly got not only prize money but also significant "presents" from grateful local Indian princes. Despite the efforts of the directors of the East India Company and of a "reforming" Parliament to reduce "private trading" by Englishmen in India, many military officers, like their civilian counterparts, also engaged in economically rewarding private enterprise. Thus, "a man who reached the rank of major in Bengal could expect with rea-

sonable luck to make his fortune" (Marshall, *East Indian Fortunes,* p. 213). One Indian notable complained about what seemed to him to be the custom of the English in India—a custom "which every one of these emigrants holds to be a Divine obligation, I mean of grasping together as much money in this country as they can, and carrying it in immense sums to the kingdom of England" (Kahn in Marshall, *Oxford History,* p. 514).

India and the East India Company provided economic resources for the Austen family. Jane Austen's great-uncle Frank acted as agent for one of the company's surgeons in India, helping to repatriate the profits of his private trading. Philadelphia Austen, Jane's aunt, lacking a portion that would have made her attractive on the English marriage market, ventured out to India in 1752 to marry this rich surgeon, a man 20 years older than she, sight-unseen. (Spinsters so desperate that they traveled to India for husbands were a frequent object of contemporary ridicule.) Philadelphia's daughter, Eliza Hancock, was the goddaughter of Warren Hastings, the governor-general. Hastings, who was suspected of being Philadelphia's biological father, settled £10,000 on her. The family connection to India continued. In 1809-10 Jane's brother Frank, as captain of the British naval vessel *Saint Albans,* convoyed East India ships. Delivering 93 chests of gold and treasure to the Company in England, he gained over £3,000 in reward money and agent fees. *Sense and Sensibility* idealizes the quiet, rural English life that Elinor and Edward are to live, having "nothing to wish for, but . . . rather better pasturage for their cows" (*Sense and Sensibility*, p. 363). Yet, from her own experience, Austen knew that in many gentry and pseudo-gentry families, lives of such tranquil financial independence sometimes were made possible only by money earned in dangerous—and perhaps disreputable—adventures abroad.

Literary context. Most critics, from Austen's time to the present, have considered Austen more sympathetic to the conservative than to the radical side in the ideological wars of her day. Particularly in the 1790s, English writers frequently declared their political allegiances in no uncertain terms. Novelists such as Robert Bage, William Godwin, and Thomas Holcroft showed interest in and sympathy for the radical principles of the French Revolution and challenged the traditional political and social order of England. In Bage's *Hermsprong, or Man as He is Not* (1796),

THE AGE OF SENSIBILITY

Novelists and philosophers alike took ideologically fraught positions on "sensibility," a key term in Austen's title. Philosophically, sensibility was understood to be a faculty or capacity of sensation and emotion, as distinguished from reason (the capacity of cognition). Interest in sensibility began early in the eighteenth century. Philosophers like the third earl of Shaftesbury in *Characteristics of Man, Manners, Opinions, Times* (1711) turned away from the doctrine of original sin to postulate that human nature was benign and people had an innate power of sympathy for others and a natural capacity for virtue. At mid-century David Hume in *The Treatise of Human Nature* (1739-40) and Adam Smith in *A Theory of Moral Sentiments* (1759) carefully explored the psychological operations of the mind and the emotions, especially sympathy, seeking to offer secular foundations for morality. By the late eighteenth century, sensibility had become both fashionable and controversial. It became fashionable to present oneself as a person of exquisite sensibility, blessed with the capacity for acute feelings and an innate sense of virtue; heroes and heroines of sensibility quivered with feeling and shed frequent tears in novels and poems of sentiment and sensibility. At the same time, although most thinkers agreed that there was an important relation between sensibility and virtuous action, critics worried that the external marks of sensibility, increasingly conventionalized—the sigh, the quick responsiveness, the tear, speaking in praise of nature and poetry, the melancholy languishing look—could all too easily be imitated by an insensible person, bereft of a real moral sense or true sympathy (like the novel's Willoughby). Critics also worried that the pleasures of sensibility were becoming narcissistic, selfish pleasures, cultivated for their own sake and for the egoistic gratification of imagining oneself as a superior person, instead of producing—as originally theorized—a sympathy that bound an individual to others in the community and motivated active charity. Elinor's attentive nursing of her sick sister is a sign of true sensibility and Marianne's lovesick moping is a mark of sensibility run amuck. Austen and many other writers agreed that sensibility alone is not a sufficient ground of virtuous action, that reason and principle were also necessary, and that distinguishing between true and false sensibility could be challenging.

for instance, Lord Grondale has his daughter's suitor, the hero Hermsprong, tried for sedition because he has criticized the British constitution and read Thomas Paine's *The Rights of Man* (for which Paine was convicted of sedition). Such novelists were considered English radicals, or Jacobins, a terms that had initially been used for the members of a French political club established in 1789 to promote democracy and the equality of man.

Female novelists too, including Mary Hays in *The Memoirs of Emma Courtney* (1796) and *The Victim of Prejudice* (1799) and Mary Wollstonecraft in the posthumously published *Wrongs of Woman* (1798), showed sympathies for radical causes, and some vigorously attacked the con-

ventional socialization of women, demanding new rights for women, and notoriously pursuing love outside the bounds of matrimony. Clearly, *Sense and Sensibility* is at a considerable remove from such bold critiques. Many critics have even supposed Jane Austen followed in the conservative footsteps of the so-called Antijacobins, like Jane West, the author of *Advantages of Education* (1793) and *A Tale of the Times* (1799), in which a supporter of the French Revolution proves to be a libertine seducer. Yet Austen did not admire the humourless didacticism of the writer Hannah More, whose *Coelebs in Search of a Wife* (1809) Austen refused to read. And, as critics have also noted, Austen does offer a scathing account of the ways in which patriarchy is unjust to women, and a sharp dramatization of the kind of male narcissism and foolishness that patriarchal privilege can produce in men such as John Dashwood, Robert Ferrars, and John Willoughby.

Reception. The publication of *Sense and Sensibility* in 1811 attracted little notice, which is hardly surprising, given that it was the first published work of an author who at that point was without any literary reputation. Indeed, like all of Austen's novels, *Sense and Sensibility* was published without Austen's name on the title page. The title page indicated only that the work was "By a Lady." Moreover, the eighteenth-century idea that novels generally were only a kind of subliterature continued to dominate the reviews. Reviewers often expressed annoyance at having to read so many bad novels, condescended to the genre, and considered that one of their principal duties in reviewing a novel was to report whether it was likely to corrupt or to improve the morals of young readers, especially young female readers. Novels were blamed for encouraging young women to adopt foolish, even dangerous ideas, especially about men. In their review, critics vigorously attacked novels they thought inculcated unrealistic, even absurd, romantic standards of male behavior and female expectations.

Only the *Critical Review* and the *British Critic* noticed the publication of *Sense and Sensibility,* both finding it above the common level of novels and both pronouncing that it had a useful moral. *The Critical Review* thought the "chief merit" of the novel lay in its portrayal of Marianne and Willoughby:

> [That] furnishes a most excellent lesson to young ladies to curb that violent sensibility that too often leads to misery, and always to inconvenience and ridicule. To young men who make a point of playing with a young woman's affections, it will be no less useful, as it shows in strong colors the folly and criminality of

sporting with the feelings of those whom their conduct tends to wound and render miserable.
>
> (Southam, p. 38)

The British Critic agreed that "our female friends . . . may peruse these volumes not only with satisfaction but with real benefits, for they may learn from them, if they please, many sober and salutary maxims for the Conduct of life, exemplified in a very pleasing and entertaining narrative" (Southam, p. 40)

—Susan Staves

For More Information

Austen, Jane. *Sense and Sensibility.* Harmondsworth, Middlesex: Penguin, 1969.

Butler, Marilyn. *Jane Austen and the War of Ideas.* Oxford: Clarendon, 1975.

Collins, Irene. *Jane Austen and the Clergy.* London: Hambledon, 1993.

Copeland, Edward, and Juliet McMaster. *The Cambridge Companion to Jane Austen.* Cambridge: Cambridge University Press, 1997.

Gilson, David. *A Bibliography of Jane Austen.* New Castle, Del.: Oak Knoll, 1997.

Johnson, Claudia L. *Jane Austen: Women, Politics and the Novel.* Chicago: University of Chicago Press, 1988.

Marshall, Peter, and Alaine Low, eds. *The Eighteenth Century.* Vol. 2 of *The Oxford History of the British Empire.* Oxford: Oxford University Press, 1998.

Marshall, P. J. *East Indian Fortunes: The British in Bengal in the Eighteenth Century.* Oxford: Clarendon Press, 1976.

Nokes, David. *Jane Austen: A Life.* New York: Farrar, Strauss, and Giroux, 1997.

Smith, Adam. *An Inquiry into the Nature and Causes of the Wealth of Nations.* Ed. Edwin Cannon. 2 vols. in 1. Chicago: University of Chicago Press, 1976.

Southam, B. C. *Jane Austen: The Critical Heritage.* London: Routledge & Kegan Paul, 1968.

Vickery, Amanda. *The Gentleman's Daughter: Women's Lives in Georgian England.* New Haven: Yale University Press, 1998.

She Stoops to Conquer

by
Oliver Goldsmith

Oliver Goldsmith, the son of an Anglican clergyman, was born in Ireland in 1728. Sent to Trinity College, Dublin, as a sizar—a student who performed menial tasks for other students in return for an allowance from the college—Goldsmith did not apply himself seriously to his studies, though he attained his undergraduate degree in 1749. After several false starts in choosing a career, he decided to pursue medicine. With the financial assistance of a generous uncle, Goldsmith attended the University of Edinburgh, but dropped out to travel on the European continent for several years. In 1756 he returned to England with a mysteriously acquired medical degree, but his attempts at finding employment as a physician were ultimately unsuccessful. Goldsmith then became a hack writer, working for Ralph Griffiths—proprietor of the *Monthly Review*—and later for the publisher Edward Newbury. After the 1759 publication of his *An Enquiry into the Present State of Polite Learning in Europe* (a treatise on the decline of fine arts in eighteenth-century Europe), Goldsmith became increasingly well-known as an author. Other successful works followed—a collection of essays known as *Citizen of the World* (1760-1761); a novel, *The Vicar of Wakefield* (1767); and the poems *The Traveller* (1764) and *The Deserted Village* (1770). Meanwhile, he wrote his first play, *The Good-Natur'd Man* (1768), followed in 1773 by perhaps his greatest triumph, *She Stoops to Conquer*, a lively comedy that provided contemporary audiences with a bracing alternative to the heavy-handed sentimental dramas of the day.

THE LITERARY WORK

A play, set in rural England, during the late eighteenth century; first performed and published in 1773.

SYNOPSIS

A well-bred young lady masquerades as a servant to encourage boldness in her timid suitor.

Events in History at the Time of the Play

Marriage in the eighteenth century. Wholly domestic in its scope, *She Stoops to Conquer* deals mainly with love and marriage, popular subjects in many eighteenth-century comedies. Marriage as an institution was undergoing significant changes at the time of the play. Since the Middle Ages, the parents of the prospective bride and groom had been the ones to arrange marriages, especially when property, money, and even political inclinations were to be considered. The wealthier the family, the more care was taken that the children of that family married someone of equal or higher social status, especially since divorces were rare and difficult to obtain. In the upper classes, children themselves had little say in the matter; nearly all of them were financially dependent on their parents and had been raised to comply with the judgments of their elders. Recalcitrant children whose attention strayed from their parents' marital choice for them could usually be brought back in line by the threat of disinheritance if they wed without their parents' consent.

By the time of *She Stoops to Conquer,* however, significant sociological changes, such as the consolidation of the nuclear family, had caused the balance of power to shift. Although the most aristocratic families still exerted a strong influence over their children's marriages, families that were a few rungs down on the social ladder had by now become more receptive to the prospect of marriages based on affection and physical attraction between spouses, as well as wealth and property. Parents still expected a say in selecting a possible spouse, but children too were allowed to exercise their judgment. On the whole, society supported various ways of making marital matches:

> In the eighteenth century, there developed in England several types of marriage, each most characteristic of a particular sector of society and each definable by a series of different variables. The first variable . . . was intergenerational conflict about the selection of a particular spouse. This might be decided by the parents, kin and "friends" without consulting the bride and groom. Or it might be decided by parents, kin and "friends," but the groom, and by extension also the bride, was granted the right to reject someone whom he or she found at first sight to be physically or temperamentally wholly incompatible. Or choice was made by the spouses themselves, their parents retaining the right of veto to reject someone they regarded as unsuitable, usually on social or economic grounds. . . . Finally, the individual spouses might make their own choices, their parents being merely informed of what had been decided and asked for their formal blessing.
>
> (Stone, pp. 390-391)

Among the gentry or "squirearchy," the order to which the play's Hardcastle family might be said to belong, "the choice of a spouse was increasingly left in the hands of the children themselves and was based mainly on temperamental compatibility with the aim of lasting companionship" (Stone, p. 392).

Actually, Goldsmith presents several variations on the eighteenth-century marriage model in *She Stoops to Conquer.* Although Mr. Hardcastle selects young Marlow as Kate Hardcastle's prospective husband, and even arranges a meeting between them, he nonetheless reassures his daughter, "I'll never control your choice" (Goldsmith, *She Stoops to Conquer,* p. 56). Later Mar-

low's apparent impudence offends Mr. Hardcastle, which no doubt makes the young man seem less ideal, yet the father allows Kate to explore her suitor's character further. By contrast, Tony Lumpkin, Kate's half-brother, is at odds with his domineering mother, Mrs. Hardcastle, who is determined that he marry her ward, Constance Neville, to keep the girl's fortune in the family. Only after Tony reaches his majority at 21 can he officially refuse to wed the bride chosen for him. Meanwhile, Constance exercises her own choice by deciding to elope with her preferred suitor, Hastings, returning only to secure her fortune and ask for Mr. Hardcastle's blessing.

Parent-child relationships. One of the more unusual features of Goldsmith's play is his depiction of affectionate—if conflicted—relationships between parents and children. Society at the time was undergoing a change in attitudes toward child rearing. Although numerous theories on child rearing abounded in the seventeenth and eighteenth centuries, two models—one proposed by English philosopher John Locke, the other by Swiss intellectual Jean-Jacques Rousseau—tended to predominate. Locke held that the child's mind was a *tabula rasa,* or "blank page," at birth, that his or her thoughts and disposition were to be formed and educated by the parents. Rousseau, on the other hand, argued that a child was born naturally good and was corrupted only by his or her experience in society. Clearly the models were different, yet both advocated a more affectionate and somewhat more permissive style of child rearing. In *Some Thoughts upon Education,* Locke proposed that "fear and awe ought to give [parents] the first power over [children's] minds, and love and friendship in riper years to hold it. . . . you shall have him your obedient subject (as is fit) whilst he is a child, and your affectionate friend when he is a man" (Locke in Stone, p. 407).

While Locke's ideas soon found a receptive audience, the new permissiveness in child rearing seemed occasionally to backfire, resulting in spoiled, overindulged children. Around the 1730s, contemporary thinkers worried that the new type of parenting was spoiling the English nobility, making them soft and sheltering them to an excessive degree. Mothers fawned over their children, having them educated at home until the early teens. Whereas concerned adults once protested the rough and repressive behavior of the father, now they blamed mothers for being too lax with their children.

In *She Stoops to Conquer,* Goldsmith presents contrasting examples of the new permissive style of child rearing in the relationships between Mr. Hardcastle and Kate and Mrs. Hardcastle and Tony Lumpkin. Although Mr. Hardcastle adores his daughter, whom he refers to as "my pretty darling," he nonetheless insists on his will in some matters, such as the plain clothes she must wear at night (*She Stoops to Conquer*, p. 54). For her part, Kate complies with her father's decree but she has also negotiated an agreement with him that enables her to wear what she pleases during the day. Their mutual respect and affection allow them to formulate such agreements. By contrast, Mrs. Hardcastle alternately indulges and bullies Tony, her son from her first marriage. Reared at home because his mother considered him too sickly to attend school, Tony chafes at his boundaries and resents his mother's attempts to rule his life even as a young man: "If I'm a man, let me have my fortin [fortune]. Ecod! I'll not be made a fool of no longer [*sic*]" (*She Stoops to Conquer,* p. 93). Mrs. Hardcastle exercises a similar tyranny over Constance Neville, who has been placed under Hardcastle's guardianship until adulthood.

Class attitudes. During the eighteenth century, English society was essentially hierarchical and rigidly stratified according to class. Royalty and the nobility—dukes, marquises, earls, viscounts, barons—were at the top of the pyramid; below them, in descending order, were the landed gentry, physicians and lawyers, yeoman farmers who owned property, bankers, merchants, artisans, and finally factory and other urban workers, and farm laborers. Significantly, this fixed social order was rarely questioned at the time. As one historian contends, there was a "usually unstated but accepted recognition that a hierarchical society was the best of all possible worlds and that the people at the top of that hierarchy should be left to get on with governing it" (Cannadine, p. 53).

Despite the widespread acceptance of a hierarchical social structure, the upper and lower classes were not without their prejudices toward one another. At their most inimical, the lower orders regarded their social superiors as selfish, corrupt and effete, while the upper classes dismissed those far beneath them as uncivilized rabble. In *She Stoops to Conquer*, Goldsmith explores a milder but still questionable form of class prejudice in the somewhat problematic character of young Marlow, the London gentleman who comes to the Hardcastles' country home to court Kate, the daughter of the house. Awkward and diffident around women of his own class, Marlow becomes a flirtatious dandy around lower-

Lillie Langtry as Kate Hardcastle in the theatrical debut of *She Stoops to Conquer,* performed at London's Haymarket Theater in 1881.

class servant girls. Unable even to converse with Kate in her proper guise as Miss Hardcastle, Marlow has no difficulty making advances toward her when he mistakes her for a barmaid and raves to his friend Hastings about "the tempting, brisk, lovely little thing, that runs about the house with a bunch of keys to its girdle" (*She Stoops to Conquer,* p. 118). When Hastings, who knows of Kate's masquerade, cautions Marlow not "to rob a woman of her honor," Marlow retorts, "We all know the honor of a barmaid of an inn. . . . There's nothing in this house that I shan't honestly pay for" (*She Stoops to Conquer,* p. 118).

Marlow's sarcasm about the so-called honor of a barmaid reflects a prejudice of 1700s England. It was mostly a permissive century, in which men of the upper classes commonly had sexual affairs before and after marriage. The pecking order for mistresses moved from respectable married women, to actresses, to high-class prostitutes in brothels, to streetwalkers, and, finally, to amateurs—"the ubiquitous maids, waiting on masters and guests in lodgings, in the home, in inns; young girls whose virtue was always uncertain and was constantly under attack. . . . These last were the most exploited, and most defenceless, of the various kinds of women whose sexual services might be obtained by a man of quality in eighteenth-century England" (Stone, p. 601).

A lady and her suitor exhibiting the formalities of eighteenth-century courtship, which Goldsmith merrily derided in his classic comedy.

On learning that Kate is not a barmaid but still believing her to be a poor relation of the Hardcastles and his social inferior, Marlow abandons his seduction plans but informs her that "the difference of our birth, fortune, and education, make an honorable connection impossible" (*She Stoops to Conquer*, pp. 124-125). Marlow must be stripped of his class prejudices and taught to recognize merit in a woman regardless of social status before Kate can accept him as a husband. This recognition occurs, a reflection of changes in real life at the time. Marlow does an about-face and, still thinking Kate poor, proposes out of love, a motivation that was gradually displacing the aim to preserve family status and fortune.

The Play in Focus

Plot summary. The play begins with an argument between a long-married couple, Mr. and Mrs. Hardcastle. Mr. Hardcastle, a contented country gentleman, sees no reason to change his comfortable existence, but his wife, Dorothy, longs for a more elegant lifestyle that would include visits to London. The couple's squabble turns to the subject of their children, especially Mrs. Hardcastle's overindulgence of her son by her first marriage, Tony Lumpkin. Mrs. Hardcastle defends her cosseting of Tony by claiming

he is sickly; Mr. Hardcastle, however, views his stepson as a hard-drinking, mischievous rascal. Tony himself appears at that moment to inform his mother that he is meeting friends at the local alehouse. Mrs. Hardcastle protests her son's choice of companions and tries to prevent him from going, but Tony is adamant. Mother and son exit, wrangling, while Mr. Hardcastle shakes his head over their relationship.

Just then, Kate, the Hardcastles' daughter, enters. Mr. Hardcastle greets her fondly, teasing her about her fine clothes. Kate reminds him that they have an agreement: in the morning, she dresses like a fashionable lady, but in the evening, she puts on plain clothes to please her father. Mr. Hardcastle acknowledges their bargain, then informs Kate that he has selected the son of his old friend Sir Charles Marlow as a possible husband for her and that the young man will be visiting that very evening. Initially startled by the news, Kate is pleased to hear that her suitor is brave, generous, and handsome but is less pleased to learn that he is also shy and reserved. As she wonders whether or not she can cure the young man of his timidity, Constance Neville, her best friend and Mrs. Hardcastle's ward, enters. The two women quickly confide in each other about the latest developments in their lives. Constance wishes to marry her longtime admirer, Mr. Hastings, but Mrs. Hardcastle, who controls Constance's fortune, wants to arrange a marriage between her ward and her son, even though Constance and Tony detest each other. Kate then relates the news about her own suitor; Constance tells her that young Marlow is Mr. Hastings' closest friend and "a very singular character. . . . Among women of reputation he is the most modest man alive; but his acquaintances give him a very different character among creatures of another stamp" (*She Stoops to Conquer*, p. 58). Kate surmises that young Marlow behaves differently depending on what class of woman he is with.

Meanwhile, at the alehouse, Tony drinks and carouses with his friends. In the midst of their merrymaking, Hastings and Marlow arrive. Both of them are seriously out-of-temper because they have gotten lost en route to the Hardcastles' house. Tony, whom they do not know, soon learns that these men are to be guests of his stepfather. Incensed after hearing the unknowing Marlow refer to him as "an awkward booby," Tony decides to play a prank on everyone by directing Hastings and Marlow toward a nearby "inn"—which is, in reality, the Hardcastles' home (*She Stoops to Conquer*, p. 64).

Arriving at the "inn," Hastings and Marlow are greeted by Mr. Hardcastle, who welcomes them as his honored guests. Believing him to be an innkeeper, the two young men are displeased by his apparent overfamiliarity. Hardcastle, in turn, finds their behavior brusque and rude, and decides that Sir Charles Marlow must not perceive the true character of his own son. Hastings soon realizes he has been duped when he sees his love, Constance, at the "inn" and she informs him of Tony's mischiefmaking ways. The two lovers resolve to elope to France at the first opportunity, but Constance is determined to obtain her fortune—mainly jewels—from Mrs. Hardcastle. Constance and Hastings decide not to tell Marlow of Tony's prank, fearing that Marlow will insist on leaving once he learns of his mistake. Hastings informs Marlow of Miss Hardcastle's presence at the "inn," but on meeting Kate, clad in her fine daytime clothes, Marlow loses his composure, fleeing the room after an awkward attempt at conversation. Kate again wonders how to instill confidence in this bashful young man.

Meanwhile, Hastings ingratiates himself with Mrs. Hardcastle but secretly confides in Tony about his desire to marry Constance. A relieved Tony promises to help the lovers by securing Constance's jewels for her. Tony later slips into his mother's room, steals the jewels, and gives them to Hastings. Unaware of their plan, however, Constance has asked Mrs. Hardcastle for her jewels. Tony quickly whispers to his mother to tell Constance the jewels truly are lost, a suggestion Mrs. Hardcastle immediately adopts. Tony then privately informs Constance that the jewels are in Hastings' possession. Unfortunately, Mrs. Hardcastle discovers that the jewels really are lost and raises a great alarm throughout the house.

Meanwhile, Kate, now changed into her plain dress, discusses Marlow with her father. Displeased by Marlow's earlier impudence, Mr. Hardcastle is astonished to hear of the young man's diffidence on meeting Kate. Kate vows to discover her would-be suitor's true nature. Later, she learns of Tony's prank and laughs to discover the reason for Marlow's lordly behavior in the Hardcastle home. On hearing that Marlow has seen her in her housekeeping dress and mistaken her for a barmaid, Kate mischievously decides not to reveal her true identity. When Marlow enters and sees Kate in her plain clothes, he immediately begins to flirt with her. Attempting to steal a kiss, Marlow flees when Mr. Hardcastle, ignorant of his daughter's ruse, enters the room.

Furious with Marlow's manhandling of his daughter, Mr. Hardcastle resolves to throw him out of the house, but then allows Kate a little more time to prove Marlow has a character pleasing to both father and daughter. At their next meeting, however, Marlow's condescending behavior toward the "innkeeper" so enrages Mr. Hardcastle that he orders the astonished young man to leave. Kate, still attired simply, then informs Marlow of the true nature of his surroundings, but allows him to believe she is actually a poor relation of the Hardcastles. Mortified, Marlow apologizes profusely for his earlier conduct toward her and promises not to take advantage of her innocence. Pleased by Marlow's humility and gentleness, Kate resolves to help mend matters between him and her father.

Elsewhere, Hastings and Constance prepare to elope but learn, to their dismay, that Marlow, to whom Hastings entrusted the casket of jewels, has given the casket back to Mrs. Hardcastle, still believing her at that point to be the innkeeper's wife. To make matters worse, Hastings's letter to Tony about the elopement plans has ended up in Mrs. Hardcastle's hands. Enraged, Mrs. Hardcastle plans to send Constance to her tyrannical aunt Pedigree as punishment. Hastings, Marlow, and Constance all blame Tony for the prank that has resulted in their discomfiture, but the young squire comes up with another plan to set everything right. Ordered by his mother to accompany her and Constance to Aunt Pedigree, Tony guides the carriage in a circle for three hours until Mrs. Hardcastle thinks they are lost. Meeting up with Hastings in the back garden, Tony tells him where to find Constance, then distracts his overwrought mother, who does not recognize her own home in the dark and believes Tony's story that they are now on Crack-skull Common, a dangerous place favored by wandering robbers and highwaymen. After Mr. Hardcastle encounters his wife and stepson in the garden, however, Mrs. Hardcastle realizes she has been tricked and berates Tony.

Sir Charles Marlow, young Marlow's father, has now arrived for a visit and been apprised of Tony's prank and his own son's odd behavior. Having taken a liking to Kate, the elder Marlow worries that she might not want to marry his son. Kate reassures him, then bids him and Mr. Hardcastle to hide themselves and witness young Marlow's behavior toward her. Marlow enters and, still believing Kate to be poor, confesses his love for her and proposes marriage. Greatly astonished by the young man's ardor, Sir Charles and Mr. Hardcastle leave their hiding place, and

Marlow learns to his chagrin that he has been flirting with Miss Hardcastle all this time. Both fathers enjoy a hearty laugh, while Kate teases her new betrothed mercilessly.

The other members of the family then enter the room, with Hastings and Constance intending to ask for Mr. Hardcastle's assistance in retrieving her jewels. Mrs. Hardcastle, however, asserts that she still has control over her ward's fortune unless Tony refuses to marry Constance when he is of age. Mr. Hardcastle then reveals that Tony has been of age for the last three months but the news was deliberately kept from him by his mother for her own purposes. A delighted Tony declares his independence from his mother and officially refuses Constance, who is now free to marry Hastings. Marlow, recovered from his embarrassment, proposes again to Kate, this time in her true guise, and is accepted. The play ends on a jovial note as Mr. Hardcastle bestows his blessing on both couples and invites everyone in to supper.

Town and country. One of the more striking features of *She Stoops to Conquer* is Goldsmith's inversion of the classic conflict between town and country values. The Restoration comedies of manners had taken their tone from the festive, splendid, but dissolute court of King Charles II, who brought a measure of French pomp and gaiety with him when he ascended to the English throne after years of exile in France. Plays such as William Wycherley's *The Country Wife* (1675), George Etherege's *The Man of Mode* (1676), and William Congreve's **The Way of the World** (1700; also in *WLAIT 3: British and Irish Literature and Its Times*) dealt with the manners of the town: witty, sophisticated, cynical, even somewhat corrupt. The heroes and heroines of such comedies were usually those who displayed the highest degrees of wit and grace and who could successfully navigate the often treacherous waters of society. Significantly, when characters from the country appeared in these plays, they tended to be either naive innocents who needed to be educated in the ways of the town, or crude buffoons whose behavior was a source of ridicule to the sophisticated town wits.

By contrast, *She Stoops to Conquer* opens with a condemnation of town values as Mr. Hardcastle criticizes his neighbors who go to town "and bring back vanity and affectation to last them the whole year," adding, "I wonder why London cannot keeps its own fools at home. In my time, the follies of the town crept slowly among us, but now they travel faster than a stagecoach" (*She*

Stoops to Conquer, p. 50). An ardent lover of "old times, old friends, old manners, old books, old wines," Mr. Hardcastle has little tolerance for "the fools of the age" and the newfangled pleasures of town (*She Stoops to Conquer*, pp. 51, 54).

Goldsmith continually depicts the country as triumphing over the town. In the most comic of these victories, the irrepressible Tony Lumpkin—whom earlier Restoration comedies would have depicted as a foolish country bumpkin—successfully tricks Hastings and Marlow, two sophisticated men of the world, about their accommodations. Weary, irritable, and unwary, these two gentlemen stumble into Tony's trap. Marlow, in particular, becomes ridiculous, unabashedly pursuing Kate when he mistakes her for a barmaid and bragging to her of his many romantic conquests "at the Ladies' Club in town" (*She Stoops to Conquer*, p. 110).

But if Hastings and Marlow face humiliation and discomfiture in the country, they ultimately receive assistance, acceptance, and even forgiveness from the very people they considered their social inferiors. On learning of Tony's prank, Mr. Hardcastle pardons Marlow for his apparent impudence and attempted seduction of Kate, who accepts the young man as her husband—though not without tormenting him a little first. She ultimately, however, views his faults as temporary—"he has only the faults that will pass off with time, and the virtues that will improve with time" (*She Stoops to Conquer*, pp. 114). Moreover, Marlow's sojourn in the country prompts him to abandon the artificial manner he had assumed in order to court Miss Hardcastle; struck by Kate's charms in her plain dress, Marlow begins to behave more naturally, if not always commendably, as he enthusiastically pursues her. Meanwhile, Hastings acquires a staunch ally in Tony Lumpkin, who freely aids the elopement with Constance. Tony, the supposedly awkward rustic, is even permitted to administer a deserved rebuke for ingratitude to the polished town gentleman:

> Ay, now it's dear friend, noble Squire. Just now, it was all idiot, cub, and run me through the guts. Damn your way of fighting, I say. After we take a knock in this part of the country, we kiss and be friends. But if you had run me through the guts, then I should be dead, and you might go kiss the hangman.
> (*She Stoops to Conquer*, pp. 140-141)

Goldsmith's affection for the country and its people reflects an increasing fondness for nature among his contemporaries. While their immediate predecessors tended to prefer nature tamed and disciplined by man, mid- and late-eighteenth-century artists and thinkers began to appreciate the beauty of nature untamed and in the wild. This appreciation would flourish especially at the very end of the eighteenth century in the poetry of **Lyrical Ballads** (also in *WLAIT 3: British and Irish Literature and Its Times*).

In the 1770s, when *She Stoops to Conquer* was written, the appreciation for nature may have stemmed in part from a growing nostalgia for a way of life that had begun to disappear. The Industrial Revolution was gaining momentum; in 1765 James Watt had introduced the steam engine, an invention whose repercussions would be felt throughout the remainder of the century and well into the next. Meanwhile, the English countryside was undergoing visible changes, with open fields and communal farmlands being fenced off and enclosed as separate, privately owned agricultural lots. "After the third decade of the Eighteenth Century, the work [of enclosure] began to be carried on by a new and more wholesale procedure: private Acts of Parliament were passed which overrode the resistance of individual proprietors to enclosure. . . . The pace of the enclosure of land grew more rapid every decade from 1740 onwards, and was fastest of all at the turn of the century" (Trevelyan, pp. 80-81). Thus, Mr. Hardcastle, who is devoted to his crumbling country mansion and reveres the past, partly embodies a dying age.

Sources and literary context. Goldsmith drew from a variety of sources, mainly other French and English plays, to create *She Stoops to Conquer*. George Farquhar's popular comedy of manners, *The Beaux' Stratagem* (1707), provided the premise of two London gentlemen visiting a country estate and falling in love with the women of the household. One of Goldsmith's friends even suggested Goldsmith call his own play *The Belle's Stratagem* as an homage to Farquhar. Goldsmith refused but he did have his heroine, Kate, refer to a character in *The Beaux' Stratagem* while donning her plain housekeeping gown: "Don't you think I look something like Cherry [the innkeeper's daughter] in *The Beaux' Stratagem?*" (*She Stoops to Conquer*, p. 106). Goldsmith's other sources included Isaac Bickerstaff's *Love in a Village* (1762)—which featured a country bumpkin, Hodge, the inspiration perhaps for Tony Lumpkin. Also Florent Dancourt's play *Maison de campagne* (1688) included an old house that was mistaken for an inn. Unlikely as this premise seems, Goldsmith had made just such an error himself as a youth in Ireland. Some have even pointed

to Shakespeare's comedies as influencing *She Stoops to Conquer,* particularly his *The Taming of the Shrew* (c. 1594).

Although Goldsmith made use of the works of his literary precursors and contemporaries, he also reacted against the theatrical trends of his day, especially the taste for sentimental comedies, which had become so popular with the predominantly middle-class audiences. Those sentimental comedies were themselves a reaction against the bawdy, cynical Restoration comedies of the previous generation. As typified by Sir

---

THE COUNTRY SQUIRE

"Squire," derived from the French "esquier" (shield), was a term frequently applied to landowners—usually among the gentry—who had long inhabited a particular area of the country. At the time of Goldsmith's play, squires could wield considerable power and influence in their community. E. W. Bovill states,

> In the eighteenth century the squires . . . were still in full enjoyment of a monopoly of power and wealth. Parliament was composed almost entirely of themselves or their nominees. . . . [I]n the country where, as Justices of the Peace, they performed all the functions of local government as well as most of those of the judicature, they were politically and, of course, socially supreme.
>
> (Bovill, p. 61)

G. M. Trevelyan, however, places the squire at the lower end of the scale, several rungs removed from landowning peers. A country squire was usually "reckoned to be worth two or three hundred [pounds] a year," spent his days "farming a part of his own land, speaking the broadest provincial dialect but [was] distinguished from the yeomen, among whom he mingled almost on equal terms, by a small sporting establishment, by a coat of arms, and by the respect which all paid to him as a 'gentleman'" (Trevelyan, p. 13). In *She Stoops to Conquer*, Tony Lumpkin, the heir of the late Squire Lumpkin, exhibits just those qualities, enjoying great popularity in the local village, mingling comfortably with Dick Muggins the exciseman, Jack Slang the horse doctor, little Aminadab that grinds the music box, and Tom Twist that spins the pewter plate. Not yet a squire, Tony is a squire-in-waiting. He cannot assert his authority as an adult or claim his inheritance of 1500 pounds a year until he reaches the legal age of 21.

Richard Steele's *The Conscious Lovers* (1722) and Richard Cumberland's *The West Indian* (1771), sentimental comedy featured virtuous, benevolent middle-class heroes and heroines. Given to morally uplifting speeches, these heroes and heroines suffered numerous trials and tribulations—designed to wring sympathetic tears from the audience—before being rewarded with happy endings. In 1773, Goldsmith essentially declared war on the genre with "An Essay on the Theatre; or, A Comparison between Laughing and Sentimental Comedy." His essay argues the following:

> Comedy is defined by Aristotle to be a picture of the frailties of the lower part of mankind, to distinguish it from tragedy, which is an exhibition of the misfortunes of the great. When comedy, therefore, ascends to produce the characters of princes or generals upon the stage, it is out of its walk, since low life and middle life are entirely its object. . . . [W]hich deserves the preference—the weeping sentimental comedy so much in fashion at present, or the laughing, and even low comedy, which seems to have been last exhibited by [early eighteenth-century playwrights] Vanbrugh and Cibber?
>
> (Goldsmith in McMillin, p. 387)

Denouncing sentimental comedy, Goldsmith complained of the genre's not doing justice to its "opposite parents"—comedy and tragedy. The comedy was not funny, the tragedy not exalted enough. In his view, sentimental comedy had all "the defects of its opposite parents," was "marked with sterility," and threatened havoc: "If we are permitted to make comedy weep, we have an equal right to make tragedy laugh and to set down in blank verse the jests and repartees of all the attendants in a funeral procession" (Goldsmith in McMillin, p. 389).

Goldsmith's position was further clarified in a prologue written by theatre manager David Garrick and spoken by comic actor Edward Woodward, which lamented how "the Comic Muse, long sick, is now a-dying" but prescribed the new play *She Stoops to Conquer* as a possible cure for comedy's ills (*She Stoops to Conquer*, p. 47). The prologue may have somewhat overstated the case regarding the impending demise of the Comic Muse, for other eighteenth-century dramatists, including Hugh Kelly, Samuel Foote, and Garrick himself were still creating "laughing comedies." Still, *She Stoops to Conquer* brought a freshness and lively sense of fun to the genre, even though it was by no means wholly unaffected by the sentimental comedies that Goldsmith

claimed to disdain. This is especially true in the play's presentation of a flawed but fundamentally good-natured cast of characters. As literary scholar Richard Bevis says,

> *She Stoops to Conquer* is a peace treaty between the various comic traditions. Diverse and hitherto contradictory elements are brought together, not simply to be maintained in balance or wary truce . . . but for fusion into an integral structure. Benevolence and satire on sentimental absurdities, farce, romance, and Restoration comedy mingle harmoniously.
>
> (Bevis, *The Laughing Tradition*, p. 206)

Reception. Opening on March 15, 1773, *She Stoops to Conquer* was greeted with a mixed reception. William Woodfall, writing for the *Monthly Review,* complained of the various plot contrivances: "The Fable of *She Stoops to Conquer* is a series of blunders, which the Author calls the *Mistakes of a Night* [a subtitle]; but they are such mistakes as never were made, and, we believe, never could have been committed" (Woodfall in Rousseau, p. 116). An unsigned review in *London Magazine* expressed similar reservations: "The fable (a fault too peculiar to the hasty productions of the modern Comic Muse) is twisted into incidents not naturally arising from the subject, in order to make things meet; and consistency is repeatedly violated for the sake of humour. . . . in lieu of comedy [the author] has sometimes presented us with farce" (Rousseau, p. 122). Horace Walpole, the famous author, was even more severe, writing in a letter to a friend that Goldsmith's comedy was "the lowest of all farces. . . . The drift tends to no moral, no edification of any kind. . . . But what disgusts me most is that though the characters are very low, and aim at low humour, not one of them says a sentence that is natural or marks any character at all. It is set up in opposition to sentimental comedy, and is as bad as the worst of them" (Walpole in Rousseau, pp. 118-119).

Significantly, however, none of these critics could deny that *She Stoops to Conquer* did, in fact, succeed as a "laughing" comedy. Woodfall grudgingly admitted that Goldsmith "certainly has a great share of the *vis comica* [comic force]; and when he has thrust his people into a situation, he makes them talk very *funnily* [sic]. His merit is in that sort of dialogue which lies on a level with the most common understandings; and in that low mischief and mirth which we laugh at, while we are reading to despise ourselves for so doing" (Woodfall in Rousseau, p. 118; italics in original). Walpole likewise conceded that "the [play's] situations are well-imagined, and make one laugh in spite of the grossness of the dialogue, the forced witticisms, and total improbability of the whole plan and conduct" (Walpole in Rousseau, p. 119).

On a more positive note, an anonymous article in *Critical Review* recognized and commended Goldsmith's attempt to "revive the dying art [of comedy]," adding,

> The author's well-deserved and unprecedented success, has shewn how ready mankind are to welcome back a favorite mistress, even after she had been guilty of a long elopement. . . . To conclude; the utmost severity of criticism could detract but little from the uncommon merit of this performance; and the most laboured encomiums could add as little to the general and judicious applause with which it still continues to be received.
>
> (Rousseau, pp. 124-125)

Also, Samuel Johnson, to whom Goldsmith dedicated the published version of *She Stoops to Conquer*, declared, "I know of no comedy for many years that has so much exhilarated an audience, that has answered so much the great end of comedy, making an audience merry" (Johnson in Forster, IV, p. 111). Goldsmith himself seemed particularly anxious about whether his play succeeded in being funny, asking a friend, Northcote, after the performance, "Did it make you laugh?"

"Exceedingly," Northcote replied.

"Then that is all I require," Goldsmith declared, promsing Northcote six more tickets (Goldsmith and Northcote in Forster, IV, p. 112).

—Pamela S. Loy

For More Information

Bevis, Richard. *The Laughing Tradition: Stage Comedy in Garrick's Day*. Athens: University of Georgia Press, 1980.

——. "Oliver Goldsmith." In *Dictionary of Literary Biography*. Vol. 89. Edited by Paula R. Backscheider. Detroit: Gale Research, 1989.

Bovill, E. W. *English Country Life 1780-1830*. London: Oxford University Press, 1962.

Cannadine, David. *The Rise and Fall of Class in Britain*. New York: Columbia University Press, 1999.

Forster, John. *The Life and Times of Oliver Goldsmith*. Vols. 1-4. New York: Harper & Brothers, 1900.

Goldsmith, Oliver. *She Stoops to Conquer*. New York: Barron's Educational Series, 1958.

McMillin, Scott, ed. *Restoration and Eighteenth-Century Comedy*. New York: W. W. Norton & Company, 1973.

Rousseau, G. S., ed. *Goldsmith: The Critical Heritage*. London: Routledge & Kegan Paul, 1974.

Stone, Lawrence. *The Family, Sex and Marriage in England 1500-1800*. New York: Harper & Row, 1977.

Trevelyan, G. M. *Illustrated English Social History*. Vol. 3. London: Longmans, Green, 1942.

Worth, Katharine. *Sheridan and Goldsmith*. New York: St. Martin's Press, 1992.

Sir Gawain and the Green Knight

as translated by
Marie Boroff

The origin of *Sir Gawain and the Green Knight* is obscure. Although nothing is known about the author, a number of educated guesses can be made based on the one surviving manuscript of the poem. It is written in the language of the northwest midlands of England in the latter half of the fourteenth century, and the physical characteristics of the manuscript itself indicate that it was produced at a time very near 1400. Details in the poem support this date; the dress of the characters, the architecture of Bertilak's castle, and the general emphasis on the luxurious splendor of courtly life all suggest that it was composed c. 1350-1400. An intimate knowledge of the habits and dress of the noble classes is evident as well, which probably means that the poet was in a position to attend aristocratic social events, such as banquets, holiday festivities, and hunting expeditions. The *Sir Gawain* manuscript also contains three other poems by the same author, involving Christian history and doctrine. Most scholars conclude from this that the actions of Gawain should be evaluated not only from the standpoint of knightly duty, but religious orthodoxy as well. The poem's "beheading game" is relatively simple, but integrated with it are elements of chivalric romance, moral theology, Arthurian myth, and otherworldly magic that provide clues to traditions and values during the poet's own era.

Events in History at the Time of the Poem

The Age of King Arthur. The familiar story of King Arthur and the knights of the Round Table,

---

THE LITERARY WORK

A long poem in Middle English set in the mythic days of King Arthur; composed in the late fourteenth century, but not published until 1839.

SYNOPSIS

Sir Gawain agrees to play a beheading "game" with a mysterious green knight; the knight magically survives the loss of his head, and a year later Gawain faces his own imminent beheading.

---

a wholly literary creation, did not begin to take a form that would have been recognizable to the *Gawain* poet until the twelfth century in Geoffrey of Monmouth's *History of the Kings of Britain* (c. 1136). It is uncertain where Geoffrey obtained his material on Arthur, but many scholars believe that he simply made it up. Not until the end of the eighth century did Arthur make his first appearance, in the British chronicler Nennius's *The History of the Britons* (c. 796), which refers to Arthur as a "commander" who "with all the kings and military force of Britain, fought against the Saxons" in 452 (Giles, p. 408). Nennius lists 12 battles in which Arthur led the British forces; in the last, he supposedly killed 940 men by his own hand. Thus even the earliest account of Arthur bears the unmistakable stamp of legend. Over the next four centuries little was added to the Arthur histories, until Geoffrey of Monmouth

The medieval English valued the chivalry and knightly honor embodied in the legend of King Arthur and the knights of the Round Table.

drew on them to create the Arthurian myth. It was Geoffrey who, for the first time, presented Arthur as a king, with a court, a castle, and a retinue of armored knights. This Arthur boasted power that stretched across Europe, subduing even Rome's emperor, but bore little resemblance to the local warlord of the earlier chronicles.

The historical Arthur, if he existed at all, seems to have been a relatively obscure fifth- or sixth-century general who helped defend what remained of Roman civilization in Britain against the invading Germanic peoples—the Angles (from whom comes the name "England"), the Saxons, and the Jutes. His career may have been brilliant (if there is even a germ of truth in what Nennius writes), but his gains were short-lived—the Germanic invaders soon gained complete mastery

of England, and the native Romano-British population was either absorbed or retreated to outlying regions such as Wales or Cornwall. Virtually everything now associated with Arthur derives not from the realities of this era, but from the fertile invention of Geoffrey and later authors.

Gawain appears in Geoffrey of Monmouth as Arthur's nephew and one of his knights. He figures prominently in major battles and serves as Arthur's ambassador to the Roman emperor. However, he bears little resemblance to the Gawain of later romances; he is neither a knight who seeks or achieves a personal reputation for chivalric valor, nor a legendary lover who engages in amorous pursuits with ladies. In Geoffrey's history, he is eventually killed by Mordred.

"**Golden Age.**" It is no accident that *Sir Gawain* begins with a reference to the destruction of the ancient city of Troy around 1200 B.C.E. For England in the fourteenth century C.E., Arthur's Camelot was a high point, a Golden Age when the glory of British knighthood and imperial power was at its zenith. However, this Golden Age harked back more than 2,000 years to another Golden Age—that of the same Troy from which the Romans derived their own foundational myth. According to one Roman tradition, the Trojan refugee Aeneas founded Rome, and thus the city's imperial and political legitimacy was linked to the glory of Troy. According to medieval tradition, Aeneas's great-grandson Brutus founded Britain, with the result that Britain's own national legitimacy was put on an equal footing with that of the ancient Romans, whose Golden Age the English saw as a model to be emulated. The view placed Arthur's achievements in a larger context of imperial succession, his Golden Age becoming one that repeated itself throughout history.

Looking back to Arthur's time from the fourteenth century, medieval writers did not attempt to reflect the past with detailed historical accuracy. Rather they set out to project contemporary values and concerns back onto a past that was seen as noble and glorious. When medieval authors portrayed the unity, stability, or noble purposefulness of King Arthur's court, it was because they thought such virtues were important (and perhaps lacking) in their own time. Fourteenth-century England valued chivalry and knightly honor, and so Arthur's knights were depicted as unmatched in these respects. By looking back to this legendary Golden Age of exemplary knighthood, writers and audiences of the later Middle Ages could see ideals of chivalry that reflected the way they thought things ought to be in their own time.

Chivalry. The word "chivalry" denotes a broad spectrum of behavior considered essential to the office of medieval knighthood. In fact the word itself comes from the Old French word for "knight." A chivalric knight exhibited qualities in five main areas of activity—in aristocratic company he was expected to be polite, witty, courteous, deferential to ladies and his superiors, and exemplary in the social graces; in love he was faithful to his lady, and bound to obey and please her to the best of his abilities; in the world at large he defended the weak (especially women and the elderly), bore himself with grace and humility, and upheld the standards of righteousness; in battle he was strong, brave, adept at the use of weapons, loyal to his lord, and merciful to his foe; and in regard to Christian morality and institutions he was to defend the interests of the Church against its enemies, and avoid sin. However noble in theory, these standards of conduct could make life somewhat complex for a knight, because they tended to contradict each other in practice. For example, all knights were in the service of a lord—there were no independent knights (or no good independent knights, at any rate). The rules of chivalry dictated that a knight obey his lord. They also dictated that he keep his word. If one obligation ran counter to another, the knight was in a quandary; what was he to do if his lord ordered him to break an oath, or if he made a promise that ran counter to his lord's wishes? Further, insofar as the entire notion of chivalry was intimately bound with obedience to both sacred and secular authorities, a knight could find himself with divided loyalties. In the Middle Ages the people who occupied positions of power in the Church were often members of noble families, with vast landholdings, territorial ambitions, and various other preoccupations of an entirely secular nature. Thus, a knight might very well be in the service of a lord who was involved in a dispute with another lord who happened to also be a bishop. To whom did

---

ARTHUR IN GEOFFREY OF MONMOUTH'S *THE HISTORY OF THE KINGS OF BRITAIN*—AN EXCERPT

"Arthur then began to increase his personal entourage by inviting very distinguished men from far-distant kingdoms to join it. In this way he developed such a code of courtliness in his household that he inspired peoples living far away to imitate him. The result was that even the man of noblest birth, once he was roused to rivalry, thought nothing at all of himself unless he wore his arms and dressed in the same way as Arthur's knights. At last the fame of Arthur's generosity and bravery spread to the very ends of the earth; and the kings of countries far across the sea trembled at the thought that they might be attacked and invaded by him, and so lose control of the lands under their dominion. They were so harassed by these tormenting anxieties that they rebuilt their towns and the towers in their towns, and then went so far as to construct castles on carefully-chosen sites, so that, if invasion should bring Arthur against them, they might have refuge in their time of need."

(Geoffrey of Monmouth, p. 222)

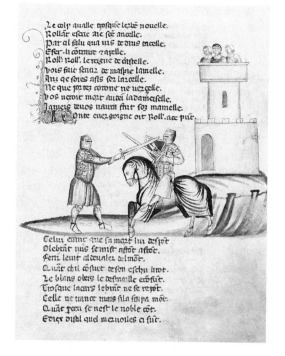

Two knights duel for a lady's hand in this manuscript illustration, which depicts an aspect of chivalry.

the knight owe loyalty? Complicating the situation still further was a knight's problematic relationship to women. Knights were bound to defend and protect women, as part of their larger obligation to protect the weak and defenseless. A knight in love with a lady could declare himself her servant, similar to his declaration of obedience to his lord. Chivalry would then dictate that he make every effort to please her, and make himself worthy of her regard. But it is not difficult to image a scenario in which a knight could run afoul of his other knightly obligations by pledging his love to a lady. In fact, he could violate all of them. For example, the archetypal adulterous liaison of the Middle Ages—that between Lancelot and Guinevere—resulted in Lancelot's breaking virtually all of his vows of chivalry. In becoming a knight of the Round Table, he had sworn to defend the honor of King Arthur—a vow he broke by committing adultery with the king's wife and by later engaging in open warfare with him. He also failed in his duty to defend the weak, as his actions led to a series of devastating wars that brought great harm to the common people. As a Christian knight, he was not supposed to sin, and yet he did, again with Guinevere. And in his efforts to escape temptation, he would often leave Camelot to engage in tournaments, quests, and other activities appro-

priate to a knight—activities that ran against the wishes of Guinevere, who wanted him to stay at court.

Lancelot was an active and willing participant in his adultery with Guinevere, but a knight could easily find himself in a no-win situation of a similar kind, and yet be entirely blameless. Chivalric literature abounds with instances in which a knight, with laudable knightly generosity, puts himself at the disposal of a lord and lady who have done him a good turn, such as giving him lodging for the night. Such an offer of service is a serious obligation that cannot be lightly cast aside. What ought a knight to do, then, if the lady makes an adulterous proposal? On the one hand, his obligation as a Christian knight to avoid the sin of adultery, and his obligation in the lord's service to avoid dishonoring him, would dictate that he refuse. On the other hand, his obligation in courtesy to the lady would demand that, at the very least, he treat her advances with respect and discretion. How can he obey the wishes of the wife without dishonoring the husband? A similar conflict could arise in the case of a knight bound in service to two lords. If these lords made war on each other, to whom should he be loyal? Thus, a medieval knight was often faced with a complex web of conflicting demands upon his sense of chivalric honor, with no practical way to resolve them.

Medieval knighthood. The literary depictions of chivalric activity in the Arthurian romances do not accurately reflect the reality of knighthood in the Middle Ages, especially in the late fourteenth century. Though the romances emphasized the chivalry, courtliness, and manners of its heroic knights, the medieval knight was first and foremost a soldier, whose existence bore an intimate connection to the medieval institution known as feudalism—a term denoting the rigid social structure devised in the early Middle Ages to impose order on a vulnerable and essentially agricultural society. This system (though it was less systematic in practice than in theory) consisted of mutual military obligation between the rich landowner-noble and the knights who defended his interests. A lord would have in his retinue knights who were his vassals—they received land and protection from the lord in exchange for their military service to him. This arrangement was sealed with an oath of fealty; each was bound by a solemn promise to maintain the status of the other. A lord, in turn, could be the vassal of another lord, and all would theoretically be vassals of the king—who was often the vassal of another king. These obligations were not always honored, and accusations of treachery and oath-breaking were commonplace. Knights went to war on a regular basis, bound as they were to defend their lords' territorial ambitions in the ever-present disputes (local and international) over land that fueled medieval warfare.

Feudal society was thus essentially militaristic in nature; those who had political authority and military strength generally wished to possess more, and maintaining a cadre of well-trained and heavily armored knights was one way to accomplish this. Knights were brought up from boyhood to serve as warriors; years of training in horsemanship, swordplay, and jousting was followed by additional service as a squire (an apprentice of sorts who learned the finer points of knighthood by serving an experienced knight) before they could join the elite ranks of full-fledged knighthood. Certain recreations were practiced as well, and proficiency in these was considered just as much a part of knighthood as expertise in warfare. The forests of medieval England were essentially vast game preserves, off-limits to all but the aristocracy. Hunting (whether with hounds or hawks) was the favored leisure-time activity for the nobility, and knights were expected to know the sport inside and out.

By the time *Sir Gawain and the Green Knight* was written, the feudal system had long been dying. Oaths between lord and vassal were still made, but only for form's sake; knights served as mercenaries, and fought for whomever paid them the most. Chivalry lived on in poetry and romance, but chroniclers and moralists repeatedly lamented that chivalry was dead. Knights no longer protected the poor as they once had, but now robbed them. In fact, whether or not knights had ever behaved with exemplary chivalry is uncertain; the bulk of the evidence is literary, authored by poets who promoted ideal behavior, rather than reflected actual practice.

Illicit love. In the earlier Arthurian material women hardly appear at all; the emphasis is exclusively on military valor. With the twelfth-century French poet Chrétien de Troyes, Arthur's knights begin to fall into romantic entanglements that serve as motivating forces for their deeds on the battlefield—the knight as lover was as important as the knight as warrior. Certain conventions had to be observed; the lady was obeyed and venerated almost at all costs, and the knight's wartime exploits were as much for her honor as his. In some narratives, adulterous love was accepted without comment—for example, in Chré-

tien's *Lancelot* (also called "The Knight of the Cart"), Guinevere is abducted from Arthur's court by an evil knight, and Lancelot goes off to save her. His success owes as much to his intense love for her as to his knightly prowess, yet the tale never refers to the adulterous nature of this love. Later versions of the Lancelot-Guinevere story do take their sin into account, and they must do penance, but the manner of their love is always presented as a characteristic instance of chivalric passion, however wrong. Another famous lover, Sir Tristan, is somewhat exonerated of his guilt for committing adultery with Isolde (the wife of King Mark) by the fact that his love is involuntary—he and Isolde are given a love potion by Isolde's servant. Gawain is the knightly lover *par excellence*; in some versions of the account of the last days of Camelot, when Gawain is killed by Lancelot, there is a vast outpouring of grief by women far and wide who bewail the loss of the greatest lover the world had ever known.

The Poem in Focus

Plot summary. The poem begins not in England but in Troy, at the end of the Trojan war—close to 2,000 years before the Age of Arthur. Aeneas flees the ruins of his native city, and founds the city of Rome. His descendants and followers also establish kingdoms, among them Tuscany, Lombardy, and Britain.

The heroic lineage of Arthur's kingdom being established, the story opens during the Christmas season at Camelot. The entire court celebrates with feasting, jousting, and dancing. Arthur, however, is not satisfied—he vows that he will not eat until something wondrous appears, either in fact or in the form of a tale. His desire is immediately granted with the appearance of "an unknown rider, / One of the greatest on ground in growth of his frame" (*Sir Gawain*, lines 136-37). Enormous and handsome, the knight is richly arrayed in the finest of clothing. More remarkable is his color—his skin, hair, and clothing are all green, as are his horse, saddle, and stirrups. Riding up to the platform on which Arthur sits, he demands to know who is in charge. Learning that it is Arthur, he says that the widespread fame of the king's court has prompted him to come play a game. He proposes to submit to a single blow with his own green axe, wielded by a knight of Camelot, who will also get to keep the axe. The Camelot knight will then accept his own blow in return, in exactly one year and one day's time. The Green Knight's proposal astounds the court so much that no one responds, whereupon the Green Knight resorts to mockery:

> "What, is this Arthur's house," said that
>   horseman then,
> "Whose fame is so fair in far realms and wide
> Where is now your arrogance and your
>   awesome deeds,
> Your valor and your victories and your
>   vaunting words?"
> (*Sir Gawain and the Green Knight*, lines 309-312)

Shamed, Arthur takes up the Green Knight's axe.

Arthur's nephew Gawain then asks permission to respond to the challenge himself, arguing that his own life, unlike Arthur's, would not be much missed. The members of the court all agree to let

MAGIC, CHIVALRY, AND THE LAW

The exemplar of chivalry in Arthur's court, Gawain needs no excuse to step in and offer to take the king's place in the Green Knight's beheading game; he is bound by oath to defend the king, and the game clearly represents a threat to the king's life. More problematic is the nature of the Green Knight himself. If the knight's proposal is a "game," the manner in which it developed is serious; Gawain chops off the head of another man who offers no resistance. Thus, Gawain's chivalry could be called into question at the outset, when he gives a blow that he thinks will kill someone who does not deserve it. On the other hand, the knight had offered a challenge that honor demanded be met, and (to put it simply) he was green, and presumably knew what he was doing. His color makes it clear to Arthur's court from the outset that he is a figure from the otherworld, possessed of supernatural powers. He survives the beheading game, but magically, which means (at least as far as medieval English law is concerned) that Gawain need not uphold his commitment to appear before the Green Knight in a year's time. Using magic in any adversarial situation in the *Gawain* poet's time was an offense, both civil and ecclesiastical, and invalidated the result. But Gawain had given his word as a knight to receive a blow in return, and so is resolved to follow through.

Gawain face the knight, who makes Gawain swear that, in one year's time, he will seek him out for the return blow. Gawain agrees, and brings the axe down swiftly on the knight's bared

neck. The Green Knight's head rolls on the floor; blood bursts from his body, but he remains standing. The body walks steadily towards the head, snatches it up, and then swings onto the green horse. Holding the head aloft by the hair, the body points it toward the royal dais. The eyes of the head are open, and the mouth reminds Gawain of his oath, instructing him to come to the Green Chapel the following New Year's morning or be known as a coward.

Winter, spring, and summer pass, and with the coming of autumn Gawain begins to prepare for departure. The members of the court feign good cheer while Gawain dresses and arms himself. Like the Green Knight, he is dressed splendidly, but unlike him he is armed to the teeth. Most prominent among his accessories is a gleaming red shield, adorned with a golden pentangle—a five-pointed star. As Gawain rides away, members of the court bemoan his likely fate.

Passing through desolate and monster-infested wastelands, Gawain asks everyone he meets about the Green Chapel, but no one has heard of it. Far from home, he must fight for his very survival:

> Now with serpents he wars, now with savage
>   wolves,
> Now with wild men of the woods, that
>   watched from the rocks,
> Both with bulls and with bears, and with
>   boars besides,
> And giants that came gibbering from the
>   jagged steeps.
> (*Sir Gawain*, lines 720-23)

He journeys day after day until Christmas Eve arrives, and begins to fear that he will not make his appointed meeting with the Green Knight. He prays to Mary that he might find lodging where he can attend Mass, and upon crossing himself three times, he sees nearby a moated castle. Knocking at the door, he is admitted to a sumptuously furnished interior, and the lord of the castle welcomes him with enthusiasm, telling him that he may stay as long as he wishes. The castle is full of noble guests, who have come to celebrate Christmas the following day. Even before revealing his name, Gawain is treated with great honor—he is clothed in the finest robes and served a splendid feast. When he does reveal his identity, the entire castle rejoices; men say to each other that now that the most honored knight in the world has arrived, they will be treated to a rare display of knightly behavior in its full perfection. At midnight Mass, Gawain is seated at a place of honor by his host's side. When the Mass is over, the lord's wife appears. Gawain thinks her beauty beyond praise, exceeding that of Guinevere herself. With her is another woman who is as old and ugly as the lady is young and beautiful. Gawain approaches, greets and kisses the lady of the castle, and proclaims himself at her service. During the lavish feast that follows, he sits deep in conversation with her.

The celebrations continue for three days, whereupon the guests begin to depart. Gawain announces that he too must go, and holds firm despite his host's entreaties that he stay. When Gawain explains that he must meet the Green Knight of the Green Chapel on New Year's day (he does not say why), the lord tells him that the chapel is not two miles away, and that he should remain for three more days—on the fourth, he promises, Gawain will be led to the chapel. Grateful, Gawain promises to stay and to do anything the host asks. This elicits a proposal from the host: that the following day Gawain sleep in and be at his leisure, while the lord and his knights go hunting at dawn; the lord's wife will entertain Gawain with her company throughout the day, and, when the day is over, "whatever I win in the woods I will give you at eve, / And all that you have earned you must offer to me" (*Sir Gawain*, lines 1106-07). Gawain consents.

Well before dawn the next morning, the lord and his men set out to hunt. The quarry is deer, and the hunt is a great success. Meanwhile, Gawain has awakened in his room to the sound of his door opening; pretending to be asleep, he sees the lady of the castle creep in and come to his bedside. She pulls aside the bed curtains and sits near him until he pretends to awaken, whereupon she begins to flirt with him aggressively, finally offering him her body. He declines with as much grace as he can muster, but as she prepares to leave, she tells him that a knight of Gawain's reputation, "had he lain so long at a lady's side / Would have claimed a kiss" (*Sir Gawain*, lines 1299-1300). Gawain agrees, and the lady leans down and kisses him. When the lord returns that night with his venison, the two men make the exchange: Gawain receives all that was taken in the hunt, and the lord is kissed by Gawain in return. The lord asks Gawain where he came by the kiss, but Gawain refuses to tell him—this, he explains, was not part of the agreement. The next day the events are repeated; this time Gawain is given the fine boar the men have taken, while the lord gets the two kisses that Gawain has received from the increasingly importunate lady.

The events are repeated one final day, during which the lord's wife, again at Gawain's bedside, asks him to give her something to remember him by; when he replies that he has nothing suitable to give her, she instead offers him a rich gold ring with a sparkling stone. When Gawain adamantly refuses to accept something so fine, the wife offers him instead her girdle (a sash worn about the waist) of green silk. Again Gawain refuses—until, that is, the wife explains that the girdle is magic: as long as a man is wearing it, "there is no hand under heaven that could hew him down" (*Sir Gawain*, line 1853). Her only condition is that he not tell anyone about it, lest her husband find out. Gawain accepts the girdle (as he had accepted three kisses from the lady that morning), and then seeks out a priest, wishing to confess his sins. This accomplished, he joins the ladies of the castle in dancing and merriment.

During his exchange with the lord that night, he does not mention the girdle; instead he accepts the spoils of the lord's third hunt (a fox)

HUNTING IN THE MIDDLE AGES

When not fighting, nobles and knights spent most of their free time in the warlike activities of hunting and hawking. All upper-class households kept horses and hounds expressly for this purpose, hunting regularly whenever a war was not already in progress, and sometimes when it was. Hunting was an almost ritualistic affair, in which a knight could show off his skill in horsemanship, tracking, and dressing the freshly-killed game. Elaborate rules dictated exactly how each of these activities should be performed, and a knight's standing in court was often substantially influenced by his reputation as a hunter. That Gawain would agree to stay in bed while the lord of the castle went hunting with all the other guests is highly uncharacteristic of a medieval knight, but it serves a literary purpose. So unusual is Gawain's inactivity at such a time that it draws attention to his being the one "hunted" here—by Bertilak's wife.

and in return gives the lord three kisses, claiming "all that I here owe is openly paid" (*Sir Gawain*, line 1941). A final evening of feasting and revelry ensues, and the next morning Gawain takes his leave (not forgetting to wear his green girdle), accompanied by one of the lord's men, who will lead him to the Green Chapel.

As Gawain and the man accompanying him approach the Green Chapel, the escort becomes more and more frightened, urging Gawain to turn back:

> You are rushing into risks that you reck not of:
> There is a villain in yon valley, the veriest on earth,
> For he is rugged and rude, and ready with his fists,
> And most immense in his mold of mortals alive,
> And his body bigger than the best four
> That are in Arthur's house. . . ."
>
> (*Sir Gawain*, lines 2097-2102)

Gawain replies that he cannot turn back—he has given his word to appear, and to do less would be the act of a coward, something that could not be excused. His escort leaves after pointing out the last leg of the journey—a narrow path leading down into a deep valley. After commending himself to God, Gawain heads down the path.

At the bottom he finds not a chapel, but a small hill by a stream—a strange hollow hill, with a hole in the front, and one on each side. He is perplexed and appalled; it seems to him a hellish place, where "might / The devil himself be seen" (*Sir Gawain*, lines 2186-87). Then he hears a loud grinding noise, horrible and grating. Echoing the Green Knight's initial challenge at Camelot (i.e., demanding to know who is in charge), he calls out for whoever has power over the place to show himself. The source of the noise is soon revealed; it is the Green Knight, sharpening an enormous axe on a grindstone. He greets Gawain, and after commending him on being true to his word, asks that he remove his helmet to receive the blow. Gawain exposes his neck, and, feigning cheerful indifference, waits for the Green Knight to strike. As the axe descends, Gawain flinches; the knight chides Gawain, who vows not to flinch again. The second blow is a mere feint; only the third time does the Green Knight bring down the axe with full force, but purposely turns the blow aside, leaving no more than a nick on the side of Gawain's neck. Dripping blood, Gawain leaps back and throws on his helmet. Drawing his sword, he exclaims: "Have done with your hacking—harry me no more! / I have borne, as behooved, one blow in this place; / If you make another move I shall meet it midway / And promptly, I promise you" (*Sir Gawain*, lines 2322-25). The Green Knight responds by revealing his identity and purpose: he is the lord from whose castle Gawain has just left, and the three blows were in response to Gawain's conduct at the castle. The first blow was for the first day, when Gawain carried out the initial agreement faithfully. The second was for the second day, when Gawain truthfully exchanged two kisses for the lord's boar. The third blow, however, was in punishment for Gawain's duplicity on the third day in withholding from the lord the green girdle, which by rights should have been surrendered to him the evening after he obtained it. The mildness of the punishment, says the knight, was because Gawain withheld the girdle out of simple fear: "Yet you lacked, sir, a little in loyalty there, / But the cause was not cunning, nor courtship either, / But that you loved your own life; the less, then, to blame (*Sir Gawain*, lines 2366-68).

GAWAIN AND CHRISTIANITY

Gawain is a mighty warrior, but in this poem one of his most prominent characteristics is his piety. Believing that he will meet his doom at the Green Chapel, he makes sure that before he leaves the castle he receives the sacrament of confession. By confessing his sins to a priest and asking God for forgiveness, Gawain exhibits hope that he will achieve heaven after death, since damnation could result from any unconfessed major sin (called "mortal" sin for this reason) after death. Religious devotion is never far from his mind; before he finds the lord's castle, he prays fervently that he might find lodging—not for comfort's sake, but so that he can attend Christmas Mass. He is especially devoted to the Virgin Mary, and even has her image painted on the inside of his shield, so that when "his look on it lighted, he never lost heart" (*Sir Gawain*, line 650). On the front of his shield is his emblem: a five-pointed star, or pentangle. The poet explains the significance of the star in some detail—it was "a sign by Solomon sagely devised / To be a token of truth," and specifically indicated the chivalric and devotional qualities of Gawain himself (*Sir Gawain*, lines 625-26). First, he was faultless in his five senses; second, his five fingers never failed; third, he was given to meditating on the five wounds of Christ on the cross; fourth, he attributed his knightly prowess to the five joys of the Virgin Mary (the annunciation of the angel Gabriel that she would bear the son of God, Christ's birth, his resurrection, his ascension, and Mary's own assumption into heaven); and fifth, he possessed five noble virtues—boundless beneficence, brotherly love, pure mind, pure manners, and compassion.

Overcome with fury and shame, Gawain cries out that he has been proved guilty of cowardice and covetousness, and asks how he can regain favor in the knight's eyes. The lord responds that Gawain has already done penance at the point of his axe, and so is fully cleansed of his guilt—he even gives Gawain the girdle, and asks him to return to the castle with him and celebrate the New Year. With great courtesy Gawain refuses, and asks that the knight send his regards to the lady of the castle. The girdle he gladly accepts, vowing to treasure it not for its beauty, but because it will remind him of his failure and keep him from thinking too highly of himself. At this point he asks the knight his name and is told that it is Bertilak de Hautdesert, and that he maintains his power through the sorcery of Morgan le Fay, who lodges with him. Morgan (presumably the ugly old woman in Bertilak's castle) is Arthur's half-sister and Gawain's aunt; jealous of the majesty of Camelot, she sought to undermine it. The whole beheading game enterprise was her idea, to afflict the pride of Arthur's court and annoy her longtime rival Guinevere.

After kissing Bertilak goodbye, Gawain returns to Camelot, where he speaks of his exploits to Arthur and the other knights, and explains why he will always wear the green girdle. Arthur and the rest of the court console Gawain, laughing at his discomfiture. They then decide that each knight of the Round Table will also wear a green girdle in Gawain's honor. The poem concludes as it began, by invoking Britain's ancient heritage and the fall of Troy.

Trawthe. Of all the knightly virtues, none was more prominent than what the poet calls *trawthe*, a Middle English word translated variously as "troth," "truth," "truthfulness," "devotion," and "fidelity." It involved not only keeping one's word, but also maintaining fidelity to the vows taken at the ceremony of knighthood, and so it carried with it the entire body of chivalric obligations, both secular and religious. This is a critical concept to *Sir Gawain and the Green Knight,* since its whole narrative energy stems from Gawain's quest to keep his trawthe, even unto death.

The importance of this idea is indicated in the poem's opening lines, when reference is made to the "knight that had knotted the nets of deceit" (*Sir Gawain,* line 3). This knight is Aeneas himself, who was believed in the Middle Ages to have betrayed Troy to its enemy, the Greeks, in order to save his own life. His apparent failure to maintain trawthe is, by implicit comparison, set against Gawain's struggle to uphold it. When Gawain gives his word to the Green Knight that he will appear at the Green Chapel in a year's time, he considers this promise inviolable, and undergoes significant physical hardship to keep his word. His only slip in this regard is when he involuntarily flinches at the first swing of the Green Knight's axe, and he is mortified when the knight jeers at him. His promise to stand still for the second blow is expressed with a resoluteness that recalls his original promise to appear in the first place: "I shall stand to the stroke and stir not an inch / Till your axe has hit home—on my honor I swear it!" (*Sir Gawain,* lines 2286-87). And stand he does, though he believes he will lose his head.

It is also important to note that Gawain's only deliberate misdeed in the poem is an offense against trawthe: he fails to surrender the green girdle to the lord of the castle, despite his formal promise to do so. Bertilak, after revealing himself, judges Gawain and so Gawain judges himself back at Camelot. Explaining the significance of the green girdle, he refers to both the flinching and the deception:

This is the blazon of the blemish that I bear
    on my neck;
This is the sign of sore loss that I have
    suffered there
For the cowardice and coveting that I came to
    there;
This is the badge of false faith that I was
    found in there
And I must bear it on my body till I breathe
    my last.
                    (*Sir Gawain,* lines 2506-10)

Gawain's sense of trawthe was fundamental to his self-image as a knight, and his failure (however minor) in this regard was a bitter blow.

The reputation of Sir Gawain—high and low. In *Sir Gawain and the Green Knight* Sir Gawain is the very model of knightly virtue, but in medieval Arthurian romance as a whole his reputation was quite varied. In earlier materials he is generally without peer—noble, strong, and fearless, a paragon among Arthur's knights. In such narratives Gawain was often paired with Sir Kay; Sir Kay would invariably fail through impetuousness, discourtesy, or some other such chivalric transgression, and then Gawain would show him how a true knight should act. However, with the advent of later, more elaborate narratives (especially those involving Lancelot), he grew less exemplary. Lancelot was now the premiere knight, and Gawain was relegated to a secondary position: still brave and formidable, but possessed of certain character flaws, such as a propensity towards seducing maidens and killing people with hotheaded abandon. Towards the end of the Middle Ages he even appeared in lowbrow, farcical poems, where he was treated as a comic figure; a good example is the late-fifteenth century *The Wedding of Sir Gawain and Dame Ragnell,* in which Gawain is coerced into marrying a hag. This makes the character of Gawain in *Sir Gawain and the Green Knight* something of an anomaly in that the poet (writing in the late fourteenth century) gives Gawain a preeminent stature at Camelot, a stature at that time usually reserved for Lancelot. Still, Gawain had never entirely lost his appeal to English audiences. Lancelot was, after all, a knight of French origin, and this doubtless contributed to the perennial popularity of Gawain—a thoroughly British knight—in Arthurian poetry in England.

Literary context. *Sir Gawain and the Green Knight* was written in an alliterative style that had its roots in the ancient poetry of the Germanic peoples. Rhyme was rare in this poetry; instead, each line would normally be divided into two halflines, each of which would contain two dominant stresses, with a varying number of unstressed elements. Three of these four stressed words or syllables would alliterate with each other, beginning with the same letter or sound. All Old English poetry (such as **Beowulf** and **The Battle of Maldon**—also in *WLAIT 3: British and Irish Literature and Its Times*) was written in this manner, and some early Middle English poetry as well. With the Norman conquest of England in 1066, French replaced English as the favored language of the ruling classes, and the majority of the surviving poetry written in England from this era is in Anglo-Norman, a French dialect spoken by the English aristocracy that had its roots in the French spoken by England's Norman conquerors. Along with the ascendancy of the French language in England came new, French styles of versification. In the fourteenth century the old alliterative poetic mode, which almost certainly never died out among the native English-speaking population, revived. Important examples from this "alliterative revival" include William Langland's **Piers Plowman** (also in *WLAIT 3: British and Irish Literature and Its Times*) and the four poems by the *Gawain* poet. At its peak when *Sir Gawain and the Green Knight* was written, the alliterative revival would not last more than a few decades into the fifteenth century.

A direct source for the narrative content of *Sir Gawain and the Green Knight* has never been convincingly identified. Virtually all of the characters and themes of the poem may be found in earlier materials, but the specific form in which they appear is the poet's own; for example, it is the only poem where the "beheading game" and the "temptations in the bedroom" motifs appear together. Moreover, these two motifs (each of which possesses its own lengthy pedigree in folklore) are so seamlessly wedded that *Sir Gawain and the Green Knight* has long been viewed as an original work rather than a versified collection of source texts.

The "beheading game" makes an early appearance in Celtic literature, in the Middle Irish *Fled Bricrend* ("Bricriu's Feast"), probably composed c. 1100, where the hero Cú Chulainn on two separate occasions must behead a shapeshifting aggressor, and then submit to a return blow from his still-living foe. Each (as in *Sir Gawain and the Green Knight*) ends happily, with Cú Chulainn given only a token blow and complimented for his bravery. Elements from Celtic folklore (such as the knight's green color, symbolizing the "otherworld" of fairy magic) have been recognized as well. Analogues of the beheading game, the temptation scene, and the exchange of winnings motif also appear in French Arthurian sources, which probably influenced the *Gawain* poet. *Perlesvaus* (c. 1250), for example, contains a scene in which Lancelot is challenged by a knight with an axe; when Lancelot beheads him, he disappears. When Lancelot arrives a year later for his return blow, he finds the knight's brother sharpening an axe. Lancelot flinches at the first blow, and the second is never delivered, due to the intercession of a lady. Other French romances have variations on the temptation scene in which Gawain variously accepts or refuses the advances of ladies; in *Le Chevalier a l'Epee,* Gawain tries to make love to the daughter of his host, but is thwarted by a magic sword, which twice wounds him. His host later informs him that it was all a test; Gawain was not killed because the sword could not kill the best knight (Vantuono, p. 266).

Reception and impact. The text of the poem survives in only one medieval manuscript (Cotton Nero A.x.), which sat for centuries in private libraries before first appearing in print. The first known owner of the manuscript was Henry Savile of Bank (1568-1617), a Yorkshire gentleman. From him it passed to Sir Robert Cotton (1571-1631), the famous book collector and antiquary, whose library (donated in 1700 to the British government) caught fire in 1731. Fortunately the manuscript containing *Sir Gawain and the Green Knight* was spared, though other medieval manuscripts (like *Beowulf*) were lost or seriously damaged in the flames.

Sir Gawain and the Green Knight disappeared from the literary scene shortly after its composition, not to reappear until its first printed edition in 1839. It had no immediate influence, possibly because the Middle English dialect in which it is written had grown more difficult to read as the years passed. The three poems ("Pearl," "Cleanness," and "Patience") that are bound in the same manuscript as *Sir Gawain and the Green Knight* suffered similar neglect. The poem has since emerged as one of the most admired works in English literature, in large part because the editions of Israel Gollancz (1897) and J.R.R. Tolkien (1925) carefully explained the poem's many difficult words and passages. A much-admired verse translation into modern English by Marie Borroff (1967) preserved the poem's beauty in a form accessible to the general reader.

The continuing appeal of *Sir Gawain and the Green Knight* doubtless owes much to the fact that its concerns are, quite simply, those of the human condition; a distinguished modern critic of the poem perhaps put it best: "[t]hat the poem still has meaning for the reader today is because, though the vocabulary has changed, the conflict between ideal codes and human limitation still persists" (Benson, p. 248).

—Matthew Brosamer

For More Information

Benson, Larry D. *Art and Tradition in Sir Gawain and the Green Knight*. New Brunswick: Rutgers University Press, 1965.

Brewer, Elizabeth, ed. *Sir Gawain and the Green Knight: Sources and Analogues*. London: D. S. Brewer, 1992.

Geoffrey of Monmouth. *The History of the Kings of Britain*. Trans. Lewis Thorpe. New York: Penguin, 1966.

Giles, John Allen, ed. and trans. *Six Old English Chronicles*. London: Henry G. Bohn, 1848.

Kieckhefer, Richard. *Magic in the Middle Ages*. Cambridge, England: Cambridge University Press, 1990.

Putter, Ad. *An Introduction to the Gawain-Poet*. London: Longman, 1996.

———. *Sir Gawain and the Green Knight and French Arthurian Romance*. Oxford: Clarendon Press, 1995.

Rogers, Gillian, et al. "Folk Romance." In *The Arthur of the English*. Ed. W. R. J. Barron. Cardiff: University of Wales Press, 1999.

Sir Gawain and the Green Knight. Trans. Marie Boroff. New York: W. W. Norton, 1967.

Sir Gawain and the Green Knight. J. R. R. Tolkien and E. V. Gordon. 2nd ed. Revised by Norman Davis. Oxford: Clarendon Press, 1967.

Vantuono, William, ed. and trans. *Sir Gawain and the Green Knight*. 2nd ed. Notre Dame: University of Notre Dame Press, 1999.

White, Richard. "Introduction." In *King Arthur in Legend and History*. Ed. Richard White. New York: Routledge, 1997.

Songs and Sonnets

by
John Donne

John Donne (1572-1631) was born in London to Roman Catholic parents; his father, a successful hardware merchant, died when Donne was four, and Donne's mother, who was descended from the English Catholic martyr Sir Thomas More, married a doctor who raised the boy and his five brothers and sisters. After attending Oxford and probably Cambridge, Donne returned to London, converted from Catholicism to Anglicanism, and sought a career at court. He served on two privateering expeditions against the Spanish and in 1597 won a position as secretary to the English courtier Sir Thomas Egerton, a job that he performed successfully for several years and that promised a good chance of future advancement. In 1601, however, Donne secretly married 17-year-old Anne More, the niece of Egerton's wife. This transgression cost him his job, his enraged employer's trust, and ultimately the secular public career for which he had longed. Virtually unemployed thereafter, Donne became an Anglican priest in 1615. His literary skills soon made him one of England's leading preachers, and in 1621 King James I appointed him dean of St. Paul's Cathedral in London. Many of his sermons survive; aside from these prose works, Donne's poetic writings include satires, elegies, and religious poems. Only two of the *Songs and Sonnets* were published during his lifetime, and few of them can be dated with confidence. They are thought to have been written starting sometime in the 1590s up to about 1617, when Donne's wife died.

THE LITERARY WORK

A group of 55 love poems probably written between c. 1590 and c. 1617; first published in London in 1633.

SYNOPSIS

Embodying a series of often contradictory statements about love, Donne's poems express attitudes ranging from indifferent lust to transcendent marital devotion.

Events in History at the Time the Poems Were Written

Catholics in Elizabethan England. To be a Catholic in England in the 1590s was to belong to a persecuted minority among an Anglican majority. Conversely, to leave the Catholic Church for the Anglican Church was viewed by Catholics as damnable. Sometime in the 1590s, John Donne abandoned Catholicism, an event that critics generally view as central to Donne's life and thought.

The Church of England or Anglican Church was founded in 1534, when Henry VIII (ruled 1509-47) removed the English Church from the control of the Pope in order to legitimize his divorce from Catherine of Aragon. During the long reign of Henry's daughter, Queen Elizabeth I (1558-1603), the Anglican Church was transformed from the immediate solution to a king's marital problems into the centerpiece of a new

One of England's leading preachers, John Donne was honored with this marble effigy, fashioned shortly before his death.

Protestant English establishment. Yet many English clung to "the old faith," or Catholicism, and decades of hostility between Catholics and their Protestant compatriots led to bloodshed on both sides. Under Elizabeth's Catholic half-sister, Queen Mary (ruled 1553-58), some 300 Protestants had been burned at the stake, earning her the nickname "Bloody Mary." At the beginning of her own reign, the Protestant queen Elizabeth, tolerant by nature and hesitant to interfere in people's beliefs, resisted calls from England's by-then Protestant majority for anti-Catholic repression. In the 1570s and 1580s such calls became too strong for Elizabeth to defy, as an atmosphere of anti-Catholic hostility and fear came to dominate the land.

Indeed, this fear, while often exaggerated, reflected a genuine threat. In 1571, for example, the government uncovered the Ridolfi Plot, in which Spanish troops were to invade England and replace Elizabeth with her Catholic cousin, Mary Queen of Scots. Also several Popes called on English Catholics to disobey their queen, and Jesuit priests infiltrated England with the aim of subverting English Catholics' loyalty to Elizabeth. In the 1580s, such threats led the government to enact new anti-Catholic laws. An act of 1581 imposed the heavy fine of £20 (about a year's wage for many families) on Catholics for each time they were absent from Anglican services, and an act of 1585 declared that any English Catholic priest who remained in the land was automatically guilty of treason and therefore liable to the death penalty.

By the end of Elizabeth's reign in 1603, 183 Catholics had been executed, most of them priests. In many cases, execution was preceded by torture and consisted of disemboweling the still living victim. Several of John Donne's relatives were executed for their activity in the Catholic Church. Donne was just 12 years old when he visited one of them, his uncle Jasper Heywood, in prison at the Tower of London shortly before the execution. Like Donne's maternal ancestor Sir Thomas More (executed in 1535), the victims of these grisly deaths were considered to be martyrs by their fellow Catholics. In families like Donne's, martyrdom was viewed with pride and children were taught that it was a noble goal to be eagerly sought. Other laws, milder but still repressive, set out to prevent Catholics from taking part in public life or from obtaining the education necessary for doing so. One law required university students age 16 and up to subscribe to the Thirty-nine Articles, which set out the beliefs of the Anglican Church. In order to evade the law, well-to-do Catholic families often sent their male children to university when very young. John Donne and his brother Henry, for example, went to Oxford at ages 12 and 11, respectively.

Despite such common everyday circumvention, brutality and terror remained simple facts of life for Catholics in England. By the early 1590s, when John Donne was about 20, he and Henry were studying law together in London. In 1593 a man named William Harrington was arrested in Henry's rooms on suspicion of being a Catholic priest. Harrington denied it, but Henry was arrested as well. Under threat of torture he betrayed the man, confirming that Harrington was indeed a priest who had been hearing his confessions. Early the following year, Harrington was disemboweled alive. Henry Donne himself was sent to prison, where he died of plague before he could come to trial on the felony charge of harboring a priest. The events surrounding Henry Donne's death must have heightened the pangs of conscience that John Donne would have felt as he wrestled with the idea of leaving the Catholic Church for the Church of England. The decision

Francis Drake—knighted in 1581 by Queen Elizabeth—was a commander of the English fleet that triumphed over the Spanish Armada.

would help advance his career but leave him open to charges of self-interest and betrayal.

Rivalry with Catholic Spain. At the end of the sixteenth century, Spain, an aggressively Catholic nation, was Europe's leading international power. Spanish participation in conspiracies like the Ridolfi Plot continually reinforced the link between Catholicism and Spanish domination in the English mind. In addition, the two powers had also become rivals on the high seas, where since the 1560s English privateers (pirates operating with royal approval) had raided Spanish ports and attacked ships loaded with treasure from Spain's colonies in the Americas. In 1588 a large invasion force, the Spanish Armada, was launched from Spain and from the Spanish-controlled Netherlands to bring the English to heel. But after suffering defeat by the English fleet under the command of Sir Francis Drake, Sir John Hawkins, and others, the Armada was savaged by storms on its return voyage; consequently only about 80 of the original 130 ships reached home. The Armada was the great crisis of Elizabeth's reign, and the English took the victory and its aftermath as a sign of God's favor.

Yet English attempts in the 1590s to capitalize on the Armada's defeat met with only mixed success. In 1596, the earl of Essex and Sir Wal-

ter Raleigh led a successful raid on the Spanish port of Cadiz, hindering Spanish preparations for a second Armada. But Essex and Raleigh were less fortunate in a subsequent raid of 1597, encountering a storm in which many ships and lives were lost. Later that year their fleet nearly met with disaster when it was becalmed for two days off the Azore Islands midway across the Atlantic. John Donne served on the Cadiz expedition as well as that of 1597. In order to participate, he would probably have had to convert to Anglicanism, so his conversion, again an important event in Donne's life, is likely to have occurred some time between his brother's death in 1593 and the Cadiz expedition of 1596.

Donne recorded his shipboard experiences during this expedition in his descriptive poems "The Storme" and "The Calme." Ships and nautical images figure prominently in the love poetry of "Songs and Sonnets" as well. In "Confined Love," for example, the poet protests against the expectation that he will remain true to one love: "Who e'er rigged fair ship to lie in harbors, / And not to seek new lands . . . ?" (Donne, "Confined Love," lines 15-16).

Elizabethan love poetry. The last decade of the sixteenth century and the first decade of the seventeenth were a period of unparalleled creativity in English letters. A major focus of this literary output was the love poem, whose English practitioners drew on and reacted against conventions established earlier by the Italian poet and humanist scholar Francesco Petrarca ("Petrarch" in English) (1304-74). Such conventions included flowery, extravagant language, lush praise of the beloved's beauty, and a stock supply of metaphors and other images. Love, for example, might be likened to a storm-tossed ship at sea; the beloved's cheeks bloom like roses and her teeth are like pearls; oceans of tears drown the poem's speaker if his love is unrequited.

Elizabethan love poetry found its most characteristic expression in the sonnet, a 14-line poetic form made popular by Petrarch and adapted

AN AGE OF DISCOVERY

Along with such maritime feats as Sir Francis Drake's circumnavigation of the world from 1577–80, Donne's lifetime saw new advances in astronomy, map-making, medicine, anatomy, and other sciences. Donne was intensely interested in such intellectual matters and kept up to date on the latest ideas. He also incorporated his wide reading into the "Songs and Sonnets." In "Love's Alchemy," for example, he pokes fun at alchemy (a blend of magic and science whose object was to turn base metals into gold), and dismisses it contemptuously. Similarly, in "The Sun Rising" he alludes to Copernicus's heliocentric theory that the earth revolves around the sun, a theory that was slowly replacing the older geocentric model of the medieval Ptolemaic system.

by Elizabethan poets such as Sir Philip Sidney, Edmund Spenser, and William Shakespeare. Sidney's sonnet sequence *Astrophel and Stella*, published in 1591, revived the Petrarchan tradition and inaugurated the sonnet's popularity in England. By the time Donne was writing, scores of young upper-class and upper-middle-class Englishmen were composing sonnets in the Petrarchan vein. While accomplished poets such as Spenser and Shakespeare brought power and originality to their treatment of the sonnet, many other Elizabethan gentlemen who did not share their genius still produced competent verse. Until recently, most poems written by these young men were thought to have been intended for poetry lovers rather than for actual female addressees. Upper-class marriages were usually

arranged by parents to ensure a financially or socially advantageous match, and therefore courtship seemed to be orchestrated by one's elders rather than undertaken by a young man in love. But the fashion for writing love sonnets among upper-class young men has been adduced as evidence that some young men actually did use poetry to court women. Another probable venue for such poetry was the royal court. In an age where wit and verbal showmanship was highly prized, the ability to compose artful verse could be an important means to social and even political advancement.

John Donne's courtship of Anne More, which lasted for several years before their marriage in 1601, was a secret love match that, far from being arranged, resulted in Donne's disgrace. Whether Donne courted her with his poems remains unknown. Donne went against the grain in poetry as in love, for in contrast with the prevailing taste of the sonnet-writers, Donne's language and tone tend to be conversational rather than flowery, and he eschews physical description, preferring instead to develop dramatic and intellectually elaborate arguments. His technique can be seen partly as a reaction against the poetic fashion: while Donne does use Petrarchan conventions, he most often undermines or distorts them in some way. For example, the poetic conceit (an extended metaphor; see below) is a Petrarchan element that Donne exaggerates to the point that it dominates his work.

Court life and patronage under James I. In 1603 the English throne passed to King James VI of Scotland, the Protestant son of Mary Queen of Scots, who became James I of England. Elizabeth's expensive wars had left the Crown saddled with a huge debt of £400,000, so one of James's first priorities was peace, which he concluded with Spain in 1604. However, savings brought by peace abroad were more than canceled by James's lavish spending at home. In addition to the extravagant entertainments, banquets, and other expensive features of his court, James freely dispensed pensions and other subsidies to his personal favorites. By 1618, James's debt stood at £900,000. Competition between favorites was nothing new to court life, but James's largesse raised the stakes among the nobles who vied for royal patronage—and among those lower on the social scale who vied for the patronage of the royal favorites themselves.

As in Elizabeth's reign, the problems with Spain and English Catholics continued to add to the complex mix of personal interest and kinship affiliation that determined the shape of court factions. A pro-Spanish faction, grouped around the influential Howard family, pressed for better relations with Spain and greater tolerance of English Catholics. Opposing the Howards was an anti-Spanish faction centered around James's wife Queen Anne; George Abbot, the Archbishop of Canterbury; and William Herbert, the earl of Pembroke. This faction desired a strongly Protestant foreign policy and generally supported stricter measures against English Catholics (though Anne herself was Catholic). In 1605, early in James's reign, anti-Catholic feeling was roused to fever pitch by the infamous Gunpowder Plot, in which a Catholic convert named Guy Fawkes was discovered in an attempt to blow up both Parliament and the entire royal family. For the rest of his reign, James's natural sympathies toward the Catholics were to be sharply checked by the deep fears this episode aroused in the English people.

John Donne was among the ambitious who sought the patronage of both the king and others during these years. Having lost his position with Sir Thomas Egerton after his secret marriage to Egerton's ward, Anne More, in 1601, Donne found himself at 30 with a rapidly growing family (his wife, Anne, would bear 12 children) and no means of support. Although he was able to obtain intermittent gifts from wealthy lovers of poetry, Egerton's unremitting hostility prevented him from securing a permanent position at court. In 1610, Donne published a prose work called *Pseudo-Martyr,* in which he attacks those Catholics who refused to swear an oath of allegiance to the king, as required since the Gunpowder Plot. James was pleased with the work, and commanded Oxford University to award Donne an honorary master of arts degree, but for the moment that was the extent of his appreciation. By 1614, Donne had managed to gain the support of Somerset, who reported back that the king insisted on Donne's taking holy orders before any position would be forthcoming. Donne did so in early 1615, becoming an Anglican priest—only in time to see Somerset fall from power. Later, in 1621, he would approach George Villiers, the king's new favorite, who interceded with the king to help Donne gain his post as dean of St. Paul's.

The Poems in Focus

Contents summary. The 55 love poems that make up the "Songs and Sonnets" are technically neither songs nor sonnets; the title was a conventional one and simply meant a selection of short lyrical love poems. The poems have no clear logical sequence and were published in different orders in the earliest editions of Donne's poetry. Rather than focusing simply on sexual love's physical and aesthetic pleasures, or even on its emotional qualities, they explore as well its deeper intellectual, psychological, and moral ambiguities.

POETIC REVOLT

By Donne's day, the body of Petrarchan imagery had become so commonplace that a vogue for "anti-Petrarchanism" set in. Such poetry was addressed to a woman characterized as unattractive, promiscuous, and so forth; in other words, she embodied the opposite qualities of the Petrarchan beloved. While Shakespeare's sonnet "My mistress' eyes are nothing like the sun" is perhaps the best-known example of anti-Petrarchanism, many of Donne's love poems also reflect its influence.

Despite wide variations, the poems share important features. The poet commonly addresses his lover directly, developing a detailed argument of some kind—whether he wants her to yield to him sexually or to celebrate their love's spiritual purity. Also, his argument is often based on a "conceit," an extended metaphorical comparison between two seemingly unrelated objects or ideas. Though other Elizabethan poets—like poets of other ages—employed the conceit, this literary device is Donne's most distinctive stylistic mark, particularly in the extent to which he elaborates on his ornate comparisons.

A Valediction: Forbidding Mourning

As virtuous men pass mildly away,
    And whisper to their souls, to go,
Whilst some of their sad friends do say,
    "The breath goes now," and some say, "No:"

So let us melt, and make no noise,
    No tear-floods, nor sigh-tempests move;
'Twere profanation of our joys
    To tell the laity our love.

Moving of th' earth brings harms and fears;
    Men reckon what it did, and meant;
But trepidation of the spheres,
    Though greater far, is innocent.

Dull sublunary lover's love
    (Whose soul is sense) cannot admit

Absence, because it doth remove
　　Those things which elemented it.
But we, by a love so much refin'd
　　That ourselves know not what it is,
Inter-assured of the mind,
　　Care less, eyes, lips, and hands to miss.

Our two souls therefore, which are one,
　　Though I must go, endure not yet
A breach, but an expansion,
　　Like gold to airy thinness beat.

If they be two, they are two so
　　As stiff twin compasses are two:
Thy soul, the fix'd foot, makes no show
　　To move, but doth, if th' other do;

And though it in the centre sit,
　　Yet when the other far doth roam,
It leans, and hearkens after it,
　　And grows erect, as that comes home.

Such wilt thou be to me, who must,
　　Like the other foot, obliquely run;
Thy firmness makes my circle just,
　　And makes me end where I begun.

In "A Valediction: Forbidding Mourning," the speaker tells his love not to be sad as they part, since their souls will remain connected by their love. "As virtuous men pass mildly away, / And whisper to their souls to go," the speaker begins, so too should the lovers part quietly from each other, without "tear-floods" or "sigh-tempests" ("A Valediction: Forbidding Mourning," lines 1-6). The lover's souls expand as much as needed to fill the physical gap between them, just as beaten gold becomes a thin film under the hammer of a goldsmith. Their two souls, the speaker argues, are really one by virtue of this capacity for infinite expansion. The parting lover's souls are then compared to the two legs of a drawing compass, which lean towards each other while one remains anchored in the center and the other circles it. However far into the world the speaker roams, his beloved will always remain fixed in the center, providing a point of orientation to which he can return. The dense and highly intellectual argument of the first six stanzas is thus brought to a climax by the extended conceit of the last three.

A Valediction: Of Weeping

　　　　Let me pour forth
My tears before thy face, whilst I stay here,
For thy face coins them, and thy stamp they
　　bear,
And by this mintage they are something worth,
　　　　For thus they be
　　　　Pregnant of thee;
Fruits of much grief they are, emblems of
　　more,

When a tear falls, that thou falls which it
　　bore,
So thou and I are nothing then, when on a
　　diverse shore.

　　　　On a round ball
A workman that hath copies by, can lay
An Europe, Africa, and an Asia,
And quickly make that, which was nothing, All;
　　　　So doth each tear
　　　　Which thee doth wear,
A globe, yea world, by that impression grow,
Till thy tears mix'd with mine do overflow
This world; by waters sent from thee, my
　　heaven dissolved so.

　　　　O more than moon,
Draw not up seas to drown me in thy sphere,
Weep me not dead, in thine arms, but forbear
To teach the sea what it may do too soon;
　　　　Let not the wind
　　　　Example find,
To do me more harm than it purposeth;
Since thou and I sigh one another's breath,
Whoe'er sighs most is cruellest, and hastes
　　the other's death.

"A Valediction: Of Weeping" treats the same conventional subject—the lover's parting—from a more pessimistic angle. "Let me pour forth / My tears before thy face" the speaker begins, "For thy face coins them, and thy stamp they bear" ("A Valediction: Of Weeping," lines 1-3). The speaker's tears are caused by his lover and carry her (reflected) image in them, like coins minted by a monarch. When one of them falls, the little image that it carries falls, too, bringing their relationship to nothing when they are apart. In the second stanza the speaker compares his tears to "a round ball" on which a workman can lay copies of maps to make a globe of the world— and thus "quickly make that, which was nothing, All" ("A Valediction: Of Weeping," lines 10-13). The weeping speaker then likens his love to the moon, asking her to be merciful in restraining the sea of tears in which he might drown. By comparing his lover to the moon, a standard poetic symbol of inconstancy, Donne's speaker also hints at a hidden fear that their parting will lead to her infidelity.

A Nocturnal upon St. Lucy's Day

'Tis the year's midnight, and it is the day's,
Lucy's, who scarce seven hours herself
　　unmasks;
　　　　The sun is spent, and now his flasks
　　　　Send forth light squibs, no constant rays;
　　　　The world's whole sap is sunk;
The general balm the hydroptic earth hath
　　drunk,

Whither, as to the bed's feet, life is shrunk,
Dead and interr'd; yet all these seem to laugh,
Compar'd with me, who am their epitaph.

Study me then, you who shall lovers be
At the next world, that is, at the next spring:
   For I am every dead thing,
    In whom Love wrought new alchemy.
      For his art did express
A quintessence even from nothingness,
From dull privations, and lean emptiness;
He ruin'd me, and I am re-begot
Of absence, darkness, death; things which are
   not.

All others, from all things, draw all that's
   good,
Life, soul, form, spirit, whence they being
   have;
   I, by Love's limbeck, am the grave
    Of all that's nothing. Oft a flood
      Have we two wept, and so
Drown'd the whole world, us two; oft did we
   grow
To be two chaoses, when we did show
Care to aught else; and often absences
Withdrew our souls, and made us carcasses.

But I am by her death (which word wrongs
   her)
Of the first nothing the elixir grown;
   Were I a man, that I were one
    I needs must know; I should prefer,
      If I were any beast,
Some ends, some means; yea plants, yea
   stones detest,
And love; all, all some properties invest;
If I an ordinary nothing were,
As shadow, a light and body must be here.

But I am none; nor will my Sun renew.
You lovers, for whose sake the lesser sun
   At this time to the Goat is run
    To fetch new lust, and give it you,
      Enjoy your summer all;
Since she enjoys her long night's festival,
Let me prepare towards her, and let me call
This hour her vigil, and her eve, since this
Both the year's, and the day's deep midnight is.

In "A Nocturnal upon St. Lucy's Day," set after sunset on the shortest day of the year, the speaker's lover has died and he is completely overcome by despair. This speaker is even more negative than that of "A Valediction: Of Weeping." In the Julian calendar (England did not adopt the Gregorian calendar until 1751), St. Lucy's Day fell very close to the winter solstice (now December 21), and the poem's nighttime setting immediately doubles this dark day's darkness: "'Tis the year's midnight," the speaker begins, "and it is the day's" ("A Nocturnal upon St. Lucy's Day," line 1). Images of darkness and life-lessness fill the first stanza: exhausted sun, withered nature, dried up earth, even life itself is "Dead and interred; yet all these seem to laugh, / Compared with me, who am their epitaph" ("A Nocturnal upon St. Lucy's Day," lines 8-9). The second stanza focuses darkness as if through a lens and then projects it: "I am every dead thing," the speaker declares, "a quintessence even from nothingness" that has been annihilated and "re-begot / Of absence, darkness, death; things which are not" ("A Nocturnal upon St. Lucy's Day," lines 12-18). Darkness thus takes on its own creative power, becoming not just the un-lit but almost a kind of anti-light in itself. It is love, the speaker says, that brought him to this state. His lover's death, which he mentions almost casually at the beginning of the fourth stanza, has made him into the very essence of the first nothing from which God created the world. His sun (that is, his lover) will never return, but the "lesser sun" will bring a new lusty springtime to other lovers, who will then enjoy their summer. The speaker, though, will keep a vigil for his love on this shortest day, which "Both the year's, and the day's deep midnight is" ("A Nocturnal upon St. Lucy's Day," lines 38-45).

The Good-Morrow

I wonder by my troth, what thou and I
Did, till we lov'd? Were we not wean'd till
   then,
But suck'd on country pleasures, childishly?
Or snorted we in the seven sleepers' den?
'Twas so; but this, all pleasures fancies be.
If ever any beauty I did see,
Which I desir'd, and got, 'Twas but a dream
   of thee.

And now good morrow to our waking souls,
Which watch not one another out of fear;
For love, all love of other sights controls,
And makes one little room, an everywhere.
Let sea-discoverers to new worlds have gone,
Let maps to other, worlds on worlds have
   shown,
Let us possess one world, each hath one, and
   is one.

My face in thine eye, thine in mine appears,
And true plain hearts do in the faces rest;
Where can we find two better hemispheres,
Without sharp north, without declining west?
Whatever dies, was not mix'd equally;
If our two loves be one, or, thou and I
Love so alike, that none do slacken, none can
   die.

In stark contrast to the deep midnight of "A Nocturnal upon St. Lucy's Day" stands the bright sunlit world of "The Good Morrow," whose seemingly lighthearted speaker celebrates awakening with his beloved. In some ways the two poems are mirror images. Just as his loss has created the speaker's nothingness in "A Nocturnal upon St. Lucy's Day," so has the lover's union created a constantly renewed world of fullness for the speaker in "The Good Morrow." Even time itself seems not to have existed before their love: "I wonder, by my troth, what thou and I / Did, till we loved?" he begins ("The Good Morrow," lines 1-2). Except for their love, all pleasures are imaginary; any other beauty the speaker has ever seen, desired, or possessed was only a dream of his lover.

The lover's union awakens their souls and offers a world of discovery, yet as in "A Nocturnal upon St. Lucy's Day," the speaker's one-sided view is subtly undermined by the mention of its opposite; just as the downcast speaker in the former poem admits that a new summer of lust will come for other lovers, so the optimistic speaker in "The Good Morrow" brings fear to our attention by his very denial of it. The idea of the lovers watching each other out of fear suggests a need to monitor his lover's loyalty that the speaker cannot admit openly. The third and final stanza cloaks a similar ambiguity. Anything that dies, the speaker concludes, was not balanced equally. (According to a Renaissance theory, decay occurs when elements are unequally mixed.) In other words, the speaker says, if our loves are one, or

if we love each other equally, our love will never die.

Faith and fidelity in Donne's life and poetry. As these readings of a few of the "Songs and Sonnets" indicate, anxiety over a lover's fidelity is a major issue in Donne's love poetry, even if it is often obscured by the poet's subtlety and the range of the voices he adopts. At times, this anxiety is expressed openly: "Nowhere / Lives a woman true, and faire," complains one speaker ("Song: Go and Catch a Falling Star," lines 17-18). "She that, oh, broke her faith," asserts another, "would soon break thee" ("A Jet Ring Sent," line 12). The critic John Carey has argued that this preoccupation with betrayal, with broken faith, can be seen as springing at least partly from the circumstances of Donne's life, specifically from his own abandonment of "the old faith" of his family, Roman Catholicism. "The love poems," Carey suggests, "are a veil for religious perturbations" (Carey, p. 24).

Whether we see one as a "veil" for another, clearly love and religion are entwined in Donne's work. On the most basic level, they are the two main subjects on which he was moved to write; and while Donne's love poems brim with religious language and images, his religious verses often sound like love poems. Furthermore, poems like "The Canonization" and "The Relic" (both from the "Songs and Sonnets") take their titles and central images from practices associated with Catholicism, not Protestantism—namely, the cultivation of saints and their relics. The religion that Donne left behind continued to inform his poetic imagination—but, as Carey points out, so did the uncomfortable fact that he had left it behind—by creating a general unease with the idea of betrayal that applied to personal relationships as well as to religion.

In a larger sense, Donne's preoccupation with religious and personal fidelity was shared by his society, as shown by the Elizabethan and Jacobean laws that attempted to enforce either Anglican practice or personal loyalty to the monarch (for example, the oath of loyalty to James I after the Gunpowder Plot). Historical circumstances thus made the poet's concerns those of his age.

Sources and literary context. Although none of the "Songs and Sonnets" can be firmly linked to events in Donne's life, critics have engaged in plausible speculation. Donne's first biographer, Izaak Walton, claims that "A Valediction: Forbidding Mourning" was composed when Donne traveled to France for an extended period in

JACK DONNE VS. DR. DONNE

The traditional view of Donne's life was that as young man he was a womanizing rake and love poet, while after becoming a priest he settled into a quiet, contemplative life and wrote religious poetry. Donne himself helped give rise to this interpretation, referring to his younger self as "Jack Donne" and his older self as "Dr. Donne" (Donne in Carey, p. xi). More recently, this division has been abandoned as simplistic, though it may reflect a gradual change in emphasis. A friend from Oxford, Sir Richard Baker, who also knew Donne as a young law student in London, describes him as "a great visitor of Ladies, a great frequenter of Playes, a great writer of conceited Verses" during this period (Baker in Bald, p. 72). (The word "conceited" refers to the literary device known as the conceit, which Donne employs frequently.) Clearly, like most young students, Donne was also engaged in lighter pursuits, probably turning some of these experiences into the poems in *Songs and Sonnets.*

1611-12. "A Nocturnal upon St. Lucy's Day" may have been written for one of Donne's patrons, Lucy, countess of Bedford, after either an illness in 1612-13 or her death in 1627; Anne Donne's death in 1617 has also been suggested as a possible occasion for the poem. Similarly, critics have put forward Donne's marriage and subsequent banishment from public life as a possible occasion for "The Canonization," which seems to scorn the public world in favor of the private realm of love. On the testimony of his letters, Donne was deeply in love with his wife, and she may well have provided the inspiration for many of his poems, though they need not have been based on any actual incident or situation.

The Petrarchan tradition that dominated Elizabethan love poetry included works such as Sir Philip Sidney's *Astrophel and Stella* (1591), Edmund Spencer's sonnet sequence *Amoretti* (1595), and many of Shakespeare's *Sonnets* (1609). As discussed above, Donne's love poetry often stands in contrast to this background. Rather than declaring his love and describing it or his lover's beauty in smoothly metrical lines, Donne often jolts the reader with broken lines that reflect the emotional intensity of an immediate dramatic situation, and often the woman to whom the poem is addressed seems less than perfect. Where other Elizabethan love poets tend to write about their lovers, Donne almost always addresses his directly, plunging the reader into a confrontation of some sort. "For God's sake, hold your tongue, and let me love," the speaker of "The Canonization" bursts out at the beginning of the poem ("The Canonization," line 1). Donne is also original in the use to which he puts such situations, taking them as a point of departure for an elaborate argument based on one or more conceits.

Publication and impact. Only two of the "Songs and Sonnets," "The Expiration" and "Breake of Day," were published during Donne's lifetime, in poetry collections of 1609 and 1612, respectively. However, many of them circulated in manuscript form among his patrons and friends. The first collection of Donne's poetry was published under the title *Poems* in 1633, with several new poems added in the second edition of 1635, when the heading *Songs and Sonnets* was first used for the love lyrics. Added to the group in the mid-seventeenth century were two poems, "The Token" and "Selfe-Love," that may not have been written by Donne at all. The friends who read Donne's work during his lifetime included the poet and playwright Ben Jonson. According to Jonson's friend William Drummond, Jonson "esteemeth John Done [sic] the first poet of the world in some things" but found his rough meter deficient: "for not keeping of accent" Jonson thought that Donne "deserved hanging" (Drummond in Donne, p. 139). Donne helped give rise to a genre later called "metaphysical poetry," in which religion and love are common themes and which rely heavily on conceits in the manner that Donne perfected. Donne's contemporary Thomas Carew, considered one of the metaphysical poets, wrote an elegy praising Donne after Donne's death in 1631.

> Can we not force from widowed poetry,
> Now thou art dead, great Donne, one elegy
> To crown thy hearse? . . .
> . . . Didst thou dispense
> Through all our language both the words and
>   sense?
>
>   (Carew, p. 1640)

—Colin Wells

For More Information

Ashley, Maurice. *England in the Seventeenth Century.* Harmondsworth: Penguin, 1977.

Bald, R.C. *John Donne: A Life.* Oxford: Oxford University Press, 1970.

Carew, Thomas. "An Elegy upon the Death of the Dean of Paul's, Dr. John Donne." In *The Norton Anthology of English Literature.* Vol. 1. 5th ed. New York: W. W. Norton, 1986.

Carey, John. *John Donne: Life, Mind and Art.* London: Faber and Faber, 1990.

Donne, John. *John Donne's Poetry.* Ed. Arthur L. Clements. New York: Norton, 1996.

Leishman, J. B. *The Monarch of Wit: An Analytical and Comparative Study of the Poetry of John Donne.* London: Hutchinson, 1965.

Lockyer, Roger. *Tudor & Stuart Britain 1471-1714.* Harlow, England: Longman, 1964.

Parfitt, George. *John Donne: A Literary Life.* London: Macmillan, 1989.

Parker, Derek. *John Donne and His World.* London: Thames and Hudson, 1975.

Songs of Innocence and of Experience;

Shewing the Two Contrary States of the Human Soul

by

William Blake

William Blake was born in 1757 in London, a place that would leave its mark on all his work. His father, a tradesman who sold hosiery, handed down to Blake a heritage of religious and political dissent. Disdainful of the restrictions of school, Blake was self-educated, until he began drawing lessons at the age of 10. After a seven-year apprenticeship as an engraver, Blake supported himself by engraving while he attended the Royal Academy. His study here, however, was short-lived because his iconoclasm conflicted with the academy's orthodoxy. In 1782 Blake married Catherine Boucher, forming an artistic partnership with her that would last a lifetime; two years later he opened his own printing business. Blake's distinctive style, the product of his visionary imagination and his varied artistic influences, was set with *Songs of Innocence,* the first of his books to interweave poetry and etchings. That only a few copies could be painstakingly produced was compensated for by the complete control that Blake exercised. In *Songs of Innocence and of Experience,* Blake describes society both as he sees it and as he believes it should be. He laments the alienation of the large city in "London," condemns child labor in two poems called "The Chimney Sweeper," and looks with sorrow on the subjection of Africans in "The Little Black Boy."

Events in History at the Time of the Poems

A revolutionary era. Revolutions—political, economic, and social—marked the second half

---

THE LITERARY WORK

A collection of engraved poems set mainly in England during the late eighteenth century, but also in timeless mythical places; *Songs of Innocence* was printed in 1789 and combined with *Songs of Experience* in 1794.

SYNOPSIS

Two complementary collections of lyric poems, *Songs of Innocence and of Experience* depict a state of joyous engagement with the world and a bitter detachment from the world.

---

of the eighteenth century. The French Revolution, which began with the storming of the Bastille in 1789, sent shock waves across the English Channel. At least initially, it inspired the liberal-minded because of its roots in Enlightenment thought, while frightening conservatives, who worried about the stability of English society and the rule of law. Rumblings of discontent had, in fact, been heard throughout the 1780s in England. William Blake was never an ideological follower, but as a young man in the 1780s he had associated with political radicals in London, who were critical of the British government. Two events in 1780 indicate the political turbulence of the times. During the Gordon Riots (named for Lord George Gordon, the leader), the volatile populace, ostensibly protesting the extension of property rights to Roman Catholics, went on a burning spree in London, attacking not only the

THE POET AS REVOLUTIONARY: FROM BLAKE'S "PREFACE" TO HIS POEM *MILTON*

And did those feet in ancient time,
Walk upon Englands mountains green:
And was the holy Lamb of god,
On Englands pleasant pastures seen!

And did the Countenance Divine,
Shine forth upon our clouded hills?
And was Jerusalem builded here,
Among these dark Satanic Mills?

Bring me my Bow of burning gold:
Bring me my Arrows of desire:
Bring me my Spear: O clouds unfold!
Bring me my Chariot of fire!

I will not cease from Mental fight,
Nor shall my Sword sleep in my hand:
Till we have built Jerusalem,
In Englands green & pleasant Land.

(Blake in Johnson and Grant,
"Preface" to *Milton,* lines 1-16)

plied. Increased profits and urbanization resulted as industries moved into factories, and people moved to the cities to work in them. Standards of living rose and England became a great exporter of goods, but alongside this increased wealth came increased crowding and pollution. Workers afraid of being displaced by technology protested, and sometimes destroyed, new equipment. Blake despised the mills; it is possible to see in Blake's own laborious method of printing a model of unalienated labor.

London. Eighteenth-century London seethed with energy. Crime and high culture coexisted as every class and occupation jostled together on the city's crowded streets. By the time Blake was born, the metropolis stretched far beyond the original Roman walls dating from the first century C.E. The fashionable moved to the rapidly developing West End; the poor lived in the East End; artisans continued to live in and adjacent to the old city. Blake himself was born above his parent's hosiery shop in Soho (the West End), a respectable neighborhood of craftsmen and merchants that would decline during his lifetime.

London was the United Kingdom's center of government, of commercial and colonial expansion, and of national mythology. As Samuel Johnson wrote in 1777, "When a man is tired of London, he is tired of life" (Johnson in Porter, p. 165). On its way to becoming the world's largest city, London dominated the nation: a tenth of the English and Welsh lived in London. It is no surprise that such a city was both celebrated and denounced. To Blake, London was Babylon and also Jerusalem—a place of confusion and conflict, but also of spiritual potential. The independent nature of its populace provided fruitful grounds for all types of political expression, from riots to reform. Blake's "London" in *Songs of Experience* focuses on the city's institutional power and the victims of that power: children forced to clean chimneys while even churches averted their gaze, soldiers assigned to control London's mobs or fight against revolutionary France, prostitutes (there were 50,000 in London) suffering under a society's hypocrisy.

Reform—the child chimney sweep. No one kept track of the number of London's destitute children. Arguably the worst off were those who, as young as four years old, cleaned the narrow chimneys that spat coal smoke into the London sky. These "climbing boys" crawled into flues measuring only seven inches square—flues that might contain still-burning soot. The master

homes of supposed Catholic sympathizers but also symbols of authority such as the Bank of England. Blake himself was swept along by a mob and witnessed the burning of London's infamous prison, Newgate. The same year, Blake and two companions, out on a sketching expedition, were briefly taken prisoner by British soldiers who accused them of being spies for the French. Britain, intermittently at war with France throughout the eighteenth century, was in the midst of conflict with the French that ended temporarily with the Treaty of Paris in 1783. When the French Revolution began, Blake, like many of his class in London, was a republican sympathizer with prorevolutionary sentiments. He began, though never finished or published, a lengthy epic poem entitled *The French Revolution,* in which monarchical France is depicted as sick and slumbering.

Revolution was not confined to politics, however. What we now call the "Industrial Revolution" steamed ahead in the second half of the eighteenth century, building on such inventions as Hargreaves's spinning jenny (1766), Arkwright's spinning frame (1768), and Cartwright's power loom (1785-90), all of which contributed to mechanizing the cotton industry; new technologies for making iron and steel also multi-

sweep who controlled them "encouraged" the boys to climb higher by pricking their feet, or lighting fires beneath them. Some were permitted the luxury of a wash once a year; some every five years. Sweeps often died from burns or suffocation; cancer and deformity shortened their unhappy lives.

Where did these children come from? Desperate parents apprenticed their children to master sweeps for 20 to 30 shillings. Parishes sold dependent orphaned children. Sympathy, when it existed, conflicted with self-interest. Londoners, with their narrow chimney flues, demanded the services of the tiny sweeps. Furthermore, there was no general sentiment against child labor at the time. Children were regarded as the possessions of their parents and as contributors to the family income.

Tireless reformers, however, pressed their cause. The most notable, Jonas Hanway, kept up a barrage of writing and committee forming. "These poor black urchins," he wrote, "have no protectors and are treated worse than a humane person would treat a dog" (Hanway in Cunningham, p. 53). Hanway's efforts culminated in the Act for the Better Regulation of Chimney Sweepers and their Apprentices, passed in 1788, the year before Blake's first published poem on the chimney sweep. Designed to combat some abuses by raising the minimum age for sweeps to eight years old and adding a primitive licensing system, Hanway's Act was often circumvented. Not until the latter part of the nineteenth century would regulations be properly enforced.

Reformers, appealing to the English belief in fairness and liberty, used the image of the black slave to forward their cause. Both sweeps and slaves were black, in bondage, and working in horrific conditions. The chimney sweepers, though, were slaves on English soil, their presence an everyday affront to the values of their country.

Slavery and the abolition movement. During the late eighteenth century, the largest slave trading country in the world was the United Kingdom. In the 1790s, the British trafficked in 45,000 slaves per year. The public had an insatiable appetite for the products of slave labor (especially sugar) from Britain's holdings in the West Indies and Caribbean. It also appreciated the wealth that accrued from slavery, both to English plantation owners and port cities, including London. Slave labor produced raw materials that could be refined in England and shipped to Britain's growing empire.

The Chimney Sweep, an 1863 painting by Jonathan Eastman Johnson, evokes Blake's tragic image of young boys forced to clean the chimneys of London.

During the decade of Blake's *Songs of Innocence and of Experience,* slavery and the slave trade were matters of constant debate. Religious forces combined to press the charge that England could not be a moral leader if it continued to traffic in human beings. Several prominent cases put the issue squarely in the public eye, the most sensational of which was that of the slave-carrying ship, the *Zong.* Fearing a shortage of water, and believing he would not collect insurance if slaves died on board, the shipmaster ordered 133 people thrown into the sea. The ship's owners then attempted to claim insurance for their lost property—each slave that had been murdered. The case galvanized and unified reformers. In 1787, Thomas Clarkson founded, in London, the Committee for Effecting the Abolition of the Slave Trade. This association turned the abolitionist movement into a national cause.

No doubt Blake would have been familiar with the situation of former slaves, 15,000 of whom made their home in London. One of them, Ottobah Cugoano, published his successful *Thoughts and Sentiments on the Evil and Wicked Traffic of Slavery* in 1787. Blake's knowledge dramatically increased, when, in the early 1790s, he worked on the engravings for John Stedman's *Narrative of Surinam,* which describes some of the horrors of slavery. Though Stedman's book ultimately supports the existence of the slave trade, Blake's plates display a frightening brutality. Several engravers worked on Stedman's book, but Blake's three engravings of tortured slaves, "A Negro Hung Alive by the Ribs to a Gallows," "Flagellation of a Female Samboe Slave," and "The Execution of Breaking on the Rack," are the most graphic and moving. Stedman's *Narrative* provided Blake with extraordinary images that fueled his conceptions of liberty and enslavement in such poems as *Visions of the Daughters of Albion* (1793) and *America: A Prophecy* (1793).

ENGLISH ABOLITION MOVEMENT: A CHRONOLOGY

1730 From this time until 1807, the United Kingdom is the world's largest slave trader

1772 *Mansfield* decision holds that slavery is not legal within England

1781 Murder of 133 slaves (thrown overboard) on the *Zong*

1783 Insurance claim for the *Zong* slaves

1783 First anti-slavery petition to Parliament

1787 Society for Effecting the Abolition of the Slave Trade founded by Quakers in London; publication of Ottobah Cugoano's *Thoughts and Sentiments on the Evil and Wicked Traffic of Slavery*

1788 Dolberi's Act limits number of slaves transported on ships

1792 Blake's first engravings for Stedman's *Narrative of Surinam*

1807 Slave trading abolished in British Empire

1833 Emancipation Act frees slaves (with conditions) in the West Indies

1838 Full freedom for slaves in the British Colonies

1840 First International Anti-Slavery Convention (London)

The Poems in Focus

Contents summary. *Songs of Innocence and of Experience* are "poem-pictures," engraved poems always meant to be read with their surrounding illustrations (Keynes, p. 10). When *Songs of Innocence* was first issued in 1789, it consisted of 23 engraved poems. *Songs of Experience*, which was issued together with *Songs of Innocence* in 1794, would eventually contain 26 engraved poems, including four ("The Little Girl Lost," "The Little Girl Found," "The School Boy," and "The Voice of the Ancient Bard") transferred there from *Songs of Innocence* because of their darker

mood. Blake's poems portray and complicate the meanings of "innocence" and "experience," linking them not only to stages of life, but also to place and perspective.

The keynotes of *Songs of Innocence* are presented in the first poem, or "Introduction." The lyric speaker, "piping down the valleys wild," is implored by an angelic child to "pipe a song about a Lamb" (Blake, "Introduction," *Innocence*, lines 1,5). With its pastoral imagery, "valleys wild," and Pan-like speaker, this first poem also locates the ideal setting for innocence (Pan, the Greek god of flocks and shepherds, invented the musical reed pipe). Many of the poems in *Songs of Innocence* are pastoral, and take place among green hills and spring meadows in the company of lambs and shepherds. Those that are not set in the countryside often invoke it, so that little Tom in "The Chimney Sweeper" dreams of the country and the orphans of "Holy Thursday" are "flowers of London town" ("Holy Thursday," *Innocence*, line 5). In *Songs of Innocence* children are usually protected by caring adults, and God himself is incarnate and concerned. Just as a mother cannot "sit and hear / An infant groan, an infant fear," so God, who "becomes an infant small" mourns along with humans ("On Another's Sorrow," *Innocence*, lines 10-11, 26). The reigning image once again is of shepherd and sheep, and of God as both shepherd and lamb.

In the fallen world of *Songs of Experience*, even children have lost their innocence, and it is far less certain that the adult or even God is interested in the plight of the weak. Selfishness and cynicism have replaced concern and belief. Even virtue is questioned, as in the social critique of "The Human Abstract":

> Pity would be no more,
> If we did not make somebody Poor:
> And Mercy no more could be,
> If all were as happy as we;
> (Blake, "The Human Abstract," *Experience*,
> lines 1-4)

In the world of *Songs of Experience*, the idealized pastoral landscape appears far less often. The companion piece to *Songs of Innocence*'s "Holy Thursday," for example, tells us that for poor children, "their sun does never shine. / And their fields are bleak & bare" ("Holy Thursday," *Experience*, lines 9-10). When the setting is the countryside, as in *Experience*'s "Nurse's Song," corruption and jealousy have replaced laughter and joy.

Songs of Innocence and of Experience are linked by similar stylistic devices that initially may suggest that children are the poems' intended readers. Blake's use of a paratactic syntax, such as the "And" . . . "And" . . . "And" of his first poem, contributes to the seeming simplicity of his work. Blake often employs both repetition and trochaic meter (a stressed followed by an unstressed syllable), both of which are standard in children's verse. Alongside these techniques, however, Blake employs such sophisticated devices as paradox and irony, even within the "Introduction" to *Innocence*. "And I stain'd the water clear," states the speaker ("Introduction," *Innocence*, line 18). The writer dips his pen in ink, but he also uses his writing to make matters clear. Or, perhaps, he muddies the seeming clarity of the water, showing his readers the folly in what had only appeared true. Blake is a master of the paradoxical aphorism. "Without Contraries," he wrote in *The Marriage of Heaven and Hell*, "is no progression. Attraction and Repulsion, Reason and Energy, Love and Hate, are necessary to Human existence" (Blake in Johnson and Grant, *The Marriage of Heaven and Hell*, Plate 3). To these we might add "innocence" and "experience," what Blake calls in his subtitle, "the Two Contrary States of the Human Soul." His intended readers, therefore, are certainly not just children.

"London." The narrator of "London" (*Songs of Experience*) wanders through the streets of the city, telling us what he sees and hears. He encounters regulation, prohibition, suffering, and oppression. The streets and the river Thames he describes as "charter'd," a word that signifies the city's ancient liberties, codified in documents like the Magna Carta, as well as the restrictions imposed by city government and corporations, both of which are established by charter ("London," *Experience*, line 2). The denizens of the city feel only the restrictions. As he walks, the narrator passes other individuals who, like him, are alienated and sorrowful, marked, like so many wandering Cains, by "weakness" and "woe" ("London," *Experience*, line 4).

The speaker blames this condition on matters both internal and external that lead to people's imprisonment in "mind-forg'd manacles" ("London," *Experience*, line 8). The oppressors are institutions—the Church, the government, the legal institution of marriage. In each case, the voices of the victims become visible to the narrator: the chimney sweeper's cry changes the church, which implicitly condones child labor, from a refuge into a tomb; the sigh of the soldier

turns to blood; the curse of the prostitute becomes the venereal disease that destroys marriages and blinds infants.

The narrator's terrifying vision presents us with a city far removed from the pastoral idylls found in *Songs of Innocence*. In this view of London, we are left with hypocrisy and a "hearse" ("London," *Experience*, line 16). The experienced speaker can generalize about social misery. Yet he is both horrified by and detached from a world that seems inescapable.

The top third of Blake's engraved poem "London" shows a young boy leading an old crippled man past a closed door. Further down the page, the young boy, alone, warms his hands at a fire.

"AUTHOR & PRINTER"

Blake signed his works "Author & Printer." Integral to the *Songs of Innocence and Experience* is their medium, "illuminated printing." John Thomas Smith gave the following account in 1828 of Blake's mystical discovery of this labor-intensive method of engraving:

Blake, after deeply perplexing himself as to the mode of accomplishing the publication of his illustrated songs, without their being subject to the expense of letter-press, his brother Robert stood before him in one of his visionary imaginations, and so decidedly directed him in the way in which he ought to proceed, that he immediately followed his advice, by writing his poetry, and drawing his marginal subjects of embellishments in outline upon the copper-plate with an impervious liquid, and then eating the plain parts or lights away with aquafortis considerably below them, so that the outlines were left as a stereotype. The plates in this state were then printed in any tint that he wished, to enable him or Mrs. Blake to colour the marginal figures up by hand in an imitation of drawings.

(Smith in Johnson and Grant, pp. 485-86)

These two homeless wanderers are shut out of indoor comfort and warmth. Perhaps, the old man, decrepit and helpless, incarnates London itself (Thompson in Wolfreys, p. 46).

"The Chimney Sweeper." Blake wrote two poems on the plight of the chimney sweeps; one for *Songs of Innocence*, the other for *Songs of Experience*. In both cases, he gives us the perspective of the child sweep. The little boy in *Songs of Innocence* is cheerful and resigned. He presents his

Illustration by Blake from "London," in *Songs of Experience.*

POETIC COUNTERPARTS IN *SONGS OF INNOCENCE* AND *OF EXPERIENCE*

The following *Songs* illuminate each other:

Innocence	Experience
"The Lamb"	"The Tyger"
"The Chimney Sweeper"	"The Chimney Sweeper"
"The Divine Image"	"The Human Abstract"
"Holy Thursday"	"Holy Thursday"
"Nurse's Song"	"Nurse's Song"
"Infant Joy"	"Infant Sorrow"

all the sweeps are released from their "coffins of black," the narrow death chutes of the chimneys, and find themselves in heaven ("The Chimney Sweeper," *Innocence,* line 12). In a pastoral land-scape, they wash themselves and run naked. It is this part of the poem that forms Blake's accompanying illustration. We see Christ releasing a boy from his coffin to a green countryside full of naked playing children. Just before Tom wakes, an angel tells him that "if he'd be a good boy, / He'd have God for a father & never want joy" ("The Chimney Sweeper," *Innocence,* lines 19-20). Tom awakes in the dark and, sustained by his vision, returns to work. The poem ends with the speaker saying that "if all do their duty, they need not fear harm" ("The Chimney Sweeper," *Innocence,* line 24).

"The Chimney Sweeper" from *Songs of Experience* contains no comforting vision. The tone is not resignation but resentment. This little boy knows that he has been mistreated. Soliciting work on the Sabbath, the boy speaks with contempt of his guardians. The poem trades on the contrast between the boy's past and present life, his appearance and thoughts, and his life and that of his parents. Once he had been happy, but then his parents conscripted him to a life of woe. Outwardly he may still "dance & sing," but inwardly, he has been corrupted. While he works on Sunday, his parents sit in church. As in "London," this poem condemns a trinity of institutions, here "God & his Priest & King" ("The Chimney Sweeper," *Experience,* line 11), who encourage the downtrodden to wait for a better life in heaven. State and Church collude in the practice of child labor. The official message is similar to that in Tom Dacre's vision. But now the child sees the hypocrisy and understands that only some have to wait for their happiness.

Blake's illustration reinforces the contrasts found in the verse. The sweep is described as "a little black thing among the snow" ("The Chimney Sweeper," *Experience,* line 1). He used to take delight in the snow, but then was "clothed . . . in the clothes of death" ("The Chimney Sweeper," *Experience,* line 6). The engraving itself is almost no more than black and white. The dark sweep stands out, an incongruous being in the white snowstorm. His blackness marks him as a type of slave.

"The Little Black Boy." The black child who speaks in "The Little Black Boy" (*Songs of Innocence*) was born in "the southern wild" ("The Little Black Boy," *Innocence,* line 1). Addressing the

situation forthrightly. His mother is dead, and his father sold him to a master sweep while he was a tiny boy. He was so young that he could barely say "weep weep weep weep," a lisping version of the sweep's street call ("sweep sweep"), but also a touching indication of the sorrow within the labor ("The Chimney Sweeper," *Innocence,* line 3). (See verse on next page.)

The poem shifts from harsh reality to the dream vision of a fellow sweep. In Tom's dream,

English people, he declares that although he is black, "as if bereav'd of light," his "soul is white" ("The Little Black Boy," *Innocence*, lines 2, 4). His mother has taught him that his black body protects him from the strength of God's shining love, and that eventually souls are freed from their bodies to stand directly in God's presence. The little black boy then tells the little white boy that one day they both will play "round the tent of God like lambs" ("The Little Black Boy," *Innocence*, line 24). In fact, the black child offers to shade the white one until he too can bear the heat.

The text and the images link whiteness with souls, angels, and Christ himself. But these ideas coexist with the mother's positive reading of the black body—that it provides protection from the sun. Eventually, she says, bodies will not matter. In the boy's imagination, he becomes a teacher of the white child, repeating and expanding on his mother's lesson. Both will eventually part from their bodies—"I from black and he from white cloud free" ("The Little Black Boy," *Innocence*, line 23). When the two are alike, the English boy will love the black boy: "And then I'll stand and stroke his silver hair, / And be like him and he will then love me" ("The Little Black Boy," *Innocence*, lines 27-28).

In the pastoral heaven that Blake engraved with the poem, the white child stands in supplication before Christ, with the black child behind the white. The white boy and Christ look into each other's eyes, while the little black boy stands slightly to the side, as if he were a servant. Blake changed his coloring of this plate. Originally, the black child was depicted as white; later, he was colored black. Black or white, as David Bindman states, this child is removed from the loving pair of Christ and the white child (Bindman, p. 377).

Blake and the Romantic child. Blake's poetic children form part of a newly evolving Romantic discourse of the child as spiritually wise, and of childhood as a phase that should be protected, nurtured, and revered. In a 1799 letter, Blake proclaimed his belief in the wisdom of childhood:

> But I am Happy to find a Great Majority of Fellow Mortals who can Elucidate My Visions, & Particularly they have been Elucidated by Children, who have taken a greater delight in contemplating my Pictures than I even hoped. Neither Youth nor Childhood is Folly or Incapacity. Some Children are Fools & so are some Old Men. But There is a vast Majority on

the side of Imagination or Spiritual Sensation. (Blake in Keynes, *The Letters of William Blake*, p. 30)

Prior to the seventeenth century, children were commonly seen as little adults, creatures

"THE CHIMNEY SWEEPER" (*SONGS OF INNOCENCE*)

When my mother died I was very young,
And my father sold me while yet my tongue
Could scarcely cry weep weep weep weep.
So your chimneys I sweep & in soot I sleep.

There's little Tom Dacre, who cried when his head
That curl'd like a lamb's back, was shav'd, so I said,
"Hush Tom never mind it, for when your head's bare,
You know that the soot cannot spoil your white hair."

And so he was quiet, & that very night,
As Tom was a sleeping he had such a sight,
That thousands of sweepers Dick, Joe, Ned & Jack
Were all of them lock'd up in coffins of black.

And by came an Angel who had a bright key,
And he open'd the coffins & set them all free.
Then down a green plain leaping laughing they run
And wash in a river and shine in the Sun.

Then naked & white, all their bags left behind,
They rise upon clouds, and sport in the wind.
And the Angel told Tom if he'd be a good boy,
He'd have God for his father & never want joy.

And so Tom awoke and we rose in the dark
And got with our bags & our brushes to work.
Tho' the morning was cold, Tom was happy & warm,
So if all do their duty, they need not fear harm.

"THE CHIMNEY SWEEPER" (*SONGS OF EXPERIENCE*)

A little black thing among the snow:
Crying weep, weep, in notes of woe!
"Where are thy father & mother" say
"They are both gone up to the church to pray.

"Because I was happy upon the heath,
And smil'd among the winter's snow:
They clothed me in the clothes of death,
And taught me to sing the notes of woe.

"And because I am happy, & dance & sing,
They think they have done me no injury:
And are gone to praise God & his Priest & King
Who make up a heaven of our misery."

who needed to be civilized, weaned from their base instincts, and led to God. They were also expected to contribute to the family income. For poor children, little changed in the eighteenth century. Starting at the age of four or five, these children worked long hours on farms and in cottage industries and the new factories. If they ran afoul of the law and were older than seven, they could furthermore be charged as adults and hung or transported to a colony.

Life, in short, was difficult for the majority of children. But the eighteenth century saw efforts to contest child labor and to provide schooling for the poor. Criticism of child labor in cotton mills began in the 1780s, and, as mentioned above, a bill to regulate the employment of chimney sweeps passed in 1788. Charitable schools for the poor, many set up by the Society for the Propagation of Christian Knowledge (established in 1699), multiplied in the eighteenth century. Yet, despite these attempts, two-thirds of poor children received no schooling whatever. Those schools that did exist were intent on producing obedient workers, and so often combined education and employment. All the attempts at reform notwithstanding, it would be another 100 years before child labor was effectively controlled in England.

THE CRITICAL VOICE BEHIND "THE CHIMNEY SWEEPER"

"The Chimney Sweeper" relies on an adult reader, who feels the condemnation not of the boy, but of the poet. "*Your* chimneys I sweep & in soot I sleep," says the boy, implicating the reader in his fate. ("The Chimney Sweeper," *Innocence*, line 4, italics added). Little Tom Dacre's last name indicates that he was sold by the poorhouse (Lady Dacre Almshouse) that had taken him in (Ackroyd, p. 126). Not only the sweep but the reader should weep, and it is the reader who should feel the irony of the poem's moralism. The "angel" tells the child to obey authority; the speaker repeats pat phrases about "duty." Yet Tom, with his lamblike curls, signifies that children are as innocent as lambs, and created in God's image. The dereliction of duty on the part of adults has condemned these children to a painful and shortened existence.

Even in Blake's day, though, one could see the perception of the child beginning to change. From the seventeenth century onward, in the middle and upper classes, adults showed signs of an increased attention to children and how their minds worked (see **Essay on Human Understanding** by John Locke, also in *WLAIT 3: British and Irish Literature and Its Times*). More mothers breastfed their babies instead of sending them to wet nurses. Children's toys and books multiplied. Especially for boys, childhood became a stage marked by schooling, and some parents took great interest in the emerging field of childhood development. One of the most popular texts in England was Jean-Jacques Rousseau's *Emile: or, On Education* (1762), which advocates that children be allowed to develop "naturally," through their contact with the natural world and in accord with their own instincts.

Blake's poems promote and extend these new attitudes to children. The frontispiece to *Songs of Innocence,* in which two children study at the lap of their nurse or mother and the title forms itself from the bending branches of a tree, suggests that the education of children should take place in nature. The proper activity of the child, *Songs of Innocence* shows, is outdoor play: "the little ones leaped & shouted & laugh'd / And all the hills ecchoed" ("Nurse's Song," *Innocence*, lines 15-16). Most importantly, innocence is not ignorance, but responsiveness and optimism. Children, moreover, possess an instinctive spirituality.

> He [Christ] is meek & he is mild,
> He became a little child:
> I a child & thou a lamb,
> We are called by his name.
> ("The Lamb," *Innocence*, lines 15-18)

The problem with the children in *Songs of Experience* is that they have grown up too soon. The babe of *Experience*, who struggles and sulks after being born into "the dangerous world" is already weary and petulant ("Infant Sorrow," *Experience*, line 2). The cynicism and despair of such children condemns the adult world, which has exploited rather than protected its young. The child chimney sweep is the most flagrant example, but also critiqued is the curbing of children's natural thoughts and desires, the imposition of orthodoxy. In "A Little Boy Lost," the child who speaks his mind and says that it is impossible to love anyone else more than the self, is martyred by the priest, "bound . . . in an iron chain," and "burn'd" ("A Little Boy Lost," *Experience*, lines 20, 21). In "The School-Boy," a young boy pleads to spend his time outdoors instead of in the prison of a schoolroom. The poem compares him to a bird born for joy but forced to sit in a cage. His incarceration, because it robs his childhood of pleasure, will stunt his adulthood. Through such charges Blake complicates the contemporary dialog on children.

Literary context. Blake's *Songs of Innocence and of Experience* revise the traditionally didactic songs for children that were popular in the eighteenth century, such as Isaac Watts's *Divine Songs for the Use of Children* (1715), John Newberry's *A Little Pretty Pocket-Book* (1744), and Anna Barbauld's *Hymns in Prose for Children* (1781). Watts's *Divine Songs,* which went through many editions, are overtly didactic. Alongside songs glorifying God are many that illustrate the consequences of bad behavior. Watts's famous "Against Idleness and Mischief," with its ever busy bee, counsels children not to waste time, "for Satan finds some mischief still / For idle hands to do" (Watts, "Against Idleness and Mischief," lines 11-12). Blake's poems, by contrast, extol the virtues of play.

Songs of Innocence and of Experience also holds a central place in the emerging Romantic literature. As with William Wordsworth's and Samuel Taylor Coleridge's **Lyrical Ballads** (1798; also in *WLAIT 3: British and Irish Literature and Its Times*), Blake's *Songs* represent a democratization of poetry's subject matter. In his "Preface" to *Lyrical Ballads,* Wordsworth writes that he wants to represent "incidents of common life" in a language "near to the language of men" (Wordsworth in Mellor, pp. 574, 576). Like Blake, Wordsworth found in children an innate spirituality, best articulated in his "Ode" of 1807, when he declared that "Heaven lies about us in our infancy!" (Wordsworth in Mellor, "Ode," p. 604).

Reception. Because of Blake's labor-intensive method of printing, few copies of *Songs of Innocence and of Experience* were circulated during his lifetime. This illuminated book was his most successful, yet only 28 copies of the combined *Songs* exist. Blake's work was not completely unknown, however. "Holy Thursday" and "The Chimney Sweeper" from *Songs of Innocence* were anthologized while he lived. William Wordsworth, Samuel Taylor Coleridge, and Charles Lamb all appreciated the *Songs;* of the three, Lamb paid Blake the highest praise, referring to him in 1824 as one of the most extraordinary persons of his time. At his death in 1827, Blake was considered primarily an artist (and a mad artist at that), not a poet. Children especially appreciated his "visions," a development that delighted him.

Blake's reputation was resuscitated in the mid-nineteenth century by Alexander Gilchrist's biography (1863), by the Pre-Raphaelites, who were also painter-poets, and later by W. B. Yeats, who, like Blake, was a poet-mythmaker.

READING RACE IN "THE LITTLE BLACK BOY"

As with the *Songs of Innocence's* chimney sweep, the little black boy is a figure of innocence in part because he has imbibed conventional thought, in this case, European racism. The black boy's statement, therefore, that he is black "as if bereav'd of light" reflects the perceptions of the "civilizing" nations ("The Little Black Boy," *Innocence,* line 4). The boy's naïve desire for reconciliation also comments upon the intransigent racism of the English mind: the black boy cannot be loved as himself, but only when he resembles the white English boy. The black child has assumed a position of inferiority, even in his vision of heaven. Perhaps his "mind forg'd manacles" reflect missionary Christianity ("London," *Experience,* line 8). D. L. Macdonald claims that "a poem on such a subject, issued in such a year, must be interpreted in the light of the abolition movement" (Macdonald, p. 166). Blake implies that those "bereav'd of light" or reason are not the mother and child in the poem, but the proponents of slavery who continued to deny humanity to Africans.

—Danielle E. Price

For More Information

Ackroyd, Peter. *Blake: A Biography.* New York: Knopf, 1996.

Bindman, David. "Blake's Vision of Slavery Revisited." *Huntington Library Quarterly* 58, nos. 3 & 4 (1996): 373-382.

Blake, William. *Songs of Innocence and of Experience.* In *Blake's Poetry and Designs.* Ed. Mary Lynn Johnson and John E. Grant. New York: Norton, 1979.

Cunningham, Hugh. *The Children of the Poor: Representations of Childhood Since the Seventeenth Century.* Oxford: Basil Blackwell, 1991.

Johnson, Mary Lynn and John E. Grant, eds. *Blake's Poetry and Designs.* New York: Norton, 1979.

Keynes, Geoffrey, ed. "Introduction." *Songs of Innocence and of Experience,* by William Blake. London: Oxford University Press, 1977.

———. *The Letters of William Blake.* Cambridge, Mass.: Harvard University Press, 1960.

Macdonald, D. L. "Pre-Romantic and Romantic Abolitionism: Cowper and Blake." *European Romantic Review* 4 (1994): 163-82.

Mellor, Anne K., and Richard E. Matlak. *British Literature 1780-1830.* Fort Worth, Tex.: Harcourt, 1996.

Porter, Roy. *London: A Social History.* Cambridge, Mass.: Harvard University Press, 1994.

Watts, Isaac. "Divine Songs for Children." In *The Poetical Works of Isaac Watts and Henry Kirke White.* Boston: Houghton Mifflin, 1910.

Wolfreys, Julian. *Writing London: The Trace of the Urban Text from Blake to Dickens.* London: Macmillan, 1998.

The Spanish Tragedy

by
Thomas Kyd

~

Thomas Kyd (1558-94) is the most shadowy, least-known member of the first generation of great English dramatists, the generation that featured Christopher Marlowe and William Shakespeare. The son of a London scrivener (essentially, a legal secretary), Kyd was educated at Merchant Taylors' School, where the poet Edmund Spenser was among his classmates. He seems to have joined the theatrical world in the 1580s after finishing school. Although he presumably wrote a number of plays, his fame rests on *The Spanish Tragedy*, one of the first popular triumphs of the emerging London theater.

THE LITERARY WORK

A play set in Spain in the sixteenth century; first performed around 1586; first published anonymously in 1592.

SYNOPSIS

A personal vendetta unfolds against a backdrop of military tension between Spain and Portugal.

Events in History at the Time the Play Takes Place

Imperial Spain. In the sixteenth century, Spain was arguably the most powerful country in the world; certainly, it dominated Europe. Kyd's play does not attempt a treatment of actual Spanish politics or history; indeed, his scenario of war with Portugal is invented. However, his original audiences no doubt thrilled to the presentation of a bloody drama set in the court of the magnificent, threatening, but little-known Spanish empire, which Elizabethan England would have viewed in much the same way that Americans of the 1960s looked upon the Soviet Union.

Spain's rise to political supremacy in Europe surged in 1492. This was the year that the Catholic monarchs Ferdinand and Isabella drove out the Moors, who had ruled vast parts of Spain for centuries, and established a unified country.

More importantly, the Spanish-backed expedition of Christopher Columbus brought Europeans into contact with the so-called New World: the Americas. By virtue of this discovery, Spain had a giant head start in the plunder that followed; for a century and a half, Spanish aspirations would be financed by South American gold.

The empire exercised authority in Europe, too, over more than just Spain. The intricate spider web of European royal lineages meant that Ferdinand and Isabella's successor, Charles V, controlled the Low Countries (Netherlands, Belgium, and Luxembourg), Austria, and large parts of Italy and pieces of France. Little could be done, politically or otherwise, without Spain's approval—at least not without risking great danger. Martin Luther inaugurated the Protestant Rebellion in Germany in 1517, after which Spain became even more important. As the most powerful Catholic country, it was expected to defend

Catholic monarchs Ferdinand and Isabella contributed greatly to Spain's rise to European political supremacy in 1492.

the faith worldwide, and its pious emperors—both Charles and his son, Philip II—took this duty very seriously. It was the era of the Inquisition, the tribunal assembled to prosecute heresy against the Catholic faith, which unified Spain religiously by burning all heretics. Spain's influence expanded even further in 1518, when Charles V was named the Holy Roman Emperor.

In the end, however, the role of defender of the faith was to be Spain's undoing as a global power. Philip II, who took the throne in 1558, inherited a complex, even baffling situation. His holdings in the New World were secure, as was his grip on Italy, and his family connections to the Habsburgs secured peace with Austria (until the next century). But England was rising to prominence, harrying Spanish galleons and stealing gold; more immediately, militant Protestants in the Low Countries were agitating for independence. This agitation escalated into war near the end of the century. A costly proposition for Spain, the war ended in failure shortly before Philip's death in 1598, with the majority of the Low Countries becoming Protestant and self-governing, though they officially remained under Spain's control. To make matters worse, Spain had to counter the emergence of a Catholic rival, France. Beset by enemies on the Continent, by continued wars with Turks in the eastern Mediterranean, and by strife in the New World, Spain entered the seventeenth century still preeminent, but almost exhausted. By 1800, it would be a hollow shell of its former self.

On the other hand, the sixteenth century saw the peak of Spanish culture. More than the plunder-laden galleons that returned from the Americas, it was the achievement of artists like El Greco, writers like Cervantes and Lope de Vega, and clerics like Ignatius of Loyola that made this Spain's "Golden Century." Ironically, in view of their political rivalry, England and Spain occupied similar positions culturally. Both were removed from the established literary and artistic trendsetters in France and Italy. Both seemed, however, to depend on French and Italian models, even as they developed innovative forms of their own that would dominate the future of literature: Cervantes established the genre of the novel just as England's Shakespeare revolutionized drama. *The Spanish Tragedy* alludes to this cultural brilliance only in the episodes of the protagonist Hieronimo's plays within the play; not surprisingly, Kyd is more interested in the scheming and machinations of a wicked court.

Spain and England. Kyd's play appeared at a moment of historical transition. Spain, the dominant power of the sixteenth century, was in the process of giving way to England, a small nation that by the end of the next century would be the chief Western power. A portent of the future occurred shortly after the play probably first appeared: a huge Spanish fleet intent on conquering England failed, victimized by bad luck, storms, and the quicker vessels of the English. Actually, the defeat of the Spanish Armada in 1588 was the culmination of a century of rivalry between the two countries.

The first moment of contention occurred during the reign of the English king Henry VIII. Henry was dissatisfied with his first wife, the Spanish Catherine of Aragon, because she had not produced a male heir. He attempted to annul their marriage and was opposed by the Pope (who was heavily indebted to Spain). This controversy led directly to the loss of England as a Catholic country; Henry removed his realm from under the Pope's spiritual authority so that he could take a new wife.

Catherine of Aragon was forgotten by the early 1550s, but the religious dispensation of England remained a topic of hot dispute. After Henry VIII's young son died, the English throne fell to Queen Mary, the only surviving child of Catherine and Henry. Mary was half-Spanish, and all

Catholic: her primary aim as queen was to reestablish Catholicism as the religion of England. To effect this, she launched the persecutions that earned her the nickname "Bloody Mary"; under her reign some 300 Protestants were burned alive. She also made a decision that sparked four unsuccessful attempts at rebellion: she married the fanatically Catholic Philip II, her second cousin and ruler of the Spanish empire. The English rebels feared this marriage would make England a pawn on Spain's chessboard, even though the marriage contract specified that Philip would lose all rights to England if Mary died childless. To make England a pawn probably was Philip's intention, but Mary died without an heir. Her anti-Protestant persecution, however, combined with the growing legend of how brutal the Inquisition was, left England with an enduring legacy of suspicion of the Spanish.

After Mary's death in 1558, the political tide turned in favor of English Protestants. Elizabeth, Henry's daughter by Ann Boleyn, was a confirmed Protestant who firmly established the Anglican Church; more important, she was an astute politician with canny advisors who exploited the weaknesses in mighty Spain's position. By the early 1560s, Philip needed England to counterbalance his losses in the strategically critical Low Countries. And he needed an alliance with Elizabeth because her chief rival, Mary Queen of Scots, was in league with Spain's Catholic rival, France. Elizabeth exploited this situation; her pirates raided Spanish ships with relative impunity, and Philip helped delay papal excommunication of Elizabeth for the vital first years of her monarchy. As long as he feared France more, he had to indulge England; he even offered to marry Elizabeth as he had married her half-sister, and Elizabeth pretended to consider that option.

By the time a rapprochement with France (in 1572) allowed Philip to treat England as a Protestant enemy, it was too late to hope for an easy victory over the island nation. Elizabeth's reign had seen a strengthening economy and a military build-up; English morale was such that the country was unlikely to fear even this redoubtable enemy. Raids on Spanish galleons continued, and tensions increased. The climax was the ill-fated Spanish Armada; the Spanish fleet's destruction buoyed English hopes and remained a high point of the nation's achievements for generations. It hardly mattered that the Armada was defeated as much by the weather as by the English. In a battle described as a conflict between Catholic and Protestant,

the weather itself seemed to prove that God was a Protestant.

The changing face of warfare. *The Spanish Tragedy* hinges on two points of conduct that may seem strange to modern readers. In the first scene, Don Andrea complains that his death must be avenged, even though he was killed in battle, not murdered. In the second scene, Balthazar is brought in as a captive of war; the next time he appears, he and the man who imprisoned him are the closest of friends.

SPAIN AND PORTUGAL

Kyd's play is based on the idea that Portugal has rebelled against Spain, been defeated in battle, and must now resume paying tribute as a state under Spanish control. This scenario is based, to some extent, on real history; but Kyd either did not know or did not care that he was mangling the facts of the case. *The Spanish Tragedy* assumes that Portugal had long been under Spanish control before its rebellion. Portugal was an independent country before the Spanish-initiated war of 1582. After this, Portugal was briefly ruled by Spain and did pay tribute, as in Kyd's play. However, the playwright has the viceroy of Portugal agree to marry his son to the Spanish king's niece, in an effort to knit relations between the two countries. In reality, such a marriage would have been unnecessary and incestuous—the Portuguese viceroy was Philip II's brother.

These odd moments arise because *The Spanish Tragedy* is situated at a moment when the nature of warfare was changing. Don Andrea feels that his death deserves avenging because he died in a hail of gunfire from Balthazar's troops, and not in single combat with a noble opponent. On the other hand, Balthazar and Lorenzo can become friends because, at least in this instance, they adhere to an older model of warfare, conducted according to rules very different from those of modern war.

During the height of the Middle Ages, war was conducted by groups of soldiers under the command of nobles who owed allegiance to a commanding king, and not by drafted or standing armies. At the heart of an army was its mounted knights, who would charge the enemy and then dismount, if necessary. Such battles were likely to devolve into a mass of single combats; and, because knights wore individual markings,

The fleet that comprised the Spanish Armada. In defending itself, England waged the first naval battles to be fought only with heavy guns, one of the changing facets of sixteenth-century warfare.

combatants often chose opponents based on social rank or personal ambition. Under these conditions, with small groups of socially prominent men—who were often very well acquainted with each other, or even related—fighting in individual combat, it is not surprising that warfare was conducted according to strict rules. To mob a single opponent was forbidden. A man who was defeated was rarely killed; he was much more valuable for the ransom his family would pay to release him from captivity—which is what happens to Balthazar in Kyd's play. But if this chivalric type of war was very personal, it was in one significant way impersonal: usually no offense was taken between enemies. Once hostilities ended, the two sides were likely to interact, if not always with the affection of Lorenzo and Balthazar, then always with cordiality. War was waged for political ends; as long as it was conducted according to the rules, there was no need for anyone to take it personally.

A number of developments obliterated this form of warfare. First, the British, Flemish, and Swiss began experimenting with massed infantry—soldiers of lower social status who wielded bows, spears, or halberds (a weapon with an axelike blade). This technique wreaked havoc on the traditional cavalry charge, especially when arrows were replaced with guns ca-

pable of piercing a knight's plate armor. Heavier artillery also limited the effectiveness of armored cavalry. In and of themselves, these changes were profound; but the biggest change lay in the nature of armies themselves. Feudalism—the social construct that characterized most of the European Middle Ages—presupposes mutual support between the king who grants land and the nobles who provide military aid. Monarchs depended for their power on proud aristocrats with armies, which meant that they often occupied a very unstable throne. By the end of the fifteenth century, many European monarchs had switched to standing armies that could be counted on in their loyalty; they sometimes also employed mercenaries from other countries. Instead of chivalric personal combat, these armies emphasized tactics and superior weaponry. Nor did professional soldiers from the lower orders of society care whom they killed, or what they might get in ransom for a captive; they were more concerned with pillage and booty.

The switch was neither immediate nor absolute; some contend that the ideal of chivalry did not die completely until World War I. And the sixteenth century was in many ways the epicenter of the confusion, the time at which both codes, the old and the new, were almost fully operational. Thus, it is possible for Balthazar to call on both codes: to supervise the craven murder of Don Andrea at one moment, but accept the chivalric largesse of Lorenzo at the next.

The Play in Focus

Plot summary. *The Spanish Tragedy* opens not in Spain but in hell: not the Christian hell, but a classical hell complete with the immortals Charon, Cerberus, and Pluto. The first speaker is Don Andrea, who avows that he is a Spanish nobleman recently killed in a war between Spain and Portugal. He cannot rest yet; Pluto has sent him to view the demise of the man who killed him—the Portuguese prince, Balthazar.

Despite Don Andrea's death, the Spaniards won the war; they have subjected the rebellious Portuguese and imprisoned Balthazar. He is carried to the Spanish court, where there is a brief argument over who was responsible for his capture: Lorenzo, the king's nephew, or Horatio, the son of the marshal Hieronimo. Horatio is of lower rank than Lorenzo, but is distinguished by his recent valor. The king resolves this dispute amicably, but the peace is only temporary: soon, new quarrels will pit Horatio against Balthazar and Lorenzo.

Horatio visits Bel-imperia, Lorenzo's sister, who loved Don Andrea. She is forlorn at Andrea's death, but overjoyed to hear that Horatio had, at great personal danger, managed to bury her dead lover. Horatio also informs her how Balthazar killed Andrea: not in honorable single combat, but with a troop of his men. This shameful murder seals Bel-imperia's hatred of Balthazar, and her love of Horatio.

Unfortunately Balthazar and Lorenzo have become friends, and Balthazar has fallen in love with Bel-imperia. She rebuffs him, but Lorenzo heartens his spurned friend, telling him that his sister will be his, no matter what it costs. They take their first step by suborning Pedringano, Bel-imperia's servant. They cajole, threaten, and finally bribe him; at last he admits that Bel-imperia loves Horatio and leads them to where the two lovers are exchanging tender words. They plan to meet in Hieronimo's garden later that night; Lorenzo and Balthazar make their own plans to meet the lovers there.

When the lovers steal into the garden, they find themselves betrayed: Balthazar and Lorenzo burst in, accompanied by servants who hang Horatio from a tree and stab him to death while the two ignoble noblemen kidnap Bel-imperia. Hieronimo and his wife emerge to find their son

dead. Hieronimo is shocked almost to insanity and vows revenge.

Hieronimo (speaking to the body of his son):
Oh speak, if any spark of life remain:
I am thy father; who hath slain my son?
What savage monster, not of humankind,
Hath here been glutted with thy harmless
    blood,
And left thy bloody corpse dishonoured here,
    for me, amidst these dark and deathful
    shades,
To drown thee with an ocean of my tears?
    (Kyd, *The Spanish Tragedy* 2.4.78-84)

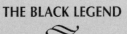

THE BLACK LEGEND

In real terms, Spain probably did not rule any more brutally than other states of Renaissance times. The Spanish Inquisition is still a byword for fanatical brutality; but in fact, the torture and burning of supposed heretics was common to almost all countries of Europe at the time, both Catholic and Protestant. Similarly, Spain's kings earned a reputation for ruthless autocracy, which, if fair standards were applied, would also blacken the reputations of every other European monarchy. While Spain's *conquistadores* are legendary for their violent destruction of the native Americans they encountered, the main difference between Spain and its neighbors on this score is that Spain arrived first, and was therefore the first to do what the English and French would also do in the next century.

These images of Spain are part of what is called the "Black Legend," a longstanding historical stereotype of Spain as oppressive, violent, and fanatical. Modern historians have revised this legend, putting Spain's actions back in their historical context, and pointing out that the conquistadores' pillaging of the New World met with vigorous attempts to stop it by Spanish clerics and legislators.

In fact, the "Black Legend" arose precisely because Spain was so powerful; its preeminence incited its many enemies to take any opportunity to slander it. This type of propaganda is visible in *The Spanish Tragedy*, which presents the Spanish court as a place of sin, illicit desire, and brazen power-plays.

The long third act pushes the intrigue nearly to its conclusion. Hieronimo receives a letter from Bel-imperia, telling him who killed his son; when he seeks her out, he finds that Lorenzo has imprisoned her. Meanwhile, Lorenzo tells Pedringano that one of the servant murderers is ready to betray the plot; Lorenzo charges Pedringano with killing this traitor. Eager for gold and wholly trusting, Pedringano complies; but the night watch, which Lorenzo has dispatched to the area, catches and imprisons Pedringano. Pedringano is nonchalant, believing that Lorenzo will save him. And Lorenzo promises to do so; he dispatches a page with what is said to be a pardon, but is in fact a blank paper. Pedringano jokes with the hangman until the very minute he is dragged off to be executed; when he realizes he is betrayed, he gives the executioner a letter that implicates Lorenzo in Horatio's death.

THE RENAISSANCE OF PAGANISM

The Spanish Tragedy seamlessly mingles Christian and pagan cosmologies; the play concerns Christians, but, once dead, Don Andrea finds himself in the ancient Greek afterworld, fully furnished with the pleasures and punishment of that place, and presided over by Pluto, the classical god of death. Kyd pursues this mixed religion without any sense of its obvious contradiction; in the last words of the play, Don Andrea makes plans to feast the friends, and torment the enemies, who will soon be joining him. In Christian theology, good people go to heaven, bad people to hell. In Kyd's play, however, there is only one afterlife where everyone goes, the bad people to be punished and the good people to be rewarded. Thus, Don Andrea looks forward to other worldly recompense of both friend and foe.

This further proof spurs Hieronimo even closer to madness; he craves revenge, but does not know how to get it. His behavior is erratic: he tries to take his complaint to the king, but is intercepted by Lorenzo; he tries to go about his business, but is always pulled back into thoughts of his dead son. Neither is Bel-imperia able to forget; Lorenzo frees her, after which she displays a seemingly milder attitude to Balthazar, but this is merely a cover for her continued hate. Unfortunately for her, the king has already agreed to Balthazar's request for her hand in marriage; he feels that the marriage of the Portuguese prince to his niece will cement the new peace between the countries. Meanwhile, Hieronimo reaches his wits' end; the court, it seems, will not administer justice: "Where shall I run abroad to breathe

my woes, / My woes, whose weight has wearied the earth? / Or mine exclaims, that have surcharged the air, / With ceaseless plaints for my deceased son?" (*Spanish Tragedy,* 3.7.1-4).

Hieronimo, after strange interludes of madness, resolves himself: he realizes that he must counterfeit his aim, and pretend friendship with his foes. Lorenzo's father, the duke of Castile (who knows nothing of the murder), oversees their reconciliation. Soon enough, this new friendship gives Hieronomo his chance. Lorenzo asks him to compose a play to entertain the guests at Bel-imperia and Balthazar's wedding. Hieronimo confides that he has just "rediscovered" a tragedy he composed in his youth. He thinks it will be the perfect play for the wedding, but he insists that the nobles themselves play the parts.

Hieronimo's tragedy is based on the story of Soliman and Perseda. Perseda was married to a knight of Rhodes, but was beloved by the more powerful Soliman. Soliman confided his love to his Bashaw, or subordinate, who tried to corrupt Perseda. When he realized he could not, he slew Perseda's husband. Perseda, grieving and enraged, stabbed Soliman and then herself. The penitent Bashaw hanged himself. In other words, the story will mirror the action of *The Spanish Tragedy* itself. Rather naively, the guilty men agree to the plan. Lorenzo will play Perseda's husband; Balthazar, Soliman; Hieronimo, the Bashaw; and Bel-imperia, Perseda.

The play is short, but (apparently) well acted. The audience is still applauding when Hieronimo reveals that the play was no play: the daggers were real, and Lorenzo, Balthazar, and Bel-imperia are, in fact, dead. He launches into a long speech that outlines the whole truth, and then attempts to escape into an inner room to hang himself. The king of Spain and the viceroy of Portugal stop him, hoping to make him reveal more—but, of course, he has nothing left to reveal. Indeed, he refuses to speak any further, and literally chews out his own tongue. The nobles ask him to write his confession. He asks for a knife to sharpen his pen; when they give him one, he promptly stabs Lorenzo's father and then kills himself. The scene closes as the mourning viceroy and king exit, carrying their dead kin.

The play ends as it begins: Don Andrea comments on the action. Indeed, his final speech extends the violence into the afterlife, as he promises to torment the villains there, even as he will feast the heroes who avenged his murder by becoming murderers themselves.

Plays, masques, and play-worlds. *The Spanish Tragedy* is filled with actors and audiences: Hieronimo directs not one but two courtly entertainments; characters must feign their emotions throughout, either to hide their intentions or to conceal their role in past crimes; and the whole play is watched, not only by its real audience, but also by the ghost of Don Andrea. It would seem that the Spanish court is a place of audiences and spectators. In fact, Kyd is exploring popular cultural ideas on a number of levels. From the curiosity of commoners about the nature of court entertainment, to the dramatic experiments of Kyd's generation, to Christian ideals of the world as a stage, the "idea of a play" was in the air.

In the broadest of ways, England had two venues for dramatic entertainment, the courtly and the popular. Court entertainments had been around for centuries. Jousts, masques, pageants, and dances were prepared to commemorate any important occasion: weddings, deaths, royal visits and birthdays. Such entertainments were likely to be elaborately planned and gorgeously outfitted; their authors (among them John Skelton, Sir Philip Sidney, and Ben Jonson) used the occasion to flatter, persuade, or cajole the monarch whom they entertained.

Beginning in the 1560s, these royal entertainments were joined by the noncourtly delights of popular theater for the masses. London theaters such as the Swan and the Red Bull catered to a wide variety of people, from threadbare apprentices to rich merchants; one of the few characteristics that this diverse audience shared was that hardly any of them had access to court. Needless to say, many members of these audiences would have been quite curious about the manner of life and the types of diversion common among their rulers.

The theatrical world was both willing and able to cater to this curiosity. A quirk of English law classified actors with vagrants; to prevent their being arrested for vagrancy, they had to secure patronage from an aristocrat. This led, in some cases, to a close relationship between an acting troupe and an aristocrat. More directly, many authors who made their living on the popular stage also wrote court entertainments, and by Shakespeare's day monarchs frequently ordered performances of popular plays for the select audience at court. Kyd is one of the first English dramatists to exploit this crossover to satisfy the curiosity of his public. *The Spanish Tragedy* contains two courtly entertainments. When the sub-jected viceroy of Portugal arrives at the Spanish court, Hieronimo directs a pantomime that presents the assembled courtiers with scenes from the Spanish and Portuguese past. More important is the play of Soliman and Perseda that brings the dramatic action to a climax.

These two plays-within-plays differ from their surrounding context in important ways. They are obscure and learned: they require both thought and education to be understood ("Soliman and Perseda" is actually performed in several different languages). This is quite different from the rest of the play, which remains simple, melodramatic, and crowd-pleasing. It was, in fact, a characteristic of court entertainments that they presented obscure lessons in an allegorical, indirect way; the authors meant to show off their learning and flatter their audience's sense of its own intelligence. These are not characteristics of the popular stage, the audience for which was less well educated. Nevertheless, this popular audience wanted to see what their nobles saw, at least in part; and Kyd was happy to oblige.

Kyd's was one of the first in a long line of plays that blurred the class-coded nature of Elizabethan entertainment. Shakespeare used the internal play for various purposes in a range of comedies and dramas. From *A Midsummer Night's Dream* to *The Tempest*, one of these purposes is to mimic the courtly entertainment. By the early eighteenth century, popular plays would be dipping into the store of royal entertainment in various ways, borrowing freely from court-masques, for example, or transferring songs from court to theater.

There were also more abstract, philosophical reasons for Kyd's interest in the idea of a play. One of the oldest tropes of Christianity is that this temporal world is simply a preparation for the permanent life that follows death. A natural extension of this idea is that the events of this world are, in some important way, unreal, mere acting before an audience composed of God alone. This notion introduces relativity to human affairs: even the most important roles played (parent, spouse) are temporary, and of limited importance, compared to the thought of eternity. An individual plays parts that determine his or her fate, and can choose to be a hero or a villain; the judgment of the performance will come only after death.

The most famous articulation of this idea is by Shakespeare in *As You Like It*, where Jaques opines, "All the world's a stage, / And all the men and women merely players" (*As You Like It*,

2.7.139-140). But different versions of the idea permeate Christian culture wherever and whenever it has existed. The idea, though simple enough, should not be underestimated. If an individual life is composed of many roles, and there is a holy audience to judge the performance, then it becomes critical to play them well. Conversely, if life is a play, then it has an author; if one believes that author loves his characters, then the believer can see any pain or misfortune as a temporary plot twist that will make the happy ending all the sweeter. In *The Spanish Tragedy* Hieronimo takes comfort in the fact that even though he must feign friendship with Lorenzo, this is a role that he will cast off at the proper time; and, as Don Andrea's comments reveal, the real conclusion of the play will occur in the torments and delights of the afterworld.

TREASON AND ATHEISM

In 1593, Kyd found himself in hot water with the law. He had been under suspicion for slander, in connection with anonymous pamphlets that mocked foreign workmen living in London. In the course of this investigation, police searched his premises and found heretical, atheistic papers. Kyd was arrested and (he claims in a letter to a friend) tortured. He argued that the papers belonged to playwright Christopher Marlowe, his roommate and one of the most scandalous figures of the 1590s in England. This was convenient, no doubt, since Marlowe had already been stabbed to death in a bar brawl. But it was also quite likely true: Marlowe's plays reveal a much greater interest in questions of religious belief than do Kyd's. It is a character of Marlowe's who suggests that the pagan Elysium may be the actual afterlife (in **Dr. Faustus,** also covered in *WLAIT 3: British and Irish Literature and Its Times*). While Kyd's drama presents that afterlife, he is at least as interested in the Christian morals of his characters. More to the point, the charge of atheism was leveled at Marlowe continually throughout his life. At any rate, Kyd seems to have been cleared of all charges. Apparently the incident lost him some noble patronage and also, perhaps, some popular esteem. It certainly embittered and weakened him: he died the next year, well before his fortieth birthday.

All these strands come together when Hieronimo breaks the dramatic illusion at the end of his court play. Addressing an audience that

has seen real murder and thought it counterfeit, and an audience that knows these murders are, like Horatio's, false, he says:

> Haply you think, but bootless are your
>   thoughts,
> That this is fabulously counterfeit,
> And that we do as all tragedians do:
> To die today for fashioning our scene
> The death of Ajax, or some Roman peer,
> And in a minute starting up again,
> Revive to please tomorrow's audience.
> No, princes.
>
> (*Spanish Tragedy*, 4.4.77-83)

For a second, in this self-referential speech, the effect is startling. Hieronomo announces to his courtly audience that his drama, which seemed to be staged, is in fact real: the knives were real and so were the deaths. This abrupt break in the dramatic illusion tends to produce, even if only for a second, an effect as jarring to the reader as it no doubt was to the courtly audience within the play: however, briefly, readers may be convinced that Hieronomo is addressing them.

Sources and literary context. No source has been identified for the plot of *The Spanish Tragedy*. This does not mean, however, that Kyd was one of the few Renaissance dramatists to work from original stories, for the basic elements and a number of his devices are very directly derived from the Roman playwright Seneca. Seneca was the great Latin playwright of revenge tragedy; his plays feature wicked tyrants, venal courtiers, bloody crimes, and outraged avengers. In other words, all the ingredients of Kyd's play can be found in Seneca, even the choric ghost of Don Andrea—with an important difference. Kyd's play did not simply narrate the blood and gore; it staged these aspects of the drama, showing the gruesome violence to the audience.

Kyd is indebted to other classical writers for other details: the ancient Roman poet Virgil's description of the underworld in the *Aeneid*, for instance, informs Andrea's opening monologue. Among other details, Kyd's play, like Virgil's poem, presents Pluto's lieutenant Minos as a judge of the underworld. For his favored stylistic method—the long speech—Kyd could have found models closer to home, in the dilated rants popular in the more primitively constructed English plays of the earlier sixteenth century. For what is truly distinctive about the play—its quick pace and unified structure—no native analog can be found; even more than Marlowe, Kyd brought these qualities to the English stage.

In crucial ways, Renaissance Europe was actually a split culture, in which Christianity was joined on almost an equal footing by the knowledge and cultural forms of ancient Greece and Rome. When it came to religious practice, Christianity was supreme; no one worshipped Zeus or Minerva. But in nearly every other arena, classical precedent held the day. Renaissance philosophy, ethics, medicine, aesthetics, political philosophy, and natural science were ruled by Greek and Roman authorities. Looking back over history, many Renaissance critics saw (inaccurately) a vast swath of monastic darkness; before that, and before Christianity, shone the example of the classical world, with its reason, method, and artistic vibrancy.

It was the band of such critics—men like Petrarch in Italy, Erasmus in Holland, and Ascham in England—that turned this general sense of awe into a program to ensure that young scholars would grow up with a living belief in the greatness of classical texts. Education centered on reading, translating, and copying classical writers, both major and minor; advanced training, even in theology, meant deep study of philosophers and scientists like Galen, Lucretius, and Aristotle. The result of this educational emphasis was generations of writers whose primary points of reference were as much pagan as Christian. In the theater, the phenomenon resulted in a public stage whose key writers were Seneca for tragedy, and Plautus and Terence for comedy. From 1580 to the closing of the theaters in 1642, hardly a significant play was produced that did not owe some debt to these classical writers, whom the playwrights learned about thoroughly in grade school. That *Renaissance* means "rebirth" is well known; but the full context of that word may not be. It was no simple revival of interest in pagan texts but, in all points except the religious, an exaltation of ancient culture.

Reviews. Alongside Christopher Marlowe's *Tamburlaine*, Kyd's *The Spanish Tragedy* is a founding text of the English stage. Produced at the moment when the London theaters were growing more stable and prosperous, Kyd's work lifted English dramatic craftsmanship to a new level, rising above such plays as Thomas Preston's *Cambyses* and Thomas Norton and Thomas Sackville's *Gorboduc*. With its tense dramatic pacing, consistency of character, and unity of action, *The Spanish Tragedy* was a breakthrough.

Kyd's play was an unparalleled hit for a decade after it first appeared, and a consistent part of the general repertoire until the theaters were closed in 1642. Its popularity can be gauged in several ways: the play was reprinted frequently; it was revised (to give it continued interest); it began a

JONSON'S REVISIONS

In 1602, a slightly revised version of *The Spanish Tragedy* was published. This version included all the scenes of the original, but it had been lengthened by more than 500 lines. Kyd had died in 1594; these additions were by Kyd's younger contemporary Ben Jonson, who had once played the role of Hieronomo in the play. In a few years, Jonson would be famous as the greatest comedic dramatist of the Stuart period. In the first years of the seventeenth century, he was known primarily for a group of entertaining but relatively slight comedies; his only masterpiece produced by 1600 was *Every Man Out of His Humour.*

Jonson had not written a tragedy yet, and he would never become an especially brilliant tragedian. His involvement with *The Spanish Tragedy* reveals a number of things about the way in which plays were produced at the time. First, no one had any sense that a playwright might have had a specific intention that needed to be respected; if a producer felt a work was lacking in any area, he would find a way to remedy that lack. Second, the person found to do the revision was likely to be another playwright of note, but not necessarily one with any sympathy for the play (Jonson's later comedies contain glancing sneers at *The Spanish Tragedy* as an abhorrent piece of work). Third, producers revised plays to keep them current. By 1602, Kyd's play was venerable, but something of a chestnut; Jonson's additions provided the audience with something new to enjoy in the play, although they did not fundamentally alter its meaning or progress of events.

Jonson's additions work in several ways. He created a new speech for Hieronimo on discovering his son's death; this speech accentuates the strain on the father by pushing him, for a moment or two, into actual insanity. Jonson also highlights this interpretation by slighter additions to Hieronimo's later scenes with the king and Lorenzo. Apart from this point of characterization, Jonson's revisions are mostly touch-ups: new dialogue for Hieronimo's servants, some lines added to Pedringano's parts. The Romantic critic Charles Lamb saw the additions as the best things about the play; but most modern critics disagree, and remove Jonson's handiwork to footnotes or to an appendix.

popular craze for tragedies of revenge (that led to Shakespeare's *Hamlet*); and it is frequently referred to in the works of other playwrights.

This last fact hints at the play's eventual fate. By around 1600, English drama had outgrown Kyd: other playwrights, notably Shakespeare and Ben Jonson, had pushed the craft beyond *The Spanish Tragedy*. What had been a sophisticated triumph now seemed crude and barbaric; in the seventeenth century, a reference to Kyd is likely to be patronizing, if not downright dismissive (this was in spite of, or perhaps because of, his continued popularity with less sophisticated audiences). After the theaters were reopened in 1660, *The Spanish Tragedy* seemed like a relic from another era: a crude, bloody melodrama. The play was forgotten, except by literary historians, and it has remained somewhat obscure ever since. In the twentieth century, although occasional claims were made for the brilliance of some aspects of Kyd's work (especially his sense of dramatic pacing), most critics and readers were interested in the play for what it could reveal about the history and development of the great age of English dramaturgy.

—Jacob Littleton

For More Information

Atkinson, William. *A History of Spain and Portugal*. Baltimore: Penguin, 1960.

Descola, Jean. *A History of Spain*. New York: Knopf, 1963.

Hall, Bert. *Weapons and Warfare in Renaissance Europe*. Baltimore: Johns Hopkins University Press, 1997.

Kyd, Thomas. *The Spanish Tragedy*. Ed. Philip Edwards. London: Methuen, 1959.

Lewis, C. S. *English Literature in the Sixteenth Century*. Oxford: Oxford University Press, 1945.

Vale, Malcolm. *War and Chivalry*. London: Duckworth, 1981.

The Spectator

by

Joseph Addison and Sir Richard Steele

Joseph Addison (1672-1719) and Richard Steele (1672-1729) became friends as schoolboys in London. Later they both attended Oxford University, though Steele left for a career in the army before graduating, while the more academic Addison stayed on, earning his Masters degree in 1693. By 1705 Steele had left the army and Addison had ended a decade of teaching and then travel. Both were living in London and pursuing writing, Steele for *The London Gazette*, the government's official newspaper, and Addison as an adjunct to a civil service career. In 1709 Steele started *The Tatler*, a thrice-weekly periodical featuring commentary on cultural and political issues to which Addison soon became a regular contributor. Two months after *The Tatler* ceased publication in January 1711, the two friends jointly launched *The Spectator*, in which they perfected the blend of casual style, light-hearted cultural commentary, and moral instruction that they had developed in *The Tatler*. In contrast to *The Tatler*, however, *The Spectator* pointedly avoided partisan political content, affirming instead such values as refinement, humor, civility, and politeness.

Events in History at the Time of the Essays

Political and social divisions. When she came to the throne in 1702, Queen Anne, England's last Stuart monarch, faced the legacy left by a century of civil war, revolution, and social tur-

---

THE LITERARY WORK

A series of periodical essays published in London from 1711 to 1714.

SYNOPSIS

The Spectator ostensibly records the activities of the Spectator Club, which is made up of several fictional characters, each representing a distinct segment of society. Through the eyes of Mr. Spectator, a shy observer of the others and of London society, the authors comment on social and cultural issues.

---

moil. In choosing the ministers who would make up her government, she also faced the bitter partisan strife that had dominated English politics since the 1680s. That decade saw the rise of the nation's first political parties, the Whigs and the Tories, which had originated in conflicts over the succession of Anne's father, James II. While highly contentious in itself, this political dissension merely reflected the deeper discord that had wracked English society for decades. By the end of Anne's reign in 1714, however, English society had begun to formulate a response to this enduring discord. Nowhere is this response better represented than in the optimistic, good-natured, and avowedly apolitical pages of *The Spectator*.

During the latter half of the seventeenth century, profound economic changes had intensified the nation's disunity. Before 1660, the English economy had relied on the manufacture and ex-

Richard Steele

port of a single commodity, wool. Over the next 50 years, however, English trade expanded rapidly, so that by the early eighteenth century London had become Europe's most important commercial center. Sugar from the West Indies, tobacco from America, and cotton from the Middle East were among the many products made available cheaply and abundantly as England accelerated the building of a global colonial trade empire. While this expansion brought strength to the nation and prosperity to its people, it also brought tensions, as a new social group of influential merchants and others vied with the gentry for political power and social status. This new social group, which found its earliest voice in such publications as *The Spectator,* would begin to emerge over the course of the eighteenth century as the growing middle class.

In politics, the liberal, reforming Whigs promoted this rising commercial interest, while the more conservative Tories defended the relatively declining influence of the Crown and the country gentry. The political landscape was highly complex, but in general the Whigs stood for the following:

- "Money" interests, i.e., merchants and others whose wealth was based on cash, not land (represented by the character of "Sir Andrew Freeport" in *The Spectator*).
- The incorporated City of London as a political entity, backed by its mercantile and professional population.
- A strong Parliament, with rights to limit the monarch's power and to decide the succession of the Crown.
- Religious tolerance of Low-Church Anglicans (who were less conservative than High-Church Anglicans) and of Dissenters, or Protestants who did not conform to the Anglican Church.
- Aggressive foreign policy, and use of the navy to support British trade.

Tories, by contrast, embraced the following:

- The "squirearchy" or country gentry, whose wealth was based on smaller estates (represented by the character of "Sir Roger de Coverley" in *The Spectator*).
- The royal court as a center of power and influence in London.
- A strong Crown, backed by the principle of a single legitimate line of succession whatever the heir's religious faith.
- Religious uniformity and the government-supported Anglican Church (Church of England).
- Less aggressive foreign policy and fewer foreign entanglements.

The spread of literary culture. Just as the rising commercial class now claimed a share of the political power previously held by the royal court, so too it asserted a right to the cultural fruits that had previously been a court monopoly. As a recent historian notes, by the beginning of the eighteenth century, high culture—painting, music, theater, and especially literature—had "slipped out of the palace and into the coffee houses, reading societies, debating clubs,

---

ADDISON ON BRITISH COMMERCE

❧

"There is no Place in the Town which I so much like to frequent as the *Royal-Exchange,*" writes Joseph Addison in an early *Spectator* essay celebrating this busy center of London trading. He continues:

It gives me a secret Satisfaction, and in some measure gratifies my Vanity, as I am an *Englishman,* to see so rich an Assembly of Countrymen and Foreigners consulting together upon the private Business of Mankind, and making this Metropolis a kind of *Emporium* for the whole Earth.

(*Spectator* 69, vol. 1, pp. 259-60)

---

assembly rooms, galleries and concert halls; ceasing to be the handmaiden of royal politics, it became the partner of commerce" (Brewer, p. 3). It was in exactly such newly expanded public spaces in London, and particularly in the many coffee houses, that English gentlemen might be found perusing the latest issue of *The Spectator* before passing it to the next eager customer.

Literature was the most pervasive and thus the most influential of the cultural products seized on by the new commercial class. In the past, printing had been rigorously controlled by the government. In 1696, however, the government allowed the Licensing Act of 1663, under which state censorship had been enforced, to lapse. Over the next two decades, the relaxation of censorship combined with a highly charged political environment (there were 10 general elections between 1695 and 1715) to produce an intense outburst of political journalism. Much of this writing was published in the form of single-issue pamphlets, but in 1704 a versatile Whig writer named Daniel Defoe began issuing thrice-weekly essays of political opinion called *The Review* (1704-13). In this early periodical Defoe, best known today for his novel *Robinson Crusoe* (1719), is credited with inventing the editorial article. Newspapers also expanded, from one or two official summaries of foreign affairs (such as *The London Gazette,* where Steele worked in the early 1700s) to a growing number of private dailies and weeklies. Some carried domestic news, while others took on the important task of supplying financial information to the growing business community. *Lloyd's News,* one of the earliest, was published briefly in 1696—from Edward Lloyd's London coffee house—and carried shipping information for the new marine insurance company that would become Lloyd's of London. (The paper would be resumed in 1736.)

Women comprised another major audience for the new literary media, particularly in London. While literacy rates in general were rising, those among London women climbed most sharply of all groups measured, from an estimated 22 percent in the 1670s to 66 percent in the 1720s (Brewer, p. 168). While written from a male perspective, Defoe's *Review, The Tatler,* and *The Spectator* all deliberately included material directed at women, most of it moralizing or instructive (as was much of the material directed at men). Indeed, as Addison writes in an early *Spectator* essay, "there are none to whom this Paper will be more useful than to the female World" (Addison and Steele, *The Spectator* 10, vol. 1, p.

Joseph Addison

43). Among the many imitations of *The Tatler* and *The Spectator* were two that aimed more exclusively at women, *The Female Tatler* (1709-10) and, later, *The Female Spectator* (1744-46).

Addison and Steele: forging a civil society. Two specific issues bitterly divided the Whigs and the Tories during Queen Anne's reign (1702-14). The first was the same as that which had created the parties in the 1680s: the succession of the throne. Now it was Anne's succession that was to be decided, not her father's. The Whigs wished to settle the throne on Princess Sophia of Hanover (the nearest Protestant Stuart relative) or her heir, while some Tories favored Anne's Catholic younger brother, James, as the legitimate heir to the throne, despite his Catholicism. Although the Whigs had seemingly secured victory with the Act of Settlement in 1701, by which Parliament gave Sophia or her heir title to the throne, the succession continued to be controversial. It grew more so, first as the ill and, at this point, childless Anne approached death during the years of *The Spectator's* publication, and then after Sophia predeceased Anne in 1714, leaving her German son George as her designated heir. While most Tories approved the Act of Settlement, many did so with strong reservations, for they disliked the idea of a German king on the British throne. Others opposed it outright. Nevertheless, on Anne's death Sophie's German son acceded to the British throne as George I. Tory supporters of the Catholic Stuarts—called Jacobites, from *Jacobus,* Latin for James—would revolt twice against the Whig-supported Hanoverian dynasty, in 1715 and 1745.

COFFEE HOUSES AND CLUBS

London in the early eighteenth century was a city in which public places were taking on an increasingly important social role. For men, the most common meeting place was the coffee house, a type of establishment that had begun appearing in London in the late seventeenth century. By 1714 there were nearly 700 coffee houses in the city. In these dirty, smoke-filled rooms men of all classes could mix and enjoy a cup of coffee while reading a newspaper (provided by the coffee house) or chatting about politics. Later in the century, the coffee house would be partly replaced by the gentlemen's club, which had begun making an appearance by the time of Addison and Steele. The two essayists were members of the famous Kitcat Club, where Whig publisher Jacob Tonson hosted writers and Whig leaders.

The second major divisive issue was the War of the Spanish Succession (1701-14), which pitted Britain, the Netherlands, and their allies against France and Spain. Because the Whigs had called for the war over strenuous Tory opposition, early victories under the Whig leader and British commander John Churchill, duke of Marlborough, helped the Whigs keep control of the government in the first part of Anne's reign. Both Addison and Steele were committed Whigs, and in 1704 Whig leaders invited Addison to celebrate Marlborough's brilliant victory at Blenheim by writing a poem about it. The result, *The Campaign,* was a success that led to lucrative positions for Addison in the Whig administration. Beginning in 1709 Steele's *The Tatler,* too, while often self-consciously trivial in subject matter and always casual in style, explicitly supported the war and other Whig policies. Tory periodicals battled openly with *The Tatler,* the leading example being *The Examiner,* which was edited by the Tory leader Henry St. John and (from October 1710 to June 1711) by the Irish satirist Jonathan Swift (see **Gulliver's Travels,** also covered in *WLAIT 3: British and Irish Literature and Its Times*).

In the second part of Anne's reign, the war began going less smoothly for Britain and her allies, and in 1710 the Whig government was ousted from power—temporarily, as it turned out. The brief hiatus (1710-14) would be followed by five decades of Whig ascendancy after the accession of George I. But during the hiatus, Addison lost his job in government, Steele lost his with *The London Gazette,* and political pressure contributed also perhaps to the folding of *The Tatler* in January 1711. (Steele's political attacks in *The Tatler* had often targeted the Tory leader Robert Harley, who now ran the government.) The stage was set, therefore, for the two friends to launch a joint venture.

Steele's editorial influence had shaped *The Tatler,* but Addison's would dominate *The Spectator,* though to a lesser degree. For one thing, Steele devoted much of his time to other projects during *The Spectator's* publication, becoming the leading writer for the Whigs in opposition. In contrast to his highly partisan output for the Whigs, Steele, the more political writer, allowed his non-partisan instincts to come to the fore in his *Spectator* essays. For instance, both men supported the Hanoverian succession, but in *The Spectator* Addison avoids this controversial topic altogether while Steele mentions it only once (in issue 384). Though political content was common in *The Tatler,* it was rare in its successor, for Addison's outlook guided his friend's.

While *The Spectator's* non-partisan content no doubt reflects the evolving aims of both writers, it especially reflects those of Joseph Addison. No greater ill can befall a people, Addison writes, than partisan strife, which divides a single nation into two hostile camps:

> The Effects of such a Division are pernicious to the last degree, not only with regard to those advantages which they give the Common Enemy, but to those private Evils which they produce in the Heart of almost every particular Person. . . . . A furious Party Spirit, when it rages in its full Violence . . . fills a Nation with Spleen and Rancour, and extinguishes all the Seeds of Good-Nature, Compassion and Humanity.
>
> (*Spectator* 125, vol. 1, p. 441)

More than any other writer of his time, Addison in his *Spectator* essays helped formulate a cohesive response to these ills: an emerging ideal of a civil society in which "Good-Nature, Compassion and Humanity" might outweigh partisan division. While never fully attained, this ideal would be immensely powerful in shaping British social values over the remainder of the eighteenth century and beyond.

The Essays in Focus

Contents summary. *The Spectator* comprises 555 issues published daily (except Sunday) from March 1, 1711, to December 6, 1712, plus 80 further numbered issues published thrice weekly by Addison alone from June 18 to December 20, 1714. Of the original 555 issues, Steele was responsible for 251 and Addison for 274; the remaining essays were contributed by other writers, including Alexander Pope, the leading poet of the age (see **The Rape of the Lock,** also in *WLAIT 3: British and Irish Literature and Its Times*). All issues were signed only with a single code letter. The signing scheme was complex, since each essayist might use more than one letter. Addison, for example, signed his essays C, L, I, or O at various times, making up the word "Clio." (In Greek mythology, Clio was the muse of history.) In addition, both Addison and Steele regularly incorporated material submitted by correspondents, though Steele did this far more frequently than Addison (perhaps two-thirds of Steele's issues consist of such submissions). The original 555 issues were numbered, bound, and sold in seven volumes; the 80 issues that Addison published in 1714 were bound and sold as volume eight.

Except for the issues including correspondence, which might consist mainly of one or more letters, most issues are made up of a single brief essay two to five pages in length. The majority of these essays adhere to the fictional premise of the Spectator Club and speak through the imaginary character of the Spectator, though some depart from this formula and seem to be written in the author's own voice (for example, Addison's critical essays on *Paradise Lost*).

In *Spectator* 1 (March 1, 1711), Addison introduces the Spectator character himself, a Londoner who has studied literature and traveled widely but who has remained almost totally silent for all his life. The only place where he opens his mouth is in his own club. "Thus I live in the world, rather as a Spectator of Mankind, than as one of the Species," he declares (*Spectator* 1, vol. 1, p. 8). His role as Spectator allows him to become familiar with many different aspects of society without ever taking part—and especially without taking sides in the disputes between Whigs and Tories.

In the next issue, Steele describes the other members of the Spectator's Club. Sir Roger de Coverley is an old-fashioned but hearty and good-natured country gentleman, a bachelor whose heart was broken many years ago and who has worn the same style of clothes ever since, so that (as he boasts) his clothes have been in and out of fashion 12 times since then. Kind but naïve, he is loved rather than respected, and people take advantage of him. Sir Andrew Freeport is "a Merchant of great Eminence in the City of London: A Person of indefatigable Industry, strong Reason, and great Experience. His Notions of Trade are noble and generous, and . . . he calls the Sea the *British Common*" (*Spectator* 2, vol. 1, p. 13). He often repeats "frugal Maxims, amongst which the greatest Favourite is 'A Penny saved is a Penny got'" (*Spectator* 2, vol. 1, p. 13). Next to Sir Andrew sits Captain Sentry, a brave but modest soldier, who will advance no further in rank because he lacks the desire to flatter his superiors. Will Honeycomb, a handsome older man-about-town who preserves the appearance of energetic youth, knows all the in's and out's of ladies' fashions and always turns the conversation to the subject of women. Two other members are briefly described but unnamed: a lawyer who knows more about ancient Greek and Latin literature than about English law, and a clergyman, infirm but wise, who (the Spectator says) rarely visits the club.

In *Spectator* 10 Addison elaborates upon the periodical's twin aims: edification and entertainment. Wishing to make his readers' "instruction agreeable and their diversion useful," the Spectator declares that he "shall endeavor to enliven Morality with Wit, and to temper Wit with Morality" (*Spectator* 10, vol. 1, p. 41). He aspires to a role in society similar to that played by the ancient Greek philosopher, Socrates:

> It was said of Socrates, that he brought Philosophy down from Heaven, to inhabit among men; and I shall be ambitious to have it said of me, that I brought Philosophy out of Closets and Libraries, Schools and Colleges, to dwell in Clubs and Assemblies, at Tea-Tables and in Coffee-houses.
>
> (*Spectator* 10, vol. 1, p. 42)

Accordingly, the essays' fluid, informal style and broad range of subject matter deliberately recall the sorts of conversations commonly found in such social settings.

Relations between the sexes interest the imaginary Spectator greatly, and many papers include his often whimsical observations on ladies' fashions from a male perspective, on love and marriage, and on the differences between men and women. Yet their generally light approach does not prevent the essayists from probing darker aspects of such topics. Steele devotes several essays to prostitution, for example, relating how he began thinking about the subject after being accosted by a young prostitute one evening. Beneath the teenaged girl's "forced Wantonness," he sees the reality of her hunger and cold and he gives her some money (*Spectator* 266, vol. 2, p. 209). Much more offensive to him than prostitutes are women who harshly condemn them without compassion. When people are "too warmly provoked at other People's personal sins," he writes, it "often makes me a little apt to suspect the Sincerity of their Virtue" (*Spectator* 266, vol. 2, p. 208). "Will Honeycomb," he continues, keeping to the fictional premise of the Spectator Club, "calls these over-offended Ladies, the Outragiously [sic] Virtuous" (*Spectator* 266, vol. 2, p. 208). A number of other essays explore the situations of those who exist, like the prostitutes, both within English society yet outside it in some definable way: examples include Jews, Gypsies, beggars, and servants.

In a follow-up essay, Steele discusses the role of male customers and pimps (as well as madams) in perpetuating prostitution. Steele's treatment of prostitution thus exemplifies another technique common in *The Spectator* over the nearly two years of publication. Both Steele and Addison make discursive forays into areas that catch their attention, devoting two or more issues to it before moving on. Often the issues are not consecutive, so that the essayist returns to a subject after writing about another, and often he includes correspondence from a reader who has a point to raise about what was said earlier (as Steele did in his follow-up on prostitution). Favorite subjects repeatedly explored from new angles in this way include love and marriage, religion, manners, the theatre, and the nature of wit (a perennial concern of both writers). The fictional format facilitates these excursions, as when the eccentric and somewhat crusty Sir Roger tells the Spectator the story of how his heart was broken as a young man by a beautiful widow who lived near his country estate. At the end of the essay (by Steele), the Spectator observes that Sir Roger's broken heart helps to explain "all that Inconsistency which appears in some Parts of my Friend's Discourse" (*Spectator* 113, vol. 1, p. 404).

Woven into nearly all of these scenarios is a central concern to which both essayists return over and over: literature. Seemingly extempora-

neous references to literary works abound in the essays. After relating his encounter with the young prostitute, for instance, Steele smoothly moves on to examine the depiction of a prostitute in a play, *The Humourous Lieutenant,* by the Jacobean playwright John Fletcher (1579-1625). Similarly, after Sir Roger's story about his broken heart, Steele has the Spectator conclude the essay by quoting in full an appropriate poem by the Latin poet Martial (first century B.C.E.).

While both writers incorporate critical observations about literary works into their essays, Addison does so more methodically than the relatively breezy Steele. Repeatedly, Addison devotes several separate issues (consecutive or otherwise) to self-contained interludes of literary criticism. The best known of Addison's critical series are:

- His seven Saturday essays on Milton's *Paradise Lost* (nos. 267, 273, 279, 285, 291, 297, 303).
- His two essays on the old English ballad *Chevy Chase* (nos. 70, 74).
- The 11 consecutive essays of his "Pleasures of the Imagination Series" (nos. 411-21).

In this last series Addison discusses the origins and workings of the imagination, and its capacity to transform human experience. In describing the force of imagination he writes:

> We have already seen the Influence that one Man has over the Fancy of another, and with what ease he conveys into it a Variety of Imagery; how great a Power then may we suppose lodged in him, who knows all the ways of affecting the Imagination, who can infuse what Ideas he pleases, and fill those Ideas with Terrour [sic] and Delight to what Degree he thinks fit?
>
> (*Spectator* 421, vol. 3, p. 12)

Addison includes art and architecture as well as natural beauty among the aesthetic experiences that stimulate the imagination. He makes special reference to literature in this regard, examining not only poetry but also historical and scientific writing.

As he bids his readers goodbye in the last issue of the first *Spectator* (no. 555), Steele explains the purpose of the fictional Spectator Club and of the authors' anonymity:

> It is much more difficult to converse with the World in a real than in a personated Character. That might pass for Humour in the *Spectator,* which would look like Arrogance in a Writer who sets his Name to his work.
>
> (*Spectator* 555, vol. 3, p. 439)

Before signing his name to the essay, he praises his partner; while not giving Addison's name, he lists the titles of other works that Addison was known to have written and alerts the reader to the letters Addison used to sign his pieces (see above). Steele does name some of the other contributors, thanking them and saying that it is now "high time" for the Spectator to take his leave (*Spectator* 555, vol. 3, p. 439).

The ideal of politeness. "I shall endeavor as much as possible to establish among us a Taste of polite Writing," Addison proclaims in one essay (*Spectator* 58, vol. 1, p. 217). Politeness, for Addison and Steele, as well as those who followed them, was an ideal that meant much more than etiquette. In its emphasis on politeness—on manners, but also on morality and aesthetic appreciation—*The Spectator* proposed a coherent response to the partisan wrangling and civic discord that had long characterized English society. As historian John Brewer writes:

> The aim of politeness was . . . to replace political zeal and religious bigotry with mutual tolerance and understanding. The means of achieving this was a manner of conversing and dealing with people which, by teaching one to regulate one's passions and to cultivate good taste, would enable a person to realize what was in the public interest and for the public good.
>
> (Brewer, p. 102)

Both Addison and Steele viewed the social and political strife they abhorred as springing from human passions, yet they also recognized that passions cannot be eradicated. "The entire Conquest of our Passions is such a difficult work," Steele writes, that we should "only attempt to regulate them" (*Spectator* 71, vol. 1, p. 268). The essayists believed that only the "pleasures of the imagination" could "regulate" the passions in this way. But those were sophisticated pleasures that had previously been available only to the upper class. To bring them to the emerging middle class (and to reinforce them in the upper class) was the job of the new politeness, and thus the job that Addison and Steele set out to achieve with *The Spectator*.

A measure of their success in this campaign to forge a civil society is that "politeness" provided the same sort of civic lubricant for the eighteenth century that its descendant, "respectability," would provide for the nineteenth. As this ideal took hold over the decades following its publication, *The Spectator* would continue to be read widely, its essays representing "the very embodiment of politeness" for their readers (Brewer, p. 100).

Sources and literary context. Addison and Steele select brief, apropos quotations from classical poets—given in the original Greek or Latin—at the beginning of each issue. Among their favorite sources for these epigraphs are the lyric poet Horace (Latin; first century B.C.E.), and the epic poets Virgil (Latin; first century B.C.E.), and Homer (Greek; c. eighth century B.C.E.).

The essay as a literary form can be defined as a short, personal, monothematic, nonfictional prose piece. It has been around since classical times, when it was practiced by authors such as Plutarch (Greek; first to second century C.E.), Cicero (Latin; first century B.C.E.), and Seneca (Latin; first century C.E.). The term *essai* (French for "attempt") was not used, however, until the Renaissance, when the influential French writer Michel de Montaigne (1533-92) applied it to his own works; like Addison, Montaigne too strove to emulate the spirit of Socrates in his writing. Shortly after Montaigne, the English scientist and writer Francis Bacon (1561-1626) was the first to write essays in English. In their own essays, Addison and Steele cite Plutarch, Cicero, Seneca, Montaigne, and Bacon as models.

STAMP ACT

In 1712 the Tory government passed the Stamp Act, which taxed all printed matter and was aimed at controlling the press. At a penny per issue, the tax effectively doubled the price of *The Spectator*. Though it kept up for several months, in the end (like many other periodicals) *The Spectator* was forced to fold because of the tax. Steele explains this in the final issue (no. 555).

Closer contemporary inspiration can be found in the early periodicals of Daniel Defoe and others. Defoe's *Review* was generally partisan, but at the end of each issue Defoe included light or humorous material under the heading "The Scandalous Club." While Defoe did not populate his "club" with imaginary characters, it can be viewed as a direct ancestor of Addison and Steele's Spectator Club. Also some of the Spectator Club's members have a basis in real-life models. The Tory knight Sir John Pakington, for example, is said to have inspired the Club's eccentric but affable Sir Roger.

Reception. The *Tatler's* popularity supplied a ready-made audience for *The Spectator,* which rapidly enjoyed an even greater success than its predecessor. By the tenth issue, Addison could claim that his publisher was distributing 3,000 copies daily and that each copy was being read by 20 people (which he thought a conservative estimate). While these copies sold at the inexpensive price of one penny each, in 1712 the publisher of the collected issues paid Addison and Steele £1,150, a small fortune, for the copyright. *The Spectator* was read throughout Britain and its colonies, from Scotland to America, where Benjamin Franklin modeled his own prose style on it. According to one count, it inspired more than 600 imitations. By 1750, it was considered a classic, and any educated English speaker would have been familiar with at least some of the essays. They have been reprinted in schoolbooks, anthologies, style manuals, and other literary collections from the eighteenth century on; they were especially widely read in the Victorian era.

At the time of publication, however, knowing of Steele's participation, the Tory press blasted *The Spectator.* Two anonymous Tory pamphlets were printed in 1711, for example: "A Spy upon the Spectator" and "The Spectator Inspected," both harshly critical. Yet by 1716, in his "Essay Upon Wit," the poet and physician Sir Richard Blackmore praised the periodical for having "all the Perfection of Writing, and all the advantages of Wit and Humour, that are required to enter-tain and instruct the People" (Blackmore in Bloom and Bloom, p. 253). While Steele was considered the greater writer during *The Spectator's* publication, Addison's reputation as an essayist has eclipsed his friend's among later critics. Yet Steele's easy warmth and approachability continue to be seen as a perfect counterpart to Addison's drier, weightier style.

—Colin Wells

For More Information

Addison, Joseph, and Sir Richard Steele. *The Spectator.* Ed. Henry Morley. 3 vols. London: George Routledge and Sons, 1891.

Becker, Marvin B. *The Emergence of Civil Society in the Eighteenth Century: A Privileged Moment in the History of England, Scotland, and France.* Bloomington and Indianapolis, Indiana: University of Indiana Press, 1994.

Bloom, Edward A., and Lillian D. Bloom. *Addison and Steele: the Critical Heritage.* London: Routledge & Kegan Paul, 1980.

Brewer, John. *The Pleasures of the Imagination: English Culture in the Eighteenth Century.* London: HarperCollins, 1997.

Downie, J. A. *Robert Harley and the Press: Propaganda and Public Opinion in the Age of Swift and Defoe.* Cambridge: Cambridge University Press, 1979.

Olsen, Kirsten. *Daily Life in 18th-Century England.* Westport, Conn.: Greenwood, 1999.

Speck, W. A. *Society and Literature in England 1700-60.* Dublin: Gill and Macmillan, 1983.

The Táin
(The Cattle Raid of Cooley)

as translated by
Thomas Kinsella

Drawn from Irish oral tradition, the *Táin Bó Cúailnge*, or "Cattle-Raid of Cúailnge" (often anglicized as "Cooley"), invokes stories that may have been circulating since pre-Christian times (pre-fifth century C.E.). The manuscript based on these oral tales survives, albeit fragmentarily, in the *Book of the Dun Cow* (Lebor na hUidre), which was produced in the midlands of Ireland at the monastery of Clonmacnois in the late eleventh century. Portions of this version of the text, written in Old and Middle Irish, are datable to as early as the eighth or ninth century. A later version figures in the twelfth-century manuscript known as the *Book of Leinster*, and even later versions appear in post-twelfth-century manuscripts. Clearly *The Táin*, as the text is commonly called, was prized by the learned community of medieval Ireland; references to the work, and the story that it features, appear in other literature produced in the early Middle Ages. The fact that the manuscript appears in different versions reflects the oral tradition from which it emanates. Traditional Irish-speaking storytellers, as well as those of western Scotland (where Scottish Gaelic is spoken, a cousin to Irish), were well-known for their extraordinary memories and their abilities to regale an audience with stories, some of which could last an entire evening or longer. The stories these tradition bearers told were not so much memorized as creatively recomposed upon each performance. This was certainly true of their highly prized *Táin*—some of whose early characters and episodes would live on in the manuscript, as well

THE LITERARY WORK

A prose narrative with poetic inserts set in Ireland in the first century C.E.; composed in stages from the eighth through the twelfth century in Irish (as *Táin Bó Cúailnge*); translated into English in the nineteenth century.

SYNOPSIS

The hero Cú Chulainn stages a superhuman defense of Ulster from the invading forces of Medb, the queen of Connacht, who is in search of the great bull of the Ulstermen.

as in the oral tradition of succeeding centuries. Embodied in *The Táin*, for example, are traces of a longstanding Celtic myth having to do with the creation of the world out of supernatural bulls, and with a primeval struggle between semidivine men and women.

Events in History at the Time the Narrative Takes Place

Reconstructing early Irish history. Literacy and the motivation to produce a literature came to Ireland with Christianity, beginning in the fifth century. The Irish of the "prehistoric" period (that is, before Christianity) left no literary record. According to the chronology of the past that was developed by medieval Irish writers, the

Medb, the Queen of Connacht

cattle raid of Cooley took place in the early first century, C.E. (A separate tale, having to do with the death of Conchobar, the king of Ulster province at the time in which the story of the cattle raid is set, claims that it was brought about after he heard of the sad death of Jesus Christ, his contemporary.)

Arguably, *The Táin*, in at least some of its details, reflects a world even earlier than that: perhaps Ireland of the late first millennium, B.C.E., of which we know very little from classical (ancient Greek and Roman) sources. These same sources, however, tell us a good deal about the Celtic peoples of the European continent and of Britain as they lived and interacted with their neighbors in the period 400 B.C.E.-200 C.E. The Romans, in particular, had the opportunity to observe the Celts firsthand, for, with the exception of Ireland, which Roman legions never invaded—they conquered all of Celtic Europe, an area that extended from Iberia to today's Turkey. Much of this information from classical authors is useful in reconstructing life in ancient Ireland, which was populated by Celts. However, it is important to keep in mind that *Celtic*, as used by the ancient Greeks and Romans, and even as used today, is a broad category, precise only in refer-

ence to a subset of languages (including Irish, Scottish Gaelic, Welsh, and Breton) within the larger Indo-European set of languages (including English, Greek, Latin, Persian, and other tongues from India to Europe). Furthermore, the Irish who produced the text of *The Táin* were in many respects as removed from their own ancient, pre-Christian, Irish past as we are, so, while the story, and the tradition that generated it, may preserve elements reflecting earlier stages of culture and society, it can hardly be viewed as a straightforward window on the past.

Given these circumstances, there is a question of whether the "world" of *The Táin* can be reconstructed. One strategy has been to find the intersections of sociocultural detail between medieval Irish literature (such as *The Táin* and other texts and stories belonging to the Ulster cycle) and the classical writings on the Celts in general. This overlap is compared with what we can learn from the archaeology of premedieval Ireland and then a cautious reconstruction of a historical context for the adventures of Cú Chulainn and the other Ulster heroes is generated, keeping in mind that this is only one of the contexts that has given rise to the elements of *The Táin*.

Early Irish life and society. What kind of picture of Ireland emerges through this process of mixing and matching different bodies of data? It is a world of ringforts (round-shaped settlements, often on hills), the traces of which still dot the Irish countryside; of nobles proud of their ancestors, bloodlines, and the number of their dependents; of cattle in profusion, susceptible to raiding in the strategic games played out among nobles and kingdoms; and of artistic creativity in relation to material goods, as displayed in museums throughout the world. The early Irish lived in small communities protected by surrounding ditches or earthen banks, in circular houses or huts that sheltered extended families, in which elder males (grandfathers or even great-grandfathers) held the ultimate decisionmaking authority. Typically, a person was born, lived his or her life, and died all in the same tribal territory or kingdom (*túath* in later Irish).

It was a highly class-conscious society. Kings inherited their thrones, although contention frequently erupted among members of dynastic families, or between different families, each claiming a right to kingship. The sons of nobles were brought up to be warriors and proud possessors, as well as generous dispensers, of goods (the early Irish did not use money). The daughters of nobles were raised to be managers of households and, in their roles as wives and mothers, important players in familial and political alliances. (Queen Medb's participation in warfare, as featured in the *Táin*, does not appear to have been typical of early Irish female activities.) Children of the upper classes normally did not live with their biological parents but with foster parents—neighbors, kinsfolk, or patrons who assumed responsibility for the raising and social training of their fosterlings, in return for a fee from the actual parents. The institution of fosterage served as a vital kind of social glue, as reflected in *The Táin*, in which some of the most tragic confrontations occur between foster brothers, or between foster son and foster father.

The servile classes produced what the ruling classes consumed, although artisans who fashioned items in metal, stone, or wood (such as weapons, jewelry, carved monuments, and musical instruments) constituted a respectable class of their own, with rights and privileges. Lords acquired clients, other nobles or freemen. In return for the loan of cattle and the prestige of being associated with the cream of the social crop, these clients would provide the lords with food, services, and military assistance. Clients, in fact, helped increase the status of a lord, constituting (along with cows) the basic standard for measuring rank and status in society. Agriculture and herding were the primary means by which both the free and the unfree could obtain food and wealth, the accumulation of which made it possible for individuals to ascend into the ranks of the nobility. Given this social structure, there was little need for professional warriors or standing armies, though warfare certainly preoccupied the menfolk in times of conflict. The ancient Irish, like their descendants, placed a high value on martial achievement.

According to a venerable tradition, the island was divided into provinces, called in Irish *coiceda* ("fifths"): Ulster, Leinster, Munster, and Connacht. (The identity of the mysterious fifth province, sometimes said to be Meath, was a matter of considerable confusion and debate for medieval Irish writers.) These divisions, still maintained in Ireland today, corresponded to genuine territorial, political, and perhaps even cultural differences. A man who lived within a province occasionally aspired to be king of the province, or perhaps even king over more than one province. In medieval literature, traits and relationships are traditionally ascribed to these distinct territories. (Munster, for example, seems much closer to or imbued with the supernatural world than the other provinces.) Within the Ulster cycle of stories, Ulster and Connacht are hostile to one another, although the Ulstermen's relationships with the Leinstermen and the Munstermen are not exactly friendly either.

ON THE MEANING OF *TÁIN*

The Irish term *táin*, usually translated "cattle raid," actually means "driving toward." The same verbal root is used to describe the act of driving a ball in a game, for example, and there were in fact strong elements of sport and ritual in the activity of cattle raiding, as it was practiced in Ireland and western Scotland down to early modern times. Cattle were symbols of wealth, and, among the aristocratic owners of cattle, to steal cows from a rival's herd—especially a prized bull—was a perfectly respectable, if cheeky, sign of challenge, or even an assertion of kingliness. The traditional response of the aggrieved party was to recover the stolen animals or steal from the cattle raider's herd, in turn.

Poets and other possessors of lore. Much artistry and sophisticated technology went into the making of weapons (swords, spears) and armor, which were vital status symbols. However, words—particularly poetic or sung words—were arguably the most powerful weapons of all, just as poets and other masters of verbal lore were the most highly respected of all artists. Unlike the typical member of society, who, as described above, lived a rather circumscribed life, poets and other high-status artists (such as harpists) could travel from kingdom to kingdom, plying their trades in the confidence that their semi-sacred status and value to society would assure their safety. Local kings (usually members of families with traditional claims to kingship in an area), overkings (including kings of provinces), and the nobility in general (from which these royal dynastic families emerged) all relied upon the services of poets. The poets would sing a noble's praises, thereby raising the great man or woman's social standing. Or, if need be, the poets would correct the excesses of the noble's behavior or exact due payment (cows, treasure, or other valuables) for their own poetic performances by threatening the noble with satire, the sinister "reverse image" of praise poetry. Making themselves

A druid issues a warning.

indispensable as guardians of culture, poets developed, conserved, and conveyed legal, genealogical, and narrative lore as parts of their repertoire.

Druids—a Celtic term meaning "those who know or see a great deal"—played a role in this ancient pre-Christian, Irish society. They were advisers who foretold the future and mediated between this world and the supernatural realms beyond, which were often located, in popular imagination, beyond the sea, under the ground, or in the wildernesses, bogs, and forests that covered much of premedieval Ireland. In a famous scene from *The Táin*, Medb, the queen of Connacht, who is leading the cattle raid, and her army encounter a female prophetess (a druidess, in effect) who tells them of her vision and rhapsodically predicts disaster for the expedition. Later in *The Táin*, when Sualtaim (the father of the hero Cú Chulainn) is warning the Ulstermen and trying to rouse them to action, he is said to be violating a sacred rule, according to which only druids are allowed to speak before the king initiates conversation. The supernatural female known as the Morrígan—the closest we come to a divinity in *The Táin*—herself behaves like a superdruid, changing shape, predicting outcomes, and seemingly exerting a mystical influence on those outcomes, and on men's minds.

A few things are known about the religious beliefs of the ancient Irish: they offered precious objects, and possibly even human victims, to their gods in sacrifice; they associated the sacred with springs and other bodies of water; they established Celtic sites (perhaps, for example, Emain Macha, the "capital" of Ulster in *The Táin*); and they thought of kingship as a sacred marriage to a divine protectress of the kingdom. There is little else that can be determined with certainty from the archaeological or literary record about the practices and beliefs of pre-Christian, Irish religious tradition. It does appear, however, that the pre-Christian Irish conceptualized their gods and goddesses in terms of related but separate, even competing, pantheons (such as the Tribes of the Goddess Danu, *Túatha Dé Danann*).

The Narrative in Focus

Plot summary. For a text that is a centerpiece of medieval Irish literature, *The Táin* tells a seemingly rambling story, at least by modern literary standards. It is also not a story complete in itself; both the *Book of the Dun Cow* and the *Book of Leinster* provide a dossier of "foretales," or "prequels," to go along with *The Táin*. The earliest version begins as the province of Ulster is being attacked by the forces of the king and queen of the province of Connacht. This royal pair, Ailill and Medb, seek to capture the famed Brown Bull of Cúailnge (an area in modern County Louth), as well as to wreak havoc on their traditional enemies, the Ulstermen. The *Book of Leinster* provides a humorous pretext for this invasion.

Queen Medb and King Ailill, says this source, were arguing in bed over which of them was wealthier and had more status. As a result of this exchange, Medb decided that she needed to obtain the Brown Bull of Cooley, in order to match Ailill's mighty bull, the Finnbennach ("White-Horned"). The Brown Bull was the prize possession of the Ulsterman Dáire mac Fiachna, but had originally belonged to Medb: having a mind of its own, it had decided to leave her, unwilling to continue as the possession of a woman.

Despite the fact that she has offered to have sex with Dáire as part of the negotiation process, Medb cannot reclaim the Brown Bull peacefully. She thus decides to take it by force, with her husband and the Connachtmen honor-bound to assist her. The timing of the winter invasion is fortuitous because the menfolk of Ulster, including their king, are suffering from mysteriously debilitating pangs that (according to one of the "prequels") were inflicted on them as punishment by a supernatural female whom they abused. This affliction tends to overtake them just when they need to be at their martial best. Fortunately, the "hound of the Ulstermen" (as he is sometimes called in the text), the hero Cú Chulainn, does not suffer from these pangs, and so is available to ward off the invaders. Unfortunately, he is committed to a tryst with one of his many lovers, and allows deep penetration of his province by the invading army (which includes not only Connachtmen but also "the men of Ireland," meaning presumably warriors from the other provinces, Leinster and Munster). Returning from his assignation, Cú Chulainn embarks on a campaign of guerilla warfare, slaughtering the advance parties sent by the invaders and harassing the main army from afar with his deadly slingshot.

Among the invaders is a contingent of Ulstermen in exile, who left their king, Conchobar, in protest against his treatment of his errant mistress Deirdriu and her lover Noísiu.

Chief among the Ulster exiles is Fergus mac Roig (a name meaning "Manly Strength, son of Big Horse"), one of Cú Chulainn's beloved foster fathers and mentors, who feels torn between his loyalty to his province (of which he was once king) and his hatred of Conchobar. Consequently, throughout the expedition, he is both helping and hindering the invaders. At the beginning it is Fergus who interprets the traces left by Cú Chulainn for the invaders as omens of the difficulties they will encounter in trying to overcome or avoid this opponent. Fergus and the other Ulstermen, in a famous flashback section early on in the text, brief the invaders on the formidable reputation of the youthful hero, telling them of his incredible boyhood deeds.

Through Fergus's intervention, a truce of sorts is arranged between the invaders and Cú Chulainn, whereby Medb and Ailill stay where they are, sending out a different champion to fight with Cú Chulainn every day. These champions, before and after the truce, challenge the formidable Ulster hero in order to win glory, to fulfill their obligations to Medb and Ailill, or to win the prize of their daughter Finnabair (or, in some cases, Medb herself). Of course, these challengers prove to be nothing more than "cannon fodder." They range from the supernaturally tinged Fróech—whose corpse is borne away by lament-

ing otherworldly females in a scene reminiscent of the death of the British King Arthur—to the brash Etarcomol, who provokes the hero into slicing him in two, to the hapless Láréne ("Little Mare"), the only man to walk away alive from his encounter with Cú Chulainn. (As a result, however, of the intense shaking that Cú Chulainn gives him, Láréne is never again able to digest or defecate properly).

THE DEIRDRIU STORY—A PREQUEL AND A SOURCE

One of the most popular stories told throughout Europe in the Middle Ages was the tragic tale of the doomed love of Tristan and Isolde, the wife of the king of Cornwall (Tristan's uncle, Mark). The lovers are attracted to each other through the influence of a magic love potion, of which they both unwittingly drink. While the story of Tristan and Isolde comes from British Celtic sources, the existence of Irish Celtic stories such as that of the fatal love of Deirdriu and the young warrior Noísiu shows us that the romantic triangle was a basic plot device, perhaps of mythic significance, in Celtic storytelling in general. Deirdriu—who, according to the earliest extant telling of the story, is the beautiful "possession" of Conchobar—finds a handsome Ulsterman, Noisiu, and forces him to elope with her. The lovers' idyllic existence comes to an end when Conchobar treacherously slays Noisiu and reclaims Deirdriu. She ultimately rebels against her life as Conchobar's mistress and commits suicide, while a contingent of distinguished Ulstermen abandon Conchobar for Connacht in protest against his slaying of Noisiu. Hence, as this "prequel" to *The Táin* explains, some of the staunchest warriors of Ulster accompany Medb and Ailill at the time when the raid commences.

As the story of the cattle raid unfolds, Cú Chulainn has to cope with the opposition of the Morrígan ("Nightmare Queen"), a supernatural female who hovers over battlefields like the Norse Valkyrie, and with whom Cú Chulainn, here and in other texts, enjoys a remarkably ambivalent relationship. Coming to him in the disguise of an attractive human female, the Morrígan offers herself to the hero, only to be rejected. Angered, she later attacks Cú Chulainn while he is engaged in one of his most desperate fights (in the waters of a ford, a typical setting for these duels). The Morrígan assaults him first in the form of an eel that coils itself around the hero's feet; then in the form of a wolf that drives the cattle already captured by the invaders against Cú Chulainn; and finally, in the form of a hornless red heifer that stampedes its bovine colleagues against the beleaguered hero. Cú Chulainn manages to wound and drive off these animal incarnations of the Morrígan (who typically appears as a crow) and also to slay his opponent-of-the-day, Lóch the horn-skinned. Faced with Lóch's magical invulnerability, Cú Chulainn resorts to the use of his secret weapon, the *gae bolga*—a mysterious spear that has to be launched at an opponent's back in the water, enters through the anus, and seemingly permeates its victim's body. Cú Chulainn learned to handle the weapon from his foster mother, Scáthach ("Spectral"), the mistress of martial arts.

The truce breaks down temporarily, on account of the treacherous attacks of the invaders, but Cú Chulainn manages to fend off their attacks nonetheless. The hero's supernatural father, Lug, comes to his aid, inducing a healing sleep and taking Cú Chulainn's place as defender of the province. During the hero's rest, the sons of the Ulster nobles launch their attack on the invaders, but all the youths are slain. Upon waking to this news, the restored but distraught Cú Chulainn goes berserk and wreaks enormous damage on the enemy army. The truce is restored, and at the end of the series of single combats, Cú Chulainn comes face to face with his greatest challenge, another of Scáthach's fosterlings and trainees, the hero Fer Día (a name that tellingly means "One of Two"). Fer Día, like the hero's previous opponent Lóch, is horn-skinned and can be killed only with the aforementioned gae bolga. Cú Chulainn's prolonged combat with Fer Día, extending over several days and mingled with scenes of cordial exchange as well as bitter recrimination, decimates the Ulster defender both physically and emotionally. Forced to retire from the battlefield and recuperate, Cú Chulainn is replaced for a while by a series of comical Ulster veterans. Then, with the coming of spring, the Ulstermen ready themselves to resume the battle.

Cú Chulainn sends his fosterfather Sualtaim to alert Conchobar and his warriors at Emain Macha to the impending invasion, a task that Sualtaim accomplishes, even though he loses his head doing so (he falls on his shield and is decapitated). The Ulster forces assemble and confront the invaders, just as Medb is about to order her forces to withdraw, having found the Brown Bull and collected enough plunder. The

armies clash, and the Ulster exile Fergus—equipped with the sword stolen from him earlier by King Ailill after he found Fergus making love to Medb—attacks the Ulster king, Conchobar with gusto, striking Conchobar's shield repeatedly. Conchobar's son convinces Fergus to vent his rage on three nearby hills instead, the crests of which are subsequently lopped off by Fergus. The din awakens Cú Chulainn, who enters the battle and reminds Fergus of his oath to withdraw from combat upon Cú Chulainn's request—the hero having earlier done the same favor for Fergus. After Fergus and the rest of the Ulster exiles depart, the invading force collapses.

Medb, having already sent ahead the Brown Bull, oversees the invaders' withdrawal but pauses to urinate, much to the chagrin of Fergus. Cú Chulainn comes upon her as she is relieving herself, with the flow of her urine creating ditches and leaving its traces on the landscape, as, explains the text, can still be seen today. Not being a slayer of women (or so the text says, despite previous instances of Cú Chulainn's slaying members of the opposite sex), the hero lets her go and "decapitates" three hills instead, matching Fergus's earlier feat.

The text concludes with a climactic duel between the Brown Bull and the White-Horned Bull, who fight all day and night throughout Ireland and are watched eagerly by the weary human combatants. In the morning, the Brown Bull emerges from a lake in Connacht with the remains of Ailill's Finnbenach ("white-horned" bull) on its horns. It heads back toward Ulster, dropping along the way pieces of its opponent (after which those places are later named). Upon reaching its own province, the Brown Bull dies. Peace is concluded between the victorious Ulstermen and the Connachtmen, and Cú Chulainn keeps Finnabair, Ailill, and Medb's daughter, as a prize.

The battle of the sexes. Cú Chulainn is hardly the most disruptive element in *The Táin.* According to Fergus, the moral of the story is: "It is the usual thing for a herd led by a mare to be strayed and destroyed" (*Táin*, p. 251). Even in the earliest extant version of the text, which does not contain the "prequel" episode detailing the contentious pillow talk between Medb and her husband Ailill, it is clear throughout that Medb is the driving force behind the destructive cattle raid. Moreover, although the army of invaders withdraws in defeat from Ulster in the end, the expedition has not been a total loss, at least for Medb. She does obtain the desired bull, and with the climactic fight between the two bovines that ends in their death, the difference in property between Medb and her husband, which was the cause of their argument in the first place, is eliminated. As for Ailill's control over his wife, it is virtually nonexistent. While he arranges for the theft of her lover Fergus's sword and mocks him with its absence, he has seemingly no choice but to be cuckolded. Medb and what she represents are too powerful even for Cú Chulainn to assault. (Medb's name means "drunken" or "intoxicating one," perhaps in reference to her association with kingship, the prize of which is often conceptualized in Irish tradition as potable.) Meanwhile, what Medb has to offer (her own sexual favors, or those of her hapless daughter) are of interest to the hero. The text ends with the statement that Finnabair, Medb's daughter, stayed with Cú Chulainn after the cattle raid drew to a close.

The Táin, for all of its detailing of single combat between males, seems at heart interested most of all in the battles involving women. Woman is matched against woman in the episode of the invading army's encounter with the female seer Fedelm, who warns of the destruction awaiting Medb and her forces at the hands of Cú Chulainn, and whose prophetic authority proves hard for Medb to challenge. In the "Boyhood Deeds" section of the text, which defines the character of Cú Chulainn as he operates through the rest of the tale, women loom large at both the beginning and the end of his heroic quest for adult identity and social recognition. He goes forth from his mother, who warns him about the dangers he will face from the Ulstermen; on his first expedition beyond the borders of Ulster, he is finally driven back by the cry of a woman lamenting her sons, slain by the ferocious young warrior; and upon his return to Emain Macha in a condition of such white-hot ferocity that he would be capable of attacking his own people, Cú Chulainn meets the women of Ulster, who slyly bear their breasts to him—giving the Ulstermen the opportunity to grab the diverted hero and dunk him in vats of cold water to "cool him off."

These powerful females—who are unafraid to stand up to their menfolk or to each other and who virtually use their female traits as weapons—are, to some extent, vestiges of Celtic goddesses (whose names are still preserved in many of the river names of Ireland, Britain, and Europe in general—such as the Shannon, the Severn, and the Danube). However, the change in women's status in medieval Irish society be-

tween the sixth and twelfth centuries is also worth factoring in. Historians, for instance, have noted that women of the aristocratic and higher free classes appeared to have gained rights as owners and marital partners during this period. Society was still dominated by males, but the coming of Christianity and then the turbulence of the Viking era brought changes in sexual, as well as social, politics. There are modern critics who characterize The Táin as a misogynistic text, but they perhaps go too far. After all, men are hardly less ridiculous in the world of the story than women. Still, The Táin is ambivalent about mythic stereotypes of women and of the increasing role played by queens and other powerfully placed women in the society of early medieval Ireland.

FEMALE PROPHET

Early in The Táin, Medb and her forces encounter a supernaturally gifted poetess, whose prediction bodes ill for their expedition. The detailed description of the inspired girl's appearance is typical of medieval Irish literatures, as is the motif of the poetess's ability, upon request, to conjure a vision of the future or of the past, and to put it into words—not unlike what the authors of this and other medieval Irish texts are able to do:

> They saw a young grown girl in front of them. She had yellow hair. She wore a speckled cloak fastened around her with a gold pin, a red-embroidered hooded tunic and sandals with gold clasps. Her brow was broad, her jaw narrow, her two eyebrows pitch black, with delicate dark lashes casting shadows half way down her cheeks. You would think her lips were inset with Parthian scarlet. Her teeth were like an array of jewels between the lips. She had hair in three tresses: two wound upward on her head and the third hanging down her back, brushing her calves. She held a light gold weaving-rod in her hands, with gold inlay. Her eyes had triple irises. Two black horses drew her chariot, and she was armed. "What is your name?" Medb said to the girl. "I am Fedelm, and I am a woman poet of Connacht." "Where have you come from?" Medb said. "From learning verse and vision in Alba [Britain or perhaps Scotland]," the girl said. "Have you the *imbas forasnai*, the light of Foresight?" Medb said. "Yes, I have," the girl said. "Then look for me and see what will become of my army." So the girl looked. Medb said, "Fedelm, prophetess; how seest though the host?" Fedelm said in reply: "I see it crimson, I see it red."
>
> (Kinsella, *Táin*, pp. 60-61)

Sources and literary context. The world of the author(s) of *The Táin* (which probably went through several stages of development between the eighth and eleventh centuries) was similar in most respects to that of ancient Ireland. There were, however, some important differences. The most important of these was Christianity, which came to Ireland from Britain (the most famous missionary to Ireland, Saint Patrick, was British), and perhaps also from the Continent, in the fifth century C.E. The Irish embrace of the new religion was doubtless a slow, gradual process among the lower ranks of society (about whom, given the nature of the historical evidence, we know less than we do about the upper ranks), but the élite, including nobles and poets, quickly became supporters, patrons, and even leaders of the early Irish Church.

EXCERPT FROM WILLIAM BUTLER YEATS'S DRAMA *ON BAILE'S STRAND* (1903) INVOKES *THE TÁIN*

~

In Yeats's drama, an older, disgruntled Cú Chulainn refers back to the events of the cattle raid in his talk with Conchobar, king of Ulster:

> And I must be obedient in all things;
> Give up my will to yours, go where you please,
> Come where you will, sit at the council-board
> Among the unshapely bodies of old men!
> I, whose mere name has kept this country safe,
> I, that in early days have driven out
> Maeve [Medb] of Cruachan.
>
> (Yeats, pp. 145-46)

The form of Christianity that succeeded in Ireland was monastic—that is, centered on communities of men and women who dedicated their lives to prayer and to the collective good of the monastery, and who prided themselves on being the followers of the saintly founder of the community. Monasteries begat other monasteries, which formed elaborate networks both in Ireland and western Europe, throughout which Irish monks went on pilgrimages, and where they often settled down as advisers to kings and scholars, and as members of ecclesiastical communities.

The major churches and monasteries of early Christian Ireland, such as Armagh, Derry (and its Scottish offshoot Iona), Clonmacnois, and Kil-

dare, grew into powerful, city-like communities, the foci of economic, political, and cultural activities. Among these activities were the production of elaborately detailed and decorated manuscripts, mostly in Latin, the language of western Christianity; the development of a written form of Irish, based on the Latin alphabet, and usable for practical as well as artistic purposes; the creation of an Irish-language literature through the fusion of the vernacular oral tradition with the learned community's knowledge of Christian and classical Latin texts; and the writing of massive manuscripts (like the *Book of the Dun Cow* and the *Book of Leinster*) that preserve such "native" literature.

Hence, the author(s) of *The Táin* were not traditional poets, druids, or storytellers, but religious men educated in scripture and in the classics, as these were available to the West in the early Middle Ages. They were keenly aware of the cultural and political statement they were making by composing in their native tongue (a practice hardly widespread in Europe at that time) and aware also of the tension between their fascination with the Irish past and its ongoing traditions and their allegiance to a more cosmopolitan tradition of learning. The literature of medieval Ireland is full of dialogues—between angels and humans, between ancients and later humans, and between representatives of oral tradition and those of the written—just as the literature itself resulted from a dynamic conversation between different periods, cultures, and priorities.

Events in History at the Time the Narrative Was Written

Parallel invasions. The *Táin* is informed by the "backward look" (as the modern Irish writer and critic Frank O'Connor termed it) of its eighth-through twelfth-century writers. The tortuous itinerary of the raid itself, resulting in the coining of seemingly innumerable place-names, the heroism of Cú Chulainn as he withstands challenge after challenge, and the profound crisis that casts a shadow over the province of Ulster—all are presented by the author(s) of *The Táin* as elements of an ancient tribal history. They are also, however, the makings of an epic as this classical genre was understood in the medieval era. These competing motivations, which create a rather rowdy textual dialogue, should be kept in mind when attempting to understand medieval Irish works such as *The Táin*.

An important new ingredient in Irish society and culture of the ninth through eleventh centuries is the expanded scope of kingship. This institution developed considerably in the second half of the first millennium, C.E., as the Irish, along with the rest of western Europe, cultivated a nostalgic view of the once-glorious Roman Empire. This came about through extensive contact with the empire-building Merovingian and Carolingian kings of early medieval France and Germany. Another contributing factor was the response of Irish kings and ecclesiastics to the Viking incursions of the ninth and tenth centuries.

During this period, many of the invaders and traders from Scandinavia actually settled down in Ireland, forming what would become the major port cities of the country (Dublin, Limerick, Galway, Waterford, and Wexford). The wars between the Vikings and the Irish, and among the Irish kings themselves, resulted in kings and kingdoms striving aggressively to extend their power and build up their military might in the eleventh and twelfth centuries. A bold move on the part of Diarmaid mac Murchadha, a contender for the throne of Leinster, led in 1166 to the invasion of Ireland by the Anglo-Normans from England—an event that would prove over the course of the next several centuries, to be the beginning of the end for Irish political independence.

Because the earliest extant text of *The Táin* that has come down to us was produced in the midst of this turbulent and dynamic period, we would be justified in seeing reflections of this history in the massive scale of the cattle raid—surely more an invasion than a "raid"—and in Medb's ambition as monarch. The entrance of the Vikings onto the Irish political scene seemed to exacerbate the struggles among Irish political forces, and even to encourage entrepreneurial moves on the part of those desirous of greater power and dominion. Likewise in *The Táin* the enemy who comes pillaging across the border exposes the tensions among kinsmen, old acquaintances, and even fellow countrymen.

Reception. *The Táin* was translated from the Irish in the second half of the nineteenth century—a period in which the study of medieval Celtic literature grew into a scholarly field as well as a source of inspiration and fascination for many readers and artists throughout Europe. At the time, the story of Cú Chulainn's heroic defense of the province of Ulster against invading forces served as an emblem for nationalistic leaders of Ireland's own struggle to gain independence from its English conquerors. In the early twentieth century, activists in Northern Ireland (still part of the United Kingdom), who resisted reunification with the Irish Republic, used Cú Chulainn as a symbol of their cause as well.

Cú Chulainn, Medb, and other characters from the Ulster cycle of heroic tales, as well as the situations depicted therein, are echoed in the works of modern Irish writers such as J. M. Synge, W. B. Yeats, James Joyce, James Stephens, Thomas Kinsella, and Seamus Heaney. A visitor to modern-day Ireland cannot avoid references to these characters and heroic episodes in place-names, as well as the public sculpture, decorative arts, and popular culture of the country. Although *The Táin* certainly did not start out as a national epic, in many respects it has come to serve as such for the people of modern Ireland.
—Joseph F. Nagy

For More Information

Kinsella, Thomas, trans. The Táin, *Translated from the Irish Epic* Táin Bó Cúailinge. Dublin: Dolmen Press and Oxford University Press, 1970.

MacCurtain, Margaret, and Donncha Ó Corráin, eds. *Women in Irish Society: The Historical Dimension*. Westport, Conn.: Greenwood, 1979.

Mallory, James P., ed. *Aspects of the Táin*. Belfast: December Publications, 1992.

Mallory, James, and Gerard Stockman, eds. *Ulidia. Proceedings of the First International Conference on the Ulster Cycle of Tales, Belfast and Emain Macha, 8-12 April 1994*. Belfast: December Publications, 1994.

O'Connor, Frank. *A Backward Look: A Short History of Irish Literature*. New York: Putnam, 1967.

Ó Cróinín, Dáibhí. *Early Medieval Ireland, 400-1200*. London: Longman, 1995.

———. "Prehistoric and Early Christian Ireland." In *The Oxford Illustrated History of Ireland*. Ed. R. F. Foster. Oxford: Oxford University Press 1989).

O'Rahilly, Cecile, ed. and trans. *Táin Bó Cúailnge from the Book of Leinster*. Dublin: Dublin Institute for Advanced Studies, 1967.

———. *Táin Bó Cúailnge: Recension I*. Dublin: Dublin Institute for Advanced Studies, 1976.

Radner, Joan. "Fury Destroys the World: Historical Strategy in Ireland's Ulster Epic." *Mankind Quarterly* 23 (1982):41-60

Yeats, William Butler. *Yeats's Poetry, Drama, and Prose*. Ed. James Pethica. New York and London: W. W. Norton, 2000.

Vanity Fair

by
William Makepeace Thackeray

Born in Calcutta, India, in 1811, William Makepeace Thackeray was the only son of Anne Becher and Richmond Thackeray, who worked for the East India Company. After his father's death in 1815, the young Thackeray was sent back to England to be educated at the Charterhouse School in London and, later, at Trinity College, Cambridge. Believing himself not destined for academic success, Thackeray left Cambridge without a degree and spent several years traveling in Europe, where he met Isabella Shawe, whom he married in 1836. The newly-weds moved to England, after which Thackeray became a successful journalist, contributing articles and satiric sketches to, for example, *Fraser's Magazine* and *Punch*. After the birth of her third child, Isabella suffered a mental breakdown and ultimately lapsed into permanent insanity. Thackeray used the profits from his work to pay for her care. He progressed to writing longer prose pieces that were first published serially: *Catherine* (1839-40), *The Luck of Barry Lyndon* (1844), and finally his masterpiece *Vanity Fair* (1847-1848), a scathing satire on English society.

Events in History at the Time the Novel Takes Place

The Regency period—an overview. Much of *Vanity Fair* takes place during the period in English history known as the Regency (1811-1820). King George III, who had suffered a mysterious outbreak of madness in 1788, experienced a re-

---

lapse in 1810, from which there was to be no recovery. On February 5, 1811, the British Parliament passed a bill that allowed the royal heir, George, the Prince of Wales, to rule England as Prince Regent in his father's stead.

Overall the Regency was a period of social and political extremes. The Industrial and French Revolutions had each left their mark on the age. In the eighteenth century the Industrial Revolution led to the construction of mills and factories, and the growth of a new laboring population whose members migrated to the city from rural areas in search of work. As the century drew to a close, the effects of the French Revolution manifested themselves in harsh, repressive measures. Unnerved by the savagery of the 1793-94 Reign of Terror (in which thousands of suspected anti-revolutionaries were executed in France) and fearful of similar developments in England, the British government legally prohibited public meetings and suspended habeas corpus—a citizen's right to obtain a common-law writ to appear before a court as protection against being illegally imprisoned. This seriously affected the population at large, especially because the government often charged those who advocated even moderate political reform in time of war with high treason (England had been at war with France since 1793 and, except for a brief period of peace, was to remain so until 1815).

PRESENTATION AT COURT

O f all the major rituals in nineteenth-century English society, presentation at court was the most eagerly sought by the socially ambitious. Most upper-class young ladies—and young men, for that matter—automatically went through this ritual when they first came out in fashionable society. Debutantes made their appearances at a set of drawing rooms (their male counterparts attended "levees") at St. James's Palace, where they were duly escorted into the Presence Chamber to make their curtseys to the king, queen, and whichever other members of the royal family were present. A special costume for the presentees was required: men wore buckle shoes, knee breeches, and a sword; women wore gowns with three-yard trains, and feathers in their hair. "The requirements for presentation were very strict. Persons of rank could be presented; so, too, could the wives of clergy, military men, naval officers, physicians, and barristers, 'these being the aristocratic professions.' Wives of general practitioners, solicitors, businessmen, or merchants (except bankers) could not be presented" (Pool, *What Jane Austen Ate*, p. 71). In *Vanity Fair*, Becky Crawley (formerly Sharp) successfully schemes to have her aristocratic sister-in-law, Lady Jane, sponsor her presentation at court, which will give Becky the cachet of respectability she craves: "If she did not wish to lead a virtuous life, at least she desired to enjoy a character for virtue, and we know that no lady in the genteel world can possess this desideratum, until she has put on a train and feathers, and has been presented to her sovereign at Court" (*Vanity Fair*, p. 598).

Not surprisingly, it was the poor who suffered most during this period. The overall cost of living had increased steadily since the war had begun; grain, in particular, became very expensive because it could no longer be imported from Europe. "The war had also the effect of shutting out the supply of European corn, which had at last become necessary to steady food prices in our thickly populated island. . . . The poor, both in town and country, suffered terribly" (Trevelyan, p. 3).

Nor did peace bring a respite. During the two decades of war, farmers adapted to the high price of grain. Therefore, when peace came and the price of grain fell, many found themselves unable to pay rent and faced ruin. The Corn Law of 1815, which levied a tariff on low-cost, imported grain, attempted to protect British farmers from foreign competition. But its passage aggravated a split in society, enraging town dwellers of all classes and widening the growing chasm between urban and rural populations.

While the rural and urban poor struggled to make ends meet in the farms and factories, the wealthy—some of whom had made their fortunes through trade and industry—and the aristocratic enjoyed an era of seemingly boundless prosperity and comfort. The upper classes took their cue from the Prince Regent, emulating his taste for lavish display and expensive entertainment. Men and women of high society wore fine clothes, dined on sumptuous food, attended extravagant parties, planned advantageous marriages for their children, devoured the most recent popular novels or epic poems, and avidly dissected the latest scandals surrounding their social circle: "It is true that there has seldom been a period when so much flair and imagination has been spent on the arts, or a society which put such a high premium on civilized living. But it is also true that [Regency] Society managed to behave at times with amazing vulgarity" (Murray, p. 1).

In *Vanity Fair*, Thackeray portrays the paradoxical nature of the Regency era through the parallel destinies of Amelia Sedley and Becky Sharp. Amelia, a rich merchant's daughter, finds herself an impoverished young widow after her father's financial ruin and her husband's death. When Mr. Sedley's business acquaintances refuse to recognize him after his misfortune, Amelia and her mother are forced to sell whatever valuables they possess to provide for their family and preserve some illusion of gentility. Meanwhile, Becky, though born poor, has married into the wealthy, propertied Crawley family, and is presented at court and introduced into "the very greatest circles of the London fashion," where her sole occupation is "to procure . . . the prettiest new dresses and ornaments; to drive to fine dinner parties" (Thackery, *Vanity Fair*, p. 637).

Napoleon and Waterloo. Although England had been at war with France since 1793, Napoleon

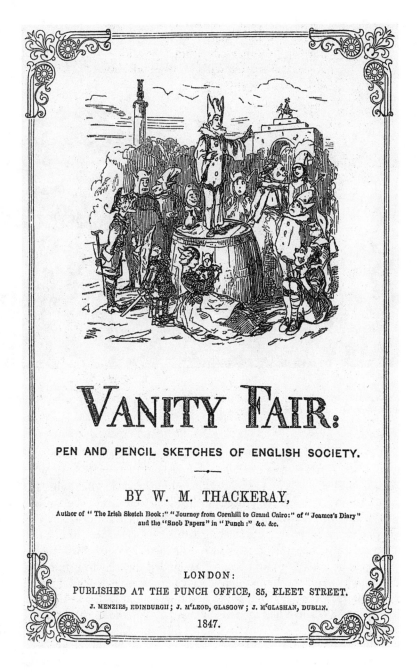

VANITY FAIR.

PEN AND PENCIL SKETCHES OF ENGLISH SOCIETY.

BY W. M. THACKERAY,

Author of " The Irish Sketch Book:" "Journey from Cornhill to Grand Cairo:" of " Jeames's Diary "
and the "Snob Papers" in " Punch :" &c. &c.

LONDON:
PUBLISHED AT THE PUNCH OFFICE, 85, FLEET STREET.

J. MENZIES, EDINBURGH; J. M'LEOD, GLASGOW; J. M'GLASHAN, DUBLIN.

1847.

Title page of the 1847 edition of *Vanity Fair*.

Bonaparte's rise to power further inflamed hostilities between the two nations. In 1804 Napoleon became Emperor of France, then spent the next decade establishing himself as master of Europe. Under Napoleon's command, the French army seized Rome, Amsterdam, and Hamburg. Although England's Admiral Horatio Nelson defeated the French navy at sea in the Battle of Trafalgar in 1805, many believed Napoleon to be invincible on land, and most English lived in dread of an invasion by France.

In 1812 Napoleon made a costly error by sending French troops to Moscow, where they fell victim to the rigors of a Russian winter. Napoleon's power base was further weakened by several defeats on land, including the Battle of Leipzig—fought in October 1813—in which Austrian troops crushed the French, who retreated across the Rhine, effectively ending Napoleon's power east of that river. Early the following year, troops from England, Russia, Prussia, and Austria successfully invaded Paris, which

Throngs of mourners attend the funeral of the Duke of Wellington, who commanded the British troops that defeated Napoleon at the battle of Waterloo.

fell to these allied powers in March 1814. Louis XVIII was restored to the French throne, while Napoleon was exiled to Elba.

The tiny island, however, ultimately proved too small to hold him. In February 1815, Napoleon managed to escape his guards and steal on board a ship bound for France, then received a hero's welcome when he landed at Cannes on March 1. Marching northward, the former emperor gathered supporters by the day, reentering Paris on March 20. Louis XVIII had fled the city on hearing of Napoleon's return.

Realizing that allied troops were mobilizing against him, Napoleon gathered together an army of 200,000 loyal men and marched into Belgium in June 1815. Meanwhile, the duke of Wellington, commander of the British forces, assembled an allied army of about 90,000 men (one-third of these were British; the remaining two-thirds were Belgian or German). On June 18, 1815, allied and French troops engaged in battle near Waterloo, a small town just south of Brussels, Belgium. Fighting lasted all day, with heavy casualties on both sides, but the arrival of the Prussian reinforcements set the seal on an allied victory. Beset by the English forces on one side and the Prussians on the other, Napoleon's army was crushed and Napoleon himself fled the battlefield in his carriage. He

was apprehended six days later and exiled to the island of Saint Helena, where he remained until his death in 1821. His "Hundred Days" of freedom were over. The Battle of Waterloo became one of the most famous battles in England's history, as well as one of the costliest. An estimated 25,000 allied men were killed or wounded that day in contrast to Napoleon's far greater losses of 250,000 killed or wounded. An additional 8,000 of Napoleon's men were taken prisoner (Chandler, p. 171).

In *Vanity Fair*, Thackeray interweaves the fortunes of his main characters with those of Napoleon. Amelia's father, John Sedley, loses what is left of his money when Napoleon escapes from Elba: "In March, Anno Domini 1815, Napoleon landed at Cannes, and Louis XVIII fled, and all Europe was in alarm, and the funds fell, and old John Sedley was ruined" (*Vanity Fair*, p. 214). The Battle of Waterloo has an even more dramatic impact on Thackeray's characters. In Brussels at the time, Becky and her companions experience the panic and confusion that overtakes civilians in a war zone, while Amelia's husband, an English infantry officer, becomes one of Waterloo's many casualties: "No more firing was heard at Brussels—the pursuit rolled miles away. Darkness came down on the field and city: and Amelia was praying for George, who was lying on his face, dead, with a bullet through his heart" (*Vanity Fair*, p. 406).

Class attitudes. Nineteenth-century English society was organized on an earlier foundation of rigid class stratification. Royalty and the nobility—dukes, marquises, earls, viscounts, and barons—occupied the topmost rung (baronetcies were hereditary titles reserved for commoners, and the far less prestigious knighthoods were nonhereditary titles conferred by the sovereign). Beneath the aristocracy, in descending order of importance, were the landed gentry; members of the respectable professions—the church, law, and, to a lesser extent, medicine; yeoman farmers with independent land holdings; bankers; merchants; artisans; factory workers; and poor urban and farm laborers.

The social hierarchy seemed fixed, but as the century progressed, significant changes took place. In 1811 the National Society for Promoting the Education of the Poor in the Principles of the Established Church was formed, with the intent of teaching children of the lower classes to read the Bible. Sunday schools were subsequently established, and gradually these institutions developed into weekday elementary schools, which by 1839 Parliament was supporting with annual grants of 30,000 pounds. These "national schools" represented the best chance for poor people to receive an education, a means toward upward social mobility. Access to education contributed to the growth of a more learned, professionally skilled middle class.

Even more dramatic were the changes wrought by successful merchants and industrialists, who found themselves in a position to compete, at least on a monetary basis, with the aristocracy. From industry and manufacturing came new sources of wealth that rivaled landholding, although industrialists often had to invest some of their wealth into ownership of a country estate for society to really accept them. Owning land—and the more of it the better—automatically raised one's status in the eyes of the world, as did being able to claim a distinguished family pedigree and a title. Few wealthy industrialists could make such claims, but they could nonetheless acquire some of the accoutrements of superior social status, including parcels of land, their own carriages, the stately country home, enough servants to manage the everyday business of running the household, and, on occasion, even a title. Gentlemen were not supposed to soil their hands with manual labor or make their living by "trade"—the business of buying and selling—but rather to live upon the rents collected from tenant farmers on their country estates. Thus, these nouveau riche industrialists were frequently not accepted as "true" gentlemen by the highest ranks of society, although some did, through their business successes, attain the honor of knighthood.

During the 1820s and 1830s, wealth acquired through trade and industry became less despised, and power shifted gradually from the upper to the middle classes. "A different England was emerging based on industry, not land; on the middle class, not the aristocracy. . . . Power was no longer limited to a tiny minority of the elite but extended to the provinces and the manufacturing towns" (Murray, pp. 288-289). In *Vanity Fair*, Thackeray traces these shifts in power through events in his characters' lives. Early in the novel, young William Dobbin, a grocer's son, is taunted by snobbish schoolmates "who rightly considered that the selling of goods by retail is a shameful and infamous practice, meriting the contempt and scorn of all real gentlemen" (*Vanity Fair*, pp. 48-49). Dobbin, however, ends the novel as a gentleman of leisure living on a country estate. Similarly, the opportunistic Becky Sharp experiences a meteoric rise and fall in Regency society, only to reinvent herself at the end of the novel as a middle-class philanthropist in the 1830s, as the powers of the aristocracy wane: "She busies herself in works of piety. . . . Her name is in all the Charity Lists. The Destitute Orange-girl, the Neglected Washerwoman, the Distressed Muffin-man, find in her a fast and generous friend. She is always having stalls at Fancy Fairs for the benefit of these hapless beings" (*Vanity Fair*, p. 877).

The Novel in Focus

Plot summary. The novel begins with two pupils, Amelia Sedley and Becky Sharp, leaving Miss Pinkerton's Academy for Young Ladies at Chiswick Mall, where pupils are taught music, dancing, spelling, and some geography and French. Amelia, a rich merchant's daughter, receives affectionate farewells from her schoolmates, while the departure of Becky, the impoverished orphan of an artist and a French opera dancer, goes virtually unnoticed. As the two young ladies ride away in a carriage, Becky throws a copy of Johnson's Dictionary, grudgingly bestowed upon her by Miss Pinkerton as a farewell present, out the window.

Despite their different backgrounds and personalities, Amelia and Becky have become good

George Osborne, dressed in his soldier's regalia, assists his wife Amelia into her carriage in this illustration from the original edition of *Vanity Fair*.

friends while at school, and Becky has been invited to stay for a few weeks at Amelia's home before taking up a position as a governess for the Crawley family. At the Sedleys' house in Russell Square, London, Becky meets Amelia's older brother, Joseph (Jos), an awkward but wealthy man who is home on leave from military service in India. Determined to snare a rich, socially respectable husband, Becky sets out to captivate Joseph, who easily succumbs to her charms. Romantic Amelia tries to encourage the relationship by arranging a party at Vauxhill Gardens—a public pleasure-spot—that will provide an opportunity for Jos to propose. Jos, Becky, Amelia, Amelia's own suitor Lieutenant George Osborne, and George's old school friend and fellow army officer, William Dobbin, all attend this party, but a nervous Jos gets drunk and makes a public spectacle of himself. The next morning, ill and embarrassed, he decides to return to India and writes a letter asking Becky to forget everything that has passed between them. George Osborne is secretly pleased that he will not be marrying into a family containing a nobody like Becky, who senses his satisfaction and blames him for her disappointed hopes.

Unable to remain any longer at Russell Square, Becky takes up her position as a governess at Queen's Crawley, a country estate. The family consists of Sir Pitt Crawley, a cantankerous old miser; his spiritless second wife, Lady Crawley; their children, Becky's pupils; and Sir Pitt's adult sons from a previous marriage, Pitt and Rawdon. Becky soon manages to ingratiate herself with the Crawley men, especially Sir Pitt and his younger son, Rawdon, a dashing army captain. Witty Becky also captivates Miss Mathilda Crawley, a rich, elderly spinster aunt of the family, who arrives at Queen's Crawley for a visit. After Miss Crawley falls ill during her visit and must return to London for her health, she demands that Becky accompany her as her nurse and companion.

Ensconced in Miss Crawley's household, Becky quickly establishes her ascendancy over the rest of the staff. Rawdon, a favorite nephew of Miss Crawley's and the main contender to inherit her vast fortune, calls frequently to visit his aunt and pay secret court to Becky. Meanwhile, back at Queen's Crawley, Lady Crawley falls ill and dies. A few days later, Sir Pitt Crawley turns up at Miss Crawley's London house and proposes to an astonished Becky, who stuns everyone by confessing that she is already married. Although Becky initially tries to conceal her husband's identity, it is soon discovered that she is married to Rawdon. Becky decamps from Miss Crawley's house to go live with her husband. Sir Pitt is outraged, and Miss Crawley, incensed to learn of Becky's low parentage, disinherits her nephew and takes to her sickbed again.

Meanwhile, the Sedley family has fallen on hard times. Mr. Sedley finds himself bankrupt after a succession of poor business deals. George Osborne's tyrannical father orders his son to break his engagement to Amelia and marry a wealthy mulatto heiress instead. But William Dobbin, himself secretly in love with Amelia for years and deeply affected by her pining over George, persuades his somewhat weak-willed friend to defy his father and marry Amelia. Not knowing of Dobbin's involvement, Amelia worships her husband all the more for marrying her in her impoverished state. Dobbin tries to reconcile Mr. Osborne to his son's marriage, but the furious father refuses to listen and makes plans to disinherit George.

While honeymooning in Brighton, George and Amelia meet Becky and Rawdon, living extravagantly, despite having little money. Soon after, Dobbin arrives in Brighton himself with the depressing news about Mr. Osborne's intransigence and the far more alarming report that the regiment has been ordered to Belgium following Napoleon's escape from Elba.

The newlywed couples meet again at Brussels, where Rawdon is now a military aide to General Tufto. Becky dazzles many officers with her wit and beauty; even George falls victim to her charms. Miserable over her husband's infatuation with Becky, Amelia hardly notices Dobbin's steadfast attendance on her. Meanwhile, more English troops arrive in Brussels in preparation for the impending battle with the French. Jos Sedley, returned from India, also resurfaces in Brussels, but as a civilian. Parties and balls, despite the military tension, continue unabated; on the 15th of June, the duchess of Richmond gives an elaborate ball, attended by the cream of Brussels society. Becky outshines many of the women there, and George secretly slips a note into her bouquet. A depressed Amelia leaves the ball early. After her departure, the officers receive their marching orders: Napoleon has entered Belgium.

Returning home, George and Rawdon bid farewell to their wives before joining their regiments. As the Battle of Waterloo rages and the wounded are borne back to Brussels, many civilians panic and flee the city, including Jos Sedley. Amelia remains behind, frantic for news of George, while Becky calmly makes preparations for her own survival should Rawdon fall. Rawdon returns safely, but George is killed.

After the war, Becky and Rawdon, now promoted to lieutenant-colonel, go to live in Paris. Becky becomes the toast of Parisian society and bears Rawdon a son and heir. The widowed Amelia, meanwhile, returns to her parents in England. Almost out of her mind with grief, Amelia rallies after the birth of her son, whom she names after his father, George. Dobbin, who also survived Waterloo, tries to mend the breach between the Sedleys and Osbornes, but again, the embittered Mr. Osborne refuses. After providing what financial assistance he can to the Sedleys, Dobbin, himself now a major, leaves for India. Amelia, doting on her infant son and idolizing George's memory, fails to discern Dobbin's love for her.

Elsewhere in England, Miss Crawley dies, leaving the bulk of her fortune to Rawdon's brother, Pitt, who has now succeeded their father as baronet. Rawdon and Becky quickly leave France—without paying their bills—to make peace with the new head of the family. Becky quickly ingratiates herself with her brother-in-law, to the dismay of Sir Pitt's well-bred wife, Lady Jane. The Rawdon Crawleys continue to live extravagantly on credit, and Becky is even presented at court. Now moving in the topmost circles of London society, Becky attracts a higher class of admirers, chiefly Lord Steyne, a wealthy, powerful marquis. Captivated by Steyne's money and influence, Becky neglects Rawdon and ignores their son altogether. Matters come to a head when Rawdon is arrested for debt; writing to Becky, he asks her to bail him out, but she claims to have no money to free him. Lady Jane, however, comes to Rawdon's rescue. Returning home, Rawdon finds Becky, resplendent in jewels, entertaining Lord Steyne. Furious, Rawdon tears off his wife's jewels, knocks down Lord Steyne, and flings a brooch at the nobleman, scarring him for life. On discovering that Becky has been hoarding a secret cache of money, the disillusioned Rawdon leaves her, entrusting care of his son to Lady Jane and taking a post as governor of Coventry Island. Repudiated by the other Crawleys, Becky flees to the Continent.

Meanwhile, Amelia has been tending to her aging parents and struggling to give her son the best of everything, despite their poverty. Old Mr. Osborne finally relents enough to propose to raise young George as his heir, while allowing him to see his mother occasionally. After some consideration, Amelia sadly agrees. Old Osborne spoils his grandson, as he did his father before him, but the worst of the damage is prevented by Dobbin's return to England after 12 years. Accompanied by Jos, who has become a wealthy man, Dobbin sets about improving the Sedleys' circumstances. Mrs. Sedley has died, but Jos insists on moving his father and sister into a more comfortable home and providing for their needs. In time, Mr. Sedley and old Mr. Osborne die, the latter having become reconciled to Amelia before his death. In his will, Osborne leaves most of his fortune to George and appoints Amelia as her son's guardian. Dobbin confesses his love to Amelia, but she is determined to remain faithful to George's memory.

Uncomfortable in society, despite her improved social status, Amelia agrees to take a short trip abroad with Jos, George, and Dobbin. While staying in the German town of Pumpernickel, the Sedleys meet Becky, who has been leading a vagabond existence since being cast off by Rawdon and the Crawley family. Becky's hard-luck story wins over Jos and Amelia, but Dobbin continues to distrust her, reminding Amelia of Becky's flirtation with George. Infuriated, Amelia quarrels outright with Dobbin, who announces that he is no longer going to waste his life pining for her love and leaves Germany.

Shocked, then saddened by her suitor's desertion, Amelia finally writes to Dobbin, entreating his forgiveness. Meanwhile, Becky, who respects Dobbin as a worthy adversary, shows Amelia the note George gave her all those years ago in Brussels, in which he asked Becky to elope with him. Having lost her illusions about George, Amelia is now free to love and marry Dobbin. Becky sets her sights on Jos again, accompanying him wherever he goes. Jos later dies under somewhat mysterious circumstances, and Becky inherits most of the proceeds of his life insurance policy.

As the years pass, Amelia and Dobbin have a daughter, Jane, and develop a cordial friendship with the Crawleys of Queen's Crawley. Dobbin no longer worships Amelia, but he is still a kind and considerate husband. Young Rawdon, Becky's neglected son, succeeds to the baronetcy after the deaths of his father—who succumbs to yellow fever at Coventry Island—and his uncle. He pays a liberal allowance to his mother, Becky, now living in England again, but refuses to see her. Acquiring a reputation for piety, Becky presents herself as a virtuous, much-injured widow who performs charitable deeds. The novel concludes with the melancholy questions: "Which of us is happy in this world? Which of us has his desire? or, having it, is satisfied?" (*Vanity Fair*, p. 878).

Women, marriage, and money. While *Vanity Fair* is often described as a panoramic novel, covering a wide range of topics, it returns most frequently to the subject of marriage, especially from a woman's perspective. In the early 1800s, respectable or would-be respectable women had few options beyond making advantageous marriages, a circumstance reflected in the parallel matrimonial journeys of Amelia Sedley and Becky Sharp. Raised in comfort as a rich merchant's daughter, Amelia can initially afford to be complacent: her parents and old Mr. Osborne arranged her future marriage to George Osborne when she was still a child. By contrast, Becky, the poor orphan, must scheme to escape the drudgery of a governess's life: "Of what else have young ladies to think, but husbands? Of what else do their dear mammas think? 'I must be my own mamma,' said Rebecca" (*Vanity Fair*, p. 108).

What the sentimental Amelia does not realize, however, and the calculating Becky is all too aware of, is the extent to which marriage, money, and position are intertwined. Devoted to George, Amelia is shattered when his family terminates the engagement after her father loses his wealth: "She lived in her past life. . . . [George's] looks and tones, his dress, what he said and how—these relics and remembrances of dead affection were all that were left her in the world" (*Vanity Fair*, p. 217). Amelia is not the only woman to suffer from the mercenary nature of the marriage market. The eldest daughter of the Osborne family, who once loved an artist her father considered unsuitable, is forced to remain single, lest she forfeit the sizable inheritance old Osborne intends to leave her on his death. Lady Crawley, who began life as an ironmonger's daughter, has a similarly tragic history, having sacrificed the man she loved for Sir Pitt Crawley's title and estate:

> When her husband was rude to her she was apathetic: whenever he struck her she cried. . . . Oh, Vanity Fair!—Vanity Fair! This might have been, but for you, a cheery lass; Peter Butt and Rose a happy man and wife, in a snug farm, with a hearty family, and an honest portion of pleasures, cares, hopes, and struggles:—but a title and a coach and four [horses] are toys more precious than happiness in Vanity Fair.
> (*Vanity Fair*, p. 98)

While Becky suffers none of the heartache endured by Amelia and other female characters in the novel, her relentless self-interest still backfires on her. Having captivated both old Sir Pitt Crawley and his younger son, Rawdon, Becky elopes with Rawdon, only to be stunned by his now-widowed father's marriage proposal: "Rebecca thought to herself, in all the woes of repentance—and I might have been my lady! I might have led that old man whither I would. . . . I would have had the handsomest carriage in London, and a box at the opera; and I would have been presented next season" (*Vanity Fair*, p. 186).

Thackeray's cynical depiction of the marriage market reflects both the times in which *Vanity Fair* takes place and those in which it was written. Late-seventeenth- to eighteenth-century attitudes toward love, marriage, and child rearing had become increasingly permissive, but late-eighteenth- to nineteenth-century attitudes saw the pendulum swing back in the opposite direction. Parents reasserted their authority over their children's futures, especially their choice of careers and marriage partners. Young girls were expected to be obedient daughters and to become subservient wives. Regency author Hannah More suggested in such works as *Coelebs in Search of a Wife* (1809) that the ideal woman should be "devoted to domestic duties, religious, modest in dress, silent unless spoken to, deferential to men, and devoted to good works" (Stone, p. 670). Legally, women owned nothing once they were married—a circumstance that would not be altered until the passage of the Married Women's Property Acts in 1870 and 1882—which may have made Becky's secret hoarding of money from her husband understandable, if shocking, to Thackeray's readers.

To a degree, sons also lived under the thumbs of their domineering fathers during the 1800s: "At this period, middle- and upper-class sons were financially dependent on their parents well into their adult life, as the expense and duration of training for a professional career grew longer and longer" (Stone, p. 671). In *Vanity Fair*, old Mr. Osborne disowns his only son, George, after the latter disobeys him by marrying the penniless Amelia instead of the wealthy heiress selected as his bride.

Sources and literary context. Thackeray's famous title was derived from John Bunyan's **The Pilgrim's Progress** (1678; also in *WLAIT 3: British and Irish Literature and Its Times*), which relates the allegorical journey of the pilgrim, Christian, through such places as the Slough of Despond and the Valley of the Shadow until he reaches the Celestial City (Heaven). In Bunyan's story, Christian and his traveling companion, Faithful, visit Vanity Fair, described as "a fair wherein should be sold all sorts of vanity . . . houses, lands, trades, places, honours, preferments, titles, countries, kingdoms, lusts, pleasures; and delights of all sorts, as whores, bawds, wives, husbands, children, masters, servants, lives, blood, bodies, souls, silver, gold, pearls, precious stones and what not" (Bunyan, pp. 96-97). Moreover, in Bunyan's Vanity Fair, "there is at all times to be seen jugglings, cheats, games, plays, fools, apes, knaves, and rogues, and that of every kind" (Bunyan, p. 97).

In "Before the Curtain," his famous prologue to *Vanity Fair*, Thackeray extends Bunyan's metaphor, describing how "the Manager of the Performance" presides over plays featuring "a great quantity of eating and drinking, making love and jilting, laughing and the contrary, smoking, cheating, fighting, dancing, and fiddling . . . Yes, this is VANITY FAIR: not a moral place certainly; nor a merry one, though very noisy" (*Vanity Fair*, p. 1). Thackeray depicts his own characters as puppets in a show, performing their antics before "the very best company in this empire," adding, "The famous little Becky Puppet has been pronounced to be uncommonly flexible in the joints, and lively on the wire: the Amelia Doll, though it has had a smaller circle of admirers, has yet been carved and dressed with the greatest care by the artist" (*Vanity Fair*, p. 2).

Despite Thackeray's apparent dismissal of his characters as mere marionettes, he did actually draw upon real-life friends and acquaintances for inspiration. Becky Sharp, for example, was partly based on Theresa Reviss; a willful, capricious little beauty with aspirations to become an opera singer, Teresa was the illegitimate daughter of Thackeray's friend, Charles Buller. Likewise, meek Amelia Sedley, the novel's other female protagonist, shared her frailty and artless nature with Isabella Shawe, Thackeray's "poor little wife" (Thackeray in Ferris, p. 8). Thackeray was less tender with his mother-in-law, who had resented her son-in-law and displayed little sympathy toward her mentally ill daughter; Mrs. Shawe served as the model for several unpleasant older women in *Vanity Fair*, including the embittered Mrs. Sedley and the domineering Lady Southdown.

When creating his male characters, George Osborne and William Osborne, however, Thackeray drew not upon his personal life but upon English history. George, whom Becky terms a "padded booby" and "low-bred Cockney dandy," shares his name with the king Thackeray most detested: the dissolute George IV, who served as Prince Regent during the era in which *Vanity Fair* takes place (Vanity Fair, p. 866).

Vanity Fair may be said to operate on several levels: as a historical novel that intertwines the destinies of its fictional characters with real-life people and events from history; as a satire that reveals the ultimate pettiness and "vanity" of English society; and as a domestic comedy rooted in the everyday problems of a predominantly mercantile class. Unlike novelist Charles Dickens, his contemporary and rival, Thackeray eschewed flamboyance and theatricality in favor of the ordinary and commonplace, arguing: "The Art of Novels *is* to represent Nature, to convey as strongly as possible the sentiment of reality . . . in a drawing-room drama a coat is a coat and a poker a poker; and must be nothing else according to my ethics, not an embroidered tunic nor a great red-hot instrument like the Pantomime weapon" (Thackeray in Ferris, p. 36).

Events in History at the Time the Novel Was Written

England in the 1840s. The early years of the Victorian Age (1837-1901) were fraught with difficulties. The Reform Bill of 1832 had ushered in dramatic changes, extending the right to vote to all males who owned property worth 10 pounds or more in annual rent. Moreover, the bill dismantled the longstanding electoral system that allowed "rotten boroughs" (depopulated communities) to elect candidates chosen by the local squire, while new industrial cities went underrepresented in Parliament. Political power thus shifted from the conservative landowners to the rising middle class. Thackeray notes this transition toward the end of *Vanity Fair*: Sir Pitt Crawley the Younger is forced to abandon his political career and return to Queen's Crawley "after the passing of the Reform Bill. . . . All idea of a peerage was out of the question, the baronet's two seats in Parliament being lost. He was both out of pocket and out of spirits by that catastrophe, failed in his health, and prophesied the speedy ruin of the Empire" (*Vanity Fair*, p. 872).

While the "speedy ruin" foreseen by Sir Pitt did not materialize, the decade after the passage of the Reform Bill nonetheless brought many problems: a severe economic depression, widespread unemployment, increasingly abysmal working conditions in mines and factories, and serious crop failures in England and the outbreak of the potato famine in Ireland in 1845. It is little wonder, then, that this period came to be known as the Hungry 1840s. Sir Robert Peel, the Tory Prime Minister, came to believe that, under such conditions, traditional protectionism of British agricultural interests was unfeasible, and the Corn Laws were repealed by Parliament in 1846. A system of free trade that permitted the importation of goods requiring only minimal tariff duties was soon introduced, relieving the worst of the Victorian economic crises. While the Chartists—a large organization of workingmen calling for such legislative reforms as further extending the voting franchise and using a secret ballot—staged demonstrations and gave fiery speeches that caused some anxieties among the general public, their agitation did not erupt into violent conflict. Unlike France and Italy, which were experiencing armed protests and revolts in the late 1840s, England was at peace and was soon to enjoy two decades of tranquil prosperity.

While the threat of revolutionary violence was ultimately avoided in England during the 1840s,

contemporary writers were nonetheless affected by the hardships and injustices they experienced or witnessed. A new tone of moral indignation crept into their works; many authors launched outright attacks on what they saw as the shortcomings and hypocrisies of Victorian society. Charles Dickens, arguably Thackeray's most famous contemporary and literary rival, attacked the abuses that took place in orphanages and workhouses in *Oliver Twist* (1839) and urban squalor in *Hard Times* (1854). In *Vanity Fair*, Thackeray himself employs a similarly inflammatory tone toward the spendthrift upper classes when he scathingly describes how Becky and her husband Rawdon Crawley manage to live lavishly in London on virtually "nothing a year," ruining their landlord, Raggles, in the process:

> Crawley got his house for nothing; for though Raggles had to pay taxes and rates, and the interest of the mortgage . . . and the insurance of his life; and the charges for his children at school and the value of the meat and drink which his own family—and for a time that of Colonel Crawley too—consumed; and though the poor wretch was utterly ruined by this transaction, his children being flung on the streets, and himself driven into the Fleet Prison: yet somebody must pay even for gentleman who live for nothing a year—and so it was this unlucky Raggles was made the representative of Colonel Crawley's defective capital.
>
> (*Vanity Fair*, p. 466)

Positions of women after 1830. During the Victorian Age, women's issues became an increasingly important concern. Although embryonic stirrings of feminism had been noted as early as the late eighteenth century with the publication of Mary Wollstonecraft's **A Vindication of the Rights of Woman** (1792; also in *WLAIT 3: British and Irish Literature and Its Times*), it was not until the mid-nineteenth century that the women's movement acquired a definite shape and agenda. As women left the domestic sphere to work outside the home—whether in factory jobs or more genteel professions like teaching and nursing—they became ever more conscious of sexual inequality in public and private life. Politically, women were second-class citizens, who could not vote or hold public office. Petitions advocating women's suffrage were submitted to Parliament as early as the 1840s but were unsuccessful. Nineteenth-century feminists also pushed for larger educational opportunities for women; in 1837, the year Victoria ascended to the throne, women were still denied admission to England's universities. In 1848, however, the first women's college was established in London.

Despite these efforts, employment prospects for most middle- and lower-class women remained limited during the first half of the century. To begin with, there was an imbalance in the population: the women significantly outnumbered the men, resulting in a surplus of unmarried women, all in search of livelihoods. Thousands of lower-class women took factory jobs, but the terrible working conditions and nationwide economic depression drove many into prostitution.

Middle-class women likewise found few respectable employment opportunities, other than becoming a governess to the children of middle- or upper-class families. Such a position usually lasted only until the children were old enough to go away to school or, in the case of the daughters, to be brought out into society. Moreover, governesses were often poorly paid and shabbily treated, patronized by their employers and shunned by the other servants. A governess's status in a household was usually ambiguous—she was too genteel to be classed with the cook or maids but too "low" to be considered a member of the family who employed her. If a governess was good-looking, she might become the object of unwelcome attentions from the men in the household, a development that could easily lead to her dismissal.

The plight of the governess was a popular subject among nineteenth-century novels, the most famous of these being *Jane Eyre* by Charlotte Brontë, who worked—unhappily—as a governess for several years before achieving success as a writer. Thackeray's *Vanity Fair* is also considered a "governess novel" to some extent; early in the story, Becky Sharp complains to Amelia Sedley of her own humble station as governess to the Crawley children at Queen's Crawley: "I am to be treated as one of the family, except on company days when the young ladies and I are to dine upstairs" (*Vanity Fair*, p. 91). Moreover, George Osborne, Amelia's suitor, displays the snobbery often directed at governesses by their "betters" when he tries to thwart Jos Sedley's courtship of Becky: "Who's this little schoolgirl that is ogling and making love to him? Hang it, the family's low enough already, without *her*. A governess is all very well, but I'd rather have a lady for my sister-in-law. . . . I've proper pride, and know my own station: let her know hers" (*Vanity Fair*, p. 71).

Reviews. Thackery was held in high regard by fellow novelists—in the preface to the second edition of *Jane Eyre*, Charlotte Brontë described him as the first social regenerator of the day. Critics of the time expressed admiration for *Vanity Fair's* keen wit and satire. Comparing Thackeray favorably to eighteenth-century novelists Henry Fielding and Samuel Richardson, John Forster wrote in the *Examiner*: "*Vanity Fair* is the work of a mind, at once accomplished and subtle, which has enjoyed opportunities of observing many and varied circles of society. Its author is endowed with penetrating discrimination and just appreciation of character, and with a rare power of graphic delineation" (Forster in Tillotson, p. 54). Among Thackeray's large cast of characters, William Dobbin, called "a noble portrait of awkward devoted affection," and Becky Sharp, who "commits every conceivable wickedness . . . without in the least losing those smart, good-tempered, sensible manners and ways, which ingratiate her with the reader," were singled out for particular praise (Forster in Tillotson, pp. 55-56). Robert Stephen Rintoul of the *Spectator* called Becky "a very wonderfully-drawn picture," adding, "As a creation or character, we know not where Rebecca can be matched in prose fiction" (Rintoul in Tillotson, p. 60).

Simultaneously, Thackeray's critics expressed certain reservations about the completeness of his portrayal of English society. Forster complained that "the atmosphere of the work is overloaded with these exhalations of human folly and wickedness. We gasp for a more liberal alternation of refreshing breezes of unsophisticated honesty. . . . But the stifling ingredients are administered by Mr. Thackeray to excess, without the necessary relief" (Forster in Tillotson, p. 57). Robert Bell, writing for *Fraser's Magazine,* was even more severe, calling Thackeray's characters "as vicious and odious as a clever condensation of the vilest qualities can make them. . . . Cunning, low pride, selfishness, envy, malice, and all uncharitableness, are scattered amongst them with impartial liberality. It does not enter into the design of *Vanity Fair* to qualify these bitter ingredients with a little sweetness now and then" (Bell in Tillotson, p. 63). Like Forster, Bell believed that "more light and air would have rendered [*Vanity Fair*] more agreeable and more healthy. The author's genius takes him off too much in the direction of satire" (Bell in Tillotson, p. 65). Bell nonetheless acknowledged the novel's strengths, conceding, "The originality of the treatment, the freshness and fluency of the style . . . inspire *[Vanity Fair]* with the charm of perpetual variety" (Bell in Tillotson, p. 67).

Significantly, Thackeray himself felt compelled to respond to Bell's criticisms. Thanking the critic for his "excellent article," Thackeray went on to defend his work, arguing,

> If I had put in more fresh air as you call it my object would have been defeated—It is to indicate, in cheerful terms, that we are for the most part an abominably foolish and selfish people "desperately wicked" and all eager after vanities.
>
> (Thackeray in Williams, p. 60)

—Pamela S. Loy

For More Information

Bunyan, John. *The Pilgrim's Progress: From this World to that which is to Come.* 1678. Reprint, New York: Fleming H. Revell, 1903.

Chandler, David. *Waterloo: The Hundred Days* . New York: Macmillan, 1980.

Clarke, Micael M. *Thackeray and Women.* De Kalb: Northern Illinois University Press, 1995.

Ferris, Ina. *William Makepeace Thackeray.* Boston: Twayne, 1983.

Murray, Venetia. *An Elegant Madness: High Society in Regency England.* New York: Viking Penguin, 1999.

Pool, Daniel. *Dickens' Fur Coat and Charlotte's Unanswered Letters: The Rows and Romances of England's Great Victorian Novelists.* New York: HarperPerennial, 1998.

————. *What Jane Austen Ate and Charles Dickens Knew: From Fox-Hunting to Whist—the Facts of Daily Life in 19th-Century England.* New York: Touchstone, 1993.

Stone, Lawrence. *The Family, Sex and Marriage in England 1500-1800.* New York: Harper & Row, 1977.

Thackeray, William Makepeace. *Vanity Fair: A Novel without a Hero.* Oxford: Oxford University Press, 1983.

Tillotson, Geoffrey, and Donald Hawes, eds. *Thackeray: The Critical Heritage.* London: Routledge & Kegan Paul, 1968.

Trevelyan, G. M. *Illustrated English Social History.* Vol 4. London: Longmans, Green, 1942.

Williams, Ioan M. *Thackeray* . New York: Arco, 1969.

A Vindication of the Rights of Woman

by
Mary Wollstonecraft

Born April 27, 1759, Mary Wollstonecraft became one of the most influential intellectuals of late eighteenth-century Britain. In her short but turbulent career, she worked as a governess, a teacher, a book reviewer, a political essayist, a historical and travel writer, and a novelist. Her most widely known work is *A Vindication of the Rights of Woman*. A product of the Enlightenment tradition, which stressed the importance of reason, Wollstonecraft sought to elevate women from their dependence on men through "a revolution in female manners" (Wollstonecraft, *A Vindication of the Rights of Woman*, p. 192). Inspired by the rational ideals put forth by the supporters of the French Revolution and her own life experiences, Wollstonecraft wrote passionately throughout the 1790s about the suffering of women and men of various classes. In 1790 she published *A Vindication of the Rights of Men*, which, like Thomas Paine's *Rights of Man (1791-92)*, asserted that there are "rights" that "men inherit at their birth" (Wollstonecraft, *Vindications: Rights of Men*, p. 43). In *A Vindication of the Rights of Woman* she shifts the focus to women. Women, she argues, have to become more independent and rational, and better educated. Such changes will make them finer companions for men, better tutors to their children, and generally more useful in society. Influenced by personal as well as political events, Wollstonecraft reached these conclusions based on her own experience and on turbulent developments in France and England during the early 1790s.

THE LITERARY WORK

A treatise on female education written and published in 1792.

SYNOPSIS

Written shortly after the French Revolution of 1789, Wollstonecraft's treatise argues for a cultural and social revolution to improve the minds, the character, and the conditions of women.

Events in History at the Time of the Treatise

Wollstonecraft's life. Mary Wollstonecraft was the second of seven children. Her father, unsuccessful at farming, consoled himself by drinking to excess and tyrannizing his timid wife. Mary's mother provided her with no more support than her father. Pampering her eldest son, Elizabeth Wollstonecraft was unusually severe with and neglectful of her other children. Consequently, Mary sought affection elsewhere, forming close ties with her sister, Eliza, and with her friend, Fanny Blood, both of whom she attempted to support financially and emotionally.

Intending to support her sister and herself, Wollstonecraft started a school with Fanny in 1784. The school was combined with a boarding house for women and their children, but in order for it to succeed, Wollstonecraft had to abide by traditional notions of "respectability,"

Mary Wollstonecraft

which called for girls to be educated for the marriage market. Dancing and French should be mandatory subjects, and music and drawing are recommended, declares Hester Chapone in *Letters on the Improvement of the Mind addressed to a Young Lady* (1773). On the other hand, "the classics and 'abstruce sciences'," should be "avoided at all costs because of 'the danger of pedantry'" in women (Chapone in Fletcher, p. 375). A few schools with a more academic curriculum for girls opened as the century wore on, especially in London, but most of the increasing number of girls' schools continued to feature subjects that would make their students desirable wives and mothers. Not only did Wollstonecraft have to be subservient to clients in the running of her school; she also had to manage most of the business aspects, and as a result, she found the whole enterprise a bit tiresome. Yet when the venture failed, after Fanny married and died in childbirth in 1786, Wollstonecraft grew severely depressed.

Until 1787 Wollstonecraft worked as a governess for an aristocratic family, the Kingsboroughs, in Ireland, after which she joined Joseph Johnson's circle of artists and intellectuals in London. This association with the radical Dissenting publisher was a fruitful one—by 1788 Wollstonecraft had become a regular contributor to Johnson's *Analytical Review,* critiquing novels, books for children, and essays on education. In

1787 Johnson published Wollstonecraft's *Thoughts on the Education of Daughters,* which questioned many traditional pedagogical methods and gave sensible, practical advice about raising girls. Like her *Original Stories from Real Life* (1788), a book of tales for children written about the same time, *Education of Daughters* tends to be severe and moralistic. Her first novel, *Mary, a Fiction* (1788), is less rigid; it reveals the difficulties of practicing some of the idealistic principles Wollstonecraft proclaims. With her published tract, *A Vindication of the Rights of Men* (1790), Wollstonecraft became a minor celebrity: when the first, anonymous edition of the work appeared, people thought it was written by one of the ablest men in London. A month later when the second edition appeared with Wollstonecraft's name, critics were surprised to find that it had been authored by a woman. The subject matter and the success of the piece inspired Wollstonecraft to write her most famous work, *A Vindication of the Rights of Woman* (1792), in which she argues on behalf of women's moral and rational worth.

The French Revolution. The storming of the Bastille, a political prison in Paris that stood as a symbol of despotism, not only led to the Declaration of the Rights of Man in France, but to a whole series of transformative events, including the proclamation of a French Republic in 1792 and the dissolution of the French monarchy. King Louis XVI and his wife, Marie Antoinette, were guillotined in 1793, and many priests and nobility were removed from their powerful positions. The Declaration, proclaiming *liberté, égalité, fraternité* (personal liberty, equality before the law, the brotherhood of man), was initially viewed by many—in France and elsewhere—as a turning point, marking the beginning of a new age. In Britain, the events of the French Revolution began a decade of lively controversy about the rights and liberties of women and men.

The controversy began when Dr. Richard Price, a Dissenting minister, delivered a sermon called "On the Love of Our Country" on November 4, 1789, to The Revolution Society in London (an organization originally formed to celebrate the Glorious Revolution of 1688). The Dissenters were already unconventional in that they dissented from the forms and rituals established by the Church of England. Comprised largely of lower-middle-class merchants, Dissenters disapproved of aristocratic frivolity and ecclesiastical pomp and tended to rely more on rational thought than on rituals in religion. Thus, Price's support of the French Revolution was hardly surprising. In his speech, he praised the underlying principles of this revolution and claimed that the desire for liberty was spreading. His praise of the French National Assembly alarmed supporters of the status quo, who felt that his words threatened the English king and the Church of England. Within a few weeks, presses were publishing incensed replies, one of the most important of which was Edmund Burke's *Reflections on the Revolution in France* (1790). Burke wished to rally English sentiment and patriotism in support of the existing aristocratic system of government. He linked political stability with the orderly running of the English family:

> Burke apotheosizes the patriarchal ideal and the social and sentimental structures which enforce it: the retired life of the country gentleman, the orderly transmission of property, the stabilizing principle of generational continuity, the grateful deference of youth to venerable age, and of course the chastity of wives and daughters which alone can guarantee the social identity of men and heirs. (Johnson, p. 5).

For Burke, the Revolution was an unnatural event, for it overturned laws. He portrayed the French revolutionaries as a mob of bloodthirsty ruffians seeking to break with time-honored traditions of family and kingdom.

Wollstonecraft's *A Vindication of the Rights of Men*, written in less than 30 days and published anonymously, was the first of many replies to Burke. In this work she counters Burke on such subjects as the nature of the French Revolution and its reception in England, the definition of rights, the nature of the British constitution, and the character and condition of the aristocracy and the poor. *A Vindication of the Rights of Men* gave Wollstonecraft confidence in writing a form of political disquisition thought unsuitable for women at the time. It also forced her to think about the relationship between privilege, education, and 'natural' birthright, and about property, moral worth, and individualism. She began, because of the experience, "to see both what complicated connections exist between the interests of women and those of the aspiring middle classes and how thoroughly the categories by which women are taught to estimate their worth emerge from the special needs of those who rule" (Poovey, p. 63).

Debates about women's education. The political and social crises caused by the French Revolution brought gender identity and the family under intense scrutiny. In late eighteenth-century Europe, there was much written about female propriety, femininity, and the proper roles for women in society. Novels, conduct books, and educational treatises represented women as delicate creatures, modest, chaste, dutiful, and self-effacing. One good example can be seen in *A Gossip's Story* by novelist Jane West (1758-1852). The ideal heroine, Louisa, is described as "tall and elegant, her eyes expressed intelligence and ingenuous modesty" (West, I:18). Louisa dedicates her whole life to the service of her father, whom she obeys without question. Her favorite amusements are "her books, her needle, her music, her garden, the society of her beloved father, and those active exertions of charity. . . . She visited the sick, consoled the afflicted, instructed the ignorant, and reproved the idle" (West, II:61-62). This dutiful character is eventually rewarded by a happy marriage to a worthy man after her father dies. To be sure, such novels presented an image of the ideal woman, but this image was contradictory: "Women are presented as both naturally virtuous, and in particular need of instruction; feminine virtue is celebrated both for its own sake, and because it makes a woman desirable; it is uniquely powerful, yet women are constantly vulnerable" (Jones, p. vii).

IMPORTANT DATES IN WOLLSTONECRAFT'S LIFE

1759 Born the second of seven children to middle-class parents.

1784 Persuades her sister Eliza to flee her husband and infant; starts a school at Newington Green.

1786 Works as governess for Lord and Lady Kingsborough.

1787 Publishes *Thoughts on the Education of Daughters*.

1788 Publishes *Original Stories from Real Life* and *Mary, A Fiction;* contributes to the *Analytical Review*.

1790 Publishes *A Vindication of the Rights of Men*.

1792 Publishes *A Vindication of the Rights of Woman*.

1793 Begins affair with Gilbert Imlay.

1794 Has a daughter, Fanny Imlay.

1795 Discovers Gilbert Imlay's infidelity; attempts suicide twice.

1796 Meets William Godwin; becomes pregnant by him.

1797 Publishes *Letters from Sweden;* marries Godwin; dies from giving birth to their daughter, Mary.

Inspired by women's activism in France during the French Revolution, Wollstonecraft hoped her essay would bring about a nonviolent revolution for women's rights.

Some of the most influential voices on the education of girls in the period came from French philosopher Jean-Jacques Rousseau, whose *Emile, or On Education* was first published in 1762, and Dr. John Gregory, who wrote *A Father's Legacy to His Daughters* in 1774. Rousseau's *Emile* is an extended tract on education. It reads like a philosophical essay about the nature of human beings, like an advice handbook for parents, and like a series of short stories. The text traces the growth of Emile from infancy to adulthood and ends with a discussion of the education of "Sophie," an ideal wife for Emile. Early in *Emile,* Rousseau is concerned with the physical well-being of the child. He writes of the need to teach the male child to "preserve himself," to "exercise his body, his organs, his senses, his strength," and to learn through questioning and experience rather than coercion and force (Rousseau, pp. 42, 94). This concern with the early years and the development of the child was influenced by such philosophers as John Locke. In **An Essay Concerning Human Understanding** (1689; also in *WLAIT 3: British and Irish Literature and Its Times*) Locke argues that human understanding originates from the world through the senses. Human behavior and character result from interacting with the environment and from education, rather than from innate nature. Rousseau echoes these ideas when he says: "Nature . . . is only habit. . . . We are born with the use of our senses, and from our birth we are affected in various ways by the objects surrounding us" (Rousseau, p. 39). Through his observations and his senses, Emile learns to love himself, and then learns to love others because he needs and depends on them.

In contrast to the boy's carefully planned education, Rousseau reveals a patriarchal and condescending attitude towards the upbringing of a girl. Rousseau believes that the sexes are different: "one [the male] ought to be active and strong, the other [the female] passive and weak" (Rousseau, p. 358). For Rousseau, a woman "is made specially to please man" and "ought to make herself agreable to man instead of arousing him" (Rousseau, p. 358). His scheme of education for girls follows his conviction that they are best suited to be wives and mothers. He believes women are naturally more docile and modest than men, but nonetheless stresses that gentleness and modesty must be cultivated and learned. It is not enough that a woman be "modest, attentive, reserved—she must also "give evidence of her virtue to the eyes of others as well as to her own conscience" (Rousseau, p. 361). In *A Vindication of the Rights* of *Woman*, Wollstonecraft takes issue with these somewhat contradictory views about women's nature.

Dr. John Gregory espoused similar ideas in a treatise addressed to his daughters. Like Rousseau, Gregory believed that women possessed a stronger sense of delicacy and modesty, along with "natural softness and sensibility" (Gregory, p. 4). He asserted that a woman ought to cultivate this modesty by being "silent in company," by being "even cautious of displaying . . . good sense," and by keeping her learning "a profound secret" in order to prevent others from supposing that she thought herself superior (Gregory, p. 13). Many women were thus placed in the difficult situation of having to assume or adopt a position of docility and submission in order to fit in with society's expectations of them.

Like Rousseau, Gregory felt that a woman's province consisted entirely of "the domestic economy of a family" (Gregory, p. 21). Her education should thus focus on such skills as dress, dancing, music, and drawing, along with needlework and reading to pass all the solitary hours that women must spend at home. Such a prescription for a woman's education was, unsurprisingly, scorned by many female thinkers. Catherine Macaulay, author of *Letters on Education* (1790), writes that this system of instruction corrupts and debilitates women's minds and bodies. Like Wollstonecraft, Macaulay argued against the encouragement of coquetry and deception in women, by which girls pretend to be the modest creatures Rousseau and Gregory want them to be. She conceded that women are inferior in corporal strength, but believed women's foibles and vices follow only from their situation and education.

The culture of sensibility. Sensibility—associated with refined emotionalism, melancholy, distress, and expressed by, for example, crying and swooning—was a key social term in the second half of the eighteenth century. According to experts of the day, sensibility stemmed from the nervous system. Physician Dr. George Cheyne (1671-1743) popularized the belief that fibers, including those of the muscles, the bone, and the more delicate membranes, tendons, and nerves, all carry sensations to the brain. These fibers are elastic and the more they are compressed, the greater the degree of one's sensibility. In time, people invested the term with spiritual and moral values; the word "sensibility" became correlated with conscious awareness, feeling, and ultimately with gender-specific traits. Because of their sup-

posed delicacy, women were associated with the so-called "cult of sensibility."

In literature, sensibility (or sentimentalism) expresses itself in conventional situations that arouse strong emotions in readers. Some of these situations and stock characters include the deathbed scene of an aged, tender father bidding farewell to his children, a distressed woman surrounded by helpless infants, and depictions of the penniless and otherwise unfortunate. Such scenes were meant to evoke socially connected emotions—compassion, benevolence, and pity, for example—as opposed to selfishness. Sentimental literature tended to value country charms, simplicity, candor, and sincerity, and was suspicious of wealth, materialism, imperialism, and power. The cult of sensibility worked well with the aims of the humanitarian reformers of the late eighteenth century. Being preoccupied with the pain and suffering of others alerted women and sentimental men to the plight of distressed groups, from the poor and the sick, to mistreated children, exploited animals, the insane, slaves, prisoners, and exiles.

There were negative and disturbing effects of sensibility, however: "Men and women of sensibility (actual or fictional) frequently drive themselves to emotional extremes (or chronic states) like hysteria or melancholy, only to be temporarily stopped by mental or physical exhaustion" (Conger, p. xv). The point is that the language of sensibility not only describes emotions, it also creates states of feeling (like anxiety and desire) and can inspire or intensify emotional conditions such as ecstasy, love, or melancholy. By the 1790s, excessive sensibility was being attacked and satirized because it led to immoral and eccentric behavior, including suicide, religious despair, and infidelity. Jane Austen's ***Sense and Sensibility*** (also in *WLAIT 3: British and Irish Literature and Its Times*) was the best-known of a spate of novels that examined the detrimental effects of sensibility on young women. Others include Elizabeth Inchbald's *A Simple Story* (1791), Ann Radcliffe's ***The Mysteries of Udolpho*** (1794; also in *WLAIT 3: British and Irish Literature and Its Times*), Jane West's *A Gossip's Story* (1796), and Frances Burney's *Camilla* (1796).

Wollstonecraft's own views on sensibility changed over the course of the 1790s. At the beginning of her writing career she was extremely enthusiastic about it, but by the time she wrote her last novel, *Wrongs of Woman*, she was more cautious about its power. Sensibility could make women become too emotional and too weak. By

1797, what Wollstonecraft wanted was for women to use sensibility primarily to emancipate themselves and to promote social change.

The Treatise in Focus

Contents summary. Divided into 13 chapters, *A Vindication of the Rights of Woman* is dedicated to Charles Maurice de Talleyrand-Périgord, who had written a report on public education for the French National Assembly in 1791. In this report, Talleyrand-Périgord recommended a state-supported system of public education available to all. Boys would be taught the entire range of knowledge, which would enable them to function in the public world, while girls would learn mainly domestic skills in order for them to fulfill their maternal and domestic roles. Wollstonecraft objects passionately to this plan, which would "force all women, by denying them civil and political rights, to remain immured in their families groping in the dark" (*Rights of Woman*, p. 5). She agrees with Talleyrand-Périgord that everyone should have access to education but disagrees with his specific plans. Her treatise argues that the whole system of education must change, for under the existing system, women cannot develop their full potential.

In the introduction to *A Vindication of the Rights of Women*, Wollstonecraft points out that the "conduct and manners of women . . . prove that their minds are not in a healthy state" (*Rights of Woman*, p. 7). Their "strength and usefulness" have been sacrificed to "beauty" through "a false system of education" (*Rights of Woman*, p. 7). She attributes the fault to men, who have been more interested in making women "alluring mistresses than affectionate wives and rational mothers" (*Rights of Woman*, p. 7). She is angry and impatient at the way women have been raised to be "weak, artificial beings" concerned with their "*fascinating* graces," their beauty and appearance, instead of becoming rational creatures: "I wish to persuade women to endeavour to acquire strength, both of mind and body, and to convince them that the soft phrases, susceptibility of heart, delicacy of sentiment, and refinement of taste, are almost synonymous with epithets of weakness" (*Rights of Woman*, p. 9). In the first three chapters of the treatise, Wollstonecraft reviews some of the ideas of male writers with whom she disagrees: Jean-Jacques Rousseau, John Gregory, and John Milton. She objects to Milton's description of Eve in ***Paradise Lost*** (also in *WLAIT 3: British and Irish Literature and Its

Times*) because he does not highlight her intelligence or moral capacity. As Wollstonecraft saw it, Milton expected Eve to obey God and Adam without question, like a child, rather than expecting an adult woman to think for herself.

Wollstonecraft notes that people are distinguished from brutes by "degree of reason, virtue, and knowledge"; to improve society, both men and women must be allowed to cultivate these traits in a social setting (*Rights of Woman*, p. 12). In contrast to Rousseau and Gregory, who propose to keep women ignorant in order to preserve their "innocence," Wollstonecraft predicts that "till women are more rationally educated, the progress of human virtue and improvement in knowledge must receive continual checks" (*Rights of Woman*, p. 40). For her, it is the duty of all human beings to endeavour to rise in moral and intellectual stature.

In Chapters 2 and 3, Wollstonecraft explains that "innocence" is not the same as "ignorance." Milton, Rousseau, and Gregory try to keep women soft, pleasing, and innocent or virtuous by sheltering them, by making them dependent on men. This is counter-productive, argues Wollstonecraft. Virtue can come only when a woman understands her choices and the consequences of her actions. Furthermore, a woman cannot rely on her physical beauties, for these are transitory: "the woman who has only been taught to please will soon find that her charms are oblique sunbeams, and that they cannot have much effect on her husband's heart when they are seen every day, when the summer is passed and gone" (*Rights of Woman*, p. 27). Wollstonecraft wants women to become productive wives and partners by using their minds: "the woman who strengthens her body and exercises her mind will, by managing her family and practising various virtues, become the friend, and not the humble dependent of her husband" (*Rights of Woman*, p. 29). Further, women who learn practical and useful skills will be able to survive on their own if they should remain unmarried.

In Chapters 4 and 5, Wollstonecraft examines the causes that have led women to a "state of degradation" (*Rights of Woman*, p. 52). She notes that "understanding has been denied to woman; and instinct, sublimated into wit and cunning, . . . has been substituted in its stead" (*Rights of Woman*, pp. 54-55). Because they have been taught only to be attractive, women have become "creatures of sensation" through their exposure to "novels, music, poetry, and gallantry" (*Rights of Woman*, p. 61). It is not so much that Wollstonecraft objects to arts; it is that the excessive sensibility in contemporary culture does not make a woman "a rational creature useful to others" (*Rights of Woman*, p. 61).

Wollstonecraft stresses that women are weak not because they are born that way but because education has made them "romantic and inconstant" (*Rights of Woman*, p. 75). Her plan of education is utilitarian: instead of spending so much time on needlework, women should learn "gardening, experimental philosophy, and literature" (*Rights of Woman*, p. 75). In Chapter 5, Wollstonecraft analyzes the language of *Emile*, the sermons of Dr. James Fordyce, and Gregory's letters, and finds that these texts employ a chivalric discourse in their discussions of women. She disapproves of the way these men refer to women as objects of desire, as if they were speaking of their lovers rather than of human beings or useful citizens. In her criticism of Fordyce, she notes, "Florid appeals are made to heaven, and to the beauteous innocents, the fairest images of heaven here below, whilst sober sense is left far behind" (*Rights of Woman*, p. 94). While these moralists were supposed to sketch a plan of education for girls, what actually happens is that they project their fantasies about the ideal woman onto their texts. Wollstonecraft points out that while a virtuous man may "have a choleric or a sanguine constitution, be gay or grave . . . be firm . . . or weakly submissive . . . all women are to be levelled, by meekness and docility, into one character of yielding softness and gentle compliance" (*Rights of Woman*, p. 95). In short, in contrast to men, women are to have no individuality, no needs, no opinions, no desires. According to writers like Rousseau, Fordyce, and Gregory, women exist only to please men.

In Chapters 6 to 12, Wollstonecraft explores some of the most common characteristics and behaviors attributed to women of her time. Following Locke, Wollstonecraft starts by arguing that human beings mature and develop as a result of the impressions received through their senses. She demonstrates that women rely on their emotions and place their hopes and aspirations on love and romance because their education overemphasizes sensibility: "Till women are led to exercise their understandings, they should not be satirized for their attachment to rakes; or even for being rakes at heart, when it appears to be the inevitable consequence of their education" (*Rights of Woman*, p. 119). Again she focuses on reason, "for it is the right use of reason alone which makes us independent of every thing" (*Rights of Woman*, p. 121).

In Chapter 7 Wollstonecraft distinguishes between two meanings of modesty: one that comes from purity, and one that is synonymous with humility. Women are expected to possess the first kind of modesty, but again Wollstonecraft notes that this quality is not inherent in woman. Prostitutes, for example, from whom she takes great pains to distance herself, are shameless and do not possess modesty. Modesty must be cultivated by both men and women, and for women, modesty needs the right kind of environment:

> The woman who has dedicated a considerable portion of her time to pursuits purely intellectual, and whose affections have been exercised by humane plans of usefulness, must have more purity of mind, as a natural consequence, than the ignorant beings whose time and thoughts have been occupied by gay pleasure or schemes to conquer hearts. (*Rights of Woman*, p. 123)

Unlike most of her contemporaries, who fear women's desires, Wollstonecraft believes that

THE ENLIGHTENMENT

The eighteenth century has been called the Age of Enlightenment and the Age of Reason. In fact, a broader time span, 1660-1800, was marked by a change of values from those of the Renaissance, when life was strongly centered on the court and on the Church. From 1660 on, England became more secularized: philosophical, scientific, and natural knowledge challenged old religious beliefs, and the royal court no longer enjoyed the social and financial power it had once commanded. In the eighteenth century, society became identified with a preference for good sense, a belief in reason and moderation, and a return to the classical ideals of ancient Greece and imperial Rome. Enlightened thinkers did not necessarily reject Christianity, but they began to rely more on their senses, their experience, and their mental powers for explanations of how the world worked.

"women as well as men ought to have the common appetites and passions of their nature, they are only brutal when unchecked by reason" (*Rights of Woman*, p. 130).

Most harmful for women, says the treatise, is the fact that the reputation for chastity has taken the place of chastity itself. In Chapter 8, Wollstonecraft points out that because a woman's reputation is so highly regarded, women acquire "an artificial mode of behaviour" in order to preserve that reputation (*Rights of Woman*, p. 131). She criticizes men who are led by their appetites but want their women to be chaste. Everyone, she says, must cultivate noble virtues, no matter what their gender is, an idea influenced by the egalitarian views of the French Revolution.

WOMEN AND THE IMPACT OF THE FRENCH REVOLUTION

The Girondists were the members of the French Legislative Assembly who represented the propertied bourgeoisie and who called for equality before the law. Although women initially played an active role in the French Revolution and expected equality, once the Republicans set up their government, it became a "brotherhood" of men. Women who acted in the public sphere of politics were described as transgressing sexual boundaries. Two of the most famous female participants of the Revolution, Olympe de Gouges and Madame Roland, were guillotined in 1793 and held up as examples of mixed-gender beings. After 1793, French women were encouraged more and more to devote their time to motherhood and domestic occupations. In 1804 a new French civil code would severely curtail women's rights, especially those of married women.

Similarly, in Chapter 9, Wollstonecraft's criticism of class distinctions comes from the ideals of the revolutionary decade. She observes that the "respect paid to property" has caused "most of the evils and vices which render this world such a dreary scene to the contemplative mind" (*Rights of Woman*, p. 140). Wollstonecraft argues passionately against privileges that do not arise from merit, and is particularly critical of a system that places one group of people, whether it be aristocrats or men, over another group, be it the lower classes or women. Instead of living as dependents, she wishes women to make better use of their intelligence and abilities, lamenting "How many women thus waste life away . . . who might have practised as physicians, regulated a farm, managed a shop" (*Rights of Woman*, 149). Her wish is for men to "snap" the chains of women, in order that women can be "more observant daughters, more affectionate sisters, more faithful wives, more reasonable mothers . . . better citizens" (*Rights of Woman*, p. 150).

Two short chapters follow on duty to parents. Again Wollstonecraft is critical of blind obedience to authority and believes that women should have more freedom, particularly in their choices of husbands. It was still customary in the eighteenth century for parents of the upper classes to choose husbands for their daughters. Frequently these choices were based on economic considerations rather than on individual merit or affection. This leads Wollstonecraft to link "respect for parents" to "a selfish respect for property" (*Rights of Woman*, p. 154). She herself had felt the negative effects of tyrannical parents and did not believe that parents ought to have unquestioned power over their children.

At the end of the *Vindication of the Rights of Woman* Wollstonecraft comes back to the subject of education. In Chapter 12, she proposes a public system of education in which girls and boys would be educated together to become good citizens. This idea in itself was radical for its day. Yet in another way the essay is conservative: it returns repeatedly to the notion that a woman's primary duty is to her family. "Make women rational creatures, and free citizens," advises Wollstonecraft, "and they will quickly become good wives, and mothers; that is if men do not neglect the duties of husbands and fathers" (*Rights of Woman*, p. 178).

In the last chapter Wollstonecraft reiterates a number of feminine follies that result from the way women are brought up. Some of the practices Wollstonecraft condemns include upper-class women's tendency to believe in fortunetellers; the tendency of women in general to be sentimental because of the romances they read; and their fondness for dress, pleasure, and sway—that is, fondness for power or influence, mostly over men. As Wollstonecraft criticizes, she also gives advice. For example, she tells women to take more responsibility in their children's upbringing and to spend less time displaying finery, playing cards, and attending balls. What the treatise calls for, in short, is a "[r]evolution in female manners" (*Rights of Woman*, p. 192).

Wollstonecraft's feminist legacy. Women had long been conceived of as the weaker sex. In his *Treatise on the Education of Daughters* (translated into English in 1707), François Fenelon wrote, "Women . . . possess a weaker but more inquisitive mind. . . . [T]heir bodies as well as minds are less strong and energetic" (Fenelon in Fletcher, p. 366). A few men disputed this opinion; the English cleric Vicessimus Knox argued as early as 1739 that a boy's education was perhaps the only reason for his subsequent superiority. His was an unpopular view, yet he ventured it, as did Wollstonecraft, whose essay advanced the view greatly. Women could no longer be simply dismissed as appendages of men because of inherent deficiencies. It was education, the Wollstonecraft essay had demonstrated, that made the difference in whether women became weak creatures or useful participants in society. Anne Mellor notes that Wollstonecraft's feminism is

> what we would now define as 'liberal' feminism, one that is committed to a model of equality rather than difference. . . . Wollstonecraft's moral vision diverges profoundly from the ideology both of the British Enlightenment and of the Girondist leaders of the French Revolution in its insistence on the rationality and equality of the female and on the primary importance of the domestic affections and the family.
>
> (Mellor, p. 38)

Wollstonecraft placed her hopes on the rational, educated woman, while demonstrating through her own life that women were also subject to strong emotions, passions, and desires.

Sources. Words in her treatise such as "rights," "freedom," "equality" and "revolution" reveal the influence on Wollstonecraft of the French Revolution and the belief in the dawning of a new age. She would have heard of Olympe de Gouges, who published *A Declaration of the Rights of Woman* (1790) as a response to France's *Declaration of the Rights of Man and Citizen* (1789). She was also familiar with works such as Thomas Paine's *The Rights of Man* which appeared in 1791 (Part I) and in 1792 (Part II). Her views on education were inspired by Catherine Macaulay, whose *Letters on Education* (1790) Wollstonecraft had discussed in the *Analytical Review*. She was prompted to discuss her own views in response to men like Rousseau, Gregory, Fordyce, and Talleyrand-Périgord, who had all published writings on education. What is extraordinary about Wollstonecraft's *A Vindication of the Rights of Woman* is its firm voice and its crossing of public and private boundaries: it is both a philosophical essay and a personal reflection drawing on observation, memory, and current experience.

Reception. Initially, the response to *A Vindication of the Rights of Woman* was positive. Because of its revolutionary undertones, it was even translated into French and German. The *Ana-lytical Review* of 1792 agreed with Wollstonecraft's recommendations, saying, "if the bulk of the great truths which this publication contains were reduced to practice, the nation would be better, wiser and happier than it is upon the wretched, trifling, useless and absurd system of education which is now prevalent" (*Analytical Review*, in Wollstonecraft, *The Vindications*, p. 431). However, after her death in 1797, sympathy for her ideas lessened considerably. In 1798 her philosopher husband, William Godwin, wrote and published *Memoirs of the Author of "A Vindication of the Rights of Woman,"* in which he gave details of Wollstonecraft's two attempts at suicide; of her illegitimate child, Fanny, who was the daughter of American Gilbert Imlay; and of Wollstonecraft's intimate relationship with Godwin even before they were married. The public reacted with outrage at such immoral and unconventional be-

---

CONTEMPORARY REACTIONS TO MARY WOLLSTONECRAFT

After Godwin published his *Memoirs*, Mary Wollstonecraft's reputation and revolutionary ideas suffered badly. Even those who were somewhat sympathetic to her views withdrew their support. One writer, Amelia Opie, who knew Wollstonecraft and Godwin, wrote a novel called *Adeline Mowbray* (1804), which was loosely modeled on the lives of her radical friends. In the novel, the heroine, Adeline, based on Wollstonecraft, attempts to live her life according to the philosophies of Glenmurray, a character based on William Godwin. Godwin was publicly known for his disapproval of the institution of marriage. Defying the customs of the time, Adeline and Glenmurray live together without the sanctity of marriage, and she incurs the mockery and condemnation of the people around her. Opie's novel exposes the shortcomings of Godwin's tenets when women attempt to live by them. Women could not, as Godwin had proposed, live a life based solely on reason because their bodies were invested with sexuality, vulnerability, and maternal energy. Unlike men, they were judged not according to their intellectual achievements, but according to how well they fulfilled the prescribed roles of daughter, mother, and wife. Opie's fictional response to Wollstonecraft's text can be read as a satire of the revolutionary principles it tenders, or else as a criticism of the double standards still operating in early-nineteenth-century society.

havior. Wollstonecraft's name became associated with debased and licentious behavior, and her book, with its practical and intelligent observations about women's education and role in society, lost favor with the public. In the nineteenth century, the work regained favor, in conjunction with the rise of feminist and suffrage movements in Great Britain and the United States. It has remained an influential text on women's rights ever since.

—Eleanor Ty

For More Information

Conger, Syndy McMillen. *Mary Wollstonecraft and the Language of Sensibility*. Cranbury, N.J.: Associated University Presses, 1994.

Fletcher, Anthony. *Gender, Sex, and Subordination in England 1500-1800*. New Haven: Yale University Press, 1995.

Gregory, John. *A Father's Legacy to His Daughters*. Reprinted in *The Young Lady's Pocket Library, or Parental Monitor*. Introduction by Vivien Jones. Bristol: Thoemmes, 1995.

Johnson, Claudia L. *Jane Austen: Women, Politics, and the Novel*. Chicago: Chicago University Press, 1988.

Jones, Vivien, ed. *The Young Lady's Pocket Library, Or Parental Monitor*. Bristol: Thoemmes, 1995.

Mellor, Anne K. *Romanticism and Gender*. New York: Routledge, 1993.

Poovey, Mary. *The Proper Lady and the Woman Writer: Ideology as Style in the Works of Mary Wollstonecraft, Mary Shelley, and Jane Austen*. Chicago: University of Chicago Press, 1984.

Rousseau, Jean-Jacques. *Emile, or On Education*. Trans. Allan Bloom. New York: HarperCollins Basic Books, 1979.

Ty, Eleanor. *Unsex'd Revolutionaries: Five Women Novelists of the 1790s*. Toronto: University of Toronto Press, 1993.

Wardle, Ralph M. *Introduction to Collected Letters of Mary Wollstonecraft*. Ed. Ralph M. Wardle. Ithaca & London: Cornell University Press, 1979.

West, Jane. *A Gossip's Story and a Legendary Tale*. 2 vols. London: T. N. Longman & O. Rees, 1797.

Wollstonecraft, Mary. *A Vindication of the Rights of Woman*. Ed. Carol H. Poston. New York: Norton, 1975/1988.

Wollstonecraft, Mary. *The Vindications: The Rights of Men and The Rights of Woman*. Eds. D.L. Macdonald & Kathleen Scherf. Peterborough, Ont.: Broadview Literary Texts, 1997.

Volpone

by
Ben Jonson

⌇

Ben Jonson, by common consensus the greatest Renaissance playwright after Shakespeare, was born the stepson of a bricklayer in 1573. In the late 1590s after some years in the occupation of a bricklayer himself and of a soldier, Jonson turned to literature. His comedies satirizing contemporary London earned him popular acclaim, while his lyric poetry won him friends and patrons in aristocratic circles. By the 1610s, Jonson was King James I's favorite playwright, largely on account of the splendid entertainments, called masques, that he produced for the court. Embittered by a decline in his popularity, and enfeebled by a stroke, Jonson died in 1640, leaving behind a body of highly lauded poems and comedies. *Volpone* is generally regarded as the pinnacle of his achievement. He wrote the play at a feverish heat, taking a mere five weeks in 1605 to produce the comic masterpiece.

Events in History at the Time the Play Takes Place

Venice, commercial crossroads. Jonson set most of his comedies in contemporary London. However, he had a reason for making an exception in the case of *Volpone*. The play is his most extended attack on the way greed corrupts people—and such a theme could not have had a better setting than Venice. This city distinguished itself as the center of the financial world in the sixteenth century; foreigners, especially the English, imagined the city to be a place whose citizens would commit almost inconceivable crimes in the name of money.

Venice's unusual history marked it for success as a center of trade. The city was founded in the fourth century C.E., during the decline of the Roman Empire. As wave after wave of eastern invaders ravaged the area, residents of what is today's northwest corner of Italy made a bold move: they established a city on the marshes of the Adriatic Sea. In this location, both secluded and inhospitable, they rode out the chaos around them in relative peace.

The city's maritime location practically forced its inhabitants to become expert seamen. Venice's environs yielded only two usable commodities: salt and fish. The city had to trade for anything else that it needed, and trading meant sailing. Thus, as early as the eighth century, Venice had the most powerful fleet in the Mediterranean Sea. Its merchants plied waters from the Middle East to Spain, and its military vessels ably defended the merchants' interests.

This early maritime dominance grew ever stronger with the passing of the centuries. Remaining sheltered in its location, Venice established itself as a relatively safe, stable place for merchants of all nations to conduct business. More importantly, the city stood at the crossroads of east and west, north and south. It was a natural landfall for a Mediterranean merchant bringing goods to central Europe; if he sailed into port elsewhere in the surrounding country, he would have to transport his goods overland, through numerous separate principalities. Venice profited even more from its location at the western end of the great trade routes with the Middle and Far East. Since the time of Marco Polo in the thirteenth century (at the latest), the city had maintained active ties with eastern ports, becoming involved in the lion's share of the trade in commodities such as silks and spices. This trade grew more important to Europe with each passing year, and the city's coffers swelled with the profits.

Venice's success resulted in its being both envied and feared by the rest of Europe. The city possessed a mystique similar to that of New York in the present-day United States: it was the site of the most cutthroat competition, the place where games were played for the highest stakes, and the commercial crossroads of the world. Any given day in Venice, one could find denizens of all the corners of the world there; and it was as likely as not that these far-flung visitors had business of great importance to conduct in the city. The unique government of Venice contributed to this impression.

Renaissance Venice has been described as a joint-stock company whose business was trade. The city government consisted of the board of directors, and the citizens of Venice constituted the shareholders. The city was in effect an oligarchy: it organized all adult male nobles over the age of 25 into a Grand Council of 1,000 to 2,000 members, a Senate of Sixty, a Council of Forty, and an all-powerful Council of Ten. Among these nobleman was an elected chief, the doge of Venice, who was treated like a prince but had limited powers. The system enabled the city to manage its affairs quickly and flexibly. Indeed, so efficient was the city government that it earned a justifiable reputation for self-serving ruthlessness. In crime, the two elite councils could arrest, try, and execute people at will. In trade, Venice regularly used its unique location to enforce outrageously favorable deals with foreign traders, requiring, for instance, these traders to do two-thirds of their business with Venetians.

Yet, although few realized it at the time, Venice in 1600 was a city in decline. The Turkish Empire posed a threat on one side; yes, Venice won significant battles at Lepanto and Aleppo in the fifteenth century, but the Turks were slowly choking the city's access to the East. More importantly, these eastern routes lost significance in the eyes of the European merchants. Columbus sailed west in 1492 to break Venice's hold on the East. If in the short term, he failed, his landfall in America threw the balance of power westward. A few years later, in 1498, Portuguese explorer Vasco da Gama sailed around Africa to reach India from Europe, and vigorous trade along this route began. As long as the Mediterranean was the hub of European trade, Venice was bound to play a major role. With the opening of new trade routes, Venice slowly but surely reverted to its original position as a backwater community.

Venice, city of pleasure. If Venice signified trade and commerce, it also distinguished itself as a center of refined pleasures, especially those of the flesh. Venetian nobles were, on the whole, a serious group: they conducted business with an economic acumen unusual for aristocrats and tended to shun the extravagance and fecklessness of their peers in other regions. However, discipline cannot be confused with asceticism. Like all port cities, where travelers look for fleeting pleasures to accompany business, Venice boasted a high rate of prostitution. Venetian courtesans enjoyed a continent-wide reputation for beauty, wit, and (sometimes) cunning. Jonson alludes to their habit of propositioning men from gondolas while dressed in men's clothes when he has his character Lady Would-be mistake Peregrine (a man) for a prostitute in drag. Venice's prostitutes gained such a stellar reputation that, during the reign of Charles II, an enterprising bawd transported some to London, where they were quite successful.

Venice gained a reputation for other corrupt pleasures too. Its famous masked balls, it was said, allowed all sorts of illicit assignations to be made in full view of the public, and never more frenetically than during the Carnival (one of the grandest in the Catholic world) that preceded Lent. Apparently, Venice's reputation for sin reached an apotheosis in one man: Pietro Aretino. Born in 1492, Aretino was to pornography what Michelangelo was to art: he combined classical precepts with modern energy so proficiently that one is hard-pressed to say whether his poems on such subjects as sodomy and prostitutes are not more graceful than filthy. His books—often graced with a veneer of classicism and always accompanied by smutty drawings—swept through Europe like syphilis: it is not mere courtesy to her Venetian host that prompts *Volpone*'s Lady Would-be to list Aretino with Dante and Petrarch—"only his pictures be a little obscene" (Jonson, *Volpone* 3.4.98). Aretino's writings express a cynical, even misogynistic perspective on women that may well explain his choice of profession as a purveyor of pornography. In a letter to a friend, Aretino remarks:

> Vanity and lewdness are so inherent a part of their being that they do not even know what discretion and what chastity are. . . . This is my conclusion: it would be well if women died when they were still young, for there is no doubt that they are good and innocent when they are tender babes.
>
> (Aretino in Chubb, pp. 304-305)

The English traveler. Englishmen of the sixteenth and seventeenth centuries experienced a welter of contradictory feelings about Italy. On the one hand, Italy was both admirable and enviable: the center of art, science, and fashion. On the other hand, it was not only a Catholic land, but the very home of the pope—enough in itself to make the region hateful to Protestant England. The pope furthermore had close ties to Spain, England's great political enemy, which only aggravated England's antipathy towards Italy. Englishmen were forbidden to travel in certain areas (Rome, Naples), although many traveled to these regions in disguise. English travelers faced dangers even when they stepped into an acceptable region of the country. Still, the pull of Italy was too powerful for many Englishmen to ignore: the danger merely added spice to the life-expanding experience.

English travelers were a continual feature of Italy in the Renaissance. In addition to embassies in Venice and Turin, there were permanent English colonies in Venice (merchants) and Padua (students). Apart from these two populations, most English visitors behaved as tourists, visiting major cities to see famous works of art and to experience local culture, just like their modern counterparts. Since travel during the Renaissance was usually reserved for the well-to-do or influential, tourists in Italy could commonly engage in extravagant activities: a nobleman might return from his trip with a shipload of expensive paintings or statues, for example. Italy's role as a prime center for many forms of

learning also made visits there essential for anyone wishing to become familiar with the latest developments in, for example, astronomy, philosophy, or art. Prominent Englishmen such as the architect Inigo Jones, philosopher Thomas Hobbes, and poet John Milton profited from stays in Italy.

The dangers of Italy were at least as great as the attractions. For most of the sixteenth century, tensions between Protestants and Catholics ran so high that the two sides were effectively at war: the slightest misstep on foreign turf could have fatal consequences for the Protestant traveler, and perhaps political ramifications for his nation. Whether rightly or wrongly, the English tended to view Italy (and especially Florence and Venice) as a land of bottomless intrigue and deception: they imagined that the country was crawling with spies ready to betray or traduce unwary Protestants. And the traveler could not even trust his countrymen, since many English people living abroad were recalcitrant Catholics. In his treatise *The Schoolmaster* (1570), Roger Ascham—tutor, and later, Latin secretary to Elizabeth I—railed against what he called the

> Englishman Italianated . . . he that by living and traveling in Italy bringeth home into England out of Italy the religion, the learning, the policy, the experience, the manners of Italy. That is to say, for religion, papistry or worse; for learning, less, commonly, than they carried out with them, for policy, a factious heart, a discoursing head, a mind to meddle in all men's matters; for experience, plenty of new mischiefs never known in England before; for manners, variety of vanities and change of filthy living.
>
> (Ascham in Abrams, p. 1027)

Ascham greatly feared the effect of Italian influences on "simple and innocent wits," and even opposed Englishmen reading "fond books, of late translated out of Italian into English, sold in every shop in London, commended by honest titles the sooner to corrupt honest manners" (Ascham in Abrams, p. 1027).

English travelers oftentimes responded to these perceived threats to their morals, persons, or faith by attempting to outmaneuver the Italians. Tact was essential, and either pretending to be Catholic, or tacitly accepting the hated papists, helped one fit into Italian society. False papers and assumed identities were common, especially for travelers who wished to visit the Spanish-allied Papal States, with which England was more or less at war. The effectiveness of the disguise varied from person to person, however:

In 1594, at Voghera in the duchy of Milan an English traveler (a gentleman disguised as a poor man going on foot) reached the inn at evening, and sitting down to a meal found among the company a merchant, who said that he was from Germany. On trial of his German, which was wretched, the man explained that he hailed from territory on the frontiers of France; but then, after speaking together in French, which the merchant could hardly manage, they talked again in Italian but his Italian also sounded strange, for in fact both these travelers, Fynes Morison and the merchant, were Englishmen in disguise.

(Munter, p. 72)

Women in Renaissance Italy. Overall, *Volpone* is a very masculine play, focusing on the greed, deceit, and chicanery of a Venetian gentleman and his various dupes. Yet the presence of women is not wholly ignored—allusions are made to the famous courtesans of Venice; Volpone numbers a foolish Englishwoman, Lady Politic Would-be, among his dupes; and the play's main plot hinges on Volpone's attempted seduction of Celia, the virtuous wife of the merchant Corvino.

Of all the women in the play, Celia is by far the most helpless, a circumstance that accurately reflects the inferior status of women in Renaissance Italy. Although a small proportion of women born into the aristocracy managed to achieve power and influence through their family's wealth or an advantageous marriage, most women remained second-class citizens all their lives—the property of their fathers and husbands. Parents generally chose their daughters' future husbands, betrothing them in childhood and marrying them off in early adolescence. Historians Bonnie S. Anderson and Judith P. Zinsser write:

> According to traditions as old as the laws and customs of the Roman, Hebrew, Celtic, and Germanic peoples, by her marriage a young woman passed from the guardianship of one male to the guardianship of another . . . from the thirteenth to the seventeenth centuries, the laws of the towns and of the new royal dynasties gave more and more authority to the husband—authority over any money or property she might have in her own right or that the couple might have acquired together.
>
> (Anderson and Zinsser, p. 400)

In Renaissance Italy, men controlled—indeed, were expected to control—not only women's money and property but their bodies as well: "Prevailing values tied men's honor to control over their womenfolk's sexuality; in practice, that limited women's approved gender roles to wifehood or enclosure in a convent" (Chojnacki in Migiel and Schiesari, p. 143). Women, for their part, were expected to be chaste, modest, and obedient to the will of their menfolk. Historian Sidney Alexander sums up the situation: "[Most Italian women] were mothers. They were good wives. They supervised the household. They did not enter into the man's world. They were definitely subordinate. This was the role of most women in the Renaissance" (Alexander, p. 339). Moreover, a double standard regarding adultery prevailed, sanctioned by law and the Church: "If a man committed adultery he could not be punished unless he set up a separate household: what was known as concubinage. But if a woman committed adultery she was subject to criminal charges" (Alexander, p. 337).

In *Volpone*, Corvino torments the hapless Celia with his excessive jealousy, resolving to confine her to the back of the house and even forcing her to wear a chastity belt: "Then, here's a lock which I shall hang upon thee; / And now I think on't, I will keep thee backwards: / Thy lodging shall be backwards, thy walks backwards, / Thy prospect—all be backwards, and no pleasure / That thou shalt know but backwards" (*Volpone*, pp. 169-170). Yet Corvino does not scruple to prostitute Celia when he believes Volpone will make him his heir; when Celia balks at this scheme, Corvino threatens to "rip up / Thy mouth unto thine ears, and slit thy nose" (*Volpone*, p. 202). Although Celia ultimately gains her freedom from her tyrannical husband and her dowry is tripled, it is again an accurate and sobering reflection of the time that she must be sent back to her father's house, still the property of a man rather than her own person.

The Play in Focus

Plot summary. The play opens at daybreak as Volpone, a wealthy Venetian grandee (gentleman), welcomes the morning as he always does: by admiring his great heaps of gold. As he and his servant Mosca discuss the virtues of wealth, they also reveal their unusual means of acquiring it. Volpone, who is actually in the prime of life, pretends to be a sick old man with no heirs to whom he can bequeath his fortune. Wealthy citizens of Venice, hoping to be made Volpone's heir, increase his wealth by plying him with gifts on the assumption that he will soon die, and all will be returned to them.

After admiring his ill-gotten gains, Volpone calls for entertainment from his private troupe, composed of a dwarf, a eunuch, and a bisexual hermaphrodite, who amuse him with a comical discourse based on the idea of reincarnation.

Volpone's entertainment is interrupted by the arrival, in turn, of his three principal dupes. Volpone puts on his sickbed disguise and lets Mosca handle his visitors. From Voltore, a lawyer, Mosca accepts an antique plate; he tells the hopeful suitor that Volpone thinks only of him. Corbaccio comes next: his greed is made doubly monstrous because he is both old and already rich. Mosca suggests that if Corbaccio makes Volpone his heir, then Volpone will surely reciprocate. Corbaccio instantly decides to disinherit his only son, Bonario. Corvino, a merchant, is the third visitor: Mosca tells him Volpone thinks only of him. After Corvino leaves, the two confidence-men discuss Corvino's stunningly beautiful wife, Celia; Volpone vows to see her, even though the pathologically jealous Corvino keeps her guarded from all male eyes.

Elsewhere in the city, Sir Politic Would-be, an English expatriate who has lived in Venice for a number of years, converses with Peregrine, an English tourist who arrived in the city that morning. Ironically, Peregrine already knows more about the city than the older man, for Sir Politic, though fancying himself deep in the current of political and economic life, is actually a self-deluding fool. He suggests that a whale seen in England's Thames River was sent there by Spain, and that a famous fool was actually a spy who sent messages in roast beef. Peregrine toys with Sir Politic, whose foolishness manifests itself when he spies a mountebank (a seller of quack medicines) entering the street to hawk his wares. Peregrine instantly recognizes the scam: the mountebank (actually Volpone in disguise) claims that his medicine has cured all the great people of Europe, yet he will sell it for the equivalent of a few pennies. Sir Politic is completely taken in by the ruse.

Volpone has disguised himself to see Celia. He persuades her to drop a handkerchief from her upstairs window. On discovering this exchange, Corvino drags Celia away, then beats the disguised Volpone, who flees. Back at his house, the love-struck Volpone devises a plan with Mosca that will enable Volpone to see Celia. Meanwhile, Corvino jealously swears that Celia will not be allowed even to look out the window and threatens to confine her to the back of his house. Mosca arrives, telling Corvino that Volpone is on the

Frontispiece for the 1898 edition of the play, illustrated by Aubrey Beardsley. The frontispiece depicts the overwhelming ambition for wealth that motivates characters in *Volpone*.

verge of an amazing recovery, thanks to Voltore and Corbaccio giving him the mountebank's oil. Now, doctors say, the only thing that will cure him completely is to sleep with a beautiful, innocent young woman. Whoever supplies this woman will be confirmed in Volpone's love: Corvino quickly decides that Celia must be the woman to lie with Volpone.

On the way home, Mosca is accosted by Corbaccio's son, Bonario, who scorns him as an immoral social parasite. But Mosca's protestations of sincerity soon deceive Bonario, especially after Mosca tells him of his father's plan to disinherit him and promises to bring him where he may see his father with his lawyers. Meanwhile, the "bedridden" Volpone is suffering the well-meant but endlessly irritating attention of Lady Politic Would-be who fancies herself an intellectual. She wearies him with her conversation of books and medicine. Fortunately, Mosca arrives and rescues Volpone by telling Lady Politic he has seen her husband consorting with a prostitute; she hurries away enraged.

Now that all the plots are laid, they comically go awry. Corvino brings Celia earlier than expected, then must force his horrified wife to go through with his plan, despite her tears and pleas for deliverance. The instant Corvino leaves, Volpone springs out of his sickbed and attempts to woo her with visions of the wealth they will share. When she refuses, begging him to kill her instead, he attempts to rape her. She screams, alerting Bonario, who has been waiting in a room

---

PRECISE BROTHERS
~

Volpone's hermaphrodite entertains him with a recounting of all the various peregrinations of his soul; this allows Jonson to amuse his audience with a satiric portrait of an English Puritan. The hermaphrodite recalls when he was

A very strange beast, by some writers called an ass;
By others a precise, pure, illuminate brother,
Of those devour flesh, and sometimes one another;
And will drop you forth a libel, or a sanctified lie,
Betwixt every spoonful of a nativity-pie.

(Volpone, 1.2.42-46)

This "strange beast" is a Puritan, one of those religious sectarians who refused to acknowledge the Anglican Church until it was "purified" of all Catholic elements, and who believed that they alone knew the way of righteousness. The word "precise" automatically signifies "Puritan," or more exactly for Puritans themselves, the group's holiness. It meant careful attention to the law of God, and a precise observance of holiness in all things. For their opponents, "precise" was less flattering. It referred to the Puritan habit of spending hour upon hour discussing minute points of permissible behavior: a habit that, according to anti-Puritans, allowed the precise brothers to follow the letter of the law at the expense of its spirit, and to find scriptural justification for anything they wished to do. Puritans, in short, were commonly viewed as hypocrites. Thus, the "illuminate" brother referred to above slanders and lies without feeling he is doing anything wrong. He remains true to his conviction, in a superficial way, substituting the word "nativity" for "Christmas," because the latter word reminds him of the Catholic Mass. In 1606, the Puritans were still a minority in England, albeit a sizeable one. In the habit of proclaiming their own righteous superiority, they were exposed to the hostility of a hundred attacks. Jonson would have counted on appreciative chuckles at the hermaphrodite's lines. But he also had a personal reason to dislike the Puritans, for this group hated the public theater and wished to shut it down.

---

nearby: he rescues Celia and the two of them flee to the police.

While a frightened Volpone and Mosca hatch a plot to save themselves, Peregrine and Sir Politic continue to talk. Sir Politic praises the virtues of secrecy and proceeds to tell this recent acquaintance all of his secret plans for making money. Luckily for Sir Politic, his ideas are as weak as his discretion: they include a plan for detecting the plague with onions and an attempt to reach the elite Council of Ten by means of a common street-watchman. Lady Politic enters, leaps to the conclusion that Peregrine is a prostitute in disguise—the courtesan Mosca spoke of—and begins to berate him as such; even more ridiculously, Sir Politic believes her! Peregrine is saved from her tirade by Mosca, who sets the foolish lady straight.

By the time Mosca appears in court (Volpone has stayed home), their plan to save themselves is in place. Voltore represents them and falsely informs the judges that Celia and Bonario were lovers—Corvino knew about the affair but loved his wife too much to punish her. On the other hand, Corbaccio decided to disinherit Bonario because of his affair with Celia. Voltore also testifies that Bonario, learning of his disinheritance, plotted to accuse his father's new heir of rape. As the finishing touch, Mosca produces Lady Politic, who swears that Celia is the woman she saw with her husband. These disclosures undermine Celia and Bonario's testimony; Volpone and Mosca are exonerated while Bonario and Celia are arrested.

As the grand finale to his jest, Volpone writes his actual will, with Mosca as his heir, and Mosca goes out to announce to everyone that Volpone has died of grief over his false accusation. The three dupes and Lady Would-be appear. Mosca, who had previously flattered each in turn, scornfully ejects them all from the house. Volpone, who has watched all this from hiding, decides he wants to continue the game; disguised as a policeman, he goes out to ridicule his victims.

Peregrine, meanwhile, has laid his own trap for Sir Politic; disguising himself as a merchant, he tells the knight that the Englishman he met earlier was no traveler, but a Venetian spy. This man has now denounced Sir Politic to the Senate, and soldiers are on their way to arrest and torture the hapless knight. Sir Politic hides himself in a tortoise shell. Peregrine and his three accomplices beat on the shell, force Sir Politic to crawl, and finally uncover him. Peregrine then leaves his "politic tortoise" with this lesson on better secrecy.

Ben Kingsley as Mosca in a 1977 production of *Volpone*.

Meanwhile, the disguised Volpone taunts Corvino, Corbaccio, and Voltore by congratulating each on his good fortune in inheriting the estate. He points out that the sins each have committed are justified by the fortune that resulted. However, he pushes Voltore too far; the lawyer decides to make a full confession to the court, ruining himself to bring down Mosca. All are called back to the courtroom; Volpone, still disguised, is sent to fetch Mosca. At home, he finds that his friend has turned on him; Volpone is locked out of his own house. Determined to scheme his way out of this disaster, Volpone returns to the court, where Voltore is explaining each deception. Corvino tries to persuade the court that Voltore is possessed by demons. Volpone whispers to the lawyer that Volpone is still alive and his "death" was a ruse to test Voltore's faithfulness.

Voltore recants his truthful testimony at once. Taking his hint from Corvino, he pretends to fall into a fit. When he arises, he disavows any knowledge of what he confessed before. The judges are still considering this when Mosca enters, dressed as an aristocrat (one of the judges contemplates marrying him to his daughter). Mosca addresses the court while carrying on a whispered conversation with Volpone. He wants half the estate; Volpone at first demurs, and when he accepts, Mosca has changed his mind. He wants it all. He tells the judges that this officer has disrespected him; Volpone is seized and carried off to be whipped. Realizing that he has no choice, Volpone makes a bold decision. He casts off his disguise and reveals all to the court: "Reverend fathers, since we all can hope/ Nought but a sentence, let's not now despair it" (*Volpone*, 5.12.93-95). The judges are brief. Mosca is to be whipped, then sentenced to life imprisonment on a prison-ship. Volpone, a gentleman by birth, cannot be punished so. But all his wealth is given to a hospital, and he too must face a lengthy prison term. Voltore is banished from Venice, and Corbaccio is sent to a monastery (Bonario gets his money). Corvino is to be publicly humiliated—rowed through the canals of Venice wearing asses' ears (symbolizing his stupidity), then put in the pillory, where the people of Venice will amuse themselves by pelting him with rotten fruit. Finally, Celia is set free. Corvino must return her to her father with her dowry tripled. The judges' verdict ends the play: "Let all that see these vices thus rewarded/ Take heart, and study 'em. Mischiefs feed/ Like beasts, til they be fat, and then they bleed" (*Volpone*, 5.13.148-151).

Renaissance trickery. Jonson took the story of *Volpone* from a variety of sources, most of which were classical. However, if the inspiration for the play was largely Latin and Greek, Jonson was nevertheless catering to a taste very popular in his own day. Renaissance Englishmen were fascinated by tales of chicanery and guile, and especially loved hearing about foolish or greedy people getting a well-deserved beguiling at the hands of a clever rogue. Jonson's dark comedy offers a full complement of rogues, tricksters, and fools: the scheming Volpone and Mosca entangle Voltore, Corbaccio, and Corvino in a web of their own avarice, making it is easy to overlook virtuous characters like Celia and Bonario.

The taste for rogues on stage begins, oddly enough, in the morality plays. These rather primitive plays produced in the early sixteenth century told moral tales centered around the tribulations of a good-hearted but misguided central character. (Prominent examples of such central characters include *Everyman* and *Mankind*.) Morality plays often included a "Vice" character, who embodied everything the hero had to reject and who often led that hero into comical mischief or played fairly simple practical jokes on him. That the Vice was a popular character is attested to by the fact that his role grows larger in later morality plays: he is sometimes given an entire subplot. Towards the end of the century, the Vice character was elevated as playwrights combined elements of the Vice with borrowings from classical comedy: specifically, the wily servant who tricks fools with a variety of clever subterfuges and disguises. Such characters as Sir Toby Belch in Shakespeare's *Twelfth Night* and Brainworm in Jonson's *Every Man in his Humour* display this combination.

The attraction to trickery extended beyond the stage. By the late 1580s England's readers were showing avid interest in written accounts of criminal behavior. These slender tomes are grouped under the term "cony-catching" pamphlets: a "cony" means a rabbit, and thus any simple, easily-tricked person. The most important cony-catching pamphlets were Thomas Harman's *Caveat for Common Cursitors*, Thomas Dekker's *Lanthorn and Candlelight*, and the small library of pamphlets by Robert Greene. The cony-catching pamphlets discussed a remarkable variety of scams and tricks, from simple pocket-picking to schemes that involved a large number of thieves, elaborate disguises, and implausible cover stories. One story, repeated in pamphlet after pamphlet, reaches a summit of intrigue. Resolving to steal the purse of a certain man, a pickpocket lodges a formal complaint against him. When the sheriffs arrive to arrest the victim, the thief is there: he and a confederate begin a quarrel with the sheriffs on their cony's behalf, and when the quarrel becomes violent, the two men steal away with the man's purse. Later, when the victim and the sheriffs are attempting to sort out the chaos, a note from the "complainant" arrives: he wants the complaint withdrawn, as it was a case of mistaken identity.

According to the authors of these cony-catching pamphlets, there was hardly such a thing as unorganized crime: any crime that could make money was, they claimed, controlled by a hierarchical racket that met regularly to discuss new prospects for secret fleecing, the latest law enforcement tactics, and new stratagems. The pamphleteers seemed to suggest that law-abiding citizens were in the clutches of an inescapable criminal network that would rob them to the poorhouse as soon as they let their guard down. These criminals loved to prey on altruism; one common scam had two thieves pretending to fight: whatever honest citizen tried to make peace would lose his purse.

However, the pamphleteers' favorite targets, by far, were the stupid and greedy. In the majority of tales, the victim is the much-ridiculed country bumpkin (often rich) who has come to London to shop or to participate in a legal case. This fellow, easily identifiable by clothes or accent, is soon beset by a plausible-sounding stranger offering his services, or asking for some small favor, or suggesting a quick way to make a tidy profit. The end is always the same: the country gull returns home poorer but wiser, and the crook makes a clean escape. The moral of the story is also invariable: do not trust in appearances, mistrust strangers, and assume the worst. The greedy, who are second only to the naive as victims of crime, get a different set of lessons: curb your desire for wealth, do not assume you have mastered a game, and do not count on luck to carry you through.

The vogue for cony-catching pamphlets lasted from the last two decades of the sixteenth century well into the second decade of the seventeenth. In a way, they were themselves a kind of cheat. Usually, the author began by frightening prospective readers into believing their personal security depended on knowing what the book contained. Then, he would pretend to inner knowledge of the criminal world: the pamphlets were replete with supposedly specialized terms used by criminals to communicate without their victims knowing. This claim to inside knowledge was nearly always fraudulent: the main sources for the stories contained in the cony-catching pamphlets were earlier pamphlets, folklore and urban-set legends, and the author's own fertile imagination.

The popularity of cony-catching pamphlets indicates that tales of trickery were likely to find an appreciative audience, especially when combined with masterfully dramatic storytelling. Certainly Volpone's ruse in Jonson's play is more elaborate and more ambitious than anything recounted in these pamphlets. However, the parallel is clear. Volpone and Mosca inhabit a world of their own creation, into which they draw fundamentally law-abiding citizens, whom they exploit and over whom—but for their own overconfidence—they might have triumphed just as the tricksters in the cony-catching pamphlets did.

Sources and literary context. There is no single source for *Volpone*. As in his other comedies, Jonson draws from his vast command of classical literature. He is most clearly influenced by Roman satires on the subject of legacy hunters. Horace's *Satire 2.5*, a number of attacks on fortune-hunters in Lucan's *Dialogues of the Dead*, and stories from Petronius's *Satyricon* appear to have been primary sources of inspiration. Petronius's work probably inspired Volpone's scam, although the equivalent character in the *Satyricon* is old but not sick. Along with this theme, which he fleshed out with a Renaissance interest in trickery, Jonson's play echoes individual lines or poems from antiquity: the song Volpone sings to woo Celia is modeled on the Roman poetry of Catullus. For the character of Lady Would-be, Jonson drew heavily on the Roman poet Juvenal's *Satire VI*, an attack on women who pretend to learning.

While modern scholars freely acknowledge the play's satiric roots, some also classify *Volpone* as a prime example of an increasingly popular genre of the time: the Jacobean city comedy, which satirizes city life and city values. Frequently English playwrights, including Jonson himself, chose London as the setting for such comedies. As others have noted, the decision to set *Volpone* in Venice, along with his painstaking use of local color, allowed Jonson to employ a darker tone and express stringent criticism of Italian—and by implication, English—city values:

> Volpone's Venice . . . is a society devoted to commerce, mercantile capitalism, and ruthlessly unprincipled competition. Nothing is grown in this version of a society exclusively devoted to trade and composed of warehouses, vaults and granaries, docks, banks, merchants' palaces, prisons, and, now and then, a church. The self-governing political system of Renaissance Venice furnished an apt and ironic analogy to the mercantile government of the city of London, with its guilds, companies, lord mayor and officials, so that as well as displaying his cosmopolitanism Jonson is making pointed satire . . . on the English when he emphasizes so carefully the exact location of *Volpone* in Venice.
>
> (Gibbons, p. 94)

THE BEAST FABLE

For his character's names, Jonson drew on another tradition: the beast fable, a type of story in which animals have certain human characteristics. Each of the main characters in the play has a name derived from the Italian word for the animal that he most resembles:

Volpone: Fox—known for wily and deceptive behavior.
Corvino: Crow—an animal known to feed on carrion and commonly imagined to mate for life: an ironic comment on Corvino's willingness to prostitute his wife.
Corbaccio: Raven—a scavenger bird, like a crow: known for long life, their croaking is also a portent of death, which makes this the perfect name for a doddering old man.
Voltore: Vulture—the largest of the scavenging birds, sometimes used as a symbol for persuasiveness.
Mosca: Fly—Mosca is a parasite: he feeds off Volpone, as a fly was thought to feed off blood.

To make sure his audience understands these allusions, Jonson has his characters refer to their animal "natures" in the play. Upon hearing the judgment against him, for example, Volpone exclaims, "This is called the mortifying of a fox" (*Volpone*, 5.13.125).

Reception. *Volpone* is almost universally considered Jonson's finest comedy. It seems to have been an instant success, published the year after its first performance and played for the king the same year it debuted. Jonson's friends and contemporaries were vocal in their praise of *Volpone*;

many composed verse epigrams expressing their satisfaction with the work and its author. The playwright Francis Beaumont declared to his friend, "All sorts should equally approve the wit / Of this thy even work, whose growing fame / Shall raise thee high, and thou it with thy name" (Beaumont in Jonson, p. 80). Beaumont went on to commend Jonson's mastery of "the rules of time, of place, / And other rites, delivered with the grace / Of comic style, which, only, is far more / Than any English stage has shown before" (Beaumont in Jonson, p. 81). Likewise, George Chapman, another poet and playwright, wrote of Jonson's roguish protagonist:

> Thou hast no earth, thou hunt'st the Milk-
>   white Way, And through th'Elysian fields
>   dost make thy train . . .
> So thou shalt be advanced and made a star
> Pole to all wits, believed in for thy craft;
> In which the scene's both mark and mystery
> Is hit and sounded, to please best and worst;
> To all which, since thou makest so sweet a
>   cry
> Take all thy *best fare,* and be nothing *curst*
>   (Chapman in Jonson, pp. 82-83)

Esmé Stuart—Lord Aubigny and Jonson's patron—also praised *Volpone*, declaring pithily yet prophetically, "The Fox will live, when all his hounds be dead" (Stuart in Jonson, p. 83). Indeed, *Volpone* would be performed with some regularity in the seventeenth century and has remained popular since. In the early nineteenth century, the poet Samuel Taylor Coleridge said *Volpone* had one of the most perfectly constructed plots in Western literature: this has stood as a kind of general consensus about the play's qualities.

Perhaps the only aspect of *Volpone* that has been questioned is its brutality, especially at the conclusion. Critics have suggested that a milder tone and more active roles for Celia and Bonario would have made the play more pleasant. However, in an epistle attached to the published play, Jonson points out the harshness of the conclusion is made necessary by the criminal nature of his characters. Modern literary scholar Alexander Leggatt even defends Celia and Bonario: "He shows us genuine virtue adrift in a hostile world, made vulnerable and even laughable by its context, but not despicable in itself" (Leggatt, p.140).

—Jacob Littleton

For More Information

Abrams, M. H., ed. *The Norton Anthology of English Literature.* Vol. 1. 5th ed. New York: W. W. Norton, 1986.

Alexander, Sidney. *Lions and Foxes: Men and Ideas of the Italian Renaissance.* New York: Macmillan, 1974.

Anderson, Bonnie S. and Judith P. Zinsser. *A History of Their Own: Women in Europe from Prehistory to the Present.* Vol. 1. New York: Harper & Row, 1988.

Brown, Horatio. *Studies in the History of Venice.* New York: Dutton, 1907.

Chubb, Thomas Caldecot. *The Letters of Pietro Aretino.* Hamden: Archon, 1967.

Gibbons, Brian. *Jacobean City Comedy.* London: Methuen, 1980.

Jonson, Ben. *Volpone.* Ed. R. B. Parker. Manchester: Manchester University Press, 1983.

Kertzer, David I., and Richard P. Saller, eds. *The Family in Italy from Antiquity to the Present.* New Haven: Yale University Press, 1991.

Leggatt, Alexander. *Ben Jonson: His Vision and His Art.* London: Methuen, 1974.

Migiel, Marilyn, and Juliana Schiesari, eds. *Refiguring Women: Perspectives on Gender and the Italian Renaissance.* Ithaca: Cornell University Press, 1991.

Munter, Robert. *Englishmen Abroad.* New York: Mellen, 1986.

The Way of the World

by

William Congreve

Born in 1670 in England but reared and educated in Ireland, William Congreve became a popular figure in the London literary circle of the late 1680s. After publishing a work of prose fiction, *Incognita* (1692), and several well-received translations of classical poetry, he achieved success on the London stage when his first play, *The Old Bachelor,* ran for two weeks in the spring of 1693. Congreve wrote another three successful plays before presenting *The Way of the World* to a lukewarm reception. Though he never wrote another play, he continued to compose literary works: poems, translations of classical works, operatic songs, and journal articles. Throughout his writings, and especially in *The Way of the World,* Congreve critiqued English society by showing how greed, artificiality, and dishonesty infected social interactions and family life.

Events in History at the Time of the Play

The Glorious Revolution. Scholar Derek Hughes says that "[i]t is well known that Congreve's last two comedies [*Love for Love* and *The Way of the World*] recapitulate the Revolution by showing the containment of parental or marital tyranny by law and contract" (Hughes, p. 380). The Revolution to which Hughes refers is alternately called the Glorious Revolution or the Bloodless Revolution, and it involved the 1688 accession to the English throne of William of Orange and his English wife, Mary, who was the Protestant daughter of England's Catholic king,

---

THE LITERARY WORK

A play set in London at the end of the seventeenth century; first performed in 1700 and published the same year.

SYNOPSIS

A reformed ladies' man schemes to convince a vain, rich widow to let him marry her niece.

James II. The reasons for this "revolution" reach back to 1660, the year in which the Stuart dynasty was restored to the English throne. The civil war of the 1640s had culminated in the triumph of the Puritans and other people dissatisfied with the Anglican Church and the monarchy. Led by Oliver Cromwell, this coalition had taken over Parliament, executed King Charles I, and instituted its own government, first called a "Commonwealth" and then a "Protectorate." When Charles II, who had taken the throne in 1660, died in 1685, his brother James, a professed Catholic, became king of a determinedly Protestant England and reigned as King James II. In 1688 James's Italian Catholic wife bore a son, and both Parliament and the English people became nervous at the renewed prospect of what they thought of as Catholic tyranny and the suppression of Protestantism. Some people saw Mary, James's adult Protestant daughter, and her husband William of Orange (a province in what is now the Netherlands) as the only hope against a renewed Catholicism. For this reason, leading

Protestants invited William to come to England and investigate the circumstances surrounding the birth of James's son. William arrived with an army on the English shore, and James fled to France with his wife and son. Declaring that by this action James had abdicated his throne, Parliament invited William and Mary jointly to become king and queen of England and they accepted. Mary died on December 28, 1694, and upon William's death in 1702 the monarchy passed into the hands of Anne, Mary's younger—and equally Protestant—sister.

The Bloodless Revolution of 1688, in which William and Mary had, with the approval of a majority of the English population, acceded to the throne, ushered in a period of political stability. Prior to this period, in the turbulent 1680s, rumors of Catholic plots against the state had run rampant and struggles had occurred over the rightful succession to the throne. The Bloodless Revolution succeeded in quelling fears of Catholic tyranny. It did not, however, completely destroy the belief in secret plots and meetings. Nearly 20 years after the unveiling in 1681 of a "Popish Plot" against the government and people of England, tensions still ran high about the possibility of secret actions and subversive plotting against authorities. This concern is reflected in the elegant dramatic environment of *The Way of the World*: characters constantly hatch plans in secret, and much of the comedic action revolves around the fact that certain figures do not know that they are being duped.

Probably the most important result of the Bloodless Revolution was the development of a constitutional monarchy, a system in which the monarch and Parliament jointly shared responsibility for governing. A so-called "Bill of Rights" in 1689 limited the Crown's authority and affirmed parliamentary power. Another law, the Toleration Act, also promulgated in 1689, granted religious freedom to Dissenters—those who refused to worship in accordance with all the principles of the Anglican Church. Toleration, however, had its limits: the Act did not change the exclusion of these same Dissenters (as well as Roman Catholics and Jews) from political participation and from universities.

The creation of a constitutional monarchy also resulted in the growth of a party system of government. Many of the English believed in a divine-right monarchy, that is, in the idea that the right to rule is God-given. Supporters of divine-right monarchy and of the Established Church came to be called "Tories," whereas those who believed in contractual government and freedom of worship were dubbed "Whigs." Generally speaking, country or landed interests predominated in the Tory party, while commercial interests figured prominently in the Whig party.

Philosophical ideas of the early Enlightenment. Significantly, the 1680s and 1690s were the first decades of the European philosophical, scientific, and political movement frequently referred to as the Enlightenment. Thinkers began to examine religion and politics in the light of individual freedoms, "natural" laws, and knowledge gained through human reason. In England, Isaac Newton's influential *Principia* (1687) portrayed the natural world as an orderly place dependent on universal mathematical principles. A few years later (1690) John Locke produced a couple of major works: *Two Treatises on Government* and the **Essay Concerning Human Understanding** (also in *WLAIT 3: British and Irish Literature and Its Times*). These writings stressed reason, empirical knowledge, liberty, and the contractual nature of government, but they also warned of the limitations of human comprehension and the need to keep liberty from developing into harmful and disorderly license.

Such early Enlightenment ideas owed a great debt to the skepticism of previous seventeenth-century thinkers and writers, including Michel de Montaigne (1533-1592) in France and John Wilmot (1647-1680), the earl of Rochester, in Restoration-era England. These skeptics questioned both dogma and absolute authority, and emphasized the needs and desires of individual human beings. Their skepticism influenced libertinism, a philosophical outlook that found expression in many Restoration comedies, including a play by Thomas Shadwell called *The Libertine* (1675). Libertines viewed the human being as essentially animal—that is, possessed of desires that were "natural" and therefore productive of good. Those entities, such as governments and religious hierarchies, that attempted to control such desires were viewed with suspicion. Libertine notions were often crystallized on the Restoration stage in the elegant, dangerous figure of the "rake." The rake, usually a gentleman rather than a commoner, sought personal satisfaction first and foremost, especially in terms of sexuality. He seduced both married and unmarried women and tricked men through his intelligence and ready wit. In *The Way of the World*, Mirabell is a particularly witty rake undergoing the humiliating process of reform by love. Earlier in life, when Mrs. Fainall was a young widow,

St. James's Park in London provided a fashionable setting for conversation between men and women of the eighteenth century.

Mirabell had desired—and found—sexual pleasure with her. But now, at the beginning of the play, he wishes to marry Mrs. Fainall's beautiful, rich, and virginal cousin—Millamant. The one-time rake, in other words, is undergoing a transformation of sorts. Mirabell seems perfectly in line with an important change in libertine philosophy that occurred in the 1690s: the libertine adopted new goals, exchanging sexual excess for "moderate pleasure, retirement, love of art and gardens; skepticism; and refinement of manners" (Novak, p. 43).

Development of a public sphere. The Restoration period and the early eighteenth century also witnessed the growth of what some historians refer to as the "public sphere." This phrase refers not only to physical spaces that were removed from the private domestic world of homes but also to new methods of social communication that frequently made private lives the subject of public discussion. London from 1650 to 1750 was a city of newspapers, pamphlets, and clubs. People congregated in political clubs, social clubs, and coffee houses. There was also the "chocolate house," a shop that sold chocolate and coffee, and served as a place where gentlemen could play cards, smoke tobacco, and discuss literature, the theater, women, and other matters.

In keeping with the times, Congreve's play opens in a chocolate house.

Whereas the coffee houses provided social connections only for men, other sites in London offered occasions for conversation between men and women. Besides the theaters, there were bowling greens, shopping arcades, and public parks. St. James's Park was especially fashionable, and Congreve chose it as the setting of the important conversations that take place between two former lovers, Mrs. Fainall and Mirabell, and two current lovers, Mr. Fainall and Mrs. Marwood.

The publishing of pamphlets, newspapers, and periodical publications that approximated modern magazines flourished during the late seventeenth century. Pamphlets, small booklets that were cheap and easy to produce, had been popular with the public for some time because they usually dealt with controversial political, religious, or social matters. Several thrice-weekly newspapers started up at the end of the century, and the first daily newspaper in England appeared in 1702, just two years after the production of *The Way of the World*. Some periodicals with a question-and-answer format began to be published: one example is the *Ladies Mercury,* a paper that claimed to deal with questions of "love etc. . . . with the zeal and softness becoming the sex" (Handover, p. 120). In addition to its other news, critical commentary on literature or the theater, and advice on proper social conduct, the early periodical press frequently printed stories of political or sexual intrigue. Mrs. Marwood, a villain in Congreve's play, makes this historical fact abundantly clear when she warns Lady Wishfort that forcing her son-in-law to prove in a court of law his claims about his wife's earlier shameful behavior would subject the entire family to ridicule in the newspapers: "[I]t must after this be consigned by the shorthand writers to the public press; and from thence be transferred to the hands, nay into the throats and lungs of the hawkers" (*The Way of the World*, p. 209).

AN UNMARRIED MRS.?

In the seventeenth century, "Mrs." did not denote a married woman. Shorthand for "mistress," it designated a woman of some standing who had a degree of control over a household, usually one that included servants. The title was therefore applied to both married and unmarried women. Gradually its usage shifted, until by 1745 it had become associated only with married women. While the exact date of the shift is unclear, it seems to have occurred during Congreve's lifetime (1670-1729). The title "Miss" during this era was used to designate a young girl of good breeding.

Status and rank. In late seventeenth-century England, social rank was of paramount importance, and the characters in *The Way of the World* represent several different levels of society. Within the hereditary nobility, a strict hierarchy existed, with the king and queen at the top, followed by the duke, marquis, and others, down to the lowest level of the nobility, the baronet (whose wife would be called a "lady"). Below the hereditary ranks came positions of honor that were often accompanied by landed wealth but that could not be inherited. The most important of these ranks was the knight, or squire. Generally speaking, the rest of the population fell under the heading "commoners," a rank that included people of varying prestige and power depending on occupation, geographic area, and other considerations. Among these commoners were the few who comprised the professional classes, such as doctors and lawyers, as well as a

considerable—and growing—class of merchants and tradesmen. Outnumbering both these classes was the majority of the English population, the very large class that still engaged in agriculture. There was also a sizable servant class in the cities.

Though economic and social divisions in society mattered greatly to many people, in actuality they were far from inflexible. Many families found themselves either moving upward or downward on the scales of wealth and social respectability, especially since wealth and status did not always match up perfectly. During this time, for instance, many merchants got rich from their trading ventures and other commercial activities, while some members of the nobility experienced a diminution in their wealth due to the depreciation of land. Derek Hughes has pointed out that Congreve was acutely aware of this possibility of downward mobility. In the play, points out Hughes, "Lady Wishfort has total and arbitrary power to displace her servant Foible from a location of genteel security into a landscape of poverty and squalor, yet her own comfort and respectability exist perilously on the brink of ruin and scandal" (Hughes, p. 416).

Courtship and marriage. Unlike most of the other Protestant Churches created during the Reformation, the Church of England—often called the Anglican Church—did not modify or reinterpret Catholic guidelines regarding marriage. Thus, rules laid out by the Catholic hierarchy centuries earlier still governed marriage at the time of *The Way of the World*. Not until 1754 would major changes in marriage policy and law take place, but in retrospect behavior of the time shows that such changes were in the offing. The period represented in Congreve's play witnessed the beginnings of important transformations in the way courtships and marriages were conducted. For instance, among wealthy people, the idea that a young person should have a say in the choice of his or her marriage partner was just beginning to mount a serious challenge to the social understanding that parents or guardians were best suited to decide upon the proper spouse. With only a few exceptions, by 1700 most young people had the ability to say "no" to a partner chosen by their parents, even if they could not yet actively seek out and decide upon a life partner on their own. A few parents were beginning to allow their children free rein in the matter, but such parents were decidedly in the minority. At the other end of the spectrum were parents and guardians like Lady Wishfort in *The Way of the World*, who threatened to withhold property or money from their children or wards if they did not obey their directives concerning the choice of a marriage partner

In the following passage, historian Lawrence Stone provides a clear and concise summation of the steps usually taken by "persons of property" in the late seventeenth century who wished to marry:

> The first [step] was a written legal contract between the parents concerning the financial arrangements. The second was the spousals (also called a contract), the formal exchange, usually before witnesses, of oral promises. The third step was the public proclamation of banns in church, three times, the purpose of which was to allow claims of pre-contract to be heard. . . . The fourth step was the wedding in church, in which mutual consent was publicly verified, and the union received the formal blessing of the church. The fifth and final step was the sexual consummation.
>
> (Stone, p. 31)

People without property generally skipped the first step, since there was no need for financial contracts. Actually many couples were unwilling to go through all of the steps, whether because they were marrying without family approval or because they wanted to get married quickly. Luckily for them, there were loopholes. As Stone explains, a "brisk trade [was] carried on by unscrupulous clergymen, operating in districts which were immune from superior ecclesiastical supervision, who would marry anyone for a fee, no questions asked" (Stone, p. 33). Paradoxically, though Church and state declared such irregular weddings illegal, they also declared the marriages binding and valid if they were followed by sexual consummation. Congreve's play contains one such irregular marriage, the union between the two servants Waitwell and Foible. Plot complications demand that Waitwell and Foible be married without delay so they must find a priest who will marry them without the banns having been said or a special license having been procured. They wind up at St. James's Church. In fact, St. James's Church was one of the most popular sites of quick marriages in the late 1600s; historians estimate that about 40,000 weddings took place there between 1664 and 1691. When Mirabell asks "So, so, you are sure they are married?" the footman shows that he is aware that sexual consummation is necessary when he responds, "Married and bedded, sir. I am witness" (Congreve, *The Way of the World*, p. 159).

There were two main types of engagement contracts, or "spousals." The contract *per verba de futuro* was an oral promise before witnesses to marry in the future. If there was no consummation the engagement could be legally broken. But, if consummation had occurred, the marriage was legally binding. The contract *per verba de praesenti* involved an exchange of vows before witnesses and, under Church law, was irrevocable. This distinction is of critical importance at the end of the play. In the concluding scenes, Millamant promises to marry Sir Willful Witwoud in the future, which appears to be enough to satisfy Lady Wishfort's stipulation that Millamant marry only with her approval. As it turns out, her promise to marry in the future is just a ploy: ultimately Sir Wilfull and Millamant decide by mutual consent to call off the marriage and Millamant is free to marry Mirabell.

Because a marriage meant the amalgamation of two families, middle- and upper-class marriage negotiations continued to center on financial and political considerations. It is also true, however, that the notion of "companionate marriage" began to develop in the late seventeenth century. The term refers to a marriage whose partners are well-suited to each other in areas such as intelligence, humor, religious beliefs, and temperament. Some people were even beginning to see sexual attraction to the other person as an important marker of compatibility. As Richard Steele said in a newspaper called *The Tatler* in 1709, "A generous and constant passion in an agreeable lover, where there is not too great disparity in other circumstances, is the greatest happiness that can befall the person beloved" (Steele in Stone, p. 276). *The Way of the World* contains a classic example of a companionate love relationship in its portrayal of Mirabell and Millamant, who are equally charming, intelligent, well-spoken, and physically attractive. The "proviso" scene, in which they decide in advance upon the principles that will rule their marriage, shows that they both value freedom, constancy, and truthfulness.

Women and property. Seventeenth-century Englishwomen were mostly dependent upon men for their economic livelihood. For women in the propertied classes, marriage was usually the only "career" choice, especially since the Protestant Reformation had closed the convents that housed nuns. However, marriage was frequently fraught with negative economic consequences because the laws of couverture dictated that anything a woman owned became her husband's property upon marriage. These laws also stipulated that a husband had a right to any prop-

The Way of the World

erty or money that came into his wife's hands during the marriage. Congreve's play critiques this state of affairs in its representation of the servant couple, Waitwell and Foible. When Mirabell gives the servant woman Foible money as his thanks for her participation in his scheme, Waitwell immediately turns to Foible and says, "Spouse." This indicates that he expects her to hand him the coin because her property is now rightfully his. Mirabell prevents this extortion, however, by saying, "Stand off, sir, not a penny. Go on and prosper, Foible" (*World,* p. 178).

Increasingly during Congreve's lifetime, women of the propertied classes were finding ways around these restrictive laws. Assisted by lawyers and their parents or guardians, some women insisted upon making legal settlements before marriage that would guarantee them an allowance of "pocket-money" as well as control over some, if not all, of their existing property. In addition, some women, especially landowning widows, were conveying their property to other responsible persons in trust to protect once they were married. At the conclusion of the play, it is revealed that just such a conveyance of property, performed years earlier, will enable Mrs. Fainall to prevent her unscrupulous husband from gaining access to her property. Mirabell presents the written document of this transaction to Fainall, who then cries "Damnation" before reading it aloud with astonishment and disappointment: "A deed of conveyance of the whole estate real of Arabella Languish, widow, in trust to Edward Mirabell" (*World,* p. 215).

The Play in Focus

Plot summary. *The Way of the World* begins in a London chocolate-house. Two men named Mirabell and Fainall wittily converse about women and love as they finish a card game. Mirabell informs Fainall of the difficulties he has encountered while trying to persuade Fainall's mother-in-law, the rich 55-year-old widow, Lady Wishfort, to let him wed her niece and ward, an attractive, wealthy, never-married young woman called Mrs. Millamant. Lady Wishfort controls Millamant's fortune of 12,000 English pounds, half of which her niece must forfeit if she marries without her aunt's consent. Looking upon the matter with worldly practicality, Mirabell considers this sum absolutely necessary for the marriage. Therefore, he has been busy trying to trick Lady Wishfort into agreeing to the match. His first scheme did not succeed: he pretended

to have a romantic interest in Lady Wishfort herself in order to gain private access to Mrs. Millamant, but Fainall's wife's friend, Mrs. Marwood, spoiled the plot by revealing it to the dowager. Mirabell has now invented a new plan, but he declines to reveal the details of it to Fainall. There is a brief interlude in which a footman secretly tells Mirabell that his servant, Waitwell, has that morning married Lady Wishfort's maid, Foible. Afterward Mirabell discourses on the type of love he has for Millamant. He says that for a "discerning" man he is perhaps "too passionate a lover," for he "like[s] her with all her faults, nay, like[s] her for her faults" (*World,* p. 160). He adds that because he has spent so much time analyzing her weaknesses they "are now grown as familiar to me as my own frailties and in all probability in a little time longer I shall like 'em as well" (*World,* p. 160).

A messenger enters the room with a letter for a Mr. Witwoud—a foolish nephew of Lady Wishfort; the letter comes from his half-brother, Sir Wilfull Witwoud, a country squire visiting London on his way to the Continent. Mr. Witwoud, whose very name indicates his unsuccessful pretensions to cleverness, then enters the chocolate-house, and becomes the unwitting butt of Fainall and Mirabell's wordplay. The men are next joined by Witwoud's friend and fellow fool, Petulant, who habitually tries to seem popular by paying servants to claim that ladies desire to speak to him. In the ensuing conversation between all the men, Petulant shares what he has learned the night before at Lady Wishfort's house: Mirabell's rich uncle has lately come to London. Disliking his nephew intensely, the uncle reportedly wishes to marry soon and have a child so that Mirabell will be disinherited. Witwoud concludes that Lady Wishfort might be a perfect match for Mirabell's uncle because she too hates Mirabell and would be happy to see him disinherited.

In the next act the scene shifts to St. James's Park, where Mrs. Fainall and Mrs. Marwood are conversing about how much they hate men. They also rail against marriage: Mrs. Fainall states that she hates her husband "most transcendently," and Mrs. Marwood says that she would be induced to "undergo the violence" of a wedding ceremony only if she could find a man who loved her and would accept being ill treated (*World,* p. 168). The fact, however, that each woman blushes when Mirabell's name comes up in conversation reveals to the audience that beneath this façade of hatred for men, both women harbor a secret liking for Mirabell.

Soon the two women are joined by Fainall and Mirabell, and, as they walk about the park, the foursome splits into two couples—Mrs. Marwood with Fainall, and Mirabell with Mrs. Fainall. The audience learns that Fainall hates his wife and is having an affair with Mrs. Marwood, whom he berates for having told Lady Wishfort of Mirabell's plot. Mrs. Marwood should not have interfered, thinks Fainall. They could have become rich if she had let things progress to the point where Mirabell and Millamant had successfully eloped. Millamant would have forfeited half her fortune to Lady Wishfort, who in turn would have transferred it to her own daughter, Mrs. Fainall. As Mrs. Fainall's husband, he would have gained possession over the fortune and used it to please himself and his mistress. He urges Mrs. Marwood to help him plan to rob his wife "of all she's worth" and "retire somewhere, anywhere, to another world" (*World*, p. 172).

Meanwhile, Mirabell and Mrs. Fainall discuss their past relationship and Mirabell's newest plan to force Lady Wishfort to let him marry her niece. It seems that Mirabell and Mrs. Fainall were lovers after her first husband, Mr. Languish, died. Later, when she feared—wrongly, it turned out—that she was pregnant, Mirabell persuaded her to marry Fainall so that she would remain respectable. Mirabell explains why he chose his friend Fainall to be the husband: "A better man ought not to have been sacrificed to the occasion; a worse had not answered to the purpose" (*World*, p. 172). He then informs Mrs. Fainall of the details of his new plot. He has directed his servant, Waitwell, to disguise himself as his rich uncle and to court Lady Wishfort. Once Lady Wishfort has publicly contracted herself to marry the supposed uncle, "Sir Rowland," Mirabell will reveal that the man is really a servant. Mirabell will then tell Lady Wishfort that he will produce a document that will release her from her promise—and therefore save her from public humiliation—if she allows him to marry Millamant.

At the end of this conversation, the former lovers are joined by Witwoud and Mrs. Millamant. The scene that follows makes clear the intellectual and psychological affinities between Mirabell and the woman he wishes to marry. They exchange witty thoughts about love and beauty and, when they are alone, graduate to a more direct discussion of their feelings for each other. Millamant pretends to be not so deeply in love with Mirabell as he is with her, though she does say to him, "[I]f ever you will win me, woo me now" (*World*, p. 176). He attempts to share

Fritz Weaver and Nancy Wickwire in a stage production of *The Way of the World*.

with her the details of the scheme against her aunt, but she cuts him off by saying that she already knows all about it. Without telling him how she heard about the plan, she leaves him alone to contemplate what he sees as the whims or vagaries of a woman's heart.

Act 3 opens with Lady Wishfort in her boudoir, as she attempts to look younger and more attractive by way of cosmetics and alcoholic drinks. She decides that her best means of defense against her enemy Mirabell will be to marry his uncle and get him disinherited. Mrs. Fainall appears on the scene, and she and Foible, Lady Wishfort's maid, discuss Mirabell's plot in the hallway. Little do they know that Mrs. Marwood is secretly listening behind a door. Now aware of Mirabell's plans, Mrs. Marwood tries to counter them by encouraging Lady Wishfort to make a match between her niece and nephew—Mrs. Millamant and Sir Wilfull Witwoud. When Millamant enters the room and laments the fact that "one has not the liberty of choosing one's acquaintance as one does one's clothes," Mrs. Marwood suggests that Millamant is actually a hypocrite (*World*, p. 184). Marwood implies that Millamant enjoys being surrounded by fools like Witwoud and Petulant because it enables her to hide the fact that she is in love with Mirabell. Knowing that she herself has a plan that may foil

Millamant's desire to wed Mirabell, Marwood says to her, "Your merry note may be changed sooner than you think" (*World*, p. 185).

Fainall and Mrs. Marwood talk about how best to stop Mirabell. Upset by Mrs. Marwood's news that his wife once had an affair with Mirabell, Fainall vows to get even with her. Mrs. Marwood suggests that he avenge himself by telling Lady Wishfort about his wife's part in Mirabell's scheme to fool the dowager. Fainall agrees to this idea and reveals that if "the worst come to the worst" he can always "turn [his] wife to grass"—meaning divorce her or separate from her—because he has previously "wheedled" out of her a "deed of settlement" on "the best" part of her estate (*World*, p. 192).

The next act includes three wooing scenes—two are ridiculous; one is genuine and successful. First, Sir Wilfull Witwoud fails miserably to match wits with Mrs. Millamant, the woman whom his aunt, Lady Wishfort, desires that he marry. After Sir Witwoud flees the room, Mirabell enters and asks whether or not the "chase" can now come to an end. Millamant replies in the negative, saying that she wishes to be "solicited to the very last, nay and afterwards" (*World*, p. 195). She poses some objections to the marriage, which he dismisses by saying that she need not worry about losing her freedom because he will try to please her always. After she presents her "conditions," he brings up some of his own in a discourse that is filled with legalistic language: "*Imprimis* then, I covenant, that your acquaintance be general; that you admit no sworn confidante or intimate of your own sex; no she-friend to screen her affairs under your countenance and tempt you to make trial of a mutual secrecy" (*World*, p. 197). In stating her provisos, Millamant seems most interested in having control over the domestic sphere and keeping a good reputation in society. Mirabell, in contrast, states that his wife must be both faithful to him and natural in her appearance and tastes. His concern even extends to his progeny; he says, "I denounce against all strait lacing, squeezing for a shape, till you mold my boy's head like a sugar loaf; and instead of a man-child make me father to a crooked billet [a piece of firewood]" (*World*, p. 197). After agreeing to accept each other's provisos, they become officially engaged.

In the third wooing scene, Waitwell, disguised as Sir Rowland, courts Lady Wishfort in front of most of the other characters. Suddenly a servant presents to Lady Wishfort a letter from Mrs. Mar-

wood warning her that "he who pretends to be Sir Rowland is a cheat and a rascal" (*World*, p. 203). Worried about the potential impact of this letter, Waitwell, still in the person of Sir Rowland, cleverly convinces Lady Wishfort that the letter has actually been sent by Mirabell in an attempt to keep from being disinherited through his uncle's marriage. Lady Wishfort then agrees that she will meet Sir Rowland later that night to draw up a "contract" of engagement.

Act 5 presents a total reversal of the plot elements that ended Act 4. It now appears that Lady Wishfort is well aware of Sir Rowland's being a fictional character dreamed up by Mirabell, and she dismisses her maid Foible for participating in the scheme. We learn that Fainall has had Waitwell arrested for imposture, and Mrs. Marwood has told Lady Wishfort not only about the plan but also about Mrs. Fainall's earlier relationship with Mirabell. The true nature of Fainall's relationship with Mrs. Marwood is exposed. Foible alerts Mrs. Fainall to the fact that her husband has been conducting a secret affair with Mrs. Marwood. Mrs. Marwood and Mr. Fainall then try to blackmail Lady Wishfort by saying that they will take pains to hush up the scandal if she agrees to three conditions: 1) she must never marry without Fainall's approval; 2) she must make her daughter settle on Fainall the rest of her fortune; and 3) she must make over to him the half of Mrs. Millamant's fortune that Millamant has forfeited by consenting to marry Mirabell. Lady Wishfort asks for time to consider these harsh conditions.

Fainall and Mrs. Marwood's plan is soon spoiled. When they return to get Lady Wishfort's signature on the articles, they discover that Millamant has reversed her position and verbally agreed to engage herself to marry Sir Wilfull, as Lady Wishfort wants. Fainall realizes that he won't be able to get Millamant's fortune, but he insists that Lady Wishfort still agree to the first two conditions. At this point, Mirabell offers to save Lady Wishfort from such an awful fate; and in her gratefulness Lady Wishfort promises that if he comes to her aid, she will let him marry her niece. Mirabell then calls in Foible and another servant-woman, Mincing, who both testify that they discovered Fainall in an illicit embrace with Mrs. Marwood some time before. Mirabell then completes his triumph over Fainall and Mrs. Marwood by presenting a document, signed much earlier by Mrs. Fainall, that had conveyed her whole estate "in trust to Edward Mirabell" (*World*, p. 215). Because this prior deed makes null and void the later deed of settlement that Fainall persuaded his wife to sign, Fainall now has no right to any part of his wife's estate. Sir Wilfull announces that he freely releases Millamant from her pledge. Thankful for Mirabell's aid, Lady Wishfort says he may marry her niece. The play ends with a dance, followed by Mirabell's wise advice to the audience: "From hence let those be warned, who mean to wed; / Lest mutual falsehood stain the bridal bed: / For each deceiver to his cost may find, / That marriage frauds too oft are paid in kind" (*World,* p. 217).

Appearance versus reality. One central tension runs through all the intricacies of plot, the witty exchanges, and the character sketches in *The Way of the World*: the contrast between appearance and reality. Evoking a tension that is faithful to the philosophical ideas of the time, the play critiques artificiality by contrasting nature and art. People are often not who they seem to be in the treacherous world portrayed by Congreve. The servant Waitwell pretends to be Mirabell's rich uncle, Sir Rowland. Witwoud pretends to be a witty man-about-town, and his friend Petulant so desperately desires to be seen as popular that he often secretly leaves the chocolate-house only to return in a disguise and call for himself. And the three young women of fashion—Mrs. Fainall, Mrs. Millamant, and Mrs. Marwood—all voice their hatred for men even though they secretly pine after Mirabell. The issue becomes complicated in relation to secret plots, however, for not all those who practice deception are punished. Ultimately those who plot for good reasons—for example, Mirabell, who wishes to marry a suitable woman—are rewarded, while those who scheme out of evil intentions—such as Mr. Fainall and Mrs. Marwood—have their dreams crushed.

The scenes involving the aging Lady Wishfort most perfectly illustrate the motif of nature versus art. She constantly applies cosmetics to make herself more beautiful, but according to Congreve she only makes herself look worse. Once, when Lady Wishfort expresses anxiety about her appearance, Foible tells her, "Your ladyship has frowned a little too rashly, indeed, madam. There are some cracks discernible in the white varnish" (*World,* p. 181). Lady Wishfort then looks in a mirror and cries, "Cracks, say'st thou? Why I am arrantly flayed; I look like an old peeled wall. Thou must repair me, Foible, before Sir Rowland comes, or I shall never keep up to my picture" (*World,* p. 181). At the end of the play, Lady

Wishfort must undergo a humbling punishment: this woman who has hidden her true self, her true body, in an attempt to impress Sir Rowland, discovers that she has been the victim of a fraud because Sir Rowland turns out to be a servant in disguise.

Sources and literary context. The restoration of Charles II to the throne of England in 1660 also restored the theater to the glory it earlier enjoyed under Elizabeth I and James I. After the execution of Charles I, Puritan leaders, convinced that drama was immoral and politically inflammatory, had shut the London theaters. Once Charles II reopened the theaters and commissioned two acting companies, drama flowered in London. Some important changes were instituted in the theater spaces themselves: women appeared on stage as actresses for the first time; theaters became enclosed spaces rather than open-air arenas; and moveable, often opulent pictorial scenery replaced the flat images used for earlier stage settings. Also, unlike their predecessors, comic playwrights at the end of the seventeenth century began to focus almost exclusively on contemporary England, as Congreve does in *The Way of the World*. Playwrights came to rely less on foreign drama and earlier English plays for their characters, plots, settings, and dialogue.

A TASTE OF SIR JOHN SUCKLING—FROM "THE DEFORMED MISTRESS"

~

I know there are some Fools that care
Not for the body, so the face be faire . . .
Each man his humor hath; and faith 'tis mine
To love that woman which I now define . . .
Her Nose I'de have a foote long, not above,
With pimples embroder'd, for those I love;
And at the end a comely Pearl of Snot,
Considering whether it should fall or not . . .

(Suckling, p. 33)

Numerous literary allusions in Congreve's play indicate its indebtedness to writings by Geoffrey Chaucer, William Shakespeare, Ben Johnson, Cervantes, Molière, and Sir John Suckling. Sometimes the allusions serve to create dramatic irony. Characters make garbled references to pieces of literature, making it abundantly clear to the more knowledgeable audience members that they are truly ignorant of culture. For example, in the play Millamant sings songs by Sir John Suckling in the presence of Sir Wilfull Witwoud, who is alarmed by the poet's name and unfamiliar with his poems; the audience, on the other hand, would have been well aware of their sexual content.

Besides a number of important allusions, a few particular plot elements and scenes in *The Way of the World* reflect Congreve's familiarity with earlier drama. For example, the subplot concerning Mrs. Fainall's conveyance of her estate in trust to Mirabell may have been inspired by the

UNREASONABLE AND DANGEROUS

William and Mary's accession has sometimes been referred to as a "moral revolution" (Love, p. 2). Their somewhat sober lifestyles contrasted markedly with the dissipation of Charles II and his court. Strict piety was emphasized and vice discouraged in the Nonconformist religious literature that flourished during their reign, and the 1690s witnessed the birth of several groups dedicated to spreading moral behavior and Christian thought. A concern with protecting morality found expression in several written attacks on the theater, the most famous of which was called "A Short View of the Immorality and Profaneness of the English Stage." Published in 1698 by a clergyman named Jeremy Collier, "A Short View" criticized the playwrights of his day for their "smuttiness of expression; their swearing, profaneness and lewd application of Scripture; [and] their abuse of the clergy" (Collier in McMillin, p. 391). Collier attacked Congreve's plays directly, accusing the playwright of creating "foul and nauseous" characters (Collier in McMillin, p. 392). Congreve published a rebuttal in 1698, detailing the reasons why particular passages and characters that Collier had found offensive were actually beneficial and instructive to the audience. More importantly, however, Congreve used *The Way of the World* to satirize the clergyman. One of the play's most foolish and hypocritical characters, Lady Wishfort, recommends Collier's "Short View of the Stage" to Mrs. Marwood, the villain of the piece, for the latter's entertainment. Congreve also states in his prologue to the play that his intention is to "delight" the audience. Collier had argued that "to make delight the main business of comedy is an unreasonable and dangerous principle" because it "opens the way to all licentiousness" (Collier in McMillin, p. 403).

main plot of Ben Jonson's play *The Devil is an Ass* (1616). Indeed, Congreve may be bringing attention to his source when he has Mrs. Marwood say "the devil's an ass: If I were a painter, I would draw him like an idiot, a driveler with a bib and bells" (*World,* p. 182). It also seems likely that Congreve borrowed the name of his hero, "Mirabell," from John Fletcher's 1621 play, *The Wild-Goose Chase,* which contains a character named "Mirabel" (Novak, p. 48). Furthermore, the witty repartee between Mirabell and Millamant, who attempt early on to disguise their true love for each other through pretended animosity, mirrors similarly spirited dialogue between Beatrice and Benedick in Shakespeare's *Much Ado About Nothing* (c. 1598). Structurally, one of the most entertaining and famous scenes in *The Way of the World*, that in which Mirabell and Millamant establish the terms of their future marriage, has forerunners in a great number of "proviso" scenes in earlier Restoration comedy. Amusing, psychologically revealing, and even poignant, Congreve's provisos themselves are, however, original to his play.

Reception. When first performed, *The Way of the World* was neither a success nor a complete failure. As John Dryden, a contemporary and friend of Congreve's as well as an influential Restoration poet, put it: "Congreve's New Play has had but moderate success[,] though it deserves much better" (Novak, p. 138). Despite its lackluster opening run, *The Way of the World* went on to become a mainstay in the mid- and late-eighteenth-century theater. The play enjoyed 126 performances between 1714 and 1747 and another 110 performances between 1747 and 1779 (Kavenik, pp. 119, 163). Although performed less frequently in the nineteenth century, the play rebounded in the 1920s and has been performed numerous times since then in the United States and Great Britain.

The play's critical reception has followed a somewhat similar trajectory. Along with most other contemporary comedies, it was either denigrated or ignored by learned critics throughout the 1700s and 1800s. Samuel Johnson complained in his *Lives of the English Poets* (1781) that Congreve "formed a peculiar idea of comic excellence. . . . His comedies . . . surprise rather than divert, and raise admiration oftener than merriment" (Johnson in Novak, p. 138). Serious scholarly work on Congreve began only in the 1920s, when Montague Summers edited Congreve's *Complete Works.* In subsequent years, many scholars have come to view *The Way of the*

World not only as Congreve's highest achievement but also as the premiere example of the late-seventeenth-century comedy of manners.

—Laura Franey

For More Information

Burns, William. "Coffee Houses." In *Historical Dictionary of Stuart England, 1603-1689*. Ed. Ronald H. Fritze and William B. Robison. Westport, Conn.: Greenwood, 1996.

Congreve, William. *The Way of the World*. In *Restoration and Eighteenth-Century Comedy*. Norton Critical Edition. Ed. Scott McMillin. New York: Norton, 1973.

Handover, P. M. *Printing in London from 1476 to Modern Times*. Cambridge, Mass.: Harvard University Press, 1960.

Hughes, Derek. *English Drama 1660-1700*. Oxford: Clarendon, 1996.

Hunter, Michael. *Science and Society in Restoration England*. New York: Cambridge University Press, 1981.

Kavenik, Frances M. *British Drama, 1660-1779: A Critical History*. New York: Twayne, 1995.

Love, Harold, *Restoration Literature: Critical Approaches*. London: Methuen, 1972.

McMillin, Scott, ed. *Restoration and Eighteenth-Century Comedy*. New York: Norton, 1973.

Novak, Maximilian. *William Congreve*. New York: Twayne, 1971.

Stone, Lawrence. *The Family, Sex and Marriage in England, 1500-1800*. London: Weidenfeld and Nicolson, 1977.

Suckling, Sir John. *The Works of Sir John Suckling: The Non-Dramatic Works*. Ed. Thomas Clayton. Oxford: Clarendon Press, 1971.

Wuthering Heights

by

Emily Brontë

~

Wuthering Heights is the only novel by Emily Brontë (1818-48), one of three sisters whose literary productions caused a minor sensation when they began appearing in the late 1840s. Born to Patrick Brontë, a Yorkshire clergyman, and his wife Maria, Emily, Anne, and Charlotte Brontë were precocious readers and writers. The three sisters spent years writing for their own pleasure and amusement, then published a volume of poetry in 1846. Fearing that the volume's reception would be biased if the authors were known to be women, the sisters adopted the names of Ellis (Emily), Acton (Anne), and Currer (Charlotte) Brontë. Their poems did not sell well but garnered some positive reviews—Ellis Bell's poems were said by one critic to demonstrate "a fine quaint spirit . . . which may have things to speak that man will be glad to hear" (Allott, p. 61). The following year Wuthering Heights was published as the first two volumes of a three-volume set, which also included Anne Brontë's *Agnes Grey*. Wuthering Heights was initially overshadowed by the greater acclaim that greeted Charlotte Brontë's *Jane Eyre*, published earlier that same year, but has since been recognized as a great work in its own right. Emily Brontë died of tuberculosis in December 1848, barely a year after the publication of *Wuthering Heights*. Her novel, recognized as an original masterpiece soon after her death, involves issues of slavery, family relationships, and gender in ways that remain fresh and provocative.

THE LITERARY WORK

A novel set in the West Riding of Yorkshire at the turn of the nineteenth century; published in 1847.

SYNOPSIS

Two families become entangled in a web of interrelations through blood and marriage over a 30-year period.

Events in History at the Time the Novel Takes Place

The chaos of revolution. *Wuthering Heights* takes place between 1771 and 1802, an era that saw rapid political, social, and economic change in England as well as the development of Romantic literature. Politically, the period experienced the momentous American and French Revolutions. While England's loss of its 13 American colonies and its subsequent struggle to contain the threat of the French Revolution have no direct analogues in *Wuthering Heights*, there is an indirect influence. The increasing social mobility and democratization associated with these political movements evoke anxiety in the novel's landed gentry, among whom Heathcliff may be seen as an almost allegorical figure for the chaos of revolution. Equally significant to the novel are the slow abolition of slavery in England and a

The Brontë family's parsonage and adjoining cemetery.

shifting understanding of the nature of marriage and the family.

Social mobility. The basis of the English class system before the nineteenth century was land, which conveyed both money and status. Society protected the commodity through the dual practices of primogeniture and entail. Primogeniture, the inheritance of land by the eldest son (or closest male relative) in a family, ensured that estates would remain intact and within the family. Entail restricted an heir's disposal of an estate, usually through a legal contract that prohibited two generations of heirs from selling off the land they inherited. Primogeniture ensures that the *Wuthering Heights* character Edgar Linton will inherit Thrushcross Grange on his father's death, and that on his own subsequent death the estate will pass to his nephew, Linton Heathcliff, rather than to his own daughter. Conversely, the lack of an entail allows another character, the unrelated Heathcliff, to acquire Wuthering Heights before two generations pass. In the first generation, the son apparently mortgages the property to Heathcliff in payment of gambling debts; when the son dies with the debt unpaid, the unentailed property passes to Heathcliff.

Over the course of the eighteenth century new means to wealth began to develop through industry and manufacturing. The value attached to land shifted with the ascendancy of those new

means, with land becoming more a marker of status than the path to one's fortune. The increased social mobility of the late eighteenth and early nineteenth centuries produced anxiety among the landed gentry, who saw their status as social leaders challenged—and, sometimes, their land acquired—by the newly wealthy capitalists. In the novel Heathcliff becomes mysteriously wealthy during his time away from Wuthering Heights, then consolidates his wealth and status by acquiring the property after Hindley Earnshaw's death. With Heathcliff's acquisition of the land comes the status of gentleman that the narrator unhesitatingly accords him.

Slavery. Although African slavery was never as significant to the English domestic economy as to the plantation economies of the Americas, England had been a dominant player in the slave trade since the mid-1600s. Liverpool, the port city where Mr. Earnshaw picks up Heathcliff at the beginning of the novel, was a major participant in the slave trade, with more than three-quarters of the English traffic in slaves (which comprised at least 55 percent of the worldwide market) passing through its port by the turn of the nineteenth century. In the "Liverpool Triangle," manufactured goods from England were traded for West African slaves, who were, in turn, traded to the Caribbean for sugar, molasses, and rum.

Emily Brontë drew upon her native Haworth, Yorkshire, for the setting of *Wuthering Heights.*

In 1772—just after the action of *Wuthering Heights* begins—the abolitionist movement marked one of its first legal victories in England with the Mansfield decision. A slave named James Somerset, who had fought his forcible return to the colonies, was granted the right to remain in England. While the decision did not abolish slavery, Lord Chief Justice Mansfield's claim that slavery was inconsistent with English law began the process. The abolitionist movement gained ground in England in the later eighteenth century; part of a larger religious awakening, the movement was influenced especially by the Society of Friends (Quakers), who presented the first petition for abolishing the slave trade to Parliament in 1783, and by Methodism, which broke away from the Church of England to form a separate denomination in 1784. Slavery continued to exist through the time of the novel. It would not be abolished until 1833, after England had abolished the slave trade in 1807. In *Wuthering Heights* the unknown origins of Heathcliff, his mysteriously dark complexion, and his position within the Earnshaw family all suggest that he may be a freed slave or the child of a slave, brought to the forbidding Yorkshire moors by Mr. Earnshaw.

The family. During the eighteenth century in England the shape of the family was changing considerably. In England's precapitalist aristocratic and feudal society, the family had been seen as a network of obligations, beginning with the members of a household or an estate, but often including more distant relatives and connections, even servants. While ties of blood and marriage formed the basis of the family, they were not determinative; a male child, for example, could be adopted and made heir. In the eighteenth and early nineteenth centuries, the development of industrial capitalism and the growth of Protestantism, with its emphasis on the individual, encouraged a new way of thinking about the family. Capitalism increased the potential for social mobility, so the family decreased in importance as an instrument of class movement. Therefore, marriage, adoption, and fosterage, which had previously been among the few means of social ascent, lost some of their significance as building blocks of society. At the same time, the concept of romantic love as a basis for marriage became increasingly viable. With the rise of the middle class, and a social system not based exclusively on land holdings to be preserved or increased through marriage, love gained a more prominent role in the development of family. During the eighteenth century, then, the family began to contract into our more contemporary way of thinking about it as a nuclear group, bound primarily by blood and love rather than law and obligation.

Wuthering Heights involves a shifting sense of both family and marriage. The waif Heathcliff is brought into the family by Mr. Earnshaw, a representative of the older generation, who might be expected to think of the family as expansive, able to incorporate new members easily; on Earnshaw's death, the family constricts to a smaller, nuclear group, expelling Heathcliff and relegating him to the status of servant. Perhaps more importantly, the issue of love matches dominates the plot, from Hindley's surprise marriage to Frances, to Heathcliff's "romantic" elopement with Isabella, to Catherine Linton's marriage to

Hareton. Catherine Earnshaw embodies the shift: romantically attracted to Heathcliff, she prudently and contractually marries Edgar Linton instead, hoping that marriage and love can be kept separate. In her case they cannot, with tragic consequences.

The Novel in Focus

Plot summary. As the novel begins, Lockwood, a Londoner, has rented a house—"Thrushcross Grange"—in a rural area in Yorkshire. He rents it from a Mr. Heathcliff, who lives at a house some four miles distant, Wuthering Heights. Lockwood visits his landlord at Wuthering Heights and is forced to stay the night when a snowstorm obscures the guideposts along his route home. Intrigued by some books he finds in his bedroom, he dreams of the girl who owned them; she seems to be variously named Catherine Earnshaw, Catherine Heathcliff, or Catherine Linton. Suddenly Lockwood screams at the apparition of a child; his nightmare awakens the household, and Heathcliff turns him out of the room. Returning to the Grange the next day, Lockwood enlists the housekeeper, Nelly Dean, to tell him Catherine's story. The bulk of the novel consists of Nelly's tale.

As Lockwood learns, Catherine Earnshaw (Cathy I) was the daughter of Nelly's late master, a Mr. Earnshaw, former owner of Wuthering Heights. Earnshaw had adopted Heathcliff as a child, after encountering him on the streets of Liverpool. Catherine and Heathcliff become inseparable as children, and Heathcliff displaces Catherine's brother, Hindley, in their father's affections as well. Their idyllic childhood is interrupted, however, first by the father's death and then by Catherine's sojourn at the Grange, where she meets Edgar and Isabella Linton.

Hindley Earnshaw, now grown, returns for his father's funeral, inheriting Wuthering Heights. His wife gives birth to a son, Hareton, and dies, after which Hindley grows increasingly dissolute. Under Hindley's regime, Heathcliff and Catherine go their separate ways. While he is relegated to servitude, she becomes increasingly "gentrified"; she dresses in fine clothes and worries about keeping her hands clean, rather than running wild on the moors like before. Her association with the Lintons—their manners, dress, and education—draws Catherine away from Heathcliff, who leaves Wuthering Heights when he overhears her telling Nelly the housekeeper that Edgar has proposed to her. What he does

---

THE SOMERSET CASE

Purchased in Virginia, the slave James Somerset accompanied his owner, Charles Stewart, to England in 1769. After two years in England, Somerset left Stewart's service without permission and refused to return. Incensed, Stewart had Somerset seized and remanded to a ship's commander to be conveyed to Jamaica for sale there. Somerset's friends complained to the English court system that the slave was confined in chains onboard a ship ready to sail for Jamaica, and the case became a cause célébre. A writ of habeas corpus was brought against the captain, forcing him to release Somerset and bring him to court. On the fifth day of the trial Lord Mansfield delivered the decision:

> No master ever was allowed here to take a slave by force to be sold abroad because he deserted from his service, or for any other reason whatever; we cannot say, the cause set forth by this return is allowed or approved by the laws of this Kingdom, and therefore the man must be discharged.
>
> (Mansfield in Shyllon, pp. 109-10)

Public opinion rested on the side of Somerset. His lawyer got a standing ovation at the end of the trial, while during it the opposing lawyer was jeered—but slavery in England continued: "blacks were still hunted and kidnapped in the streets of London, Bristol, and Liverpool; hateful advertisements still appeared in the papers for the sale of blacks" (Shyllon, p. 174).

GENEALOGY OF *WUTHERING HEIGHTS*

~

*W*uthering Heights includes potentially confusing sets of names, both identical (Catherine I and II) and similar (Hindley, Hareton, Heathcliff). This confusion is compounded by the two Catherines' marital choices: Catherine Earnshaw (Cathy I) becomes Catherine Linton; her daughter, Catherine Linton (Cathy II), becomes Catherine Heathcliff and, prospectively by the novel's end, Catherine Earnshaw. The following developments outline the eighteenth-century Earnshaw family history:

Parents—Mr. and Mrs. Earnshaw

Son Hindley	Daughter Catherine	Foster son Heathcliff
(1757-84) marries Francis and they have a son named Hareton	(1765-84) marries Edgar Linton and has a daughter, Catherine Linton	(b. 1764; adopted 1771) marries Isabella Linton and they have a son named Linton Heathcliff

Catherine Linton marries her cousin Linton Heathcliff in 1801; he dies soon after. Her marriage to her other cousin, Hareton Earnshaw, is projected for New Year's Day of 1803. (Adapted from Sanger in Sale and Dunn, p. 331)

not catch is her assertion that she and Heathcliff will always be one; she considers her planned marriage irrelevant to her feelings for Heathcliff.

Three years pass, during which we hear nothing of Heathcliff's whereabouts. Nelly raises Hindley's son, Hareton, then moves to the Grange with Catherine on her marriage to Edgar. Heathcliff returns, as mysteriously as he has disappeared, and disrupts both families. He becomes a divisive force between Edgar and Catherine, and lives at the Heights with Hindley and Hareton Earnshaw. Rumor has it that he has won property from Hindley by gambling with him. Edgar's sister, Isabella, finds herself attracted to Heathcliff, though Catherine warns her against him. Disregarding the warning, Isabella elopes with Heathcliff and, after two months, they return to take up residence at Wuthering Heights.

Isabella grows almost immediately disillusioned with her choice. Heathcliff proves brutal and cruel; he has clearly married her because she is her brother's heir. When Catherine dies giving birth to a daughter, Catherine Linton (Cathy II), Isabella escapes from Heathcliff and flees to London, where she gives birth to a son, Linton Heathcliff. Although divorce was rare and extremely difficult in the period, and children of separated parents were legally the property of the father, Heathcliff does not pursue his wife, and Edgar presumably helps to support Isabella in

hiding. Soon after Linton's birth, Hindley dies, and Heathcliff acquires Wuthering Heights through the mortgage he has held in payment of Hindley's gambling debts.

Almost 13 years pass. Nelly continues as a servant at the Grange, where Edgar is raising his daughter in relative isolation. At about 13, Cathy II is out rambling on the moors when she meets her cousin Hareton for the first time. Shortly thereafter, a report of Isabella's death reaches Edgar, who goes to London to bring Linton Heathcliff, her son, back to the Grange. Heathcliff demands to raise the child himself, and after a brief meeting of the cousins at the Grange, Linton is returned to the Heights.

Almost three years pass before the cousins see each other again. Linton is an invalid who has received little care at the Heights, but Heathcliff encourages him to correspond with Catherine II. Though Edgar disapproves, the correspondence continues in secret. When Nelly falls ill, and is thus unable to monitor Catherine's movements, Catherine begins to visit the Heights every evening, developing a deeper connection with Linton. By this time, Edgar's health is failing; clearly Heathcliff is trying to engineer a marriage between Catherine and Linton so that when Edgar dies, Linton (as Catherine's husband) will inherit Edgar's property, making it part of Linton's holdings, holdings that sickly Linton has already willed to his father. When the cousins meet, however, Linton is querulous and selfish.

Catherine comes for a final visit, chaperoned by Nelly. Locking Nelly into an upper room, Heathcliff prevents Catherine from returning home until she marries Linton. She does so, and Heathcliff releases Nelly, who returns to the Grange to find Edgar dying. Catherine escapes and meets her father one last time before his death; she then returns to Wuthering Heights to nurse her new husband. Nelly remains at the Grange as housekeeper.

Linton Heathcliff dies within months of his marriage, and all his property (including the Grange) passes to Heathcliff. This, then, is the situation at the beginning of the narrative: Heathcliff owns both houses, occupying one and renting the other to Lockwood. Hareton and Catherine live at the Heights, relegated by Heathcliff to servant status, as he had earlier been by Hareton's father, Hindley. Nelly's whole narrative stirs a romantic interest in Lockwood for Catherine, but, dissuaded by both her temper and the forbidding nature of the landscape, he returns to London.

Almost a year later, Lockwood takes a hunting trip to the area and decides to stay briefly at the Grange. Surprised not to find Nelly there, he learns that she now lives at Wuthering Heights. He ambles over to find the place considerably changed: flowers are growing in the yard, the kitchen is bright, and Cathy II and Hareton are sharing a book. He hears the conclusion of the story from Nelly: Heathcliff has died, apparently willing himself to death in order to join Cathy I, whose ghost haunted Lockwood on his first arrival but seemingly never appeared to Heathcliff. He has been buried next to her. Cathy II has taken an interest in Hareton, and through their shared opposition to Heathcliff and interest in books (she has taught him to read) they have forged a bond that will end, Nelly triumphantly informs Lockwood, in a marriage that will reunite the two households.

Who is Heathcliff? *Wuthering Heights* can best be viewed through the lens of Heathcliff's identity. He enters the novel as a foundling, carried under Mr. Earnshaw's coat from Liverpool with no history, no name, no language: "a dirty, ragged, black-haired child; big enough both to walk and talk . . . [repeating] over and over again some gibberish that nobody could understand" (Brontë, *Wuthering Heights*, pp. 36-37). Earnshaw gives him the name of a son who had died, thus

marking him as a member of the family; significantly, however, Earnshaw does not give the boy the family surname as well. Thus, like a slave or a pet, Heathcliff has only one name.

As suggested, critics have recently posited that Heathcliff may not be just like a slave, he may literally be one, or a freed slave. After all, he is picked up in Liverpool, a major port on the slave trade, and he is consistently described as physically dark, mysterious, and "other" than the Earnshaws and Lintons among whom he lives. He is "black and cross" in Catherine Earnshaw's eyes, and Nelly compares him to "a regular black" (*Wuthering Heights*, pp. 53, 57). His dark skin suggests some other genealogies as well: he is referred to as a "Lascar," a "gipsy," and "an American or Spanish castaway"; the latter reference to castaways may again refer to the slave trade (*Wuthering Heights*, p. 50).

But it is not only Heathcliff's looks and his provenance that suggest an originally African heritage. The language of ownership and property permeates the novel, as when Catherine, in her dying delirium, says "that is not *my* Heathcliff," or when old Mr. Linton refers to him as "that strange acquisition my late neighbor made in his journey to Liverpool" (*Wuthering Heights*, pp. 159, 50). And when Isabella Linton asks Nelly, "Is Mr. Heathcliff a man?" her language reflects the tendency of the nineteenth-century English to question the humanity of their African slaves (*Wuthering Heights*, p. 134). Identifying Heathcliff as a slave allows us to see in Brontë's novel a critique of the practice of slavery, still legal, as pointed out, at the time the novel is set. One central argument against slavery was that the practice degraded not only the slave, but also the master, both by association with a racial "inferior" and by the unjust exercise of power. In this case, Heathcliff's presence clearly degrades both Hindley and Hindley's son Hareton, who are not only under his thumb, but rendered "savage" by their constant association with him; Heathcliff takes pride in his manipulation and destruction of the father and his near-ruin of the son. His own son, Linton, furthermore, has all sorts of congenital weaknesses. There was a widespread belief at the time that children of interracial relationships, or miscegenation, were intellectually and physically weaker than the general population.

Actually, from an 1840s perspective, Heathcliff may be as much Irish as he is African. During this decade, Liverpool became a magnet for Irish refugees, who began flooding the city in

1845 during the Great Famine (1845-49). Emily's older brother, Branwell Brontë, had visited Liverpool in August 1845, just before she began writing the novel, and would have returned to Haworth with tales of the ragged Irish children pouring into the city. Nineteenth-century English stereotypes about the Irish are strikingly similar to those of the African—both, for example, were thought of as dark, curly-haired, and passionate. The Irish, like Africans, functioned as a racial "other" to the Victorian English. Thus, Heathcliff's "otherness" may stem as much from the Liverpool that Brontë heard about after her brother's sojourn as from the Liverpool of earlier years, as much from working-class Irish emigration as from the African slave trade.

There is a question not only of Heathcliff's background but also of his genuine role in the novel. Absent for three years, he returns a wealthy and polished young man, soon insinuating himself into the Linton household as well as gaining possession of Wuthering Heights. Could he be the father of the child Cathy I dies after bearing? As Nelly makes clear, Catherine Linton (Cathy II), is born just about seven months after Heathcliff's return. This would make Cathy II illegitimate and (if so) her marriage to Linton Heathcliff, Heathcliff's son by Isabella, incestuous—for he would be her half-brother.

Speculations about identity are necessary for an understanding of the tightly structured narrative, which doubles back on itself and returns, again and again, to the same few characters, the same few questions. Brontë's novel does not, ever, explicitly condemn African slavery, bemoan the increasingly restricted structure of the family, or name a father or a race for Heathcliff. Yet by focusing the action of the novel on this mysterious creature, this "cuckoo," as Nelly calls him, the novel insistently forces our attention to these issues (*Wuthering Heights*, p. 35).

Heathcliff represents a threat to the orderly society of Wuthering Heights. His status—as servant or slave, family member or interloper—is continually at issue in the novel. Brontë represents the anxiety of the gentry over the period's new social mobility in the Lintons' distaste for Heathcliff. Ultimately, however, the little society of the novel is able to accommodate change, as indeed the larger English society did at the time, through slow generational shifts rather than revolutionary upheaval. England in the nineteenth century prided itself on the prudent constitutional and social change that helped it avoid the revolutions that swept the continent, beginning with the French Revolution and continuing through the 1840s; the society of Wuthering Heights and Thrushcross Grange reenacts this evolutionary change in microcosm.

Sources and literary context. Emily Brontë was surprisingly well read for the daughter of a country clergyman whose forebears were illiterate Irish peasants. She and her sisters were particularly fond of the English Romantic poet George Gordon, Lord Byron, whose poems (see **Don Juan**, also in *WLAIT 3: British and Irish Literature and It Times*) feature alienated heroes often thought to be precursors to Heathcliff. Byron's poem "Manfred" may be a particularly apt precursor, as the protagonist's alienation stems at least in part from his remorse over what appears to be an incestuous relationship with his sister, Astarte, who may have killed herself. Manfred's dark brooding marks him as a prototypical "Byronic hero," a character type that quickly became a target of both imitation and parody in early-nineteenth-century writing. Brontë's Heathcliff in many ways demonstrates the dangers of Byronism: her Heathcliff seems less remorseful, indeed less sympathetic generally, than any of Byron's heroes, and his actions are directly or indirectly responsible for the deaths of at least four characters in the novel, not including himself.

The Romantic movement generally privileged feelings above logic or reason, and often emphasized the individual's emotional response to the environment. Emily Brontë has gained a reputation in this regard for being the most "Romantic" of the Brontë sisters because her novel is firmly rooted in a specific landscape that provides more than simple "local color." The Yorkshire landscape that animates *Wuthering Heights* is grim and foreboding, like many of the people who inhabit it.

A folklore revival in the eighteenth century affected the Romantic movement, and evidence of it surfaces in *Wuthering Heights*, which has sources in local legend and lore. Brontë absorbed these sources especially from the family servant, Tabitha Aykroyd (known as Tabby). Critics have noted parallels between certain familiar ballads and the themes of the novel, especially those ballads that take up the doomed passion of highborn ladies for "gypsy lovers" and other outcast souls. One such ballad, "Johnny Faa," involves a woman who abandons her husband for her gypsy lover, claiming—like Cathy I on her deathbed—"my lord shall nae mair come near me" (Smith, p. 507). Since ballads, unlike the realistic novels of mid-century England, easily incorporate the supernatural, the links are compelling. Cathy I appears to Lockwood as a ghost, and one of Nelly's closing comments to Lockwood is that the ghosts of Cathy I and Heathcliff have been spotted—she reports that a little boy has told her "They's Heathcliff and a woman, yonder" (*Wuthering Heights*, p. 333). These supernatural elements enter the novel without extensive commentary or apology, and unlike many "supernatural" occurrences in the Gothic fiction of the time, they are not explained away by later events. Though Nelly dismisses the boy's report, she admits that she, like him, fears to pass the site where the ghosts have been seen.

Events in History at the Time the Novel Was Written

The working class. Throughout the early part of the nineteenth century the growth and development of industrial capitalism brought about the beginnings of a working-class movement. In England, the People's Charter (1838) and the associated movement known as Chartism called for working-class political rights: the right to vote, to organize, to strike. While the Reform Bill of 1832 had extended the franchise to allow some middle-class males (white property-owners only) to vote, the People's Charter demanded universal suffrage and posed a serious threat to middle-class stability. Heathcliff's unknown origins and his original status as a servant mark him as a member of this threatening class, and indeed his presence does pose a significant threat to the stability of life at both Wuthering Heights and the Grange. As Daniel Pool notes, Yorkshire's isolated farmsteads were among the last in England to give up the practice of having servants actually live with the family, as Nelly and Heathcliff do (Pool, p. 159). From an 1845 point of view, Heathcliff at least can be seen as a disgruntled worker whose residence in the household increases the class anxiety already evidenced in the novel.

Gender in Victorian England. The Victorian period saw the birth of the women's movement, a response to the overwhelming legal and social strictures under which women labored in the nineteenth century. Yet England from the period of 1837 to 1901 was governed by a queen. This central paradox informs all ideas about gender in the nineteenth century. Although it is true that the most powerful person in the realm was

a woman, she was the exception to prove the rule. In fact, in 1847, women, especially married women, had almost no legal standing whatsoever. They could not vote, own property, testify in court, or, in most cases, retain custody of their children in the unlikely event of separation or divorce. Divorce was extremely rare for middle-class women, requiring an act of Parliament or a religious annulment, and marriage was one of the few "occupations" open to them, besides writer, teacher, or governess (all of which the Brontës tried).

From being the ward of her father, the female became almost literally the possession of her husband after marriage. English marriage law determined that a woman's personal property became her husband's on marriage. Her own political person was absorbed into her husband's by the practice of "coverture," in which the wife is metaphorically "covered" by her husband, making them, in the language of the marriage service, "one flesh." Her children were, legally, the property of her husband (until 1839, when limited custody rights were granted to women). These legal issues are raised implicitly throughout the novel. Most obviously, Heathcliff imprisons Cathy II at the Heights in order to force her marriage to his son, whom he controls, so that her property will become Linton's and eventually his. Soon after the marriage Linton boasts to Nelly, "Catherine always spoke of it [the Grange] as *her* house. It isn't hers! It's mine—papa says everything she has is mine" (*Wuthering Heights*, p. 177).

The legal oppression of women in the period was matched, however, by a growing cultural idealization of them. Coventry Patmore's "The Angel in the House," a poem of the 1850s, embodies the mid-Victorian ideal of woman: proper, domestic, and utterly devoted to hearth, home, and husband. Nineteenth-century women were furthermore regarded as moral arbiters and guides, placed on a pedestal of piety. But a woman's political and legal rights were considered irrelevant, the conviction being that they were amply represented by her husband, while he relied on her to regulate his household and moral status.

Brontë's novel steers a middle course between Catherine's uninhibited behavior and her daughter's domestic imprisonment, between freedom from propriety and the status of property. Cathy II is not a domestic "angel," as Victorian ideology of Brontë's own time would have her be; her porridge has lumps in it, and she is a hostile hostess at best. Yet she "domesticates" Hareton, teaching him to read and encouraging him to help her plant flowers. And, significantly, she safeguards home and hearth, a primary duty for the Victorian woman, for she restores her family's property. Married to Hareton, Cathy II will once again inhabit the family home of Wuthering Heights. As maternal teacher and domestic beautifier, Catherine II steps into the socially sanctioned roles for the Victorian woman, stopping short of chafing at her limitations, as her mother so clearly did.

Reception. Early reviews of *Wuthering Heights* were mixed. Most praised the originality and power of the novel, but condemned its coarseness, vulgarity, and even depravity. Typical of these mixed responses is an unsigned review in the *Examiner:* "This is a strange book. It is not without evidences of considerable power: but, as a whole, it is wild, confused, disjointed, and improbable; and the people who make up the drama, which is tragic enough in its consequences, are savages ruder than those who lived before the days of Homer" (Allott, p. 220). The same critic, like many others, focuses on Heathcliff as "the hero of the book, if a hero there be. He is an incarnation of evil qualities; implacable hate, ingratitude, cruelty, falsehood, selfishness, and revenge" (Allott, p. 220). Early critics frequently noted connections to Byron, to "those irregular German tales in which the writers, giving the reins to their fancy, represent personages as swayed and impelled to evil by supernatural influences" (Allott, pp. 220, 223).

After Emily's death, Charlotte Brontë published a new edition of *Wuthering Heights* in 1850; in this edition she wrote a note that set the tone for new appraisals of the novel thereafter. She emphasizes the "rude and strange" qualities of the work, but defends them as appropriate to the Yorkshire setting and the genius of her sister (C. Brontë in Allott, p. 284). Later critics like W.C. Roscoe concur, claiming, "in force of genius, in the power of conceiving and uttering intensity of passion, Emily surpassed her sister Charlotte. On the other hand, her range seems to have been still more confined" (Roscoe in Allott, p. 348). Poet Dante Gabriel Rossetti wrote to a friend that it was "the first novel I've read for an age, and the best (as regards power and sound style) for two ages, except *Sidonia* [by

Johann Wilhelm Meinhold, translated into English in 1844]" (Rossetti in Allott, p. 300). Matthew Arnold's 1855 elegy for Emily Brontë, "Haworth Churchyard," provides a fitting final commentary on the novel and its author:

> . . . She—
> (How shall I sing her?)—whose soul
> Knew no fellow for might,
> Passion, vehemence, grief,
> Daring, since Byron died,
> That world-fam'd Son of Fire; She who sank
> Baffled, unknown, self-consum'd;
> Whose too-bold dying song
> Shook, like a clarion blast, my soul.
> (Arnold in Allott, pp. 309-10)

—Elisabeth Rose Gruner

For More Information

Allott, Miriam, ed. *The Brontës: The Critical Heritage.* London: Routledge & Kegan Paul, 1974.

Ariés, Philippe. *Centuries of Childhood: A Social History of Family Life.* Trans. Robert Baldick. New York: Vintage, 1962.

Brontë, Emily. *Wuthering Heights.* 1847. London: Penguin, 1995.

Eagleton, Terry. *Heathcliff and the Great Hunger.* London: Verso, 1995.

Gérin, Winifred. *Emily Brontë: A Biography.* Oxford: Clarendon, 1971.

Meyer, Susan. *Imperialism and Home: Race and Victorian Women's Fiction.* Ithaca: Cornell University Press, 1996.

Michie, Elsie B. *Outside the Pale: Cultural Exclusion, Gender Difference, and the Victorian Woman Writer.* Ithaca: Cornell University Press, 1993.

Pool, Daniel. *What Jane Austen Ate and Charles Dickens Knew: From Fox-Hunting to Whist—the Facts of Daily Life in 19th-Century England.* New York: Simon and Schuster, 1993.

Sale, W. M., and Richard J. Dunn, eds. *Wuthering Heights: Authoritative Text, Backgrounds, Criticism.* 3d. ed. New York: W. W. Norton, 1990.

Shyllon, F. O. *Black Slaves in Britain.* London: Oxford University Press, 1974.

Smith, Sheila. "At Once Strong and Eerie: The Supernatural in *Wuthering Heights* and its Debt to the Traditional Ballad." *Review of English Studies* 43, no. 172 (Nov. 1992): 498-517.

Von Sneidern, Maja-Lisa. "*Wuthering Heights* and the Liverpool Slave Trade." *English Literary History* 62, no. 1 (spring 1995): 171-96.

Index